# THE OFFICIAL
# 1987 PRICE GUIDE TO

# BASEBALL
# CARDS

### BY
### DR. JAMES BECKETT

**SIXTH EDITION**

**THE HOUSE OF COLLECTIBLES**
**NEW YORK, NEW YORK 10022**

© 1986 Dr. James Beckett

Published by: The House of Collectibles
201 East 50th Street
New York, New York 10022

Distributed by Ballantine Books, a division of Random House, Inc., New York and simultaneously in Canada by Random House of Canada Limited, Toronto.

Manufactured in the United States of America

Library of Congress Catalog Card Number: 84-645496

ISBN: 0-87637-509-3

10 9 8 7 6 5 4 3 2

# TABLE OF CONTENTS

# ABOUT THE AUTHOR

Jim Beckett, the leading authority on sports card values in the United States, maintains a wide range of activities in the world of sports. He possesses one of the finest collections of sports cards and autographs in the world, has made numerous appearances on radio and television, and has been frequently cited in many national publications. Dr. Beckett has been the recipient of the first Special Achievement Award for Contribution to the Hobby from the National Sports Collectors Convention in 1980 and the Jock-Jasperson Award for Hobby Dedication in 1983. He is the author of *The Sport Americana Football, Hockey, Basketball and Boxing Price Guide, The Official Price Guide to Football Cards, The Sport Americana Baseball Card Price Guide, The Official Price Guide to Baseball Cards, The Sport Americana Baseball Memorabilia and Autograph Price Guide,* and *The Sport Americana Alphabetical Baseball Card Checklist.* In addition, he is the founder, author, and editor of *Beckett Baseball Card Monthly,* a magazine dedicated to the card collecting hobby.

Jim Beckett received his Ph.D. in Statistics from Southern Methodist University in 1975. He resides in Dallas with his wife and his daughters, while actively pursuing his writing and consultancy services.

# ACKNOWLEDGMENTS

This edition of the *Price Guide* contains new sets and, of course, completely revised prices on all the cards. A great deal of hard work went into this volume, and it could not have been done without a considerable amount of help from many people. Our thanks are extended to each and every one of you.

First, we owe a special acknowledgment to Dennis W. Eckes, Mr. Sport Americana, who had the vision to see where the hobby was going and the perseverance and drive to help it get there. The success of the *Beckett Price Guides* has been the result of a team effort. Although Denny has chosen no longer to be a co-author on price guides—in order to devote more time to his business, Den's Collector's Den—he is still on board as a special consultant.

Those who have worked closely with us on this and many other books have again proven themselves invaluable in every aspect of producing this book—Cartophilium (Andrew Pywowarczuk), Mike Cramer (Pacific Trading Cards), Bill and Diane Dodge, Gervise Ford, Larry and Jeff Fritsch, Tony Galovich, Mike and Howie Gordon, John Greenwald, Wayne Grove, Bill Haber, Danny Hitt, Stewart Jones, Alan Kaye (Baseball Card News), Lew Lipset, Ralph Nozaki, Jack Pollard, Dick Reuss, Gavin Riley, John Rumierz, John Spalding, Sports Collector's Digest (Bob Lemke), and Murvin Sterling.

Special thanks are extended to the Donruss Company, The Fleer Corporation, and the Topps Chewing Gum Company, who have consistently provided checklists and visual materials in order that the *Price Guide* could be complete.

Many other individuals have provided price input, illustrative material, checklist verifications, errata, and/or background information. At the risk of inadvertently overlooking or omitting these many contributors, we should like to personally thank Ab D Cards (Dale Wesolewski), Jerry Adamic, Bob Alexander, Dennis Anderson, Lee Anderson, Mike Aronstein (TCMA), Robert Bansley, Frank and Vivian Barning, Ed Barry (Ed's Collectibles), Bob Bartosz, Baseball Card Shop, Bay State Cards (Lenny DeAngelico), Chris Benjamin, Beulah Sports, Big Andy's, Tim Bond, Joe Borte, Bill Bossert (Mid-Atlantic Coin Exchange), Larry Calder, Murray Calder, California Card Co., Cards and Comics, Burdette M. Cattley, Ira Cetron, Dwight Chapin, Chriss Christiansen, Barry Colla, Collection de Sport AZ, Kevin Cormier, Taylor Crane, James Critzer, Alan Custer, Dame Dame, Dixie Dugout, Guy Downs, Dave Dryden, Charles Dugre, Doak Ewing, David and Mark Federman, David Festberg, Bill Finneran, Bob Fletcher, Frank Fox (The Card Shop), Steve Freedman, Dick Goddard, Steve Gold (AU Sports), Jeff Goldstein, Grand Slam Sports Collectibles, Julie Grove, Clayton Gum, Dave Hadeler, Dean Haley, Ronald Haley, Charley Hall, Hall's Nostalgia, Ernie Hammond, Hershell Hanks, Joel Hellman (JJ's Budget Baseball Cards), Bill Henderson, Ryan Hurba, James Johnston, Dave and Rosie Jones, Dave Jurgensmeier, Jim Kelley, Rick Keplinger, Tom Kiecker, Jim Knowler, Thomas Kunnecke, Dan Lavin, Greg Lawton, Morley Leeking, Irv Lerner, Liberty Hobby Shop, LNW Sports, Chris Lockwood, Chuck Lombardo, Mike London, Jim Macie, Paul Marchant, Raymond May, Mike McDonald (Sports Page), J. McElroy, Mendal Mearkle, John Mehlin, Joe Michalowicz, Wayne Miller, Dick Millerd, Ashby Milstead, Brian Morris, Dick Mueller, Ray Murphy, Edward Nazzaro (The Collector), Chip Nelson, Murry Nelson, North Conway Baseball Card Shop, Mike O'Brien, Carl Olsen (Baseball Card Express), Clay Pasternack, Nancy Paterson, Bill Pekarik (Pastime Hobbies), Michael Perrotta, Gerald Perry, Tom Pfirrmann, Rick Rapa (Atlanta Sports Cards), Bill Reed, Gordon Reid, Tom Reid, Owen Ricker, Dave Ring, Alan Rosen (Mr. Mint), Clifton Rouse, Terry Sack, Jennifer Salems, John Salsido, Ang Savelli, Robert Scagnelli, Don Schlaff, David Shannon, Gerry Shebib, Chris Shore, State Video and Comics, Dave Steckling, Don Steinbach, Jack Stowe, Strikeout Sports Cards, Richard Strobino, Barrie Sullivan, Tony Taggio, Darius Tandon, Ian Taylor, Lyle Telfer, Lee Temanson, 20th Century Collectibles, Rich Unruh, Kurt Utley, John Vanden Beek, John Vangen, Bill Wesslund, Richard West, Bob Wilke (The Shoe Box), Jeff Williams, Kit Young, and Ted Zanidakis.

Finally, writing this book would have been a very unpleasant experience without the understanding and cooperation of my wife, Patti, and daughters, Christina and Rebecca. I thank them and promise them that I will pay them back for all those hours. While on the subject of family, my sister, Claire Beckett, who is my full-time assistant on *Beckett Monthly*, put in extensive overtime carrying the administrative load on the magazine singlehandedly during the time that I was working on this book. Those of you who subscribe to the *Monthly* already know what a super job Claire is doing. Thank you, everyone.

# ADDITIONAL ACKNOWLEDGMENTS

We have appreciated all of the help we have received over the years from collectors across the country and, indeed, throughout the world. Because we made active solicitations to individuals and groups for input to this year's edition, we are particularly appreciative of help provided for this volume. While we receive many inquiries, comments, and questions regarding material within this book—and, in fact, each and every one is read and digested—time constraints prevent us from replying to all but a few such letters. We hope that the letters will continue, and that even though no reply is received, you will feel that you are making significant contributions, with your interest and comments, to the hobby.

# ERRATA

There are thousands of names, over 100,000 prices, and untold other words in this book. There are going to be a few typographical errors, a few misspellings, and possibly, a number or two out of order. If you catch a blooper, drop me a note directly or in care of the publisher, and we will fix it up in the next year's issue.

# INTRODUCTION

Isn't it great? Every year this book gets bigger and bigger with all the new sets coming out. But even more exciting is that every year there are more collectors, more shows, more stores, and more interest in the cards we love so much. This edition has been enhanced and expanded from the previous edition. The cards you collect—who they are of, what they look like, where they are from, and (most importantly to many of you) what their current values are—are enumerated within. Many of the features contained in the other *Beckett Price Guides* have been incorporated into this volume since condition grading, nomenclature, and many other aspects of collecting are common to card collecting in general. We hope you find the book both interesting and useful in your collecting pursuits.

*The Beckett Guide* has been successful where other attempts have failed because it is complete, current, and valid. This price guide contains not just one, but three prices, by condition, for all the baseball cards in the issues listed. This accounts for almost all the baseball cards in existence. The prices were added to the card lists just prior to the printing of this book and reflect not the author's opinions or desires but the going retail prices for each card, based on the marketplace (sports memorabilia conventions and shows, hobby papers, current mail order catalogs, local club meetings, auction results, and other first hand reportings of actual realized prices).

To facilitate your use of this book, read the complete introductory section in the pages following before going to the pricing pages. Every collectible field has its own terminology; we've tried to capture most of these terms and definitions in our glossary. Please read carefully the section on grading and the condition of your cards as you will not be able to determine which price column is appropriate for a given card without first knowing its condition.

Welcome to the world of baseball cards.

*Sincerely, Dr. James Beckett*

# HISTORY OF BASEBALL CARDS

Today's version of the baseball card, with its color front and statistic laden back, is a far cry from its earliest ancestors. The institution of baseball cards began in the mid-1800's, more than a century ago. Early issues, generally printed on heavy cardboard, were of poor quality, with photography, drawing, and printing far behind today's standards. The issue as to which was the very first baseball card ever produced still remains cloudy.

Goodwin & Co., of New York, makers of Gypsy Queen, Old Judge, and other cigarette brands is considered by many to be the first issuer of baseball cards. Their issues, predominantly in the 1½″ by 2½″ size, generally consisted of photographs of baseball players, boxers, wrestlers, and other subjects mounted on stiff cardboard stock. Over 2000 different photos of baseball players alone have been identified. These "Old Judges," a collective name commonly used for the Goodwin & Co. cards, were issued from 1886 to 1890 and are treasured parts of many collections. Among the other cigarette companies issuing baseball cards which still command attention today are Allen & Ginter, D. Buchner & Co. (Gold Coin Chewing Tobacco) and P. H. Mayo & Brother. The first two companies issued colored line-drawing cards while the Mayo's were sepia photographs on black cardboard. In addition to the small-sized cards from this era, several tobacco companies issued cabinet-sized baseball cards. These "cabinets" were considerably larger than the small cards, usually about 4¼″ by 6½″, and were printed on heavy stock. Goodwin & Co.'s Old Judge cabinets and the National Tobacco Works' "Newsboy" baseball photos are two that remain popular today. By 1895 the American Tobacco Company began to dominate its competition. They discontinued baseball card inserts to their cigarette packages (actually slide boxes in those days). The lack of competition in the cigarette market had made the inserts unnecessary. This marked the end of the first era of the baseball card.

At the dawn of the twentieth century only a few baseball cards were being issued. Once again, the cigarette companies—particularly, the American Tobacco Company—and to a lesser extent the candy and gum makers, began to issue baseball cards, thus reviving the institution. The bulk of these cards, identified by the American Card Catalog as T and E cards (designated hereafter as ACC for twentieth century "Tobacco" issues and "Early Candy and Gum" issues, respectively) were released from 1909 to 1915.

This romantic and popular era of baseball card collecting produced many popular items. The most outstanding was the fabled T–206 Honus Wagner card. Other perennial favorites among collectors are the T–206 Eddie Plank card, long the second most valuable card (only recently relinquishing its number two position to the more distinctive and aesthetically pleasing Napoleon Lajoie card from the 1933–34 Goudey Gum series); and the T–206 Magee error card (Magee was misspelled Magie on the card), the most famous and valuable blooper card.

The ingenuity and distinctiveness of this era has yet to be surpassed. The T–202 Hassan Triple-folders, one of the best looking and the most distinctive card ever issued; the durable T–201 Mecca double folders, one of the first sets with the player's records on the back; the T–3 Turkey Reds, collecting's most popular cabinet card; the E–145 Cracker Jacks, the only major set containing Federal League player cards; and the T–204 Ramlys, with their distinctive black and white oval photos and ornate gold borders, were but a few of the variety of cards issued during this period. While the American Tobacco Company dominated the field, several other tobacco companies, clothing manufacturers, newspapers and periodicals, game makers, and companies whose identities remain anonymous also issued cards during this period. In fact, The Collins-McCarthy Candy Company, makers of Zeenuts Pacific Coast League baseball cards, issued cards every year from 1911 to 1938. This record for continuous yearly production of cards has been exceeded only by the Topps Chewing Gum Company.

The last of tobacco cards, with the exception of the Red Man chewing tobacco sets produced from 1952–1955, occurred with the onset of World War I.

The next flurry of card issues began in the roaring and prosperous 1920's, the era of the E card. The caramel companies (National Caramel, American Caramel, York Caramel) were the lead distributors of the E card. In addition, the strip card, a continuous strip with several cards separated by dotted lines or other sectioning features, flourished during this time. While the E cards and the strip cards are generally considered less imaginative than the T cards or the recent candy and gum issues, they are still sought after by many advanced collectors.

Another significant event of the 1920's was the introduction of the arcade card. Taking its designation from its issuer, the Exhibit Supply Company of Chicago, it is usually known as the "Exhibit" card. The Exhibit machines, once a trademark of the penny arcades, amusement parks, and county fairs across the country, dispensed for one penny a large (close to the size of a postcard) picture card on thick stock of one's favorite cowboy, actor, actress, or baseball player. The Exhibit Supply (or one of its associated companies) produced baseball cards over a longer span of years, although discontinuous, than any other manufacturer. Its first cards were produced in 1921 while the last Exhibit issue was in 1966. In 1979, the Exhibit Supply Company was bought and somewhat revived by a collector/dealer who has since issued other Exhibit cards, reprinted from Exhibit photos of the past.

If the T-card period, from 1909 to 1915, can be said to be the Golden Age of baseball card collecting, then with the introduction of the Big League Gum series, consisting of 239 cards issued in 1933 (the forerunner of today's baseball gum cards), the Goudey Gum Company of Boston ushered in the Silver Age of card collecting. This era spanned the period from the Depression days in 1933 until America's formal involvement in World War II in 1941. Goudey's attractive cards, in full color with line drawings on thick card stock, had a great influence on other cards being issued at this time. As a result, the most attractive and popular cards in the history of collecting were produced in the Silver Age. The 1933 Goudey Big League Gum series is also popular since it contains over 40 Hall of Fame players, including four cards of Babe Ruth and two of Lou Gehrig. Goudey's reign continued into 1934 when they issued a 96-card set, in color, together with the single remaining card in the 1933 series, #106, the Napoleon Lajoie card.

In addition to Goudey, several other bubble gum manufacturers issued baseball cards during this era. DeLong Gum Company issued an extremely attractive set in 1933. National Chicle Company's 192-card "Batter-Up" series of 1934–36 became the largest die-cut set in card history. In addition, they offered the popular "Diamond Stars" series during the same period. Other popular sets included the "Tattoo Orbit" set of 60 color cards issued in 1933 and Gum Products' 75-card "Double Play" set, a sepia colored set consisting of two players per card.

In 1939, Gum Inc., which later became Bowman Gum, replaced Goudey Gum as the leading baseball card producer. Between 1939 and 1940 they issued two important sets of black and white cards. In 1939, the set entitled "Play Ball America" consisted of 162 cards. The 240 cards called "Play Ball" issued in 1940 are still considered by many to be the most attractive black and white cards ever produced. They introduced their only color set in 1941, consisting of 72 cards entitled "Play Ball Sports Hall of Fame." Many of the poses were colored repeats of the 1940 series.

In addition to regular gum cards, many manufacturers distributed premium issues during the 1930's. These premiums were printed on paper or photographic stock, rather than card stock. They were much larger than the regular cards and were sold across the counter with gum (which was packaged separately from the premium) for a penny. They were often redeemed at the store or through the mail in exchange for the wrappers of previously purchased gum cards, a la proof-of-purchase box-top premiums of today. The premiums are scarcer than the card issues of the 1930's and, in most cases, no manufacturer's identification is present. Thin, postcard-sized premiums (known as "fine pen" and "wide pen" depending on the boldness of the autograph facsimiles) were offered in sepia (4" by 6¼") and in black and white (4¾" by 7⁵⁄₁₆") by Goudey Gum Company with Diamond Star Gum. Diamond Star premiums were issued anonymously by National Chicle Company.

World War II brought an end to this popular era of card collecting. Paper and rubber shortages curtailed the production of bubble gum baseball cards until they were resurrected again in 1948 by the Bowman Gum Company (the direct descendant of Gum, Inc.). This marked the beginning of the modern era of card collecting.

In 1948, Bowman Gum issued a 48-card set in black and white consisting of one card and one slab of gum in every one-cent pack. That same year, the Leaf Gum Company also issued a set of cards. Although the quality was rather poor, these cards were issued in color. A squabble over the rights to use players' pictures developed between Bowman and Leaf, and eventually Leaf dropped out of the card market—but not before it had left a lasting impression on the hobby by issuing some of the rarest cards now in existence. Leaf's baseball card series of 1948–49 contained 98 cards, skip numbered to #168 (not all numbers were printed). Of these 98 cards, 49 are relatively plentiful. However, the other 49 are rare and quite valuable.

Bowman continued its production of cards in 1949 with a color series of 240 cards. Because its "high numbers" are both numerous and scarce, this series remains the most difficult Bowman regular issue to complete. Although the set was printed in color and commands great interest due to its scarcity, it is considered aesthetically inferior to the Goudey and National Chicle issues of the 1930's. In addition to the regular issue of 1949, Bowman also issued a set of 36 Pacific Coast League players. While this was not a regular issue, it is still prized by collectors. In fact, it has become the most valuable Bowman issue.

In 1950, Bowman's one-year monopoly of the baseball card market, the company began a string of top-quality cards and which it continued to produce until its demise in 1955. The 1950 series was itself something of an oddity because the "low numbers," rather than the traditional high numbers, were the more difficult numbers to obtain.

The year 1951 marked the beginning of the most competitive, and perhaps the highest quality, period of baseball card production. It was in this year that Topps Chewing Gum Company of Brooklyn entered the market. Topps' 1951 series consisted of two sets of 52 cards each, one set with red backs and the other with blue backs. In addition, Topps also issued 31 insert cards, three of which remain the rarest Topps cards ("Current All—Stars" Konstanty, Roberts, and Stanky). The 1951 Topps cards were unattractive and paled in comparison to the 1951 Bowman issues; however, they were successful. Topps continued to produce cards—and has done so ever since. In 1952, Topps issued a larger and much more attractive card. The size was to be the standard for the next five years. (Bowman followed with larger-size baseball cards in 1953.) The 1952 Topps set has become, like the 1933 Goudey series and the T—206 white border series, the classic set of its era. The 407-card set is a collector's dream of scarcities, rarities, errors, and variations. It also contains the first Topps issues of Mickey Mantle and Willie Mays.

As with Bowman and Leaf in the late 1940's, competition over player rights arose. Ensuing court battles occurred between Topps and Bowman. The market split due to stiff competition, and in January 1956, Topps bought out Bowman. Topps remained relatively unchallenged as the primary producer of baseball cards through 1980. So, the story of major baseball card sets from 1956 through 1980 is by and large the story of Topps issues, with a few exceptions. Fleer Gum produced small sets in 1959, 1960, 1961, and 1963, several cartoon sets in the 1970's, and recently Kelloggs Cereal and Hostess Cakes have issued baseball cards to promote their products.

A court decision in 1980 paved the way for two other large gum companies to enter, or re-enter, the baseball card arena. The Fleer Corporation and the Donruss Company (a division of General Mills) secured rights to produce baseball cards of current players. Each company issued major card sets in 1981 with bubble gum products. A higher court decision in that year revoked the earlier ruling against Topps, and it appeared that Topps had regained its position as the number one producer of baseball cards. Undaunted by the revocation ruling, Fleer and Donruss continued to issue cards in 1982 but without bubble gum or any other edible product. Fleer issued its current player baseball cards with "team logo stickers," while Donruss issued their cards with a piece of a baseball jigsaw puzzle.

Since 1981, these three major baseball card producers have all thrived, sharing equal recognition. Each has steadily increased its involvement in terms of number of issues per year. What the competition has generated, to the delight of the collector, are novel and, in some cases, exceptional issues of current major league baseball players. These major producers have become increasingly aware of the organized hobby market. While the corner candy store remains a big marketplace for card sales, an increasing number of issues have been directed to the organized market. In fact, many of these issues have been distributed exclusively through hobby channels. Although no one can ever say what the future will bring, one can only surmise that the hobby market will play a significant role in future plans of all the major baseball card producers.

The above has been a thumbnail sketch of card collecting from its inception in the 1880's to the present. It is difficult to tell the whole story in just a few pages—there are several other good sources of information. Serious collectors should subscribe to at least one of the excellent hobby magazines or papers. You might also try to attend a sports collectibles convention in your area, if possible. Card collecting is still a young and informal hobby—the chances are good that you will run into one or more of the "experts" in the field, who are usually more than happy to share their knowledge with you.

# HOW TO COLLECT

There are no set rules on how to collect cards. Card collecting is a hobby, a leisure pastime. What you collect, how much you collect, and how much time and money you spend collecting are entirely up to you; the funds you have available for collecting, and your own personal taste, should determine how you collect. The information and ideas presented here are intended to help you get the most enjoyment from this hobby.

It is impossible to collect every card ever produced. Therefore, collectors usually specialize their collecting in some way. One of the reasons this hobby is popular is that individual collectors can define and tailor their collecting methods to match their own tastes. To give you some ideas on the various approaches to collecting, we mention here some of the more popular areas of specialization.

Many collectors select complete sets from particular years. For example, they may concentrate on assembling complete sets from all the years since their birth or since they became an avid sports fan. They may try to collect a card for every player during that specified period of time.

Many collectors wish to acquire only certain players. Usually the players are the superstars of the sport, but occasionally a collector will specialize in all the cards of players who attended a certain college or came from a certain town. Some collectors are only interested in the first card or rookie card of a certain player.

Another fun way to collect cards is by the team. Most fans have a favorite team, and it is natural for that loyalty to be translated into a desire for cards of the players on that favorite team. For most of the recent years, team sets (all the cards from a given team for that year) are readily available at a reasonable price.

# COLLECTING/INVESTING

Collecting individual players and collecting complete sets are both popular vehicles for investment and speculation. Most investors and speculators stock up on complete sets or on quantities of players they think have good investment potential. There is obviously no guarantee in this book, or anywhere else for that matter, that cards will outperform the stock market in the future. After all, there are no quarterly dividends with baseball cards. Nevertheless, investors have noticed a favorable trend in the past performance of baseball and other sports collectibles, and certain cards and sets have outperformed just about any other investment in some years. Some of the obvious questions are: Which cards? When to buy? When to sell? The best investment you can make is in your education. The more you know about your collection and the hobby, the better the decisions you will be able to make. We're not selling investment tips. We're selling information about the current value of baseball cards. It's up to you to use the information contained herein to your best advantage.

# OBTAINING CARDS

Several avenues are open to card collectors. Cards can be purchased in the traditional way at the local candy, grocery, or drug store, with the bubble gum or other products included. It is also possible to purchase complete sets of baseball cards through mail order advertisers found in sports media publications, such as *The Sporting News, Baseball Digest, Street & Smith's Year-*

*books,* and others. Many collectors will begin by subscribing to at least one of the monthly hobby publications, all with good up-to-date information; in fact, subscription offers can be found in the advertising section of this book. Most serious card collectors obtain old (and new) cards from one or more of the following three sources: (1) trading or buying from other collectors or dealers; (2) responding to sale or auction ads in the monthly hobby papers; and/or (3) attending sports collectibles shows or conventions. We advise that you try all three methods, as each has its own distinct advantages: (1) trading is a great way to make some new friends; (2) monthly hobby papers help you keep up with what's going on in the hobby (and tell you when and where the conventions are happening); and (3) shows provide enjoyment and the opportunity to see millions of collectibles under one roof, along with hundreds or even thousands of other collectors attending who all share a common interest.

# DETERMINING VALUE

Why are some cards more valuable than others? Obviously, the economic law of supply and demand is applicable to card collecting just as it is to any other field where a commodity is bought, sold, or traded.

Supply—the number of cards available on the market—is less than the total number of cards produced as a certain percentage of the cards are typically thrown away, destroyed, or otherwise lost. This percentage is smaller today than it has been in the past, since more and more people have become increasingly aware of the value of their cards. For those who collect only "mint" condition cards, the supply of older cards can be quite scarce indeed. Until recently, collectors were not conscious of the need to preserve the condition of their cards. For this reason, it is difficult to know exactly how many 1953 Topps are currently available, mint or otherwise. It is generally accepted that there are fewer 1953 Topps in circulation than 1963, 1973, or 1983 Topps cards. If demand were equal for each of these sets, the law of supply and demand would raise the price for the least available set. Demand, however, is not equal for all sets, and this complicates matters further.

The demand for a card is influenced by many factors, among them being: (1) the age of the card; (2) the number of cards printed; (3) the player(s) portrayed on the card; (4) the attractiveness and popularity of the set; and perhaps most important, (5) the physical condition of the card.

In general, the older the card, the lower the quantity of the card printed, the more famous the player, the more attractive and popular the set, or the better the condition of the card—the higher the value of the card. There are exceptions to all but one of these factors: the condition of the card. Given two cards similar in all respects except condition, the one in the best condition will always be valued higher.

While there are certain guidelines that help to establish the value of a card, the exceptions and peculiarities make any simple mathematical formula to determine value impossible.

# REGIONAL VARIATION

Although prices may vary from the East to the West, or from the Southwest to the Midwest, the prices in this guide are nonetheless presented as a consensus of all sections of this large and diverse country. Likewise, the prices for a particular player's cards may well show a higher price in his home team's area. Sometimes even common player cards command a higher price to hometown collectors than in other parts of the country.

Two types of price variations exist among the sections of the country where a card is bought or sold. The first is the general price variation on all cards bought and sold in one geographical area as compared to another. Card prices are slightly higher on the East and West coasts, and slightly lower in the middle of the country. The second is the specific price variation for a player card found in a certain geographical area and not found in another. For example, the demand for an Al Kaline card is higher in Detroit than in Cincinnati because Kaline played in Detroit; therefore, the value of an Al Kaline card would be higher in Detroit than it is in Cincinnati. On the other hand, a Johnny Bench card would be priced higher in Cincinnati than in Detroit for similar reasons.

# SET PRICES

A somewhat paradoxical situation exists in the price of a complete set versus the combined cost of the individual cards in the set, especially prevalent in the cards of the past few years. In nearly every case, the sum of the prices for the individual cards is higher than the cost for the complete set. The reasons behind this apparent anomaly lie in the habits of collectors and in the carrying costs of dealers. Each card in a set is normally produced in the same quantity as all others in its set (scarcities and rare series notwithstanding). However, many collectors pick up only stars, superstars and particular teams. As a result, the dealer is left with a shortage of certain player cards and an abundance of others; therefore, he incurs an expense in simply "carrying" these cards. On the other hand, if he sells a complete set, he gets rid of a large number of cards at one time. For this reason, he is often willing to receive less money for a complete set. By doing this, he recovers all of his costs and also receives some profit.

The disparity between the price for the complete set and that for the sum of the individual cards has also been influenced by the fact that the major manufacturers are now pre-collating card sets. Since "pulling" individual cards from the sets of all three manufacturers involves a specific type of labor (and cost), the singles or star card market does not benefit significantly from pre-collation.

# SCARCE SERIES

The term "scarce series" is derived from the fact that cards issued before 1974 were made available to the public in more than one series, each of a finite number of cards, rather than all cards of the set being available for purchase at one time. At some point during the year, usually near the end of the baseball season, interest in baseball cards of that year wanes; consequently, the manufacturers produce a smaller number of these later series of cards. Nearly all national issues from the post-World War II manufacturers (1948 to 1973) can be recognized in series. For example, Bowman used 36 cards on its standard printed sheets. (While the number of cards on printed sheets is usually the same as the number of cards in a particular series, such is not always the case, as will be explained below.) Topps series have comprised many different numbers of cards, including 55, 66, 80, 88, and others. Recently Topps has settled on what is now their standard sheet size of 132 cards.

While we have stated that the number of cards within a particular series usually has the same number of cards as the number of cards on one printed sheet, this is not always the case. As early as 1948, Bowman substituted 12 cards during later print runs of its 1948 baseball cards. Twelve of the cards from the initial sheet of 36 cards were removed and replaced by 12 different cards giving, in effect, a first series of 36 cards and a second series of 12 new cards. This replacement phenomenon in the 1948 Bowman series produced a scarcity of 24 cards in the series—the 12 cards removed from the original sheet and the 12 new cards added to the sheet. A full sheet of 1948 Bowman cards (second printing) shows that card numbers 37 through 48 have replaced 12 of the cards on the first printing sheet. The Topps Gum Company has also created scarcities and/or excesses of certain cards in many of their sets. Topps, however, has most frequently used the double-printing procedure. The double-printing procedure causes an abundance of cards of the players who are on the same sheet more than one time. During the years between 1978 and 1981, Topps double-printed 66 cards out of their large 726-card set. The Topps practice of double-printing cards in earlier years is the most logical explanation for the known scarcities of particular cards in some of the Topps sets.

# PRESERVING YOUR CARDS

Cards are fragile. They must be handled properly in order that they retain their value. Careless handling can easily result in a creased or bent card. It is, however, not recommended that tweezers or tongs be used to pick up your cards, as this might indent or mar the surface, which would reduce a mint card to excellent condition. In general, your cards should be directly handled as little as possible—easy to say but hard to do. A collection stored in plastic pages in a three-ring album allows you to view your collection at any time without the need to touch the card itself. Plastic sheets are the preferred method of storing cards, although there are still many who use custom boxes, storage trays, or even shoe boxes. For a large collection, some collectors may use a combination of the above methods. When purchasing plastic sheets for your cards, be sure that you find the pocket size that fits your cards snugly; don't put your 1951 Bowmans in a sheet designed to fit 1981 Topps. Most hobby and collectible shops, and virtually all collectors' conventions, will have these plastic pages available in quantity for the various sizes available.

Damp, sunny, and hot—this is not a weather forecast—these are three conditions to avoid in excess if you are interested in preserving your collection. Too much (or too little) humidity can cause gradual deterioration in the condition of a card. Direct, bright sun (or fluorescent light) over time will bleach out the color of a card. Extreme heat accelerates the decomposition of the paper the card is printed on. On the other hand, cards have lasted over the past 50 years without much scientific intervention. The above factors typically only present a problem when carried to an extreme—but it never hurts to be cautious.

# SELLING YOUR CARDS

Just about every collector sells cards or will sell cards some day. You may be interested in selling your duplicates or, maybe, your whole collection. You may sell to other collectors, friends, or dealers. You may even sell cards you purchased from a certain dealer back to that same dealer. In any event, it helps to know some of the mechanics of the typical transaction between buyer and seller.

Dealers will buy cards in order to resell them to other collectors who might be interested in the cards. Dealers will always pay a larger percentage for items which (in the dealer's opinion) can be resold quickly, and a much smaller percentage for those items which are perceived as having a low demand and are slow-moving. In either case, dealers must buy at a price that allows for the expense of doing business and a fair margin of profit. Virtually all dealers are interested in older complete sets and superstar cards in excellent condition. If you have cards for sale, the best advice we can give is that you get three offers for your cards and take the best offer, all things considered. Note that the best offer may not be the one with the highest dollar amount. And remember, if a dealer really wants your cards, he won't let you get away without making his best competitive offer. Another alternative is to take your cards to the next convention nearby and either auction them off in the show auction or offer them for sale to some of the dealers present.

Many people think nothing of going into a department store and paying $15 for an item of clothing for which the store paid $5. But, if you were selling your $15 card to a dealer and he offered you only $5 for it, you might think his mark-up unreasonable. To complete the analogy: most department stores (and card dealers) that pay $10 for $15 items eventually go out of business. An exception to this is when the dealer knows that a willing buyer for the merchandise you are attempting to sell is only a phone call away. Then an offer of two-thirds or maybe 70% of the book value will still allow the dealer a reasonable profit due to the short time he will need to hold the card. Nevertheless most cards and collections will bring offers in the range of 25% to 50% of the true value. Material from the past five to ten years or so is very plentiful. Don't be surprised if your best offer is only 20% of the book value for these recent years.

# NOMENCLATURE

Each hobby has its own nomenclature to describe the collectibles of that particular hobby. The nomenclature traditionally used for trading cards is derived from the *American Card Catalog*, published in 1960 by Nostalgia Press. This catalog, written by Jefferson Burdick (who is called the Father of Card Collecting for his pioneering work), uses letter and number descriptions for each separate set of cards.

The letter used in the ACC number refers to the generic type of card. While both sport and non-sport issues are classified in the ACC, we shall confine ourselves in this description to the sport issues. The following list defines the letters and their meanings as used by the *American Card Catalog*.

(none) or N—Nineteenth Century U.S. Tobacco
B—Blankets
D—Bakery Inserts Including Bread
E—Early Candy and Gum
F—Food Inserts
H—Advertising
M—Periodicals

PC—Postcards
R—Candy and Gum Cards 1930 to Present
T—Twentieth Century U.S. Tobacco
UO—Gas and Oil Inserts
V—Canadian Candy
W—Exhibits, Strip Cards, Team Issues

Following the letter designation and an optional hyphen are one-, two-, or three-digit numerical descriptors which typically represent the company or entity issuing the cards, i.e., numbers 1–999. In several cases, the ACC number is further extended by an additional hyphen and an additional one- or two-digit numerical descriptor. For example, the 1957 Topps regular series baseball card issue carries an ACC designation of R414-11. The "R" indicates a candy or gum card produced after 1929. The "414" is the ACC designation for Topps Chewing Gum baseball card issues. And, the "11" is the ACC designation for the 1957 regular issue (Topps eleventh baseball set).

Like other traditional methods of identification, this system provides order to the process of cataloging cards; however, most serious collectors learn the ACC designation of the popular sets by repetitive use and familiarity, rather than by attempting to "figure out" what they might or should be.

From 1948 forward, all sets are normally referred to by their year, maker, type of issue, or any other distinguishing characteristics. An example of such a characteristic could be an unusual issue or one of several regular issues put out by a specific maker in a single year. Regional issues are usually referred to by year, maker, and sometimes by title or theme of the set.

# GLOSSARY/LEGEND

Our glossary defines common terms frequently used in the card collecting hobby. Many of the terms are also common to other types of sports memorabilia collecting. There are exceptions to some of the definitions presented. However, listing all these exceptions would confuse the reader and detract from the usefulness of the glossary.

**AAS.** Action All Stars, a postcard-sized set issued by the Donruss Company.

**ACC.** Acronym for American Card Catalog.

**AD CARD.** See Display Card.

**AL.** Abbreviation for American League or American Leaguer.

**ALL STAR CARD.** A card portraying an All Star player of the previous year that says "All Star" on its face.

**ALPH.** Alphabetical.

**AS.** Abbreviation for All Star (card).

**ATG.** All Time Great card.

**AUTOGRAPHED CARD.** A card that has been signed (usually on the front of the card) by the player portrayed on the card with a fountain pen, felt tip, magic marker, or ball-point pen. This term does not include stamped or facsimile autographed cards.

**BLANKET.** A felt square (normally 5" to 6") portraying a baseball player.

**BOX.** A card issued on a box or a card depicting a boxer.

**BRICK.** A group of cards, usually 50 or more and having some common characteristics, that is intended to be bought, sold, or traded as a unit.

**C.** Abbreviation for catcher.

**CABINETS.** Very popular and highly valuable cards on thick card stock produced in the nineteenth and early twentieth century.

**CF.** Abbreviation for centerfielder.

**CHECKLIST.** A list of the cards contained in a particular set. The list is always in numerical order if the cards are numbered. Some unnumbered sets are artificially numbered in alphabetical order, or by team and alphabetical within the team for convenience.

**CHECKLIST CARD.** A card which lists in order the cards and players in the set or series. Older checklist cards in mint condition which have not been checked off are very desirable.

**CL.** Abbreviation for checklist.

**COA.** Abbreviation for coach.

**COIN.** A small disc of metal or plastic portraying a player in its center.

**COLLECTOR.** A person who engages in the hobby of collecting cards primarily for his own enjoyment, with any profit motive being secondary.

**COLLECTOR ISSUE.** A set produced for the sake of the card itself, with no product or service sponsor. It derives its name from the fact that most of these sets are produced by collectors/dealers.

**COMBINATION CARD.** A single card depicting two or more players (but not a team card).

**COMMON CARD.** The typical card of any set; it has no premium value accruing from subject matter, numerical scarcity, popular demand, or anomaly.

**COMP.** A card issued by the (Post Cereal) Company through their mail in offer.

**CONVENTION.** A large weekend gathering at one location of dealers and collectors for the purpose of buying, selling, and sometimes trading of sports memorabilia items. Conventions are open to the public and sometimes feature celebrities, door prizes, films, contests, etc.

**CONVENTION ISSUE.** A set produced in conjunction with a sports collectibles convention to commemorate or promote the show.

**COR.** Correct or corrected card.

**COUPON.** See Tab.

**CREASE.** A wrinkle on the card, usually caused by bending the card. Creases are a common defect in cards usually caused by careless collectors.

**CY.** Cy Young Award.

**DEALER.** A person who engages in buying, selling, and trading sports collectibles or supplies. A dealer may also be a collector but, as a dealer, he anticipates a profit.

**DH.** Double Header (1955 Topps) or Designated Hitter.

**DIE-CUT.** A card on which the stock is partially cut, allowing one or more parts to be folded or removed. After removal or appropriate folding, the remaining part of the card can frequently be made to stand up.

**DISC.** A circular shaped card.

**DISPLAY CARD.** A sheet, usually containing three to nine cards, that is printed and used by the manufacturer to advertise and/or display the packages containing his products and cards. The backs of display cards are blank or contain advertisements.

**DK.** Diamond King (artwork produced by Perez-Steele for Donruss).

**DP.** Double Print. A card which was printed in double the quantity compared to the other cards in the same series.

**E CARD.** A candy or gum card produced and issued prior to 1930.

**ERA.** Earned Run Average.

**ERR.** Error card (see also COR).

**ERROR CARD.** A card with erroneous information, spelling, or depiction on either side of the card. Note that not all errors are corrected by the producing card company.

**EXHIBIT.** The generic name given to thick stock, postcard-sized cards with single color, obverse pictures. The name is derived from the Exhibit Supply Co. of Chicago, the principal manufacturer of this type of card. These are also known as Arcade cards, as they were found in many arcades.

**FDP.** First Draft Pick (see 1985 Topps Baseball).

**FULL SHEET.** (Also called an uncut sheet.) A complete sheet of cards that has not been cut up into individual cards by the manufacturer.

**HALL OF FAMER.** (HOF'er) A card which portrays a player who has been inducted into the Hall of Fame.

**HIGH NUMBER.** The cards in the last series of numbers in a year in which these higher-numbered cards were printed or distributed in significantly lesser amounts than the lower numbered cards. The high-number designation refers to a scarcity of the high-numbered cards. Not all years have high numbers in terms of this definition.

**HL.** Highlight card.

**HOC.** House of Collectibles.

**HOF.** Acronym for Hall of Fame.

**HOR.** Horizontal pose on card as opposed to the more standard vertical orientation found on most cards.

**HR.** Abbreviation for home run.

**IA.** In Action (type of card).

**INF.** Abbreviation for infielder.

**INSERT.** A card of a different type, e.g., a poster, or any other sports collectible contained and sold in the same package along with a card or cards of a major set.

**ISSUE.** Synonymous with set, but usually used in conjunction with a manufacturer, e.g., a Topps issue.

**KP.** Kid Picture (a sub-series issued in the Topps baseball sets of 1972 and 1973).

**LAYERING.** The separation or peeling of one or more layers of the card stock, usually at the corner of the card.

**LEGITIMATE ISSUE.** A set produced to promote or boost sales of a product or service, e.g., bubble gum, cereal, cigarettes, etc. Most collector issues are not legitimate issues in this sense.

**LHP.** Left Handed Pitcher.

**LID.** A circular (possibly with tab) shaped card that forms the top of the container for the product being promoted.

**LL.** Living Legends (Donruss 1984) or large letters.

**MAJOR SET.** A set produced by a national manufacturer of cards containing a large number of cards. Usually 100 or more different cards are in the set.

**MGR.** Abbreviation for manager.

**MINI.** A small card; specifically, a Topps baseball card of identical design but smaller dimensions than the regular Topps issue of 1975.

**MISCUT.** A card that has been cut particularly unevenly at the manufacturer's cutting stage.

**ML.** Major League.

**MVP.** Most Valuable Player.

**N CARD.** A tobacco card produced and issued during the nineteenth century.

**NL.** National League.

**NNOF.** No Name on Front (see 1949 Bowman).

**NOF.** Name on Front (see 1949 Bowman).

**NON-SPORT CARD.** A card from a set whose major theme is a subject other than a sports subject. A card of a sports figure or event that is part of a non-sport set is still a non-sport card, e.g., while the Look 'N' See non-sport card set contains a card of Babe Ruth, a sports figure, the card is a non-sport card.

**NOTCHING.** The grooving of the edge of a card, usually caused by the fingernail, rubber bands, or bumping the edge against another object.

**NY.** New York.

**OBVERSE.** The front, face, or pictured side of the card.

**OF.** Outfielder.

**OLY.** Olympics (see 1985 Topps Baseball; the members of the 1984 U.S. Olympic Baseball team were a featured sub-series).

**OPT.** Option.

**P.** Pitcher or Pitching pose.

**P1.** First printing.

**P2.** Second printing.

**P3.** Third printing.

**PANEL.** An extended card that is composed of two or more individual cards. Often the panel forms the back part of the container for the product being promoted, e.g., a Hostess panel, a Bazooka panel, an Esskay Meat panel.

**PCL.** Pacific Coast League.

**PG.** Price Guide.

**PLASTIC SHEET.** A clear, vinyl, plastic page which is punched for insertion into a binder with standard 3-ring spacing, containing pockets for insertion of cards. Many different styles of sheets exist with pockets of varying sizes to hold the many different sizes of cards.

**PREMIUM.** A card, sometimes on photographic stock, that is purchased or obtained in conjunction with, or redemption for, another card or product. The premium is not packaged in the same unit as the primary item.

**PUZZLE CARD.** A card whose back contains a part of a picture which, when joined correctly with other puzzle cards, forms the complete picture.

**PUZZLE PIECE.** An actual die-cut piece designed to interlock with similar pieces.

**R CARD.** A candy or gum card produced and issued after 1930.

**RARE.** A card or series of cards of very limited availability. Unfortunately, rare is a subjective term sometimes used indiscriminately. Rare cards are harder to obtain than scarce cards.

**RB.** Record Breaker card.

**RBI.** Runs Batted In.

**REGIONAL.** A card issued and distributed only in a limited area of the country. The producer is not a major, national producer of trading cards.

**REPRINT.** A reproduction of an original card, usually produced by a maker other than the original manufacturer from a source other than the original artwork or negative.

**REVERSE.** The back or narrative side of the card.

**RHP.** Right Handed Pitcher.

**ROOKIE CARD.** The first regular card of a particular player or a card which portrays one or more players, with the notation on the card that these players are rookies.

**ROY.** Acronym for Rookie of the Year.

**RR.** Rated Rookies, a subset featured in the Donruss baseball sets.

**SA.** Super Action or Sport Americana.

**SASE.** Self-Addressed Stamped Envelope.

**SB.** Stolen Bases.

**SCARCE.** A card or series of cards of limited availability. This subjective term is sometimes used indiscriminately to promote or hype value. Scarce cards are not as difficult to obtain as rare cards.

**SCR.** Script name on back (see 1949 Bowman Baseball).

**SEMI-HIGH.** A card from the next to last series of a sequentially issued set. It has more value than an average card and generally has less value than a high number. A card is not called a semi-high unless the next to last series in which it exists has an additional premium attached to it.

**SERIES.** The entire set of cards issued by a particular producer in a particular year, e.g., the 1971 Topps series. Also, within a particular set, series can refer to a group of consecutively numbered cards printed at the same time, e.g., the first series of the 1957 Topps issue (numbers 1 through 88).

**SET.** One each of the entire run of cards of the same type produced by a particular manufacturer during a single year. In other words, if you have a complete set of 1976 Topps, then you have every card from number 1 up through number 660, i.e., all the different cards that were produced.

**SF.** San Francisco.

**SKIP-NUMBERED.** A set that has many card numbers not issued between the lowest number in the set and the highest number in the set, e.g., the 1948 Leaf baseball set contains 98 cards skip-numbered from number 1 to number 168. A major set in which a few numbers were not printed is not considered to be skip-numbered.

**SO.** Strikeouts.

**SP.** Single or Short Print. A card which was printed in lesser quantity compared to the other cards in the same series; see also DP and TP.

**SPECIAL CARD.** A card that portrays something other than a single player or team, e.g., a card that portrays the previous year's statistical leaders or the results from the previous year's post-season action.

**SS.** Abbreviation for shortstop.

**STAMP.** Adhesive-backed papers depicting a player. The stamp may be individual or in a sheet of many stamps. Moisture must be applied to the adhesive in order for the stamp to be attached to another surface.

**STAR CARD.** A card that portrays a player of some repute, usually determined by his ability, although sometimes referring to sheer popularity.

**STICKER.** A card with a removable layer that can be adhered to another surface.

**STOCK.** The cardboard or paper on which the card is printed.

**STRIP CARDS.** A sheet or strip of cards, particularly popular in the 1920's and 1930's, with the individual cards usually separated by a broken or dotted line.

**SUPERSTAR CARD.** A card that portrays a superstar, e.g., a Hall of Fame member or a certain future Hall of Fame member.

**SV.** Super Veteran.

**T CARD.** A tobacco card produced and issued during the twentieth century.

**TAB.** A part of a card set off from the rest of the card, usually with perforations, that may be removed without damaging the central character or event depicted by the card.

**TBC.** Turn Back the Clock cards.

**TEAM CARD.** A card which depicts an entire team.

**TEST SET.** A set, usually containing a small number of cards, issued by a national card producer and distributed in a limited section or sections of the country. Presumably, the purpose of a test set is to test market appeal for this particular type of card.

**TL.** Team Leader card.

**TP.** Triple Print. A card which was printed in triple the quantity compared to the other cards in the same series.

**TR.** Trade or Traded.

**TRIMMED.** A card cut down from its original size. Trimmed cards are undesirable to most collectors.

**UMP.** Umpire (see 1955 Bowman Baseball last series).

**VARIATION.** One of two or more cards from the same series with the same number (or player with identical pose if the series is unnumbered) differing from one another by some aspect, the different feature stemming from the printing or stock of the card, not from an alteration. This can be caused when the manufacturer of the cards notices an error in one (or more) of the cards, makes the changes, and then resumes the print run. In this case there will be two versions or variations of the same card. Sometimes one of the variations is relatively scarce.

**VERT.** Vertical pose on card.

**W CARD.** A card grouped within a general miscellaneous category by the ACC. Included in this category are exhibits, strip cards, team issues, and those issues which do not conveniently fall into other established categories.

**WASH.** Washington.

**WL.** White Letters (see 1969 Topps Baseball).

**WS.** World Series card.

**YL.** Yellow Letters (see 1958 Topps Baseball).

**YT.** Yellow Team (see 1958 Topps Baseball).

**1B.** First Base or First Baseman.

**2B.** Second Base or Second Baseman.

**3B.** Third Base or Third Baseman.

# ADDITIONAL READING

Other literature on the collecting hobby can be divided into two categories: books and periodicals. We have furnished a listing for both books and periodicals that we feel would further your knowledge and enjoyment.

## BOOKS AVAILABLE

Many of the reference books listed below have stood the test of time and are considered useful by collectors in spite of the elapsed years since their publication.

### The Encyclopedia of Baseball Cards, Volume I: 19th Century Cards.
Author and Publisher: Lew Lipset, released 1983. Everything you ever wanted to know about nineteenth century cards.

### The Encyclopedia of Baseball Cards, Volume II: Early Gum and Candy Cards.
Author and Publisher: Lew Lipset, released 1984. Everything you ever wanted to know about early candy and gum cards.

### Hockey Card Checklist and Price Guide, Fifth Edition.
Author and Publisher: Cartophilium (Andrew Pywowarczuk). This book contains the most complete list of hockey card checklists ever assembled, including a listing of Bee Hive photos.

### The Official Price Guide to Football Cards.
Dr. James Beckett, Third Edition, $4.95, released 1985, published by House of Collectibles. *The Official Price Guide* is an abridgement of the *Sport Americana Price Guide* in a convenient pocket-size format, providing Dr. Beckett's pricing of the major football sets since 1948.

### The Sport Americana Alphabetical Baseball Card Checklist.
Dr. James Beckett and Dennis W. Eckes, Second Edition, co-published by Den's Collectors Den and Edgewater Book Company. An illustrated, alphabetical listing, by the last name of the player portrayed on the card, of virtually all baseball cards produced up to 1983.

### The Sport Americana Baseball Address List.
Jack Smalling and Dennis W. Eckes, Third Edition, released 1984, co-published by Den's Collectors Den and Edgewater Book Company. This third edition is the definitive guide for autograph hunters giving addresses and deceased information for virtually all major league baseball players past and present.

### The Sport Americana Baseball Card Team Checklist.
Jeff Fritsch and Dennis W. Eckes, co-published by Den's Collectors Den and Edgewater Book Company. Includes all Topps, Bowman, Fleer, Play Ball, Goudey, and Donruss cards, with the players portrayed on the cards listed with the teams for whom they played. The book is invaluable to the collector who specializes in an individual team, as it is the most complete baseball card team checklist available.

### The Sport Americana Baseball Memorabilia and Autograph Price Guide.
Dr. James Beckett and Dennis W. Eckes, First Edition, co-published by Den's Collectors Den and Edgewater Book Company. This book is the most defini-

tive book ever produced on baseball memorabilia other than baseball cards. Over one year in the making, this book attempts to present in an illustrated, logical fashion information on baseball memorabilia and autographs which had been heretofore not available to the collector.

### The Sport Americana Football, Hockey, Basketball and Boxing Card Price Guide.

Dr. James Beckett, Fourth Edition, $11.95, released 1985, published by Edgewater Book Company. *The Sport Americana Football Card Price Guide* is the most comprehensive price guide/checklist ever issued on football cards. No serious hobbyist should be without it.

### The Sport Americana Price Guide to the Non-Sports Cards.

Christopher Benjamin and Dennis W. Eckes, Second Edition, released 1983, co-published by Den's Collectors Den and Edgewater Book Company. This second edition is the definitive guide on all popular non-sports American tobacco and bubble gum cards. In addition to cards, illustrations and prices for wrappers are also included.

## PERIODICALS AVAILABLE

There are several magazines and periodicals about the card collecting hobby which are published monthly, bi-weekly, quarterly, etc. One (or more) of those listed below should be just right for you.

### Baseball Cards.

Published by Krause Publications. A sharp-looking quarterly magazine with interior color and mix of features and ads.

### Baseball Card News.

Published by Krause Publications. A monthly tabloid format with good mix of editorials, features, and ads.

### Baseball Hobby News.

Published by Frank and Vivian Barning. A monthly tabloid newspaper format with good mix of news, editorials, features, and ads.

### Beckett Baseball Card Monthly.

Authored and edited by Dr. James Beckett. Contains the most extensive and accepted monthly price guide, feature articles, who's hot and who's not section, convention calendar, numerous letters to and from the editor. It is the hobby's fastest-growing magazine.

### Sports Collectors Digest.

Published by Krause Publications. A bi-weekly tabloid issue loaded with ads.

# GRADING YOUR CARDS

Each hobby has its own grading terminology—stamps, coins, comic books, beer cans, right down the line. The collectors of sports cards are no exception. The one absolute criterion for determining the value of a card is its condition: the better the condition of the card, the more valuable it is. However, condition grading is very subjective. Individual card dealers and collectors differ in the strictness of their grading. The stated condition of a card should be determined without regard to whether it is being bought or sold.

The physical defects which lower the condition of a card are usually quite apparent, but each individual places his own value (negative value in this case) on the defects. We present the condition guide for use in determining values listed in this price guide.

The defects listed in the condition guide below are those either placed in the card at the time of printing—uneven borders, out of focus pictures—or those defects that occur to a card under normal handling—corner sharpness, gloss, edge wear—and finally, environmental conditions—browning. Other defects found on cards are inflicted by human carelessness and in all cases should be noted separately and in addition to the condition grade. Among the more common alterations are tape, tape stains, rubber-band marks, water damage, smoke damage, trimming, paste, tears, writing, pin or tack holes, any back damage, and missing parts (tabs, tops, coupons, backgrounds).

Rather than confuse the issue further let us present the Condition Guide used for values in this Price Guide.

# CONDITION GUIDE

**MINT (M OR MT).** A card with no defects. The card has sharp corners, even borders, original gloss or shine on the surface, sharp focus of the picture, smooth edges, no signs of wear, and white borders. There is no allowance made for the age of the card.

**EXCELLENT (EX OR E).** A card with very minor defects. Any of the following qualities would be sufficient to lower the grade of a card from mint to the excellent category: very slight rounding or layering at some of the corners, a very small amount of the original gloss lost, minor wear on the edges, slight unevenness of the borders, slight wear visible only on close inspection, slight off-whiteness of the borders.

**VERY GOOD (VG).** A card that has been handled but not abused. Some rounding at all corners, slight layering or scuffing at one or two corners, slight notching on edges, gloss lost from the surface but not scuffed, borders might be somewhat uneven but some white is visible on all borders, noticeable yellowing or browning of borders, pictures may be slightly off focus.

**GOOD (G).** A well-handled card, rounding and some layering at the corners, scuffing at the corners and minor scuffing on the face, borders noticeably uneven and browning, loss of gloss on the face, notching on the edges.

**FAIR (F).** Round and layering corners, brown and dirty borders, frayed edges, noticeable scuffing on the face, white not visible on one or more borders, cloudy focus.

**POOR (P).** An abused card, the lowest grade of card, frequently some major physical alteration has been performed on the card, collectible only as a fill-in until a better condition replacement can be obtained.

Categories between these major condition grades are frequently used, such as very good to excellent (VG-E), fair to good (F-G), etc. The grades indicate a card with all qualities at least in the lower of the two categories, but with several qualities in the higher of the two categories.

The most common physical defect in a trading card is the crease or wrinkle. The crease may vary from a slight crease barely noticeable at one corner of the card to a major crease across the entire card. Therefore, the degree that a crease lowers the value of the card depends on the type and number of creases. On giving the condition of a card, creases should be noted separately. If the crease is noticeable only upon close inspection under bright light, an otherwise mint card could be called excellent; whereas noticeable but light creases would lower most otherwise mint cards into the VG category. A heavily creased card could be classified fair at best.

# PRICES IN THIS BOOK

Prices found in this guide reflect current retail rates just prior to the printing of this book. They do not reflect the FOR SALE prices of the author, the publisher, the distributors, the advertisers or any card dealers associated with this guide. No one is any way obligated to buy, sell, or trade his or her cards based on these prices. The price listings were compiled by the author from actual buy/sell transactions at sports conventions, buy/sell advertisements in the hobby papers, for sale prices from dealer catalogs and price lists, and discussions with leading hobbyists in the United States and Canada. All prices are U.S. prices in U.S. dollars.

# INTERESTING NOTES

The numerical first card of an issue is the single card most likely to obtain excessive wear; consequently, you will typically find the price on the number one card somewhat higher than its inherent status would seem to justify. Similarly, but to a lesser extent, the numerical last card in an issue is also prone to abnormal wear, because the first and last cards are exposed to the elements (human element included) more than any other cards. They are generally end cards in any brick formations, rubber bandings, stackings on wet surfaces, and the like.

Sports cards have no intrinsic value. The value of a card, like the value of other collectibles, can only be assessed by you and your enjoyment in viewing and possessing these cardboard swatches.

Remember, you, the buyer, ultimately determine the price of each baseball card. You are the determining price factor in that you have ability to say "no" to the price of any card by not exchanging your hard-earned money for a given card. When the cost of a trading card exceeds the enjoyment or utility you will receive from it, your answer should be "no." We assess and report the prices. You set them!

We are always interested in receiving price input from collectors and dealers from around the country; we happily credit major contributions. We welcome your opinions; your contributions assist us in ensuring a better guide each year. If you would like to join our survey list for the next edition of this book, and others authored by Dr. Beckett, please send your name and address to Dr. James Beckett, 4214 Spring Valley, Dallas, Texas 75244.

# ADVERTISING

Within the *Price Guide*, you will find advertisements for sports memorabilia material, mail order, and retail sports collectibles establishments. All advertisements were accepted in good faith based on the reputation of the advertiser; however, neither the author, the publisher, the distributors, nor the other advertisers in the *Price Guide* accept any responsibility for any particular advertiser not complying with the terms of his or her ad.

Should you come into contact with any of the advertisers in this guide as a result of their advertisement herein, please mention to them this source as your contact.

# 1952 TOPPS

The cards in this 407 card set measure 2⅝" by 3¾". The 1952 Topps set is Topps" first truly major set. Card numbers 1 to 80 were issued with red or black backs, both of which are less plentiful than card numbers 81 to 250. Card number 48 (Joe Page) and number 49 (Johnny Sain) can be found with each other's write-up on their back. Card numbers 251 to 310 are somewhat scarce and numbers 311 to 407 are quite scarce. Cards 281–300 were single-printed compared to the other cards in the next to last series. Cards 311–313 were double-printed on the last high number printing sheet.

COMPLETE SET: M-15000.00; VG-E-7000.00;
F-G-1500.00

|  | MINT | VG-E | F-G |
|---|---|---|---|
| Common Player (1–80) . . . . | 8.00 | 3.00 | .75 |
| Common Player (81–250) . . . . . . . . . . | 5.50 | 2.25 | .50 |
| Common Player (251–280) . . . . . . . . . . | 12.00 | 5.00 | 1.25 |
| Common Player (281–300) . . . . . . . . . . | 18.00 | 7.50 | 1.75 |
| Common Player (301–310) . . . . . . . . . . | 12.00 | 5.00 | 1.25 |
| Common Player (311–407) . . . . . . . . . . | 65.00 | 27.00 | 6.00 |

|  |  | MINT | VG-E | F-G |
|---|---|---|---|---|
| ☐ | 1 Andy Pafko . . . . . . . . . | 225.00 | 10.00 | 2.00 |
| ☐ | 2 James Runnels . . . . . . | 9.00 | 4.25 | .90 |
| ☐ | 3 Henry Thompson . . . . | 9.00 | 4.25 | .90 |
| ☐ | 4 Don Lenhardt . . . . . . . | 8.00 | 3.00 | .75 |
| ☐ | 5 Larry Jansen . . . . . . . . | 8.00 | 3.00 | .75 |
| ☐ | 6 Grady Hatton . . . . . . . | 8.00 | 3.00 | .75 |
| ☐ | 7 Wayne Terwilliger . . . | 8.00 | 3.00 | .75 |
| ☐ | 8 Fred Marsh . . . . . . . . . | 8.00 | 3.00 | .75 |
| ☐ | 9 Robert Hogue . . . . . . . | 8.00 | 3.00 | .75 |
| ☐ | 10 Al Rosen . . . . . . . . . . | 12.00 | 5.50 | 1.20 |
| ☐ | 11 Phil Rizzuto . . . . . . . . | 30.00 | 14.00 | 3.00 |
| ☐ | 12 Romanus Basgall . . . | 8.00 | 3.00 | .75 |
| ☐ | 13 Johnny Wyrostek . . . | 8.00 | 3.00 | .75 |
| ☐ | 14 Bob Elliott . . . . . . . . | 9.00 | 4.25 | .90 |
| ☐ | 15 Johnny Pesky . . . . . . | 9.00 | 4.25 | .90 |
| ☐ | 16 Gene Hermanski . . . . | 8.00 | 3.00 | .75 |
| ☐ | 17 Jim Hegan . . . . . . . . . | 9.00 | 4.25 | .90 |
| ☐ | 18 Merrill Combs . . . . . . | 8.00 | 3.00 | .75 |
| ☐ | 19 Johnny Bucha . . . . . . | 8.00 | 3.00 | .75 |
| ☐ | 20 Billy Loes . . . . . . . . . | 9.00 | 4.25 | .90 |
| ☐ | 21 Ferris Fain . . . . . . . . | 9.00 | 4.25 | .90 |
| ☐ | 22 Dom DiMaggio . . . . . | 12.00 | 5.50 | 1.20 |
| ☐ | 23 Billy Goodman . . . . . | 9.00 | 4.25 | .90 |
| ☐ | 24 Luke Easter . . . . . . . | 9.00 | 4.25 | .90 |
| ☐ | 25 John Groth . . . . . . . . | 8.00 | 3.00 | .75 |
| ☐ | 26 Monte Irvin . . . . . . . | 14.00 | 6.50 | 1.40 |
| ☐ | 27 Sam Jethroe . . . . . . . | 8.00 | 3.00 | .75 |
| ☐ | 28 Jerry Priddy . . . . . . . | 8.00 | 3.00 | .75 |
| ☐ | 29 Ted Kluszewski . . . . . | 12.00 | 5.50 | 1.20 |
| ☐ | 30 Mel Parnell . . . . . . . . | 9.00 | 4.25 | .90 |
| ☐ | 31 Gus Zernial . . . . . . . . | 9.00 | 4.25 | .90 |
| ☐ | 32 Eddie Robinson . . . . . | 8.00 | 3.00 | .75 |
| ☐ | 33 Warren Spahn . . . . . . | 30.00 | 14.00 | 3.00 |
| ☐ | 34 Elmer Valo . . . . . . . . | 8.00 | 3.00 | .75 |
| ☐ | 35 Hank Sauer . . . . . . . . | 10.00 | 4.75 | 1.00 |
| ☐ | 36 Gil Hodges . . . . . . . . | 25.00 | 11.00 | 2.50 |
| ☐ | 37 Duke Snider . . . . . . . | 45.00 | 20.00 | 4.50 |
| ☐ | 38 Wally Westlake . . . . . | 8.00 | 3.00 | .75 |
| ☐ | 39 Dizzy Trout . . . . . . . | 8.00 | 3.00 | .75 |
| ☐ | 40 Irv Noren . . . . . . . . . | 8.00 | 3.00 | .75 |
| ☐ | 41 Bob Wellman . . . . . . | 8.00 | 3.00 | .75 |
| ☐ | 42 Lou Kretlow . . . . . . . | 8.00 | 3.00 | .75 |
| ☐ | 43 Ray Scarborough . . . | 8.00 | 3.00 | .75 |
| ☐ | 44 Con Dempsey . . . . . . | 8.00 | 3.00 | .75 |
| ☐ | 45 Eddie Joost . . . . . . . | 8.00 | 3.00 | .75 |
| ☐ | 46 Gordon Goldsberry . . | 8.00 | 3.00 | .75 |
| ☐ | 47 Willie Jones . . . . . . . | 8.00 | 3.00 | .75 |
| ☐ | 48 A Joe Page COR . . . . | 12.00 | 5.50 | 1.20 |
| ☐ | 48 B Joe Page ERR . . . . | 90.00 | 42.00 | 9.00 |
| ☐ | 49 A Johnny Sain COR . . | 14.00 | 6.50 | 1.40 |
| ☐ | 49 B Johnny Sain ERR . . | 90.00 | 42.00 | 9.00 |
| ☐ | 50 Marv Rickert . . . . . . | 8.00 | 3.00 | .75 |
| ☐ | 51 Jim Russell . . . . . . . . | 8.00 | 3.00 | .75 |
| ☐ | 52 Don Mueller . . . . . . . | 9.00 | 4.25 | .90 |
| ☐ | 53 Chris Van Cuyk . . . . | 8.00 | 3.00 | .75 |
| ☐ | 54 Leo Kiely . . . . . . . . . | 8.00 | 3.00 | .75 |
| ☐ | 55 Ray Boone . . . . . . . . | 9.00 | 4.25 | .90 |

| | MINT | VG-E | F-G |
|---|---|---|---|
| 56 Thomas Glaviano | 8.00 | 3.00 | .75 |
| 57 Ed Lopat | 12.00 | 5.50 | 1.20 |
| 58 Bob Mahoney | 8.00 | 3.00 | .75 |
| 59 Robin Roberts | 20.00 | 9.00 | 2.00 |
| 60 Sid Hudson | 8.00 | 3.00 | .75 |
| 61 Tookie Gilbert | 8.00 | 3.00 | .75 |
| 62 Chuck Stobbs | 8.00 | 3.00 | .75 |
| 63 Howie Pollett | 8.00 | 3.00 | .75 |
| 64 Roy Sievers | 9.00 | 4.25 | .90 |
| 65 Enos Slaughter | 20.00 | 9.00 | 2.00 |
| 66 Preacher Roe | 12.00 | 5.50 | 1.20 |
| 67 Allie Reynolds | 12.00 | 5.50 | 1.20 |
| 68 Cliff Chambers | 8.00 | 3.00 | .75 |
| 69 Virgil Stallcup | 8.00 | 3.00 | .75 |
| 70 Al Zarilla | 8.00 | 3.00 | .75 |
| 71 Tom Upton | 8.00 | 3.00 | .75 |
| 72 Karl Olson | 8.00 | 3.00 | .75 |
| 73 William Werle | 8.00 | 3.00 | .75 |
| 74 Andy Hansen | 8.00 | 3.00 | .75 |
| 75 Wes Westrum | 8.00 | 3.00 | .75 |
| 76 Eddie Stanky | 9.00 | 4.25 | .90 |
| 77 Bob Kennedy | 9.00 | 4.25 | .90 |
| 78 Ellis Kinder | 8.00 | 3.00 | .75 |
| 79 Gerald Staley | 8.00 | 3.00 | .75 |
| 80 Herman Wehmeier | 8.00 | 3.00 | .75 |
| 81 Vernon Law | 6.50 | 3.00 | .65 |
| 82 Duane Pillette | 5.50 | 2.25 | .50 |
| 83 Billy Johnson | 5.50 | 2.25 | .50 |
| 84 Vern Stephens | 6.50 | 3.00 | .65 |
| 85 Bob Kuzava | 5.50 | 2.25 | .50 |
| 86 Ted Gray | 5.50 | 2.25 | .50 |
| 87 Dale Coogan | 5.50 | 2.25 | .50 |
| 88 Bob Feller | 30.00 | 14.00 | 3.00 |
| 89 Johnny Lipon | 5.50 | 2.25 | .50 |
| 90 Mickey Grasso | 5.50 | 2.25 | .50 |
| 91 Red Schoendienst | 8.00 | 3.75 | .80 |
| 92 Dale Mitchell | 6.50 | 3.00 | .65 |
| 93 Al Sima | 5.50 | 2.25 | .50 |
| 94 Sam Mele | 5.50 | 2.25 | .50 |
| 95 Ken Holcombe | 5.50 | 2.25 | .50 |
| 96 Willard Marshall | 5.50 | 2.25 | .50 |
| 97 Earl Torgeson | 5.50 | 2.25 | .50 |
| 98 Billy Pierce | 6.50 | 3.00 | .65 |
| 99 Gene Woodling | 6.50 | 3.00 | .65 |
| 100 Del Rice | 5.50 | 2.25 | .50 |
| 101 Max Lanier | 5.50 | 2.25 | .50 |
| 102 Bill Kennedy | 5.50 | 2.25 | .50 |
| 103 Cliff Mapes | 5.50 | 2.25 | .50 |
| 104 Don Kolloway | 5.50 | 2.25 | .50 |
| 105 John Pramesa | 5.50 | 2.25 | .50 |
| 106 Mickey Vernon | 6.50 | 3.00 | .65 |
| 107 Connie Ryan | 5.50 | 2.25 | .50 |
| 108 Jim Konstanty | 6.50 | 3.00 | .65 |

| | MINT | VG-E | F-G |
|---|---|---|---|
| 109 Ted Wilks | 5.50 | 2.25 | .50 |
| 110 Dutch Leonard | 5.50 | 2.25 | .50 |
| 111 Peanuts Lowrey | 5.50 | 2.25 | .50 |
| 112 Henry Majeski | 5.50 | 2.25 | .50 |
| 113 Dick Sisler | 5.50 | 2.25 | .50 |
| 114 Willard Ramsdell | 5.50 | 2.25 | .50 |
| 115 Red Munger | 5.50 | 2.25 | .50 |
| 116 Carl Scheib | 5.50 | 2.25 | .50 |
| 117 Sherman Lollar | 6.50 | 3.00 | .65 |
| 118 Ken Raffensberger | 5.50 | 2.25 | .50 |
| 119 Mickey McDermott | 5.50 | 2.25 | .50 |
| 120 Bob Chakales | 5.50 | 2.25 | .50 |
| 121 Gus Niarhos | 5.50 | 2.25 | .50 |
| 122 Jackie Jensen | 10.00 | 4.75 | 1.00 |
| 123 Eddie Yost | 6.50 | 3.00 | .65 |
| 124 Monte Kennedy | 5.50 | 2.25 | .50 |
| 125 Bill Rigney | 5.50 | 2.25 | .50 |
| 126 Fred Hutchinson | 6.50 | 3.00 | .65 |
| 127 Paul Minner | 5.50 | 2.25 | .50 |
| 128 Don Bollweg | 5.50 | 2.25 | .50 |
| 129 Johnny Mize | 16.00 | 7.50 | 1.60 |
| 130 Sheldon Jones | 5.50 | 2.25 | .50 |
| 131 Morris Martin | 5.50 | 2.25 | .50 |
| 132 Clyde Klutz | 5.50 | 2.25 | .50 |
| 133 Al Widmar | 5.50 | 2.25 | .50 |
| 134 Joe Tipton | 5.50 | 2.25 | .50 |
| 135 Dixie Howell | 5.50 | 2.25 | .50 |
| 136 Johnny Schmitz | 5.50 | 2.25 | .50 |
| 137 Roy McMillan | 5.50 | 2.25 | .50 |
| 138 Bill MacDonald | 5.50 | 2.25 | .50 |
| 139 Ken Wood | 5.50 | 2.25 | .50 |
| 140 Johnny Antonelli | 6.50 | 3.00 | .65 |
| 141 Clint Hartung | 5.50 | 2.25 | .50 |
| 142 Harry Perkowski | 5.50 | 2.25 | .50 |
| 143 Les Moss | 5.50 | 2.25 | .50 |
| 144 Ed Blake | 5.50 | 2.25 | .50 |
| 145 Joe Haynes | 5.50 | 2.25 | .50 |
| 146 Frank House | 5.50 | 2.25 | .50 |
| 147 Bob Young | 5.50 | 2.25 | .50 |
| 148 Johnny Klippstein | 5.50 | 2.25 | .50 |
| 149 Dick Kryhoski | 5.50 | 2.25 | .50 |
| 150 Ted Beard | 5.50 | 2.25 | .50 |
| 151 Wally Post | 5.50 | 2.25 | .50 |
| 152 Al Evans | 5.50 | 2.25 | .50 |
| 153 Bob Rush | 5.50 | 2.25 | .50 |
| 154 Joe Muir | 5.50 | 2.25 | .50 |
| 155 Frank Overmire | 5.50 | 2.25 | .50 |
| 156 Frank Hiller | 5.50 | 2.25 | .50 |
| 157 Bob Usher | 5.50 | 2.25 | .50 |
| 158 Eddie Waitkus | 5.50 | 2.25 | .50 |
| 159 Saul Rogovin | 5.50 | 2.25 | .50 |
| 160 Owen Friend | 5.50 | 2.25 | .50 |
| 161 Bud Byerly | 5.50 | 2.25 | .50 |

| | MINT | VG-E | F-G |
|---|---|---|---|
| ☐ 162 Del Crandall | 6.50 | 3.00 | .65 |
| ☐ 163 Stan Rojek | 5.50 | 2.25 | .50 |
| ☐ 164 Walt Dubiel | 5.50 | 2.25 | .50 |
| ☐ 165 Eddie Kazak | 5.50 | 2.25 | .50 |
| ☐ 166 Paul LaPalme | 5.50 | 2.25 | .50 |
| ☐ 167 Bill Howerton | 5.50 | 2.25 | .50 |
| ☐ 168 Charlie Silvera | 5.50 | 2.25 | .50 |
| ☐ 169 Howie Judson | 5.50 | 2.25 | .50 |
| ☐ 170 Gus Bell | 6.50 | 3.00 | .65 |
| ☐ 171 Ed Erautt | 5.50 | 2.25 | .50 |
| ☐ 172 Eddie Miksis | 5.50 | 2.25 | .50 |
| ☐ 173 Roy Smalley | 5.50 | 2.25 | .50 |
| ☐ 174 Clarence Marshall | 5.50 | 2.25 | .50 |
| ☐ 175 Billy Martin | 40.00 | 18.00 | 4.00 |
| ☐ 176 Hank Edwards | 5.50 | 2.25 | .50 |
| ☐ 177 Bill Wight | 5.50 | 2.25 | .50 |
| ☐ 178 Cass Michaels | 5.50 | 2.25 | .50 |
| ☐ 179 Frank Smith | 5.50 | 2.25 | .50 |
| ☐ 180 Charley Maxwell | 5.50 | 2.25 | .50 |
| ☐ 181 Bob Swift | 5.50 | 2.25 | .50 |
| ☐ 182 Billy Hitchcock | 5.50 | 2.25 | .50 |
| ☐ 183 Erv Dusak | 5.50 | 2.25 | .50 |
| ☐ 184 Bob Ramazotti | 5.50 | 2.25 | .50 |
| ☐ 185 Bill Nicholson | 5.50 | 2.25 | .50 |
| ☐ 186 Walt Masterson | 5.50 | 2.25 | .50 |
| ☐ 187 Bob Miller | 5.50 | 2.25 | .50 |
| ☐ 188 Clarence Podbielan | 5.50 | 2.25 | .50 |
| ☐ 189 Pete Reiser | 6.50 | 3.00 | .65 |
| ☐ 190 Don Johnson | 5.50 | 2.25 | .50 |
| ☐ 191 Yogi Berra | 55.00 | 25.00 | 5.50 |
| ☐ 192 Myron Ginsberg | 5.50 | 2.25 | .50 |
| ☐ 193 Harry Simpson | 5.50 | 2.25 | .50 |
| ☐ 194 Joe Hatton | 5.50 | 2.25 | .50 |
| ☐ 195 Minnie Minoso | 12.00 | 5.50 | 1.20 |
| ☐ 196 Solly Hemus | 5.50 | 2.25 | .50 |
| ☐ 197 George Strickland | 5.50 | 2.25 | .50 |
| ☐ 198 Phil Haugstad | 5.50 | 2.25 | .50 |
| ☐ 199 George Zuverink | 5.50 | 2.25 | .50 |
| ☐ 200 Ralph Houk | 12.00 | 5.50 | 1.20 |
| ☐ 201 Alex Kellner | 5.50 | 2.25 | .50 |
| ☐ 202 Joe Collins | 6.50 | 3.00 | .65 |
| ☐ 203 Curt Simmons | 6.50 | 3.00 | .65 |
| ☐ 204 Ron Northey | 5.50 | 2.25 | .50 |
| ☐ 205 Clyde King | 6.50 | 3.00 | .65 |
| ☐ 206 Joe Ostrowski | 5.50 | 2.25 | .50 |
| ☐ 207 Mickey Harris | 5.50 | 2.25 | .50 |
| ☐ 208 Marlin Stuart | 5.50 | 2.25 | .50 |
| ☐ 209 Howie Fox | 5.50 | 2.25 | .50 |
| ☐ 210 Dick Fowler | 5.50 | 2.25 | .50 |
| ☐ 211 Ray Coleman | 5.50 | 2.25 | .50 |
| ☐ 212 Ned Garver | 5.50 | 2.25 | .50 |
| ☐ 213 Nippy Jones | 5.50 | 2.25 | .50 |
| ☐ 214 Johnny Hopp | 6.50 | 3.00 | .65 |
| ☐ 215 Hank Bauer | 10.00 | 4.75 | 1.00 |
| ☐ 216 Richie Ashburn | 14.00 | 6.50 | 1.40 |
| ☐ 217 Snuffy Stirnweiss | 6.50 | 3.00 | .65 |
| ☐ 218 Clyde McCullough | 5.50 | 2.25 | .50 |
| ☐ 219 Bobby Shantz | 8.50 | 4.00 | .85 |
| ☐ 220 Joe Presko | 5.50 | 2.25 | .50 |
| ☐ 221 Granny Hamner | 5.50 | 2.25 | .50 |
| ☐ 222 Hoot Evers | 5.50 | 2.25 | .50 |
| ☐ 223 Del Ennis | 6.50 | 3.00 | .65 |
| ☐ 224 Bruce Edwards | 5.50 | 2.25 | .50 |
| ☐ 225 Frank Baumholtz | 5.50 | 2.25 | .50 |
| ☐ 226 Dave Philley | 5.50 | 2.25 | .50 |
| ☐ 227 Joe Garagiola | 18.00 | 8.50 | 1.80 |
| ☐ 228 Al Brazle | 5.50 | 2.25 | .50 |
| ☐ 229 Gene Bearden | 5.50 | 2.25 | .50 |
| ☐ 230 Matt Batts | 5.50 | 2.25 | .50 |
| ☐ 231 Sam Zoldak | 5.50 | 2.25 | .50 |
| ☐ 232 Billy Cox | 6.50 | 3.00 | .65 |
| ☐ 233 Bob Friend | 6.50 | 3.00 | .65 |
| ☐ 234 Steve Souchock | 5.50 | 2.25 | .50 |
| ☐ 235 Walt Dropo | 5.50 | 2.25 | .50 |
| ☐ 236 Ed Fitzgerald | 5.50 | 2.25 | .50 |
| ☐ 237 Jerry Coleman | 6.50 | 3.00 | .65 |
| ☐ 238 Art Houtteman | 5.50 | 2.25 | .50 |
| ☐ 239 Rocky Bridges | 5.50 | 2.25 | .50 |
| ☐ 240 Jack Phillips | 5.50 | 2.25 | .50 |
| ☐ 241 Tommy Byrne | 6.50 | 3.00 | .65 |
| ☐ 242 Tom Poholsky | 5.50 | 2.25 | .50 |
| ☐ 243 Larry Doby | 10.00 | 4.75 | 1.00 |
| ☐ 244 Vic Wertz | 6.50 | 3.00 | .65 |
| ☐ 245 Sherry Robertson | 5.50 | 2.25 | .50 |
| ☐ 246 George Kell | 15.00 | 7.00 | 1.50 |
| ☐ 247 Randy Gumpert | 5.50 | 2.25 | .50 |
| ☐ 248 Frank Shea | 5.50 | 2.25 | .50 |
| ☐ 249 Bobby Adams | 5.50 | 2.25 | .50 |
| ☐ 250 Carl Erskine | 12.00 | 5.50 | 1.20 |
| ☐ 251 Chico Carrasquel | 12.00 | 5.00 | 1.25 |
| ☐ 252 Vern Bickford | 12.00 | 5.00 | 1.25 |
| ☐ 253 Johnny Berardino | 12.00 | 5.00 | 1.25 |
| ☐ 254 Joe Dobson | 12.00 | 5.00 | 1.25 |
| ☐ 255 Clyde Vollmer | 12.00 | 5.00 | 1.25 |
| ☐ 256 Pete Suder | 12.00 | 5.00 | 1.25 |
| ☐ 257 Bobby Avila | 12.00 | 5.00 | 1.25 |
| ☐ 258 Steve Gromek | 12.00 | 5.00 | 1.25 |
| ☐ 259 Bob Addis | 12.00 | 5.00 | 1.25 |
| ☐ 260 Pete Castiglione | 12.00 | 5.00 | 1.25 |
| ☐ 261 Willie Mays | 450.00 | 175.00 | 40.00 |
| ☐ 262 Virgil Trucks | 12.00 | 5.00 | 1.25 |
| ☐ 263 Harry Brecheen | 12.00 | 5.00 | 1.25 |
| ☐ 264 Roy Hartsfield | 12.00 | 5.00 | 1.25 |
| ☐ 265 Chuck Diering | 12.00 | 5.00 | 1.25 |
| ☐ 266 Murry Dickson | 12.00 | 5.00 | 1.25 |
| ☐ 267 Sid Gordon | 12.00 | 5.00 | 1.25 |

|  | MINT | VG-E | F-G |
|---|---|---|---|
| ☐ 268 Bob Lemon | 55.00 | 25.00 | 5.50 |
| ☐ 269 Willard Nixon | 12.00 | 5.00 | 1.25 |
| ☐ 270 Lou Brissie | 12.00 | 5.00 | 1.25 |
| ☐ 271 Jim Delsing | 12.00 | 5.00 | 1.25 |
| ☐ 272 Mike Garcia | 14.00 | 6.50 | 1.40 |
| ☐ 273 Erv Palica | 12.00 | 5.00 | 1.25 |
| ☐ 274 Ralph Branca | 14.00 | 6.50 | 1.40 |
| ☐ 275 Pat Mullin | 12.00 | 5.00 | 1.25 |
| ☐ 276 Jim Wilson | 12.00 | 5.00 | 1.25 |
| ☐ 277 Early Wynn | 60.00 | 27.00 | 6.00 |
| ☐ 278 Al Clark | 12.00 | 5.00 | 1.25 |
| ☐ 279 Ed Stewart | 12.00 | 5.00 | 1.25 |
| ☐ 280 Cloyd Boyer | 12.00 | 5.00 | 1.25 |
| ☐ 281 Tommy Brown SP | 18.00 | 7.50 | 1.75 |
| ☐ 282 Birdie Tebbetts SP | 18.00 | 7.50 | 1.75 |
| ☐ 283 Philip Masi SP | 18.00 | 7.50 | 1.75 |
| ☐ 284 Hank Arft SP | 18.00 | 7.50 | 1.75 |
| ☐ 285 Cliff Fannin SP | 18.00 | 7.50 | 1.75 |
| ☐ 286 Joe DeMaestri SP | 18.00 | 7.50 | 1.75 |
| ☐ 287 Steve Bilko SP | 18.00 | 7.50 | 1.75 |
| ☐ 288 Chet Nichols SP | 18.00 | 7.50 | 1.75 |
| ☐ 289 Tommy Holmes SP | 18.00 | 7.50 | 1.75 |
| ☐ 290 Joe Astroth SP | 18.00 | 7.50 | 1.75 |
| ☐ 291 Gil Coan SP | 18.00 | 7.50 | 1.75 |
| ☐ 292 Floyd Baker SP | 18.00 | 7.50 | 1.75 |
| ☐ 293 Sibby Sisti SP | 18.00 | 7.50 | 1.75 |
| ☐ 294 Walker Cooper SP | 18.00 | 7.50 | 1.75 |
| ☐ 295 Phil Cavarretta SP | 18.00 | 7.50 | 1.75 |
| ☐ 296 Red Rolfe SP | 18.00 | 7.50 | 1.75 |
| ☐ 297 Andy Seminick SP | 18.00 | 7.50 | 1.75 |
| ☐ 258 Bob Ross SP | 18.00 | 7.50 | 1.75 |
| ☐ 299 Ray Murray SP | 18.00 | 7.50 | 1.75 |
| ☐ 300 Barney McCosky SP | 18.00 | 7.50 | 1.75 |
| ☐ 301 Bob Porterfield | 12.00 | 5.00 | 1.25 |
| ☐ 302 Max Surkont | 12.00 | 5.00 | 1.25 |
| ☐ 303 Harry Dorish | 12.00 | 5.00 | 1.25 |
| ☐ 304 Sam Dente | 12.00 | 5.00 | 1.25 |
| ☐ 305 Paul Richards | 14.00 | 6.50 | 1.40 |
| ☐ 306 Lou Sleater | 12.00 | 5.00 | 1.25 |
| ☐ 307 Frank Campos | 12.00 | 5.00 | 1.25 |
| ☐ 308 Luis Aloma | 12.00 | 5.00 | 1.25 |
| ☐ 309 Jim Busby | 12.00 | 5.00 | 1.25 |
| ☐ 310 George Metkovich | 12.00 | 5.00 | 1.25 |
| ☐ 311 Mickey Mantle DP | 2900.00 | 900.00 | 250.00 |
| ☐ 312 Jackie Robinson DP | 350.00 | 150.00 | 35.00 |
| ☐ 313 Bobby Thomson DP | 75.00 | 35.00 | 7.50 |
| ☐ 314 Roy Campanella | 450.00 | 200.00 | 45.00 |
| ☐ 315 Leo Durocher | 125.00 | 57.00 | 12.50 |
| ☐ 316 Dave Williams | 65.00 | 27.00 | 6.00 |
| ☐ 317 Conrado Marrerro | 65.00 | 27.00 | 6.00 |
| ☐ 318 Harold Gregg | 65.00 | 27.00 | 6.00 |
| ☐ 319 Al Walker | 65.00 | 27.00 | 6.00 |
| ☐ 320 John Rutherford | 65.00 | 27.00 | 6.00 |
| ☐ 321 Joe Black | 75.00 | 35.00 | 7.50 |
| ☐ 322 Randy Jackson | 65.00 | 27.00 | 6.00 |
| ☐ 323 Bubba Church | 65.00 | 27.00 | 6.00 |
| ☐ 324 Warren Hacker | 65.00 | 27.00 | 6.00 |
| ☐ 325 Bill Serena | 65.00 | 27.00 | 6.00 |
| ☐ 326 George Shuba | 65.00 | 27.00 | 6.00 |
| ☐ 327 Al Wilson | 65.00 | 27.00 | 6.00 |
| ☐ 328 Bob Borkowski | 65.00 | 27.00 | 6.00 |
| ☐ 329 Ike Delock | 65.00 | 27.00 | 6.00 |
| ☐ 330 Turk Lown | 65.00 | 27.00 | 6.00 |
| ☐ 331 Tom Morgan | 65.00 | 27.00 | 6.00 |
| ☐ 332 Anthony Bartirome | 65.00 | 27.00 | 6.00 |
| ☐ 333 Pee Wee Reese | 275.00 | 120.00 | 27.00 |
| ☐ 334 Wilmer Mizell | 65.00 | 27.00 | 6.00 |
| ☐ 335 Ted Lepcio | 65.00 | 27.00 | 6.00 |
| ☐ 336 Dave Koslo | 65.00 | 27.00 | 6.00 |
| ☐ 337 Jim Hearn | 65.00 | 27.00 | 6.00 |
| ☐ 338 Sal Yvars | 65.00 | 27.00 | 6.00 |
| ☐ 339 Russ Meyer | 65.00 | 27.00 | 6.00 |
| ☐ 340 Bob Hooper | 65.00 | 27.00 | 6.00 |
| ☐ 341 Hal Jeffcoat | 65.00 | 27.00 | 6.00 |
| ☐ 342 Clem Labine | 75.00 | 35.00 | 7.50 |
| ☐ 343 Dick Gernert | 65.00 | 27.00 | 6.00 |
| ☐ 344 Ewell Blackwell | 75.00 | 35.00 | 7.50 |
| ☐ 345 Charles White | 65.00 | 27.00 | 6.00 |
| ☐ 346 George Spencer | 65.00 | 27.00 | 6.00 |
| ☐ 347 Joe Adcock | 75.00 | 35.00 | 7.50 |
| ☐ 348 Robert Kelly | 65.00 | 27.00 | 6.00 |
| ☐ 349 Bob Cain | 65.00 | 27.00 | 6.00 |
| ☐ 350 Cal Abrams | 65.00 | 27.00 | 6.00 |
| ☐ 351 Alvin Dark | 75.00 | 35.00 | 7.50 |
| ☐ 352 Karl Drews | 65.00 | 27.00 | 6.00 |
| ☐ 353 Bobby Del Greco | 65.00 | 27.00 | 6.00 |
| ☐ 354 Fred Hatfield | 65.00 | 27.00 | 6.00 |
| ☐ 355 Bobby Morgan | 65.00 | 27.00 | 6.00 |
| ☐ 356 Toby Atwell | 65.00 | 27.00 | 6.00 |
| ☐ 357 Smokey Burgess | 75.00 | 35.00 | 7.50 |
| ☐ 358 John Kucab | 65.00 | 27.00 | 6.00 |
| ☐ 359 Dee Fondy | 65.00 | 27.00 | 6.00 |
| ☐ 360 George Crowe | 65.00 | 27.00 | 6.00 |
| ☐ 361 William Posedel | 65.00 | 27.00 | 6.00 |
| ☐ 362 Ken Heintzelman | 65.00 | 27.00 | 6.00 |
| ☐ 363 Dick Rozek | 65.00 | 27.00 | 6.00 |
| ☐ 364 Clyde Sukeforth | 65.00 | 27.00 | 6.00 |
| ☐ 365 Cookie Lavagetto | 65.00 | 27.00 | 6.00 |
| ☐ 366 Dave Madison | 65.00 | 27.00 | 6.00 |
| ☐ 367 Ben Thorpe | 65.00 | 27.00 | 6.00 |
| ☐ 368 Ed Wright | 65.00 | 27.00 | 6.00 |
| ☐ 369 Dick Groat | 125.00 | 57.00 | 12.50 |
| ☐ 370 Billy Hoeft | 65.00 | 27.00 | 6.00 |
| ☐ 371 Bobby Hofman | 65.00 | 27.00 | 6.00 |
| ☐ 372 Gil McDougald | 125.00 | 57.00 | 12.50 |
| ☐ 373 Jim Turner | 65.00 | 27.00 | 6.00 |

| | | MINT | VG-E | F-G |
|---|---|---|---|---|
| ☐ 374 | John Benton | 65.00 | 27.00 | 6.00 |
| ☐ 375 | John Merson | 65.00 | 27.00 | 6.00 |
| ☐ 376 | Faye Throneberry | 65.00 | 27.00 | 6.00 |
| ☐ 377 | Chuck Dressen | 75.00 | 35.00 | 7.50 |
| ☐ 378 | Leroy Fusselman | 65.00 | 27.00 | 6.00 |
| ☐ 379 | Joseph Rossi | 65.00 | 27.00 | 6.00 |
| ☐ 380 | Clem Koshorek | 65.00 | 27.00 | 6.00 |
| ☐ 381 | Milton Stock | 65.00 | 27.00 | 6.00 |
| ☐ 382 | Sam Jones | 65.00 | 27.00 | 6.00 |
| ☐ 383 | Del Wilber | 65.00 | 27.00 | 6.00 |
| ☐ 384 | Frank Crosetti | 125.00 | 57.00 | 12.50 |
| ☐ 385 | Herman Franks | 75.00 | 35.00 | 7.50 |
| ☐ 386 | John Yuhas | 65.00 | 27.00 | 6.00 |
| ☐ 387 | William Meyer | 65.00 | 27.00 | 6.00 |
| ☐ 388 | Bob Chipman | 65.00 | 27.00 | 6.00 |
| ☐ 389 | Ben Wade | 65.00 | 27.00 | 6.00 |
| ☐ 390 | Glenn Nelson | 65.00 | 27.00 | 6.00 |
| ☐ 391 | Ben Chapman (photo actually Sam Nahem) | 65.00 | 27.00 | 6.00 |
| ☐ 392 | Hoyt Wilhelm | 200.00 | 90.00 | 20.00 |
| ☐ 393 | Ebba St. Claire | 65.00 | 27.00 | 6.00 |
| ☐ 394 | Billy Herman | 100.00 | 45.00 | 10.00 |
| ☐ 395 | Jake Pitler | 65.00 | 27.00 | 6.00 |
| ☐ 396 | Dick Williams | 85.00 | 40.00 | 8.50 |
| ☐ 397 | Forrest Main | 65.00 | 27.00 | 6.00 |
| ☐ 398 | Hal Rice | 65.00 | 27.00 | 6.00 |
| ☐ 399 | Jim Fridley | 65.00 | 27.00 | 6.00 |
| ☐ 400 | Bill Dickey COACH | 275.00 | 120.00 | 27.00 |
| ☐ 401 | Bob Schultz | 65.00 | 27.00 | 6.00 |
| ☐ 402 | Earl Harrist | 65.00 | 27.00 | 6.00 |
| ☐ 403 | Bill Miller | 65.00 | 27.00 | 6.00 |
| ☐ 404 | Dick Brodowski | 65.00 | 27.00 | 6.00 |
| ☐ 405 | Ed Pellagrini | 65.00 | 27.00 | 6.00 |
| ☐ 406 | Joe Nuxhall | 75.00 | 35.00 | 7.50 |
| ☐ 407 | Eddie Mathews | 500.00 | 175.00 | 30.00 |

### 1953 TOPPS

The cards in this 274 card set measure 2⅝″ by 3¾″. Although the last card is numbered 280, there are only 274 cards in the set since numbers 253, 261, 267, 268, 271, and 275 were never issued. The 1953 Topps series contains line drawings of players in full color. The name and team panel at the card base is easily damaged, making it very difficult to complete a mint set. The high number series, 221 to 280, is scarce.

COMPLETE SET: M-2200.00; VG-E-900.00; F-G-150.00

| | | MINT | VG-E | F-G |
|---|---|---|---|---|
| | Common Player (1–165) | 3.25 | 1.25 | .30 |
| | Common Player (166–220) | 2.25 | .90 | .20 |
| | Common Player (221–280) | 14.00 | 6.00 | 1.50 |

| | | MINT | VG-E | F-G |
|---|---|---|---|---|
| ☐ 1 | Jackie Robinson | 80.00 | 20.00 | 5.00 |
| ☐ 2 | Luke Easter | 3.25 | 1.25 | .30 |
| ☐ 3 | George Crowe | 3.25 | 1.25 | .30 |
| ☐ 4 | Ben Wade | 3.25 | 1.25 | .30 |
| ☐ 5 | Joe Dobson | 3.25 | 1.25 | .30 |
| ☐ 6 | Sam Jones | 3.25 | 1.25 | .30 |
| ☐ 7 | Bob Borkowski | 3.25 | 1.25 | .30 |
| ☐ 8 | Clem Koshorek | 3.25 | 1.25 | .30 |
| ☐ 9 | Joe Collins | 3.75 | 1.40 | .35 |
| ☐ 10 | Smokey Burgess | 3.75 | 1.40 | .35 |
| ☐ 11 | Sal Yvars | 3.25 | 1.25 | .30 |
| ☐ 12 | Howie Judson | 3.25 | 1.25 | .30 |
| ☐ 13 | Connie Marrero | 3.25 | 1.25 | .30 |
| ☐ 14 | Clem Labine | 3.75 | 1.40 | .35 |
| ☐ 15 | Bobo Newsom | 3.75 | 1.40 | .35 |
| ☐ 16 | Peanuts Lowrey | 3.25 | 1.25 | .30 |
| ☐ 17 | Billy Hitchcock | 3.25 | 1.25 | .30 |
| ☐ 18 | Ted Lepcio | 3.25 | 1.25 | .30 |
| ☐ 19 | Mel Parnell | 3.75 | 1.40 | .35 |
| ☐ 20 | Hank Thompson | 3.75 | 1.40 | .35 |
| ☐ 21 | Billy Johnson | 3.25 | 1.25 | .30 |
| ☐ 22 | Howie Fox | 3.25 | 1.25 | .30 |
| ☐ 23 | Toby Atwell | 3.25 | 1.25 | .30 |
| ☐ 24 | Ferris Fain | 3.75 | 1.40 | .35 |
| ☐ 25 | Ray Boone | 3.75 | 1.40 | .35 |
| ☐ 26 | Dale Mitchell | 3.75 | 1.40 | .35 |
| ☐ 27 | Roy Campanella | 42.00 | 15.00 | 4.00 |
| ☐ 28 | Eddie Pellagrini | 3.25 | 1.25 | .30 |
| ☐ 29 | Hal Jeffcoat | 3.25 | 1.25 | .30 |
| ☐ 30 | Willard Nixon | 3.25 | 1.25 | .30 |
| ☐ 31 | Ewell Blackwell | 3.75 | 1.40 | .35 |
| ☐ 32 | Clyde Vollmer | 3.25 | 1.25 | .30 |
| ☐ 33 | Bob Kennedy | 3.25 | 1.25 | .30 |

| | MINT | VG-E | F-G | | MINT | VG-E | F-G |
|---|---|---|---|---|---|---|---|
| ☐ 34 George Shuba | 3.75 | 1.40 | .35 | ☐ 87 Ed Lopat | 6.50 | 3.00 | .65 |
| ☐ 35 Irv Noren | 3.25 | 1.25 | .30 | ☐ 88 Willie Jones | 3.25 | 1.25 | .30 |
| ☐ 36 Johnny Groth | 3.25 | 1.25 | .30 | ☐ 89 Chuck Stobbs | 3.25 | 1.25 | .30 |
| ☐ 37 Ed Mathews | 16.00 | 7.50 | 1.60 | ☐ 90 Hank Edwards | 3.25 | 1.25 | .30 |
| ☐ 38 Jim Hearn | 3.25 | 1.25 | .30 | ☐ 91 Ebba St. Claire | 3.25 | 1.25 | .30 |
| ☐ 39 Eddie Miksis | 3.25 | 1.25 | .30 | ☐ 92 Paul Minner | 3.25 | 1.25 | .30 |
| ☐ 40 John Lipon | 3.25 | 1.25 | .30 | ☐ 93 Hal Rice | 3.25 | 1.25 | .30 |
| ☐ 41 Enos Slaughter | 10.00 | 4.75 | 1.00 | ☐ 94 Bill Kennedy | 3.25 | 1.25 | .30 |
| ☐ 42 Gus Zernial | 3.75 | 1.40 | .35 | ☐ 95 Willard Marshall | 3.25 | 1.25 | .30 |
| ☐ 43 Gil McDougald | 5.00 | 2.35 | .50 | ☐ 96 Virgil Trucks | 3.75 | 1.75 | .37 |
| ☐ 44 Ellis Kinder | 3.25 | 1.25 | .30 | ☐ 97 Don Kolloway | 3.25 | 1.25 | .30 |
| ☐ 45 Grady Hatton | 3.25 | 1.25 | .30 | ☐ 98 Cal Abrams | 3.25 | 1.25 | .30 |
| ☐ 46 Johnny Klippstein | 3.25 | 1.25 | .30 | ☐ 99 Dave Madison | 3.25 | 1.25 | .30 |
| ☐ 47 Bubba Church | 3.25 | 1.25 | .30 | ☐ 100 Bill Miller | 3.25 | 1.25 | .30 |
| ☐ 48 Bob Del Greco | 3.25 | 1.25 | .30 | ☐ 101 Ted Wilks | 3.25 | 1.25 | .30 |
| ☐ 49 Faye Throneberry | 3.25 | 1.25 | .30 | ☐ 102 Connie Ryan | 3.25 | 1.25 | .30 |
| ☐ 50 Chuck Dressen | 3.75 | 1.40 | .35 | ☐ 103 Joe Astroth | 3.25 | 1.25 | .30 |
| ☐ 51 Frank Campos | 3.25 | 1.25 | .30 | ☐ 104 Yogi Berra | 40.00 | 18.00 | 4.00 |
| ☐ 52 Ted Gray | 3.25 | 1.25 | .30 | ☐ 105 Joe Nuxhall | 3.75 | 1.40 | .35 |
| ☐ 53 Sherman Lollar | 3.75 | 1.40 | .35 | ☐ 106 Johnny Antonelli | 3.75 | 1.40 | .35 |
| ☐ 54 Bob Feller | 24.00 | 8.00 | 2.25 | ☐ 107 Danny O'Connell | 3.25 | 1.25 | .30 |
| ☐ 55 Maurice McDermott | 3.25 | 1.25 | .30 | ☐ 108 Bob Porterfield | 3.25 | 1.25 | .30 |
| ☐ 56 Gerry Staley | 3.25 | 1.25 | .30 | ☐ 109 Alvin Dark | 4.50 | 2.10 | .45 |
| ☐ 57 Carl Scheib | 3.25 | 1.25 | .30 | ☐ 110 Herman Wehmeier | 3.25 | 1.25 | .30 |
| ☐ 58 George Metkovich | 3.25 | 1.25 | .30 | ☐ 111 Hank Sauer | 3.75 | 1.40 | .35 |
| ☐ 59 Karl Drews | 3.25 | 1.25 | .30 | ☐ 112 Ned Garver | 3.25 | 1.25 | .30 |
| ☐ 60 Cloyd Boyer | 3.25 | 1.25 | .30 | ☐ 113 Jerry Priddy | 3.25 | 1.25 | .30 |
| ☐ 61 Early Wynn | 11.00 | 4.00 | 1.00 | ☐ 114 Phil Rizzuto | 21.00 | 8.00 | 2.00 |
| ☐ 62 Monte Irvin | 8.00 | 3.00 | .80 | ☐ 115 George Spencer | 3.25 | 1.25 | .30 |
| ☐ 63 Gus Niarhos | 3.25 | 1.25 | .30 | ☐ 116 Frank Smith | 3.25 | 1.25 | .30 |
| ☐ 64 Dave Philley | 3.25 | 1.25 | .30 | ☐ 117 Sid Gordon | 3.25 | 1.25 | .30 |
| ☐ 65 Earl Harrist | 3.25 | 1.25 | .30 | ☐ 118 Gus Bell | 3.75 | 1.40 | .35 |
| ☐ 66 Minnie Minoso | 5.50 | 2.60 | .55 | ☐ 119 John Sain | 6.00 | 2.80 | .60 |
| ☐ 67 Roy Sievers | 3.75 | 1.40 | .35 | ☐ 120 Davey Williams | 3.75 | 1.40 | .35 |
| ☐ 68 Del Rice | 3.25 | 1.25 | .30 | ☐ 121 Walter Dropo | 3.25 | 1.25 | .30 |
| ☐ 69 Dick Brodowski | 3.25 | 1.25 | .30 | ☐ 122 Elmer Valo | 3.25 | 1.25 | .30 |
| ☐ 70 Ed Yuhas | 3.25 | 1.25 | .30 | ☐ 123 Tommy Byrne | 3.75 | 1.40 | .35 |
| ☐ 71 Tony Bartirome | 3.25 | 1.25 | .30 | ☐ 124 Sibby Sisti | 3.25 | 1.25 | .30 |
| ☐ 72 Fred Hutchison | 3.75 | 1.40 | .35 | ☐ 125 Dick Williams | 3.75 | 1.40 | .35 |
| ☐ 73 Eddie Robinson | 3.25 | 1.25 | .30 | ☐ 126 Bill Connelly | 3.25 | 1.25 | .30 |
| ☐ 74 Joe Rossi | 3.25 | 1.25 | .30 | ☐ 127 Clint Courtney | 3.25 | 1.25 | .30 |
| ☐ 75 Mike Garcia | 3.75 | 1.40 | .35 | ☐ 128 Wilmer Mizell | 3.25 | 1.25 | .30 |
| ☐ 76 Peewee Reese | 22.00 | 8.00 | 2.00 | ☐ 129 Keith Thomas | 3.25 | 1.25 | .30 |
| ☐ 77 John Mize | 11.00 | 4.50 | 1.00 | ☐ 130 Turk Lown | 3.25 | 1.25 | .30 |
| ☐ 78 Al (Red) Schoendienst | 5.00 | 2.35 | .50 | ☐ 131 Harry Byrd | 3.25 | 1.25 | .30 |
| ☐ 79 Johnny Wyrostek | 3.25 | 1.25 | .30 | ☐ 132 Tom Morgan | 3.25 | 1.25 | .30 |
| ☐ 80 Jim Hegan | 3.75 | 1.40 | .35 | ☐ 133 Gil Coan | 3.25 | 1.25 | .30 |
| ☐ 81 Joe Black | 3.75 | 1.40 | .35 | ☐ 134 Rube Walker | 3.75 | 1.40 | .35 |
| ☐ 82 Mickey Mantle | 375.00 | 125.00 | 35.00 | ☐ 135 Al Rosen | 8.50 | 4.00 | .85 |
| ☐ 83 Howie Pollet | 3.25 | 1.25 | .30 | ☐ 136 Ken Heintzelman | 3.25 | 1.25 | .30 |
| ☐ 84 Bob Hooper | 3.25 | 1.25 | .30 | ☐ 137 John Rutherford | 3.25 | 1.25 | .30 |
| ☐ 85 Bobby Morgan | 3.25 | 1.25 | .30 | ☐ 138 George Kell | 10.00 | 4.00 | 1.00 |
| ☐ 86 Billy Martin | 18.00 | 7.00 | 2.00 | ☐ 139 Sammy White | 3.25 | 1.25 | .30 |

| | MINT | VG-E | F-G |
|---|---|---|---|
| ☐ 140 Tommy Glaviano | 3.25 | 1.25 | .30 |
| ☐ 141 Allie Reynolds | 6.50 | 3.00 | .65 |
| ☐ 142 Vic Wertz | 3.75 | 1.40 | .35 |
| ☐ 143 Billy Pierce | 4.50 | 2.10 | .45 |
| ☐ 144 Bob Schultz | 3.25 | 1.25 | .30 |
| ☐ 145 Harry Dorish | 3.25 | 1.25 | .30 |
| ☐ 146 Granny Hamner | 3.25 | 1.25 | .30 |
| ☐ 147 Warren Spahn | 21.00 | 8.00 | 2.00 |
| ☐ 148 Mickey Grasso | 3.25 | 1.25 | .30 |
| ☐ 149 Dom DiMaggio | 9.00 | 3.50 | .80 |
| ☐ 150 Harry Simpson | 3.25 | 1.25 | .30 |
| ☐ 151 Hoyt Wilhelm | 10.00 | 4.00 | 1.00 |
| ☐ 152 Bob Adams | 3.25 | 1.25 | .30 |
| ☐ 153 Andy Seminick | 3.25 | 1.25 | .30 |
| ☐ 154 Dick Groat | 4.50 | 2.10 | .45 |
| ☐ 155 Dutch Leonard | 3.25 | 1.25 | .30 |
| ☐ 156 Jim Rivera | 3.25 | 1.25 | .30 |
| ☐ 157 Bob Addis | 3.25 | 1.25 | .30 |
| ☐ 158 John Logan | 3.75 | 1.75 | .37 |
| ☐ 159 Wayne Terwilliger | 3.25 | 1.25 | .30 |
| ☐ 160 Bob Young | 3.25 | 1.25 | .30 |
| ☐ 161 Vern Bickford | 3.25 | 1.25 | .30 |
| ☐ 162 Ted Kluszewski | 6.00 | 2.80 | .60 |
| ☐ 163 Fred Hatfield | 3.25 | 1.25 | .30 |
| ☐ 164 Frank Shea | 3.25 | 1.25 | .30 |
| ☐ 165 Billy Hoeft | 3.25 | 1.25 | .30 |
| ☐ 166 Bill Hunter | 2.25 | .90 | .20 |
| ☐ 167 Art Schult | 2.25 | .90 | .20 |
| ☐ 168 Willard Schmidt | 2.25 | .90 | .20 |
| ☐ 169 Dizzy Trout | 2.25 | .90 | .20 |
| ☐ 170 Bill Werle | 2.25 | .90 | .20 |
| ☐ 171 Bill Glynn | 2.25 | .90 | .20 |
| ☐ 172 Rip Repulski | 2.25 | .90 | .20 |
| ☐ 173 Preston Ward | 2.25 | .90 | .20 |
| ☐ 174 Billy Loes | 2.75 | 1.25 | .27 |
| ☐ 175 Ronnie Kline | 2.25 | .90 | .20 |
| ☐ 176 Don Hoak | 2.75 | 1.25 | .27 |
| ☐ 177 Jim Dyck | 2.25 | .90 | .20 |
| ☐ 178 Jim Waugh | 2.25 | .90 | .20 |
| ☐ 179 Gene Hermanski | 2.25 | .90 | .20 |
| ☐ 180 Virgil Stallcup | 2.25 | .90 | .20 |
| ☐ 181 Al Zarilla | 2.25 | .90 | .20 |
| ☐ 182 Bobby Hofman | 2.25 | .90 | .20 |
| ☐ 183 Stu Miller | 2.25 | .90 | .20 |
| ☐ 184 Hal Brown | 2.25 | .90 | .20 |
| ☐ 185 Jim Pendleton | 2.25 | .90 | .20 |
| ☐ 186 Charlie Bishop | 2.25 | .90 | .20 |
| ☐ 187 Jim Fridley | 2.25 | .90 | .20 |
| ☐ 188 Andy Carey | 2.75 | 1.25 | .27 |
| ☐ 189 Ray Jablonski | 2.25 | .90 | .20 |
| ☐ 190 Dixie Walker | 2.25 | .90 | .20 |
| ☐ 191 Ralph Kiner | 12.00 | 5.50 | 1.20 |
| ☐ 192 Wally Westlake | 2.25 | .90 | .20 |

| | MINT | VG-E | F-G |
|---|---|---|---|
| ☐ 193 Mike Clark | 2.25 | .90 | .20 |
| ☐ 194 Eddie Kazak | 2.25 | .90 | .20 |
| ☐ 195 Ed McGhee | 2.25 | .90 | .20 |
| ☐ 196 Bob Keegan | 2.25 | .90 | .20 |
| ☐ 197 Del Crandall | 2.75 | 1.25 | .27 |
| ☐ 198 Forrest Main | 2.25 | .90 | .20 |
| ☐ 199 Marion Fricano | 2.25 | .90 | .20 |
| ☐ 200 Gordon Goldsberry | 2.25 | .90 | .20 |
| ☐ 201 Paul LaPalme | 2.25 | .90 | .20 |
| ☐ 202 Carl Sawatski | 2.25 | .90 | .20 |
| ☐ 203 Cliff Fannin | 2.25 | .90 | .20 |
| ☐ 204 Dick Bokelman | 2.25 | .90 | .20 |
| ☐ 205 Vern Benson | 2.25 | .90 | .20 |
| ☐ 206 Ed Bailey | 2.75 | 1.25 | .27 |
| ☐ 207 Whitey Ford | 20.00 | 9.00 | 2.00 |
| ☐ 208 Jim Wilson | 2.25 | .90 | .20 |
| ☐ 209 Jim Greengrass | 2.25 | .90 | .20 |
| ☐ 210 Bob Cerv | 2.75 | 1.25 | .27 |
| ☐ 211 J.W. Porter | 2.25 | .90 | .20 |
| ☐ 212 Jack Dittmer | 2.25 | .90 | .20 |
| ☐ 213 Ray Scarborough | 2.25 | .90 | .20 |
| ☐ 214 Bill Bruton | 2.75 | 1.25 | .27 |
| ☐ 215 Gene Conley | 2.75 | 1.25 | .27 |
| ☐ 216 Jim Hughes | 2.25 | .90 | .20 |
| ☐ 217 Murray Wall | 2.25 | .90 | .20 |
| ☐ 218 Les Fusselman | 2.25 | .90 | .20 |
| ☐ 219 Pete Runnels | 2.75 | 1.25 | .27 |
| ☐     (Photo actually | | | |
| ☐     Don Johnson) | | | |
| ☐ 220 Satchel Paige | 60.00 | 27.00 | 6.00 |
| ☐ 221 Bob Milliken | 14.00 | 6.00 | 1.50 |
| ☐ 222 Vic Janowicz | 16.00 | 7.50 | 1.60 |
| ☐ 223 Johnny O'Brien | 14.00 | 6.00 | 1.50 |
| ☐ 224 Lou Sleater | 14.00 | 6.00 | 1.50 |
| ☐ 225 Bobby Shantz | 18.00 | 8.50 | 1.80 |
| ☐ 226 Ed Erautt | 14.00 | 6.00 | 1.50 |
| ☐ 227 Morris Martin | 14.00 | 6.00 | 1.50 |
| ☐ 228 Hal Newhouser | 25.00 | 11.00 | 2.50 |
| ☐ 229 Rockey Krsnich | 14.00 | 6.00 | 1.50 |
| ☐ 230 Johnny Lindell | 14.00 | 6.00 | 1.50 |
| ☐ 231 Solly Hemus | 14.00 | 6.00 | 1.50 |
| ☐ 232 Dick Kokos | 14.00 | 6.00 | 1.50 |
| ☐ 233 Al Aber | 14.00 | 6.00 | 1.50 |
| ☐ 234 Ray Murray | 14.00 | 6.00 | 1.50 |
| ☐ 235 John Hetki | 14.00 | 6.00 | 1.50 |
| ☐ 236 Harry Perkowski | 14.00 | 6.00 | 1.50 |
| ☐ 237 Bud Podbielan | 14.00 | 6.00 | 1.50 |
| ☐ 238 Cal Hogue | 14.00 | 6.00 | 1.50 |
| ☐ 239 Jim Delsing | 14.00 | 6.00 | 1.50 |
| ☐ 240 Freddie Marsh | 14.00 | 6.00 | 1.50 |
| ☐ 241 Al Sima | 14.00 | 6.00 | 1.50 |
| ☐ 242 Charlie Silvera | 14.00 | 6.00 | 1.50 |
| ☐ 243 Carlos Bernier | 14.00 | 6.00 | 1.50 |

| | MINT | VG-E | F-G |
|---|---|---|---|
| ☐ 244 Willie Mays | 500.00 | 150.00 | 40.00 |
| ☐ 245 Bill Norman | 14.00 | 6.00 | 1.50 |
| ☐ 246 Roy Face | 18.00 | 8.50 | 1.80 |
| ☐ 247 Mike Sandlock | 14.00 | 6.00 | 1.50 |
| ☐ 248 Gene Stephens | 14.00 | 6.00 | 1.50 |
| ☐ 249 Eddie O'Brien | 14.00 | 6.00 | 1.50 |
| ☐ 250 Bob Wilson | 14.00 | 6.00 | 1.50 |
| ☐ 251 Sid Hudson | 14.00 | 6.00 | 1.50 |
| ☐ 252 Henry Foiles | 14.00 | 6.00 | 1.50 |
| ☐ 254 Preacher Roe | 21.00 | 9.50 | 2.10 |
| ☐ 255 Dixie Howell | 14.00 | 6.00 | 1.50 |
| ☐ 256 Les Peden | 14.00 | 6.00 | 1.50 |
| ☐ 257 Bob Boyd | 14.00 | 6.00 | 1.50 |
| ☐ 258 Jim Gilliam | 65.00 | 30.00 | 6.50 |
| ☐ 259 Roy McMillan | 14.00 | 6.00 | 1.50 |
| ☐ 260 Sam Calderone | 14.00 | 6.00 | 1.50 |
| ☐ 262 Bob Oldis | 14.00 | 6.00 | 1.50 |
| ☐ 263 Johnny Podres | 45.00 | 20.00 | 4.50 |
| ☐ 264 Gene Woodling | 21.00 | 9.50 | 2.10 |
| ☐ 265 Jackie Jensen | 30.00 | 14.00 | 3.00 |
| ☐ 266 Bob Cain | 14.00 | 6.00 | 1.50 |
| ☐ 269 Duane Pillette | 14.00 | 6.00 | 1.50 |
| ☐ 270 Vern Stephens | 16.00 | 7.50 | 1.60 |
| ☐ 272 Bill Antonello | 14.00 | 6.00 | 1.50 |
| ☐ 273 Harvey Haddix | 16.00 | 7.50 | 1.60 |
| ☐ 274 John Riddle | 14.00 | 6.00 | 1.50 |
| ☐ 276 Ken Raffensberger | 14.00 | 6.00 | 1.50 |
| ☐ 277 Don Lund | 14.00 | 6.00 | 1.50 |
| ☐ 278 Willie Miranda | 14.00 | 6.00 | 1.50 |
| ☐ 279 Joe Coleman | 14.00 | 6.00 | 1.50 |
| ☐ 280 Milt Bolling | 50.00 | 10.00 | 2.00 |

## 1954 TOPPS

TOM LASORDA
THOMAS CHARLES LASORDA  *pitcher*  Brooklyn Dodgers
TOPPS 132

The cards in this 250 card set measure 2⅝" by 3¾". Each of the cards in the 1954 Topps set contains a large "head" shot of a player plus a smaller full length photo (both are black and white pictures set against a color background). This series contains the rookie cards of Hank Aaron, Ernie Banks, and Al Kaline and two separate cards of Ted Williams (number 1 and number 250).

COMPLETE SET: M-1100.00; VG-E-450.00; F-G-100.00

| | MINT | VG-E | F-G |
|---|---|---|---|
| Common Player (1- 50) | 1.25 | .60 | .12 |
| Common Player (51-75) | 3.00 | 1.25 | .30 |
| Common Player (76-250) | 1.50 | .70 | .15 |

| | | MINT | VG-E | F-G |
|---|---|---|---|---|
| ☐ | 1 Ted Williams | 85.00 | 25.00 | 6.00 |
| ☐ | 2 Gus Zernial | 1.25 | .60 | .12 |
| ☐ | 3 Monte Irvin | 5.00 | 2.35 | .50 |
| ☐ | 4 Hank Sauer | 1.50 | .70 | .15 |
| ☐ | 5 Ed Lopat | 3.25 | 1.50 | .32 |
| ☐ | 6 Pete Runnels | 1.50 | .70 | .15 |
| ☐ | 7 Ted Kluszewski | 3.50 | 1.65 | .35 |
| ☐ | 8 Bob Young | 1.25 | .60 | .12 |
| ☐ | 9 Harvey Haddix | 1.50 | .70 | .15 |
| ☐ | 10 Jackie Robinson | 36.00 | 15.00 | 3.50 |
| ☐ | 11 Paul Leslie Smith | 1.25 | .60 | .12 |
| ☐ | 12 Del Crandall | 1.50 | .70 | .15 |
| ☐ | 13 Billy Martin | 16.00 | 7.50 | 1.60 |
| ☐ | 14 Preacher Roe | 3.25 | 1.50 | .32 |
| ☐ | 15 Al Rosen | 4.00 | 1.85 | .40 |
| ☐ | 16 Vic Janowicz | 1.50 | .70 | .15 |
| ☐ | 17 Phil Rizzuto | 16.00 | 7.50 | 1.60 |
| ☐ | 18 Walt Dropo | 1.25 | .60 | .12 |
| ☐ | 19 Johnny Lipon | 1.25 | .60 | .12 |
| ☐ | 20 Warren Spahn | 16.00 | 7.50 | 1.60 |
| ☐ | 21 Bobby Shantz | 1.50 | .70 | .15 |
| ☐ | 22 Jim Greengrass | 1.25 | .60 | .12 |
| ☐ | 23 Luke Easter | 1.25 | .60 | .12 |
| ☐ | 24 Granny Hamner | 1.25 | .60 | .12 |
| ☐ | 25 Harvey Kuenn | 4.50 | 2.10 | .45 |
| ☐ | 26 Ray Jablonski | 1.25 | .60 | .12 |
| ☐ | 27 Ferris Fain | 1.50 | .70 | .15 |
| ☐ | 28 Paul Minner | 1.25 | .60 | .12 |
| ☐ | 29 Jim Hegan | 1.25 | .60 | .12 |
| ☐ | 30 Ed Mathews | 14.00 | 6.50 | 1.40 |
| ☐ | 31 Johnny Klippstein | 1.25 | .60 | .12 |
| ☐ | 32 Duke Snider | 30.00 | 14.00 | 3.00 |
| ☐ | 33 Johnny Schmitz | 1.25 | .60 | .12 |
| ☐ | 34 Jim Rivera | 1.25 | .60 | .12 |
| ☐ | 35 Jim Gilliam | 3.25 | 1.50 | .32 |
| ☐ | 36 Hoyt Wilhelm | 7.00 | 3.25 | .70 |
| ☐ | 37 Whitey Ford | 16.00 | 7.50 | 1.60 |
| ☐ | 38 Eddie Stanky | 1.50 | .70 | .15 |
| ☐ | 39 Sherm Lollar | 1.50 | .70 | .15 |
| ☐ | 40 Mel Parnell | 1.50 | .70 | .15 |
| ☐ | 41 Willie Jones | 1.25 | .60 | .12 |

| | | MINT | VG-E | F-G | | | MINT | VG-E | F-G |
|---|---|---|---|---|---|---|---|---|---|
| ☐ | 42 Don Mueller | 1.50 | .70 | .15 | ☐ | 95 Hal Rice | 1.50 | .70 | .15 |
| ☐ | 43 Dick Groat | 2.50 | 1.15 | .25 | ☐ | 96 Charlie Silvera | 1.50 | .70 | .15 |
| ☐ | 44 Ned Garver | 1.25 | .60 | .12 | ☐ | 97 Jerald Hal Lane | 1.50 | .70 | .15 |
| ☐ | 45 Richie Ashburn | 4.50 | 2.10 | .45 | ☐ | 98 Joe Black | 2.00 | .90 | .20 |
| ☐ | 46 Ken Raffensberger | 1.25 | .60 | .12 | ☐ | 99 Bobby Hofman | 1.50 | .70 | .15 |
| ☐ | 47 Ellis Kinder | 1.25 | .60 | .12 | ☐ | 100 Bob Keegan | 1.50 | .70 | .15 |
| ☐ | 48 William Hunter | 1.25 | .60 | .12 | ☐ | 101 Gene Woodling | 2.00 | .90 | .20 |
| ☐ | 49 Ray Murray | 1.25 | .60 | .12 | ☐ | 102 Gil Hodges | 16.00 | 7.50 | 1.60 |
| ☐ | 50 Yogi Berra | 30.00 | 14.00 | 3.00 | ☐ | 103 Jim Lemon | 1.75 | .85 | .17 |
| ☐ | 51 Johnny Lindell | 3.00 | 1.25 | .30 | ☐ | 104 Mike Sandlock | 1.50 | .70 | .15 |
| ☐ | 52 Vic Power | 3.00 | 1.25 | .30 | ☐ | 105 Andy Carey | 1.75 | .85 | .17 |
| ☐ | 53 Jack Dittmar | 3.00 | 1.25 | .30 | ☐ | 106 Dick Kokos | 1.50 | .70 | .15 |
| ☐ | 54 Vern Stephens | 3.00 | 1.25 | .30 | ☐ | 107 Duane Pillette | 1.50 | .70 | .15 |
| ☐ | 55 Phil Cavarretta | 3.00 | 1.25 | .30 | ☐ | 108 Thornton Kipper | 1.50 | .70 | .15 |
| ☐ | 56 Willie Miranda | 3.00 | 1.25 | .30 | ☐ | 109 Bill Bruton | 1.50 | .70 | .15 |
| ☐ | 57 Luis Aloma | 3.00 | 1.25 | .30 | ☐ | 110 Harry Dorish | 1.50 | .70 | .15 |
| ☐ | 58 Bob Wilson | 3.00 | 1.25 | .30 | ☐ | 111 Jim Delsing | 1.50 | .70 | .15 |
| ☐ | 59 Gene Conley | 3.00 | 1.25 | .30 | ☐ | 112 Bill Renna | 1.50 | .70 | .15 |
| ☐ | 60 Frank Baumholtz | 3.00 | 1.25 | .30 | ☐ | 113 Bob Boyd | 1.50 | .70 | .15 |
| ☐ | 61 Bob Cain | 3.00 | 1.25 | .30 | ☐ | 114 Dean Stone | 1.50 | .70 | .15 |
| ☐ | 62 Eddie Robinson | 3.00 | 1.25 | .30 | ☐ | 115 Rip Repulski | 1.50 | .70 | .15 |
| ☐ | 63 Johnny Pesky | 3.00 | 1.25 | .30 | ☐ | 116 Steve Bilko | 1.50 | .70 | .15 |
| ☐ | 64 Hank Thompson | 3.00 | 1.25 | .30 | ☐ | 117 Solly Hemus | 1.50 | .70 | .15 |
| ☐ | 65 Bob Swift | 3.00 | 1.25 | .30 | ☐ | 118 Carl Scheib | 1.50 | .70 | .15 |
| ☐ | 66 Thad Lepcio | 3.00 | 1.25 | .30 | ☐ | 119 Johnny Antonelli | 2.00 | .90 | .20 |
| ☐ | 67 Jim Willis | 3.00 | 1.25 | .30 | ☐ | 120 Roy McMillan | 1.50 | .70 | .15 |
| ☐ | 68 Sam Calderone | 3.00 | 1.25 | .30 | ☐ | 121 Clem Labine | 2.00 | .90 | .20 |
| ☐ | 69 Bud Podbielan | 3.00 | 1.25 | .30 | ☐ | 122 Johnny Logan | 1.75 | .85 | .17 |
| ☐ | 70 Larry Doby | 6.00 | 2.75 | .60 | ☐ | 123 Bobby Adams | 1.50 | .70 | .15 |
| ☐ | 71 Frank Smith | 3.00 | 1.25 | .30 | ☐ | 124 Marion Fricano | 1.50 | .70 | .15 |
| ☐ | 72 Preston Ward | 3.00 | 1.25 | .30 | ☐ | 125 Harry Perkowski | 1.50 | .70 | .15 |
| ☐ | 73 Wayne Terwilliger | 3.00 | 1.25 | .30 | ☐ | 126 Ben Wade | 1.50 | .70 | .15 |
| ☐ | 74 Bill Taylor | 3.00 | 1.25 | .30 | ☐ | 127 Steve O'Neill | 1.50 | .70 | .15 |
| ☐ | 75 Fred Haney | 3.00 | 1.25 | .30 | ☐ | 128 Hank Aaron | 225.00 | 75.00 | 20.00 |
| ☐ | 76 Bob Scheffing | 1.50 | .70 | .15 | ☐ | 129 Forrest Jacobs | 1.50 | .70 | .15 |
| ☐ | 77 Ray Boone | 1.50 | .70 | .15 | ☐ | 130 Hank Bauer | 3.50 | 1.65 | .35 |
| ☐ | 78 Ted Kazanski | 1.50 | .70 | .15 | ☐ | 131 Reno Bertoia | 1.50 | .70 | .15 |
| ☐ | 79 Andy Pafko | 1.50 | .70 | .15 | ☐ | 132 Tom Lasorda | 9.00 | 4.25 | .90 |
| ☐ | 80 Jackie Jensen | 2.75 | 1.25 | .27 | ☐ | 133 Dave Baker | 1.50 | .70 | .15 |
| ☐ | 81 Dave Hoskins | 1.50 | .70 | .15 | ☐ | 134 Cal Hogue | 1.50 | .70 | .15 |
| ☐ | 82 Milt Bolling | 1.50 | .70 | .15 | ☐ | 135 Joe Presko | 1.50 | .70 | .15 |
| ☐ | 83 Joe Collins | 1.50 | .70 | .15 | ☐ | 136 Connie Ryan | 1.50 | .70 | .15 |
| ☐ | 84 Dick Cole | 1.50 | .70 | .15 | ☐ | 137 Wally Moon | 2.75 | 1.25 | .27 |
| ☐ | 85 Bob Turley | 3.75 | 1.75 | .37 | ☐ | 138 Bob Borkowski | 1.50 | .70 | .15 |
| ☐ | 86 Billy Herman | 2.75 | 1.25 | .27 | ☐ | 139 The O'Brien's | 3.25 | 1.50 | .32 |
| ☐ | 87 Roy Face | 2.00 | .90 | .20 | |    Johnny O'Brien | | | |
| ☐ | 88 Matt Batts | 1.50 | .70 | .15 | |    Eddie O'Brien | | | |
| ☐ | 89 Howie Pollet | 1.50 | .70 | .15 | ☐ | 140 Tom Wright | 1.50 | .70 | .15 |
| ☐ | 90 Willie Mays | 110.00 | 50.00 | 11.00 | ☐ | 141 Joe Jay | 1.75 | .85 | .17 |
| ☐ | 91 Bob Oldis | 1.50 | .70 | .15 | ☐ | 142 Tom Poholsky | 1.50 | .70 | .15 |
| ☐ | 92 Wally Westlake | 1.50 | .70 | .15 | ☐ | 143 Ralston Hemsley | 1.50 | .70 | .15 |
| ☐ | 93 Sid Hudson | 1.50 | .70 | .15 | ☐ | 144 Bill Werle | 1.50 | .70 | .15 |
| ☐ | 94 Ernie Banks | 65.00 | 30.00 | 6.50 | ☐ | 145 Elmer Valo | 1.50 | .70 | .15 |

| | MINT | VG-E | F-G |
|---|---|---|---|
| ☐ 146 Don Johnson | 1.50 | .70 | .15 |
| ☐ 147 Johnny Riddle | 1.50 | .70 | .15 |
| ☐ 148 Bob Trice | 1.50 | .70 | .15 |
| ☐ 149 Al Robertson | 1.50 | .70 | .15 |
| ☐ 150 Dick Kryhoski | 1.50 | .70 | .15 |
| ☐ 151 Alex Grammas | 1.50 | .70 | .15 |
| ☐ 152 Michael Blyzka | 1.50 | .70 | .15 |
| ☐ 153 Al Walker | 1.50 | .70 | .15 |
| ☐ 154 Mike Fornieles | 1.50 | .70 | .15 |
| ☐ 155 Bob Kennedy | 1.50 | .70 | .15 |
| ☐ 156 Joe Coleman | 1.50 | .70 | .15 |
| ☐ 157 Don Lenhardt | 1.50 | .70 | .15 |
| ☐ 158 Peanuts Lowrey | 1.50 | .70 | .15 |
| ☐ 159 Dave Philley | 1.50 | .70 | .15 |
| ☐ 160 Ralph Kress | 1.50 | .70 | .15 |
| ☐ 161 John Hetki | 1.50 | .70 | .15 |
| ☐ 162 Herman Wehmeier | 1.50 | .70 | .15 |
| ☐ 163 Frank House | 1.50 | .70 | .15 |
| ☐ 164 Stu Miller | 1.50 | .70 | .15 |
| ☐ 165 Jim Pendleton | 1.50 | .70 | .15 |
| ☐ 166 Johnny Podres | 3.25 | 1.50 | .32 |
| ☐ 167 Don Lund | 1.50 | .70 | .15 |
| ☐ 168 Morrie Martin | 1.50 | .70 | .15 |
| ☐ 169 Jim Hughes | 1.50 | .70 | .15 |
| ☐ 170 James (Dusty) Rhodes | 1.75 | .85 | .17 |
| ☐ 171 Leo Kiely | 1.50 | .70 | .15 |
| ☐ 172 Harold Brown | 1.50 | .70 | .15 |
| ☐ 173 Jack Harshman | 1.50 | .70 | .15 |
| ☐ 174 Tom Qualters | 1.50 | .70 | .15 |
| ☐ 175 Frank Leja | 1.50 | .70 | .15 |
| ☐ 176 Robert Keeley | 1.50 | .70 | .15 |
| ☐ 177 Bob Milliken | 1.50 | .70 | .15 |
| ☐ 178 Bill Glynn | 1.50 | .70 | .15 |
| ☐ 179 Gair Allie | 1.50 | .70 | .15 |
| ☐ 180 Wes Westrum | 1.50 | .70 | .15 |
| ☐ 181 Mel Roach | 1.50 | .70 | .15 |
| ☐ 182 Chuck Harmon | 1.50 | .70 | .15 |
| ☐ 183 Earle Combs | 2.75 | 1.25 | .27 |
| ☐ 184 Ed Bailey | 1.50 | .70 | .15 |
| ☐ 185 Chuck Stobbs | 1.50 | .70 | .15 |
| ☐ 186 Karl Olson | 1.50 | .70 | .15 |
| ☐ 187 Henry Manush | 2.75 | 1.25 | .27 |
| ☐ 188 Dave Jolly | 1.50 | .70 | .15 |
| ☐ 189 Floyd Ross | 1.50 | .70 | .15 |
| ☐ 190 Ray Herbert | 1.50 | .70 | .15 |
| ☐ 191 John (Dick) Schofield | 1.75 | .85 | .17 |
| ☐ 192 Ellis Deal | 1.50 | .70 | .15 |
| ☐ 193 Johnny Hopp | 1.50 | .70 | .15 |
| ☐ 194 Bill Sarni | 1.50 | .70 | .15 |
| ☐ 195 Bill Consolo | 1.50 | .70 | .15 |
| ☐ 196 Stanley Jok | 1.50 | .70 | .15 |
| ☐ 197 Lynwood Rowe | 1.75 | .85 | .17 |
| ☐ 198 Carl Sawatski | 1.50 | .70 | .15 |

| | MINT | VG-E | F-G |
|---|---|---|---|
| ☐ 199 Glenn (Rocky) Nelson | 1.50 | .70 | .15 |
| ☐ 200 Larry Jansen | 1.50 | .70 | .15 |
| ☐ 201 Al Kaline | 75.00 | 35.00 | 7.50 |
| ☐ 202 Bob Purkey | 1.50 | .70 | .15 |
| ☐ 203 Harry Brecheen | 1.50 | .70 | .15 |
| ☐ 204 Angel Scull | 1.50 | .70 | .15 |
| ☐ 205 Johnny Sain | 3.50 | 1.65 | .35 |
| ☐ 206 Ray Crone | 1.50 | .70 | .15 |
| ☐ 207 Tom Oliver | 1.50 | .70 | .15 |
| ☐ 208 Grady Hatton | 1.50 | .70 | .15 |
| ☐ 209 Chuck Thompson | 1.50 | .70 | .15 |
| ☐ 210 Bob Buhl | 1.75 | .85 | .17 |
| ☐ 211 Don Hoak | 1.50 | .70 | .15 |
| ☐ 212 Bob Micelotta | 1.50 | .70 | .15 |
| ☐ 213 Johnny Fitzpatrick | 1.50 | .70 | .15 |
| ☐ 214 Arnie Portocarrero | 1.50 | .70 | .15 |
| ☐ 215 Warren McGhee | 1.50 | .70 | .15 |
| ☐ 216 Al Sima | 1.50 | .70 | .15 |
| ☐ 217 Paul Schreiber | 1.50 | .70 | .15 |
| ☐ 218 Fred Marsh | 1.50 | .70 | .15 |
| ☐ 219 Chuck Kress | 1.50 | .70 | .15 |
| ☐ 220 Ruben Gomez | 1.50 | .70 | .15 |
| ☐ 221 Dick Brodowski | 1.50 | .70 | .15 |
| ☐ 222 Bill Wilson | 1.50 | .70 | .15 |
| ☐ 223 Joe Haynes | 1.50 | .70 | .15 |
| ☐ 224 Dick Weik | 1.50 | .70 | .15 |
| ☐ 225 Don Liddle | 1.50 | .70 | .15 |
| ☐ 226 Jehosie Heard | 1.50 | .70 | .15 |
| ☐ 227 Colonel Mills | 1.50 | .70 | .15 |
| ☐ 228 Gene Hermanski | 1.50 | .70 | .15 |
| ☐ 229 Robert Talbot | 1.50 | .70 | .15 |
| ☐ 230 Bob Kuzava | 1.50 | .70 | .15 |
| ☐ 231 Roy Smalley | 1.50 | .70 | .15 |
| ☐ 232 Lou Limmer | 1.50 | .70 | .15 |
| ☐ 233 Augie Galan | 1.50 | .70 | .15 |
| ☐ 234 Jerry Lynch | 1.75 | .85 | .17 |
| ☐ 235 Vernon Law | 2.00 | .90 | .20 |
| ☐ 236 Paul Penson | 1.50 | .70 | .15 |
| ☐ 237 Dominic Ryba | 1.50 | .70 | .15 |
| ☐ 238 Al Aber | 1.50 | .70 | .15 |
| ☐ 239 Bill Skowron | 4.00 | 1.85 | .40 |
| ☐ 240 Sam Mele | 1.50 | .70 | .15 |
| ☐ 241 Robert Miller | 1.50 | .70 | .15 |
| ☐ 242 Curt Roberts | 1.50 | .70 | .15 |
| ☐ 243 Ray Blades | 1.50 | .70 | .15 |
| ☐ 244 Leroy Wheat | 1.50 | .70 | .15 |
| ☐ 245 Roy Sievers | 1.75 | .85 | .17 |
| ☐ 246 Howie Fox | 1.50 | .70 | .15 |
| ☐ 247 Ed Mayo | 1.50 | .70 | .15 |
| ☐ 248 Alphonse Smith | 1.75 | .85 | .17 |
| ☐ 249 Wilmer Mizell | 1.50 | .70 | .15 |
| ☐ 250 Ted Williams | 80.00 | 25.00 | 6.00 |

# 1955 TOPPS

The cards in this 206 card set measure 2⅝" by 3¾". Both the large "head" shot and the smaller full-length photos used on each card of the 1955 Topps set are in color. The card fronts were designed horizontally for the first time in Topps' history. The first card features Dusty Rhodes, hitting star for the Giants 1954 World Series sweep over the Indians. A "high" series, 161 to 210, is more difficult to find than cards 1 to 160. Numbers 175, 186, 203, and 209 were never issued. To fill in for the four cards not issued in the high number series, Topps double-printed four players, those appearing on cards 170, 172, 184, and 188.

COMPLETE SET: M-850.00; VG-E-375.00; F-G-75.00

| | MINT | VG-E | F-G |
|---|---|---|---|
| Common Player (1–150) | 1.25 | .60 | .12 |
| Common Player (151–160) | 2.50 | 1.15 | .25 |
| Common Player (161–210) | 3.75 | 1.75 | .37 |

| | | MINT | VG-E | F-G |
|---|---|---|---|---|
| ☐ | 1 Dusty Rhodes | 4.50 | 1.00 | .30 |
| ☐ | 2 Ted Williams | 45.00 | 20.00 | 4.50 |
| ☐ | 3 Art Fowler | 1.25 | .60 | .12 |
| ☐ | 4 Al Kaline | 18.00 | 8.50 | 1.80 |
| ☐ | 5 Jim Gilliam | 2.75 | 1.25 | .27 |
| ☐ | 6 Stan Hack | 1.25 | .60 | .12 |
| ☐ | 7 Jim Hegan | 1.25 | .60 | .12 |
| ☐ | 8 Harold Smith | 1.25 | .60 | .12 |
| ☐ | 9 Robert Miller | 1.25 | .60 | .12 |
| ☐ | 10 Bob Keegan | 1.25 | .60 | .12 |
| ☐ | 11 Ferris Fain | 1.25 | .60 | .12 |
| ☐ | 12 Vernon Thies | 1.25 | .60 | .12 |
| ☐ | 13 Fred Marsh | 1.25 | .60 | .12 |
| ☐ | 14 Jim Finigan | 1.25 | .60 | .12 |
| ☐ | 15 Jim Pendleton | 1.25 | .60 | .12 |
| ☐ | 16 Roy Sievers | 1.50 | .70 | .15 |
| ☐ | 17 Bobby Hofman | 1.25 | .60 | .12 |
| ☐ | 18 Russ Kemmerer | 1.25 | .60 | .12 |
| ☐ | 19 Billy Herman | 2.50 | 1.15 | .25 |
| ☐ | 20 Andy Carey | 1.50 | .70 | .15 |
| ☐ | 21 Alex Grammas | 1.25 | .60 | .12 |
| ☐ | 22 Bill Skowron | 2.75 | 1.25 | .27 |
| ☐ | 23 Jack Parks | 1.25 | .60 | .12 |
| ☐ | 24 Hal Newhouser | 2.25 | 1.00 | .22 |
| ☐ | 25 John Podres | 2.25 | 1.00 | .22 |
| ☐ | 26 Dick Groat | 2.00 | .90 | .20 |
| ☐ | 27 Bill Gardner | 1.50 | .70 | .15 |
| ☐ | 28 Ernie Banks | 16.00 | 7.50 | 1.60 |
| ☐ | 29 Herman Wehmeier | 1.25 | .60 | .12 |
| ☐ | 30 Vic Power | 1.25 | .60 | .12 |
| ☐ | 31 Warren Spahn | 12.00 | 5.50 | 1.20 |
| ☐ | 32 Warren McGhee | 1.25 | .60 | .12 |
| ☐ | 33 Tom Qualters | 1.25 | .60 | .12 |
| ☐ | 34 Wayne Terwilliger | 1.25 | .60 | .12 |
| ☐ | 35 Dave Jolly | 1.25 | .60 | .12 |
| ☐ | 36 Leo Kiely | 1.25 | .60 | .12 |
| ☐ | 37 Joe Cunningham | 1.50 | .70 | .15 |
| ☐ | 38 Bob Turley | 2.25 | 1.00 | .22 |
| ☐ | 39 Bill Glynn | 1.25 | .60 | .12 |
| ☐ | 40 Don Hoak | 1.25 | .60 | .12 |
| ☐ | 41 Chuck Stobbs | 1.25 | .60 | .12 |
| ☐ | 42 John (Windy) McCall | 1.25 | .60 | .12 |
| ☐ | 43 Harvey Haddix | 1.50 | .70 | .15 |
| ☐ | 44 Harold Valentine | 1.25 | .60 | .12 |
| ☐ | 45 Hank Sauer | 1.50 | .70 | .15 |
| ☐ | 46 Ted Kazanski | 1.25 | .60 | .12 |
| ☐ | 47 Hank Aaron | 50.00 | 22.00 | 5.00 |
| ☐ | 48 Bob Kennedy | 1.25 | .60 | .12 |
| ☐ | 49 J.W. Porter | 1.25 | .60 | .12 |
| ☐ | 50 Jackie Robinson | 35.00 | 16.50 | 3.50 |
| ☐ | 51 Jim Hughes | 1.25 | .60 | .12 |
| ☐ | 52 Bill Tremel | 1.25 | .60 | .12 |
| ☐ | 53 Bill Taylor | 1.25 | .60 | .12 |
| ☐ | 54 Lou Limmer | 1.25 | .60 | .12 |
| ☐ | 55 Rip Repulski | 1.25 | .60 | .12 |
| ☐ | 56 Ray Jablonski | 1.25 | .60 | .12 |
| ☐ | 57 Bill O'Dell | 1.25 | .60 | .12 |
| ☐ | 58 Jim Rivera | 1.25 | .60 | .12 |
| ☐ | 59 Gair Allie | 1.25 | .60 | .12 |
| ☐ | 60 Dean Stone | 1.25 | .60 | .12 |
| ☐ | 61 Forrest Jacobs | 1.25 | .60 | .12 |
| ☐ | 62 Thornton Kipper | 1.25 | .60 | .12 |
| ☐ | 63 Joe Collins | 1.50 | .70 | .15 |
| ☐ | 64 Gus Triandos | 1.50 | .70 | .15 |
| ☐ | 65 Ray Boone | 1.25 | .60 | .12 |
| ☐ | 66 Ron Jackson | 1.25 | .60 | .12 |

|  | MINT | VG-E | F-G |
|---|---|---|---|
| ☐ 67 Wally Moon | 1.50 | .70 | .15 |
| ☐ 68 Jim Davis | 1.25 | .60 | .12 |
| ☐ 69 Ed Bailey | 1.25 | .60 | .12 |
| ☐ 70 Al Rosen | 3.25 | 1.50 | .32 |
| ☐ 71 Ruben Gomez | 1.25 | .60 | .12 |
| ☐ 72 Karl Olson | 1.25 | .60 | .12 |
| ☐ 73 Jack Shepard | 1.25 | .60 | .12 |
| ☐ 74 Robert Borkowski | 1.25 | .60 | .12 |
| ☐ 75 Sandy Amoros | 1.75 | .85 | .17 |
| ☐ 76 Howie Pollet | 1.25 | .60 | .12 |
| ☐ 77 Arnold Portocarrero | 1.25 | .60 | .12 |
| ☐ 78 Gordon Jones | 1.25 | .60 | .12 |
| ☐ 79 Clyde Schell | 1.25 | .60 | .12 |
| ☐ 80 Bob Grim | 1.75 | .85 | .17 |
| ☐ 81 Gene Conley | 1.25 | .60 | .12 |
| ☐ 82 Chuck Harmon | 1.25 | .60 | .12 |
| ☐ 83 Tom Brewer | 1.25 | .60 | .12 |
| ☐ 84 Camilo Pascual | 1.50 | .70 | .15 |
| ☐ 85 Don Mossi | 1.75 | .85 | .17 |
| ☐ 86 Bill Wilson | 1.25 | .60 | .12 |
| ☐ 87 Frank House | 1.25 | .60 | .12 |
| ☐ 88 Bob Skinner | 1.50 | .70 | .15 |
| ☐ 89 Joe Frazier | 1.25 | .60 | .12 |
| ☐ 90 Karl Spooner | 1.50 | .70 | .15 |
| ☐ 91 Milt Bolling | 1.25 | .60 | .12 |
| ☐ 92 Don Zimmer | 2.50 | 1.15 | .25 |
| ☐ 93 Steve Bilko | 1.25 | .60 | .12 |
| ☐ 94 Reno Bertoia | 1.25 | .60 | .12 |
| ☐ 95 Preston Ward | 1.25 | .60 | .12 |
| ☐ 96 Chuck Bishop | 1.25 | .60 | .12 |
| ☐ 97 Carlos Paula | 1.25 | .60 | .12 |
| ☐ 98 John Riddle | 1.25 | .60 | .12 |
| ☐ 99 Frank Leja | 1.25 | .60 | .12 |
| ☐ 100 Monte Irvin | 4.50 | 2.10 | .45 |
| ☐ 101 Johnny Gray | 1.25 | .60 | .12 |
| ☐ 102 Wally Westlake | 1.25 | .60 | .12 |
| ☐ 103 Chuck White | 1.25 | .60 | .12 |
| ☐ 104 Jack Harshman | 1.25 | .60 | .12 |
| ☐ 105 Chuck Diering | 1.25 | .60 | .12 |
| ☐ 106 Frank Sullivan | 1.25 | .60 | .12 |
| ☐ 107 Curt Roberts | 1.25 | .60 | .12 |
| ☐ 108 Al Walker | 1.25 | .60 | .12 |
| ☐ 109 Ed Lopat | 2.50 | 1.15 | .25 |
| ☐ 110 Gus Zernial | 1.50 | .70 | .15 |
| ☐ 111 Bob Milliken | 1.25 | .60 | .12 |
| ☐ 112 Nelson King | 1.25 | .60 | .12 |
| ☐ 113 Harry Brecheen | 1.25 | .60 | .12 |
| ☐ 114 Louis Ortiz | 1.25 | .60 | .12 |
| ☐ 115 Ellis Kinder | 1.25 | .60 | .12 |
| ☐ 116 Tom Hurd | 1.25 | .60 | .12 |
| ☐ 117 Mel Roach | 1.25 | .60 | .12 |
| ☐ 118 Bob Purkey | 1.25 | .60 | .12 |
| ☐ 119 Bob Lennon | 1.25 | .60 | .12 |

|  | MINT | VG-E | F-G |
|---|---|---|---|
| ☐ 120 Ted Kluszewski | 3.00 | 1.40 | .30 |
| ☐ 121 Bill Renna | 1.25 | .60 | .12 |
| ☐ 122 Carl Sawatski | 1.25 | .60 | .12 |
| ☐ 123 Sandy Koufax | 80.00 | 37.00 | 8.00 |
| ☐ 124 Harmon Killebrew | 40.00 | 18.00 | 4.00 |
| ☐ 125 Ken Boyer | 5.00 | 2.35 | .50 |
| ☐ 126 Dick Hall | 1.25 | .60 | .12 |
| ☐ 127 Dale Long | 1.50 | .70 | .15 |
| ☐ 128 Ted Lepcio | 1.25 | .60 | .12 |
| ☐ 129 Elvin Tappe | 1.25 | .60 | .12 |
| ☐ 130 Mayo Smith | 1.25 | .60 | .12 |
| ☐ 131 Grady Hatton | 1.25 | .60 | .12 |
| ☐ 132 Bob Trice | 1.25 | .60 | .12 |
| ☐ 133 Dave Hoskins | 1.25 | .60 | .12 |
| ☐ 134 Joe Jay | 1.25 | .60 | .12 |
| ☐ 135 Johnny O'Brien | 1.25 | .60 | .12 |
| ☐ 136 Vernon Stewart | 1.25 | .60 | .12 |
| ☐ 137 Harry Elliott | 1.25 | .60 | .12 |
| ☐ 138 Ray Herbert | 1.25 | .60 | .12 |
| ☐ 139 Steve Kraly | 1.25 | .60 | .12 |
| ☐ 140 Mel Parnell | 1.50 | .70 | .15 |
| ☐ 141 Tom Wright | 1.25 | .60 | .12 |
| ☐ 142 Gerry Lynch | 1.25 | .60 | .12 |
| ☐ 143 John (Dick) Schofield | 1.25 | .60 | .12 |
| ☐ 144 John (Joe) Amalfitano | 1.25 | .60 | .12 |
| ☐ 145 Elmer Valo | 1.25 | .60 | .12 |
| ☐ 146 Dick Donovan | 1.25 | .60 | .12 |
| ☐ 147 Hugh Pepper | 1.25 | .60 | .12 |
| ☐ 148 Hector Brown | 1.25 | .60 | .12 |
| ☐ 149 Ray Crone | 1.25 | .60 | .12 |
| ☐ 150 Michael Higgins | 1.25 | .60 | .12 |
| ☐ 151 Ralph Kress | 2.50 | 1.15 | .25 |
| ☐ 152 Harry Agganis | 3.75 | 1.75 | .37 |
| ☐ 153 Bud Podbielan | 2.50 | 1.15 | .25 |
| ☐ 154 Willie Miranda | 2.50 | 1.15 | .25 |
| ☐ 155 Eddie Mathews | 12.50 | 5.75 | 1.25 |
| ☐ 156 Joe Black | 3.75 | 1.75 | .37 |
| ☐ 157 Robert Miller | 2.50 | 1.15 | .25 |
| ☐ 158 Tommy Carroll | 3.00 | 1.40 | .30 |
| ☐ 159 Johnny Schmitz | 2.50 | 1.15 | .25 |
| ☐ 160 Ray Narleski | 3.00 | 1.40 | .30 |
| ☐ 161 Chuck Tanner | 4.50 | 2.10 | .45 |
| ☐ 162 Joe Coleman | 3.75 | 1.75 | .37 |
| ☐ 163 Faye Throneberry | 3.75 | 1.75 | .37 |
| ☐ 164 Roberto Clemente | 135.00 | 60.00 | 13.50 |
| ☐ 165 Don Johnson | 3.75 | 1.75 | .37 |
| ☐ 166 Hank Bauer | 7.50 | 3.50 | .75 |
| ☐ 167 Thomas Casagrande | 3.75 | 1.75 | .37 |
| ☐ 168 Duane Pillette | 3.75 | 1.75 | .37 |
| ☐ 169 Bob Oldis | 3.75 | 1.75 | .37 |
| ☐ 170 Jim Pearce DP | 1.50 | .70 | .15 |
| ☐ 171 Dick Brodowski | 3.75 | 1.75 | .37 |
| ☐ 172 Frank Baumholtz DP | 1.50 | .70 | .15 |

| | | MINT | VG-E | F-G |
|---|---|---|---|---|
| ☐ 173 | Johnny Kline | 3.75 | 1.75 | .37 |
| ☐ 174 | Rudy Minarcin | 3.75 | 1.75 | .37 |
| ☐ 176 | Norm Zauchin | 3.75 | 1.75 | .37 |
| ☐ 177 | Al Robertson | 3.75 | 1.75 | .37 |
| ☐ 178 | Bobby Adams | 3.75 | 1.75 | .37 |
| ☐ 179 | Jim Bolger | 3.75 | 1.75 | .37 |
| ☐ 180 | Clem Labine | 4.50 | 2.10 | .45 |
| ☐ 181 | Roy McMillan | 3.75 | 1.75 | .37 |
| ☐ 182 | Humberto Robinson | 3.75 | 1.75 | .37 |
| ☐ 183 | Anthony Jacobs | 3.75 | 1.75 | .37 |
| ☐ 184 | Harry Perkowski DP | 1.50 | .70 | .15 |
| ☐ 185 | Don Ferrarese | 3.75 | 1.75 | .37 |
| ☐ 187 | Gil Hodges | 35.00 | 16.50 | 3.50 |
| ☐ 188 | Charlie Silvera DP | 1.50 | .70 | .15 |
| ☐ 189 | Phil Rizzuto | 30.00 | 14.00 | 3.00 |
| ☐ 190 | Gene Woodling | 4.50 | 2.10 | .45 |
| ☐ 191 | Eddie Stanky | 4.50 | 2.10 | .45 |
| ☐ 192 | Jim Delsing | 3.75 | 1.75 | .37 |
| ☐ 193 | Johnny Sain | 5.50 | 2.60 | .55 |
| ☐ 194 | Willie Mays | 160.00 | 75.00 | 16.00 |
| ☐ 195 | Ed Roebuck | 3.75 | 1.75 | .37 |
| ☐ 196 | Gale Wade | 3.75 | 1.75 | .37 |
| ☐ 197 | Al Smith | 3.75 | 1.75 | .37 |
| ☐ 198 | Yogi Berra | 45.00 | 20.00 | 4.50 |
| ☐ 199 | Odbert Hamrick | 3.75 | 1.75 | .37 |
| ☐ 200 | Jackie Jensen | 5.00 | 2.35 | .50 |
| ☐ 201 | Sherman Lollar | 4.25 | 2.00 | .42 |
| ☐ 202 | Jim Owens | 3.75 | 1.75 | .37 |
| ☐ 204 | Frank Smith | 3.75 | 1.75 | .37 |
| ☐ 205 | Gene Freese | 3.75 | 1.75 | .37 |
| ☐ 206 | Pete Daley | 3.75 | 1.75 | .37 |
| ☐ 207 | Bill Consolo | 3.75 | 1.75 | .37 |
| ☐ 208 | Ray Moore | 3.75 | 1.75 | .37 |
| ☐ 210 | Duke Snider | 125.00 | 40.00 | 12.00 |

## 1956 TOPPS

The cards in this 340 card set measure 2⅝" by 3¾". Following up with another horizontally oriented card in 1956, Topps improved the format by layering the color "head" shot onto an actual action sequence involving the player. Cards 1 to 180 come with either white or gray backs: in the 1 to 100 sequence, gray backs are less common (worth about 10% more) and in the 101 to 180 sequence, white backs are less common (worth 30% more). The team cards used for the first time in a regular set by Topps are found dated 1955, or undated, with the team name appearing on either side. The two unnumbered checklist cards are highly prized (must be unmarked to qualify as excellent or mint).

COMPLETE SET: M-850.00; VG-E-375.00; F-G-85.00

| | | MINT | VG-E | F-G |
|---|---|---|---|---|
| | Common Player (1–100) | .85 | .40 | .08 |
| | Common Player (101–180) | 1.15 | .45 | .10 |
| | Common Player (181–260) | 2.25 | 1.00 | .25 |
| | Common Player (261–340) | 1.30 | .65 | .13 |
| ☐ 1 | William Harridge (AL President) | 9.00 | 2.50 | .75 |
| ☐ 2 | Warren Giles (NL President) | 2.50 | 1.15 | .25 |
| ☐ 3 | Elmer Valo | .85 | .40 | .08 |
| ☐ 4 | Carlos Paula | .85 | .40 | .08 |
| ☐ 5 | Ted Williams | 40.00 | 18.00 | 4.00 |
| ☐ 6 | Ray Boone | .85 | .40 | .08 |
| ☐ 7 | Ron Negray | .85 | .40 | .08 |
| ☐ 8 | Walter Alston MGR | 4.00 | 1.85 | .40 |
| ☐ 9 | Ruben Gomez | .85 | .40 | .08 |
| ☐ 10 | Warren Spahn | 9.00 | 4.25 | .90 |
| ☐ 11 A | Chicago Cubs (centered) | 2.25 | 1.00 | .22 |
| ☐ 11 B | Cubs Team (dated 1955) | 8.50 | 4.00 | .85 |
| ☐ 11 C | Cubs Team (name at far left) | 2.50 | 1.15 | .25 |
| ☐ 12 | Andy Carey | 1.10 | .50 | .11 |
| ☐ 13 | Roy Face | 1.25 | .60 | .12 |
| ☐ 14 | Ken Boyer | 2.50 | 1.15 | .25 |
| ☐ 15 | Ernie Banks | 11.00 | 5.25 | 1.10 |
| ☐ 16 | Hector Lopez | .85 | .40 | .08 |
| ☐ 17 | Gene Conley | .85 | .40 | .08 |
| ☐ 18 | Dick Donovan | .85 | .40 | .08 |
| ☐ 19 | Chuck Diering | .85 | .40 | .08 |
| ☐ 20 | Al Kaline | 14.00 | 6.50 | 1.40 |

| | MINT | VG-E | F-G |
|---|---|---|---|
| ☐ 21 Joe Collins | 1.10 | .50 | .11 |
| ☐ 22 Jim Finigan | .85 | .40 | .08 |
| ☐ 23 Freddie Marsh | .85 | .40 | .08 |
| ☐ 24 Dick Groat | 1.75 | .85 | .17 |
| ☐ 25 Ted Kluszewski | 2.50 | 1.15 | .25 |
| ☐ 26 Grady Hatton | .85 | .40 | .08 |
| ☐ 27 Nelson Burbrink | .85 | .40 | .08 |
| ☐ 28 Bobby Hofman | .85 | .40 | .08 |
| ☐ 29 Jack Harshman | .85 | .40 | .08 |
| ☐ 30 Jackie Robinson | 33.00 | 15.00 | 3.00 |
| ☐ 31 Hank Aaron | 45.00 | 20.00 | 4.50 |
| ☐ 32 Frank House | .85 | .40 | .08 |
| ☐ 33 Roberto Clemente | 33.00 | 15.00 | 3.00 |
| ☐ 34 Tom Brewer | .85 | .40 | .08 |
| ☐ 35 Al Rosen | 2.50 | 1.15 | .25 |
| ☐ 36 Rudy Minarcin | .85 | .40 | .08 |
| ☐ 37 Alex Grammas | .85 | .40 | .08 |
| ☐ 38 Bob Kennedy | .85 | .40 | .08 |
| ☐ 39 Don Mossi | 1.25 | .60 | .12 |
| ☐ 40 Bob Turley | 1.75 | .85 | .17 |
| ☐ 41 Hank Sauer | 1.10 | .50 | .11 |
| ☐ 42 Sandy Amoros | 1.10 | .50 | .11 |
| ☐ 43 Ray Moore | .85 | .40 | .08 |
| ☐ 44 Windy McCall | .85 | .40 | .08 |
| ☐ 45 Gus Zernial | .85 | .40 | .08 |
| ☐ 46 Gene Freese | .85 | .40 | .08 |
| ☐ 47 Art Fowler | .85 | .40 | .08 |
| ☐ 48 Jim Hegan | .85 | .40 | .08 |
| ☐ 49 Pedro Ramos | .85 | .40 | .08 |
| ☐ 50 Dusty Rhodes | 1.10 | .50 | .11 |
| ☐ 51 Ernie Oravetz | .85 | .40 | .08 |
| ☐ 52 Bob Grim | 1.10 | .50 | .11 |
| ☐ 53 Arnie Portocarrero | .85 | .40 | .08 |
| ☐ 54 Bob Keegan | .85 | .40 | .08 |
| ☐ 55 Wally Moon | 1.10 | .50 | .11 |
| ☐ 56 Dale Long | .85 | .40 | .08 |
| ☐ 57 Duke Maas | .85 | .40 | .08 |
| ☐ 58 Ed Roebuck | .85 | .40 | .08 |
| ☐ 59 Jose Santiago | .85 | .40 | .08 |
| ☐ 60 Mayo Smith | .85 | .40 | .08 |
| ☐ 61 Bill Skowron | 2.50 | 1.15 | .25 |
| ☐ 62 Hal Smith | .85 | .40 | .08 |
| ☐ 63 Roger Craig | 2.00 | .90 | .20 |
| ☐ 64 Luis Arroyo | 1.10 | .50 | .11 |
| ☐ 65 Johnny O'Brien | .85 | .40 | .08 |
| ☐ 66 Bob Speake | .85 | .40 | .08 |
| ☐ 67 Vic Power | .85 | .40 | .08 |
| ☐ 68 Chuck Stobbs | .85 | .40 | .08 |
| ☐ 69 Chuck Tanner | 1.10 | .50 | .11 |
| ☐ 70 Jim Rivera | .85 | .40 | .08 |
| ☐ 71 Frank Sullivan | .85 | .40 | .08 |
| ☐ 72 A Phillies Team (centered) | 2.25 | 1.00 | .22 |
| ☐ 72 B Phillies Team (dated 1955) | 8.50 | 4.00 | .85 |
| ☐ 72 C Phillies Team (name at far left) | 2.50 | 1.15 | .25 |
| ☐ 73 Wayne Terwilliger | .85 | .40 | .08 |
| ☐ 74 Jim King | .85 | .40 | .08 |
| ☐ 75 Roy Sievers | 1.10 | .50 | .11 |
| ☐ 76 Ray Crone | .85 | .40 | .08 |
| ☐ 77 Harvey Haddix | 1.10 | .50 | .11 |
| ☐ 78 Herman Wehmeier | .85 | .40 | .08 |
| ☐ 79 Sandy Koufax | 33.00 | 15.00 | 3.00 |
| ☐ 80 Gus Triandos | 1.10 | .50 | .11 |
| ☐ 81 Wally Westlake | .85 | .40 | .08 |
| ☐ 82 Bill Renna | .85 | .40 | .08 |
| ☐ 83 Karl Spooner | 1.10 | .50 | .11 |
| ☐ 84 Babe Birrer | .85 | .40 | .08 |
| ☐ 85 A Cleveland Indians (centered) | 2.25 | 1.00 | .22 |
| ☐ 85 B Indians Team (dated 1955) | 8.50 | 4.00 | .85 |
| ☐ 85 C Indians Team (name at far left) | 2.50 | 1.15 | .25 |
| ☐ 86 Ray Jablonski | .85 | .40 | .08 |
| ☐ 87 Dean Stone | .85 | .40 | .08 |
| ☐ 88 Johnny Kucks | 1.10 | .50 | .11 |
| ☐ 89 Norm Zauchin | .85 | .40 | .08 |
| ☐ 90 A Cincinnati Redlegs Team (centered) | 2.25 | 1.00 | .22 |
| ☐ 90 B Reds Team (dated 1955) | 8.50 | 4.00 | .85 |
| ☐ 90 C Reds Team (name at far left) | 2.50 | 1.15 | .25 |
| ☐ 91 Gail Harris | .85 | .40 | .08 |
| ☐ 92 Bob (Red) Wilson | .85 | .40 | .08 |
| ☐ 93 George Susce | .85 | .40 | .08 |
| ☐ 94 Ronnie Kline | .85 | .40 | .08 |
| ☐ 95 A Milwaukee Braves Team (centered) | 2.25 | 1.00 | .22 |
| ☐ 95 B Braves Team (dated 1955) | 8.50 | 4.00 | .85 |
| ☐ 95 C Braves Team (name) (at far left) | 2.50 | 1.15 | .25 |
| ☐ 96 Bill Tremel | .85 | .40 | .08 |
| ☐ 97 Jerry Lynch | .85 | .40 | .08 |
| ☐ 98 Camilo Pascual | 1.10 | .50 | .11 |
| ☐ 99 Don Zimmer | 1.50 | .70 | .15 |
| ☐ 100 A Baltimore Orioles Team (centered) | 2.25 | 1.00 | .22 |
| ☐ 100 B Orioles Team (dated 1955) | 8.50 | 4.00 | .85 |
| ☐ 100 C Orioles Team (at far left) | 2.50 | 1.15 | .25 |
| ☐ 101 Roy Campanella | 30.00 | 14.00 | 3.00 |

| | MINT | VG-E | F-G | | MINT | VG-E | F-G |
|---|---|---|---|---|---|---|---|
| ☐ 102 Jim Davis | 1.15 | .45 | .10 | ☐ 155 Harvey Kuenn | 2.00 | .90 | .20 |
| ☐ 103 Willie Miranda | 1.15 | .45 | .10 | ☐ 156 Wes Westrum | 1.15 | .45 | .10 |
| ☐ 104 Bob Lennon | 1.15 | .45 | .10 | ☐ 157 Dick Brodowski | 1.15 | .45 | .10 |
| ☐ 105 Al Smith | 1.15 | .45 | .10 | ☐ 158 Wally Post | 1.15 | .45 | .10 |
| ☐ 106 Joe Astroth | 1.15 | .45 | .10 | ☐ 159 Clint Courtney | 1.15 | .45 | .10 |
| ☐ 107 Ed Mathews | 9.00 | 4.25 | .90 | ☐ 160 Billy Pierce | 1.50 | .70 | .15 |
| ☐ 108 Laurin Pepper | 1.15 | .45 | .10 | ☐ 161 Joe DeMaestri | 1.15 | .45 | .10 |
| ☐ 109 Enos Slaughter | 6.00 | 2.80 | .60 | ☐ 162 Dave (Gus) Bell | 1.50 | .70 | .15 |
| ☐ 110 Yogi Berra | 21.00 | 9.50 | 2.10 | ☐ 163 Gene Woodling | 1.50 | .70 | .15 |
| ☐ 111 Boston Red Sox Team | 2.50 | 1.15 | .25 | ☐ 164 Harmon Killebrew | 16.00 | 7.50 | 1.60 |
| ☐ 112 Dee Fondy | 1.15 | .45 | .10 | ☐ 165 Red Schoendienst | 2.00 | .90 | .20 |
| ☐ 113 Phil Rizzuto | 12.50 | 5.75 | 1.25 | ☐ 166 Brooklyn Dodgers Team | 18.00 | 8.50 | 1.80 |
| ☐ 114 Jim Owens | 1.15 | .45 | .10 | ☐ 167 Harry Dorish | 1.15 | .45 | .10 |
| ☐ 115 Jackie Jensen | 2.25 | 1.00 | .22 | ☐ 168 Sammy White | 1.15 | .45 | .10 |
| ☐ 116 Eddie O'Brien | 1.15 | .45 | .10 | ☐ 169 Bob Nelson | 1.15 | .45 | .10 |
| ☐ 117 Virgil Trucks | 1.15 | .45 | .10 | ☐ 170 Bill Virdon | 2.00 | .90 | .20 |
| ☐ 118 Nelson Fox | 3.50 | 1.65 | .35 | ☐ 171 Jim Wilson | 1.15 | .45 | .10 |
| ☐ 119 Larry Jackson | 1.15 | .45 | .10 | ☐ 172 Frank Torre | 1.15 | .45 | .10 |
| ☐ 120 Richie Ashburn | 3.75 | 1.75 | .37 | ☐ 173 Johnny Podres | 2.25 | 1.00 | .22 |
| ☐ 121 Pirates Team | 2.25 | 1.00 | .22 | ☐ 174 Glen Gorbous | 1.15 | .45 | .10 |
| ☐ 122 Willard Nixon | 1.15 | .45 | .10 | ☐ 175 Del Crandall | 1.50 | .70 | .15 |
| ☐ 123 Roy McMillan | 1.15 | .45 | .10 | ☐ 176 Alex Kellner | 1.15 | .45 | .10 |
| ☐ 124 Don Kaiser | 1.15 | .45 | .10 | ☐ 177 Hank Bauer | 2.25 | 1.00 | .22 |
| ☐ 125 Minnie Minoso | 2.75 | 1.25 | .27 | ☐ 178 Joe Black | 1.50 | .70 | .15 |
| ☐ 126 Jim Brady | 1.15 | .45 | .10 | ☐ 179 Harry Chiti | 1.15 | .45 | .10 |
| ☐ 127 Willie Jones | 1.15 | .45 | .10 | ☐ 180 Robin Roberts | 8.50 | 4.00 | .85 |
| ☐ 128 Eddie Yost | 1.15 | .45 | .10 | ☐ 181 Billy Martin | 12.50 | 5.75 | 1.25 |
| ☐ 129 Jake Martin | 1.15 | .45 | .10 | ☐ 182 Paul Minner | 2.25 | 1.00 | .25 |
| ☐ 130 Willie Mays | 50.00 | 22.00 | 5.00 | ☐ 183 Stan Lopata | 2.25 | 1.00 | .25 |
| ☐ 131 Bob Roselli | 1.15 | .45 | .10 | ☐ 184 Don Bessent | 2.25 | 1.00 | .25 |
| ☐ 132 Bobby Avila | 1.15 | .45 | .10 | ☐ 185 Bill Bruton | 2.25 | 1.00 | .25 |
| ☐ 133 Ray Narleski | 1.15 | .45 | .10 | ☐ 186 Ron Jackson | 2.25 | 1.00 | .25 |
| ☐ 134 Cardinals Team | 2.50 | 1.15 | .25 | ☐ 187 Early Wynn | 10.00 | 4.75 | 1.00 |
| ☐ 135 Mickey Mantle | 120.00 | 55.00 | 12.00 | ☐ 188 White Sox Team | 4.00 | 1.85 | .40 |
| ☐ 136 Johnny Logan | 1.50 | .70 | .15 | ☐ 189 Ned Garver | 2.25 | 1.00 | .25 |
| ☐ 137 Al Silvera | 1.15 | .45 | .10 | ☐ 190 Carl Furillo | 5.00 | 2.35 | .50 |
| ☐ 138 Johnny Antonelli | 1.50 | .70 | .15 | ☐ 191 Frank Lary | 2.50 | 1.15 | .25 |
| ☐ 139 Tommy Carroll | 1.15 | .45 | .10 | ☐ 192 Smokey Burgess | 2.25 | 1.00 | .22 |
| ☐ 140 Herb Score | 2.75 | 1.25 | .27 | ☐ 193 Wilmer Mizell | 2.25 | 1.00 | .25 |
| ☐ 141 Joe Frazier | 1.15 | .45 | .10 | ☐ 194 Monte Irvin | 7.00 | 3.25 | .70 |
| ☐ 142 Gene Baker | 1.15 | .45 | .10 | ☐ 195 George Kell | 8.00 | 3.75 | .80 |
| ☐ 143 Jim Piersall | 2.00 | .90 | .20 | ☐ 196 Tom Poholsky | 2.25 | 1.00 | .25 |
| ☐ 144 Leroy Powell | 1.15 | .45 | .10 | ☐ 197 Granny Hamner | 2.25 | 1.00 | .25 |
| ☐ 145 Gil Hodges | 12.00 | 5.50 | 1.20 | ☐ 198 Ed Fitzgerald | 2.25 | 1.00 | .25 |
| ☐ 146 Washington Team | 2.25 | 1.00 | .22 | ☐ 199 Hank Thompson | 2.25 | 1.00 | .25 |
| ☐ 147 Earl Torgeson | 1.15 | .45 | .10 | ☐ 200 Bob Feller | 20.00 | 9.00 | 2.00 |
| ☐ 148 Al Dark | 1.75 | .85 | .17 | ☐ 201 Rip Repulski | 2.25 | 1.00 | .25 |
| ☐ 149 Dixie Howell | 1.15 | .45 | .10 | ☐ 202 Jim Hearn | 2.25 | 1.00 | .25 |
| ☐ 150 Duke Snider | 30.00 | 14.00 | 3.00 | ☐ 203 Bill Tuttle | 2.25 | 1.00 | .25 |
| ☐ 151 Spook Jacobs | 1.15 | .45 | .10 | ☐ 204 Art Swanson | 2.25 | 1.00 | .25 |
| ☐ 152 Billy Hoeft | 1.15 | .45 | .10 | ☐ 205 Whitey Lockman | 2.25 | 1.00 | .25 |
| ☐ 153 Frank Thomas | 1.15 | .45 | .10 | ☐ 206 Erv Palica | 2.25 | 1.00 | .25 |
| ☐ 154 David Pope | 1.15 | .45 | .10 | ☐ 207 Jim Small | 2.25 | 1.00 | .25 |

| | MINT | VG-E | F-G | | MINT | VG-E | F-G |
|---|---|---|---|---|---|---|---|
| 208 Elston Howard | 6.50 | 3.00 | .65 | 261 Bobby Shantz | 1.75 | .85 | .17 |
| 209 Max Surkont | 2.25 | 1.00 | .25 | 262 Howie Pollett | 1.30 | .65 | .13 |
| 210 Mike Garcia | 3.00 | 1.40 | .30 | 263 Bob Miller | 1.30 | .65 | .13 |
| 211 Murry Dickson | 2.25 | 1.00 | .25 | 264 Ray Monzant | 1.30 | .65 | .13 |
| 212 Johnny Temple | 3.00 | 1.40 | .30 | 265 Sandy Consuegra | 1.30 | .65 | .13 |
| 213 Detroit Tigers Team | 6.00 | 2.80 | .60 | 266 Don Ferrarese | 1.30 | .65 | .13 |
| 214 Bob Rush | 2.25 | 1.00 | .25 | 267 Bob Nieman | 1.30 | .65 | .13 |
| 215 Tommy Byrne | 2.25 | 1.00 | .25 | 268 Dale Mitchell | 1.75 | .85 | .17 |
| 216 Jerry Schoonmaker | 2.25 | 1.00 | .25 | 269 Jack Meyer | 1.30 | .65 | .13 |
| 217 Billy Klaus | 2.25 | 1.00 | .25 | 270 Billy Loes | 1.75 | .85 | .17 |
| 218 Joe Nuxhall (Nuxall) | 3.00 | 1.40 | .30 | 271 Foster Castleman | 1.30 | .65 | .13 |
| 219 Lew Burdette | 4.00 | 1.85 | .40 | 272 Danny O'Connell | 1.30 | .65 | .13 |
| 220 Del Ennis | 3.00 | 1.40 | .30 | 273 Walker Cooper | 1.30 | .65 | .13 |
| 221 Bob Friend | 3.00 | 1.40 | .30 | 274 Frank Baumholtz | 1.30 | .65 | .13 |
| 222 Dave Philley | 2.25 | 1.00 | .25 | 275 Jim Greengrass | 1.30 | .65 | .13 |
| 223 Randy Jackson | 2.25 | 1.00 | .25 | 276 George Zuverink | 1.30 | .65 | .13 |
| 224 Bud Podbielan | 2.25 | 1.00 | .25 | 277 Daryl Spencer | 1.30 | .65 | .13 |
| 225 Gil McDougald | 6.00 | 2.80 | .60 | 278 Chet Nichols | 1.30 | .65 | .13 |
| 226 Giants Team | 9.00 | 4.25 | .90 | 279 Johnny Groth | 1.30 | .65 | .13 |
| 227 Russ Meyer | 2.25 | 1.00 | .25 | 280 Jim Gilliam | 3.50 | 1.65 | .35 |
| 228 Mickey Vernon | 3.00 | 1.40 | .30 | 281 Art Houtteman | 1.30 | .65 | .13 |
| 229 Harry Brecheen | 2.25 | 1.00 | .25 | 282 Warren Hacker | 1.30 | .65 | .13 |
| 230 Chico Carrasquel | 2.25 | 1.00 | .25 | 283 Hal Smith | 1.30 | .65 | .13 |
| 231 Bob Hale | 2.25 | 1.00 | .25 | 284 Ike Delock | 1.30 | .65 | .13 |
| 232 Toby Atwell | 2.25 | 1.00 | .25 | 285 Eddie Miksis | 1.30 | .65 | .13 |
| 233 Carl Erskine | 6.00 | 2.80 | .60 | 286 Bill Wight | 1.30 | .65 | .13 |
| 234 Pete Runnels | 3.00 | 1.40 | .30 | 287 Bobby Adams | 1.30 | .65 | .13 |
| 235 Don Newcombe | 9.00 | 4.25 | .90 | 288 Bob Cerv | 1.75 | .85 | .17 |
| 236 Athletics Team | 4.00 | 1.85 | .40 | 289 Hal Jeffcoat | 1.30 | .65 | .13 |
| 237 Jose Valdivielso | 2.25 | 1.00 | .25 | 290 Curt Simmons | 1.75 | .85 | .17 |
| 238 Walt Dropo | 2.25 | 1.00 | .25 | 291 Frank Kellert | 1.30 | .65 | .13 |
| 239 Harry Simpson | 2.25 | 1.00 | .25 | 292 Luis Aparicio | 20.00 | 9.00 | 2.00 |
| 240 Whitey Ford | 18.00 | 8.50 | 1.80 | 293 Stu Miller | 1.30 | .65 | .13 |
| 241 Don Mueller | 2.25 | 1.00 | .25 | 294 Ernie Johnson | 1.30 | .65 | .13 |
| 242 Hershell Freeman | 2.25 | 1.00 | .25 | 295 Clem Labine | 1.75 | .85 | .17 |
| 243 Sherm Lollar | 2.25 | 1.00 | .25 | 296 Andy Seminick | 1.30 | .65 | .13 |
| 244 Bob Buhl | 2.25 | 1.00 | .25 | 297 Bob Skinner | 1.50 | .70 | .15 |
| 245 Billy Goodman | 3.00 | 1.40 | .30 | 298 Johnny Schmitz | 1.30 | .65 | .13 |
| 246 Tom Gorman | 2.25 | 1.00 | .25 | 299 Charley Neal | 1.75 | .85 | .17 |
| 247 Bill Sarni | 2.25 | 1.00 | .25 | 300 Vic Wertz | 1.50 | .70 | .15 |
| 248 Bob Porterfield | 2.25 | 1.00 | .25 | 301 Marv Grissom | 1.30 | .65 | .13 |
| 249 Johnny Klippstein | 2.25 | 1.00 | .25 | 302 Eddie Robinson | 1.30 | .65 | .13 |
| 250 Larry Doby | 5.00 | 2.35 | .50 | 303 Jim Dyck | 1.30 | .65 | .13 |
| 251 Yankees Team | 20.00 | 9.00 | 2.00 | 304 Frank Malzone | 1.75 | .85 | .17 |
| 252 Vernon Law | 3.00 | 1.40 | .30 | 305 Brooks Lawrence | 1.30 | .65 | .13 |
| 253 Irv Noren | 2.25 | 1.00 | .25 | 306 Curt Roberts | 1.30 | .65 | .13 |
| 254 George Crowe | 2.25 | 1.00 | .25 | 307 Hoyt Wilhelm | 8.00 | 3.75 | .80 |
| 255 Bob Lemon | 10.00 | 4.75 | 1.00 | 308 Chuck Harmon | 1.30 | .65 | .13 |
| 256 Tom Hurd | 2.25 | 1.00 | .25 | 309 Don Blasingame | 1.50 | .70 | .15 |
| 257 Bobby Thomson | 4.00 | 1.85 | .40 | 310 Steve Gromek | 1.30 | .65 | .13 |
| 258 Art Ditmar | 2.25 | 1.00 | .25 | 311 Hal Naragon | 1.30 | .65 | .13 |
| 259 Sam Jones | 2.25 | 1.00 | .25 | 312 Andy Pafko | 1.50 | .70 | .15 |
| 260 Pee Wee Reese | 18.00 | 8.50 | 1.80 | 313 Gene Stephens | 1.30 | .65 | .13 |

| | | MINT | VG-E | F-G |
|---|---|---|---|---|
| ☐ | 314 Hobie Landrith | 1.30 | .65 | .13 |
| ☐ | 315 Milt Bolling | 1.30 | .65 | .13 |
| ☐ | 316 Jerry Coleman | 1.75 | .85 | .17 |
| ☐ | 317 Al Aber | 1.30 | .65 | .13 |
| ☐ | 318 Fred Hatfield | 1.30 | .65 | .13 |
| ☐ | 319 John Crimian | 1.30 | .65 | .13 |
| ☐ | 320 Joe Adcock | 1.75 | .85 | .17 |
| ☐ | 321 Jim Konstanty | 1.50 | .70 | .15 |
| ☐ | 322 Karl Olson | 1.30 | .65 | .13 |
| ☐ | 323 Willard Schmidt | 1.30 | .65 | .13 |
| ☐ | 324 Rocky Bridges | 1.30 | .65 | .13 |
| ☐ | 325 Don Liddle | 1.30 | .65 | .13 |
| ☐ | 326 Connie Johnson | 1.30 | .65 | .13 |
| ☐ | 327 Bob Wiesler | 1.30 | .65 | .13 |
| ☐ | 328 Preston Ward | 1.30 | .65 | .13 |
| ☐ | 329 Lou Berberet | 1.30 | .65 | .13 |
| ☐ | 330 Jim Busby | 1.30 | .65 | .13 |
| ☐ | 331 Dick Hall | 1.30 | .65 | .13 |
| ☐ | 332 Don Larsen | 3.50 | 1.65 | .35 |
| ☐ | 333 Rube Walker | 1.50 | .70 | .15 |
| ☐ | 334 Bob Miller | 1.30 | .65 | .13 |
| ☐ | 335 Don Hoak | 1.30 | .65 | .13 |
| ☐ | 336 Ellis Kinder | 1.30 | .65 | .13 |
| ☐ | 337 Bobby Morgan | 1.30 | .65 | .13 |
| ☐ | 338 Jim Delsing | 1.30 | .65 | .13 |
| ☐ | 339 Rance Pless | 1.30 | .65 | .13 |
| ☐ | 340 Mickey McDermott | 3.00 | 1.00 | .30 |

**UNNUMBERED CHECKLISTS**

| | | MINT | VG-E | F-G |
|---|---|---|---|---|
| ☐ | 341 Checklist 1/3 | 65.00 | 10.00 | 2.00 |
| ☐ | 342 Checklist 2/4 | 65.00 | 10.00 | 2.00 |

## 1957 TOPPS

The cards in this 407 card set measure 2½″ by 3½″. In 1957, Topps returned to the vertical obverse, adopted what we now call the standard card size, and used a large, uncluttered color photo for the first time since 1952. Cards in the series 265 to 352 and the unnumbered checklist cards are scarcer than other cards in the set. The first star combination cards (Numbers 400 and 407) featured Yankees and Dodgers.

COMPLETE SET: M-1050.00; VG-E-450.00; F-G-100.00

| | MINT | VG-E | F-G |
|---|---|---|---|
| Common Player (1–264) | .75 | .35 | .07 |
| Common Player (265–352) | 3.75 | 1.60 | .40 |
| Common Player (353–407) | 1.00 | .45 | .10 |

| | | MINT | VG-E | F-G |
|---|---|---|---|---|
| ☐ | 1 Ted Williams | 70.00 | 17.00 | 4.00 |
| ☐ | 2 Yogi Berra | 17.00 | 8.00 | 1.70 |
| ☐ | 3 Dale Long | .75 | .35 | .07 |
| ☐ | 4 Johnny Logan | .90 | .40 | .09 |
| ☐ | 5 Sal Maglie | 2.00 | .90 | .20 |
| ☐ | 6 Hector Lopez | .75 | .35 | .07 |
| ☐ | 7 Luis Aparicio | 5.00 | 2.35 | .50 |
| ☐ | 8 Don Mossi | .90 | .40 | .09 |
| ☐ | 9 Johnny Temple | .90 | .40 | .09 |
| ☐ | 10 Willie Mays | 40.00 | 18.00 | 4.00 |
| ☐ | 11 George Zuverink | .75 | .35 | .07 |
| ☐ | 12 Dick Groat | 1.50 | .70 | .15 |
| ☐ | 13 Wally Burnette | .75 | .35 | .07 |
| ☐ | 14 Bob Nieman | .75 | .35 | .07 |
| ☐ | 15 Robin Roberts | 6.00 | 2.80 | .60 |
| ☐ | 16 Walt Moryn | .75 | .35 | .07 |
| ☐ | 17 Billy Gardner | .90 | .40 | .09 |
| ☐ | 18 Don Drysdale | 25.00 | 11.00 | 2.50 |
| ☐ | 19 Bob Wilson | .75 | .35 | .07 |
| ☐ | 20 Hank Aaron (reverse negative photo on front) | 45.00 | 20.00 | 4.50 |
| ☐ | 21 Frank Sullivan | .75 | .35 | .07 |
| ☐ | 22 Jerry Snyder (photo actually Ed Fitzgerald) | .75 | .35 | .07 |
| ☐ | 23 Sherm Lollar | .90 | .40 | .09 |
| ☐ | 24 Bill Mazeroski | 4.00 | 1.85 | .40 |
| ☐ | 25 Whitey Ford | 10.00 | 4.75 | 1.00 |
| ☐ | 26 Bob Boyd | .75 | .35 | .07 |
| ☐ | 27 Ted Kazanski | .75 | .35 | .07 |
| ☐ | 28 Gene Conley | .75 | .35 | .07 |
| ☐ | 29 Whitey Herzog | 1.75 | .85 | .17 |
| ☐ | 30 Pee Wee Reese | 12.00 | 5.50 | 1.20 |
| ☐ | 31 Ron Northey | .75 | .35 | .07 |
| ☐ | 32 Hershell Freeman | .75 | .35 | .07 |
| ☐ | 33 Jim Small | .75 | .35 | .07 |
| ☐ | 34 Tom Sturdivant | .75 | .35 | .07 |

| | | MINT | VG-E | F-G |
|---|---|---|---|---|
| ☐ 35 | Frank Robinson | 36.00 | 15.00 | 3.00 |
| ☐ 36 | Bob Grim | .90 | .40 | .09 |
| ☐ 37 | Frank Torre | .90 | .40 | .09 |
| ☐ 38 | Nelson Fox | 2.75 | 1.25 | .27 |
| ☐ 39 | Al Worthington | .75 | .35 | .07 |
| ☐ 40 | Early Wynn | 6.00 | 2.80 | .60 |
| ☐ 41 | Hal W. Smith | .75 | .35 | .07 |
| ☐ 42 | Dee Fondy | .75 | .35 | .07 |
| ☐ 43 | Connie Johnson | .75 | .35 | .07 |
| ☐ 44 | Joe DeMaestri | .75 | .35 | .07 |
| ☐ 45 | Carl Furillo | 2.75 | 1.25 | .27 |
| ☐ 46 | Robert J. Miller | .75 | .35 | .07 |
| ☐ 47 | Don Blasingame | .75 | .35 | .07 |
| ☐ 48 | Bill Bruton | .75 | .35 | .07 |
| ☐ 49 | Daryl Spencer | .75 | .35 | .07 |
| ☐ 50 | Herb Score | 1.50 | .70 | .15 |
| ☐ 51 | Clint Courtney | .75 | .35 | .07 |
| ☐ 52 | Lee Walls | .75 | .35 | .07 |
| ☐ 53 | Clem Labine | 1.00 | .45 | .10 |
| ☐ 54 | Elmer Valo | .75 | .35 | .07 |
| ☐ 55 | Ernie Banks | 11.00 | 5.25 | 1.10 |
| ☐ 56 | Dave Sisler | .75 | .35 | .07 |
| ☐ 57 | Jim Lemon | .90 | .40 | .09 |
| ☐ 58 | Ruben Gomez | .75 | .35 | .07 |
| ☐ 59 | Dick Williams | .90 | .40 | .09 |
| ☐ 60 | Billy Hoeft | .75 | .35 | .07 |
| ☐ 61 | James Rhodes | .90 | .40 | .09 |
| ☐ 62 | Billy Martin | 9.00 | 4.25 | .90 |
| ☐ 63 | Ike Delock | .75 | .35 | .07 |
| ☐ 64 | Pete Runnels | .90 | .40 | .09 |
| ☐ 65 | Wally Moon | .90 | .40 | .09 |
| ☐ 66 | Brooks Lawrence | .75 | .35 | .07 |
| ☐ 67 | Chico Carrasquel | .75 | .35 | .07 |
| ☐ 68 | Ray Crone | .75 | .35 | .07 |
| ☐ 69 | Roy McMillan | .75 | .35 | .07 |
| ☐ 70 | Richie Ashburn | 3.00 | 1.40 | .30 |
| ☐ 71 | Murry Dickson | .75 | .35 | .07 |
| ☐ 72 | Bill Tuttle | .75 | .35 | .07 |
| ☐ 73 | George Crowe | .75 | .35 | .07 |
| ☐ 74 | Vito Valentinetti | .75 | .35 | .07 |
| ☐ 75 | Jim Piersall | 1.75 | .85 | .17 |
| ☐ 76 | Roberto Clemente | 23.00 | 10.50 | 2.30 |
| ☐ 77 | Paul Foytack | .75 | .35 | .07 |
| ☐ 78 | Vic Wertz | .90 | .40 | .09 |
| ☐ 79 | Lindy McDaniel | .90 | .40 | .09 |
| ☐ 80 | Gil Hodges | 10.00 | 4.75 | 1.00 |
| ☐ 81 | Herman Wehmeier | .75 | .35 | .07 |
| ☐ 82 | Elston Howard | 2.75 | 1.25 | .27 |
| ☐ 83 | Lou Skizas | .75 | .35 | .07 |
| ☐ 84 | Moe Drabowsky | .90 | .40 | .09 |
| ☐ 85 | Larry Doby | 1.75 | .85 | .17 |
| ☐ 86 | Bill Sarni | .75 | .35 | .07 |
| ☐ 87 | Tom Gorman | .75 | .35 | .07 |

| | | MINT | VG-E | F-G |
|---|---|---|---|---|
| ☐ 88 | Harvey Kuenn | 1.75 | .85 | .17 |
| ☐ 89 | Roy Sievers | .90 | .40 | .09 |
| ☐ 90 | Warren Spahn | 10.00 | 4.75 | 1.00 |
| ☐ 91 | Mack Burk | .75 | .35 | .07 |
| ☐ 92 | Mickey Vernon | .90 | .40 | .09 |
| ☐ 93 | Hal Jeffcoat | .75 | .35 | .07 |
| ☐ 94 | Bobby Del Greco | .75 | .35 | .07 |
| ☐ 95 | Mickey Mantle | 110.00 | 50.00 | 11.00 |
| ☐ 96 | Hank Aguirre | .75 | .35 | .07 |
| ☐ 97 | New York Yankees Team | 6.00 | 2.80 | .60 |
| ☐ 98 | Alvin Dark | 1.50 | .70 | .15 |
| ☐ 99 | Bob Keegan | .75 | .35 | .07 |
| ☐ 100 | Giles and Harridge League Presidents | 2.00 | .90 | .20 |
| ☐ 101 | Chuck Stobbs | .75 | .35 | .07 |
| ☐ 102 | Ray Boone | .75 | .35 | .07 |
| ☐ 103 | Joe Nuxhall | .90 | .40 | .09 |
| ☐ 104 | Hank Foiles | .75 | .35 | .07 |
| ☐ 105 | Johnny Antonelli | 1.00 | .45 | .10 |
| ☐ 106 | Ray Moore | .75 | .35 | .07 |
| ☐ 107 | Jim Rivera | .75 | .35 | .07 |
| ☐ 108 | Tommy Byrne | .90 | .40 | .09 |
| ☐ 109 | Hank Thompson | .90 | .40 | .09 |
| ☐ 110 | Bill Virdon | 1.75 | .85 | .17 |
| ☐ 111 | Hal R. Smith | .75 | .35 | .07 |
| ☐ 112 | Tom Brewer | .75 | .35 | .07 |
| ☐ 113 | Wilmer Mizell | .75 | .35 | .07 |
| ☐ 114 | Milwaukee Braves Team | 2.25 | 1.00 | .22 |
| ☐ 115 | Jim Gilliam | 2.25 | 1.00 | .22 |
| ☐ 116 | Mike Fornieles | .75 | .35 | .07 |
| ☐ 117 | Joe Adcock | 1.50 | .70 | .15 |
| ☐ 118 | Bob Porterfield | .75 | .35 | .07 |
| ☐ 119 | Stan Lopata | .75 | .35 | .07 |
| ☐ 120 | Bob Lemon | 5.00 | 2.35 | .50 |
| ☐ 121 | Cletis Boyer | 1.50 | .70 | .15 |
| ☐ 122 | Ken Boyer | 2.25 | 1.00 | .22 |
| ☐ 123 | Steve Ridzik | .75 | .35 | .07 |
| ☐ 124 | Dave Philley | .75 | .35 | .07 |
| ☐ 125 | Al Kaline | 11.00 | 5.25 | 1.10 |
| ☐ 126 | Bob Wiesler | .75 | .35 | .07 |
| ☐ 127 | Bob Buhl | .75 | .35 | .07 |
| ☐ 128 | Ed Bailey | .75 | .35 | .07 |
| ☐ 129 | Saul Rogovin | .75 | .35 | .07 |
| ☐ 130 | Don Newcombe | 3.00 | 1.40 | .30 |
| ☐ 131 | Milt Bolling | .75 | .35 | .07 |
| ☐ 132 | Art Ditmar | .75 | .35 | .07 |
| ☐ 133 | Del Crandall | .90 | .40 | .09 |
| ☐ 134 | Don Kaiser | .75 | .35 | .07 |
| ☐ 135 | Bill Skowron | 2.50 | 1.15 | .25 |
| ☐ 136 | Jim Hegan | .90 | .40 | .09 |
| ☐ 137 | Bob Rush | .75 | .35 | .07 |
| ☐ 138 | Minnie Minoso | 2.50 | 1.15 | .25 |
| ☐ 139 | Lou Kretlow | .75 | .35 | .07 |

|  | MINT | VG-E | F-G |  | MINT | VG-E | F-G |
|---|---|---|---|---|---|---|---|
| ☐ 140 Frank Thomas | .75 | .35 | .07 | ☐ 193 Del Rice | .75 | .35 | .07 |
| ☐ 141 Al Aber | .75 | .35 | .07 | ☐ 194 Hal Brown | .75 | .35 | .07 |
| ☐ 142 Charley Thompson | .75 | .35 | .07 | ☐ 195 Bobby Avila | .75 | .35 | .07 |
| ☐ 143 Andy Pafko | .75 | .35 | .07 | ☐ 196 Larry Jackson | .75 | .35 | .07 |
| ☐ 144 Ray Narleski | .75 | .35 | .07 | ☐ 197 Hank Sauer | .90 | .40 | .09 |
| ☐ 145 Al Smith | .75 | .35 | .07 | ☐ 198 Detroit Tigers Team | 2.50 | 1.15 | .25 |
| ☐ 146 Don Ferrarese | .75 | .35 | .07 | ☐ 199 Vern Law | 1.00 | .45 | .10 |
| ☐ 147 Al Walker | .75 | .35 | .07 | ☐ 200 Gil McDougald | 2.25 | 1.00 | .22 |
| ☐ 148 Don Mueller | .90 | .40 | .09 | ☐ 201 Sandy Amoros | 1.00 | .45 | .10 |
| ☐ 149 Bob Kennedy | .75 | .35 | .07 | ☐ 202 Dick Gernert | .75 | .35 | .07 |
| ☐ 150 Bob Friend | 1.00 | .45 | .10 | ☐ 203 Hoyt Wilhelm | 5.00 | 2.35 | .50 |
| ☐ 151 Willie Miranda | .75 | .35 | .07 | ☐ 204 Athletics Team | 1.75 | .85 | .17 |
| ☐ 152 Jack Harshman | .75 | .35 | .07 | ☐ 205 Charlie Maxwell | .75 | .35 | .07 |
| ☐ 153 Karl Olson | .75 | .35 | .07 | ☐ 206 Willard Schmidt | .75 | .35 | .07 |
| ☐ 154 Red Schoendienst | 1.75 | .85 | .17 | ☐ 207 Gordon (Billy) Hunter | .75 | .35 | .07 |
| ☐ 155 Jim Brosnan | .90 | .40 | .09 | ☐ 208 Lou Burdette | 2.00 | .90 | .20 |
| ☐ 156 Gus Triandos | .90 | .40 | .09 | ☐ 209 Bob Skinner | .90 | .40 | .09 |
| ☐ 157 Wally Post | .75 | .35 | .07 | ☐ 210 Roy Campanella | 22.00 | 10.00 | 2.20 |
| ☐ 158 Curt Simmons | 1.00 | .45 | .10 | ☐ 211 Camilo Pascual | .90 | .40 | .09 |
| ☐ 159 Solly Drake | .75 | .35 | .07 | ☐ 212 Rocco Colavito | 4.00 | 1.85 | .40 |
| ☐ 160 Billy Pierce | 1.50 | .70 | .15 | ☐ 213 Les Moss | .75 | .35 | .07 |
| ☐ 161 Pirates Team | 1.75 | .85 | .17 | ☐ 214 Phillies Team | 1.75 | .85 | .17 |
| ☐ 162 Jack Meyer | .75 | .35 | .07 | ☐ 215 Enos Slaughter | 4.50 | 2.10 | .45 |
| ☐ 163 Sammy White | .75 | .35 | .07 | ☐ 216 Marv Grissom | .75 | .35 | .07 |
| ☐ 164 Tommy Carroll | .75 | .35 | .07 | ☐ 217 Gene Stephens | .75 | .35 | .07 |
| ☐ 165 Ted Kluszewski | 2.50 | 1.15 | .25 | ☐ 218 Ray Jablonski | .75 | .35 | .07 |
| ☐ 166 Elroy Face | 1.25 | .60 | .12 | ☐ 219 Tom Acker | .75 | .35 | .07 |
| ☐ 167 Vic Power | .90 | .40 | .09 | ☐ 220 Jackie Jensen | 1.75 | .85 | .17 |
| ☐ 168 Frank Lary | .90 | .40 | .09 | ☐ 221 Dixie Howell | .75 | .35 | .07 |
| ☐ 169 Herb Plews | .75 | .35 | .07 | ☐ 222 Alex Grammas | .75 | .35 | .07 |
| ☐ 170 Duke Snider | 21.00 | 9.50 | 2.10 | ☐ 223 Frank House | .75 | .35 | .07 |
| ☐ 171 Boston Red Sox Team | 1.75 | .85 | .17 | ☐ 224 Marv Blaylock | .75 | .35 | .07 |
| ☐ 172 Gene Woodling | .90 | .40 | .09 | ☐ 225 Hank Simpson | .75 | .35 | .07 |
| ☐ 173 Roger Craig | 1.25 | .60 | .12 | ☐ 226 Preston Ward | .75 | .35 | .07 |
| ☐ 174 Willie Jones | .75 | .35 | .07 | ☐ 227 Gene Staley | .75 | .35 | .07 |
| ☐ 175 Don Larsen | 2.25 | 1.00 | .22 | ☐ 228 Smokey Burgess | .90 | .40 | .09 |
| ☐ 176 Gene Baker | .75 | .35 | .07 | ☐ 229 George Susce | .75 | .35 | .07 |
| ☐ 177 Eddie Yost | .90 | .40 | .09 | ☐ 230 George Kell | 4.50 | 2.10 | .45 |
| ☐ 178 Don Bessent | .75 | .35 | .07 | ☐ 231 Solly Hemus | .75 | .35 | .07 |
| ☐ 179 Ernie Oravetz | .75 | .35 | .07 | ☐ 232 Whitey Lockman | .90 | .40 | .09 |
| ☐ 180 Dave (Gus) Bell | .90 | .40 | .09 | ☐ 233 Art Fowler | .75 | .35 | .07 |
| ☐ 181 Dick Donovan | .75 | .35 | .07 | ☐ 234 Dick Cole | .75 | .35 | .07 |
| ☐ 182 Hobie Landrith | .75 | .35 | .07 | ☐ 235 Tom Poholsky | .75 | .35 | .07 |
| ☐ 183 Chicago Cubs Team | 1.75 | .85 | .17 | ☐ 236 Joe Ginsberg | .75 | .35 | .07 |
| ☐ 184 Tito Francona | .90 | .40 | .09 | ☐ 237 Foster Castleman | .75 | .35 | .07 |
| ☐ 185 Johnny Kucks | .90 | .40 | .09 | ☐ 238 Eddie Robinson | .75 | .35 | .07 |
| ☐ 186 Jim King | .75 | .35 | .07 | ☐ 239 Tom Morgan | .75 | .35 | .07 |
| ☐ 187 Virgil Trucks | .75 | .35 | .07 | ☐ 240 Hank Bauer | 2.50 | 1.15 | .25 |
| ☐ 188 Felix Mantilla | .75 | .35 | .07 | ☐ 241 Joe Lonnett | .75 | .35 | .07 |
| ☐ 189 Willard Nixon | .75 | .35 | .07 | ☐ 242 Charlie Neal | .90 | .40 | .09 |
| ☐ 190 Randy Jackson | .75 | .35 | .07 | ☐ 243 Cardinals Team | 2.00 | .90 | .20 |
| ☐ 191 Joe Margoneri | .75 | .35 | .07 | ☐ 244 Billy Loes | .90 | .40 | .09 |
| ☐ 192 Gerry Coleman | .90 | .40 | .09 | ☐ 245 Rip Repulski | .75 | .35 | .07 |

| | MINT | VG-E | F-G |
|---|---|---|---|
| ☐ 246 Jose Valdivielso | .75 | .35 | .07 |
| ☐ 247 Turk Lown | .75 | .35 | .07 |
| ☐ 248 Jim Finigan | .75 | .35 | .07 |
| ☐ 249 Dave Pope | .75 | .35 | .07 |
| ☐ 250 Ed Mathews | 7.50 | 3.50 | .75 |
| ☐ 251 Orioles Team | 2.00 | .90 | .20 |
| ☐ 252 Carl Erskine | 2.50 | 1.15 | .25 |
| ☐ 253 Gus Zernial | .90 | .40 | .09 |
| ☐ 254 Ron Negray | .75 | .35 | .07 |
| ☐ 255 Charlie Silvera | .75 | .35 | .07 |
| ☐ 256 Ron Kline | .75 | .35 | .07 |
| ☐ 257 Walt Dropo | .75 | .35 | .07 |
| ☐ 258 Steve Gromek | .75 | .35 | .07 |
| ☐ 259 Eddie O'Brien | .75 | .35 | .07 |
| ☐ 260 Del Ennis | .90 | .40 | .09 |
| ☐ 261 Bob Chakales | .75 | .35 | .07 |
| ☐ 262 Bobby Thomson | 1.75 | .85 | .17 |
| ☐ 263 George Strickland | .75 | .35 | .07 |
| ☐ 264 Bob Turley | 2.00 | .90 | .20 |
| ☐ 265 Harvey Haddix | 4.00 | 1.85 | .40 |
| ☐ 266 Ken Kuhn | 3.75 | 1.60 | .40 |
| ☐ 267 Danny Kravitz | 3.75 | 1.60 | .40 |
| ☐ 268 Joe Collum | 3.75 | 1.60 | .40 |
| ☐ 269 Bob Cerv | 4.00 | 1.85 | .40 |
| ☐ 270 Washington Team | 6.00 | 2.80 | .60 |
| ☐ 271 Danny O'Connell | 3.75 | 1.60 | .40 |
| ☐ 272 Bobby Shantz | 9.00 | 4.25 | .90 |
| ☐ 273 Jim Davis | 3.75 | 1.60 | .40 |
| ☐ 274 Don Hoak | 3.75 | 1.60 | .40 |
| ☐ 275 Indians Team | 6.00 | 2.80 | .60 |
| ☐ 276 Jim Pyburn | 3.75 | 1.60 | .40 |
| ☐ 277 Johnny Podres | 13.00 | 6.00 | 1.30 |
| ☐ 278 Fred Hatfield | 3.75 | 1.60 | .40 |
| ☐ 279 Bob Thurman | 3.75 | 1.60 | .40 |
| ☐ 280 Alex Kellner | 3.75 | 1.60 | .40 |
| ☐ 281 Gail Harris | 3.75 | 1.60 | .40 |
| ☐ 282 Jack Dittmar | 3.75 | 1.60 | .40 |
| ☐ 283 Wes Covington | 4.50 | 2.10 | .45 |
| ☐ 284 Don Zimmer | 4.50 | 2.10 | .45 |
| ☐ 285 Ned Garver | 3.75 | 1.60 | .40 |
| ☐ 286 Bobby Richardson | 18.00 | 8.50 | 1.80 |
| ☐ 287 Sam Jones | 3.75 | 1.60 | .40 |
| ☐ 288 Ted Lepcio | 3.75 | 1.60 | .40 |
| ☐ 289 Jim Bolger | 3.75 | 1.60 | .40 |
| ☐ 290 Andy Carey | 4.50 | 2.10 | .45 |
| ☐ 291 Jim McCall | 3.75 | 1.60 | .40 |
| ☐ 292 Billy Klaus | 3.75 | 1.60 | .40 |
| ☐ 293 Tom Abernathy | 3.75 | 1.60 | .40 |
| ☐ 294 Rocky Bridges | 3.75 | 1.60 | .40 |
| ☐ 295 Joe Collins | 4.50 | 2.10 | .45 |
| ☐ 296 Johnny Klippstein | 3.75 | 1.60 | .40 |
| ☐ 297 Jim Crimian | 3.75 | 1.60 | .40 |
| ☐ 298 Irv Noren | 3.75 | 1.60 | .40 |
| ☐ 299 Chuck Harmon | 3.75 | 1.60 | .40 |
| ☐ 300 Mike Garcia | 4.50 | 2.10 | .45 |
| ☐ 301 Sammy Esposito | 3.75 | 1.60 | .40 |
| ☐ 302 Sandy Koufax | 85.00 | 40.00 | 8.50 |
| ☐ 303 Billy Goodman | 4.50 | 2.10 | .45 |
| ☐ 304 Joe Cunningham | 4.50 | 2.10 | .45 |
| ☐ 305 Willie Fernandez | 3.75 | 1.60 | .40 |
| ☐ 306 Darrell Johnson | 3.75 | 1.60 | .40 |
| ☐ 307 J.D. (Bubba) Phillips | 3.75 | 1.60 | .40 |
| ☐ 308 Richard Hall | 3.75 | 1.60 | .40 |
| ☐ 309 Jim Busby | 3.75 | 1.60 | .40 |
| ☐ 310 Max Surkont | 3.75 | 1.60 | .40 |
| ☐ 311 Al Pilarcik | 3.75 | 1.60 | .40 |
| ☐ 312 Tony Kubek | 21.00 | 9.50 | 2.10 |
| ☐ 313 Mel Parnell | 4.50 | 2.10 | .45 |
| ☐ 314 Ed Bouchee | 3.75 | 1.60 | .40 |
| ☐ 315 Lou Berberet | 3.75 | 1.60 | .40 |
| ☐ 316 Billy O'Dell | 3.75 | 1.60 | .40 |
| ☐ 317 New York Giants Team | 15.00 | 7.00 | 1.50 |
| ☐ 318 Mickey McDermott | 3.75 | 1.60 | .40 |
| ☐ 319 Gino Cimoli | 3.75 | 1.60 | .40 |
| ☐ 320 Neil Chrisley | 3.75 | 1.60 | .40 |
| ☐ 321 John (Red) Murff | 3.75 | 1.60 | .40 |
| ☐ 322 Cincinnati Team | 15.00 | 7.00 | 1.50 |
| ☐ 323 Wes Westrum | 3.75 | 1.60 | .40 |
| ☐ 324 Brooklyn Dodgers Team | 25.00 | 11.00 | 2.50 |
| ☐ 325 Frank Bolling | 3.75 | 1.60 | .40 |
| ☐ 326 Pedro Ramos | 3.75 | 1.60 | .40 |
| ☐ 327 Jim Pendleton | 3.75 | 1.60 | .40 |
| ☐ 328 Brooks Robinson | 95.00 | 40.00 | 9.00 |
| ☐ 329 White Sox Team | 9.00 | 4.25 | .90 |
| ☐ 330 Jim Wilson | 3.75 | 1.60 | .40 |
| ☐ 331 Ray Katt | 3.75 | 1.60 | .40 |
| ☐ 332 Bob Bowman | 3.75 | 1.60 | .40 |
| ☐ 333 Ernie Johnson | 3.75 | 1.60 | .40 |
| ☐ 334 Jerry Schoonmaker | 3.75 | 1.60 | .40 |
| ☐ 335 Granny Hamner | 3.75 | 1.60 | .40 |
| ☐ 336 Haywood Sullivan | 4.50 | 2.10 | .45 |
| ☐ 337 Rene Valdes | 3.75 | 1.60 | .40 |
| ☐ 338 Jim Bunning | 18.00 | 8.50 | 1.80 |
| ☐ 339 Bob Speake | 3.75 | 1.60 | .40 |
| ☐ 340 Bill Wight | 3.75 | 1.60 | .40 |
| ☐ 341 Don Gross | 3.75 | 1.60 | .40 |
| ☐ 342 Gene Mauch | 6.00 | 2.80 | .60 |
| ☐ 343 Taylor Phillips | 3.75 | 1.60 | .40 |
| ☐ 344 Paul LaPalme | 3.75 | 1.60 | .40 |
| ☐ 345 Paul Smith | 3.75 | 1.60 | .40 |
| ☐ 346 Dick Littlefield | 3.75 | 1.60 | .40 |
| ☐ 347 Hal Naragon | 3.75 | 1.60 | .40 |
| ☐ 348 Jim Hearn | 3.75 | 1.60 | .40 |
| ☐ 349 Nellie King | 3.75 | 1.60 | .40 |
| ☐ 350 Eddie Miksis | 3.75 | 1.60 | .40 |
| ☐ 351 Dave Hillman | 3.75 | 1.60 | .40 |

|  | MINT | VG-E | F-G |
|---|---|---|---|
| ☐ 352 Ellis Kinder | 3.75 | 1.60 | .40 |
| ☐ 353 Cal Neeman | 1.00 | .45 | .10 |
| ☐ 354 W. (Rip) Coleman | 1.00 | .45 | .10 |
| ☐ 355 Frank Malzone | 1.25 | .60 | .12 |
| ☐ 356 Faye Throneberry | 1.00 | .45 | .10 |
| ☐ 357 Earl Torgeson | 1.00 | .45 | .10 |
| ☐ 358 Gerry Lynch | 1.00 | .45 | .10 |
| ☐ 359 Tom Cheney | 1.00 | .45 | .10 |
| ☐ 360 Johnny Groth | 1.00 | .45 | .10 |
| ☐ 361 Curt Barclay | 1.00 | .45 | .10 |
| ☐ 362 Roman Mejias | 1.00 | .45 | .10 |
| ☐ 363 Eddie Kasko | 1.00 | .45 | .10 |
| ☐ 364 Cal McLish | 1.00 | .45 | .10 |
| ☐ 365 Ozzie Virgil | 1.00 | .45 | .10 |
| ☐ 366 Ken Lehman | 1.00 | .45 | .10 |
| ☐ 367 Ed Fitzgerald | 1.00 | .45 | .10 |
| ☐ 368 Bob Purkey | 1.00 | .45 | .10 |
| ☐ 369 Milt Graff | 1.00 | .45 | .10 |
| ☐ 370 Warren Hacker | 1.00 | .45 | .10 |
| ☐ 371 Bob Lennon | 1.00 | .45 | .10 |
| ☐ 372 Norm Zauchin | 1.00 | .45 | .10 |
| ☐ 373 Pete Whisenant | 1.00 | .45 | .10 |
| ☐ 374 Don Cardwell | 1.00 | .45 | .10 |
| ☐ 375 Jim Landis | 1.00 | .45 | .10 |
| ☐ 376 Don Elston | 1.00 | .45 | .10 |
| ☐ 377 Andre Rodgers | 1.00 | .45 | .10 |
| ☐ 378 Elmer Singleton | 1.00 | .45 | .10 |
| ☐ 379 Don Lee | 1.00 | .45 | .10 |
| ☐ 380 Walker Cooper | 1.00 | .45 | .10 |
| ☐ 381 Dean Stone | 1.00 | .45 | .10 |
| ☐ 382 Jim Brideweser | 1.00 | .45 | .10 |
| ☐ 383 Juan Pizarro | 1.00 | .45 | .10 |
| ☐ 384 Bobby G. Smith | 1.00 | .45 | .10 |
| ☐ 385 Art Houtteman | 1.00 | .45 | .10 |
| ☐ 386 Lyle Luttrell | 1.00 | .45 | .10 |
| ☐ 387 Jack Sanford | 1.50 | .70 | .15 |
| ☐ 388 Pete Daley | 1.00 | .45 | .10 |
| ☐ 389 Dave Jolly | 1.00 | .45 | .10 |
| ☐ 390 Reno Bertoia | 1.00 | .45 | .10 |
| ☐ 391 Ralph Terry | 1.50 | .70 | .15 |
| ☐ 392 Chuck Tanner | 1.25 | .60 | .12 |
| ☐ 393 Raul Sanchez | 1.00 | .45 | .10 |
| ☐ 394 Luis Arroyo | 1.25 | .60 | .12 |
| ☐ 395 J.M. (Bubba) Phillips | 1.00 | .45 | .10 |
| ☐ 396 K. (Casey) Wise | 1.00 | .45 | .10 |
| ☐ 397 Roy Smalley | 1.00 | .45 | .10 |
| ☐ 398 Al Cicotte | 1.00 | .45 | .10 |
| ☐ 399 Bill Consolo | 1.00 | .45 | .10 |
| ☐ 400 Dodgers' Sluggers: | 25.00 | 11.00 | 2.50 |
|     Carl Furillo | | | |
|     Gil Hodges | | | |
|     Roy Campanella | | | |
|     Duke Snyder | | | |

|  | MINT | VG-E | F-G |
|---|---|---|---|
| ☐ 401 Earl Battey | 1.00 | .45 | .10 |
| ☐ 402 Jim Pisani | 1.00 | .45 | .10 |
| ☐ 403 Richard Hyde | 1.00 | .45 | .10 |
| ☐ 404 Harry Anderson | 1.00 | .45 | .10 |
| ☐ 405 Duke Maas | 1.00 | .45 | .10 |
| ☐ 406 Bob Hale | 1.00 | .45 | .10 |
| ☐ 407 Yankee Power Hitters: | 30.00 | 14.00 | 3.00 |
|     Mickey Mantle | | | |
|     Yogi Berra | | | |
|     UNNUMBERED | | | |
|     CHECKLISTS | | | |
| ☐ 408 Checklist ½ | 25.00 | 11.00 | 2.50 |
| ☐ 409 Checklist ⅔ | 35.00 | 16.50 | 3.50 |
| ☐ 410 Checklist ¾ | 80.00 | 37.00 | 8.00 |
| ☐ 411 Checklist ⅘ | 100.00 | 45.00 | 10.00 |

## 1958 TOPPS

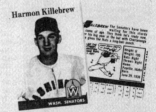

The cards in this 494 card set measure 2½" by 3½". Although the last card is numbered 495, number 145 was not issued, bringing the total to 494 cards. The 1958 Topps set contains the first Sport Magazine All-Star selection series (475–495) and expanded use of combination cards. The team cards carried series checklists on back (Milwaukee, Detroit, Baltimore, and Cincinnati are also found with players listed alphabetically. Cards with the scarce yellow name (YL) or team (YT) lettering as opposed to the common white lettering are noted in the checklist. In the last series cards of Stan Musial and Mickey Mantle were triple printed; the cards they replaced (443, 446, 450, and 462) on the printing sheet were hence printed in shorter supply than other cards *in the last series and are marked with an SP in the list below.*

Complete Set: M-650.00; VG-E-275.00; F-G-50.00

| | MINT | VG-E | F-G |
|---|---|---|---|
| Common Player (1–110) | .75 | .35 | .07 |
| Common Player (111–198) | .60 | .28 | .06 |
| Common Player (199–440) | .50 | .22 | .05 |
| Common Player (441–474) | .45 | .20 | .04 |
| Common Player (475–495) | .60 | .28 | .06 |

| | | MINT | VG-E | F-G |
|---|---|---|---|---|
| ☐ | 1 Ted Williams | 75.00 | 20.00 | 5.00 |
| ☐ | 2 A Bob Lemon | 4.50 | 2.10 | .45 |
| ☐ | 2 B Bob Lemon YT | 13.50 | 6.00 | 1.25 |
| ☐ | 3 Alex Kellner | .75 | .35 | .07 |
| ☐ | 4 Hank Foiles | .75 | .35 | .07 |
| ☐ | 5 Willie Mays | 32.00 | 15.00 | 3.20 |
| ☐ | 6 George Zuverink | .75 | .35 | .07 |
| ☐ | 7 Dale Long | .75 | .35 | .07 |
| ☐ | 8 A Eddie Kasko | .75 | .35 | .07 |
| ☐ | 8 B Eddie Kasko YL | 9.00 | 4.25 | .90 |
| ☐ | 9 Hank Bauer | 1.50 | .70 | .15 |
| ☐ | 10 Lou Burdette | 1.50 | .70 | .15 |
| ☐ | 11 A Jim Rivera | .75 | .35 | .07 |
| ☐ | 11 B Jim Rivera YT | 6.00 | 2.80 | .60 |
| ☐ | 12 George Crowe | .75 | .35 | .07 |
| ☐ | 13 A Billy Hoeft | .75 | .35 | .07 |
| ☐ | 13 B Billy Hoeft YL | 9.00 | 4.25 | .90 |
| ☐ | 14 Rip Repulski | .75 | .35 | .07 |
| ☐ | 15 Jim Lemon | .90 | .40 | .09 |
| ☐ | 16 Charley Neal | .90 | .40 | .09 |
| ☐ | 17 Felix Mantilla | .75 | .35 | .07 |
| ☐ | 18 Frank Sullivan | .75 | .35 | .07 |
| ☐ | 19 New York Giants Team | 2.75 | .75 | .20 |
| ☐ | 20 A Gil McDougald | 2.00 | .90 | .20 |
| ☐ | 20 B Gil McDougald YL | 12.50 | 5.75 | 1.25 |
| ☐ | 21 Curt Barclay | .75 | .35 | .07 |
| ☐ | 22 Hal Naragon | .75 | .35 | .07 |
| ☐ | 23 A Bill Tuttle | .75 | .35 | .07 |
| ☐ | 23 B Bill Tuttle YL | 9.00 | 4.25 | .90 |
| ☐ | 24 A Hobie Landrith | .75 | .35 | .07 |
| ☐ | 24 B Hobie Landrith YL | 9.00 | 4.25 | .90 |
| ☐ | 25 Don Drysdale | 7.50 | 3.50 | .75 |
| ☐ | 26 Ron Jackson | .75 | .35 | .07 |
| ☐ | 27 Bud Freeman | .75 | .35 | .07 |
| ☐ | 28 Jim Busby | .75 | .35 | .07 |
| ☐ | 29 Ted Lepcio | .75 | .35 | .07 |
| ☐ | 30 A Hank Aaron | 32.00 | 15.00 | 3.20 |
| ☐ | 30 B Hank Aaron YL | 75.00 | 35.00 | 7.50 |
| ☐ | 31 Tex Clevenger | .75 | .35 | .07 |
| ☐ | 32 A J. W. Porter | .75 | .35 | .07 |
| ☐ | 32 B J. W. Porter YL | 9.00 | 4.25 | .90 |
| ☐ | 33 A Cal Neeman | .75 | .35 | .07 |
| ☐ | 33 B Cal Neeman YT | 6.00 | 2.80 | .60 |
| ☐ | 34 Bob Thurman | .75 | .35 | .07 |
| ☐ | 35 A Don Mossi | .90 | .40 | .09 |
| ☐ | 35 B Don Mossi YT | 7.00 | 3.25 | .70 |
| ☐ | 36 Ted Kazanski | .75 | .35 | .07 |
| ☐ | 37 Mike McCormick (photo actually Ray Monzant) | 1.00 | .45 | .10 |
| ☐ | 38 Dick Gernert | .75 | .35 | .07 |
| ☐ | 39 Bob Martyn | .75 | .35 | .07 |
| ☐ | 40 George Kell | 3.50 | 1.65 | .35 |
| ☐ | 41 Dave Hillman | .75 | .35 | .07 |
| ☐ | 42 John Roseboro | 1.50 | .70 | .15 |
| ☐ | 43 Sal Maglie | 1.50 | .70 | .15 |
| ☐ | 44 Wash. Senators Team | 1.50 | .50 | .15 |
| ☐ | 45 Dick Groat | 1.50 | .70 | .15 |
| ☐ | 46 A Lou Sleater | .75 | .35 | .07 |
| ☐ | 46 B Lou Sleater YL | 9.00 | 4.25 | .90 |
| ☐ | 47 Roger Maris | 27.00 | 12.00 | 2.70 |
| ☐ | 48 Chuck Harmon | .75 | .35 | .07 |
| ☐ | 49 Smokey Burgess | .90 | .40 | .09 |
| ☐ | 50 A Billy Pierce | 1.50 | .70 | .15 |
| ☐ | 50 B Billy Pierce YT | 9.00 | 4.25 | .90 |
| ☐ | 51 Del Rice | .75 | .35 | .07 |
| ☐ | 52 A Bob Clemente | 18.00 | 8.50 | 1.80 |
| ☐ | 52 B Bob Clemente YT | 45.00 | 20.00 | 4.50 |
| ☐ | 53 A Morrie Martin | .75 | .35 | .07 |
| ☐ | 53 B Morrie Martin YL | 9.00 | 4.25 | .90 |
| ☐ | 54 Norm Siebern | .75 | .35 | .07 |
| ☐ | 55 Chico Carrasquel | .75 | .35 | .07 |
| ☐ | 56 Bill Fischer | .75 | .35 | .07 |
| ☐ | 57 A Tim Thompson | .75 | .35 | .07 |
| ☐ | 57 B Tim Thompson YL | 9.00 | 4.25 | .90 |
| ☐ | 58 A Art Schult | .75 | .35 | .07 |
| ☐ | 58 B Art Schult YT | 6.00 | 2.80 | .60 |
| ☐ | 59 Dave Sisler | .75 | .35 | .07 |
| ☐ | 60 A Del Ennis | .90 | .40 | .09 |
| ☐ | 60 B Del Ennis YL | 9.00 | 4.25 | .90 |
| ☐ | 61 A Darrell Johnson | .90 | .40 | .09 |
| ☐ | 61 B Darrell Johnson YL | 9.00 | 4.25 | .90 |
| ☐ | 62 Joe DeMaestri | .75 | .35 | .07 |
| ☐ | 63 Joe Nuxhall | .90 | .40 | .09 |
| ☐ | 64 Joe Lonnett | .75 | .35 | .07 |
| ☐ | 65 A Von McDaniel | .75 | .35 | .07 |
| ☐ | 65 B Von McDaniel YL | 9.00 | 4.25 | .90 |
| ☐ | 66 Lee Walls | .75 | .35 | .07 |
| ☐ | 67 Joe Ginsberg | .75 | .35 | .07 |
| ☐ | 68 Daryl Spencer | .75 | .35 | .07 |
| ☐ | 69 Wally Burnette | .75 | .35 | .07 |
| ☐ | 70 A Al Kaline | 10.00 | 4.75 | 1.00 |

| | MINT | VG-E | F-G |
|---|---|---|---|
| 70 B Al Kaline YL | 40.00 | 18.00 | 4.00 |
| 71 Dodgers Team | 3.75 | 1.25 | .30 |
| 72 Bud Byerly | .75 | .35 | .07 |
| 73 Pete Daley | .75 | .35 | .07 |
| 74 Roy Face | 1.00 | .45 | .10 |
| 75 Gus Bell | .90 | .40 | .09 |
| 76 A Dick Farrell | .90 | .40 | .09 |
| 76 B Dick Farrell YT | 6.00 | 2.80 | .60 |
| 77 A Don Zimmer | 1.25 | .60 | .12 |
| 77 B Don Zimmer YT | 7.00 | 3.25 | .70 |
| 78 A Ernie Johnson | .75 | .35 | .07 |
| 78 B Ernie Johnson YL | 9.00 | 4.25 | .90 |
| 79 A Dick Williams | 1.25 | .60 | .12 |
| 79 B Dick Williams YT | 7.00 | 3.25 | .70 |
| 80 Dick Drott | .75 | .35 | .07 |
| 81 A Steve Boros | .90 | .40 | .09 |
| 81 B Steve Boros YT | 6.50 | 3.00 | .65 |
| 82 Ronnie Kline | .75 | .35 | .07 |
| 83 Bob Hazle | .75 | .35 | .07 |
| 84 Billy O'Dell | .75 | .35 | .07 |
| 85 A Luis Aparicio | 4.50 | 2.00 | .40 |
| 85 B Luis Aparicio YT | 15.00 | 7.00 | 1.50 |
| 86 Valmy Thomas | .75 | .35 | .07 |
| 87 Johnny Kucks | .75 | .35 | .07 |
| 88 Duke Snider | 12.50 | 5.75 | 1.25 |
| 89 Billy Klaus | .75 | .35 | .07 |
| 90 Robin Roberts | 5.00 | 2.35 | .50 |
| 91 Chuck Tanner | 1.25 | .60 | .12 |
| 92 A Clint Courtney | .75 | .35 | .07 |
| 92 B Clint Courtney YL | 9.00 | 4.25 | .90 |
| 93 Sandy Amoros | .90 | .40 | .09 |
| 94 Bob Skinner | .75 | .35 | .07 |
| 95 Frank Bolling | .75 | .35 | .07 |
| 96 Joe Durham | .75 | .35 | .07 |
| 97 A Larry Jackson | .75 | .35 | .07 |
| 97 B Larry Jackson YL | 9.00 | 4.25 | .90 |
| 98 A Billy Hunter | .75 | .35 | .07 |
| 98 B Billy Hunter YL | 9.00 | 4.00 | .85 |
| 99 Bobby Adams | .75 | .35 | .07 |
| 100 A Early Wynn | 4.50 | 2.10 | .45 |
| 100 B Early Wynn YT | 12.50 | 5.75 | 1.25 |
| 101 A Bobby Richardson | 2.50 | 1.15 | .25 |
| 101 B Bobby Richardson YL | 12.50 | 5.75 | 1.25 |
| 102 George Strickland | .75 | .35 | .07 |
| 103 Jerry Lynch | .75 | .35 | .07 |
| 104 Jim Pendleton | .75 | .35 | .07 |
| 105 Billy Gardner | .90 | .40 | .09 |
| 106 Dick Schofield | .75 | .35 | .07 |
| 107 Ossie Virgil | .75 | .35 | .07 |
| 108 A Jim Landis | .75 | .35 | .07 |
| 108 B Jim Landis YT | 6.00 | 2.80 | .60 |
| 109 Herb Plews | .75 | .35 | .07 |
| 110 Johnny Logan | .90 | .40 | .09 |

| | MINT | VG-E | F-G |
|---|---|---|---|
| 111 Stu Miller | .60 | .28 | .06 |
| 112 Gus Zernial | .75 | .35 | .07 |
| 113 Jerry Walker | .60 | .28 | .06 |
| 114 Irv Noren | .60 | .28 | .06 |
| 115 Jim Bunning | 2.50 | 1.15 | .25 |
| 116 Dave Philley | .60 | .28 | .06 |
| 117 Frank Torre | .75 | .35 | .07 |
| 118 Harvey Haddix | .90 | .40 | .09 |
| 119 Harry Chiti | .60 | .28 | .06 |
| 120 Johnny Podres | 1.75 | .85 | .17 |
| 121 Eddie Miksis | .60 | .28 | .06 |
| 122 Walt Moryn | .60 | .28 | .06 |
| 123 Dick Tomanek | .60 | .28 | .06 |
| 124 Bobby Usher | .60 | .28 | .06 |
| 125 Al Dark | 1.25 | .60 | .12 |
| 126 Stan Palys | .60 | .28 | .06 |
| 127 Tom Sturdivant | .75 | .35 | .07 |
| 128 Willie Kirkland | .60 | .28 | .06 |
| 129 Jim Derrington | .60 | .28 | .06 |
| 130 Jackie Jensen | 2.25 | 1.00 | .22 |
| 131 Bob Henrich | .60 | .28 | .06 |
| 132 Vernon Law | .75 | .35 | .07 |
| 133 Russ Nixon | .60 | .28 | .06 |
| 134 Phillies Team | 1.75 | .60 | .15 |
| 135 Mike (Moe) Drabowsky | .60 | .28 | .06 |
| 136 Jim Finigan | .60 | .28 | .06 |
| 137 Russ Kemmerer | .60 | .28 | .06 |
| 138 Earl Torgeson | .60 | .28 | .06 |
| 139 George Brunet | .60 | .28 | .06 |
| 140 Wes Covington | .75 | .35 | .07 |
| 141 Ken Lehman | .60 | .28 | .06 |
| 142 Enos Slaughter | 3.50 | 1.65 | .35 |
| 143 Billy Muffett | .60 | .28 | .06 |
| 144 Bobby Morgan | .60 | .28 | .06 |
| 145 Never issued | .00 | .00 | .00 |
| 146 Dick Gray | .60 | .28 | .06 |
| 147 Don McMahon | .75 | .35 | .07 |
| 148 Billy Consolo | .60 | .28 | .06 |
| 149 Tom Acker | .60 | .28 | .06 |
| 150 Mickey Mantle | 75.00 | 30.00 | 6.00 |
| 151 Buddy Pritchard | .60 | .28 | .06 |
| 152 Johnny Antonelli | .90 | .40 | .09 |
| 153 Les Moss | .60 | .28 | .06 |
| 154 Harry Byrd | .60 | .28 | .06 |
| 155 Hector Lopez | .60 | .28 | .06 |
| 156 Dick Hyde | .60 | .28 | .06 |
| 157 Dee Fondy | .60 | .28 | .06 |
| 158 Indians Team | 1.50 | .50 | .15 |
| 159 Taylor Phillips | .60 | .28 | .06 |
| 160 Don Hoak | .60 | .28 | .06 |
| 161 Don Larsen | 1.75 | .85 | .17 |
| 162 Gil Hodges | 7.50 | 3.50 | .75 |
| 163 Jim Wilson | .60 | .28 | .06 |

| | MINT | VG-E | F-G | | MINT | VG-E | F-G |
|---|---|---|---|---|---|---|---|
| ☐ 164 Bob Taylor | .60 | .28 | .06 | ☐ 214 Willard Schmidt | .50 | .22 | .05 |
| ☐ 165 Bob Nieman | .60 | .28 | .06 | ☐ 215 Jim Gilliam | 2.00 | .90 | .20 |
| ☐ 166 Danny O'Connell | .60 | .28 | .06 | ☐ 216 Cardinals Team | 1.75 | .60 | .15 |
| ☐ 167 Frank Baumann | .60 | .28 | .06 | ☐ 217 Jack Harshman | .50 | .22 | .05 |
| ☐ 168 Joe Cunningham | .75 | .35 | .07 | ☐ 218 Dick Rand | .50 | .22 | .05 |
| ☐ 169 Ralph Terry | .90 | .40 | .09 | ☐ 219 Camilo Pascual | .65 | .30 | .05 |
| ☐ 170 Vic Wertz | .75 | .35 | .07 | ☐ 220 Tom Brewer | .50 | .22 | .05 |
| ☐ 171 Harry Anderson | .60 | .28 | .06 | ☐ 221 Jerry Kindall | .50 | .22 | .05 |
| ☐ 172 Don Gross | .60 | .28 | .06 | ☐ 222 Bud Daley | .50 | .22 | .05 |
| ☐ 173 Eddie Yost | .60 | .28 | .06 | ☐ 223 Andy Pafko | .50 | .22 | .05 |
| ☐ 174 Athletics Team | 1.50 | .50 | .15 | ☐ 224 Bob Grim | .75 | .35 | .07 |
| ☐ 175 Marv Throneberry | 1.75 | .85 | .17 | ☐ 225 Billy Goodman | .60 | .28 | .06 |
| ☐ 176 Bob Buhl | .60 | .28 | .06 | ☐ 226 Bob Smith | .50 | .22 | .05 |
| ☐ 177 Al Smith | .60 | .28 | .06 | ☐ 227 Gene Stephens | .50 | .22 | .05 |
| ☐ 178 Ted Kluszewski | 2.00 | .90 | .20 | ☐ 228 Duke Maas | .50 | .22 | .05 |
| ☐ 179 Willie Miranda | .60 | .28 | .06 | ☐ 229 Frank Zupo | .50 | .22 | .05 |
| ☐ 180 Lindy McDaniel | .60 | .28 | .06 | ☐ 230 Richie Ashburn | 2.50 | 1.15 | .25 |
| ☐ 181 Willie Jones | .60 | .28 | .06 | ☐ 231 Lloyd Merritt | .50 | .22 | .05 |
| ☐ 182 Joe Caffie | .60 | .28 | .06 | ☐ 232 Reno Bertoia | .50 | .22 | .05 |
| ☐ 183 Dave Jolly | .60 | .28 | .06 | ☐ 233 Mickey Vernon | .75 | .35 | .07 |
| ☐ 184 Elvin Tappe | .60 | .28 | .06 | ☐ 234 Carl Sawatski | .50 | .22 | .05 |
| ☐ 185 Ray Boone | .60 | .28 | .06 | ☐ 235 Tom Gorman | .50 | .22 | .05 |
| ☐ 186 Jack Meyer | .60 | .28 | .06 | ☐ 236 Ed Fitzgerald | .50 | .22 | .05 |
| ☐ 187 Sandy Koufax | 21.00 | 9.50 | 2.10 | ☐ 237 Bill Wight | .50 | .22 | .05 |
| ☐ 188 Milt Bolling | .60 | .28 | .06 | ☐ 238 Bill Mazeroski | 2.00 | .90 | .20 |
| (photo actually | | | | ☐ 239 Chuck Stobbs | .50 | .22 | .05 |
| Lou Berberet) | | | | ☐ 240 Moose Skowron | 2.00 | .90 | .20 |
| ☐ 189 George Susce | .60 | .28 | .06 | ☐ 241 Dick Littlefield | .50 | .22 | .05 |
| ☐ 190 Red Schoendienst | 1.25 | .60 | .12 | ☐ 242 Johnny Klippstein | .50 | .22 | .05 |
| ☐ 191 Art Ceccarelli | .60 | .28 | .06 | ☐ 243 Larry Raines | .50 | .22 | .05 |
| ☐ 192 Milt Graff | .60 | .28 | .06 | ☐ 244 Don Demeter | .50 | .22 | .05 |
| ☐ 193 Jerry Lumpe | .75 | .35 | .07 | ☐ 245 Frank Lary | .75 | .35 | .07 |
| ☐ 194 Roger Craig | .90 | .40 | .09 | ☐ 246 Yankees Team | 5.00 | 1.50 | .30 |
| ☐ 195 Whitey Lockman | .75 | .35 | .07 | ☐ 247 Casey Wise | .50 | .22 | .05 |
| ☐ 196 Mike Garcia | .75 | .35 | .07 | ☐ 248 Herm Wehmeier | .50 | .22 | .05 |
| ☐ 197 Haywood Sullivan | .75 | .35 | .07 | ☐ 249 Ray Moore | .50 | .22 | .05 |
| ☐ 198 Bill Virdon | 1.25 | .60 | .12 | ☐ 250 Roy Sievers | .75 | .35 | .07 |
| ☐ 199 Don Blasingame | .50 | .22 | .05 | ☐ 251 Warren Hacker | .50 | .22 | .05 |
| ☐ 200 Bob Keegan | .50 | .22 | .05 | ☐ 252 Bob Trowbridge | .50 | .22 | .05 |
| ☐ 201 Jim Bolger | .50 | .22 | .05 | ☐ 253 Don Mueller | .60 | .28 | .06 |
| ☐ 202 Woody Held | .50 | .22 | .05 | ☐ 254 Alex Grammas | .50 | .22 | .05 |
| ☐ 203 Al Walker | .50 | .22 | .05 | ☐ 255 Bob Turley | 2.00 | .90 | .20 |
| ☐ 204 Leo Kiely | .50 | .22 | .05 | ☐ 256 White Sox Team | 1.50 | .50 | .15 |
| ☐ 205 Johnny Temple | .60 | .28 | .06 | ☐ 257 Hal Smith | .50 | .22 | .05 |
| ☐ 206 Bob Shaw | .50 | .22 | .05 | ☐ 258 Carl Erskine | 2.00 | .90 | .20 |
| ☐ 207 Solly Hemus | .50 | .22 | .05 | ☐ 259 Al Pilarcik | .50 | .22 | .05 |
| ☐ 208 Cal McLish | .50 | .22 | .05 | ☐ 260 Frank Malzone | .75 | .35 | .07 |
| ☐ 209 Bob Anderson | .50 | .22 | .05 | ☐ 261 Turk Lown | .50 | .22 | .05 |
| ☐ 210 Wally Moon | .75 | .35 | .07 | ☐ 262 Johnny Groth | .50 | .22 | .05 |
| ☐ 211 Pete Burnside | .50 | .22 | .05 | ☐ 263 Eddie Bressoud | .50 | .22 | .05 |
| ☐ 212 Bubba Phillips | .50 | .22 | .05 | ☐ 264 Jack Sanford | .60 | .28 | .06 |
| ☐ 213 Red Wilson | .50 | .22 | .05 | ☐ 265 Pete Runnels | .65 | .30 | .06 |

| | MINT | VG-E | F-G |
|---|---|---|---|
| ☐ 266 Connie Johnson | .50 | .22 | .05 |
| ☐ 267 Sherm Lollar | .65 | .30 | .06 |
| ☐ 268 Granny Hamner | .50 | .22 | .05 |
| ☐ 269 Paul Smith | .50 | .22 | .05 |
| ☐ 270 Warren Spahn | 7.50 | 3.50 | .75 |
| ☐ 271 Billy Martin | 3.00 | 1.40 | .30 |
| ☐ 272 Ray Crone | .50 | .22 | .05 |
| ☐ 273 Hal Smith | .50 | .22 | .05 |
| ☐ 274 Rocky Bridges | .50 | .22 | .05 |
| ☐ 275 Elston Howard | 2.25 | 1.00 | .22 |
| ☐ 276 Bobby Avila | .60 | .28 | .06 |
| ☐ 277 Virgil Trucks | .60 | .28 | .06 |
| ☐ 278 Mack Burk | .50 | .22 | .05 |
| ☐ 279 Bob Boyd | .50 | .22 | .05 |
| ☐ 280 Jim Piersall | 1.50 | .70 | .15 |
| ☐ 281 Sam Taylor | .50 | .22 | .05 |
| ☐ 282 Paul Foytack | .50 | .22 | .05 |
| ☐ 283 Ray Shearer | .50 | .22 | .05 |
| ☐ 284 Ray Katt | .50 | .22 | .05 |
| ☐ 285 Frank Robinson | 10.00 | 4.75 | 1.00 |
| ☐ 286 Gino Cimoli | .50 | .22 | .05 |
| ☐ 287 Sam Jones | .60 | .28 | .06 |
| ☐ 288 Harmon Killebrew | 10.00 | 4.75 | 1.00 |
| ☐ 289 Series Hurling Rivals: | 1.25 | .60 | .12 |
| Lou Burdette | | | |
| Bobby Shantz | | | |
| ☐ 290 Dick Donovan | .50 | .22 | .05 |
| ☐ 291 Don Landrum | .50 | .22 | .05 |
| ☐ 292 Ned Garver | .50 | .22 | .05 |
| ☐ 293 Gene Freese | .50 | .22 | .05 |
| ☐ 294 Hal Jeffcoat | .50 | .22 | .05 |
| ☐ 295 Minnie Minoso | 2.00 | .90 | .20 |
| ☐ 296 Ryne Duren | 1.25 | .60 | .12 |
| ☐ 297 Don Buddin | .50 | .22 | .05 |
| ☐ 298 Jim Hearn | .50 | .22 | .05 |
| ☐ 299 Harry Simpson | .50 | .22 | .05 |
| ☐ 300 Harridge and Giles | 1.75 | .85 | .17 |
| League Presidents | | | |
| ☐ 301 Randy Jackson | .50 | .22 | .05 |
| ☐ 302 Mike Baxes | .50 | .22 | .05 |
| ☐ 303 Neil Chrisley | .50 | .22 | .05 |
| ☐ 304 Tigers' Big Bats: | 2.50 | 1.15 | .25 |
| Harvey Kuenn | | | |
| Al Kaline | | | |
| ☐ 305 Clem Labine | .75 | .35 | .07 |
| ☐ 306 Whammy Douglas | .50 | .22 | .05 |
| ☐ 307 Brooks Robinson | 12.50 | 5.75 | 1.25 |
| ☐ 308 Paul Giel | .50 | .22 | .05 |
| ☐ 309 Gail Harris | .50 | .22 | .05 |
| ☐ 310 Ernie Banks | 11.00 | 5.25 | 1.10 |
| ☐ 311 Bob Purkey | .50 | .22 | .05 |
| ☐ 312 Boston Red Sox Team | 2.00 | .60 | .20 |

| | MINT | VG-E | F-G |
|---|---|---|---|
| ☐ 313 Bob Rush | .50 | .22 | .05 |
| ☐ 314 Dodgers' Boss and | 4.50 | 2.10 | .45 |
| Power: Duke Snider | | | |
| Walt Alston | | | |
| ☐ 315 Bob Friend | .75 | .35 | .07 |
| ☐ 316 Tito Francona | .60 | .28 | .06 |
| ☐ 317 Albie Pearson | .75 | .35 | .07 |
| ☐ 318 Frank Housee | .50 | .22 | .05 |
| ☐ 319 Lou Skizas | .50 | .22 | .05 |
| ☐ 320 Whitey Ford | 9.00 | 4.25 | .90 |
| ☐ 321 Sluggers Supreme: | 5.00 | 2.35 | .50 |
| Ted Kluszewski | | | |
| Ted Williams | | | |
| ☐ 322 Harding Peterson | .60 | .28 | .06 |
| ☐ 323 Elmer Valo | .50 | .22 | .05 |
| ☐ 324 Hoyt Wilhelm | 4.00 | 1.85 | .40 |
| ☐ 325 Joe Adcock | 1.25 | .60 | .12 |
| ☐ 326 Bob Miller | .50 | .22 | .05 |
| ☐ 327 Chicago Cubs Team | 1.75 | .60 | .20 |
| ☐ 328 Ike Delock | .50 | .22 | .05 |
| ☐ 329 Bob Cerv | .60 | .28 | .06 |
| ☐ 330 Ed Bailey | .60 | .28 | .06 |
| ☐ 331 Pedro Ramos | .50 | .22 | .05 |
| ☐ 332 Jim King | .50 | .22 | .05 |
| ☐ 333 Andy Carey | .65 | .30 | .06 |
| ☐ 334 Mound Aces: | 1.00 | .45 | .10 |
| Bob Friend | | | |
| Billy Pierce | | | |
| ☐ 335 Ruben Gomez | .50 | .22 | .05 |
| ☐ 336 Bert Hamric | .50 | .22 | .05 |
| ☐ 337 Hank Aguirre | .50 | .22 | .05 |
| ☐ 338 Walt Dropo | .50 | .22 | .05 |
| ☐ 339 Fred Hatfield | .50 | .22 | .05 |
| ☐ 340 Don Newcombe | 2.00 | .90 | .20 |
| ☐ 341 Pirates Team | 1.50 | .50 | .10 |
| ☐ 342 Jim Brosnan | .50 | .22 | .05 |
| ☐ 343 Orlando Cepeda | 8.00 | 3.75 | .80 |
| ☐ 344 Bob Porterfield | .50 | .22 | .05 |
| ☐ 345 Jim Hegan | .60 | .28 | .06 |
| ☐ 346 Steve Bilko | .50 | .22 | .05 |
| ☐ 347 Don Rudolph | .50 | .22 | .05 |
| ☐ 348 Chico Fernandez | .50 | .22 | .05 |
| ☐ 349 Murry Dickson | .50 | .22 | .05 |
| ☐ 350 Ken Boyer | 2.00 | .90 | .20 |
| ☐ 351 Braves Fence Busters: | 5.50 | 2.60 | .55 |
| Del Crandall | | | |
| Eddie Mathews | | | |
| Hank Aaron | | | |
| Joe Adcock | | | |
| ☐ 352 Herb Score | 1.25 | .60 | .12 |
| ☐ 353 Stan Lopata | .50 | .22 | .05 |
| ☐ 354 Art Ditmar | .60 | .28 | .06 |

| | MINT | VG-E | F-G |
|---|---|---|---|
| ☐ 355 Bill Bruton | .50 | .22 | .05 |
| ☐ 356 Bob Malkmus | .50 | .22 | .05 |
| ☐ 357 Danny McDevitt | .50 | .22 | .05 |
| ☐ 358 Gene Baker | .50 | .22 | .05 |
| ☐ 359 Billy Loes | .50 | .22 | .05 |
| ☐ 360 Roy McMillan | .50 | .22 | .05 |
| ☐ 361 Mike Fornieles | .50 | .22 | .05 |
| ☐ 362 Ray Jablonski | .50 | .22 | .05 |
| ☐ 363 Don Elston | .50 | .22 | .05 |
| ☐ 364 Earl Battey | .60 | .28 | .06 |
| ☐ 365 Tom Morgan | .50 | .22 | .05 |
| ☐ 366 Gene Green | .50 | .22 | .05 |
| ☐ 367 Jack Urban | .50 | .22 | .05 |
| ☐ 368 Rocky Colavito | 2.00 | .90 | .20 |
| ☐ 369 Ralph Lumenti | .50 | .22 | .05 |
| ☐ 370 Yogi Berra | 11.00 | 5.25 | 1.10 |
| ☐ 371 Marty Keough | .50 | .22 | .05 |
| ☐ 372 Don Cardwell | .50 | .22 | .05 |
| ☐ 373 Joe Pignatano | .60 | .28 | .06 |
| ☐ 374 Brooks Lawrence | .50 | .22 | .05 |
| ☐ 375 Pee Wee Reese | 9.00 | 4.25 | .90 |
| ☐ 376 Charley Rabe | .50 | .22 | .05 |
| ☐ 377 A Milwaukee Team<br>alphabetical | 1.75 | .50 | .15 |
| ☐ 377 B Milwaukee Team<br>numerical | 11.00 | 2.00 | .50 |
| ☐ 378 Hank Sauer | .65 | .30 | .06 |
| ☐ 379 Ray Herbert | .50 | .22 | .05 |
| ☐ 380 Charley Maxwell | .50 | .22 | .05 |
| ☐ 381 Hal Brown | .50 | .22 | .05 |
| ☐ 382 Al Cicotte | .65 | .30 | .06 |
| ☐ 383 Lou Berberet | .50 | .22 | .05 |
| ☐ 384 John Goryl | .50 | .22 | .05 |
| ☐ 385 Wilmer Mizell | .50 | .22 | .05 |
| ☐ 386 Birdie's Sluggers:<br>Ed Bailey<br>Birdie Tebbetts<br>Frank Robinson | 1.50 | .70 | .15 |
| ☐ 387 Wally Post | .50 | .22 | .05 |
| ☐ 388 Billy Moran | .50 | .22 | .05 |
| ☐ 389 Bill Taylor | .50 | .22 | .05 |
| ☐ 390 Del Crandall | .75 | .35 | .07 |
| ☐ 391 Dave Melton | .50 | .22 | .05 |
| ☐ 392 Bennie Daniels | .50 | .22 | .05 |
| ☐ 393 Tony Kubek | 3.00 | 1.40 | .30 |
| ☐ 394 Jim Grant | .50 | .22 | .05 |
| ☐ 395 Willard Nixon | .50 | .22 | .05 |
| ☐ 396 Dutch Dotterer | .50 | .22 | .05 |
| ☐ 397 A Detroit Team<br>alphabetical | 1.75 | .50 | .15 |
| ☐ 397 B Detroit Team<br>numerical | 11.00 | 2.00 | .50 |

| | MINT | VG-E | F-G |
|---|---|---|---|
| ☐ 398 Gene Woodling | .75 | .35 | .07 |
| ☐ 399 Marv Grissom | .50 | .22 | .05 |
| ☐ 400 Nellie Fox | 2.25 | 1.00 | .22 |
| ☐ 401 Don Bessent | .60 | .28 | .06 |
| ☐ 402 Bobby Gene Smith | .50 | .22 | .05 |
| ☐ 403 Steve Korcheck | .50 | .22 | .05 |
| ☐ 404 Curt Simmons | .75 | .35 | .07 |
| ☐ 405 Ken Aspromonte | .50 | .22 | .05 |
| ☐ 406 Vic Power | .60 | .28 | .06 |
| ☐ 407 Carlton Willey | .50 | .22 | .05 |
| ☐ 408 A Baltimore Team<br>alphabetical | 1.75 | .50 | .15 |
| ☐ 408 B Baltimore Team<br>numerical | 11.00 | 2.00 | .50 |
| ☐ 409 Frank Thomas | .60 | .28 | .06 |
| ☐ 410 Murray Wall | .50 | .22 | .05 |
| ☐ 411 Tony Taylor | .50 | .22 | .05 |
| ☐ 412 Jerry Staley | .50 | .22 | .05 |
| ☐ 413 Jim Davenport | .75 | .35 | .07 |
| ☐ 414 Sammy White | .50 | .22 | .05 |
| ☐ 415 Bob Bowman | .50 | .22 | .05 |
| ☐ 416 Foster Castleman | .50 | .22 | .05 |
| ☐ 417 Carl Furillo | 2.00 | .90 | .20 |
| ☐ 418 World Series Batting<br>Foes: Mickey Mantle<br>Hank Aaron | 18.00 | 8.50 | 1.80 |
| ☐ 419 Bobby Shantz | 1.25 | .60 | .12 |
| ☐ 420 Vada Pinson | 3.50 | 1.65 | .35 |
| ☐ 421 Dixie Howell | .50 | .22 | .05 |
| ☐ 422 Norm Zauchin | .50 | .22 | .05 |
| ☐ 423 Phil Clark | .50 | .22 | .05 |
| ☐ 424 Larry Doby | 1.50 | .70 | .15 |
| ☐ 425 Sam Esposito | .50 | .22 | .05 |
| ☐ 426 Johnny O'Brien | .50 | .22 | .05 |
| ☐ 427 Al Worthington | .50 | .22 | .05 |
| ☐ 428 A Cincinnati Team<br>alphabetical | 1.75 | .50 | .15 |
| ☐ 428 B Cincinnati Team<br>numerical | 11.00 | 2.00 | .50 |
| ☐ 429 Gus Triandos | .75 | .35 | .07 |
| ☐ 430 Bobby Thomson | 1.25 | .60 | .12 |
| ☐ 431 Gene Conley | .50 | .22 | .05 |
| ☐ 432 John Powers | .50 | .22 | .05 |
| ☐ 433 A Pancho Herrera COR | .65 | .30 | .06 |
| ☐ 433 B Pancho Herrer ERR | 6.50 | 3.00 | .65 |
| ☐ 434 Harvey Kuenn | 1.50 | .70 | .15 |
| ☐ 435 Ed Roebuck | .60 | .28 | .06 |
| ☐ 436 Rival Fence Busters:<br>Willie Mays<br>Duke Snider | 12.00 | 5.50 | 1.20 |
| ☐ 437 Bob Speake | .50 | .22 | .05 |
| ☐ 438 Whitey Herzog | .75 | .35 | .07 |

|  | MINT | VG-E | F-G |
|---|---|---|---|
| ☐ 439 Ray Narleski | .50 | .22 | .05 |
| ☐ 440 Ed Mathews | 7.00 | 3.25 | .70 |
| ☐ 441 Jim Marshall | .45 | .20 | .04 |
| ☐ 442 Phil Paine | .45 | .20 | .04 |
| ☐ 443 Billy Harrell SP | 4.00 | 1.85 | .40 |
| ☐ 444 Danny Kravitz | .45 | .20 | .04 |
| ☐ 445 Bob Smith | .45 | .20 | .04 |
| ☐ 446 Carroll Hardy SP | 4.00 | 1.85 | .40 |
| ☐ 447 Ray Monzant | .45 | .20 | .04 |
| ☐ 448 Charlie Lau | .75 | .35 | .07 |
| ☐ 449 Gene Fodge | .45 | .20 | .04 |
| ☐ 450 Preston Ward SP | 4.00 | 1.85 | .40 |
| ☐ 451 Joe Taylor | .45 | .20 | .04 |
| ☐ 452 Roman Mejias | .45 | .20 | .04 |
| ☐ 453 Tom Qualters | .45 | .20 | .04 |
| ☐ 454 Harry Hanebrink | .45 | .20 | .04 |
| ☐ 455 Hal Griggs | .45 | .20 | .04 |
| ☐ 456 Dick Brown | .45 | .20 | .04 |
| ☐ 457 Milt Pappas | 1.00 | .45 | .10 |
| ☐ 458 Julio Becquer | .45 | .20 | .04 |
| ☐ 459 Ron Blackburn | .45 | .20 | .04 |
| ☐ 460 Chuck Essegian | .45 | .20 | .04 |
| ☐ 461 Ed Mayer | .45 | .20 | .04 |
| ☐ 462 Gary Geiger SP | 4.00 | 1.85 | .40 |
| ☐ 463 Vito Valentinetti | .45 | .20 | .04 |
| ☐ 464 Curt Flood | 2.50 | 1.15 | .25 |
| ☐ 465 Arnie Portocarrero | .45 | .20 | .04 |
| ☐ 466 Pete Whisenant | .45 | .20 | .04 |
| ☐ 467 Glen Hobbie | .45 | .20 | .04 |
| ☐ 468 Bob Schmidt | .45 | .20 | .04 |
| ☐ 469 Don Ferrarese | .45 | .20 | .04 |
| ☐ 470 R.C. Stevens | .45 | .20 | .04 |
| ☐ 471 Lenny Green | .45 | .20 | .04 |
| ☐ 472 Joe Jay | .45 | .20 | .04 |
| ☐ 473 Bill Renna | .45 | .20 | .04 |
| ☐ 474 Roman Semproch | .45 | .20 | .04 |
| ALL-STAR SELECTIONS (475-495) | | | |
| ☐ 475 Haney/Stengel AS (checklist back) | 3.50 | 1.00 | .25 |
| ☐ 476 Stan Musial AS TP | 4.50 | 2.10 | .45 |
| ☐ 477 Bill Skowron AS | .75 | .35 | .07 |
| ☐ 478 Johnny Temple AS | .60 | .28 | .06 |
| ☐ 479 Nellie Fox AS | 1.50 | .70 | .15 |
| ☐ 480 Eddie Mathews AS | 2.75 | 1.25 | .27 |
| ☐ 481 Frank Malzone AS | .60 | .28 | .06 |
| ☐ 482 Ernie Banks AS | 3.50 | 1.65 | .35 |
| ☐ 483 Luis Aparicio AS | 2.75 | .1.25 | .27 |
| ☐ 484 Frank Robinson AS | 3.50 | 1.65 | .35 |
| ☐ 485 Ted Williams AS | 9.00 | 4.25 | .90 |
| ☐ 486 Willie Mays AS | 7.50 | 3.50 | .75 |
| ☐ 487 Mickey Mantle AS TP | 7.50 | 3.50 | .75 |

|  | MINT | VG-E | F-G |
|---|---|---|---|
| ☐ 488 Hank Aaron AS | 7.50 | 3.50 | .75 |
| ☐ 489 Jackie Jensen AS | .75 | .35 | .07 |
| ☐ 490 Ed Bailey AS | .60 | .28 | .06 |
| ☐ 491 Sherm Lollar AS | .60 | .28 | .06 |
| ☐ 492 Bob Friend AS | .60 | .28 | .06 |
| ☐ 493 Bob Turley AS | .75 | .35 | .07 |
| ☐ 494 Warren Spahn AS | 2.75 | 1.25 | .27 |
| ☐ 495 Herb Score AS | 1.00 | .45 | .10 |

## 1959 TOPPS

The cards in this 572 card set measure 2½" by 3½". The 1959 Topps set contains bust pictures of the players in a colored circle. Card numbers 551 to 572 are The Sporting News All-Star selections. High numbers 507 to 572 have the card number in a black background on the reverse rather than a green background as in the lower numbers. The high numbers are more difficult to obtain. Several cards in the 300's exist with or without an extra traded or option line on the back of the card. Cards 199 to 286 exist with either white or gray backs. Cards 461 to 470 contain "Highlights" while cards 116 to 146 give an alphabetically ordered listing of "Rookie Prospects."

Complete Set: M-575.00; VG-E-225.00; F-G-50.00

| | MINT | VG-E | F-G |
|---|---|---|---|
| Common Player (1–110) | .50 | .22 | .05 |
| Common Player (111–506) | .40 | .18 | .04 |
| Common Player (507–572) | 2.00 | .90 | .20 |

|  | | MINT | VG-E | F-G |
|---|---|---|---|---|
| ☐ | 1 Ford Frick | 3.50 | 1.00 | .25 |
| ☐ | 2 Eddie Yost | .50 | .22 | .05 |
| ☐ | 3 Don McMahon | .50 | .22 | .05 |
| ☐ | 4 Albie Pearson | .50 | .22 | .05 |
| ☐ | 5 Dick Donovan | .50 | .22 | .05 |
| ☐ | 6 Alex Grammas | .50 | .22 | .05 |
| ☐ | 7 Al Pilarcik | .50 | .22 | .05 |
| ☐ | 8 Phillies Team | 1.50 | .50 | .15 |
| ☐ | 9 Paul Giel | .50 | .22 | .05 |
| ☐ | 10 Mickey Mantle | 60.00 | 27.00 | 6.00 |
| ☐ | 11 Billy Hunter | .50 | .22 | .05 |
| ☐ | 12 Vern Law | .60 | .28 | .06 |
| ☐ | 13 Dick Gernert | .50 | .22 | .05 |
| ☐ | 14 Pete Whisenant | .50 | .22 | .05 |
| ☐ | 15 Dick Drott | .50 | .22 | .05 |
| ☐ | 16 Joe Pignatano | .50 | .22 | .05 |
| ☐ | 17 Danny's Stars | .75 | .35 | .07 |
|  | Frank Thomas | | | |
|  | Danny Murtaugh | | | |
|  | Ted Kluszewski | | | |
| ☐ | 18 Jack Urban | .50 | .22 | .05 |
| ☐ | 19 Eddie Bressoud | .50 | .22 | .05 |
| ☐ | 20 Duke Snider | 10.00 | 4.75 | 1.00 |
| ☐ | 21 Connie Johnson | .50 | .22 | .05 |
| ☐ | 22 Al Smith | .50 | .22 | .05 |
| ☐ | 23 Murry Dickson | .50 | .22 | .05 |
| ☐ | 24 Red Wilson | .50 | .22 | .05 |
| ☐ | 25 Don Hoak | .50 | .22 | .05 |
| ☐ | 26 Chuck Stobbs | .50 | .22 | .05 |
| ☐ | 27 Andy Pafko | .50 | .22 | .05 |
| ☐ | 28 Ray Worthington | .50 | .22 | .05 |
| ☐ | 29 Jim Bolger | .50 | .22 | .05 |
| ☐ | 30 Nellie Fox | 2.25 | 1.00 | .22 |
| ☐ | 31 Ken Lehman | .50 | .22 | .05 |
| ☐ | 32 Don Buddin | .50 | .22 | .05 |
| ☐ | 33 Ed Fitzgerald | .50 | .22 | .05 |
| ☐ | 34 Pitchers Beware | 2.00 | .90 | .20 |
|  | Al Kaline | | | |
|  | Charley Maxwell | | | |
| ☐ | 35 Ted Kluszewski | 1.50 | .70 | .15 |
| ☐ | 36 Hank Aguirre | .50 | .22 | .05 |
| ☐ | 37 Gene Green | .50 | .22 | .05 |
| ☐ | 38 Morrie Martin | .50 | .22 | .05 |
| ☐ | 39 Ed Bouchee | .50 | .22 | .05 |
| ☐ | 40 Warren Spahn | 7.50 | 3.50 | .75 |
| ☐ | 41 Bob Martyn | .50 | .22 | .05 |
| ☐ | 42 Murray Wall | .50 | .22 | .05 |
| ☐ | 43 Steve Bilko | .50 | .22 | .05 |
| ☐ | 44 Vito Valentinetti | .50 | .22 | .05 |
| ☐ | 45 Andy Carey | .60 | .28 | .06 |
| ☐ | 46 R. Henry | .50 | .22 | .05 |
| ☐ | 47 Jim Finigan | .50 | .22 | .05 |
| ☐ | 48 Orioles Team | 1.50 | .50 | .15 |
| ☐ | 49 Bill Hall | .50 | .22 | .05 |

|  | | MINT | VG-E | F-G |
|---|---|---|---|---|
| ☐ | 50 Willie Mays | 27.00 | 12.00 | 2.70 |
| ☐ | 51 Rip Coleman | .50 | .22 | .05 |
| ☐ | 52 Coot Veal | .50 | .22 | .05 |
| ☐ | 53 Stan Williams | .50 | .22 | .05 |
| ☐ | 54 Mel Roach | .50 | .22 | .05 |
| ☐ | 55 Tom Brewer | .50 | .22 | .05 |
| ☐ | 56 Carl Sawatski | .50 | .22 | .05 |
| ☐ | 57 Al Cicotte | .60 | .28 | .06 |
| ☐ | 58 Eddie Miksis | .50 | .22 | .05 |
| ☐ | 59 Irv Noren | .50 | .22 | .05 |
| ☐ | 60 Bob Turley | 1.25 | .60 | .12 |
| ☐ | 61 Dick Brown | .50 | .22 | .05 |
| ☐ | 62 Tony Taylor | .50 | .22 | .05 |
| ☐ | 63 Jim Hearn | .50 | .22 | .05 |
| ☐ | 64 Joe DeMaestri | .50 | .22 | .05 |
| ☐ | 65 Frank Torre | .60 | .28 | .06 |
| ☐ | 66 Joe Ginsberg | .50 | .22 | .05 |
| ☐ | 67 Brooks Lawrence | .50 | .22 | .05 |
| ☐ | 68 Dick Schofield | .50 | .22 | .05 |
| ☐ | 69 Giants Team | 1.50 | .50 | .15 |
| ☐ | 70 Harvey Kuenn | 1.50 | .70 | .15 |
| ☐ | 71 Don Bessent | .50 | .22 | .05 |
| ☐ | 72 Bill Renna | .50 | .22 | .05 |
| ☐ | 73 Ron Jackson | .50 | .22 | .05 |
| ☐ | 74 Directing Power | .60 | .28 | .06 |
|  | Jim Lemon | | | |
|  | Cookie Lavagetto | | | |
|  | Roy Sievers | | | |
| ☐ | 75 Sam Jones | .60 | .28 | .06 |
| ☐ | 76 Bobby Richardson | 2.25 | 1.00 | .22 |
| ☐ | 77 John Goryl | .50 | .22 | .05 |
| ☐ | 78 Pedro Ramos | .50 | .22 | .05 |
| ☐ | 79 Harry Chiti | .50 | .22 | .05 |
| ☐ | 80 Minnie Minoso | 1.75 | .85 | .17 |
| ☐ | 81 Hal Jeffcoat | .50 | .22 | .05 |
| ☐ | 82 Bob Boyd | .50 | .22 | .05 |
| ☐ | 83 Bob Smith | .50 | .22 | .05 |
| ☐ | 84 Reno Bertoia | .50 | .22 | .05 |
| ☐ | 85 Harry Anderson | .50 | .22 | .05 |
| ☐ | 86 Bob Keegan | .50 | .22 | .05 |
| ☐ | 87 Danny O'Connell | .50 | .22 | .05 |
| ☐ | 88 Herb Score | .90 | .40 | .09 |
| ☐ | 89 Billy Gardner | .60 | .28 | .06 |
| ☐ | 90 Bill Skowron | 2.00 | .90 | .20 |
| ☐ | 91 Herb Moford | .50 | .22 | .05 |
| ☐ | 92 Dave Philley | .50 | .22 | .05 |
| ☐ | 93 Julio Becquer | .50 | .22 | .05 |
| ☐ | 94 White Sox Team | 1.50 | .50 | .15 |
| ☐ | 95 Carl Willey | .50 | .22 | .05 |
| ☐ | 96 Lou Berberet | .50 | .22 | .05 |
| ☐ | 97 Jerry Lynch | .50 | .22 | .05 |
| ☐ | 98 Arnie Portocarrero | .50 | .22 | .05 |
| ☐ | 99 Ted Kazanski | .50 | .22 | .05 |
| ☐ | 100 Bob Cerv | .60 | .28 | .06 |

| | MINT | VG-E | F-G |
|---|---|---|---|
| □ 101 Alex Kellner | .50 | .22 | .05 |
| □ 102 Felipe Alou | 1.75 | .85 | .17 |
| □ 103 Billy Goodman | .60 | .28 | .06 |
| □ 104 Del Rice | .50 | .22 | .05 |
| □ 105 Lee Walls | .50 | .22 | .05 |
| □ 106 Hal Woodeshick | .50 | .22 | .05 |
| □ 107 Norm Larker | .50 | .22 | .05 |
| □ 108 Zack Monroe | .50 | .22 | .05 |
| □ 109 Bob Schmidt | .50 | .22 | .05 |
| □ 110 George Witt | .50 | .22 | .05 |
| □ 111 Redlegs Team | 1.50 | .50 | .15 |
| □ 112 Billy Consolo | .40 | .18 | .04 |
| □ 113 Taylor Phillips | .40 | .18 | .04 |
| □ 114 Earl Battey | .40 | .18 | .04 |
| □ 115 Mickey Vernon | .50 | .22 | .05 |
| ROOKIE PROSPECTS (116-146) | | | |
| □ 116 Bob Allison | 2.00 | .90 | .20 |
| □ 117 John Blanchard | .60 | .28 | .06 |
| □ 118 John Buzhardt | .40 | .18 | .04 |
| □ 119 John Callison | 1.50 | .70 | .15 |
| □ 120 Chuck Coles | .40 | .18 | .04 |
| □ 121 Bob Conley | .40 | .18 | .04 |
| □ 122 Bennie Daniels | .40 | .18 | .04 |
| □ 123 Don Dillard | .40 | .18 | .04 |
| □ 124 Dan Dobbek | .40 | .18 | .04 |
| □ 125 Ron Fairly | 1.25 | .60 | .12 |
| □ 126 Ed Haas | .60 | .28 | .06 |
| □ 127 Kent Hadley | .40 | .18 | .04 |
| □ 128 Bob Hartman | .40 | .18 | .04 |
| □ 129 Frank Herrera | .40 | .18 | .04 |
| □ 130 Lou Jackson | .40 | .18 | .04 |
| □ 131 Deron Johnson | .50 | .22 | .05 |
| □ 132 Don Lee | .40 | .18 | .04 |
| □ 133 Bob Lillis | .75 | .35 | .07 |
| □ 134 Jim McDaniel | .40 | .18 | .04 |
| □ 135 Gene Oliver | .40 | .18 | .04 |
| □ 136 Jim O'Toole | .50 | .22 | .05 |
| □ 137 Dick Ricketts | .40 | .18 | .04 |
| □ 138 John Romano | .40 | .18 | .04 |
| □ 139 Ed Sadowski | .40 | .18 | .04 |
| □ 140 Charlie Secrest | .40 | .18 | .04 |
| □ 141 Joe Shipley | .40 | .18 | .04 |
| □ 142 Dick Stigman | .40 | .18 | .04 |
| □ 143 Willie Tasby | .40 | .18 | .04 |
| □ 144 Jerry Walker | .40 | .18 | .04 |
| □ 145 Dom Zanni | .40 | .18 | .04 |
| □ 146 Jerry Zimmerman | .40 | .18 | .04 |
| □ 147 Cubs Clubbers | 2.00 | .90 | .20 |
| Dale Long | | | |
| Ernie Banks | | | |
| Walt Moryn | | | |
| □ 148 Mike McCormick | .50 | .22 | .05 |

| | MINT | VG-E | F-G |
|---|---|---|---|
| □ 149 Jim Bunning | 2.25 | 1.00 | .22 |
| □ 150 Stan Musial | 16.00 | 7.50 | 1.60 |
| □ 151 Bob Malkmus | .40 | .18 | .04 |
| □ 152 John Klippstein | .40 | .18 | .04 |
| □ 153 Jim Marshall | .40 | .18 | .04 |
| □ 154 Ray Herbert | .40 | .18 | .04 |
| □ 155 Enos Slaughter | 3.00 | 1.40 | .30 |
| □ 156 Ace Hurlers | 1.25 | .60 | .12 |
| Billy Pierce | | | |
| Robin Roberts | | | |
| □ 157 Felix Mantilla | .40 | .18 | .04 |
| □ 158 Walt Dropo | .40 | .18 | .04 |
| □ 159 Bob Shaw | .40 | .18 | .04 |
| □ 160 Dick Groat | 1.25 | .60 | .12 |
| □ 161 Frank Baumann | .40 | .18 | .04 |
| □ 162 Bobby G. Smith | .40 | .18 | .04 |
| □ 163 Sandy Koufax | 20.00 | 9.00 | 2.00 |
| □ 164 Johnny Groth | .40 | .18 | .04 |
| □ 165 Bill Bruton | .40 | .18 | .04 |
| □ 166 Destruction Crew | .75 | .35 | .07 |
| Minnie Minoso | | | |
| Rocky Colavito | | | |
| Larry Doby | | | |
| □ 167 Duke Maas | .40 | .18 | .04 |
| □ 168 Carroll Hardy | .40 | .18 | .04 |
| □ 169 Ted Abernathy | .40 | .18 | .04 |
| □ 170 Gene Woodling | .50 | .22 | .05 |
| □ 171 Willard Schmidt | .40 | .18 | .04 |
| □ 172 Athletics Team | 1.25 | .40 | .15 |
| □ 173 Bill Monbouquette | .40 | .18 | .04 |
| □ 174 Jim Pendleton | .40 | .18 | .04 |
| □ 175 Dick Farrell | .40 | .18 | .04 |
| □ 176 Preston Ward | .40 | .18 | .04 |
| □ 177 John Briggs | .40 | .18 | .04 |
| □ 178 Ruben Amaro | .40 | .18 | .04 |
| □ 179 Don Rudolph | .40 | .18 | .04 |
| □ 180 Yogi Berra | 10.00 | 4.75 | 1.00 |
| □ 181 Bob Porterfield | .40 | .18 | .04 |
| □ 182 Milt Graff | .40 | .18 | .04 |
| □ 183 Stu Miller | .40 | .18 | .04 |
| □ 184 Harvey Haddix | .60 | .28 | .06 |
| □ 185 Jim Busby | .40 | .18 | .04 |
| □ 186 Mudcat Grant | .40 | .18 | .04 |
| □ 187 Bubba Phillips | .40 | .18 | .04 |
| □ 188 Juan Pizzaro | .40 | .18 | .04 |
| □ 189 Neil Chrisley | .40 | .18 | .04 |
| □ 190 Bill Virdon | 1.00 | .45 | .10 |
| □ 191 Russ Kemmerer | .40 | .18 | .04 |
| □ 192 Charlie Beamon | .40 | .18 | .04 |
| □ 193 Sammy Taylor | .40 | .18 | .04 |
| □ 194 Jim Brosnan | .50 | .22 | .05 |
| □ 195 Rip Repulski | .40 | .18 | .04 |
| □ 196 Billy Moran | .40 | .18 | .04 |

| | MINT | VG-E | F-G |
|---|---|---|---|
| ☐ 197 Ray Semproch | .40 | .18 | .04 |
| ☐ 198 Jim Davenport | .60 | .28 | .06 |
| ☐ 199 Leo Kiely | .40 | .18 | .04 |
| ☐ 200 Warren Giles | 1.50 | .70 | .15 |
| (NL President) | | | |
| ☐ 201 Tom Acker | .40 | .18 | .04 |
| ☐ 202 Roger Maris | 8.00 | 3.75 | .80 |
| ☐ 203 Ossie Virgil | .40 | .18 | .04 |
| ☐ 204 Casey Wise | .40 | .18 | .04 |
| ☐ 205 Don Larsen | 1.50 | .70 | .15 |
| ☐ 206 Carl Furillo | 1.50 | .70 | .15 |
| ☐ 207 George Strickland | .40 | .18 | .04 |
| ☐ 208 Willie Jones | .40 | .18 | .04 |
| ☐ 209 Lenny Green | .40 | .18 | .04 |
| ☐ 210 Ed Bailey | .40 | .18 | .04 |
| ☐ 211 Bob Blaylock | .40 | .18 | .04 |
| ☐ 212 Fence Busters | 5.00 | 2.35 | .50 |
| Hank Aaron | | | |
| Eddie Mathews | | | |
| ☐ 213 Jim Rivera | .40 | .18 | .04 |
| ☐ 214 Marcelino Solis | .40 | .18 | .04 |
| ☐ 215 Jim Lemon | .50 | .22 | .05 |
| ☐ 216 Andre Rodgers | .40 | .18 | .04 |
| ☐ 217 Carl Erskine | 1.50 | .70 | .15 |
| ☐ 218 Roman Mejias | .40 | .18 | .04 |
| ☐ 219 George Zuverink | .40 | .18 | .04 |
| ☐ 220 Frank Malzone | .50 | .22 | .05 |
| ☐ 221 Bob Bowman | .40 | .18 | .04 |
| ☐ 222 Bobby Shantz | .75 | .35 | .07 |
| ☐ 223 Cardinals Team | 1.35 | .45 | .15 |
| ☐ 224 Claude Osteen | .90 | .40 | .09 |
| ☐ 225 Johnny Logan | .50 | .22 | .05 |
| ☐ 226 Art Ceccarelli | .40 | .18 | .04 |
| ☐ 227 Hal W. Smith | .40 | .18 | .04 |
| ☐ 228 Don Gross | .40 | .18 | .04 |
| ☐ 229 Vic Power | .40 | .18 | .04 |
| ☐ 230 Bill Fischer | .40 | .18 | .04 |
| ☐ 231 Ellis Burton | .40 | .18 | .04 |
| ☐ 232 Eddie Kasko | .40 | .18 | .04 |
| ☐ 233 Paul Foytack | .40 | .18 | .04 |
| ☐ 234 Chuck Tanner | .60 | .28 | .06 |
| ☐ 235 Valmy Thomas | .40 | .18 | .04 |
| ☐ 236 Ted Bowsfield | .40 | .18 | .04 |
| ☐ 237 Run Preventers | 1.25 | .60 | .12 |
| Gil McDougald | | | |
| Bob Turley | | | |
| Bobby Richardson | | | |
| ☐ 238 Gene Baker | .40 | .18 | .04 |
| ☐ 239 Bob Trowbridge | .40 | .18 | .04 |
| ☐ 240 Hank Bauer | 1.25 | .60 | .12 |
| ☐ 241 Billy Muffett | .40 | .18 | .04 |
| ☐ 242 Ron Samford | .40 | .18 | .04 |
| ☐ 243 Marv Grissom | .40 | .18 | .04 |

| | MINT | VG-E | F-G |
|---|---|---|---|
| ☐ 244 Ted Gray | .40 | .18 | .04 |
| ☐ 245 Ned Garver | .40 | .18 | .04 |
| ☐ 246 J.W. Porter | .40 | .18 | .04 |
| ☐ 247 Don Ferrarese | .40 | .18 | .04 |
| ☐ 248 Red Sox Team | 1.35 | .45 | .15 |
| ☐ 249 Bobby Adams | .40 | .18 | .04 |
| ☐ 250 Billy O'Dell | .40 | .18 | .04 |
| ☐ 251 Cletis Boyer | .60 | .28 | .06 |
| ☐ 252 Ray Boone | .40 | .18 | .04 |
| ☐ 253 Seth Morehead | .40 | .18 | .04 |
| ☐ 254 Zeke Bella | .40 | .18 | .04 |
| ☐ 255 Del Ennis | .50 | .22 | .05 |
| ☐ 256 Jerry Davie | .40 | .18 | .04 |
| ☐ 257 Leon Wagner | .50 | .22 | .05 |
| ☐ 258 Fred Kipp | .40 | .18 | .04 |
| ☐ 259 Jim Pisoni | .40 | .18 | .04 |
| ☐ 260 Early Wynn | 3.50 | 1.65 | .35 |
| ☐ 261 Gene Stephens | .40 | .18 | .04 |
| ☐ 262 Hitters' Foes | 1.25 | .60 | .12 |
| Johnny Podres | | | |
| Clem Labine | | | |
| Don Drysdale | | | |
| ☐ 263 B. Daley | .40 | .18 | .04 |
| ☐ 264 Chico Carrasquel | .40 | .18 | .04 |
| ☐ 265 Ron Kline | .40 | .18 | .04 |
| ☐ 266 Woody Held | .40 | .18 | .04 |
| ☐ 267 John Romonosky | .40 | .18 | .04 |
| ☐ 268 Tito Francona | .50 | .22 | .05 |
| ☐ 269 Jack Mayer | .40 | .18 | .04 |
| ☐ 270 Gil Hodges | 4.00 | 1.85 | .40 |
| ☐ 271 Orlando Pena | .40 | .18 | .04 |
| ☐ 272 Jerry Lumpe | .40 | .18 | .04 |
| ☐ 273 Joey Jay | .40 | .18 | .04 |
| ☐ 274 Jerry Kindall | .40 | .18 | .04 |
| ☐ 275 Jack Sanford | .40 | .18 | .04 |
| ☐ 276 Pete Daley | .40 | .18 | .04 |
| ☐ 277 Turk Lown | .40 | .18 | .04 |
| ☐ 278 Chuck Essegian | .40 | .18 | .04 |
| ☐ 279 Ernie Johnson | .40 | .18 | .04 |
| ☐ 280 Frank Bolling | .40 | .18 | .04 |
| ☐ 281 Walt Craddock | .40 | .18 | .04 |
| ☐ 282 R.C. Stevens | .40 | .18 | .04 |
| ☐ 283 Russ Heman | .40 | .18 | .04 |
| ☐ 284 Steve Korcheck | .40 | .18 | .04 |
| ☐ 285 Joe Cunningham | .40 | .18 | .04 |
| ☐ 286 Dean Stone | .40 | .18 | .04 |
| ☐ 287 Don Zimmer | .75 | .35 | .07 |
| ☐ 288 Dutch Dotterer | .40 | .18 | .04 |
| ☐ 289 Johnny Kucks | .50 | .22 | .05 |
| ☐ 290 Wes Covington | .50 | .22 | .05 |
| ☐ 291 Pitching Partners | .50 | .22 | .05 |
| Pedro Ramos | | | |
| Camilo Pascual | | | |

| | MINT | VG-E | F-G |
|---|---|---|---|
| ☐ 292 Dick Williams | .50 | .22 | .05 |
| ☐ 293 Ray Moore | .40 | .18 | .04 |
| ☐ 294 Hank Foiles | .40 | .18 | .04 |
| ☐ 295 Billy Martin | 2.25 | 1.00 | .22 |
| ☐ 296 Ernie Broglio | .50 | .22 | .05 |
| ☐ 297 Jackie Brandt | .40 | .18 | .04 |
| ☐ 298 Tex Clevenger | .40 | .18 | .04 |
| ☐ 299 B. Klaus | .40 | .18 | .04 |
| ☐ 300 Richie Ashburn | 2.25 | 1.00 | .22 |
| ☐ 301 Earl Averill | .40 | .18 | .04 |
| ☐ 302 Don Mossi | .50 | .22 | .05 |
| ☐ 303 Marty Keough | .40 | .18 | .04 |
| ☐ 304 Cubs Team | 1.35 | .45 | .15 |
| ☐ 305 Curt Raydon | .40 | .18 | .04 |
| ☐ 306 Jim Gilliam | 1.50 | .70 | .15 |
| ☐ 307 Curt Barclay | .40 | .18 | .04 |
| ☐ 308 Norm Siebern | .40 | .18 | .04 |
| ☐ 309 Sal Maglie | .75 | .35 | .07 |
| ☐ 310 Luis Aparicio | 3.50 | 1.65 | .35 |
| ☐ 311 Norm Zauchin | .40 | .18 | .04 |
| ☐ 312 Don Newcombe | 1.10 | .50 | .11 |
| ☐ 313 Frank House | .40 | .18 | .04 |
| ☐ 314 Don Cardwell | .40 | .18 | .04 |
| ☐ 315 Joe Adcock | 1.00 | .45 | .10 |
| ☐ 316 A Ralph Lumenti (Opt.) . (photo actually Camilo Pascual) | .50 | .22 | .05 |
| ☐ 316 B Ralph Lumenti (No Option) (photo actually Camilo Pascual) | 20.00 | 9.00 | 2.00 |
| ☐ 317 Hitting Kings: Willie Mays Richie Ashburn | 4.00 | 1.85 | .40 |
| ☐ 318 Rocky Bridges | .40 | .18 | .04 |
| ☐ 319 Dave Hillmann | .40 | .18 | .04 |
| ☐ 320 Bob Skinner | .40 | .18 | .04 |
| ☐ 321 A Bob Giallombardo (Option) | .50 | .22 | .05 |
| ☐ 321 B Bob Giallombardo (No Option) | 20.00 | 9.00 | 2.00 |
| ☐ 322 A Harry Hanebrink (Traded) | .50 | .22 | .05 |
| ☐ 322 B Harry Hanebrink (No Trade) | 20.00 | 9.00 | 2.00 |
| ☐ 323 Frank Sullivan | .40 | .18 | .04 |
| ☐ 324 Don Demeter | .40 | .18 | .04 |
| ☐ 325 Ken Boyer | 1.50 | .70 | .15 |
| ☐ 326 Marv Throneberry | 1.25 | .60 | .12 |
| ☐ 327 Gary Bell | .40 | .18 | .04 |
| ☐ 328 Lou Skizas | .40 | .18 | .04 |
| ☐ 329 Tigers Team | 1.35 | .45 | .15 |
| ☐ 330 Gus Triandos | .50 | .22 | .05 |
| ☐ 331 Steve Boros | .50 | .22 | .05 |
| ☐ 332 Ray Monzant | .40 | .18 | .04 |
| ☐ 333 Harry Simpson | .40 | .18 | .04 |
| ☐ 334 Glen Hobbie | .40 | .18 | .04 |
| ☐ 335 Johnny Temple | .50 | .22 | .05 |
| ☐ 336 A Billy Loes (with traded line) | .50 | .22 | .05 |
| ☐ 336 B Billy Loes (no trade) | 20.00 | 9.00 | 2.00 |
| ☐ 337 George Crowe | .40 | .18 | .04 |
| ☐ 338 Sparky Anderson | 2.50 | 1.15 | .25 |
| ☐ 339 Roy Face | .75 | .35 | .07 |
| ☐ 340 Roy Sievers | .50 | .22 | .05 |
| ☐ 341 Tom Qualters | .40 | .18 | .04 |
| ☐ 342 Ray Jablonski | .50 | .22 | .05 |
| ☐ 343 Bill Hoeft | .40 | .18 | .04 |
| ☐ 344 Russ Nixon | .40 | .18 | .04 |
| ☐ 345 Gil McDougald | 1.50 | .70 | .15 |
| ☐ 346 Batter Bafflers Dave Sisler Tom Brewer | .50 | .22 | .05 |
| ☐ 347 Bob Buhl | .40 | .18 | .04 |
| ☐ 348 Ted Lepcio | .40 | .18 | .04 |
| ☐ 349 Hoyt Wilhelm | 3.00 | 1.40 | .30 |
| ☐ 350 Ernie Banks | 9.00 | 4.25 | .90 |
| ☐ 351 Earl Torgeson | .40 | .18 | .04 |
| ☐ 352 Robin Roberts | 3.50 | 1.65 | .35 |
| ☐ 353 Curt Flood | 1.25 | .60 | .12 |
| ☐ 354 Pete Burnside | .40 | .18 | .04 |
| ☐ 355 Jim Piersall | 1.10 | .50 | .11 |
| ☐ 356 Bob Mabe | .40 | .18 | .04 |
| ☐ 357 Dick Stuart | .75 | .35 | .07 |
| ☐ 358 Ralph Terry | .50 | .22 | .05 |
| ☐ 359 Bill White | 1.50 | .70 | .15 |
| ☐ 360 Al Kaline | 8.00 | 3.75 | .80 |
| ☐ 361 Willard Nixon | .40 | .18 | .04 |
| ☐ 362 A Dolan Nichols (with option line) | .50 | .22 | .05 |
| ☐ 362 B Dolan Nichols (no option) | 20.00 | 9.00 | 2.00 |
| ☐ 363 Bobby Avila | .40 | .18 | .04 |
| ☐ 364 Danny McDevitt | .40 | .18 | .04 |
| ☐ 365 Gus Bell | .50 | .22 | .05 |
| ☐ 366 Humberto Robinson | .40 | .18 | .04 |
| ☐ 367 Cal Neeman | .40 | .18 | .04 |
| ☐ 368 Don Mueller | .50 | .22 | .05 |
| ☐ 369 Dick Tomanek | .40 | .18 | .04 |
| ☐ 370 Pete Runnels | .50 | .22 | .05 |
| ☐ 371 Dick Brodowski | .40 | .18 | .04 |
| ☐ 372 Jim Hegan | .40 | .18 | .04 |
| ☐ 373 Herb Plews | .40 | .18 | .04 |
| ☐ 374 Art Ditmar | .40 | .18 | .04 |
| ☐ 375 Bob Nieman | .40 | .18 | .04 |

| | MINT | VG-E | F-G |
|---|---|---|---|
| ☐ 376 Hal Naragon | .40 | .18 | .04 |
| ☐ 377 John Antonelli | .60 | .28 | .06 |
| ☐ 378 Gail Harris | .40 | .18 | .04 |
| ☐ 379 Bob Miller | .40 | .18 | .04 |
| ☐ 380 Hank Aaron | 23.00 | 10.50 | 2.30 |
| ☐ 381 Mike Baxes | .40 | .18 | .04 |
| ☐ 382 Curt Simmons | .50 | .22 | .05 |
| ☐ 383 Words of Wisdom | 1.50 | .70 | .15 |
| Don Larsen | | | |
| Casey Stengel | | | |
| ☐ 384 Dave Sisler | .40 | .18 | .04 |
| ☐ 385 Sherm Lollar | .50 | .22 | .05 |
| ☐ 386 Jim Delsing | .40 | .18 | .04 |
| ☐ 387 Don Drysdale | 5.50 | 2.60 | .55 |
| ☐ 388 Bob Will | .40 | .18 | .04 |
| ☐ 389 Joe Nuxhall | .50 | .22 | .05 |
| ☐ 390 Orlando Cepeda | 2.00 | .90 | .20 |
| ☐ 391 Milt Pappas | .50 | .22 | .05 |
| ☐ 392 Whitey Herzog | .75 | .35 | .07 |
| ☐ 393 Frank Lary | .50 | .22 | .05 |
| ☐ 394 Randy Jackson | .40 | .18 | .04 |
| ☐ 395 Elston Howard | 1.75 | .85 | .17 |
| ☐ 396 Bob Rush | .40 | .18 | .04 |
| ☐ 397 Senators Team | 1.25 | .40 | .15 |
| ☐ 398 Wally Post | .40 | .18 | .04 |
| ☐ 399 Larry Jackson | .40 | .18 | .04 |
| ☐ 400 Jackie Jensen | .75 | .35 | .07 |
| ☐ 401 Ron Blackburn | .40 | .18 | .04 |
| ☐ 402 Hector Lopez | .40 | .18 | .04 |
| ☐ 403 Clem Labine | .50 | .22 | .05 |
| ☐ 404 Hank Sauer | .50 | .22 | .05 |
| ☐ 405 Roy McMillan | .40 | .18 | .04 |
| ☐ 406 S. Drake | .40 | .18 | .04 |
| ☐ 407 Moe Drabowsky | .40 | .18 | .04 |
| ☐ 408 Keystone Combo | 1.75 | .85 | .17 |
| Nellie Fox | | | |
| Luis Aparicio | | | |
| ☐ 409 Gus Zernial | .50 | .22 | .05 |
| ☐ 410 Billy Pierce | .75 | .35 | .07 |
| ☐ 411 Whitey Lockman | .50 | .22 | .05 |
| ☐ 412 Stan Lopata | .40 | .18 | .04 |
| ☐ 413 Camilo Pascual | .50 | .22 | .05 |
| ☐ 414 Dale Long | .40 | .18 | .04 |
| ☐ 415 Bill Mazeroski | 1.50 | .70 | .15 |
| ☐ 416 Haywood Sullivan | .50 | .22 | .05 |
| ☐ 417 Virgil Trucks | .40 | .18 | .04 |
| ☐ 418 Gino Cimoli | .40 | .18 | .04 |
| ☐ 419 Braves Team | 1.50 | .50 | .15 |
| ☐ 420 Rocky Colavito | 1.50 | .70 | .15 |
| ☐ 421 Herm Wehmeier | .40 | .18 | .04 |
| ☐ 422 Hobie Landrith | .40 | .18 | .04 |
| ☐ 423 Bob Grim | .50 | .22 | .05 |

| | MINT | VG-E | F-G |
|---|---|---|---|
| ☐ 424 Ken Aspromonte | .40 | .18 | .04 |
| ☐ 425 Del Crandall | .50 | .22 | .05 |
| ☐ 426 Jerry Staley | .40 | .18 | .04 |
| ☐ 427 Charlie Neal | .50 | .22 | .05 |
| ☐ 428 Buc Hill Aces | .75 | .35 | .07 |
| Ron Kline | | | |
| Bob Friend | | | |
| Vernon Law | | | |
| Roy Face | | | |
| ☐ 429 Bobby Thomson | .75 | .35 | .07 |
| ☐ 430 Whitey Ford | 8.00 | 3.75 | .80 |
| ☐ 431 Whammy Douglas | .40 | .18 | .04 |
| ☐ 432 Smokey Burgess | .50 | .22 | .05 |
| ☐ 433 Billy Harrell | .40 | .18 | .04 |
| ☐ 434 Hal Griggs | .40 | .18 | .04 |
| ☐ 435 Frank Robinson | 8.00 | 3.75 | .80 |
| ☐ 436 Granny Hamner | .40 | .18 | .04 |
| ☐ 437 Ike Delock | .40 | .18 | .04 |
| ☐ 438 Sam Esposito | .40 | .18 | .04 |
| ☐ 439 Brooks Robinson | 10.00 | 4.75 | 1.00 |
| ☐ 440 Lou Burdette (Lefty) | 2.00 | .90 | .20 |
| ☐ 441 John Roseboro | .65 | .30 | .06 |
| ☐ 442 Ray Narleski | .40 | .18 | .04 |
| ☐ 443 Daryl Spencer | .40 | .18 | .04 |
| ☐ 444 Ron Hansen | .40 | .18 | .04 |
| ☐ 445 Cal McLish | .40 | .18 | .04 |
| ☐ 446 Rocky Nelson | .40 | .18 | .04 |
| ☐ 447 Bob Anderson | .40 | .18 | .04 |
| ☐ 448 Vada Pinson | 1.50 | .70 | .15 |
| ☐ 449 Tom Gorman | .40 | .18 | .04 |
| ☐ 450 Ed Mathews | 5.00 | 2.35 | .50 |
| ☐ 451 Jimmy Constable | .40 | .18 | .04 |
| ☐ 452 Chico Fernandez | .40 | .18 | .04 |
| ☐ 453 Les Moss | .40 | .18 | .04 |
| ☐ 454 Phil Clark | .40 | .18 | .04 |
| ☐ 455 Larry Doby | 1.25 | .60 | .12 |
| ☐ 456 Jerry Casale | .40 | .18 | .04 |
| ☐ 457 Dodgers Team | 3.00 | 1.00 | .25 |
| ☐ 458 Gordon Jones | .40 | .18 | .04 |
| ☐ 459 Bill Tuttle | .40 | .18 | .04 |
| ☐ 460 Bob Friend | .50 | .22 | .05 |
| HIGHLIGHTS (461–470) | | | |
| ☐ 461 Mantle Hits Homer | 5.50 | 2.60 | .55 |
| ☐ 462 Colavito's Catch | .75 | .35 | .07 |
| ☐ 463 Kaline Batting Champ | 2.00 | .90 | .20 |
| ☐ 464 Mays' Series Catch | 3.75 | 1.75 | .37 |
| ☐ 465 Sievers Sets Mark | .55 | .25 | .05 |
| ☐ 466 Pierce All-Star | .55 | .25 | .05 |
| ☐ 467 Aaron Clubs Homer | 3.25 | 1.50 | .32 |
| ☐ 468 Snider's Play | 3.00 | 1.40 | .30 |
| ☐ 469 Hustler Banks | 2.00 | .90 | .20 |
| ☐ 470 Musial's 3000 Hit | 3.00 | 1.40 | .30 |

| | MINT | VG-E | F-G |
|---|---|---|---|
| ☐ 471 Tom Sturdivant | .40 | .18 | .04 |
| ☐ 472 Gene Freese | .40 | .18 | .04 |
| ☐ 473 Mike Fornieles | .40 | .18 | .04 |
| ☐ 474 Moe Thacker | .40 | .18 | .04 |
| ☐ 475 Jack Harshman | .40 | .18 | .04 |
| ☐ 476 Indians Team | 1.25 | .40 | .15 |
| ☐ 477 Barry Latman | .40 | .18 | .04 |
| ☐ 478 Bob Clemente | 12.50 | 5.75 | 1.25 |
| ☐ 479 Lindy McDaniel | .40 | .18 | .04 |
| ☐ 480 Red Schoendienst | 1.10 | .50 | .11 |
| ☐ 481 Charlie Maxwell | .40 | .18 | .04 |
| ☐ 482 Russ Meyer | .40 | .18 | .04 |
| ☐ 483 Clint Courtney | .40 | .18 | .04 |
| ☐ 484 Willie Kirkland | .40 | .18 | .04 |
| ☐ 485 Ryne Duren | .75 | .35 | .07 |
| ☐ 486 Sam White | .40 | .18 | .04 |
| ☐ 487 H. Brown | .40 | .18 | .04 |
| ☐ 488 Walt Moryn | .40 | .18 | .04 |
| ☐ 489 John Powers | .40 | .18 | .04 |
| ☐ 490 Frank Thomas | .50 | .22 | .05 |
| ☐ 491 Don Blasingame | .40 | .18 | .04 |
| ☐ 492 Gene Conley | .40 | .18 | .04 |
| ☐ 493 Jim Landis | .40 | .18 | .04 |
| ☐ 494 Don Pavletich | .40 | .18 | .04 |
| ☐ 495 John Podres | 1.25 | .60 | .12 |
| ☐ 496 Wayne Terwilliger | .40 | .18 | .04 |
| ☐ 497 Hal R. Smith | .40 | .18 | .04 |
| ☐ 498 Dick Hyde | .40 | .18 | .04 |
| ☐ 499 John O'Brien | .40 | .18 | .04 |
| ☐ 500 Vic Wertz | .50 | .22 | .05 |
| ☐ 501 Bob Tiefenauer | .40 | .18 | .04 |
| ☐ 502 Alvin Dark | .75 | .35 | .07 |
| ☐ 503 Jim Owens | .40 | .18 | .04 |
| ☐ 504 Ossie Alvarez | .40 | .18 | .04 |
| ☐ 505 Tony Kubek | 2.00 | .90 | .20 |
| ☐ 506 Bob Purkey | .40 | .18 | .04 |
| ☐ 507 Bob Hale | 2.00 | .90 | .20 |
| ☐ 508 Art Fowler | 2.00 | .90 | .20 |
| ☐ 509 Norm Cash | 4.00 | 1.85 | .40 |
| ☐ 510 Yankees Team | 8.00 | 2.00 | .40 |
| ☐ 511 George Susce | 2.00 | .90 | .20 |
| ☐ 512 George Altman | 2.00 | .90 | .20 |
| ☐ 513 Tommy Carroll | 2.00 | .90 | .20 |
| ☐ 514 Bob Gibson | 36.00 | 15.00 | 3.00 |
| ☐ 515 Harmon Killebrew | 18.00 | 8.50 | 1.80 |
| ☐ 516 Mike Garcia | 2.50 | 1.15 | .25 |
| ☐ 517 Joe Koppe | 2.00 | .90 | .20 |
| ☐ 518 Mike Cueller | 3.00 | 1.40 | .30 |
| (sic, Cuellar) | | | |
| ☐ 519 Infield Power | 2.50 | 1.15 | .25 |
| Pete Runnels | | | |
| Dick Gernert | | | |
| Frank Malzone | | | |
| ☐ 520 Don Elston | 2.00 | .90 | .20 |
| ☐ 521 Gary Geiger | 2.00 | .90 | .20 |
| ☐ 522 Gene Snyder | 2.00 | .90 | .20 |
| ☐ 523 Harry Bright | 2.00 | .90 | .20 |
| ☐ 524 Larry Osborne | 2.00 | .90 | .20 |
| ☐ 525 Jim Coates | 2.00 | .90 | .20 |
| ☐ 526 Bob Speake | 2.00 | .90 | .20 |
| ☐ 527 Solly Hemus | 2.00 | .90 | .20 |
| ☐ 528 Pirates Team | 4.00 | 1.25 | .40 |
| ☐ 529 George Bamberger | 4.00 | 1.85 | .40 |
| ☐ 530 Wally Moon | 2.50 | 1.15 | .25 |
| ☐ 531 Ray Webster | 2.00 | .90 | .20 |
| ☐ 532 Mark Freeman | 2.00 | .90 | .20 |
| ☐ 533 Darrell Johnson | 2.50 | 1.15 | .25 |
| ☐ 534 Faye Throneberry | 2.00 | .90 | .20 |
| ☐ 535 Ruben Gomez | 2.00 | .90 | .20 |
| ☐ 536 Danny Kravitz | 2.00 | .90 | .20 |
| ☐ 537 Rudolph Arias | 2.00 | .90 | .20 |
| ☐ 538 Chick King | 2.00 | .90 | .20 |
| ☐ 539 Gary Blaylock | 2.00 | .90 | .20 |
| ☐ 540 Willie Miranda | 2.00 | .90 | .20 |
| ☐ 541 Bob Thurman | 2.00 | .90 | .20 |
| ☐ 542 Jim Perry | 4.00 | 1.85 | .40 |
| ☐ 543 Corsair Trio | 9.00 | 4.25 | .90 |
| Bob Skinner | | | |
| Bill Virdon | | | |
| Roberto Clemente | | | |
| ☐ 544 Lee Tate | 2.00 | .90 | .20 |
| ☐ 545 Tom Morgan | 2.00 | .90 | .20 |
| ☐ 546 Al Schroll | 2.00 | .90 | .20 |
| ☐ 547 Jim Baxes | 2.00 | .90 | .20 |
| ☐ 548 Elmer Singleton | 2.00 | .90 | .20 |
| ☐ 549 Howie Nunn | 2.00 | .90 | .20 |
| ☐ 550 Roy Campanella | 25.00 | 11.00 | 2.50 |
| (Symbol of Courage) | | | |
| ALL-STAR | | | |
| SELECTIONS (551–572) | | | |
| ☐ 551 Fred Haney MGR AS | 2.00 | .90 | .20 |
| ☐ 552 Casey Stengel MGR AS | 4.00 | 1.85 | .40 |
| ☐ 553 Orlando Cepeda AS | 2.25 | 1.00 | .22 |
| ☐ 554 Bill Skowron AS | 2.25 | 1.00 | .22 |
| ☐ 555 Bill Mazeroski AS | 2.25 | 1.00 | .22 |
| ☐ 556 Nellie Fox AS | 2.50 | 1.15 | .25 |
| ☐ 557 Ken Boyer AS | 2.25 | 1.00 | .22 |
| ☐ 558 Frank Malzone AS | 2.00 | .90 | .20 |
| ☐ 559 Ernie Banks AS | 7.50 | 3.50 | .75 |
| ☐ 560 Luis Aparicio AS | 4.50 | 2.10 | .45 |
| ☐ 561 Hank Aaron AS | 18.00 | 8.50 | 1.80 |
| ☐ 562 Al Kaline AS | 7.50 | 3.50 | .75 |
| ☐ 563 Willie Mays AS | 18.00 | 8.50 | 1.80 |
| ☐ 564 Mickey Mantle AS | 30.00 | 14.00 | 3.00 |

| | | MINT | VG-E | F-G |
|---|---|---|---|---|
| ☐ 565 | Wes Covington AS | 2.00 | .90 | .20 |
| ☐ 566 | Roy Sievers AS | 2.00 | .90 | .20 |
| ☐ 567 | Del Crandall AS | 2.00 | .90 | .20 |
| ☐ 568 | Gus Triandos AS | 2.00 | .90 | .20 |
| ☐ 569 | Bob Friend AS | 2.00 | .90 | .20 |
| ☐ 570 | Bob Turley AS | 2.25 | 1.00 | .22 |
| ☐ 571 | Warren Spahn AS | 5.00 | 2.35 | .50 |
| ☐ 572 | Billy Pierce AS | 2.50 | 1.15 | .25 |

## 1960 TOPPS

The cards in this 572 card set measure 2½" by 3½". The 1960 Topps set is the only Topps standard size issue to use a horizontally oriented front. World Series cards appeared for the first time (385 to 391), and there is a Rookie series (117 to 149) and a Sport Magazine All-Star Selection series (553 to 572). Cards 375 to 440 come with either gray or white backs, and the high series (507 to 572) were printed on a more limited basis than the rest of the set. The team cards have series checklists on the reverse.

Complete Set: M-550.00; VG-E-225.00; F-G-50.00

| | | MINT | VG-E | F-G |
|---|---|---|---|---|
| | Common Player (1–440) | .35 | .15 | .03 |
| | Common Player (441–506) | .55 | .25 | .05 |
| | Common Player (507–552) | 1.75 | .85 | .17 |
| | Common Player (553–572) | 2.00 | .90 | .18 |
| ☐ 1 | Early Wynn | 4.50 | 1.50 | .50 |
| ☐ 2 | Roman Mejias | .35 | .15 | .03 |
| ☐ 3 | Joe Adcock | .80 | .40 | .08 |
| ☐ 4 | Bob Purkey | .35 | .15 | .03 |

| | | MINT | VG-E | F-G |
|---|---|---|---|---|
| ☐ 5 | Wally Moon | .45 | .20 | .04 |
| ☐ 6 | Lou Berberet | .35 | .15 | .03 |
| ☐ 7 | Master and Mentor: Willie Mays Bill Rigney | 3.00 | 1.40 | .30 |
| ☐ 8 | Bud Daley | .35 | .15 | .03 |
| ☐ 9 | Faye Throneberry | .35 | .15 | .03 |
| ☐ 10 | Ernie Banks | 5.00 | 2.35 | .50 |
| ☐ 11 | Norm Siebern | .35 | .15 | .03 |
| ☐ 12 | Milt Pappas | .45 | .20 | .04 |
| ☐ 13 | Wally Post | .35 | .15 | .03 |
| ☐ 14 | Jim Grant | .35 | .15 | .03 |
| ☐ 15 | Pete Runnels | .45 | .20 | .04 |
| ☐ 16 | Ernie Broglio | .35 | .15 | .03 |
| ☐ 17 | Johnny Callison | .50 | .22 | .05 |
| ☐ 18 | Dodgers Team | 2.25 | .75 | .20 |
| ☐ 19 | Felix Mantilla | .35 | .15 | .03 |
| ☐ 20 | Roy Face | .75 | .35 | .07 |
| ☐ 21 | Dutch Dotterer | .35 | .15 | .03 |
| ☐ 22 | Rocky Bridges | .35 | .15 | .03 |
| ☐ 23 | Eddie Fisher | .35 | .15 | .03 |
| ☐ 24 | Dick Gray | .35 | .15 | .03 |
| ☐ 25 | Roy Sievers | .50 | .22 | .05 |
| ☐ 26 | Wayne Terwilliger | .35 | .15 | .03 |
| ☐ 27 | Dick Drott | .35 | .15 | .03 |
| ☐ 28 | Brooks Robinson | 9.00 | 4.25 | .90 |
| ☐ 29 | Clem Labine | .45 | .20 | .04 |
| ☐ 30 | Tito Francona | .45 | .20 | .04 |
| ☐ 31 | Sammy Esposito | .35 | .15 | .03 |
| ☐ 32 | Sophomore Stalwarts: Jim O'Toole Vada Pinson | .50 | .22 | .05 |
| ☐ 33 | Tom Morgan | .35 | .15 | .03 |
| ☐ 34 | George Anderson | 1.10 | .50 | .11 |
| ☐ 35 | Whitey Ford | 6.00 | 2.80 | .60 |
| ☐ 36 | Russ Nixon | .35 | .15 | .03 |
| ☐ 37 | Bill Bruton | .35 | .15 | .03 |
| ☐ 38 | Jerry Casale | .35 | .15 | .03 |
| ☐ 39 | Earl Averill | .35 | .15 | .03 |
| ☐ 40 | Joe Cunningham | .35 | .15 | .03 |
| ☐ 41 | Barry Latman | .35 | .15 | .03 |
| ☐ 42 | Hobie Landrith | .35 | .15 | .03 |
| ☐ 43 | Senators Team | 1.25 | .40 | .15 |
| ☐ 44 | Bob Locke | .35 | .15 | .03 |
| ☐ 45 | Roy McMillan | .35 | .15 | .03 |
| ☐ 46 | Jerry Fisher | .35 | .15 | .03 |
| ☐ 47 | Don Zimmer | .65 | .30 | .06 |
| ☐ 48 | Hal W. Smith | .35 | .15 | .03 |
| ☐ 49 | Curt Raydon | .35 | .15 | .03 |
| ☐ 50 | Al Kaline | 6.50 | 3.00 | .65 |
| ☐ 51 | Jim Coates | .35 | .15 | .03 |
| ☐ 52 | Dave Philley | .35 | .15 | .03 |
| ☐ 53 | Jackie Brandt | .35 | .15 | .03 |

| | MINT | VG-E | F-G |
|---|---|---|---|
| ☐ 54 Mike Fornieles | .35 | .15 | .03 |
| ☐ 55 Bill Mazeroski | 1.25 | .60 | .12 |
| ☐ 56 Steve Korcheck | .35 | .15 | .03 |
| ☐ 57 Win Savers | .45 | .20 | .04 |
| Turk Lown | | | |
| Jerry Staley | | | |
| ☐ 58 Gino Cimoli | .35 | .15 | .03 |
| ☐ 59 Juan Pizarro | .35 | .15 | .03 |
| ☐ 60 Gus Triandos | .45 | .20 | .04 |
| ☐ 61 Eddie Kasko | .35 | .15 | .03 |
| ☐ 62 Roger Craig | .50 | .22 | .05 |
| ☐ 63 George Strickland | .35 | .15 | .03 |
| ☐ 64 Jack Meyer | .35 | .15 | .03 |
| ☐ 65 Elston Howard | 1.50 | .70 | .15 |
| ☐ 66 Bob Trowbridge | .35 | .15 | .03 |
| ☐ 67 Jose Pagan | .35 | .15 | .03 |
| ☐ 68 Dave Hillman | .35 | .15 | .03 |
| ☐ 69 Billy Goodman | .45 | .20 | .04 |
| ☐ 70 Lew Burdette | 1.10 | .50 | .11 |
| ☐ 71 Marty Keough | .35 | .15 | .03 |
| ☐ 72 Tigers Team | 1.35 | .45 | .15 |
| ☐ 73 Bob Gibson | 6.00 | 2.80 | .60 |
| ☐ 74 Walt Moryn | .35 | .15 | .03 |
| ☐ 75 Vic Power | .35 | .15 | .03 |
| ☐ 76 Bill Fischer | .35 | .15 | .03 |
| ☐ 77 Hank Foiles | .35 | .15 | .03 |
| ☐ 78 Bob Grim | .35 | .15 | .03 |
| ☐ 79 Walt Dropo | .35 | .15 | .03 |
| ☐ 80 Johnny Antonelli | .50 | .22 | .05 |
| ☐ 81 Russ Snyder | .35 | .15 | .03 |
| ☐ 82 Ruben Gomez | .35 | .15 | .03 |
| ☐ 83 Tony Kubek | 1.50 | .70 | .15 |
| ☐ 84 Hal R. Smith | .35 | .15 | .03 |
| ☐ 85 Frank Lary | .45 | .20 | .04 |
| ☐ 86 Dick Gernert | .35 | .15 | .03 |
| ☐ 87 John Romonosky | .35 | .15 | .03 |
| ☐ 88 John Roseboro | .45 | .20 | .04 |
| ☐ 89 Hal Brown | .35 | .15 | .03 |
| ☐ 90 Bobby Avila | .35 | .15 | .03 |
| ☐ 91 Bennie Daniels | .35 | .15 | .03 |
| ☐ 92 Whitey Herzog | .75 | .35 | .07 |
| ☐ 93 Art Schult | .35 | .15 | .03 |
| ☐ 94 Leo Kiely | .35 | .15 | .03 |
| ☐ 95 Frank Thomas | .35 | .15 | .03 |
| ☐ 96 Ralph Terry | .50 | .22 | .05 |
| ☐ 97 Ted Lepcio | .35 | .15 | .03 |
| ☐ 98 Gordon Jones | .35 | .15 | .03 |
| ☐ 99 Lenny Green | .35 | .15 | .03 |
| ☐ 100 Nellie Fox | 1.50 | .70 | .15 |
| ☐ 101 Bob Miller | .35 | .15 | .03 |
| ☐ 102 Kent Hadley | .35 | .15 | .03 |
| ☐ 103 Dick Farrell | .35 | .15 | .03 |
| ☐ 104 Dick Schofield | .35 | .15 | .03 |

| | MINT | VG-E | F-G |
|---|---|---|---|
| ☐ 105 Larry Sherry | .65 | .30 | .06 |
| ☐ 106 Billy Gardner | .45 | .20 | .04 |
| ☐ 107 Carlton Willey | .35 | .15 | .03 |
| ☐ 108 Pete Daley | .35 | .15 | .03 |
| ☐ 109 Clete Boyer | .50 | .22 | .05 |
| ☐ 110 Cal McLish | .35 | .15 | .03 |
| ☐ 111 Vic Wertz | .45 | .20 | .04 |
| ☐ 112 Jack Harshman | .35 | .15 | .03 |
| ☐ 113 Bob Skinner | .35 | .15 | .03 |
| ☐ 114 Ken Aspromonte | .35 | .15 | .03 |
| ☐ 115 Fork and Knuckler: | 1.25 | .60 | .12 |
| Roy Face | | | |
| Hoyt Wilhelm | | | |
| ☐ 116 Jim Rivera | .35 | .15 | .03 |
| ROOKIE PROSPECTS | | | |
| (117–148) | | | |
| ☐ 117 Tom Borland | .35 | .15 | .03 |
| ☐ 118 Bob Bruce | .35 | .15 | .03 |
| ☐ 119 Chico Cardenas | .50 | .22 | .05 |
| ☐ 120 Duke Carmel | .35 | .15 | .03 |
| ☐ 121 Camilo Carreon | .35 | .15 | .03 |
| ☐ 122 Don Dillard | .35 | .15 | .03 |
| ☐ 123 Dan Dobbek | .35 | .15 | .03 |
| ☐ 124 Jim Donohue | .35 | .15 | .03 |
| ☐ 125 Dick Ellsworth | .55 | .25 | .05 |
| ☐ 126 Chuck Estrada | .75 | .35 | .07 |
| ☐ 127 Ron Hansen | .50 | .22 | .05 |
| ☐ 128 Bill Harris | .35 | .15 | .03 |
| ☐ 129 Bob Hartman | .35 | .15 | .03 |
| ☐ 130 Frank Herrera | .35 | .15 | .03 |
| ☐ 131 Ed Hobaugh | .35 | .15 | .03 |
| ☐ 132 Frank Howard | 2.50 | 1.00 | .25 |
| ☐ 133 Manuel (Julian) Javier | .50 | .22 | .05 |
| ☐ 134 Deron Johnson | .50 | .22 | .05 |
| ☐ 135 Ken Johnson | .35 | .15 | .03 |
| ☐ 136 Jim Kaat | 7.50 | 3.50 | .75 |
| ☐ 137 Lou Klimchock | .35 | .15 | .03 |
| ☐ 138 Art Mahaffey | .50 | .22 | .05 |
| ☐ 139 Carl Mathias | .35 | .15 | .03 |
| ☐ 140 Julio Navarro | .35 | .15 | .03 |
| ☐ 141 Jim Proctor | .35 | .15 | .03 |
| ☐ 142 Bill Short | .35 | .15 | .03 |
| ☐ 143 Al Spangler | .35 | .15 | .03 |
| ☐ 144 Al Stieglitz | .35 | .15 | .03 |
| ☐ 145 Jim Umbricht | .35 | .15 | .03 |
| ☐ 146 Ted Wieand | .35 | .15 | .03 |
| ☐ 147 Bob Will | .35 | .15 | .03 |
| ☐ 148 Carl Yastrzemski | 100.00 | 45.00 | 10.00 |
| ☐ 149 Bob Nieman | .35 | .15 | .03 |
| ☐ 150 Billy Pierce | .75 | .35 | .07 |
| ☐ 151 Giants Team | 1.25 | .40 | .15 |
| ☐ 152 Gail Harris | .35 | .15 | .03 |
| ☐ 153 Bobby Thomson | .75 | .35 | .07 |

|  | MINT | VG-E | F-G |
|---|---|---|---|
| ☐ 154 Jim Davenport | .50 | .22 | .05 |
| ☐ 155 Charlie Neal | .45 | .20 | .04 |
| ☐ 156 Art Ceccarelli | .35 | .15 | .03 |
| ☐ 157 Rocky Nelson | .35 | .15 | .03 |
| ☐ 158 Wes Covington | .45 | .20 | .04 |
| ☐ 159 Jim Piersall | .75 | .35 | .07 |
| ☐ 160 Rival All-Stars: | 5.00 | 2.35 | .50 |
| Mickey Mantle | | | |
| Ken Boyer | | | |
| ☐ 161 Ray Narleski | .35 | .15 | .03 |
| ☐ 162 Sammy Taylor | .35 | .15 | .03 |
| ☐ 163 Hector Lopez | .35 | .15 | .03 |
| ☐ 164 Reds Team | 1.35 | .45 | .15 |
| ☐ 165 Jack Sanford | .45 | .20 | .04 |
| ☐ 166 Chuck Essegian | .35 | .15 | .03 |
| ☐ 167 Valmy Thomas | .35 | .15 | .03 |
| ☐ 168 Alex Grammas | .35 | .15 | .03 |
| ☐ 169 Jake Striker | .35 | .15 | .03 |
| ☐ 170 Del Crandall | .50 | .22 | .05 |
| ☐ 171 Johnny Groth | .35 | .15 | .03 |
| ☐ 172 Willie Kirkland | .35 | .15 | .03 |
| ☐ 173 Billy Martin | 2.00 | .90 | .20 |
| ☐ 174 Indians Team | 1.25 | .40 | .15 |
| ☐ 175 Pete Ramos | .35 | .15 | .03 |
| ☐ 176 Vada Pinson | 1.25 | .60 | .12 |
| ☐ 177 Johnny Kucks | .35 | .15 | .03 |
| ☐ 178 Woody Held | .35 | .15 | .03 |
| ☐ 179 Rip Coleman | .35 | .15 | .03 |
| ☐ 180 Harry Simpson | .35 | .15 | .03 |
| ☐ 181 Billy Loes | .35 | .15 | .03 |
| ☐ 182 Glen Hobbie | .35 | .15 | .03 |
| ☐ 183 Eli Grba | .35 | .15 | .03 |
| ☐ 184 Gary Geiger | .35 | .15 | .03 |
| ☐ 185 Jim Owens | .35 | .15 | .03 |
| ☐ 186 Dave Sisler | .35 | .15 | .03 |
| ☐ 187 Jay Hook | .35 | .15 | .03 |
| ☐ 188 Dick Williams | .50 | .22 | .05 |
| ☐ 189 Don McMahon | .35 | .15 | .03 |
| ☐ 190 Gene Woodling | .45 | .20 | .04 |
| ☐ 191 John Klippstein | .35 | .15 | .03 |
| ☐ 192 Danny O'Connell | .35 | .15 | .03 |
| ☐ 193 Dick Hyde | .35 | .15 | .03 |
| ☐ 194 Bobby Gene Smith | .35 | .15 | .03 |
| ☐ 195 Lindy McDaniel | .35 | .15 | .03 |
| ☐ 196 Andy Carey | .45 | .20 | .04 |
| ☐ 197 Ron Kline | .35 | .15 | .03 |
| ☐ 198 Jerry Lynch | .35 | .15 | .03 |
| ☐ 199 Dick Donovan | .35 | .15 | .03 |
| ☐ 200 Willie Mays | 24.00 | 11.00 | 2.40 |
| ☐ 201 Larry Osborne | .35 | .15 | .03 |
| ☐ 202 Fred Kipp | .35 | .15 | .03 |
| ☐ 203 Sam White | .35 | .15 | .03 |

|  | MINT | VG-E | F-G |
|---|---|---|---|
| ☐ 204 Ryne Duren | .75 | .35 | .07 |
| ☐ 205 John Logan | .50 | .22 | .05 |
| ☐ 206 Claude Osteen | .50 | .22 | .05 |
| ☐ 207 Bob Boyd | .35 | .15 | .03 |
| ☐ 208 White Sox Team | 1.25 | .40 | .15 |
| ☐ 209 Ron Blackburn | .35 | .15 | .03 |
| ☐ 210 Harmon Killebrew | 5.00 | 2.35 | .50 |
| ☐ 211 Taylor Phillips | .35 | .15 | .03 |
| MANAGER CARDS | | | |
| (212–227) | | | |
| ☐ 212 Walt Alston MGR | 1.50 | .70 | .15 |
| ☐ 213 Chuck Dressen MGR | .50 | .22 | .05 |
| ☐ 214 Jimmy Dykes MGR | .50 | .22 | .05 |
| ☐ 215 Bob Elliott MGR | .35 | .15 | .03 |
| ☐ 216 Joe Gordon MGR | .50 | .22 | .05 |
| ☐ 217 Charlie Grimm MGR | .50 | .22 | .05 |
| ☐ 218 Solly Hemus MGR | .35 | .15 | .03 |
| ☐ 219 Fred Hutchinson MGR | .50 | .22 | .05 |
| ☐ 220 Billy Jurges MGR | .35 | .15 | .03 |
| ☐ 221 Cookie Lavagetto MGR | .35 | .15 | .03 |
| ☐ 222 Al Lopez MGR | 1.25 | .60 | .12 |
| ☐ 223 Danny Murtaugh MGR | .50 | .22 | .05 |
| ☐ 224 Paul Richards MGR | .50 | .22 | .05 |
| ☐ 225 Bill Rigney MGR | .35 | .15 | .03 |
| ☐ 226 Eddie Sawyer MGR | .35 | .15 | .03 |
| ☐ 227 Casey Stengel MGR | 4.00 | 1.85 | .40 |
| ☐ 228 Ernie Johnson | .35 | .15 | .03 |
| ☐ 229 Joe M. Morgan | .35 | .15 | .03 |
| ☐ 230 Mound Magicians: | 2.00 | .90 | .20 |
| Lou Burdette | | | |
| Warren Spahn | | | |
| Bob Buhl | | | |
| ☐ 231 Hal Naragon | .35 | .15 | .03 |
| ☐ 232 Jim Busby | .35 | .15 | .03 |
| ☐ 233 Don Elston | .35 | .15 | .03 |
| ☐ 234 Don Demeter | .35 | .15 | .03 |
| ☐ 235 Gus Bell | .45 | .20 | .04 |
| ☐ 236 Dick Ricketts | .35 | .15 | .03 |
| ☐ 237 Elmer Valo | .35 | .15 | .03 |
| ☐ 238 Danny Kravitz | .35 | .15 | .03 |
| ☐ 239 Joe Shipley | .35 | .15 | .03 |
| ☐ 240 Luis Aparicio | 3.25 | 1.50 | .32 |
| ☐ 241 Albie Pearson | .35 | .15 | .03 |
| ☐ 242 Cardinals Team | 1.25 | .40 | .15 |
| ☐ 243 Bubba Phillips | .35 | .15 | .03 |
| ☐ 244 Hal Griggs | .35 | .15 | .03 |
| ☐ 245 Ed Yost | .35 | .15 | .03 |
| ☐ 246 Lee Maye | .35 | .15 | .03 |
| ☐ 247 Gil McDougald | 1.25 | .60 | .12 |
| ☐ 248 Del Rice | .35 | .15 | .03 |
| ☐ 249 Earl Wilson | .35 | .15 | .03 |
| ☐ 250 Stan Musial | 12.50 | 5.75 | 1.25 |

| | MINT | VG-E | F-G |
|---|---|---|---|
| ☐ 251 Bob Malkmus | .35 | .15 | .03 |
| ☐ 252 Ray Herbert | .35 | .15 | .03 |
| ☐ 253 Eddie Bressoud | .35 | .15 | .03 |
| ☐ 254 Arnie Portocarrero | .35 | .15 | .03 |
| ☐ 255 Jim Gilliam | 1.50 | .70 | .15 |
| ☐ 256 Dick Brown | .35 | .15 | .03 |
| ☐ 257 Gordy Coleman | .50 | .22 | .05 |
| ☐ 258 Dick Groat | 1.50 | .70 | .15 |
| ☐ 259 George Altman | .35 | .15 | .03 |
| ☐ 260 Power Plus | .50 | .22 | .05 |
|     Rocky Colavito | | | |
|     Tito Francona | | | |
| ☐ 261 Pete Burnside | .35 | .15 | .03 |
| ☐ 262 Hank Bauer | .75 | .35 | .07 |
| ☐ 263 Darrell Johnson | .50 | .22 | .05 |
| ☐ 264 Robin Roberts | 3.50 | 1.65 | .35 |
| ☐ 265 Rip Repulski | .35 | .15 | .03 |
| ☐ 266 Joe Jay | .35 | .15 | .03 |
| ☐ 267 Jim Marshall | .35 | .15 | .03 |
| ☐ 268 Al Worthington | .35 | .15 | .03 |
| ☐ 269 Gene Green | .35 | .15 | .03 |
| ☐ 270 Bob Turley | .75 | .35 | .07 |
| ☐ 271 Julio Becquer | .35 | .15 | .03 |
| ☐ 272 Fred Green | .35 | .15 | .03 |
| ☐ 273 Neil Chrisley | .35 | .15 | .03 |
| ☐ 274 Tom Acker | .35 | .15 | .03 |
| ☐ 275 Curt Flood | .90 | .40 | .09 |
| ☐ 276 Ken McBride | .35 | .15 | .03 |
| ☐ 277 Harry Bright | .35 | .15 | .03 |
| ☐ 278 Stan Williams | .35 | .15 | .03 |
| ☐ 279 Chuck Tanner | .50 | .22 | .05 |
| ☐ 280 Frank Sullivan | .35 | .15 | .03 |
| ☐ 281 Ray Boone | .35 | .15 | .03 |
| ☐ 282 Joe Nuxhall | .50 | .22 | .05 |
| ☐ 283 John Blanchard | .35 | .15 | .03 |
| ☐ 284 Don Gross | .35 | .15 | .03 |
| ☐ 285 Harry Anderson | .35 | .15 | .03 |
| ☐ 286 Ray Semproch | .35 | .15 | .03 |
| ☐ 287 Felipe Alou | .60 | .28 | .06 |
| ☐ 288 Bob Mabe | .35 | .15 | .03 |
| ☐ 289 Willie Jones | .35 | .15 | .03 |
| ☐ 290 Jerry Lumpe | .35 | .15 | .03 |
| ☐ 291 Bob Keegan | .35 | .15 | .03 |
| ☐ 292 Dodger Backstops | .50 | .22 | .05 |
|     Joe Pignatano | | | |
|     John Roseboro | | | |
| ☐ 293 Gene Conley | .35 | .15 | .03 |
| ☐ 294 Tony Taylor | .35 | .15 | .03 |
| ☐ 295 Gil Hodges | 4.00 | 1.85 | .40 |
| ☐ 296 Nelson Chittum | .35 | .15 | .03 |
| ☐ 297 Reno Bertoia | .35 | .15 | .03 |
| ☐ 298 George Witt | .35 | .15 | .03 |
| ☐ 299 Earl Torgeson | .35 | .15 | .03 |
| ☐ 300 Hank Aaron | 24.00 | 10.00 | 2.50 |
| ☐ 301 Jerry Davie | .35 | .15 | .03 |
| ☐ 302 Phillies Team | 1.25 | .40 | .15 |
| ☐ 303 Billy O'Dell | .35 | .15 | .03 |
| ☐ 304 Joe Ginsberg | .35 | .15 | .03 |
| ☐ 305 Richie Ashburn | 1.75 | .85 | .17 |
| ☐ 306 Frank Baumann | .35 | .15 | .03 |
| ☐ 307 Gene Oliver | .35 | .15 | .03 |
| ☐ 308 Dick Hall | .35 | .15 | .03 |
| ☐ 309 Bob Hale | .35 | .15 | .03 |
| ☐ 310 Frank Malzone | .45 | .20 | .04 |
| ☐ 311 Raul Sanchez | .35 | .15 | .03 |
| ☐ 312 Charley Lau | .45 | .20 | .04 |
| ☐ 313 Turk Lown | .35 | .15 | .03 |
| ☐ 314 Chico Fernandez | .35 | .15 | .03 |
| ☐ 315 Bobby Shantz | .75 | .35 | .07 |
| ☐ 316 Willie McCovey | 30.00 | 14.00 | 3.00 |
| ☐ 317 Pumpsie Green | .35 | .15 | .03 |
| ☐ 318 Jim Baxes | .35 | .15 | .03 |
| ☐ 319 Joe Koppe | .35 | .15 | .03 |
| ☐ 320 Bob Allison | .50 | .22 | .05 |
| ☐ 321 Ron Fairly | .50 | .22 | .05 |
| ☐ 322 Willie Tasby | .35 | .15 | .03 |
| ☐ 323 John Romano | .35 | .15 | .03 |
| ☐ 324 Jim Perry | .75 | .35 | .07 |
| ☐ 325 Jim O'Toole | .50 | .22 | .05 |
| ☐ 326 Bob Clemente | 14.00 | 6.50 | 1.40 |
| ☐ 327 Ray Sadecki | .35 | .15 | .03 |
| ☐ 328 Earl Battey | .35 | .15 | .03 |
| ☐ 329 Zack Monroe | .35 | .15 | .03 |
| ☐ 330 Harvey Kuenn | 1.10 | .50 | .11 |
| ☐ 331 Henry Mason | .35 | .15 | .03 |
| ☐ 332 Yankees Team | 5.00 | 1.25 | .30 |
| ☐ 333 Danny McDevitt | .35 | .15 | .03 |
| ☐ 334 Ted Abernathy | .35 | .15 | .03 |
| ☐ 335 Red Schoendienst | 1.00 | .45 | .10 |
| ☐ 336 Ike Delock | .35 | .15 | .03 |
| ☐ 337 Cal Neeman | .35 | .15 | .03 |
| ☐ 338 Ray Monzant | .35 | .15 | .03 |
| ☐ 339 Harry Chiti | .35 | .15 | .03 |
| ☐ 340 Harvey Haddix | .60 | .28 | .06 |
| ☐ 341 Carroll Hardy | .35 | .15 | .03 |
| ☐ 342 Casey Wise | .35 | .15 | .03 |
| ☐ 343 Sandy Koufax | 12.50 | 5.75 | 1.25 |
| ☐ 344 Clint Courtney | .35 | .15 | .03 |
| ☐ 345 Don Newcombe | .75 | .35 | .07 |
| ☐ 346 J. C. Martin | .35 | .15 | .03 |
|     (face actually | | | |
|     Gary Peters) | | | |
| ☐ 347 Ed Bouchee | .35 | .15 | .03 |
| ☐ 348 Barry Shetrone | .35 | .15 | .03 |

| | MINT | VG-E | F-G | | | MINT | VG-E | F-G |
|---|---|---|---|---|---|---|---|---|
| 349 Moe Drabowsky | .35 | .15. | .03 | 391 World Series Summary | 1.25 | .60 | .12 |
| 350 Mickey Mantle | 50.00 | 22.00 | 5.00 | The Champs Celebrate | | | |
| 351 Don Nottebart | .35 | .15 | .03 | 392 Tex Clevenger | .35 | .15 | .03 |
| 352 Cincy Clouters | 1.50 | .70 | .15 | 393 Smokey Burgess | .50 | .22 | .05 |
| Gus Bell | | | | 394 Norm Larker | .35 | .15 | .03 |
| Frank Robinson | | | | 395 Hoyt Wilhelm | 3.00 | 1.40 | .30 |
| Jerry Lynch | | | | 396 Steve Bilko | .35 | .15 | .03 |
| 353 Don Larsen | .75 | .35 | .07 | 397 Don Blasingame | .35 | .15 | .03 |
| 354 Bob Lillis | .45 | .20 | .04 | 398 Mike Cuellar | .50 | .22 | .05 |
| 355 Bill White | .50 | .22 | .05 | 399 Young Hill Stars | .50 | .22 | .05 |
| 356 Joe Amalfitano | .35 | .15 | .03 | Milt Pappas | | | |
| 357 Al Schroll | .35 | .15 | .03 | Jack Fisher | | | |
| 358 Joe DeMaestri | .35 | .15 | .03 | Jerry Walker | | | |
| 359 Buddy Gilbert | .35 | .15 | .03 | 400 Rocky Colavito | 1.10 | .50 | .11 |
| 360 Herb Score | .60 | .28 | .06 | 401 Bob Duliba | .35 | .15 | .03 |
| 361 Bob Oldis | .35 | .15 | .03 | 402 Dick Stuart | .50 | .22 | .05 |
| 362 Russ Kemmerer | .35 | .15 | .03 | 403 Ed Sadowski | .35 | .15 | .03 |
| 363 Gene Stephens | .35 | .15 | .03 | 404 Bob Rush | .35 | .15 | .03 |
| 364 Paul Foytack | .35 | .15 | .03 | 405 Bobby Richardson | 1.50 | .70 | .15 |
| 365 Minnie Minoso | 1.25 | .60 | .12 | 406 Billy Klaus | .35 | .15 | .03 |
| 366 Dallas Green | 1.25 | .60 | .12 | 407 Gary Peters | .75 | .35 | .07 |
| 367 Bill Tuttle | .35 | .15 | .03 | (face actually | | | |
| 368 Daryl Spencer | .35 | .15 | .03 | J. C. Martin) | | | |
| 369 Billy Hoeft | .35 | .15 | .03 | 408 Carl Furillo | 1.50 | .70 | .15 |
| 370 Bill Skowron | 1.50 | .70 | .15 | 409 Ron Samford | .35 | .15 | .03 |
| 371 Bud Byerly | .35 | .15 | .03 | 410 Sam Jones | .35 | .15 | .03 |
| 372 Frank House | .35 | .15 | .03 | 411 Ed Bailey | .35 | .15 | .03 |
| 373 Don Hoak | .35 | .15 | .03 | 412 Bob Anderson | .35 | .15 | .03 |
| 374 Bob Buhl | .35 | .15 | .03 | 413 Athletics Team | 1.25 | .40 | .15 |
| 375 Dale Long | .35 | .15 | .03 | 414 Don Williams | .35 | .15 | .03 |
| 376 John Briggs | .35 | .15 | .03 | 415 Bob Cerv | .35 | .15 | .03 |
| 377 Roger Maris | 11.00 | 5.25 | 1.10 | 416 Humberto Robinson | .35 | .15 | .03 |
| 378 Stu Miller | .35 | .15 | .03 | 417 Chuck Cottier | .75 | .35 | .07 |
| 379 Red Wilson | .35 | .15 | .03 | 418 Don Mossi | .45 | .20 | .04 |
| 380 Bob Shaw | .35 | .15 | .03 | 419 George Crowe | .35 | .15 | .03 |
| 381 Braves Team | 1.35 | .45 | .15 | 420 Ed Mathews | 4.00 | 1.85 | .40 |
| 382 Ted Bowsfield | .35 | .15 | .03 | 421 Duke Maas | .35 | .15 | .03 |
| 383 Leon Wagner | .35 | .15 | .03 | 422 John Powers | .35 | .15 | .03 |
| 384 Don Cardwell | .35 | .15 | .03 | 423 Ed Fitzgerald | .35 | .15 | .03 |
| WORLD SERIES | | | | 424 Pete Whisenant | .35 | .15 | .03 |
| CARDS (385–391) | | | | 425 John Podres | 1.10 | .50 | .11 |
| 385 World Series Game 1 | 1.25 | .60 | .12 | 426 Ron Jackson | .35 | .15 | .03 |
| Neal Steals Second | | | | 427 Al Grunwald | .35 | .15 | .03 |
| 386 World Series Game 2 | 1.25 | .60 | .12 | 428 Al Smith | .35 | .15 | .03 |
| Neal Belts 2nd Homer | | | | 429 AL Kings | 1.10 | .50 | .11 |
| 387 World Series Game 3 | 1.25 | .60 | .12 | Nellie Fox | | | |
| Furillo Breaks Game | | | | Harvey Kuenn | | | |
| 388 World Series Game 4 | 1.75 | .85 | .17 | 430 Art Ditmar | .35 | .15 | .03 |
| Hodges' Winning Homer | | | | 431 Andre Rodgers | .35 | .15 | .03 |
| 389 World Series Game 5 | 1.75 | .85 | .17 | 432 Chuck Stobbs | .35 | .15 | .03 |
| Luis Swipes Base | | | | 433 Irv Noren | .35 | .15 | .03 |
| 390 World Series Game 6 | 1.25 | .60 | .12 | 434 Brooks Lawrence | .35 | .15 | .03 |
| Scrambling After Ball | | | | 435 Gene Freese | .35 | .15 | .03 |

| | MINT | VG-E | F-G |
|---|---|---|---|
| ☐ 436 Marv Throneberry | 1.10 | .50 | .11 |
| ☐ 437 Bob Friend | .50 | .22 | .05 |
| ☐ 438 Jim Coker | .35 | .15 | .03 |
| ☐ 439 Tom Brewer | .35 | .15 | .03 |
| ☐ 440 Jim Lemon | .45 | .20 | .04 |
| ☐ 441 Gary Bell | .60 | .28 | .06 |
| ☐ 442 Joe Pignatano | .60 | .28 | .06 |
| ☐ 443 Charley Maxwell | .60 | .28 | .06 |
| ☐ 444 Jerry Kindall | .60 | .28 | .06 |
| ☐ 445 Warren Spahn | 6.50 | 3.00 | .65 |
| ☐ 446 Ellis Burton | .60 | .28 | .06 |
| ☐ 447 Ray Moore | .60 | .28 | .06 |
| ☐ 448 Jim Gentile | .90 | .40 | .09 |
| ☐ 449 Jim Brosnan | .75 | .35 | .07 |
| ☐ 450 Orlando Cepeda | 2.25 | 1.00 | .22 |
| ☐ 451 Curt Simmons | .75 | .35 | .07 |
| ☐ 452 Ray Webster | .60 | .28 | .06 |
| ☐ 453 Vern Law | 1.10 | .50 | .11 |
| ☐ 454 Hal Woodeshick | .60 | .28 | .06 |
| ☐ 455 Baltimore Coaches | .75 | .35 | .07 |
|     Eddie Robinson | | | |
|     Harry Brecheen | | | |
|     Harris | | | |
| ☐ 456 Red Sox Coaches | 1.10 | .50 | .11 |
|     Rudy York | | | |
|     Billy Herman | | | |
|     Sal Maglie | | | |
|     Del Baker | | | |
| ☐ 457 Cubs Coaches | .75 | .35 | .07 |
|     Charlie Root | | | |
|     Lou Klein | | | |
|     Elvin Tappe | | | |
| ☐ 458 White Sox Coaches | .75 | .35 | .07 |
|     Johnny Cooney | | | |
|     Don Gutteridge | | | |
|     Tony Cuccinello | | | |
|     Ray Berres | | | |
| ☐ 459 Reds Coaches | .75 | .35 | .07 |
|     Reggie Otero | | | |
|     Cot Deal | | | |
|     Wally Moses | | | |
| ☐ 460 Indians Coaches | 1.10 | .50 | .11 |
|     Mel Harder | | | |
|     White | | | |
|     Bob Lemon | | | |
|     Kress | | | |
| ☐ 461 Tigers Coaches | 1.10 | .50 | .11 |
|     Tom Ferrick | | | |
|     Luke Appling | | | |
|     Billy Hitchcock | | | |
| ☐ 462 Athletics Coaches | .75 | .35 | .07 |
|     Fitzsimmons | | | |
|     Don Heffner | | | |
|     Cooper | | | |
| ☐ 463 Coaches—Dodgers | .90 | .40 | .09 |
|     Bobby Bragan | | | |
|     Pete Reiser | | | |
|     Joe Becker | | | |
|     Mulleavy | | | |
| ☐ 464 Coaches—Braves | .75 | .35 | .07 |
|     Bob Scheffing | | | |
|     Whitlow Wyatt | | | |
|     Andy Pafko | | | |
|     George Myatt | | | |
| ☐ 465 Yankees Coaches | 1.75 | .85 | .17 |
|     Billy Dickey | | | |
|     Ralph Houk | | | |
|     Frank Crosetti | | | |
|     Ed Lopat | | | |
| ☐ 466 Coaches—Phillies | .75 | .35 | .07 |
|     Ken Silvestri | | | |
|     Carter | | | |
|     Cohen | | | |
| ☐ 467 Coaches - Pirates | .75 | .35 | .07 |
|     Mickey Vernon | | | |
|     Frank Oceak | | | |
|     Sam Narron | | | |
|     Bill Burwell | | | |
| ☐ 468 Cardinals Coaches | .75 | .35 | .07 |
|     Johnny Keane | | | |
|     Howie Pollett | | | |
|     Ray Katt | | | |
|     Harry Walker | | | |
| ☐ 469 Giants Coaches | .75 | .35 | .07 |
|     Wes Westrum | | | |
|     Salty Parker | | | |
|     Bill Posedel | | | |
| ☐ 470 Senators Coaches | .75 | .35 | .07 |
|     Bob Swift | | | |
|     Ellis Clary | | | |
|     Sam Mele | | | |
| ☐ 471 Ned Garver | .60 | .28 | .06 |
| ☐ 472 Al Dark | .90 | .40 | .09 |
| ☐ 473 Al Cicotte | .60 | .28 | .06 |
| ☐ 474 Haywood Sullivan | .75 | .35 | .07 |
| ☐ 475 Don Drysdale | 6.50 | 3.00 | .65 |
| ☐ 476 Lou Johnson | .60 | .28 | .06 |
| ☐ 477 Don Ferrarese | .60 | .28 | .06 |
| ☐ 478 Frank Torre | .60 | .28 | .06 |
| ☐ 479 Georges Maranda | .60 | .28 | .06 |
| ☐ 480 Yogi Berra | 9.00 | 4.25 | .90 |
| ☐ 481 Wes Stock | .90 | .40 | .09 |
| ☐ 482 Frank Bolling | .60 | .28 | .06 |
| ☐ 483 Camilo Pascual | .75 | .35 | .07 |
| ☐ 484 Pirates Team | 3.25 | 1.00 | .25 |
| ☐ 485 Ken Boyer | 1.75 | .85 | .17 |

| | MINT | VG-E | F-G |
|---|---|---|---|
| ☐ 486 Bobby Del Greco | .60 | .28 | .06 |
| ☐ 487 Tom Sturdivant | .60 | .28 | .06 |
| ☐ 488 Norm Cash | 1.75 | .85 | .17 |
| ☐ 489 Steve Ridzik | .60 | .28 | .06 |
| ☐ 490 Frank Robinson | 8.00 | 3.75 | .80 |
| ☐ 491 Mel Roach | .60 | .28 | .06 |
| ☐ 492 Larry Jackson | .60 | .28 | .06 |
| ☐ 493 Duke Snider | 10.00 | 4.75 | 1.00 |
| ☐ 494 Orioles Team | 2.00 | .60 | .20 |
| ☐ 495 Sherm Lollar | .75 | .35 | .07 |
| ☐ 496 Bill Virdon | 1.10 | .50 | .11 |
| ☐ 497 John Tsitouris | .60 | .28 | .06 |
| ☐ 498 Al Pilarcik | .60 | .28 | .06 |
| ☐ 499 Johnny James | .60 | .28 | .06 |
| ☐ 500 Johnny Temple | .75 | .35 | .07 |
| ☐ 501 Bob Schmidt | .60 | .28 | .06 |
| ☐ 502 Jim Bunning | 2.25 | 1.00 | .22 |
| ☐ 503 Don Lee | .60 | .28 | .06 |
| ☐ 504 Seth Morehead | .60 | .28 | .06 |
| ☐ 505 Ted Kluszewski | 1.50 | .70 | .15 |
| ☐ 506 Lee Walls | .60 | .28 | .06 |
| ☐ 507 Dick Stigman | 1.75 | .85 | .17 |
| ☐ 508 Bill Consolo | 1.75 | .85 | .17 |
| ☐ 509 Tommy Davis | 4.50 | 2.10 | .45 |
| ☐ 510 Jerry Staley | 1.75 | .85 | .17 |
| ☐ 511 Ken Walters | 1.75 | .85 | .17 |
| ☐ 512 Joe Gibbon | 1.75 | .85 | .17 |
| ☐ 513 Cubs Team | 3.75 | 1.25 | .35 |
| ☐ 514 Steve Barber | 2.00 | .90 | .20 |
| ☐ 515 Stan Lopata | 1.75 | .85 | .17 |
| ☐ 516 Marty Kutyna | 1.75 | .85 | .17 |
| ☐ 517 Charlie James | 1.75 | .85 | .17 |
| ☐ 518 Tony Gonzales | 1.75 | .85 | .17 |
| ☐ 519 Ed Roebuck | 2.00 | .90 | .20 |
| ☐ 520 Don Buddin | 1.75 | .85 | .17 |
| ☐ 521 Mike Lee | 1.75 | .85 | .17 |
| ☐ 522 Ken Hunt | 1.75 | .85 | .17 |
| ☐ 523 Clay Dalrymple | 1.75 | .85 | .17 |
| ☐ 524 Bill Henry | 1.75 | .85 | .17 |
| ☐ 525 Marv Breeding | 1.75 | .85 | .17 |
| ☐ 526 Paul Giel | 1.75 | .85 | .17 |
| ☐ 527 Jose Valdivielso | 1.75 | .85 | .17 |
| ☐ 528 Ben Johnson | 1.75 | .85 | .17 |
| ☐ 529 Norm Sherry | 2.00 | .90 | .20 |
| ☐ 530 Mike McCormick | 2.00 | .90 | .20 |
| ☐ 531 Sandy Amoros | 2.00 | .90 | .20 |
| ☐ 532 Mike Garcia | 2.00 | .90 | .20 |
| ☐ 533 Lou Clinton | 1.75 | .85 | .17 |
| ☐ 534 Ken Mackenzie | 1.75 | .85 | .17 |
| ☐ 535 Whitey Lockman | 2.00 | .90 | .20 |
| ☐ 536 Wynn Hawkins | 1.75 | .85 | .17 |
| ☐ 537 Red Sox Team | 3.75 | 1.25 | .30 |
| ☐ 538 Frank Barnes | 1.75 | .85 | .17 |

| | MINT | VG-E | F-G |
|---|---|---|---|
| ☐ 539 Gene Baker | 1.75 | .85 | .17 |
| ☐ 540 Jerry Walker | 1.75 | .85 | .17 |
| ☐ 541 Tony Curry | 1.75 | .85 | .17 |
| ☐ 542 Ken Hamlin | 1.75 | .85 | .17 |
| ☐ 543 Elio Chacon | 1.75 | .85 | .17 |
| ☐ 544 Bill Monbouquette | 1.75 | .85 | .17 |
| ☐ 545 Carl Sawatski | 1.75 | .85 | .17 |
| ☐ 546 Hank Aguirre | 1.75 | .85 | .17 |
| ☐ 547 Bob Aspromonte | 1.75 | .85 | .17 |
| ☐ 548 Don Mincher | 2.25 | 1.00 | .22 |
| ☐ 549 John Buzhardt | 1.75 | .85 | .17 |
| ☐ 550 Jim Landis | 1.75 | .85 | .17 |
| ☐ 551 Ed Rakow | 1.75 | .85 | .17 |
| ☐ 552 Walt Bond | 1.75 | .85 | .17 |
| ALL-STARS (553-572) | | | |
| ☐ 553 Bill Skowron AS | 2.00 | .90 | .20 |
| ☐ 554 Willie McCovey AS | 11.00 | 5.25 | 1.10 |
| ☐ 555 Nellie Fox AS | 3.00 | 1.40 | .30 |
| ☐ 556 Charlie Neal AS | 2.00 | .90 | .20 |
| ☐ 557 Frank Malzone AS | 2.00 | .90 | .20 |
| ☐ 558 Eddie Mathews AS | 5.50 | 2.60 | .55 |
| ☐ 559 Luis Aparicio AS | 4.50 | 2.10 | .45 |
| ☐ 560 Ernie Banks AS | 7.50 | 3.50 | .75 |
| ☐ 561 Al Kaline AS | 7.50 | 3.50 | .75 |
| ☐ 562 Joe Cunningham AS | 2.00 | .90 | .20 |
| ☐ 563 Mickey Mantle AS | 30.00 | 14.00 | 3.00 |
| ☐ 564 Willie Mays AS | 18.00 | 8.50 | 1.80 |
| ☐ 565 Roger Maris AS | 7.50 | 3.50 | .75 |
| ☐ 566 Hank Aaron AS | 18.00 | 8.50 | 1.80 |
| ☐ 567 Sherm Lollar AS | 2.00 | .90 | .20 |
| ☐ 568 Del Crandall AS | 2.00 | .90 | .20 |
| ☐ 569 Camilo Pascual AS | 2.00 | .90 | .20 |
| ☐ 570 Don Drysdale AS | 5.50 | 2.60 | .55 |
| ☐ 571 Billy Pierce AS | 2.00 | .90 | .20 |
| ☐ 572 Johnny Antonelli AS | 2.50 | 1.15 | .25 |

**1961 TOPPS**

ROGER MARIS
Outfield

The cards in this 587 card set measure 2½" by 3½". In 1961, Topps returned to the vertical obverse format. Introduced for the first time were "League Leaders" (41 to 50) and separate, numbered checklist cards. Two number 463's exist: the Braves team card carrying that number was meant to be number 426. There are series of Baseball Thrills (401 to 410), previous MVP's (471 to 486) and Sporting News All-Stars (566 to 589). The usual last series scarcity (523 to 589) exists. The set actually totals 587 cards since numbers 587 and 588 were never issued.

Complete Set: M-925.00; VG-E-400.00; F-G-80.00

|  | MINT | VG-E | F-G |
|---|---|---|---|
| Common Player (1–370) | .33 | .15 | .03 |
| Common Player (371–522) | .40 | .18 | .04 |
| Common Player (523–565) | 6.00 | 2.80 | .60 |
| Common Player (566–589) | 6.50 | 3.00 | .65 |

|  | MINT | VG-E | F-G |
|---|---|---|---|
| ☐ 1 Dick Groat | 2.75 | .65 | .15 |
| ☐ 2 Roger Maris | 12.00 | 4.00 | 1.00 |
| ☐ 3 John Buzhardt | .33 | .15 | .03 |
| ☐ 4 Lenny Green | .33 | .15 | .03 |
| ☐ 5 John Romano | .33 | .15 | .03 |
| ☐ 6 Ed Roebuck | .33 | .15 | .03 |
| ☐ 7 White Sox Team | .85 | .40 | .08 |
| ☐ 8 Dick Williams | .45 | .20 | .04 |
| ☐ 9 Bob Purkey | .33 | .15 | .03 |
| ☐ 10 Brooks Robinson | 7.00 | 3.25 | .70 |
| ☐ 11 Curt Simmons | .45 | .20 | .04 |
| ☐ 12 Moe Thacker | .33 | .15 | .03 |
| ☐ 13 Chuck Cottier | .45 | .20 | .04 |
| ☐ 14 Don Mossi | .45 | .20 | .04 |
| ☐ 15 Willie Kirkland | .33 | .15 | .03 |
| ☐ 16 Billy Muffett | .33 | .15 | .03 |
| ☐ 17 Checklist 1 | 1.75 | .40 | .10 |
| ☐ 18 Jim Grant | .33 | .15 | .03 |
| ☐ 19 Cletis Boyer | .50 | .22 | .05 |
| ☐ 20 Robin Roberts | 3.00 | 1.40 | .30 |
| ☐ 21 Zorro Versalles | .45 | .20 | .04 |
| ☐ 22 Clem Labine | .45 | .20 | .04 |
| ☐ 23 Don Demeter | .33 | .15 | .03 |
| ☐ 24 Ken Johnson | .33 | .15 | .03 |
| ☐ 25 Reds' Heavy Artillery | 1.25 | .60 | .12 |
| Vada Pinson | | | |
| Gus Bell | | | |
| Frank Robinson | | | |

|  | MINT | VG-E | F-G |
|---|---|---|---|
| ☐ 26 Wes Stock | .45 | .20 | .04 |
| ☐ 27 Jerry Kindall | .33 | .15 | .03 |
| ☐ 28 Hector Lopez | .33 | .15 | .03 |
| ☐ 29 Don Nottebart | .33 | .15 | .03 |
| ☐ 30 Nellie Fox | 1.75 | .85 | .17 |
| ☐ 31 Bob Schmidt | .33 | .15 | .03 |
| ☐ 32 Ray Sadecki | .33 | .15 | .03 |
| ☐ 33 Gary Geiger | .33 | .15 | .03 |
| ☐ 34 Wynn Hawkins | .33 | .15 | .03 |
| ☐ 35 Ron Santo | 2.25 | 1.00 | .22 |
| ☐ 36 Jack Kralick | .33 | .15 | .03 |
| ☐ 37 Charley Maxwell | .33 | .15 | .03 |
| ☐ 38 Bob Lillis | .45 | .20 | .04 |
| ☐ 39 Leo Posada | .33 | .15 | .03 |
| ☐ 40 Bob Turley | .75 | .35 | .07 |
| ☐ 41 NL Batting Leaders | 1.25 | .60 | .12 |
| Dick Groat | | | |
| Norm Larker | | | |
| Willie Mays | | | |
| Robert Clemente | | | |
| ☐ 42 AL Batting Leaders | .75 | .35 | .07 |
| Pete Runnels | | | |
| Al Smith | | | |
| Minnie Minoso | | | |
| Bill Skowron | | | |
| ☐ 43 NL Home Run Leaders | 1.25 | .60 | .12 |
| Ernie Banks | | | |
| Hank Aaron | | | |
| Ed Mathews | | | |
| Ken Boyer | | | |
| ☐ 44 AL Home Run Leaders | 2.50 | 1.15 | .25 |
| Mickey Mantle | | | |
| Roger Maris | | | |
| Jim Lemon | | | |
| Rocky Colavito | | | |
| ☐ 45 NL ERA Leaders | .75 | .35 | .07 |
| Mike McCormick | | | |
| Ernie Broglio | | | |
| Don Drysdale | | | |
| Bob Friend | | | |
| Stan Williams | | | |
| ☐ 46 AL ERA Leaders | .75 | .35 | .07 |
| Frank Baumann | | | |
| Jim Bunning | | | |
| Art Ditmar | | | |
| H. Brown | | | |
| ☐ 47 NL Pitching Leaders | .75 | .35 | .07 |
| Ernie Broglio | | | |
| Warren Spahn | | | |
| Vern Law | | | |
| Lou Burdette | | | |

| | | MINT | VG-E | F-G |
|---|---|---|---|---|
| ☐ 48 | AL Pitching Leaders .... | .75 | .35 | .07 |
| | Chuck Estrada | | | |
| | Jim Perry | | | |
| | Bud Daley | | | |
| | Art Ditmar | | | |
| | Frank Lary | | | |
| | Milt Pappas | | | |
| ☐ 49 | NL Strikeout Leaders ... | 1.25 | .60 | .12 |
| | Don Drysdale | | | |
| | Sandy Koufax | | | |
| | Sam Jones | | | |
| | Ernie Broglio | | | |
| ☐ 50 | AL Strikeout Leaders ... | .75 | .35 | .07 |
| | Jim Bunning | | | |
| | Pedro Ramos | | | |
| | Early Wynn | | | |
| | Frank Lary | | | |
| ☐ 51 | Tigers Team .......... | .85 | .40 | .08 |
| ☐ 52 | George Crowe ......... | .33 | .15 | .03 |
| ☐ 53 | Russ Nixon ........... | .33 | .15 | .03 |
| ☐ 54 | Earl Francis .......... | .33 | .15 | .03 |
| ☐ 55 | Jim Davenport ........ | .50 | .22 | .05 |
| ☐ 56 | Russ Kemmerer ....... | .33 | .15 | .03 |
| ☐ 57 | Marv Throneberry ..... | .85 | .40 | .08 |
| ☐ 58 | Joe Schaffernoth ...... | .33 | .15 | .03 |
| ☐ 59 | Jim Woods ........... | .33 | .15 | .03 |
| ☐ 60 | Woodie Held .......... | .33 | .15 | .03 |
| ☐ 61 | Ron Piche ............ | .33 | .15 | .03 |
| ☐ 62 | Al Pilarcik ........... | .33 | .15 | .03 |
| ☐ 63 | Jim Kaat ............. | 2.25 | 1.00 | .22 |
| ☐ 64 | Alex Grammas ........ | .33 | .15 | .03 |
| ☐ 65 | Ted Kluszewski ....... | 1.10 | .50 | .11 |
| ☐ 66 | Billy Henry ........... | .33 | .15 | .03 |
| ☐ 67 | Ossie Virgil .......... | .33 | .15 | .03 |
| ☐ 68 | Deron Johnson ........ | .33 | .15 | .03 |
| ☐ 69 | Earl Wilson .......... | .33 | .15 | .03 |
| ☐ 70 | Bill Virdon ........... | .75 | .35 | .07 |
| ☐ 71 | Jerry Adair ........... | .33 | .15 | .03 |
| ☐ 72 | Stu Miller ............ | .33 | .15 | .03 |
| ☐ 73 | Al Spangler .......... | .33 | .15 | .03 |
| ☐ 74 | Joe Pignatano ........ | .33 | .15 | .03 |
| ☐ 75 | Lindy Shows Larry ..... | .50 | .22 | .05 |
| | Lindy McDaniel | | | |
| | Larry Jackson | | | |
| ☐ 76 | Harry Anderson ....... | .33 | .15 | .03 |
| ☐ 77 | Dick Stigman ......... | .33 | .15 | .03 |
| ☐ 78 | Lee Walls ............ | .33 | .15 | .03 |
| ☐ 79 | Joe Ginsberg ......... | .33 | .15 | .03 |
| ☐ 80 | Harmon Killebrew ..... | 4.25 | 2.00 | .42 |
| ☐ 81 | Tracy Stallard ........ | .33 | .15 | .03 |
| ☐ 82 | Joe Christopher ....... | .33 | .15 | .03 |
| ☐ 83 | Bob Bruce ........... | .33 | .15 | .03 |
| ☐ 84 | Lee Maye ............ | .33 | .15 | .03 |

| | | MINT | VG-E | F-G |
|---|---|---|---|---|
| ☐ 85 | Jerry Walker .......... | .33 | .15 | .03 |
| ☐ 86 | Dodgers Team ........ | 1.25 | .60 | .12 |
| ☐ 87 | Joe Amalfitano ....... | .33 | .15 | .03 |
| ☐ 88 | Richie Ashburn ....... | 1.75 | .85 | .17 |
| ☐ 89 | Billy Martin .......... | 2.00 | .90 | .20 |
| ☐ 90 | Jerry Staley ......... | .33 | .15 | .03 |
| ☐ 91 | Walt Moryn ........... | .33 | .15 | .03 |
| ☐ 92 | Hal Naragon ......... | .33 | .15 | .03 |
| ☐ 93 | Tony Gonzalez ....... | .33 | .15 | .03 |
| ☐ 94 | John Kucks ........... | .33 | .15 | .03 |
| ☐ 95 | Norm Cash ........... | 1.25 | .60 | .12 |
| ☐ 96 | Bill O'Dell .......... | .33 | .15 | .03 |
| ☐ 97 | Jerry Lynch .......... | .33 | .15 | .03 |
| ☐ 98 | Checklist 2 .......... | 1.60 | .40 | .10 |
| ☐ 99 | Don Buddin ........... | .33 | .15 | .03 |
| ☐ 100 | Harvey Haddix ....... | .55 | .25 | .05 |
| ☐ 101 | Bubba Phillips ....... | .33 | .15 | .03 |
| ☐ 102 | Gene Stephens ....... | .33 | .15 | .03 |
| ☐ 103 | Ruben Amaro ......... | .33 | .15 | .03 |
| ☐ 104 | John Blanchard ....... | .50 | .22 | .05 |
| ☐ 105 | Carl Willey .......... | .33 | .15 | .03 |
| ☐ 106 | Whitey Herzog ........ | .55 | .25 | .05 |
| ☐ 107 | Seth Morehead ....... | .33 | .15 | .03 |
| ☐ 108 | Dan Dobbek .......... | .33 | .15 | .03 |
| ☐ 109 | John Podres .......... | 1.25 | .60 | .12 |
| ☐ 110 | Vada Pinson ......... | 1.25 | .60 | .12 |
| ☐ 111 | Jack Meyer ........... | .33 | .15 | .03 |
| ☐ 112 | Chico Fernandez ..... | .33 | .15 | .03 |
| ☐ 113 | Mike Fornieles ....... | .33 | .15 | .03 |
| ☐ 114 | Hobie Landrith ....... | .33 | .15 | .03 |
| ☐ 115 | Johnny Antonelli ..... | .50 | .22 | .05 |
| ☐ 116 | Joe DeMaestri ....... | .33 | .15 | .03 |
| ☐ 117 | Dale Long ........... | .33 | .15 | .03 |
| ☐ 118 | Chris Cannizzaro ..... | .33 | .15 | .03 |
| ☐ 119 | A's Big Armor ........ | .50 | .22 | .05 |
| | Norm Siebern | | | |
| | Hank Bauer | | | |
| | Jerry Lumpe | | | |
| ☐ 120 | Ed Mathews .......... | 4.00 | 1.85 | .40 |
| ☐ 121 | Eli Grba ............. | .33 | .15 | .03 |
| ☐ 122 | Cubs Team ........... | .80 | .40 | .08 |
| ☐ 123 | Billy Gardner ........ | .45 | .20 | .04 |
| ☐ 124 | J. C. Martin ......... | .33 | .15 | .03 |
| ☐ 125 | Steve Barber ........ | .33 | .15 | .03 |
| ☐ 126 | Dick Stuart .......... | .50 | .22 | .05 |
| ☐ 127 | Ron Kline ........... | .33 | .15 | .03 |
| ☐ 128 | Rip Repulski ......... | .33 | .15 | .03 |
| ☐ 129 | Ed Hobaugh .......... | .33 | .15 | .03 |
| ☐ 130 | Norm Larker ......... | .33 | .15 | .03 |
| | MANAGERS (131–139) | | | |
| ☐ 131 | Paul Richards MGR .... | .50 | .22 | .05 |
| ☐ 132 | Al Lopez MGR ........ | 1.25 | .60 | .12 |
| ☐ 133 | Ralph Houk MGR ...... | .80 | .40 | .08 |

| | MINT | VG-E | F-G | | | MINT | VG-E | F-G |
|---|---|---|---|---|---|---|---|---|
| ☐ 134 Mickey Vernon MGR ... | .50 | .22 | .05 | ☐ 182 Dave Nicholson ........ | .33 | .15 | .03 |
| ☐ 135 Fred Hutchinson MGR .. | .50 | .22 | .05 | ☐ 183 Andre Rodgers ......... | .33 | .15 | .03 |
| ☐ 136 Walt Alston MGR ...... | 1.50 | .70 | .15 | ☐ 184 Steve Bilko ........... | .33 | .15 | .03 |
| ☐ 137 Chuck Dressen MGR .. | .50 | .22 | .05 | ☐ 185 Herb Score ........... | .50 | .22 | .05 |
| ☐ 138 Danny Murtaugh MGR . | .50 | .22 | .05 | ☐ 186 Elmer Valo .......... | .33 | .15 | .03 |
| ☐ 139 Solly Hemus MGR ..... | .33 | .15 | .03 | ☐ 187 Billy Klaus .......... | .33 | .15 | .03 |
| ☐ 140 Gus Triandos ........ | .45 | .20 | .04 | ☐ 188 Jim Marshall ......... | .33 | .15 | .03 |
| ☐ 141 Billy Williams ....... | 10.00 | 4.75 | 1.00 | ☐ 189 Checklist 3 ......... | 1.60 | .40 | .10 |
| ☐ 142 Luis Arroyo ......... | .50 | .22 | .05 | ☐ 190 Stan Williams ....... | .33 | .15 | .03 |
| ☐ 143 Russ Snyder ........ | .33 | .15 | .03 | ☐ 191 Mike De La Hoz ..... | .33 | .15 | .03 |
| ☐ 144 Jim Coker .......... | .33 | .15 | .03 | ☐ 192 Dick Brown ......... | .33 | .15 | .03 |
| ☐ 145 Bob Buhl .......... | .33 | .15 | .03 | ☐ 193 Gene Conley ........ | .33 | .15 | .03 |
| ☐ 146 Marty Keough ....... | .33 | .15 | .03 | ☐ 194 Gordy Coleman ...... | .33 | .15 | .03 |
| ☐ 147 Ed Rakow .......... | .33 | .15 | .03 | ☐ 195 Jerry Casale ........ | .33 | .15 | .03 |
| ☐ 148 Julian Javier ....... | .33 | .15 | .03 | ☐ 196 Ed Bouchee ........ | .33 | .15 | .03 |
| ☐ 149 Bob Oldis ......... | .33 | .15 | .03 | ☐ 197 Dick Hall ......... | .33 | .15 | .03 |
| ☐ 150 Willie Mays ........ | 21.00 | 9.50 | 2.10 | ☐ 198 Carl Sawatski ...... | .33 | .15 | .03 |
| ☐ 151 Jim Donohue ....... | .33 | .15 | .03 | ☐ 199 Bob Boyd .......... | .33 | .15 | .03 |
| ☐ 152 Earl Torgeson ...... | .33 | .15 | .03 | ☐ 200 Warren Spahn ...... | 5.00 | 2.35 | .50 |
| ☐ 153 Don Lee .......... | .33 | .15 | .03 | ☐ 201 Pete Whisenant ..... | .33 | .15 | .03 |
| ☐ 154 Bobby Del Greco .... | .33 | .15 | .03 | ☐ 202 Al Neiger .......... | .33 | .15 | .03 |
| ☐ 155 John Temple ....... | .33 | .15 | .03 | ☐ 203 Eddie Bressoud ..... | .33 | .15 | .03 |
| ☐ 156 Ken Hunt .......... | .33 | .15 | .03 | ☐ 204 Bob Skinner ....... | .33 | .15 | .03 |
| ☐ 157 Cal McLish ........ | .33 | .15 | .03 | ☐ 205 Bill Pierce ........ | .75 | .35 | .07 |
| ☐ 158 Pete Daley ........ | .33 | .15 | .03 | ☐ 206 Gene Green ....... | .33 | .15 | .03 |
| ☐ 159 Orioles Team ...... | .80 | .40 | .08 | ☐ 207 Dodger Southpaws ... | 2.50 | 1.15 | .25 |
| ☐ 160 Whitey Ford ....... | 7.00 | 3.25 | .70 |     Sandy Koufax | | | |
| ☐ 161 Sherman Jones ..... | .33 | .15 | .03 |     Johnny Podres | | | |
|     (photo actually | | | | ☐ 208 Larry Osborne ...... | .33 | .15 | .03 |
|     Eddie Fisher) | | | | ☐ 209 Ken McBride ...... | .33 | .15 | .03 |
| ☐ 162 Jay Hook ......... | .33 | .15 | .03 | ☐ 210 Pete Runnels ...... | .45 | .20 | .04 |
| ☐ 163 Ed Sadowski ...... | .33 | .15 | .03 | ☐ 211 Bob Gibson ....... | 5.00 | 2.35 | .50 |
| ☐ 164 Felix Mantilla ..... | .33 | .15 | .03 | ☐ 212 Haywood Sullivan ... | .45 | .20 | .04 |
| ☐ 165 Gino Cimoli ....... | .33 | .15 | .03 | ☐ 213 Billy Stafford ..... | .45 | .20 | .04 |
| ☐ 166 Danny Kravitz ..... | .33 | .15 | .03 | ☐ 214 Danny Murphy ..... | .33 | .15 | .03 |
| ☐ 167 Giants Team ...... | .80 | .40 | .08 | ☐ 215 Gus Bell ......... | .45 | .20 | .04 |
| ☐ 168 Tommy Davis ...... | 1.10 | .50 | .11 | ☐ 216 Ted Bowsfield ..... | .33 | .15 | .03 |
| ☐ 169 Don Elston ....... | .33 | .15 | .03 | ☐ 217 Mel Roach ........ | .33 | .15 | .03 |
| ☐ 170 Al Smith ......... | .33 | .15 | .03 | ☐ 218 Hal Brown ........ | .33 | .15 | .03 |
| ☐ 171 Paul Foytack ...... | .33 | .15 | .03 |     MANAGERS (219–226) | | | |
| ☐ 172 Don Dillard ....... | .33 | .15 | .03 | ☐ 219 Gene Mauch MGR .... | .50 | .22 | .05 |
| ☐ 173 Beantown Bombers .. | .50 | .22 | .05 | ☐ 220 Al Dark MGR ...... | .50 | .22 | .05 |
|     Frank Malzone | | | | ☐ 221 Mike Higgins MGR ... | .33 | .15 | .03 |
|     Vic Wertz | | | | ☐ 222 Jimmie Dykes MGR ... | .45 | .20 | .04 |
|     Jackie Jensen | | | | ☐ 223 Bob Scheffing MGR ... | .33 | .15 | .03 |
| ☐ 174 Ray Semproch ..... | .33 | .15 | .03 | ☐ 224 Joe Gordon MGR ..... | .45 | .20 | .04 |
| ☐ 175 Gene Freese ...... | .33 | .15 | .03 | ☐ 225 Bill Rigney MGR ..... | .33 | .15 | .03 |
| ☐ 176 Ken Aspromonte ... | .33 | .15 | .03 | ☐ 226 Harry Lavagetto MGR .. | .33 | .15 | .03 |
| ☐ 177 Don Larsen ....... | .50 | .22 | .05 | ☐ 227 Juan Pizarro ....... | .33 | .15 | .03 |
| ☐ 178 Bob Nieman ....... | .33 | .15 | .03 | ☐ 228 Yankees Team ...... | 3.50 | 1.65 | .35 |
| ☐ 179 Joe Koppe ........ | .33 | .15 | .03 | ☐ 229 Rudy Hernandez .... | .33 | .15 | .03 |
| ☐ 180 Bobby Richardson .. | 1.50 | .70 | .15 | ☐ 230 Don Hoak ......... | .33 | .15 | .03 |
| ☐ 181 Fred Green ....... | .33 | .15 | .03 | ☐ 231 Dick Drott ........ | .33 | .15 | .03 |

| | | MINT | VG-E | F-G |
|---|---|---|---|---|
| ☐ 232 | Bill White | .50 | .22 | .05 |
| ☐ 233 | Joe Jay | .33 | .15 | .03 |
| ☐ 234 | Ted Lepcio | .33 | .15 | .03 |
| ☐ 235 | Camilo Pascual | .45 | .20 | .04 |
| ☐ 236 | Don Gile | .33 | .15 | .03 |
| ☐ 237 | Billy Loes | .33 | .15 | .03 |
| ☐ 238 | Jim Gilliam | 1.50 | .70 | .15 |
| ☐ 239 | Dave Sisler | .33 | .15 | .03 |
| ☐ 240 | Ron Hansen | .33 | .15 | .03 |
| ☐ 241 | Al Cicotte | .45 | .20 | .04 |
| ☐ 242 | Hal Smith | .33 | .15 | .03 |
| ☐ 243 | Frank Lary | .45 | .20 | .04 |
| ☐ 244 | Chico Cardenas | .33 | .15 | .03 |
| ☐ 245 | Joe Adcock | .90 | .40 | .09 |
| ☐ 246 | Bob Davis | .33 | .15 | .03 |
| ☐ 247 | Billy Goodman | .45 | .20 | .04 |
| ☐ 248 | Ed Keegan | .33 | .15 | .03 |
| ☐ 249 | Reds Team | 1.10 | .50 | .11 |
| ☐ 250 | Buc Hill Aces: | .50 | .22 | .05 |
| | Vern Law | | | |
| | Roy Face | | | |
| ☐ 251 | Bill Bruton | .33 | .15 | .03 |
| ☐ 252 | Bill Short | .33 | .15 | .03 |
| ☐ 253 | Sammy Taylor | .33 | .15 | .03 |
| ☐ 254 | Ted Sadowski | .33 | .15 | .03 |
| ☐ 255 | Vic Power | .33 | .15 | .03 |
| ☐ 256 | Billy Hoeft | .33 | .15 | .03 |
| ☐ 257 | Carroll Hardy | .33 | .15 | .03 |
| ☐ 258 | Jack Sanford | .33 | .15 | .03 |
| ☐ 259 | John Schaive | .33 | .15 | .03 |
| ☐ 260 | Don Drysdale | 4.00 | 1.85 | .40 |
| ☐ 261 | Charlie Lau | .50 | .22 | .05 |
| ☐ 262 | Tony Curry | .33 | .15 | .03 |
| ☐ 263 | Ken Hamlin | .33 | .15 | .03 |
| ☐ 264 | Glen Hobbie | .33 | .15 | .03 |
| ☐ 265 | Tony Kubek | 2.00 | .90 | .20 |
| ☐ 266 | Lindy McDaniel | .33 | .15 | .03 |
| ☐ 267 | Norm Siebern | .33 | .15 | .03 |
| ☐ 268 | Ike Delock | .33 | .15 | .03 |
| ☐ 269 | Harry Chiti | .33 | .15 | .03 |
| ☐ 270 | Bob Friend | .50 | .22 | .05 |
| ☐ 271 | Jim Landis | .33 | .15 | .03 |
| ☐ 272 | Tom Morgan | .33 | .15 | .03 |
| ☐ 273 | Checklist 4 | 1.60 | .40 | .10 |
| ☐ 274 | Gary Bell | .33 | .15 | .03 |
| ☐ 275 | Gene Woodling | .45 | .20 | .04 |
| ☐ 276 | Ray Rippelmeyer | .33 | .15 | .03 |
| ☐ 277 | Hank Foiles | .33 | .15 | .03 |
| ☐ 278 | Don McMahon | .33 | .15 | .03 |
| ☐ 279 | Jose Pagan | .33 | .15 | .03 |
| ☐ 280 | Frank Howard | 1.25 | .60 | .12 |
| ☐ 281 | Frank Sullivan | .33 | .15 | .03 |
| ☐ 282 | Faye Throneberry | .33 | .15 | .03 |

| | | MINT | VG-E | F-G |
|---|---|---|---|---|
| ☐ 283 | Bob Anderson | .33 | .15 | .03 |
| ☐ 284 | Dick Gernert | .33 | .15 | .03 |
| ☐ 285 | Sherm Lollar | .45 | .20 | .04 |
| ☐ 286 | George Witt | .33 | .15 | .03 |
| ☐ 287 | Carl Yastrzemski | 50.00 | 22.00 | 5.00 |
| ☐ 288 | Albie Pearson | .33 | .15 | .03 |
| ☐ 289 | Ray Moore | .33 | .15 | .03 |
| ☐ 290 | Stan Musial | 12.00 | 5.50 | 1.20 |
| ☐ 291 | Tex Clevenger | .33 | .15 | .03 |
| ☐ 292 | Jim Baumer | .33 | .15 | .03 |
| ☐ 293 | Tom Sturdivant | .33 | .15 | .03 |
| ☐ 294 | Don Blasingame | .33 | .15 | .03 |
| ☐ 295 | Milt Pappas | .45 | .20 | .04 |
| ☐ 296 | Wes Covington | .33 | .15 | .03 |
| ☐ 297 | Athletics Team | .75 | .35 | .07 |
| ☐ 298 | Jim Golden | .33 | .15 | .03 |
| ☐ 299 | Clay Dalrymple | .33 | .15 | .03 |
| ☐ 300 | Mickey Mantle | 45.00 | 20.00 | 4.50 |
| ☐ 301 | Chet Nichols | .33 | .15 | .03 |
| ☐ 302 | Al Heist | .33 | .15 | .03 |
| ☐ 303 | Gary Peters | .45 | .20 | .04 |
| ☐ 304 | Rocky Nelson | .33 | .15 | .03 |
| ☐ 305 | Mike McCormick | .50 | .22 | .05 |
| | WORLD SERIES | | | |
| | CARDS (306–313) | | | |
| ☐ 306 | World Series Game 1 | 1.50 | .70 | .15 |
| | Virdon Saves Game | | | |
| ☐ 307 | World Series Game 2 | 4.50 | 2.10 | .45 |
| | Mantle 2 Homers | | | |
| ☐ 308 | World Series Game 3 | 1.50 | .70 | .15 |
| | Richardson Is Hero | | | |
| ☐ 309 | World Series Game 4 | 1.50 | .70 | .15 |
| | Cimoli Safe | | | |
| ☐ 310 | World Series Game 5 | 1.50 | .70 | .15 |
| | Face Saves the Day | | | |
| ☐ 311 | World Series Game 6 | 2.00 | .90 | .20 |
| | Ford Second Shutout | | | |
| ☐ 312 | World Series Game 7 | 2.00 | .90 | .20 |
| | Mazeroski's Homer | | | |
| ☐ 313 | World Series Summary | 1.50 | .70 | .15 |
| | Pirates Celebrate | | | |
| ☐ 314 | Bob Miller | .33 | .15 | .03 |
| ☐ 315 | Earl Battey | .33 | .15 | .03 |
| ☐ 316 | Bobby Gene Smith | .33 | .15 | .03 |
| ☐ 317 | Jim Brewer | .33 | .15 | .03 |
| ☐ 318 | Danny O'Connell | .33 | .15 | .03 |
| ☐ 319 | Valmy Thomas | .33 | .15 | .03 |
| ☐ 320 | Lou Burdette | 1.10 | .50 | .11 |
| ☐ 321 | Marv Breeding | .33 | .15 | .03 |
| ☐ 322 | Bill Kunkel | .45 | .20 | .04 |
| ☐ 323 | Sammy Esposito | .33 | .15 | .03 |
| ☐ 324 | Hank Aguirre | .33 | .15 | .03 |
| ☐ 325 | Wally Moon | .50 | .22 | .05 |

| | MINT | VG-E | F-G |
|---|---|---|---|
| ☐ 326 Dave Hillman | .33 | .15 | .03 |
| ☐ 327 Matty Alou | 1.10 | .50 | .11 |
| ☐ 328 Jim O'Toole | .45 | .20 | .04 |
| ☐ 329 Julio Becquer | .33 | .15 | .03 |
| ☐ 330 Rocky Colavito | 1.25 | .60 | .12 |
| ☐ 331 Ned Garver | .33 | .15 | .03 |
| ☐ 332 Dutch Dotterer | .45 | .20 | .04 |
| (photo actually Tommy Dotterer, Dutch's brother) | | | |
| ☐ 333 Fritz Brickell | .33 | .15 | .03 |
| ☐ 334 Walt Bond | .33 | .15 | .03 |
| ☐ 335 Frank Bolling | .33 | .15 | .03 |
| ☐ 336 Don Mincher | .45 | .20 | .04 |
| ☐ 337 Al's Aces | 1.50 | .70 | .15 |
| Early Wynn Al Lopez Herb Score | | | |
| ☐ 338 Don Landrum | .33 | .15 | .03 |
| ☐ 339 Gene Baker | .33 | .15 | .03 |
| ☐ 340 Vic Wertz | .45 | .20 | .04 |
| ☐ 341 Jim Owens | .33 | .15 | .03 |
| ☐ 342 Clint Courtney | .33 | .15 | .03 |
| ☐ 343 Earl Robinson | .33 | .15 | .03 |
| ☐ 344 Sandy Koufax | 12.00 | 5.50 | 1.20 |
| ☐ 345 Jim Piersall | .75 | .35 | .07 |
| ☐ 346 Howie Nunn | .33 | .15 | .03 |
| ☐ 347 Cardinals Team | .80 | .40 | .08 |
| ☐ 348 Steve Boros | .45 | .20 | .04 |
| ☐ 349 Danny McDevitt | .33 | .15 | .03 |
| ☐ 350 Ernie Banks | 5.50 | 2.60 | .55 |
| ☐ 351 Jim King | .33 | .15 | .03 |
| ☐ 352 Bob Shaw | .33 | .15 | .03 |
| ☐ 353 Howie Bedell | .33 | .15 | .03 |
| ☐ 354 Billy Harrell | .33 | .15 | .03 |
| ☐ 355 Bob Allison | .50 | .22 | .05 |
| ☐ 356 Ryne Duren | .75 | .35 | .07 |
| ☐ 357 Daryl Spencer | .33 | .15 | .03 |
| ☐ 358 Earl Averill | .33 | .15 | .03 |
| ☐ 359 Dallas Green | .75 | .35 | .07 |
| ☐ 360 Frank Robinson | 8.50 | 4.00 | .85 |
| ☐ 361 A Checklist 5 | 2.00 | .60 | .20 |
| (no ad on back) | | | |
| ☐ 361 B Checklist 5 | 3.25 | .75 | .25 |
| (Special Feature ad on back) | | | |
| ☐ 362 Frank Funk | .33 | .15 | .03 |
| ☐ 363 John Roseboro | .50 | .22 | .05 |
| ☐ 364 Moe Drabowski | .33 | .15 | .03 |
| ☐ 365 Jerry Lumpe | .33 | .15 | .03 |
| ☐ 366 Eddie Fisher | .33 | .15 | .03 |
| ☐ 367 Jim Rivera | .33 | .15 | .03 |
| ☐ 368 Bennie Daniels | .33 | .15 | .03 |

| | MINT | VG-E | F-G |
|---|---|---|---|
| ☐ 369 Dave Philley | .33 | .15 | .03 |
| ☐ 370 Roy Face | .80 | .40 | .08 |
| ☐ 371 Bill Skowron | 2.00 | .90 | .20 |
| ☐ 372 Bob Hendley | .40 | .18 | .04 |
| ☐ 373 Red Sox Team | .85 | .40 | .08 |
| ☐ 374 Paul Giel | .40 | .18 | .04 |
| ☐ 375 Ken Boyer | 2.00 | .90 | .20 |
| ☐ 376 Mike Roarke | .40 | .18 | .04 |
| ☐ 377 Ruben Gomez | .40 | .18 | .04 |
| ☐ 378 Wally Post | .40 | .18 | .04 |
| ☐ 379 Bobby Shantz | .85 | .40 | .08 |
| ☐ 380 Minnie Minoso | 1.25 | .60 | .12 |
| ☐ 381 Dave Wickersham | .40 | .18 | .04 |
| ☐ 382 Frank Thomas | .40 | .18 | .04 |
| ☐ 383 Frisco First Liners | .50 | .22 | .05 |
| Mike McCormick Jack Sanford Billy O'Dell | | | |
| ☐ 384 Chuck Essegian | .40 | .18 | .04 |
| ☐ 385 Jim Perry | .85 | .40 | .08 |
| ☐ 386 Joe Hicks | .40 | .18 | .04 |
| ☐ 387 Duke Maas | .40 | .18 | .04 |
| ☐ 388 Bob Clemente | 12.50 | 5.75 | 1.25 |
| ☐ 389 Ralph Terry | .75 | .35 | .07 |
| ☐ 390 Del Crandall | .50 | .22 | .05 |
| ☐ 391 Winston Brown | .40 | .18 | .04 |
| ☐ 392 Reno Bertoia | .40 | .18 | .04 |
| ☐ 393 Batter Bafflers | .50 | .22 | .05 |
| Don Cardwell Glen Hobbie | | | |
| ☐ 394 Ken Walters | .40 | .18 | .04 |
| ☐ 395 Chuck Estrada | .50 | .22 | .05 |
| ☐ 396 Bob Aspromonte | .40 | .18 | .04 |
| ☐ 397 Hal Woodeschick | .40 | .18 | .04 |
| ☐ 398 Hank Bauer | .75 | .35 | .07 |
| ☐ 399 Cliff Cook | .40 | .18 | .04 |
| ☐ 400 Vern Law | .75 | .35 | .07 |
| BASEBALL THRILLS (401–410) | | | |
| ☐ 401 Ruth 60th Homer | 4.50 | 2.10 | .45 |
| ☐ 402 Perfect Game (Larsen) | 1.50 | .70 | .15 |
| ☐ 403 26 Inning Tie | .75 | .35 | .07 |
| ☐ 404 Hornsby .424 Average | 1.25 | .60 | .12 |
| ☐ 405 Gehrig's Streak | 3.50 | 1.65 | .35 |
| ☐ 406 Mantle 565 Ft. Homer | 4.50 | 2.10 | .45 |
| ☐ 407 Chesbro Wins 41 | .75 | .35 | .07 |
| ☐ 408 Mathewson Fans 267 | 1.75 | .85 | .17 |
| ☐ 409 Johnson Shutouts | 1.75 | .85 | .17 |
| ☐ 410 Haddix 12 Perfect Inn. | .75 | .35 | .07 |
| ☐ 411 Tony Taylor | .40 | .18 | .04 |
| ☐ 412 Larry Sherry | .50 | .22 | .05 |
| ☐ 413 Eddie Yost | .40 | .18 | .04 |
| ☐ 414 Dick Donovan | .40 | .18 | .04 |

| | MINT | VG-E | F-G |
|---|---|---|---|
| ☐ 415 Hank Aaron | 25.00 | 11.00 | 2.50 |
| ☐ 416 Dick Howser | 1.25 | .60 | .12 |
| ☐ 417 Juan Marichal | 27.00 | 12.00 | 2.70 |
| ☐ 418 Ed Bailey | .40 | .18 | .04 |
| ☐ 419 Tom Borland | .40 | .18 | .04 |
| ☐ 420 Ernie Broglio | .50 | .22 | .05 |
| ☐ 421 Ty Cline | .40 | .18 | .04 |
| ☐ 422 Bud Daley | .40 | .18 | .04 |
| ☐ 423 Charlie Neal | .50 | .22 | .05 |
| ☐ 424 Turk Lown | .40 | .18 | .04 |
| ☐ 425 Yogi Berra | 10.00 | 4.75 | 1.00 |
| ☐ 426 Braves Team (463) | 2.00 | .90 | .20 |
| ☐ 427 Dick Ellsworth | .50 | .22 | .05 |
| ☐ 428 Ray Barker | .40 | .18 | .04 |
| ☐ 429 Al Kaline | 7.00 | 3.25 | .70 |
| ☐ 430 Bill Mazeroski | 1.50 | .70 | .15 |
| ☐ 431 Chuck Stobbs | .40 | .18 | .04 |
| ☐ 432 Coot Veal | .40 | .18 | .04 |
| ☐ 433 Art Mahaffey | .40 | .18 | .04 |
| ☐ 434 Tom Brewer | .40 | .18 | .04 |
| ☐ 435 Orlando Cepeda | 2.00 | .90 | .20 |
| ☐ 436 Jim Maloney | 1.00 | .45 | .10 |
| ☐ 437 Checklist 6 | 1.60 | .40 | .10 |
| ☐ 438 Curt Flood | 1.00 | .45 | .10 |
| ☐ 439 Phil Regan | .50 | .22 | .05 |
| ☐ 440 Luis Aparicio | 3.00 | 1.40 | .30 |
| ☐ 441 Dick Bertell | .40 | .18 | .04 |
| ☐ 442 Gordon Jones | .40 | .18 | .04 |
| ☐ 443 Duke Snider | 7.50 | 3.50 | .75 |
| ☐ 444 Joe Nuxhall | .50 | .22 | .05 |
| ☐ 445 Frank Malzone | .50 | .22 | .05 |
| ☐ 446 Bob Taylor | .40 | .18 | .04 |
| ☐ 447 Harry Bright | .40 | .18 | .04 |
| ☐ 448 Del Rice | .40 | .18 | .04 |
| ☐ 449 Bob Bolin | .40 | .18 | .04 |
| ☐ 450 Jim Lemon | .50 | .22 | .05 |
| ☐ 451 Power for Ernie | .50 | .22 | .05 |
| Daryl Spencer | | | |
| Bill White | | | |
| Ernie Broglio | | | |
| ☐ 452 Bob Allen | .40 | .18 | .04 |
| ☐ 453 Dick Schofield | .40 | .18 | .04 |
| ☐ 454 Pumpsie Green | .40 | .18 | .04 |
| ☐ 455 Early Wynn | 3.00 | 1.40 | .30 |
| ☐ 456 Hal Bevan | .40 | .18 | .04 |
| ☐ 457 John James | .40 | .18 | .04 |
| ☐ 458 Willie Tasby | .40 | .18 | .04 |
| ☐ 459 Terry Fox | .40 | .18 | .04 |
| ☐ 460 Gil Hodges | 3.75 | 1.75 | .37 |
| ☐ 461 Smoky Burgess | .50 | .22 | .05 |
| ☐ 462 Lou Klimchock | .40 | .18 | .04 |
| ☐ 463 Jack Fisher | .50 | .22 | .05 |
| (See also 426) | | | |

| | MINT | VG-E | F-G |
|---|---|---|---|
| ☐ 464 Leroy Thomas | .40 | .18 | .04 |
| ☐ 465 Roy McMillan | .40 | .18 | .04 |
| ☐ 466 Ron Moeller | .40 | .18 | .04 |
| ☐ 467 Indians Team | .85 | .40 | .08 |
| ☐ 468 John Callison | .50 | .22 | .05 |
| ☐ 469 Ralph Lumenti | .40 | .18 | .04 |
| ☐ 470 Roy Sievers | .50 | .22 | .05 |
| AL MVP's (471-478) | | | |
| ☐ 471 Phil Rizzuto MVP | 3.50 | 1.65 | .35 |
| ☐ 472 Yogi Berra MVP | 4.50 | 2.10 | .45 |
| ☐ 473 Bob Shantz MVP | .75 | .35 | .07 |
| ☐ 474 Al Rosen MVP | 1.00 | .45 | .10 |
| ☐ 475 Mickey Mantle MVP | 12.00 | 5.50 | 1.20 |
| ☐ 476 Jackie Jensen MVP | .75 | .35 | .07 |
| ☐ 477 Nellie Fox MVP | 1.10 | .50 | .11 |
| ☐ 478 Roger Maris MVP | 4.00 | 1.85 | .40 |
| NL MVP's (479-486) | | | |
| ☐ 479 Jim Konstanty MVP | .75 | .35 | .07 |
| ☐ 480 Roy Campanella MVP | 7.50 | 3.50 | .75 |
| ☐ 481 Hank Sauer MVP | .75 | .35 | .07 |
| ☐ 482 Willie Mays MVP | 7.50 | 3.50 | .75 |
| ☐ 483 Don Newcombe MVP | .75 | .35 | .07 |
| ☐ 484 Hank Aaron MVP | 7.50 | 3.50 | .75 |
| ☐ 485 Ernie Banks MVP | 3.50 | 1.65 | .35 |
| ☐ 486 Dick Groat MVP | .75 | .35 | .07 |
| ☐ 487 Gene Oliver | .40 | .18 | .04 |
| ☐ 488 Joe McClain | .40 | .18 | .04 |
| ☐ 489 Walt Dropo | .40 | .18 | .04 |
| ☐ 490 Jim Bunning | 1.75 | .85 | .17 |
| ☐ 491 Phillies Team | .85 | .40 | .08 |
| ☐ 492 Ron Fairly | .50 | .22 | .05 |
| ☐ 493 Don Zimmer | .65 | .30 | .06 |
| ☐ 494 Tom Cheney | .40 | .18 | .04 |
| ☐ 495 Elston Howard | 1.75 | .85 | .17 |
| ☐ 496 Ken Mackenzie | .40 | .18 | .04 |
| ☐ 497 Willie Jones | .40 | .18 | .04 |
| ☐ 498 Ray Herbert | .40 | .18 | .04 |
| ☐ 499 Chuck Schilling | .40 | .18 | .04 |
| ☐ 500 Harvey Kuenn | 1.10 | .50 | .11 |
| ☐ 501 John DeMerit | .40 | .18 | .04 |
| ☐ 502 Clarence Coleman | .40 | .18 | .04 |
| ☐ 503 Tito Francona | .50 | .22 | .05 |
| ☐ 504 Billy Consolo | .40 | .18 | .04 |
| ☐ 505 Red Schoendienst | 1.00 | .45 | .10 |
| ☐ 506 Willie Davis | 1.50 | .70 | .15 |
| ☐ 507 Pete Burnside | .40 | .18 | .04 |
| ☐ 508 Rocky Bridges | .40 | .18 | .04 |
| ☐ 509 Camilo Carreon | .40 | .18 | .04 |
| ☐ 510 Art Ditmar | .40 | .18 | .04 |
| ☐ 511 Joe Morgan | .40 | .18 | .04 |
| ☐ 512 Bob Will | .40 | .18 | .04 |
| ☐ 513 Jim Brosnan | .50 | .22 | .05 |
| ☐ 514 Jake Wood | .40 | .18 | .04 |

| | MINT | VG-E | F-G |
|---|---|---|---|
| ☐ 515 Jackie Brandt | .40 | .18 | .04 |
| ☐ 516 Checklist 7 | 1.75 | .45 | .10 |
| ☐ 517 Willie McCovey | 9.00 | 4.25 | .90 |
| ☐ 518 Andy Carey | .40 | .18 | .04 |
| ☐ 519 Jim Pagliaroni | .40 | .18 | .04 |
| ☐ 520 Joe Cunningham | .40 | .18 | .04 |
| ☐ 521 Brother Battery | .50 | .22 | .05 |
|     Norm Sherry | | | |
|     Larry Sherry | | | |
| ☐ 522 Dick Farrell | .40 | .18 | .04 |
| ☐ 523 Joe Gibbon | 6.00 | 2.80 | .60 |
| ☐ 524 John Logan | 6.50 | 3.00 | .65 |
| ☐ 525 Ron Perranoski | 7.00 | 3.25 | .70 |
| ☐ 526 R.C. Stevens | 6.00 | 2.80 | .60 |
| ☐ 527 Gene Leek | 6.00 | 2.80 | .60 |
| ☐ 528 Pedro Ramos | 6.00 | 2.80 | .60 |
| ☐ 529 Bob Roselli | 6.00 | 2.80 | .60 |
| ☐ 530 Bob Malkmus | 6.00 | 2.80 | .60 |
| ☐ 531 Jim Coates | 6.00 | 2.80 | .60 |
| ☐ 532 Bob Hale | 6.00 | 2.80 | .60 |
| ☐ 533 Jack Curtis | 6.00 | 2.80 | .60 |
| ☐ 534 Eddie Kasko | 6.00 | 2.80 | .60 |
| ☐ 535 Larry Jackson | 6.00 | 2.80 | .60 |
| ☐ 536 Bill Tuttle | 6.00 | 2.80 | .60 |
| ☐ 537 Bobby Locke | 6.00 | 2.80 | .60 |
| ☐ 538 Chuck Hiller | 6.00 | 2.80 | .60 |
| ☐ 539 John Klippstein | 6.00 | 2.80 | .60 |
| ☐ 540 Jackie Jensen | 7.50 | 3.50 | .75 |
| ☐ 541 Roland Sheldon | 6.00 | 2.80 | .60 |
| ☐ 542 Minnesota Twins Team | 10.00 | 4.75 | 1.00 |
| ☐ 543 Roger Craig | 8.50 | 4.00 | .85 |
| ☐ 544 George Thomas | 6.00 | 2.80 | .60 |
| ☐ 545 Hoyt Wilhelm | 18.00 | 8.50 | 1.80 |
| ☐ 546 Marty Kutyna | 6.00 | 2.80 | .60 |
| ☐ 547 Leon Wagner | 6.00 | 2.80 | .60 |
| ☐ 548 Ted Wills | 6.00 | 2.80 | .60 |
| ☐ 549 Hal R. Smith | 6.00 | 2.80 | .60 |
| ☐ 550 Frank Baumann | 6.00 | 2.80 | .60 |
| ☐ 551 George Altman | 6.00 | 2.80 | .60 |
| ☐ 552 Jim Archer | 6.00 | 2.80 | .60 |
| ☐ 553 Bill Fischer | 6.00 | 2.80 | .60 |
| ☐ 554 Pirates Team | 8.00 | 3.75 | .80 |
| ☐ 555 Sam Jones | 6.50 | 3.00 | .65 |
| ☐ 556 Ken R. Hunt | 6.00 | 2.80 | .60 |
| ☐ 557 Jose Valdivielso | 6.00 | 2.80 | .60 |
| ☐ 558 Don Ferrarese | 6.00 | 2.80 | .60 |
| ☐ 559 Jim Gentile | 6.50 | 3.00 | .65 |
| ☐ 560 Barry Latman | 6.00 | 2.80 | .60 |
| ☐ 561 Charley James | 6.00 | 2.80 | .60 |
| ☐ 562 Bill Monbouquette | 6.00 | 2.80 | .60 |
| ☐ 563 Bob Cerv | 6.50 | 3.00 | .65 |
| ☐ 564 Don Cardwell | 6.00 | 2.80 | .60 |

| | MINT | VG-E | F-G |
|---|---|---|---|
| ☐ 565 Felipe Alou ALL-STARS (566–589) | 7.00 | 3.25 | .70 |
| ☐ 566 Paul Richards MGR AS | 6.50 | 3.00 | .65 |
| ☐ 567 Danny Murtaugh MGR AS | 6.50 | 3.00 | .65 |
| ☐ 568 Bill Skowron AS | 7.00 | 3.25 | .70 |
| ☐ 569 Frank Herrera AS | 6.50 | 3.00 | .65 |
| ☐ 570 Nellie Fox AS | 10.00 | 4.75 | 1.00 |
| ☐ 571 Bill Mazeroski AS | 7.00 | 3.25 | .70 |
| ☐ 572 Brooks Robinson AS | 21.00 | 9.50 | 2.10 |
| ☐ 573 Ken Boyer AS | 8.00 | 3.75 | .80 |
| ☐ 574 Luis Aparicio AS | 15.00 | 7.00 | 1.50 |
| ☐ 575 Ernie Banks AS | 21.00 | 9.50 | 2.10 |
| ☐ 576 Roger Maris AS | 21.00 | 9.50 | 2.10 |
| ☐ 577 Hank Aaron AS | 50.00 | 22.00 | 5.00 |
| ☐ 578 Mickey Mantle AS | 90.00 | 42.00 | 9.00 |
| ☐ 579 Willie Mays AS | 50.00 | 22.00 | 5.00 |
| ☐ 580 Al Kaline AS | 21.00 | 9.50 | 2.10 |
| ☐ 581 Frank Robinson AS | 21.00 | 9.50 | 2.10 |
| ☐ 582 Earl Battey AS | 6.50 | 3.00 | .65 |
| ☐ 583 Del Crandall AS | 6.50 | 3.00 | .65 |
| ☐ 584 Jim Perry AS | 6.50 | 3.00 | .65 |
| ☐ 585 Bob Friend AS | 6.50 | 3.00 | .65 |
| ☐ 586 Whitey Ford AS | 21.00 | 9.50 | 2.10 |
| ☐ 587 Does not exist | 0.00 | 0.00 | 0.00 |
| ☐ 588 Does not exist | 0.00 | 0.00 | 0.00 |
| ☐ 589 Warren Spahn AS | 21.00 | 9.50 | 2.10 |

## 1962 TOPPS

The cards in this 598 card set measure 2½" by 3½". The 1962 Topps set contains a mini-series spotlighting Babe Ruth (135 to 144). Card number 139 exists as A: Babe Ruth Special card, B: Hal Reniff with arms over head, or C: Hal Reniff in the same pose as card number 159. In addi-

*tion, two poses exist for players depicted on card numbers 129, 132, 134, 147, 174, 176, and 190. The high number series, 523 to 598, is somewhat more difficult to obtain than other cards in the set. The set price listed does not include the pose variations (see checklist for individual values).*

**Complete Set: M-650.00; VG-E-250.00; F-G-50.00**

|  | MINT | VG-E | F-G |
|---|---|---|---|
| Common Player (1–370) | .30 | .12 | .03 |
| Common Player (371–522) | .50 | .22 | .05 |
| Common Player (523–590) | 2.00 | .90 | .20 |
| Common Player (591–598) | 4.50 | 2.10 | .45 |
| 1 Roger Maris | 22.00 | 4.50 | 1.25 |
| 2 Jim Brosnan | .40 | .18 | .04 |
| 3 Pete Runnels | .40 | .18 | .04 |
| 4 John DeMerit | .30 | .12 | .03 |
| 5 Sandy Koufax | 13.00 | 6.00 | 1.30 |
| 6 Marv Breeding | .30 | .12 | .03 |
| 7 Frank Thomas | .30 | .12 | .03 |
| 8 Ray Herbert | .30 | .12 | .03 |
| 9 Jim Davenport | .40 | .18 | .04 |
| 10 Bob Clemente | 13.00 | 6.00 | 1.30 |
| 11 Tom Morgan | .30 | .12 | .03 |
| 12 Harry Craft MGR | .30 | .12 | .03 |
| 13 Dick Howser | .50 | .22 | .05 |
| 14 Bill White | .50 | .22 | .05 |
| 15 Dick Donovan | .30 | .12 | .03 |
| 16 Darrell Johnson | .40 | .18 | .04 |
| 17 John Callison | .40 | .18 | .04 |
| 18 Managers' Dream: | 16.00 | 7.50 | 1.60 |
| Mickey Mantle | | | |
| Willie Mays | | | |
| 19 Ray Washburn | .30 | .12 | .03 |
| 20 Rocky Colavito | 1.00 | .45 | .10 |
| 21 Jim Kaat | 1.50 | .70 | .15 |
| 22 A Checklist 1 COR | 1.50 | .40 | .10 |
| 22 B Checklist 1 ERR (121–176 on back) | 1.75 | .45 | .10 |
| 23 Norm Larker | .30 | .12 | .03 |
| 24 Tigers Team | .75 | .35 | .07 |
| 25 Ernie Banks | 5.00 | 2.35 | .50 |
| 26 Chris Cannizzaro | .30 | .12 | .03 |
| 27 Chuck Cottier | .40 | .18 | .04 |
| 28 Minnie Minoso | 1.00 | .45 | .10 |
| 29 Casey Stengel | 3.50 | 1.65 | .35 |
| 30 Ed Mathews | 3.50 | 1.65 | .35 |
| 31 Tom Tresh | 1.75 | .85 | .17 |

|  | MINT | VG-E | F-G |
|---|---|---|---|
| 32 John Roseboro | .40 | .18 | .04 |
| 33 Don Larsen | .50 | .22 | .05 |
| 34 Johnny Temple | .30 | .12 | .03 |
| 35 Don Schwall | .30 | .12 | .03 |
| 36 Don Leppert | .30 | .12 | .03 |
| 37 Tribe Hill Trio | .40 | .18 | .04 |
| Barry Latman | | | |
| Dick Stigman | | | |
| Jim Perry | | | |
| 38 Gene Stephens | .30 | .12 | .03 |
| 39 Joe Koppe | .30 | .12 | .03 |
| 40 Orlando Cepeda | 1.50 | .70 | .15 |
| 41 Cliff Cook | .30 | .12 | .03 |
| 42 Jim King | .30 | .12 | .03 |
| 43 Dodgers Team | 1.00 | .45 | .10 |
| 44 Don Taussig | .30 | .12 | .03 |
| 45 Brooks Robinson | 7.00 | 3.25 | .70 |
| 46 Jack Baldschun | .30 | .12 | .03 |
| 47 Bob Will | .30 | .12 | .03 |
| 48 Ralph Terry | .50 | .22 | .05 |
| 49 Hal Jones | .30 | .12 | .03 |
| 50 Stan Musial | 13.00 | 6.00 | 1.30 |
| 51 AL Batting Leaders | .75 | .35 | .07 |
| Norm Cash | | | |
| Jim Piersall | | | |
| Al Kaline | | | |
| Elston Howard | | | |
| 52 NL Batting Leaders | .75 | .35 | .07 |
| Bob Clemente | | | |
| Vada Pinson | | | |
| Ken Boyer | | | |
| Wally Moon | | | |
| 53 AL Home Run Leaders | 2.50 | 1.15 | .25 |
| Roger Maris | | | |
| Mickey Mantle | | | |
| Jim Gentile | | | |
| Harmon Killebrew | | | |
| 54 NL Home Run Leaders | 1.00 | .45 | .10 |
| Orlando Cepeda | | | |
| Willie Mays | | | |
| Frank Robinson | | | |
| 55 AL ERA Leaders | .75 | .35 | .07 |
| Dick Donovan | | | |
| Bill Stafford | | | |
| Don Mossi | | | |
| Milt Pappas | | | |
| 56 NL ERA Leaders | .75 | .35 | .07 |
| Warren Spahn | | | |
| Jim O'Toole | | | |
| Curt Simmons | | | |
| Mike McCormick | | | |

|  | MINT | VG-E | F-G |
|---|---|---|---|
| ☐ 57 AL Wins Leaders ...... | .75 | .35 | .07 |
| Whitey Ford | | | |
| Frank Lary | | | |
| Steve Barber | | | |
| Jim Bunning | | | |
| ☐ 58 NL Wins Leaders ...... | .75 | .35 | .07 |
| Warren Spahn | | | |
| Joe Jay | | | |
| Jim O'Toole | | | |
| ☐ 59 AL Strikeout Leaders ... | .75 | .35 | .07 |
| Camilo Pascual | | | |
| Whitey Ford | | | |
| Jim Bunning | | | |
| Juan Pizzaro | | | |
| ☐ 60 NL Strikeout Leaders ... | 1.25 | .60 | .12 |
| Sandy Koufax | | | |
| Stan Williams | | | |
| Don Drysdale | | | |
| Jim O'Toole | | | |
| ☐ 61 Cardinals Team ........ | .75 | .35 | .07 |
| ☐ 62 Steve Boros ........... | .40 | .18 | .04 |
| ☐ 63 Tony Cloninger ........ | .30 | .12 | .03 |
| ☐ 64 Russ Snyder .......... | .30 | .12 | .03 |
| ☐ 65 Bobby Richardson ..... | 1.50 | .70 | .15 |
| ☐ 66 Cuno Barragon ........ | .30 | .12 | .03 |
| ☐ 67 Harvey Haddix ........ | .40 | .18 | .04 |
| ☐ 68 Ken Hunt ............. | .30 | .12 | .03 |
| ☐ 69 Phil Ortega ........... | .30 | .12 | .03 |
| ☐ 70 Harmon Killebrew ..... | 3.75 | 1.75 | .37 |
| ☐ 71 Dick Le May .......... | .30 | .12 | .03 |
| ☐ 72 Bob's Pupils ......... | .40 | .18 | .04 |
| Steve Boros | | | |
| Bob Scheffing | | | |
| Jake Wood | | | |
| ☐ 73 Nellie Fox ............ | 1.50 | .70 | .15 |
| ☐ 74 Bob Lillis ............ | .40 | .18 | .04 |
| ☐ 75 Milt Pappas .......... | .40 | .18 | .04 |
| ☐ 76 Howie Bedell ......... | .30 | .12 | .03 |
| ☐ 77 Tony Taylor .......... | .30 | .12 | .03 |
| ☐ 78 Gene Green ........... | .30 | .12 | .03 |
| ☐ 79 Ed Hobaugh .......... | .30 | .12 | .03 |
| ☐ 80 Vada Pinson .......... | 1.00 | .45 | .10 |
| ☐ 81 Jim Pagliaroni ........ | .30 | .12 | .03 |
| ☐ 82 Deron Johnson ....... | .30 | .12 | .03 |
| ☐ 83 Larry Jackson ........ | .30 | .12 | .03 |
| ☐ 84 Lenny Green .......... | .30 | .12 | .03 |
| ☐ 85 Gil Hodges ........... | 3.50 | 1.65 | .35 |
| ☐ 86 Donn Clendennon ..... | .65 | .30 | .06 |
| ☐ 87 Mike Roarke .......... | .30 | .12 | .03 |
| ☐ 88 Ralph Houk .......... | .75 | .35 | .07 |
| ☐ 89 Barney Schultz ....... | .30 | .12 | .03 |
| ☐ 90 Jim Piersall ......... | .70 | .32 | .07 |
| ☐ 91 J.C. Martin .......... | .30 | .12 | .03 |

|  | MINT | VG-E | F-G |
|---|---|---|---|
| ☐ 92 Sam Jones ........... | .30 | .12 | .03 |
| ☐ 93 John Blanchard ....... | .40 | .18 | .04 |
| ☐ 94 Jay Hook ............ | .30 | .12 | .03 |
| ☐ 95 Don Hoak ........... | .30 | .12 | .03 |
| ☐ 96 Eli Grba ............. | .30 | .12 | .03 |
| ☐ 97 Tito Francona ........ | .40 | .18 | .04 |
| ☐ 98 Checklist 2 .......... | 1.50 | .40 | .10 |
| ☐ 99 John (Boog) Powell ... | 2.75 | 1.25 | .27 |
| ☐ 100 Warren Spahn ....... | 4.00 | 1.85 | .40 |
| ☐ 101 Carroll Hardy ........ | .30 | .12 | .03 |
| ☐ 102 Al Schroll .......... | .30 | .12 | .03 |
| ☐ 103 Don Blasingame ..... | .30 | .12 | .03 |
| ☐ 104 Ted Savage ......... | .30 | .12 | .03 |
| ☐ 105 Don Mossi .......... | .50 | .22 | .05 |
| ☐ 106 Carl Sawatski ....... | .30 | .12 | .03 |
| ☐ 107 Mike McCormick ..... | .50 | .22 | .05 |
| ☐ 108 Willie Davis ........ | .75 | .35 | .07 |
| ☐ 109 Bob Shaw .......... | .30 | .12 | .03 |
| ☐ 110 Bill Skowron ........ | 1.50 | .70 | .15 |
| ☐ 111 Dallas Green ........ | .45 | .20 | .04 |
| ☐ 112 Hank Foiles ......... | .30 | .12 | .03 |
| ☐ 113 White Sox Team ..... | .75 | .35 | .07 |
| ☐ 114 Howie Koplitz ....... | .30 | .12 | .03 |
| ☐ 115 Bob Skinner ........ | .30 | .12 | .03 |
| ☐ 116 Herb Score ......... | .50 | .22 | .05 |
| ☐ 117 Gary Geiger ........ | .30 | .12 | .03 |
| ☐ 118 Julian Javier ....... | .40 | .18 | .04 |
| ☐ 119 Danny Murphy ...... | .30 | .12 | .03 |
| ☐ 120 Bob Purkey ......... | .30 | .12 | .03 |
| ☐ 121 Billy Hitchcock ..... | .30 | .12 | .03 |
| ☐ 122 Norm Bass ......... | .30 | .12 | .03 |
| ☐ 123 Mike De La Hoz ..... | .30 | .12 | .03 |
| ☐ 124 Bill Pleis .......... | .30 | .12 | .03 |
| ☐ 125 Gene Woodling ...... | .40 | .18 | .04 |
| ☐ 126 Al Cicotte .......... | .30 | .12 | .03 |
| ☐ 127 Pride of A's: ........ | .40 | .18 | .04 |
| Norm Siebern | | | |
| Hank Bauer | | | |
| Jerry Lumpe | | | |
| ☐ 128 Art Fowler .......... | .30 | .12 | .03 |
| ☐ 129 A Lee Walls ........ | .60 | .28 | .06 |
| (facing right) | | | |
| ☐ 129 B Lee Walls ........ | 4.00 | 1.85 | .40 |
| (face left) | | | |
| ☐ 130 Frank Bolling ....... | .30 | .12 | .03 |
| ☐ 131 Pete Richert ........ | .30 | .12 | .03 |
| ☐ 132 A Angels Team ...... | 1.00 | .45 | .10 |
| (without photo) | | | |
| ☐ 132 B Angels Team ...... | 4.00 | 1.85 | .40 |
| (with photo) | | | |
| ☐ 133 Felipe Alou ........ | .50 | .22 | .05 |
| ☐ 134 A Billy Hoeft ....... | .60 | .28 | .06 |
| (facing right) | | | |

| | MINT | VG-E | F-G |
|---|---|---|---|
| ☐ 134 B Billy Hoeft .......... (facing straight) | 4.00 | 1.85 | .40 |
| BABE RUTH SPECIALS (135–144) | | | |
| ☐ 135 Babe Ruth Special 1 ... Babe as a boy | 3.50 | 1.65 | .35 |
| ☐ 136 Babe Ruth Special 2 ... Babe Joins Yanks | 3.50 | 1.65 | .35 |
| ☐ 137 Babe Ruth Special 3 ... Babe with Huggins | 3.50 | 1.65 | .35 |
| ☐ 138 Babe Ruth Special 4 ... Famous Slugger | 3.50 | 1.65 | .35 |
| ☐ 139 A Babe Ruth Special 5 . | 4.50 | 2.10 | .45 |
| ☐ 139 B Hal Reniff PORT ..... | 6.50 | 3.00 | .65 |
| ☐ 139 C Hal Reniff .......... (pitching) | 24.00 | 11.00 | 2.40 |
| ☐ 140 Babe Ruth Special 6 ... Gehrig and Ruth | 4.00 | 1.85 | .40 |
| ☐ 141 Babe Ruth Special 7 ... Twilight Years | 3.50 | 1.65 | .35 |
| ☐ 142 Babe Ruth Special 8 ... Coaching Dodgers | 3.50 | 1.65 | .35 |
| ☐ 143 Babe Ruth Special 9 ... Greatest Sports Hero | 3.50 | 1.65 | .35 |
| ☐ 144 Babe Ruth Special 10 .. Farewell Speech | 3.50 | 1.65 | .35 |
| ☐ 145 Barry Latman .......... | .30 | .12 | .03 |
| ☐ 146 Don Demeter .......... | .30 | 12. | .03 |
| ☐ 147 A Bill Kunkel PORT .... | .60 | .28 | .06 |
| ☐ 147 B Bill Kunkel .......... (pitching pose) | 4.00 | 1.85 | .40 |
| ☐ 148 Wally Post ............ | .30 | .12 | .03 |
| ☐ 149 Bob Duliba ............ | .30 | .12 | .03 |
| ☐ 150 Al Kaline ............. | 5.50 | 2.60 | .55 |
| ☐ 151 Johnny Klippstein ..... | .30 | .12 | .03 |
| ☐ 152 Mickey Vernon ........ | .40 | .18 | .04 |
| ☐ 153 Pumpsie Green ........ | .30 | .12 | .03 |
| ☐ 154 Lee Thomas .......... | .30 | .12 | .03 |
| ☐ 155 Stu Miller ............ | .30 | .12 | .03 |
| ☐ 156 Merritt Ranew ......... | .30 | .12 | .03 |
| ☐ 157 Wes Covington ........ | .30 | .12 | .03 |
| ☐ 158 Braves Team .......... | .75 | .35 | .07 |
| ☐ 159 Hal Reniff ............ | .65 | .30 | .06 |
| ☐ 160 Dick Stuart ........... | .50 | .22 | .05 |
| ☐ 161 Frank Baumann ........ | .30 | .12 | .03 |
| ☐ 162 Sammy Drake ......... | .30 | .12 | .03 |
| ☐ 163 Hot Corner Guard ...... Billy Gardner Cletis Boyer | .50 | .22 | .05 |
| ☐ 164 Hal Naragon .......... | .30 | .12 | .03 |
| ☐ 165 Jackie Brandt ......... | .30 | .12 | .03 |
| ☐ 166 Don Lee .............. | .30 | .12 | .03 |

| | MINT | VG-E | F-G |
|---|---|---|---|
| ☐ 167 Tim McCarver ......... | 2.00 | .90 | .20 |
| ☐ 168 Leo Posada ........... | .30 | .12 | .03 |
| ☐ 169 Bob Cerv ............. | .30 | .12 | .03 |
| ☐ 170 Ron Santo ............ | 1.00 | .45 | .10 |
| ☐ 171 Dave Sisler ........... | .30 | .12 | .03 |
| ☐ 172 Fred Hutchinson ....... | .50 | .22 | .05 |
| ☐ 173 Chico Fernandez ...... | .30 | .12 | .03 |
| ☐ 174 A Carl Willey .......... (capless) | .60 | .28 | .06 |
| ☐ 174 B Carl Willey .......... (with cap) | 4.00 | 1.85 | .40 |
| ☐ 175 Frank Howard ......... | 1.00 | .45 | .10 |
| ☐ 176 A Eddie Yost PORT .... | .60 | .28 | .06 |
| ☐ 176 B Eddie Yost BATTING . | 4.00 | 1.85 | .40 |
| ☐ 177 Bobby Shantz ......... | .50 | .22 | .05 |
| ☐ 178 Cam Carreon ......... | .30 | .12 | .03 |
| ☐ 179 Tom Sturdivant ....... | .30 | .12 | .03 |
| ☐ 180 Bob Allison .......... | .50 | .22 | .05 |
| ☐ 181 Paul Brown ........... | .30 | .12 | .03 |
| ☐ 182 Bob Nieman .......... | .30 | .12 | .03 |
| ☐ 183 Roger Craig .......... | .50 | .22 | .05 |
| ☐ 184 Haywood Sullivan ..... | .40 | .18 | .04 |
| ☐ 185 Roland Sheldon ....... | .30 | .12 | .03 |
| ☐ 186 Mack Jones .......... | .30 | .12 | .03 |
| ☐ 187 Gene Conley .......... | .30 | .12 | .03 |
| ☐ 188 Chuck Hiller .......... | .30 | .12 | .03 |
| ☐ 189 Dick Hall ............ | .30 | .12 | .03 |
| ☐ 190 A Wally Moon PORT ... | .60 | .28 | .06 |
| ☐ 190 B Wally Moon BATTING | 4.00 | 1.85 | .40 |
| ☐ 191 Jim Brewer ........... | .30 | .12 | .03 |
| ☐ 192 A Checklist 3 ......... (without comma) | 1.50 | .40 | .10 |
| ☐ 192 B Checklist 3 ......... (comma after Checklist) | 1.75 | .45 | .10 |
| ☐ 193 Eddie Kasko .......... | .30 | .12 | .03 |
| ☐ 194 Dean Chance ......... | .50 | .22 | .05 |
| ☐ 195 Joe Cunningham ...... | .30 | .12 | .03 |
| ☐ 196 Terry Fox ............ | .30 | .12 | .03 |
| ☐ 197 Daryl Spencer ........ | .30 | .12 | .03 |
| ☐ 198 Johnny Keane MGR .... | .40 | .18 | .04 |
| ☐ 199 Gaylord Perry ........ | 27.00 | 12.00 | 2.70 |
| ☐ 200 Mickey Mantle ........ | 50.00 | 22.00 | 5.00 |
| ☐ 201 Ike Delock ........... | .30 | .12 | .03 |
| ☐ 202 Carl Warwick ......... | .30 | .12 | .03 |
| ☐ 203 Jack Fisher .......... | .30 | .12 | .03 |
| ☐ 204 Johnny Weekly ........ | .30 | .12 | .03 |
| ☐ 205 Gene Freese ......... | .30 | .12 | .03 |
| ☐ 206 Senators Team ........ | .70 | .32 | .07 |
| ☐ 207 Pete Burnside ........ | .30 | .12 | .03 |
| ☐ 208 Billy Martin .......... | 1.75 | .85 | .17 |
| ☐ 209 Jim Fregosi .......... | 1.25 | .60 | .12 |
| ☐ 210 Roy Face ............ | .75 | .35 | .07 |

| | MINT | VG-E | F-G |
|---|---|---|---|
| ☐ 211 Midway Masters: | .40 | .18 | .04 |
| Frank Bolling | | | |
| Roy McMillan | | | |
| ☐ 212 Jim Owens | .30 | .12 | .03 |
| ☐ 213 Richie Ashburn | 1.25 | .60 | .12 |
| ☐ 214 Dom Zanni | .30 | .12 | .03 |
| ☐ 215 Woody Held | .30 | .12 | .03 |
| ☐ 216 Ron Kline | .30 | .12 | .03 |
| ☐ 217 Walt Alston MGR | 1.25 | .60 | .12 |
| ☐ 218 Joe Torre | 4.00 | 1.85 | .40 |
| ☐ 219 Al Downing | .50 | .22 | .05 |
| ☐ 220 Roy Sievers | .40 | .18 | .04 |
| ☐ 221 Bill Short | .30 | .12 | .03 |
| ☐ 222 Jerry Zimmerman | .30 | .12 | .03 |
| ☐ 223 Alex Grammas | .30 | .12 | .03 |
| ☐ 224 Don Rudolph | .30 | .12 | .03 |
| ☐ 225 Frank Malzone | .40 | .18 | .04 |
| ☐ 226 Giants Team | .75 | .35 | .07 |
| ☐ 227 Bob Tiefenauer | .30 | .12 | .03 |
| ☐ 228 Dale Long | .30 | .12 | .03 |
| ☐ 229 Jesus McFarlane | .30 | .12 | .03 |
| ☐ 230 Camilo Pascual | .40 | .18 | .04 |
| ☐ 231 Ernie Bowman | .30 | .12 | .03 |
| WORLD SERIES | | | |
| CARDS (232–237) | | | |
| ☐ 232 World Series Game 1 | 1.25 | .60 | .12 |
| Yanks win opener | | | |
| ☐ 233 World Series Game 2 | 1.25 | .60 | .12 |
| Jay ties it up | | | |
| ☐ 234 World Series Game 3 | 2.25 | 1.00 | .22 |
| Maris wins in 9th | | | |
| ☐ 235 World Series Game 4 | 2.25 | 1.00 | .22 |
| Ford sets new mark | | | |
| ☐ 236 World Series Game 5 | 1.25 | .60 | .12 |
| Yanks crush Reds | | | |
| ☐ 237 World Series Summary | 1.25 | .60 | .12 |
| Yanks celebrate. | | | |
| ☐ 238 Norm Sherry | .40 | .18 | .04 |
| ☐ 239 Cecil Butler | .30 | .12 | .03 |
| ☐ 240 George Altman | .30 | .12 | .03 |
| ☐ 241 Johnny Kucks | .30 | .12 | .03 |
| ☐ 242 Mel McGaha | .30 | .12 | .03 |
| ☐ 243 Robin Roberts | 2.75 | 1.25 | .27 |
| ☐ 244 Don Gile | .30 | .12 | .03 |
| ☐ 245 Ron Hansen | .30 | .12 | .03 |
| ☐ 246 Art Ditmar | .30 | .12 | .03 |
| ☐ 247 Joe Pignatano | .30 | .12 | .03 |
| ☐ 248 Bob Aspromonte | .30 | .12 | .03 |
| ☐ 249 Ed Keegan | .30 | .12 | .03 |
| ☐ 250 Norm Cash | 1.00 | .45 | .10 |
| ☐ 251 New York Yankees Team | 2.50 | 1.15 | .25 |
| ☐ 252 Earl Francis | .30 | .12 | .03 |

| | MINT | VG-E | F-G |
|---|---|---|---|
| ☐ 253 Harry Chiti | .30 | .12 | .03 |
| ☐ 254 Gordon Windhom | .30 | .12 | .03 |
| ☐ 255 Juan Pizzarro | .30 | .12 | .03 |
| ☐ 256 Elio Chacon | .30 | .12 | .03 |
| ☐ 257 Jack Spring | .30 | .12 | .03 |
| ☐ 258 Marty Keough | .30 | .12 | .03 |
| ☐ 259 Lou Klimchock | .30 | .12 | .03 |
| ☐ 260 Bill Pierce | .75 | .35 | .07 |
| ☐ 261 George Alusik | .30 | .12 | .03 |
| ☐ 262 Bob Schmidt | .30 | .12 | .03 |
| ☐ 263 The Right Pitch | .40 | .18 | .04 |
| Bob Purkey | | | |
| Jim Turner | | | |
| Joe Jay | | | |
| ☐ 264 Dick Ellsworth | .40 | .18 | .04 |
| ☐ 265 Joe Adcock | .75 | .35 | .07 |
| ☐ 266 John Anderson | .30 | .12 | .03 |
| ☐ 267 Dan Dobbek | .30 | .12 | .03 |
| ☐ 268 Ken McBride | .30 | .12 | .03 |
| ☐ 269 Bob Oldis | .30 | .12 | .03 |
| ☐ 270 Dick Groat | 1.00 | .45 | .10 |
| ☐ 271 Ray Rippelmeyer | .30 | .12 | .03 |
| ☐ 272 Earl Robinson | .30 | .12 | .03 |
| ☐ 273 Gary Bell | .30 | .12 | .03 |
| ☐ 274 Sammy Taylor | .30 | .12 | .03 |
| ☐ 275 Norm Siebern | .30 | .12 | .03 |
| ☐ 276 Hal Kolstad | .30 | .12 | .03 |
| ☐ 277 Checklist 4 | 1.35 | .40 | .10 |
| ☐ 278 Ken Johnson | .30 | .12 | .03 |
| ☐ 279 Hobie Landrith | .30 | .12 | .03 |
| ☐ 280 Johnny Podres | 1.00 | .45 | .10 |
| ☐ 281 Jake Gibbs | .40 | .18 | .04 |
| ☐ 282 Dave Hillman | .30 | .12 | .03 |
| ☐ 283 Charlie Smith | .30 | .12 | .03 |
| ☐ 284 Ruben Amaro | .30 | .12 | .03 |
| ☐ 285 Curt Simmons | .40 | .18 | .04 |
| ☐ 286 Al Lopez MGR | 1.00 | .45 | .10 |
| ☐ 287 George Witt | .30 | .12 | .03 |
| ☐ 288 Billy Williams | 3.00 | 1.40 | .30 |
| ☐ 289 Mike Krsnich | .30 | .12 | .03 |
| ☐ 290 Jim Gentile | .50 | .22 | .05 |
| ☐ 291 Hal Stowe | .30 | .12 | .03 |
| ☐ 292 Jerry Kindall | .30 | .12 | .03 |
| ☐ 293 Bob Miller | .30 | .12 | .03 |
| ☐ 294 Phillies Team | .75 | .35 | .07 |
| ☐ 295 Vern Law | .50 | .22 | .05 |
| ☐ 296 Ken Hamlin | .30 | .12 | .03 |
| ☐ 297 Ron Perranoski | .50 | .22 | .05 |
| ☐ 298 Bill Tuttle | .30 | .12 | .03 |
| ☐ 299 Don Wert | .30 | .12 | .03 |
| ☐ 300 Willie Mays | 30.00 | 14.00 | 3.00 |
| ☐ 301 Galen Cisco | .40 | .18 | .04 |

| | | MINT | VG-E | F-G |
|---|---|---|---|---|
| ☐ 302 | John Edwards | .30 | .12 | .03 |
| ☐ 303 | Frank Torre | .30 | .12 | .03 |
| ☐ 304 | Dick Farrell | .30 | .12 | .03 |
| ☐ 305 | Jerry Lumpe | .30 | .12 | .03 |
| ☐ 306 | Redbird Rippers | .40 | .18 | .04 |
| | Lindy McDaniel | | | |
| | Larry Jackson | | | |
| ☐ 307 | Jim Grant | .30 | .12 | .03 |
| ☐ 308 | Neil Chrisley | .30 | .12 | .03 |
| ☐ 309 | Moe Morhardt | .30 | .12 | .03 |
| ☐ 310 | Whitey Ford | 5.00 | 2.35 | .50 |
| | IN ACTION CARDS | | | |
| | (311–319) | | | |
| ☐ 311 | Tony Kubek IA | .75 | .35 | .07 |
| ☐ 312 | Warren Spahn IA | 1.75 | .85 | .17 |
| ☐ 313 | Roger Maris IA | 2.25 | 1.00 | .22 |
| ☐ 314 | Rocky Colavito IA | .75 | .35 | .07 |
| ☐ 315 | Whitey Ford IA | 2.00 | .90 | .20 |
| ☐ 316 | Harmon Killebrew IA | 1.75 | .85 | .17 |
| ☐ 317 | Stan Musial IA | 2.75 | 1.25 | .27 |
| ☐ 318 | Mickey Mantle IA | 5.50 | 2.60 | .55 |
| ☐ 319 | Mike McCormick IA | .50 | .22 | .05 |
| ☐ 320 | Hank Aaron | 30.00 | 14.00 | 3.00 |
| ☐ 321 | Lee Stange | .30 | .12 | .03 |
| ☐ 322 | Al Dark | .50 | .22 | .05 |
| ☐ 323 | Don Landrum | .30 | .12 | .03 |
| ☐ 324 | Joe McClain | .30 | .12 | .03 |
| ☐ 325 | Luis Aparicio | 3.00 | 1.40 | .30 |
| ☐ 326 | Tom Parsons | .30 | .12 | .03 |
| ☐ 327 | Ozzie Virgil | .30 | .12 | .03 |
| ☐ 328 | Ken Walters | .30 | .12 | .03 |
| ☐ 329 | Bob Bolin | .30 | .12 | .03 |
| ☐ 330 | John Romano | .30 | .12 | .03 |
| ☐ 331 | Moe Drabowsky | .30 | .12 | .03 |
| ☐ 332 | Don Buddin | .30 | .12 | .03 |
| ☐ 333 | Frank Cipriani | .30 | .12 | .03 |
| ☐ 334 | Red Sox Team | .75 | .35 | .07 |
| ☐ 335 | Bill Bruton | .30 | .12 | .03 |
| ☐ 336 | Billy Muffett | .30 | .12 | .03 |
| ☐ 337 | Jim Marshall | .30 | .12 | .03 |
| ☐ 338 | Billy Gardner | .40 | .18 | .04 |
| ☐ 339 | Jose Valdivielso | .30 | .12 | .03 |
| ☐ 340 | Don Drysdale | 6.00 | 2.80 | .60 |
| ☐ 341 | Mike Hershberger | .30 | .12 | .03 |
| ☐ 342 | Ed Rakow | .30 | .12 | .03 |
| ☐ 343 | Albie Pearson | .30 | .12 | .03 |
| ☐ 344 | Ed Bauta | .30 | .12 | .03 |
| ☐ 345 | Chuck Schilling | .30 | .12 | .03 |
| ☐ 346 | Jack Kralick | .30 | .12 | .03 |
| ☐ 347 | Chuck Hinton | .30 | .12 | .03 |
| ☐ 348 | Larry Burright | .30 | .12 | .03 |
| ☐ 349 | Paul Foytack | .30 | .12 | .03 |
| ☐ 350 | Frank Robinson | 6.50 | 3.00 | .65 |

| | | MINT | VG-E | F-G |
|---|---|---|---|---|
| ☐ 351 | Braves' Backstops | .60 | .28 | .06 |
| | Joe Torre | | | |
| | Del Crandall | | | |
| ☐ 352 | Frank Sullivan | .30 | .12 | .03 |
| ☐ 353 | Bill Mazeroski | 1.00 | .45 | .10 |
| ☐ 354 | Roman Mejias | .30 | .12 | .03 |
| ☐ 355 | Steve Barber | .30 | .12 | .03 |
| ☐ 356 | Tom Haller | .30 | .12 | .03 |
| ☐ 357 | Jerry Walker | .30 | .12 | .03 |
| ☐ 358 | Tommy Davis | 1.00 | .45 | .10 |
| ☐ 359 | Bobby Locke | .30 | .12 | .03 |
| ☐ 360 | Yogi Berra | 8.50 | 4.00 | .85 |
| ☐ 361 | Bob Hendley | .30 | .12 | .03 |
| ☐ 362 | Ty Cline | .30 | .12 | .03 |
| ☐ 363 | Bob Roselli | .30 | .12 | .03 |
| ☐ 364 | Ken Hunt | .30 | .12 | .03 |
| ☐ 365 | Charley Neal | .50 | .22 | .05 |
| ☐ 366 | Phil Regan | .30 | .12 | .03 |
| ☐ 367 | Checklist 5 | 1.60 | .40 | .10 |
| ☐ 368 | Bob Tillman | .30 | .12 | .03 |
| ☐ 369 | Ted Bowsfield | .30 | .12 | .03 |
| ☐ 370 | Ken Boyer | 1.50 | .70 | .15 |
| ☐ 371 | Earl Battey | .50 | .22 | .05 |
| ☐ 372 | Jack Curtis | .50 | .22 | .05 |
| ☐ 373 | Al Heist | .50 | .22 | .05 |
| ☐ 374 | Gene Mauch | .60 | .28 | .06 |
| ☐ 375 | Ron Fairly | .60 | .28 | .06 |
| ☐ 376 | Bud Daley | .50 | .22 | .05 |
| ☐ 377 | John Orsino | .50 | .22 | .05 |
| ☐ 378 | Bennie Daniels | .50 | .22 | .05 |
| ☐ 379 | Chuck Essegian | .50 | .22 | .05 |
| ☐ 380 | Lou Burdette | 1.00 | .45 | .10 |
| ☐ 381 | Chico Cardenas | .50 | .22 | .05 |
| ☐ 382 | Dick Williams | .60 | .28 | .06 |
| ☐ 383 | Ray Sadecki | .50 | .22 | .05 |
| ☐ 384 | K. C. Athletics Team | .80 | .40 | .08 |
| ☐ 385 | Early Wynn | 3.00 | 1.40 | .30 |
| ☐ 386 | Don Mincher | .50 | .22 | .05 |
| ☐ 387 | Lou Brock | 35.00 | 16.50 | 3.50 |
| ☐ 388 | Ryne Duren | .75 | .32 | .07 |
| ☐ 389 | Smokey Burgess | .70 | .35 | .07 |
| | NL ALL-STARS | | | |
| | (390–399) | | | |
| ☐ 390 | Orlando Cepeda AS | 1.00 | .45 | .10 |
| ☐ 391 | Bill Mazeroski AS | .75 | .35 | .07 |
| ☐ 392 | Ken Boyer AS | .75 | .35 | .07 |
| ☐ 393 | Roy McMillan AS | .50 | .22 | .05 |
| ☐ 394 | Hank Aaron AS | 8.00 | 3.75 | .80 |
| ☐ 395 | Willie Mays AS | 8.00 | 3.75 | .80 |
| ☐ 396 | Frank Robinson AS | 3.50 | 1.65 | .35 |
| ☐ 397 | John Roseboro AS | .60 | .28 | .06 |
| ☐ 398 | Don Drysdale AS | 2.75 | 1.25 | .27 |
| ☐ 399 | Warren Spahn AS | 2.75 | 1.25 | .27 |

| | MINT | VG-E | F-G |
|---|---|---|---|
| ☐ 400 Elston Howard | 1.50 | .70 | .15 |
| ☐ 401 AL/NL Homer Kings | 4.00 | 1.85 | .40 |
| Roger Maris | | | |
| Orlando Cepeda | | | |
| ☐ 402 Gino Cimoli | .50 | .22 | .05 |
| ☐ 403 Chet Nichols | .50 | .22 | .05 |
| ☐ 404 Tim Harkness | .50 | .22 | .05 |
| ☐ 405 Jim Perry | 1.00 | .45 | .10 |
| ☐ 406 Bob Taylor | .50 | .22 | .05 |
| ☐ 407 Hank Aguirre | .50 | .22 | .05 |
| ☐ 408 Gus Bell | .60 | .28 | .06 |
| ☐ 409 Pirates Team | .90 | .40 | .09 |
| ☐ 410 Al Smith | .50 | .22 | .05 |
| ☐ 411 Danny O'Connell | .50 | .22 | .05 |
| ☐ 412 Charlie James | .50 | .22 | .05 |
| ☐ 413 Matty Alou | .65 | .30 | .06 |
| ☐ 414 Joe Gaines | .50 | .22 | .05 |
| ☐ 415 Bill Virdon | .75 | .35 | .07 |
| ☐ 416 Bob Scheffing | .50 | .22 | .05 |
| ☐ 417 Joe Azcue | .50 | .22 | .05 |
| ☐ 418 Andy Carey | .50 | .22 | .05 |
| ☐ 419 Bob Bruce | .50 | .22 | .05 |
| ☐ 420 Gus Triandos | .60 | .28 | .06 |
| ☐ 421 Ken Mackenzie | .50 | .22 | .05 |
| ☐ 422 Steve Bilko | .50 | .22 | .05 |
| ☐ 423 Rival League | 1.50 | .70 | .15 |
| Relief Aces: | | | |
| Roy Face | | | |
| Hoyt Wilhelm | | | |
| ☐ 424 Al McBean | .50 | .22 | .05 |
| ☐ 425 Carl Yastrzemski | 75.00 | 35.00 | 7.50 |
| ☐ 426 Bob Farley | .50 | .22 | .05 |
| ☐ 427 Jake Wood | .50 | .22 | .05 |
| ☐ 428 Joe Hicks | .50 | .22 | .05 |
| ☐ 429 Billy O'Dell | .50 | .22 | .05 |
| ☐ 430 Tony Kubek | 3.00 | 1.40 | .30 |
| ☐ 431 Bob Rodgers | .50 | .22 | .05 |
| ☐ 432 Jim Pendleton | .50 | .22 | .05 |
| ☐ 433 Jim Archer | .50 | .22 | .05 |
| ☐ 434 Clay Dalrymple | .50 | .22 | .05 |
| ☐ 435 Larry Sherry | .60 | .28 | .06 |
| ☐ 436 Felix Mantilla | .50 | .22 | .05 |
| ☐ 437 Ray Moore | .50 | .22 | .05 |
| ☐ 438 Dick Brown | .50 | .22 | .05 |
| ☐ 439 Jerry Buchek | .50 | .22 | .05 |
| ☐ 440 Joe Jay | .50 | .22 | .05 |
| ☐ 441 Checklist 6 | 1.80 | .40 | .10 |
| ☐ 442 Wes Stock | .60 | .28 | .06 |
| ☐ 443 Del Crandall | .65 | .30 | .06 |
| ☐ 444 Ted Wills | .50 | .22 | .05 |
| ☐ 445 Vic Power | .50 | .22 | .05 |
| ☐ 446 Don Elston | .50 | .22 | .05 |
| ☐ 447 Willie Kirkland | .50 | .22 | .05 |

| | MINT | VG-E | F-G |
|---|---|---|---|
| ☐ 448 Joe Gibbon | .50 | .22 | .05 |
| ☐ 449 Jerry Adair | .50 | .22 | .05 |
| ☐ 450 Jim O'Toole | .50 | .22 | .05 |
| ☐ 451 Jose Tartabull | .50 | .22 | .05 |
| ☐ 452 Earl Averill | .50 | .22 | .05 |
| ☐ 453 Cal McLish | .50 | .22 | .05 |
| ☐ 454 Floyd Robinson | .50 | .22 | .05 |
| ☐ 455 Luis Arroyo | .60 | .28 | .06 |
| ☐ 456 Joe Amalfitano | .50 | .22 | .05 |
| ☐ 457 Lou Clinton | .50 | .22 | .05 |
| ☐ 458 A Bob Buhl | .60 | .28 | .06 |
| (Braves cap emblem) | | | |
| ☐ 458 B Bob Buhl | 12.00 | 5.50 | 1.20 |
| (no emblem on cap) | | | |
| ☐ 459 Ed Bailey | .50 | .22 | .05 |
| ☐ 460 Jim Bunning | 2.00 | .90 | .20 |
| ☐ 461 Ken Hubbs | 2.00 | .90 | .20 |
| ☐ 462 A Willie Tasby | .60 | .28 | .06 |
| (Senators cap emblem) | | | |
| ☐ 462 B Willie Tasby | 12.00 | 5.50 | 1.20 |
| (no emblem on cap) | | | |
| ☐ 463 Hank Bauer | .60 | .28 | .06 |
| ☐ 464 Al Jackson | .50 | .22 | .05 |
| ☐ 465 Reds Team | 1.00 | .45 | .10 |
| AL ALL-STARS | | | |
| (466-475) | | | |
| ☐ 466 Norm Cash AS | .75 | .35 | .07 |
| ☐ 467 Chuck Schilling AS | .50 | .22 | .05 |
| ☐ 468 Brooks Robinson AS | 4.00 | 1.85 | .40 |
| ☐ 469 Luis Aparicio AS | 1.75 | .85 | .17 |
| ☐ 470 Al Kaline AS | 4.00 | 1.85 | .40 |
| ☐ 471 Mickey Mantle AS | 15.00 | 7.00 | 1.50 |
| ☐ 472 Rocky Colavito AS | .75 | .35 | .07 |
| ☐ 473 Elston Howard AS | .75 | .35 | .07 |
| ☐ 474 Frank Lary AS | .50 | .22 | .05 |
| ☐ 475 Whitey Ford AS | 3.50 | 1.65 | .35 |
| ☐ 476 Orioles Team | 1.00 | .45 | .10 |
| ☐ 477 Andre Rodgers | .50 | .22 | .05 |
| ☐ 478 Don Zimmer | .60 | .28 | .06 |
| ☐ 479 Joel Horlen | .75 | .35 | .07 |
| ☐ 480 Harvey Kuenn | 1.00 | .45 | .10 |
| ☐ 481 Vic Wertz | .50 | .22 | .05 |
| ☐ 482 Sam Mele | .50 | .22 | .05 |
| ☐ 483 Don McMahon | .50 | .22 | .05 |
| ☐ 484 Dick Schofield | .50 | .22 | .05 |
| ☐ 485 Pedro Ramos | .50 | .22 | .05 |
| ☐ 486 Jim Gilliam | 2.50 | 1.15 | .25 |
| ☐ 487 Jerry Lynch | .50 | .22 | .05 |
| ☐ 488 Hal Brown | .50 | .22 | .05 |
| ☐ 489 Julio Gotay | .50 | .22 | .05 |
| ☐ 490 Clete Boyer | 1.75 | .85 | .17 |
| ☐ 491 Leon Wagner | .50 | .22 | .05 |
| ☐ 492 Hal W. Smith | .50 | .22 | .05 |

| | MINT | VG-E | F-G |
|---|---|---|---|
| ☐ 493 Danny McDevitt | .50 | .22 | .05 |
| ☐ 494 Sammy White | .50 | .22 | .05 |
| ☐ 495 Don Cardwell | .50 | .22 | .05 |
| ☐ 496 Wayne Causey | .50 | .22 | .05 |
| ☐ 497 Ed Bouchee | .50 | .22 | .05 |
| ☐ 498 Jim Donohue | .50 | .22 | .05 |
| ☐ 499 Zoilo Versalles | .50 | .22 | .05 |
| ☐ 500 Duke Snider | 10.00 | 4.75 | 1.00 |
| ☐ 501 Claude Osteen | .60 | .28 | .06 |
| ☐ 502 Hector Lopez | .50 | .22 | .05 |
| ☐ 503 Danny Murtaugh | .50 | .22 | .05 |
| ☐ 504 Eddie Bressoud | .50 | .22 | .05 |
| ☐ 505 Juan Marichal | 9.00 | 4.25 | .90 |
| ☐ 506 Charlie Maxwell | .50 | .22 | .05 |
| ☐ 507 Ernie Broglio | .50 | .22 | .05 |
| ☐ 508 Gordy Coleman | .50 | .22 | .05 |
| ☐ 509 Dave Giusti | .60 | .28 | .06 |
| ☐ 510 Jim Lemon | .50 | .22 | .05 |
| ☐ 511 Bubba Phillips | .50 | .22 | .05 |
| ☐ 512 Mike Fornieles | .50 | .22 | .05 |
| ☐ 513 Whitey Herzog | .75 | .35 | .07 |
| ☐ 514 Sherm Lollar | .60 | .28 | .06 |
| ☐ 515 Stan Williams | .50 | .22 | .05 |
| ☐ 516 Checklist 7 | 2.25 | .50 | .10 |
| ☐ 517 Dave Wickersham | .50 | .22 | .05 |
| ☐ 518 Lee Maye | .50 | .22 | .05 |
| ☐ 519 Bob Johnson | .50 | .22 | .05 |
| ☐ 520 Bob Friend | .60 | .28 | .06 |
| ☐ 521 Jacke Davis | .50 | .22 | .05 |
| ☐ 522 Lindy McDaniel | .50 | .22 | .05 |
| ☐ 523 Russ Nixon | 2.00 | .90 | .20 |
| ☐ 524 Howie Nunn | 2.00 | .90 | .20 |
| ☐ 525 George Thomas | 2.00 | .90 | .20 |
| ☐ 526 Hal Woodeschick | 2.00 | .90 | .20 |
| ☐ 527 Dick McAuliffe | 2.25 | 1.00 | .22 |
| ☐ 528 Turk Lown | 2.00 | .90 | .20 |
| ☐ 529 John Schaive | 2.00 | .90 | .20 |
| ☐ 530 Bob Gibson | 30.00 | 14.00 | 3.00 |
| ☐ 531 Bobby G. Smith | 2.00 | .90 | .20 |
| ☐ 532 Dick Stigman | 2.00 | .90 | .20 |
| ☐ 533 Charley Lau | 2.00 | .90 | .20 |
| ☐ 534 Tony Gonzalez | 2.00 | .90 | .20 |
| ☐ 535 Ed Roebuck | 2.00 | .90 | .20 |
| ☐ 536 Dick Gernert | 2.00 | .90 | .20 |
| ☐ 537 Indians Team | 4.00 | 1.85 | .40 |
| ☐ 538 Jack Sanford | 2.00 | .90 | .20 |
| ☐ 539 Billy Moran | 2.00 | .90 | .20 |
| ☐ 540 Jim Landis | 2.00 | .90 | .20 |
| ☐ 541 Don Nottebart | 2.00 | .90 | .20 |
| ☐ 542 Dave Philley | 2.00 | .90 | .20 |
| ☐ 543 Bob Allen | 2.00 | .90 | .20 |
| ☐ 544 Willie McCovey | 30.00 | 14.00 | 3.00 |
| ☐ 545 Hoyt Wilhelm | 12.00 | 5.50 | 1.20 |

| | MINT | VG-E | F-G |
|---|---|---|---|
| ☐ 546 Moe Thacker | 2.00 | .90 | .20 |
| ☐ 547 Don Ferrarese | 2.00 | .90 | .20 |
| ☐ 548 Bobby Del Greco | 2.00 | .90 | .20 |
| ☐ 549 Bill Rigney | 2.00 | .90 | .20 |
| ☐ 550 Art Mahaffey | 2.00 | .90 | .20 |
| ☐ 551 Harry Bright | 2.00 | .90 | .20 |
| ☐ 552 Chicago Cubs Team | 4.00 | 1.85 | .40 |
| ☐ 553 Jim Coates | 2.00 | .90 | .20 |
| ☐ 554 Bubba Morton | 2.00 | .90 | .20 |
| ☐ 555 John Buzhardt | 2.00 | .90 | .20 |
| ☐ 556 Al Spangler | 2.00 | .90 | .20 |
| ☐ 557 Bob Anderson | 2.00 | .90 | .20 |
| ☐ 558 John Goryl | 2.00 | .90 | .20 |
| ☐ 559 Mike Higgins | 2.00 | .90 | .20 |
| ☐ 560 Chuck Estrada | 2.00 | .90 | .20 |
| ☐ 561 Gene Oliver | 2.00 | .90 | .20 |
| ☐ 562 Bill Henry | 2.00 | .90 | .20 |
| ☐ 563 Ken Aspromonte | 2.00 | .90 | .20 |
| ☐ 564 Bob Grim | 2.00 | .90 | .20 |
| ☐ 565 Jose Pagan | 2.00 | .90 | .20 |
| ☐ 566 Marty Kutyna | 2.00 | .90 | .20 |
| ☐ 567 Tracy Stallard | 2.00 | .90 | .20 |
| ☐ 568 Jim Golden | 2.00 | .90 | .20 |
| ☐ 569 Ed Sadowski | 2.00 | .90 | .20 |
| ☐ 570 Bill Stafford | 2.00 | .90 | .20 |
| ☐ 571 Billy Klaus | 2.00 | .90 | .20 |
| ☐ 572 B.G. Miller | 2.00 | .90 | .20 |
| ☐ 573 Johnny Logan | 2.00 | .90 | .20 |
| ☐ 574 Dean Stone | 2.00 | .90 | .20 |
| ☐ 575 Red Schoendienst | 3.00 | 1.40 | .30 |
| ☐ 576 Russ Kemmerer | 2.00 | .90 | .20 |
| ☐ 577 Dave Nicholson | 2.00 | .90 | .20 |
| ☐ 578 Jim Duffalo | 2.00 | .90 | .20 |
| ☐ 579 Jim Schaffer | 2.00 | .90 | .20 |
| ☐ 580 Bill Monbouquette | 2.00 | .90 | .20 |
| ☐ 581 Mel Roach | 2.00 | .90 | .20 |
| ☐ 582 Ron Piche | 2.00 | .90 | .20 |
| ☐ 583 Larry Osborne | 2.00 | .90 | .20 |
| ☐ 584 Minnesota Twins Team | 4.00 | 1.85 | .40 |
| ☐ 585 Glen Hobbie | 2.00 | .90 | .20 |
| ☐ 586 Sam Esposito | 2.00 | .90 | .20 |
| ☐ 587 Frank Funk | 2.00 | .90 | .20 |
| ☐ 588 Birdie Tebbetts | 2.00 | .90 | .20 |
| ☐ 589 Bob Turley | 2.50 | 1.15 | .25 |
| ☐ 590 Curt Flood | 3.50 | 1.65 | .35 |
| ROOKIE CARDS (591–598) | | | |
| ☐ 591 Rookie Pitchers | 6.00 | 2.80 | .60 |
| Sam McDowell | | | |
| Ron Taylor | | | |
| Ron Nischwitz | | | |
| Art Quirk | | | |
| Dick Radatz | | | |

| | | MINT | VG-E | F-G |
|---|---|---|---|---|
| ☐ 592 | Rookie Pitchers | 8.00 | 3.75 | .80 |
| | Dan Pfister | | | |
| | Bo Belinsky | | | |
| | Dave Stenhouse | | | |
| | Jim Bouton | | | |
| | Joe Bonikowski | | | |
| ☐ 593 | Rookie Pitchers | 4.50 | 2.10 | .45 |
| | Jack Lamabe | | | |
| | Craig Anderson | | | |
| | Jack Hamilton | | | |
| | Bob Moorhead | | | |
| | Bob Veale | | | |
| ☐ 594 | Rookie Catchers | 13.00 | 6.00 | 1.30 |
| | Doc Edwards | | | |
| | Ken Retzer | | | |
| | Bob Uecker | | | |
| | Doug Camilli | | | |
| | Don Pavletich | | | |
| ☐ 595 | Rookie Catchers | 4.50 | 2.10 | .45 |
| | Bob Sadowski | | | |
| | Felix Torres | | | |
| | Marlan Coughtry | | | |
| | Ed Charles | | | |
| ☐ 596 | Rookie Infielders | 8.00 | 3.75 | .80 |
| | Bernie Allen | | | |
| | Joe Pepitone | | | |
| | Phil Linz | | | |
| | Rich Rollins | | | |
| ☐ 597 | Rookie Infielders | 4.50 | 2.10 | .45 |
| | Jim McKnight | | | |
| | Rod Kanehl | | | |
| | Amado Samuel | | | |
| | Denis Menke | | | |
| ☐ 598 | Rookie Outfielders | 6.00 | 2.80 | .60 |
| | Al Luplow | | | |
| | Danny Jimenez | | | |
| | Howie Goss | | | |
| | Jim Hickman | | | |
| | Ed Olivares | | | |

**1963 TOPPS**

*The cards in this 576 card set measure 2½" by 3½". The sharp color photographs of the 1963 set are a vivid contrast to the drab pictures of 1962. In addition to the "Leaders" series (1 to 10) and the World Series cards (142 to 148), the seventh and last series of cards (507 to 576) contains seven rookie cards (each depicting four players).*

Complete Set: M-975.00; VG-E-425.00; F-G-85.00

| | | MINT | VG-E | F-G |
|---|---|---|---|---|
| | Common Player (1–196) | .22 | .10 | .02 |
| | Common Player (197–446) | .35 | .15 | .03 |
| | Common Player (447–506) | 2.00 | .90 | .20 |
| | Common Player (507–576) | 1.60 | .80 | .16 |
| ☐ 1 | NL Batting Leaders | 2.75 | .60 | .15 |
| | Tommy Davis | | | |
| | Frank Robinson | | | |
| | Stan Musial | | | |
| | Hank Aaron | | | |
| | Bill White | | | |
| ☐ 2 | AL Batting Leaders | 1.75 | .85 | .17 |
| | Pete Runnels | | | |
| | Mickey Mantle | | | |
| | Floyd Robinson | | | |
| | Norm Siebern | | | |
| | Chuck Hinton | | | |
| ☐ 3 | NL Home Run Leaders | 2.00 | .90 | .20 |
| | Willie Mays | | | |
| | Hank Aaron | | | |
| | Frank Robinson | | | |
| | Orlando Cepeda | | | |
| | Ernie Banks | | | |
| ☐ 4 | AL Home Run Leaders | 1.00 | .45 | .10 |
| | Harmon Killebrew | | | |
| | Norm Cash | | | |
| | Rocky Colavito | | | |
| | Roger Maris | | | |
| | Jim Gentile | | | |
| | Leon Wagner | | | |
| ☐ 5 | NL ERA Leaders | 1.30 | .65 | .13 |
| | Sandy Koufax | | | |
| | Bob Shaw | | | |
| | Bob Purkey | | | |
| | Bob Gibson | | | |
| | Don Drysdale | | | |

| | MINT | VG-E | F-G |
|---|---|---|---|
| ☐ 6 AL ERA Leaders ....... | 1.00 | .45 | .10 |
|    Hank Aguirre | | | |
|    Robin Roberts | | | |
|    Whitey Ford | | | |
|    Eddie Fisher | | | |
|    Dean Chance | | | |
| ☐ 7 AL Pitching Leaders .... | 1.00 | .45 | .10 |
|    Don Drysdale | | | |
|    Jack Sanford | | | |
|    Bob Purkey | | | |
|    Billy O'Dell | | | |
|    Art Mahaffey | | | |
|    Joe Jay | | | |
| ☐ 8 AL Pitching Leaders .... | .75 | .35 | .07 |
|    Ralph Terry | | | |
|    Dick Donovan | | | |
|    Ray Herbert | | | |
|    Jim Bunning | | | |
|    Camilo Pascual | | | |
| ☐ 9 NL Strikeout Leaders ... | 1.30 | .65 | .13 |
|    Don Drysdale | | | |
|    Sandy Koufax | | | |
|    Bob Gibson | | | |
|    Billy O'Dell | | | |
|    Dick Farrell | | | |
| ☐ 10 AL Strikeout Leaders ... | .75 | .35 | .07 |
|    Camilo Pascual | | | |
|    Jim Bunning | | | |
|    Ralph Terry | | | |
|    Juan Pizarro | | | |
|    Jim Kaat | | | |
| ☐ 11 Lee Walls ............ | .22 | .10 | .02 |
| ☐ 12 Steve Barber .......... | .22 | .10 | .02 |
| ☐ 13 Phillies Team .......... | .60 | .28 | .06 |
| ☐ 14 Pedro Ramos .......... | .22 | .10 | .02 |
| ☐ 15 Ken Hubbs ............ | .90 | .40 | .09 |
| ☐ 16 Al Smith ............. | .22 | .10 | .02 |
| ☐ 17 Ryne Duren ........... | .30 | .12 | .03 |
| ☐ 18 Buc Blasters ......... | 1.50 | .70 | .15 |
|    Smoky Burgess | | | |
|    Dick Stuart | | | |
|    Bob Clemente | | | |
|    Bob Skinner | | | |
| ☐ 19 Pete Burnside ......... | .22 | .10 | .02 |
| ☐ 20 Tony Kubek ........... | 1.50 | .70 | .15 |
| ☐ 21 Marty Keough ......... | .22 | .10 | .02 |
| ☐ 22 Curt Simmons ........ | .30 | .12 | .03 |
| ☐ 23 Ed Lopat ............ | .50 | .22 | .05 |
| ☐ 24 Bob Bruce ........... | .22 | .10 | .02 |
| ☐ 25 Al Kaline ............ | 5.00 | 2.35 | .50 |
| ☐ 26 Ray Moore ........... | .22 | .10 | .02 |
| ☐ 27 Choo Choo Coleman ... | .22 | .10 | .02 |
| ☐ 28 Mike Fornieles ........ | .22 | .10 | .02 |

| | MINT | VG-E | F-G |
|---|---|---|---|
| ☐ 29 A 1963 Rookie Stars ... | .35 | .15 | .03 |
|    Sammy Ellis | | | |
|    Ray Culp | | | |
|    John Boozer | | | |
|    Jesse Gonder | | | |
| ☐ 29 B 1962 Rookie Stars ... | 1.75 | .85 | .17 |
|    Sammy Ellis | | | |
|    Ray Culp | | | |
|    John Boozer | | | |
|    Jesse Gonder | | | |
| ☐ 30 Harvey Kuenn ......... | .60 | .28 | .06 |
| ☐ 31 Cal Koonce ........... | .22 | .10 | .02 |
| ☐ 32 Tony Gonzalez ........ | .22 | .10 | .02 |
| ☐ 33 Bo Belinski ........... | .30 | .12 | .03 |
| ☐ 34 Dick Schofield ........ | .22 | .10 | .02 |
| ☐ 35 John Buzhardt ........ | .22 | .10 | .02 |
| ☐ 36 Jerry Kindall .......... | .22 | .10 | .02 |
| ☐ 37 Jerry Lynch ........... | .22 | .10 | .02 |
| ☐ 38 Bud Daley ............ | .22 | .10 | .02 |
| ☐ 39 Angels Team .......... | .60 | .28 | .06 |
| ☐ 40 Vic Power ............ | .22 | .10 | .02 |
| ☐ 41 Charley Lau ........... | .30 | .12 | .03 |
| ☐ 42 Stan Williams ......... | .22 | .10 | .02 |
| ☐ 43 Veteran Masters ....... | 1.25 | .60 | .12 |
|    Casey Stengel | | | |
|    Gene Woodling | | | |
| ☐ 44 Terry Fox ............ | .22 | .10 | .02 |
| ☐ 45 Bob Aspromonte ...... | .22 | .10 | .02 |
| ☐ 46 Tommy Aaron ......... | .30 | .12 | .03 |
| ☐ 47 Don Lock ............ | .22 | .10 | .02 |
| ☐ 48 Birdie Tebbetts ....... | .22 | .10 | .02 |
| ☐ 49 Dal Maxvill ........... | .22 | .10 | .02 |
| ☐ 50 Billy Pierce .......... | .60 | .28 | .06 |
| ☐ 51 George Alusik ........ | .22 | .10 | .02 |
| ☐ 52 Chuck Schilling ....... | .22 | .10 | .02 |
| ☐ 53 Joe Moeller .......... | .22 | .10 | .02 |
| ☐ 54 A 1963 Rookie Stars ... | 2.25 | 1.00 | .22 |
|    Nelson Mathews | | | |
|    Harry Fanok | | | |
|    Jack Cullen | | | |
|    Dave DeBusschere | | | |
| ☐ 54 B 1962 Rookie Stars ... | 3.25 | 1.50 | .32 |
|    Nelson Mathews | | | |
|    Harry Fanok | | | |
|    Jack Cullen | | | |
|    Dave DeBusschere | | | |
| ☐ 55 Bill Virdon ........... | .80 | .40 | .08 |
| ☐ 56 Dennis Bennett ....... | .22 | .10 | .02 |
| ☐ 57 Billy Moran ........... | .22 | .10 | .02 |
| ☐ 58 Bob Will ............. | .22 | .10 | .02 |
| ☐ 59 C. Anderson ......... | .22 | .10 | .02 |
| ☐ 60 Elston Howard ........ | 1.75 | .85 | .17 |
| ☐ 61 Ernie Bowman ........ | .22 | .10 | .02 |

| | MINT | VG-E | F-G |
|---|---|---|---|
| ☐ 62 Bob Hendley | .22 | .10 | .02 |
| ☐ 63 Reds Team | .60 | .28 | .06 |
| ☐ 64 Dick McAuliffe | .22 | .10 | .02 |
| ☐ 65 Jackie Brandt | .22 | .10 | .02 |
| ☐ 66 Mike Joyce | .22 | .10 | .02 |
| ☐ 67 Ed Charles | .22 | .10 | .02 |
| ☐ 68 Friendly Foes | 3.00 | 1.40 | .30 |
| Duke Snider | | | |
| Gil Hodges | | | |
| ☐ 69 Bud Ziplel | .22 | .10 | .02 |
| ☐ 70 Jim O'Toole | .22 | .10 | .02 |
| ☐ 71 Bobby Wine | .22 | .10 | .02 |
| ☐ 72 Johnny Romano | .22 | .10 | .02 |
| ☐ 73 Bob Bragan | .22 | .10 | .02 |
| ☐ 74 Denny Lemaster | .22 | .10 | .02 |
| ☐ 75 Bob Allison | .30 | .12 | .03 |
| ☐ 76 Earl Wilson | .22 | .10 | .02 |
| ☐ 77 Al Spangler | .22 | .10 | .02 |
| ☐ 78 Marv Throneberry | .60 | .28 | .06 |
| ☐ 79 1st Series Checklist | 1.35 | .40 | .10 |
| ☐ 80 Jim Gilliam | 1.35 | .60 | .12 |
| ☐ 81 Jim Schaffer | .22 | .10 | .02 |
| ☐ 82 Ed Rakow | .22 | .10 | .02 |
| ☐ 83 Charley James | .22 | .10 | .02 |
| ☐ 84 Ron Kline | .22 | .10 | .02 |
| ☐ 85 Tom Haller | .22 | .10 | .02 |
| ☐ 86 Charley Maxwell | .22 | .10 | .02 |
| ☐ 87 Bob Veale | .30 | .12 | .03 |
| ☐ 88 Ron Hansen | .22 | .10 | .02 |
| ☐ 89 Dick Stigman | .22 | .10 | .02 |
| ☐ 90 Gordy Coleman | .22 | .10 | .02 |
| ☐ 91 Dallas Green | .30 | .12 | .03 |
| ☐ 92 Hector Lopez | .22 | .10 | .02 |
| ☐ 93 Galen Cisco | .22 | .10 | .02 |
| ☐ 94 Bob Schmidt | .22 | .10 | .02 |
| ☐ 95 Larry Jackson | .22 | .10 | .02 |
| ☐ 96 Lou Clinton | .22 | .10 | .02 |
| ☐ 97 Bob Duliba | .22 | .10 | .02 |
| ☐ 98 George Thomas | .22 | .10 | .02 |
| ☐ 99 Jim Umbricht | .22 | .10 | .02 |
| ☐ 100 Joe Cunningham | .22 | .10 | .02 |
| ☐ 101 Joe Gibbon | .22 | .10 | .02 |
| ☐ 102 A Checklist 2 | 1.25 | .40 | .10 |
| (red on yellow) | | | |
| ☐ 102 B Checklist 2 | 1.75 | .40 | .10 |
| (white on red) | | | |
| ☐ 103 Chuck Essegian | .22 | .10 | .02 |
| ☐ 104 Lew Krausse | .22 | .10 | .02 |
| ☐ 105 Ron Fairly | .30 | .12 | .03 |
| ☐ 106 Bobby Bolin | .22 | .10 | .02 |
| ☐ 107 Jim Hickman | .22 | .10 | .02 |
| ☐ 108 Hoyt Wilhelm | 2.50 | 1.15 | .25 |
| ☐ 109 Lee Maye | .22 | .10 | .02 |

| | MINT | VG-E | F-G |
|---|---|---|---|
| ☐ 110 Rich Rollins | .22 | .10 | .02 |
| ☐ 111 Al Jackson | .22 | .10 | .02 |
| ☐ 112 Dick Brown | .22 | .10 | .02 |
| ☐ 113 Don Landrum | .30 | .12 | .03 |
| (photo actually | | | |
| Ron Santo) | | | |
| ☐ 114 Dan Osinski | .22 | .10 | .02 |
| ☐ 115 Carl Yastrzemski | 30.00 | 14.00 | 3.00 |
| ☐ 116 Jim Brosnan | .30 | .12 | .03 |
| ☐ 117 Jacke Davis | .22 | .10 | .02 |
| ☐ 118 Sherm Lollar | .30 | .12 | .03 |
| ☐ 119 Bob Lillis | .30 | .12 | .03 |
| ☐ 120 Roger Maris | 6.00 | 2.80 | .60 |
| ☐ 121 Jim Hannan | .22 | .10 | .02 |
| ☐ 122 Julio Gotay | .22 | .10 | .02 |
| ☐ 123 Frank Howard | .90 | .40 | .09 |
| ☐ 124 Dick Howser | .35 | .15 | .03 |
| ☐ 125 Robin Roberts | 2.50 | 1.15 | .25 |
| ☐ 126 Bob Uecker | 2.75 | 1.25 | .27 |
| ☐ 127 Bill Tuttle | .22 | .10 | .02 |
| ☐ 128 Matty Alou | .30 | .12 | .03 |
| ☐ 129 Gary Bell | .22 | .10 | .02 |
| ☐ 130 Dick Groat | .60 | .28 | .06 |
| ☐ 131 Senators Team | .60 | .28 | .06 |
| ☐ 132 Jack Hamilton | .22 | .10 | .02 |
| ☐ 133 Gene Freese | .22 | .10 | .02 |
| ☐ 134 Bob Scheffing | .22 | .10 | .02 |
| ☐ 135 Richie Ashburn | 1.40 | .70 | .14 |
| ☐ 136 Ike Delock | .22 | .10 | .02 |
| ☐ 137 Mack Jones | .22 | .10 | .02 |
| ☐ 138 Pride Of N.L. | 6.00 | 2.80 | .60 |
| Willie Mays | | | |
| Stan Musial | | | |
| ☐ 139 Earl Averill | .22 | .10 | .02 |
| ☐ 140 Frank Lary | .30 | .12 | .03 |
| ☐ 141 Manny Mota | 1.50 | .70 | .15 |
| WORLD SERIES | | | |
| CARDS (142–148) | | | |
| ☐ 142 World Series Game 1 | 2.00 | .90 | .20 |
| Ford wins | | | |
| series opener | | | |
| ☐ 143 World Series Game 2 | 1.30 | .65 | .13 |
| Sanford flashes | | | |
| shutout magic | | | |
| ☐ 144 World Series Game 3 | 2.00 | .90 | .20 |
| Maris sparks | | | |
| Yankee rally | | | |
| ☐ 145 World Series Game 4 | 1.30 | .65 | .13 |
| Hiller blasts | | | |
| grand slammer | | | |
| ☐ 146 World Series Game 5 | 1.30 | .65 | .13 |
| Tresh's homer | | | |
| defeats Giants | | | |

| | MINT | VG-E | F-G |
|---|---|---|---|
| ☐ 147 World Series Game 6 .. Pierce stars in 3 hit victory | 1.30 | .65 | .13 |
| ☐ 148 World Series Game 7 .. Yanks celebrate as Terry wins | 1.30 | .65 | .13 |
| ☐ 149 Marv Breeding | .22 | .10 | .02 |
| ☐ 150 John Podres | .90 | .40 | .09 |
| ☐ 151 Pirates Team | .60 | .28 | .06 |
| ☐ 152 Ron Nischwitz | .22 | .10 | .02 |
| ☐ 153 Hal Smith | .22 | .10 | .02 |
| ☐ 154 Walt Alston MGR | 1.00 | .45 | .10 |
| ☐ 155 Bill Stafford | .22 | .10 | .02 |
| ☐ 156 Roy McMillan | .22 | .10 | .02 |
| ☐ 157 Diego Segui | .22 | .10 | .02 |
| ☐ 158 Rookie Stars Rogelio Alvares Dave Roberts Tommy Harper Bob Saverine | .35 | .15 | .03 |
| ☐ 159 Jim Pagliaroni | .22 | .10 | .02 |
| ☐ 160 Juan Pizarro | .22 | .10 | .02 |
| ☐ 161 Frank Torre | .22 | .10 | .02 |
| ☐ 162 Twins Team | .60 | .28 | .06 |
| ☐ 163 Don Larsen | .35 | .15 | .03 |
| ☐ 164 Bubba Morton | .22 | .10 | .02 |
| ☐ 165 Jim Kaat | 1.50 | .70 | .15 |
| ☐ 166 Johnny Keane MGR | .30 | .12 | .03 |
| ☐ 167 Jim Fregosi | .35 | .15 | .03 |
| ☐ 168 Russ Nixon | .22 | .10 | .02 |
| ☐ 169 Rookie Stars Dick Egan Julio Navarro Tommie Sisk Gaylord Perry | 6.00 | 2.80 | .60 |
| ☐ 170 Joe Adcock | .35 | .15 | .03 |
| ☐ 171 Steve Hamilton | .22 | .10 | .02 |
| ☐ 172 Gene Oliver | .22 | .10 | .02 |
| ☐ 173 Bombers' Best Tom Tresh Mickey Mantle Bobby Richardson | 5.00 | 2.35 | .50 |
| ☐ 174 Larry Burright | .22 | .10 | .02 |
| ☐ 175 Bob Buhl | .22 | .10 | .02 |
| ☐ 176 Jim King | .22 | .10 | .02 |
| ☐ 177 Bubba Phillips | .22 | .10 | .02 |
| ☐ 178 Johnny Edwards | .22 | .10 | .02 |
| ☐ 179 Ron Piche | .22 | .10 | .02 |
| ☐ 180 Bill Skowron | .75 | .35 | .07 |
| ☐ 181 Sammy Esposito | .22 | .10 | .02 |
| ☐ 182 Albie Pearson | .22 | .10 | .02 |
| ☐ 183 Joe Pepitone | .60 | .28 | .06 |
| ☐ 184 Vern Law | .35 | .15 | .03 |
| ☐ 185 Chuck Hiller | .22 | .10 | .02 |

| | MINT | VG-E | F-G |
|---|---|---|---|
| ☐ 186 Jerry Zimmerman | .22 | .10 | .02 |
| ☐ 187 Willie Kirkland | .22 | .10 | .02 |
| ☐ 188 Eddie Bressoud | .22 | .10 | .02 |
| ☐ 189 Dave Giusti | .22 | .10 | .02 |
| ☐ 190 Minnie Minoso | .90 | .40 | .09 |
| ☐ 191 3rd Series Checklist | 1.30 | .35 | .10 |
| ☐ 192 Clay Dalrymple | .22 | .10 | .02 |
| ☐ 193 Andre Rodgers | .22 | .10 | .02 |
| ☐ 194 Joe Nuxhall | .30 | .12 | .03 |
| ☐ 195 Manny Jimenez | .22 | .10 | .02 |
| ☐ 196 Doug Camilli | .22 | .10 | .02 |
| ☐ 197 Roger Craig | .45 | .20 | .04 |
| ☐ 198 Lenny Green | .35 | .15 | .03 |
| ☐ 199 Joe Amalfitano | .35 | .15 | .03 |
| ☐ 200 Mickey Mantle | 45.00 | 20.00 | 4.50 |
| ☐ 201 Cecil Butler | .35 | .15 | .03 |
| ☐ 202 Red Sox Team | .85 | .40 | .08 |
| ☐ 203 Chico Cardenas | .35 | .15 | .03 |
| ☐ 204 Don Nottebart | .35 | .15 | .03 |
| ☐ 205 Luis Aparicio | 3.00 | 1.40 | .30 |
| ☐ 206 Ray Washburn | .35 | .15 | .03 |
| ☐ 207 Ken Hunt | .35 | .15 | .03 |
| ☐ 208 Rookie Stars Ron Herbel John Miller Wally Wolf Ron Taylor | .35 | .15 | .03 |
| ☐ 209 Hobie Landrith | .35 | .15 | .03 |
| ☐ 210 Sandy Koufax | 21.00 | 9.50 | 2.10 |
| ☐ 211 Fred Whitfield | .35 | .15 | .03 |
| ☐ 212 Glen Hobbie | .35 | .15 | .03 |
| ☐ 213 Billy Hitchcock MGR | .35 | .15 | .03 |
| ☐ 214 Orlando Pena | .35 | .15 | .03 |
| ☐ 215 Bob Skinner | .35 | .15 | .03 |
| ☐ 216 Gene Conley | .35 | .15 | .03 |
| ☐ 217 Joe Christopher | .35 | .15 | .03 |
| ☐ 218 Tiger Twirlers Frank Lary Don Mossi Jim Bunning | .65 | .30 | .06 |
| ☐ 219 Chuck Cottier | .45 | .20 | .04 |
| ☐ 220 Camilo Pascual | .45 | .20 | .04 |
| ☐ 221 Cookie Rojas | .35 | .15 | .03 |
| ☐ 222 Cubs Team | .85 | .40 | .08 |
| ☐ 223 Eddie Fisher | .35 | .15 | .03 |
| ☐ 224 Mike Roarke | .35 | .15 | .03 |
| ☐ 225 Joe Jay | .35 | .15 | .03 |
| ☐ 226 Julian Javier | .35 | .15 | .03 |
| ☐ 227 Jim Grant | .35 | .15 | .03 |
| ☐ 228 Rookie Stars Max Alvis Bob Bailey Pedro Oliva Ed Kranepool | 6.00 | 2.80 | .60 |

|  | MINT | VG-E | F-G |
|---|---|---|---|
| ☐ 229 Willie Davis | .60 | .28 | .06 |
| ☐ 230 Pete Runnels | .45 | .20 | .04 |
| ☐ 231 Eli Grba | .45 | .20 | .04 |
| (large photo is Ryne Duren) | | | |
| ☐ 232 Frank Malzone | .45 | .20 | .04 |
| ☐ 233 Casey Stengel | 3.50 | 1.65 | .35 |
| ☐ 234 Dave Nicholson | .35 | .15 | .03 |
| ☐ 235 Bill O'Dell | .35 | .15 | .03 |
| ☐ 236 Bill Bryan | .35 | .15 | .03 |
| ☐ 237 Jim Coates | .35 | .15 | .03 |
| ☐ 238 Lou Johnson | .35 | .15 | .03 |
| ☐ 239 Harvey Haddix | .45 | .20 | .04 |
| ☐ 240 Rocky Colavito | 1.00 | .45 | .10 |
| ☐ 241 Bob Smith | .35 | .15 | .03 |
| ☐ 242 Power Plus | 4.50 | 2.10 | .45 |
| Ernie Banks Hank Aaron | | | |
| ☐ 243 Don Leppert | .35 | .15 | .03 |
| ☐ 244 John Tsitouris | .35 | .15 | .03 |
| ☐ 245 Gil Hodges | 3.00 | 1.40 | .30 |
| ☐ 246 Lee Stange | .35 | .15 | .03 |
| ☐ 247 Yankees Team | 2.75 | 1.25 | .27 |
| ☐ 248 Tito Francona | .45 | .20 | .04 |
| ☐ 249 Leo Burke | .35 | .15 | .03 |
| ☐ 250 Stan Musial | 14.00 | 6.50 | 1.40 |
| ☐ 251 Jack Lamabe | .35 | .15 | .03 |
| ☐ 252 Ron Santo | 1.00 | .45 | .10 |
| ☐ 253 Rookie Stars | .45 | .20 | .04 |
| Len Gabrielson Pete Jernigan John Wojcik Deacon Jones | | | |
| ☐ 254 Mike Hershberger | .35 | .15 | .03 |
| ☐ 255 Bob Shaw | .35 | .15 | .03 |
| ☐ 256 Jerry Lumpe | .35 | .15 | .03 |
| ☐ 257 Hank Aguirre | .35 | .15 | .03 |
| ☐ 258 Al Dark | .60 | .28 | .06 |
| ☐ 259 John Logan | .45 | .20 | .04 |
| ☐ 260 Jim Gentile | .45 | .20 | .04 |
| ☐ 261 Bob Miller | .35 | .15 | .03 |
| ☐ 262 Ellis Burton | .35 | .15 | .03 |
| ☐ 263 Dave Stenhouse | .35 | .15 | .03 |
| ☐ 264 Phil Linz | .35 | .15 | .03 |
| ☐ 265 Vada Pinson | 1.00 | .45 | .10 |
| ☐ 266 Bob Allen | .35 | .15 | .03 |
| ☐ 267 Carl Sawatski | .35 | .15 | .03 |
| ☐ 268 Don Demeter | .35 | .15 | .03 |
| ☐ 269 Don Mincher | .35 | .15 | .03 |
| ☐ 270 Felipe Alou | .55 | .25 | .05 |
| ☐ 271 Dean Stone | .35 | .15 | .03 |
| ☐ 272 Danny Murphy | .35 | .15 | .03 |
| ☐ 273 Sammy Taylor | .35 | .15 | .03 |
| ☐ 274 4th Series Checklist | 1.40 | .35 | .10 |

|  | MINT | VG-E | F-G |
|---|---|---|---|
| ☐ 275 Eddie Mathews | 4.50 | 2.10 | .45 |
| ☐ 276 Barry Shetrone | .35 | .15 | .03 |
| ☐ 277 Dick Farrell | .35 | .15 | .03 |
| ☐ 278 Chico Fernandez | .35 | .15 | .03 |
| ☐ 279 Wally Moon | .45 | .20 | .04 |
| ☐ 280 Bob Rodgers | .35 | .15 | .03 |
| ☐ 281 Tom Sturdivant | .35 | .15 | .03 |
| ☐ 282 Bobby Del Greco | .35 | .15 | .03 |
| ☐ 283 Roy Sievers | .45 | .20 | .04 |
| ☐ 284 Dave Sisler | .35 | .15 | .03 |
| ☐ 285 Dick Stuart | .45 | .20 | .04 |
| ☐ 286 Stu Miller | .35 | .15 | .03 |
| ☐ 287 Dick Bertell | .35 | .15 | .03 |
| ☐ 288 White Sox Team | .85 | .40 | .08 |
| ☐ 289 Hal Brown | .35 | .15 | .03 |
| ☐ 290 Bill White | .45 | .20 | .04 |
| ☐ 291 Don Rudolph | .35 | .15 | .03 |
| ☐ 292 Pumpsie Green | .35 | .15 | .03 |
| ☐ 293 Bill Pleis | .35 | .15 | .03 |
| ☐ 294 Bill Rigney MGR | .35 | .15 | .03 |
| ☐ 295 Ed Roebuck | .35 | .15 | .03 |
| ☐ 296 Doc Edwards | .35 | .15 | .03 |
| ☐ 297 Jim Golden | .35 | .15 | .03 |
| ☐ 298 Don Dillard | .35 | .15 | .03 |
| ☐ 299 Rookie Stars | .35 | .15 | .03 |
| Dave Morehead Bob Dustal Tom Butters Dan Schneider | | | |
| ☐ 300 Willie Mays | 32.00 | 15.00 | 3.20 |
| ☐ 301 Bill Fischer | .35 | .15 | .03 |
| ☐ 302 Whitey Herzog | .75 | .35 | .07 |
| ☐ 303 Earl Francis | .35 | .15 | .03 |
| ☐ 304 Harry Bright | .35 | .15 | .03 |
| ☐ 305 Don Hoak | .35 | .15 | .03 |
| ☐ 306 Star Receivers | .80 | .40 | .08 |
| Earl Battey Elston Howard | | | |
| ☐ 307 Chet Nichols | .35 | .15 | .03 |
| ☐ 308 Camilo Carreon | .35 | .15 | .03 |
| ☐ 309 Jim Brewer | .35 | .15 | .03 |
| ☐ 310 Tommy Davis | .90 | .40 | .09 |
| ☐ 311 Joe McClain | .35 | .15 | .03 |
| ☐ 312 Colts Team | 2.50 | 1.15 | .25 |
| ☐ 313 Ernie Broglio | .35 | .15 | .03 |
| ☐ 314 John Goryl | .35 | .15 | .03 |
| ☐ 315 Ralph Terry | .45 | .20 | .04 |
| ☐ 316 Norm Sherry | .35 | .15 | .03 |
| ☐ 317 Sam McDowell | .55 | .25 | .05 |
| ☐ 318 Gene Mauch | .60 | .28 | .06 |
| ☐ 319 Joe Gaines | .35 | .15 | .03 |
| ☐ 320 Warren Spahn | 6.00 | 2.80 | .60 |
| ☐ 321 Gino Cimoli | .35 | .15 | .03 |
| ☐ 322 Bob Turley | .60 | .28 | .06 |

| | MINT | VG-E | F-G |
|---|---|---|---|
| ☐ 323 Bill Mazeroski | .90 | .40 | .09 |
| ☐ 324 Rookie Stars | .70 | .32 | .07 |
| George Williams | | | |
| Pete Ward | | | |
| Phil Ward | | | |
| Vic Davalillo | | | |
| ☐ 325 Jack Sanford | .35 | .15 | .03 |
| ☐ 326 Hank Foiles | .35 | .15 | .03 |
| ☐ 327 Paul Foytack | .35 | .15 | .03 |
| ☐ 328 Dick Williams | .60 | .28 | .06 |
| ☐ 329 Lindy McDaniel | .35 | .15 | .03 |
| ☐ 330 Chuck Hinton | .35 | .15 | .03 |
| ☐ 331 Series Foes | .45 | .20 | .04 |
| Bill Stafford | | | |
| Bill Pierce | | | |
| ☐ 332 Joel Horlen | .45 | .20 | .04 |
| ☐ 333 Carl Warwick | .35 | .15 | .03 |
| ☐ 334 Wynn Hawkins | .35 | .15 | .03 |
| ☐ 335 Leon Wagner | .35 | .15 | .03 |
| ☐ 336 Ed Bauta | .35 | .15 | .03 |
| ☐ 337 Dodgers Team | 2.00 | .90 | .20 |
| ☐ 338 Russ Kemmerer | .35 | .15 | .03 |
| ☐ 339 Ted Bowsfield | .35 | .15 | .03 |
| ☐ 340 Yogi Berra | 11.00 | 5.25 | 1.10 |
| ☐ 341 Jack Baldschun | .35 | .15 | .03 |
| ☐ 342 Gene Woodling | .45 | .20 | .04 |
| ☐ 343 Johnny Pesky | .45 | .20 | .04 |
| ☐ 344 Don Schwall | .35 | .15 | .03 |
| ☐ 345 Brooks Robinson | 11.00 | 5.25 | 1.10 |
| ☐ 346 Billy Hoeft | .35 | .15 | .03 |
| ☐ 347 Joe Torre | 1.75 | .85 | .17 |
| ☐ 348 Vic Wertz | .45 | .20 | .04 |
| ☐ 349 Zoilo Versailles | .45 | .20 | .04 |
| ☐ 350 Bob Purkey | .35 | .15 | .03 |
| ☐ 351 Al Luplow | .35 | .15 | .03 |
| ☐ 352 Ken Johnson | .35 | .15 | .03 |
| ☐ 353 Billy Williams | 2.50 | 1.15 | .25 |
| ☐ 354 Dom Zanni | .35 | .15 | .03 |
| ☐ 355 Dean Chance | .45 | .20 | .04 |
| ☐ 356 John Schaive | .35 | .15 | .03 |
| ☐ 357 George Altman | .35 | .15 | .03 |
| ☐ 358 Milt Pappas | .45 | .20 | .04 |
| ☐ 359 Haywood Sullivan | .45 | .20 | .04 |
| ☐ 360 Don Drysdale | 5.50 | 2.60 | .55 |
| ☐ 361 Cletis Boyer | .70 | .32 | .07 |
| ☐ 362 5th Series Checklist | 1.50 | .40 | .10 |
| ☐ 363 Dick Radatz | .45 | .20 | .04 |
| ☐ 364 Howie Goss | .35 | .15 | .03 |
| ☐ 365 Jim Bunning | 2.00 | .90 | .20 |
| ☐ 366 Tony Taylor | .35 | .15 | .03 |
| ☐ 367 Tony Cloninger | .35 | .15 | .03 |
| ☐ 368 Ed Bailey | .35 | .15 | .03 |

| | MINT | VG-E | F-G |
|---|---|---|---|
| ☐ 369 Jim Lemon | .35 | .15 | .03 |
| ☐ 370 Dick Donovan | .35 | .15 | .03 |
| ☐ 371 Rod Kanehl | .35 | .15 | .03 |
| ☐ 372 Don Lee | .35 | .15 | .03 |
| ☐ 373 Jim Campbell | .35 | .15 | .03 |
| ☐ 374 Claude Osteen | .45 | .20 | .04 |
| ☐ 375 Ken Boyer | 1.50 | .70 | .15 |
| ☐ 376 John Wyatt | .35 | .15 | .03 |
| ☐ 377 Orioles Team | .85 | .40 | .08 |
| ☐ 378 Bill Henry | .35 | .15 | .03 |
| ☐ 379 Bob Anderson | .35 | .15 | .03 |
| ☐ 380 Ernie Banks | 12.00 | 5.50 | 1.20 |
| ☐ 381 Frank Baumann | .35 | .15 | .03 |
| ☐ 382 Ralph Houk MGR | .65 | .30 | .06 |
| ☐ 383 Pete Richert | .35 | .15 | .03 |
| ☐ 384 Bob Tillman | .35 | .15 | .03 |
| ☐ 385 Art Mahaffey | .35 | .15 | .03 |
| ☐ 386 Rookie Stars | .50 | .22 | .05 |
| Ed Kirkpatrick | | | |
| John Bateman | | | |
| Larry Bearnarth | | | |
| Garry Roggenburk | | | |
| ☐ 387 Al McBean | .35 | .15 | .03 |
| ☐ 388 Jim Davenport | .50 | .22 | .05 |
| ☐ 389 Frank Sullivan | .35 | .15 | .03 |
| ☐ 390 Hank Aaron | 32.00 | 15.00 | 3.20 |
| ☐ 391 B. Dailey | .35 | .15 | .03 |
| ☐ 392 Tribe Thumpers | .45 | .20 | .04 |
| Johnny Romano | | | |
| Tito Francona | | | |
| ☐ 393 Ken MacKenzie | .35 | .15 | .03 |
| ☐ 394 Tim McCarver | .75 | .35 | .07 |
| ☐ 395 Don McMahon | .35 | .15 | .03 |
| ☐ 396 Joe Koppe | .35 | .15 | .03 |
| ☐ 397 K.C. Athletics Team | .70 | .32 | .07 |
| ☐ 398 Boog Powell | 1.75 | .85 | .17 |
| ☐ 399 Dick Ellsworth | .35 | .15 | .03 |
| ☐ 400 Frank Robinson | 12.00 | 5.50 | 1.20 |
| ☐ 401 Jim Bouton | 1.40 | .70 | .14 |
| ☐ 402 Mickey Vernon | .45 | .20 | .04 |
| ☐ 403 Ron Perranoski | .45 | .20 | .04 |
| ☐ 404 Bob Oldis | .35 | .15 | .03 |
| ☐ 405 Floyd Robinson | .35 | .15 | .03 |
| ☐ 406 Howie Koplitz | .35 | .15 | .03 |
| ☐ 407 Rookie Stars | .35 | .15 | .03 |
| Frank Kostro | | | |
| Chico Ruiz | | | |
| Larry Elliot | | | |
| Dick Simpson | | | |
| ☐ 408 Billy Gardner | .45 | .20 | .04 |
| ☐ 409 Roy Face | .65 | .30 | .06 |
| ☐ 410 Earl Battey | .35 | .15 | .03 |

| | MINT | VG-E | F-G | | | MINT | VG-E | F-G |
|---|---|---|---|---|---|---|---|---|
| ☐ 411 Jim Constable | .35 | .15 | .03 | ☐ 457 Tex Clevenger | 2.00 | .90 | .20 |
| ☐ 412 Dodger Big Three | 6.00 | 2.80 | .60 | ☐ 458 Al Lopez | 4.00 | 1.85 | .40 |
|    Johnny Podres | | | | ☐ 459 Dick Lemay | 2.00 | .90 | .20 |
|    Don Drysdale | | | | ☐ 460 Del Crandall | 2.50 | 1.15 | .25 |
|    Sandy Koufax | | | | ☐ 461 Norm Bass | 2.00 | .90 | .20 |
| ☐ 413 Jerry Walker | .35 | .15 | .03 | ☐ 462 Wally Post | 2.00 | .90 | .20 |
| ☐ 414 Ty Cline | .35 | .15 | .03 | ☐ 463 Joe Schaffernoth | 2.00 | .90 | .20 |
| ☐ 415 Bob Gibson | 11.00 | 5.25 | 1.10 | ☐ 464 Ken Aspromonte | 2.00 | .90 | .20 |
| ☐ 416 Alex Grammas | .35 | .15 | .03 | ☐ 465 Chuck Estrada | 2.25 | 1.00 | .22 |
| ☐ 417 Giants Team | .90 | .40 | .09 | ☐ 466 Rookie Stars | 3.50 | 1.65 | .35 |
| ☐ 418 John Orsino | .35 | .15 | .03 |    Nate Oliver | | | |
| ☐ 419 Tracy Stallard | .35 | .15 | .03 |    Tony Martinez | | | |
| ☐ 420 Bobby Richardson | 1.75 | .85 | .17 |    Bill Freehan | | | |
| ☐ 421 Tom Morgan | .35 | .15 | .03 |    Jerry Robinson | | | |
| ☐ 422 Fred Hutchinson | .50 | .22 | .05 | ☐ 467 Phil Ortega | 2.00 | .90 | .20 |
| ☐ 423 Ed Hobaugh | .35 | .15 | .03 | ☐ 468 Carroll Hardy | 2.00 | .90 | .20 |
| ☐ 424 Charley Smith | .35 | .15 | .03 | ☐ 469 Jay Hook | 2.00 | .90 | .20 |
| ☐ 425 Smokey Burgess | .45 | .20 | .04 | ☐ 470 Tom Tresh | 10.00 | 4.75 | 1.00 |
| ☐ 426 Barry Latman | .35 | .15 | .03 | ☐ 471 Ken Retzer | 2.00 | .90 | .20 |
| ☐ 427 Bernie Allen | .35 | .15 | .03 | ☐ 472 Lou Brock | 45.00 | 18.00 | 4.00 |
| ☐ 428 Carl Boles | .35 | .15 | .03 | ☐ 473 Mets Team | 5.00 | 2.35 | .50 |
| ☐ 429 Lou Burdette | .90 | .40 | .09 | ☐ 474 Jack Fisher | 2.00 | .90 | .20 |
| ☐ 430 Norm Siebern | .35 | .15 | .03 | ☐ 475 Gus Triandos | 2.25 | 1.00 | .22 |
| ☐ 431 A Checklist 6 | 1.50 | .40 | .10 | ☐ 476 Frank Funk | 2.00 | .90 | .20 |
|    (white on red) | | | | ☐ 477 Donn Clendenon | 2.25 | 1.00 | .22 |
| ☐ 431 B Checklist 6 | 2.25 | .50 | .10 | ☐ 478 Paul Brown | 2.00 | .90 | .20 |
|    (black on orange) | | | | ☐ 479 Ed Brinkman | 2.00 | .90 | .20 |
| ☐ 432 Roman Mejias | .35 | .15 | .03 | ☐ 480 Bill Monbouquette | 2.00 | .90 | .20 |
| ☐ 433 Denis Menke | .35 | .15 | .03 | ☐ 481 Bill Taylor | 2.00 | .90 | .20 |
| ☐ 434 John Callison | .45 | .20 | .04 | ☐ 482 Frank Torre | 2.00 | .90 | .20 |
| ☐ 435 Woody Held | .35 | .15 | .03 | ☐ 483 Jim Owens | 2.00 | .90 | .20 |
| ☐ 436 Tim Harkness | .35 | .15 | .03 | ☐ 484 Dale Long | 2.00 | .90 | .20 |
| ☐ 437 Bill Bruton | .35 | .15 | .03 | ☐ 485 Jim Landis | 2.00 | .90 | .20 |
| ☐ 438 Wes Stock | .45 | .20 | .04 | ☐ 486 Ray Sadecki | 2.00 | .90 | .20 |
| ☐ 439 Don Zimmer | .55 | .25 | .05 | ☐ 487 John Roseboro | 2.25 | 1.00 | .22 |
| ☐ 440 Juan Marichal | 5.00 | 2.35 | .50 | ☐ 488 Jerry Adair | 2.00 | .90 | .20 |
| ☐ 441 Lee Thomas | .35 | .15 | .03 | ☐ 489 Paul Toth | 2.00 | .90 | .20 |
| ☐ 442 J.C. Hartman | .35 | .15 | .03 | ☐ 490 Willie McCovey | 27.00 | 12.00 | 2.70 |
| ☐ 443 Jim Piersall | .85 | .40 | .08 | ☐ 491 Harry Craft | 2.00 | .90 | .20 |
| ☐ 444 Jim Maloney | .70 | .32 | .07 | ☐ 492 Dave Wickersham | 2.00 | .90 | .20 |
| ☐ 445 Norm Cash | 1.50 | .70 | .15 | ☐ 493 Walt Bond | 2.00 | .90 | .20 |
| ☐ 446 Whitey Ford | 9.00 | 4.25 | .90 | ☐ 494 Phil Regan | 2.00 | .90 | .20 |
| ☐ 447 Felix Mantilla | 2.00 | .90 | .20 | ☐ 495 Frank Thomas | 2.00 | .90 | .20 |
| ☐ 448 Jack Kralick | 2.00 | .90 | .20 | ☐ 496 Rookie Stars | 2.00 | .90 | .20 |
| ☐ 449 Jose Tartabull | 2.00 | .90 | .20 |    Steve Dalkowski | | | |
| ☐ 450 Bob Friend | 2.25 | 1.00 | .22 |    Fred Newman | | | |
| ☐ 451 Indians Team | 3.50 | 1.65 | .35 |    Jack Smith | | | |
| ☐ 452 Buddy Schultz | 2.00 | .90 | .20 |    Carl Bouldin | | | |
| ☐ 453 Jake Wood | 2.00 | .90 | .20 | ☐ 497 Bennie Daniels | 2.00 | .90 | .20 |
| ☐ 454 Art Fowler | 2.00 | .90 | .20 | ☐ 498 Ed Kasko | 2.00 | .90 | .20 |
| ☐ 455 Ruben Amaro | 2.00 | .90 | .20 | ☐ 499 J.C. Martin | 2.00 | .90 | .20 |
| ☐ 456 Jim Coker | 2.00 | .90 | .20 | ☐ 500 Harmon Killebrew | 20.00 | 9.00 | 2.00 |

| | MINT | VG-E | F-G |
|---|---|---|---|
| ☐ 501 Joe Azcue | 2.00 | .90 | .20 |
| ☐ 502 Daryl Spencer | 2.00 | .90 | .20 |
| ☐ 503 Braves Team | 3.50 | 1.65 | .35 |
| ☐ 504 B. Johnson | 2.00 | .90 | .20 |
| ☐ 505 Curt Flood | 5.00 | 2.35 | .50 |
| ☐ 506 Gene Green | 2.00 | .90 | .20 |
| ☐ 507 Rollie Sheldon | 1.60 | .80 | .16 |
| ☐ 508 Ted Savage | 1.60 | .80 | .16 |
| ☐ 509 7th Series Checklist | 4.50 | 1.00 | .25 |
| ☐ 510 Ken McBride | 1.60 | .80 | .16 |
| ☐ 511 Charlie Neal | 1.80 | .90 | .18 |
| ☐ 512 Cal McLish | 1.60 | .80 | .16 |
| ☐ 513 Gary Geiger | 1.60 | .80 | .16 |
| ☐ 514 Larry Osborne | 1.60 | .80 | .16 |
| ☐ 515 Don Elston | 1.60 | .80 | .16 |
| ☐ 516 Purnell Goldy | 1.60 | .80 | .16 |
| ☐ 517 Hal Woodeshick | 1.60 | .80 | .16 |
| ☐ 518 Don Blasingame | 1.60 | .80 | .16 |
| ☐ 519 Claude Raymond | 1.60 | .80 | .16 |
| ☐ 520 Orlando Cepeda | 5.00 | 2.35 | .50 |
| ☐ 521 Dan Pfister | 1.60 | .80 | .16 |
| ☐ 522 Rookie Stars | 2.00 | .90 | .20 |
| Mel Nelson | | | |
| Gary Peters | | | |
| Jim Roland | | | |
| Art Quirk | | | |
| ☐ 523 Bill Kunkel | 1.60 | .80 | .16 |
| ☐ 524 Cards Team | 3.50 | 1.65 | .35 |
| ☐ 525 Nellie Fox | 3.50 | 1.65 | .35 |
| ☐ 526 Dick Hall | 1.60 | .80 | .16 |
| ☐ 527 Ed Sadowski | 1.60 | .80 | .16 |
| ☐ 528 Carl Willey | 1.60 | .80 | .16 |
| ☐ 529 Wes Covington | 1.60 | .80 | .16 |
| ☐ 530 Don Mossi | 1.80 | .90 | .18 |
| ☐ 531 Sam Mele | 1.60 | .80 | .16 |
| ☐ 532 Steve Boros | 1.80 | .90 | .18 |
| ☐ 533 Bobby Shantz | 2.00 | .90 | .20 |
| ☐ 534 Ken Walters | 1.60 | .80 | .16 |
| ☐ 535 Jim Perry | 2.00 | .90 | .20 |
| ☐ 536 Norm Larker | 1.60 | .80 | .16 |
| ☐ 537 Rookie Stars | 450.00 | 175.00 | 35.00 |
| Pedro Gonzales | | | |
| Ken McMullen | | | |
| Al Weis | | | |
| Pete Rose | | | |
| ☐ 538 George Brunet | 1.60 | .80 | .16 |
| ☐ 539 Wayne Causey | 1.60 | .80 | .16 |
| ☐ 540 Bob Clemente | 45.00 | 20.00 | 4.50 |
| ☐ 541 Ron Moeller | 1.60 | .80 | .16 |
| ☐ 542 Lou Klimchock | 1.60 | .80 | .16 |
| ☐ 543 Russ Snyder | 1.60 | .80 | .16 |

| | MINT | VG-E | F-G |
|---|---|---|---|
| ☐ 544 Rookie Stars | 10.00 | 4.75 | 1.00 |
| Duke Carmel | | | |
| Bill Haas | | | |
| Rusty Staub | | | |
| Dick Phillips | | | |
| ☐ 545 Jose Pagan | 1.60 | .80 | .16 |
| ☐ 546 Hal Reniff | 1.60 | .80 | .16 |
| ☐ 547 Gus Bell | 1.80 | .90 | .18 |
| ☐ 548 Tom Satriano | 1.60 | .80 | .16 |
| ☐ 549 Rookie Stars | 1.60 | .80 | .16 |
| Marcelino Lopez | | | |
| Pete Lovrich | | | |
| Paul Ratliff | | | |
| Elmo Plaskett | | | |
| ☐ 550 Duke Snider | 21.00 | 9.50 | 2.10 |
| ☐ 551 B. Klaus | 1.60 | .80 | .16 |
| ☐ 552 Tigers Team | 4.50 | 2.10 | .45 |
| ☐ 553 Rookie Stars | 45.00 | 18.00 | 4.00 |
| Brock Davis | | | |
| Jim Gosger | | | |
| Willie Stargell | | | |
| John Hermstein | | | |
| ☐ 554 Hank Fischer | 1.60 | .80 | .16 |
| ☐ 555 John Blanchard | 1.60 | .80 | .16 |
| ☐ 556 Al Worthington | 1.60 | .80 | .16 |
| ☐ 557 Cuno Barragan | 1.60 | .80 | .16 |
| ☐ 558 Rookie Stars | 1.60 | .80 | .16 |
| Bill Faul | | | |
| Ron Hunt | | | |
| Al Moran | | | |
| Bob Lipski | | | |
| ☐ 559 Danny Murtaugh | 1.60 | .80 | .16 |
| ☐ 560 Ray Herbert | 1.60 | .80 | .16 |
| ☐ 561 Mike De La Hoz | 1.60 | .80 | .16 |
| ☐ 562 Rookie Stars | 3.00 | 1.40 | .30 |
| Randy Cardinal | | | |
| Dave McNally | | | |
| Ken Rowe | | | |
| Don Rowe | | | |
| ☐ 563 Mike McCormick | 2.00 | .90 | .20 |
| ☐ 564 George Banks | 1.60 | .80 | .16 |
| ☐ 565 Larry Sherry | 2.00 | .90 | .20 |
| ☐ 566 Cliff Cook | 1.60 | .80 | .16 |
| ☐ 567 Jim Duffalo | 1.60 | .80 | .16 |
| ☐ 568 Bob Sadowski | 1.60 | .80 | .16 |
| ☐ 569 Luis Arroyo | 1.80 | .90 | .18 |
| ☐ 570 Frank Bolling | 1.60 | .80 | .16 |
| ☐ 571 John Klippstein | 1.60 | .80 | .16 |
| ☐ 572 Jack Spring | 1.60 | .80 | .16 |
| ☐ 573 Coot Veal | 1.60 | .80 | .16 |
| ☐ 574 Hal Kolstad | 1.60 | .80 | .16 |
| ☐ 575 Don Cardwell | 1.60 | .80 | .16 |
| ☐ 576 Johnny Temple | 2.50 | 1.15 | .25 |

**1964 TOPPS**

WARREN SPAHN

The cards in this 587 card set measure
2½" by 3½". Players in the 1964 Topps
baseball series were easy to sort by team
due to the giant block lettering found at the
top of each card. The name and position of
the player are found underneath the picture and the card is numbered in a ball
design on the orange-colored back. The
usual last series scarcity holds for this set
(523 to 587).

Complete Set: M-525.00; VG-E-225.00; F-G-50.00

|  | MINT | VG-E | F-G |
|---|---|---|---|
| Common Player (1–370) | .24 | .10 | .02 |
| Common Player (371–522) | .36 | .15 | .03 |
| Common Player (523–587) | .85 | .40 | .08 |
| ☐ 1 NL ERA Leaders | 2.25 | .65 | .15 |
| Sandy Koufax | | | |
| Dick Ellsworth | | | |
| Bob Friend | | | |
| ☐ 2 AL ERA Leaders | .75 | .35 | .07 |
| Gary Peters | | | |
| Juan Pizarro | | | |
| Camilo Pascual | | | |
| ☐ 3 NL Pitching Leaders | 1.75 | .85 | .17 |
| Sandy Koufax | | | |
| Juan Marichal | | | |
| Warren Spahn | | | |
| Jim Maloney | | | |
| ☐ 4 AL Pitching Leaders | 1.25 | .60 | .12 |
| Whitey Ford | | | |
| Camilo Pascual | | | |
| Jim Bouton | | | |

| | | MINT | VG-E | F-G |
|---|---|---|---|---|
| ☐ 5 | NL Strikeout Leaders | 1.75 | .85 | .17 |
| | Sandy Koufax | | | |
| | Jim Maloney | | | |
| | Don Drysdale | | | |
| ☐ 6 | AL Strikeout Leaders | .75 | .35 | .07 |
| | Camilo Pascual | | | |
| | Jim Bunning | | | |
| | Dick Stigman | | | |
| ☐ 7 | NL Batting Leaders | 1.25 | .60 | .12 |
| | Tommy Davis | | | |
| | Bob Clemente | | | |
| | Dick Groat | | | |
| | Hank Aaron | | | |
| ☐ 8 | AL Batting Leaders | 1.75 | .85 | .17 |
| | Carl Yastrzemski | | | |
| | Al Kaline | | | |
| | Rich Rollins | | | |
| ☐ 9 | NL Home Run Leaders | 2.25 | 1.00 | .22 |
| | Hank Aaron | | | |
| | Willie McCovey | | | |
| | Willie Mays | | | |
| | Orlando Cepeda | | | |
| ☐ 10 | AL Home Run Leaders | .90 | .40 | .09 |
| | Harmon Killebrew | | | |
| | Dick Stuart | | | |
| | Bob Allison | | | |
| ☐ 11 | NL RBI Leaders | .90 | .40 | .09 |
| | Hank Aaron | | | |
| | Ken Boyer | | | |
| | Bill White | | | |
| ☐ 12 | AL RBI Leaders | .90 | .40 | .09 |
| | Dick Stuart | | | |
| | Al Kaline | | | |
| | Harmon Killebrew | | | |
| ☐ 13 | Hoyt Wilhelm | 2.25 | 1.00 | .22 |
| ☐ 14 | Dodgers Rookies: | .24 | .10 | .02 |
| | Dick Nen | | | |
| | Nick Willhite | | | |
| ☐ 15 | Zoilo Versalles | .24 | .10 | .02 |
| ☐ 16 | John Boozer | .24 | .10 | .02 |
| ☐ 17 | Willie Kirkland | .24 | .10 | .02 |
| ☐ 18 | Billy O'Dell | .24 | .10 | .02 |
| ☐ 19 | Don Wert | .24 | .10 | .02 |
| ☐ 20 | Bob Friend | .35 | .15 | .03 |
| ☐ 21 | Yogi Berra | 6.50 | 3.00 | .65 |
| ☐ 22 | Jerry Adair | .24 | .10 | .02 |
| ☐ 23 | Chris Zachary | .24 | .10 | .02 |
| ☐ 24 | Carl Sawatski | .24 | .10 | .02 |
| ☐ 25 | Bill Monbouquette | .24 | .10 | .02 |
| ☐ 26 | Gino Cimoli | .24 | .10 | .02 |
| ☐ 27 | Mets Team | .85 | .40 | .08 |
| ☐ 28 | Claude Osteen | .35 | .15 | .03 |
| ☐ 29 | Lou Brock | 10.00 | 4.75 | 1.00 |

| | MINT | VG-E | F-G |
|---|---|---|---|
| ☐ 30 Ron Perranoski | .35 | .15 | .03 |
| ☐ 31 Dave Nicholson | .24 | .10 | .02 |
| ☐ 32 Dean Chance | .35 | .15 | .03 |
| ☐ 33 Reds Rookies: | .24 | .10 | .02 |
|   Sammy Ellis | | | |
|   Mel Queen | | | |
| ☐ 34 Jim Perry | .35 | .15 | .03 |
| ☐ 35 Ed Mathews | 3.00 | 1.40 | .30 |
| ☐ 36 Hal Reniff | .24 | .10 | .02 |
| ☐ 37 Smokey Burgess | .35 | .15 | .03 |
| ☐ 38 Jim Wynn | .60 | .28 | .06 |
| ☐ 39 Hank Aguirre | .24 | .10 | .02 |
| ☐ 40 Dick Groat | .60 | .28 | .06 |
| ☐ 41 Friendly Foes | 1.00 | .45 | .10 |
|   Willie McCovey | | | |
|   Leon Wagner | | | |
| ☐ 42 Moe Drabowski | .24 | .10 | .02 |
| ☐ 43 Roy Sievers | .35 | .15 | .03 |
| ☐ 44 Duke Carmel | .24 | .10 | .02 |
| ☐ 45 Milt Pappas | .35 | .15 | .03 |
| ☐ 46 Ed Brinkman | .24 | .10 | .02 |
| ☐ 47 Giants Rookies: | .35 | .15 | .03 |
|   Jesus Alou | | | |
|   Ron Herbel | | | |
| ☐ 48 Bob Perry | .24 | .10 | .02 |
| ☐ 49 Bill Henry | .24 | .10 | .02 |
| ☐ 50 Mickey Mantle | 36.00 | 15.00 | 3.50 |
| ☐ 51 Pete Richert | .24 | .10 | .02 |
| ☐ 52 Chuck Hinton | .24 | .10 | .02 |
| ☐ 53 Denis Menke | .24 | .10 | .02 |
| ☐ 54 Sam Mele | .24 | .10 | .02 |
| ☐ 55 Ernie Banks | 4.50 | 2.10 | .45 |
| ☐ 56 Hal Brown | .24 | .10 | .02 |
| ☐ 57 Tim Harkness | .24 | .10 | .02 |
| ☐ 58 Don Demeter | .24 | .10 | .02 |
| ☐ 59 Ernie Broglio | .24 | .10 | .02 |
| ☐ 60 Frank Malzone | .35 | .15 | .03 |
| ☐ 61 Angel Backstops | .35 | .15 | .03 |
|   Bob Rodgers | | | |
|   Ed Sadowski | | | |
| ☐ 62 Ted Savage | .24 | .10 | .02 |
| ☐ 63 Johnny Orsino | .24 | .10 | .02 |
| ☐ 64 Ted Abernathy | .24 | .10 | .02 |
| ☐ 65 Felipe Alou | .35 | .15 | .03 |
| ☐ 66 Eddie Fisher | .24 | .10 | .02 |
| ☐ 67 Tigers Team | .65 | .30 | .06 |
| ☐ 68 Willie Davis | .55 | .25 | .05 |
| ☐ 69 Clete Boyer | .35 | .15 | .03 |
| ☐ 70 Joe Torre | .90 | .40 | .09 |
| ☐ 71 Jack Spring | .24 | .10 | .02 |
| ☐ 72 Chico Cardenas | .24 | .10 | .02 |
| ☐ 73 Jimmie Hall | .24 | .10 | .02 |
| ☐ 74 Pirates Rookies: | .24 | .10 | .02 |
|   Bob Priddy | | | |
|   Tom Butters | | | |
| ☐ 75 Wayne Causey | .24 | .10 | .02 |
| ☐ 76 1st Series Checklist | 1.25 | .35 | .10 |
| ☐ 77 Jerry Walker | .24 | .10 | .02 |
| ☐ 78 Merritt Ranew | .24 | .10 | .02 |
| ☐ 79 Bob Heffner | .24 | .10 | .02 |
| ☐ 80 Vada Pinson | .90 | .40 | .09 |
| ☐ 81 All-Star Vets | 2.25 | 1.00 | .22 |
|   Nellie Fox | | | |
|   Harmon Killebrew | | | |
| ☐ 82 Jim Davenport | .35 | .15 | .03 |
| ☐ 83 Gus Triandos | .35 | .15 | .03 |
| ☐ 84 Carl Willey | .24 | .10 | .02 |
| ☐ 85 Pete Ward | .24 | .10 | .02 |
| ☐ 86 Al Downing | .35 | .15 | .03 |
| ☐ 87 Cardinals Team | .65 | .30 | .06 |
| ☐ 88 John Roseboro | .35 | .15 | .03 |
| ☐ 89 Boog Powell | .90 | .40 | .09 |
| ☐ 90 Earl Battey | .35 | .15 | .03 |
| ☐ 91 Bob Bailey | .24 | .10 | .02 |
| ☐ 92 Steve Ridzik | .24 | .10 | .02 |
| ☐ 93 Gary Geiger | .24 | .10 | .02 |
| ☐ 94 Braves Rookies: | .24 | .10 | .02 |
|   Jim Britton | | | |
|   Larry Maxie | | | |
| ☐ 95 George Altman | .24 | .10 | .02 |
| ☐ 96 Bob Buhl | .24 | .10 | .02 |
| ☐ 97 Jim Fregosi | .35 | .15 | .03 |
| ☐ 98 Bill Bruton | .24 | .10 | .02 |
| ☐ 99 Al Stanek | .24 | .10 | .02 |
| ☐ 100 Elston Howard | 1.25 | .60 | .12 |
| ☐ 101 Walt Alston MGR | .90 | .40 | .09 |
| ☐ 102 2nd Series Checklist | 1.20 | .30 | .08 |
| ☐ 103 Curt Flood | .75 | .35 | .07 |
| ☐ 104 Art Mahaffey | .24 | .10 | .02 |
| ☐ 105 Woody Held | .24 | .10 | .02 |
| ☐ 106 Joe Nuxhall | .35 | .15 | .03 |
| ☐ 107 White Sox Rookies | .24 | .10 | .02 |
|   Bruce Howard | | | |
|   Frank Kreutzer | | | |
| ☐ 108 John Wyatt | .24 | .10 | .02 |
| ☐ 109 Rusty Staub | 1.75 | .85 | .17 |
| ☐ 110 Albie Pearson | .24 | .10 | .02 |
| ☐ 111 Don Elston | .24 | .10 | .02 |
| ☐ 112 Bob Tillman | .24 | .10 | .02 |
| ☐ 113 Grover Powell | .24 | .10 | .02 |
| ☐ 114 Don Lock | .24 | .10 | .02 |
| ☐ 115 Frank Bolling | .24 | .10 | .02 |
| ☐ 116 Twins Rookies: | 2.50 | 1.15 | .25 |

| | MINT | VG-E | F-G | | | MINT | VG-E | F-G |
|---|---|---|---|---|---|---|---|---|
| ☐ 117 Earl Francis | .24 | .10 | .02 | ☐ 159 Charlie Dees | .24 | .10 | .02 |
| ☐ 118 John Blanchard | .24 | .10 | .02 | ☐ 160 Ken Boyer | 1.75 | .85 | .17 |
| ☐ 119 Gary Kolb | .24 | .10 | .02 | ☐ 161 Dave McNally | .65 | .30 | .06 |
| ☐ 120 Don Drysdale | 4.00 | 1.85 | .40 | ☐ 162 Hitting Area | .35 | .15 | .03 |
| ☐ 121 Pete Runnels | .35 | .15 | .03 | Dick Sisler | | | |
| ☐ 122 Don McMahon | .24 | .10 | .02 | Vada Pinson | | | |
| ☐ 123 Jose Pagan | .24 | .10 | .02 | ☐ 163 Donn Clendenon | .35 | .15 | .03 |
| ☐ 124 Orlando Pena | .24 | .10 | .02 | ☐ 164 Bud Daley | .24 | .10 | .02 |
| ☐ 125 Pete Rose | 100.00 | 45.00 | 10.00 | ☐ 165 Jerry Lumpe | .24 | .10 | .02 |
| ☐ 126 Russ Snyder | .24 | .10 | .02 | ☐ 166 Marty Keough | .24 | .10 | .02 |
| ☐ 127 Angels Rookies: | .24 | .10 | .02 | ☐ 167 Rookies (Senators) | 4.50 | 2.10 | .45 |
| Aubrey Gatewood | | | | Mike Brumley | | | |
| Dick Simpson | | | | Lou Piniella | | | |
| ☐ 128 Mickey Lolich | 2.50 | 1.15 | .25 | ☐ 168 Al Weis | .24 | .10 | .02 |
| ☐ 129 Amado Samuel | .24 | .10 | .02 | ☐ 169 Del Crandall | .35 | .15 | .03 |
| ☐ 130 Gary Peters | .35 | .15 | .03 | ☐ 170 Dick Radatz | .35 | .15 | .03 |
| ☐ 131 Steve Boros | .35 | .15 | .03 | ☐ 171 Ty Cline | .24 | .10 | .02 |
| ☐ 132 Braves Team | .65 | .30 | .06 | ☐ 172 Indians Team | .65 | .30 | .06 |
| ☐ 133 Jim Grant | .24 | .10 | .02 | ☐ 173 Ryne Duren | .35 | .15 | .03 |
| ☐ 134 Don Zimmer | .55 | .25 | .05 | ☐ 174 Doc Edwards | .24 | .10 | .02 |
| ☐ 135 Johnny Callison | .35 | .15 | .03 | ☐ 175 Billy Williams | 2.00 | .90 | .20 |
| WORLD SERIES | | | | ☐ 176 Tracy Stallard | .24 | .10 | .02 |
| CARDS (136–140) | | | | ☐ 177 Harmon Killebrew | 3.75 | 1.75 | .37 |
| ☐ 136 World Series Game 1 | 2.50 | 1.15 | .25 | ☐ 178 Hank Bauer | .35 | .15 | .03 |
| Koufax strikes out 15 | | | | ☐ 179 Carl Warwick | .24 | .10 | .02 |
| ☐ 137 World Series Game 2 | 1.25 | .60 | .12 | ☐ 180 Tommy Davis | .60 | .28 | .06 |
| Davis sparks rally | | | | ☐ 181 Dave Wickersham | .24 | .10 | .02 |
| ☐ 138 World Series Game 3 | 1.25 | .60 | .12 | ☐ 182 Sox Sockers | 2.50 | 1.15 | .25 |
| LA 3 straight | | | | Carl Yastrzemski | | | |
| ☐ 139 World Series Game 4 | 1.25 | .60 | .12 | Chuck Schilling | | | |
| Sealing Yanks doom | | | | ☐ 183 Ron Taylor | .24 | .10 | .02 |
| ☐ 140 World Series Summary | 1.25 | .60 | .12 | ☐ 184 Al Luplow | .24 | .10 | .02 |
| Dodgers celebrate | | | | ☐ 185 Jim O'Toole | .24 | .10 | .02 |
| ☐ 141 Danny Murtaugh MGR | .24 | .10 | .02 | ☐ 186 Roman Mejias | .24 | .10 | .02 |
| ☐ 142 John Bateman | .24 | .10 | .02 | ☐ 187 Ed Roebuck | .24 | .10 | .02 |
| ☐ 143 Bubba Phillips | .24 | .10 | .02 | ☐ 188 3rd Series Checklist | 1.30 | .35 | .08 |
| ☐ 144 Al Worthington | .24 | .10 | .02 | ☐ 189 Bob Hendley | .24 | .10 | .02 |
| ☐ 145 Norm Siebern | .24 | .10 | .02 | ☐ 190 Bob Richardson | 1.00 | .45 | .10 |
| ☐ 146 Indians Rookies | 9.00 | 4.25 | .90 | ☐ 191 Clay Darymple | .24 | .10 | .02 |
| Tommy John | | | | ☐ 192 Cubs Rookies: | .24 | .10 | .02 |
| Bob Chance | | | | John Boccabella | | | |
| ☐ 147 Ray Sadecki | .24 | .10 | .02 | Billy Cowan | | | |
| ☐ 148 J.C. Martin | .24 | .10 | .02 | ☐ 193 Jerry Lynch | .24 | .10 | .02 |
| ☐ 149 Paul Foytack | .24 | .10 | .02 | ☐ 194 John Goryl | .24 | .10 | .02 |
| ☐ 150 Willie Mays | 21.00 | 9.50 | 2.10 | ☐ 195 Floyd Robinson | .24 | .10 | .02 |
| ☐ 151 Athletics Team | .60 | .28 | .06 | ☐ 196 Jim Gentile | .35 | .15 | .03 |
| ☐ 152 Denver LeMaster | .24 | .10 | .02 | ☐ 197 Frank Lary | .35 | .15 | .03 |
| ☐ 153 Dick Williams | .35 | .15 | .03 | ☐ 198 Len Gabrielson | .24 | .10 | .02 |
| ☐ 154 Dick Tracewski | .24 | .10 | .02 | ☐ 199 Joe Azcue | .24 | .10 | .02 |
| ☐ 155 Duke Snider | 5.50 | 2.60 | .55 | ☐ 200 Sandy Koufax | 13.00 | 6.00 | 1.30 |
| ☐ 156 Bill Dailey | .24 | .10 | .02 | ☐ 201 Orioles Rookies: | .35 | .15 | .03 |
| ☐ 157 Gene Mauch | .35 | .15 | .03 | Sam Bowens | | | |
| ☐ 158 Ken Johnson | .24 | .10 | .02 | Wally Bunker | | | |

| | MINT | VG-E | F-G | | MINT | VG-E | F-G |
|---|---|---|---|---|---|---|---|
| ☐ 202 Galen Cisco | .24 | .10 | .02 | ☐ 248 Johnny Pesky | .35 | .15 | .03 |
| ☐ 203 John Kennedy | .24 | .10 | .02 | ☐ 249 Doug Camilli | .24 | .10 | .02 |
| ☐ 204 Matty Alou | .35 | .15 | .03 | ☐ 250 Al Kaline | 5.00 | 2.35 | .50 |
| ☐ 205 Nellie Fox | 1.25 | .60 | .12 | ☐ 251 Choo Choo Coleman | .24 | .10 | .02 |
| ☐ 206 Steve Hamilton | .24 | .10 | .02 | ☐ 252 Ken Aspromonte | .24 | .10 | .02 |
| ☐ 207 Fred Hutchinson | .35 | .15 | .03 | ☐ 253 Wally Post | .24 | .10 | .02 |
| ☐ 208 Wes Covington | .24 | .10 | .02 | ☐ 254 Don Hoak | .24 | .10 | .02 |
| ☐ 209 Bob Allen | .24 | .10 | .02 | ☐ 255 Lee Thomas | .24 | .10 | .02 |
| ☐ 210 Carl Yastrzemski | 27.00 | 12.00 | 2.70 | ☐ 256 Johnny Weekly | .24 | .10 | .02 |
| ☐ 211 Jim Coker | .24 | .10 | .02 | ☐ 257 Giants Team | .60 | .28 | .06 |
| ☐ 212 Pete Lovrich | .24 | .10 | .02 | ☐ 258 Garry Roggenburk | .24 | .10 | .02 |
| ☐ 213 Angels Team | .60 | .28 | .06 | ☐ 259 Harry Bright | .24 | .10 | .02 |
| ☐ 214 Ken McMullen | .35 | .15 | .03 | ☐ 260 Frank Robinson | 4.50 | 2.10 | .45 |
| ☐ 215 Ray Herbert | .24 | .10 | .02 | ☐ 261 Jim Hannan | .24 | .10 | .02 |
| ☐ 216 Mike De La Hoz | .24 | .10 | .02 | ☐ 262 Cards Rookies | .80 | .40 | .08 |
| ☐ 217 Jim King | .24 | .10 | .02 | Mike Shannon | | | |
| ☐ 218 Hank Fischer | .24 | .10 | .02 | Harry Fanok | | | |
| ☐ 219 Young Aces | .35 | .15 | .03 | ☐ 263 Chuck Estrada | .35 | .15 | .03 |
| Al Downing | | | | ☐ 264 Jim Landis | .24 | .10 | .02 |
| Jim Bouton | | | | ☐ 265 Jim Bunning | 1.25 | .60 | .12 |
| ☐ 220 Dick Ellsworth | .35 | .15 | .03 | ☐ 266 Gene Freese | .24 | .10 | .02 |
| ☐ 221 Bob Saverine | .24 | .10 | .02 | ☐ 267 Wilbur Wood | .50 | .22 | .05 |
| ☐ 222 Billy Pierce | .60 | .28 | .06 | ☐ 268 Bill's Got It | .35 | .15 | .03 |
| ☐ 223 George Banks | .24 | .10 | .02 | Danny Murtaugh | | | |
| ☐ 224 Tommie Sisk | .24 | .10 | .02 | Bill Virdon | | | |
| ☐ 225 Roger Maris | 5.00 | 2.35 | .50 | ☐ 269 Ellis Burton | .24 | .10 | .02 |
| ☐ 226 Colts Rookies: | .35 | .15 | .03 | ☐ 270 Rich Rollins | .24 | .10 | .02 |
| Gerald Grote | | | | ☐ 271 Bob Sadowski | .24 | .10 | .02 |
| Larry Yellen | | | | ☐ 272 Jake Wood | .24 | .10 | .02 |
| ☐ 227 Barry Latman | .24 | .10 | .02 | ☐ 273 Mel Nelson | .24 | .10 | .02 |
| ☐ 228 Felix Mantilla | .24 | .10 | .02 | ☐ 274 4th Series Checklist | 1.25 | .35 | .08 |
| ☐ 229 Charley Lau | .35 | .15 | .03 | ☐ 275 John Tsitouris | .24 | .10 | .02 |
| ☐ 230 Brooks Robinson | 8.00 | 3.75 | .80 | ☐ 276 Jose Tartabull | .24 | .10 | .02 |
| ☐ 231 Dick Calmus | .24 | .10 | .02 | ☐ 277 Ken Retzer | .24 | .10 | .02 |
| ☐ 232 Al Lopez MGR | 1.00 | .45 | .10 | ☐ 278 Bobby Shantz | .35 | .15 | .03 |
| ☐ 233 Hal Smith | .24 | .10 | .02 | ☐ 279 Joe Koppe (glove | .24 | .10 | .02 |
| ☐ 234 Gary Bell | .24 | .10 | .02 | on wrong hand) | | | |
| ☐ 235 Ron Hunt | .24 | .10 | .02 | ☐ 280 Juan Marichal | 3.50 | 1.65 | .35 |
| ☐ 236 Bill Faul | .24 | .10 | .02 | ☐ 281 Yankees Rookies | .35 | .15 | .03 |
| ☐ 237 Cubs Team | .60 | .28 | .06 | Jake Gibbs | | | |
| ☐ 238 Roy McMillan | .24 | .10 | .02 | Tom Metcalf | | | |
| ☐ 239 Herm Starrette | .24 | .10 | .02 | ☐ 282 Bob Bruce | .24 | .10 | .02 |
| ☐ 240 Bill White | .35 | .15 | .03 | ☐ 283 Tommy McCraw | .24 | .10 | .02 |
| ☐ 241 Jim Owens | .24 | .10 | .02 | ☐ 284 Dick Schofield | .24 | .10 | .02 |
| ☐ 242 Harvey Kuenn | .60 | .28 | .06 | ☐ 285 Robin Roberts | 2.50 | 1.15 | .25 |
| ☐ 243 Phillies Rookies: | 3.50 | 1.65 | .35 | ☐ 286 Don Landrum | .24 | .10 | .02 |
| Richie Allen | | | | ☐ 287 Red Sox Rookies | 2.00 | .90 | .20 |
| John Herrnstein | | | | Tony Conigliaro | | | |
| ☐ 244 Tony LaRussa | .75 | .35 | .07 | Bill Spanswick | | | |
| ☐ 245 Dick Stigman | .24 | .10 | .02 | ☐ 288 Al Moran | .24 | .10 | .02 |
| ☐ 246 Manny Mota | .60 | .28 | .06 | ☐ 289 Frank Funk | .24 | .10 | .02 |
| ☐ 247 Dave DeBusschere | 1.25 | .60 | .12 | ☐ 290 Bob Allison | .35 | .15 | .03 |

| | | MINT | VG-E | F-G |
|---|---|---|---|---|
| ☐ 291 | Phil Ortega | .24 | .10 | .02 |
| ☐ 292 | Mike Roarke | .24 | .10 | .02 |
| ☐ 293 | Phillies Team | .60 | .28 | .06 |
| ☐ 294 | Kent Hunt | .24 | .10 | .02 |
| ☐ 295 | Roger Craig | .35 | .15 | .03 |
| ☐ 296 | Ed Kirkpatrick | .24 | .10 | .02 |
| ☐ 297 | Ken MacKenzie | .24 | .10 | .02 |
| ☐ 298 | Harry Craft | .24 | .10 | .02 |
| ☐ 299 | Bill Stafford | .24 | .10 | .02 |
| ☐ 300 | Hank Aaron | 21.00 | 9.50 | 2.10 |
| ☐ 301 | Larry Brown | .24 | .10 | .02 |
| ☐ 302 | Dan Pfister | .24 | .10 | .02 |
| ☐ 303 | Jim Campbell | .24 | .10 | .02 |
| ☐ 304 | Bob Johnson | .24 | .10 | .02 |
| ☐ 305 | Jack Lamabe | .24 | .10 | .02 |
| ☐ 306 | Giant Gunners | 4.00 | 1.85 | .40 |
| | Willie Mays | | | |
| | Orlando Cepeda | | | |
| ☐ 307 | Joe Gibbon | .24 | .10 | .02 |
| ☐ 308 | Gene Stephens | .24 | .10 | .02 |
| ☐ 309 | Paul Toth | .24 | .10 | .02 |
| ☐ 310 | Jim Gilliam | 1.25 | .60 | .12 |
| ☐ 311 | Tom Brown | .24 | .10 | .02 |
| ☐ 312 | Tigers Rookies: | .24 | .10 | .02 |
| | Fritz Fisher | | | |
| | Fred Gladding | | | |
| ☐ 313 | Chuck Hiller | .24 | .10 | .02 |
| ☐ 314 | Jerry Buchek | .24 | .10 | .02 |
| ☐ 315 | Bo Belinski | .35 | .15 | .03 |
| ☐ 316 | Gene Oliver | .24 | .10 | .02 |
| ☐ 317 | Al Smith | .24 | .10 | .02 |
| ☐ 318 | Twins Team | .60 | .28 | .06 |
| ☐ 319 | Paul Brown | .24 | .10 | .02 |
| ☐ 320 | Rocky Colavito | .90 | .40 | .09 |
| ☐ 321 | Bob Lillis | .35 | .15 | .03 |
| ☐ 322 | George Brunet | .24 | .10 | .02 |
| ☐ 323 | John Buzhardt | .24 | .10 | .02 |
| ☐ 324 | Casey Stengel MGR | 3.50 | 1.65 | .35 |
| ☐ 325 | Hector Lopez | .24 | .10 | .02 |
| ☐ 326 | Ron Brand | .24 | .10 | .02 |
| ☐ 327 | Don Blasingame | .24 | .10 | .02 |
| ☐ 328 | Bob Shaw | .24 | .10 | .02 |
| ☐ 329 | Russ Nixon | .24 | .10 | .02 |
| ☐ 330 | Tommy Harper | .35 | .15 | .03 |
| ☐ 331 | AL Bombers: | 10.00 | 4.50 | 1.00 |
| | Roger Maris | | | |
| | Norm Cash | | | |
| | Mickey Mantle | | | |
| | Al Kaline | | | |
| ☐ 332 | Ray Washburn | .24 | .10 | .02 |
| ☐ 333 | Billy Moran | .24 | .10 | .02 |
| ☐ 334 | Lew Krausse | .24 | .10 | .02 |
| ☐ 335 | Don Mossi | .35 | .15 | .03 |
| ☐ 336 | Andre Rodgers | .24 | .10 | .02 |
| ☐ 337 | Dodgers Rookies: | .45 | .20 | .04 |
| | Al Ferrara | | | |
| | Jeff Torborg | | | |
| ☐ 338 | Jack Kralick | .24 | .10 | .02 |
| ☐ 339 | Walt Bond | .24 | .10 | .02 |
| ☐ 340 | Joe Cunningham | .24 | .10 | .02 |
| ☐ 341 | Jim Roland | .24 | .10 | .02 |
| ☐ 342 | Willie Stargell | 6.50 | 3.00 | .65 |
| ☐ 343 | Senators Team | .60 | .28 | .06 |
| ☐ 344 | Phil Linz | .24 | .10 | .02 |
| ☐ 345 | Frank Thomas | .24 | .10 | .02 |
| ☐ 346 | Joe Jay | .24 | .10 | .02 |
| ☐ 347 | Bobby Wine | .24 | .10 | .02 |
| ☐ 348 | Ed Lopat | .50 | .22 | .05 |
| ☐ 349 | Art Fowler | .24 | .10 | .02 |
| ☐ 350 | Willie McCovey | 6.00 | 2.80 | .60 |
| ☐ 351 | Dan Schneider | .24 | .10 | .02 |
| ☐ 352 | Eddie Bressoud | .24 | .10 | .02 |
| ☐ 353 | Wally Moon | .35 | .15 | .03 |
| ☐ 354 | Dave Giusti | .35 | .15 | .03 |
| ☐ 355 | Vic Power | .24 | .10 | .02 |
| ☐ 356 | Reds Rookies: | .35 | .15 | .03 |
| | Bill McCool | | | |
| | Chico Ruiz | | | |
| ☐ 357 | Charley James | .24 | .10 | .02 |
| ☐ 358 | Ron Kline | .24 | .10 | .02 |
| ☐ 359 | Jim Schaffer | .24 | .10 | .02 |
| ☐ 360 | Joe Pepitone | .60 | .28 | .06 |
| ☐ 361 | Jay Hook | .24 | .10 | .02 |
| ☐ 362 | 5th Series Checklist | 1.35 | .35 | .08 |
| ☐ 363 | Dick McAuliffe | .24 | .10 | .02 |
| ☐ 364 | Joe Gaines | .24 | .10 | .02 |
| ☐ 365 | Cal McLish | .24 | .10 | .02 |
| ☐ 366 | Nelson Mathews | .24 | .10 | .02 |
| ☐ 367 | Fred Whitfield | .24 | .10 | .02 |
| ☐ 368 | White Sox Rookies: | .35 | .15 | .03 |
| | Fritz Ackley | | | |
| | Don Buford | | | |
| ☐ 369 | Jerry Zimmerman | .24 | .10 | .02 |
| ☐ 370 | Hal Woodeschick | .24 | .10 | .02 |
| ☐ 371 | Frank Howard | 1.25 | .60 | .12 |
| ☐ 372 | Howie Koplitz | .36 | .15 | .03 |
| ☐ 373 | Pirates Team | .85 | .40 | .08 |
| ☐ 374 | Bobby Bolin | .36 | .15 | .03 |
| ☐ 375 | Ron Santo | .90 | .40 | .09 |
| ☐ 376 | Dave Morehead | .36 | .15 | .03 |
| ☐ 377 | Bob Skinner | .36 | .15 | .03 |
| ☐ 378 | Braves Rookies: | .36 | .15 | .03 |
| | Woody Woodward | | | |
| | Jack Smith | | | |

|  | MINT | VG-E | F-G |
|---|---|---|---|
| ☐ 379 Tony Gonzalez | .36 | .15 | .03 |
| ☐ 380 Whitey Ford | 6.50 | 3.00 | .65 |
| ☐ 381 Bob Taylor | .36 | .15 | .03 |
| ☐ 382 Wes Stock | .45 | .20 | .04 |
| ☐ 383 Bill Rigney MGR | .36 | .15 | .03 |
| ☐ 384 Ron Hansen | .36 | .15 | .03 |
| ☐ 385 Curt Simmons | .55 | .25 | .05 |
| ☐ 386 Lenny Green | .36 | .15 | .03 |
| ☐ 387 Terry Fox | .36 | .15 | .03 |
| ☐ 388 A's Rookies | .36 | .15 | .03 |
|     John O'Donoghue | | | |
|     George Williams | | | |
| ☐ 389 Jim Umbricht | .36 | .15 | .03 |
| ☐ 390 Orlando Cepeda | 1.75 | .85 | .17 |
| ☐ 391 Sam McDowell | .65 | .30 | .06 |
| ☐ 392 Jim Pagliaroni | .36 | .15 | .03 |
| ☐ 393 Casey Teaches | 1.75 | .85 | .17 |
|     Casey Stengel | | | |
|     Ed Kranepool | | | |
| ☐ 394 Bob Miller | .36 | .15 | .03 |
| ☐ 395 Tom Tresh | 1.00 | .45 | .10 |
| ☐ 396 Dennis Bennett | .36 | .15 | .03 |
| ☐ 397 Chuck Cottier | .60 | .28 | .06 |
| ☐ 398 Mets Rookies | .36 | .15 | .03 |
|     Bill Haas | | | |
|     Dick Smith | | | |
| ☐ 399 Jackie Brandt | .36 | .15 | .03 |
| ☐ 400 Warren Spahn | 6.50 | 3.00 | .65 |
| ☐ 401 Charlie Maxwell | .36 | .15 | .03 |
| ☐ 402 Tom Sturdivant | .36 | .15 | .03 |
| ☐ 403 Reds Team | .90 | .40 | .09 |
| ☐ 404 Tony Martinez | .36 | .15 | .03 |
| ☐ 405 Ken McBride | .36 | .15 | .03 |
| ☐ 406 Al Spangler | .36 | .15 | .03 |
| ☐ 407 Bill Freehan | 1.00 | .45 | .10 |
| ☐ 408 Cubs Rookies: | .36 | .15 | .03 |
|     Jim Stewart | | | |
|     Fred Burdette | | | |
| ☐ 409 Bill Fischer | .36 | .15 | .03 |
| ☐ 410 Dick Stuart | .60 | .28 | .06 |
| ☐ 411 Lee Walls | .36 | .15 | .03 |
| ☐ 412 Ray Culp | .36 | .15 | .03 |
| ☐ 413 Johnny Keane MGR | .45 | .20 | .04 |
| ☐ 414 Jack Sanford | .45 | .20 | .04 |
| ☐ 415 Tony Kubek | 2.00 | .90 | .20 |
| ☐ 416 Lee Maye | .36 | .15 | .03 |
| ☐ 417 Don Cardwell | .36 | .15 | .03 |
| ☐ 418 Orioles Rookies | .60 | .28 | .06 |
|     Darold Knowles | | | |
|     Les Narum | | | |
| ☐ 419 Ken Harrelson | 2.00 | .90 | .20 |
| ☐ 420 Jim Maloney | .65 | .30 | .06 |
| ☐ 421 Camilo Carreon | .36 | .15 | .03 |

|  | MINT | VG-E | F-G |
|---|---|---|---|
| ☐ 422 Jack Fisher | .36 | .15 | .03 |
| ☐ 423 Tops in N.L. | 10.00 | 4.75 | 1.00 |
|     Hank Aaron | | | |
|     Willie Mays | | | |
| ☐ 424 Dick Bertell | .36 | .15 | .03 |
| ☐ 425 Norm Cash | 1.00 | .45 | .10 |
| ☐ 426 Bob Rodgers | .36 | .15 | .03 |
| ☐ 427 Don Rudolph | .36 | .15 | .03 |
| ☐ 428 Red Sox Rookies: | .36 | .15 | .03 |
|     Archie Skeen | | | |
|     Pete Smith | | | |
| ☐ 429 Tim McCarver | .80 | .40 | .08 |
| ☐ 430 Juan Pizarro | .36 | .15 | .03 |
| ☐ 431 George Alusik | .36 | .15 | .03 |
| ☐ 432 Ruben Amaro | .36 | .15 | .03 |
| ☐ 433 Yankees Team | 2.50 | 1.15 | .25 |
| ☐ 434 Don Nottebart | .36 | .15 | .03 |
| ☐ 435 Vic Davalillo | .45 | .20 | .04 |
| ☐ 436 Charlie Neal | .36 | .15 | .03 |
| ☐ 437 Ed Bailey | .36 | .15 | .03 |
| ☐ 438 6th Series Checklist | 1.50 | .35 | .08 |
| ☐ 439 Harvey Haddix | .55 | .25 | .05 |
| ☐ 440 Bob Clemente | 15.00 | 7.00 | 1.50 |
| ☐ 441 Bob Duliba | .36 | .15 | .03 |
| ☐ 442 Pumpsie Green | .36 | .15 | .03 |
| ☐ 443 Chuck Dressen MGR | .36 | .15 | .03 |
| ☐ 444 Larry Jackson | .36 | .15 | .03 |
| ☐ 445 Bill Skowron | .90 | .40 | .09 |
| ☐ 446 Julian Javier | .45 | .20 | .04 |
| ☐ 447 Ted Bowsfield | .36 | .15 | .03 |
| ☐ 448 Cookie Rojas | .45 | .20 | .04 |
| ☐ 449 Deron Johnson | .45 | .20 | .04 |
| ☐ 450 Steve Barber | .36 | .15 | .03 |
| ☐ 451 Joe Amalfitano | .36 | .15 | .03 |
| ☐ 452 Giants Rookies | .90 | .40 | .09 |
|     Gil Garrido | | | |
|     Jim Ray Hart | | | |
| ☐ 453 Frank Baumann | .36 | .15 | .03 |
| ☐ 454 Tommie Aaron | .50 | .22 | .05 |
| ☐ 455 Bernie Allen | .36 | .15 | .03 |
| ☐ 456 Dodgers Rookies | .90 | .40 | .09 |
|     Wes Parker | | | |
|     John Werhas | | | |
| ☐ 457 Jesse Gonder | .36 | .15 | .03 |
| ☐ 458 Ralph Terry | .55 | .25 | .05 |
| ☐ 459 Red Sox Rookies | .36 | .15 | .03 |
|     Pete Charton | | | |
|     Dalton Jones | | | |
| ☐ 460 Bob Gibson | 7.00 | 3.25 | .70 |
| ☐ 461 George Thomas | .36 | .15 | .03 |
| ☐ 462 Birdie Tebbetts | .36 | .15 | .03 |
| ☐ 463 Don Leppert | .36 | .15 | .03 |
| ☐ 464 Dallas Green | .65 | .30 | .06 |

|  | MINT | VG-E | F-G |
|---|---|---|---|
| ☐ 465 Mike Hershberger | .36 | .15 | .03 |
| ☐ 466 A's Rookies: | .36 | .15 | .03 |
|     Dick Green | | | |
|     Aurelio Monteagudo | | | |
| ☐ 467 Bob Aspromonte | .36 | .15 | .03 |
| ☐ 468 Gaylord Perry | 7.00 | 3.25 | .70 |
| ☐ 469 Cubs Rookies: | .55 | .25 | .05 |
|     Fred Norman | | | |
|     Sterling Slaughter | | | |
| ☐ 470 Jim Bouton | 1.00 | .45 | .10 |
| ☐ 471 Gates Brown | .90 | .40 | .09 |
| ☐ 472 Vern Law | .65 | .30 | .06 |
| ☐ 473 Orioles Team | .90 | .40 | .09 |
| ☐ 474 Larry Sherry | .45 | .20 | .04 |
| ☐ 475 Ed Charles | .36 | .15 | .03 |
| ☐ 476 Braves Rookies: | 2.25 | 1.00 | .22 |
|     Rico Carty | | | |
|     Dick Kelley | | | |
| ☐ 477 Mike Joyce | .36 | .15 | .03 |
| ☐ 478 Dick Howser | .75 | .35 | .07 |
| ☐ 479 Cardinals Rookies: | .36 | .15 | .03 |
|     Dave Bakenhaster | | | |
|     Johnny Lewis | | | |
| ☐ 480 Bob Purkey | .36 | .15 | .03 |
| ☐ 481 Chuck Schilling | .36 | .15 | .03 |
| ☐ 482 Phillies Rookies | .55 | .25 | .05 |
|     John Briggs | | | |
|     Danny Cater | | | |
| ☐ 483 Fred Valentine | .36 | .15 | .03 |
| ☐ 484 Bill Pleis | .36 | .15 | .03 |
| ☐ 485 Tom Haller | .45 | .20 | .04 |
| ☐ 486 Bob Kennedy | .36 | .15 | .03 |
| ☐ 487 Mike McCormick | .45 | .20 | .04 |
| ☐ 488 Yankees Rookies: | .36 | .15 | .03 |
|     Pete Mikkelsen | | | |
|     Bob Meyer | | | |
| ☐ 489 Julio Navarro | .36 | .15 | .03 |
| ☐ 490 Ron Fairly | .55 | .25 | .05 |
| ☐ 491 Ed Rakow | .36 | .15 | .03 |
| ☐ 492 Colts Rookies | .36 | .15 | .03 |
|     Jim Beauchamp | | | |
|     Mike White | | | |
| ☐ 493 Don Lee | .36 | .15 | .03 |
| ☐ 494 Al Jackson | .36 | .15 | .03 |
| ☐ 495 Bill Virdon | .85 | .40 | .08 |
| ☐ 496 White Sox Team | .85 | .40 | .08 |
| ☐ 497 Jeoff Long | .36 | .15 | .03 |
| ☐ 498 Dave Stenhouse | .36 | .15 | .03 |
| ☐ 499 Indians Rookies | .36 | .15 | .03 |
|     Chico Salmon | | | |
|     Gordon Seyfried | | | |
| ☐ 500 Camilo Pascual | .55 | .25 | .05 |
| ☐ 501 Bob Veale | .45 | .20 | .04 |

|  | MINT | VG-E | F-G |
|---|---|---|---|
| ☐ 502 Angels Rookies: | .36 | .15 | .03 |
|     Bobby Knoop | | | |
|     Bob Lee | | | |
| ☐ 503 Earl Wilson | .36 | .15 | .03 |
| ☐ 504 Claude Raymond | .36 | .15 | .03 |
| ☐ 505 Stan Williams | .36 | .15 | .03 |
| ☐ 506 Bobby Bragan | .36 | .15 | .03 |
| ☐ 507 John Edwards | .36 | .15 | .03 |
| ☐ 508 Diego Segui | .36 | .15 | .03 |
| ☐ 509 Pirates Rookies: | .75 | .35 | .07 |
|     Gene Alley | | | |
|     Orlando McFarlane | | | |
| ☐ 510 Lindy McDaniel | .45 | .20 | .04 |
| ☐ 511 Lou Jackson | .36 | .15 | .03 |
| ☐ 512 Tigers Rookies: | 1.75 | .85 | .17 |
|     Willie Horton | | | |
|     Joe Sparma | | | |
| ☐ 513 Don Larsen | .60 | .28 | .06 |
| ☐ 514 Jim Hickman | .36 | .15 | .03 |
| ☐ 515 Johnny Romano | .36 | .15 | .03 |
| ☐ 516 Twins Rookies: | .36 | .15 | .03 |
|     Jerry Arrigo | | | |
|     Dwight Siebler | | | |
| ☐ 517 A Checklist 7 COR | 2.00 | .50 | .10 |
|     (correct numbering | | | |
|     on back) | | | |
| ☐ 517 B Checklist 7 ERR | 3.25 | .60 | .10 |
|     (incorrect numbering | | | |
|     sequence on back) | | | |
| ☐ 518 Carl Bouldin | .36 | .15 | .03 |
| ☐ 519 Charlie Smith | .36 | .15 | .03 |
| ☐ 520 Jack Baldschun | .36 | .15 | .03 |
| ☐ 521 Tom Satriano | .36 | .15 | .03 |
| ☐ 522 Bob Tiefenauer | .36 | .15 | .03 |
| ☐ 523 Lou Burdette | 1.75 | .85 | .17 |
|     (pitching lefty) | | | |
| ☐ 524 Rookies (Reds) | .85 | .40 | .08 |
|     Jim Dickson | | | |
|     Bobby Klaus | | | |
| ☐ 525 Al McBean | .85 | .40 | .08 |
| ☐ 526 Lou Clinton | .85 | .40 | .08 |
| ☐ 527 Larry Bearnarth | .85 | .40 | .08 |
| ☐ 528 A's Rookies: | 1.00 | .45 | .10 |
|     Dave Duncan | | | |
|     Tom Reynolds | | | |
| ☐ 529 Al Dark | 1.00 | .45 | .10 |
| ☐ 530 Leon Wagner | .85 | .40 | .08 |
| ☐ 531 Dodgers Team | 2.25 | 1.00 | .22 |
| ☐ 532 Twins Rookies | .85 | .40 | .08 |
|     Bud Bloomfield | | | |
|     (Bloomfield photo | | | |
|     actually Jay Ward) | | | |
|     Joe Nossek | | | |

| | MINT | VG-E | F-G |
|---|---|---|---|
| ☐ 533 John Klippstein | .85 | .40 | .08 |
| ☐ 534 Gus Bell | 1.00 | .45 | .10 |
| ☐ 535 Phil Regan | .85 | .40 | .08 |
| ☐ 536 Mets Rookies: | .85 | .40 | .08 |
| Larry Elliot | | | |
| John Stephenson | | | |
| ☐ 537 Dan Osinski | .85 | .40 | .08 |
| ☐ 538 Minnie Minoso | 1.75 | .85 | .17 |
| ☐ 539 Roy Face | 1.35 | .60 | .13 |
| ☐ 540 Luis Aparicio | 4.50 | 2.10 | .45 |
| ☐ 541 Rookies (Braves) | 30.00 | 14.00 | 3.00 |
| Phil Roof | | | |
| Phil Niekro | | | |
| ☐ 542 Don Mincher | 1.00 | .45 | .10 |
| ☐ 543 Bob Uecker | 5.00 | 2.35 | .50 |
| ☐ 544 Colts Rookies: | .85 | .40 | .08 |
| Steve Hertz | | | |
| Joe Hoerner | | | |
| ☐ 545 Max Alvis | .85 | .40 | .08 |
| ☐ 546 Joe Christopher | .85 | .40 | .08 |
| ☐ 547 Gil Hodges | 4.00 | 1.85 | .40 |
| ☐ 548 NL Rookies | .85 | .40 | .08 |
| Wayne Schurr | | | |
| Paul Speckenbach | | | |
| ☐ 549 Joe Moeller | .85 | .40 | .08 |
| ☐ 550 Ken Hubbs | 3.00 | 1.40 | .30 |
| (in memoriam) | | | |
| ☐ 551 Billy Hoeft | .85 | .40 | .08 |
| ☐ 552 Indians Rookies | 1.00 | .45 | .10 |
| Tom Kelley | | | |
| Sonny Siebert | | | |
| ☐ 553 Jim Brewer | .85 | .40 | .08 |
| ☐ 554 Hank Foiles | .85 | .40 | .08 |
| ☐ 555 Lee Stange | .85 | .40 | .08 |
| ☐ 556 Mets Rookies | .85 | .40 | .08 |
| Steve Dillon | | | |
| Ron Locke | | | |
| ☐ 557 Leo Burke | .85 | .40 | .08 |
| ☐ 558 Don Schwall | .85 | .40 | .08 |
| ☐ 559 Dick Phillips | .85 | .40 | .08 |
| ☐ 560 Dick Farrell | .85 | .40 | .08 |
| ☐ 561 Phillies Rookies | 1.50 | .70 | .15 |
| Dave Bennett | | | |
| (19 . . . is 18) | | | |
| Rick Wise | | | |
| ☐ 562 Pedro Ramos | .85 | .40 | .08 |
| ☐ 563 Dal Maxvill | .85 | .40 | .08 |
| ☐ 564 AL Rookies | .85 | .40 | .08 |
| Joe McCabe | | | |
| Jerry McNertney | | | |
| ☐ 565 Stu Miller | .85 | .40 | .08 |
| ☐ 566 Ed Kranepool | 1.25 | .60 | .12 |
| ☐ 567 Jim Kaat | 3.00 | 1.40 | .30 |

| | MINT | VG-E | F-G |
|---|---|---|---|
| ☐ 568 NL Rookies | .85 | .40 | .08 |
| Phil Gagliano | | | |
| Cap Peterson | | | |
| ☐ 569 Fred Newman | .85 | .40 | .08 |
| ☐ 570 Bill Mazeroski | 1.75 | .85 | .17 |
| ☐ 571 Gene Conley | .85 | .40 | .08 |
| ☐ 572 AL Rookies | .85 | .40 | .08 |
| Dave Gray | | | |
| Dick Egan | | | |
| ☐ 573 Jim Duffalo | .85 | .40 | .08 |
| ☐ 574 Manny Jimenez | .85 | .40 | .08 |
| ☐ 575 Tony Cloninger | .85 | .40 | .08 |
| ☐ 576 Mets Rookies: | .85 | .40 | .08 |
| Jerry Hinsley | | | |
| Bill Wakefield | | | |
| ☐ 577 Gordy Coleman | .85 | .40 | .08 |
| ☐ 578 Glen Hobbie | .85 | .40 | .08 |
| ☐ 579 Red Sox Team | 1.75 | .85 | .17 |
| ☐ 580 Johnny Podres | 1.75 | .85 | .17 |
| ☐ 581 Yankees Rookies | .85 | .40 | .08 |
| Pedro Gonzales | | | |
| Archie Moore | | | |
| ☐ 582 Rod Kanehl | .85 | .40 | .08 |
| ☐ 583 Tito Francona | 1.00 | .45 | .10 |
| ☐ 584 Joel Horlen | 1.00 | .45 | .10 |
| ☐ 585 Tony Taylor | .85 | .40 | .08 |
| ☐ 586 Jim Piersall | 1.25 | .60 | .12 |
| ☐ 587 Bennie Daniels | 1.00 | .45 | .10 |

## 1965 TOPPS

*The cards in this 598 card set measure 2½″ by 3½″. The cards comprising the 1965 Topps set have team names located within a distinctive pennant design below the picture. The cards have blue borders on the reverse and were issued by series.*

*Cards 523 to 598 are more difficult to obtain than all other series. In addition, the sixth series (447-522) is more difficult to obtain than series one through five.*
Complete Set: M-550.00; VG-E-250.00; F-G-55.00

| | MINT | VG-E | F-G |
|---|---|---|---|
| Common Player (1-198) | .20 | .09 | .02 |
| Common Player (199-446) | .26 | .11 | .02 |
| Common Player (447-522) | .50 | .22 | .05 |
| Common Player (523-598) | .70 | .32 | .07 |

| | | MINT | VG-E | F-G |
|---|---|---|---|---|
| ☐ | 1 AL Batting Leaders | 2.00 | .50 | .15 |
| | Tony Oliva | | | |
| | Elston Howard | | | |
| | Brooks Robinson | | | |
| ☐ | 2 NL Batting Leaders | 1.75 | .85 | .17 |
| | Bob Clemente | | | |
| | Hank Aaron | | | |
| | Rico Carty | | | |
| ☐ | 3 AL Home Run Leaders | 1.75 | .85 | .17 |
| | Harmon Killebrew | | | |
| | Mickey Mantle | | | |
| | Boog Powell | | | |
| ☐ | 4 NL Home Run Leaders | 1.50 | .70 | .15 |
| | Willie Mays | | | |
| | Billy Williams | | | |
| | Jim Ray Hart | | | |
| | Orlando Cepeda | | | |
| | Johnny Callison | | | |
| ☐ | 5 AL RBI Leaders | 1.75 | .85 | .17 |
| | Brooks Robinson | | | |
| | Harmon Killebrew | | | |
| | Mickey Mantle | | | |
| | Dick Stuart | | | |
| ☐ | 6 NL RBI Leaders | .90 | .40 | .09 |
| | Ken Boyer | | | |
| | Willie Mays | | | |
| | Ron Santo | | | |
| ☐ | 7 AL ERA Leaders | .65 | .30 | .06 |
| | Dean Chance | | | |
| | Joel Horlen | | | |
| ☐ | 8 NL ERA Leaders | 1.75 | .85 | .17 |
| | Sandy Koufax | | | |
| | Don Drysdale | | | |
| ☐ | 9 AL Pitching Leaders | .65 | .30 | .06 |
| | Dean Chance | | | |
| | Gary Peters | | | |
| | Dave Wickersham | | | |
| | Juan Pizarro | | | |
| | Wally Bunker | | | |

| | | MINT | VG-E | F-G |
|---|---|---|---|---|
| ☐ | 10 NL Pitching Leaders | .65 | .30 | .06 |
| | Larry Jackson | | | |
| | Ray Sadecki | | | |
| | Juan Marichal | | | |
| ☐ | 11 AL Strikeout Leaders | .65 | .30 | .06 |
| | Al Downing | | | |
| | Dean Chance | | | |
| | Camilo Pascual | | | |
| ☐ | 12 NL Strikeout Leaders | .90 | .40 | .09 |
| | Bob Veale | | | |
| | Don Drysdale | | | |
| | Bob Gibson | | | |
| ☐ | 13 Pedro Ramos | .20 | .09 | .02 |
| ☐ | 14 Len Gabrielson | .20 | .09 | .02 |
| ☐ | 15 Robin Roberts | 2.50 | 1.15 | .25 |
| ☐ | 16 Houston Rookies: | 12.50 | 5.75 | 1.25 |
| | Joe Morgan | | | |
| | Sonny Jackson | | | |
| ☐ | 17 John Romano | .20 | .09 | .02 |
| ☐ | 18 Bill McCool | .20 | .09 | .02 |
| ☐ | 19 Gates Brown | .25 | .10 | .02 |
| ☐ | 20 Jim Bunning | 1.25 | .60 | .12 |
| ☐ | 21 Don Blasingame | .20 | .09 | .02 |
| ☐ | 22 Charlie Smith | .20 | .09 | .02 |
| ☐ | 23 Bob Tiefenauer | .20 | .09 | .02 |
| ☐ | 24 Twins Team | .85 | .40 | .08 |
| ☐ | 25 Al McBean | .20 | .09 | .02 |
| ☐ | 26 Bob Knoop | .20 | .09 | .02 |
| ☐ | 27 Dick Bertell | .20 | .09 | .02 |
| ☐ | 28 Barney Schultz | .20 | .09 | .02 |
| ☐ | 29 Felix Mantilla | .20 | .09 | .02 |
| ☐ | 30 Jim Bouton | .60 | .28 | .06 |
| ☐ | 31 Mike White | .20 | .09 | .02 |
| ☐ | 32 Herman Franks | .20 | .09 | .02 |
| ☐ | 33 Jackie Brandt | .20 | .09 | .02 |
| ☐ | 34 Cal Koonce | .20 | .09 | .02 |
| ☐ | 35 Ed Charles | .20 | .09 | .02 |
| ☐ | 36 Bob Wine | .20 | .09 | .02 |
| ☐ | 37 Fred Gladding | .20 | .09 | .02 |
| ☐ | 38 Jim King | .20 | .09 | .02 |
| ☐ | 39 Gerry Arrigo | .20 | .09 | .02 |
| ☐ | 40 Frank Howard | .85 | .40 | .08 |
| ☐ | 41 White Sox Rookies | .20 | .09 | .02 |
| | Bruce Howard | | | |
| | Marv Staehle | | | |
| ☐ | 42 Earl Wilson | .20 | .09 | .02 |
| ☐ | 43 Mike Shannon | .45 | .20 | .04 |
| ☐ | 44 Wade Blasingame | .20 | .09 | .02 |
| ☐ | 45 Roy McMillan | .20 | .09 | .02 |
| ☐ | 46 Bob Lee | .20 | .09 | .02 |
| ☐ | 47 Tom Harper | .35 | .15 | .03 |
| ☐ | 48 Claude Raymond | .20 | .09 | .02 |

|  |  | MINT | VG-E | F-G |
|---|---|---|---|---|
| ☐ 49 | Orioles Rookies ....... | .45 | .20 | .04 |
| | Curt Blefary | | | |
| | John Miller | | | |
| ☐ 50 | Juan Marichal ......... | 3.00 | 1.40 | .30 |
| ☐ 51 | Bill Bryan ............. | .20 | .09 | .02 |
| ☐ 52 | Ed Roebuck ........... | .20 | .09 | .02 |
| ☐ 53 | Dick McAuliffe ........ | .25 | .10 | .02 |
| ☐ 54 | Joe Gibbon ........... | .20 | .09 | .02 |
| ☐ 55 | Tony Conigliaro ....... | .80 | .40 | .08 |
| ☐ 56 | Ron Kline ............. | .20 | .09 | .02 |
| ☐ 57 | Cardinals Team ....... | .60 | .28 | .06 |
| ☐ 58 | Fred Talbot ........... | .20 | .09 | .02 |
| ☐ 59 | Nate Oliver ........... | .20 | .09 | .02 |
| ☐ 60 | Jim O'Toole ........... | .20 | .09 | .02 |
| ☐ 61 | Chris Cannizzaro ...... | .20 | .09 | .02 |
| ☐ 62 | Jim Katt (sic, Kaat) .... | 1.75 | .85 | .17 |
| ☐ 63 | Ty Cline .............. | .20 | .09 | .02 |
| ☐ 64 | Lou Burdette .......... | .65 | .30 | .06 |
| ☐ 65 | Tony Kubek ........... | 1.25 | .55 | .12 |
| ☐ 66 | Bill Rigney ........... | .20 | .09 | .02 |
| ☐ 67 | Harvey Haddix ........ | .30 | .12 | .03 |
| ☐ 68 | Del Crandall .......... | .30 | .12 | .03 |
| ☐ 69 | Bill Virdon ........... | .55 | .25 | .05 |
| ☐ 70 | Bill Skowron .......... | .55 | .25 | .05 |
| ☐ 71 | John O'Donoghue ..... | .20 | .09 | .02 |
| ☐ 72 | Tony Gonzalez ........ | .20 | .09 | .02 |
| ☐ 73 | Dennis Ribant ........ | .20 | .09 | .02 |
| ☐ 74 | Red Sox Rookies ...... | 1.00 | .45 | .10 |
| | Rico Petrocelli | | | |
| | Jerry Stephenson | | | |
| ☐ 75 | Deron Johnson ........ | .25 | .10 | .02 |
| ☐ 76 | Sam McDowell ........ | .35 | .15 | .03 |
| ☐ 77 | Doug Camilli ......... | .20 | .09 | .02 |
| ☐ 78 | Dal Maxvill ........... | .20 | .09 | .02 |
| ☐ 79 | 1st Series Checklist .... | 1.25 | .25 | .05 |
| ☐ 80 | Turk Farrell .......... | .20 | .09 | .02 |
| ☐ 81 | Don Buford ........... | .20 | .09 | .02 |
| ☐ 82 | Braves Rookies: ....... | .25 | .10 | .02 |
| | Santos Alomar | | | |
| | John Braun | | | |
| ☐ 83 | George Thomas ....... | .20 | .09 | .02 |
| ☐ 84 | Ron Herbel ........... | .20 | .09 | .02 |
| ☐ 85 | Willie Smith .......... | .20 | .09 | .02 |
| ☐ 86 | Les Narum ........... | .20 | .09 | .02 |
| ☐ 87 | Nelson Mathews ....... | .20 | .09 | .02 |
| ☐ 88 | Jack Lamabe ......... | .20 | .09 | .02 |
| ☐ 89 | Mike Hershberger ..... | .20 | .09 | .02 |
| ☐ 90 | Rich Rollins .......... | .20 | .09 | .02 |
| ☐ 91 | Cubs Team ........... | .60 | .28 | .06 |
| ☐ 92 | Dick Howser .......... | .40 | .18 | .04 |
| ☐ 93 | Jack Fisher ........... | .20 | .09 | .02 |
| ☐ 94 | Charlie Lau ........... | .30 | .12 | .03 |
| ☐ 95 | Bill Mazeroski ........ | .90 | .40 | .09 |

|  |  | MINT | VG-E | F-G |
|---|---|---|---|---|
| ☐ 96 | Sonny Siebert ......... | .25 | .10 | .02 |
| ☐ 97 | Pedro Gonzalez ....... | .20 | .09 | .02 |
| ☐ 98 | Bob Miller ............ | .20 | .09 | .02 |
| ☐ 99 | Gil Hodges ........... | 2.50 | 1.15 | .25 |
| ☐ 100 | Ken Boyer ............ | 1.25 | .60 | .12 |
| ☐ 101 | Fred Newman ......... | .20 | .09 | .02 |
| ☐ 102 | Steve Boros .......... | .30 | .12 | .03 |
| ☐ 103 | Harvey Kuenn ........ | .55 | .25 | .05 |
| ☐ 104 | 2nd Series Checklist ... | 1.10 | .20 | .05 |
| ☐ 105 | Chico Salmon ......... | .20 | .09 | .02 |
| ☐ 106 | Gene Oliver .......... | .20 | .09 | .02 |
| ☐ 107 | Phillies Rookies ...... | .60 | .28 | .06 |
| | Pat Corrales | | | |
| | Costen Shockley | | | |
| ☐ 108 | Don Mincher .......... | .25 | .10 | .02 |
| ☐ 109 | Walt Bond ............ | .20 | .09 | .02 |
| ☐ 110 | Ron Santo ............ | .75 | .35 | .07 |
| ☐ 111 | Lee Thomas .......... | .20 | .09 | .02 |
| ☐ 112 | Derrell Griffith ....... | .20 | .09 | .02 |
| ☐ 113 | Steve Barber ......... | .20 | .09 | .02 |
| ☐ 114 | Jim Hickman .......... | .20 | .09 | .02 |
| ☐ 115 | Bob Richardson ....... | 1.00 | .45 | .10 |
| ☐ 116 | Cardinals Rookies: .... | .40 | .18 | .04 |
| | Dave Dowling | | | |
| | Bob Tolan | | | |
| ☐ 117 | Wes Stock ........... | .25 | .10 | .02 |
| ☐ 118 | Hal Lanier ........... | .35 | .15 | .03 |
| ☐ 119 | John Kennedy ........ | .20 | .09 | .02 |
| ☐ 120 | Frank Robinson ....... | 4.25 | 2.00 | .42 |
| ☐ 121 | Gene Alley ........... | .25 | .10 | .02 |
| ☐ 122 | Bill Pleis ............ | .20 | .09 | .02 |
| ☐ 123 | Frank Thomas ........ | .25 | .10 | .02 |
| ☐ 124 | Tom Satriano ......... | .20 | .09 | .02 |
| ☐ 125 | Juan Pizarro ......... | .20 | .09 | .02 |
| ☐ 126 | Dodgers Team ........ | .90 | .40 | .09 |
| ☐ 127 | Frank Lary ........... | .25 | .10 | .02 |
| ☐ 128 | Vic Davalillo ......... | .25 | .10 | .02 |
| ☐ 129 | Bennie Daniels ....... | .20 | .09 | .02 |
| ☐ 130 | Al Kaline ............ | 4.50 | 2.10 | .45 |
| ☐ 131 | John Keane MGR ..... | .30 | .12 | .03 |
| | WORLD SERIES | | | |
| | CARDS (132–139) | | | |
| ☐ 132 | World Series Game 1 .. | 1.00 | .45 | .10 |
| | Cards take opener | | | |
| ☐ 133 | World Series Game 2 .. | 1.00 | .45 | .10 |
| | Stottlemyre wins | | | |
| ☐ 134 | World Series Game 3 .. | 4.00 | 1.85 | .40 |
| | Mantle's clutch homer | | | |
| ☐ 135 | World Series Game 4 .. | 1.25 | .60 | .12 |
| | Boyer's grand-slam | | | |
| ☐ 136 | World Series Game 5 .. | 1.00 | .45 | .10 |
| | 10th inning triumph | | | |
| ☐ 137 | World Series Game 6 .. | 1.25 | .60 | .12 |
| | Bouton wins again | | | |

| | | MINT | VG-E | F-G |
|---|---|---|---|---|
| ☐ 138 | World Series Game 7 ..<br>Gibson wins finale | 2.00 | .90 | .20 |
| ☐ 139 | World Series Summary .<br>Cards celebrate | 1.00 | .45 | .10 |
| ☐ 140 | Dean Chance ......... | .25 | .10 | .02 |
| ☐ 141 | Charlie James ........ | .20 | .09 | .02 |
| ☐ 142 | Bill Monbouquette .... | .20 | .09 | .02 |
| ☐ 143 | Pirates Rookies:<br>John Gelnar<br>Jerry May | .20 | .09 | .02 |
| ☐ 144 | Ed Kranepool ........ | .30 | .12 | .03 |
| ☐ 145 | Luis Tiant .......... | 2.50 | 1.15 | .25 |
| ☐ 146 | Ron Hansen ......... | .20 | .09 | .02 |
| ☐ 147 | Dennis Bennett ...... | .20 | .09 | .02 |
| ☐ 148 | Willie Kirkland ...... | .20 | .09 | .02 |
| ☐ 149 | Wayne Schurr ....... | .20 | .09 | .02 |
| ☐ 150 | Brooks Robinson ..... | 5.00 | 2.35 | .50 |
| ☐ 151 | Athletics Team ...... | .60 | .28 | .06 |
| ☐ 152 | Phil Ortega ......... | .20 | .09 | .02 |
| ☐ 153 | Norm Cash .......... | .85 | .40 | .08 |
| ☐ 154 | Bob Humphreys ...... | .20 | .09 | .02 |
| ☐ 155 | Roger Maris ......... | 4.50 | 2.10 | .45 |
| ☐ 156 | Bob Sadowski ....... | .20 | .09 | .02 |
| ☐ 157 | Zoilo Versalles ...... | .50 | .22 | .05 |
| ☐ 158 | Dick Sisler ......... | .20 | .09 | .02 |
| ☐ 159 | Jim Duffalo ......... | .20 | .09 | .02 |
| ☐ 160 | Bob Clemente ....... | 9.50 | 4.50 | .95 |
| ☐ 161 | Frank Baumann ...... | .20 | .09 | .02 |
| ☐ 162 | Russ Nixon ......... | .20 | .09 | .02 |
| ☐ 163 | John Briggs ......... | .20 | .09 | .02 |
| ☐ 164 | Al Spangler ......... | .20 | .09 | .02 |
| ☐ 165 | Dick Ellsworth ...... | .20 | .09 | .02 |
| ☐ 166 | Indians Rookies .....<br>George Culver<br>Tommie Agee | .35 | .15 | .03 |
| ☐ 167 | Bill Wakefield ....... | .20 | .09 | .02 |
| ☐ 168 | Dick Green .......... | .20 | .09 | .02 |
| ☐ 169 | Dave Vineyard ...... | .20 | .09 | .02 |
| ☐ 170 | Hank Aaron ......... | 18.00 | 8.50 | 1.80 |
| ☐ 171 | Jim Roland ......... | .20 | .09 | .02 |
| ☐ 172 | Jim Piersall ........ | .55 | .25 | .05 |
| ☐ 173 | Tigers Team ........ | .65 | .30 | .06 |
| ☐ 174 | Joe Jay ............ | .20 | .09 | .02 |
| ☐ 175 | Bob Aspromonte ..... | .20 | .09 | .02 |
| ☐ 176 | Willie McCovey ...... | 4.50 | 2.10 | .45 |
| ☐ 177 | Pete Mikkelsen ...... | .20 | .09 | .02 |
| ☐ 178 | Dalton Jones ........ | .20 | .09 | .02 |
| ☐ 179 | Hal Woodeschick ..... | .20 | .09 | .02 |
| ☐ 180 | Bob Allison ......... | .35 | .15 | .03 |
| ☐ 181 | Senators Rookies .....<br>Don Loun<br>Joe McCabe | .20 | .09 | .02 |
| ☐ 182 | Mike De La Hoz ...... | .20 | .09 | .02 |
| ☐ 183 | Dave Nicholson ....... | .20 | .09 | .02 |
| ☐ 184 | John Boozer ......... | .20 | .09 | .02 |
| ☐ 185 | Max Alvis .......... | .20 | .09 | .02 |
| ☐ 186 | Bill Cowan .......... | .20 | .09 | .02 |
| ☐ 187 | Casey Stengel ....... | 3.25 | 1.50 | .32 |
| ☐ 188 | Sam Bowens ........ | .20 | .09 | .02 |
| ☐ 189 | 3rd Series Checklist .. | 1.00 | .20 | .05 |
| ☐ 190 | Bill White .......... | .30 | .12 | .03 |
| ☐ 191 | Phil Regan ......... | .25 | .10 | .02 |
| ☐ 192 | Jim Coker .......... | .20 | .09 | .02 |
| ☐ 193 | Gaylord Perry ....... | 3.50 | 1.65 | .35 |
| ☐ 194 | Rookie Stars ........<br>Bill Kelso<br>Rick Reichardt | .25 | .10 | .02 |
| ☐ 195 | Bob Veale .......... | .30 | .12 | .03 |
| ☐ 196 | Ron Fairly .......... | .30 | .12 | .03 |
| ☐ 197 | Diego Segui ........ | .20 | .09 | .02 |
| ☐ 198 | Smoky Burgess ...... | .30 | .12 | .03 |
| ☐ 199 | Bob Heffner ........ | .26 | .11 | .02 |
| ☐ 200 | Joe Torre .......... | 1.00 | .45 | .10 |
| ☐ 201 | Twins Rookies .......<br>Sandy Valdespino<br>Cesar Tovar | .35 | .15 | .03 |
| ☐ 202 | Leo Burke .......... | .26 | .11 | .02 |
| ☐ 203 | Dallas Green ........ | .35 | .15 | .03 |
| ☐ 204 | Russ Snyder ........ | .26 | .11 | .02 |
| ☐ 205 | Warren Spahn ....... | 4.00 | 1.85 | .40 |
| ☐ 206 | Willie Horton ....... | .55 | .25 | .05 |
| ☐ 207 | Pete Rose .......... | 100.00 | 40.00 | 8.00 |
| ☐ 208 | Tommy John ........ | 2.25 | 1.00 | .22 |
| ☐ 209 | Pirates Team ....... | .65 | .30 | .06 |
| ☐ 210 | Jim Fregosi ........ | .35 | .15 | .03 |
| ☐ 211 | Steve Ridzik ........ | .26 | .11 | .02 |
| ☐ 212 | Ron Brand .......... | .26 | .11 | .02 |
| ☐ 213 | Jim Davenport ...... | .35 | .15 | .03 |
| ☐ 214 | Bob Purkey ......... | .26 | .11 | .02 |
| ☐ 215 | Pete Ward .......... | .26 | .11 | .02 |
| ☐ 216 | Al Worthington ...... | .26 | .11 | .02 |
| ☐ 217 | Walt Alston ......... | .90 | .40 | .09 |
| ☐ 218 | Dick Schofield ...... | .26 | .11 | .02 |
| ☐ 219 | Bob Meyer .......... | .26 | .11 | .02 |
| ☐ 220 | Bill Williams ........ | 2.00 | .90 | .20 |
| ☐ 221 | John Tsitouris ....... | .26 | .11 | .02 |
| ☐ 222 | Bob Tillman ........ | .26 | .11 | .02 |
| ☐ 223 | Dan Osinski ........ | .26 | .11 | .02 |
| ☐ 224 | Bob Chance ......... | .26 | .11 | .02 |
| ☐ 225 | Bo Belinsky ........ | .35 | .15 | .03 |
| ☐ 226 | Yankees Rookies .....<br>Elvio Jimenez<br>Jake Gibbs | .35 | .15 | .03 |
| ☐ 227 | Bob Klaus .......... | .26 | .11 | .02 |
| ☐ 228 | Jack Sanford ........ | .26 | .11 | .02 |
| ☐ 229 | Lou Clinton ......... | .26 | .11 | .02 |

| | MINT | VG-E | F-G |
|---|---|---|---|
| ☐ 230 Ray Sadecki | .26 | .11 | .02 |
| ☐ 231 Jerry Adair | .26 | .11 | .02 |
| ☐ 232 Steve Blass | .55 | .25 | .05 |
| ☐ 233 Don Zimmer | .55 | .25 | .05 |
| ☐ 234 White Sox Team | .65 | .30 | .06 |
| ☐ 235 Chuck Hinton | .26 | .11 | .02 |
| ☐ 236 Dennis McLain | 2.25 | 1.00 | .22 |
| ☐ 237 Bernie Allen | .26 | .11 | .02 |
| ☐ 238 Joe Moeller | .26 | .11 | .02 |
| ☐ 239 Doc Edwards | .26 | .11 | .02 |
| ☐ 240 Bob Bruce | .26 | .11 | .02 |
| ☐ 241 Mack Jones | .26 | .11 | .02 |
| ☐ 242 George Brunet | .26 | .11 | .02 |
| ☐ 243 Reds Rookies | .35 | .15 | .03 |
|     Ted Davidson | | | |
|     Tommy Helms | | | |
| ☐ 244 Lindy McDaniel | .26 | .11 | .02 |
| ☐ 245 Joe Pepitone | .55 | .25 | .05 |
| ☐ 246 Tom Butters | .26 | .11 | .02 |
| ☐ 247 Wally Moon | .35 | .15 | .03 |
| ☐ 248 Gus Triandos | .35 | .15 | .03 |
| ☐ 249 Dave McNally | .60 | .28 | .06 |
| ☐ 250 Willie Mays | 20.00 | 9.00 | 2.00 |
| ☐ 251 Billy Herman | .90 | .40 | .09 |
| ☐ 252 Pete Richert | .26 | .11 | .02 |
| ☐ 253 Danny Cater | .26 | .11 | .02 |
| ☐ 254 Roland Sheldon | .26 | .11 | .02 |
| ☐ 255 Camilo Pascual | .35 | .15 | .03 |
| ☐ 256 Tito Francona | .35 | .15 | .03 |
| ☐ 257 Jim Wynn | .55 | .25 | .05 |
| ☐ 258 Larry Bearnarth | .26 | .11 | .02 |
| ☐ 259 Tigers Rookies | .45 | .20 | .04 |
|     Jim Northrup | | | |
|     Ray Oyler | | | |
| ☐ 260 Don Drysdale | 3.75 | 1.75 | .37 |
| ☐ 261 Duke Carmel | .26 | .11 | .02 |
| ☐ 262 Bud Daley | .26 | .11 | .02 |
| ☐ 263 Marty Keough | .26 | .11 | .02 |
| ☐ 264 Bob Buhl | .26 | .11 | .02 |
| ☐ 265 Jim Pagliaroni | .26 | .11 | .02 |
| ☐ 266 Bert Campaneris | 1.25 | .60 | .12 |
| ☐ 267 Senators Team | .60 | .28 | .06 |
| ☐ 268 Ken McBride | .26 | .11 | .02 |
| ☐ 269 Frank Bolling | .26 | .11 | .02 |
| ☐ 270 Milt Pappas | .35 | .15 | .03 |
| ☐ 271 Don Wert | .26 | .11 | .02 |
| ☐ 272 Chuck Schilling | .26 | .11 | .02 |
| ☐ 273 4th Series Checklist | 1.10 | .20 | .05 |
| ☐ 274 Lum Harris MGR | .26 | .11 | .02 |
| ☐ 275 Dick Groat | .55 | .25 | .05 |
| ☐ 276 Hoyt Wilhelm | 2.25 | 1.00 | .22 |
| ☐ 277 John Lewis | .26 | .11 | .02 |
| ☐ 278 Ken Retzer | .26 | .11 | .02 |

| | MINT | VG-E | F-G |
|---|---|---|---|
| ☐ 279 Dick Tracewski | .26 | .11 | .02 |
| ☐ 280 Dick Stuart | .35 | .15 | .03 |
| ☐ 281 Bill Stafford | .26 | .11 | .02 |
| ☐ 282 Giants Rookies | .50 | .22 | .05 |
|     Dick Estelle | | | |
|     Masanori Murakami | | | |
| ☐ 283 Fred Whitfield | .26 | .11 | .02 |
| ☐ 284 Nick Willhite | .26 | .11 | .02 |
| ☐ 285 Ron Hunt | .26 | .11 | .02 |
| ☐ 286 Athletics Rookies | .26 | .11 | .02 |
|     Jim Dickson | | | |
|     Aurelio Monteagudo | | | |
| ☐ 287 Gary Kolb | .26 | .11 | .02 |
| ☐ 288 Jack Hamilton | .26 | .11 | .02 |
| ☐ 289 Gordy Coleman | .26 | .11 | .02 |
| ☐ 290 Wally Bunker | .26 | .11 | .02 |
| ☐ 291 Jerry Lynch | .26 | .11 | .02 |
| ☐ 292 Larry Yellen | .26 | .11 | .02 |
| ☐ 293 Angels Team | .60 | .28 | .06 |
| ☐ 294 Tim McCarver | .65 | .30 | .06 |
| ☐ 295 Dick Radatz | .35 | .15 | .03 |
| ☐ 296 Tony Taylor | .26 | .11 | .02 |
| ☐ 297 Dave Debusschere | 1.25 | .60 | .12 |
| ☐ 298 Jim Stewart | .26 | .11 | .02 |
| ☐ 299 Jerry Zimmerman | .26 | .11 | .02 |
| ☐ 300 Sandy Koufax | 13.00 | 6.00 | 1.30 |
| ☐ 301 Birdie Tebbetts | .26 | .11 | .02 |
| ☐ 302 Al Stanek | .26 | .11 | .02 |
| ☐ 303 John Orsino | .26 | .11 | .02 |
| ☐ 304 Dave Stenhouse | .26 | .11 | .02 |
| ☐ 305 Rico Carty | .65 | .30 | .06 |
| ☐ 306 Bubba Phillips | .26 | .11 | .02 |
| ☐ 307 Barry Latman | .26 | .11 | .02 |
| ☐ 308 Mets Rookies | .35 | .15 | .03 |
|     Cleon Jones | | | |
|     Tom Parsons | | | |
| ☐ 309 Steve Hamilton | .26 | .11 | .02 |
| ☐ 310 John Callison | .35 | .15 | .03 |
| ☐ 311 Orlando Pena | .26 | .11 | .02 |
| ☐ 312 Joe Nuxhall | .35 | .15 | .03 |
| ☐ 313 Jim Schaffer | .26 | .11 | .02 |
| ☐ 314 Sterling Slaughter | .26 | .11 | .02 |
| ☐ 315 Frank Malzone | .35 | .15 | .03 |
| ☐ 316 Reds Team | .65 | .30 | .06 |
| ☐ 317 Don McMahon | .26 | .11 | .02 |
| ☐ 318 Matty Alou | .35 | .15 | .03 |
| ☐ 319 Ken McMullen | .26 | .11 | .02 |
| ☐ 320 Bob Gibson | 3.75 | 1.75 | .37 |
| ☐ 321 Rusty Staub | 1.50 | .70 | .15 |
| ☐ 322 Rick Wise | .35 | .15 | .03 |
| ☐ 323 Hank Bauer | .35 | .15 | .03 |
| ☐ 324 Bob Locke | .26 | .11 | .02 |
| ☐ 325 Donn Clendenon | .26 | .11 | .02 |

| | MINT | VG-E | F-G |
|---|---|---|---|
| ☐ 326 Dwight Siebler | .26 | .11 | .02 |
| ☐ 327 Dennis Menke | .35 | .15 | .03 |
| ☐ 328 Eddie Fisher | .26 | .11 | .02 |
| ☐ 329 Hawk Taylor | .26 | .11 | .02 |
| ☐ 330 Whitey Ford | 4.50 | 2.10 | .45 |
| ☐ 331 Dodgers Rookies | .35 | .15 | .03 |
| Al Ferrara | | | |
| John Purdin | | | |
| ☐ 332 Ted Abernathy | .26 | .11 | .02 |
| ☐ 333 Tom Reynolds | .26 | .11 | .02 |
| ☐ 334 Vic Roznovsky | .26 | .11 | .02 |
| ☐ 335 Mickey Lolich | 1.25 | .60 | .12 |
| ☐ 336 Woody Held | .26 | .11 | .02 |
| ☐ 337 Mike Cuellar | .35 | .15 | .03 |
| ☐ 338 Phillies Team | .65 | .30 | .06 |
| ☐ 339 Ryne Duren | .35 | .15 | .03 |
| ☐ 340 Tony Oliva | 2.00 | .90 | .20 |
| ☐ 341 Bob Bolin | .26 | .11 | .02 |
| ☐ 342 Bob Rodgers | .26 | .11 | .02 |
| ☐ 343 Mike McCormick | .35 | .15 | .03 |
| ☐ 344 Wes Parker | .35 | .15 | .03 |
| ☐ 345 Floyd Robinson | .26 | .11 | .02 |
| ☐ 346 Bob Bragan | .26 | .11 | .02 |
| ☐ 347 Roy Face | .45 | .20 | .04 |
| ☐ 348 George Banks | .26 | .11 | .02 |
| ☐ 349 Larry Miller | .26 | .11 | .02 |
| ☐ 350 Mickey Mantle | 45.00 | 20.00 | 4.50 |
| ☐ 351 Jim Perry | .45 | .20 | .04 |
| ☐ 352 Alex Johnson | .35 | .15 | .03 |
| ☐ 353 Jerry Lumpe | .26 | .11 | .02 |
| ☐ 354 Cubs Rookies | .26 | .11 | .02 |
| Billy Ott | | | |
| Jack Warner | | | |
| ☐ 355 Vada Pinson | .90 | .40 | .09 |
| ☐ 356 Bill Spanswick | .26 | .11 | .02 |
| ☐ 357 Carl Warwick | .26 | .11 | .02 |
| ☐ 358 Albie Pearson | .26 | .11 | .02 |
| ☐ 359 Ken Johnson | .26 | .11 | .02 |
| ☐ 360 Orlando Cepeda | 1.75 | .85 | .17 |
| ☐ 361 5th Series Checklist | 1.20 | .20 | .05 |
| ☐ 362 Don Schwall | .26 | .11 | .02 |
| ☐ 363 Bob Johnson | .26 | .11 | .02 |
| ☐ 364 Galen Cisco | .26 | .11 | .02 |
| ☐ 365 Jim Gentile | .35 | .15 | .03 |
| ☐ 366 Dan Schneider | .26 | .11 | .02 |
| ☐ 367 Leon Wagner | .26 | .11 | .02 |
| ☐ 368 White Sox Rookies | .35 | .15 | .03 |
| Ken Berry | | | |
| Joel Gibson | | | |
| ☐ 369 Phil Linz | .35 | .14 | .03 |
| ☐ 370 Tommy Davis | .60 | .28 | .06 |
| ☐ 371 Frank Kreutzer | .26 | .11 | .02 |
| ☐ 372 Clay Dalrymple | .26 | .11 | .02 |

| | MINT | VG-E | F-G |
|---|---|---|---|
| ☐ 373 Curt Simmons | .35 | .15 | .03 |
| ☐ 374 Angels Rookies | .40 | .18 | .04 |
| Jose Cardenal | | | |
| Dick Simpson | | | |
| ☐ 375 Dave Wickersham | .26 | .11 | .02 |
| ☐ 376 Jim Landis | .26 | .11 | .02 |
| ☐ 377 Willie Stargell | 4.00 | 1.85 | .40 |
| ☐ 378 Chuck Estrada | .35 | .15 | .03 |
| ☐ 379 Giants Team | .65 | .30 | .06 |
| ☐ 380 Rocky Colavito | .90 | .40 | .09 |
| ☐ 381 Al Jackson | .26 | .11 | .02 |
| ☐ 382 J.C. Martin | .26 | .11 | .02 |
| ☐ 383 Felipe Alou | .35 | .15 | .03 |
| ☐ 384 John Klippstein | .26 | .11 | .02 |
| ☐ 385 Carl Yastrzemski | 30.00 | 14.00 | 3.00 |
| ☐ 386 Cubs Rookies | .35 | .15 | .03 |
| Paul Jaeckel | | | |
| Fred Norman | | | |
| ☐ 387 John Podres | .85 | .40 | .08 |
| ☐ 388 John Blanchard | .35 | .15 | .03 |
| ☐ 389 Don Larsen | .40 | .18 | .04 |
| ☐ 390 Bill Freehan | .75 | .35 | .07 |
| ☐ 391 Mel McGaha | .26 | .11 | .02 |
| ☐ 392 Bob Friend | .35 | .15 | .03 |
| ☐ 393 Ed Kirkpatrick | .26 | .11 | .02 |
| ☐ 394 Jim Hannan | .26 | .11 | .02 |
| ☐ 395 Jim Ray Hart | .35 | .15 | .03 |
| ☐ 396 Frank Bertaina | .26 | .11 | .02 |
| ☐ 397 Jerry Buchek | .26 | .11 | .02 |
| ☐ 398 Reds Rookies | .26 | .11 | .02 |
| Dan Neville | | | |
| Art Shamsky | | | |
| ☐ 399 Ray Herbert | .26 | .11 | .02 |
| ☐ 400 Harmon Killebrew | 4.50 | 2.10 | .45 |
| ☐ 401 Carl Willey | .26 | .11 | .02 |
| ☐ 402 Joe Amalfitano | .26 | .11 | .02 |
| ☐ 403 Red Sox Team | .65 | .30 | .06 |
| ☐ 404 Stan Williams | .26 | .11 | .02 |
| ☐ 405 John Roseboro | .35 | .15 | .03 |
| ☐ 406 Ralph Terry | .35 | .15 | .03 |
| ☐ 407 Lee Maye | .26 | .11 | .02 |
| ☐ 408 Larry Sherry | .35 | .15 | .03 |
| ☐ 409 Astros Rookies | .40 | .18 | .04 |
| Jim Beauchamp | | | |
| Larry Dierker | | | |
| ☐ 410 Luis Aparicio | 2.50 | 1.15 | .25 |
| ☐ 411 Roger Craig | .40 | .18 | .04 |
| ☐ 412 Bob Bailey | .26 | .11 | .02 |
| ☐ 413 Hal Reniff | .26 | .11 | .02 |
| ☐ 414 Al Lopez | 1.00 | .45 | .10 |
| ☐ 415 Curt Flood | .70 | .32 | .07 |
| ☐ 416 Jim Brewer | .26 | .11 | .02 |
| ☐ 417 Ed Brinkman | .26 | .11 | .02 |

|  | MINT | VG-E | F-G |
|---|---|---|---|
| ☐ 418 John Edwards | .26 | .11 | .02 |
| ☐ 419 Ruben Amaro | .26 | .11 | .02 |
| ☐ 420 Larry Jackson | .26 | .11 | .02 |
| ☐ 421 Twins Rookies | .26 | .11 | .02 |
| Gary Dotter | | | |
| Jay Ward | | | |
| ☐ 422 Aubrey Gatewood | .26 | .11 | .02 |
| ☐ 423 Jesse Gonder | .26 | .11 | .02 |
| ☐ 424 Gary Bell | .26 | .11 | .02 |
| ☐ 425 Wayne Causey | .26 | .11 | .02 |
| ☐ 426 Braves Team | .65 | .30 | .06 |
| ☐ 427 Bob Saverine | .26 | .11 | .02 |
| ☐ 428 Bob Shaw | .26 | .11 | .02 |
| ☐ 429 Don Demeter | .26 | .11 | .02 |
| ☐ 430 Gary Peters | .35 | .15 | .03 |
| ☐ 431 Cards Rookies | .40 | .18 | .04 |
| Nelson Briles | | | |
| Wayne Spiezio | | | |
| ☐ 432 Jim Grant | .26 | .11 | .02 |
| ☐ 433 John Bateman | .26 | .11 | .02 |
| ☐ 434 Dave Morehead | .26 | .11 | .02 |
| ☐ 435 Willie Davis | .55 | .25 | .05 |
| ☐ 436 Don Elston | .26 | .11 | .02 |
| ☐ 437 Chico Cardenas | .26 | .11 | .02 |
| ☐ 438 Harry Walker | .26 | .11 | .02 |
| ☐ 439 Moe Drabowski | .26 | .11 | .02 |
| ☐ 440 Tom Tresh | .65 | .30 | .06 |
| ☐ 441 Denny LeMaster | .26 | .11 | .02 |
| ☐ 442 Vic Power | .26 | .11 | .02 |
| ☐ 443 6th Series Checklist | 1.25 | .20 | .05 |
| ☐ 444 Bob Hendley | .26 | .11 | .02 |
| ☐ 445 Don Lock | .26 | .11 | .02 |
| ☐ 446 Art Mahaffey | .26 | .11 | .02 |
| ☐ 447 Julian Javier | .50 | .22 | .05 |
| ☐ 448 Lee Stange | .50 | .22 | .05 |
| ☐ 449 Mets Rookies | .50 | .22 | .05 |
| Jerry Hinsley | | | |
| Gary Kroll | | | |
| ☐ 450 Elston Howard | 1.75 | .85 | .17 |
| ☐ 451 Jim Owens | .50 | .22 | .05 |
| ☐ 452 Gary Geiger | .50 | .22 | .05 |
| ☐ 453 Dodgers Rookies | .65 | .30 | .06 |
| Willie Crawford | | | |
| John Werhas | | | |
| ☐ 454 Ed Rakow | .50 | .22 | .05 |
| ☐ 455 Norm Siebern | .50 | .22 | .05 |
| ☐ 456 Bill Henry | .50 | .22 | .05 |
| ☐ 457 Bob Kennedy | .50 | .22 | .05 |
| ☐ 458 John Buzhardt | .50 | .22 | .05 |
| ☐ 459 Frank Kostro | .50 | .22 | .05 |
| ☐ 460 Richie Allen | 1.75 | .85 | .17 |
| ☐ 461 Braves Rookies | 8.50 | 4.00 | .85 |
| Clay Carroll | | | |
| Phil Niekro | | | |

|  | MINT | VG-E | F-G |
|---|---|---|---|
| ☐ 462 Lew Krausse | .50 | .22 | .05 |
| (photo actually | | | |
| Pete Lovrich) | | | |
| ☐ 463 Manny Mota | .70 | .32 | .07 |
| ☐ 464 Ron Piche | .50 | .22 | .05 |
| ☐ 465 Tom Haller | .50 | .22 | .05 |
| ☐ 466 Senators Rookies | .50 | .22 | .05 |
| Pete Craig | | | |
| Dick Nen | | | |
| ☐ 467 Ray Washburn | .50 | .22 | .05 |
| ☐ 468 Larry Brown | .50 | .22 | .05 |
| ☐ 469 Don Nottebart | .50 | .22 | .05 |
| ☐ 470 Yogi Berra | 9.00 | 4.00 | .80 |
| ☐ 471 Bill Hoeft | .50 | .22 | .05 |
| ☐ 472 Don Pavletich | .50 | .22 | .05 |
| ☐ 473 Orioles Rookies | 2.75 | 1.25 | .27 |
| Paul Blair | | | |
| Dave Johnson | | | |
| ☐ 474 Cookie Rojas | .50 | .22 | .05 |
| ☐ 475 Clete Boyer | .75 | .35 | .07 |
| ☐ 476 Billy O'Dell | .50 | .22 | .05 |
| ☐ 477 Cards Rookies | 100.00 | 45.00 | 10.00 |
| Fritz Ackley | | | |
| Steve Carlton | | | |
| ☐ 478 Wilbur Wood | .70 | .32 | .07 |
| ☐ 479 Ken Harrelson | 1.50 | .70 | .15 |
| ☐ 480 Joel Horlen | .65 | .30 | .06 |
| ☐ 481 Indians Team | .90 | .40 | .09 |
| ☐ 482 Bob Priddy | .50 | .22 | .05 |
| ☐ 483 George Smith | .50 | .22 | .05 |
| ☐ 484 Ron Perranoski | .75 | .35 | .07 |
| ☐ 485 Nellie Fox | 1.75 | .85 | .17 |
| ☐ 486 Angels Rookies | .50 | .22 | .05 |
| Tom Egan | | | |
| Pat Rogan | | | |
| ☐ 487 Woody Woodward | .50 | .22 | .05 |
| ☐ 488 Ted Wills | .50 | .22 | .05 |
| ☐ 489 Gene Mauch MGR | .65 | .30 | .06 |
| ☐ 490 Earl Battey | .50 | .22 | .05 |
| ☐ 491 Tracy Stallard | .50 | .22 | .05 |
| ☐ 492 Gene Freese | .50 | .22 | .05 |
| ☐ 493 Tigers Rookies | .50 | .22 | .05 |
| Bill Roman | | | |
| Bruce Brubaker | | | |
| ☐ 494 Jay Ritchie | .50 | .22 | .05 |
| ☐ 495 Joe Christopher | .50 | .22 | .05 |
| ☐ 496 Joe Cunningham | .50 | .22 | .05 |
| ☐ 497 Giants Rookies | .60 | .28 | .06 |
| Ken Henderson | | | |
| Jack Hiatt | | | |
| ☐ 498 Gene Stephens | .50 | .22 | .05 |
| ☐ 499 Stu Miller | .50 | .22 | .05 |
| ☐ 500 Ed Mathews | 5.50 | 2.60 | .55 |

|  | MINT | VG-E | F-G |
|---|---|---|---|
| 501 Indians Rookies ........ | .50 | .22 | .05 |
| Ralph Gagliano | | | |
| Jim Rittwage | | | |
| 502 Don Cardwell .......... | .50 | .22 | .05 |
| 503 Phil Gagliano .......... | .50 | .22 | .05 |
| 504 Jerry Grote ........... | .50 | .22 | .05 |
| 505 Ray Culp ............. | .50 | .22 | .05 |
| 506 Sam Mele ............. | .50 | .22 | .05 |
| 507 Sam Ellis ............. | .50 | .22 | .05 |
| 508 7th Series Checklist ..... | 1.50 | .25 | .05 |
| 509 Red Sox Rookies ..... | .50 | .22 | .05 |
| Bob Guindon | | | |
| Gerry Vezendy | | | |
| 510 Ernie Banks .......... | 12.00 | 5.50 | 1.20 |
| 511 Ron Locke ........... | .50 | .22 | .05 |
| 512 Cap Peterson ......... | .50 | .22 | .05 |
| 513 Yankees Team ......... | 2.00 | .90 | .20 |
| 514 Joe Azcue ........... | .50 | .22 | .05 |
| 515 Vern Law ............ | .65 | .30 | .06 |
| 516 Al Weis .............. | .50 | .22 | .05 |
| 517 Angels Rookies ....... | .50 | .22 | .05 |
| Paul Schaal | | | |
| Jack Warner | | | |
| 518 Ken Rowe ............ | .50 | .22 | .05 |
| 519 Bob Uecker .......... | 4.50 | 2.10 | .45 |
| 520 Tony Cloninger ....... | .50 | .22 | .05 |
| 521 Phillies Rookies ...... | .50 | .22 | .05 |
| Dave Bennett | | | |
| Morrie Stevens | | | |
| 522 Hank Aguirre ......... | .50 | .22 | .05 |
| 523 Mike Brumley ........ | .70 | .32 | .07 |
| 524 Dave Giusti .......... | .70 | .32 | .07 |
| 525 Ed Bressoud ......... | .70 | .32 | .07 |
| 526 Athletics Rookies ..... | 12.50 | 5.75 | 1.25 |
| Rene Lachemann | | | |
| Johnny Odom | | | |
| Jim Hunter | | | |
| Skip Lockwood | | | |
| 527 Jeff Torborg ......... | .70 | .32 | .07 |
| 528 George Altman ....... | .70 | .32 | .07 |
| 529 Jerry Fosnow ........ | .70 | .32 | .07 |
| 530 Jim Maloney ......... | .90 | .40 | .09 |
| 531 Chuck Hiller ......... | .70 | .32 | .07 |
| 532 Hector Lopez ........ | .70 | .32 | .07 |
| 533 Mets Rookies ........ | 4.50 | 2.10 | .45 |
| Dan Napoleon | | | |
| Ron Swoboda | | | |
| Tug McGraw | | | |
| Jim Bethke | | | |
| 534 John Herrnstein ...... | .70 | .32 | .07 |
| 535 Jack Kralick ......... | .70 | .32 | .07 |
| 536 Andre Rodgers ....... | .70 | .32 | .07 |
| 537 Angels Rookies ........ | .90 | .40 | .09 |
| Marcelino Lopes | | | |
| Phil Roof | | | |
| Rudy May | | | |
| 538 Chuck Dressen ........ | .70 | .32 | .07 |
| 539 Herm Starrette ....... | .70 | .32 | .07 |
| 540 Lou Brock ........... | 12.00 | 5.50 | 1.20 |
| 541 White Sox Rookies ..... | .70 | .32 | .07 |
| Greg Bollo | | | |
| Bob Locker | | | |
| 542 Lou Klimchock ........ | .70 | .32 | .07 |
| 543 Ed Connolly .......... | .70 | .32 | .07 |
| 544 Howie Reed .......... | .70 | .32 | .07 |
| 545 Jesus Alou .......... | .70 | .32 | .07 |
| 546 Indians Rookies ....... | .70 | .32 | .07 |
| Bill Davis | | | |
| Mike Hedlund | | | |
| Ray Barker | | | |
| Floyd Weaver | | | |
| 547 Jake Wood ........... | .70 | .32 | .07 |
| 548 Dick Stigman ......... | .70 | .32 | .07 |
| 549 Cubs Rookies ........ | 1.25 | .60 | .12 |
| Roberto Pena | | | |
| Glenn Beckert | | | |
| 550 Mel Stottlemyre ...... | 3.25 | 1.50 | .32 |
| 551 Mets Team .......... | 1.75 | .85 | .17 |
| 552 Julio Gotay .......... | .70 | .32 | .07 |
| 553 Astros Rookies ....... | .70 | .32 | .07 |
| Gene Ratliff | | | |
| Jack McClure | | | |
| 554 Chico Ruiz .......... | .70 | .32 | .07 |
| 555 Jack Baldschun ....... | .70 | .32 | .07 |
| 556 Red Schoendienst ..... | 1.50 | .70 | .15 |
| 557 Jose Santiago ........ | .70 | .32 | .07 |
| 558 Tom Sisk ........... | .70 | .32 | .07 |
| 559 Ed Bailey ........... | .70 | .32 | .07 |
| 560 Boog Powell ......... | 1.75 | .85 | .17 |
| 561 Dodgers Rookies ...... | 1.50 | .70 | .15 |
| Dennis Daboll | | | |
| Mike Kekich | | | |
| Hector Valle | | | |
| Jim Lefebvre | | | |
| 562 Bill Moran ........... | .70 | .32 | .07 |
| 563 Julio Navarro ........ | .70 | .32 | .07 |
| 564 Mel Nelson .......... | .70 | .32 | .07 |
| 565 Ernie Broglio ......... | .70 | .32 | .07 |
| 566 Yankees Rookies ...... | .70 | .32 | .07 |
| Gil Blanco | | | |
| Ross Moschitto | | | |
| Art Lopez | | | |
| 567 Tommie Aaron ........ | .90 | .40 | .09 |
| 568 Ron Taylor .......... | .70 | .32 | .07 |
| 569 Gino Cimoli .......... | .70 | .32 | .07 |

|  | MINT | VG-E | F-G |
|---|---|---|---|
| ☐ 570 Claude Osteen ......... | .90 | .40 | .09 |
| ☐ 571 Ossie Virgil ........... | .70 | .32 | .07 |
| ☐ 572 Orioles Team .......... | 1.35 | .60 | .15 |
| ☐ 573 Red Sox Rookies ...... | 1.75 | .85 | .17 |
|    Jim Lonborg | | | |
|    Gerry Moses | | | |
|    Bill Schlesinger | | | |
|    Mike Ryan | | | |
| ☑ 574 Roy Sievers ........... | .90 | .40 | .09 |
| ☐ 575 Jose Pagan ........... | .70 | .32 | .07 |
| ☐ 576 Terry Fox ............. | .70 | .32 | .07 |
| ☐ 577 AL Rookie Stars ....... | .70 | .32 | .07 |
|    Darold Knowles | | | |
|    Don Buschhorn | | | |
|    Richie Scheinblum | | | |
| ☐ 578 Cam Carreon .......... | .70 | .32 | .07 |
| ☐ 579 Dick Smith ........... | .70 | .32 | .07 |
| ☐ 580 Jim Hall ............. | .70 | .32 | .07 |
| ☐ 581 NL Rookie Stars ....... | 11.00 | 5.25 | 1.10 |
|    Tony Perez | | | |
|    Dave Ricketts | | | |
|    Kevin Collins | | | |
| ☐ 582 Bob Schmidt .......... | .70 | .32 | .07 |
| ☐ 583 Wes Covington ........ | .70 | .32 | .07 |
| ☐ 584 Harry Bright .......... | .70 | .32 | .07 |
| ☐ 585 Hank Fischer ......... | .70 | .32 | .07 |
| ☐ 586 Tom McCraw .......... | .70 | .32 | .07 |
| ☐ 587 Joe Sparma ........... | .70 | .32 | .07 |
| ☐ 588 Len Green ............ | .70 | .32 | .07 |
| ☐ 589 Giants Rookies ........ | .70 | .32 | .07 |
|    Frank Linzy | | | |
|    B. Schroder | | | |
| ☐ 590 John Wyatt ........... | .70 | .32 | .07 |
| ☐ 591 Bob Skinner .......... | .70 | .32 | .07 |
| ☐ 592 Frank Bork ........... | .70 | .32 | .07 |
| ☐ 593 Tigers Rookies ........ | .90 | .40 | .09 |
|    Jackie Moore | | | |
|    John Sullivan | | | |
| ☐ 594 Joe Gaines ........... | .70 | .32 | .07 |
| ☐ 595 Don Lee ............. | .70 | .32 | .07 |
| ☐ 596 Don Landrum ......... | .70 | .32 | .07 |
| ☐ 597 Twins Rookies ........ | .70 | .32 | .07 |
|    Joe Nossek | | | |
|    John Sevcik | | | |
|    Dick Reese | | | |
| ☐ 598 Al Downing ........... | 1.00 | .45 | .10 |

## 1966 TOPPS

pitcher

The cards in this 598 card set measure 2½" by 3½". There are the same number of cards as in the 1966 set. Once again, the seventh series cards (523 to 598) are considered more difficult to obtain than any other series' cards in the set.

Complete Set: M-700.00; VG-E-320.00; F-G-70.00

|  | MINT | VG-E | F-G |
|---|---|---|---|
| Common Player (1–110) | .18 | .08 | .01 |
| Common Player (111–446) | .24 | .10 | .02 |
| Common Player (447–522) | .55 | .25 | .05 |
| Common Player (523–598) | 3.50 | 1.65 | .35 |
| ☐ 1 Willie Mays ........... | 33.00 | 9.00 | 2.00 |
| ☐ 2 Ted Abernathy ......... | .18 | .08 | .01 |
| ☐ 3 Sam Mele ............. | .18 | .08 | .01 |
| ☐ 4 Ray Culp ............. | .18 | .08 | .01 |
| ☐ 5 Jim Fregosi ........... | .30 | .12 | .03 |
| ☐ 6 Chuck Schilling ........ | .18 | .08 | .01 |
| ☐ 7 Tracy Stallard ......... | .18 | .08 | .01 |
| ☐ 8 Floyd Robinson ........ | .18 | .08 | .01 |
| ☐ 9 Clete Boyer ........... | .30 | .12 | .03 |
| ☐ 10 Tony Cloninger ........ | .18 | .08 | .01 |
| ☐ 11 Senators Rookies ...... | .18 | .08 | .01 |
|    Brant Alyea | | | |
|    Pete Craig | | | |
| ☐ 12 John Tsitouris ......... | .18 | .08 | .01 |
| ☐ 13 Lou Johnson .......... | .18 | .08 | .01 |
| ☐ 14 Norm Siebern ......... | .18 | .08 | .01 |
| ☐ 15 Vern Law ............ | .30 | .12 | .03 |
| ☐ 16 Larry Brown .......... | .18 | .08 | .01 |
| ☐ 17 John Stephenson ...... | .18 | .08 | .01 |
| ☐ 18 Roland Sheldon ....... | .18 | .08 | .01 |
| ☐ 19 Giants Team .......... | .55 | .25 | .05 |

| | | MINT | VG-E | F-G |
|---|---|---|---|---|
| ☐ 20 | Willie Horton | .45 | .20 | .04 |
| ☐ 21 | Don Nottebart | .18 | .08 | .01 |
| ☐ 22 | Joe Nossek | .18 | .08 | .01 |
| ☐ 23 | Jack Sanford | .18 | .08 | .01 |
| ☐ 24 | Don Kessinger | .55 | .25 | .05 |
| ☐ 25 | Pete Ward | .18 | .08 | .01 |
| ☐ 26 | Ray Sadecki | .18 | .08 | .01 |
| ☐ 27 | Orioles Rookies | .25 | .10 | .02 |
| | Darold Knowles | | | |
| | Andy Etchebarren | | | |
| ☐ 28 | Phil Niekro | 4.00 | 1.85 | .40 |
| ☐ 29 | Mike Brumley | .18 | .08 | .01 |
| ☐ 30 | Pete Rose | 35.00 | 16.50 | 3.50 |
| ☐ 31 | Jack Cullen | .18 | .08 | .01 |
| ☐ 32 | Adolfo Phillips | .18 | .08 | .01 |
| ☐ 33 | Jim Pagliaroni | .18 | .08 | .01 |
| ☐ 34 | 1st Series Checklist | 1.00 | .20 | .05 |
| ☐ 35 | Ron Swoboda | .18 | .08 | .01 |
| ☐ 36 | Jim Hunter | 3.50 | 1.65 | .35 |
| ☐ 37 | Billy Herman | .75 | .35 | .07 |
| ☐ 38 | Ron Nischwitz | .18 | .08 | .01 |
| ☐ 39 | Ken Henderson | .18 | .08 | .01 |
| ☐ 40 | Jim Grant | .18 | .08 | .01 |
| ☐ 41 | Don LeJohn | .18 | .08 | .01 |
| ☐ 42 | Aubrey Gatewood | .18 | .08 | .01 |
| ☐ 43 | Don Landrum | .18 | .08 | .01 |
| ☐ 44 | Indians Rookies | .18 | .08 | .01 |
| | Bill Davis | | | |
| | Tom Kelley | | | |
| ☐ 45 | Jim Gentile | .30 | .12 | .03 |
| ☐ 46 | Howie Koplitz | .18 | .08 | .01 |
| ☐ 47 | J.C. Martin | .18 | .08 | .01 |
| ☐ 48 | Paul Blair | .30 | .12 | .03 |
| ☐ 49 | Woody Woodward | .18 | .08 | .01 |
| ☐ 50 | Mickey Mantle | 32.00 | 14.00 | 3.20 |
| ☐ 51 | Gordon Richardson | .18 | .08 | .01 |
| ☐ 52 | Power Plus | .25 | .10 | .02 |
| | Wes Covington | | | |
| | Johnny Callison | | | |
| ☐ 53 | Bob Duliba | .18 | .08 | .01 |
| ☐ 54 | Jose Pagan | .18 | .08 | .01 |
| ☐ 55 | Ken Harrelson | .75 | .35 | .07 |
| ☐ 56 | Sandy Valdespino | .18 | .08 | .01 |
| ☐ 57 | Jim Lefebvre | .25 | .10 | .02 |
| ☐ 58 | Dave Wickersham | .18 | .08 | .01 |
| ☐ 59 | Reds Team | .55 | .25 | .05 |
| ☐ 60 | Curt Flood | .55 | .25 | .05 |
| ☐ 61 | Bob Bolin | .18 | .08 | .01 |
| ☐ 62 A | Merritt Ranew | .25 | .10 | .02 |
| | (with sold line) | | | |
| ☐ 62 B | Merritt Ranew | 5.00 | 2.35 | .50 |
| | (without sold line) | | | |
| ☐ 63 | Jim Stewart | .18 | .08 | .01 |

| | | MINT | VG-E | F-G |
|---|---|---|---|---|
| ☐ 64 | Bob Bruce | .18 | .08 | .01 |
| ☐ 65 | Leon Wagner | .18 | .08 | .01 |
| ☐ 66 | Al Weis | .18 | .08 | .01 |
| ☐ 67 | Mets Rookies | .25 | .10 | .02 |
| | Cleon Jones | | | |
| | Dick Selma | | | |
| ☐ 68 | Hal Reniff | .18 | .08 | .01 |
| ☐ 69 | Ken Hamlin | .18 | .08 | .01 |
| ☐ 70 | Carl Yastrzemski | 24.00 | 11.00 | 2.40 |
| ☐ 71 | Frank Carpin | .18 | .08 | .01 |
| ☐ 72 | Tony Perez | 3.00 | 1.40 | .30 |
| ☐ 73 | Jerry Zimmerman | .18 | .08 | .01 |
| ☐ 74 | Don Mossi | .25 | .10 | .02 |
| ☐ 75 | Tommy Davis | .50 | .22 | .05 |
| ☐ 76 | Red Schoendienst | .45 | .20 | .04 |
| ☐ 77 | Johnny Orsino | .18 | .08 | .01 |
| ☐ 78 | Frank Linzy | .18 | .08 | .01 |
| ☐ 79 | Joe Pepitone | .50 | .22 | .05 |
| ☐ 80 | Richie Allen | 1.00 | .45 | .10 |
| ☐ 81 | Ray Oyler | .18 | .08 | .01 |
| ☐ 82 | Bob Hendley | .18 | .08 | .01 |
| ☐ 83 | Albie Pearson | .18 | .08 | .01 |
| ☐ 84 | Braves Rookies | .18 | .08 | .01 |
| | Jim Beauchamp | | | |
| | Dick Kelley | | | |
| ☐ 85 | Eddie Fisher | .18 | .08 | .01 |
| ☐ 86 | John Bateman | .18 | .08 | .01 |
| ☐ 87 | Dan Napoleon | .18 | .08 | .01 |
| ☐ 88 | Fred Whitfield | .18 | .08 | .01 |
| ☐ 89 | Ted Davidson | .18 | .08 | .01 |
| ☐ 90 | Luis Aparicio | 2.25 | 1.00 | .22 |
| ☐ 91 A | Bob Uecker | 3.00 | 1.40 | .30 |
| | (with traded line) | | | |
| ☐ 91 B | Bob Uecker | 9.00 | 4.25 | .90 |
| | (no traded line) | | | |
| ☐ 92 | Yankees Team | 1.10 | .50 | .11 |
| ☐ 93 | Jim Lonborg | .50 | .22 | .05 |
| ☐ 94 | Matty Alou | .30 | .12 | .03 |
| ☐ 95 | Pete Richert | .18 | .08 | .01 |
| ☐ 96 | Felipe Alou | .30 | .12 | .03 |
| ☐ 97 | Jim Merritt | .18 | .08 | .01 |
| ☐ 98 | Don Demeter | .18 | .08 | .01 |
| ☐ 99 | Buc Belters | 1.10 | .50 | .11 |
| | Willie Stargell | | | |
| | Donn Clendenon | | | |
| ☐ 100 | Sandy Koufax | 11.00 | 5.25 | 1.10 |
| ☐ 101 A | Checklist 2 | 1.35 | .25 | .05 |
| | (115 Bill Henry) | | | |
| ☐ 101 B | Checklist 2 | 4.25 | .60 | .10 |
| | (115 W. Spahn) | | | |
| ☐ 102 | Ed Kirkpatrick | .18 | .08 | .01 |
| ☐ 103 A | Dick Groat | .50 | .22 | .05 |
| | (with traded line) | | | |

| | MINT | VG-E | F-G |
|---|---|---|---|
| ☐ 103 **B** Dick Groat | 7.50 | 3.50 | .75 |
| (no traded line) | | | |
| ☐ 104 **A** Alex Johnson | .40 | .18 | .04 |
| (with traded line) | | | |
| ☐ 104 **B** Alex Johnson | 7.00 | 3.25 | .70 |
| (no traded line) | | | |
| ☐ 105 Milt Pappas | .30 | .12 | .03 |
| ☐ 106 Rusty Staub | 1.00 | .45 | .10 |
| ☐ 107 A's Rookies | .18 | .08 | .01 |
| Larry Stahl | | | |
| Ron Tompkins | | | |
| ☐ 108 Bobby Klaus | .18 | .08 | .01 |
| ☐ 109 Ralph Terry | .30 | .12 | .03 |
| ☐ 110 Ernie Banks | 4.00 | 1.85 | .40 |
| ☐ 111 Gary Peters | .35 | .15 | .03 |
| ☐ 112 Manny Mota | .35 | .15 | .03 |
| ☐ 113 Hank Aguirre | .24 | .10 | .02 |
| ☐ 114 Jim Gosger | .24 | .10 | .02 |
| ☐ 115 Bill Henry | .24 | .10 | .02 |
| ☐ 116 Walt Alston | .80 | .40 | .08 |
| ☐ 117 Jake Gibbs | .24 | .10 | .02 |
| ☐ 118 Mike McCormick | .35 | .15 | .03 |
| ☐ 119 Art Shamsky | .24 | .10 | .02 |
| ☐ 120 Harmon Killebrew | 3.75 | 1.75 | .37 |
| ☐ 121 Ray Herbert | .24 | .10 | .02 |
| ☐ 122 Joe Gaines | .24 | .10 | .02 |
| ☐ 123 Pirates Rookies | .24 | .10 | .02 |
| Frank Bork | | | |
| Jerry May | | | |
| ☐ 124 Tug McGraw | 1.10 | .50 | .11 |
| ☐ 125 Lou Brock | 5.00 | 2.35 | .50 |
| ☐ 126 Jim Palmer | 30.00 | 14.00 | 3.00 |
| ☐ 127 Ken Berry | .24 | .10 | .02 |
| ☐ 128 Jim Landis | .24 | .10 | .02 |
| ☐ 129 Jack Kralick | .24 | .10 | .02 |
| ☐ 130 Joe Torre | .75 | .35 | .07 |
| ☐ 131 Angels Team | .55 | .25 | .05 |
| ☐ 132 Orlando Cepeda | 1.25 | .60 | .12 |
| ☐ 133 Don McMahon | .24 | .10 | .02 |
| ☐ 134 Wes Parker | .35 | .15 | .03 |
| ☐ 135 Dave Morehead | .24 | .10 | .02 |
| ☐ 136 Woody Held | .24 | .10 | .02 |
| ☐ 137 Pat Corrales | .30 | .12 | .03 |
| ☐ 138 Roger Repoz | .24 | .10 | .02 |
| ☐ 139 Cubs Rookies | .24 | .10 | .02 |
| Byron Browne | | | |
| Don Young | | | |
| ☐ 140 Jim Maloney | .35 | .15 | .03 |
| ☐ 141 Tom McCraw | .24 | .10 | .02 |
| ☐ 142 Don Dennis | .24 | .10 | .02 |
| ☐ 143 Jose Tartabull | .24 | .10 | .02 |
| ☐ 144 Don Schwall | .24 | .10 | .02 |
| ☐ 145 Bill Freehan | .50 | .22 | .05 |

| | MINT | VG-E | F-G |
|---|---|---|---|
| ☐ 146 George Altman | .24 | .10 | .02 |
| ☐ 147 Lum Harris | .24 | .10 | .02 |
| ☐ 148 Bob Johnson | .24 | .10 | .02 |
| ☐ 149 Dick Nen | .24 | .10 | .02 |
| ☐ 150 Rocky Colavito | .80 | .40 | .08 |
| ☐ 151 Gary Wagner | .24 | .10 | .02 |
| ☐ 152 Frank Malzone | .35 | .15 | .03 |
| ☐ 153 Rico Carty | .60 | .28 | .06 |
| ☐ 154 Chuck Hiller | .24 | .10 | .02 |
| ☐ 155 Marcelino Lopez | .24 | .10 | .02 |
| ☐ 156 Double Play Combo | .35 | .15 | .03 |
| Dick Schofield | | | |
| Hal Lanier | | | |
| ☐ 157 Rene Lachemann | .35 | .15 | .03 |
| ☐ 158 Jim Brewer | .24 | .10 | .02 |
| ☐ 159 Chico Ruiz | .24 | .10 | .02 |
| ☐ 160 Whitey Ford | 4.00 | 1.85 | .40 |
| ☐ 161 Jerry Lumpe | .24 | .10 | .02 |
| ☐ 162 Lee Maye | .24 | .10 | .02 |
| ☐ 163 Tito Francona | .35 | .15 | .03 |
| ☐ 164 White Sox Rookies | .35 | .15 | .03 |
| Tommie Agee | | | |
| Marv Staehle | | | |
| ☐ 165 Don Lock | .24 | .10 | .02 |
| ☐ 166 Chris Krug | .24 | .10 | .02 |
| ☐ 167 Boog Powell | .90 | .40 | .09 |
| ☐ 168 Dan Osinski | .24 | .10 | .02 |
| ☐ 169 Duke Sims | .24 | .10 | .02 |
| ☐ 170 Cookie Rojas | .24 | .10 | .02 |
| ☐ 171 Nick Willhite | .24 | .10 | .02 |
| ☐ 172 Mets Team | .75 | .35 | .07 |
| ☐ 173 Al Spangler | .24 | .10 | .02 |
| ☐ 174 Ron Taylor | .24 | .10 | .02 |
| ☐ 175 Bert Campaneris | .50 | .22 | .05 |
| ☐ 176 Jim Davenport | .35 | .15 | .03 |
| ☐ 177 Hector Lopez | .24 | .10 | .02 |
| ☐ 178 Bob Tillman | .24 | .10 | .02 |
| ☐ 179 Cards Rookies | .35 | .15 | .03 |
| Dennis Aust | | | |
| Bob Tolan | | | |
| ☐ 180 Vada Pinson | .80 | .40 | .08 |
| ☐ 181 Al Worthington | .24 | .10 | .02 |
| ☐ 182 Jerry Lynch | .24 | .10 | .02 |
| ☐ 183 3rd Series Checklist | 1.10 | .20 | .05 |
| ☐ 184 Denis Menke | .24 | .10 | .02 |
| ☐ 185 Bob Buhl | .24 | .10 | .02 |
| ☐ 186 Ruben Amaro | .24 | .10 | .02 |
| ☐ 187 Chuck Dressen | .24 | .10 | .02 |
| ☐ 188 Al Luplow | .24 | .10 | .02 |
| ☐ 189 John Roseboro | .35 | .15 | .03 |
| ☐ 190 Jimmie Hall | .24 | .10 | .02 |
| ☐ 191 Darrell Sutherland | .24 | .10 | .02 |
| ☐ 192 Vic Power | .24 | .10 | .02 |

| | MINT | VG-E | F-G | | MINT | VG-E | F-G |
|---|---|---|---|---|---|---|---|
| ☐ 193 Dave McNally | .35 | .15 | .03 | ☐ 221 NL ERA Leaders: | 1.50 | .70 | .15 |
| ☐ 194 Senators Team | .55 | .25 | .05 | Sandy Koufax | | | |
| ☐ 195 Joe Morgan | 4.25 | 2.00 | .42 | Juan Marichal | | | |
| ☐ 196 Don Pavletich | .24 | .10 | .02 | Vern Law | | | |
| ☐ 197 Sonny Siebert | .35 | .15 | .03 | ☐ 222 AL ERA Leaders: | .75 | .35 | .07 |
| ☐ 198 Mickey Stanley | .50 | .22 | .05 | Sam McDowell | | | |
| ☐ 199 Chisox Clubbers | .35 | .15 | .03 | Eddie Fisher | | | |
| Bill Skowron | | | | Sonny Siebert | | | |
| Johnny Romano | | | | ☐ 223 NL Pitching Leaders: | 1.50 | .70 | .15 |
| Floyd Robinson | | | | Sandy Koufax | | | |
| ☐ 200 Eddie Mathews | 3.00 | 1.40 | .30 | Tony Cloninger | | | |
| ☐ 201 Jim Dickson | .24 | .10 | .02 | Don Drysdale | | | |
| ☐ 202 Clay Dalrymple | .24 | .10 | .02 | ☐ 224 AL Pitching Leaders: | .75 | .35 | .07 |
| ☐ 203 Jose Santiago | .24 | .10 | .02 | Jim Grant | | | |
| ☐ 204 Cubs Team | .55 | .25 | .05 | Mel Stottlemyre | | | |
| ☐ 205 Tom Tresh | .55 | .25 | .05 | Jim Kaat | | | |
| ☐ 206 Alvin Jackson | .24 | .10 | .02 | ☐ 225 NL Strikeout Leaders: | 1.50 | .70 | .15 |
| ☐ 207 Frank Quilici | .24 | .10 | .02 | Sandy Koufax | | | |
| ☐ 208 Bob Miller | .24 | .10 | .02 | Bob Veale | | | |
| ☐ 209 Tigers Rookies | .60 | .28 | .06 | Bob Gibson | | | |
| Fritz Fisher | | | | ☐ 226 AL Strikeout Leaders: | .75 | .35 | .07 |
| John Hiller | | | | Sam McDowell | | | |
| ☐ 210 Bill Mazeroski | .75 | .35 | .07 | Mickey Lolich | | | |
| ☐ 211 Frank Kreutzer | .24 | .10 | .02 | Dennis McLain | | | |
| ☐ 212 Ed Kranepool | .35 | .15 | .03 | Sonny Siebert | | | |
| ☐ 213 Fred Newman | .24 | .10 | .02 | ☐ 227 Russ Nixon | .24 | .10 | .02 |
| ☐ 214 Tommy Harper | .35 | .15 | .03 | ☐ 228 Larry Dierker | .24 | .10 | .02 |
| ☐ 215 NL Batting Leaders: | 3.00 | 1.40 | .30 | ☐ 229 Hank Bauer | .35 | .15 | .03 |
| Bob Clemente | | | | ☐ 230 John Callison | .35 | .15 | .03 |
| Hank Aaron | | | | ☐ 231 Floyd Weaver | .24 | .10 | .02 |
| Willie Mays | | | | ☐ 232 Glenn Beckert | .35 | .15 | .03 |
| ☐ 216 AL Batting Leaders: | 1.25 | .60 | .12 | ☐ 233 Dom Zanni | .24 | .10 | .02 |
| Tony Oliva | | | | ☐ 234 Yankees Rookies | 1.50 | .70 | .15 |
| Carl Yastrzemski | | | | Rich Beck | | | |
| Vic Davalillo | | | | Roy White | | | |
| ☐ 217 NL Home Run Leaders: | 1.75 | .85 | .17 | ☐ 235 Don Cardwell | .24 | .10 | .02 |
| Willie Mays | | | | ☐ 236 Mike Hershberger | .24 | .10 | .02 |
| Willie McCovey | | | | ☐ 237 Billy O'Dell | .24 | .10 | .02 |
| Billy Williams | | | | ☐ 238 Dodgers Team | .85 | .40 | .08 |
| ☐ 218 AL Home Run Leaders: | .75 | .35 | .07 | ☐ 239 Orlando Pena | .24 | .10 | .02 |
| Tony Conigliaro | | | | ☐ 240 Earl Battey | .24 | .10 | .02 |
| Norm Cash | | | | ☐ 241 Dennis Ribant | .24 | .10 | .02 |
| Willie Horton | | | | ☐ 242 Jesus Alou | .24 | .10 | .02 |
| ☐ 219 NL RBI Leaders: | 1.25 | .60 | .12 | ☐ 243 Nelson Briles | .24 | .10 | .02 |
| Deron Johnson | | | | ☐ 244 Astros Rookies | .24 | .10 | .02 |
| Frank Robinson | | | | Chuck Harrison | | | |
| Willie Mays | | | | Sonny Jackson | | | |
| ☐ 220 AL RBI Leaders: | .75 | .35 | .07 | ☐ 245 John Buzhardt | .24 | .10 | .02 |
| Rocky Colavito | | | | ☐ 246 Ed Bailey | .24 | .10 | .02 |
| Willie Horton | | | | ☐ 247 Carl Warwick | .24 | .10 | .02 |
| Tony Oliva | | | | ☐ 248 Pete Mikkelsen | .24 | .10 | .02 |
| | | | | ☐ 249 Bill Rigney | .24 | .10 | .02 |
| | | | | ☐ 250 Sam Ellis | .24 | .10 | .02 |

| | MINT | VG-E | F-G |
|---|---|---|---|
| ☐ 251 Ed Brinkman | .24 | .10 | .02 |
| ☐ 252 Denny Lemaster | .24 | .10 | .02 |
| ☐ 253 Don Wert | .24 | .10 | .02 |
| ☐ 254 Phillies Rookies | 11.00 | 5.25 | 1.10 |
| Ferguson Jenkins | | | |
| Bill Sorrell | | | |
| ☐ 255 Willie Stargell | 4.00 | 1.85 | .40 |
| ☐ 256 Lew Krausse | .24 | .10 | .02 |
| ☐ 257 Jeff Torborg | .35 | .15 | .03 |
| ☐ 258 Dave Giusti | .24 | .10 | .02 |
| ☐ 259 Red Sox Team | .55 | .25 | .05 |
| ☐ 260 Bob Shaw | .24 | .10 | .02 |
| ☐ 261 Ron Hansen | .24 | .10 | .02 |
| ☐ 262 Jack Hamilton | .24 | .10 | .02 |
| ☐ 263 Tom Egan | .24 | .10 | .02 |
| ☐ 264 Twins Rookies | .24 | .10 | .02 |
| Andy Kosco | | | |
| Ted Uhlaender | | | |
| ☐ 265 Stu Miller | .24 | .10 | .02 |
| ☐ 266 Pedro Gonzalez | .24 | .10 | .02 |
| ☐ 267 Joe Sparma | .24 | .10 | .02 |
| ☐ 268 John Blanchard | .24 | .10 | .02 |
| ☐ 269 Don Heffner | .24 | .10 | .02 |
| ☐ 270 Claude Osteen | .35 | .15 | .03 |
| ☐ 271 Hal Lanier | .40 | .18 | .04 |
| ☐ 272 Jack Baldschun | .24 | .10 | .02 |
| ☐ 273 Astro Aces | .45 | .20 | .04 |
| Bob Aspromonte | | | |
| Rusty Staub | | | |
| ☐ 274 Buster Narum | .24 | .10 | .02 |
| ☐ 275 Tim McCarver | .65 | .30 | .06 |
| ☐ 276 Jim Bouton | .55 | .25 | .05 |
| ☐ 277 George Thomas | .24 | .10 | .02 |
| ☐ 278 Calvin Koonce | .24 | .10 | .02 |
| ☐ 279 4th Series Checklist | 1.10 | .20 | .05 |
| ☐ 280 Bobby Knoop | .24 | .10 | .02 |
| ☐ 281 Bruce Howard | .24 | .10 | .02 |
| ☐ 282 Johnny Lewis | .24 | .10 | .02 |
| ☐ 283 Jim Perry | .40 | .18 | .04 |
| ☐ 284 Bobby Wine | .35 | .15 | .03 |
| ☐ 285 Luis Tiant | 1.00 | .45 | .10 |
| ☐ 286 Gary Geiger | .24 | .10 | .02 |
| ☐ 287 Jack Aker | .24 | .10 | .02 |
| ☐ 288 Dodgers Rookies | 16.00 | 7.50 | 1.60 |
| Bill Singer | | | |
| Don Sutton | | | |
| ☐ 289 Larry Sherry | .35 | .15 | .03 |
| ☐ 290 Ron Santo | .65 | .30 | .06 |
| ☐ 291 Moe Drabowsky | .24 | .10 | .02 |
| ☐ 292 Jim Coker | .24 | .10 | .02 |
| ☐ 293 Mike Shannon | .45 | .20 | .04 |
| ☐ 294 Steve Ridzik | .24 | .10 | .02 |
| ☐ 295 Jim Ray Hart | .35 | .15 | .03 |
| ☐ 296 Johnny Keane MGR | .35 | .15 | .03 |
| ☐ 297 Jim Owens | .24 | .10 | .02 |
| ☐ 298 Rico Petrocelli | .35 | .15 | .03 |
| ☐ 299 Lou Burdette | .55 | .25 | .05 |
| ☐ 300 Bob Clemente | 16.00 | 7.50 | 1.60 |
| ☐ 301 Greg Bollo | .24 | .10 | .02 |
| ☐ 302 Ernie Bowman | .24 | .10 | .02 |
| ☐ 303 Indians Team | .55 | .25 | .05 |
| ☐ 304 John Herrnstein | .24 | .10 | .02 |
| ☐ 305 Camilo Pascual | .35 | .15 | .03 |
| ☐ 306 Ty Cline | .24 | .10 | .02 |
| ☐ 307 Clay Carroll | .24 | .10 | .02 |
| ☐ 308 Tom Haller | .24 | .10 | .02 |
| ☐ 309 Diego Segui | .24 | .10 | .02 |
| ☐ 310 Frank Robinson | 9.00 | 4.25 | .90 |
| ☐ 311 Reds Rookies | .35 | .15 | .03 |
| Tommy Helms | | | |
| Dick Simpson | | | |
| ☐ 312 Bob Saverine | .24 | .10 | .02 |
| ☐ 313 Chris Zachary | .24 | .10 | .02 |
| ☐ 314 Hector Valle | .24 | .10 | .02 |
| ☐ 315 Norm Cash | .85 | .40 | .08 |
| ☐ 316 Jack Fisher | .24 | .10 | .02 |
| ☐ 317 Dalton Jones | .24 | .10 | .02 |
| ☐ 318 Harry Walker | .24 | .10 | .02 |
| ☐ 319 Gene Freese | .24 | .10 | .02 |
| ☐ 320 Bob Gibson | 4.25 | 2.00 | .42 |
| ☐ 321 Rick Reichardt | .24 | .10 | .02 |
| ☐ 322 Bill Faul | .24 | .10 | .02 |
| ☐ 323 Ray Barker | .24 | .10 | .02 |
| ☐ 324 John Boozer | .24 | .10 | .02 |
| ☐ 325 Vic Davalillo | .24 | .10 | .02 |
| ☐ 326 Braves Team | .55 | .25 | .05 |
| ☐ 327 Bernie Allen | .24 | .10 | .02 |
| ☐ 328 Jerry Grote | .24 | .10 | .02 |
| ☐ 329 Pete Charton | .24 | .10 | .02 |
| ☐ 330 Ron Fairly | .35 | .15 | .03 |
| ☐ 331 Ron Herbel | .24 | .10 | .02 |
| ☐ 332 Billy Bryan | .24 | .10 | .02 |
| ☐ 333 Senators Rookies | .24 | .10 | .02 |
| Joe Coleman | | | |
| Jim French | | | |
| ☐ 334 Marty Keough | .24 | .10 | .02 |
| ☐ 335 Juan Pizarro | .24 | .10 | .02 |
| ☐ 336 Gene Alley | .40 | .18 | .04 |
| ☐ 337 Fred Gladding | .24 | .10 | .02 |
| ☐ 338 Dal Maxvill | .24 | .10 | .02 |
| ☐ 339 Del Crandall | .35 | .15 | .03 |
| ☐ 340 Dean Chance | .35 | .15 | .03 |
| ☐ 341 Wes Westrum | .24 | .10 | .02 |
| ☐ 342 Bob Humphreys | .24 | .10 | .02 |

|  | MINT | VG-E | F-G |
|---|---|---|---|
| ☐ 343 Joe Christopher | .24 | .10 | .02 |
| ☐ 344 Steve Blass | .35 | .15 | .03 |
| ☐ 345 Bob Allison | .35 | .15 | .03 |
| ☐ 346 Mike De La Hoz | .24 | .10 | .02 |
| ☐ 347 Phil Regan | .35 | .15 | .03 |
| ☐ 348 Orioles Team | .55 | .25 | .05 |
| ☐ 349 Cap Peterson | .24 | .10 | .02 |
| ☐ 350 Mel Stottlemyre | .65 | .30 | .06 |
| ☐ 351 Fred Valentine | .24 | .10 | .02 |
| ☐ 352 Bob Aspromonte | .24 | .10 | .02 |
| ☐ 353 Al McBean | .24 | .10 | .02 |
| ☐ 354 Smoky Burgess | .35 | .15 | .03 |
| ☐ 355 Wade Blasingame | .24 | .10 | .02 |
| ☐ 356 Red Sox Rookies | .24 | .10 | .02 |
|     Owen Johnson |  |  |  |
|     Ken Sanders |  |  |  |
| ☐ 357 Gerry Arrigo | .24 | .10 | .02 |
| ☐ 358 Charlie Smith | .24 | .10 | .02 |
| ☐ 359 Johnny Briggs | .24 | .10 | .02 |
| ☐ 360 Ron Hunt | .24 | .10 | .02 |
| ☐ 361 Tom Satriano | .24 | .10 | .02 |
| ☐ 362 Gates Brown | .35 | .15 | .03 |
| ☐ 363 5th Series Checklist | 1.10 | .20 | .05 |
| ☐ 364 Nate Oliver | .24 | .10 | .02 |
| ☐ 365 Roger Maris | 4.50 | 2.10 | .45 |
| ☐ 366 Wayne Causey | .24 | .10 | .02 |
| ☐ 367 Mel Nelson | .24 | .10 | .02 |
| ☐ 368 Charlie Lau | .35 | .15 | .03 |
| ☐ 369 Jim King | .24 | .10 | .02 |
| ☐ 370 Chico Cardenas | .24 | .10 | .02 |
| ☐ 371 Lee Stange | .24 | .10 | .02 |
| ☐ 372 Harvey Kuenn | .50 | .22 | .05 |
| ☐ 373 Giants Rookies | .24 | .10 | .02 |
|     Jack Hiatt |  |  |  |
|     Dick Estelle |  |  |  |
| ☐ 374 Bob Locker | .24 | .10 | .02 |
| ☐ 375 Donn Clendenon | .35 | .15 | .03 |
| ☐ 376 Paul Schaal | .24 | .10 | .02 |
| ☐ 377 Turk Farrell | .24 | .10 | .02 |
| ☐ 378 Dick Tracewski | .24 | .10 | .02 |
| ☐ 379 Cardinal Team | .55 | .25 | .05 |
| ☐ 380 Tony Conigliaro | .75 | .35 | .07 |
| ☐ 381 Hank Fischer | .24 | .10 | .02 |
| ☐ 382 Phil Roof | .24 | .10 | .02 |
| ☐ 383 Jack Brandt | .24 | .10 | .02 |
| ☐ 384 Al Downing | .35 | .15 | .03 |
| ☐ 385 Ken Boyer | 1.25 | .60 | .12 |
| ☐ 386 Gil Hodges | 2.50 | 1.15 | .25 |
| ☐ 387 Howie Reed | .24 | .10 | .02 |
| ☐ 388 Don Mincher | .24 | .10 | .02 |
| ☐ 389 Jim O'Toole | .24 | .10 | .02 |
| ☐ 390 Brooks Robinson | 5.00 | 2.35 | .50 |
| ☐ 391 Chuck Hinton | .24 | .10 | .02 |
| ☐ 392 Cubs Rookies | .35 | .15 | .03 |
|     Bill Hands |  |  |  |
|     Randy Hundley |  |  |  |
| ☐ 393 George Brunet | .24 | .10 | .02 |
| ☐ 394 Ron Brand | .24 | .10 | .02 |
| ☐ 395 Len Gabrielson | .24 | .10 | .02 |
| ☐ 396 J. Stephenson | .24 | .10 | .02 |
| ☐ 397 Bill White | .35 | .15 | .03 |
| ☐ 398 Danny Cater | .24 | .10 | .02 |
| ☐ 399 Ray Washburn | .24 | .10 | .02 |
| ☐ 400 Zoilo Versalles | .35 | .15 | .03 |
| ☐ 401 Ken McMullen | .24 | .10 | .02 |
| ☐ 402 Jim Hickman | .24 | .10 | .02 |
| ☐ 403 Fred Talbot | .24 | .10 | .02 |
| ☐ 404 Pirates Team | .55 | .25 | .05 |
| ☐ 405 Elston Howard | 1.25 | .60 | .12 |
| ☐ 406 Joe Jay | .24 | .10 | .02 |
| ☐ 407 John Kennedy | .24 | .10 | .02 |
| ☐ 408 Lee Thomas | .24 | .10 | .02 |
| ☐ 409 Billy Hoeft | .24 | .10 | .02 |
| ☐ 410 Al Kaline | 4.50 | 2.10 | .45 |
| ☐ 411 Gene Mauch | .35 | .15 | .03 |
| ☐ 412 Sam Bowens | .24 | .10 | .02 |
| ☐ 413 John Romano | .24 | .10 | .02 |
| ☐ 414 Dan Coombs | .24 | .10 | .02 |
| ☐ 415 Max Alvis | .24 | .10 | .02 |
| ☐ 416 Phil Ortega | .24 | .10 | .02 |
| ☐ 417 Angels Rookies | .35 | .15 | .03 |
|     Jim McGlothlin |  |  |  |
|     Ed Sukla |  |  |  |
| ☐ 418 Phil Gagliano | .24 | .10 | .02 |
| ☐ 419 Mike Ryan | .24 | .10 | .02 |
| ☐ 420 Juan Marichal | 3.50 | 1.65 | .35 |
| ☐ 421 Roy McMillan | .24 | .10 | .02 |
| ☐ 422 Ed Charles | .24 | .10 | .02 |
| ☐ 423 Ernie Broglio | .24 | .10 | .02 |
| ☐ 424 Reds Rookies | 1.00 | .45 | .10 |
|     Lee May |  |  |  |
|     Darrell Osteen |  |  |  |
| ☐ 425 Bob Veale | .35 | .15 | .03 |
| ☐ 426 White Sox Team | .55 | .25 | .05 |
| ☐ 427 John Miller | .24 | .10 | .02 |
| ☐ 428 Sandy Alomar | .24 | .10 | .02 |
| ☐ 429 Bill Monbouquette | .24 | .10 | .02 |
| ☐ 430 Don Drysdale | 3.50 | 1.65 | .35 |
| ☐ 431 Walt Bond | .24 | .10 | .02 |
| ☐ 432 Bob Heffner | .24 | .10 | .02 |
| ☐ 433 Alvin Dark | .35 | .15 | .03 |
| ☐ 434 Willie Kirkland | .24 | .10 | .02 |
| ☐ 435 Jim Bunning | 1.25 | .60 | .12 |
| ☐ 436 Julian Javier | .35 | .15 | .03 |

| | MINT | VG-E | F-G |
|---|---|---|---|
| ☐ 437 Al Stanek | .24 | .10 | .02 |
| ☐ 438 Willie Smith | .24 | .10 | .02 |
| ☐ 439 Pedro Ramos | .24 | .10 | .02 |
| ☐ 440 Deron Johnson | .24 | .10 | .02 |
| ☐ 441 Tommie Sisk | .24 | .10 | .02 |
| ☐ 442 Orioles Rookies | .24 | .10 | .02 |
|     Ed Barnowski | | | |
|     Eddie Watt | | | |
| ☐ 443 Bill Wakefield | .24 | .10 | .02 |
| ☐ 444 6th Series Checklist | 1.25 | .25 | .05 |
| ☐ 445 Jim Kaat | 1.75 | .85 | .17 |
| ☐ 446 Mack Jones | .24 | .10 | .02 |
| ☐ 447 Dick Ellsworth | .65 | .30 | .06 |
|     (photo actually | | | |
|     Ken Hubbs) | | | |
| ☐ 448 Eddie Stanky | .65 | .30 | .06 |
| ☐ 449 Joe Moeller | .55 | .25 | .05 |
| ☐ 450 Tony Oliva | 1.75 | .85 | .17 |
| ☐ 451 Barry Latman | .55 | .25 | .05 |
| ☐ 452 Joe Azcue | .55 | .25 | .05 |
| ☐ 453 Ron Kline | .55 | .25 | .05 |
| ☐ 454 Jerry Buchek | .55 | .25 | .05 |
| ☐ 455 Mickey Lolich | 1.25 | .60 | .12 |
| ☐ 456 Red Sox Rookies | .55 | .25 | .05 |
|     Darrell Brandon | | | |
|     Joe Foy | | | |
| ☐ 457 Joe Gibbon | .55 | .25 | .05 |
| ☐ 458 Manny Jiminez | .55 | .25 | .05 |
| ☐ 459 Bill McCool | .55 | .25 | .05 |
| ☐ 460 Curt Blefary | .55 | .25 | .05 |
| ☐ 461 Roy Face | .85 | .40 | .08 |
| ☐ 462 Bob Rodgers | .55 | .25 | .05 |
| ☐ 463 Phillies Team | .90 | .40 | .09 |
| ☐ 464 Larry Bearnarth | .55 | .25 | .05 |
| ☐ 465 Don Buford | .55 | .25 | .05 |
| ☐ 466 Ken Johnson | .55 | .25 | .05 |
| ☐ 467 Vic Roznovsky | .55 | .25 | .05 |
| ☐ 468 Johnny Podres | 1.10 | .50 | .11 |
| ☐ 469 Yankees Rookies | 4.25 | 2.00 | .42 |
|     Bobby Murcer | | | |
|     Dooley Womack | | | |
| ☐ 470 Sam McDowell | .75 | .35 | .07 |
| ☐ 471 Bob Skinner | .65 | .30 | .06 |
| ☐ 472 Terry Fox | .55 | .25 | .05 |
| ☐ 473 Rich Rollins | .55 | .25 | .05 |
| ☐ 474 Dick Schofield | .55 | .25 | .05 |
| ☐ 475 Dick Radatz | .65 | .30 | .06 |
| ☐ 476 Bobby Bragan | .55 | .25 | .05 |
| ☐ 477 Steve Barber | .55 | .25 | .05 |
| ☐ 478 Tony Gonzalez | .55 | .25 | .05 |
| ☐ 479 Jim Hannan | .55 | .25 | .05 |
| ☐ 480 Dick Stuart | .65 | .30 | .06 |
| ☐ 481 Bob Lee | .55 | .25 | .05 |

| | MINT | VG-E | F-G |
|---|---|---|---|
| ☐ 482 Cubs Rookies | .55 | .25 | .05 |
|     John Boccabella | | | |
|     Dave Dowling | | | |
| ☐ 483 Joe Nuxhall | .65 | .30 | .06 |
| ☐ 484 Wes Covington | .55 | .25 | .05 |
| ☐ 485 Bob Bailey | .55 | .25 | .05 |
| ☐ 486 Tommy John | 2.50 | 1.15 | .25 |
| ☐ 487 Al Ferrara | .65 | .30 | .06 |
| ☐ 488 George Banks | .55 | .25 | .05 |
| ☐ 489 Curt Simmons | .65 | .30 | .06 |
| ☐ 490 Bobby Richardson | 2.25 | 1.00 | .22 |
| ☐ 491 Dennis Bennett | .55 | .25 | .05 |
| ☐ 492 Athletics Team | .85 | .40 | .08 |
| ☐ 493 John Klippstein | .55 | .25 | .05 |
| ☐ 494 Gordon Coleman | .55 | .25 | .05 |
| ☐ 495 Dick McAuliffe | .65 | .30 | .06 |
| ☐ 496 Lindy McDaniel | .55 | .25 | .05 |
| ☐ 497 Chris Cannizzaro | .55 | .25 | .05 |
| ☐ 498 Pirates Rookies | .65 | .30 | .06 |
|     Luke Walker | | | |
|     Woody Fryman | | | |
| ☐ 499 Wally Bunker | .55 | .25 | .05 |
| ☐ 500 Hank Aaron | 20.00 | 9.00 | 2.00 |
| ☐ 501 John O'Donoghue | .55 | .25 | .05 |
| ☐ 502 Lenny Green | .55 | .25 | .05 |
| ☐ 503 Steve Hamilton | .55 | .25 | .05 |
| ☐ 504 Grady Hatton | .55 | .25 | .05 |
| ☐ 505 Jose Cardenal | .55 | .25 | .05 |
| ☐ 506 Bo Belinsky | .65 | .30 | .06 |
| ☐ 507 John Edwards | .55 | .25 | .05 |
| ☐ 508 Steve Hargan | .55 | .25 | .05 |
| ☐ 509 Jake Wood | .55 | .25 | .05 |
| ☐ 510 Hoyt Wilhelm | 3.75 | 1.75 | .37 |
| ☐ 511 Giants Rookies | .55 | .25 | .05 |
|     Bob Barton | | | |
|     Tito Fuentes | | | |
| ☐ 512 Dick Stigman | .55 | .25 | .05 |
| ☐ 513 Camilo Carreon | .55 | .25 | .05 |
| ☐ 514 Hal Woodeschick | .55 | .25 | .05 |
| ☐ 515 Frank Howard | 1.50 | .70 | .15 |
| ☐ 516 Eddie Bressoud | .55 | .25 | .05 |
| ☐ 517 7th Series Checklist | 3.25 | .60 | .10 |
| ☐ 518 Braves Rookies | .55 | .25 | .05 |
|     Herb Hippauf | | | |
|     Arnie Umbach | | | |
| ☐ 519 Bob Friend | .65 | .30 | .06 |
| ☐ 520 Jim Wynn | .65 | .30 | .06 |
| ☐ 521 John Wyatt | .55 | .25 | .05 |
| ☐ 522 Phil Linz | .65 | .30 | .06 |
| ☐ 523 Bob Sadowski | 3.50 | 1.65 | .35 |
| ☐ 524 Giants Rookies | 3.50 | 1.65 | .35 |
|     Ollie Brown | | | |
|     Don Mason | | | |

| | MINT | VG-E | F-G |
|---|---|---|---|
| ☐ 525 Gary Bell | 3.50 | 1.65 | .35 |
| ☐ 526 Twins Team | 8.00 | 3.75 | .80 |
| ☐ 527 Julio Navarro | 3.50 | 1.65 | .35 |
| ☐ 528 Jesse Gonder | 3.50 | 1.65 | .35 |
| ☐ 529 White Sox Rookies | 4.50 | 2.10 | .45 |
|     Lee Elia | | | |
|     Dennis Higgins | | | |
|     Bill Voss | | | |
| ☐ 530 Robin Roberts | 12.50 | 5.75 | 1.25 |
| ☐ 531 Joe Cunningham | 4.00 | 1.85 | .40 |
| ☐ 532 Aurelio Monteagudo | 3.50 | 1.65 | .35 |
| ☐ 533 Jerry Adair | 3.50 | 1.65 | .35 |
| ☐ 534 Mets Rookies | 3.50 | 1.65 | .35 |
|     Dave Eilers | | | |
|     Rob Gardner | | | |
| ☐ 535 Willie Davis | 4.50 | 2.10 | .45 |
| ☐ 536 Dick Egan | 3.50 | 1.65 | .35 |
| ☐ 537 Herman Franks | 3.50 | 1.65 | .35 |
| ☐ 538 Bob Allen | 3.50 | 1.65 | .35 |
| ☐ 539 Astros Rookies | 3.50 | 1.65 | .35 |
|     Bill Heath | | | |
|     Carroll Sembera | | | |
| ☐ 540 Denny McLain | 12.00 | 5.50 | 1.20 |
| ☐ 541 Gene Oliver | 3.50 | 1.65 | .35 |
| ☐ 542 George Smith | 3.50 | 1.65 | .35 |
| ☐ 543 Roger Craig | 5.00 | 2.35 | .50 |
| ☐ 544 Cardinals Rookies | 3.50 | 1.65 | .35 |
|     Joe Hoerner | | | |
|     George Kernek | | | |
|     Jimmy Williams | | | |
| ☐ 545 Dick Green | 3.50 | 1.65 | .35 |
| ☐ 546 Dwight Siebler | 3.50 | 1.65 | .35 |
| ☐ 547 Horace Clarke | 4.50 | 2.10 | .45 |
| ☐ 548 Gary Kroll | 3.50 | 1.65 | .35 |
| ☐ 549 Senators Rookies | 3.50 | 1.65 | .35 |
|     Al Closter | | | |
|     Casey Cox | | | |
| ☐ 550 Willie McCovey | 40.00 | 18.00 | 4.00 |
| ☐ 551 Bob Purkey | 3.50 | 1.65 | .35 |
| ☐ 552 Birdie Tebbetts | 3.50 | 1.65 | .35 |
| ☐ 553 Rookie Stars | 3.50 | 1.65 | .35 |
|     Pat Garrett | | | |
|     Jackie Warner | | | |
| ☐ 554 Jim Northrup | 4.50 | 2.10 | .45 |
| ☐ 555 Ron Perranoski | 4.50 | 2.10 | .45 |
| ☐ 556 Mel Queen | 3.50 | 1.65 | .35 |
| ☐ 557 Felix Mantilla | 3.50 | 1.65 | .35 |
| ☐ 558 Red Sox Rookies | 7.50 | 3.50 | .75 |
|     Guido Grilli | | | |
|     Pete Magrini | | | |
|     George Scott | | | |
| ☐ 559 Roberto Pena | 3.50 | 1.65 | .35 |
| ☐ 560 Joel Horlen | 4.50 | 2.10 | .45 |

| | MINT | VG-E | F-G |
|---|---|---|---|
| ☐ 561 Choo Choo Coleman | 3.50 | 1.65 | .35 |
| ☐ 562 Russ Snyder | 3.50 | 1.65 | .35 |
| ☐ 563 Twins Rookies | 4.50 | 2.10 | .45 |
|     Pete Cimino | | | |
|     Cesar Tovar | | | |
| ☐ 564 Bob Chance | 3.50 | 1.65 | .35 |
| ☐ 565 Jimmy Piersall | 6.00 | 2.80 | .60 |
| ☐ 566 Mike Cuellar | 4.50 | 2.10 | .45 |
| ☐ 567 Dick Howser | 4.50 | 2.10 | .45 |
| ☐ 568 Athletics Rookies | 4.50 | 2.10 | .45 |
|     Paul Lindblad | | | |
|     Rod Stone | | | |
| ☐ 569 Orlando McFarlane | 3.50 | 1.65 | .35 |
| ☐ 570 Art Mahaffey | 4.00 | 1.85 | .40 |
| ☐ 571 Dave Roberts | 3.50 | 1.65 | .35 |
| ☐ 572 Bob Priddy | 3.50 | 1.65 | .35 |
| ☐ 573 Derrell Griffith | 3.50 | 1.65 | .35 |
| ☐ 574 Mets Rookies | 3.50 | 1.65 | .35 |
|     Bill Hepler | | | |
|     Bill Murphy | | | |
| ☐ 575 Earl Wilson | 3.50 | 1.65 | .35 |
| ☐ 576 Dave Nicholson | 3.50 | 1.65 | .35 |
| ☐ 577 Jack Lamabe | 3.50 | 1.65 | .35 |
| ☐ 578 Chi Chi Olivo | 3.50 | 1.65 | .35 |
| ☐ 579 Orioles Rookies | 4.00 | 1.85 | .40 |
|     Frank Bertaina | | | |
|     Gene Brabender | | | |
|     Dave Johnson | | | |
| ☐ 580 Billy Williams | 11.00 | 5.25 | 1.10 |
| ☐ 581 Tony Martinez | 3.50 | 1.65 | .35 |
| ☐ 582 Garry Roggenburk | 3.50 | 1.65 | .35 |
| ☐ 583 Tigers Team | 12.00 | 5.50 | 1.20 |
| ☐ 584 Yankees Rookies | 4.00 | 1.85 | .40 |
|     Frank Fernandez | | | |
|     Fritz Peterson | | | |
| ☐ 585 Tony Taylor | 3.50 | 1.65 | .35 |
| ☐ 586 Claude Raymond | 3.50 | 1.65 | .35 |
| ☐ 587 Dick Bertell | 3.50 | 1.65 | .35 |
| ☐ 588 Athletics Rookies | 3.50 | 1.65 | .35 |
|     Chuck Dobson | | | |
|     Ken Suarez | | | |
| ☐ 589 Lou Klimchock | 3.50 | 1.65 | .35 |
| ☐ 590 Bill Skowron | 6.00 | 2.80 | .60 |
| ☐ 591 N.L. Rookies | 4.50 | 2.10 | .45 |
|     Bart Shirley | | | |
|     Grant Jackson | | | |
| ☐ 592 Andre Rodgers | 3.50 | 1.65 | .35 |
| ☐ 593 Doug Camilli | 3.50 | 1.65 | .35 |
| ☐ 594 Chico Salmon | 3.50 | 1.65 | .35 |
| ☐ 595 Larry Jackson | 3.50 | 1.65 | .35 |
| ☐ 596 Astros Rookies | 4.50 | 2.10 | .45 |
|     Nate Colbert | | | |
|     Greg Sims | | | |

|  | MINT | VG-E | F-G |
|---|---|---|---|
| ☐ 597 John Sullivan | 3.50 | 1.65 | .35 |
| ☐ 598 Gaylord Perry | 65.00 | 25.00 | 5.00 |

## 1967 TOPPS

The cards in this 609 card set measure 2½" by 3½". The 1967 Topps series is considered by some collectors to be one of the company's finest accomplishments in baseball card production. Excellent color photographs are combined with easy to read backs. Cards 458 to 533 are slightly harder to find than numbers 1 to 457, and the inevitable (difficult to find) high series (534 to 609) exists. Each checklist card features a small circular picture of a popular player included in that series. Printing discrepancies resulted in some high series cards being in short supply.

Complete Set: M-925.00; VG-E-375.00; F-G-75.00

|  | | | |
|---|---|---|---|
| Common Player (1---370) | .24 | .10 | .02 |
| Common Player (371---457) | .30 | .12 | .03 |
| Common Player (458---533) | .70 | .32 | .07 |
| Common Player (534---609) | 2.00 | .90 | .20 |
| ☐ 1 The Champs: Frank Robinson Hank Bauer Brooks Robinson | 3.00 | .75 | .15 |
| ☐ 2 Jack Hamilton | .24 | .10 | .02 |
| ☐ 3 Duke Sims | .24 | .10 | .02 |
| ☐ 4 Hal Lanier | .35 | .15 | .03 |

|  | MINT | VG-E | F-G |
|---|---|---|---|
| ☐ 5 Whitey Ford | 4.25 | 2.00 | .42 |
| ☐ 6 Dick Simpson | .24 | .10 | .02 |
| ☐ 7 Don McMahon | .24 | .10 | .02 |
| ☐ 8 Chuck Harrison | .24 | .10 | .02 |
| ☐ 9 Ron Hansen | .24 | .10 | .02 |
| ☐ 10 Matty Alou | .35 | .15 | .03 |
| ☐ 11 Barry Moore | .24 | .10 | .02 |
| ☐ 12 Dodgers Rookies Jim Campanis Bill Singer | .35 | .15 | .03 |
| ☐ 13 Joe Sparma | .24 | .10 | .02 |
| ☐ 14 Phil Linz | .24 | .10 | .02 |
| ☐ 15 Earl Battey | .24 | .10 | .02 |
| ☐ 16 Bill Hands | .24 | .10 | .02 |
| ☐ 17 Jim Gosger | .24 | .10 | .02 |
| ☐ 18 Gene Oliver | .24 | .10 | .02 |
| ☐ 19 Jim McGlothlin | .24 | .10 | .02 |
| ☐ 20 Orlando Cepeda | 1.75 | .85 | .17 |
| ☐ 21 Dave Bristol | .24 | .10 | .02 |
| ☐ 22 Gene Brabender | .24 | .10 | .02 |
| ☐ 23 Larry Elliot | .24 | .10 | .02 |
| ☐ 24 Bob Allen | .24 | .10 | .02 |
| ☐ 25 Elston Howard | 1.10 | .50 | .11 |
| ☐ 26 A Bob Priddy (with traded line) | .24 | .10 | .02 |
| ☐ 26 B Bob Priddy (no traded line) | 6.00 | 2.50 | .50 |
| ☐ 27 Bob Saverine | .24 | .10 | .02 |
| ☐ 28 Barry Latman | .24 | .10 | .02 |
| ☐ 29 Tommy McCraw | .24 | .10 | .02 |
| ☐ 30 Al Kaline | 4.00 | 1.85 | .40 |
| ☐ 31 Jim Brewer | .24 | .10 | .02 |
| ☐ 32 Bob Bailey | .24 | .10 | .02 |
| ☐ 33 Athletic Rookies Sal Bando Randy Schwartz | .80 | .40 | .08 |
| ☐ 34 Pete Cimino | .24 | .10 | .02 |
| ☐ 35 Rico Carty | .55 | .25 | .05 |
| ☐ 36 Bob Tillman | .24 | .10 | .02 |
| ☐ 37 Rick Wise | .35 | .15 | .03 |
| ☐ 38 Bob Johnson | .24 | .10 | .02 |
| ☐ 39 Curt Simmons | .35 | .15 | .03 |
| ☐ 40 Rick Reichardt | .24 | .10 | .02 |
| ☐ 41 Joe Hoerner | .24 | .10 | .02 |
| ☐ 42 Mets Team | .75 | .35 | .07 |
| ☐ 43 Chico Salmon | .24 | .10 | .02 |
| ☐ 44 Joe Nuxhall | .35 | .15 | .03 |
| ☐ 45 Roger Maris | 4.00 | 1.85 | .40 |
| ☐ 46 Lindy McDaniel | .24 | .10 | .02 |
| ☐ 47 Ken McMullen | .24 | .10 | .02 |
| ☐ 48 Bill Freehan | .55 | .25 | .05 |
| ☐ 49 Roy Face | .45 | .20 | .04 |

| | | MINT | VG-E | F-G |
|---|---|---|---|---|
| ☐ 50 | Tony Oliva | 1.10 | .50 | .11 |
| ☐ 51 | Astros Rookies | .24 | .10 | .02 |
| | Dave Adlesh | | | |
| | Wes Bales | | | |
| ☐ 52 | Dennis Higgins | .24 | .10 | .02 |
| ☐ 53 | Clay Dalrymple | .24 | .10 | .02 |
| ☐ 54 | Dick Green | .24 | .10 | .02 |
| ☐ 55 | Don Drysdale | 3.50 | 1.65 | .35 |
| ☐ 56 | Jose Tartabull | .24 | .10 | .02 |
| ☐ 57 | Pat Jarvis | .24 | .10 | .02 |
| ☐ 58 | Paul Schaal | .24 | .10 | .02 |
| ☐ 59 | Ralph Terry | .35 | .15 | .03 |
| ☐ 60 | Luis Aparicio | 2.25 | 1.00 | .22 |
| ☐ 61 | Gordy Coleman | .24 | .10 | .02 |
| ☐ 62 | 1st Checklist | 1.20 | .25 | .05 |
| | Frank Robinson | | | |
| ☐ 63 | Cards' Clubbers | 1.50 | .70 | .15 |
| | Lou Brock | | | |
| | Curt Flood | | | |
| ☐ 64 | Fred Valentine | .24 | .10 | .02 |
| ☐ 65 | Tom Haller | .24 | .10 | .02 |
| ☐ 66 | Manny Mota | .35 | .15 | .03 |
| ☐ 67 | Ken Berry | .24 | .10 | .02 |
| ☐ 68 | Bob Buhl | .24 | .10 | .02 |
| ☐ 69 | Vic Davalillo | .24 | .10 | .02 |
| ☐ 70 | Ron Santo | .60 | .28 | .06 |
| ☐ 71 | Camilo Pascual | .35 | .15 | .03 |
| ☐ 72 | Tigers Rookies | .24 | .10 | .02 |
| | George Korince (photo | | | |
| | actually John Brown) | | | |
| | John (Tom) Matchick | | | |
| ☐ 73 | Rusty Staub | 1.00 | .45 | .10 |
| ☐ 74 | Wes Stock | .35 | .15 | .03 |
| ☐ 75 | George Scott | .35 | .15 | .03 |
| ☐ 76 | Jim Barbieri | .24 | .10 | .02 |
| ☐ 77 | Dooley Womack | .24 | .10 | .02 |
| ☐ 78 | Pat Corrales | .35 | .15 | .03 |
| ☐ 79 | Bubba Morton | .24 | .10 | .02 |
| ☐ 80 | Jim Maloney | .35 | .15 | .03 |
| ☐ 81 | Eddie Stanky | .35 | .15 | .03 |
| ☐ 82 | Steve Barber | .24 | .10 | .02 |
| ☐ 83 | Ollie Brown | .24 | .10 | .02 |
| ☐ 84 | Tommie Sisk | .24 | .10 | .02 |
| ☐ 85 | Johnny Callison | .35 | .15 | .03 |
| ☐ 86 A | Mike McCormick | .35 | .15 | .03 |
| | (with traded line) | | | |
| ☐ 86 B | Mike McCormick | 6.00 | 2.80 | .60 |
| | (no traded line) | | | |
| ☐ 87 | George Altman | .24 | .10 | .02 |
| ☐ 88 | Mickey Lolich | .80 | .40 | .08 |
| ☐ 89 | Felix Millan | .35 | .15 | .03 |
| ☐ 90 | Jim Nash | .24 | .10 | .02 |

| | | MINT | VG-E | F-G |
|---|---|---|---|---|
| ☐ 91 | Johnny Lewis | .24 | .10 | .02 |
| ☐ 92 | Ray Washburn | .24 | .10 | .02 |
| ☐ 93 | Yankees Rookies | 1.25 | .60 | .12 |
| | Stan Bahnsen | | | |
| | Bobby Murcer | | | |
| ☐ 94 | Ron Fairly | .35 | .15 | .03 |
| ☐ 95 | Sonny Siebert | .35 | .15 | .03 |
| ☐ 96 | Art Shamsky | .24 | .10 | .02 |
| ☐ 97 | Mike Cuellar | .35 | .15 | .03 |
| ☐ 98 | Rich Rollins | .24 | .10 | .02 |
| ☐ 99 | Lee Stange | .24 | .10 | .02 |
| ☐ 100 | Frank Robinson | 3.75 | 1.75 | .37 |
| ☐ 101 | Ken Johnson | .24 | .10 | .02 |
| ☐ 102 | Phillies Team | .55 | .25 | .05 |
| ☐ 103 | 2nd Checklist | 1.75 | .35 | .05 |
| | Mickey Mantle | | | |
| ☐ 104 | Minnie Rojas | .24 | .10 | .02 |
| ☐ 105 | Ken Boyer | .80 | .40 | .08 |
| ☐ 106 | Randy Hundley | .35 | .15 | .03 |
| ☐ 107 | Joel Horlen | .35 | .15 | .03 |
| ☐ 108 | Alex Johnson | .35 | .15 | .03 |
| ☐ 109 | Tribe Thumpers | .35 | .15 | .03 |
| | Rocky Colavito | | | |
| | Leon Wagner | | | |
| ☐ 110 | Jack Aker | .24 | .10 | .02 |
| ☐ 111 | John Kennedy | .24 | .10 | .02 |
| ☐ 112 | Dave Wickersham | .24 | .10 | .02 |
| ☐ 113 | Dave Nicholson | .24 | .10 | .02 |
| ☐ 114 | Jack Baldschun | .24 | .10 | .02 |
| ☐ 115 | Paul Casanova | .24 | .10 | .02 |
| ☐ 116 | Herman Franks | .24 | .10 | .02 |
| ☐ 117 | Darrell Brandon | .24 | .10 | .02 |
| ☐ 118 | Bernie Allen | .24 | .10 | .02 |
| ☐ 119 | Wade Blasingame | .24 | .10 | .02 |
| ☐ 120 | Floyd Robinson | .24 | .10 | .02 |
| ☐ 121 | Ed Bressoud | .24 | .10 | .02 |
| ☐ 122 | George Brunet | .24 | .10 | .02 |
| ☐ 123 | Pirates Rookies | .24 | .10 | .02 |
| | Jim Price | | | |
| | Luke Walker | | | |
| ☐ 124 | Jim Stewart | .24 | .10 | .02 |
| ☐ 125 | Moe Drabowsky | .24 | .10 | .02 |
| ☐ 126 | Tony Taylor | .24 | .10 | .02 |
| ☐ 127 | John O'Donoghue | .24 | .10 | .02 |
| ☐ 128 | Ed Spiezio | .24 | .10 | .02 |
| ☐ 129 | Phil Roof | .24 | .10 | .02 |
| ☐ 130 | Phil Regan | .35 | .15 | .03 |
| ☐ 131 | Yankees Team | .80 | .40 | .08 |
| ☐ 132 | Ozzie Virgil | .24 | .10 | .02 |
| ☐ 133 | Ron Kline | .24 | .10 | .02 |
| ☐ 134 | Gates Brown | .35 | .15 | .03 |
| ☐ 135 | Deron Johnson | .24 | .10 | .02 |

| | MINT | VG-E | F-G |
|---|---|---|---|
| ☐ 136 Carroll Sembera | .24 | .10 | .02 |
| ☐ 137 Twins Rookies | .24 | .10 | .02 |
| Ron Clark | | | |
| Jim Ollum | | | |
| ☐ 138 Dick Kelley | .24 | .10 | .02 |
| ☐ 139 Dalton Jones | .24 | .10 | .02 |
| ☐ 140 Willie Stargell | 4.00 | 1.85 | .40 |
| ☐ 141 John Miller | .24 | .10 | .02 |
| ☐ 142 Jackie Brandt | .24 | .10 | .02 |
| ☐ 143 Sox Sockers | .35 | .15 | .03 |
| Pete Ward | | | |
| Don Buford | | | |
| ☐ 144 Bill Hepler | .24 | .10 | .02 |
| ☐ 145 Larry Brown | .24 | .10 | .02 |
| ☐ 146 Steve Carlton | 30.00 | 14.00 | 3.00 |
| ☐ 147 Tom Egan | .24 | .10 | .02 |
| ☐ 148 Adolfo Phillips | .24 | .10 | .02 |
| ☐ 149 Joe Moeller | .24 | .10 | .02 |
| ☐ 150 Mickey Mantle | 35.00 | 16.50 | 3.50 |
| ☐ 151 World Series Game 1 | .90 | .40 | .09 |
| Moe mows down 11 | | | |
| ☐ 152 World Series Game 2 | 1.75 | .85 | .17 |
| Palmer blanks Dodgers | | | |
| ☐ 153 World Series Game 3 | .90 | .40 | .09 |
| Blair's homer | | | |
| defeats L.A. | | | |
| ☐ 154 World Series Game 4 | .90 | .40 | .09 |
| Orioles 4 straight | | | |
| ☐ 155 World Series Summary | 1.10 | .50 | .11 |
| Winners celebrate | | | |
| ☐ 156 Ron Herbel | .24 | .10 | .02 |
| ☐ 157 Danny Cater | .24 | .10 | .02 |
| ☐ 158 Jimmie Coker | .24 | .10 | .02 |
| ☐ 159 Bruce Howard | .24 | .10 | .02 |
| ☐ 160 Willie Davis | .50 | .22 | .05 |
| ☐ 161 Dick Williams | .35 | .15 | .03 |
| ☐ 162 Billy O'Dell | .24 | .10 | .02 |
| ☐ 163 Vic Roznovsky | .24 | .10 | .02 |
| ☐ 164 Dwight Siebler | .24 | .10 | .02 |
| ☐ 165 Cleon Jones | .24 | .10 | .02 |
| ☐ 166 Ed Mathews | 2.75 | 1.25 | .27 |
| ☐ 167 Senators Rookies | .24 | .10 | .02 |
| Joe Coleman | | | |
| Tim Cullen | | | |
| ☐ 168 Ray Culp | .24 | .10 | .02 |
| ☐ 169 Horace Clarke | .24 | .10 | .02 |
| ☐ 170 Dick McAuliffe | .35 | .15 | .03 |
| ☐ 171 Calvin Koonce | .24 | .10 | .02 |
| ☐ 172 Bill Heath | .24 | .10 | .02 |
| ☐ 173 Cardinals Team | .55 | .25 | .05 |
| ☐ 174 Dick Radatz | .35 | .15 | .03 |
| ☐ 175 Bobby Knoop | .24 | .10 | .02 |
| ☐ 176 Sammy Ellis | .24 | .10 | .02 |

| | MINT | VG-E | F-G |
|---|---|---|---|
| ☐ 177 Tito Fuentes | .24 | .10 | .02 |
| ☐ 178 John Buzhardt | .24 | .10 | .02 |
| ☐ 179 Braves Rookies | .24 | .10 | .02 |
| Charles Vaughan | | | |
| Cecil Upshaw | | | |
| ☐ 180 Curt Blefary | .24 | .10 | .02 |
| ☐ 181 Terry Fox | .24 | .10 | .02 |
| ☐ 182 Ed Charles | .24 | .10 | .02 |
| ☐ 183 Jim Pagliaroni | .24 | .10 | .02 |
| ☐ 184 George Thomas | .24 | .10 | .02 |
| ☐ 185 Ken Holtzman | .75 | .35 | .07 |
| ☐ 186 Mets Maulers | .35 | .15 | .03 |
| Ed Kranepool | | | |
| Ron Swoboda | | | |
| ☐ 187 Pedro Ramos | .24 | .10 | .02 |
| ☐ 188 Ken Harrelson | .75 | .35 | .07 |
| ☐ 189 Chuck Hinton | .24 | .10 | .02 |
| ☐ 190 Turk Farrell | .24 | .10 | .02 |
| ☐ 191 A Checklist 3 | 1.25 | .25 | .05 |
| (214 Tom Kelley) | | | |
| (Willie Mays) | | | |
| ☐ 191 B Checklist 3 | 4.00 | .60 | .10 |
| (214 Dick Kelley) | | | |
| (Willie Mays) | | | |
| ☐ 192 Fred Gladding | .24 | .10 | .02 |
| ☐ 193 Jose Cardenal | .24 | .10 | .02 |
| ☐ 194 Bob Allison | .35 | .15 | .03 |
| ☐ 195 Al Jackson | .24 | .10 | .02 |
| ☐ 196 Johnny Romano | .24 | .10 | .02 |
| ☐ 197 Ron Perranoski | .35 | .15 | .03 |
| ☐ 198 Chuck Hiller | .24 | .10 | .02 |
| ☐ 199 Billy Hitchcock | .24 | .10 | .02 |
| ☐ 200 Willie Mays | 18.00 | 8.50 | 1.80 |
| ☐ 201 Hal Reniff | .24 | .10 | .02 |
| ☐ 202 Johnny Edwards | .24 | .10 | .02 |
| ☐ 203 Al McBean | .24 | .10 | .02 |
| ☐ 204 Orioles Rookies | .35 | .15 | .03 |
| Mike Epstein | | | |
| Tom Phoebus | | | |
| ☐ 205 Dick Groat | .50 | .22 | .05 |
| ☐ 206 Dennis Bennett | .24 | .10 | .02 |
| ☐ 207 John Orsino | .24 | .10 | .02 |
| ☐ 208 Jack Lamabe | .24 | .10 | .02 |
| ☐ 209 Joe Nossek | .24 | .10 | .02 |
| ☐ 210 Bob Gibson | 3.50 | 1.65 | .35 |
| ☐ 211 Twins Team | .55 | .25 | .05 |
| ☐ 212 Chris Zachary | .24 | .10 | .02 |
| ☐ 213 Jay Johnstone | .35 | .15 | .03 |
| ☐ 214 Dick Kelley | .24 | .10 | .02 |
| ☐ 215 Ernie Banks | 3.50 | 1.65 | .35 |
| ☐ 216 Bengal Belters | 1.75 | .85 | .17 |
| Norm Cash | | | |
| Al Kaline | | | |

| | MINT | VG-E | F-G |
|---|---|---|---|
| ☐ 217 Rob Gardner | .24 | .10 | .02 |
| ☐ 218 Wes Parker | .35 | .15 | .03 |
| ☐ 219 Clay Carroll | .24 | .10 | .02 |
| ☐ 220 Jim Ray Hart | .35 | .15 | .03 |
| ☐ 221 Woody Fryman | .24 | .10 | .02 |
| ☐ 222 Reds Rookies | .45 | .20 | .04 |
| Darrell Osteen | | | |
| Lee May | | | |
| ☐ 223 Mike Ryan | .24 | .10 | .02 |
| ☐ 224 Walt Bond | .24 | .10 | .02 |
| ☐ 225 Mel Stottlemyre | .65 | .30 | .06 |
| ☐ 226 Julian Javier | .35 | .15 | .03 |
| ☐ 227 Paul Lindblad | .24 | .10 | .02 |
| ☐ 228 Gil Hodges | 2.25 | 1.00 | .22 |
| ☐ 229 Larry Jackson | .24 | .10 | .02 |
| ☐ 230 Boog Powell | .85 | .40 | .08 |
| ☐ 231 John Bateman | .24 | .10 | .02 |
| ☐ 232 Don Buford | .24 | .10 | .02 |
| ☐ 233 AL ERA Leaders: | .75 | .35 | .07 |
| Gary Peters | | | |
| Joel Horlen | | | |
| Steve Hargan | | | |
| ☐ 234 NL ERA Leaders: | 2.00 | .90 | .20 |
| Sandy Koufax | | | |
| Mike Cuellar | | | |
| Juan Marichal | | | |
| ☐ 235 AL Pitching Leaders: | .75 | .35 | .07 |
| Jim Kaat | | | |
| Denny McLain | | | |
| Earl Wilson | | | |
| ☐ 236 NL Pitching Leaders: | 2.75 | 1.25 | .27 |
| Sandy Koufax | | | |
| Juan Marichal | | | |
| Bob Gibson | | | |
| Gaylord Perry | | | |
| ☐ 237 AL Strikeout Leaders: | .75 | .35 | .07 |
| Sam McDowell | | | |
| Jim Kaat | | | |
| Earl Wilson | | | |
| ☐ 238 NL Strikeout Leaders: | 1.25 | .60 | .12 |
| Sandy Koufax | | | |
| Jim Bunning | | | |
| Bob Veale | | | |
| ☐ 239 AL Batting Leaders: | 1.50 | .70 | .15 |
| Frank Robinson | | | |
| Tony Oliva | | | |
| Al Kaline | | | |
| ☐ 240 NL Batting Leaders: | .75 | .35 | .07 |
| Matty Alou | | | |
| Felipe Alou | | | |
| Rico Carty | | | |

| | MINT | VG-E | F-G |
|---|---|---|---|
| ☐ 241 AL RBI Leaders: | 1.50 | .70 | .15 |
| Frank Robinson | | | |
| Harmon Killebrew | | | |
| Boog Powell | | | |
| ☐ 242 NL RBI Leaders: | 1.50 | .70 | .15 |
| Hank Aaron | | | |
| Bob Clemente | | | |
| Richie Allen | | | |
| ☐ 243 AL Home Run Leaders: | 1.50 | .70 | .15 |
| Frank Robinson | | | |
| Harmon Killebrew | | | |
| Boog Powell | | | |
| ☐ 244 NL Home Run Leaders: | 1.50 | .70 | .15 |
| Hank Aaron | | | |
| Richie Allen | | | |
| Willie Mays | | | |
| ☐ 245 Curt Flood | .55 | .25 | .05 |
| ☐ 246 Jim Perry | .45 | .20 | .04 |
| ☐ 247 Jerry Lumpe | .24 | .10 | .02 |
| ☐ 248 Gene Mauch MGR | .35 | .15 | .03 |
| ☐ 249 Nick Willhite | .24 | .10 | .02 |
| ☐ 250 Hank Aaron | 18.00 | 8.50 | 1.80 |
| ☐ 251 Woody Held | .24 | .10 | .02 |
| ☐ 252 Bob Bolin | .24 | .10 | .02 |
| ☐ 253 Indians Rookies | .24 | .10 | .02 |
| Bill Davis | | | |
| Gus Gil | | | |
| ☐ 254 Milt Pappas | .35 | .15 | .03 |
| ☐ 255 Frank Howard | .80 | .40 | .08 |
| ☐ 256 Bob Hendley | .24 | .10 | .02 |
| ☐ 257 Charlie Smith | .24 | .10 | .02 |
| ☐ 258 Lee Maye | .24 | .10 | .02 |
| ☐ 259 Don Dennis | .24 | .10 | .02 |
| ☐ 260 Jim Lefebvre | .35 | .15 | .03 |
| ☐ 261 John Wyatt | .24 | .10 | .02 |
| ☐ 262 Athletics Team | .55 | .25 | .05 |
| ☐ 263 Hank Aguirre | .24 | .10 | .02 |
| ☐ 264 Ron Swoboda | .24 | .10 | .02 |
| ☐ 265 Lou Burdette | .50 | .22 | .05 |
| ☐ 266 Pitt Power | 1.25 | .60 | .12 |
| Willie Stargell | | | |
| Donn Clendenon | | | |
| ☐ 267 Don Schwall | .24 | .10 | .02 |
| ☐ 268 John Briggs | .24 | .10 | .02 |
| ☐ 269 Don Nottebart | .24 | .10 | .02 |
| ☐ 270 Zoilo Versalles | .24 | .10 | .02 |
| ☐ 271 Eddie Watt | .24 | .10 | .02 |
| ☐ 272 Cubs Rookies | .24 | .10 | .02 |
| Bill Connors | | | |
| Dave Dowling | | | |
| ☐ 273 Dick Lines | .24 | .10 | .02 |
| ☐ 274 Bob Aspromonte | .24 | .10 | .02 |
| ☐ 275 Fred Whitfield | .24 | .10 | .02 |

|  | MINT | VG-E | F-G |
|---|---|---|---|
| ☐ 276 Bruce Brubaker | .24 | .10 | .02 |
| ☐ 277 Steve Whitaker | .24 | .10 | .02 |
| ☐ 278 Checklist 4 | .85 | .15 | .04 |
| Jim Kaat |  |  |  |
| ☐ 279 Frank Linzy | .24 | .10 | .02 |
| ☐ 280 Tony Conigliaro | .65 | .30 | .06 |
| ☐ 281 Bob Rodgers | .24 | .10 | .02 |
| ☐ 282 Johnny Odom | .24 | .10 | .02 |
| ☐ 283 Gene Alley | .35 | .15 | .03 |
| ☐ 284 Johnny Podres | .50 | .22 | .05 |
| ☐ 285 Lou Brock | 4.25 | 2.00 | .42 |
| ☐ 286 Wayne Causey | .24 | .10 | .02 |
| ☐ 287 Mets Rookies | .24 | .10 | .02 |
| Greg Goossen |  |  |  |
| Bart Shirley |  |  |  |
| ☐ 288 Denny Lemaster | .24 | .10 | .02 |
| ☐ 289 Tom Tresh | .45 | .20 | .04 |
| ☐ 290 Bill White | .40 | .18 | .04 |
| ☐ 291 Jim Hannan | .24 | .10 | .02 |
| ☐ 292 Don Pavletich | .24 | .10 | .02 |
| ☐ 293 Ed Kirkpatrick | .24 | .10 | .02 |
| ☐ 294 Walt Alston | .85 | .40 | .08 |
| ☐ 295 Sam McDowell | .40 | .18 | .04 |
| ☐ 296 Glenn Beckert | .40 | .18 | .04 |
| ☐ 297 Dave Morehead | .24 | .10 | .02 |
| ☐ 298 Ron Davis | .24 | .10 | .02 |
| ☐ 299 Norm Siebern | .24 | .10 | .02 |
| ☐ 300 Jim Kaat | 1.10 | .50 | .11 |
| ☐ 301 Jesse Gonder | .24 | .10 | .02 |
| ☐ 302 Orioles Team | .55 | .25 | .05 |
| ☐ 303 Gil Blanco | .24 | .10 | .02 |
| ☐ 304 Phil Gagliano | .24 | .10 | .02 |
| ☐ 305 Earl Wilson | .24 | .10 | .02 |
| ☐ 306 Bud Harrelson | .35 | .15 | .03 |
| ☐ 307 Jim Beauchamp | .24 | .10 | .02 |
| ☐ 308 Al Downing | .24 | .10 | .02 |
| ☐ 309 Hurlers Beware | .45 | .20 | .04 |
| Johnny Callison |  |  |  |
| Richie Allen |  |  |  |
| ☐ 310 Gary Peters | .35 | .15 | .03 |
| ☐ 311 Ed Brinkman | .24 | .10 | .02 |
| ☐ 312 Don Mincher | .24 | .10 | .02 |
| ☐ 313 Bob Lee | .24 | .10 | .02 |
| ☐ 314 Red Sox Rookies | 1.50 | .70 | .15 |
| Mike Andrews |  |  |  |
| Reggie Smith |  |  |  |
| ☐ 315 Billy Williams | 1.75 | .85 | .17 |
| ☐ 316 Jack Kralick | .24 | .10 | .02 |
| ☐ 317 Cesar Tovar | .24 | .10 | .02 |
| ☐ 318 Dave Giusti | .24 | .10 | .02 |
| ☐ 319 Paul Blair | .35 | .15 | .03 |
| ☐ 320 Gaylord Perry | 3.00 | 1.40 | .30 |
| ☐ 321 Mayo Smith | .24 | .10 | .02 |

|  | MINT | VG-E | F-G |
|---|---|---|---|
| ☐ 322 Jose Pagan | .24 | .10 | .02 |
| ☐ 323 Mike Hershberger | .24 | .10 | .02 |
| ☐ 324 Hal Woodeschick | .24 | .10 | .02 |
| ☐ 325 Chico Cardenas | .24 | .10 | .02 |
| ☐ 326 Bob Uecker | 2.25 | 1.00 | .22 |
| ☐ 327 Angels Team | .55 | .25 | .05 |
| ☐ 328 Clete Boyer | .35 | .15 | .03 |
| ☐ 329 Charlie Lau | .35 | .15 | .03 |
| ☐ 330 Claude Osteen | .35 | .15 | .03 |
| ☐ 331 Joe Foy | .24 | .10 | .02 |
| ☐ 332 Jesus Alou | .24 | .10 | .02 |
| ☐ 333 Fergie Jenkins | 1.50 | .70 | .15 |
| ☐ 334 Twin Terrors | 1.50 | .70 | .15 |
| Bob Allison |  |  |  |
| Harmon Killebrew |  |  |  |
| ☐ 335 Bob Veale | .35 | .15 | .03 |
| ☐ 336 Joe Azcue | .24 | .10 | .02 |
| ☐ 337 Joe Morgan | 2.75 | 1.25 | .27 |
| ☐ 338 Bob Locker | .24 | .10 | .02 |
| ☐ 339 Chico Ruiz | .24 | .10 | .02 |
| ☐ 340 Joe Pepitone | .45 | .20 | .04 |
| ☐ 341 Giants Rookies | .24 | .10 | .02 |
| Dick Dietz |  |  |  |
| Bill Sorrell |  |  |  |
| ☐ 342 Hank Fischer | .24 | .10 | .02 |
| ☐ 343 Tom Satriano | .24 | .10 | .02 |
| ☐ 344 Ossie Chavarria | .24 | .10 | .02 |
| ☐ 345 Stu Miller | .24 | .10 | .02 |
| ☐ 346 Jim Hickman | .24 | .10 | .02 |
| ☐ 347 Grady Hatton | .24 | .10 | .02 |
| ☐ 348 Tug McGraw | .75 | .35 | .07 |
| ☐ 349 Bob Chance | .24 | .10 | .02 |
| ☐ 350 Joe Torre | .75 | .35 | .07 |
| ☐ 351 Vern Law | .35 | .15 | .03 |
| ☐ 352 Ray Oyler | .24 | .10 | .02 |
| ☐ 353 Bill McCool | .24 | .10 | .02 |
| ☐ 354 Cubs Team | .55 | .25 | .05 |
| ☐ 355 Carl Yastrzemski | 35.00 | 16.50 | 3.50 |
| ☐ 356 Larry Jaster | .24 | .10 | .02 |
| ☐ 357 Bill Skowron | .50 | .22 | .05 |
| ☐ 358 Ruben Amaro | .24 | .10 | .02 |
| ☐ 359 Dick Ellsworth | .35 | .15 | .03 |
| ☐ 360 Leon Wagner | .24 | .10 | .02 |
| ☐ 361 Checklist 5 | 1.15 | .20 | .05 |
| Roberto Clemente |  |  |  |
| ☐ 362 Darold Knowles | .24 | .10 | .02 |
| ☐ 363 Dave Johnson | .40 | .18 | .04 |
| ☐ 364 Claude Raymond | .24 | .10 | .02 |
| ☐ 365 John Roseboro | .35 | .15 | .03 |
| ☐ 366 Andy Kosco | .24 | .10 | .02 |
| ☐ 367 Angels Rookies | .24 | .10 | .02 |
| Bill Kelso |  |  |  |
| Don Wallace |  |  |  |

|   |   | MINT | VG-E | F-G |
|---|---|---|---|---|
| ☐ 368 | Jack Hiatt | .24 | .10 | .02 |
| ☐ 369 | Jim Hunter | 2.50 | 1.15 | .25 |
| ☐ 370 | Tommy Davis | .50 | .22 | .05 |
| ☐ 371 | Jim Lonborg | .80 | .40 | .08 |
| ☐ 372 | Mike De La Hoz | .30 | .12 | .03 |
| ☐ 373 | White Sox Rookies | .30 | .12 | .03 |
|   | Duane Josephson | | | |
|   | Fred Klages | | | |
| ☐ 374 | Mel Queen | .30 | .12 | .03 |
| ☐ 375 | Jake Gibbs | .30 | .12 | .03 |
| ☐ 376 | Don Lock | .30 | .12 | .03 |
| ☐ 377 | Luis Tiant | .85 | .40 | .08 |
| ☐ 378 | Tigers Team | .85 | .40 | .08 |
| ☐ 379 | Jerry May | .30 | .12 | .03 |
| ☐ 380 | Dean Chance | .30 | .12 | .03 |
| ☐ 381 | Dick Schofield | .30 | .12 | .03 |
| ☐ 382 | Dave McNally | .60 | .28 | .06 |
| ☐ 383 | Ken Henderson | .30 | .12 | .03 |
| ☐ 384 | Cardinals Rookies | .30 | .12 | .03 |
|   | Jim Cosman | | | |
|   | Dick Hughes | | | |
| ☐ 385 | Jim Fregosi | .45 | .20 | .04 |
|   | (batting wrong) | | | |
| ☐ 386 | Dick Selma | .30 | .12 | .03 |
| ☐ 387 | Cap Peterson | .30 | .12 | .03 |
| ☐ 388 | Arnold Earley | .30 | .12 | .03 |
| ☐ 389 | Al Dark | .40 | .18 | .04 |
| ☐ 390 | Jim Wynn | .50 | .22 | .05 |
| ☐ 391 | Wilbur Wood | .50 | .22 | .05 |
| ☐ 392 | Tommy Harper | .40 | .18 | .04 |
| ☐ 393 | Jim Bouton | .85 | .40 | .08 |
| ☐ 394 | Jake Wood | .30 | .12 | .03 |
| ☐ 395 | Chris Short | .30 | .12 | .03 |
| ☐ 396 | Atlanta Aces | .40 | .18 | .04 |
|   | Denis Menke | | | |
|   | Tony Cloninger | | | |
| ☐ 397 | Willie Smith | .30 | .12 | .03 |
| ☐ 398 | Jeff Torborg | .40 | .18 | .04 |
| ☐ 399 | Al Worthington | .30 | .12 | .03 |
| ☐ 400 | Bob Clemente | 13.00 | 6.00 | 1.30 |
| ☐ 401 | Jim Coates | .30 | .12 | .03 |
| ☐ 402 | Phillies Rookies | .40 | .18 | .04 |
|   | Grant Jackson | | | |
|   | Billy Wilson | | | |
| ☐ 403 | Dick Nen | .30 | .12 | .03 |
| ☐ 404 | Nelson Briles | .30 | .12 | .03 |
| ☐ 405 | Russ Snyder | .30 | .12 | .03 |
| ☐ 406 | Lee Elia | .30 | .12 | .03 |
| ☐ 407 | Reds Rookies | .75 | .35 | .07 |
| ☐ 408 | Jim Northrup | .40 | .18 | .04 |
| ☐ 409 | Ray Sadecki | .30 | .12 | .03 |
| ☐ 410 | Lou Johnson | .30 | .12 | .03 |
| ☐ 411 | Dick Howser | .55 | .25 | .05 |

|   |   | MINT | VG-E | F-G |
|---|---|---|---|---|
| ☐ 412 | Astros Rookies | .75 | .35 | .07 |
|   | Norm Miller | | | |
|   | Doug Rader | | | |
| ☐ 413 | Jerry Grote | .30 | .12 | .03 |
| ☐ 414 | Casey Cox | .30 | .12 | .03 |
| ☐ 415 | Sonny Jackson | .30 | .12 | .03 |
| ☐ 416 | Roger Repoz | .30 | .12 | .03 |
| ☐ 417 | Bob Bruce | .30 | .12 | .03 |
| ☐ 418 | Sam Mele | .30 | .12 | .03 |
| ☐ 419 | Don Kessinger | .50 | .22 | .05 |
| ☐ 420 | Denny McLain | 1.10 | .50 | .11 |
| ☐ 421 | Dal Maxvill | .30 | .12 | .03 |
| ☐ 422 | Hoyt Wilhelm | 2.50 | 1.15 | .25 |
| ☐ 423 | Fence Busters | 4.50 | 2.10 | .45 |
|   | Willie Mays | | | |
|   | Willie McCovey | | | |
| ☐ 424 | Pedro Gonzales | .30 | .12 | .03 |
| ☐ 425 | Pete Mikkelsen | .30 | .12 | .03 |
| ☐ 426 | Lou Clinton | .30 | .12 | .03 |
| ☐ 427 | Ruben Gomez | .30 | .12 | .03 |
| ☐ 428 | Dodgers Rookies | .50 | .22 | .05 |
|   | Tom Hutton | | | |
|   | Gene Michael | | | |
| ☐ 429 | Garry Roggenburk | .30 | .12 | .03 |
| ☐ 430 | Pete Rose | 40.00 | 18.00 | 4.00 |
| ☐ 431 | Ted Uhlaender | .30 | .12 | .03 |
| ☐ 432 | Jimmie Hall | .30 | .12 | .03 |
| ☐ 433 | Al Luplow | .30 | .12 | .03 |
| ☐ 434 | Eddie Fisher | .30 | .12 | .03 |
| ☐ 435 | Mack Jones | .30 | .12 | .03 |
| ☐ 436 | Pete Ward | .30 | .12 | .03 |
| ☐ 437 | Senators Team | .55 | .25 | .05 |
| ☐ 438 | Chuck Dobson | .30 | .12 | .03 |
| ☐ 439 | Byron Browne | .30 | .12 | .03 |
| ☐ 440 | Steve Hargan | .30 | .12 | .03 |
| ☐ 441 | Jim Davenport | .55 | .25 | .05 |
| ☐ 442 | Yankees Rookies | .50 | .22 | .05 |
|   | Bill Robinson | | | |
|   | Joe Verbanic | | | |
| ☐ 443 | Tito Francona | .45 | .20 | .04 |
| ☐ 444 | George Smith | .30 | .12 | .03 |
| ☐ 445 | Don Sutton | 3.00 | 1.40 | .30 |
| ☐ 446 | Russ Nixon | .30 | .12 | .03 |
| ☐ 447 | Bo Belinsky | .30 | .12 | .03 |
| ☐ 448 | Harry Walker | .30 | .12 | .03 |
| ☐ 449 | Orlando Pena | .30 | .12 | .03 |
| ☐ 450 | Richie Allen | 1.25 | .60 | .12 |
| ☐ 451 | Fred Newman | .30 | .12 | .03 |
| ☐ 452 | Ed Kranepool | .50 | .22 | .05 |
| ☐ 453 | Aurelio Monteagudo | .30 | .12 | .03 |
| ☐ 454 | Checklist 6 | 1.20 | .20 | .05 |
|   | Juan Marichal | | | |
| ☐ 455 | Tommy Agee | .30 | .12 | .03 |

| | MINT | VG-E | F-G |
|---|---|---|---|
| ☐ 456 Phil Niekro | 3.00 | 1.40 | .30 |
| ☐ 457 Andy Etchebarren | .30 | .12 | .03 |
| ☐ 458 Lee Thomas | .70 | .32 | .07 |
| ☐ 459 Senators Rookies | .70 | .32 | .07 |
| Dick Bosman | | | |
| Pete Craig | | | |
| ☐ 460 Harmon Killebrew | 6.00 | 2.80 | .60 |
| ☐ 461 Bob Miller | .70 | .32 | .07 |
| ☐ 462 Bob Barton | .70 | .32 | .07 |
| ☐ 463 Hill Aces | .80 | .40 | .08 |
| Sam McDowell | | | |
| Sonny Siebert | | | |
| ☐ 464 Dan Coombs | .70 | .32 | .07 |
| ☐ 465 Willie Horton | .80 | .40 | .08 |
| ☐ 466 Bobby Wine | .75 | .35 | .07 |
| ☐ 467 Jim O'Toole | .70 | .32 | .07 |
| ☐ 468 Ralph Houk MGR | .85 | .40 | .08 |
| ☐ 469 Len Gabrielson | .70 | .32 | .07 |
| ☐ 470 Bob Shaw | .70 | .32 | .07 |
| ☐ 471 Rene Lachemann | .80 | .40 | .08 |
| ☐ 472 Rookies Pirates | .70 | .32 | .07 |
| John Gelnar | | | |
| George Spriggs | | | |
| ☐ 473 Jose Santiago | .70 | .32 | .07 |
| ☐ 474 Bob Tolan | .75 | .35 | .07 |
| ☐ 475 Jim Palmer | 11.00 | 5.25 | 1.10 |
| ☐ 476 Tony Perez SP | 11.00 | 5.25 | 1.10 |
| ☐ 477 Braves Team | 1.00 | .45 | .10 |
| ☐ 478 Bob Humphreys | .70 | .32 | .07 |
| ☐ 479 Gary Bell | .70 | .32 | .07 |
| ☐ 480 Willie McCovey | 7.50 | 3.50 | .75 |
| ☐ 481 Leo Durocher | 1.10 | .50 | .11 |
| ☐ 482 Bill Monbouquette | .70 | .32 | .07 |
| ☐ 483 Jim Landis | .70 | .32 | .07 |
| ☐ 484 Jerry Adair | .70 | .32 | .07 |
| ☐ 485 Tim McCarver | 1.25 | .60 | .12 |
| ☐ 486 Twins Rookies | .70 | .32 | .07 |
| Rich Reese | | | |
| Bill Whitby | | | |
| ☐ 487 Tommie Reynolds | .70 | .32 | .07 |
| ☐ 488 Gerry Arrigo | .70 | .32 | .07 |
| ☐ 489 Doug Clemens | .70 | .32 | .07 |
| ☐ 490 Tony Cloninger | .70 | .32 | .07 |
| ☐ 491 Sam Bowens | .70 | .32 | .07 |
| ☐ 492 Pirates Team | 1.00 | .45 | .10 |
| ☐ 493 Phil Ortega | .70 | .32 | .07 |
| ☐ 494 Bill Rigney | .70 | .32 | .07 |
| ☐ 495 Fritz Peterson | .70 | .32 | .07 |
| ☐ 496 Orlando McFarlane | .70 | .32 | .07 |
| ☐ 497 Ron Campbell | .70 | .32 | .07 |
| ☐ 498 Larry Dierker | .85 | .40 | .08 |

| | MINT | VG-E | F-G |
|---|---|---|---|
| ☐ 499 Indians Rookies | .70 | .32 | .07 |
| George Culver | | | |
| Jose Vidal | | | |
| ☐ 500 Juan Marichal | 4.50 | 2.10 | .45 |
| ☐ 501 Jerry Zimmerman | .70 | .32 | .07 |
| ☐ 502 Derrell Griffith | .70 | .32 | .07 |
| ☐ 503 Dodgers Team | 1.75 | .85 | .17 |
| ☐ 504 Orlando Martinez | .70 | .32 | .07 |
| ☐ 505 Tommy Helms | .75 | .35 | .07 |
| ☐ 506 Smokey Burgess | .85 | .40 | .08 |
| ☐ 507 Orioles Rookies | .70 | .32 | .07 |
| Ed Barnowski | | | |
| Larry Haney | | | |
| ☐ 508 Dick Hall | .70 | .32 | .07 |
| ☐ 509 Jim King | .70 | .32 | .07 |
| ☐ 510 Bill Mazeroski | 1.25 | .60 | .12 |
| ☐ 511 Don Wert | .70 | .32 | .07 |
| ☐ 512 Red Schoendienst | 1.00 | .45 | .10 |
| ☐ 513 Marcelino Lopez | .70 | .32 | .07 |
| ☐ 514 John Werhas | .70 | .32 | .07 |
| ☐ 515 Bert Campaneris | 1.00 | .45 | .10 |
| ☐ 516 Giants Team | 1.00 | .45 | .10 |
| ☐ 517 Fred Talbot | .70 | .32 | .07 |
| ☐ 518 Denis Menke | .70 | .32 | .07 |
| ☐ 519 Ted Davidson | .70 | .32 | .07 |
| ☐ 520 Max Alvis | .70 | .32 | .07 |
| ☐ 521 Bird Bombers | .85 | .40 | .08 |
| Boog Powell | | | |
| Curt Blefary | | | |
| ☐ 522 John Stephenson | .70 | .32 | .07 |
| ☐ 523 Jim Merritt | .70 | .32 | .07 |
| ☐ 524 Felix Mantilla | .70 | .32 | .07 |
| ☐ 525 Ron Hunt | .70 | .32 | .07 |
| ☐ 526 Tigers Rookies | 1.00 | .45 | .10 |
| Pat Dobson | | | |
| George Korince | | | |
| (See 67T—72) | | | |
| ☐ 527 Dennis Ribant | .70 | .32 | .07 |
| ☐ 528 Rico Petrocelli | 1.00 | .45 | .10 |
| ☐ 529 Gary Wagner | .70 | .32 | .07 |
| ☐ 530 Felipe Alou | 1.00 | .45 | .10 |
| ☐ 531 Checklist 7 | 3.00 | .45 | .10 |
| Brooks Robinson | | | |
| ☐ 532 Jim Hicks | .70 | .32 | .07 |
| ☐ 533 Jack Fisher | .70 | .32 | .07 |
| ☐ 534 Hank Aguirre | 2.75 | 1.25 | .27 |
| ☐ 535 Donn Clendenon | 2.75 | 1.25 | .27 |
| ☐ 536 Cubs Rookies | 4.25 | 2.00 | .42 |
| Joe Niekro | | | |
| Paul Popovich | | | |
| ☐ 537 Chuck Estrada | 2.25 | 1.00 | .22 |
| ☐ 538 J. C. Martin | 2.00 | .90 | .20 |
| ☐ 539 Dick Egan | 2.00 | .90 | .20 |

| | MINT | VG-E | F-G | | MINT | VG-E | F-G |
|---|---|---|---|---|---|---|---|
| ☐ 540 Norm Cash | 7.50 | 3.50 | .75 | ☐ 579 Bill Henry | 2.00 | .90 | .20 |
| ☐ 541 Joe Gibbon | 2.00 | .90 | .20 | ☐ 580 Rocky Colavito | 9.00 | 4.25 | .90 |
| ☐ 542 Athletics Rookies | 3.50 | 1.65 | .35 | ☐ 581 Mets Rookies | 135.00 | 60.00 | 13.50 |
| Rick Monday | | | | Bill Denehy | | | |
| Tony Pierce | | | | Tom Seaver | | | |
| ☐ 543 Dan Schneider | 2.00 | .90 | .20 | ☐ 582 Jim Owens | 2.00 | .90 | .20 |
| ☐ 544 Indians Team | 4.00 | 1.85 | .40 | ☐ 583 Ray Barker | 2.00 | .90 | .20 |
| ☐ 545 Jim Grant | 2.00 | .90 | .20 | ☐ 584 Jim Piersall | 6.00 | 2.80 | .60 |
| ☐ 546 Woody Woodward | 2.00 | .90 | .20 | ☐ 585 Wally Bunker | 2.00 | .90 | .20 |
| ☐ 547 Red Sox Rookies | 2.00 | .90 | .20 | ☐ 586 Manny Jimenez | 2.00 | .90 | .20 |
| Russ Gibson | | | | ☐ 587 N.L. Rookies | 2.00 | .90 | .20 |
| Bill Rohr | | | | Don Shaw | | | |
| ☐ 548 Tony Gonzalez | 2.00 | .90 | .20 | Gary Sutherland | | | |
| ☐ 549 Jack Sanford | 2.00 | .90 | .20 | ☐ 588 Johnny Klippstein | 2.00 | .90 | .20 |
| ☐ 550 Vada Pinson | 3.00 | 1.40 | .30 | ☐ 589 Dave Ricketts | 2.00 | .90 | .20 |
| ☐ 551 Doug Camilli | 2.00 | .90 | .20 | ☐ 590 Pete Richert | 2.00 | .90 | .20 |
| ☐ 552 Ted Savage | 2.00 | .90 | .20 | ☐ 591 Ty Cline | 2.00 | .90 | .20 |
| ☐ 553 Yankees Rookies | 4.00 | 1.85 | .40 | ☐ 592 N.L. Rookies | 2.00 | .90 | .20 |
| Mike Hegan | | | | Jim Shellenback | | | |
| Thad Tillotson | | | | Ron Willis | | | |
| ☐ 554 Andre Rodgers | 2.00 | .90 | .20 | ☐ 593 Wes Westrum | 2.00 | .90 | .20 |
| ☐ 555 Don Cardwell | 2.00 | .90 | .20 | ☐ 594 Dan Osinski | 2.00 | .90 | .20 |
| ☐ 556 Al Weis | 2.00 | .90 | .20 | ☐ 595 Cookie Rojas | 2.00 | .90 | .20 |
| ☐ 557 Al Ferrara | 2.00 | .90 | .20 | ☐ 596 Galen Cisco | 2.00 | .90 | .20 |
| ☐ 558 Orioles Rookies | 5.00 | 2.35 | .50 | ☐ 597 Ted Abernathy | 2.00 | .90 | .20 |
| Mark Belanger | | | | ☐ 598 White Sox Rookies | 2.00 | .90 | .20 |
| Bill Dillman | | | | Walt Williams | | | |
| ☐ 559 Dick Tracewski | 2.00 | .90 | .20 | Ed Stroud | | | |
| ☐ 560 Jim Bunning | 10.00 | 4.75 | 1.00 | ☐ 599 Bob Duliba | 2.00 | .90 | .20 |
| ☐ 561 Sandy Alomar | 2.00 | .90 | .20 | ☐ 600 Brooks Robinson | 100.00 | 45.00 | 10.00 |
| ☐ 562 Steve Blass | 2.25 | 1.00 | .22 | ☐ 601 Bill Bryan | 2.00 | .90 | .20 |
| ☐ 563 Joe Adcock | 5.00 | 2.35 | .50 | ☐ 602 Juan Pizarro | 2.00 | .90 | .20 |
| ☐ 564 Astros Rookies | 2.00 | .90 | .20 | ☐ 603 Athletics Rookies | 2.00 | .90 | .20 |
| Alonzo Harris | | | | Tim Talton | | | |
| Aaron Pointer | | | | Ramon Webster | | | |
| ☐ 565 Lew Krausse | 2.00 | .90 | .20 | ☐ 604 Red Sox Team | 8.00 | 3.75 | .80 |
| ☐ 566 Gary Geiger | 2.00 | .90 | .20 | ☐ 605 Mike Shannon | 3.00 | 1.40 | .30 |
| ☐ 567 Steve Hamilton | 2.00 | .90 | .20 | ☐ 606 Ron Taylor | 2.00 | .90 | .20 |
| ☐ 568 John Sullivan | 2.00 | .90 | .20 | ☐ 607 Mickey Stanley | 2.00 | .90 | .20 |
| ☐ 569 A.L. Rookies | 90.00 | 42.00 | 9.00 | ☐ 608 Cubs Rookies | 2.00 | .90 | .20 |
| Rod Carew | | | | Rich Nye | | | |
| Hank Allen | | | | John Upham | | | |
| ☐ 570 Maury Wills | 50.00 | 22.00 | 5.00 | ☐ 609 Tommy John | 28.00 | 8.00 | 2.00 |
| ☐ 571 Larry Sherry | 2.00 | .90 | .20 | | | | |
| ☐ 572 Don Demeter | 2.00 | .90 | .20 | | | | |
| ☐ 573 White Sox Team | 4.50 | 2.10 | .45 | | | | |
| ☐ 574 Jerry Buchek | 2.00 | .90 | .20 | | | | |
| ☐ 575 Dave Boswell | 2.00 | .90 | .20 | | | | |
| ☐ 576 N.L. Rookies | 2.00 | .90 | .20 | | | | |
| Ramon Hernandez | | | | | | | |
| Norm Gigon | | | | | | | |
| ☐ 577 Bill Short | 2.00 | .90 | .20 | | | | |
| ☐ 578 John Boccabella | 2.00 | .90 | .20 | | | | |

# 1968 TOPPS

WILLIE MAYS

The cards in this 598 card set measure
2½″ by 3½″. The 1968 Topps set includes
The Sporting News All-Star selections as
card numbers 361 to 380. The front of
each checklist card features a picture of a
popular player inside a circle. High numbers 534 to 598 are slightly more difficult
to obtain.

**Complete Set: M-450.00; VG-E-200.00; F-G-45.00**

|  | MINT | VG-E | F-G |
|---|---|---|---|
| Common Player (1---457) | .20 | .09 | .02 |
| Common Player (458---533) | .27 | .11 | .02 |
| Common Player (534---598) | .27 | .11 | .02 |
| ☐ 1 NL Batting Leaders .... Bob Clemente Matty Alou | 2.25 | .60 | .15 |
| ☐ 2 AL Batting Leaders ..... Carl Yastrzemski Frank Robinson Al Kaline | 1.50 | .70 | .15 |
| ☐ 3 NL RBI Leaders ....... Orlando Cepeda Bob Clemente Hank Aaron | 1.50 | .70 | .15 |
| ☐ 4 AL RBI Leaders ....... Carl Yastrzemski Harmon Killebrew Frank Robinson | 1.50 | .70 | .15 |
| ☐ 5 NL Home Run Leaders . Hank Aaron Jim Wynn Ron Santo Willie McCovey | 1.50 | .70 | .15 |
| ☐ 6 NL Home Run Leaders . Carl Yastrzemski Harmon Killebrew Frank Howard | 1.50 | .70 | .15 |
| ☐ 7 NL ERA Leaders ....... Phil Niekro Jim Bunning Chris Short | .75 | .35 | .07 |
| ☐ 8 AL ERA Leaders ....... Joe Horlen Gary Peters Sonny Siebert | .50 | .22 | .05 |
| ☐ 9 NL Pitching Leaders .... Mike McCormick Ferguson Jenkins Jim Bunning Claude Osteen | .65 | .30 | .06 |
| ☐ 10 AL Pitching Leaders .... Jim Lonborg Earl Wilson Dean Chance | .50 | .22 | .05 |
| ☐ 11 NL Strikeout Leaders ... Jim Bunning Ferguson Jenkins Gaylord Perry | 1.00 | .45 | .10 |
| ☐ 12 AL Strikeout Leaders ... Jim Lonborg Sam McDowell Dean Chance | .50 | .22 | .05 |
| ☐ 13 Chuck Hartenstein .... | .20 | .09 | .02 |
| ☐ 14 Jerry McNertney ....... | .20 | .09 | .02 |
| ☐ 15 Ron Hunt ............ | .20 | .09 | .02 |
| ☐ 16 Indians Rookies ....... Lou Piniella Richie Scheinblum | 1.00 | .45 | .10 |
| ☐ 17 Dick Hall ............ | .20 | .09 | .02 |
| ☐ 18 Mike Hershberger ..... | .20 | .09 | .02 |
| ☐ 19 Juan Pizarro ......... | .20 | .09 | .02 |
| ☐ 20 Brooks Robinson ...... | 4.25 | 2.00 | .42 |
| ☐ 21 Ron Davis ........... | .20 | .09 | .02 |
| ☐ 22 Pat Dobson .......... | .30 | .12 | .03 |
| ☐ 23 Chico Cardenas ...... | .20 | .09 | .02 |
| ☐ 24 Bobby Locke ......... | .20 | .09 | .02 |
| ☐ 25 Julian Javier ......... | .20 | .09 | .02 |
| ☐ 26 Darrell Brandon ...... | .20 | .09 | .02 |
| ☐ 27 Gil Hodges .......... | 2.00 | .90 | .20 |
| ☐ 28 Ted Uhlaender ....... | .20 | .09 | .02 |
| ☐ 29 Joe Verbanic ........ | .20 | .09 | .02 |
| ☐ 30 Joe Torre ........... | .75 | .35 | .07 |
| ☐ 31 Ed Stroud ........... | .20 | .09 | .02 |
| ☐ 32 Joe Gibbon .......... | .20 | .09 | .02 |
| ☐ 33 Pete Ward ........... | .20 | .09 | .02 |
| ☐ 34 Al Ferrara ........... | .20 | .09 | .02 |

| | | MINT | VG-E | F-G |
|---|---|---|---|---|
| ☐ | 35 Steve Hargan | .20 | .09 | .02 |
| ☐ | 36 Pirates Rookies | .30 | .12 | .03 |
| | Bob Moose | | | |
| | Bob Robertson | | | |
| ☐ | 37 Billy Williams | 1.50 | .70 | .15 |
| ☐ | 38 Tony Pierce | .20 | .09 | .02 |
| ☐ | 39 Cookie Rojas | .20 | .09 | .02 |
| ☐ | 40 Denny McLain | 1.50 | .70 | .15 |
| ☐ | 41 Julio Gotay | .20 | .09 | .02 |
| ☐ | 42 Larry Haney | .20 | .09 | .02 |
| ☐ | 43 Gary Bell | .20 | .09 | .02 |
| ☐ | 44 Frank Kostro | .20 | .09 | .02 |
| ☐ | 45 Tom Seaver | 18.00 | 8.50 | 1.80 |
| ☐ | 46 Dave Ricketts | .20 | .09 | .02 |
| ☐ | 47 Ralph Houk MGR | .35 | .15 | .03 |
| ☐ | 48 Ted Davidson | .20 | .09 | .02 |
| ☐ | 49 Ed Brinkman | .20 | .09 | .02 |
| ☐ | 50 Willie Mays | 14.00 | 6.50 | 1.40 |
| ☐ | 51 Bob Locker | .20 | .09 | .02 |
| ☐ | 52 Hawk Taylor | .20 | .09 | .02 |
| ☐ | 53 Gene Alley | .25 | .10 | .02 |
| ☐ | 54 Stan Williams | .20 | .09 | .02 |
| ☐ | 55 Felipe Alou | .30 | .12 | .03 |
| ☐ | 56 Orioles Rookies | .20 | .09 | .02 |
| | Dave Leonhard | | | |
| | Dave May | | | |
| ☐ | 57 Dan Schneider | .20 | .09 | .02 |
| ☐ | 58 Ed Mathews | 2.50 | 1.15 | .25 |
| ☐ | 59 Don Lock | .20 | .09 | .02 |
| ☐ | 60 Ken Holtzman | .35 | .15 | .03 |
| ☐ | 61 Reggie Smith | .70 | .32 | .07 |
| ☐ | 62 Chuck Dobson | .20 | .09 | .02 |
| ☐ | 63 Dick Kenworthy | .20 | .09 | .02 |
| ☐ | 64 Jim Merritt | .20 | .09 | .02 |
| ☐ | 65 John Roseboro | .30 | .12 | .03 |
| ☐ | 66 A Casey Cox | .30 | .12 | .03 |
| | (Team name in white) | | | |
| ☐ | 66 B Casey Cox | 5.00 | 2.35 | .50 |
| | (Team name in yellow) | | | |
| ☐ | 67 Checklist 1 | .90 | .20 | .05 |
| | Jim Kaat | | | |
| ☐ | 68 Ron Willis | .20 | .09 | .02 |
| ☐ | 69 Tom Tresh | .40 | .18 | .04 |
| ☐ | 70 Bob Veale | .25 | .10 | .02 |
| ☐ | 71 Vern Fuller | .20 | .09 | .02 |
| ☐ | 72 Tommy John | 1.50 | .70 | .15 |
| ☐ | 73 Jim Ray Hart | .30 | .12 | .03 |
| ☐ | 74 Milt Pappas | .30 | .12 | .03 |
| ☐ | 75 Don Mincher | .20 | .09 | .02 |
| ☐ | 76 Braves Rookies | .30 | .12 | .03 |
| | Jim Britton | | | |
| | Ron Reed | | | |
| ☐ | 77 Don Wilson | .20 | .09 | .02 |

| | | MINT | VG-E | F-G |
|---|---|---|---|---|
| ☐ | 78 Jim Northrup | .25 | .10 | .02 |
| ☐ | 79 Ted Kubiak | .20 | .09 | .02 |
| ☐ | 80 Rod Carew | 16.00 | 7.50 | 1.60 |
| ☐ | 81 Larry Jackson | .20 | .09 | .02 |
| ☐ | 82 Sam Bowens | .20 | .09 | .02 |
| ☐ | 83 John Stephenson | .20 | .09 | .02 |
| ☐ | 84 Bob Tolan | .20 | .09 | .02 |
| ☐ | 85 Gaylord Perry | 2.50 | 1.15 | .25 |
| ☐ | 86 Willie Stargell | 3.00 | 1.40 | .30 |
| ☐ | 87 Dick Williams | .30 | .12 | .03 |
| ☐ | 88 Phil Regan | .25 | .10 | .02 |
| ☐ | 89 Jake Gibbs | .20 | .09 | .02 |
| ☐ | 90 Vada Pinson | .70 | .32 | .07 |
| ☐ | 91 Jim Ollom | .20 | .09 | .02 |
| ☐ | 92 Ed Kranepool | .25 | .10 | .02 |
| ☐ | 93 Tony Cloninger | .20 | .09 | .02 |
| ☐ | 94 Lee Maye | .20 | .09 | .02 |
| ☐ | 95 Bob Aspromonte | .20 | .09 | .02 |
| ☐ | 96 Senator Rookies | .20 | .09 | .02 |
| | Frank Coggins | | | |
| | Dick Nold | | | |
| ☐ | 97 Tom Phoebus | .20 | .09 | .02 |
| ☐ | 98 Gary Sutherland | .20 | .09 | .02 |
| ☐ | 99 Rocky Colavito | .70 | .32 | .07 |
| ☐ | 100 Bob Gibson | 4.00 | 1.85 | .40 |
| ☐ | 101 Glenn Beckert | .30 | .12 | .03 |
| ☐ | 102 Jose Cardenal | .20 | .09 | .02 |
| ☐ | 103 Don Sutton | 1.50 | .70 | .15 |
| ☐ | 104 Dick Dietz | .20 | .09 | .02 |
| ☐ | 105 Al Downing | .20 | .09 | .02 |
| ☐ | 106 Dalton Jones | .20 | .09 | .02 |
| ☐ | 107 Checklist 2 | .80 | .20 | .04 |
| | Juan Marichal | | | |
| ☐ | 108 Don Pavletich | .20 | .09 | .02 |
| ☐ | 109 Bert Campaneris | .30 | .12 | .03 |
| ☐ | 110 Hank Aaron | 13.00 | 6.00 | 1.30 |
| ☐ | 111 Rich Reese | .20 | .09 | .02 |
| ☐ | 112 Woody Fryman | .20 | .09 | .02 |
| ☐ | 113 Tigers Rookies | .20 | .09 | .02 |
| | Tom Matchick | | | |
| | Daryl Patterson | | | |
| ☐ | 114 Ron Swoboda | .20 | .09 | .02 |
| ☐ | 115 Sam McDowell | .30 | .12 | .03 |
| ☐ | 116 Ken McMullen | .20 | .09 | .02 |
| ☐ | 117 Larry Jaster | .20 | .09 | .02 |
| ☐ | 118 Mark Belanger | .30 | .12 | .03 |
| ☐ | 119 Ted Savage | .20 | .09 | .02 |
| ☐ | 120 Mel Stottlemyre | .35 | .15 | .03 |
| ☐ | 121 Jimmie Hall | .20 | .09 | .02 |
| ☐ | 122 Gene Mauch MGR | .30 | .12 | .03 |
| ☐ | 123 Jose Santiago | .20 | .09 | .02 |
| ☐ | 124 Nate Oliver | .20 | .09 | .02 |
| ☐ | 125 Joe Horlen | .25 | .10 | .02 |

| | MINT | VG-E | F-G |
|---|---|---|---|
| ☐ 126 Bob Etheridge ......... | .20 | .09 | .02 |
| ☐ 127 Paul Lindblad ......... | .20 | .09 | .02 |
| ☐ 128 Astros Rookies ......... | .20 | .09 | .02 |
|     Tom Dukes | | | |
|     Alonzo Harris | | | |
| ☐ 129 Mickey Stanley ......... | .25 | .10 | .02 |
| ☐ 130 Tony Perez ......... | 1.75 | .85 | .17 |
| ☐ 131 Frank Bertaina ......... | .20 | .09 | .02 |
| ☐ 132 Bud Harrelson ......... | .20 | .09 | .02 |
| ☐ 133 Fred Whitfield ......... | .20 | .09 | .02 |
| ☐ 134 Pat Jarvis ......... | .20 | .09 | .02 |
| ☐ 135 Paul Blair ......... | .30 | .12 | .03 |
| ☐ 136 Randy Hundley ......... | .20 | .09 | .02 |
| ☐ 137 Twins Team ......... | .45 | .20 | .04 |
| ☐ 138 Ruben Amaro ......... | .20 | .09 | .02 |
| ☐ 139 Chris Short ......... | .20 | .09 | .02 |
| ☐ 140 Tony Conigliaro ......... | .60 | .28 | .06 |
| ☐ 141 Dal Maxvill ......... | .20 | .09 | .02 |
| ☐ 142 White Sox Rookies ...... | .20 | .09 | .02 |
|     Buddy Bradford | | | |
|     Bill Voss | | | |
| ☐ 143 Pete Cimino ......... | .20 | .09 | .02 |
| ☐ 144 Joe Morgan ......... | 2.25 | 1.00 | .22 |
| ☐ 145 Don Drysdale ......... | 2.75 | 1.25 | .27 |
| ☐ 146 Sal Bando ......... | .45 | .20 | .04 |
| ☐ 147 Frank Linzy ......... | .20 | .09 | .02 |
| ☐ 148 Dave Bristol ......... | .20 | .09 | .02 |
| ☐ 149 Bob Saverine ......... | .20 | .09 | .02 |
| ☐ 150 Bob Clemente ......... | 9.00 | 4.25 | .90 |
| ☐ 151 World Series Game 1: .. | 2.00 | .90 | .20 |
|     Brock socks 4 hits | | | |
|     in opener | | | |
| ☐ 152 World Series Game 2: .. | 2.50 | 1.15 | .25 |
|     Yaz smashes 2 homers | | | |
| ☐ 153 World Series Game 3: .. | 1.00 | .45 | .10 |
|     Briles cools | | | |
|     off Boston | | | |
| ☐ 154 World Series Game 4: .. | 2.00 | .90 | .20 |
|     Gibson hurls shutout | | | |
| ☐ 155 World Series Game 5: .. | 1.00 | .45 | .10 |
|     Lonborg wins again | | | |
| ☐ 156 World Series Game 6: .. | 1.00 | .45 | .10 |
|     Petrocelli 2 homers | | | |
| ☐ 157 World Series Game 7: .. | 1.00 | .45 | .10 |
|     St. Louis wins it | | | |
| ☐ 158 World Series Summary . | 1.00 | .45 | .10 |
|     Cardinals celebrate | | | |
| ☐ 159 Don Kessinger ......... | .30 | .12 | .03 |
| ☐ 160 Earl Wilson ......... | .20 | .09 | .02 |
| ☐ 161 Norm Miller ......... | .20 | .09 | .02 |
| ☐ 162 Cards Rookies ......... | .55 | .25 | .05 |
|     Hal Gilson | | | |
|     Mike Torrez | | | |

| | MINT | VG-E | F-G |
|---|---|---|---|
| ☐ 163 Gene Brabender ...... | .20 | .09 | .02 |
| ☐ 164 Ramon Webster ...... | .20 | .09 | .02 |
| ☐ 165 Tony Oliva ......... | 1.00 | .45 | .10 |
| ☐ 166 Claude Raymond ...... | .20 | .09 | .02 |
| ☐ 167 Elston Howard ......... | 1.00 | .45 | .10 |
| ☐ 168 Dodgers Team ......... | .75 | .35 | .07 |
| ☐ 169 Bob Bolin ......... | .20 | .09 | .02 |
| ☐ 170 Jim Fregosi ......... | .30 | .12 | .03 |
| ☐ 171 Don Nottebart ......... | .20 | .09 | .02 |
| ☐ 172 Walt Williams ......... | .20 | .09 | .02 |
| ☐ 173 John Boozer ......... | .20 | .09 | .02 |
| ☐ 174 Bob Tillman ......... | .20 | .09 | .02 |
| ☐ 175 Maury Wills ......... | 1.00 | .45 | .10 |
| ☐ 176 Bob Allen ......... | .20 | .09 | .02 |
| ☐ 177 Mets Rookies ......... | 50.00 | 22.00 | 5.00 |
|     Jerry Koosman | | | |
|     Nolan Ryan | | | |
| ☐ 178 Don Wert ......... | .20 | .09 | .02 |
| ☐ 179 Bill Stoneman ......... | .20 | .09 | .02 |
| ☐ 180 Curt Flood ......... | .50 | .22 | .05 |
| ☐ 181 Jerry Zimmerman ...... | .20 | .09 | .02 |
| ☐ 182 Dave Guisti ......... | .20 | .09 | .02 |
| ☐ 183 Ken Boyer ......... | .20 | .09 | .02 |
| ☐ 184 Lou Johnson ......... | .20 | .09 | .02 |
| ☐ 185 Tom Haller ......... | .20 | .09 | .02 |
| ☐ 186 Eddie Watt ......... | .20 | .09 | .02 |
| ☐ 187 Sonny Jackson ......... | .20 | .09 | .02 |
| ☐ 188 Cap Peterson ......... | .20 | .09 | .02 |
| ☐ 189 Bill Landis ......... | .20 | .09 | .02 |
| ☐ 190 Bill White ......... | .30 | .12 | .03 |
| ☐ 191 Dan Frisella ......... | .20 | .09 | .02 |
| ☐ 192 Checklist 3 ......... | 1.10 | .20 | .04 |
|     Carl Yastrzemski | | | |
| ☐ 193 Jack Hamilton ......... | .20 | .09 | .02 |
| ☐ 194 Don Buford ......... | .20 | .09 | .02 |
| ☐ 195 Joe Pepitone ......... | .30 | .12 | .03 |
| ☐ 196 Gary Nolan ......... | .20 | .09 | .02 |
| ☐ 197 Larry Brown ......... | .20 | .09 | .02 |
| ☐ 198 Roy Face ......... | .35 | .15 | .03 |
| ☐ 199 A's Rookies ......... | .20 | .09 | .02 |
|     Roberto Rodriguez | | | |
|     Darrell Osteen | | | |
| ☐ 200 Orlando Cepeda ...... | 1.40 | .70 | .14 |
| ☐ 201 Mike Marshall ......... | .75 | .35 | .07 |
| ☐ 202 Adolfo Phillips ......... | .20 | .09 | .02 |
| ☐ 203 Dick Kelley ......... | .20 | .09 | .02 |
| ☐ 204 Andy Etchebarren ...... | .20 | .09 | .02 |
| ☐ 205 Juan Marichal ......... | 2.50 | 1.15 | .25 |
| ☐ 206 Cal Ermer ......... | .20 | .09 | .02 |
| ☐ 207 Carroll Sembera ...... | .20 | .09 | .02 |
| ☐ 208 Willie Davis ......... | .45 | .20 | .04 |
| ☐ 209 Tim Cullen ......... | .20 | .09 | .02 |
| ☐ 210 Gary Peters ......... | .25 | .10 | .02 |

| | MINT | VG-E | F-G |
|---|---|---|---|
| ☐ 211 J. C. Martin | .20 | .09 | .02 |
| ☐ 212 Dave Morehead | .20 | .09 | .02 |
| ☐ 213 Chico Ruiz | .20 | .09 | .02 |
| ☐ 214 Yankees Rookies | .30 | .12 | .03 |
| Stan Bahnsen | | | |
| Frank Fernandez | | | |
| ☐ 215 Jim Bunning | 1.25 | .60 | .12 |
| ☐ 216 Bubba Morton | .20 | .09 | .02 |
| ☐ 217 Turk Farrell | .20 | .09 | .02 |
| ☐ 218 Ken Suarez | .20 | .09 | .02 |
| ☐ 219 Rob Gardner | .20 | .09 | .02 |
| ☐ 220 Harmon Killebrew | 3.25 | 1.50 | .32 |
| ☐ 221 Braves Team | .50 | .22 | .05 |
| ☐ 222 Jim Hardin | .20 | .09 | .02 |
| ☐ 223 Ollie Brown | .20 | .09 | .02 |
| ☐ 224 Jack Aker | .20 | .09 | .02 |
| ☐ 225 Richie Allen | .75 | .35 | .07 |
| ☐ 226 Jimmie Price | .20 | .09 | .02 |
| ☐ 227 Joe Hoerner | .20 | .09 | .02 |
| ☐ 228 Dodgers Rookies | .25 | .10 | .02 |
| Jack Billingham | | | |
| Jim Fairey | | | |
| ☐ 229 Fred Klages | .20 | .09 | .02 |
| ☐ 230 Pete Rose | 33.00 | 15.00 | 3.00 |
| ☐ 231 Dave Baldwin | .20 | .09 | .02 |
| ☐ 232 Denis Menke | .20 | .09 | .02 |
| ☐ 233 George Scott | .30 | .12 | .03 |
| ☐ 234 Bill Monbouquette | .20 | .09 | .02 |
| ☐ 235 Ron Santo | .55 | .25 | .05 |
| ☐ 236 Tug McGraw | .70 | .32 | .07 |
| ☐ 237 Alvin Dark | .30 | .12 | .03 |
| ☐ 238 Tom Satriano | .20 | .09 | .02 |
| ☐ 239 Bill Henry | .20 | .09 | .02 |
| ☐ 240 Al Kaline | 4.00 | 1.85 | .40 |
| ☐ 241 Felix Millan | .20 | .09 | .02 |
| ☐ 242 Moe Drabowsky | .20 | .09 | .02 |
| ☐ 243 Rich Rollins | .20 | .09 | .02 |
| ☐ 244 John Donaldson | .20 | .09 | .02 |
| ☐ 245 Tony Gonzalez | .20 | .09 | .02 |
| ☐ 246 Fritz Peterson | .20 | .09 | .02 |
| ☐ 247 Reds Rookies | 50.00 | 22.00 | 5.00 |
| Johnny Bench | | | |
| Ron Tompkins | | | |
| ☐ 248 Fred Valentine | .20 | .09 | .02 |
| ☐ 249 Bill Singer | .20 | .09 | .02 |
| ☐ 250 Carl Yastrzemski | 17.00 | 8.00 | 1.70 |
| ☐ 251 Manny Sanguillen | .65 | .30 | .06 |
| ☐ 252 Angels Team | .45 | .20 | .04 |
| ☐ 253 Dick Hughes | .20 | .09 | .02 |
| ☐ 254 Cleon Jones | .20 | .09 | .02 |
| ☐ 255 Dean Chance | .25 | .10 | .02 |
| ☐ 256 Norm Cash | .75 | .35 | .07 |
| ☐ 257 Phil Niekro | 2.00 | .90 | .20 |

| | MINT | VG-E | F-G |
|---|---|---|---|
| ☐ 258 Cubs Rookies | .20 | .09 | .02 |
| Jose Arcia | | | |
| Bill Schlesinger | | | |
| ☐ 259 Ken Boyer | .70 | .32 | .07 |
| ☐ 260 Jim Wynn | .45 | .20 | .04 |
| ☐ 261 Dave Duncan | .20 | .09 | .02 |
| ☐ 262 Rick Wise | .30 | .12 | .03 |
| ☐ 263 Horace Clarke | .20 | .09 | .02 |
| ☐ 264 Ted Abernathy | .20 | .09 | .02 |
| ☐ 265 Tommy Davis | .40 | .18 | .04 |
| ☐ 266 Paul Popovich | .20 | .09 | .02 |
| ☐ 267 Herman Franks | .20 | .09 | .02 |
| ☐ 268 Bob Humphreys | .20 | .09 | .02 |
| ☐ 269 Bob Tiefenauer | .20 | .09 | .02 |
| ☐ 270 Matty Alou | .30 | .12 | .03 |
| ☐ 271 Bobby Knoop | .20 | .09 | .02 |
| ☐ 272 Ray Culp | .20 | .09 | .02 |
| ☐ 273 Dave Johnson | .35 | .15 | .03 |
| ☐ 274 Mike Cuellar | .30 | .12 | .03 |
| ☐ 275 Tim McCarver | .40 | .18 | .04 |
| ☐ 276 Jim Roland | .20 | .09 | .02 |
| ☐ 277 Jerry Buchek | .20 | .09 | .02 |
| ☐ 278 Checklist 4 | .75 | .15 | .03 |
| Orlando Cepeda | | | |
| ☐ 279 Bill Hands | .20 | .09 | .02 |
| ☐ 280 Mickey Mantle | 28.00 | 12.50 | 2.80 |
| ☐ 281 Jim Campanis | .20 | .09 | .02 |
| ☐ 282 Rick Monday | .40 | .18 | .04 |
| ☐ 283 Mel Queen | .20 | .09 | .02 |
| ☐ 284 John Briggs | .20 | .09 | .02 |
| ☐ 285 Dick McAuliffe | .25 | .10 | .02 |
| ☐ 286 Cecil Upshaw | .20 | .09 | .02 |
| ☐ 287 White Sox Rookies | .20 | .09 | .02 |
| Mickey Abarbanel | | | |
| Cisco Carlos | | | |
| ☐ 288 Dave Wickersham | .20 | .09 | .02 |
| ☐ 289 Woody Held | .20 | .09 | .02 |
| ☐ 290 Willie McCovey | 3.50 | 1.65 | .35 |
| ☐ 291 Dick Lines | .20 | .09 | .02 |
| ☐ 292 Art Shamsky | .20 | .09 | .02 |
| ☐ 293 Bruce Howard | .20 | .09 | .02 |
| ☐ 294 Red Schoendienst | .40 | .18 | .04 |
| ☐ 295 Sonny Siebert | .25 | .10 | .02 |
| ☐ 296 Byron Browne | .20 | .09 | .02 |
| ☐ 297 Russ Gibson | .20 | .09 | .02 |
| ☐ 298 Jim Brewer | .20 | .09 | .02 |
| ☐ 299 Gene Michael | .25 | .10 | .02 |
| ☐ 300 Rusty Staub | .70 | .32 | .07 |
| ☐ 301 Twins Rookies | .20 | .09 | .02 |
| George Mitterwald | | | |
| Rick Renick | | | |
| ☐ 302 Gerry Arrigo | .20 | .09 | .02 |
| ☐ 303 Dick Green | .20 | .09 | .02 |

| | MINT | VG-E | F-G |
|---|---|---|---|
| ☐ 304 Sandy Valdespino | .20 | .09 | .02 |
| ☐ 305 Minnie Rojas | .20 | .09 | .02 |
| ☐ 306 Mike Ryan | .20 | .09 | .02 |
| ☐ 307 John Hiller | .30 | .12 | .03 |
| ☐ 308 Pirates Team | .45 | .20 | .04 |
| ☐ 309 Ken Henderson | .20 | .09 | .02 |
| ☐ 310 Luis Aparicio | 2.00 | .90 | .20 |
| ☐ 311 Jack Lamabe | .20 | .09 | .02 |
| ☐ 312 Curt Blefary | .20 | .09 | .02 |
| ☐ 313 Al Weis | .20 | .09 | .02 |
| ☐ 314 Red Sox Rookies | .20 | .09 | .02 |
|     Bill Rohr | | | |
|     George Spriggs | | | |
| ☐ 315 Zoilo Versalles | .20 | .09 | .02 |
| ☐ 316 Steve Barber | .20 | .09 | .02 |
| ☐ 317 Ron Brand | .20 | .09 | .02 |
| ☐ 318 Chico Salmon | .20 | .09 | .02 |
| ☐ 319 George Culver | .20 | .09 | .02 |
| ☐ 320 Frank Howard | .75 | .35 | .07 |
| ☐ 321 Leo Durocher | .75 | .35 | .07 |
| ☐ 322 Dave Boswell | .20 | .09 | .02 |
| ☐ 323 Deron Johnson | .20 | .09 | .02 |
| ☐ 324 Jim Nash | .20 | .09 | .02 |
| ☐ 325 Manny Mota | .30 | .12 | .03 |
| ☐ 326 Denny Ribant | .20 | .09 | .02 |
| ☐ 327 Tony Taylor | .20 | .09 | .02 |
| ☐ 328 Angels Rookies | .20 | .09 | .02 |
|     Chuck Vinson | | | |
|     Jim Weaver | | | |
| ☐ 329 Duane Josephson | .20 | .09 | .02 |
| ☐ 330 Roger Maris | 3.50 | 1.65 | .35 |
| ☐ 331 Dan Osinski | .20 | .09 | .02 |
| ☐ 332 Doug Rader | .30 | .12 | .03 |
| ☐ 333 Ron Herbel | .20 | .09 | .02 |
| ☐ 334 Orioles Team | .50 | .22 | .05 |
| ☐ 335 Bob Allison | .30 | .12 | .03 |
| ☐ 336 John Purdin | .20 | .09 | .02 |
| ☐ 337 Bill Robinson | .20 | .09 | .02 |
| ☐ 338 Bob Johnson | .20 | .09 | .02 |
| ☐ 339 Rich Nye | .20 | .09 | .02 |
| ☐ 340 Max Alvis | .20 | .09 | .02 |
| ☐ 341 Jim Lemon | .20 | .09 | .02 |
| ☐ 342 Ken Johnson | .20 | .09 | .02 |
| ☐ 343 Jim Gosger | .20 | .09 | .02 |
| ☐ 344 Donn Clendenon | .20 | .09 | .02 |
| ☐ 345 Bob Hendley | .20 | .09 | .02 |
| ☐ 346 Jerry Adair | .20 | .09 | .02 |
| ☐ 347 George Brunet | .20 | .09 | .02 |
| ☐ 348 Phillies Rookies | .20 | .09 | .02 |
|     Larry Colton | | | |
|     Dick Thoenen | | | |
| ☐ 349 Ed Spiezio | .20 | .09 | .02 |

| | MINT | VG-E | F-G |
|---|---|---|---|
| ☐ 350 Hoyt Wilhelm | 2.00 | .90 | .20 |
| ☐ 351 Bob Barton | .20 | .09 | .02 |
| ☐ 352 Jackie Hernandez | .20 | .09 | .02 |
| ☐ 353 Mack Jones | .20 | .09 | .02 |
| ☐ 354 Pete Richert | .20 | .09 | .02 |
| ☐ 355 Ernie Banks | 3.50 | 1.65 | .35 |
| ☐ 356 Checklist 5 | .75 | .15 | .04 |
|     Ken Holtzman | | | |
| ☐ 357 Len Gabrielson | .20 | .09 | .02 |
| ☐ 358 Mike Epstein | .20 | .09 | .02 |
| ☐ 359 Joe Moeller | .20 | .09 | .02 |
| ☐ 360 Willie Horton | .45 | .20 | .04 |
|     ALL-STAR | | | |
|     SELECTIONS (361-380) | | | |
| ☐ 361 Harmon Killebrew AS | 1.50 | .70 | .15 |
| ☐ 362 Orlando Cepeda AS | .75 | .35 | .07 |
| ☐ 363 Rod Carew AS | 3.00 | 1.40 | .30 |
| ☐ 364 Joe Morgan AS | 1.25 | .60 | .12 |
| ☐ 365 Brooks Robinson AS | 2.50 | 1.15 | .25 |
| ☐ 366 Ron Santo AS | .40 | .18 | .04 |
| ☐ 367 Jim Fregosi AS | .30 | .12 | .03 |
| ☐ 368 Gene Alley AS | .30 | .12 | .03 |
| ☐ 369 Carl Yastrzemski AS | 3.75 | 1.75 | .37 |
| ☐ 370 Hank Aaron AS | 3.75 | 1.75 | .37 |
| ☐ 371 Tony Oliva AS | .45 | .20 | .04 |
| ☐ 372 Lou Brock AS | 2.50 | 1.15 | .25 |
| ☐ 373 Frank Robinson AS | 2.50 | 1.15 | .25 |
| ☐ 374 Bob Clemente AS | 3.25 | 1.50 | .32 |
| ☐ 375 Bill Freehan AS | .30 | .12 | .03 |
| ☐ 376 Tim McCarver AS | .30 | .12 | .03 |
| ☐ 377 Joe Horlen AS | .30 | .12 | .03 |
| ☐ 378 Bob Gibson AS | 2.25 | 1.00 | .22 |
| ☐ 379 Gary Peters AS | .30 | .12 | .03 |
| ☐ 380 Ken Holtzman AS | .30 | .12 | .03 |
| ☐ 381 Boog Powell | .70 | .32 | .07 |
| ☐ 382 Ramon Hernandez | .20 | .09 | .02 |
| ☐ 383 Steve Whitaker | .20 | .09 | .02 |
| ☐ 384 Reds Rookies | 2.00 | .90 | .20 |
|     Bill Henry | | | |
|     Hal McRae | | | |
| ☐ 385 Jim Hunter | 2.25 | 1.00 | .22 |
| ☐ 386 Greg Goossen | .20 | .09 | .02 |
| ☐ 387 Joe Foy | .20 | .09 | .02 |
| ☐ 388 Ray Washburn | .20 | .09 | .02 |
| ☐ 389 Jay Johnstone | .25 | .10 | .02 |
| ☐ 390 Bill Mazeroski | .45 | .20 | .04 |
| ☐ 391 Bob Priddy | .20 | .09 | .02 |
| ☐ 392 Grady Hatton | .20 | .09 | .02 |
| ☐ 393 Jim Perry | .35 | .15 | .03 |
| ☐ 394 Tommie Aaron | .25 | .10 | .02 |
| ☐ 395 Camilo Pascual | .25 | .10 | .02 |
| ☐ 396 Bobby Wine | .25 | .10 | .02 |

| | MINT | VG-E | F-G |
|---|---|---|---|
| ☐ 397 Vic Davalillo | .20 | .09 | .02 |
| ☐ 398 Jim Grant | .20 | .09 | .02 |
| ☐ 399 Ray Oyler | .20 | .09 | .02 |
| ☐ 400 Mike McCormick | .25 | .10 | .02 |
| ☐ 401 Mets Team | .70 | .32 | .07 |
| ☐ 402 Mike Hegan | .20 | .09 | .02 |
| ☐ 403 John Buzhardt | .20 | .09 | .02 |
| ☐ 404 Floyd Robinson | .20 | .09 | .02 |
| ☐ 405 Tommy Helms | .20 | .09 | .02 |
| ☐ 406 Dick Ellsworth | .20 | .09 | .02 |
| ☐ 407 Gary Kolb | .20 | .09 | .02 |
| ☐ 408 Steve Carlton | 22.00 | 10.00 | 2.20 |
| ☐ 409 Orioles Rookies | .20 | .09 | .02 |
| Frank Peters | | | |
| Don Stone | | | |
| ☐ 410 Ferguson Jenkins | 1.50 | .70 | .15 |
| ☐ 411 Ron Hansen | .20 | .09 | .02 |
| ☐ 412 Clay Carroll | .20 | .09 | .02 |
| ☐ 413 Tommy McGraw | .20 | .09 | .02 |
| ☐ 414 Mickey Lolich | 1.00 | .45 | .10 |
| ☐ 415 Johnny Callison | .30 | .12 | .03 |
| ☐ 416 Bill Rigney | .20 | .09 | .02 |
| ☐ 417 Willie Crawford | .20 | .09 | .02 |
| ☐ 418 Eddie Fisher | .20 | .09 | .02 |
| ☐ 419 Jack Hiatt | .20 | .09 | .02 |
| ☐ 420 Cesar Tovar | .20 | .09 | .02 |
| ☐ 421 Ron Taylor | .20 | .09 | .02 |
| ☐ 422 Rene Lachemann | .30 | .12 | .03 |
| ☐ 423 Fred Gladding | .20 | .09 | .02 |
| ☐ 424 White Sox Team | .45 | .20 | .04 |
| ☐ 425 Jim Maloney | .35 | .15 | .03 |
| ☐ 426 Hank Allen | .20 | .09 | .02 |
| ☐ 427 Dick Calmus | .20 | .09 | .02 |
| ☐ 428 Vic Roznovsky | .20 | .09 | .02 |
| ☐ 429 Tommie Sisk | .20 | .09 | .02 |
| ☐ 430 Rico Petrocelli | .30 | .12 | .03 |
| ☐ 431 Dooley Womack | .20 | .09 | .02 |
| ☐ 432 Indians Rookies | .20 | .09 | .02 |
| Bill Davis | | | |
| Jose Vidal | | | |
| ☐ 433 Bob Rodgers | .20 | .09 | .02 |
| ☐ 434 Ricardo Joseph | .20 | .09 | .02 |
| ☐ 435 Ron Perranoski | .30 | .12 | .03 |
| ☐ 436 Hal Lanier | .30 | .12 | .03 |
| ☐ 437 Don Cardwell | .20 | .09 | .02 |
| ☐ 438 Lee Thomas | .20 | .09 | .02 |
| ☐ 439 Luman Harris | .20 | .09 | .02 |
| ☐ 440 Claude Osteen | .30 | .12 | .03 |
| ☐ 441 Alex Johnson | .25 | .10 | .02 |
| ☐ 442 Dick Bosman | .20 | .09 | .02 |
| ☐ 443 Joe Azcue | .20 | .09 | .02 |
| ☐ 444 Jack Fisher | .20 | .09 | .02 |

| | MINT | VG-E | F-G |
|---|---|---|---|
| ☐ 445 Mike Shannon | .35 | .15 | .03 |
| ☐ 446 Ron Kline | .20 | .09 | .02 |
| ☐ 447 Tigers Rookies | .20 | .09 | .02 |
| George Korince | | | |
| Fred Lasher | | | |
| ☐ 448 Gary Wagner | .20 | .09 | .02 |
| ☐ 449 Gene Oliver | .20 | .09 | .02 |
| ☐ 450 Jim Kaat | 1.25 | .60 | .12 |
| ☐ 451 Al Spangler | .20 | .09 | .02 |
| ☐ 452 Jesus Alou | .20 | .09 | .02 |
| ☐ 453 Sammy Ellis | .20 | .09 | .02 |
| ☐ 454 Checklist 6 | .90 | .20 | .04 |
| Frank Robinson | | | |
| ☐ 455 Rico Carty | .45 | .20 | .04 |
| ☐ 456 John O'Donoghue | .20 | .09 | .02 |
| ☐ 457 Jim Lefebvre | .25 | .10 | .02 |
| ☐ 458 Lew Krausse | .27 | .11 | .02 |
| ☐ 459 Dick Simpson | .27 | .11 | .02 |
| ☐ 460 Jim Lonborg | .45 | .20 | .04 |
| ☐ 461 Chuck Hiller | .27 | .11 | .02 |
| ☐ 462 Barry Moore | .27 | .11 | .02 |
| ☐ 463 Jim Schaffer | .27 | .11 | .02 |
| ☐ 464 Don McMahon | .27 | .11 | .02 |
| ☐ 465 Tommie Agee | .27 | .11 | .02 |
| ☐ 466 Bill Dillman | .27 | .11 | .02 |
| ☐ 467 Dick Howser | .45 | .20 | .04 |
| ☐ 468 Larry Sherry | .27 | .11 | .02 |
| ☐ 469 Ty Cline | .27 | .11 | .02 |
| ☐ 470 Bill Freehan | .55 | .25 | .05 |
| ☐ 471 Orlando Pena | .27 | .11 | .02 |
| ☐ 472 Walt Alston | .80 | .40 | .08 |
| ☐ 473 Al Worthington | .27 | .11 | .02 |
| ☐ 474 Paul Schaal | .27 | .11 | .02 |
| ☐ 475 Joe Niekro | 1.00 | .45 | .10 |
| ☐ 476 Woody Woodward | .27 | .11 | .02 |
| ☐ 477 Phillies Team | .55 | .25 | .05 |
| ☐ 478 Dave McNally | .55 | .25 | .05 |
| ☐ 479 Phil Gagliano | .27 | .11 | .02 |
| ☐ 480 Manager's Dream | 4.25 | 2.00 | .42 |
| Tony Oliva | | | |
| Chico Cardenas | | | |
| Bob Clemente | | | |
| ☐ 481 John Wyatt | .27 | .11 | .02 |
| ☐ 482 Jose Pagan | .27 | .11 | .02 |
| ☐ 483 Darold Knowles | .27 | .11 | .02 |
| ☐ 484 Phil Roof | .27 | .11 | .02 |
| ☐ 485 Ken Berry | .27 | .11 | .02 |
| ☐ 486 Cal Koonce | .27 | .11 | .02 |
| ☐ 487 Lee May | .45 | .20 | .04 |
| ☐ 488 Dick Tracewski | .27 | .11 | .02 |
| ☐ 489 Wally Bunker | .27 | .11 | .02 |

| | MINT | VG-E | F-G |
|---|---|---|---|
| ☐ 490 Super Stars: | 10.00 | 4.75 | 1.00 |
| Harmon Killebrew | | | |
| Willie Mays | | | |
| Mickey Mantle | | | |
| ☐ 491 Denny LeMaster | .27 | .11 | .02 |
| ☐ 492 Jeff Torborg | .27 | .11 | .02 |
| ☐ 493 Jim McGlothlin | .27 | .11 | .02 |
| ☐ 494 Ray Sadecki | .27 | .11 | .02 |
| ☐ 495 Leon Wagner | .27 | .11 | .02 |
| ☐ 496 Steve Hamilton | .27 | .11 | .02 |
| ☐ 497 Cards Team | .75 | .35 | .07 |
| ☐ 498 Bill Bryan | .27 | .11 | .02 |
| ☐ 499 Steve Blass | .35 | .15 | .03 |
| ☐ 500 Frank Robinson | 4.50 | 2.10 | .45 |
| ☐ 501 John Odom | .27 | .11 | .02 |
| ☐ 502 Mike Andrews | .27 | .11 | .02 |
| ☐ 503 Al Jackson | .27 | .11 | .02 |
| ☐ 504 Russ Snyder | .27 | .11 | .02 |
| ☐ 505 Joe Sparma | .27 | .11 | .02 |
| ☐ 506 Clarence Jones | .27 | .11 | .02 |
| ☐ 507 Wade Blasingame | .27 | .11 | .02 |
| ☐ 508 Duke Sims | .27 | .11 | .02 |
| ☐ 509 Dennis Higgins | .27 | .11 | .02 |
| ☐ 510 Ron Fairly | .35 | .15 | .03 |
| ☐ 511 Bill Kelso | .27 | .11 | .02 |
| ☐ 512 Grant Jackson | .27 | .11 | .02 |
| ☐ 513 Hank Bauer | .35 | .15 | .03 |
| ☐ 514 Al McBean | .27 | .11 | .02 |
| ☐ 515 Russ Nixon | .27 | .11 | .02 |
| ☐ 516 Pete Mikkelsen | .27 | .11 | .02 |
| ☐ 517 Diego Segui | .27 | .11 | .02 |
| ☐ 518 A Checklist 7 | 1.25 | .25 | .05 |
| (539 ML Rookies) | | | |
| (Clete Boyer) | | | |
| ☐ 518 B Checklist 7 | 4.00 | .50 | .10 |
| (539 AL Rookies) | | | |
| (Clete Boyer) | | | |
| ☐ 519 Jerry Stephenson | .27 | .11 | .02 |
| ☐ 520 Lou Brock | 4.50 | 2.10 | .45 |
| ☐ 521 Don Shaw | .27 | .11 | .02 |
| ☐ 522 Wayne Causey | .27 | .11 | .02 |
| ☐ 523 John Tsitouris | .27 | .11 | .02 |
| ☐ 524 Andy Kosco | .27 | .11 | .02 |
| ☐ 525 Jim Davenport | .40 | .18 | .04 |
| ☐ 526 Bill Denehy | .27 | .11 | .02 |
| ☐ 527 Tito Francona | .35 | .15 | .03 |
| ☐ 528 Tigers Team | 2.00 | .90 | .20 |
| ☐ 529 Bruce Von Hoff | .27 | .11 | .02 |
| ☐ 530 Bird Belters: | 3.25 | 1.50 | .32 |
| Brooks Robinson | | | |
| Frank Robinson | | | |
| ☐ 531 Chuck Hinton | .27 | .11 | .02 |
| ☐ 532 Luis Tiant | .75 | .35 | .07 |
| ☐ 533 Wes Parker | .45 | .20 | .04 |
| ☐ 534 Bob Miller | .27 | .11 | .02 |
| ☐ 535 Danny Cater | .27 | .11 | .02 |
| ☐ 536 Bill Short | .27 | .11 | .02 |
| ☐ 537 Norm Siebern | .27 | .11 | .02 |
| ☐ 538 Manny Jimenez | .27 | .11 | .02 |
| ☐ 539 Major League Rookies | .35 | .15 | .03 |
| Jim Ray | | | |
| Mike Ferraro | | | |
| ☐ 540 Nelson Briles | .27 | .11 | .02 |
| ☐ 541 Sandy Alomar | .27 | .11 | .02 |
| ☐ 542 John Boccabella | .27 | .11 | .02 |
| ☐ 543 Bob Lee | .27 | .11 | .02 |
| ☐ 544 Mayo Smith | .27 | .11 | .02 |
| ☐ 545 Lindy McDaniel | .27 | .11 | .02 |
| ☐ 546 Roy White | .45 | .20 | .04 |
| ☐ 547 Dan Coombs | .27 | .11 | .02 |
| ☐ 548 Bernie Allen | .27 | .11 | .02 |
| ☐ 549 Orioles Rookies | .27 | .11 | .02 |
| Curt Motton | | | |
| Roger Nelson | | | |
| ☐ 550 Clete Boyer | .45 | .20 | .04 |
| ☐ 551 Darrell Sutherland | .27 | .11 | .02 |
| ☐ 552 Ed Kirkpatrick | .27 | .11 | .02 |
| ☐ 553 Hank Aguirre | .27 | .11 | .02 |
| ☐ 554 A's Team | .75 | .35 | .07 |
| ☐ 555 Jose Tartabull | .27 | .11 | .02 |
| ☐ 556 Dick Selma | .27 | .11 | .02 |
| ☐ 557 Frank Quilici | .27 | .11 | .02 |
| ☐ 558 John Edwards | .27 | .11 | .02 |
| ☐ 559 Pirates Rookies | .27 | .11 | .02 |
| Carl Taylor | | | |
| Luke Walker | | | |
| ☐ 560 Paul Casanova | .27 | .11 | .02 |
| ☐ 561 Lee Elia | .27 | .11 | .02 |
| ☐ 562 Jim Bouton | .75 | .35 | .07 |
| ☐ 563 Ed Charles | .27 | .11 | .02 |
| ☐ 564 Ed Stanky | .35 | .15 | .03 |
| ☐ 565 Larry Dierker | .35 | .15 | .03 |
| ☐ 566 Ken Harrelson | .75 | .35 | .07 |
| ☐ 567 Clay Dalrymple | .27 | .11 | .02 |
| ☐ 568 Willie Smith | .27 | .11 | .02 |
| ☐ 569 N.L. Rookies | .27 | .11 | .02 |
| Ivan Murrell | | | |
| Les Rohr | | | |
| ☐ 570 Rick Reichardt | .27 | .11 | .02 |
| ☐ 571 Tony LaRussa | .45 | .20 | .04 |
| ☐ 572 Don Bosch | .27 | .11 | .02 |
| ☐ 573 Joe Coleman | .27 | .11 | .02 |
| ☐ 574 Reds Team | .75 | .35 | .07 |
| ☐ 575 Jim Palmer | 6.50 | 3.00 | .65 |
| ☐ 576 Dave Adlesh | .27 | .11 | .02 |
| ☐ 577 Fred Talbot | .27 | .11 | .02 |

|  | MINT | VG-E | F-G |
|---|---|---|---|
| ☐ 578 Orlando Martinez | .27 | .11 | .02 |
| ☐ 579 N.L. Rookies | .70 | .32 | .07 |
| Larry Hisle | | | |
| Mike Lum | | | |
| ☐ 580 Bob Bailey | .27 | .11 | .02 |
| ☐ 581 Garry Roggenburk | .27 | .11 | .02 |
| ☐ 582 Jerry Grote | .27 | .11 | .02 |
| ☐ 583 Gates Brown | .35 | .15 | .03 |
| ☐ 584 Larry Shepard | .27 | .11 | .02 |
| ☐ 585 Wilbur Wood | .35 | .15 | .03 |
| ☐ 586 Jim Pagliaroni | .27 | .11 | .02 |
| ☐ 587 Roger Repoz | .27 | .11 | .02 |
| ☐ 588 Dick Schofield | .27 | .11 | .02 |
| ☐ 589 Twins Rookies | .27 | .11 | .02 |
| Ron Clark | | | |
| Moe Ogier | | | |
| ☐ 590 Tommy Harper | .35 | .15 | .03 |
| ☐ 591 Dick Nen | .27 | .11 | .02 |
| ☐ 592 John Bateman | .27 | .11 | .02 |
| ☐ 593 Lee Stange | .27 | .11 | .02 |
| ☐ 594 Phil Linz | .27 | .11 | .02 |
| ☐ 595 Phil Ortega | .27 | .11 | .02 |
| ☐ 596 Charlie Smith | .27 | .11 | .02 |
| ☐ 597 Bill McCool | .27 | .11 | .02 |
| ☐ 598 Jerry May | .45 | .20 | .04 |

## 1969 TOPPS

The cards in this 664 card set measure 2½" by 3½". The 1969 Topps set includes The Sporting News All-Star selections as card numbers 416 to 435. The fifth series contains several variations; the more difficult variety consists of cards with the player's whole name in white letters, which are designated in the checklist below by WL. Each checklist card features a dif-

ferent popular player's picture inside a circle on the front of the checklist card. Two different poses of Clay Dalrymple and Donn Clendenon exist as indicated in the checklist.

Complete Set: M-475.00; VG-E-200.00; F-G-45.00

|  | MINT | VG-E | F-G |
|---|---|---|---|
| Common Player (1–218) | .20 | .09 | .02 |
| Common Player (219–327) | .35 | .15 | .03 |
| Common Player (328–512) | .20 | .09 | .02 |
| Common Player (513–664) | .25 | .10 | .02 |
| ☐ 1 AL Batting Leaders | 2.25 | .75 | .15 |
| Carl Yastrzemski | | | |
| Danny Cater | | | |
| Tony Oliva | | | |
| ☐ 2 NL Batting Leaders | 1.50 | .70 | .15 |
| Pete Rose | | | |
| Matty Alou | | | |
| Felipe Alou | | | |
| ☐ 3 AL RBI Leaders | .65 | .30 | .06 |
| Ken Harrelson | | | |
| Frank Howard | | | |
| Jim Northrup | | | |
| ☐ 4 NL RBI Leaders | .75 | .35 | .07 |
| Willie McCovey | | | |
| Ron Santo | | | |
| Billy Williams | | | |
| ☐ 5 AL Home Run Leaders | .65 | .30 | .06 |
| Frank Howard | | | |
| Willie Horton | | | |
| Ken Harrelson | | | |
| ☐ 6 NL Home Run Leaders | 1.00 | .45 | .10 |
| Willie McCovey | | | |
| Richie Allen | | | |
| Ernie Banks | | | |
| ☐ 7 AL ERA Leaders | .50 | .22 | .05 |
| Luis Tiant | | | |
| Sam McDowell | | | |
| Dave McNally | | | |
| ☐ 8 NL ERA Leaders | .65 | .30 | .06 |
| Bob Gibson | | | |
| Bobby Bolin | | | |
| Bob Veale | | | |
| ☐ 9 AL Pitching Leaders | .50 | .22 | .05 |
| Denny McLain | | | |
| Dave McNally | | | |
| Luis Tiant | | | |
| Mel Stottlemyre | | | |

| | | MINT | VG-E | F-G |
|---|---|---|---|---|
| ☐ 10 | NL Pitching Leaders .... | 1.25 | .60 | .12 |
| | Juan Marichal | | | |
| | Bob Gibson | | | |
| | Fergie Jenkins | | | |
| ☐ 11 | AL Strikeout Leaders ... | .50 | .22 | .05 |
| | Sam McDowell | | | |
| | Denny McLain | | | |
| | Luis Tiant | | | |
| ☐ 12 | NL Strikeout Leaders ... | .75 | .35 | .07 |
| | Bob Gibson | | | |
| | Fergie Jenkins | | | |
| | Bill Singer | | | |
| ☐ 13 | Mickey Stanley | .25 | .10 | .02 |
| ☐ 14 | Al McBean | .20 | .09 | .02 |
| ☐ 15 | Boog Powell | .70 | .32 | .07 |
| ☐ 16 | Giants Rookies | .20 | .09 | .02 |
| | Cesar Gutierrez | | | |
| | Rich Robertson | | | |
| ☐ 17 | Mike Marshall | .45 | .20 | .04 |
| ☐ 18 | Dick Schofield | .20 | .09 | .02 |
| ☐ 19 | Ken Suarez | .20 | .09 | .02 |
| ☐ 20 | Ernie Banks | 3.25 | 1.50 | .32 |
| ☐ 21 | Jose Santiago | .20 | .09 | .02 |
| ☐ 22 | Jesus Alou | .20 | .09 | .02 |
| ☐ 23 | Lew Krausse | .20 | .09 | .02 |
| ☐ 24 | Walt Alston | .75 | .35 | .07 |
| ☐ 25 | Roy White | .30 | .12 | .03 |
| ☐ 26 | Clay Carroll | .20 | .09 | .02 |
| ☐ 27 | Bernie Allen | .20 | .09 | .02 |
| ☐ 28 | Mike Ryan | .20 | .09 | .02 |
| ☐ 29 | Dave Morehead | .20 | .09 | .02 |
| ☐ 30 | Bob Allison | .30 | .12 | .03 |
| ☐ 31 | Mets Rookies | .85 | .40 | .08 |
| | Gary Gentry | | | |
| | Amos Otis | | | |
| ☐ 32 | Sammy Ellis | .20 | .09 | .02 |
| ☐ 33 | Wayne Causey | .20 | .09 | .02 |
| ☐ 34 | Gary Peters | .25 | .10 | .02 |
| ☐ 35 | Joe Morgan | 2.25 | 1.00 | .22 |
| ☐ 36 | Luke Walker | .20 | .09 | .02 |
| ☐ 37 | Curt Motton | .20 | .09 | .02 |
| ☐ 38 | Zoilo Versalles | .20 | .09 | .02 |
| ☐ 39 | Dick Hughes | .20 | .09 | .02 |
| ☐ 40 | Mayo Smith | .20 | .09 | .02 |
| ☐ 41 | Bob Barton | .20 | .09 | .02 |
| ☐ 42 | Tommy Harper | .30 | .12 | .03 |
| ☐ 43 | Joe Niekro | .55 | .25 | .05 |
| ☐ 44 | Danny Cater | .20 | .09 | .02 |
| ☐ 45 | Maury Wills | 1.00 | .45 | .10 |
| ☐ 46 | Fritz Peterson | .20 | .09 | .02 |
| ☐ 47 A | Paul Popovich | .25 | .10 | .02 |
| | (no emblem on helmet) | | | |

| | | MINT | VG-E | F-G |
|---|---|---|---|---|
| ☐ 47 B | Paul Popovich | 5.00 | 2.35 | .50 |
| | (C emblem on helmet) | | | |
| ☐ 48 | Brant Alyea | .20 | .09 | .02 |
| ☐ 49 A | Royals Rookies | .25 | .10 | .02 |
| | Steve Jones | | | |
| | E. Rodriguez "g" | | | |
| ☐ 49 B | Royals Rookies | 6.00 | 2.80 | .60 |
| | Steve Jones | | | |
| | E. Rodriguez "q" | | | |
| ☐ 50 | Bob Clemente | 9.00 | 4.25 | .90 |
| ☐ 51 | Woody Fryman | .20 | .09 | .02 |
| ☐ 52 | Mike Andrews | .20 | .09 | .02 |
| ☐ 53 | Sonny Jackson | .20 | .09 | .02 |
| ☐ 54 | Cisco Carlos | .20 | .09 | .02 |
| ☐ 55 | Jerry Grote | .20 | .09 | .02 |
| ☐ 56 | Rich Reese | .20 | .09 | .02 |
| ☐ 57 | Checklist 1 | .80 | .15 | .04 |
| | Denny McLain | | | |
| ☐ 58 | Fred Gladding | .20 | .09 | .02 |
| ☐ 59 | Jay Johnstone | .25 | .10 | .02 |
| ☐ 60 | Nelson Briles | .20 | .09 | .02 |
| ☐ 61 | Jimmie Hall | .20 | .09 | .02 |
| ☐ 62 | Chico Salmon | .30 | .12 | .03 |
| ☐ 63 | Jim Hickman | .20 | .09 | .02 |
| ☐ 64 | Bill Monbouquette | .20 | .09 | .02 |
| ☐ 65 | Willie Davis | .45 | .20 | .04 |
| ☐ 66 | Orioles Rookies | .30 | .12 | .03 |
| | Mike Adamson | | | |
| | Merv Rettenmund | | | |
| ☐ 67 | Bill Stoneman | .20 | .09 | .02 |
| ☐ 68 | Dave Duncan | .20 | .09 | .02 |
| ☐ 69 | Steve Hamilton | .20 | .09 | .02 |
| ☐ 70 | Tommy Helms | .20 | .09 | .02 |
| ☐ 71 | Steve Whitaker | .20 | .09 | .02 |
| ☐ 72 | Ron Taylor | .20 | .09 | .02 |
| ☐ 73 | Johnny Briggs | .20 | .09 | .02 |
| ☐ 74 | Preston Gomez | .20 | .09 | .02 |
| ☐ 75 | Luis Aparicio | 2.00 | .90 | .20 |
| ☐ 76 | Norm Miller | .20 | .09 | .02 |
| ☐ 77 A | Ron Perranoski | .25 | .10 | .02 |
| | (no emblem on cap) | | | |
| ☐ 77 B | Ron Perranoski | 5.00 | 2.35 | .50 |
| | (LA on cap) | | | |
| ☐ 78 | Tom Satriano | .20 | .09 | .02 |
| ☐ 79 | Milt Pappas | .30 | .12 | .03 |
| ☐ 80 | Norm Cash | .75 | .35 | .07 |
| ☐ 81 | Mel Queen | .20 | .09 | .02 |
| ☐ 82 | Pirates Rookies | 14.00 | 6.50 | 1.40 |
| | Rich Hebner | | | |
| | Al Oliver | | | |
| ☐ 83 | Mike Ferraro | .25 | .10 | .02 |
| ☐ 84 | Bob Humphreys | .20 | .09 | .02 |

|  | MINT | VG-E | F-G |
|---|---|---|---|
| ☐ 85 Lou Brock | 3.75 | 1.75 | .37 |
| ☐ 86 Pete Richert | .20 | .09 | .02 |
| ☐ 87 Horace Clarke | .20 | .09 | .02 |
| ☐ 88 Rich Nye | .20 | .09 | .02 |
| ☐ 89 Russ Gibson | .20 | .09 | .02 |
| ☐ 90 Jerry Koosman | .75 | .35 | .07 |
| ☐ 91 Al Dark | .30 | .12 | .03 |
| ☐ 92 Jack Billingham | .20 | .09 | .02 |
| ☐ 93 Joe Foy | .20 | .09 | .02 |
| ☐ 94 Hank Aguirre | .20 | .09 | .02 |
| ☐ 95 Johnny Bench | 20.00 | 9.00 | 2.00 |
| ☐ 96 Denver LeMaster | .20 | .09 | .02 |
| ☐ 97 Buddy Bradford | .20 | .09 | .02 |
| ☐ 98 Dave Giusti | .20 | .09 | .02 |
| ☐ 99 Twins Rookies | 7.00 | 3.25 | .70 |
|    Danny Morris | | | |
|    Graig Nettles | | | |
| ☐ 100 Hank Aaron | 11.00 | 5.25 | 1.10 |
| ☐ 101 Daryl Patterson | .20 | .09 | .02 |
| ☐ 102 Jim Davenport | .30 | .12 | .03 |
| ☐ 103 Roger Repoz | .20 | .09 | .02 |
| ☐ 104 Steve Blass | .25 | .10 | .02 |
| ☐ 105 Rick Monday | .30 | .12 | .03 |
| ☐ 106 Jim Hannan | .20 | .09 | .02 |
| ☐ 107 A Checklist 2 | .80 | .15 | .04 |
|    (161 Jim Purdin) | | | |
|    (Bob Gibson) | | | |
| ☐ 107 B Checklist 2 | 3.00 | .50 | .07 |
|    (161 John Purdin) | | | |
|    (Bob Gibson) | | | |
| ☐ 108 Tony Taylor | .20 | .09 | .02 |
| ☐ 109 Jim Lonborg | .35 | .15 | .03 |
| ☐ 110 Mike Shannon | .35 | .15 | .03 |
| ☐ 111 Johnny Morris | .30 | .12 | .03 |
| ☐ 112 J. C. Martin | .20 | .09 | .02 |
| ☐ 113 Dave May | .20 | .09 | .02 |
| ☐ 114 Yankees Rookies | .20 | .09 | .02 |
|    Alan Closter | | | |
|    John Cumberland | | | |
| ☐ 115 Bill Hands | .20 | .09 | .02 |
| ☐ 116 Chuck Harrison | .20 | .09 | .02 |
| ☐ 117 Jim Fairey | .20 | .09 | .02 |
| ☐ 118 Stan Williams | .20 | .09 | .02 |
| ☐ 119 Doug Rader | .30 | .12 | .03 |
| ☐ 120 Pete Rose | 22.00 | 10.00 | 2.20 |
| ☐ 121 Joe Grzenda | .20 | .09 | .02 |
| ☐ 122 Ron Fairly | .30 | .12 | .03 |
| ☐ 123 Wilbur Wood | .30 | .12 | .03 |
| ☐ 124 Hank Bauer | .30 | .12 | .03 |
| ☐ 125 Ray Sadecki | .20 | .09 | .02 |
| ☐ 126 Dick Tracewski | .20 | .09 | .02 |
| ☐ 127 Kevin Collins | .20 | .09 | .02 |

|  | MINT | VG-E | F-G |
|---|---|---|---|
| ☐ 128 Tommie Aaron | .30 | .12 | .03 |
| ☐ 129 Bill McCool | .20 | .09 | .02 |
| ☐ 130 Carl Yastrzemski | 15.00 | 7.00 | 1.50 |
| ☐ 131 Chris Cannizzaro | .20 | .09 | .02 |
| ☐ 132 Dave Baldwin | .20 | .09 | .02 |
| ☐ 133 Johnny Callison | .30 | .12 | .03 |
| ☐ 134 Jim Weaver | .20 | .09 | .02 |
| ☐ 135 Tommy Davis | .45 | .20 | .04 |
| ☐ 136 Cards Rookies | .30 | .12 | .03 |
|    Steve Huntz | | | |
|    Mike Torrez | | | |
| ☐ 137 Wally Bunker | .20 | .09 | .02 |
| ☐ 138 John Bateman | .20 | .09 | .02 |
| ☐ 139 Andy Kosco | .20 | .09 | .02 |
| ☐ 140 Jim Lefebvre | .25 | .10 | .02 |
| ☐ 141 Bill Dillman | .20 | .09 | .02 |
| ☐ 142 Woody Woodward | .20 | .09 | .02 |
| ☐ 143 Joe Nossek | .20 | .09 | .02 |
| ☐ 144 Bob Hendley | .20 | .09 | .02 |
| ☐ 145 Max Alvis | .20 | .09 | .02 |
| ☐ 146 Jim Perry | .40 | .18 | .04 |
| ☐ 147 Leo Durocher | .70 | .32 | .07 |
| ☐ 148 Lee Stange | .20 | .09 | .02 |
| ☐ 149 Ollie Brown | .20 | .09 | .02 |
| ☐ 150 Denny McLain | 1.00 | .45 | .10 |
| ☐ 151 A Clay Dalrymple | .25 | .10 | .02 |
|    (Portrait) (Orioles) | | | |
| ☐ 151 B Clay Dalrymple | 4.50 | 2.10 | .45 |
|    (Catching) (Phillies) | | | |
| ☐ 152 Tommie Sisk | .20 | .09 | .02 |
| ☐ 153 Ed Brinkman | .20 | .09 | .02 |
| ☐ 154 Jim Britton | .20 | .09 | .02 |
| ☐ 155 Pete Ward | .20 | .09 | .02 |
| ☐ 156 Houston Rookies | .20 | .09 | .02 |
|    Hal Gilson | | | |
|    Leon McFadden | | | |
| ☐ 157 Bob Rodgers | .20 | .09 | .02 |
| ☐ 158 Joe Gibbon | .20 | .09 | .02 |
| ☐ 159 Jerry Adair | .20 | .09 | .02 |
| ☐ 160 Vada Pinson | .70 | .32 | .07 |
| ☐ 161 John Purdin | .20 | .09 | .02 |
| ☐ 162 World Series Game 1 | 2.00 | .90 | .20 |
|    Gibson fans 17 | | | |
| ☐ 163 World Series Game 2 | 1.00 | .45 | .10 |
|    Tiger homers | | | |
|    deck the Cards | | | |
| ☐ 164 World Series Game 3 | 1.00 | .45 | .10 |
|    McCarver's homer | | | |
| ☐ 165 World Series Game 4 | 2.00 | .90 | .20 |
|    Brock lead-off homer | | | |
| ☐ 166 World Series Game 5 | 2.25 | 1.00 | .22 |
|    Kaline's key hit | | | |

| | MINT | VG-E | F-G |
|---|---|---|---|
| ☐ 167 World Series Game 6 .. Northrup grandslam | 1.00 | .45 | .10 |
| ☐ 168 World Series Game 7 .. Lolich outduels Bob Gibson | 2.00 | .90 | .20 |
| ☐ 169 World Series Summary . Tigers celebrate | 1.00 | .45 | .10 |
| ☐ 170 Frank Howard .......... | .70 | .32 | .07 |
| ☐ 171 Glenn Beckert ......... | .30 | .12 | .03 |
| ☐ 172 Jerry Stephenson ...... | .20 | .09 | .02 |
| ☐ 173 White Sox Rookies ..... Bob Christian Gerry Nyman | .20 | .09 | .02 |
| ☐ 174 Grant Jackson ......... | .20 | .09 | .02 |
| ☐ 175 Jim Bunning .......... | .90 | .40 | .09 |
| ☐ 176 Joe Azcue ............ | .20 | .09 | .02 |
| ☐ 177 Ron Reed ............. | .20 | .09 | .02 |
| ☐ 178 Ray Oyler ............ | .25 | .10 | .02 |
| ☐ 179 Don Pavletich ......... | .20 | .09 | .02 |
| ☐ 180 Willie Horton ......... | .35 | .15 | .03 |
| ☐ 181 Mel Nelson ........... | .20 | .09 | .02 |
| ☐ 182 Bill Rigney ........... | .20 | .09 | .02 |
| ☐ 183 Don Shaw ............ | .20 | .09 | .02 |
| ☐ 184 Roberto Pena ......... | .20 | .09 | .02 |
| ☐ 185 Tom Phoebus ......... | .20 | .09 | .02 |
| ☐ 186 John Edwards ......... | .20 | .09 | .02 |
| ☐ 187 Leon Wagner .......... | .20 | .09 | .02 |
| ☐ 188 Rick Wise ............ | .30 | .12 | .03 |
| ☐ 189 Red Sox Rookies ...... Joe Lahoud John Thibodeau | .20 | .09 | .02 |
| ☐ 190 Willie Mays ........... | 11.00 | 5.25 | 1.10 |
| ☐ 191 Lindy McDaniel ....... | .20 | .09 | .02 |
| ☐ 192 Jose Pagan .......... | .20 | .09 | .02 |
| ☐ 193 Don Cardwell ......... | .20 | .09 | .02 |
| ☐ 194 Ted Uhlaender ........ | .20 | .09 | .02 |
| ☐ 195 John Odom ........... | .20 | .09 | .02 |
| ☐ 196 Lum Harris ........... | .20 | .09 | .02 |
| ☐ 197 Dick Selma ........... | .20 | .09 | .02 |
| ☐ 198 Willie Smith .......... | .20 | .09 | .02 |
| ☐ 199 Jim French ........... | .20 | .09 | .02 |
| ☐ 200 Bob Gibson ........... | 3.00 | 1.40 | .30 |
| ☐ 201 Russ Snyder .......... | .20 | .09 | .02 |
| ☐ 202 Don Wilson .......... | .20 | .09 | .02 |
| ☐ 203 Dave Johnson ........ | .35 | .15 | .03 |
| ☐ 204 Jack Hiatt ........... | .20 | .09 | .02 |
| ☐ 205 Rick Reichardt ........ | .20 | .09 | .02 |
| ☐ 206 Phillies Rookies ....... Larry Hisle Barry Lersch | .30 | .12 | .03 |
| ☐ 207 Roy Face ............ | .35 | .15 | .03 |
| ☐ 208 A Donn Clendenon ..... (Houston) | .30 | .12 | .03 |

| | MINT | VG-E | F-G |
|---|---|---|---|
| ☐ 208 B Donn Clendenon ..... (Expos) | 4.50 | 2.10 | .45 |
| ☐ 209 Larry Haney ........... (reverse negative) | .25 | .10 | .02 |
| ☐ 210 Felix Millan .......... | .20 | .09 | .02 |
| ☐ 211 Galen Cisco .......... | .20 | .09 | .02 |
| ☐ 212 Tom Tresh ........... | .35 | .15 | .03 |
| ☐ 213 Gerry Arrigo ......... | .20 | .09 | .02 |
| ☐ 214 Checklist 3 .......... With 69T deckle CL on back (no player) | .75 | .15 | .05 |
| ☐ 215 Rico Petrocelli ........ | .30 | .12 | .03 |
| ☐ 216 Don Sutton .......... | 1.50 | .70 | .15 |
| ☐ 217 John Donaldson ....... | .20 | .09 | .02 |
| ☐ 218 John Roseboro ........ | .30 | .12 | .03 |
| ☐ 219 Freddie Patek ........ | .35 | .15 | .03 |
| ☐ 220 Sam McDowell ........ | .45 | .20 | .04 |
| ☐ 221 Art Shamsky ......... | .35 | .15 | .03 |
| ☐ 222 Duane Josephson ...... | .35 | .15 | .03 |
| ☐ 223 Tom Dukes .......... | .35 | .15 | .03 |
| ☐ 224 Angels Rookies ........ Bill Harrelson Steve Kealey | .35 | .15 | .03 |
| ☐ 225 Don Kessinger ........ | .45 | .20 | .04 |
| ☐ 226 Bruce Howard ........ | .35 | .15 | .03 |
| ☐ 227 Frank Johnson ........ | .35 | .15 | .03 |
| ☐ 228 Dave Leonhard ........ | .35 | .15 | .03 |
| ☐ 229 Don Lock ............ | .35 | .15 | .03 |
| ☐ 230 Rusty Staub ......... | .75 | .35 | .07 |
| ☐ 231 Pat Dobson .......... | .45 | .20 | .04 |
| ☐ 232 Dave Ricketts ........ | .35 | .15 | .03 |
| ☐ 233 Steve Barber ......... | .45 | .20 | .04 |
| ☐ 234 Dave Bristol ......... | .35 | .15 | .03 |
| ☐ 235 Jim Hunter .......... | 2.25 | 1.00 | .22 |
| ☐ 236 Manny Mota .......... | .45 | .20 | .04 |
| ☐ 237 Bobby Cox ........... | .45 | .20 | .04 |
| ☐ 238 Ken Johnson ......... | .35 | .15 | .03 |
| ☐ 239 Bob Taylor .......... | .35 | .15 | .03 |
| ☐ 240 Ken Harrelson ........ | .75 | .35 | .07 |
| ☐ 241 Jim Brewer .......... | .35 | .15 | .03 |
| ☐ 242 Frank Kostro ......... | .35 | .15 | .03 |
| ☐ 243 Ron Kline ........... | .35 | .15 | .03 |
| ☐ 244 Indians Rookies ....... Ray Fosse George Woodson | .45 | .20 | .04 |
| ☐ 245 Ed Charles .......... | .35 | .15 | .03 |
| ☐ 246 Joe Coleman ......... | .35 | .15 | .03 |
| ☐ 247 Gene Oliver .......... | .35 | .15 | .03 |
| ☐ 248 Bob Priddy .......... | .35 | .15 | .03 |
| ☐ 249 Ed Spiezio ........... | .35 | .15 | .03 |
| ☐ 250 Frank Robinson ....... | 6.50 | 3.00 | .65 |
| ☐ 251 Ron Herbel .......... | .35 | .15 | .03 |
| ☐ 252 Chuck Cottier ........ | .45 | .20 | .04 |

| | | MINT | VG-E | F-G |
|---|---|---|---|---|
| ☐ 253 | Jerry Johnson | .35 | .15 | .03 |
| ☐ 254 | Joe Schultz | .35 | .15 | .03 |
| ☐ 255 | Steve Carlton | 22.00 | 10.00 | 2.20 |
| ☐ 256 | Gates Brown | .45 | .20 | .04 |
| ☐ 257 | Jim Ray | .35 | .15 | .03 |
| ☐ 258 | Jackie Hernandez | .35 | .15 | .03 |
| ☐ 259 | Bill Short | .35 | .15 | .03 |
| ☐ 260 | Reggie Jackson | 70.00 | 32.00 | 7.00 |
| ☐ 261 | Bob Johnson | .35 | .15 | .03 |
| ☐ 262 | Mike Kekich | .35 | .15 | .03 |
| ☐ 263 | Jerry May | .35 | .15 | .03 |
| ☐ 264 | Bill Landis | .35 | .15 | .03 |
| ☐ 265 | Chico Cardenas | .35 | .15 | .03 |
| ☐ 266 | Dodger Rookies | .35 | .15 | .03 |
| | Tom Hutton | | | |
| | Alan Foster | | | |
| ☐ 267 | Vicente Romo | .35 | .15 | .03 |
| ☐ 268 | Al Spangler | .35 | .15 | .03 |
| ☐ 269 | Al Weis | .35 | .15 | .03 |
| ☐ 270 | Mickey Lolich | 1.00 | .45 | .10 |
| ☐ 271 | Larry Stahl | .35 | .15 | .03 |
| ☐ 272 | Ed Stroud | .35 | .15 | .03 |
| ☐ 273 | Ron Willis | .35 | .15 | .03 |
| ☐ 274 | Clyde King | .35 | .15 | .03 |
| ☐ 275 | Vic Davalillo | .35 | .15 | .03 |
| ☐ 276 | Gary Wagner | .35 | .15 | .03 |
| ☐ 277 | Rod Hendricks | .35 | .15 | .03 |
| ☐ 278 | Gary Geiger | .35 | .15 | .03 |
| | (Batting wrong) | | | |
| ☐ 279 | Roger Nelson | .35 | .15 | .03 |
| ☐ 280 | Alex Johnson | .45 | .20 | .04 |
| ☐ 281 | Ted Kubiak | .35 | .15 | .03 |
| ☐ 282 | Pat Jarvis | .35 | .15 | .03 |
| ☐ 283 | Sandy Alomar | .35 | .15 | .03 |
| ☐ 284 | Expos Rookies | .35 | .15 | .03 |
| | Jerry Robertson | | | |
| | Mike Wegener | | | |
| ☐ 285 | Don Mincher | .45 | .20 | .04 |
| ☐ 286 | Dock Ellis | .35 | .15 | .03 |
| ☐ 287 | Jose Tartabull | .35 | .15 | .03 |
| ☐ 288 | Ken Holtzman | .55 | .25 | .05 |
| ☐ 289 | Bart Shirley | .35 | .15 | .03 |
| ☐ 290 | Jim Kaat | 1.50 | .70 | .15 |
| ☐ 291 | Vern Fuller | .35 | .15 | .03 |
| ☐ 292 | Al Downing | .35 | .15 | .03 |
| ☐ 293 | Dick Dietz | .35 | .15 | .03 |
| ☐ 294 | Jim Lemon | .35 | .15 | .03 |
| ☐ 295 | Tony Perez | 2.00 | .90 | .20 |
| ☐ 296 | Andy Messersmith | .55 | .25 | .05 |
| ☐ 297 | Deron Johnson | .55 | .25 | .05 |
| ☐ 298 | Dave Nicholson | .35 | .15 | .03 |
| ☐ 299 | Mark Belanger | .45 | .20 | .04 |
| ☐ 300 | Felipe Alou | .45 | .20 | .04 |

| | | MINT | VG-E | F-G |
|---|---|---|---|---|
| ☐ 301 | Darrell Brandon | .45 | .20 | .04 |
| ☐ 302 | Jim Pagliaroni | .35 | .15 | .03 |
| ☐ 303 | Cal Koonce | .35 | .15 | .03 |
| ☐ 304 | Padres Rookies | .35 | .15 | .03 |
| | Bill Davis | | | |
| | Clarence Gaston | | | |
| ☐ 305 | Dick McAuliffe | .45 | .20 | .04 |
| ☐ 306 | Jim Grant | .35 | .15 | .03 |
| ☐ 307 | Gary Kolb | .35 | .15 | .03 |
| ☐ 308 | Wade Blasingame | .35 | .15 | .03 |
| ☐ 309 | Walt Williams | .35 | .15 | .03 |
| ☐ 310 | Tom Haller | .35 | .15 | .03 |
| ☐ 311 | Sparky Lyle | 1.50 | .70 | .15 |
| ☐ 312 | Lee Elia | .45 | .20 | .04 |
| ☐ 313 | Bill Robinson | .35 | .15 | .03 |
| ☐ 314 | Checklist 4 | .85 | .15 | .04 |
| | Don Drysdale | | | |
| ☐ 315 | Eddie Fisher | .35 | .15 | .03 |
| ☐ 316 | Hal Lanier | .45 | .20 | .04 |
| ☐ 317 | Bruce Look | .35 | .15 | .03 |
| ☐ 318 | Jack Fisher | .35 | .15 | .03 |
| ☐ 319 | Ken McMullen | .35 | .15 | .03 |
| ☐ 320 | Dal Maxvill | .35 | .15 | .03 |
| ☐ 321 | Jim McAndrew | .35 | .15 | .03 |
| ☐ 322 | Jose Vidal | .45 | .20 | .04 |
| ☐ 323 | Larry Miller | .35 | .15 | .03 |
| ☐ 324 | Tiger Rookies | .35 | .15 | .03 |
| | Les Cain | | | |
| | Dave Campbell | | | |
| ☐ 325 | Jose Cardenal | .35 | .15 | .03 |
| ☐ 326 | Gary Sutherland | .35 | .15 | .03 |
| ☐ 327 | Willie Crawford | .35 | .15 | .03 |
| ☐ 328 | Joe Horlen | .25 | .10 | .02 |
| ☐ 329 | Rick Joseph | .20 | .09 | .02 |
| ☐ 330 | Tony Conigliaro | .55 | .25 | .05 |
| ☐ 331 | Braves Rookies | .20 | .09 | .02 |
| | Gil Garrido | | | |
| | Tom House | | | |
| ☐ 332 | Fred Talbot | .20 | .09 | .02 |
| ☐ 333 | Ivan Murrell | .20 | .09 | .02 |
| ☐ 334 | Phil Roof | .20 | .09 | .02 |
| ☐ 335 | Bill Mazeroski | .45 | .20 | .04 |
| ☐ 336 | Jim Roland | .20 | .09 | .02 |
| ☐ 337 | Marty Martinez | .20 | .09 | .02 |
| ☐ 338 | Del Unser | .20 | .09 | .02 |
| ☐ 339 | Reds Rookies | .20 | .09 | .02 |
| | Steve Mingori | | | |
| | Jose Pena | | | |
| ☐ 340 | Dave McNally | .40 | .18 | .04 |
| ☐ 341 | Dave Adlesh | .20 | .09 | .02 |
| ☐ 342 | Bubba Morton | .20 | .09 | .02 |
| ☐ 343 | Dan Frisella | .20 | .09 | .02 |
| ☐ 344 | Tom Matchick | .20 | .09 | .02 |

| | MINT | VG-E | F-G |
|---|---|---|---|
| ☐ 345 Frank Linzy | .20 | .09 | .02 |
| ☐ 346 Wayne Comer | .30 | .12 | .03 |
| ☐ 347 Randy Hundley | .25 | .10 | .02 |
| ☐ 348 Steve Hargan | .20 | .09 | .02 |
| ☐ 349 Dick Williams MGR | .30 | .12 | .03 |
| ☐ 350 Richie Allen | .70 | .32 | .07 |
| ☐ 351 Carroll Sembera | .20 | .09 | .02 |
| ☐ 352 Paul Schaal | .20 | .09 | .02 |
| ☐ 353 Jeff Torborg | .20 | .09 | .02 |
| ☐ 354 Nate Oliver | .20 | .09 | .02 |
| ☐ 355 Phil Niekro | 2.00 | .90 | .20 |
| ☐ 356 Frank Quilici | .20 | .09 | .02 |
| ☐ 357 Carl Taylor | .20 | .09 | .02 |
| ☐ 358 Athletics Rookies | .20 | .09 | .02 |
| George Lauzerique | | | |
| Roberto Rodriquez | | | |
| ☐ 359 Dick Kelley | .20 | .09 | .02 |
| ☐ 360 Jim Wynn | .30 | .12 | .03 |
| ☐ 361 Gary Holman | .20 | .09 | .02 |
| ☐ 362 Jim Maloney | .30 | .12 | .03 |
| ☐ 363 Russ Nixon | .20 | .09 | .02 |
| ☐ 364 Tommie Agee | .20 | .09 | .02 |
| ☐ 365 Jim Fregosi | .30 | .12 | .03 |
| ☐ 366 Bo Belinsky | .25 | .10 | .02 |
| ☐ 367 Lou Johnson | .20 | .09 | .02 |
| ☐ 368 Vic Roznovsky | .20 | .09 | .02 |
| ☐ 369 Bob Skinner | .20 | .09 | .02 |
| ☐ 370 Juan Marichal | 2.50 | 1.15 | .25 |
| ☐ 371 Sal Bando | .45 | .20 | .04 |
| ☐ 372 Adolfo Phillips | .20 | .09 | .02 |
| ☐ 373 Fred Lasher | .20 | .09 | .02 |
| ☐ 374 Bob Tillman | .20 | .09 | .02 |
| ☐ 375 Harmon Killebrew | 4.50 | 2.10 | .45 |
| ☐ 376 Royals Rookies | .20 | .09 | .02 |
| Mike Fiore | | | |
| Jim Rooker | | | |
| ☐ 377 Gary Bell | .30 | .12 | .03 |
| ☐ 378 Jose Herrera | .20 | .09 | .02 |
| ☐ 379 Ken Boyer | .75 | .35 | .07 |
| ☐ 380 Stan Bahnsen | .20 | .09 | .02 |
| ☐ 381 Ed Kranepool | .30 | .12 | .03 |
| ☐ 382 Pat Corrales | .25 | .10 | .02 |
| ☐ 383 Casey Cox | .20 | .09 | .02 |
| ☐ 384 Larry Shepard | .20 | .09 | .02 |
| ☐ 385 Orlando Cepeda | 1.20 | .55 | .12 |
| ☐ 386 Jim McGlothlin | .20 | .09 | .02 |
| ☐ 387 Bobby Klaus | .20 | .09 | .02 |
| ☐ 388 Tom McCraw | .20 | .09 | .02 |
| ☐ 389 Dan Coombs | .20 | .09 | .02 |
| ☐ 390 Bill Freehan | .45 | .20 | .04 |
| ☐ 391 Ray Culp | .20 | .09 | .02 |
| ☐ 392 Bob Burda | .20 | .09 | .02 |

| | MINT | VG-E | F-G |
|---|---|---|---|
| ☐ 393 Gene Brabender | .20 | .09 | .02 |
| ☐ 394 Pilots Rookies | 1.00 | .45 | .10 |
| Lou Piniella | | | |
| Marv Staehle | | | |
| ☐ 395 Chris Short | .20 | .09 | .02 |
| ☐ 396 Jim Campanis | .20 | .09 | .02 |
| ☐ 397 Chuck Dobson | .20 | .09 | .02 |
| ☐ 398 Tito Francona | .25 | .10 | .02 |
| ☐ 399 Bob Bailey | .20 | .09 | .02 |
| ☐ 400 Don Drysdale | 2.75 | 1.25 | .27 |
| ☐ 401 Jake Gibbs | .20 | .09 | .02 |
| ☐ 402 Ken Boswell | .20 | .09 | .02 |
| ☐ 403 Bob Miller | .20 | .09 | .02 |
| ☐ 404 Cubs Rookies | .20 | .09 | .02 |
| Vic LaRose | | | |
| Gary Ross | | | |
| ☐ 405 Lee May | .40 | .18 | .04 |
| ☐ 406 Phil Ortega | .20 | .09 | .02 |
| ☐ 407 Tom Egan | .20 | .09 | .02 |
| ☐ 408 Nate Colbert | .20 | .09 | .02 |
| ☐ 409 Bob Moose | .20 | .09 | .02 |
| ☐ 410 Al Kaline | 3.50 | 1.65 | .35 |
| ☐ 411 Larry Dierker | .25 | .10 | .02 |
| ☐ 412 Checklist 5 | 1.60 | .40 | .05 |
| Mickey Mantle | | | |
| ☐ 413 Roland Sheldon | .30 | .12 | .03 |
| ☐ 414 Duke Sims | .20 | .09 | .02 |
| ☐ 415 Ray Washburn | .20 | .09 | .02 |
| ALL-STAR | | | |
| SELECTIONS (416–436) | | | |
| ☐ 416 Willie McCovey AS | 2.00 | .90 | .20 |
| ☐ 417 Ken Harrelson AS | .30 | .12 | .03 |
| ☐ 418 Tommy Helms AS | .30 | .12 | .03 |
| ☐ 419 Rod Carew AS | 3.00 | 1.40 | .30 |
| ☐ 420 Ron Santo AS | .30 | .12 | .03 |
| ☐ 421 Brooks Robinson AS | 2.50 | 1.15 | .25 |
| ☐ 422 Don Kessinger AS | .30 | .12 | .03 |
| ☐ 423 Bert Campaneris AS | .30 | .12 | .03 |
| ☐ 424 Pete Rose AS | 5.25 | 2.50 | .50 |
| ☐ 425 Carl Yastrzemski AS | 3.75 | 1.75 | .37 |
| ☐ 426 Curt Flood AS | .30 | .12 | .03 |
| ☐ 427 Tony Oliva AS | .45 | .20 | .04 |
| ☐ 428 Lou Brock AS | 2.25 | 1.00 | .22 |
| ☐ 429 Willie Horton AS | .30 | .12 | .03 |
| ☐ 430 Johnny Bench AS | 3.25 | 1.50 | .32 |
| ☐ 431 Bill Freehan AS | .30 | .12 | .03 |
| ☐ 432 Bob Gibson AS | 2.00 | .90 | .20 |
| ☐ 433 Denny McLain AS | .40 | .18 | .04 |
| ☐ 434 Jerry Koosman AS | .30 | .12 | .03 |
| ☐ 435 Sam McDowell AS | .30 | .12 | .03 |
| ☐ 436 Gene Alley | .30 | .12 | .03 |
| ☐ 437 Luis Alcaraz | .20 | .09 | .02 |

| | MINT | VG-E | F-G |
|---|---|---|---|
| ☐ 438 Gary Waslewski | .20 | .09 | .02 |
| ☐ 439 White Sox Rookies | .20 | .09 | .02 |
|     Ed Herrmann | | | |
|     Dan Lazar | | | |
| ☐ 440 A Willie McCovey | 5.50 | 2.60 | .55 |
| ☐ 440 B Willie McCovey WL | 25.00 | 11.00 | 2.50 |
| ☐ 441 A Dennis Higgins | .25 | .10 | .02 |
| ☐ 441 B Dennis Higgins WL | 3.00 | 1.40 | .30 |
| ☐ 442 Ty Cline | .20 | .09 | .02 |
| ☐ 443 Don Wert | .20 | .09 | .02 |
| ☐ 444 A Joe Moeller | .25 | .10 | .02 |
| ☐ 445 B Joe Moeller WL | 3.00 | 1.40 | .30 |
| ☐ 445 Bobby Knoop | .20 | .09 | .02 |
| ☐ 446 Claude Raymond | .20 | .09 | .02 |
| ☐ 447 A Ralph Houk | .40 | .18 | .04 |
| ☐ 447 B Ralph Houk WL | 3.50 | 1.65 | .35 |
| ☐ 448 Bob Tolan | .20 | .09 | .02 |
| ☐ 449 Paul Lindblad | .20 | .09 | .02 |
| ☐ 450 Billy Williams | 1.50 | .70 | .15 |
| ☐ 451 A Rich Rollins | .25 | .10 | .02 |
| ☐ 451 B Rich Rollins WL | 3.00 | 1.40 | .30 |
| ☐ 452 A Al Ferrara | .25 | .10 | .02 |
| ☐ 452 B Al Ferrara WL | 3.00 | 1.40 | .30 |
| ☐ 453 Mike Cuellar | .40 | .18 | .04 |
| ☐ 454 A Phillies Rookies | .35 | .15 | .03 |
|     Larry Colton | | | |
|     Don Money | | | |
| ☐ 454 B Phillies Rookies WL | 3.25 | 1.50 | .32 |
|     Larry Colton | | | |
|     Don Money | | | |
| ☐ 455 Sonny Siebert | .25 | .10 | .02 |
| ☐ 456 Bud Harrelson | .20 | .09 | .02 |
| ☐ 457 Dalton Jones | .20 | .09 | .02 |
| ☐ 458 Curt Blefary | .20 | .09 | .02 |
| ☐ 459 Dave Boswell | .20 | .09 | .02 |
| ☐ 460 Joe Torre | .65 | .30 | .06 |
| ☐ 461 A Mike Epstein | .25 | .10 | .02 |
| ☐ 461 B Mike Epstein WL | 3.00 | 1.40 | .30 |
| ☐ 462 Red Schoendienst | .45 | .20 | .04 |
| ☐ 463 Dennis Ribant | .20 | .09 | .02 |
| ☐ 464 A Dave Marshall | .25 | .10 | .02 |
| ☐ 464 B Dave Marshall WL | 3.00 | 1.40 | .30 |
| ☐ 465 Tommy John | 1.40 | .70 | .14 |
| ☐ 466 John Boccabella | .20 | .09 | .02 |
| ☐ 467 Tom Reynolds | .20 | .09 | .02 |
| ☐ 468 A Pirates Rookies | .25 | .10 | .02 |
|     Bruce Dal Canton | | | |
|     Bob Robertson | | | |
| ☐ 468 B Pirates Rookies WL | 3.00 | 1.40 | .30 |
|     Bruce Dal Canton | | | |
|     Bob Robertson | | | |
| ☐ 469 Chico Ruiz | .20 | .09 | .02 |

| | MINT | VG-E | F-G |
|---|---|---|---|
| ☐ 470 A Mel Stottlemyre | .50 | .22 | .05 |
| ☐ 470 B Mel Stottlemyre WL | 3.50 | 1.65 | .35 |
| ☐ 471 A Ted Savage | .25 | .10 | .02 |
| ☐ 471 B Ted Savage WL | 3.00 | 1.40 | .30 |
| ☐ 472 Jim Price | .20 | .09 | .02 |
| ☐ 473 A Jose Arcia | .25 | .10 | .02 |
| ☐ 473 B Jose Arcia WL | 3.00 | 1.40 | .30 |
| ☐ 474 Tom Murphy | .20 | .09 | .02 |
| ☐ 475 Tim McCarver | .35 | .15 | .03 |
| ☐ 476 A Boston Rookies | .30 | .12 | .03 |
|     Ken Brett | | | |
|     Gerry Moses | | | |
| ☐ 476 B Boston Rookies WL | 3.00 | 1.40 | .30 |
|     Ken Brett | | | |
|     Gerry Moses | | | |
| ☐ 477 Jeff James | .20 | .09 | .02 |
| ☐ 478 Don Buford | .20 | .09 | .02 |
| ☐ 479 Richie Scheinblum | .20 | .09 | .02 |
| ☐ 480 Tom Seaver | 16.00 | 7.50 | 1.60 |
| ☐ 481 Bill Melton | .20 | .09 | .02 |
| ☐ 482 A Jim Gosger | .25 | .10 | .02 |
| ☐ 482 B Jim Gosger WL | 3.00 | 1.40 | .30 |
| ☐ 483 Ted Abernathy | .20 | .09 | .02 |
| ☐ 484 Joe Gordon | .25 | .10 | .02 |
| ☐ 485 A Gaylord Perry | 2.50 | 1.15 | .25 |
| ☐ 485 B Gaylord Perry WL | 15.00 | 7.00 | 1.50 |
| ☐ 486 A Paul Casanova | .25 | .10 | .02 |
| ☐ 486 B Paul Casanova WL | 3.00 | 1.40 | .30 |
| ☐ 487 Denis Menke | .25 | .10 | .02 |
| ☐ 488 Joe Sparma | .20 | .09 | .01 |
| ☐ 489 Clete Boyer | .35 | .15 | .03 |
| ☐ 490 Matty Alou | .30 | .12 | .03 |
| ☐ 491 A Twins Rookies | .25 | .10 | .02 |
|     Jerry Crider | | | |
|     George Mitterwald | | | |
| ☐ 491 B Twins Rookies WL | 3.00 | 1.40 | .30 |
|     Jerry Crider | | | |
|     George Mitterwald | | | |
| ☐ 492 Tony Cloninger | .20 | .09 | .02 |
| ☐ 493 A Wes Parker | .35 | .15 | .03 |
| ☐ 493 B Wes Parker WL | 3.25 | 1.50 | .32 |
| ☐ 494 Ken Berry | .20 | .09 | .02 |
| ☐ 495 Bert Campaneris | .35 | .15 | .03 |
| ☐ 496 Larry Jaster | .20 | .09 | .02 |
| ☐ 497 Julian Javier | .25 | .10 | .02 |
| ☐ 498 Juan Pizarro | .20 | .09 | .02 |
| ☐ 499 Astro Rookies | .20 | .09 | .02 |
|     Don Bryant | | | |
|     Steve Shea | | | |
| ☐ 500 A Mickey Mantle | 32.00 | 15.00 | 3.20 |
| ☐ 500 B Mickey Mantle WL | 85.00 | 40.00 | 8.50 |

|  | MINT | VG-E | F-G |
|---|---|---|---|
| □ 501 A Tony Gonzalez | .30 | .12 | .03 |
| □ 501 B Tony Gonzalez WL | 3.00 | 1.40 | .30 |
| □ 502 Minnie Rojas | .20 | .09 | .02 |
| □ 503 Larry Brown | .20 | .09 | .02 |
| □ 504 Checklist 6 | .90 | .20 | .04 |
| Brooks Robinson | | | |
| □ 505 A Bobby Bolin | .25 | .10 | .02 |
| □ 505 B Bobby Bolin WL | 3.00 | 1.40 | .30 |
| □ 506 Paul Blair | .30 | .12 | .03 |
| □ 507 Cookie Rojas | .20 | .09 | .02 |
| □ 508 Moe Drabowsky | .20 | .09 | .02 |
| □ 509 Manny Sanguillen | .35 | .15 | .03 |
| □ 510 Rod Carew | 16.00 | 7.50 | 1.60 |
| □ 511 A Diego Segui | .35 | .15 | .03 |
| □ 511 B Diego Segui WL | 3.00 | 1.40 | .30 |
| □ 512 Cleon Jones | .20 | .09 | .02 |
| □ 513 Camilo Pascual | .30 | .12 | .03 |
| □ 514 Mike Lum | .25 | .10 | .02 |
| □ 515 Dick Green | .25 | .10 | .02 |
| □ 516 Earl Weaver MGR | 1.75 | .85 | .17 |
| □ 517 Mike McCormick | .30 | .12 | .03 |
| □ 518 Fred Whitfield | .25 | .10 | .02 |
| □ 519 Yankees Rookies | .25 | .10 | .02 |
| Gerry Kenney | | | |
| Len Boehmer | | | |
| □ 520 Bob Veale | .30 | .12 | .03 |
| □ 521 George Thomas | .25 | .10 | .02 |
| □ 522 Joe Hoerner | .25 | .10 | .02 |
| □ 523 Bob Chance | .25 | .10 | .02 |
| □ 524 Expos Rookies | .25 | .10 | .02 |
| Jose Laboy | | | |
| Floyd Wicker | | | |
| □ 525 Earl Wilson | .25 | .10 | .02 |
| □ 526 Hector Torres | .25 | .10 | .02 |
| □ 527 Al Lopez | .80 | .40 | .08 |
| □ 528 Claude Osteen | .35 | .15 | .03 |
| □ 529 Ed Kirkpatrick | .25 | .10 | .02 |
| □ 530 Cesar Tovar | .25 | .10 | .02 |
| □ 531 Dick Farrell | .25 | .10 | .02 |
| □ 532 Bird Hill Aces | .45 | .20 | .04 |
| Tom Phoebus | | | |
| Jim Hardin | | | |
| Dave McNally | | | |
| Mike Cuellar | | | |
| □ 533 Nolan Ryan | 15.00 | 7.00 | 1.50 |
| □ 534 Jerry McNertney | .30 | .12 | .03 |
| □ 535 Phil Regan | .30 | .12 | .03 |
| □ 536 Padres Rookies | .25 | .10 | .02 |
| Danny Breeden | | | |
| Dave Roberts | | | |
| □ 537 Mike Paul | .25 | .10 | .02 |
| □ 538 Charlie Smith | .25 | .10 | .02 |

|  | MINT | VG-E | F-G |
|---|---|---|---|
| □ 539 Ted Shows How | 1.25 | .60 | .12 |
| Mike Epstein | | | |
| Ted Williams | | | |
| □ 540 Curt Flood | .50 | .22 | .05 |
| □ 541 Joe Verbanic | .25 | .10 | .02 |
| □ 542 Bob Aspromonte | .25 | .10 | .02 |
| □ 543 Fred Newman | .25 | .10 | .02 |
| □ 544 Tigers Rookies | .25 | .10 | .02 |
| Mike Kilkenny | | | |
| Ron Woods | | | |
| □ 545 Willie Stargell | 3.00 | 1.40 | .30 |
| □ 546 Jim Nash | .25 | .10 | .02 |
| □ 547 Billy Martin MGR | 1.00 | .45 | .10 |
| □ 548 Bob Locker | .25 | .10 | .02 |
| □ 549 Ron Brand | .25 | .10 | .02 |
| □ 550 Brooks Robinson | 5.50 | 2.60 | .55 |
| □ 551 Wayne Granger | .25 | .10 | .02 |
| □ 552 Dodgers Rookies | .40 | .18 | .04 |
| Ted Sizemore | | | |
| Bill Sudakis | | | |
| □ 553 Ron Davis | .25 | .10 | .02 |
| □ 554 Frank Bertaina | .25 | .10 | .02 |
| □ 555 Jim Ray Hart | .35 | .15 | .03 |
| □ 556 A's Stars | .45 | .20 | .04 |
| Sal Bando | | | |
| Bert Campaneris | | | |
| Danny Cater | | | |
| □ 557 Frank Fernandez | .25 | .10 | .02 |
| □ 558 Tom Burgmeier | .30 | .12 | .03 |
| □ 559 Cardinals Rookies | .25 | .10 | .02 |
| Joe Hague | | | |
| Jim Hicks | | | |
| □ 560 Luis Tiant | .70 | .32 | .07 |
| □ 561 Ron Clark | .25 | .10 | .02 |
| □ 562 Bob Watson | .90 | .40 | .09 |
| □ 563 Martin Pattin | .30 | .12 | .03 |
| □ 564 Gil Hodges MGR | 2.50 | 1.15 | .25 |
| □ 565 Hoyt Wilhelm | 2.25 | 1.00 | .22 |
| □ 566 Ron Hansen | .25 | .10 | .02 |
| □ 567 Pirates Rookies | .25 | .10 | .02 |
| Elvio Jimenez | | | |
| Jim Shellenback | | | |
| □ 568 Cecil Upshaw | .25 | .10 | .02 |
| □ 569 Billy Harris | .25 | .10 | .02 |
| □ 570 Ron Santo | .60 | .28 | .06 |
| □ 571 Cap Peterson | .25 | .10 | .02 |
| □ 572 Giants Heroes | 3.00 | 1.40 | .30 |
| Willie McCovey | | | |
| Juan Marichal | | | |
| □ 573 Jim Palmer | 6.50 | 3.00 | .65 |
| □ 574 George Scott | .35 | .15 | .03 |
| □ 575 Bill Singer | .25 | .10 | .02 |

| | MINT | VG-E | F-G |
|---|---|---|---|
| ☐ **576** Phillies Rookies | .25 | .10 | .02 |
| Ron Stone | | | |
| Bill Wilson | | | |
| ☐ **577** Mike Hegan | .30 | .12 | .03 |
| ☐ **578** Don Bosch | .25 | .10 | .02 |
| ☐ **579** Dave Nelson | .25 | .10 | .02 |
| ☐ **580** Jim Northrup | .30 | .12 | .03 |
| ☐ **581** Gary Nolan | .25 | .10 | .02 |
| ☐ **582** A Checklist 7 | .85 | .15 | .04 |
| (White circle on back) | | | |
| (Tony Oliva) | | | |
| ☐ **582** B Checklist 7 | 2.25 | .45 | .07 |
| (Red circle on back) | | | |
| (Tony Oliva) | | | |
| ☐ **583** Clyde Wright | .25 | .10 | .02 |
| ☐ **584** Don Mason | .25 | .10 | .02 |
| ☐ **585** Ron Swoboda | .35 | .15 | .03 |
| ☐ **586** Tim Cullen | .25 | .10 | .02 |
| ☐ **587** Joe Rudi | .75 | .35 | .07 |
| ☐ **588** Bill White | .35 | .15 | .03 |
| ☐ **589** Joe Pepitone | .40 | .18 | .04 |
| ☐ **590** Rico Carty | .40 | .18 | .04 |
| ☐ **591** Mike Hedlund | .25 | .10 | .02 |
| ☐ **592** Padres Rookies | .25 | .10 | .02 |
| Rafael Robles | | | |
| Al Santorini | | | |
| ☐ **593** Don Nottebart | .25 | .10 | .02 |
| ☐ **594** Dooley Womack | .25 | .10 | .02 |
| ☐ **595** Lee Maye | .25 | .10 | .02 |
| ☐ **596** Chuck Hartenstein | .25 | .10 | .02 |
| ☐ **597** A.L. Rookies | 9.00 | 4.25 | .90 |
| Bob Floyd | | | |
| Larry Burchart | | | |
| Rollie Fingers | | | |
| ☐ **598** Ruben Amaro | .25 | .10 | .02 |
| ☐ **599** John Boozer | .25 | .10 | .02 |
| ☐ **600** Tony Oliva | 1.00 | .45 | .10 |
| ☐ **601** Tug McGraw | .90 | .40 | .09 |
| ☐ **602** Cubs Rookies | .25 | .10 | .02 |
| Alec Distaso | | | |
| Don Young | | | |
| Jim Qualls | | | |
| ☐ **603** Joe Keough | .25 | .10 | .02 |
| ☐ **604** Bobby Etheridge | .25 | .10 | .02 |
| ☐ **605** Dick Ellsworth | .25 | .10 | .02 |
| ☐ **606** Gene Mauch MGR | .35 | .15 | .03 |
| ☐ **607** Dick Bosman | .25 | .10 | .02 |
| ☐ **608** Dick Simpson | .25 | .10 | .02 |
| ☐ **609** Phil Gagliano | .25 | .10 | .02 |
| ☐ **610** Jim Hardin | .25 | .10 | .02 |
| ☐ **611** Braves Rookies | .25 | .10 | .02 |
| Bob Didier | | | |
| Walt Hriniak | | | |
| Gary Neibauer | | | |

| | MINT | VG-E | F-G |
|---|---|---|---|
| ☐ **612** Jack Aker | .35 | .15 | .03 |
| ☐ **613** Jim Beauchamp | .25 | .10 | .02 |
| ☐ **614** Houston Rookies | .25 | .10 | .02 |
| Tom Griffin | | | |
| Skip Guinn | | | |
| ☐ **615** Len Gabrielson | .25 | .10 | .02 |
| ☐ **616** Don McMahon | .25 | .10 | .02 |
| ☐ **617** Jesse Gonder | .25 | .10 | .02 |
| ☐ **618** Ramon Webster | .25 | .10 | .02 |
| ☐ **619** Royals Rookies | .35 | .15 | .03 |
| Bill Butler | | | |
| Pat Kelly | | | |
| Juan Rios | | | |
| ☐ **620** Dean Chance | .30 | .12 | .03 |
| ☐ **621** Bill Voss | .25 | .10 | .02 |
| ☐ **622** Dan Osinski | .25 | .10 | .02 |
| ☐ **623** Hank Allen | .25 | .10 | .02 |
| ☐ **624** N.L. Rookies | .25 | .10 | .02 |
| Darrel Chaney | | | |
| Duffy Dyer | | | |
| Terry Harmon | | | |
| ☐ **625** Mack Jones | .25 | .10 | .02 |
| (Batting wrong) | | | |
| ☐ **626** Gene Michael | .30 | .12 | .03 |
| ☐ **627** George Stone | .25 | .10 | .02 |
| ☐ **628** Red Sox Rookies | .35 | .15 | .03 |
| Bill Conigliaro | | | |
| Syd O'Brien | | | |
| Fred Wenz | | | |
| ☐ **629** Jack Hamilton | .25 | .10 | .02 |
| ☐ **630** Bobby Bonds | 2.00 | .90 | .20 |
| ☐ **631** John Kennedy | .30 | .12 | .03 |
| ☐ **632** Jon Warden | .25 | .10 | .02 |
| ☐ **633** Harry Walker | .25 | .10 | .02 |
| ☐ **634** Andy Etchebarren | .25 | .10 | .02 |
| ☐ **635** George Culver | .25 | .10 | .02 |
| ☐ **636** Woodie Held | .25 | .10 | .02 |
| ☐ **637** Padres Rookies | .25 | .10 | .02 |
| Jerry DaVanon | | | |
| Frank Reberger | | | |
| Clay Kirby | | | |
| ☐ **638** Ed Sprague | .25 | .10 | .02 |
| ☐ **639** Barry Moore | .25 | .10 | .02 |
| ☐ **640** Fergie Jenkins | 1.50 | .70 | .15 |
| ☐ **641** N.L. Rookies | .25 | .10 | .02 |
| Bobby Darwin | | | |
| John Miller | | | |
| Tommy Dean | | | |
| ☐ **642** John Hiller | .35 | .15 | .03 |
| ☐ **643** Billy Cowan | .25 | .10 | .02 |
| ☐ **644** Chuck Hinton | .25 | .10 | .02 |
| ☐ **645** George Brunet | .25 | .10 | .02 |

| | | MINT | VG-E | F-G |
|---|---|---|---|---|
| ☐ 646 | Expos Rookies ........<br>Dan McGinn<br>Carl Morton | .25 | .10 | .02 |
| ☐ 647 | Dave Wickersham ..... | .25 | .10 | .02 |
| ☐ 648 | Bobby Wine ........... | .30 | .12 | .03 |
| ☐ 649 | Al Jackson ........... | .25 | .10 | .02 |
| ☐ 650 | Ted Williams ......... | 2.50 | 1.15 | .25 |
| ☐ 651 | Gus Gil .............. | .30 | .12 | .03 |
| ☐ 652 | Eddie Watt ........... | .25 | .10 | .02 |
| ☐ 653 | Aurelio Rodriguez ..... | 1.00 | .45 | .10 |
| | (photo actually<br>Angels' batboy) | | | |
| ☐ 654 | White Sox Rookies ... <br>Carlos May<br>Don Secrist<br>Rich Morales | .35 | .15 | .03 |
| ☐ 655 | Mike Hershberger ..... | .25 | .10 | .02 |
| ☐ 656 | Dan Schneider ........ | .25 | .10 | .02 |
| ☐ 657 | Bobby Murcer ........ | .80 | .40 | .08 |
| ☐ 658 | A.L. Rookies .........<br>Tom Hall<br>Bill Burbach<br>Jim Miles | .25 | .10 | .02 |
| ☐ 659 | Johnny Podres ........ | .55 | .25 | .05 |
| ☐ 660 | Reggie Smith ......... | .85 | .40 | .08 |
| ☐ 661 | Jim Merritt .......... | .25 | .10 | .02 |
| ☐ 662 | Royals Rookies .......<br>Dick Drago<br>George Spriggs<br>Bob Oliver | .35 | .15 | .03 |
| ☐ 663 | Dick Radatz .......... | .35 | .15 | .03 |
| ☐ 664 | Ron Hunt ............ | .50 | .22 | .05 |

## 1970 TOPPS

*Jim Palmer*    PITCHER

*The cards in this 720 card set measure
2½" by 3½". The Topps set for 1970 has
color photos surrounded by white frame
lines and gray borders. The backs have a
blue biographical section and a yellow record section. All Star selections are featured on cards 450 to 469. There are
graduations of scarcity, terminating in the
high series (634 to 720), which are out-
lined in the value summary.*
*Complete Set: M-475.00; VG-E-225.00; F-G-40.00*

| | MINT | VG-E | F-G |
|---|---|---|---|
| Common Player (1–132) | .15 | .06 | .01 |
| Common Player (133–546) | .20 | .09 | .02 |
| Common Player (547–633) | .35 | .15 | .03 |
| Common Player (634–720) | .80 | .40 | .08 |

| | | MINT | VG-E | F-G |
|---|---|---|---|---|
| ☐ 1 | New York Mets Team .. | 2.00 | .50 | .10 |
| ☐ 2 | Diego Segui .......... | .20 | .09 | .02 |
| ☐ 3 | Darrel Chaney ........ | .15 | .06 | .01 |
| ☐ 4 | Tom Egan ............ | .15 | .06 | .01 |
| ☐ 5 | Wes Parker .......... | .25 | .10 | .02 |
| ☐ 6 | Grant Jackson ........ | .15 | .06 | .01 |
| ☐ 7 | Indians Rookies ......<br>Gary Boyd<br>Russ Nagelson | .15 | .06 | .01 |
| ☐ 8 | Jose Martinez ........ | .15 | .06 | .01 |
| ☐ 9 | 1st Checklist ......... | .70 | .15 | .03 |
| ☐ 10 | Carl Yastrzemski ...... | 13.00 | 6.00 | 1.30 |
| ☐ 11 | Nate Colbert ......... | .15 | .06 | .01 |
| ☐ 12 | John Hiller .......... | .20 | .09 | .02 |
| ☐ 13 | Jack Hiatt .......... | .15 | .06 | .01 |
| ☐ 14 | Hank Allen .......... | .15 | .06 | .01 |
| ☐ 15 | Larry Dierker ........ | .20 | .09 | .02 |
| ☐ 16 | Charlie Metro ........ | .15 | .06 | .01 |
| ☐ 17 | Hoyt Wilhelm ........ | 1.75 | .85 | .17 |
| ☐ 18 | Carlos May .......... | .20 | .09 | .02 |
| ☐ 19 | John Boccabella ...... | .15 | .06 | .01 |
| ☐ 20 | Dave McNally ........ | .25 | .10 | .02 |
| ☐ 21 | A's Rookies .........<br>Vida Blue<br>Gene Tenace | 1.75 | .85 | .17 |
| ☐ 22 | Ray Washburn ........ | .15 | .06 | .01 |
| ☐ 23 | Bill Robinson ........ | .15 | .06 | .01 |
| ☐ 24 | Dick Selma .......... | .15 | .06 | .01 |
| ☐ 25 | Cesar Tovar ......... | .15 | .06 | .01 |
| ☐ 26 | Tug McGraw .......... | .60 | .28 | .06 |
| ☐ 27 | Chuck Hinton ........ | .15 | .06 | .01 |
| ☐ 28 | Billy Wilson ......... | .15 | .06 | .01 |
| ☐ 29 | Sandy Alomar ........ | .15 | .06 | .01 |
| ☐ 30 | Matty Alou .......... | .25 | .10 | .02 |
| ☐ 31 | Marty Pattin ......... | .20 | .09 | .02 |
| ☐ 32 | Harry Walker ........ | .15 | .06 | .01 |

|   |   | MINT | VG-E | F-G |
|---|---|------|------|-----|
| ☐ 33 | Don Wert .............. | .15 | .06 | .01 |
| ☐ 34 | Willie Crawford ........ | .15 | .06 | .01 |
| ☐ 35 | Joe Horlen ........... | .15 | .06 | .01 |
| ☐ 36 | Red Rookies .......... | .15 | .06 | .01 |
|   | Danny Breeden |   |   |   |
|   | Bernie Carbo |   |   |   |
| ☐ 37 | Dick Drago ........... | .15 | .06 | .01 |
| ☐ 38 | Mack Jones .......... | .15 | .06 | .01 |
| ☐ 39 | Mike Nagy ........... | .15 | .06 | .01 |
| ☐ 40 | Rich Allen ........... | .60 | .28 | .06 |
| ☐ 41 | George Lauzerique .... | .15 | .06 | .01 |
| ☐ 42 | Tito Fuentes ......... | .15 | .06 | .01 |
| ☐ 43 | Jack Aker ............ | .15 | .06 | .01 |
| ☐ 44 | Roberto Pena ........ | .15 | .06 | .01 |
| ☐ 45 | Dave Johnson ........ | .25 | .10 | .02 |
| ☐ 46 | Ken Rudolph ......... | .15 | .06 | .01 |
| ☐ 47 | Bob Miller ........... | .15 | .06 | .01 |
| ☐ 48 | Gil Garrido .......... | .15 | .06 | .01 |
| ☐ 49 | Tim Cullen ........... | .15 | .06 | .01 |
| ☐ 50 | Tommie Agee ......... | .15 | .06 | .01 |
| ☐ 51 | Bob Christian ........ | .15 | .06 | .01 |
| ☐ 52 | Bruce Dal Canton ...... | .15 | .06 | .01 |
| ☐ 53 | John Kennedy ........ | .20 | .09 | .02 |
| ☐ 54 | Jeff Torborg ......... | .15 | .06 | .01 |
| ☐ 55 | John Odom ........... | .15 | .06 | .01 |
| ☐ 56 | Phillies Rookies ....... | .15 | .06 | .01 |
|   | Joe Lis |   |   |   |
|   | Scott Reid |   |   |   |
| ☐ 57 | Pat Kelly ............ | .15 | .06 | .01 |
| ☐ 58 | Dave Marshall ........ | .15 | .06 | .01 |
| ☐ 59 | Dick Ellsworth ........ | .15 | .06 | .01 |
| ☐ 60 | Jim Wynn ............ | .25 | .10 | .02 |
| ☐ 61 | NL Batting Leaders .... | 1.75 | .85 | .17 |
|   | Pete Rose |   |   |   |
|   | Bob Clemente |   |   |   |
|   | Cleon Jones |   |   |   |
| ☐ 62 | AL Batting Leaders ..... | .75 | .35 | .07 |
|   | Rod Carew |   |   |   |
|   | Reggie Smith |   |   |   |
|   | Tony Oliva |   |   |   |
| ☐ 63 | NL RBI Leaders ....... | .75 | .35 | .07 |
|   | Willie McCovey |   |   |   |
|   | Ron Santo |   |   |   |
|   | Tony Perez |   |   |   |
| ☐ 64 | AL RBI Leaders ....... | .90 | .40 | .09 |
|   | Harmon Killebrew |   |   |   |
|   | Boog Powell |   |   |   |
|   | Reggie Jackson |   |   |   |
| ☐ 65 | NL Home Run Leaders . | 1.00 | .45 | .10 |
|   | Willie McCovey |   |   |   |
|   | Hank Aaron |   |   |   |
|   | Lee May |   |   |   |

|   |   | MINT | VG-E | F-G |
|---|---|------|------|-----|
| ☐ 66 | AL Home Run Leaders . | .75 | .35 | .07 |
|   | Harmon Killebrew |   |   |   |
|   | Frank Howard |   |   |   |
|   | Reggie Jackson |   |   |   |
| ☐ 67 | NL ERA Leaders ....... | 1.50 | .70 | .15 |
|   | Juan Marichal |   |   |   |
|   | Steve Carlton |   |   |   |
|   | Bob Gibson |   |   |   |
| ☐ 68 | AL ERA Leaders ....... | .60 | .28 | .06 |
|   | Dick Bosman |   |   |   |
|   | Jim Palmer |   |   |   |
|   | Mike Cuellar |   |   |   |
| ☐ 69 | NL Pitching Leaders .... | 1.50 | .70 | .15 |
|   | Tom Seaver |   |   |   |
|   | Phil Niekro |   |   |   |
|   | Fergie Jenkins |   |   |   |
|   | Juan Marichal |   |   |   |
| ☐ 70 | AL Pitching Leaders .... | .45 | .20 | .04 |
|   | Dennis McLain |   |   |   |
|   | Mike Cuellar |   |   |   |
|   | Dave Boswell |   |   |   |
|   | Dave McNally |   |   |   |
|   | Jim Perry |   |   |   |
|   | Mel Stottlemyre |   |   |   |
| ☐ 71 | NL Strikeout Leaders ... | .65 | .30 | .06 |
|   | Fergie Jenkins |   |   |   |
|   | Bob Gibson |   |   |   |
|   | Bill Singer |   |   |   |
| ☐ 72 | AL Strikeout Leaders ... | .45 | .20 | .04 |
|   | Sam McDowell |   |   |   |
|   | Mickey Lolich |   |   |   |
|   | Andy Messersmith |   |   |   |
| ☐ 73 | Wayne Granger ........ | .15 | .06 | .01 |
| ☐ 74 | Angels Rookies ........ | .15 | .06 | .01 |
|   | Greg Washburn |   |   |   |
|   | Wally Wolf |   |   |   |
| ☐ 75 | Jim Kaat ............. | .90 | .40 | .09 |
| ☐ 76 | Carl Taylor .......... | .15 | .06 | .01 |
| ☐ 77 | Frank Linzy .......... | .15 | .06 | .01 |
| ☐ 78 | Joe Lahoud .......... | .15 | .06 | .01 |
| ☐ 79 | Clay Kirby ........... | .15 | .06 | .01 |
| ☐ 80 | Don Kessinger ........ | .25 | .10 | .02 |
| ☐ 81 | Dave May ............ | .15 | .06 | .01 |
| ☐ 82 | Frank Fernandez ...... | .15 | .06 | .01 |
| ☐ 83 | Don Cardwell ........ | .15 | .06 | .01 |
| ☐ 84 | Paul Casanova ....... | .15 | .06 | .01 |
| ☐ 85 | Max Alvis ............ | .15 | .06 | .01 |
| ☐ 86 | Lum Harris .......... | .15 | .06 | .01 |
| ☐ 87 | Steve Renko ......... | .15 | .06 | .01 |
| ☐ 88 | Pilots Rookies ........ | .20 | .09 | .02 |
|   | Miguel Fuentes |   |   |   |
|   | Dick Baney |   |   |   |
| ☐ 89 | Juan Rios ............ | .15 | .06 | .01 |

| | | MINT | VG-E | F-G |
|---|---|---|---|---|
| ☐ 90 | Tim McCarver | .30 | .12 | .03 |
| ☐ 91 | Rich Morales | .15 | .06 | .01 |
| ☐ 92 | George Culver | .15 | .06 | .01 |
| ☐ 93 | Rick Renick | .15 | .06 | .01 |
| ☐ 94 | Fred Patek | .15 | .06 | .01 |
| ☐ 95 | Earl Wilson | .15 | .06 | .01 |
| ☐ 96 | Cardinals Rookies | 1.50 | .70 | .15 |
| | Leron Lee | | | |
| | Jerry Reuss | | | |
| ☐ 97 | Joe Moeller | .15 | .06 | .01 |
| ☐ 98 | Gates Brown | .20 | .09 | .02 |
| ☐ 99 | Bobby Pfeil | .15 | .06 | .01 |
| ☐ 100 | Mel Stottlemyre | .25 | .10 | .02 |
| ☐ 101 | Bobby Floyd | .15 | .06 | .01 |
| ☐ 102 | Joe Rudi | .30 | .12 | .03 |
| ☐ 103 | Frank Reberger | .15 | .06 | .01 |
| ☐ 104 | Gerry Moses | .15 | .06 | .01 |
| ☐ 105 | Tony Gonzalez | .15 | .06 | .01 |
| ☐ 106 | Darold Knowles | .15 | .06 | .01 |
| ☐ 107 | Bobby Etheridge | .15 | .06 | .01 |
| ☐ 108 | Tom Burgmeier | .20 | .09 | .02 |
| ☐ 109 | Expos Rookies | .20 | .09 | .02 |
| | Garry Jestadt | | | |
| | Carl Morton | | | |
| ☐ 110 | Bob Moose | .15 | .06 | .01 |
| ☐ 111 | Mike Hegan | .20 | .09 | .02 |
| ☐ 112 | Dave Nelson | .15 | .06 | .01 |
| ☐ 113 | Jim Ray | .15 | .06 | .01 |
| ☐ 114 | Gene Michael | .20 | .09 | .02 |
| ☐ 115 | Alex Johnson | .15 | .06 | .01 |
| ☐ 116 | Sparky Lyle | .45 | .20 | .04 |
| ☐ 117 | Don Young | .15 | .06 | .01 |
| ☐ 118 | George Mitterwald | .15 | .06 | .01 |
| ☐ 119 | Chuck Taylor | .15 | .06 | .01 |
| ☐ 120 | Sal Bando | .40 | .18 | .04 |
| ☐ 121 | Orioles Rookies | .15 | .06 | .01 |
| | Fred Beene | | | |
| | Terry Crowley | | | |
| ☐ 122 | George Stone | .15 | .06 | .01 |
| ☐ 123 | Don Gutteridge | .15 | .06 | .01 |
| ☐ 124 | Larry Jaster | .15 | .06 | .01 |
| ☐ 125 | Deron Johnson | .15 | .06 | .01 |
| ☐ 126 | Marty Martinez | .15 | .06 | .01 |
| ☐ 127 | Joe Coleman | .15 | .06 | .01 |
| ☐ 128 | 2nd Checklist | .55 | .15 | .03 |
| ☐ 129 | Jimmie Price | .15 | .06 | .01 |
| ☐ 130 | Ollie Brown | .15 | .06 | .01 |
| ☐ 131 | Dodgers Rookies | .15 | .06 | .01 |
| | Ray Lamb | | | |
| | Bob Stinson | | | |
| ☐ 132 | Jim McGlothlin | .15 | .06 | .01 |
| ☐ 133 | Clay Carroll | .20 | .09 | .02 |
| ☐ 134 | Danny Walton | .25 | .10 | .02 |

| | | MINT | VG-E | F-G |
|---|---|---|---|---|
| ☐ 135 | Dick Dietz | .20 | .09 | .02 |
| ☐ 136 | Steve Hargan | .20 | .09 | .02 |
| ☐ 137 | Art Shamsky | .20 | .09 | .02 |
| ☐ 138 | Joe Foy | .20 | .09 | .02 |
| ☐ 139 | Rich Nye | .20 | .09 | .02 |
| ☐ 140 | Reggie Jackson | 16.00 | 7.50 | 1.60 |
| ☐ 141 | Pirates Rookies | .30 | .12 | .03 |
| | Dave Cash | | | |
| | Johnny Jeter | | | |
| ☐ 142 | Fritz Peterson | .20 | .09 | .02 |
| ☐ 143 | Phil Gagliano | .20 | .09 | .02 |
| ☐ 144 | Ray Culp | .20 | .09 | .02 |
| ☐ 145 | Rico Carty | .40 | .18 | .04 |
| ☐ 146 | Danny Murphy | .20 | .09 | .02 |
| ☐ 147 | Angel Hermoso | .20 | .09 | .02 |
| ☐ 148 | Earl Weaver | .65 | .30 | .06 |
| ☐ 149 | Billy Champion | .20 | .09 | .02 |
| ☐ 150 | Harmon Killebrew | 2.75 | 1.25 | .27 |
| ☐ 151 | Dave Roberts | .20 | .09 | .02 |
| ☐ 152 | Ike Brown | .20 | .09 | .02 |
| ☐ 153 | Gary Gentry | .20 | .09 | .02 |
| ☐ 154 | Senators Rookies | .20 | .09 | .02 |
| | Jim Miles | | | |
| | Jan Dukes | | | |
| ☐ 155 | Denis Menke | .20 | .09 | .02 |
| ☐ 156 | Eddie Fisher | .20 | .09 | .02 |
| ☐ 157 | Manny Mota | .25 | .10 | .02 |
| ☐ 158 | Jerry McNertney | .25 | .10 | .02 |
| ☐ 159 | Tommy Helms | .20 | .09 | .02 |
| ☐ 160 | Phil Niekro | 1.75 | .85 | .17 |
| ☐ 161 | Richie Scheinblum | .20 | .09 | .02 |
| ☐ 162 | Jerry Johnson | .20 | .09 | .02 |
| ☐ 163 | Syd O'Brien | .20 | .09 | .02 |
| ☐ 164 | Ty Cline | .20 | .09 | .02 |
| ☐ 165 | Ed Kirkpatrick | .20 | .09 | .02 |
| ☐ 166 | Al Oliver | 2.50 | 1.15 | .25 |
| ☐ 167 | Bill Burbach | .20 | .09 | .02 |
| ☐ 168 | Dave Watkins | .20 | .09 | .02 |
| ☐ 169 | Tom Hall | .20 | .09 | .02 |
| ☐ 170 | Billy Williams | 1.50 | .70 | .15 |
| ☐ 171 | Jim Nash | .20 | .09 | .02 |
| ☐ 172 | Braves Rookies | .60 | .28 | .06 |
| | Garry Hill | | | |
| | Ralph Garr | | | |
| ☐ 173 | Jim Hicks | .20 | .09 | .02 |
| ☐ 174 | Ted Sizemore | .20 | .09 | .02 |
| ☐ 175 | Dick Bosman | .20 | .09 | .02 |
| ☐ 176 | Jim Ray Hart | .25 | .10 | .02 |
| ☐ 177 | Jim Northrup | .25 | .10 | .02 |
| ☐ 178 | Denny Lemaster | .20 | .09 | .02 |
| ☐ 179 | Ivan Murrell | .20 | .09 | .02 |
| ☐ 180 | Tommy John | 1.25 | .60 | .12 |
| ☐ 181 | Sparky Anderson | .40 | .18 | .04 |

| | MINT | VG-E | F-G |
|---|---|---|---|
| ☐ 182 Dick Hall | .20 | .09 | .02 |
| ☐ 183 Jerry Grote | .20 | .09 | .02 |
| ☐ 184 Ray Fosse | .20 | .09 | .02 |
| ☐ 185 Don Mincher | .25 | .10 | .02 |
| ☐ 186 Rick Joseph | .20 | .09 | .02 |
| ☐ 187 Mike Hedlund | .20 | .09 | .02 |
| ☐ 188 Manny Sanguillen | .30 | .12 | .03 |
| ☐ 189 Yankees Rookies | 17.00 | 8.00 | 1.70 |
| Thurman Munson | | | |
| Dave McDonald | | | |
| ☐ 190 Joe Torre | .55 | .25 | .05 |
| ☐ 191 Vicente Romo | .20 | .09 | .02 |
| ☐ 192 Jim Qualls | .20 | .09 | .02 |
| ☐ 193 Mike Wegener | .20 | .09 | .02 |
| ☐ 194 Chuck Manuel | .20 | .09 | .02 |
| PLAYOFFS CARDS | | | |
| (195-202) | | | |
| ☐ 195 NL Playoff Game 1 | 1.25 | .60 | .12 |
| Seaver wins opener | | | |
| ☐ 196 NL Playoff Game 2 | .65 | .30 | .06 |
| Mets show muscle | | | |
| ☐ 197 NL Playoff Game 3 | 1.25 | .60 | .12 |
| Ryan saves the day | | | |
| ☐ 198 NL Playoff Summary | .65 | .30 | .06 |
| Mets celebrate | | | |
| ☐ 199 AL Playoff Game 1 | .65 | .30 | .06 |
| Orioles win | | | |
| squeaker (Cuellar) | | | |
| ☐ 200 AL Playoff Game 2 | .65 | .30 | .06 |
| Powell scores | | | |
| winning run | | | |
| ☐ 201 AL Playoff Game 3 | .65 | .30 | .06 |
| Birds wrap it up | | | |
| ☐ 202 AL Playoff Summary | .65 | .30 | .06 |
| Orioles celebrate | | | |
| ☐ 203 Rudy May | .20 | .09 | .02 |
| ☐ 204 Len Gabrielson | .20 | .09 | .02 |
| ☐ 205 Bert Campaneris | .30 | .12 | .03 |
| ☐ 206 Clete Boyer | .25 | .10 | .02 |
| ☐ 207 Tigers Rookies | .20 | .09 | .02 |
| Norman McRae | | | |
| Bob Reed | | | |
| ☐ 208 Fred Gladding | .20 | .09 | .02 |
| ☐ 209 Ken Suarez | .20 | .09 | .02 |
| ☐ 210 Juan Marichal | 2.00 | .90 | .20 |
| ☐ 211 Ted Williams | 2.25 | 1.00 | .22 |
| ☐ 212 Al Santorini | .20 | .09 | .02 |
| ☐ 213 Andy Etchebarren | .20 | .09 | .02 |
| ☐ 214 Ken Boswell | .20 | .09 | .02 |
| ☐ 215 Reggie Smith | .70 | .32 | .07 |
| ☐ 216 Chuck Hartenstein | .20 | .09 | .02 |
| ☐ 217 Ron Hansen | .20 | .09 | .02 |
| ☐ 218 Ron Stone | .20 | .09 | .02 |

| | MINT | VG-E | F-G |
|---|---|---|---|
| ☐ 219 Jerry Kenney | .20 | .09 | .02 |
| ☐ 220 Steve Carlton | 10.00 | 4.75 | 1.00 |
| ☐ 221 Ron Brand | .20 | .09 | .02 |
| ☐ 222 Jim Rooker | .20 | .09 | .02 |
| ☐ 223 Nate Oliver | .20 | .09 | .02 |
| ☐ 224 Steve Barber | .25 | .10 | .02 |
| ☐ 225 Lee May | .35 | .15 | .03 |
| ☐ 226 Ron Perranoski | .30 | .12 | .03 |
| ☐ 227 Astros Rookies | .60 | .28 | .06 |
| John Mayberry | | | |
| Bob Watkins | | | |
| ☐ 228 Aurelio Rodriguez | .25 | .10 | .02 |
| ☐ 229 Rich Robertson | .20 | .09 | .02 |
| ☐ 230 Brooks Robinson | 3.75 | 1.75 | .37 |
| ☐ 231 Luis Tiant | .55 | .25 | .05 |
| ☐ 232 Bob Didier | .20 | .09 | .02 |
| ☐ 233 Lew Krausse | .20 | .09 | .02 |
| ☐ 234 Tommy Dean | .20 | .09 | .02 |
| ☐ 235 Mike Epstein | .20 | .09 | .02 |
| ☐ 236 Bob Veale | .25 | .10 | .02 |
| ☐ 237 Russ Gibson | .20 | .09 | .02 |
| ☐ 238 Jose Laboy | .20 | .09 | .02 |
| ☐ 239 Ken Berry | .20 | .09 | .02 |
| ☐ 240 Fergie Jenkins | 1.00 | .45 | .10 |
| ☐ 241 Royals Rookies | .20 | .09 | .02 |
| Al Fitzmorris | | | |
| Scott Northey | | | |
| ☐ 242 Walter Alston | .65 | .30 | .06 |
| ☐ 243 Joe Sparma | .20 | .09 | .02 |
| ☐ 244 3rd Checklist | .60 | .15 | .03 |
| ☐ 245 Leo Cardenas | .20 | .09 | .02 |
| ☐ 246 Jim McAndrew | .20 | .09 | .02 |
| ☐ 247 Lou Klimchock | .20 | .09 | .02 |
| ☐ 248 Jesus Alou | .20 | .09 | .02 |
| ☐ 249 Bob Locker | .25 | .10 | .02 |
| ☐ 250 Willie McCovey | 3.50 | 1.65 | .35 |
| ☐ 251 Dick Schofield | .20 | .09 | .02 |
| ☐ 252 Lowell Palmer | .20 | .09 | .02 |
| ☐ 253 Ron Woods | .20 | .09 | .02 |
| ☐ 254 Camilo Pascual | .25 | .10 | .02 |
| ☐ 255 Jim Spencer | .20 | .09 | .02 |
| ☐ 256 Vic Davalillo | .20 | .09 | .02 |
| ☐ 257 Dennis Higgins | .20 | .09 | .02 |
| ☐ 258 Paul Popovich | .20 | .09 | .02 |
| ☐ 259 Tommie Reynolds | .20 | .09 | .02 |
| ☐ 260 Claude Osteen | .25 | .10 | .02 |
| ☐ 261 Curt Motton | .20 | .09 | .02 |
| ☐ 262 Twins Rookies | .20 | .09 | .02 |
| Jerry Morales | | | |
| Jim Williams | | | |
| ☐ 263 Duane Josephson | .20 | .09 | .02 |
| ☐ 264 Rich Hebner | .25 | .10 | .02 |
| ☐ 265 Randy Hundley | .25 | .10 | .02 |

| | | MINT | VG-E | F-G |
|---|---|---|---|---|
| ☐ 266 | Wally Bunker | .20 | .09 | .02 |
| ☐ 267 | Twins Rookies | .20 | .09 | .02 |
| | Herman Hill | | | |
| | Paul Ratliff | | | |
| ☐ 268 | Claude Raymond | .20 | .09 | .02 |
| ☐ 269 | Cesar Gutierrez | .20 | .09 | .02 |
| ☐ 270 | Chris Short | .20 | .09 | .02 |
| ☐ 271 | Greg Goossen | .25 | .10 | .02 |
| ☐ 272 | Hector Torres | .20 | .09 | .02 |
| ☐ 273 | Ralph Houk | .30 | .12 | .03 |
| ☐ 274 | Gerry Arrigo | .20 | .09 | .02 |
| ☐ 275 | Duke Sims | .20 | .09 | .02 |
| ☐ 276 | Ron Hunt | .20 | .09 | .02 |
| ☐ 277 | Paul Doyle | .20 | .09 | .02 |
| ☐ 278 | Tommie Aaron | .25 | .10 | .02 |
| ☐ 279 | Bill Lee | .25 | .10 | .02 |
| ☐ 280 | Donn Clendenon | .20 | .09 | .02 |
| ☐ 281 | Casey Cox | .20 | .09 | .02 |
| ☐ 282 | Steve Huntz | .20 | .09 | .02 |
| ☐ 283 | Angel Bravo | .20 | .09 | .02 |
| ☐ 284 | Jack Baldschun | .20 | .09 | .02 |
| ☐ 285 | Paul Blair | .25 | .10 | .02 |
| ☐ 286 | Dodgers Rookies | 4.00 | 1.85 | .40 |
| | Jack Jenkins | | | |
| | Bill Buckner | | | |
| ☐ 287 | Fred Talbot | .20 | .09 | .02 |
| ☐ 288 | Larry Hisle | .30 | .12 | .03 |
| ☐ 289 | Gene Brabender | .25 | .10 | .02 |
| ☐ 290 | Rod Carew | 10.00 | 4.75 | 1.00 |
| ☐ 291 | Leo Durocher | .60 | .28 | .06 |
| ☐ 292 | Eddie Leon | .20 | .09 | .02 |
| ☐ 293 | Bob Bailey | .20 | .09 | .02 |
| ☐ 294 | Jose Azcue | .20 | .09 | .02 |
| ☐ 295 | Cecil Upshaw | .20 | .09 | .02 |
| ☐ 296 | Woody Woodward | .20 | .09 | .02 |
| ☐ 297 | Curt Blefary | .20 | .09 | .02 |
| ☐ 298 | Ken Henderson | .20 | .09 | .02 |
| ☐ 299 | Buddy Bradford | .20 | .09 | .02 |
| ☐ 300 | Tom Seaver | 12.50 | 5.75 | 1.25 |
| ☐ 301 | Chico Salmon | .20 | .09 | .02 |
| ☐ 302 | Jeff James | .20 | .09 | .02 |
| ☐ 303 | Brant Alyea | .20 | .09 | .02 |
| ☐ 304 | Bill Russell | 1.25 | .60 | .12 |
| | WORLD SERIES | | | |
| | CARDS (305-310) | | | |
| ☐ 305 | World Series Game 1 | .65 | .30 | .06 |
| | Buford leadoff homer | | | |
| ☐ 306 | World Series Game 2 | .65 | .30 | .06 |
| | Clendenon's homer | | | |
| | breaks ice | | | |
| ☐ 307 | World Series Game 3 | .65 | .30 | .06 |
| | Agee's catch | | | |
| | saves the day | | | |

| | | MINT | VG-E | F-G |
|---|---|---|---|---|
| ☐ 308 | World Series Game 4 | .65 | .30 | .06 |
| | Martin's bunt | | | |
| | ends deadlock | | | |
| ☐ 309 | World Series Game 5 | .65 | .30 | .06 |
| | Koosman shuts door | | | |
| ☐ 310 | World Series Summary | .65 | .30 | .06 |
| | Mets whoop it up | | | |
| ☐ 311 | Dick Green | .20 | .09 | .02 |
| ☐ 312 | Mike Torrez | .40 | .18 | .04 |
| ☐ 313 | Mayo Smith | .20 | .09 | .02 |
| ☐ 314 | Bill McCool | .20 | .09 | .02 |
| ☐ 315 | Luis Aparicio | 2.00 | .90 | .20 |
| ☐ 316 | Skip Guinn | .20 | .09 | .02 |
| ☐ 317 | Red Sox Rookies | .30 | .12 | .03 |
| | Billy Conigliaro | | | |
| | Luis Alvarado | | | |
| ☐ 318 | Willie Smith | .20 | .09 | .02 |
| ☐ 319 | Clay Dalrymple | .20 | .09 | .02 |
| ☐ 320 | Jim Maloney | .25 | .10 | .02 |
| ☐ 321 | Lou Piniella | .75 | .35 | .07 |
| ☐ 322 | Luke Walker | .20 | .09 | .02 |
| ☐ 323 | Wayne Comer | .25 | .10 | .02 |
| ☐ 324 | Tony Taylor | .20 | .09 | .02 |
| ☐ 325 | Dave Boswell | .20 | .09 | .02 |
| ☐ 326 | Bill Voss | .20 | .09 | .02 |
| ☐ 327 | Hal King | .20 | .09 | .02 |
| ☐ 328 | George Brunet | .20 | .09 | .02 |
| ☐ 329 | Chris Cannizzaro | .20 | .09 | .02 |
| ☐ 330 | Lou Brock | 3.25 | 1.50 | .32 |
| ☐ 331 | Chuck Dobson | .20 | .09 | .02 |
| ☐ 332 | Bobby Wine | .20 | .09 | .02 |
| ☐ 333 | Bobby Murcer | .70 | .32 | .07 |
| ☐ 334 | Phil Regan | .25 | .10 | .02 |
| ☐ 335 | Bill Freehan | .40 | .18 | .04 |
| ☐ 336 | Del Unser | .20 | .09 | .02 |
| ☐ 337 | Mike McCormick | .25 | .10 | .02 |
| ☐ 338 | Paul Schaal | .20 | .09 | .02 |
| ☐ 339 | Johnny Edwards | .20 | .09 | .02 |
| ☐ 340 | Tony Conigliaro | .45 | .20 | .04 |
| ☐ 341 | Bill Sudakis | .20 | .09 | .02 |
| ☐ 342 | Wilbur Wood | .25 | .10 | .02 |
| ☐ 343 | 4th Checklist | .60 | .15 | .04 |
| ☐ 344 | Marcelino Lopez | .20 | .09 | .02 |
| ☐ 345 | Al Ferrara | .20 | .09 | .02 |
| ☐ 346 | Red Schoendienst | .40 | .18 | .04 |
| ☐ 347 | Russ Snyder | .20 | .09 | .02 |
| ☐ 348 | Mets Rookies | .25 | .10 | .02 |
| | Mike Jorgensen | | | |
| | Jesse Hudson | | | |
| ☐ 349 | Steve Hamilton | .20 | .09 | .02 |
| ☐ 350 | Roberto Clemente | 11.00 | 5.25 | 1.10 |
| ☐ 351 | Tom Murphy | .20 | .09 | .02 |
| ☐ 352 | Bob Barton | .20 | .09 | .02 |

|  | MINT | VG-E | F-G |
|---|---|---|---|
| ☐ 353 Stan Williams | .20 | .09 | .02 |
| ☐ 354 Amos Otis | .35 | .15 | .03 |
| ☐ 355 Doug Rader | .25 | .10 | .02 |
| ☐ 356 Fred Lasher | .20 | .09 | .02 |
| ☐ 357 Bob Burda | .20 | .09 | .02 |
| ☐ 358 Pedro Borbon | .20 | .09 | .02 |
| ☐ 359 Phil Roof | .25 | .10 | .02 |
| ☐ 360 Curt Flood | .40 | .18 | .04 |
| ☐ 361 Ray Jarvis | .20 | .09 | .02 |
| ☐ 362 Joe Hague | .20 | .09 | .02 |
| ☐ 363 Tom Shopay | .20 | .09 | .02 |
| ☐ 364 Dan McGinn | .20 | .09 | .02 |
| ☐ 365 Zoilo Versalles | .20 | .09 | .02 |
| ☐ 366 Barry Moore | .20 | .09 | .02 |
| ☐ 367 Mike Lum | .20 | .09 | .02 |
| ☐ 368 Ed Herrmann | .20 | .09 | .02 |
| ☐ 369 Alan Foster | .20 | .09 | .02 |
| ☐ 370 Tommy Harper | .25 | .10 | .02 |
| ☐ 371 Rod Gaspar | .20 | .09 | .02 |
| ☐ 372 Dave Guisti | .20 | .09 | .02 |
| ☐ 373 Roy White | .25 | .10 | .02 |
| ☐ 374 Tommie Sisk | .20 | .09 | .02 |
| ☐ 375 Johnny Callison | .25 | .10 | .02 |
| ☐ 376 Lefty Phillips | .20 | .09 | .02 |
| ☐ 377 Bill Butler | .20 | .09 | .02 |
| ☐ 378 Jim Davenport | .30 | .12 | .03 |
| ☐ 379 Tom Tischinski | .20 | .09 | .02 |
| ☐ 380 Tony Perez | 1.25 | .60 | .12 |
| ☐ 381 Athletics Rookies | .20 | .09 | .02 |
| Bobby Brooks | | | |
| Mike Olivo | | | |
| ☐ 382 Jack DiLauro | .20 | .09 | .02 |
| ☐ 383 Mickey Stanley | .25 | .10 | .02 |
| ☐ 384 Gary Neibauer | .20 | .09 | .02 |
| ☐ 385 George Scott | .25 | .10 | .02 |
| ☐ 386 Bill Dillman | .20 | .09 | .02 |
| ☐ 387 Orioles Team | .65 | .30 | .06 |
| ☐ 388 Byron Browne | .20 | .09 | .02 |
| ☐ 389 Jim Shellenback | .20 | .09 | .02 |
| ☐ 390 Willie Davis | .40 | .18 | .04 |
| ☐ 391 Larry Brown | .20 | .09 | .02 |
| ☐ 392 Walt Hriniak | .20 | .09 | .02 |
| ☐ 393 John Gelnar | .25 | .10 | .02 |
| ☐ 394 Gil Hodges | 2.00 | .90 | .20 |
| ☐ 395 Walt Williams | .20 | .09 | .02 |
| ☐ 396 Steve Blass | .25 | .10 | .02 |
| ☐ 397 Roger Repoz | .20 | .09 | .02 |
| ☐ 398 Bill Stoneman | .20 | .09 | .02 |
| ☐ 399 Yankees Team | .65 | .30 | .06 |
| ☐ 400 Denny McLain | .60 | .28 | .06 |
| ☐ 401 Giants Rookies | .20 | .09 | .02 |
| John Harrell | | | |
| Bernie Williams | | | |

|  | MINT | VG-E | F-G |
|---|---|---|---|
| ☐ 402 Ellie Rodriguez | .20 | .09 | .02 |
| ☐ 403 Jim Bunning | 1.00 | .45 | .10 |
| ☐ 404 Rich Reese | .20 | .09 | .02 |
| ☐ 405 Bill Hands | .20 | .09 | .02 |
| ☐ 406 Mike Andrews | .20 | .09 | .02 |
| ☐ 407 Bob Watson | .40 | .18 | .04 |
| ☐ 408 Paul Lindblad | .20 | .09 | .02 |
| ☐ 409 Bob Tolan | .20 | .09 | .02 |
| ☐ 410 Boog Powell | 1.00 | .45 | .10 |
| ☐ 411 Dodgers Team | .65 | .30 | .06 |
| ☐ 412 Larry Burchart | .20 | .09 | .02 |
| ☐ 413 Sonny Jackson | .20 | .09 | .02 |
| ☐ 414 Paul Edmondson | .20 | .09 | .02 |
| ☐ 415 Julian Javier | .20 | .09 | .02 |
| ☐ 416 Joe Verbanic | .20 | .09 | .02 |
| ☐ 417 John Bateman | .20 | .09 | .02 |
| ☐ 418 John Donaldson | .25 | .10 | .02 |
| ☐ 419 Ron Taylor | .20 | .09 | .02 |
| ☐ 420 Ken McMullen | .20 | .09 | .02 |
| ☐ 421 Pat Dobson | .25 | .10 | .02 |
| ☐ 422 Royals Team | .45 | .20 | .04 |
| ☐ 423 Jerry May | .20 | .09 | .02 |
| ☐ 424 Mike Kilkenny | .20 | .09 | .02 |
| ☐ 425 Bobby Bonds | .70 | .32 | .07 |
| ☐ 426 Bill Rigney | .20 | .09 | .02 |
| ☐ 427 Fred Norman | .20 | .09 | .02 |
| ☐ 428 Don Buford | .20 | .09 | .02 |
| ☐ 429 Cubs Rookies | .20 | .09 | .02 |
| Randy Bobb | | | |
| Jim Cosman | | | |
| ☐ 430 Andy Messersmith | .40 | .18 | .04 |
| ☐ 431 Ron Swoboda | .25 | .10 | .02 |
| ☐ 432 5th Checklist | .65 | .15 | .04 |
| ☐ 433 Ron Bryant | .20 | .09 | .02 |
| ☐ 434 Felipe Alou | .25 | .10 | .02 |
| ☐ 435 Nelson Briles | .20 | .09 | .02 |
| ☐ 436 Phillies Team | .45 | .20 | .04 |
| ☐ 437 Danny Cater | .20 | .09 | .02 |
| ☐ 438 Pat Jarvis | .20 | .09 | .02 |
| ☐ 439 Lee Maye | .20 | .09 | .02 |
| ☐ 440 Bill Mazeroski | .40 | .18 | .04 |
| ☐ 441 John O'Donoghue | .25 | .10 | .02 |
| ☐ 442 Gene Mauch MGR | .25 | .10 | .02 |
| ☐ 443 Al Jackson | .20 | .09 | .02 |
| ☐ 444 White Sox Rookies | .20 | .09 | .02 |
| Billy Farmer | | | |
| John Matias | | | |
| ☐ 445 Vada Pinson | .60 | .28 | .06 |
| ☐ 446 Billy Grabarkewitz | .20 | .09 | .02 |
| ☐ 447 Lee Stange | .20 | .09 | .02 |
| ☐ 448 Astros Team | .45 | .20 | .04 |
| ☐ 449 Jim Palmer | 5.50 | 2.60 | .55 |

|  | | MINT | VG-E | F-G |
|---|---|---|---|---|
| | ALL-STAR | | | |
| | SELECTIONS (450–469) | | | |
| ☐ 450 | Willie McCovey AS | 2.00 | .90 | .20 |
| ☐ 451 | Boog Powell AS | .40 | .18 | .04 |
| ☐ 452 | Felix Millan AS | .25 | .10 | .02 |
| ☐ 453 | Rod Carew AS | 2.75 | 1.25 | .27 |
| ☐ 454 | Ron Santo AS | .25 | .10 | .02 |
| ☐ 455 | Brooks Robinson AS | 2.25 | 1.00 | .22 |
| ☐ 456 | Don Kessinger AS | .25 | .10 | .02 |
| ☐ 457 | Rico Petrocelli AS | .25 | .10 | .02 |
| ☐ 458 | Pete Rose AS | 5.50 | 2.60 | .55 |
| ☐ 459 | Reggie Jackson AS | 4.00 | 1.85 | .40 |
| ☐ 460 | Matty Alou AS | .25 | .10 | .02 |
| ☐ 461 | Carl Yastrzemski AS | 3.50 | 1.65 | .35 |
| ☐ 462 | Hank Aaron AS | 3.50 | 1.65 | .35 |
| ☐ 463 | Frank Robinson AS | 2.00 | .90 | .20 |
| ☐ 464 | Johnny Bench AS | 3.00 | 1.40 | .30 |
| ☐ 465 | Bill Freehan AS | .25 | .10 | .02 |
| ☐ 466 | Juan Marichal AS | 1.75 | .85 | .17 |
| ☐ 467 | Denny McLain AS | .35 | .15 | .03 |
| ☐ 468 | Jerry Koosman AS | .25 | .10 | .02 |
| ☐ 469 | Sam McDowell AS | .25 | .10 | .02 |
| ☐ 470 | Willie Stargell | 2.75 | 1.25 | .27 |
| ☐ 471 | Chris Zachary | .20 | .09 | .02 |
| ☐ 472 | Braves Team | .45 | .20 | .04 |
| ☐ 473 | Don Bryant | .25 | .10 | .02 |
| ☐ 474 | Dick Kelley | .20 | .09 | .02 |
| ☐ 475 | Dick McAuliffe | .25 | .10 | .02 |
| ☐ 476 | Don Shaw | .20 | .09 | .02 |
| ☐ 477 | Orioles Rookies | .20 | .09 | .02 |
| | Al Severinsen | | | |
| | Roger Freed | | | |
| ☐ 478 | Bob Heise | .20 | .09 | .02 |
| ☐ 479 | Dick Woodson | .20 | .09 | .02 |
| ☐ 480 | Glen Beckert | .25 | .10 | .02 |
| ☐ 481 | Jose Tartabull | .20 | .09 | .02 |
| ☐ 482 | Tom Hilgendorf | .20 | .09 | .02 |
| ☐ 483 | Gail Hopkins | .20 | .09 | .02 |
| ☐ 484 | Gary Nolan | .25 | .10 | .02 |
| ☐ 485 | Jay Johnstone | .25 | .10 | .02 |
| ☐ 486 | Terry Harmon | .20 | .09 | .02 |
| ☐ 487 | Cisco Carlos | .20 | .09 | .02 |
| ☐ 488 | J.C. Martin | .20 | .09 | .02 |
| ☐ 489 | Eddie Kasko | .20 | .09 | .02 |
| ☐ 490 | Bill Singer | .20 | .09 | .02 |
| ☐ 491 | Graig Nettles | 2.00 | .90 | .20 |
| ☐ 492 | Astros Rookies | .20 | .09 | .02 |
| | Keith Lampard | | | |
| | Scipio Spinks | | | |
| ☐ 493 | Lindy McDaniel | .20 | .09 | .02 |
| ☐ 494 | Larry Stahl | .20 | .09 | .02 |
| ☐ 495 | Dave Morehead | .20 | .09 | .02 |
| ☐ 496 | Steve Whitaker | .20 | .09 | .02 |

|  | | MINT | VG-E | F-G |
|---|---|---|---|---|
| ☐ 497 | Eddie Watt | .20 | .09 | .02 |
| ☐ 498 | Al Weis | .20 | .09 | .02 |
| ☐ 499 | Skip Lockwood | .25 | .10 | .02 |
| ☐ 500 | Hank Aaron | 11.00 | 5.25 | 1.10 |
| ☐ 501 | White Sox Team | .45 | .20 | .04 |
| ☐ 502 | Rollie Fingers | 2.50 | 1.15 | .25 |
| ☐ 503 | Dal Maxvill | .20 | .09 | .02 |
| ☐ 504 | Don Pavletich | .20 | .09 | .02 |
| ☐ 505 | Ken Holtzman | .35 | .15 | .03 |
| ☐ 506 | Ed Stroud | .20 | .09 | .02 |
| ☐ 507 | Pat Corrales | .25 | .10 | .02 |
| ☐ 508 | Joe Niekro | .45 | .20 | .04 |
| ☐ 509 | Expos Team | .45 | .20 | .04 |
| ☐ 510 | Tony Oliva | 1.00 | .45 | .10 |
| ☐ 511 | Joe Hoerner | .20 | .09 | .02 |
| ☐ 512 | Billy Harris | .20 | .09 | .02 |
| ☐ 513 | Preston Gomez | .20 | .09 | .02 |
| ☐ 514 | Steve Hovley | .25 | .10 | .02 |
| ☐ 515 | Don Wilson | .20 | .09 | .02 |
| ☐ 516 | Yankees Rookies | .20 | .09 | .02 |
| | John Ellis | | | |
| | Jim Lyttle | | | |
| ☐ 517 | Joe Gibbon | .20 | .09 | .02 |
| ☐ 518 | Bill Melton | .20 | .09 | .02 |
| ☐ 519 | Don McMahon | .20 | .09 | .02 |
| ☐ 520 | Willie Horton | .40 | .18 | .04 |
| ☐ 521 | Cal Koonce | .20 | .09 | .02 |
| ☐ 522 | Angels Team | .45 | .20 | .04 |
| ☐ 523 | Jose Pena | .20 | .09 | .02 |
| ☐ 524 | Alvin Dark | .25 | .10 | .02 |
| ☐ 525 | Jerry Adair | .20 | .09 | .02 |
| ☐ 526 | Ron Herbel | .20 | .09 | .02 |
| ☐ 527 | Don Bosch | .20 | .09 | .02 |
| ☐ 528 | Elrod Hendricks | .20 | .09 | .02 |
| ☐ 529 | Bob Aspromonte | .20 | .09 | .02 |
| ☐ 530 | Bob Gibson | 3.50 | 1.65 | .35 |
| ☐ 531 | Ron Clark | .20 | .09 | .02 |
| ☐ 532 | Danny Murtaugh | .20 | .09 | .02 |
| ☐ 533 | Buzz Stephen | .25 | .10 | .02 |
| ☐ 534 | Twins Team | .45 | .20 | .04 |
| ☐ 535 | Andy Kosco | .20 | .09 | .02 |
| ☐ 536 | Mike Kekich | .20 | .09 | .02 |
| ☐ 537 | Joe Morgan | 2.00 | .90 | .20 |
| ☐ 538 | Bob Humphreys | .20 | .09 | .02 |
| ☐ 539 | Phillies Rookies | 1.75 | .85 | .17 |
| | Dennis Doyle | | | |
| | Larry Bowa | | | |
| ☐ 540 | Gary Peters | .25 | .10 | .02 |
| ☐ 541 | Bill Heath | .20 | .09 | .02 |
| ☐ 542 | 6th Checklist | .70 | .15 | .04 |
| ☐ 543 | Clyde Wright | .20 | .09 | .02 |
| ☐ 544 | Reds Team | .70 | .32 | .07 |
| ☐ 545 | Ken Harrelson | .70 | .32 | .07 |

| | MINT | VG-E | F-G |
|---|---|---|---|
| 546 Ron Reed | .20 | .09 | .02 |
| 547 Rick Monday | .50 | .22 | .05 |
| 548 Howie Reed | .35 | .15 | .03 |
| 549 Cardinals Team | .65 | .30 | .06 |
| 550 Frank Howard | .65 | .30 | .06 |
| 551 Dock Ellis | .35 | .15 | .03 |
| 552 Royals Rookies | .35 | .15 | .03 |
|    Don O'Riley | | | |
|    Dennis Paepke | | | |
|    Fred Rico | | | |
| 553 Jim LeFebvre | .35 | .15 | .03 |
| 554 Tom Timmermann | .35 | .15 | .03 |
| 555 Orlando Cepeda | 1.75 | .85 | .17 |
| 556 Dave Bristol | .35 | .15 | .03 |
| 557 Ed Kranepool | .45 | .20 | .04 |
| 558 Vern Fuller | .35 | .15 | .03 |
| 559 Tommy Davis | .45 | .20 | .04 |
| 560 Gaylord Perry | 3.25 | 1.50 | .32 |
| 561 Tom McCraw | .35 | .15 | .03 |
| 562 Ted Abernathy | .35 | .15 | .03 |
| 563 Red Sox Team | .65 | .30 | .06 |
| 564 Johnny Briggs | .35 | .15 | .03 |
| 565 Jim Hunter | 2.50 | 1.15 | .25 |
| 566 Gene Alley | .45 | .20 | .04 |
| 567 Bob Oliver | .35 | .15 | .03 |
| 568 Stan Bahnsen | .35 | .15 | .03 |
| 569 Cookie Rojas | .35 | .15 | .03 |
| 570 Jim Fregosi | .45 | .20 | .04 |
| 571 Jim Brewer | .35 | .15 | .03 |
| 572 Frank Quilici | .35 | .15 | .03 |
| 573 Padres Rookies | .35 | .15 | .03 |
|    Mike Corkins | | | |
|    Rafael Robles | | | |
|    Ron Slocum | | | |
| 574 Bobby Bolin | .35 | .15 | .03 |
| 575 Cleon Jones | .35 | .15 | .03 |
| 576 Milt Pappas | .45 | .20 | .04 |
| 577 Bernie Allen | .35 | .15 | .03 |
| 578 Tom Griffin | .35 | .15 | .03 |
| 579 Tigers Team | .65 | .30 | .06 |
| 580 Pete Rose | 36.00 | 15.00 | 3.00 |
| 581 Tom Satriano | .35 | .15 | .03 |
| 582 Mike Paul | .35 | .15 | .03 |
| 583 Hal Lanier | .45 | .20 | .04 |
| 584 Al Downing | .35 | .15 | .03 |
| 585 Rusty Staub | 1.00 | .45 | .10 |
| 586 Rickey Clark | .35 | .15 | .03 |
| 587 Jose Arcia | .35 | .15 | .03 |
| 588 A Checklist 7 | 1.25 | .20 | .05 |
|    (666 Adolpho) | | | |
| 588 B Checklist 7 | 2.50 | .35 | .07 |
|    (666 Adolfo) | | | |
| 589 Joe Keough | .35 | .15 | .03 |
| 590 Mike Cuellar | .45 | .20 | .04 |
| 591 Mike Ryan | .35 | .15 | .03 |
| 592 Daryl Patterson | .35 | .15 | .03 |
| 593 Cubs Team | .65 | .30 | .06 |
| 594 Jake Gibbs | .35 | .15 | .03 |
| 595 Maury Wills | 1.00 | .45 | .10 |
| 596 Mike Hershberger | .35 | .15 | .03 |
| 597 Sonny Siebert | .35 | .15 | .03 |
| 598 Joe Pepitone | .45 | .20 | .04 |
| 599 Senators Rookies | .35 | .15 | .03 |
|    Dick Stelmaszek | | | |
|    Gene Martin | | | |
|    Dick Such | | | |
| 600 Willie Mays | 14.00 | 6.50 | 1.40 |
| 601 Pete Richert | .35 | .15 | .03 |
| 602 Ted Savage | .35 | .15 | .03 |
| 603 Ray Oyler | .35 | .15 | .03 |
| 604 Clarence Gaston | .35 | .15 | .03 |
| 605 Rick Wise | .45 | .20 | .04 |
| 606 Chico Ruiz | .35 | .15 | .03 |
| 607 Gary Waslewski | .35 | .15 | .03 |
| 608 Pirates Team | .65 | .30 | .06 |
| 609 Buck Martinez | .35 | .15 | .03 |
| 610 Jerry Koosman | .75 | .35 | .07 |
| 611 Norm Cash | .75 | .35 | .07 |
| 612 Jim Hickman | .35 | .15 | .03 |
| 613 Dave Baldwin | .35 | .15 | .03 |
| 614 Mike Shannon | .50 | .22 | .05 |
| 615 Mark Belanger | .50 | .22 | .05 |
| 616 Jim Merritt | .35 | .15 | .03 |
| 617 Jim French | .35 | .15 | .03 |
| 618 Billy Wynne | .35 | .15 | .03 |
| 619 Norm Miller | .35 | .15 | .03 |
| 620 Jim Perry | .85 | .40 | .08 |
| 621 Braves Rookies | 3.25 | 1.50 | .32 |
|    Mike McQueen | | | |
|    Darrell Evans | | | |
|    Rick Kester | | | |
| 622 Don Sutton | 2.00 | .90 | .20 |
| 623 Horace Clarke | .35 | .15 | .03 |
| 624 Clyde King | .35 | .15 | .03 |
| 625 Dean Chance | .35 | .15 | .03 |
| 626 Dave Ricketts | .35 | .15 | .03 |
| 627 Gary Wagner | .35 | .15 | .03 |
| 628 Wayne Garrett | .35 | .15 | .03 |
| 629 Merv Rettenmund | .35 | .15 | .03 |
| 630 Ernie Banks | 7.50 | 3.50 | .75 |
| 631 Athletics Team | .65 | .30 | .06 |
| 632 Gary Sutherland | .35 | .15 | .03 |
| 633 Roger Nelson | .35 | .15 | .03 |
| 634 Bud Harrelson | .80 | .40 | .08 |
| 635 Bob Allison | 1.00 | .45 | .10 |
| 636 Jim Stewart | .80 | .40 | .08 |

| | MINT | VG-E | F-G |
|---|---|---|---|
| ☐ 637 Indians Team | 1.50 | .70 | .15 |
| ☐ 638 Frank Bertaina | .80 | .40 | .08 |
| ☐ 639 Dave Campbell | .80 | .40 | .08 |
| ☐ 640 Al Kaline | 11.00 | 5.25 | 1.10 |
| ☐ 641 Al McBean | .80 | .40 | .08 |
| ☐ 642 Angels Rookies | .80 | .40 | .08 |
|     Greg Garrett | | | |
|     Gordon Lund | | | |
|     Jarvis Tatum | | | |
| ☐ 643 Jose Pagan | .80 | .40 | .08 |
| ☐ 644 Gerry Nyman | .80 | .40 | .08 |
| ☐ 645 Don Money | 1.00 | .45 | .10 |
| ☐ 646 Jim Britton | .80 | .40 | .08 |
| ☐ 647 Tom Matchick | .80 | .40 | .08 |
| ☐ 648 Larry Haney | .80 | .40 | .08 |
| ☐ 649 Jimmie Hall | .80 | .40 | .08 |
| ☐ 650 Sam McDowell | 1.00 | .45 | .10 |
| ☐ 651 Jim Gosger | .80 | .40 | .08 |
| ☐ 652 Rich Rollins | .80 | .40 | .08 |
| ☐ 653 Moe Drabowsky | .80 | .40 | .08 |
| ☐ 654 N.L. Rookies | 2.00 | .90 | .20 |
|     Oscar Gamble | | | |
|     Boots Day | | | |
|     Angel Mangual | | | |
| ☐ 655 John Roseboro | 1.00 | .45 | .10 |
| ☐ 656 Jim Hardin | .80 | .40 | .08 |
| ☐ 657 Padres Team | 2.25 | 1.00 | .22 |
| ☐ 658 Ken Tatum | .80 | .40 | .08 |
| ☐ 659 Pete Ward | .80 | .40 | .08 |
| ☐ 660 Johnny Bench | 50.00 | 22.00 | 5.00 |
| ☐ 661 Jerry Robertson | .80 | .40 | .08 |
| ☐ 662 Frank Lucchesi | .80 | .40 | .08 |
| ☐ 663 Tito Francona | 1.00 | .45 | .10 |
| ☐ 664 Bob Robertson | .80 | .40 | .08 |
| ☐ 665 Jim Lonborg | 1.00 | .45 | .10 |
| ☐ 666 Adolpho Phillips | .80 | .40 | .08 |
| ☐ 667 Bob Meyer | .80 | .40 | .08 |
| ☐ 668 Bob Tillman | .80 | .40 | .08 |
| ☐ 669 White Sox Rookies | .80 | .40 | .08 |
|     Bart Johnson | | | |
|     Dan Lazar | | | |
|     Mickey Scott | | | |
| ☐ 670 Ron Santo | 1.75 | .85 | .17 |
| ☐ 671 Jim Campanis | .80 | .40 | .08 |
| ☐ 672 Leon McFadden | .80 | .40 | .08 |
| ☐ 673 Ted Uhlaender | .80 | .40 | .08 |
| ☐ 674 Dave Leonhard | .80 | .40 | .08 |
| ☐ 675 Jose Cardenal | 1.00 | .45 | .10 |
| ☐ 676 Senators Team | 1.50 | .70 | .15 |
| ☐ 677 Woodie Fryman | .80 | .40 | .08 |
| ☐ 678 Dave Duncan | .80 | .40 | .08 |
| ☐ 679 Ray Sadecki | .80 | .40 | .08 |
| ☐ 680 Rico Petrocelli | 1.25 | .60 | .12 |

| | MINT | VG-E | F-G |
|---|---|---|---|
| ☐ 681 Bob Garibaldi | .80 | .40 | .08 |
| ☐ 682 Dalton Jones | .80 | .40 | .08 |
| ☐ 683 Reds Rookies | 2.00 | .90 | .20 |
|     Vern Geishert | | | |
|     Hal McRae | | | |
|     Wayne Simpson | | | |
| ☐ 684 Jack Fisher | .80 | .40 | .08 |
| ☐ 685 Tom Haller | .80 | .40 | .08 |
| ☐ 686 Jackie Hernandez | .80 | .40 | .08 |
| ☐ 687 Bob Priddy | .80 | .40 | .08 |
| ☐ 688 Ted Kubiak | .80 | .40 | .08 |
| ☐ 689 Frank Tepedino | .80 | .40 | .08 |
| ☐ 690 Ron Fairly | 1.00 | .45 | .10 |
| ☐ 691 Joe Grzenda | .80 | .40 | .08 |
| ☐ 692 Duffy Dyer | .80 | .40 | .08 |
| ☐ 693 Bob Johnson | .80 | .40 | .08 |
| ☐ 694 Gary Ross | .80 | .40 | .08 |
| ☐ 695 Bobby Knoop | .80 | .40 | .08 |
| ☐ 696 Giants Team | 1.50 | .70 | .15 |
| ☐ 697 Jim Hannan | .80 | .40 | .08 |
| ☐ 698 Tom Tresh | 1.50 | .70 | .15 |
| ☐ 699 Hank Aguirre | .80 | .40 | .08 |
| ☐ 700 Frank Robinson | 11.00 | 5.25 | 1.10 |
| ☐ 701 Jack Billingham | .80 | .40 | .08 |
| ☐ 702 AL Rookies | .80 | .40 | .08 |
|     Bob Johnson | | | |
|     Ron Klimkowski | | | |
|     Bill Zepp | | | |
| ☐ 703 Lou Marone | .80 | .40 | .08 |
| ☐ 704 Frank Baker | .80 | .40 | .08 |
| ☐ 705 Tony Cloninger | .80 | .40 | .08 |
| ☐ 706 John McNamara | 1.75 | .85 | .17 |
| ☐ 707 Kevin Collins | .80 | .40 | .08 |
| ☐ 708 Jose Santiago | .80 | .40 | .08 |
| ☐ 709 Mike Fiore | .80 | .40 | .08 |
| ☐ 710 Felix Millan | .80 | .40 | .08 |
| ☐ 711 Ed Brinkman | .80 | .40 | .08 |
| ☐ 712 Nolan Ryan | 20.00 | 9.00 | 2.00 |
| ☐ 713 Pilots Team | 5.00 | 2.35 | .50 |
| ☐ 714 Al Spangler | .80 | .40 | .08 |
| ☐ 715 Mickey Lolich | 2.00 | .90 | .20 |
| ☐ 716 Cardinals Rookies | .80 | .40 | .08 |
|     Sal Campisi | | | |
|     Reggie Cleveland | | | |
|     Santiago Guzman | | | |
| ☐ 717 Tom Phoebus | .80 | .40 | .08 |
| ☐ 718 Ed Spezio | .80 | .40 | .08 |
| ☐ 719 Jim Roland | .80 | .40 | .08 |
| ☐ 720 Rick Reichardt | 1.00 | .45 | .10 |

## 1971 TOPPS

The cards in this 752 card set measure 2½" by 3½". The 1971 Topps set is a challenge to complete in "mint" condition because the black obverse border is easily scratched and damaged. An unusual feature of this set is that the player is also pictured in black and white on the back of the card. Cards 524–643 and the last series (644–752) are somewhat scarce.

Complete Set: M-500.00; VG-E-225.00; F-G-40.00

| | MINT | VG-E | F-G |
|---|---|---|---|
| Common Player (1–523) | .22 | .09 | .02 |
| Common Player (524–643) | .40 | .18 | .04 |
| Common Player (644–752) | .90 | .40 | .09 |
| 1 Orioles Team | 1.75 | .50 | .10 |
| 2 Dock Ellis | .22 | .09 | .02 |
| 3 Dick McAuliffe | .22 | .09 | .02 |
| 4 Vic Davalillo | .22 | .09 | .02 |
| 5 Thurman Munson | 9.00 | 4.25 | .90 |
| 6 Ed Spiezio | .22 | .09 | .02 |
| 7 Jim Holt | .22 | .09 | .02 |
| 8 Mike McQueen | .22 | .09 | .02 |
| 9 George Scott | .30 | .12 | .03 |
| 10 Claude Osteen | .30 | .12 | .03 |
| 11 Elliott Maddox | .22 | .09 | .02 |
| 12 Johnny Callison | .30 | .12 | .03 |
| 13 White Sox Rookies | .22 | .09 | .02 |
| Charlie Brinkman | | | |
| Dick Moloney | | | |
| 14 Dave Concepcion | 3.50 | 1.65 | .35 |
| 15 Andy Messersmith | .30 | .12 | .03 |
| 16 Ken Singleton | 1.75 | .85 | .17 |
| 17 Billy Sorrell | .22 | .09 | .02 |
| 18 Norm Miller | .22 | .09 | .02 |
| 19 Skip Pitlock | .22 | .09 | .02 |
| 20 Reggie Jackson | 12.00 | 5.50 | 1.20 |
| 21 Dan McGinn | .22 | .09 | .02 |
| 22 Phil Roof | .22 | .09 | .02 |
| 23 Oscar Gamble | .40 | .18 | .04 |
| 24 Rich Hand | .22 | .09 | .02 |
| 25 Clarence Gaston | .22 | .09 | .02 |
| 26 Bert Blyleven | 5.00 | 2.35 | .50 |
| 27 Pirates Rookies | .22 | .09 | .02 |
| Fred Cambria | | | |
| Gene Clines | | | |
| 28 Ron Klimkowski | .22 | .09 | .02 |
| 29 Don Buford | .22 | .09 | .02 |
| 30 Phil Niekro | 1.75 | .85 | .17 |
| 31 Eddie Kasko | .22 | .09 | .02 |
| 32 Jerry Davanon | .22 | .09 | .02 |
| 33 Del Unser | .22 | .09 | .02 |
| 34 Sandy Vance | .22 | .09 | .02 |
| 35 Lou Piniella | .60 | .28 | .06 |
| 36 Dean Chance | .22 | .09 | .02 |
| 37 Rich McKinney | .22 | .09 | .02 |
| 38 Jim Colborn | .22 | .09 | .02 |
| 39 Tiger Rookies | .22 | .09 | .02 |
| Lerrin LaGrow | | | |
| Gene Lamont | | | |
| 40 Lee May | .30 | .12 | .03 |
| 41 Rick Austin | .22 | .09 | .02 |
| 42 Boots Day | .22 | .09 | .02 |
| 43 Steve Kealey | .22 | .09 | .02 |
| 44 Johnny Edwards | .22 | .09 | .02 |
| 45 Jim Hunter | 1.75 | .85 | .17 |
| 46 Dave Campbell | .22 | .09 | .02 |
| 47 Johnny Jeter | .22 | .09 | .02 |
| 48 Dave Baldwin | .22 | .09 | .02 |
| 49 Don Money | .22 | .09 | .02 |
| 50 Willie McCovey | 3.00 | 1.40 | .30 |
| 51 Steve Kline | .22 | .09 | .02 |
| 52 Braves Rookies | .30 | .12 | .03 |
| Oscar Brown | | | |
| Earl Williams | | | |
| 53 Paul Blair | .22 | .09 | .02 |
| 54 Checklist 1st Series | .60 | .12 | .02 |
| 55 Steve Carlton | 9.00 | 4.25 | .90 |
| 56 Duane Josephson | .22 | .09 | .02 |
| 57 Von Joshua | .22 | .09 | .02 |
| 58 Bill Lee | .22 | .09 | .02 |
| 59 Gene Mauch | .22 | .09 | .02 |
| 60 Dick Bosman | .22 | .09 | .02 |
| 61 AL Batting Leaders | .85 | .40 | .08 |
| Alex Johnson | | | |
| Carl Yastrzemski | | | |
| Tony Oliva | | | |

| | | MINT | VG-E | F-G |
|---|---|---|---|---|
| ☐ 62 | NL Batting Leaders .... Rico Carty Joe Torre Manny Sanguillen | .45 | .20 | .04 |
| ☐ 63 | AL RBI Leaders ....... Frank Robinson Tony Conigliaro Boog Powell | .65 | .30 | .06 |
| ☐ 64 | NL RBI Leaders ....... Johnny Bench Tony Perez Billy Williams | .65 | .30 | .06 |
| ☐ 65 | AL HR Leaders ........ Frank Howard Harmon Killebrew Carl Yastrzemski | .85 | .40 | .08 |
| ☐ 66 | NL HR Leaders ........ Johnny Bench Billy Williams Tony Perez | .65 | .30 | .06 |
| ☐ 67 | AL ERA Leaders ....... Diego Segui Jim Palmer Clyde Wright | .45 | .20 | .04 |
| ☐ 68 | NL ERA Leaders ....... Tom Seaver Wayne Simpson Luke Walker | .65 | .30 | .06 |
| ☐ 69 | AL Pitching Leaders .... Mike Cuellar Dave McNally Jim Perry | .45 | .20 | .04 |
| ☐ 70 | NL Pitching Leaders .... Bob Gibson Gaylord Perry Fergie Jenkins | 1.00 | .45 | .10 |
| ☐ 71 | AL Strikeout Leaders ... Sam McDowell Mickey Lolich Bob Johnson | .45 | .20 | .04 |
| ☐ 72 | NL Strikeout Leaders ... Tom Seaver Bob Gibson Fergie Jenkins | 1.00 | .45 | .10 |
| ☐ 73 | George Brunet .......... | .22 | .09 | .02 |
| ☐ 74 | Twins Rookies .......... Pete Hamm Jim Nettles | .22 | .09 | .02 |
| ☐ 75 | Gary Nolan ............ | .22 | .09 | .02 |
| ☐ 76 | Ted Savage ............ | .22 | .09 | .02 |
| ☐ 77 | Mike Compton .......... | .22 | .09 | .02 |
| ☐ 78 | Jim Spencer ........... | .22 | .09 | .02 |
| ☐ 79 | Wade Blasingame ...... | .22 | .09 | .02 |

| | | MINT | VG-E | F-G |
|---|---|---|---|---|
| ☐ 80 | Bill Melton ............ | .22 | .09 | .02 |
| ☐ 81 | Felix Millan ........... | .22 | .09 | .02 |
| ☐ 82 | Casey Cox ............ | .22 | .09 | .02 |
| ☐ 83 | Met Rookies .......... Tim Foli Randy Bobb | .30 | .12 | .03 |
| ☐ 84 | Marcel Lachemann ...... | .22 | .09 | .02 |
| ☐ 85 | Bill Grabarkewitz ...... | .22 | .09 | .02 |
| ☐ 86 | Mike Kilkenny ......... | .22 | .09 | .02 |
| ☐ 87 | Jack Heidemann ....... | .22 | .09 | .02 |
| ☐ 88 | Hal King ............. | .22 | .09 | .02 |
| ☐ 89 | Ken Brett ............. | .22 | .09 | .02 |
| ☐ 90 | Joe Pepitone .......... | .30 | .12 | .03 |
| ☐ 91 | Bob Lemon ........... | .75 | .35 | .07 |
| ☐ 92 | Fred Wenz ............ | .22 | .09 | .02 |
| ☐ 93 | Senators Rookies ...... Norm McRae Denny Riddleberger | .22 | .09 | .02 |
| ☐ 94 | Don Hahn ............. | .22 | .09 | .02 |
| ☐ 95 | Luis Tiant ............ | .55 | .25 | .05 |
| ☐ 96 | Joe Hague ............ | .22 | .09 | .02 |
| ☐ 97 | Floyd Wicker .......... | .22 | .09 | .02 |
| ☐ 98 | Joe Decker ........... | .22 | .09 | .02 |
| ☐ 99 | Mark Belanger ........ | .30 | .12 | .03 |
| ☐ 100 | Pete Rose ............ | 27.00 | 10.00 | 2.00 |
| ☐ 101 | Les Cain ............. | .22 | .09 | .02 |
| ☐ 102 | Astros Rookies ........ Ken Forsch Larry Howard | .40 | .18 | .04 |
| ☐ 103 | Rich Severinson ....... | .22 | .09 | .02 |
| ☐ 104 | Dan Frisella .......... | .22 | .09 | .02 |
| ☐ 105 | Tony Conigliaro ........ | .40 | .18 | .04 |
| ☐ 106 | Tom Dukes ........... | .22 | .09 | .02 |
| ☐ 107 | Roy Foster ........... | .22 | .09 | .02 |
| ☐ 108 | John Cumberland ...... | .22 | .09 | .02 |
| ☐ 109 | Steve Hovley ......... | .22 | .09 | .02 |
| ☐ 110 | Bill Mazeroski ........ | .40 | .18 | .04 |
| ☐ 111 | Yankee Rookies ....... Loyd Colson Bobby Mitchell | .22 | .09 | .02 |
| ☐ 112 | Manny Mota ........... | .30 | .12 | .03 |
| ☐ 113 | Jerry Crider .......... | .22 | .09 | .02 |
| ☐ 114 | Billy Conigliaro ....... | .22 | .09 | .02 |
| ☐ 115 | Donn Clendenon ....... | .22 | .09 | .02 |
| ☐ 116 | Ken Sanders .......... | .22 | .09 | .02 |
| ☐ 117 | Ted Simmons .......... | 4.25 | 1.75 | .40 |
| ☐ 118 | Cookie Rojas .......... | .22 | .09 | .02 |
| ☐ 119 | Frank Lucchesi ........ | .22 | .09 | .02 |
| ☐ 120 | Willie Horton .......... | .30 | .12 | .03 |
| ☐ 121 | Cubs Rookies ......... Jim Dunegan Roe Skidmore | .22 | .09 | .02 |

| | MINT | VG-E | F-G |
|---|---|---|---|
| ☐ 122 Eddie Watt | .22 | .09 | .02 |
| ☐ 123 Checklist 2nd Series | .60 | .12 | .02 |
| ☐ 124 Don Gullett | .30 | .12 | .03 |
| ☐ 125 Ray Fosse | .22 | .09 | .02 |
| ☐ 126 Danny Coombs | .22 | .09 | .02 |
| ☐ 127 Danny Thompson | .22 | .09 | .02 |
| ☐ 128 Frank Johnson | .22 | .09 | .02 |
| ☐ 129 Aurelio Monteagudo | .22 | .09 | .02 |
| ☐ 130 Denis Menke | .22 | .09 | .02 |
| ☐ 131 Curt Blefary | .22 | .09 | .02 |
| ☐ 132 Jose Laboy | .22 | .09 | .02 |
| ☐ 133 Mickey Lolich | .55 | .25 | .05 |
| ☐ 134 Jose Arcia | .22 | .09 | .02 |
| ☐ 135 Rick Monday | .30 | .12 | .03 |
| ☐ 136 Duffy Dyer | .22 | .09 | .02 |
| ☐ 137 Marcelino Lopez | .22 | .09 | .02 |
| ☐ 138 Phillies Rookies | .30 | .12 | .03 |
| Joe Lis | | | |
| Willie Montanez | | | |
| ☐ 139 Paul Casanova | .22 | .09 | .02 |
| ☐ 140 Gaylord Perry | 2.75 | 1.25 | .27 |
| ☐ 141 Frank Quilici | .22 | .09 | .02 |
| ☐ 142 Mack Jones | .22 | .09 | .02 |
| ☐ 143 Steve Blass | .30 | .12 | .02 |
| ☐ 144 Jackie Hernandez | .22 | .09 | .02 |
| ☐ 145 Bill Singer | .22 | .09 | .02 |
| ☐ 146 Ralph Houk | .30 | .12 | .03 |
| ☐ 147 Bob Priddy | .22 | .09 | .02 |
| ☐ 148 John Mayberry | .30 | .12 | .03 |
| ☐ 149 Mike Hershberger | .22 | .09 | .02 |
| ☐ 150 Sam McDowell | .30 | .12 | .03 |
| ☐ 151 Tommy Davis | .40 | .18 | .04 |
| ☐ 152 Angels Rookies | .22 | .09 | .02 |
| Lloyd Allen | | | |
| Winston Llenas | | | |
| ☐ 153 Gary Ross | .22 | .09 | .02 |
| ☐ 154 Cesar Gutierrez | .22 | .09 | .02 |
| ☐ 155 Ken Henderson | .22 | .09 | .02 |
| ☐ 156 Bart Johnson | .22 | .09 | .02 |
| ☐ 157 Bob Bailey | .22 | .09 | .02 |
| ☐ 158 Jerry Reuss | .55 | .25 | .05 |
| ☐ 159 Jarvis Tatum | .22 | .09 | .02 |
| ☐ 160 Tom Seaver | 9.00 | 4.25 | .90 |
| ☐ 161 Coin Checklist | .90 | .15 | .03 |
| ☐ 162 Jack Billingham | .22 | .09 | .02 |
| ☐ 163 Buck Martinez | .22 | .09 | .02 |
| ☐ 164 Reds Rookies: | .45 | .20 | .04 |
| Frank Duffy | | | |
| Milt Wilcox | | | |
| ☐ 165 Cesar Tovar | .22 | .09 | .02 |
| ☐ 166 Joe Hoerner | .22 | .09 | .02 |
| ☐ 167 Tom Grieve | .30 | .12 | .03 |
| ☐ 168 Bruce Dal Canton | .22 | .09 | .02 |

| | MINT | VG-E | F-G |
|---|---|---|---|
| ☐ 169 Ed Herrmann | .22 | .09 | .02 |
| ☐ 170 Mike Cuellar | .30 | .12 | .03 |
| ☐ 171 Bobby Wine | .22 | .09 | .02 |
| ☐ 172 Duke Sims | .22 | .09 | .02 |
| ☐ 173 Gil Garrido | .22 | .09 | .02 |
| ☐ 174 Dave LaRoche | .22 | .09 | .02 |
| ☐ 175 Jim Hickman | .22 | .09 | .02 |
| ☐ 176 Red Sox Rookies | .22 | .09 | .02 |
| Bob Montgomery | | | |
| Doug Griffin | | | |
| ☐ 177 Hal McRae | .40 | .18 | .04 |
| ☐ 178 Dave Duncan | .22 | .09 | .02 |
| ☐ 179 Mike Corkins | .22 | .09 | .02 |
| ☐ 180 Al Kaline | 3.25 | 1.50 | .32 |
| ☐ 181 Hal Lanier | .30 | .12 | .03 |
| ☐ 182 Al Downing | .22 | .09 | .02 |
| ☐ 183 Gil Hodges | 1.75 | .85 | .17 |
| ☐ 184 Stan Bahnsen | .22 | .09 | .02 |
| ☐ 185 Julian Javier | .22 | .09 | .02 |
| ☐ 186 Bob Spence | .22 | .09 | .02 |
| ☐ 187 Ted Abernathy | .22 | .09 | .02 |
| ☐ 188 Dodgers Rookies | .50 | .22 | .05 |
| Bob Valentine | | | |
| Mike Strahler | | | |
| ☐ 189 George Mitterwald | .22 | .09 | .02 |
| ☐ 190 Bob Tolan | .22 | .09 | .02 |
| ☐ 191 Mike Andrews | .22 | .09 | .02 |
| ☐ 192 Billy Wilson | .22 | .09 | .02 |
| ☐ 193 Bob Grich | 2.00 | .90 | .20 |
| ☐ 194 Mike Lum | .22 | .09 | .02 |
| ☐ 195 AL Playoff Game 1 | .65 | .30 | .06 |
| Powell muscles Twins | | | |
| ☐ 196 AL Playoff Game 2 | .65 | .30 | .06 |
| McNally makes it | | | |
| two straight | | | |
| ☐ 197 AL Playoff Game 3 | 1.00 | .45 | .10 |
| Palmer mows 'em down | | | |
| ☐ 198 AL Playoff Summary | .65 | .30 | .06 |
| Orioles Celebrate | | | |
| ☐ 199 NL Playoff Game 1 | .65 | .30 | .06 |
| Cline pinch-triple | | | |
| decides it | | | |
| ☐ 200 NL Playoff Game 2 | .65 | .30 | .06 |
| Tolan scores for | | | |
| third time | | | |
| ☐ 201 NL Playoff Game 3 | .65 | .30 | .06 |
| Cline scores | | | |
| winning run | | | |
| ☐ 202 NL Playoff Summary | .65 | .30 | .06 |
| Reds Celebrate | | | |
| ☐ 203 Larry Gura | .85 | .40 | .08 |

| | MINT | VG-E | F-G |
|---|---|---|---|
| ☐ 204 Brewers Rookies | .22 | .09 | .02 |
| Bernie Smith | | | |
| George Kopacz | | | |
| ☐ 205 Gerry Moses | .22 | .09 | .02 |
| ☐ 206 Checklist 3rd Series | .60 | .09 | .02 |
| ☐ 207 Alan Foster | .22 | .09 | .02 |
| ☐ 208 Billy Martin | .90 | .40 | .09 |
| ☐ 209 Steve Henko | .22 | .09 | .02 |
| ☐ 210 Rod Carew | 10.00 | 4.75 | 1.00 |
| ☐ 211 Phil Hennigan | .22 | .09 | .02 |
| ☐ 212 Rich Hebner | .22 | .09 | .02 |
| ☐ 213 Frank Baker | .22 | .09 | .02 |
| ☐ 214 Al Ferrara | .22 | .09 | .02 |
| ☐ 215 Diego Segui | .22 | .09 | .02 |
| ☐ 216 Cards Rookies | .22 | .09 | .02 |
| Reggie Cleveland | | | |
| Luis Melendez | | | |
| ☐ 217 Ed Stroud | .22 | .09 | .02 |
| ☐ 218 Tony Cloninger | .22 | .09 | .02 |
| ☐ 219 Elrod Hendricks | .22 | .09 | .02 |
| ☐ 220 Ron Santo | .45 | .20 | .04 |
| ☐ 221 Dave Morehead | .22 | .09 | .02 |
| ☐ 222 Bob Watson | .35 | .15 | .03 |
| ☐ 223 Cecil Upshaw | .22 | .09 | .02 |
| ☐ 224 Alan Gallagher | .22 | .09 | .02 |
| ☐ 225 Gary Peters | .22 | .09 | .02 |
| ☐ 226 Bill Russell | .30 | .12 | .03 |
| ☐ 227 Floyd Weaver | .22 | .09 | .02 |
| ☐ 228 Wayne Garrett | .22 | .09 | .02 |
| ☐ 229 Jim Hannan | .22 | .09 | .02 |
| ☐ 230 Willie Stargell | 2.75 | 1.25 | .27 |
| ☐ 231 Indians Rookies | .35 | .15 | .03 |
| Vince Colbert | | | |
| John Lowenstein | | | |
| ☐ 232 John Strohmayer | .22 | .09 | .02 |
| ☐ 233 Larry Bowa | .80 | .40 | .08 |
| ☐ 234 Jim Lyttle | .22 | .09 | .02 |
| ☐ 235 Nate Colbert | .22 | .09 | .02 |
| ☐ 236 Bob Humphreys | .22 | .09 | .02 |
| ☐ 237 Cesar Cedeno | 1.50 | .70 | .15 |
| ☐ 238 Chuck Dobson | .22 | .09 | .02 |
| ☐ 239 Red Schoendienst | .40 | .18 | .04 |
| ☐ 240 Clyde Wright | .22 | .09 | .02 |
| ☐ 241 Dave Nelson | .22 | .09 | .02 |
| ☐ 242 Jim Ray | .22 | .09 | .02 |
| ☐ 243 Carlos May | .22 | .09 | .02 |
| ☐ 244 Bob Tillman | .22 | .09 | .02 |
| ☐ 245 Jim Kaat | .90 | .40 | .09 |
| ☐ 246 Tony Taylor | .22 | .09 | .02 |
| ☐ 247 Royals Rookies | .40 | .18 | .04 |
| Jerry Cram | | | |
| Paul Splittorff | | | |
| ☐ 248 Hoyt Wilhelm | 1.75 | .85 | .17 |

| | MINT | VG-E | F-G |
|---|---|---|---|
| ☐ 249 Chico Salmon | .22 | .09 | .02 |
| ☐ 250 Johnny Bench | 11.00 | 5.25 | 1.10 |
| ☐ 251 Frank Reberger | .22 | .09 | .02 |
| ☐ 252 Eddie Leon | .22 | .09 | .02 |
| ☐ 253 Bill Sudakis | .22 | .09 | .02 |
| ☐ 254 Cal Koonce | .22 | .09 | .02 |
| ☐ 255 Bob Robertson | .22 | .09 | .02 |
| ☐ 256 Tony Gonzalez | .22 | .09 | .02 |
| ☐ 257 Nelson Briles | .22 | .09 | .02 |
| ☐ 258 Dick Green | .22 | .09 | .02 |
| ☐ 259 Dave Marshall | .22 | .09 | .02 |
| ☐ 260 Tommy Harper | .22 | .09 | .02 |
| ☐ 261 Darold Knowles | .22 | .09 | .02 |
| ☐ 262 Padres Rookies | .22 | .09 | .02 |
| Jim Williams | | | |
| Dave Robinson | | | |
| ☐ 263 John Ellis | .22 | .09 | .02 |
| ☐ 264 Joe Morgan | 2.00 | .90 | .20 |
| ☐ 265 Jim Northrup | .22 | .09 | .02 |
| ☐ 266 Bill Stoneman | .22 | .09 | .02 |
| ☐ 267 Rich Morales | .22 | .09 | .02 |
| ☐ 268 Phillies Team | .45 | .20 | .04 |
| ☐ 269 Gail Hopkins | .22 | .09 | .02 |
| ☐ 270 Rico Carty | .35 | .15 | .03 |
| ☐ 271 Bill Zepp | .22 | .09 | .02 |
| ☐ 272 Tommy Helms | .22 | .09 | .02 |
| ☐ 273 Pete Richert | .22 | .09 | .02 |
| ☐ 274 Ron Slocum | .22 | .09 | .02 |
| ☐ 275 Vada Pinson | .50 | .22 | .05 |
| ☐ 276 Giants Rookies | 6.50 | 3.00 | .65 |
| Mike Davison | | | |
| George Foster | | | |
| ☐ 277 Gary Waslewski | .22 | .09 | .02 |
| ☐ 278 Jerry Grote | .22 | .09 | .02 |
| ☐ 279 Lefty Phillips | .22 | .09 | .02 |
| ☐ 280 Fergie Jenkins | 1.00 | .45 | .10 |
| ☐ 281 Danny Walton | .22 | .09 | .02 |
| ☐ 282 Jose Pagan | .22 | .09 | .02 |
| ☐ 283 Dick Such | .22 | .09 | .02 |
| ☐ 284 Jim Gosger | .22 | .09 | .02 |
| ☐ 285 Sal Bando | .30 | .12 | .03 |
| ☐ 286 Jerry McNertney | .22 | .09 | .02 |
| ☐ 287 Mike Fiore | .22 | .09 | .02 |
| ☐ 288 Joe Moeller | .22 | .09 | .02 |
| ☐ 289 White Sox Team | .45 | .20 | .04 |
| ☐ 290 Tony Oliva | .90 | .40 | .09 |
| ☐ 291 George Culver | .22 | .09 | .02 |
| ☐ 292 Jay Johnstone | .30 | .12 | .02 |
| ☐ 293 Pat Corrales | .22 | .09 | .02 |
| ☐ 294 Steve Dunning | .22 | .09 | .02 |
| ☐ 295 Bobby Bonds | .60 | .28 | .06 |
| ☐ 296 Tom Timmermann | .22 | .09 | .02 |
| ☐ 297 Johnny Briggs | .22 | .09 | .02 |

|  | MINT | VG-E | F-G |
|---|---|---|---|
| ☐ 298 Jim Nelson | .22 | .09 | .02 |
| ☐ 299 Ed Kirkpatrick | .22 | .09 | .02 |
| ☐ 300 Brooks Robinson | 4.25 | 2.00 | .42 |
| ☐ 301 Earl Wilson | .22 | .09 | .02 |
| ☐ 302 Phil Gagliano | .22 | .09 | .02 |
| ☐ 303 Lindy McDaniel | .22 | .09 | .02 |
| ☐ 304 Ron Brand | .22 | .09 | .02 |
| ☐ 305 Reggie Smith | .55 | .25 | .05 |
| ☐ 306 Jim Nash | .22 | .09 | .02 |
| ☐ 307 Don Wert | .22 | .09 | .02 |
| ☐ 308 Cardinals Team | .45 | .20 | .04 |
| ☐ 309 Dick Ellsworth | .22 | .09 | .02 |
| ☐ 310 Tommie Agee | .22 | .09 | .02 |
| ☐ 311 Lee Stange | .22 | .09 | .02 |
| ☐ 312 Harry Walker | .22 | .09 | .02 |
| ☐ 313 Tom Hall | .22 | .09 | .02 |
| ☐ 314 Jeff Torborg | .22 | .09 | .02 |
| ☐ 315 Ron Fairly | .22 | .09 | .02 |
| ☐ 316 Fred Scherman | .22 | .09 | .02 |
| ☐ 317 Athletic Rookies | .22 | .09 | .02 |
| Jim Driscoll | | | |
| Angel Mangual | | | |
| ☐ 318 Rudy May | .22 | .09 | .02 |
| ☐ 319 Ty Cline | .22 | .09 | .02 |
| ☐ 320 Dave McNally | .30 | .12 | .03 |
| ☐ 321 Tom Matchick | .22 | .09 | .02 |
| ☐ 322 Jim Beauchamp | .22 | .09 | .02 |
| ☐ 323 Billy Champion | .22 | .09 | .02 |
| ☐ 324 Graig Nettles | 1.75 | .85 | .17 |
| ☐ 325 Juan Marichal | 2.25 | 1.00 | .22 |
| ☐ 326 Richie Scheinblum | .22 | .09 | .02 |
| ☐ 327 World Series Game 1 | .65 | .30 | .06 |
| Powell homers to | | | |
| opposite field | | | |
| ☐ 328 World Series Game 2 | .65 | .30 | .06 |
| Don Buford | | | |
| ☐ 329 World Series Game 3 | 1.25 | .60 | .12 |
| Frank Robinson | | | |
| shows muscle | | | |
| ☐ 330 World Series Game 4 | .65 | .30 | .06 |
| Reds stay alive | | | |
| ☐ 331 World Series Game 5 | 1.25 | .60 | .12 |
| Brooks Robinson | | | |
| commits robbery | | | |
| ☐ 332 World Series Summary | .65 | .30 | .06 |
| Orioles Celebrate | | | |
| ☐ 333 Clay Kirby | .22 | .09 | .02 |
| ☐ 334 Roberto Pena | .22 | .09 | .02 |
| ☐ 335 Jerry Koosman | .50 | .22 | .05 |
| ☐ 336 Tigers Team | .45 | .20 | .04 |
| ☐ 337 Jesus Alou | .22 | .09 | .02 |
| ☐ 338 Gene Tenace | .30 | .12 | .03 |
| ☐ 339 Wayne Simpson | .22 | .09 | .02 |

|  | MINT | VG-E | F-G |
|---|---|---|---|
| ☐ 340 Rico Petrocelli | .30 | .12 | .03 |
| ☐ 341 Steve Garvey | 35.00 | 16.50 | 3.50 |
| ☐ 342 Frank Tepedino | .22 | .09 | .02 |
| ☐ 343 Pirates Rookies | .22 | .09 | .02 |
| Ed Acosta | | | |
| Milt May | | | |
| ☐ 344 Ellie Rodriguez | .22 | .09 | .02 |
| ☐ 345 Joe Horlen | .22 | .09 | .02 |
| ☐ 346 Lum Harris | .22 | .09 | .02 |
| ☐ 347 Ted Uhlaender | .22 | .09 | .02 |
| ☐ 348 Fred Norman | .22 | .09 | .02 |
| ☐ 349 Rich Reese | .22 | .09 | .02 |
| ☐ 350 Billy Williams | 1.25 | .60 | .12 |
| ☐ 351 Jim Shellenback | .22 | .09 | .02 |
| ☐ 352 Denny Doyle | .22 | .09 | .02 |
| ☐ 353 Carl Taylor | .22 | .09 | .02 |
| ☐ 354 Don McMahon | .22 | .09 | .02 |
| ☐ 355 Bud Harrelson | .22 | .09 | .02 |
| ☐ 356 Bob Locker | .22 | .09 | .02 |
| ☐ 357 Reds Team | .65 | .30 | .06 |
| ☐ 358 Danny Cater | .22 | .09 | .02 |
| ☐ 359 Ron Reed | .22 | .09 | .02 |
| ☐ 360 Jim Fregosi | .30 | .12 | .03 |
| ☐ 361 Don Sutton | 1.10 | .50 | .11 |
| ☐ 362 Orioles Rookies | .22 | .09 | .02 |
| Mike Adamson | | | |
| Roger Freed | | | |
| ☐ 363 Mike Nagy | .22 | .09 | .02 |
| ☐ 364 Tommy Dean | .22 | .09 | .02 |
| ☐ 365 Bob Johnson | .22 | .09 | .02 |
| ☐ 366 Ron Stone | .22 | .09 | .02 |
| ☐ 367 Dalton Jones | .22 | .09 | .02 |
| ☐ 368 Bob Veale | .22 | .09 | .02 |
| ☐ 369 Checklist 4th Series | .65 | .12 | .02 |
| ☐ 370 Joe Torre | .90 | .40 | .09 |
| ☐ 371 Jack Hiatt | .22 | .09 | .02 |
| ☐ 372 Lew Krausse | .22 | .09 | .02 |
| ☐ 373 Tom McCraw | .22 | .09 | .02 |
| ☐ 374 Clete Boyer | .30 | .12 | .03 |
| ☐ 375 Steve Hargan | .22 | .09 | .02 |
| ☐ 376 Expos Rookies | .22 | .09 | .02 |
| Clyde Mashore | | | |
| Ernie McAnally | | | |
| ☐ 377 Greg Garrett | .22 | .09 | .02 |
| ☐ 378 Tito Fuentes | .22 | .09 | .02 |
| ☐ 379 Wayne Granger | .22 | .09 | .02 |
| ☐ 380 Ted Williams | 2.50 | 1.15 | .25 |
| ☐ 381 Fred Gladding | .22 | .09 | .02 |
| ☐ 382 Jake Gibbs | .22 | .09 | .02 |
| ☐ 383 Rod Gaspar | .22 | .09 | .02 |
| ☐ 384 Rollie Fingers | 1.75 | .85 | .17 |
| ☐ 385 Maury Wills | .90 | .40 | .09 |
| ☐ 386 Red Sox Team | .65 | .30 | .06 |

| | | MINT | VG-E | F-G |
|---|---|---|---|---|
| ☐ 387 | Ron Herbel | .22 | .09 | .02 |
| ☐ 388 | Al Oliver | 2.25 | 1.00 | .22 |
| ☐ 389 | Ed Brinkman | .22 | .09 | .02 |
| ☐ 390 | Glenn Beckert | .30 | .12 | .03 |
| ☐ 391 | Twins Rookies | .22 | .09 | .02 |
| | Steve Brye | | | |
| | Cotton Nash | | | |
| ☐ 392 | Grant Jackson | .22 | .09 | .02 |
| ☐ 393 | Merv Rettenmund | .22 | .09 | .02 |
| ☐ 394 | Clay Carroll | .22 | .09 | .02 |
| ☐ 395 | Roy White | .30 | .12 | .03 |
| ☐ 396 | Dick Schofield | .22 | .09 | .02 |
| ☐ 397 | Alvin Dark | .30 | .12 | .03 |
| ☐ 398 | Howie Reed | .22 | .09 | .02 |
| ☐ 399 | Jim French | .22 | .09 | .02 |
| ☐ 400 | Hank Aaron | 12.00 | 5.50 | 1.20 |
| ☐ 401 | Tom Murphy | .22 | .09 | .02 |
| ☐ 402 | Dodgers Team | .65 | .30 | .06 |
| ☐ 403 | Joe Coleman | .22 | .09 | .02 |
| ☐ 404 | Astros Rookies | .22 | .09 | .02 |
| | Buddy Harris | | | |
| | Roger Metzger | | | |
| ☐ 405 | Leo Cardenas | .22 | .09 | .02 |
| ☐ 406 | Ray Sedecki | .22 | .09 | .02 |
| ☐ 407 | Joe Rudi | .30 | .12 | .03 |
| ☐ 408 | Rafael Robles | .22 | .09 | .02 |
| ☐ 409 | Don Pavletich | .22 | .09 | .02 |
| ☐ 410 | Ken Holtzman | .35 | .15 | .03 |
| ☐ 411 | George Spriggs | .22 | .09 | .02 |
| ☐ 412 | Jerry Johnson | .22 | .09 | .02 |
| ☐ 413 | Pat Kelly | .22 | .09 | .02 |
| ☐ 414 | Woodie Fryman | .22 | .09 | .02 |
| ☐ 415 | Mike Hegan | .22 | .09 | .02 |
| ☐ 416 | Gene Alley | .22 | .09 | .02 |
| ☐ 417 | Dick Hall | .22 | .09 | .02 |
| ☐ 418 | Adolfo Phillips | .22 | .09 | .02 |
| ☐ 419 | Ron Hansen | .22 | .09 | .02 |
| ☐ 420 | Jim Merritt | .22 | .09 | .02 |
| ☐ 421 | John Stephenson | .22 | .09 | .02 |
| ☐ 422 | Frank Bertaina | .22 | .09 | .02 |
| ☐ 423 | Tigers Rookies | .22 | .09 | .02 |
| | Dennis Saunders | | | |
| | Tim Marting | | | |
| ☐ 424 | R. Rodriquez | .22 | .09 | .02 |
| ☐ 425 | Doug Rader | .30 | .12 | .03 |
| ☐ 426 | Chris Cannizzaro | .22 | .09 | .02 |
| ☐ 427 | Bernie Allen | .22 | .09 | .02 |
| ☐ 428 | Jim McAndrew | .22 | .09 | .02 |
| ☐ 429 | Chuck Hinton | .22 | .09 | .02 |
| ☐ 430 | Wes Parker | .30 | .12 | .03 |
| ☐ 431 | Tom Burgmeier | .22 | .09 | .02 |
| ☐ 432 | Bob Didier | .22 | .09 | .02 |

| | | MINT | VG-E | F-G |
|---|---|---|---|---|
| ☐ 433 | Skip Lockwood | .22 | .09 | .02 |
| ☐ 434 | Gary Sutherland | .22 | .09 | .02 |
| ☐ 435 | Jose Cardenal | .22 | .09 | .02 |
| ☐ 436 | Wilbur Wood | .30 | .12 | .03 |
| ☐ 437 | Danny Murtaugh | .22 | .09 | .02 |
| ☐ 438 | Mike McCormick | .30 | .12 | .02 |
| ☐ 439 | Phillies Rookies | 2.00 | .90 | .20 |
| | Greg Luzinski | | | |
| | Scott Reid | | | |
| ☐ 440 | Bert Campaneris | .30 | .12 | .03 |
| ☐ 441 | Milt Pappas | .30 | .12 | .03 |
| ☐ 442 | Angels Team | .45 | .20 | .04 |
| ☐ 443 | Rich Robertson | .22 | .09 | .02 |
| ☐ 444 | Jimmie Price | .22 | .09 | .02 |
| ☐ 445 | Art Shamsky | .22 | .09 | .02 |
| ☐ 446 | Bobby Bolin | .22 | .09 | .02 |
| ☐ 447 | Cesar Geronimo | .22 | .09 | .02 |
| ☐ 448 | Dave Roberts | .22 | .09 | .02 |
| ☐ 449 | Brant Alyea | .22 | .09 | .02 |
| ☐ 450 | Bob Gibson | 3.50 | 1.65 | .35 |
| ☐ 451 | Joe Keough | .22 | .09 | .02 |
| ☐ 452 | John Boccabella | .22 | .09 | .02 |
| ☐ 453 | Terry Crowley | .22 | .09 | .02 |
| ☐ 454 | Mike Paul | .22 | .09 | .02 |
| ☐ 455 | Don Kessinger | .30 | .12 | .03 |
| ☐ 456 | Bob Meyer | .22 | .09 | .02 |
| ☐ 457 | Willie Smith | .22 | .09 | .02 |
| ☐ 458 | White Sox Rookies | .22 | .09 | .02 |
| | Ron Lolich | | | |
| | Dave Lemonds | | | |
| ☐ 459 | Jim LeFebvre | .22 | .09 | .02 |
| ☐ 460 | Fritz Peterson | .22 | .09 | .02 |
| ☐ 461 | Jim Ray Hart | .30 | .12 | .02 |
| ☐ 462 | Senators Team | .45 | .20 | .04 |
| ☐ 463 | Tom Kelley | .22 | .09 | .02 |
| ☐ 464 | Aurelio Rodriguez | .22 | .09 | .02 |
| ☐ 465 | Tim McCarver | .40 | .18 | .04 |
| ☐ 466 | Ken Berry | .22 | .09 | .02 |
| ☐ 467 | Al Santorini | .22 | .09 | .02 |
| ☐ 468 | Frank Fernandez | .22 | .09 | .02 |
| ☐ 469 | Bob Aspromonte | .22 | .09 | .02 |
| ☐ 470 | Bob Oliver | .22 | .09 | .02 |
| ☐ 471 | Tom Griffin | .22 | .09 | .02 |
| ☐ 472 | Ken Rudolph | .22 | .09 | .02 |
| ☐ 473 | Gary Wagner | .22 | .09 | .02 |
| ☐ 474 | Jim Fairey | .22 | .09 | .02 |
| ☐ 475 | Ron Perranoski | .30 | .12 | .03 |
| ☐ 476 | Dal Maxvill | .22 | .09 | .02 |
| ☐ 477 | Earl Weaver | .75 | .35 | .07 |
| ☐ 478 | Bernie Carbo | .22 | .09 | .02 |
| ☐ 479 | Dennis Higgins | .22 | .09 | .02 |
| ☐ 480 | Manny Sanguillen | .35 | .15 | .03 |

| | MINT | VG-E | F-G |
|---|---|---|---|
| ☐ 481 Daryl Patterson | .22 | .09 | .02 |
| ☐ 482 Padres Team | .45 | .20 | .04 |
| ☐ 483 Gene Michael | .22 | .09 | .02 |
| ☐ 484 Don Wilson | .22 | .09 | .02 |
| ☐ 485 Ken McMullen | .22 | .09 | .02 |
| ☐ 486 Steve Huntz | .22 | .09 | .02 |
| ☐ 487 Paul Schaal | .22 | .09 | .02 |
| ☐ 488 Jerry Stephenson | .22 | .09 | .02 |
| ☐ 489 Luis Alvarado | .22 | .09 | .02 |
| ☐ 490 Deron Johnson | .22 | .09 | .02 |
| ☐ 491 Jim Hardin | .22 | .09 | .02 |
| ☐ 492 Ken Boswell | .22 | .09 | .02 |
| ☐ 493 Dave May | .22 | .09 | .02 |
| ☐ 494 Braves Rookies | .30 | .12 | .03 |
| Ralph Garr | | | |
| Rick Kester | | | |
| ☐ 495 Felipe Alou | .30 | .12 | .03 |
| ☐ 496 Woody Woodward | .22 | .09 | .02 |
| ☐ 497 Horacio Pina | .22 | .09 | .02 |
| ☐ 498 John Kennedy | .22 | .09 | .02 |
| ☐ 499 Checklist 5th Series | .65 | .12 | .02 |
| ☐ 500 Jim Perry | .45 | .20 | .04 |
| ☐ 501 Andy Etchebarren | .22 | .09 | .02 |
| ☐ 502 Cubs Team | .45 | .20 | .04 |
| ☐ 503 Gates Brown | .22 | .09 | .02 |
| ☐ 504 Ken Wright | .22 | .09 | .02 |
| ☐ 505 Ollie Brown | .22 | .09 | .02 |
| ☐ 506 Bobby Knoop | .22 | .09 | .02 |
| ☐ 507 George Stone | .22 | .09 | .02 |
| ☐ 508 Roger Repoz | .22 | .09 | .02 |
| ☐ 509 Jim Grant | .22 | .09 | .02 |
| ☐ 510 Ken Harrelson | .65 | .30 | .06 |
| ☐ 511 Chris Short | .22 | .09 | .02 |
| ☐ 512 Red Sox Rookies | .22 | .09 | .02 |
| Dick Mills | | | |
| Mike Garman | | | |
| ☐ 513 Nolan Ryan | 9.00 | 4.25 | .90 |
| ☐ 514 Ron Woods | .22 | .09 | .02 |
| ☐ 515 Carl Morton | .22 | .09 | .02 |
| ☐ 516 Ted Kubiak | .22 | .09 | .02 |
| ☐ 517 Charlie Fox | .22 | .09 | .02 |
| ☐ 518 Joe Grzenda | .22 | .09 | .02 |
| ☐ 519 Willie Crawford | .22 | .09 | .02 |
| ☐ 520 Tommy John | 1.50 | .70 | .15 |
| ☐ 521 Leron Lee | .22 | .09 | .02 |
| ☐ 522 Twins Team | .45 | .20 | .04 |
| ☐ 523 John Odom | .22 | .09 | .02 |
| ☐ 524 Mickey Stanley | .50 | .22 | .05 |
| ☐ 525 Ernie Banks | 5.50 | 2.60 | .55 |
| ☐ 526 Ray Jarvis | .40 | .18 | .04 |
| ☐ 527 Cleon Jones | .40 | .18 | .04 |
| ☐ 528 Wally Bunker | .40 | .18 | .04 |

| | MINT | VG-E | F-G |
|---|---|---|---|
| ☐ 529 NL Rookie Infielders | 2.50 | 1.15 | .25 |
| Enzo Hernandez | | | |
| Bill Buckner | | | |
| Marty Perez | | | |
| ☐ 530 Carl Yastrzemski | 14.00 | 6.50 | 1.40 |
| ☐ 531 Mike Torrez | .50 | .22 | .05 |
| ☐ 532 Bill Rigney | .40 | .18 | .04 |
| ☐ 533 Mike Ryan | .40 | .18 | .04 |
| ☐ 534 Luke Walker | .40 | .18 | .04 |
| ☐ 535 Curt Flood | .60 | .28 | .06 |
| ☐ 536 Claude Raymond | .40 | .18 | .04 |
| ☐ 537 Tom Egan | .40 | .18 | .04 |
| ☐ 538 Angel Bravo | .40 | .18 | .04 |
| ☐ 539 Larry Brown | .40 | .18 | .04 |
| ☐ 540 Larry Dierker | .50 | .22 | .05 |
| ☐ 541 Bob Burda | .40 | .18 | .04 |
| ☐ 542 Bob Miller | .40 | .18 | .04 |
| ☐ 543 Yankees Team | .90 | .40 | .09 |
| ☐ 544 Vida Blue | 2.25 | 1.00 | .22 |
| ☐ 545 Dick Dietz | .40 | .18 | .04 |
| ☐ 546 John Matias | .40 | .18 | .04 |
| ☐ 547 Pat Dobson | .60 | .28 | .06 |
| ☐ 548 Don Mason | .40 | .18 | .04 |
| ☐ 549 Jim Brewer | .40 | .18 | .04 |
| ☐ 550 Harmon Killebrew | 4.50 | 2.10 | .45 |
| ☐ 551 Frank Linzy | .40 | .18 | .04 |
| ☐ 552 Buddy Bradford | .40 | .18 | .04 |
| ☐ 553 Kevin Collins | .40 | .18 | .04 |
| ☐ 554 Lowell Palmer | .40 | .18 | .04 |
| ☐ 555 Walt Williams | .40 | .18 | .04 |
| ☐ 556 Jim McGlothlin | .40 | .18 | .04 |
| ☐ 557 Tom Satriano | .40 | .18 | .04 |
| ☐ 558 Hector Torres | .40 | .18 | .04 |
| ☐ 559 AL Rookie Pitchers | .40 | .18 | .04 |
| Terry Cox | | | |
| Bill Gogolewski | | | |
| Gary Jones | | | |
| ☐ 560 Rusty Staub | .90 | .40 | .09 |
| ☐ 561 Syd O'Brien | .40 | .18 | .04 |
| ☐ 562 Dave Guisti | .40 | .18 | .04 |
| ☐ 563 Giants Team | .90 | .40 | .09 |
| ☐ 564 Al Fitzmorris | .40 | .18 | .04 |
| ☐ 565 Jim Wynn | .60 | .28 | .06 |
| ☐ 566 Tim Cullen | .40 | .18 | .04 |
| ☐ 567 Walt Alston | 1.00 | .45 | .10 |
| ☐ 568 Sal Campisi | .40 | .18 | .04 |
| ☐ 569 Ivan Murrell | .40 | .18 | .04 |
| ☐ 570 Jim Palmer | 6.00 | 2.80 | .60 |
| ☐ 571 Ted Sizemore | .40 | .18 | .04 |
| ☐ 572 Jerry Kenney | .40 | .18 | .04 |
| ☐ 573 Ed Kranepool | .50 | .22 | .05 |
| ☐ 574 Jim Bunning | 1.10 | .50 | .11 |

| | MINT | VG-E | F-G |
|---|---|---|---|
| ☐ 575 Bill Freehan | .65 | .30 | .06 |
| ☐ 576 Cubs Rookies | .40 | .18 | .04 |
|     Adrian Garrett | | | |
|     Brock Davis | | | |
|     Garry Jestadt | | | |
| ☐ 577 Jim Lonborg | .60 | .28 | .06 |
| ☐ 578 Ron Hunt | .40 | .18 | .04 |
| ☐ 579 Marty Pattin | .40 | .18 | .04 |
| ☐ 580 Tony Perez | 1.25 | .60 | .12 |
| ☐ 581 Roger Nelson | .40 | .18 | .04 |
| ☐ 582 Dave Cash | .50 | .22 | .05 |
| ☐ 583 Ron Cook | .40 | .18 | .04 |
| ☐ 584 Indians Team | .90 | .40 | .09 |
| ☐ 585 Willie Davis | .60 | .28 | .06 |
| ☐ 586 Dick Woodson | .40 | .18 | .04 |
| ☐ 587 Sonny Jackson | .40 | .18 | .04 |
| ☐ 588 Tom Bradley | .40 | .18 | .04 |
| ☐ 589 Bob Barton | .40 | .18 | .04 |
| ☐ 590 Alex Johnson | .40 | .18 | .04 |
| ☐ 591 Jackie Brown | .40 | .18 | .04 |
| ☐ 592 Randy Hundley | .40 | .18 | .04 |
| ☐ 593 Jack Aker | .40 | .18 | .04 |
| ☐ 594 Cards Rookies | .90 | .40 | .09 |
|     Bob Chlupsa | | | |
|     Bob Stinson | | | |
|     Al Hrabosky | | | |
| ☐ 595 Dave Johnson | .90 | .40 | .09 |
| ☐ 596 Mike Jorgensen | .40 | .18 | .04 |
| ☐ 597 Ken Suarez | .40 | .18 | .04 |
| ☐ 598 Rick Wise | .60 | .28 | .06 |
| ☐ 599 Norm Cash | .90 | .40 | .09 |
| ☐ 600 Willie Mays | 15.00 | 7.00 | 1.50 |
| ☐ 601 Ken Tatum | .40 | .18 | .04 |
| ☐ 602 Marty Martinez | .40 | .18 | .04 |
| ☐ 603 Pirates Team | .90 | .40 | .09 |
| ☐ 604 John Gelnar | .40 | .18 | .04 |
| ☐ 605 Orlando Cepeda | 1.50 | .70 | .15 |
| ☐ 606 Chuck Taylor | .40 | .18 | .04 |
| ☐ 607 Paul Ratliff | .40 | .18 | .04 |
| ☐ 608 Mike Wegener | .40 | .18 | .04 |
| ☐ 609 Leo Durocher | .70 | .32 | .07 |
| ☐ 610 Amos Otis | .65 | .30 | .06 |
| ☐ 611 Tom Phoebus | .40 | .18 | .04 |
| ☐ 612 Indians Rookies | .40 | .18 | .04 |
|     Lou Camilli | | | |
|     Ted Ford | | | |
|     Steve Mingori | | | |
| ☐ 613 Pedro Borbon | .40 | .18 | .04 |
| ☐ 614 Billy Cowan | .40 | .18 | .04 |
| ☐ 615 Mel Stottlemyre | .65 | .30 | .06 |
| ☐ 616 Larry Hisle | .55 | .25 | .05 |
| ☐ 617 Clay Dalrymple | .40 | .18 | .04 |

| | MINT | VG-E | F-G |
|---|---|---|---|
| ☐ 618 Tug McGraw | .90 | .40 | .09 |
| ☐ 619 Checklist 6th Series | .90 | .15 | .03 |
| ☐ 620 Frank Howard | .90 | .40 | .09 |
| ☐ 621 Ron Bryant | .40 | .18 | .04 |
| ☐ 622 Joe LaHoud | .40 | .18 | .04 |
| ☐ 623 Pat Jarvis | .40 | .18 | .04 |
| ☐ 624 Athletics Team | .90 | .40 | .09 |
| ☐ 625 Lou Brock | 6.50 | 3.00 | .65 |
| ☐ 626 Freddie Patek | .40 | .18 | .04 |
| ☐ 627 Steve Hamilton | .40 | .18 | .04 |
| ☐ 628 John Bateman | .40 | .18 | .04 |
| ☐ 629 John Hiller | .40 | .18 | .04 |
| ☐ 630 Roberto Clemente | 12.00 | 5.50 | 1.20 |
| ☐ 631 Eddie Fisher | .40 | .18 | .04 |
| ☐ 632 Darrel Chaney | .40 | .18 | .04 |
| ☐ 633 AL Rookie Outfielders | .40 | .18 | .04 |
|     Bobby Brooks | | | |
|     Pete Koegel | | | |
|     Scott Northey | | | |
| ☐ 634 Phil Regan | .50 | .22 | .05 |
| ☐ 635 Bobby Murcer | 1.10 | .50 | .11 |
| ☐ 636 Denny LeMaster | .40 | .18 | .04 |
| ☐ 637 Dave Bristol | .40 | .18 | .04 |
| ☐ 638 Stan Williams | .40 | .18 | .04 |
| ☐ 639 Tom Haller | .40 | .18 | .04 |
| ☐ 640 Frank Robinson | 7.50 | 3.50 | .75 |
| ☐ 641 Mets Team | 1.20 | .55 | .12 |
| ☐ 642 Jim Roland | .40 | .18 | .04 |
| ☐ 643 Rick Reichardt | .40 | .18 | .04 |
| ☐ 644 Jim Stewart | .90 | .40 | .09 |
| ☐ 645 Jim Maloney | 1.10 | .50 | .11 |
| ☐ 646 Bobby Floyd | .90 | .40 | .09 |
| ☐ 647 Juan Pizarro | .90 | .40 | .09 |
| ☐ 648 Mets Rookies | 1.75 | .85 | .17 |
|     Rich Folkers | | | |
|     Ted Martinez | | | |
|     John Matlack | | | |
| ☐ 649 Sparky Lyle | 1.75 | .85 | .17 |
| ☐ 650 Rich Allen | 3.25 | 1.50 | .32 |
| ☐ 651 Jerry Robertson | .90 | .40 | .09 |
| ☐ 652 Braves Team | 1.50 | .70 | .15 |
| ☐ 653 Russ Snyder | .90 | .40 | .09 |
| ☐ 654 Don Shaw | .90 | .40 | .09 |
| ☐ 655 Mike Epstein | .90 | .40 | .09 |
| ☐ 656 Gerry Nyman | .90 | .40 | .09 |
| ☐ 657 Jose Azcue | .90 | .40 | .09 |
| ☐ 658 Paul Lindblad | .90 | .40 | .09 |
| ☐ 659 Byron Browne | .90 | .40 | .09 |
| ☐ 660 Ray Culp | .90 | .40 | .09 |
| ☐ 661 Chuck Tanner | 1.35 | .60 | .12 |
| ☐ 662 Mike Hedlund | .90 | .40 | .09 |
| ☐ 663 Marv Staehle | .90 | .40 | .09 |

| | MINT | VG-E | F-G |
|---|---|---|---|
| ☐ 664 Rookie Pitchers | .90 | .40 | .09 |
| Archie Reynolds | | | |
| Bob Reynolds | | | |
| Ken Reynolds | | | |
| ☐ 665 Ron Swoboda | .90 | .40 | .09 |
| ☐ 666 Gene Brabender | .90 | .40 | .09 |
| ☐ 667 Pete Ward | .90 | .40 | .09 |
| ☐ 668 Gary Neibauer | .90 | .40 | .09 |
| ☐ 669 Ike Brown | .90 | .40 | .09 |
| ☐ 670 Bill Hands | .90 | .40 | .09 |
| ☐ 671 Bill Voss | .90 | .40 | .09 |
| ☐ 672 Ed Crosby | .90 | .40 | .09 |
| ☐ 673 Gerry Janeski | .90 | .40 | .09 |
| ☐ 674 Expos Team | 1.75 | .85 | .17 |
| ☐ 675 Dave Boswell | .90 | .40 | .09 |
| ☐ 676 Tommie Reynolds | .90 | .40 | .09 |
| ☐ 677 Jack DiLauro | .90 | .40 | .09 |
| ☐ 678 George Thomas | .90 | .40 | .09 |
| ☐ 679 Don O'Riley | .90 | .40 | .09 |
| ☐ 680 Don Mincher | 1.10 | .50 | .11 |
| ☐ 681 Bill Butler | .90 | .40 | .09 |
| ☐ 682 Terry Harmon | .90 | .40 | .09 |
| ☐ 683 Bill Burbach | .90 | .40 | .09 |
| ☐ 684 Curt Motton | .90 | .40 | .09 |
| ☐ 685 Moe Drabowsky | .90 | .40 | .09 |
| ☐ 686 Chico Ruiz | .90 | .40 | .09 |
| ☐ 687 Ron Taylor | .90 | .40 | .09 |
| ☐ 688 Sparky Anderson MGR | 1.75 | .85 | .17 |
| ☐ 689 Frank Baker | .90 | .40 | .09 |
| ☐ 690 Bob Moose | .90 | .40 | .09 |
| ☐ 691 Bob Heise | .90 | .40 | .09 |
| ☐ 692 AL Rookie Pitchers | .90 | .40 | .09 |
| Hal Haydel | | | |
| Rogelio Moret | | | |
| Wayne Twitchell | | | |
| ☐ 693 Jose Pena | .90 | .40 | .09 |
| ☐ 694 Rick Renick | .90 | .40 | .09 |
| ☐ 695 Joe Niekro | 1.75 | .85 | .17 |
| ☐ 696 Jerry Morales | .90 | .40 | .09 |
| ☐ 697 Rickey Clark | .90 | .40 | .09 |
| ☐ 698 Brewers Team | 2.00 | .90 | .20 |
| ☐ 699 Jim Britton | .90 | .40 | .09 |
| ☐ 700 Boog Powell | 2.25 | 1.00 | .22 |
| ☐ 701 Bob Garibaldi | .90 | .40 | .09 |
| ☐ 702 Milt Ramirez | .90 | .40 | .09 |
| ☐ 703 Mike Kekich | .90 | .40 | .09 |
| ☐ 704 J.C. Martin | .90 | .40 | .09 |
| ☐ 705 Dick Selma | .90 | .40 | .09 |
| ☐ 706 Joe Foy | .90 | .40 | .09 |
| ☐ 707 Fred Lasher | .90 | .40 | .09 |
| ☐ 708 Russ Nagelson | .90 | .40 | .09 |

| | MINT | VG-E | F-G |
|---|---|---|---|
| ☐ 709 Rookie Outfielders | 13.00 | 6.00 | 1.30 |
| Dusty Baker | | | |
| Don Baylor | | | |
| Tom Paciorek | | | |
| ☐ 710 Sonny Siebert | .90 | .40 | .09 |
| ☐ 711 Larry Stahl | .90 | .40 | .09 |
| ☐ 712 Jose Martinez | .90 | .40 | .09 |
| ☐ 713 Mike Marshall | 1.35 | .60 | .12 |
| ☐ 714 Dick Williams | 1.10 | .50 | .11 |
| ☐ 715 Horace Clarke | .90 | .40 | .09 |
| ☐ 716 Dave Leonhard | .90 | .40 | .09 |
| ☐ 717 Tommie Aaron | 1.10 | .50 | .11 |
| ☐ 718 Billy Wynne | .90 | .40 | .09 |
| ☐ 719 Jerry May | .90 | .40 | .09 |
| ☐ 720 Matty Alou | 1.10 | .50 | .11 |
| ☐ 721 John Morris | .90 | .40 | .09 |
| ☐ 722 Astros Team | 1.75 | .85 | .17 |
| ☐ 723 Vicente Romo | .90 | .40 | .09 |
| ☐ 724 Tom Tischinski | .90 | .40 | .09 |
| ☐ 725 Gary Gentry | .90 | .40 | .09 |
| ☐ 726 Paul Popovich | .90 | .40 | .09 |
| ☐ 727 Ray Lamb | .90 | .40 | .09 |
| ☐ 728 NL Rookie Outfielders | .90 | .40 | .09 |
| Wayne Redmond | | | |
| Keith Lampard | | | |
| Bernie Williams | | | |
| ☐ 729 Dick Billings | .90 | .40 | .09 |
| ☐ 730 Jim Rooker | .90 | .40 | .09 |
| ☐ 731 Jim Qualls | .90 | .40 | .09 |
| ☐ 732 Bob Reed | .90 | .40 | .09 |
| ☐ 733 Lee Maye | .90 | .40 | .09 |
| ☐ 734 Rob Gardner | .90 | .40 | .09 |
| ☐ 735 Mike Shannon | 1.25 | .60 | .12 |
| ☐ 736 Mel Queen | .90 | .40 | .09 |
| ☐ 737 Preston Gomez | .90 | .40 | .09 |
| ☐ 738 Russ Gibson | .90 | .40 | .09 |
| ☐ 739 Barry Lersch | .90 | .40 | .09 |
| ☐ 740 Luis Aparicio | 4.50 | 2.10 | .45 |
| ☐ 741 Skip Guinn | .90 | .40 | .09 |
| ☐ 742 Royals Team | 1.75 | .85 | .17 |
| ☐ 743 John O'Donoghue | .90 | .40 | .09 |
| ☐ 744 Chuck Manuel | .90 | .40 | .09 |
| ☐ 745 Sandy Alomar | .90 | .40 | .09 |
| ☐ 746 Andy Kosco | .90 | .40 | .09 |
| ☐ 747 NL Rookie Pitchers | .90 | .40 | .09 |
| Al Severinsen | | | |
| Scipio Spinks | | | |
| Balor Moore | | | |
| ☐ 748 John Purdin | .90 | .40 | .09 |
| ☐ 749 Ken Szotkiewicz | .90 | .40 | .09 |
| ☐ 750 Denny McLain | 1.75 | .85 | .17 |
| ☐ 751 Al Weis | .90 | .40 | .09 |
| ☐ 752 Dick Drago | 1.10 | .50 | .11 |

## 1972 TOPPS

The cards in this 787 card set measure 2½" by 3½". The 1972 Topps set contained the most cards ever for a Topps set to that point in time. Features also appearing for the first time were "Boyhood Photos" (KP: 341–348 and 491–498), "In Action" and "Traded Cards" (TR: 751–757). The curved lines of the color picture are a departure from the rectangular designs of other years. There is a series of intermediate scarcity (526–656) and the usual high numbers (657–787).

Complete Set: M-500.00; VG-E-225.00; F-G-40.00

|  | MINT | VG-E | F-G |
|---|---|---|---|
| Common Player (1–132) | .14 | .06 | .01 |
| Common Player (133–394) | .16 | .07 | .01 |
| Common Player (395–525) | .21 | .09 | .02 |
| Common Player (526–656) | .35 | .15 | .03 |
| Common Player (657–787) | .90 | .40 | .09 |

| | | MINT | VG-E | F-G |
|---|---|---|---|---|
| ☐ | 1 Pirates Team | 1.35 | .25 | .05 |
| ☐ | 2 Ray Culp | .14 | .06 | .01 |
| ☐ | 3 Bob Tolan | .14 | .06 | .01 |
| ☐ | 4 Checklist 1st Series | .65 | .10 | .02 |
| ☐ | 5 John Bateman | .14 | .06 | .01 |
| ☐ | 6 Fred Scherman | .14 | .06 | .01 |
| ☐ | 7 Enzo Hernandez | .14 | .06 | .01 |
| ☐ | 8 Ron Swoboda | .14 | .06 | .01 |
| ☐ | 9 Stan Williams | .14 | .06 | .01 |
| ☐ | 10 Amos Otis | .30 | .12 | .03 |
| ☐ | 11 Bobby Valentine | .30 | .12 | .03 |
| ☐ | 12 Jose Cardenal | .14 | .06 | .01 |

| | | MINT | VG-E | F-G |
|---|---|---|---|---|
| ☐ | 13 Joe Grzenda | .14 | .06 | .01 |
| ☐ | 14 Phillies Rookies | .14 | .06 | .01 |
| |     Pete Koegel | | | |
| |     Mike Anderson | | | |
| |     Wayne Twitchell | | | |
| ☐ | 15 Walt Williams | .14 | .06 | .01 |
| ☐ | 16 Mike Jorgensen | .14 | .06 | .01 |
| ☐ | 17 Dave Duncan | .14 | .06 | .01 |
| ☐ | 18 Juan Pizarro | .14 | .06 | .01 |
| ☐ | 19 Billy Cowan | .14 | .06 | .01 |
| ☐ | 20 Don Wilson | .14 | .06 | .01 |
| ☐ | 21 Braves Team | .40 | .18 | .04 |
| ☐ | 22 Rob Gardner | .14 | .06 | .01 |
| ☐ | 23 Ted Kubiak | .14 | .06 | .01 |
| ☐ | 24 Ted Ford | .14 | .06 | .01 |
| ☐ | 25 Bill Singer | .14 | .06 | .01 |
| ☐ | 26 Andy Etchebarren | .14 | .06 | .01 |
| ☐ | 27 Bob Johnson | .14 | .06 | .01 |
| ☐ | 28 Twins Rookies | .14 | .06 | .01 |
| |     Bob Gebhard | | | |
| |     Steve Brye | | | |
| |     Hal Haydel | | | |
| ☐ | 29 Bill Bonham | .14 | .06 | .01 |
| ☐ | 30 Rico Petrocelli | .25 | .10 | .02 |
| ☐ | 31 Cleon Jones | .14 | .06 | .01 |
| ☐ | 32 Jones In Action | .14 | .06 | .01 |
| ☐ | 33 Billy Martin | .85 | .40 | .08 |
| ☐ | 34 Martin In Action | .50 | .22 | .05 |
| ☐ | 35 Jerry Johnson | .14 | .06 | .01 |
| ☐ | 36 Johnson In Action | .14 | .06 | .01 |
| ☐ | 37 Carl Yastrzemski | 8.00 | 3.75 | .80 |
| ☐ | 38 Yastrzemski In Action | 4.00 | 1.85 | .40 |
| ☐ | 39 Bob Barton | .14 | .06 | .01 |
| ☐ | 40 Barton In Action | .14 | .06 | .01 |
| ☐ | 41 Tommy Davis | .25 | .10 | .02 |
| ☐ | 42 Davis In Action | .20 | .09 | .02 |
| ☐ | 43 Rick Wise | .25 | .10 | .02 |
| ☐ | 44 Wise In Action | .20 | .09 | .02 |
| ☐ | 45 Glenn Beckert | .25 | .10 | .02 |
| ☐ | 46 Beckert In Action | .20 | .09 | .02 |
| ☐ | 47 John Ellis | .14 | .06 | .01 |
| ☐ | 48 Ellis In Action | .14 | .06 | .01 |
| ☐ | 49 Willie Mays | 8.00 | 3.75 | .80 |
| ☐ | 50 Mays In Action | 4.00 | 1.85 | .40 |
| ☐ | 51 Harmon Killebrew | 2.00 | .90 | .20 |
| ☐ | 52 Killebrew In Action | 1.00 | .45 | .10 |
| ☐ | 53 Bud Harrelson | .14 | .06 | .01 |
| ☐ | 54 Harrelson In Action | .14 | .06 | .01 |
| ☐ | 55 Clyde Wright | .14 | .06 | .01 |
| ☐ | 56 Rich Chiles | .14 | .06 | .01 |
| ☐ | 57 Bob Oliver | .14 | .06 | .01 |
| ☐ | 58 Ernie McAnally | .14 | .06 | .01 |
| ☐ | 59 Fred Stanley | .14 | .06 | .01 |

|  | MINT | VG-E | F-G |
|---|---|---|---|
| ☐ 60 Manny Sanguillen | .25 | .10 | .02 |
| ☐ 61 Cubs Rookies | .55 | .25 | .05 |
| Burt Hooton |  |  |  |
| Gene Hiser |  |  |  |
| Earl Stephenson |  |  |  |
| ☐ 62 Angel Mangual | .14 | .06 | .01 |
| ☐ 63 Duke Sims | .14 | .06 | .01 |
| ☐ 64 Pete Broberg | .14 | .06 | .01 |
| ☐ 65 Cesar Cedeno | .60 | .28 | .06 |
| ☐ 66 Ray Corbin | .14 | .06 | .01 |
| ☐ 67 Red Schoendienst | .30 | .12 | .03 |
| ☐ 68 Jim York | .14 | .06 | .01 |
| ☐ 69 Roger Freed | .14 | .06 | .01 |
| ☐ 70 Mike Cuellar | .20 | .09 | .02 |
| ☐ 71 Angels Team | .35 | .15 | .03 |
| ☐ 72 Bruce Kison | .45 | .20 | .04 |
| ☐ 73 Steve Huntz | .14 | .06 | .01 |
| ☐ 74 Cecil Upshaw | .14 | .06 | .01 |
| ☐ 75 Bert Campaneris | .30 | .12 | .03 |
| ☐ 76 Don Carrithers | .14 | .06 | .01 |
| ☐ 77 Ron Theobald | .14 | .06 | .01 |
| ☐ 78 Steve Arlin | .14 | .06 | .01 |
| ☐ 79 Red Sox Rookies | 16.00 | 7.50 | 1.60 |
| Mike Garman |  |  |  |
| Cecil Cooper |  |  |  |
| Carlton Fisk |  |  |  |
| ☐ 80 Tony Perez | .90 | .40 | .09 |
| ☐ 81 Mike Hedlund | .14 | .06 | .01 |
| ☐ 82 Ron Woods | .14 | .06 | .01 |
| ☐ 83 Dalton Jones | .14 | .06 | .01 |
| ☐ 84 Vince Colbert | .14 | .06 | .01 |
| ☐ 85 NL Batting Leaders: | .50 | .22 | .05 |
| Joe Torre |  |  |  |
| Ralph Garr |  |  |  |
| Glenn Beckert |  |  |  |
| ☐ 86 AL Batting Leaders: | .50 | .22 | .05 |
| Tony Oliva |  |  |  |
| Bobby Murcer |  |  |  |
| Merv Rettenmund |  |  |  |
| ☐ 87 NL RBI Leaders: | .90 | .40 | .09 |
| Joe Torre |  |  |  |
| Willie Stargell |  |  |  |
| Hank Aaron |  |  |  |
| ☐ 88 AL RBI Leaders: | .65 | .30 | .06 |
| Harmon Killebrew |  |  |  |
| Frank Robinson |  |  |  |
| Reggie Smith |  |  |  |
| ☐ 89 NL Home Run Leaders: | .90 | .40 | .09 |
| Willie Stargell |  |  |  |
| Hank Aaron |  |  |  |
| Lee May |  |  |  |

|  | MINT | VG-E | F-G |
|---|---|---|---|
| ☐ 90 AL Home Run Leaders: | .75 | .35 | .07 |
| Bill Melton |  |  |  |
| Norm Cash |  |  |  |
| Reggie Jackson |  |  |  |
| ☐ 91 NL ERA Leaders: | .65 | .30 | .06 |
| Tom Seaver |  |  |  |
| Dave Roberts |  |  |  |
| (photo actually) |  |  |  |
| Danny Coombs) |  |  |  |
| Don Wilson |  |  |  |
| ☐ 92 AL ERA Leaders: | .65 | .30 | .06 |
| Vida Blue |  |  |  |
| Wilbur Wood |  |  |  |
| Jim Palmer |  |  |  |
| ☐ 93 NL Pitching Leaders: | .90 | .40 | .09 |
| Fergie Jenkins |  |  |  |
| Steve Carlton |  |  |  |
| Al Downing |  |  |  |
| Tom Seaver |  |  |  |
| ☐ 94 AL Pitching Leaders: | .50 | .22 | .05 |
| Mickey Lolich |  |  |  |
| Vida Blue |  |  |  |
| Wilbur Wood |  |  |  |
| ☐ 95 NL Strikeout Leaders: | .65 | .30 | .06 |
| Tom Seaver |  |  |  |
| Fergie Jenkins |  |  |  |
| Bill Stoneman |  |  |  |
| ☐ 96 AL Strikeout Leaders: | .50 | .22 | .05 |
| Mickey Lolich |  |  |  |
| Vida Blue |  |  |  |
| Joe Coleman |  |  |  |
| ☐ 97 Tom Kelley | .14 | .06 | .01 |
| ☐ 98 Chuck Tanner | .25 | .10 | .02 |
| ☐ 99 Ross Grimsley | .14 | .06 | .01 |
| ☐ 100 Frank Robinson | 2.50 | 1.15 | .25 |
| ☐ 101 Astros Rookies | 1.20 | .55 | .12 |
| Bill Greif |  |  |  |
| J.R. Richard |  |  |  |
| Ray Busse |  |  |  |
| ☐ 102 Lloyd Allen | .14 | .06 | .01 |
| ☐ 103 Checklist 2nd Series | .55 | .10 | .02 |
| ☐ 104 Toby Harrah | 1.35 | .60 | .12 |
| ☐ 105 Gary Gentry | .14 | .06 | .01 |
| ☐ 106 Brewers Team | .40 | .18 | .04 |
| ☐ 107 Jose Cruz | 2.25 | 1.00 | .22 |
| ☐ 108 Gary Waslewski | .14 | .06 | .01 |
| ☐ 109 Jerry May | .14 | .06 | .01 |
| ☐ 110 Ron Hunt | .14 | .06 | .01 |
| ☐ 111 Jim Grant | .14 | .06 | .01 |
| ☐ 112 Greg Luzinski | .85 | .40 | .08 |
| ☐ 113 Rogelio Moret | .14 | .06 | .01 |
| ☐ 114 Bill Buckner | .85 | .40 | .08 |
| ☐ 115 Jim Fregosi | .25 | .10 | .02 |

|  | MINT | VG-E | F-G |
|---|---|---|---|
| ☐ 116 Ed Farmer | .20 | .09 | .02 |
| ☐ 117 Cleo James | .14 | .06 | .01 |
| ☐ 118 Skip Lockwood | .14 | .06 | .01 |
| ☐ 119 Marty Perez | .14 | .06 | .01 |
| ☐ 120 Bill Freehan | .30 | .12 | .03 |
| ☐ 121 Ed Sprague | .14 | .06 | .01 |
| ☐ 122 Larry Biittner | .14 | .06 | .01 |
| ☐ 123 Ed Acosta | .14 | .06 | .01 |
| ☐ 124 Yankees Rookies | .14 | .06 | .01 |
|     Alan Closter | | | |
|     Rusty Torres | | | |
|     Roger Hambright | | | |
| ☐ 125 Dave Nelson | .14 | .06 | .01 |
| ☐ 126 Bart Johnson | .14 | .06 | .01 |
| ☐ 127 Duffy Dyer | .14 | .06 | .01 |
| ☐ 128 Eddie Watt | .14 | .06 | .01 |
| ☐ 129 Charlie Fox | .14 | .06 | .01 |
| ☐ 130 Bob Gibson | 2.25 | 1.00 | .22 |
| ☐ 131 Jim Nettles | .14 | .06 | .01 |
| ☐ 132 Joe Morgan | 1.75 | .85 | .17 |
| ☐ 133 Joe Keough | .16 | .07 | .01 |
| ☐ 134 Carl Morton | .16 | .07 | .01 |
| ☐ 135 Vada Pinson | .35 | .15 | .03 |
| ☐ 136 Darrel Chaney | .16 | .07 | .01 |
| ☐ 137 Dick Williams | .25 | .10 | .02 |
| ☐ 138 Mike Kekich | .16 | .07 | .01 |
| ☐ 139 Tim McCarver | .30 | .12 | .03 |
| ☐ 140 Pat Dobson | .25 | .10 | .02 |
| ☐ 141 Mets Rookies | .30 | .12 | .03 |
|     Buzz Capra | | | |
|     Leroy Stanton | | | |
|     Jon Matlack | | | |
| ☐ 142 Chris Chambliss | 1.50 | .70 | .15 |
| ☐ 143 Garry Jestadt | .16 | .07 | .01 |
| ☐ 144 Marty Pattin | .16 | .07 | .01 |
| ☐ 145 Don Kessinger | .25 | .10 | .02 |
| ☐ 146 Steve Kealey | .16 | .07 | .01 |
| ☐ 147 Dave Kingman | 3.00 | 1.40 | .30 |
| ☐ 148 Dick Billings | .16 | .07 | .01 |
| ☐ 149 Gary Neibauer | .16 | .07 | .01 |
| ☐ 150 Norm Cash | .35 | .15 | .03 |
| ☐ 151 Jim Brewer | .16 | .07 | .01 |
| ☐ 152 Gene Clines | .16 | .07 | .01 |
| ☐ 153 Rick Auerbach | .16 | .07 | .01 |
| ☐ 154 Ted Simmons | 1.20 | .55 | .12 |
| ☐ 155 Larry Dierker | .25 | .10 | .02 |
| ☐ 156 Twins Team | .35 | .15 | .03 |
| ☐ 157 Don Gullett | .25 | .10 | .02 |
| ☐ 158 Jerry Kenney | .16 | .07 | .01 |
| ☐ 159 John Boccabella | .16 | .07 | .01 |
| ☐ 160 Andy Messersmith | .25 | .10 | .02 |
| ☐ 161 Brock Davis | .16 | .07 | .01 |

|  | MINT | VG-E | F-G |
|---|---|---|---|
| ☐ 162 Brewers Rookies | .85 | .40 | .08 |
|     Jerry Bell | | | |
|     Darrell Porter | | | |
|     Bob Reynolds | | | |
|     (Porter and Bell | | | |
|     photos switched) | | | |
| ☐ 163 Tug McGraw | .45 | .20 | .04 |
| ☐ 164 McGraw In Action | .25 | .10 | .02 |
| ☐ 165 Chris Speier | .16 | .07 | .01 |
| ☐ 166 Speier In Action | .16 | .07 | .01 |
| ☐ 167 Deron Johnson | .16 | .07 | .01 |
| ☐ 168 Johnson In Action | .16 | .07 | .01 |
| ☐ 169 Vida Blue | .65 | .30 | .06 |
| ☐ 170 Blue In Action | .35 | .15 | .03 |
| ☐ 171 Darrell Evans | .65 | .30 | .06 |
| ☐ 172 Evans In Action | .35 | .15 | .03 |
| ☐ 173 Clay Kirby | .16 | .07 | .01 |
| ☐ 174 Kirby In Action | .16 | .07 | .01 |
| ☐ 175 Tom Haller | .16 | .07 | .01 |
| ☐ 176 Haller In Action | .16 | .07 | .01 |
| ☐ 177 Paul Schaal | .16 | .07 | .01 |
| ☐ 178 Schaal In Action | .16 | .07 | .01 |
| ☐ 179 Dock Ellis | .16 | .07 | .01 |
| ☐ 180 Ellis In Action | .16 | .07 | .01 |
| ☐ 181 Ed Kranepool | .25 | .10 | .02 |
| ☐ 182 Kranepool In Action | .20 | .09 | .02 |
| ☐ 183 Bill Melton | .16 | .07 | .01 |
| ☐ 184 Melton In Actin | .16 | .07 | .01 |
| ☐ 185 Ron Bryant | .16 | .07 | .01 |
| ☐ 186 Bryant In Action | .16 | .07 | .01 |
| ☐ 187 Gates Brown | .20 | .09 | .02 |
| ☐ 188 Frank Lucchesi | .16 | .07 | .01 |
| ☐ 189 Gene Tenace | .25 | .10 | .02 |
| ☐ 190 Dave Giusti | .16 | .07 | .01 |
| ☐ 191 Jeff Burroughs | .45 | .20 | .04 |
| ☐ 192 Cubs Team | .40 | .18 | .04 |
| ☐ 193 Kurt Bevacqua | .16 | .07 | .01 |
| ☐ 194 Fred Norman | .16 | .07 | .01 |
| ☐ 195 Orlando Cepeda | .85 | .40 | .08 |
| ☐ 196 Mel Queen | .16 | .07 | .01 |
| ☐ 197 Johnny Briggs | .16 | .07 | .01 |
| ☐ 198 Dodgers Rookies | .40 | .18 | .04 |
|     Charlie Hough | | | |
|     Bob O'Brien | | | |
|     Mike Strahler | | | |
| ☐ 199 Mike Fiore | .16 | .07 | .01 |
| ☐ 200 Lou Brock | 2.50 | 1.15 | .25 |
| ☐ 201 Phil Roof | .16 | .07 | .01 |
| ☐ 202 Scipio Spinks | .16 | .07 | .01 |
| ☐ 203 Ron Blomberg | .16 | .07 | .01 |
| ☐ 204 Tommy Helms | .16 | .07 | .01 |
| ☐ 205 Dick Drago | .16 | .07 | .01 |

|  | | MINT | VG-E | F-G |
|---|---|---|---|---|
| ☐ 206 | Dal Maxvill | .16 | .07 | .01 |
| ☐ 207 | Tom Egan | .16 | .07 | .01 |
| ☐ 208 | Milt Pappas | .20 | .09 | .02 |
| ☐ 209 | Joe Rudi | .25 | .10 | .02 |
| ☐ 210 | Denny McLain | .50 | .22 | .05 |
| ☐ 211 | Gary Sutherland | .16 | .07 | .01 |
| ☐ 212 | Grant Jackson | .16 | .07 | .01 |
| ☐ 213 | Angels Rookies | .16 | .07 | .01 |
|  | Billy Parker | | | |
|  | Art Kusnyer | | | |
|  | Tom Silverio | | | |
| ☐ 214 | Mike McQueen | .16 | .07 | .01 |
| ☐ 215 | Alex Johnson | .16 | .07 | .01 |
| ☐ 216 | Joe Niekro | .35 | .15 | .03 |
| ☐ 217 | Roger Metzger | .16 | .07 | .01 |
| ☐ 218 | Eddie Kasko | .16 | .07 | .01 |
| ☐ 219 | Rennie Stennett | .25 | .10 | .02 |
| ☐ 220 | Jim Perry | .25 | .10 | .02 |
| ☐ 221 | NL Playoffs: | .55 | .25 | .05 |
|  | Bucs champs | | | |
| ☐ 222 | AL Playoffs: | .85 | .40 | .08 |
|  | Orioles champs | | | |
|  | (Brooks Robinson) | | | |
| ☐ 223 | World Series Game 1 | .55 | .25 | .05 |
|  | (McNally pitching) | | | |
| ☐ 224 | World Series Game 2 | .55 | .25 | .05 |
|  | (B. Robinson and | | | |
|  | Belanger) | | | |
| ☐ 225 | World Series Game 3 | .55 | .25 | .05 |
|  | (Sanguillen scoring) | | | |
| ☐ 226 | World Series Game 4 | 1.50 | .70 | .15 |
|  | (Clemente on 2nd) | | | |
| ☐ 227 | World Series Game 5 | .55 | .25 | .05 |
|  | (Briles pitching) | | | |
| ☐ 228 | World Series Game 6 | .65 | .30 | .06 |
|  | (Frank Robinson and | | | |
|  | Manny Sanguillen) | | | |
| ☐ 229 | World Series Game 7 | .55 | .25 | .05 |
|  | (Blass pitching) | | | |
| ☐ 230 | World Series Summary | .55 | .25 | .05 |
|  | Pirates celebrate | | | |
| ☐ 231 | Casey Cox | .16 | .07 | .01 |
| ☐ 232 | Giants Rookies | .16 | .07 | .01 |
|  | Chris Arnold | | | |
|  | Jim Barr | | | |
|  | Dave Rader | | | |
| ☐ 233 | Jay Johnstone | .25 | .10 | .02 |
| ☐ 234 | Ron Taylor | .16 | .07 | .01 |
| ☐ 235 | Merv Rettenmund | .16 | .07 | .01 |
| ☐ 236 | Jim McGlothlin | .16 | .07 | .01 |
| ☐ 237 | Yankees Team | .60 | .28 | .06 |
| ☐ 238 | Leron Lee | .16 | .07 | .01 |

|  | | MINT | VG-E | F-G |
|---|---|---|---|---|
| ☐ 239 | Tom Timmermann | .16 | .07 | .01 |
| ☐ 240 | Rich Allen | .90 | .40 | .09 |
| ☐ 241 | Rollie Fingers | 1.50 | .70 | .15 |
| ☐ 242 | Don Mincher | .16 | .07 | .01 |
| ☐ 243 | Frank Linzy | .16 | .07 | .01 |
| ☐ 244 | Steve Braun | .16 | .07 | .01 |
| ☐ 245 | Tommie Agee | .16 | .07 | .01 |
| ☐ 246 | Tom Burgmeier | .16 | .07 | .01 |
| ☐ 247 | Milt May | .16 | .07 | .01 |
| ☐ 248 | Tom Bradley | .16 | .07 | .01 |
| ☐ 249 | Garry Walker | .16 | .07 | .01 |
| ☐ 250 | Boog Powell | .55 | .25 | .05 |
| ☐ 251 | Checklist 3 | .55 | .10 | .02 |
| ☐ 252 | Ken Reynolds | .16 | .07 | .01 |
| ☐ 253 | Sandy Alomar | .16 | .07 | .01 |
| ☐ 254 | Boots Day | .16 | .07 | .01 |
| ☐ 255 | Jim Lonborg | .25 | .10 | .02 |
| ☐ 256 | George Foster | 1.75 | .85 | .17 |
| ☐ 257 | Tigers Rookies | .16 | .07 | .01 |
|  | Jim Foor | | | |
|  | Tim Hosley | | | |
|  | Paul Jata | | | |
| ☐ 258 | Randy Hundley | .16 | .07 | .01 |
| ☐ 259 | Sparky Lyle | .30 | .12 | .03 |
| ☐ 260 | Ralph Garr | .25 | .10 | .02 |
| ☐ 261 | Steve Mingori | .16 | .07 | .01 |
| ☐ 262 | Padres Team | .35 | .15 | .03 |
| ☐ 263 | Felipe Alou | .25 | .10 | .02 |
| ☐ 264 | Tommy John | 1.25 | .60 | .12 |
| ☐ 265 | Wes Parker | .25 | .10 | .02 |
| ☐ 266 | Bobby Bolin | .16 | .07 | .01 |
| ☐ 267 | Dave Concepcion | 1.25 | .60 | .12 |
| ☐ 268 | A's Rookies | .16 | .07 | .01 |
|  | Dwain Anderson | | | |
|  | Chris Floethe | | | |
| ☐ 269 | Don Hahn | .16 | .07 | .01 |
| ☐ 270 | Jim Palmer | 3.00 | 1.40 | .30 |
| ☐ 271 | Ken Rudolph | .16 | .07 | .01 |
| ☐ 272 | Mickey Rivers | .75 | .35 | .07 |
| ☐ 273 | Bobby Floyd | .16 | .07 | .01 |
| ☐ 274 | Al Severinsen | .16 | .07 | .01 |
| ☐ 275 | Cesar Tovar | .16 | .07 | .01 |
| ☐ 276 | Gene Mauch | .25 | .10 | .02 |
| ☐ 277 | Elliot Maddox | .16 | .07 | .01 |
| ☐ 278 | Dennis Higgins | .16 | .07 | .01 |
| ☐ 279 | Larry Brown | .16 | .07 | .01 |
| ☐ 280 | Willie McCovey | 3.00 | 1.40 | .30 |
| ☐ 281 | Bill Parsons | .16 | .07 | .01 |
| ☐ 282 | Astros Team | .35 | .15 | .03 |
| ☐ 283 | Darrell Brandon | .16 | .07 | .01 |
| ☐ 284 | Ike Brown | .16 | .07 | .01 |
| ☐ 285 | Gaylord Perry | 2.75 | 1.25 | .27 |

| | MINT | VG-E | F-G |
|---|---|---|---|
| ☐ 286 Gene Alley | .20 | .09 | .02 |
| ☐ 287 Jim Hardin | .16 | .07 | .01 |
| ☐ 288 Johnny Jeter | .16 | .07 | .01 |
| ☐ 289 Syd O'Brien | .16 | .07 | .01 |
| ☐ 290 Sonny Siebert | .16 | .07 | .01 |
| ☐ 291 Hal McRae | .35 | .15 | .03 |
| ☐ 292 McRae In Action | .20 | .09 | .02 |
| ☐ 293 Danny Frisella | .16 | .07 | .01 |
| ☐ 294 Frisella In Action | .16 | .07 | .01 |
| ☐ 295 Dick Dietz | .16 | .07 | .01 |
| ☐ 296 Dietz In Action | .16 | .07 | .01 |
| ☐ 297 Claude Osteen | .25 | .10 | .02 |
| ☐ 298 Osteen In Action | .20 | .09 | .02 |
| ☐ 299 Hank Aaron | 8.00 | 3.75 | .80 |
| ☐ 300 Aaron In Action | 4.00 | 1.85 | .40 |
| ☐ 301 George Mitterwald | .16 | .07 | .01 |
| ☐ 302 Mitterwald In Action | .16 | .07 | .01 |
| ☐ 303 Joe Pepitone | .25 | .10 | .02 |
| ☐ 304 Pepitone In Action | .20 | .09 | .02 |
| ☐ 305 Ken Boswell | .16 | .07 | .01 |
| ☐ 306 Boswell In Action | .16 | .07 | .01 |
| ☐ 307 Steve Renko | .16 | .07 | .01 |
| ☐ 308 Renko In Action | .16 | .07 | .01 |
| ☐ 309 Roberto Clemente | 7.00 | 3.25 | .70 |
| ☐ 310 Clemente In Action | 3.50 | 1.65 | .35 |
| ☐ 311 Clay Carroll | .16 | .07 | .01 |
| ☐ 312 Carroll In Action | .16 | .07 | .01 |
| ☐ 313 Luis Aparicio | 1.75 | .85 | .17 |
| ☐ 314 Aparicio In Action | .90 | .40 | .09 |
| ☐ 315 Paul Splittorff | .25 | .10 | .02 |
| ☐ 316 Cardinals Rookies | .30 | .12 | .03 |
| Jim Bibby | | | |
| Jorge Roque | | | |
| Santiago Guzman | | | |
| ☐ 317 Rich Hand | .16 | .07 | .01 |
| ☐ 318 Sonny Jackson | .16 | .07 | .01 |
| ☐ 319 Aurelio Rodriguez | .16 | .07 | .01 |
| ☐ 320 Steve Blass | .20 | .09 | .02 |
| ☐ 321 Joe LaHoud | .16 | .07 | .01 |
| ☐ 322 Jose Pena | .16 | .07 | .01 |
| ☐ 323 Earl Weaver | .35 | .15 | .03 |
| ☐ 324 Mike Ryan | .16 | .07 | .01 |
| ☐ 325 Mel Stottlemyre | .25 | .10 | .02 |
| ☐ 326 Pat Kelly | .16 | .07 | .01 |
| ☐ 327 Steve Stone | .60 | .28 | .06 |
| ☐ 328 Red Sox Team | .55 | .25 | .05 |
| ☐ 329 Roy Foster | .16 | .07 | .01 |
| ☐ 330 Jim Hunter | 1.50 | .70 | .15 |
| ☐ 331 Stan Swanson | .16 | .07 | .01 |
| ☐ 332 Buck Martinez | .16 | .07 | .01 |
| ☐ 333 Steve Barber | .16 | .07 | .01 |

| | MINT | VG-E | F-G |
|---|---|---|---|
| ☐ 334 Rangers Rookies | .16 | .07 | .01 |
| Bill Fahey | | | |
| Jim Mason | | | |
| Tom Ragland | | | |
| ☐ 335 Bill Hands | .16 | .07 | .01 |
| ☐ 336 Marty Martinez | .16 | .07 | .01 |
| ☐ 337 Mike Kilkenny | .16 | .07 | .01 |
| ☐ 338 Bob Grich | .55 | .25 | .05 |
| ☐ 339 Ron Cook | .16 | .07 | .01 |
| ☐ 340 Roy White | .25 | .10 | .02 |
| KID PICTURES | | | |
| (341–348) | | | |
| ☐ 341 KP: Joe Torre | .30 | .12 | .03 |
| ☐ 342 KP: Wilbur Wood | .20 | .09 | .02 |
| ☐ 343 KP: Willie Stargell | .50 | .22 | .05 |
| ☐ 344 KP: Dave McNally | .20 | .09 | .02 |
| ☐ 345 KP: Rick Wise | .20 | .09 | .02 |
| ☐ 346 KP: Jim Fregosi | .20 | .09 | .02 |
| ☐ 347 KP: Tom Seaver | 1.00 | .45 | .10 |
| ☐ 348 KP: Sal Bando | .20 | .09 | .02 |
| ☐ 349 Al Fitzmorris | .16 | .07 | .01 |
| ☐ 350 Frank Howard | .50 | .22 | .05 |
| ☐ 351 Braves Rookies | .16 | .07 | .01 |
| Tom House | | | |
| Rick Kester | | | |
| Jimmy Britton | | | |
| ☐ 352 Dave LaRoche | .16 | .07 | .01 |
| ☐ 353 Art Shamsky | .16 | .07 | .01 |
| ☐ 354 Tom Murphy | .16 | .07 | .01 |
| ☐ 355 Bob Watson | .30 | .12 | .03 |
| ☐ 356 Gerry Moses | .16 | .07 | .01 |
| ☐ 357 Woodie Fryman | .16 | .07 | .01 |
| ☐ 358 Sparky Anderson | .35 | .15 | .03 |
| ☐ 359 Don Pavletich | .16 | .07 | .01 |
| ☐ 360 Dave Roberts | .16 | .07 | .01 |
| ☐ 361 Mike Andrews | .16 | .07 | .01 |
| ☐ 362 Mets Team | .55 | .25 | .05 |
| ☐ 363 Ron Klimkowski | .16 | .07 | .01 |
| ☐ 364 Johnny Callison | .25 | .10 | .02 |
| ☐ 365 Dick Bosman | .16 | .07 | .01 |
| ☐ 366 Jimmy Rosario | .16 | .07 | .01 |
| ☐ 367 Mike Andrews | .16 | .07 | .01 |
| ☐ 368 Danny Thompson | .16 | .07 | .01 |
| ☐ 369 Jim LeFebvre | .16 | .07 | .01 |
| ☐ 370 Don Buford | .16 | .07 | .01 |
| ☐ 371 Denny LeMaster | .16 | .07 | .01 |
| ☐ 372 Royals Rookies | .16 | .07 | .01 |
| Lance Clemons | | | |
| Monty Montgomery | | | |
| ☐ 373 John Mayberry | .25 | .10 | .02 |
| ☐ 374 Jack Heidemann | .16 | .07 | .01 |
| ☐ 375 Reggie Cleveland | .16 | .07 | .01 |
| ☐ 376 Andy Kosco | .16 | .07 | .01 |

| | MINT | VG-E | F-G |
|---|---|---|---|
| ☐ 377 Terry Harmon | .16 | .07 | .01 |
| ☐ 378 Checklist 4th Series | .55 | .10 | .02 |
| ☐ 379 Ken Berry | .16 | .07 | .01 |
| ☐ 380 Earl Williams | .16 | .07 | .01 |
| ☐ 381 White Sox Team | .40 | .18 | .04 |
| ☐ 382 Joe Gibbon | .16 | .07 | .01 |
| ☐ 383 Brant Alyea | .16 | .07 | .01 |
| ☐ 384 Dave Campbell | .16 | .07 | .01 |
| ☐ 385 Mickey Stanley | .16 | .07 | .01 |
| ☐ 386 Jim Colborn | .16 | .07 | .01 |
| ☐ 387 Horace Clarke | .16 | .07 | .01 |
| ☐ 388 Charlie Williams | .16 | .07 | .01 |
| ☐ 389 Bill Rigney | .16 | .07 | .01 |
| ☐ 390 Willie Davis | .30 | .12 | .03 |
| ☐ 391 Ken Sanders | .16 | .07 | .01 |
| ☐ 392 Pirates Rookies | .75 | .35 | .07 |
|    Fred Cambria | | | |
|    Richie Zisk | | | |
| ☐ 393 Curt Motton | .16 | .07 | .01 |
| ☐ 394 Ken Forsch | .25 | .10 | .02 |
| ☐ 395 Matty Alou | .30 | .12 | .03 |
| ☐ 396 Paul Lindblad | .21 | .09 | .02 |
| ☐ 397 Phillies Team | .55 | .25 | .05 |
| ☐ 398 Larry Hisle | .35 | .15 | .03 |
| ☐ 399 Milt Wilcox | .25 | .10 | .02 |
| ☐ 400 Tony Oliva | 1.00 | .45 | .10 |
| ☐ 401 Jim Nash | .21 | .09 | .02 |
| ☐ 402 Bobby Heise | .21 | .09 | .02 |
| ☐ 403 John Cumberland | .21 | .09 | .02 |
| ☐ 404 Jeff Torborg | .21 | .09 | .02 |
| ☐ 405 Ron Fairly | .25 | .10 | .02 |
| ☐ 406 George Hendrick | 1.50 | .70 | .15 |
| ☐ 407 Chuck Taylor | .21 | .09 | .02 |
| ☐ 408 Jim Northrup | .25 | .10 | .02 |
| ☐ 409 Frank Baker | .21 | .09 | .02 |
| ☐ 410 Fergie Jenkins | .85 | .40 | .08 |
| ☐ 411 Bob Montgomery | .21 | .09 | .02 |
| ☐ 412 Dick Kelley | .21 | .09 | .02 |
| ☐ 413 White Sox Rookies | .21 | .09 | .02 |
|    Don Eddy | | | |
|    Dave Lemonds | | | |
| ☐ 414 Bob Miller | .21 | .09 | .02 |
| ☐ 415 Cookie Rojas | .21 | .09 | .02 |
| ☐ 416 Johnny Edwards | .21 | .09 | .02 |
| ☐ 417 Tom Hall | .21 | .09 | .02 |
| ☐ 418 Tom Shopay | .21 | .09 | .02 |
| ☐ 419 Jim Spencer | .21 | .09 | .02 |
| ☐ 420 Steve Carlton | 9.00 | 4.25 | .90 |
| ☐ 421 Ellie Rodriguez | .21 | .09 | .02 |
| ☐ 422 Ray Lamb | .21 | .09 | .02 |
| ☐ 423 Oscar Gamble | .30 | .12 | .03 |
| ☐ 424 Bill Gogolewski | .21 | .09 | .02 |
| ☐ 425 Ken Singleton | .55 | .25 | .05 |

| | MINT | VG-E | F-G |
|---|---|---|---|
| ☐ 426 Singleton In Action | .30 | .12 | .03 |
| ☐ 427 Tito Fuentes | .21 | .09 | .02 |
| ☐ 428 Fuentes In Action | .21 | .09 | .02 |
| ☐ 429 Bob Robertson | .21 | .09 | .02 |
| ☐ 430 Robertson In Action | .21 | .09 | .02 |
| ☐ 431 Clarence Gaston | .21 | .09 | .02 |
| ☐ 432 Gaston In Action | .21 | .09 | .02 |
| ☐ 433 Johnny Bench | 10.00 | 4.75 | 1.00 |
| ☐ 434 Bench In Action | 4.50 | 2.10 | .45 |
| ☐ 435 Reggie Jackson | 10.00 | 4.75 | 1.00 |
| ☐ 436 Jackson In Action | 4.50 | 2.10 | .45 |
| ☐ 437 Maury Wills | .85 | .40 | .08 |
| ☐ 438 Wills In Action | .50 | .22 | .05 |
| ☐ 439 Billy Williams | 1.25 | .60 | .12 |
| ☐ 440 Williams In Action | .65 | .30 | .06 |
| ☐ 441 Thurman Munson | 6.00 | 2.80 | .60 |
| ☐ 442 Munson In Action | 3.00 | 1.40 | .30 |
| ☐ 443 Ken Henderson | .21 | .09 | .02 |
| ☐ 444 Henderson In Action | .21 | .09 | .02 |
| ☐ 445 Tom Seaver | 8.00 | 3.75 | .80 |
| ☐ 446 Seaver In Action | 4.00 | 1.85 | .40 |
| ☐ 447 Willie Stargell | 2.50 | 1.15 | .25 |
| ☐ 448 Stargell In Action | 1.25 | .60 | .12 |
| ☐ 449 Bob Lemon | .55 | .25 | .05 |
| ☐ 450 Mickey Lolich | .55 | .25 | .05 |
| ☐ 451 Tony LaRussa | .35 | .15 | .03 |
| ☐ 452 Ed Herrmann | .21 | .09 | .02 |
| ☐ 453 Barry Lerch | .21 | .09 | .02 |
| ☐ 454 A's Team | .55 | .25 | .05 |
| ☐ 455 Tommy Harper | .25 | .10 | .02 |
| ☐ 456 Mark Belanger | .25 | .10 | .02 |
| ☐ 457 Padres Rookies | .25 | .10 | .02 |
|    Darcy Fast | | | |
|    Derrel Thomas | | | |
|    Mike Ivie | | | |
| ☐ 458 Aurelio Monteagudo | .21 | .09 | .02 |
| ☐ 459 Rick Renick | .21 | .09 | .02 |
| ☐ 460 Al Downing | .21 | .09 | .02 |
| ☐ 461 Tim Cullen | .21 | .09 | .02 |
| ☐ 462 Rickey Clark | .21 | .09 | .02 |
| ☐ 463 Bernie Carbo | .21 | .09 | .02 |
| ☐ 464 Jim Roland | .21 | .09 | .02 |
| ☐ 465 Gil Hodges | 1.50 | .70 | .15 |
| ☐ 466 Norm Miller | .21 | .09 | .02 |
| ☐ 467 Steve Kline | .21 | .09 | .02 |
| ☐ 468 Richie Scheinblum | .21 | .09 | .02 |
| ☐ 469 Ron Herbel | .21 | .09 | .02 |
| ☐ 470 Ray Fosse | .21 | .09 | .02 |
| ☐ 471 Luke Walker | .21 | .09 | .02 |
| ☐ 472 Phil Gagliano | .21 | .09 | .02 |
| ☐ 473 Dan McGinn | .21 | .09 | .02 |

| | MINT | VG-E | F-G |
|---|---|---|---|
| ☐ 474 Orioles Rookies ....... | 1.50 | .70 | .15 |
| Don Baylor | | | |
| Roric Harrison | | | |
| Johnny Oates | | | |
| ☐ 475 Gary Nolan ........... | .21 | .09 | .02 |
| ☐ 476 Lee Richard .......... | .21 | .09 | .02 |
| ☐ 477 Tom Phoebus ......... | .21 | .09 | .02 |
| ☐ 478 Checklist 5th Series .... | .60 | .10 | .02 |
| ☐ 479 Don Shaw ............ | .21 | .09 | .02 |
| ☐ 480 Lee May ............. | .30 | .12 | .03 |
| ☐ 481 Billy Conigliaro ....... | .25 | .10 | .02 |
| ☐ 482 Joe Hoerner .......... | .21 | .09 | .02 |
| ☐ 483 Ken Suarez .......... | .21 | .09 | .02 |
| ☐ 484 Lum Harris ........... | .21 | .09 | .02 |
| ☐ 485 Phil Regan ........... | .25 | .10 | .02 |
| ☐ 486 John Lowenstein ...... | .25 | .10 | .02 |
| ☐ 487 Tigers Team .......... | .60 | .28 | .06 |
| ☐ 488 Mike Nagy ........... | .21 | .09 | .02 |
| ☐ 489 Expos Rookies ........ | .21 | .09 | .02 |
| Terry Humphrey | | | |
| Keith Lampard | | | |
| ☐ 490 Dave McNally ......... | .30 | .12 | .03 |
| KID PICTURES | | | |
| (491–498) | | | |
| ☐ 491 KP: Lou Piniella ....... | .30 | .12 | .03 |
| ☐ 492 KP: Mel Stottlemyre .... | .25 | .10 | .02 |
| ☐ 493 KP: Bob Bailey ........ | .21 | .09 | .02 |
| ☐ 494 KP: Willie Horton ...... | .25 | .10 | .02 |
| ☐ 495 KP: Bill Melton ........ | .21 | .09 | .02 |
| ☐ 496 KP: Bud Harrelson ..... | .21 | .09 | .02 |
| ☐ 497 KP: Jim Perry ......... | .25 | .10 | .02 |
| ☐ 498 KP: Brooks Robinson ... | 1.00 | .45 | .10 |
| ☐ 499 Vicente Romo ......... | .21 | .09 | .02 |
| ☐ 500 Joe Torre ............ | .55 | .25 | .05 |
| ☐ 501 Pete Hamm ........... | .21 | .09 | .02 |
| ☐ 502 Jackie Hernandez ..... | .21 | .09 | .02 |
| ☐ 503 Gary Peters .......... | .25 | .10 | .02 |
| ☐ 504 Ed Spiezio ........... | .21 | .09 | .02 |
| ☐ 505 Mike Marshall ........ | .35 | .15 | .03 |
| ☐ 506 Indians Rookies ....... | .35 | .15 | .03 |
| Terry Ley | | | |
| Jim Moyer | | | |
| Dick Tidrow | | | |
| ☐ 507 Fred Gladding ........ | .21 | .09 | .02 |
| ☐ 508 Ellie Hendricks ....... | .21 | .09 | .02 |
| ☐ 509 Don McMahon ........ | .21 | .09 | .02 |
| ☐ 510 Ted Williams ......... | 3.00 | 1.40 | .30 |
| ☐ 511 Tony Taylor .......... | .21 | .09 | .02 |
| ☐ 512 Paul Popovich ........ | .21 | .09 | .02 |
| ☐ 513 Lindy McDaniel ....... | .21 | .09 | .02 |
| ☐ 514 Ted Sizemore ........ | .21 | .09 | .02 |
| ☐ 515 Bert Blyleven ........ | 1.75 | .85 | .17 |
| ☐ 516 Oscar Brown ......... | .21 | .09 | .02 |

| | MINT | VG-E | F-G |
|---|---|---|---|
| ☐ 517 Ken Brett ............ | .25 | .10 | .02 |
| ☐ 518 Wayne Garrett ....... | .21 | .09 | .02 |
| ☐ 519 Ted Abernathy ....... | .21 | .09 | .02 |
| ☐ 520 Larry Bowa .......... | .80 | .40 | .08 |
| ☐ 521 Alan Foster .......... | .21 | .09 | .02 |
| ☐ 522 Dodgers Team ....... | .85 | .40 | .08 |
| ☐ 523 Chuck Dobson ....... | .21 | .09 | .02 |
| ☐ 524 Reds Rookies ........ | .21 | .09 | .02 |
| Ed Armbrister | | | |
| Mel Behney | | | |
| ☐ 525 Carlos May .......... | .25 | .10 | .02 |
| ☐ 526 Bob Bailey .......... | .35 | .15 | .03 |
| ☐ 527 Dave Leonhard ...... | .35 | .15 | .03 |
| ☐ 528 Ron Stone .......... | .35 | .15 | .03 |
| ☐ 529 Dave Nelson ........ | .35 | .15 | .03 |
| ☐ 530 Don Sutton ......... | 1.75 | .85 | .17 |
| ☐ 531 Freddie Patek ....... | .35 | .15 | .03 |
| ☐ 532 Fred Kendall ........ | .35 | .15 | .03 |
| ☐ 533 Ralph Houk MGR ..... | .55 | .25 | .05 |
| ☐ 534 Jim Hickman ........ | .35 | .15 | .03 |
| ☐ 535 Ed Brinkman ........ | .35 | .15 | .03 |
| ☐ 536 Doug Rader ......... | .45 | .20 | .04 |
| ☐ 537 Bob Locker .......... | .35 | .15 | .03 |
| ☐ 538 Charlie Sands ....... | .35 | .15 | .03 |
| ☐ 539 Terry Forster ........ | 1.50 | .70 | .15 |
| ☐ 540 Felix Milan .......... | .35 | .15 | .03 |
| ☐ 541 Roger Repoz ........ | .35 | .15 | .03 |
| ☐ 542 Jack Billingham ...... | .35 | .15 | .03 |
| ☐ 543 Duane Josephson .... | .35 | .15 | .03 |
| ☐ 544 Ted Martinez ........ | .35 | .15 | .03 |
| ☐ 545 Wayne Granger ...... | .35 | .15 | .03 |
| ☐ 546 Joe Hague .......... | .35 | .15 | .03 |
| ☐ 547 Indians Team ........ | .60 | .28 | .06 |
| ☐ 548 Frank Reberger ...... | .35 | .15 | .03 |
| ☐ 549 Dave May ........... | .35 | .15 | .03 |
| ☐ 550 Brooks Robinson ..... | 5.00 | 2.35 | .50 |
| ☐ 551 Ollie Brown ......... | .35 | .15 | .03 |
| ☐ 552 Brown In Action ...... | .35 | .15 | .03 |
| ☐ 553 Wilbur Wood ........ | .35 | .15 | .03 |
| ☐ 554 Wood In Action ...... | .35 | .15 | .03 |
| ☐ 555 Ron Santo .......... | .70 | .32 | .07 |
| ☐ 556 Santo In Action ...... | .45 | .20 | .04 |
| ☐ 557 John Odom ......... | .35 | .15 | .03 |
| ☐ 558 Odom In Action ...... | .35 | .15 | .03 |
| ☐ 559 Pete Rose .......... | 34.00 | 15.00 | 3.00 |
| ☐ 560 Rose In Action ....... | 15.00 | 7.00 | 1.50 |
| ☐ 561 Leo Cardenas ....... | .35 | .15 | .03 |
| ☐ 562 Cardenas In Action ... | .35 | .15 | .03 |
| ☐ 563 Ray Sadecki ........ | .35 | .15 | .03 |
| ☐ 564 Sadecki In Action .... | .35 | .15 | .03 |
| ☐ 565 Reggie Smith ....... | .65 | .30 | .06 |
| ☐ 566 Smith In Action ...... | .45 | .20 | .04 |
| ☐ 567 Juan Marichal ....... | 2.50 | 1.15 | .25 |

| | MINT | VG-E | F-G |
|---|---|---|---|
| ☐ 568 Marichal In Action | 1.25 | .60 | .12 |
| ☐ 569 Ed Kirkpatrick | .35 | .15 | .03 |
| ☐ 570 Kirkpatrick In Action | .35 | .15 | .03 |
| ☐ 571 Nate Colbert | .35 | .15 | .03 |
| ☐ 572 Colbert in Action | .35 | .15 | .03 |
| ☐ 573 Fritz Peterson | .35 | .15 | .03 |
| ☐ 574 Peterson In Action | .35 | .15 | .03 |
| ☐ 575 Al Oliver | 2.00 | .90 | .20 |
| ☐ 576 Leo Durocher | .60 | .28 | .06 |
| ☐ 577 Mike Paul | .35 | .15 | .03 |
| ☐ 578 Billy Grabarkewitz | .35 | .15 | .03 |
| ☐ 579 Doyle Alexander | .90 | .40 | .09 |
| ☐ 580 Lou Piniella | 1.25 | .60 | .12 |
| ☐ 581 Wade Blasingame | .35 | .15 | .03 |
| ☐ 582 Expos Team | .65 | .30 | .06 |
| ☐ 583 Darold Knowles | .35 | .15 | .03 |
| ☐ 584 Jerry McNertney | .35 | .15 | .03 |
| ☐ 585 George Scott | .45 | .20 | .04 |
| ☐ 586 Denis Menke | .35 | .15 | .03 |
| ☐ 587 Billy Wilson | .35 | .15 | .03 |
| ☐ 588 Jim Holt | .35 | .15 | .03 |
| ☐ 589 Hal Lanier | .45 | .20 | .04 |
| ☐ 590 Graig Nettles | 1.50 | .70 | .15 |
| ☐ 591 Paul Casanova | .35 | .15 | .03 |
| ☐ 592 Lew Krausse | .35 | .15 | .03 |
| ☐ 593 Rich Morales | .35 | .15 | .03 |
| ☐ 594 Jim Beauchamp | .35 | .15 | .03 |
| ☐ 595 Nolan Ryan | 8.00 | 3.75 | .80 |
| ☐ 596 Manny Mota | .55 | .25 | .05 |
| ☐ 597 Jim Magnuson | .35 | .15 | .03 |
| ☐ 598 Hal King | .35 | .15 | .03 |
| ☐ 599 Billy Champion | .35 | .15 | .03 |
| ☐ 600 Al Kaline | 5.00 | 2.35 | .50 |
| ☐ 601 George Stone | .35 | .15 | .03 |
| ☐ 602 Dave Bristol | .35 | .15 | .03 |
| ☐ 603 Jim Ray | .35 | .15 | .03 |
| ☐ 604 Checklist 6th Series | 1.50 | .30 | .05 |
| ☐ 605 Nelson Briles | .35 | .15 | .03 |
| ☐ 606 Luis Melendez | .35 | .15 | .03 |
| ☐ 607 Frank Duffy | .35 | .15 | .03 |
| ☐ 608 Mike Corkins | .35 | .15 | .03 |
| ☐ 609 Tom Grieve | .45 | .20 | .04 |
| ☐ 610 Bill Stoneman | .35 | .15 | .03 |
| ☐ 611 Rich Reese | .35 | .15 | .03 |
| ☐ 612 Joe Decker | .35 | .15 | .03 |
| ☐ 613 Mike Ferraro | .45 | .20 | .04 |
| ☐ 614 Ted Uhlaender | .35 | .15 | .03 |
| ☐ 615 Steve Hargan | .35 | .15 | .03 |
| ☐ 616 Joe Ferguson | .55 | .25 | .05 |
| ☐ 617 Royals Team | .65 | .30 | .06 |
| ☐ 618 Rich Robertson | .35 | .15 | .03 |
| ☐ 619 Rich McKinney | .35 | .15 | .03 |
| ☐ 620 Phil Niekro | 2.00 | .90 | .20 |

| | MINT | VG-E | F-G |
|---|---|---|---|
| **AWARDS AND TROPHIES (621–626)** | | | |
| ☐ 621 Commissioners Award | .60 | .28 | .06 |
| ☐ 622 MVP Award | .60 | .28 | .06 |
| ☐ 623 Cy Young Award | .60 | .28 | .06 |
| ☐ 624 Minor League Player | .60 | .28 | .06 |
| ☐ 625 Rookie of the Year | .60 | .28 | .06 |
| ☐ 626 Babe Ruth Award | .90 | .40 | .09 |
| ☐ 627 Moe Drabowsky | .35 | .15 | .03 |
| ☐ 628 Terry Crowley | .35 | .15 | .03 |
| ☐ 629 Paul Doyle | .35 | .15 | .03 |
| ☐ 630 Rich Hebner | .35 | .15 | .03 |
| ☐ 631 John Strohmayer | .35 | .15 | .03 |
| ☐ 632 Mike Hegan | .35 | .15 | .03 |
| ☐ 633 Jack Hiatt | .35 | .15 | .03 |
| ☐ 634 Dick Woodson | .35 | .15 | .03 |
| ☐ 635 Don Money | .45 | .20 | .04 |
| ☐ 636 Bill Lee | .45 | .20 | .04 |
| ☐ 637 Preston Gomez | .35 | .15 | .03 |
| ☐ 638 Ken Wright | .35 | .15 | .03 |
| ☐ 639 J. C. Martin | .35 | .15 | .03 |
| ☐ 640 Joe Coleman | .35 | .15 | .03 |
| ☐ 641 Mike Lum | .35 | .15 | .03 |
| ☐ 642 Dennis Riddleberger | .35 | .15 | .03 |
| ☐ 643 Russ Gibson | .35 | .15 | .03 |
| ☐ 644 Bernie Allen | .35 | .15 | .03 |
| ☐ 645 Jim Maloney | .45 | .20 | .04 |
| ☐ 646 Chico Salmon | .35 | .15 | .03 |
| ☐ 647 Bob Moose | .35 | .15 | .03 |
| ☐ 648 Jim Lyttle | .35 | .15 | .03 |
| ☐ 649 Pete Richert | .35 | .15 | .03 |
| ☐ 650 Sal Bando | .55 | .25 | .05 |
| ☐ 651 Reds Team | .85 | .40 | .08 |
| ☐ 652 Marcelino Lopez | .35 | .15 | .03 |
| ☐ 653 Jim Fairey | .35 | .15 | .03 |
| ☐ 654 Horacio Pina | .35 | .15 | .03 |
| ☐ 655 Jerry Grote | .35 | .15 | .03 |
| ☐ 656 Rudy May | .35 | .15 | .03 |
| ☐ 657 Bobby Wine | 1.00 | .45 | .10 |
| ☐ 658 Steve Dunning | .90 | .40 | .09 |
| ☐ 659 Bob Aspromonte | .90 | .40 | .09 |
| ☐ 660 Paul Blair | 1.00 | .45 | .10 |
| ☐ 661 Bill Virdon | 1.35 | .60 | .12 |
| ☐ 662 Stan Bahnsen | .90 | .40 | .09 |
| ☐ 663 Fran Healy | .90 | .40 | .09 |
| ☐ 664 Bobby Knoop | .90 | .40 | .09 |
| ☐ 665 Chris Short | .90 | .40 | .09 |
| ☐ 666 Hector Torres | .90 | .40 | .09 |
| ☐ 667 Ray Newman | .90 | .40 | .09 |
| ☐ 668 Rangers Team | 2.25 | 1.00 | .22 |
| ☐ 669 Willie Crawford | .90 | .40 | .09 |
| ☐ 670 Ken Holtzman | 1.50 | .70 | .15 |
| ☐ 671 Donn Clendenon | 1.00 | .45 | .10 |

|  | MINT | VG-E | F-G |
|---|---|---|---|
| ☐ 672 Archie Reynolds | .90 | .40 | .09 |
| ☐ 673 Dave Marshall | .90 | .40 | .09 |
| ☐ 674 John Kennedy | .90 | .40 | .09 |
| ☐ 675 Pat Jarvis | .90 | .40 | .09 |
| ☐ 676 Danny Cater | .90 | .40 | .09 |
| ☐ 677 Ivan Murrell | .90 | .40 | .09 |
| ☐ 678 Steve Luebber | .90 | .40 | .09 |
| ☐ 679 Astros Rookies | .90 | .40 | .09 |
|     Bob Fenwick | | | |
|     Bob Stinson | | | |
| ☐ 680 Dave Johnson | 1.75 | .85 | .17 |
| ☐ 681 Bobby Pfeil | .90 | .40 | .09 |
| ☐ 682 Mike McCormick | 1.00 | .45 | .10 |
| ☐ 683 Steve Hovley | .90 | .40 | .09 |
| ☐ 684 Hal Breeden | .90 | .40 | .09 |
| ☐ 685 Joe Horlen | 1.00 | .45 | .10 |
| ☐ 686 Steve Garvey | 50.00 | 22.00 | 5.00 |
| ☐ 687 Del Unser | .90 | .40 | .09 |
| ☐ 688 Cardinals Team | 1.50 | .70 | .15 |
| ☐ 689 Eddie Fisher | .90 | .40 | .09 |
| ☐ 690 Willie Montanez | 1.00 | .45 | .10 |
| ☐ 691 Curt Blefary | .90 | .40 | .09 |
| ☐ 692 Blefary In Action | .90 | .40 | .09 |
| ☐ 693 Alan Gallagher | .90 | .40 | .09 |
| ☐ 694 Gallagher In Action | .90 | .40 | .09 |
| ☐ 695 Rod Carew | 50.00 | 22.00 | 5.00 |
| ☐ 696 Carew In Action | 20.00 | 9.00 | 2.00 |
| ☐ 697 Jerry Koosman | 3.50 | 1.65 | .35 |
| ☐ 698 Koosman In Action | 1.75 | .85 | .17 |
| ☐ 699 Bobby Murcer | 3.50 | 1.65 | .35 |
| ☐ 700 Murcer In Action | 1.75 | .85 | .17 |
| ☐ 701 Jose Pagan | .90 | .40 | .09 |
| ☐ 702 Pagan In Action | .90 | .40 | .09 |
| ☐ 703 Doug Griffin | .90 | .40 | .09 |
| ☐ 704 Griffin In Action | .90 | .40 | .09 |
| ☐ 705 Pat Corrales | 1.25 | .60 | .12 |
| ☐ 706 Corrales in Action | 1.00 | .45 | .10 |
| ☐ 707 Tim Foli | .90 | .40 | .09 |
| ☐ 708 Foli In Action | .90 | .40 | .09 |
| ☐ 709 Jim Kaat | 3.50 | 1.65 | .35 |
| ☐ 710 Kaat In Action | 1.50 | .70 | .15 |
| ☐ 711 Bobby Bonds | 2.75 | 1.25 | .27 |
| ☐ 712 Bonds In Action | 1.50 | .70 | .15 |
| ☐ 713 Gene Michael | 1.25 | .60 | .12 |
| ☐ 714 Michael In Action | 1.00 | .45 | .10 |
| ☐ 715 Mike Epstein | .90 | .40 | .09 |
| ☐ 716 Jesus Alou | .90 | .40 | .09 |
| ☐ 717 Bruce Dal Canton | .90 | .40 | .09 |
| ☐ 718 Del Rice | .90 | .40 | .09 |
| ☐ 719 Cesar Geronimo | .90 | .40 | .09 |
| ☐ 720 Sam McDowell | 1.25 | .60 | .12 |
| ☐ 721 Eddie Leon | .90 | .40 | .09 |
| ☐ 722 Bill Sudakis | .90 | .40 | .09 |

|  | MINT | VG-E | F-G |
|---|---|---|---|
| ☐ 723 Al Santorini | .90 | .40 | .09 |
| ☐ 724 AL Rookie Pitchers | 1.25 | .60 | .12 |
|     John Curtis | | | |
|     Rich Hinton | | | |
|     Mickey Scott | | | |
| ☐ 725 Dick McAuliffe | 1.00 | .45 | .10 |
| ☐ 726 Dick Selma | .90 | .40 | .09 |
| ☐ 727 Jose LaBoy | .90 | .40 | .09 |
| ☐ 728 Gail Hopkins | .90 | .40 | .09 |
| ☐ 729 Bob Veale | 1.00 | .45 | .10 |
| ☐ 730 Rick Monday | 1.50 | .70 | .15 |
| ☐ 731 Orioles Team | 1.50 | .70 | .15 |
| ☐ 732 George Culver | .90 | .40 | .09 |
| ☐ 733 Jim Ray Hart | 1.00 | .45 | .10 |
| ☐ 734 Bob Burda | .90 | .40 | .09 |
| ☐ 735 Diego Segui | .90 | .40 | .09 |
| ☐ 736 Bill Russell | 1.50 | .70 | .15 |
| ☐ 737 Lenny Randle | .90 | .40 | .09 |
| ☐ 738 Jim Merritt | .90 | .40 | .09 |
| ☐ 739 Don Mason | .90 | .40 | .09 |
| ☐ 740 Rico Carty | 1.25 | .60 | .12 |
| ☐ 741 Rookie First Basemen | 1.25 | .60 | .12 |
|     Tom Hutton | | | |
|     John Milner | | | |
|     Rick Miller | | | |
| ☐ 742 Jim Rooker | .90 | .40 | .09 |
| ☐ 743 Cesar Gutierrez | .90 | .40 | .09 |
| ☐ 744 Jim Slaton | 1.25 | .60 | .12 |
| ☐ 745 Julian Javier | 1.00 | .45 | .10 |
| ☐ 746 Lowell Palmer | .90 | .40 | .09 |
| ☐ 747 Jim Stewart | .90 | .40 | .09 |
| ☐ 748 Phil Hennigan | .90 | .40 | .09 |
| ☐ 749 Walter Alston MGR | 2.50 | 1.15 | .25 |
| ☐ 750 Willie Horton | 1.25 | .60 | .12 |
|     TRADED CARDS | | | |
|     (751–757) | | | |
| ☐ 751 Steve Carlton TR | 25.00 | 11.00 | 2.50 |
| ☐ 752 Joe Morgan TR | 8.00 | 3.75 | .80 |
| ☐ 753 Denny McLain TR | 2.50 | 1.15 | .25 |
| ☐ 754 Frank Robinson TR | 8.00 | 3.75 | .80 |
| ☐ 755 Jim Fregosi TR | 1.25 | .60 | .12 |
| ☐ 756 Rick Wise TR | 1.25 | .60 | .12 |
| ☐ 757 Jose Cardenal TR | 1.00 | .45 | .10 |
| ☐ 758 Gil Garrido | .90 | .40 | .09 |
| ☐ 759 Chris Cannizzaro | .90 | .40 | .09 |
| ☐ 760 Bill Mazeroski | 1.50 | .70 | .15 |
| ☐ 761 Rookie Outfielders | 12.00 | 5.50 | 1.20 |
|     Ben Oglivie | | | |
|     Ron Cey | | | |
|     Bernie Williams | | | |
| ☐ 762 Wayne Simpson | .90 | .40 | .09 |
| ☐ 763 Ron Hansen | .90 | .40 | .09 |
| ☐ 764 Dusty Baker | 2.75 | 1.25 | .27 |

| | | MINT | VG-E | F-G |
|---|---|---|---|---|
| ☐ 765 | Ken McMullen | .90 | .40 | .09 |
| ☐ 766 | Steve Hamilton | .90 | .40 | .09 |
| ☐ 767 | Tom McCraw | .90 | .40 | .09 |
| ☐ 768 | Denny Doyle | .90 | .40 | .09 |
| ☐ 769 | Jack Aker | .90 | .40 | .09 |
| ☐ 770 | Jim Wynn | 1.25 | .60 | .12 |
| ☐ 771 | Giants Team | 1.50 | .70 | .15 |
| ☐ 772 | Ken Tatum | .90 | .40 | .09 |
| ☐ 773 | Ron Brand | .90 | .40 | .09 |
| ☐ 774 | Luis Alvarado | .90 | .40 | .09 |
| ☐ 775 | Jerry Reuss | 2.25 | 1.00 | .22 |
| ☐ 776 | Bill Voss | .90 | .40 | .09 |
| ☐ 777 | Hoyt Wilhelm | 4.50 | 2.10 | .45 |
| ☐ 778 | Twins Rookies | 1.50 | .70 | .15 |
| | Vic Albury | | | |
| | Rick Dempsey | | | |
| | Jim Strickland | | | |
| ☐ 779 | Tony Cloninger | .90 | .40 | .09 |
| ☐ 780 | Dick Green | .90 | .40 | .09 |
| ☐ 781 | Jim McAndrew | .90 | .40 | .09 |
| ☐ 782 | Larry Stahl | .90 | .40 | .09 |
| ☐ 783 | Les Cain | .90 | .40 | .09 |
| ☐ 784 | Ken Aspromonte | .90 | .40 | .09 |
| ☐ 785 | Vic Davalillo | .90 | .40 | .09 |
| ☐ 786 | Chuck Brinkman | .90 | .40 | .09 |
| ☐ 787 | Ron Reed | 1.50 | .50 | .10 |

## 1973 TOPPS

The cards in this 660 card set measure 2½" by 3½". The 1973 Topps set marked the last year in which Topps marketed baseball cards in consecutive series. The last series (529–660) is more difficult to obtain. Beginning in 1974, all Topps cards were printed at the same time, thus eliminating the "high number" factor. An "All-

*Time Leaders" series (471–478) appeared for the first time in this set. Kid pictures appeared again for the second year in a row (341–346).*

Complete Set: M-250.00; VG-E-110.00; F-G-25.00

| | | MINT | VG-E | F-G |
|---|---|---|---|---|
| | Common Player (1–264) | .13 | .06 | .01 |
| | Common Player (265–396) | .16 | .07 | .01 |
| | Common Player (397–528) | .21 | .09 | .02 |
| | Common Player (529–660) | .60 | .28 | .06 |
| ☐ 1 | All-Time HR Leaders: | 5.25 | 1.50 | .30 |
| | 714 Babe Ruth | | | |
| | 673 Hank Aaron | | | |
| | 654 Willie Mays | | | |
| ☐ 2 | Rich Hebner | .13 | .06 | .01 |
| ☐ 3 | Jim Lonborg | .20 | .09 | .02 |
| ☐ 4 | John Milner | .13 | .06 | .01 |
| ☐ 5 | Ed Brinkman | .13 | .06 | .01 |
| ☐ 6 | Mac Scarce | .13 | .06 | .01 |
| ☐ 7 | Texas Rangers Team | .35 | .15 | .03 |
| ☐ 8 | Tom Hall | .13 | .06 | .01 |
| ☐ 9 | Johnny Oates | .13 | .06 | .01 |
| ☐ 10 | Don Sutton | 1.00 | .45 | .10 |
| ☐ 11 | Chris Chambliss | .35 | .15 | .03 |
| ☐ 12 | Padres Manager: | .25 | .10 | .02 |
| | Don Zimmer | | | |
| | Coaches: Dave Garcia | | | |
| | Johnny Podres | | | |
| | Bob Skinner | | | |
| | Whitey Wietelmann | | | |
| ☐ 13 | George Hendrick | .60 | .28 | .06 |
| ☐ 14 | Sonny Siebert | .13 | .06 | .01 |
| ☐ 15 | Ralph Garr | .20 | .09 | .02 |
| ☐ 16 | Steve Braun | .13 | .06 | .01 |
| ☐ 17 | Fred Gladding | .13 | .06 | .01 |
| ☐ 18 | Leroy Stanton | .13 | .06 | .01 |
| ☐ 19 | Tim Foli | .13 | .06 | .01 |
| ☐ 20 | Stan Bahnsen | .13 | .06 | .01 |
| ☐ 21 | Randy Hundley | .13 | .06 | .01 |
| ☐ 22 | Ted Abernathy | .13 | .06 | .01 |
| ☐ 23 | Dave Kingman | 1.25 | .60 | .12 |
| ☐ 24 | Al Santorini | .13 | .06 | .01 |
| ☐ 25 | Roy White | .25 | .10 | .02 |
| ☐ 26 | Pirates Team | .35 | .15 | .03 |
| ☐ 27 | Bill Gogolewski | .13 | .06 | .01 |
| ☐ 28 | Hal McRae | .35 | .15 | .03 |
| ☐ 29 | Tony Taylor | .13 | .06 | .01 |
| ☐ 30 | Tug McGraw | .50 | .22 | .05 |

| | MINT | VG-E | F-G |
|---|---|---|---|
| ☐ 31 Buddy Bell .......... | 2.50 | 1.15 | .25 |
| ☐ 32 Fred Norman .......... | .13 | .06 | .01 |
| ☐ 33 Jim Breazeale .......... | .13 | .06 | .01 |
| ☐ 34 Pat Dobson .......... | .25 | .10 | .02 |
| ☐ 35 Willie Davis .......... | .30 | .12 | .03 |
| ☐ 36 Steve Barber .......... | .13 | .06 | .01 |
| ☐ 37 Bill Robinson .......... | .13 | .06 | .01 |
| ☐ 38 Mike Epstein .......... | .13 | .06 | .01 |
| ☐ 39 Dave Roberts .......... | .13 | .06 | .01 |
| ☐ 40 Reggie Smith .......... | .50 | .22 | .05 |
| ☐ 41 Tom Walker .......... | .13 | .06 | .01 |
| ☐ 42 Mike Andrews .......... | .13 | .06 | .01 |
| ☐ 43 Randy Moffitt .......... | .13 | .06 | .01 |
| ☐ 44 Rick Monday .......... | .25 | .10 | .02 |
| ☐ 45 Ellie Rodriguez .......... | .13 | .06 | .01 |
| (photo actually | | | |
| John Felske) | | | |
| ☐ 46 Lindy McDaniel .......... | .13 | .06 | .01 |
| ☐ 47 Luis Melendez .......... | .13 | .06 | .01 |
| ☐ 48 Paul Splittorff .......... | .25 | .10 | .02 |
| ☐ 49 Minnesota Twins Mgr. .. | .25 | .10 | .02 |
| Frank Quilici | | | |
| Coaches: Vern Morgan | | | |
| Bob Rodgers | | | |
| Ralph Rowe | | | |
| Al Worthington | | | |
| ☐ 50 Roberto Clemente ..... | 6.50 | 3.00 | .65 |
| ☐ 51 Chuck Seelbach .......... | .13 | .06 | .01 |
| ☐ 52 Denis Menke .......... | .13 | .06 | .01 |
| ☐ 53 Steve Dunning .......... | .13 | .06 | .01 |
| ☐ 54 Checklist 1st Series ... | .50 | .10 | .02 |
| ☐ 55 Jon Matlack .......... | .25 | .10 | .02 |
| ☐ 56 Merv Rettenmund .......... | .13 | .06 | .01 |
| ☐ 57 Derrel Thomas .......... | .13 | .06 | .01 |
| ☐ 58 Mike Paul .......... | .13 | .06 | .01 |
| ☐ 59 Steve Yeager .......... | .45 | .20 | .04 |
| ☐ 60 Ken Holtzman .......... | .25 | .10 | .02 |
| ☐ 61 Batting Leaders .......... | .90 | .40 | .09 |
| Billy Williams | | | |
| Rod Carew | | | |
| ☐ 62 Home Run Leaders .... | .90 | .40 | .09 |
| Johnny Bench | | | |
| Dick Allen | | | |
| ☐ 63 RBI Leaders .......... | .90 | .40 | .09 |
| Johnny Bench | | | |
| Dick Allen | | | |
| ☐ 64 Stolen Base Leaders ... | .60 | .28 | .06 |
| Lou Brock | | | |
| Bert Campaneris | | | |
| ☐ 65 ERA Leaders .......... | .80 | .40 | .08 |
| Steve Carlton | | | |
| Luis Tiant | | | |

| | MINT | VG-E | F-G |
|---|---|---|---|
| ☐ 66 Victory Leaders .......... | .90 | .40 | .09 |
| Steve Carlton | | | |
| Gaylord Perry | | | |
| Wilbur Wood | | | |
| ☐ 67 Strikeout Leaders .......... | 1.75 | .85 | .17 |
| Steve Carlton | | | |
| Nolan Ryan | | | |
| ☐ 68 Leading Firemen .......... | .30 | .12 | .03 |
| Clay Carroll | | | |
| Sparky Lyle | | | |
| ☐ 69 Phil Gagliano .......... | .13 | .06 | .01 |
| ☐ 70 Milt Pappas .......... | .20 | .09 | .02 |
| ☐ 71 Johnny Briggs .......... | .13 | .06 | .01 |
| ☐ 72 Ron Reed .......... | .13 | .06 | .01 |
| ☐ 73 Ed Herrmann .......... | .13 | .06 | .01 |
| ☐ 74 Billy Champion .......... | .13 | .06 | .01 |
| ☐ 75 Vada Pinson .......... | .35 | .15 | .03 |
| ☐ 76 Doug Rader .......... | .25 | .10 | .02 |
| ☐ 77 Mike Torrez .......... | .25 | .10 | .02 |
| ☐ 78 Richie Scheinblum .......... | .13 | .06 | .01 |
| ☐ 79 Jim Willoughby .......... | .13 | .06 | .01 |
| ☐ 80 Tony Oliva .......... | .65 | .30 | .06 |
| ☐ 81 Chicago Cubs MGR .... | .35 | .15 | .03 |
| Whitey Lockman | | | |
| Coaches: Hank Aguirre | | | |
| Ernie Banks | | | |
| Larry Jansen | | | |
| Pete Reiser | | | |
| ☐ 82 Fritz Peterson .......... | .13 | .06 | .01 |
| ☐ 83 Leron Lee .......... | .13 | .06 | .01 |
| ☐ 84 Rollie Fingers .......... | 1.25 | .60 | .12 |
| ☐ 85 Ted Simmons .......... | .90 | .40 | .09 |
| ☐ 86 Tom McCraw .......... | .13 | .06 | .01 |
| ☐ 87 Ken Boswell .......... | .13 | .06 | .01 |
| ☐ 88 Mickey Stanley .......... | .13 | .06 | .01 |
| ☐ 89 Jack Billingham .......... | .13 | .06 | .01 |
| ☐ 90 Brooks Robinson .......... | 3.00 | 1.40 | .30 |
| ☐ 91 Dodgers Team .......... | .55 | .25 | .05 |
| ☐ 92 Jerry Bell .......... | .13 | .06 | .01 |
| ☐ 93 Jesus Alou .......... | .13 | .06 | .01 |
| ☐ 94 Dick Billings .......... | .13 | .06 | .01 |
| ☐ 95 Steve Blass .......... | .13 | .06 | .01 |
| ☐ 96 Doug Griffin .......... | .13 | .06 | .01 |
| ☐ 97 Willie Montanez .......... | .13 | .06 | .01 |
| ☐ 98 Dick Woodson .......... | .13 | .06 | .01 |
| ☐ 99 Carl Taylor .......... | .13 | .06 | .01 |
| ☐ 100 Hank Aaron .......... | 7.50 | 3.50 | .75 |
| ☐ 101 Ken Henderson .......... | .13 | .06 | .01 |
| ☐ 102 Rudy May .......... | .13 | .06 | .01 |
| ☐ 103 Celerino Sanchez .......... | .13 | .06 | .01 |
| ☐ 104 Reggie Cleveland .......... | .13 | .06 | .01 |
| ☐ 105 Carlos May .......... | .13 | .06 | .01 |

| | MINT | VG-E | F-G |
|---|---|---|---|
| ☐ 106 Terry Humphrey | .13 | .06 | .01 |
| ☐ 107 Phil Hennigan | .13 | .06 | .01 |
| ☐ 108 Bill Russell | .25 | .10 | .02 |
| ☐ 109 Doyle Alexander | .25 | .10 | .02 |
| ☐ 110 Bob Watson | .25 | .10 | .02 |
| ☐ 111 Dave Nelson | .13 | .06 | .01 |
| ☐ 112 Gary Ross | .13 | .06 | .01 |
| ☐ 113 Jerry Grote | .13 | .06 | .01 |
| ☐ 114 Lynn McGlothen | .13 | .06 | .01 |
| ☐ 115 Ron Santo | .35 | .15 | .03 |
| ☐ 116 Yankees Manager: | .40 | .18 | .04 |
|     Ralph Houk | | | |
|     Coaches: Jim Hegan | | | |
|     Elston Howard | | | |
|     Dick Howser | | | |
|     Jim Turner | | | |
| ☐ 117 Ramon Hernandez | .13 | .06 | .01 |
| ☐ 118 John Mayberry | .25 | .10 | .02 |
| ☐ 119 Larry Bowa | .45 | .20 | .04 |
| ☐ 120 Joe Coleman | .13 | .06 | .01 |
| ☐ 121 Dave Rader | .13 | .06 | .01 |
| ☐ 122 Jim Strickland | .13 | .06 | .01 |
| ☐ 123 Sandy Alomar | .13 | .06 | .01 |
| ☐ 124 Jim Hardin | .13 | .06 | .01 |
| ☐ 125 Ron Fairly | .20 | .09 | .02 |
| ☐ 126 Jim Brewer | .13 | .06 | .01 |
| ☐ 127 Brewers Team | .35 | .15 | .03 |
| ☐ 128 Ted Sizemore | .13 | .06 | .01 |
| ☐ 129 Terry Forster | .35 | .15 | .03 |
| ☐ 130 Pete Rose | 13.00 | 6.00 | 1.30 |
| ☐ 131 Red Sox Manager | .25 | .10 | .02 |
|     Eddie Kasko | | | |
|     Coaches: Doug Camilli | | | |
|     Don Lenhardt | | | |
|     Eddie Popowski | | | |
|     Lee Stange | | | |
| ☐ 132 Matty Alou | .20 | .09 | .02 |
| ☐ 133 Dave Roberts | .13 | .06 | .01 |
| ☐ 134 Milt Wilcox | .20 | .09 | .02 |
| ☐ 135 Lee May | .25 | .10 | .02 |
| ☐ 136 Orioles Manager | .50 | .22 | .05 |
|     Earl Weaver | | | |
|     Coaches: | | | |
|     George Bamberger | | | |
|     Jim Frey | | | |
|     Billy Hunter | | | |
|     George Staller | | | |
| ☐ 137 Jim Beauchamp | .13 | .06 | .01 |
| ☐ 138 Horacio Pina | .13 | .06 | .01 |
| ☐ 139 Carmen Fanzone | .13 | .06 | .01 |
| ☐ 140 Lou Piniella | .45 | .20 | .04 |
| ☐ 141 Bruce Kison | .25 | .10 | .02 |

| | MINT | VG-E | F-G |
|---|---|---|---|
| ☐ 142 Thurman Munson | 4.00 | 1.85 | .40 |
| ☐ 143 John Curtis | .13 | .06 | .01 |
| ☐ 144 Marty Perez | .13 | .06 | .01 |
| ☐ 145 Bobby Bonds | .35 | .15 | .03 |
| ☐ 146 Woodie Fryman | .13 | .06 | .01 |
| ☐ 147 Mike Anderson | .13 | .06 | .01 |
| ☐ 148 Dave Goltz | .20 | .09 | .02 |
| ☐ 149 Ron Hunt | .13 | .06 | .01 |
| ☐ 150 Wilbur Wood | .20 | .09 | .02 |
| ☐ 151 Wes Parker | .25 | .10 | .02 |
| ☐ 152 Dave May | .13 | .06 | .01 |
| ☐ 153 Al Hrabosky | .25 | .10 | .02 |
| ☐ 154 Jeff Torborg | .13 | .06 | .01 |
| ☐ 155 Sal Bando | .30 | .12 | .03 |
| ☐ 156 Cesar Geronimo | .13 | .06 | .01 |
| ☐ 157 Denny Riddleberger | .13 | .06 | .01 |
| ☐ 158 Astros Team | .35 | .15 | .03 |
| ☐ 159 Clarence Gaston | .13 | .06 | .01 |
| ☐ 160 Jim Palmer | 3.00 | 1.40 | .30 |
| ☐ 161 Ted Martinez | .13 | .06 | .01 |
| ☐ 162 Pete Broberg | .13 | .06 | .01 |
| ☐ 163 Vic Davalillo | .13 | .06 | .01 |
| ☐ 164 Monty Montgomery | .13 | .06 | .01 |
| ☐ 165 Luis Aparicio | 1.60 | .80 | .16 |
| ☐ 166 Terry Harmon | .13 | .06 | .01 |
| ☐ 167 Steve Stone | .30 | .12 | .03 |
| ☐ 168 Jim Northrup | .20 | .09 | .02 |
| ☐ 169 Ron Schueler | .13 | .06 | .01 |
| ☐ 170 Harmon Killebrew | 2.00 | .90 | .20 |
| ☐ 171 Bernie Carbo | .13 | .06 | .01 |
| ☐ 172 Steve Kline | .13 | .06 | .01 |
| ☐ 173 Hal Breeden | .13 | .06 | .01 |
| ☐ 174 Rich Gossage | 6.00 | 2.80 | .60 |
| ☐ 175 Frank Robinson | 2.75 | 1.25 | .27 |
| ☐ 176 Chuck Taylor | .13 | .06 | .01 |
| ☐ 177 Bill Plummer | .13 | .06 | .01 |
| ☐ 178 Don Rose | .13 | .06 | .01 |
| ☐ 179 Oakland A's MGR: | .30 | .12 | .03 |
|     Dick Williams | | | |
|     Coaches: Jerry Adair | | | |
|     Vern Hoscheit | | | |
|     Irv Noren | | | |
|     Wes Stock | | | |
| ☐ 180 Fergie Jenkins | .80 | .40 | .08 |
| ☐ 181 Jack Brohamer | .13 | .06 | .01 |
| ☐ 182 Mike Caldwell | .35 | .15 | .03 |
| ☐ 183 Don Buford | .13 | .06 | .01 |
| ☐ 184 Jerry Koosman | .35 | .15 | .03 |
| ☐ 185 Jim Wynn | .25 | .10 | .02 |
| ☐ 186 Bill Fahey | .13 | .06 | .01 |
| ☐ 187 Luke Walker | .13 | .06 | .01 |
| ☐ 188 Cookie Rojas | .13 | .06 | .01 |

|  | MINT | VG-E | F-G |
|---|---|---|---|
| ☐ 189 Greg Luzinski | .75 | .35 | .07 |
| ☐ 190 Bob Gibson | 2.25 | 1.00 | .22 |
| ☐ 191 Tigers Team | .40 | .18 | .04 |
| ☐ 192 Pat Jarvis | .13 | .06 | .01 |
| ☐ 193 Carlton Fisk | 2.50 | 1.15 | .25 |
| ☐ 194 Jorge Orta | .13 | .06 | .01 |
| ☐ 195 Clay Carroll | .13 | .06 | .01 |
| ☐ 196 Ken McMullen | .13 | .06 | .01 |
| ☐ 197 Ed Goodson | .13 | .06 | .01 |
| ☐ 198 Horace Clarke | .13 | .06 | .01 |
| ☐ 199 Bert Blyleven | .75 | .35 | .07 |
| ☐ 200 Billy Williams | 1.00 | .45 | .10 |
| ☐ 201 A.L. Playoffs | .55 | .25 | .05 |
| A's over Tigers; | | | |
| Hendrick scores | | | |
| winning run | | | |
| ☐ 202 N.L. Playoffs | .55 | .25 | .05 |
| Reds over Pirates | | | |
| Foster's run decides | | | |
| ☐ 203 World Series Game 1 | .55 | .25 | .05 |
| Tenace the Menace | | | |
| ☐ 204 World Series Game 2 | .55 | .25 | .05 |
| A's two straight | | | |
| ☐ 205 World Series Game 3 | .55 | .25 | .05 |
| Reds win squeeker | | | |
| ☐ 206 World Series Game 4 | .55 | .25 | .05 |
| Tenace singles | | | |
| in ninth | | | |
| ☐ 207 World Series Game 5 | .55 | .25 | .05 |
| Odom out at plate | | | |
| ☐ 208 World Series Game 6 | .55 | .25 | .05 |
| Red's slugging | | | |
| ties series | | | |
| ☐ 209 World Series Game 7 | .55 | .25 | .05 |
| Campy stars | | | |
| winning rally | | | |
| ☐ 210 World Series Summary | .55 | .25 | .05 |
| World champions: | | | |
| A's Win | | | |
| ☐ 211 Balor Moore | .13 | .06 | .01 |
| ☐ 212 Joe LaHoud | .13 | .06 | .01 |
| ☐ 213 Steve Garvey | 7.50 | 3.50 | .75 |
| ☐ 214 Steve Hamilton | .13 | .06 | .01 |
| ☐ 215 Dusty Baker | .65 | .30 | .06 |
| ☐ 216 Toby Harrah | .35 | .15 | .03 |
| ☐ 217 Don Wilson | .13 | .06 | .01 |
| ☐ 218 Aurelio Rodriguez | .13 | .06 | .01 |
| ☐ 219 Cardinals Team | .35 | .15 | .03 |
| ☐ 220 Nolan Ryan | 4.50 | 2.10 | .45 |
| ☐ 221 Fred Kendall | .13 | .06 | .01 |
| ☐ 222 Rob Gardner | .13 | .06 | .01 |
| ☐ 223 Bud Harrelson | .13 | .06 | .01 |

|  | MINT | VG-E | F-G |
|---|---|---|---|
| ☐ 224 Bill Lee | .20 | .09 | .02 |
| ☐ 225 Al Oliver | 1.25 | .60 | .12 |
| ☐ 226 Ray Fosse | .13 | .06 | .01 |
| ☐ 227 Wayne Twitchell | .13 | .06 | .01 |
| ☐ 228 Bobby Darwin | .13 | .06 | .01 |
| ☐ 229 Roric Harrison | .13 | .06 | .01 |
| ☐ 230 Joe Morgan | 1.60 | .80 | .16 |
| ☐ 231 Bill Parsons | .13 | .06 | .01 |
| ☐ 232 Ken Singleton | .35 | .15 | .03 |
| ☐ 233 Ed Kirkpatrick | .13 | .06 | .01 |
| ☐ 234 Bill North | .20 | .09 | .02 |
| ☐ 235 Jim Hunter | 1.25 | .60 | .12 |
| ☐ 236 Tito Fuentes | .13 | .06 | .01 |
| ☐ 237 Braves Manager: | .50 | .22 | .05 |
| Eddie Mathews | | | |
| Coaches: Lew Burdette | | | |
| Jim Busby | | | |
| Roy Hartsfield | | | |
| Ken Silvestri | | | |
| ☐ 238 Tony Muser | .13 | .06 | .01 |
| ☐ 239 Pete Richert | .13 | .06 | .01 |
| ☐ 240 Bobby Murcer | .50 | .22 | .05 |
| ☐ 241 Dwain Anderson | .13 | .06 | .01 |
| ☐ 242 George Culver | .13 | .06 | .01 |
| ☐ 243 Angels Team | .35 | .15 | .03 |
| ☐ 244 Ed Acosta | .13 | .06 | .01 |
| ☐ 245 Carl Yastrzemski | 8.00 | 3.75 | .80 |
| ☐ 246 Ken Sanders | .13 | .06 | .01 |
| ☐ 247 Del Unser | .13 | .06 | .01 |
| ☐ 248 Jerry Johnson | .13 | .06 | .01 |
| ☐ 249 Larry Biittner | .13 | .06 | .01 |
| ☐ 250 Manny Sanguillen | .25 | .10 | .02 |
| ☐ 251 Roger Nelson | .13 | .06 | .01 |
| ☐ 252 Giants Manager: | .25 | .10 | .02 |
| Charlie Fox | | | |
| Coaches: | | | |
| Joe Amalfitano | | | |
| Andy Gilbert | | | |
| Don McMahon | | | |
| John McNamara | | | |
| ☐ 253 Mark Belanger | .20 | .09 | .02 |
| ☐ 254 Bill Stoneman | .13 | .06 | .01 |
| ☐ 255 Reggie Jackson | 8.00 | 3.75 | .80 |
| ☐ 256 Chris Zachary | .13 | .06 | .01 |
| ☐ 257 N.Y. Mets Manager: | .55 | .25 | .05 |
| Yogi Berra | | | |
| Coaches: Roy McMillan | | | |
| Joe Pignatano | | | |
| Rube Walker | | | |
| Eddie Yost | | | |
| ☐ 258 Tommy John | .90 | .40 | .09 |
| ☐ 259 Jim Holt | .13 | .06 | .01 |

| | MINT | VG-E | F-G |
|---|---|---|---|
| ☐ 260 Gary Nolan | .13 | .06 | .01 |
| ☐ 261 Pat Kelly | .13 | .06 | .01 |
| ☐ 262 Jack Aker | .13 | .06 | .01 |
| ☐ 263 George Scott | .20 | .09 | .02 |
| ☐ 264 Checklist 2nd Series | .50 | .10 | .02 |
| ☐ 265 Gene Michael | .20 | .09 | .02 |
| ☐ 266 Mike Lum | .16 | .07 | .01 |
| ☐ 267 Lloyd Allen | .16 | .07 | .01 |
| ☐ 268 Jerry Morales | .16 | .07 | .01 |
| ☐ 269 Tim McCarver | .30 | .12 | .03 |
| ☐ 270 Luis Tiant | .35 | .15 | .03 |
| ☐ 271 Tom Hutton | .16 | .07 | .01 |
| ☐ 272 Ed Farmer | .16 | .07 | .01 |
| ☐ 273 Chris Speier | .16 | .07 | .01 |
| ☐ 274 Darold Knowles | .16 | .07 | .01 |
| ☐ 275 Tony Perez | .70 | .32 | .07 |
| ☐ 276 Joe Lovitto | .16 | .07 | .01 |
| ☐ 277 Bob Miller | .16 | .07 | .01 |
| ☐ 278 Orioles Team | .40 | .18 | .04 |
| ☐ 279 Mike Strahler | .16 | .07 | .01 |
| ☐ 280 Al Kaline | 2.75 | 1.25 | .27 |
| ☐ 281 Mike Jorgensen | .16 | .07 | .01 |
| ☐ 282 Steve Hovley | .16 | .07 | .01 |
| ☐ 283 Ray Sadecki | .16 | .07 | .01 |
| ☐ 284 Glenn Borgmann | .16 | .07 | .01 |
| ☐ 285 Don Kessinger | .20 | .09 | .02 |
| ☐ 286 Frank Linzy | .16 | .07 | .01 |
| ☐ 287 Eddie Leon | .16 | .07 | .01 |
| ☐ 288 Gary Gentry | .16 | .07 | .01 |
| ☐ 289 Bob Oliver | .16 | .07 | .01 |
| ☐ 290 Cesar Cedeno | .35 | .15 | .03 |
| ☐ 291 Rogelio Moret | .16 | .07 | .01 |
| ☐ 292 Jose Cruz | .65 | .30 | .06 |
| ☐ 293 Bernie Allen | .16 | .07 | .01 |
| ☐ 294 Steve Arlin | .16 | .07 | .01 |
| ☐ 295 Bert Campaneris | .30 | .12 | .03 |
| ☐ 296 Reds Manager: | .35 | .15 | .03 |
| Sparky Anderson | | | |
| Coaches: Alex Grammas | | | |
| Ted Kluszewski | | | |
| George Scherger | | | |
| Larry Shepard | | | |
| ☐ 297 Walt Williams | .16 | .07 | .01 |
| ☐ 298 Ron Bryant | .16 | .07 | .01 |
| ☐ 299 Ted Ford | .16 | .07 | .01 |
| ☐ 300 Steve Carlton | 6.50 | 3.00 | .65 |
| ☐ 301 Billy Grabarkewitz | .16 | .07 | .01 |
| ☐ 302 Terry Crowley | .16 | .07 | .01 |
| ☐ 303 Nelson Briles | .16 | .07 | .01 |
| ☐ 304 Duke Sims | .16 | .07 | .01 |
| ☐ 305 Willie Mays | 8.00 | 3.75 | .80 |
| ☐ 306 Tom Burgmeier | .16 | .07 | .01 |

| | MINT | VG-E | F-G |
|---|---|---|---|
| ☐ 307 Boots Day | .16 | .07 | .01 |
| ☐ 308 Skip Lockwood | .16 | .07 | .01 |
| ☐ 309 Paul Popovich | .16 | .07 | .01 |
| ☐ 310 Dick Allen | .40 | .18 | .04 |
| ☐ 311 Joe Decker | .16 | .07 | .01 |
| ☐ 312 Oscar Brown | .16 | .07 | .01 |
| ☐ 313 Jim Ray | .16 | .07 | .01 |
| ☐ 314 Ron Swoboda | .16 | .07 | .01 |
| ☐ 315 John Odom | .16 | .07 | .01 |
| ☐ 316 Padres Team | .40 | .18 | .04 |
| ☐ 317 Danny Cater | .16 | .07 | .01 |
| ☐ 318 Jim McGlothlin | .16 | .07 | .01 |
| ☐ 319 Jim Spencer | .16 | .07 | .01 |
| ☐ 320 Lou Brock | 2.50 | 1.15 | .25 |
| ☐ 321 Rich Hinton | .16 | .07 | .01 |
| ☐ 322 Garry Maddox | .50 | .22 | .05 |
| ☐ 323 Tigers Manager: | .50 | .22 | .05 |
| Billy Martin | | | |
| Coaches: Art Fowler | | | |
| Charlie Silvera | | | |
| Dick Tracewski | | | |
| ☐ 324 Al Downing | .16 | .07 | .01 |
| ☐ 325 Boog Powell | .50 | .22 | .05 |
| ☐ 326 Darrell Brandon | .16 | .07 | .01 |
| ☐ 327 John Lowenstein | .16 | .07 | .01 |
| ☐ 328 Bill Bonham | .16 | .07 | .01 |
| ☐ 329 Ed Kranepool | .20 | .09 | .02 |
| ☐ 330 Rod Carew | 6.00 | 2.80 | .60 |
| ☐ 331 Carl Morton | .16 | .07 | .01 |
| ☐ 332 John Felske | .16 | .07 | .01 |
| ☐ 333 Gene Clines | .16 | .07 | .01 |
| ☐ 334 Freddie Patek | .16 | .07 | .01 |
| ☐ 335 Bob Tolan | .16 | .07 | .01 |
| ☐ 336 Tom Bradley | .16 | .07 | .01 |
| ☐ 337 Dave Duncan | .16 | .07 | .01 |
| ☐ 338 Checklist 3rd Series | .50 | .10 | .02 |
| ☐ 339 Dick Tidrow | .16 | .07 | .01 |
| ☐ 340 Nate Colbert | .16 | .07 | .01 |
| KID PICTURES | | | |
| (341–346) | | | |
| ☐ 341 KP: Jim Palmer | .85 | .40 | .08 |
| ☐ 342 KP: Sam McDowell | .20 | .09 | .02 |
| ☐ 343 KP: Bobby Murcer | .25 | .10 | .02 |
| ☐ 344 KP: Jim Hunter | .50 | .22 | .05 |
| ☐ 345 KP: Chris Speier | .20 | .09 | .02 |
| ☐ 346 KP: Gaylord Perry | .55 | .25 | .05 |
| ☐ 347 Royals Team | .40 | .18 | .04 |
| ☐ 348 Rennie Stennett | .20 | .09 | .02 |
| ☐ 349 Dick McAuliffe | .20 | .09 | .02 |
| ☐ 350 Tom Seaver | 6.00 | 2.80 | .60 |
| ☐ 351 Jimmy Stewart | .16 | .07 | .01 |
| ☐ 352 Don Stanhouse | .20 | .09 | .02 |

| | MINT | VG-E | F-G |
|---|---|---|---|
| ☐ 353 Steve Brye | .16 | .07 | .01 |
| ☐ 354 Billy Parker | .16 | .07 | .01 |
| ☐ 355 Mike Marshall | .35 | .15 | .03 |
| ☐ 356 White Sox Manager | .30 | .12 | .03 |
| Chuck Tanner | | | |
| Coaches: Joe Lonnett | | | |
| Jim Mahoney | | | |
| Al Monchak | | | |
| Johnny Sain | | | |
| ☐ 357 Ross Grimsley | .16 | .07 | .01 |
| ☐ 358 Jim Nettles | .16 | .07 | .01 |
| ☐ 359 Cecil Upshaw | .16 | .07 | .01 |
| ☐ 360 Joe Rudi | .35 | .15 | .03 |
| (photo actually | | | |
| Gene Tenace) | | | |
| ☐ 361 Fran Healy | .16 | .07 | .01 |
| ☐ 362 Eddie Watt | .16 | .07 | .01 |
| ☐ 363 Jackie Hernandez | .16 | .07 | .01 |
| ☐ 364 Rick Wise | .20 | .09 | .02 |
| ☐ 365 Rico Petrocelli | .20 | .09 | .02 |
| ☐ 366 Brock Davis | .16 | .07 | .01 |
| ☐ 367 Burt Hooton | .20 | .09 | .02 |
| ☐ 368 Bill Buckner | .65 | .30 | .06 |
| ☐ 369 Lerrin LaGrow | .16 | .07 | .01 |
| ☐ 370 Willie Stargell | 2.00 | .90 | .20 |
| ☐ 371 Mike Kekich | .16 | .07 | .01 |
| ☐ 372 Oscar Gamble | .25 | .10 | .02 |
| ☐ 373 Clyde Wright | .16 | .07 | .01 |
| ☐ 374 Darrell Evans | .50 | .22 | .05 |
| ☐ 375 Larry Dierker | .20 | .09 | .02 |
| ☐ 376 Frank Duffy | .16 | .07 | .01 |
| ☐ 377 Expos Manager | .25 | .10 | .02 |
| Gene Mauch | | | |
| Coaches: Dave Bristol | | | |
| Larry Doby | | | |
| Cal McLish | | | |
| Jerry Zimmerman | | | |
| ☐ 378 Lenny Randle | .16 | .07 | .01 |
| ☐ 379 Cy Acosta | .16 | .07 | .01 |
| ☐ 380 Johnny Bench | 6.00 | 2.80 | .60 |
| ☐ 381 Vicente Romo | .16 | .07 | .01 |
| ☐ 382 Mike Hegan | .16 | .07 | .01 |
| ☐ 383 Diego Segui | .16 | .07 | .01 |
| ☐ 384 Don Baylor | .90 | .40 | .09 |
| ☐ 385 Jim Perry | .35 | .15 | .03 |
| ☐ 386 Don Money | .20 | .09 | .02 |
| ☐ 387 Jim Barr | .16 | .07 | .01 |
| ☐ 388 Ben Oglivie | .55 | .25 | .05 |
| ☐ 389 Mets Team | .90 | .40 | .09 |
| ☐ 390 Mickey Lolich | .50 | .22 | .05 |
| ☐ 391 Lee Lacy | .75 | .35 | .07 |
| ☐ 392 Dick Drago | .16 | .07 | .01 |
| ☐ 393 Jose Cardenal | .16 | .07 | .01 |

| | MINT | VG-E | F-G |
|---|---|---|---|
| ☐ 394 Sparky Lyle | .30 | .12 | .03 |
| ☐ 395 Roger Metzger | .16 | .07 | .01 |
| ☐ 396 Grant Jackson | .16 | .07 | .01 |
| ☐ 397 Dave Cash | .21 | .09 | .02 |
| ☐ 398 Rich Hand | .21 | .09 | .02 |
| ☐ 399 George Foster | 1.50 | .70 | .15 |
| ☐ 400 Gaylord Perry | 1.75 | .85 | .17 |
| ☐ 401 Clyde Mashore | .21 | .09 | .02 |
| ☐ 402 Jack Hiatt | .21 | .09 | .02 |
| ☐ 403 Sonny Jackson | .21 | .09 | .02 |
| ☐ 404 Chuck Brinkman | .21 | .09 | .02 |
| ☐ 405 Cesar Tovar | .21 | .09 | .02 |
| ☐ 406 Paul Lindblad | .21 | .09 | .02 |
| ☐ 407 Felix Millan | .21 | .09 | .02 |
| ☐ 408 Jim Colborn | .21 | .09 | .02 |
| ☐ 409 Ivan Murrell | .21 | .09 | .02 |
| ☐ 410 Willie McCovey | 2.50 | 1.15 | .25 |
| ☐ 411 Ray Corbin | .21 | .09 | .02 |
| ☐ 412 Manny Mota | .25 | .10 | .02 |
| ☐ 413 Tom Timmerman | .21 | .09 | .02 |
| ☐ 414 Ken Rudolph | .21 | .09 | .02 |
| ☐ 415 Marty Pattin | .21 | .09 | .02 |
| ☐ 416 Paul Schaal | .21 | .09 | .02 |
| ☐ 417 Scipio Spinks | .21 | .09 | .02 |
| ☐ 418 Bobby Grich | .40 | .18 | .04 |
| ☐ 419 Casey Cox | .21 | .09 | .02 |
| ☐ 420 Tommie Agee | .21 | .09 | .02 |
| ☐ 421 Angels Manager | .25 | .10 | .02 |
| Bobby Winkles | | | |
| Coaches: Tom Morgan | | | |
| Salty Parker | | | |
| Jimmie Reese | | | |
| John Roseboro | | | |
| ☐ 422 Bob Robertson | .21 | .09 | .02 |
| ☐ 423 Johnny Jeter | .21 | .09 | .02 |
| ☐ 424 Denny Doyle | .21 | .09 | .02 |
| ☐ 425 Alex Johnson | .21 | .09 | .02 |
| ☐ 426 Dave LaRoche | .21 | .09 | .02 |
| ☐ 427 Rick Auerbach | .21 | .09 | .02 |
| ☐ 428 Wayne Simpson | .21 | .09 | .02 |
| ☐ 429 Jim Fairey | .21 | .09 | .02 |
| ☐ 430 Vida Blue | .45 | .20 | .04 |
| ☐ 431 Gerry Moses | .21 | .09 | .02 |
| ☐ 432 Dan Frisella | .21 | .09 | .02 |
| ☐ 433 Willie Horton | .30 | .12 | .03 |
| ☐ 434 Giants Team | .45 | .20 | .04 |
| ☐ 435 Rico Carty | .40 | .18 | .04 |
| ☐ 436 Jim McAndrew | .21 | .09 | .02 |
| ☐ 437 John Kennedy | .21 | .09 | .02 |
| ☐ 438 Enzo Hernandez | .21 | .09 | .02 |
| ☐ 439 Eddie Fisher | .21 | .09 | .02 |
| ☐ 440 Glenn Beckert | .25 | .10 | .02 |
| ☐ 441 Gail Hopkins | .21 | .09 | .02 |

| | MINT | VG-E | F-G |
|---|---|---|---|
| ☐ 442 Dick Dietz | .21 | .09 | .02 |
| ☐ 443 Danny Thompson | .21 | .09 | .02 |
| ☐ 444 Ken Brett | .25 | .10 | .02 |
| ☐ 445 Ken Berry | .21 | .09 | .02 |
| ☐ 446 Jerry Reuss | .40 | .18 | .04 |
| ☐ 447 Joe Hague | .21 | .09 | .02 |
| ☐ 448 John Hiller | .25 | .10 | .02 |
| ☐ 449 Indians Manager | .35 | .15 | .03 |
| Ken Aspromonte | | | |
| Coaches: | | | |
| Rocky Colavito | | | |
| Joe Lutz | | | |
| Warren Spahn | | | |
| ☐ 450 Joe Torre | .55 | .25 | .05 |
| ☐ 451 John Vuckovich | .21 | .09 | .02 |
| ☐ 452 Paul Casanova | .21 | .09 | .02 |
| ☐ 453 Checklist 4th Series | .75 | .15 | .03 |
| ☐ 454 Tom Haller | .21 | .09 | .02 |
| ☐ 455 Bill Melton | .21 | .09 | .02 |
| ☐ 456 Dick Green | .21 | .09 | .02 |
| ☐ 457 John Strohmayer | .21 | .09 | .02 |
| ☐ 458 Jim Mason | .21 | .09 | .02 |
| ☐ 459 Jimmy Howarth | .21 | .09 | .02 |
| ☐ 460 Bill Freehan | .35 | .15 | .03 |
| ☐ 461 Mike Corkins | .21 | .09 | .02 |
| ☐ 462 Ron Blomberg | .21 | .09 | .02 |
| ☐ 463 Ken Tatum | .21 | .09 | .02 |
| ☐ 464 Chicago Cubs Team | .45 | .20 | .04 |
| ☐ 465 Dave Giusti | .21 | .09 | .02 |
| ☐ 466 Jose Arcia | .21 | .09 | .02 |
| ☐ 467 Mike Ryan | .21 | .09 | .02 |
| ☐ 468 Tom Griffin | .21 | .09 | .02 |
| ☐ 469 Dan Monzon | .21 | .09 | .02 |
| ☐ 470 Mike Cuellar | .25 | .10 | .02 |
| ALL-TIME LEADERS (471–478) | | | |
| ☐ 471 Hits Leaders | 2.00 | .90 | .20 |
| Ty Cobb 4191 | | | |
| ☐ 472 Grand Slam Leaders | 2.00 | .90 | .20 |
| Lou Gehrig 23 | | | |
| ☐ 473 Total Bases Leaders | 2.00 | .90 | .20 |
| Hank Aaron 6172 | | | |
| ☐ 474 RBI Leaders | 2.75 | 1.25 | .27 |
| Babe Ruth 2209 | | | |
| ☐ 475 Batting Leaders | 2.00 | .90 | .20 |
| Ty Cobb .367 | | | |
| ☐ 476 Shutout Leaders | 1.00 | .45 | .10 |
| Walter Johnson 113 | | | |
| ☐ 477 Victory Leaders | 1.00 | .45 | .10 |
| Cy Young 511 | | | |
| ☐ 478 Strikeout Leaders | 1.00 | .45 | .10 |
| Walter Johnson 3508 | | | |
| ☐ 479 Hal Lanier | .30 | .12 | .03 |

| | MINT | VG-E | F-G |
|---|---|---|---|
| ☐ 480 Juan Marichal | 1.75 | .85 | .17 |
| ☐ 481 White Sox Team | .40 | .18 | .04 |
| ☐ 482 Rick Reuschel | .85 | .40 | .08 |
| ☐ 483 Dal Maxvill | .21 | .09 | .02 |
| ☐ 484 Ernie McAnally | .21 | .09 | .02 |
| ☐ 485 Norm Cash | .40 | .18 | .04 |
| ☐ 486 Phillies Manager | .30 | .12 | .03 |
| Danny Ozark | | | |
| Coaches: | | | |
| Carroll Beringer | | | |
| Billy DeMars | | | |
| Ray Rippelmeyer | | | |
| Bobby Wine | | | |
| ☐ 487 Bruce Dal Canton | .21 | .09 | .02 |
| ☐ 488 Dave Campbell | .21 | .09 | .02 |
| ☐ 489 Jeff Burroughs | .30 | .12 | .03 |
| ☐ 490 Claude Osteen | .25 | .10 | .02 |
| ☐ 491 Bob Montgomery | .21 | .09 | .02 |
| ☐ 492 Pedro Borbon | .21 | .09 | .02 |
| ☐ 493 Duffy Dyer | .21 | .09 | .02 |
| ☐ 494 Rich Morales | .21 | .09 | .02 |
| ☐ 495 Tommy Helms | .21 | .09 | .02 |
| ☐ 496 Ray Lamb | .21 | .09 | .02 |
| ☐ 497 Cardinals Manager | .35 | .15 | .03 |
| Red Schoendienst | | | |
| Coaches: Vern Benson | | | |
| George Kissell | | | |
| Barney Schultz | | | |
| ☐ 498 Graig Nettles | 1.50 | .70 | .15 |
| ☐ 499 Bob Moose | .21 | .09 | .02 |
| ☐ 500 Oakland A's Team | .45 | .20 | .04 |
| ☐ 501 Larry Gura | .35 | .15 | .03 |
| ☐ 502 Bobby Valentine | .35 | .15 | .03 |
| ☐ 503 Phil Niekro | 1.50 | .70 | .15 |
| ☐ 504 Earl Williams | .21 | .09 | .02 |
| ☐ 505 Bob Bailey | .21 | .09 | .02 |
| ☐ 506 Bart Johnson | .21 | .09 | .02 |
| ☐ 507 Darrel Chaney | .21 | .09 | .02 |
| ☐ 508 Gates Brown | .25 | .10 | .02 |
| ☐ 509 Jim Nash | .21 | .09 | .02 |
| ☐ 510 Amos Otis | .35 | .15 | .03 |
| ☐ 511 Sam McDowell | .30 | .12 | .03 |
| ☐ 512 Dalton Jones | .21 | .09 | .02 |
| ☐ 513 Dave Marshall | .21 | .09 | .02 |
| ☐ 514 Jerry Kenney | .21 | .09 | .02 |
| ☐ 515 Andy Messersmith | .30 | .12 | .03 |
| ☐ 516 Danny Walton | .21 | .09 | .02 |
| ☐ 517 Pirates Manager | .30 | .12 | .03 |
| Bill Virdon | | | |
| Coaches: Don Leppert | | | |
| Bill Mazeroski | | | |
| Dave Ricketts | | | |
| Mel Wright | | | |

| | MINT | VG-E | F-G |
|---|---|---|---|
| ☐ 518 Bob Veale | .25 | .10 | .02 |
| ☐ 519 John Edwards | .21 | .09 | .02 |
| ☐ 520 Mel Stottlemyre | .35 | .15 | .03 |
| ☐ 521 Atlanta Braves Team | .45 | .20 | .04 |
| ☐ 522 Leo Cardenas | .21 | .09 | .02 |
| ☐ 523 Wayne Granger | .21 | .09 | .02 |
| ☐ 524 Gene Tenace | .25 | .10 | .02 |
| ☐ 525 Jim Fregosi | .30 | .12 | .03 |
| ☐ 526 Ollie Brown | .21 | .09 | .02 |
| ☐ 527 Dan McGinn | .21 | .09 | .02 |
| ☐ 528 Paul Blair | .25 | .10 | .02 |
| ☐ 529 Milt May | .60 | .28 | .06 |
| ☐ 530 Jim Kaat | 1.75 | .85 | .17 |
| ☐ 531 Ron Woods | .60 | .28 | .06 |
| ☐ 532 Steve Mingori | .60 | .28 | .06 |
| ☐ 533 Larry Stahl | .60 | .28 | .06 |
| ☐ 534 Dave Lemonds | .60 | .28 | .06 |
| ☐ 535 John Callison | .90 | .40 | .09 |
| ☐ 536 Phillies Team | 1.10 | .50 | .11 |
| ☐ 537 Bill Slayback | .60 | .28 | .06 |
| ☐ 538 Jim Ray Hart | .75 | .35 | .07 |
| ☐ 539 Tom Murphy | .60 | .28 | .06 |
| ☐ 540 Cleon Jones | .60 | .28 | .06 |
| ☐ 541 Bob Bolin | .60 | .28 | .06 |
| ☐ 542 Pat Corrales | .75 | .35 | .07 |
| ☐ 543 Alan Foster | .60 | .28 | .06 |
| ☐ 544 Von Joshua | .60 | .28 | .06 |
| ☐ 545 Orlando Cepeda | 1.50 | .70 | .15 |
| ☐ 546 Jim York | .60 | .28 | .06 |
| ☐ 547 Bobby Heise | .60 | .28 | .06 |
| ☐ 548 Don Durham | .60 | .28 | .06 |
| ☐ 549 Rangers Manager | 1.25 | .60 | .12 |
| Whitey Herzog | | | |
| Coaches: Chuck Estrada | | | |
| Chuck Hiller | | | |
| Jackie Moore | | | |
| ☐ 550 Dave Johnson | 1.50 | .70 | .15 |
| ☐ 551 Mike Kilkenny | .60 | .28 | .06 |
| ☐ 552 J. C. Martin | .60 | .28 | .06 |
| ☐ 553 Mickey Scott | .60 | .28 | .06 |
| ☐ 554 Dave Concepcion | 1.75 | .85 | .17 |
| ☐ 555 Bill Hands | .60 | .28 | .06 |
| ☐ 556 Yankees Team | 1.75 | .85 | .17 |
| ☐ 557 Bernie Williams | .60 | .28 | .06 |
| ☐ 558 Jerry May | .60 | .28 | .06 |
| ☐ 559 Barry Lersch | .60 | .28 | .06 |
| ☐ 560 Frank Howard | 1.75 | .85 | .17 |
| ☐ 561 Jim Geddes | .60 | .28 | .06 |
| ☐ 562 Wayne Garrett | .60 | .28 | .06 |
| ☐ 563 Larry Haney | .60 | .28 | .06 |
| ☐ 564 Mike Thompson | .60 | .28 | .06 |
| ☐ 565 Jim Hickman | .60 | .28 | .06 |

| | MINT | VG-E | F-G |
|---|---|---|---|
| ☐ 566 Lew Krausse | .60 | .28 | .06 |
| ☐ 567 Bob Fenwick | .60 | .28 | .06 |
| ☐ 568 Ray Newman | .60 | .28 | .06 |
| ☐ 569 Dodgers Manager | 1.50 | .70 | .15 |
| Walt Alston | | | |
| Coaches: Red Adams | | | |
| Monty Basgall | | | |
| Jim Gilliam | | | |
| Tom Lasorda | | | |
| ☐ 570 Bill Singer | .60 | .28 | .06 |
| ☐ 571 Rusty Torres | .60 | .28 | .06 |
| ☐ 572 Gary Sutherland | .60 | .28 | .06 |
| ☐ 573 Fred Beene | .60 | .28 | .06 |
| ☐ 574 Bob Didier | .60 | .28 | .06 |
| ☐ 575 Dock Ellis | .60 | .28 | .06 |
| ☐ 576 Expos Team | 1.20 | .55 | .12 |
| ☐ 577 Eric Soderholm | .60 | .28 | .06 |
| ☐ 578 Ken Wright | .60 | .28 | .06 |
| ☐ 579 Tom Grieve | .75 | .35 | .07 |
| ☐ 580 Joe Pepitone | .90 | .40 | .09 |
| ☐ 581 Steve Kealey | .60 | .28 | .06 |
| ☐ 582 Darrell Porter | 1.00 | .45 | .10 |
| ☐ 583 Bill Grief | .60 | .28 | .06 |
| ☐ 584 Chris Arnold | .60 | .28 | .06 |
| ☐ 585 Joe Niekro | 1.25 | .60 | .12 |
| ☐ 586 Bill Sudakis | .60 | .28 | .06 |
| ☐ 587 Rich McKinney | .60 | .28 | .06 |
| ☐ 588 Checklist 5th Series | 7.00 | .70 | .07 |
| ☐ 589 Ken Forsch | .75 | .35 | .07 |
| ☐ 590 Deron Johnson | .75 | .35 | .07 |
| ☐ 591 Mike Hedlund | .60 | .28 | .06 |
| ☐ 592 John Boccabella | .60 | .28 | .06 |
| ☐ 593 Royals Manager | .75 | .35 | .07 |
| Jack McKeon | | | |
| Coaches: Galen Cisco | | | |
| Harry Dunlop | | | |
| Charlie Lau | | | |
| ☐ 594 Vic Harris | .60 | .28 | .06 |
| ☐ 595 Don Gullett | .75 | .35 | .07 |
| ☐ 596 Red Sox Team | 1.25 | .60 | .12 |
| ☐ 597 Mickey Rivers | 1.25 | .60 | .12 |
| ☐ 598 Phil Roof | .60 | .28 | .06 |
| ☐ 599 Ed Crosby | .60 | .28 | .06 |
| ☐ 600 Dave McNally | .90 | .40 | .09 |
| ☐ 601 Rookie Catchers | .60 | .28 | .06 |
| Sergio Robles | | | |
| George Pena | | | |
| Rick Stelmaszek | | | |
| ☐ 602 Rookie Pitchers | .60 | .28 | .06 |
| Mel Behney | | | |
| Ralph Garcia | | | |
| Doug Rau | | | |

| | MINT | VG-E | F-G | | | MINT | VG-E | F-G |
|---|---|---|---|---|---|---|---|---|
| ☐ 603 Rookie 3rd Basemen ... | .75 | .35 | .07 | ☐ 616 Rookie Pitchers ......... | .60 | .28 | .06 |
| Terry Hughes | | | | Norm Angelini | | | |
| Bill McNulty | | | | Steve Blateric | | | |
| Ken Reitz | | | | Mike Garman | | | |
| ☐ 604 Rookie Pitchers ......... | .60 | .28 | .06 | ☐ 617 Rich Chiles ............. | .60 | .28 | .06 |
| Jesse Jefferson | | | | ☐ 618 Andy Etchebarren ...... | .60 | .28 | .06 |
| Dennis O'Toole | | | | ☐ 619 Billy Wilson ........... | .60 | .28 | .06 |
| Bob Strampe | | | | ☐ 620 Tommy Harper ......... | .70 | .32 | .07 |
| ☐ 605 Rookie 1st Basemen ... | .75 | .35 | .07 | ☐ 621 Joe Ferguson ......... | .75 | .35 | .07 |
| Enos Cabell | | | | ☐ 622 Larry Hisle ........... | .75 | .35 | .07 |
| Pat Bourque | | | | ☐ 623 Steve Renko .......... | .60 | .28 | .06 |
| Gonzalo Marquez | | | | ☐ 624 Astros Manager ...... | 1.00 | .45 | .10 |
| ☐ 606 Rookie Outfielders ..... | 3.00 | 1.40 | .30 | Leo Durocher | | | |
| Gary Matthews | | | | Coaches: Preston | | | |
| Tom Paciorek | | | | Gomez | | | |
| Jorge Roque | | | | Grady Hatton | | | |
| ☐ 607 Rookie Shortstops ...... | .60 | .28 | .06 | Hub Kittle | | | |
| Pepe Frias | | | | Jim Owens | | | |
| Ray Busse | | | | ☐ 625 Angel Mangual ....... | .60 | .28 | .06 |
| Mario Guerrero | | | | ☐ 626 Bob Barton .......... | .60 | .28 | .06 |
| ☐ 608 Rookie Pitchers ......... | .75 | .35 | .07 | ☐ 627 Luis Alvarado ....... | .60 | .28 | .06 |
| Steve Busby | | | | ☐ 628 Jim Slaton ........... | .75 | .35 | .07 |
| Dick Colpaert | | | | ☐ 629 Indians Team ........ | 1.20 | .55 | .12 |
| George Medich | | | | ☐ 630 Denny McLain ....... | 1.50 | .70 | .15 |
| ☐ 609 Rookie 2nd Basemen .. | 2.75 | 1.25 | .27 | ☐ 631 Tom Matchick ....... | .60 | .28 | .06 |
| Larvel Blanks | | | | ☐ 632 Dick Selma .......... | .60 | .28 | .06 |
| Pedro Garcia | | | | ☐ 633 Ike Brown ........... | .60 | .28 | .06 |
| Dave Lopes | | | | ☐ 634 Alan Closter ......... | .60 | .28 | .06 |
| ☐ 610 Rookie Pitchers ......... | 1.50 | .70 | .15 | ☐ 635 Gene Alley .......... | .75 | .35 | .07 |
| Jimmy Freeman | | | | ☐ 636 Rickey Clark ........ | .60 | .28 | .06 |
| Charlie Hough | | | | ☐ 637 Norm Miller ......... | .60 | .28 | .06 |
| Hank Webb | | | | ☐ 638 Ken Reynolds ....... | .60 | .28 | .06 |
| ☐ 611 Rookie Outfielders ..... | 1.50 | .70 | .15 | ☐ 639 Willie Crawford ..... | .60 | .28 | .06 |
| Rich Coggins | | | | ☐ 640 Dick Bosman ........ | .60 | .28 | .06 |
| Jim Wohlford | | | | ☐ 641 Reds Team .......... | 1.25 | .60 | .12 |
| Richie Zisk | | | | ☐ 642 Jose LaBoy ......... | .60 | .28 | .06 |
| ☐ 612 Rookie Pitchers ......... | .60 | .28 | .06 | ☐ 643 Al Fitzmorris ........ | .60 | .28 | .06 |
| Steve Lawson | | | | ☐ 644 Jack Heidemann ..... | .60 | .28 | .06 |
| Bob Reynolds | | | | ☐ 645 Bob Locker .......... | .60 | .28 | .06 |
| Brent Strom | | | | ☐ 646 Brewers Manager ..... | 1.00 | .45 | .10 |
| ☐ 613 Rookie Catchers ........ | 1.50 | .70 | .15 | Del Crandall | | | |
| Bob Boone | | | | Coaches: Harvey Kuenn | | | |
| Skip Jutze | | | | Joe Nossek | | | |
| Mike Ivie | | | | Bob Shaw | | | |
| ☐ 614 Rookie Outfielders ..... | 7.00 | 3.25 | .70 | Jim Walton | | | |
| Alonza Bumbry | | | | ☐ 647 George Stone ........ | .60 | .28 | .06 |
| Dwight Evans | | | | ☐ 648 Tom Egan ........... | .60 | .28 | .06 |
| Charlie Spikes | | | | ☐ 649 Rich Folkers ......... | .60 | .28 | .06 |
| ☐ 615 Rookie 3rd Basemen ... | 70.00 | 32.00 | 7.00 | ☐ 650 Felipe Alou ......... | .75 | .35 | .07 |
| Ron Cey | | | | ☐ 651 Don Carrithers ...... | .60 | .28 | .06 |
| John Hilton | | | | ☐ 652 Ted Kubiak .......... | .60 | .28 | .06 |
| Mike Schmidt | | | | | | | |

| | MINT | VG-E | F-G |
|---|---|---|---|
| ☐ 653 Joe Hoerner | .60 | .28 | .06 |
| ☐ 654 Twins Team | 1.20 | .55 | .12 |
| ☐ 655 Clay Kirby | .60 | .28 | .06 |
| ☐ 656 John Ellis | .60 | .28 | .06 |
| ☐ 657 Bob Johnson | .60 | .28 | .06 |
| ☐ 658 Elliott Maddox | .60 | .28 | .06 |
| ☐ 659 Jose Pagan | .60 | .28 | .06 |
| ☐ 660 Fred Scherman | .90 | .40 | .09 |

## 1974 TOPPS

The cards in this 660 card set measure
2½" by 3½". This year marked the first
time Topps issued all the cards of its baseball set at the same time rather than in
series. Some interesting variations were
created by the rumored move of the San
Diego Padres to Washington. Fifteen
cards (13 players, the team card, and the
rookie card #599) of the Padres were
printed either as "San Diego" (SD) or
"Washington." The latter are the scarcer
variety and are denoted in the checklist
below by WASH. The first six cards in the
set (1–6) feature Hank Aaron and his career.

Complete Set: M-200.00; VG-E-90.00; F-G-20.00

| | | | |
|---|---|---|---|
| Common Player (1–660) | .14 | .06 | .01 |

| | MINT | VG-E | F-G |
|---|---|---|---|
| ☐ 1 Hank Aaron | 9.00 | 3.00 | .60 |
| Complete ML record | | | |
| ☐ 2 Aaron Special 54–57 | 2.25 | 1.00 | .22 |
| Records on back | | | |
| ☐ 3 Aaron Special 58–61 | 2.25 | 1.00 | .22 |
| Most memorable homers | | | |

| | MINT | VG-E | F-G |
|---|---|---|---|
| ☐ 4 Aaron Special 62–65 | 2.25 | 1.00 | .22 |
| Life in ML's 1954–63 | | | |
| ☐ 5 Aaron Special 66–69 | 2.25 | 1.00 | .22 |
| Life in ML's 1964–73 | | | |
| ☐ 6 Aaron Special 70–73 | 2.25 | 1.00 | .22 |
| Milestone homers | | | |
| ☐ 7 Jim Hunter | 1.25 | .60 | .12 |
| ☐ 8 George Theodore | .14 | .06 | .01 |
| ☐ 9 Mickey Lolich | .35 | .15 | .03 |
| ☐ 10 Johnny Bench | 4.50 | 2.10 | .45 |
| ☐ 11 Jim Bibby | .20 | .09 | .02 |
| ☐ 12 Dave May | .14 | .06 | .01 |
| ☐ 13 Tom Hilgendorf | .14 | .06 | .01 |
| ☐ 14 Paul Popovich | .14 | .06 | .01 |
| ☐ 15 Joe Torre | .50 | .22 | .05 |
| ☐ 16 Orioles Team | .35 | .15 | .03 |
| ☐ 17 Doug Bird | .14 | .06 | .01 |
| ☐ 18 Gary Thomasson | .14 | .06 | .01 |
| ☐ 19 Gerry Moses | .14 | .06 | .01 |
| ☐ 20 Nolan Ryan | 3.50 | 1.65 | .35 |
| ☐ 21 Bob Gallagher | .14 | .06 | .01 |
| ☐ 22 Cy Acosta | .14 | .06 | .01 |
| ☐ 23 Craig Robinson | .14 | .06 | .01 |
| ☐ 24 John Hiller | .20 | .09 | .02 |
| ☐ 25 Ken Singleton | .30 | .12 | .03 |
| ☐ 26 Bill Campbell | .25 | .10 | .02 |
| ☐ 27 George Scott | .20 | .09 | .02 |
| ☐ 28 Manny Sanguillen | .20 | .09 | .02 |
| ☐ 29 Phil Niekro | 1.00 | .45 | .10 |
| ☐ 30 Bobby Bonds | .30 | .12 | .03 |
| ☐ 31 Astros Manager | .20 | .09 | .02 |
| Preston Gomez | | | |
| Coaches: Roger Craig | | | |
| Hub Kittle | | | |
| Grady Hatton | | | |
| Bob Lillis | | | |
| ☐ 32 A Johnny Grubb SD | .30 | .12 | .03 |
| ☐ 32 B Johnny Grubb WASH | 2.75 | 1.25 | .27 |
| ☐ 33 Don Newhauser | .14 | .06 | .01 |
| ☐ 34 Andy Kosco | .14 | .06 | .01 |
| ☐ 35 Gaylord Perry | 1.50 | .70 | .15 |
| ☐ 36 Cardinals Team | .35 | .15 | .03 |
| ☐ 37 Dave Sells | .14 | .06 | .01 |
| ☐ 38 Don Kessinger | .20 | .09 | .02 |
| ☐ 39 Ken Suarez | .14 | .06 | .01 |
| ☐ 40 Jim Palmer | 2.50 | 1.15 | .25 |
| ☐ 41 Bobby Floyd | .14 | .06 | .01 |
| ☐ 42 Claude Osteen | .20 | .09 | .02 |
| ☐ 43 Jim Wynn | .20 | .09 | .02 |
| ☐ 44 Mel Stottlemyre | .20 | .09 | .02 |
| ☐ 45 Dave Johnson | .25 | .10 | .02 |
| ☐ 46 Pat Kelly | .14 | .06 | .01 |

|  | | MINT | VG-E | F-G |
|---|---|---|---|---|
| ☐ 47 | Dick Ruthven | .14 | .06 | .01 |
| ☐ 48 | Dick Sharon | .14 | .06 | .01 |
| ☐ 49 | Steve Renko | .14 | .06 | .01 |
| ☐ 50 | Rod Carew | 4.50 | 2.10 | .45 |
| ☐ 51 | Bob Heise | .14 | .06 | .01 |
| ☐ 52 | Al Oliver | 1.00 | .45 | .10 |
| ☐ 53 A | Fred Kendall SD | .30 | .12 | .03 |
| ☐ 53 B | Fred Kendall WASH | 2.75 | 1.25 | .27 |
| ☐ 54 | Elias Sosa | .14 | .06 | .01 |
| ☐ 55 | Frank Robinson | 2.25 | 1.00 | .22 |
| ☐ 56 | New York Mets Team | .50 | .22 | .05 |
| ☐ 57 | Darold Knowles | .14 | .06 | .01 |
| ☐ 58 | Charlie Spikes | .14 | .06 | .01 |
| ☐ 59 | Ross Grimsley | .14 | .06 | .01 |
| ☐ 60 | Lou Brock | 2.25 | 1.00 | .22 |
| ☐ 61 | Luis Aparicio | 1.50 | .70 | .15 |
| ☐ 62 | Bob Locker | .14 | .06 | .01 |
| ☐ 63 | Bill Sudakis | .14 | .06 | .01 |
| ☐ 64 | Doug Rau | .14 | .06 | .01 |
| ☐ 65 | Amos Otis | .30 | .12 | .03 |
| ☐ 66 | Sparky Lyle | .30 | .12 | .03 |
| ☐ 67 | Tommy Helms | .14 | .06 | .01 |
| ☐ 68 | Grant Jackson | .14 | .06 | .01 |
| ☐ 69 | Del Unser | .14 | .06 | .01 |
| ☐ 70 | Dick Allen | .35 | .15 | .03 |
| ☐ 71 | Dan Frisella | .14 | .06 | .01 |
| ☐ 72 | Aurelio Rodriguez | .14 | .06 | .01 |
| ☐ 73 | Mike Marshall | .35 | .15 | .03 |
| ☐ 74 | Twins Team | .30 | .12 | .03 |
| ☐ 75 | Jim Colborn | .14 | .06 | .01 |
| ☐ 76 | Mickey Rivers | .30 | .12 | .03 |
| ☐ 77 A | Rich Troedson SD | .30 | .12 | .03 |
| ☐ 77 B | Rich Troedson WASH | 2.75 | 1.25 | .27 |
| ☐ 78 | Giants Manager | .20 | .09 | .02 |
| | Charlie Fox | | | |
| | Coaches: John | | | |
| | McNamara | | | |
| | Joe Amalfitano | | | |
| | Andy Gilbert | | | |
| | Don McMahon | | | |
| ☐ 79 | Gene Tenace | .14 | .06 | .01 |
| ☐ 80 | Tom Seaver | 4.00 | 1.85 | .40 |
| ☐ 81 | Frank Duffy | .14 | .06 | .01 |
| ☐ 82 | Dave Giusti | .14 | .06 | .01 |
| ☐ 83 | Orlando Cepeda | .50 | .22 | .05 |
| ☐ 84 | Rick Wise | .20 | .09 | .02 |
| ☐ 85 | Joe Morgan | 1.50 | .70 | .15 |
| ☐ 86 | Joe Ferguson | .20 | .09 | .02 |
| ☐ 87 | Fergie Jenkins | .75 | .35 | .07 |
| ☐ 88 | Fred Patek | .14 | .06 | .01 |
| ☐ 89 | Jackie Brown | .14 | .06 | .01 |
| ☐ 90 | Bobby Murcer | .50 | .22 | .05 |

|  | | MINT | VG-E | F-G |
|---|---|---|---|---|
| ☐ 91 | Ken Forsch | .20 | .09 | .02 |
| ☐ 92 | Paul Blair | .20 | .09 | .02 |
| ☐ 93 | Rod Gilbreath | .14 | .06 | .01 |
| ☐ 94 | Tigers Team | .35 | .15 | .03 |
| ☐ 95 | Steve Carlton | 5.00 | 2.35 | .50 |
| ☐ 96 | Jerry Hairston | .14 | .06 | .01 |
| ☐ 97 | Bob Bailey | .14 | .06 | .01 |
| ☐ 98 | Bert Blyleven | .50 | .22 | .05 |
| ☐ 99 | Brewers Manager | .30 | .12 | .03 |
| | Del Crandall | | | |
| | Coaches: Harvey Kuenn | | | |
| | Joe Nossek | | | |
| | Jim Walton | | | |
| | Al Widmar | | | |
| ☐ 100 | Willie Stargell | 1.75 | .85 | .17 |
| ☐ 101 | Bobby Valentine | .25 | .10 | .02 |
| ☐ 102 A | Bill Greif SD | .30 | .12 | .03 |
| ☐ 102 B | Bill Greif WASH | 2.75 | 1.25 | .27 |
| ☐ 103 | Sal Bando | .30 | .12 | .03 |
| ☐ 104 | Ron Bryant | .14 | .06 | .01 |
| ☐ 105 | Carlton Fisk | 1.25 | .60 | .12 |
| ☐ 106 | Harry Parker | .14 | .06 | .01 |
| ☐ 107 | Alex Johnson | .14 | .06 | .01 |
| ☐ 108 | Al Hrabosky | .20 | .09 | .02 |
| ☐ 109 | Bobby Grich | .30 | .12 | .03 |
| ☐ 110 | Billy Williams | .75 | .35 | .07 |
| ☐ 111 | Clay Carroll | .14 | .06 | .01 |
| ☐ 112 | Dave Lopes | .30 | .12 | .03 |
| ☐ 113 | Dick Drago | .14 | .06 | .01 |
| ☐ 114 | Angels Team | .30 | .12 | .03 |
| ☐ 115 | Willie Horton | .20 | .09 | .02 |
| ☐ 116 | Jerry Reuss | .30 | .12 | .03 |
| ☐ 117 | Ron Blomberg | .14 | .06 | .01 |
| ☐ 118 | Bill Lee | .20 | .09 | .02 |
| ☐ 119 | Phillies Manager | .20 | .09 | .02 |
| | Danny Ozark | | | |
| | Coaches: | | | |
| | Ray Rippelmeyer | | | |
| | Bobby Wine | | | |
| | Carroll Beringer | | | |
| | Billy DeMars | | | |
| ☐ 120 | Wilbur Wood | .20 | .09 | .02 |
| ☐ 121 | Larry Lintz | .14 | .06 | .01 |
| ☐ 122 | Jim Holt | .14 | .06 | .01 |
| ☐ 123 | Nellie Briles | .14 | .06 | .01 |
| ☐ 124 | Bobby Coluccio | .14 | .06 | .01 |
| ☐ 125 A | Nate Colbert SD | .30 | .12 | .03 |
| ☐ 125 B | Nate Colbert WASH | 2.75 | 1.25 | .27 |
| ☐ 126 | Checklist 1 | .50 | .10 | .02 |
| ☐ 127 | Tom Paciorek | .20 | .09 | .02 |
| ☐ 128 | John Ellis | .14 | .06 | .01 |
| ☐ 129 | Chris Speier | .14 | .06 | .01 |

| | MINT | VG-E | F-G |
|---|---|---|---|
| ☐ 130 Reggie Jackson | 5.00 | 2.35 | .50 |
| ☐ 131 Bob Boone | .25 | .10 | .02 |
| ☐ 132 Felix Millan | .14 | .06 | .01 |
| ☐ 133 David Clyde | .20 | .09 | .02 |
| ☐ 134 Dennis Menke | .14 | .06 | .01 |
| ☐ 135 Roy White | .20 | .09 | .02 |
| ☐ 136 Rick Reuschel | .25 | .10 | .02 |
| ☐ 137 Al Bumbry | .14 | .06 | .01 |
| ☐ 138 Eddie Brinkman | .14 | .06 | .01 |
| ☐ 139 Aurelio Monteagudo | .14 | .06 | .01 |
| ☐ 140 Darrell Evans | .35 | .15 | .03 |
| ☐ 141 Pat Bourque | .14 | .06 | .01 |
| ☐ 142 Pedro Garcia | .14 | .06 | .01 |
| ☐ 143 Dick Woodson | .14 | .06 | .01 |
| ☐ 144 Dodgers Manager | .50 | .22 | .05 |
| Walter Alston | | | |
| Coaches: Tom Lasorda | | | |
| Jim Gilliam | | | |
| Red Adams | | | |
| Monty Basgall | | | |
| ☐ 145 Dock Ellis | .14 | .06 | .01 |
| ☐ 146 Ron Fairly | .20 | .09 | .02 |
| ☐ 147 Bart Johnson | .14 | .06 | .01 |
| ☐ 148 A Dave Hilton SD | .30 | .12 | .03 |
| ☐ 148 B Dave Hilton WASH | 2.75 | 1.25 | .27 |
| ☐ 149 Mac Scarce | .14 | .06 | .01 |
| ☐ 150 John Mayberry | .20 | .09 | .02 |
| ☐ 151 Diego Segui | .14 | .06 | .01 |
| ☐ 152 Oscar Gamble | .25 | .10 | .02 |
| ☐ 153 Jon Matlack | .20 | .09 | .02 |
| ☐ 154 Astros Team | .30 | .12 | .03 |
| ☐ 155 Bert Campaneris | .30 | .12 | .03 |
| ☐ 156 Randy Moffitt | .14 | .06 | .01 |
| ☐ 157 Vic Harris | .14 | .06 | .01 |
| ☐ 158 Jack Billingham | .14 | .06 | .01 |
| ☐ 159 Jim Ray Hart | .20 | .09 | .02 |
| ☐ 160 Brooks Robinson | 2.25 | 1.00 | .22 |
| ☐ 161 Ray Burris | .35 | .15 | .03 |
| ☐ 162 Bill Freehan | .30 | .12 | .03 |
| ☐ 163 Ken Berry | .14 | .06 | .01 |
| ☐ 164 Tom House | .14 | .06 | .01 |
| ☐ 165 Willie Davis | .20 | .09 | .02 |
| ☐ 166 Royals Manager | .20 | .09 | .02 |
| Jack McKeon | | | |
| Coaches: Charlie Lau | | | |
| Harry Dunlop | | | |
| Galen Cisco | | | |
| ☐ 167 Luis Tiant | .30 | .12 | .03 |
| ☐ 168 Danny Thompson | .14 | .06 | .01 |
| ☐ 169 Steve Rogers | 1.25 | .60 | .12 |
| ☐ 170 Bill Melton | .14 | .06 | .01 |
| ☐ 171 Eduardo Rodriguez | .14 | .06 | .01 |
| ☐ 172 Gene Clines | .14 | .06 | .01 |

| | MINT | VG-E | F-G |
|---|---|---|---|
| ☐ 173 A Randy Jones SD | .45 | .20 | .04 |
| ☐ 173 B Randy Jones WASH | 3.25 | 1.50 | .32 |
| ☐ 174 Bill Robinson | .14 | .06 | .01 |
| ☐ 175 Reggie Cleveland | .14 | .06 | .01 |
| ☐ 176 John Lowenstein | .14 | .06 | .01 |
| ☐ 177 Dave Roberts | .14 | .06 | .01 |
| ☐ 178 Garry Maddox | .20 | .09 | .02 |
| ☐ 179 New York Mets Manager | .50 | .22 | .05 |
| Yogi Berra | | | |
| Coaches: Rube Walker | | | |
| Eddie Yost | | | |
| Roy McMillan | | | |
| Joe Pignatano | | | |
| ☐ 180 Ken Holtzman | .25 | .10 | .02 |
| ☐ 181 Cesar Geronimo | .14 | .06 | .01 |
| ☐ 182 Lindy McDaniel | .14 | .06 | .01 |
| ☐ 183 Johnny Oates | .14 | .06 | .01 |
| ☐ 184 Rangers Team | .30 | .12 | .03 |
| ☐ 185 Jose Cardenal | .14 | .06 | .01 |
| ☐ 186 Fred Scherman | .14 | .06 | .01 |
| ☐ 187 Don Baylor | .50 | .22 | .05 |
| ☐ 188 Rudy Meoli | .14 | .06 | .01 |
| ☐ 189 Jim Brewer | .14 | .06 | .01 |
| ☐ 190 Tony Oliva | .50 | .22 | .05 |
| ☐ 191 Al Fitzmorris | .14 | .06 | .01 |
| ☐ 192 Mario Guerrero | .14 | .06 | .01 |
| ☐ 193 Tom Walker | .14 | .06 | .01 |
| ☐ 194 Darrell Porter | .25 | .10 | .02 |
| ☐ 195 Carlos May | .14 | .06 | .01 |
| ☐ 196 Jim Fregosi | .20 | .09 | .02 |
| ☐ 197 A Vicente Romo SD | .30 | .12 | .03 |
| ☐ 197 B Vicente Romo WASH | 2.75 | 1.25 | .27 |
| ☐ 198 Dave Cash | .14 | .06 | .01 |
| ☐ 199 Mike Kekich | .14 | .06 | .01 |
| ☐ 200 Cesar Cedeno | .30 | .12 | .03 |
| ☐ 201 Batting Leaders: | 2.25 | 1.00 | .22 |
| Rod Carew | | | |
| Pete Rose | | | |
| ☐ 202 Home Run Leaders: | 1.10 | .50 | .11 |
| Reggie Jackson | | | |
| Willie Stargell | | | |
| ☐ 203 RBI Leaders: | 1.10 | .50 | .11 |
| Reggie Jackson | | | |
| Willie Stargell | | | |
| ☐ 204 Stolen Base Leaders: | .55 | .25 | .05 |
| Tommy Harper | | | |
| Lou Brock | | | |
| ☐ 205 Victory Leaders: | .30 | .12 | .03 |
| Wilbur Wood | | | |
| Ron Bryant | | | |
| ☐ 206 ERA Leaders: | 1.25 | .60 | .12 |
| Jim Palmer | | | |
| Tom Seaver | | | |

| | MINT | VG-E | F-G |
|---|---|---|---|
| ☐ 207 Strikeout Leaders: ...... | 1.25 | .60 | .12 |
| Nolan Ryan | | | |
| Tom Seaver | | | |
| ☐ 208 Leading Firemen: ...... | .30 | .12 | .03 |
| John Hiller | | | |
| Mike Marshall | | | |
| ☐ 209 Ted Sizemore ............ | .14 | .06 | .01 |
| ☐ 210 Bill Singer ............. | .14 | .06 | .01 |
| ☐ 211 Chicago Cubs Team ... | .30 | .12 | .03 |
| ☐ 212 Rollie Fingers ......... | 1.00 | .45 | .10 |
| ☐ 213 Dave Rader ............. | .14 | .06 | .01 |
| ☐ 214 Bill Grabarkewitz ...... | .14 | .06 | .01 |
| ☐ 215 Al Kaline .............. | 2.25 | 1.00 | .22 |
| ☐ 216 Ray Sadecki ........... | .14 | .06 | .01 |
| ☐ 217 Tim Foli .............. | .14 | .06 | .01 |
| ☐ 218 John Briggs ........... | .14 | .06 | .01 |
| ☐ 219 Doug Griffin .......... | .14 | .06 | .01 |
| ☐ 220 Don Sutton ........... | .85 | .40 | .08 |
| ☐ 221 White Sox Manager .... | .25 | .10 | .02 |
| Chuck Tanner | | | |
| Coaches: Jim Mahoney | | | |
| Alex Monchak | | | |
| Johnny Sain | | | |
| Joe Lonnett | | | |
| ☐ 222 Ramon Hernandez ...... | .14 | .06 | .01 |
| ☐ 223 Jeff Burroughs ......... | .35 | .15 | .03 |
| ☐ 224 Roger Metzger ......... | .14 | .06 | .01 |
| ☐ 225 Paul Splittorff ........ | .20 | .09 | .02 |
| ☐ 226 A Padres Team Card SD | .50 | .22 | .05 |
| ☐ 226 B Padres Team Card | | | |
| WASH | 3.50 | 1.65 | .35 |
| ☐ 227 Mike Lum ............. | .14 | .06 | .01 |
| ☐ 228 Ted Kubiak ........... | .14 | .06 | .01 |
| ☐ 229 Fritz Peterson ........ | .14 | .06 | .01 |
| ☐ 230 Tony Perez ........... | .50 | .22 | .05 |
| ☐ 231 Dick Tidrow .......... | .14 | .06 | .01 |
| ☐ 232 Steve Brye ........... | .14 | .06 | .01 |
| ☐ 233 Jim Barr ............. | .14 | .06 | .01 |
| ☐ 234 John Milner .......... | .14 | .06 | .01 |
| ☐ 235 Dave McNally ......... | .20 | .09 | .02 |
| ☐ 236 Cardinals Manager .... | .30 | .12 | .03 |
| Red Schoendienst | | | |
| Coaches: Barney Schultz | | | |
| George Kissell | | | |
| Johnny Lewis | | | |
| Vern Benson | | | |
| ☐ 237 Ken Brett ............. | .20 | .09 | .02 |
| ☐ 238 Fran Healy ........... | .14 | .06 | .01 |
| ☐ 239 Bill Russell .......... | .20 | .09 | .02 |
| ☐ 240 Joe Coleman .......... | .14 | .06 | .01 |
| ☐ 241 A Glenn Beckert SD .... | .30 | .12 | .03 |
| ☐ 241 B Glenn Beckert WASH | 2.75 | 1.25 | .27 |
| ☐ 242 Bill Gogolewski ....... | .14 | .06 | .01 |

| | MINT | VG-E | F-G |
|---|---|---|---|
| ☐ 243 Bob Oliver ............ | .14 | .06 | .01 |
| ☐ 244 Carl Morton .......... | .14 | .06 | .01 |
| ☐ 245 Cleon Jones .......... | .14 | .06 | .01 |
| ☐ 246 Athletics Team ....... | .30 | .12 | .03 |
| ☐ 247 Rick Miller ........... | .14 | .06 | .01 |
| ☐ 248 Tom Hall ............. | .14 | .06 | .01 |
| ☐ 249 George Mitterwald .... | .14 | .06 | .01 |
| ☐ 250 A Willie McCovey SD ... | 3.00 | 1.40 | .30 |
| ☐ 250 B Willie McCovey WASH | 15.00 | 7.00 | 1.50 |
| ☐ 251 Graig Nettles ........ | 1.25 | .60 | .12 |
| ☐ 252 Dave Parker .......... | 9.00 | 4.25 | .90 |
| ☐ 253 John Boccabella ...... | .14 | .06 | .01 |
| ☐ 254 Stan Bahnsen ........ | .14 | .06 | .01 |
| ☐ 255 Larry Bowa ........... | .35 | .15 | .03 |
| ☐ 256 Tom Griffin .......... | .14 | .06 | .01 |
| ☐ 257 Buddy Bell ........... | .75 | .35 | .07 |
| ☐ 258 Jerry Morales ........ | .14 | .06 | .01 |
| ☐ 259 Bob Reynolds ........ | .14 | .06 | .01 |
| ☐ 260 Ted Simmons ........ | .75 | .35 | .07 |
| ☐ 261 Jerry Bell ........... | .14 | .06 | .01 |
| ☐ 262 Ed Kirkpatrick ....... | .14 | .06 | .01 |
| ☐ 263 Checklist 2 .......... | .50 | .10 | .02 |
| ☐ 264 Joe Rudi ............. | .25 | .10 | .02 |
| ☐ 265 Tug McGraw ......... | .30 | .12 | .03 |
| ☐ 266 Jim Northrup ........ | .14 | .06 | .01 |
| ☐ 267 Andy Messersmith .... | .20 | .09 | .02 |
| ☐ 268 Tom Grieve .......... | .20 | .09 | .02 |
| ☐ 269 Bob Johnson ........ | .14 | .06 | .01 |
| ☐ 270 Ron Santo ........... | .35 | .15 | .03 |
| ☐ 271 Bill Hands ........... | .14 | .06 | .01 |
| ☐ 272 Paul Casanova ....... | .14 | .06 | .01 |
| ☐ 273 Checklist 3 .......... | .50 | .10 | .02 |
| ☐ 274 Fred Beene .......... | .14 | .06 | .01 |
| ☐ 275 Ron Hunt ............ | .14 | .06 | .01 |
| ☐ 276 Angels Manager ...... | .20 | .09 | .02 |
| Bobby Winkles | | | |
| Coaches: John Roseboro | | | |
| Tom Morgan | | | |
| Jimmie Reese | | | |
| Salty Parker | | | |
| ☐ 277 Gary Nolan .......... | .14 | .06 | .01 |
| ☐ 278 Cookie Rojas ........ | .14 | .06 | .01 |
| ☐ 279 Jim Crawford ........ | .14 | .06 | .01 |
| ☐ 280 Carl Yastrzemski .... | 6.50 | 3.00 | .65 |
| ☐ 281 Giants Team ......... | .30 | .12 | .03 |
| ☐ 282 Doyle Alexander ..... | .20 | .09 | .02 |
| ☐ 283 Mike Schmidt ....... | 10.50 | 5.00 | 1.00 |
| ☐ 284 Dave Duncan ........ | .14 | .06 | .01 |
| ☐ 285 Reggie Smith ........ | .35 | .15 | .03 |
| ☐ 286 Tony Muser .......... | .14 | .06 | .01 |
| ☐ 287 Clay Kirby ........... | .14 | .06 | .01 |
| ☐ 288 Gorman Thomas ..... | 2.00 | .90 | .20 |
| ☐ 289 Rick Auerbach ....... | .14 | .06 | .01 |

| | MINT | VG-E | F-G |
|---|---|---|---|
| ☐ 290 Vida Blue | .35 | .15 | .03 |
| ☐ 291 Don Hahn | .14 | .06 | .01 |
| ☐ 292 Chuck Seelbach | .14 | .06 | .01 |
| ☐ 293 Milt May | .14 | .06 | .01 |
| ☐ 294 Steve Foucault | .14 | .06 | .01 |
| ☐ 295 Rick Monday | .20 | .09 | .02 |
| ☐ 296 Ray Corbin | .14 | .06 | .01 |
| ☐ 297 Hal Breeden | .14 | .06 | .01 |
| ☐ 298 Roric Harrison | .14 | .06 | .01 |
| ☐ 299 Gene Michael | .20 | .09 | .02 |
| ☐ 300 Pete Rose | 11.00 | 5.25 | 1.10 |
| ☐ 301 Bob Montgomery | .14 | .06 | .01 |
| ☐ 302 Rudy May | .14 | .06 | .01 |
| ☐ 303 George Hendrick | .40 | .18 | .04 |
| ☐ 304 Don Wilson | .14 | .06 | .01 |
| ☐ 305 Tito Fuentes | .14 | .06 | .01 |
| ☐ 306 Orioles Manager | .45 | .20 | .04 |
| Earl Weaver | | | |
| Coaches: Jim Frey | | | |
| George Bamberger | | | |
| Billy Hunter | | | |
| George Staller | | | |
| ☐ 307 Luis Melendez | .14 | .06 | .01 |
| ☐ 308 Bruce Dal Canton | .14 | .06 | .01 |
| ☐ 309 A Dave Roberts SD | .30 | .12 | .03 |
| ☐ 309 B Dave Roberts WASH | 3.50 | 1.65 | .35 |
| ☐ 310 Terry Forster | .25 | .10 | .02 |
| ☐ 311 Jerry Grote | .14 | .06 | .01 |
| ☐ 312 Deron Johnson | .14 | .06 | .01 |
| ☐ 313 Barry Lersch | .14 | .06 | .01 |
| ☐ 314 Brewers Team | .30 | .12 | .03 |
| ☐ 315 Ron Cey | 1.00 | .45 | .10 |
| ☐ 316 Jim Perry | .25 | .10 | .02 |
| ☐ 317 Richie Zisk | .25 | .10 | .02 |
| ☐ 318 Jim Merritt | .14 | .06 | .01 |
| ☐ 319 Randy Hundley | .14 | .06 | .01 |
| ☐ 320 Dusty Baker | .45 | .20 | .04 |
| ☐ 321 Steve Braun | .14 | .06 | .01 |
| ☐ 322 Ernie McAnally | .14 | .06 | .01 |
| ☐ 323 Richie Scheinblum | .14 | .06 | .01 |
| ☐ 324 Steve Kline | .14 | .06 | .01 |
| ☐ 325 Tommy Harper | .20 | .09 | .02 |
| ☐ 326 Reds Manager | .30 | .12 | .03 |
| Sparky Anderson | | | |
| Coaches: Larry | | | |
| Shephard | | | |
| George Scherger | | | |
| Alex Grammas | | | |
| Ted Kluszewski | | | |
| ☐ 327 Tom Timmermann | .14 | .06 | .01 |
| ☐ 328 Skip Jutze | .14 | .06 | .01 |
| ☐ 329 Mark Belanger | .20 | .09 | .02 |
| ☐ 330 Juan Marichal | 1.50 | .70 | .15 |

| | MINT | VG-E | F-G |
|---|---|---|---|
| ☐ 331 All-Star Catchers: | 1.10 | .50 | .11 |
| Carlton Fisk | | | |
| Johnny Bench | | | |
| ☐ 332 All-Star 1B: | 1.10 | .50 | .11 |
| Dick Allen | | | |
| Hank Aaron | | | |
| ☐ 333 All-Star 2B: | 1.10 | .50 | .11 |
| Rod Carew | | | |
| Joe Morgan | | | |
| ☐ 334 All-Star 3B: | .80 | .40 | .08 |
| Brooks Robinson | | | |
| Ron Santo | | | |
| ☐ 335 All-Star SS: | .20 | .09 | .02 |
| Bert Campaneris | | | |
| Chris Speier | | | |
| ☐ 336 All-Star LF: | 2.00 | .90 | .20 |
| Bobby Murcer | | | |
| Pete Rose | | | |
| ☐ 337 All-Star CF: | .20 | .09 | .02 |
| Amos Otis | | | |
| Cesar Cedeno | | | |
| ☐ 338 All-Star RF: | 1.25 | .60 | .12 |
| Reggie Jackson | | | |
| Billy Williams | | | |
| ☐ 339 All-Star Pitchers: | .35 | .15 | .03 |
| Jim Hunter | | | |
| Rick Wise | | | |
| ☐ 340 Thurman Munson | 3.50 | 1.65 | .35 |
| ☐ 341 Dan Driessen | .45 | .20 | .04 |
| ☐ 342 Jim Lonborg | .20 | .09 | .02 |
| ☐ 343 Royals Team | .30 | .12 | .03 |
| ☐ 344 Mike Caldwell | .20 | .09 | .02 |
| ☐ 345 Bill North | .14 | .06 | .01 |
| ☐ 346 Ron Reed | .14 | .06 | .01 |
| ☐ 347 Sandy Alomar | .14 | .06 | .01 |
| ☐ 348 Pete Richert | .14 | .06 | .01 |
| ☐ 349 John Vukovich | .14 | .06 | .01 |
| ☐ 350 Bob Gibson | 1.75 | .85 | .17 |
| ☐ 351 Dwight Evans | 1.25 | .60 | .12 |
| ☐ 352 Bill Stoneman | .14 | .06 | .01 |
| ☐ 353 Rich Coggins | .14 | .06 | .01 |
| ☐ 354 Chicago Cubs Manager | .20 | .09 | .02 |
| Whitey Lockman | | | |
| Coaches: J.C. Martin | | | |
| Hank Aguirre | | | |
| Al Spangler | | | |
| Jim Marshall | | | |
| ☐ 355 Dave Nelson | .14 | .06 | .01 |
| ☐ 356 Jerry Koosman | .30 | .12 | .03 |
| ☐ 357 Buddy Bradford | .14 | .06 | .01 |
| ☐ 358 Dal Maxvill | .14 | .06 | .01 |
| ☐ 359 Brent Strom | .14 | .06 | .01 |
| ☐ 360 Greg Luzinski | .70 | .32 | .07 |

| | MINT | VG-E | F-G |
|---|---|---|---|
| ☐ 361 Don Carrithers | .14 | .06 | .01 |
| ☐ 362 Hal King | .14 | .06 | .01 |
| ☐ 363 Yankees Team | .50 | .22 | .05 |
| ☐ 364 A Cito Gaston SD | .30 | .12 | .03 |
| ☐ 364 B Cito Gaston WASH | 3.50 | 1.65 | .35 |
| ☐ 365 Steve Busby | .25 | .10 | .02 |
| ☐ 366 Larry Hisle | .25 | .10 | .02 |
| ☐ 367 Norm Cash | .30 | .12 | .03 |
| ☐ 368 Manny Mota | .20 | .09 | .02 |
| ☐ 369 Paul Lindblad | .14 | .06 | .01 |
| ☐ 370 Bob Watson | .30 | .12 | .03 |
| ☐ 371 Jim Slaton | .14 | .06 | .01 |
| ☐ 372 Ken Reitz | .14 | .06 | .01 |
| ☐ 373 John Curtis | .14 | .06 | .01 |
| ☐ 374 Marty Perez | .14 | .06 | .01 |
| ☐ 375 Earl Williams | .14 | .06 | .01 |
| ☐ 376 Jorge Orta | .14 | .06 | .01 |
| ☐ 377 Ron Woods | .14 | .06 | .01 |
| ☐ 378 Burt Hooton | .20 | .09 | .02 |
| ☐ 379 Rangers Manager | .50 | .22 | .05 |
| Billy Martin | | | |
| Coaches: Frank Lucchesi | | | |
| Art Fowler | | | |
| Charlie Silvera | | | |
| Jackie Moore | | | |
| ☐ 380 Bud Harrelson | .14 | .06 | .01 |
| ☐ 381 Charlie Sands | .14 | .06 | .01 |
| ☐ 382 Bob Moose | .14 | .06 | .01 |
| ☐ 383 Phillies Team | .30 | .12 | .03 |
| ☐ 384 Chris Chambliss | .30 | .12 | .03 |
| ☐ 385 Don Gullett | .20 | .09 | .02 |
| ☐ 386 Gary Matthews | .45 | .20 | .04 |
| ☐ 387 A Rich Morales SD | .30 | .12 | .03 |
| ☐ 387 B Rich Morales WASH | 3.50 | 1.65 | .35 |
| ☐ 388 Phil Roof | .14 | .06 | .01 |
| ☐ 389 Gates Brown | .20 | .09 | .02 |
| ☐ 390 Lou Piniella | .40 | .18 | .04 |
| ☐ 391 Billy Champion | .14 | .06 | .01 |
| ☐ 392 Dick Green | .14 | .06 | .01 |
| ☐ 393 Orlando Pena | .14 | .06 | .01 |
| ☐ 394 Ken Henderson | .14 | .06 | .01 |
| ☐ 395 Doug Rader | .20 | .09 | .02 |
| ☐ 396 Tommy Davis | .20 | .09 | .02 |
| ☐ 397 George Stone | .14 | .06 | .01 |
| ☐ 398 Duke Sims | .14 | .06 | .01 |
| ☐ 399 Mike Paul | .14 | .06 | .01 |
| ☐ 400 Harmon Killebrew | 1.75 | .85 | .17 |
| ☐ 401 Elliot Maddox | .14 | .06 | .01 |
| ☐ 402 Jim Rooker | .14 | .06 | .01 |

| | MINT | VG-E | F-G |
|---|---|---|---|
| ☐ 403 Red Sox Manager | .20 | .09 | .02 |
| Darrell Johnson | | | |
| Coaches: Eddie | | | |
| Popowski | | | |
| Lee Stange | | | |
| Don Zimmer | | | |
| Don Bryant | | | |
| ☐ 404 Jim Howarth | .14 | .06 | .01 |
| ☐ 405 Ellie Rodriguez | .14 | .06 | .01 |
| ☐ 406 Steve Arlin | .14 | .06 | .01 |
| ☐ 407 Jim Wohlford | .14 | .06 | .01 |
| ☐ 408 Charlie Hough | .25 | .10 | .02 |
| ☐ 409 Ike Brown | .14 | .06 | .01 |
| ☐ 410 Pedro Borbon | .14 | .06 | .01 |
| ☐ 411 Frank Baker | .14 | .06 | .01 |
| ☐ 412 Chuck Taylor | .14 | .06 | .01 |
| ☐ 413 Don Money | .20 | .09 | .02 |
| ☐ 414 Checklist 4 | .50 | .10 | .02 |
| ☐ 415 Gary Gentry | .14 | .06 | .01 |
| ☐ 416 White Sox Team | .30 | .12 | .03 |
| ☐ 417 Rich Folkers | .14 | .06 | .01 |
| ☐ 418 Walt Williams | .14 | .06 | .01 |
| ☐ 419 Wayne Twitchell | .14 | .06 | .01 |
| ☐ 420 Ray Fosse | .14 | .06 | .01 |
| ☐ 421 Dan Fife | .14 | .06 | .01 |
| ☐ 422 Gonzalo Marquez | .14 | .06 | .01 |
| ☐ 423 Fred Stanley | .14 | .06 | .01 |
| ☐ 424 Jim Beauchamp | .14 | .06 | .01 |
| ☐ 425 Pete Broberg | .14 | .06 | .01 |
| ☐ 426 Rennie Stennett | .14 | .06 | .01 |
| ☐ 427 Bobby Bolin | .14 | .06 | .01 |
| ☐ 428 Gary Sutherland | .14 | .06 | .01 |
| ☐ 429 Dick Lange | .14 | .06 | .01 |
| ☐ 430 Matty Alou | .20 | .09 | .02 |
| ☐ 431 Gene Garber | .14 | .06 | .01 |
| ☐ 432 Chris Arnold | .14 | .06 | .01 |
| ☐ 433 Lerrin LaGrow | .14 | .06 | .01 |
| ☐ 434 Ken McMullen | .14 | .06 | .01 |
| ☐ 435 Dave Concepcion | .50 | .22 | .05 |
| ☐ 436 Don Hood | .14 | .06 | .01 |
| ☐ 437 Jim Lyttle | .14 | .06 | .01 |
| ☐ 438 Ed Herrmann | .14 | .06 | .01 |
| ☐ 439 Norm Miller | .14 | .06 | .01 |
| ☐ 440 Jim Kaat | .75 | .35 | .07 |
| ☐ 441 Tom Ragland | .14 | .06 | .01 |
| ☐ 442 Alan Foster | .14 | .06 | .01 |
| ☐ 443 Tom Hutton | .14 | .06 | .01 |
| ☐ 444 Vic Davalillo | .14 | .06 | .01 |
| ☐ 445 George Medich | .20 | .09 | .02 |
| ☐ 446 Len Randle | .14 | .06 | .01 |

|  | MINT | VG-E | F-G |
|---|---|---|---|
| ☐ 447 Twins Manager ........ <br> Frank Quilici <br> Coaches: Ralph Rowe <br> Bob Rodgers <br> Vern Morgan | .20 | .09 | .02 |
| ☐ 448 Ron Hodges ......... | .14 | .06 | .01 |
| ☐ 449 Tom McCraw ........ | .14 | .06 | .01 |
| ☐ 450 Rich Hebner ......... | .14 | .06 | .01 |
| ☐ 451 Tommy John ........ | 1.00 | .45 | .10 |
| ☐ 452 Gene Hiser .......... | .14 | .06 | .01 |
| ☐ 453 Balor Moore ......... | .14 | .06 | .01 |
| ☐ 454 Kurt Bevacqua ...... | .14 | .06 | .01 |
| ☐ 455 Tom Bradley ........ | .14 | .06 | .01 |
| ☐ 456 Dave Winfield ....... | 18.00 | 8.50 | 1.80 |
| ☐ 457 Chuck Goggin ...... | .14 | .06 | .01 |
| ☐ 458 Jim Ray ............ | .14 | .06 | .01 |
| ☐ 459 Reds Team ......... | .35 | .15 | .03 |
| ☐ 460 Boog Powell ........ | .45 | .20 | .04 |
| ☐ 461 John Odom ......... | .14 | .06 | .01 |
| ☐ 462 Luis Alvarado ....... | .14 | .06 | .01 |
| ☐ 463 Pat Dobson ......... | .20 | .09 | .02 |
| ☐ 464 Jose Cruz .......... | .50 | .22 | .05 |
| ☐ 465 Dick Bosman ....... | .14 | .06 | .01 |
| ☐ 466 Dick Billings ........ | .14 | .06 | .01 |
| ☐ 467 Winston Llenas ..... | .14 | .06 | .01 |
| ☐ 468 Pepe Frias ......... | .14 | .06 | .01 |
| ☐ 469 Joe Decker ......... | .14 | .06 | .01 |
| ☐ 470 A.L. Playoffs: ...... <br> A's over Orioles <br> (Reggie Jackson) | 1.50 | .70 | .15 |
| ☐ 471 N.L. Playoffs: ...... <br> Mets over Reds <br> (Matlack pitching) | .50 | .22 | .05 |
| ☐ 472 World Series Game 1: . <br> (Knowles pitching) | .50 | .22 | .05 |
| ☐ 473 World Series Game 2: . <br> (Willie Mays batting) | 1.50 | .70 | .15 |
| ☐ 474 World Series Game 3: . <br> (Campaneris stealing) | .50 | .22 | .05 |
| ☐ 475 World Series Game 4: . <br> (Staub batting) | .50 | .22 | .05 |
| ☐ 476 World Series Game 5: . <br> (Cleon Jones scoring) | .50 | .22 | .05 |
| ☐ 477 World Series Game 6: . <br> (Reggie Jackson) | 1.50 | .70 | .15 |
| ☐ 478 World Series Game 7: . <br> (Campaneris batting) | .50 | .22 | .05 |
| ☐ 479 World Series Summary: . <br> A's Celebrate; Win <br> 2nd cons. championship | .50 | .22 | .05 |
| ☐ 480 Willie Crawford ...... | .14 | .06 | .01 |
| ☐ 481 Jerry Terrell ........ | .14 | .06 | .01 |
| ☐ 482 Bob Didier .......... | .14 | .06 | .01 |

|  | MINT | VG-E | F-G |
|---|---|---|---|
| ☐ 483 Braves Team ....... | .30 | .12 | .03 |
| ☐ 484 Carmen Fanzone ..... | .14 | .06 | .01 |
| ☐ 485 Felipe Alou ........ | .20 | .09 | .02 |
| ☐ 486 Steve Stone ........ | .20 | .09 | .02 |
| ☐ 487 Ted Martinez ....... | .14 | .06 | .01 |
| ☐ 488 Andy Etchebarren .... | .14 | .06 | .01 |
| ☐ 489 Pirates Manager ..... <br> Danny Murtaugh <br> Coaches: Don Osborn <br> Don Leppert <br> Bill Mazeroski <br> Bob Skinner | .20 | .09 | .02 |
| ☐ 490 Vada Pinson ........ | .30 | .12 | .03 |
| ☐ 491 Roger Nelson ....... | .14 | .06 | .01 |
| ☐ 492 Mike Rogodzinski .... | .14 | .06 | .01 |
| ☐ 493 Joe Hoerner ........ | .14 | .06 | .01 |
| ☐ 494 Ed Goodson ........ | .14 | .06 | .01 |
| ☐ 495 Dick McAuliffe ...... | .14 | .06 | .01 |
| ☐ 496 Tom Murphy ........ | .14 | .06 | .01 |
| ☐ 497 Bobby Mitchell ...... | .14 | .06 | .01 |
| ☐ 498 Pat Corrales ....... | .20 | .09 | .02 |
| ☐ 499 Rusty Torres ....... | .14 | .06 | .01 |
| ☐ 500 Lee May ........... | .25 | .10 | .02 |
| ☐ 501 Eddie Leon ........ | .14 | .06 | .01 |
| ☐ 502 Dave LaRoche ...... | .14 | .06 | .01 |
| ☐ 503 Eric Soderholm ..... | .14 | .06 | .01 |
| ☐ 504 Joe Niekro ......... | .30 | .12 | .03 |
| ☐ 505 Bill Buckner ........ | .50 | .22 | .05 |
| ☐ 506 Ed Farmer ......... | .14 | .06 | .01 |
| ☐ 507 Larry Stahl ......... | .14 | .06 | .01 |
| ☐ 508 Expos Team ........ | .30 | .12 | .03 |
| ☐ 509 Jesse Jefferson ..... | .14 | .06 | .01 |
| ☐ 510 Wayne Garrett ...... | .14 | .06 | .01 |
| ☐ 511 Toby Harrah ....... | .25 | .10 | .02 |
| ☐ 512 Joe Lahoud ........ | .14 | .06 | .01 |
| ☐ 513 Jim Campanis ...... | .14 | .06 | .01 |
| ☐ 514 Paul Schaal ........ | .14 | .06 | .01 |
| ☐ 515 Willie Montanez ..... | .14 | .06 | .01 |
| ☐ 516 Horacio Pina ....... | .14 | .06 | .01 |
| ☐ 517 Mike Hegan ........ | .14 | .06 | .01 |
| ☐ 518 Derrel Thomas ...... | .14 | .06 | .01 |
| ☐ 519 Bill Sharp ......... | .14 | .06 | .01 |
| ☐ 520 Tim McCarver ...... | .25 | .10 | .02 |
| ☐ 521 Indians Manager ..... <br> Ken Aspromonte <br> Coaches: Clay Bryant <br> Tony Pacheco | .20 | .09 | .02 |
| ☐ 522 J.R. Richard ........ | .45 | .20 | .04 |
| ☐ 523 Cecil Cooper ....... | 2.25 | 1.00 | .22 |
| ☐ 524 Bill Plummer ....... | .14 | .06 | .01 |
| ☐ 525 Clyde Wright ....... | .14 | .06 | .01 |
| ☐ 526 Frank Tepedino ..... | .14 | .06 | .01 |
| ☐ 527 Bobby Darwin ...... | .14 | .06 | .01 |

| | MINT | VG-E | F-G |
|---|---|---|---|
| ☐ 528 Bill Bonham | .14 | .06 | .01 |
| ☐ 529 Horace Clarke | .14 | .06 | .01 |
| ☐ 530 Mickey Stanley | .14 | .06 | .01 |
| ☐ 531 Expos Manager | .20 | .09 | .02 |
| Gene Mauch | | | |
| Coaches: Dave Bristol | | | |
| Cal McLish | | | |
| Larry Doby | | | |
| Jerry Zimmerman | | | |
| ☐ 532 Skip Lockwood | .14 | .06 | .01 |
| ☐ 533 Mike Phillips | .14 | .06 | .01 |
| ☐ 534 Eddie Watt | .14 | .06 | .01 |
| ☐ 535 Bob Tolan | .14 | .06 | .01 |
| ☐ 536 Duffy Dyer | .14 | .06 | .01 |
| ☐ 537 Steve Mingori | .14 | .06 | .01 |
| ☐ 538 Cesar Tovar | .14 | .06 | .01 |
| ☐ 539 Lloyd Allen | .14 | .06 | .01 |
| ☐ 540 Bob Robertson | .14 | .06 | .01 |
| ☐ 541 Indians Team | .30 | .12 | .03 |
| ☐ 542 Rich Gossage | 1.75 | .85 | .17 |
| ☐ 543 Danny Cater | .14 | .06 | .01 |
| ☐ 544 Ron Schueler | .14 | .06 | .01 |
| ☐ 545 Billy Conigliaro | .14 | .06 | .01 |
| ☐ 546 Mike Corkins | .14 | .06 | .01 |
| ☐ 547 Glenn Borgmann | .14 | .06 | .01 |
| ☐ 548 Sonny Siebert | .14 | .06 | .01 |
| ☐ 549 Mike Jorgensen | .14 | .06 | .01 |
| ☐ 550 Sam McDowell | .20 | .09 | .02 |
| ☐ 551 Von Joshua | .14 | .06 | .01 |
| ☐ 552 Denny Doyle | .14 | .06 | .01 |
| ☐ 553 Jim Willoughby | .14 | .06 | .01 |
| ☐ 554 Tim Johnson | .14 | .06 | .01 |
| ☐ 555 Woody Fryman | .14 | .06 | .01 |
| ☐ 556 Dave Campbell | .14 | .06 | .01 |
| ☐ 557 Jim McGlothlin | .14 | .06 | .01 |
| ☐ 558 Bill Fahey | .14 | .06 | .01 |
| ☐ 559 Darrell Chaney | .14 | .06 | .01 |
| ☐ 560 Mike Cuellar | .20 | .09 | .02 |
| ☐ 561 Ed Kranepool | .20 | .09 | .02 |
| ☐ 562 Jack Aker | .14 | .06 | .01 |
| ☐ 563 Hal McRae | .30 | .12 | .03 |
| ☐ 564 Mike Ryan | .14 | .06 | .01 |
| ☐ 565 Milt Wilcox | .20 | .09 | .02 |
| ☐ 566 Jackie Hernandez | .14 | .06 | .01 |
| ☐ 567 Red Sox Team | .30 | .12 | .03 |
| ☐ 568 Mike Torrez | .20 | .09 | .02 |
| ☐ 569 Rick Dempsey | .20 | .09 | .02 |
| ☐ 570 Ralph Garr | .20 | .09 | .02 |
| ☐ 571 Rich Hand | .14 | .06 | .01 |
| ☐ 572 Enzo Hernandez | .14 | .06 | .01 |
| ☐ 573 Mike Adams | .14 | .06 | .01 |
| ☐ 574 Bill Parsons | .14 | .06 | .01 |
| ☐ 575 Steve Garvey | 6.00 | 2.80 | .60 |

| | MINT | VG-E | F-G |
|---|---|---|---|
| ☐ 576 Scipio Spinks | .14 | .06 | .01 |
| ☐ 577 Mike Sadek | .14 | .06 | .01 |
| ☐ 578 Ralph Houk MGR | .20 | .09 | .02 |
| ☐ 579 Cecil Upshaw | .14 | .06 | .01 |
| ☐ 580 Jim Spencer | .14 | .06 | .01 |
| ☐ 581 Fred Norman | .14 | .06 | .01 |
| ☐ 582 Bucky Dent | .50 | .22 | .05 |
| ☐ 583 Marty Pattin | .14 | .06 | .01 |
| ☐ 584 Ken Rudolph | .14 | .06 | .01 |
| ☐ 585 Merv Rettenmund | .14 | .06 | .01 |
| ☐ 586 Jack Brohamer | .14 | .06 | .01 |
| ☐ 587 Larry Christenson | .14 | .06 | .01 |
| ☐ 588 Hal Lanier | .20 | .09 | .02 |
| ☐ 589 Boots Day | .14 | .06 | .01 |
| ☐ 590 Roger Moret | .14 | .06 | .01 |
| ☐ 591 Sonny Jackson | .14 | .06 | .01 |
| ☐ 592 Ed Bane | .14 | .06 | .01 |
| ☐ 593 Steve Yeager | .20 | .09 | .02 |
| ☐ 594 Lee Stanton | .14 | .06 | .01 |
| ☐ 595 Steve Blass | .14 | .06 | .01 |
| ☐ 596 Rookie Pitchers: | .30 | .12 | .03 |
| Wayne Garland | | | |
| Fred Holdsworth | | | |
| Mark Littell | | | |
| Dick Pole | | | |
| ☐ 597 Rookie Shortstops: | .75 | .35 | .07 |
| Dave Chalk | | | |
| John Gamble | | | |
| Pete MacKanin | | | |
| Manny Trillo | | | |
| ☐ 598 Rookie Outfielders: | 1.75 | .85 | .17 |
| Dave Augustine | | | |
| Ken Griffey | | | |
| Steve Ontiveros | | | |
| Jim Tyrone | | | |
| ☐ 599 A Rookie Pitchers WASH: | .75 | .35 | .07 |
| Ron Diorio | | | |
| Dave Freisleben | | | |
| Frank Riccelli | | | |
| Greg Shanahan | | | |
| ☐ 599 B Rookie Pitchers SD: (SD in large print) | 2.25 | 1.00 | .22 |
| ☐ 599 C Rookie Pitchers SD: (SD in small print) | 4.50 | 2.10 | .45 |
| ☐ 600 Rookie Infielders: | 7.00 | 3.25 | .70 |
| Ron Cash | | | |
| Jim Cox | | | |
| Bill Madlock | | | |
| Reggie Sanders | | | |

| | MINT | VG-E | F-G |
|---|---|---|---|
| ☐ **601 Rookie Outfielders:** | .75 | .35 | .07 |
| Ed Armbrister | | | |
| Rich Bladt | | | |
| Brian Downing | | | |
| Bake McBride | | | |
| ☐ **602 Rookie Pitchers:** | .40 | .18 | .04 |
| Glen Abbott | | | |
| Rick Henninger | | | |
| Craig Swan | | | |
| Dan Vossler | | | |
| ☐ **603 Rookie Catchers:** | .30 | .12 | .03 |
| Barry Foote | | | |
| Tom Lundstedt | | | |
| Charlie Moore | | | |
| Sergio Robles | | | |
| ☐ **604 Rookie Infielders:** | 2.25 | 1.00 | .22 |
| Terry Hughes | | | |
| John Knox | | | |
| Andy Thornton | | | |
| Frank White | | | |
| ☐ **605 Rookie Pitchers:** | .60 | .28 | .06 |
| Vic Albury | | | |
| Ken Frailing | | | |
| Kevin Kobel | | | |
| Frank Tanana | | | |
| ☐ **606 Rookie Outfielders:** | .20 | .09 | .02 |
| Jim Fuller | | | |
| Wilbur Howard | | | |
| Tommy Smith | | | |
| Otto Velez | | | |
| ☐ **607 Rookie Shortstops:** | .20 | .09 | .02 |
| Leo Foster | | | |
| Tom Heintzelman | | | |
| Dave Rosello | | | |
| Frank Taveras | | | |
| ☐ **608 A Rookie Pitchers: ERR** | 1.75 | .85 | .17 |
| Bob Apodaco (sic) | | | |
| Dick Baney | | | |
| John D'Acquisto | | | |
| Mike Wallace | | | |
| ☐ **608 B Rookie Pitchers: COR** | .35 | .15 | .03 |
| Bob Apodaca | | | |
| Dick Baney | | | |
| John D'Acquisto | | | |
| Mike Wallace | | | |
| ☐ 609 Rico Petrocelli | .20 | .09 | .02 |
| ☐ 610 Dave Kingman | .80 | .40 | .08 |
| ☐ 611 Rich Stelmaszek | .14 | .06 | .01 |
| ☐ 612 Luke Walker | .14 | .06 | .01 |
| ☐ 613 Dan Monzon | .14 | .06 | .01 |
| ☐ 614 Adrian Devine | .14 | .06 | .01 |
| ☐ 615 John Jeter | .14 | .06 | .01 |
| ☐ 616 Larry Gura | .25 | .10 | .02 |

| | MINT | VG-E | F-G |
|---|---|---|---|
| ☐ 617 Ted Ford | .14 | .06 | .01 |
| ☐ 618 Jim Mason | .14 | .06 | .01 |
| ☐ 619 Mike Anderson | .14 | .06 | .01 |
| ☐ 620 Al Downing | .14 | .06 | .01 |
| ☐ 621 Bernie Carbo | .14 | .06 | .01 |
| ☐ 622 Phil Gagliano | .14 | .06 | .01 |
| ☐ 623 Celerino Sanchez | .14 | .06 | .01 |
| ☐ 624 Bob Miller | .14 | .06 | .01 |
| ☐ 625 Ollie Brown | .14 | .06 | .01 |
| ☐ 626 Pirates Team | .30 | .12 | .03 |
| ☐ 627 Carl Taylor | .14 | .06 | .01 |
| ☐ 628 Ivan Murrell | .14 | .06 | .01 |
| ☐ 629 Rusty Staub | .50 | .22 | .05 |
| ☐ 630 Tommy Agee | .14 | .06 | .01 |
| ☐ 631 Steve Barber | .14 | .06 | .01 |
| ☐ 632 George Culver | .14 | .06 | .01 |
| ☐ 633 Dave Hamilton | .14 | .06 | .01 |
| ☐ **634 Braves Manager:** | .50 | .22 | .05 |
| Eddie Mathews | | | |
| Coaches: Herm Starrette | | | |
| Connie Ryan | | | |
| Jim Busby | | | |
| Ken Silvestri | | | |
| ☐ 635 John Edwards | .14 | .06 | .01 |
| ☐ 636 Dave Goltz | .20 | .09 | .02 |
| ☐ 637 Checklist 5 | .50 | .10 | .02 |
| ☐ 638 Ken Sanders | .14 | .06 | .01 |
| ☐ 639 Joe Lovitto | .14 | .06 | .01 |
| ☐ 640 Milt Pappas | .20 | .09 | .02 |
| ☐ 641 Chuck Brinkman | .14 | .06 | .01 |
| ☐ 642 Terry Harmon | .14 | .06 | .01 |
| ☐ 643 Dodgers Team | .50 | .22 | .05 |
| ☐ 644 Wayne Granger | .14 | .06 | .01 |
| ☐ 645 Ken Boswell | .14 | .06 | .01 |
| ☐ 646 George Foster | 1.50 | .70 | .15 |
| ☐ 647 Juan Beniquez | .50 | .22 | .05 |
| ☐ 648 Terry Crowley | .14 | .06 | .01 |
| ☐ 649 Fernando Gonzalez | .14 | .06 | .01 |
| ☐ 650 Mike Epstein | .14 | .06 | .01 |
| ☐ 651 Leron Lee | .14 | .06 | .01 |
| ☐ 652 Gail Hopkins | .14 | .06 | .01 |
| ☐ 653 Bob Stinson | .14 | .06 | .01 |
| ☐ 654 A Jesus Alou (outfield) | .35 | .15 | .03 |
| ☐ 654 B Jesus Alou | 4.50 | 2.10 | .45 |
| (no position) | | | |
| ☐ 655 Mike Tyson | .14 | .06 | .01 |
| ☐ 656 Adrian Garrett | .14 | .06 | .01 |
| ☐ 657 Jim Shellenback | .14 | .06 | .01 |
| ☐ 658 Lee Lacy | .25 | .10 | .02 |
| ☐ 659 Joe Lis | .14 | .06 | .01 |
| ☐ 660 Larry Dierker | .30 | .12 | .03 |

## 1974 TOPPS TRADED

The cards in this 44 card set measure 2½" by 3½". The 1974 Topps Traded set contains 43 player cards and one unnumbered checklist card. The obverses have the word "traded" in block letters and the backs are designed in newspaper style. Card numbers are the same as in the regular set except they are followed by a "T." No known scarcities exist for this set.

Complete Set: M-5.00; VG-E-2.35; F-G-.50

|  | MINT | VG-E | F-G |
|---|---|---|---|
| Common Player ....... | .10 | .04 | .01 |
| ☐ 23 T Craig Robinson ...... | .10 | .04 | .01 |
| ☐ 42 T Claude Osteen ...... | .15 | .06 | .01 |
| ☐ 43 T Jim Wynn ......... | .15 | .06 | .01 |
| ☐ 51 T Bobby Heise ....... | .10 | .04 | .01 |
| ☐ 59 T Ross Grimsley ...... | .10 | .04 | .01 |
| ☐ 62 T Bob Locker ........ | .10 | .04 | .01 |
| ☐ 63 T Bill Sudakis ....... | .10 | .04 | .01 |
| ☐ 73 T Mike Marshall ...... | .20 | .09 | .02 |
| ☐ 123 T Nelson Briles ...... | .10 | .04 | .01 |
| ☐ 139 T Aurelio Monteagudo .. | .10 | .04 | .01 |
| ☐ 151 T Diego Segui ....... | .10 | .04 | .01 |
| ☐ 165 T Willie Davis ....... | .20 | .09 | .02 |
| ☐ 175 T Reggie Cleveland ... | .10 | .04 | .01 |
| ☐ 182 T Lindy McDaniel ..... | .10 | .04 | .01 |
| ☐ 186 T Fred Scherman ..... | .10 | .04 | .01 |
| ☐ 249 T George Mitterwald ... | .10 | .04 | .01 |
| ☐ 262 T Ed Kirkpatrick ..... | .10 | .04 | .01 |
| ☐ 269 T Bob Johnson ...... | .10 | .04 | .01 |
| ☐ 270 T Ron Santo ........ | .30 | .12 | .03 |
| ☐ 313 T Barry Lersch ...... | .10 | .04 | .01 |
| ☐ 319 T Randy Hundley ..... | .15 | .06 | .01 |
| ☐ 330 T Juan Marichal ..... | 1.00 | .45 | .10 |

|  | MINT | VG-E | F-G |
|---|---|---|---|
| ☐ 348 T Pete Richert ....... | .10 | .04 | .01 |
| ☐ 373 T John Curtis ....... | .10 | .04 | .01 |
| ☐ 390 T Lou Piniella ....... | .30 | .12 | .03 |
| ☐ 428 T Gary Sutherland ... | .10 | .04 | .01 |
| ☐ 454 T Kurt Bevacqua .... | .10 | .04 | .01 |
| ☐ 458 T Jim Ray ......... | .10 | .04 | .01 |
| ☐ 485 T Felipe Alou ....... | .15 | .06 | .01 |
| ☐ 486 T Steve Stone ...... | .15 | .06 | .01 |
| ☐ 496 T Tom Murphy ...... | .10 | .04 | .01 |
| ☐ 516 T Horacio Pina ...... | .10 | .04 | .01 |
| ☐ 534 T Eddie Watt ....... | .10 | .04 | .01 |
| ☐ 538 T Cesar Tovar ...... | .10 | .04 | .01 |
| ☐ 544 T Ron Schueler ..... | .10 | .04 | .01 |
| ☐ 579 T Cecil Upshaw ..... | .10 | .04 | .01 |
| ☐ 585 T Merv Rettenmund .. | .10 | .04 | .01 |
| ☐ 612 T Luke Walker ...... | .10 | .04 | .01 |
| ☐ 616 T Larry Gura ....... | .20 | .09 | .02 |
| ☐ 618 T Jim Mason ....... | .10 | .04 | .01 |
| ☐ 630 T Tommie Agee ..... | .10 | .04 | .01 |
| ☐ 648 T Terry Crowley ..... | .10 | .04 | .01 |
| ☐ 649 T Fernando Gonzalez . | .10 | .04 | .01 |
| Traded Checklist ....... | .50 | .10 | .02 |
| (unnumbered) | | | |

## 1975 TOPPS

The cards in the 1975 Topps set were issued in two different sizes: a regular standard size and a mini size which was issued as a test in certain areas of the country. The standard size cards measure 2½" by 3½" versus 2¼" by 3⅛" for the minis. The 660 card Topps baseball set for 1975 was radically different in appearance from sets *of the preceding years. The most prominent change was the use of a two-color frame surrounding the picture area rather than a single, subdued color. A facsimile autograph appears on the picture, and the backs are printed in red and green on gray. Cards 189–212 depict the MVP's of both leagues from 1951 through 1974. The first six cards (1–6) feature players breaking records or achieving milestones during the previous season. Cards 306–313 picture league leaders in various statistical categories. Cards 459–466 depict the results of post-season action. Team cards feature a checklist back for players on that team. Topps mini's have the same checklist and are worth approximately double the prices listed below.*

**Complete Set: M–250.00; VG-E–110.00; F-G–25.00**

|  | MINT | VG-E | F-G |
|---|---|---|---|
| Common Player (1–132) | .16 | .07 | .01 |
| Common Player (133–660) | .14 | .06 | .01 |

|  |  | MINT | VG-E | F-G |
|---|---|---|---|---|
| ☐ | 1 RB: Hank Aaron Sets Homer Mark | 6.00 | 1.50 | .30 |
| ☐ | 2 RB: Lou Brock 118 Stolen Bases | 1.25 | .60 | .12 |
| ☐ | 3 RB: Bob Gibson 3000th Strikeout | 1.25 | .60 | .12 |
| ☐ | 4 RB: Al Kaline 3000 Hit Club | 1.25 | .60 | .12 |
| ☐ | 5 RB: Nolan Ryan Fans 300 for 3rd Year in a Row | 1.50 | .70 | .15 |
| ☐ | 6 RB: Mike Marshall Hurls 106 Games | .30 | .12 | .03 |
| ☐ | 7 No Hitters: Steve Busby Dick Bosman Nolan Ryan | .50 | .22 | .05 |
| ☐ | 8 Rogelio Moret | .16 | .07 | .01 |
| ☐ | 9 Frank Tepedino | .16 | .07 | .01 |
| ☐ | 10 Willie Davis | .25 | .10 | .02 |
| ☐ | 11 Bill Melton | .16 | .07 | .01 |
| ☐ | 12 David Clyde | .16 | .07 | .01 |
| ☐ | 13 Gene Locklear | .16 | .07 | .01 |
| ☐ | 14 Milt Wilcox | .20 | .09 | .02 |
| ☐ | 15 Jose Cardenal | .16 | .07 | .01 |
| ☐ | 16 Frank Tanana | .30 | .12 | .03 |
| ☐ | 17 Dave Concepcion | .50 | .22 | .05 |

|  |  | MINT | VG-E | F-G |
|---|---|---|---|---|
| ☐ | 18 Tigers: Team/Mgr. Ralph Houk | .35 | .07 | .01 |
| ☐ | 19 Jerry Koosman | .30 | .12 | .03 |
| ☐ | 20 Thurman Munson | 3.25 | 1.50 | .32 |
| ☐ | 21 Rollie Fingers | .90 | .40 | .09 |
| ☐ | 22 Dave Cash | .16 | .07 | .01 |
| ☐ | 23 Bill Russell | .20 | .09 | .02 |
| ☐ | 24 Al Fitzmorris | .16 | .07 | .01 |
| ☐ | 25 Lee May | .25 | .10 | .02 |
| ☐ | 26 Dave McNally | .20 | .09 | .02 |
| ☐ | 27 Ken Reitz | .16 | .07 | .01 |
| ☐ | 28 Tom Murphy | .16 | .07 | .01 |
| ☐ | 29 Dave Parker | 2.50 | 1.15 | .25 |
| ☐ | 30 Bert Blyleven | .50 | .22 | .05 |
| ☐ | 31 Dave Rader | .16 | .07 | .01 |
| ☐ | 32 Reggie Cleveland | .16 | .07 | .01 |
| ☐ | 33 Dusty Baker | .45 | .20 | .04 |
| ☐ | 34 Steve Renko | .16 | .07 | .01 |
| ☐ | 35 Ron Santo | .35 | .15 | .03 |
| ☐ | 36 Joe Lovitto | .16 | .07 | .01 |
| ☐ | 37 Dave Freisleben | .16 | .07 | .01 |
| ☐ | 38 Buddy Bell | .70 | .32 | .07 |
| ☐ | 39 Andy Thornton | .60 | .28 | .06 |
| ☐ | 40 Bill Singer | .16 | .07 | .01 |
| ☐ | 41 Cesar Geronimo | .16 | .07 | .01 |
| ☐ | 42 Joe Coleman | .16 | .07 | .01 |
| ☐ | 43 Cleon Jones | .16 | .07 | .01 |
| ☐ | 44 Pat Dobson | .20 | .09 | .02 |
| ☐ | 45 Joe Rudi | .20 | .09 | .02 |
| ☐ | 46 Phillies: Team/Mgr Danny Ozark | .35 | .07 | .01 |
| ☐ | 47 Tommy John | .90 | .40 | .09 |
| ☐ | 48 Freddie Patek | .16 | .07 | .01 |
| ☐ | 49 Larry Dierker | .20 | .09 | .01 |
| ☐ | 50 Brooks Robinson | 2.50 | 1.15 | .25 |
| ☐ | 51 Bob Forsch | .20 | .09 | .02 |
| ☐ | 52 Darrell Porter | .25 | .10 | .02 |
| ☐ | 53 Dave Giusti | .16 | .07 | .01 |
| ☐ | 54 Eric Soderholm | .16 | .07 | .01 |
| ☐ | 55 Bobby Bonds | .30 | .12 | .03 |
| ☐ | 56 Rick Wise | .20 | .09 | .02 |
| ☐ | 57 Dave Johnson | .25 | .10 | .02 |
| ☐ | 58 Chuck Taylor | .16 | .07 | .01 |
| ☐ | 59 Ken Henderson | .16 | .07 | .01 |
| ☐ | 60 Fergie Jenkins | .70 | .32 | .07 |
| ☐ | 61 Dave Winfield | 5.00 | 2.35 | .50 |
| ☐ | 62 Fritz Peterson | .16 | .07 | .01 |
| ☐ | 63 Steve Swisher | .16 | .07 | .01 |
| ☐ | 64 Dave Chalk | .16 | .07 | .01 |
| ☐ | 65 Don Gullett | .20 | .09 | .02 |
| ☐ | 66 Willie Horton | .20 | .09 | .02 |
| ☐ | 67 Tug McGraw | .30 | .12 | .03 |

| | | MINT | VG-E | F-G |
|---|---|---|---|---|
| ☐ 68 | Ron Blomberg | .16 | .07 | .01 |
| ☐ 69 | John Odom | .16 | .07 | .01 |
| ☐ 70 | Mike Schmidt | 9.50 | 4.50 | .95 |
| ☐ 71 | Charlie Hough | .20 | .09 | .02 |
| ☐ 72 | Royals: Team/Mgr. Jack McKeon | .35 | .07 | .01 |
| ☐ 73 | J.R. Richard | .30 | .12 | .03 |
| ☐ 74 | Mark Belanger | .20 | .09 | .02 |
| ☐ 75 | Ted Simmons | .70 | .32 | .07 |
| ☐ 76 | Ed Sprague | .16 | .07 | .01 |
| ☐ 77 | Richie Zisk | .20 | .09 | .02 |
| ☐ 78 | Ray Corbin | .16 | .07 | .01 |
| ☐ 79 | Gary Matthews | .35 | .15 | .03 |
| ☐ 80 | Carlton Fisk | 1.25 | .60 | .12 |
| ☐ 81 | Ron Reed | .16 | .07 | .01 |
| ☐ 82 | Pat Kelly | .16 | .07 | .01 |
| ☐ 83 | Jim Merritt | .16 | .07 | .01 |
| ☐ 84 | Enzo Hernandez | .16 | .07 | .01 |
| ☐ 85 | Bill Bonham | .16 | .07 | .01 |
| ☐ 86 | Joe Lis | .16 | .07 | .01 |
| ☐ 87 | George Foster | 1.50 | .70 | .15 |
| ☐ 88 | Tom Egan | .16 | .07 | .01 |
| ☐ 89 | Jim Ray | .16 | .07 | .01 |
| ☐ 90 | Rusty Staub | .35 | .15 | .03 |
| ☐ 91 | Dick Green | .16 | .07 | .01 |
| ☐ 92 | Cecil Upshaw | .16 | .07 | .01 |
| ☐ 93 | Dave Lopes | .35 | .15 | .03 |
| ☐ 94 | Jim Lonborg | .20 | .09 | .02 |
| ☐ 95 | John Mayberry | .20 | .09 | .02 |
| ☐ 96 | Mike Cosgrove | .16 | .07 | .01 |
| ☐ 97 | Earl Williams | .16 | .07 | .01 |
| ☐ 98 | Rich Folkers | .16 | .07 | .01 |
| ☐ 99 | Mike Hegan | .16 | .07 | .01 |
| ☐ 100 | Willie Stargell | 1.75 | .85 | .17 |
| ☐ 101 | Expos: Team/Mgr. Gene Mauch | .35 | .07 | .01 |
| ☐ 102 | Joe Decker | .16 | .07 | .01 |
| ☐ 103 | Rick Miller | .16 | .07 | .01 |
| ☐ 104 | Bill Madlock | 1.75 | .85 | .17 |
| ☐ 105 | Buzz Capra | .16 | .07 | .01 |
| ☐ 106 | Mike Hargrove | .50 | .22 | .05 |
| ☐ 107 | Jim Barr | .16 | .07 | .01 |
| ☐ 108 | Tom Hall | .16 | .07 | .01 |
| ☐ 109 | George Hendrick | .30 | .12 | .03 |
| ☐ 110 | Wilbur Wood | .20 | .09 | .01 |
| ☐ 111 | Wayne Garrett | .16 | .07 | .01 |
| ☐ 112 | Larry Hardy | .16 | .07 | .01 |
| ☐ 113 | Elliott Maddox | .16 | .07 | .01 |
| ☐ 114 | Dick Lange | .16 | .07 | .01 |
| ☐ 115 | Joe Ferguson | .16 | .07 | .01 |
| ☐ 116 | Lerrin LaGrow | .16 | .07 | .01 |
| ☐ 117 | Orioles: Team/Mgr. Earl Weaver | .50 | .10 | .02 |
| ☐ 118 | Mike Anderson | .16 | .07 | .01 |
| ☐ 119 | Tommy Helms | .16 | .07 | .01 |
| ☐ 120 | Steve Busby (photo actually Fran Healy) | .20 | .09 | .02 |
| ☐ 121 | Bill North | .16 | .07 | .01 |
| ☐ 122 | Al Hrabosky | .20 | .09 | .02 |
| ☐ 123 | Johnny Briggs | .16 | .07 | .01 |
| ☐ 124 | Jerry Reuss | .30 | .12 | .03 |
| ☐ 125 | Ken Singleton | .30 | .12 | .03 |
| ☐ 126 | Checklist 1–132 | .50 | .08 | .01 |
| ☐ 127 | Glenn Borgmann | .16 | .07 | .01 |
| ☐ 128 | Bill Lee | .20 | .09 | .02 |
| ☐ 129 | Rick Monday | .20 | .09 | .02 |
| ☐ 130 | Phil Niekro | 1.00 | .45 | .10 |
| ☐ 131 | Toby Harrah | .25 | .10 | .02 |
| ☐ 132 | Randy Moffitt | .16 | .07 | .01 |
| ☐ 133 | Dan Driessen | .20 | .09 | .02 |
| ☐ 134 | Ron Hodges | .14 | .06 | .01 |
| ☐ 135 | Charlie Spikes | .14 | .06 | .01 |
| ☐ 136 | Jim Mason | .14 | .06 | .01 |
| ☐ 137 | Terry Forster | .25 | .10 | .02 |
| ☐ 138 | Del Unser | .14 | .06 | .01 |
| ☐ 139 | Horacio Pina | .14 | .06 | .01 |
| ☐ 140 | Steve Garvey | 4.50 | 2.10 | .45 |
| ☐ 141 | Mickey Stanley | .14 | .06 | .01 |
| ☐ 142 | Bob Reynolds | .14 | .06 | .01 |
| ☐ 143 | Cliff Johnson | .20 | .09 | .01 |
| ☐ 144 | Jim Wohlford | .14 | .06 | .01 |
| ☐ 145 | Ken Holtzman | .20 | .09 | .02 |
| ☐ 146 | Padres: Team/Mgr. John McNamara | .35 | .07 | .01 |
| ☐ 147 | Pedro Garcia | .14 | .06 | .01 |
| ☐ 148 | Jim Rooker | .14 | .06 | .01 |
| ☐ 149 | Tim Foli | .14 | .06 | .01 |
| ☐ 150 | Bob Gibson | 1.75 | .85 | .17 |
| ☐ 151 | Steve Brye | .14 | .06 | .01 |
| ☐ 152 | Mario Guerrero | .14 | .06 | .01 |
| ☐ 153 | Rick Reuschel | .25 | .10 | .02 |
| ☐ 154 | Mike Lum | .14 | .06 | .01 |
| ☐ 155 | Jim Bibby | .20 | .09 | .02 |
| ☐ 156 | Dave Kingman | .90 | .40 | .09 |
| ☐ 157 | Pedro Borbon | .14 | .06 | .01 |
| ☐ 158 | Jerry Grote | .14 | .06 | .01 |
| ☐ 159 | Steve Arlin | .14 | .06 | .01 |
| ☐ 160 | Graig Nettles | 1.10 | .50 | .11 |
| ☐ 161 | Stan Bahnsen | .14 | .06 | .01 |
| ☐ 162 | Willie Montanez | .14 | .06 | .01 |
| ☐ 163 | Jim Brewer | .14 | .06 | .01 |
| ☐ 164 | Mickey Rivers | .20 | .09 | .02 |

|  | MINT | VG-E | F-G |
|---|---|---|---|
| ☐ 165 Doug Rader | .20 | .09 | .02 |
| ☐ 166 Woodie Fryman | .14 | .06 | .01 |
| ☐ 167 Rich Coggins | .14 | .06 | .01 |
| ☐ 168 Bill Greif | .14 | .06 | .01 |
| ☐ 169 Cookie Rojas | .14 | .06 | .01 |
| ☐ 170 Bert Campaneris | .25 | .10 | .02 |
| ☐ 171 Ed Kirkpatrick | .14 | .06 | .01 |
| ☐ 172 Red Sox: Team/Mgr. | .35 | .07 | .01 |
| Darrell Johnson | | | |
| ☐ 173 Steve Rogers | .35 | .15 | .03 |
| ☐ 174 Bake McBride | .20 | .09 | .02 |
| ☐ 175 Don Money | .14 | .06 | .01 |
| ☐ 176 Burt Hooton | .14 | .06 | .01 |
| ☐ 177 Vic Correll | .14 | .06 | .01 |
| ☐ 178 Cesar Tovar | .14 | .06 | .01 |
| ☐ 179 Tom Bradley | .14 | .06 | .01 |
| ☐ 180 Joe Morgan | 2.00 | .90 | .20 |
| ☐ 181 Fred Beene | .14 | .06 | .01 |
| ☐ 182 Don Hahn | .14 | .06 | .01 |
| ☐ 183 Mel Stottlemyre | .20 | .09 | .02 |
| ☐ 184 Jorge Orta | .14 | .06 | .01 |
| ☐ 185 Steve Carlton | 4.50 | 2.10 | .45 |
| ☐ 186 Willie Crawford | .14 | .06 | .01 |
| ☐ 187 Denny Doyle | .14 | .06 | .01 |
| ☐ 188 Tom Griffin | .14 | .06 | .01 |
| ☐ 189 1951 MVP's: | 1.00 | .45 | .10 |
| Larry (Yogi) Berra | | | |
| Roy Campanella | | | |
| (Campy never issued) | | | |
| ☐ 190 1952 MVP's: | .30 | .12 | .03 |
| Bobby Shantz | | | |
| Hank Bauer | | | |
| ☐ 191 1953 MVP's: | .55 | .25 | .05 |
| Al Rosen | | | |
| Roy Campanella | | | |
| ☐ 192 1954 MVP's: | 1.00 | .45 | .10 |
| Yogi Berra | | | |
| Willie Mays | | | |
| ☐ 193 1955 MVP's: | 1.00 | .45 | .10 |
| Yogi Berra | | | |
| Roy Campanella | | | |
| (Campy never issued) | | | |
| ☐ 194 1956 MVP's: | 1.25 | .60 | .12 |
| Mickey Mantle | | | |
| Don Newcombe | | | |
| ☐ 195 1957 MVP's: | 1.75 | .85 | .17 |
| Mickey Mantle | | | |
| Hank Aaron | | | |
| ☐ 196 1958 MVP's: | .55 | .25 | .05 |
| Jackie Jensen | | | |
| Ernie Banks | | | |
| ☐ 197 1959 MVP's: | .55 | .25 | .05 |
| Nellie Fox | | | |
| Ernie Banks | | | |

|  | MINT | VG-E | F-G |
|---|---|---|---|
| ☐ 198 1960 MVP's: | .55 | .25 | .05 |
| Roger Maris | | | |
| Dick Groat | | | |
| ☐ 199 1961 MVP's: | .75 | .35 | .07 |
| Roger Maris | | | |
| Frank Robinson | | | |
| ☐ 200 1962 MVP's: | 1.25 | .60 | .12 |
| Mickey Mantle | | | |
| Maury Wills | | | |
| (Wills never issued) | | | |
| ☐ 201 1963 MVP's: | .55 | .25 | .05 |
| Elston Howard | | | |
| Sandy Koufax | | | |
| ☐ 202 1964 MVP's: | .55 | .25 | .05 |
| Brooks Robinson | | | |
| Ken Boyer | | | |
| ☐ 203 1965 MVP's: | .55 | .25 | .05 |
| Zoilo Versalles | | | |
| Willie Mays | | | |
| ☐ 204 1966 MVP's: | .75 | .35 | .07 |
| Frank Robinson | | | |
| Bob Clemente | | | |
| ☐ 205 1967 MVP's: | .75 | .35 | .07 |
| Carl Yastrzemski | | | |
| Orlando Cepeda | | | |
| ☐ 206 1968 MVP's: | .55 | .25 | .05 |
| Denny McLain | | | |
| Bob Gibson | | | |
| ☐ 207 1969 MVP's: | .65 | .30 | .06 |
| Harmon Killebrew | | | |
| Willie McCovey | | | |
| ☐ 208 1970 MVP's: | .55 | .25 | .05 |
| Boog Powell | | | |
| Johnny Bench | | | |
| ☐ 209 1971 MVP's: | .45 | .20 | .04 |
| Vida Blue | | | |
| Joe Torre | | | |
| ☐ 210 1972 MVP's: | .55 | .25 | .05 |
| Rich Allen | | | |
| Johnny Bench | | | |
| ☐ 211 1973 MVP's: | 1.75 | .85 | .17 |
| Reggie Jackson | | | |
| Pete Rose | | | |
| ☐ 212 1974 MVP's: | .55 | .25 | .05 |
| Jeff Burroughs | | | |
| Steve Garvey | | | |
| ☐ 213 Oscar Gamble | .25 | .10 | .02 |
| ☐ 214 Harry Parker | .14 | .06 | .01 |
| ☐ 215 Bobby Valentine | .20 | .09 | .01 |
| ☐ 216 Giants: Team/Mgr. | .35 | .07 | .01 |
| Wes Westrum | | | |
| ☐ 217 Lou Piniella | .35 | .15 | .03 |
| ☐ 218 Jerry Johnson | .14 | .06 | .01 |
| ☐ 219 Ed Herrmann | .14 | .06 | .01 |

| | MINT | VG-E | F-G |
|---|---|---|---|
| ☐ 220 Don Sutton | .85 | .40 | .08 |
| ☐ 221 Aurelio Rodriguez | .14 | .06 | .01 |
| ☐ 222 Dan Spillner | .25 | .10 | .02 |
| ☐ 223 Robin Yount | 16.00 | 7.50 | 1.60 |
| ☐ 224 Ramon Hernandez | .14 | .06 | .01 |
| ☐ 225 Bob Grich | .30 | .12 | .03 |
| ☐ 226 Bill Campbell | .20 | .09 | .02 |
| ☐ 227 Bob Watson | .25 | .10 | .02 |
| ☐ 228 George Brett | 32.00 | 15.00 | 3.20 |
| ☐ 229 Barry Foote | .14 | .06 | .01 |
| ☐ 230 Jim Hunter | 1.00 | .45 | .10 |
| ☐ 231 Mike Tyson | .14 | .06 | .01 |
| ☐ 232 Diego Segui | .14 | .06 | .01 |
| ☐ 233 Billy Grabarkewitz | .14 | .06 | .01 |
| ☐ 234 Tom Grieve | .20 | .09 | .01 |
| ☐ 235 Jack Billingham | .14 | .06 | .01 |
| ☐ 236 Angels: Team/Mgr. Dick Williams | .35 | .07 | .01 |
| ☐ 237 Carl Morton | .14 | .06 | .01 |
| ☐ 238 Dave Duncan | .14 | .06 | .01 |
| ☐ 239 George Stone | .14 | .06 | .01 |
| ☐ 240 Garry Maddox | .20 | .09 | .02 |
| ☐ 241 Dick Tidrow | .14 | .06 | .01 |
| ☐ 242 Jay Johnstone | .20 | .09 | .01 |
| ☐ 243 Jim Kaat | .55 | .25 | .05 |
| ☐ 244 Bill Buckner | .50 | .22 | .05 |
| ☐ 245 Mickey Lolich | .30 | .12 | .03 |
| ☐ 246 Cardinals: Team/Mgr. Red Schoendienst | .35 | .07 | .01 |
| ☐ 247 Enos Cabell | .20 | .09 | .01 |
| ☐ 248 Randy Jones | .20 | .09 | .02 |
| ☐ 249 Danny Thompson | .14 | .06 | .01 |
| ☐ 250 Ken Brett | .20 | .09 | .01 |
| ☐ 251 Fran Healy | .14 | .06 | .01 |
| ☐ 252 Fred Scherman | .14 | .06 | .01 |
| ☐ 253 Jesus Alou | .14 | .06 | .01 |
| ☐ 254 Mike Torrez | .20 | .09 | .02 |
| ☐ 255 Dwight Evans | .70 | .32 | .07 |
| ☐ 256 Billy Champion | .14 | .06 | .01 |
| ☐ 257 Checklist: 133–264 | .40 | .08 | .01 |
| ☐ 258 Dave LaRoche | .14 | .06 | .01 |
| ☐ 259 Len Randle | .14 | .06 | .01 |
| ☐ 260 Johnny Bench | 4.00 | 1.85 | .40 |
| ☐ 261 Andy Hassler | .14 | .06 | .01 |
| ☐ 262 Rowland Office | .14 | .06 | .01 |
| ☐ 263 Jim Perry | .25 | .10 | .02 |
| ☐ 264 John Milner | .14 | .06 | .01 |
| ☐ 265 Ron Bryant | .14 | .06 | .01 |
| ☐ 266 Sandy Alomar | .14 | .06 | .01 |
| ☐ 267 Dick Ruthven | .14 | .06 | .01 |
| ☐ 268 Hal McRae | .30 | .12 | .03 |
| ☐ 269 Doug Rau | .14 | .06 | .01 |
| ☐ 270 Ron Fairly | .20 | .09 | .02 |
| ☐ 271 Jerry Moses | .14 | .06 | .01 |

| | MINT | VG-E | F-G |
|---|---|---|---|
| ☐ 272 Lynn McGlothen | .14 | .06 | .01 |
| ☐ 273 Steve Braun | .14 | .06 | .01 |
| ☐ 274 Vincente Romo | .14 | .06 | .01 |
| ☐ 275 Paul Blair | .20 | .09 | .01 |
| ☐ 276 White Sox Team/Mgr. Chuck Tanner | .35 | .07 | .01 |
| ☐ 277 Frank Taveras | .14 | .06 | .01 |
| ☐ 278 Paul Lindblad | .14 | .06 | .01 |
| ☐ 279 Milt May | .14 | .06 | .01 |
| ☐ 280 Carl Yastrzemski | 5.00 | 2.35 | .50 |
| ☐ 281 Jim Slaton | .14 | .06 | .01 |
| ☐ 282 Jerry Morales | .14 | .06 | .01 |
| ☐ 283 Steve Foucault | .14 | .06 | .01 |
| ☐ 284 Ken Griffey | .55 | .25 | .05 |
| ☐ 285 Ellie Rodriguez | .14 | .06 | .01 |
| ☐ 286 Mike Jorgensen | .14 | .06 | .01 |
| ☐ 287 Roric Harrison | .14 | .06 | .01 |
| ☐ 288 Bruce Ellingsen | .14 | .06 | .01 |
| ☐ 289 Ken Rudolph | .14 | .06 | .01 |
| ☐ 290 Jon Matlack | .20 | .09 | .02 |
| ☐ 291 Bill Sudakis | .14 | .06 | .01 |
| ☐ 292 Ron Schueler | .14 | .06 | .01 |
| ☐ 293 Dick Sharon | .14 | .06 | .01 |
| ☐ 294 Geoff Zahn | .25 | .10 | .02 |
| ☐ 295 Vada Pinson | .30 | .12 | .03 |
| ☐ 296 Alan Foster | .14 | .06 | .01 |
| ☐ 297 Craig Kusick | .14 | .06 | .01 |
| ☐ 298 Johnny Grubb | .14 | .06 | .01 |
| ☐ 299 Bucky Dent | .30 | .12 | .03 |
| ☐ 300 Reggie Jackson | 5.00 | 2.35 | .50 |
| ☐ 301 Dave Roberts | .14 | .06 | .01 |
| ☐ 302 Rick Burleson | .60 | .28 | .06 |
| ☐ 303 Grant Jackson | .14 | .06 | .01 |
| ☐ 304 Pirates: Team/Mgr. Danny Murtaugh | .35 | .07 | .01 |
| ☐ 305 Jim Colborn | .14 | .06 | .01 |
| ☐ 306 Batting Leaders: Rod Carew Ralph Garr | .55 | .25 | .05 |
| ☐ 307 Home Run Leaders: Dick Allen Mike Schmidt | .75 | .35 | .07 |
| ☐ 308 RBI Leaders: Jeff Burroughs Johnny Bench | .55 | .25 | .05 |
| ☐ 309 Stolen Base Leaders: Bill North Lou Brock | .55 | .25 | .05 |
| ☐ 310 Victory Leaders: Jim Hunter Fergie Jenkins Andy Messersmith Phil Niekro | .55 | .25 | .05 |

| | MINT | VG-E | F-G |
|---|---|---|---|
| ☐ 311 ERA Leaders: | .35 | .15 | .03 |
| Jim Hunter | | | |
| Buzz Capra | | | |
| ☐ 312 Strikeout Leaders: | 1.25 | .60 | .12 |
| Nolan Ryan | | | |
| Steve Carlton | | | |
| ☐ 313 Leading Firemen: | .30 | .12 | .03 |
| Terry Forster | | | |
| Mike Marshall | | | |
| ☐ 314 Buck Martinez | .14 | .06 | .01 |
| ☐ 315 Don Kessinger | .20 | .09 | .02 |
| ☐ 316 Jackie Brown | .14 | .06 | .01 |
| ☐ 317 Joe LaHoud | .14 | .06 | .01 |
| ☐ 318 Ernie McAnally | .14 | .06 | .01 |
| ☐ 319 Johnny Oates | .14 | .06 | .01 |
| ☐ 320 Pete Rose | 12.00 | 5.50 | 1.20 |
| ☐ 321 Rudy May | .14 | .06 | .01 |
| ☐ 322 Ed Goodson | .14 | .06 | .01 |
| ☐ 323 Fred Holdsworth | .14 | .06 | .01 |
| ☐ 324 Ed Kranepool | .20 | .09 | .02 |
| ☐ 325 Tony Oliva | .50 | .22 | .05 |
| ☐ 326 Wayne Twitchell | .14 | .06 | .01 |
| ☐ 327 Jerry Hairston | .14 | .06 | .01 |
| ☐ 328 Sonny Siebert | .14 | .06 | .01 |
| ☐ 329 Ted Kubiak | .14 | .06 | .01 |
| ☐ 330 Mike Marshall | .20 | .09 | .02 |
| ☐ 331 Indians: Team/Mgr. | .50 | .08 | .01 |
| Frank Robinson | | | |
| ☐ 332 Fred Kendall | .14 | .06 | .01 |
| ☐ 333 Dick Drago | .14 | .06 | .01 |
| ☐ 334 Greg Gross | .14 | .06 | .01 |
| ☐ 335 Jim Palmer | 2.50 | 1.15 | .25 |
| ☐ 336 Rennie Stennett | .14 | .06 | .01 |
| ☐ 337 Kevin Kobel | .14 | .06 | .01 |
| ☐ 338 Rick Stelmaszek | .14 | .06 | .01 |
| ☐ 339 Jim Fregosi | .20 | .09 | .02 |
| ☐ 340 Paul Splittorff | .20 | .09 | .02 |
| ☐ 341 Hal Breeden | .14 | .06 | .01 |
| ☐ 342 Leroy Stanton | .14 | .06 | .01 |
| ☐ 343 Danny Frisella | .14 | .06 | .01 |
| ☐ 344 Ben Oglivie | .30 | .12 | .03 |
| ☐ 345 Clay Carroll | .14 | .06 | .01 |
| ☐ 346 Bobby Darwin | .14 | .06 | .01 |
| ☐ 347 Mike Caldwell | .20 | .09 | .02 |
| ☐ 348 Tony Muser | .14 | .06 | .01 |
| ☐ 349 Ray Sadecki | .14 | .06 | .01 |
| ☐ 350 Bobby Murcer | .45 | .20 | .04 |
| ☐ 351 Bob Boone | .25 | .10 | .02 |
| ☐ 352 Darold Knowles | .14 | .06 | .01 |
| ☐ 353 Luis Melendez | .14 | .06 | .01 |
| ☐ 354 Dick Bosman | .14 | .06 | .01 |
| ☐ 355 Chris Cannizzaro | .14 | .06 | .01 |
| ☐ 356 Rico Petrocelli | .20 | .09 | .02 |

| | MINT | VG-E | F-G |
|---|---|---|---|
| ☐ 357 Ken Forsch | .14 | .06 | .01 |
| ☐ 358 Al Bumbry | .14 | .06 | .01 |
| ☐ 359 Paul Popovich | .14 | .06 | .01 |
| ☐ 360 George Scott | .20 | .09 | .02 |
| ☐ 361 Dodgers: Team/Mgr. | .50 | .10 | .02 |
| Walter Alston | | | |
| ☐ 362 Steve Hargan | .14 | .06 | .01 |
| ☐ 363 Carmen Fanzone | .14 | .06 | .01 |
| ☐ 364 Doug Bird | .14 | .06 | .01 |
| ☐ 365 Bob Bailey | .14 | .06 | .01 |
| ☐ 366 Ken Sanders | .14 | .06 | .01 |
| ☐ 367 Craig Robinson | .14 | .06 | .01 |
| ☐ 368 Vic Albury | .14 | .06 | .01 |
| ☐ 369 Merv Rettenmund | .14 | .06 | .01 |
| ☐ 370 Tom Seaver | 3.75 | 1.75 | .37 |
| ☐ 371 Gates Brown | .14 | .06 | .01 |
| ☐ 372 John D'Acquisto | .14 | .06 | .01 |
| ☐ 373 Bill Sharp | .14 | .06 | .01 |
| ☐ 374 Eddie Watt | .14 | .06 | .01 |
| ☐ 375 Roy White | .20 | .09 | .02 |
| ☐ 376 Steve Yeager | .20 | .09 | .02 |
| ☐ 377 Tom Hilgendorf | .14 | .06 | .01 |
| ☐ 378 Derrel Thomas | .14 | .06 | .01 |
| ☐ 379 Bernie Carbo | .14 | .06 | .01 |
| ☐ 380 Sal Bando | .25 | .10 | .02 |
| ☐ 381 John Curtis | .14 | .06 | .01 |
| ☐ 382 Don Baylor | .75 | .35 | .07 |
| ☐ 383 Jim York | .14 | .06 | .01 |
| ☐ 384 Brewers: Team/Mgr. | .35 | .07 | .01 |
| Del Crandall | | | |
| ☐ 385 Dock Ellis | .14 | .06 | .01 |
| ☐ 386 Checklist: 265–396 | .40 | .08 | .01 |
| ☐ 387 Jim Spencer | .14 | .06 | .01 |
| ☐ 388 Steve Stone | .20 | .09 | .02 |
| ☐ 389 Tony Solaita | .14 | .06 | .01 |
| ☐ 390 Ron Cey | .70 | .32 | .07 |
| ☐ 391 Don DeMola | .14 | .06 | .01 |
| ☐ 392 Bruce Bochte | .55 | .25 | .05 |
| ☐ 393 Gary Gentry | .14 | .06 | .01 |
| ☐ 394 Larvell Blanks | .14 | .06 | .01 |
| ☐ 395 Bud Harrelson | .14 | .06 | .01 |
| ☐ 396 Fred Norman | .14 | .06 | .01 |
| ☐ 397 Bill Freehan | .25 | .10 | .02 |
| ☐ 398 Elias Sosa | .14 | .06 | .01 |
| ☐ 399 Terry Harmon | .14 | .06 | .01 |
| ☐ 400 Dick Allen | .35 | .15 | .03 |
| ☐ 401 Mike Wallace | .14 | .06 | .01 |
| ☐ 402 Bob Tolan | .14 | .06 | .01 |
| ☐ 403 Tom Buskey | .14 | .06 | .01 |
| ☐ 404 Ted Sizemore | .14 | .06 | .01 |
| ☐ 405 John Montague | .14 | .06 | .01 |
| ☐ 406 Bob Gallagher | .14 | .06 | .01 |
| ☐ 407 Herb Washington | .14 | .06 | .01 |

| | MINT | VG-E | F-G | | MINT | VG-E | F-G |
|---|---|---|---|---|---|---|---|
| 408 Clyde Wright | .14 | .06 | .01 | 458 Ross Grimsley | .14 | .06 | .01 |
| 409 Bob Robertson | .14 | .06 | .01 | 459 1974 AL Champs: | .30 | .12 | .03 |
| 410 Mike Cueller | .20 | .09 | .02 | A's over Orioles | | | |
| (sic, Cuellar) | | | | (Second base | | | |
| 411 George Mitterwald | .14 | .06 | .01 | action pictured) | | | |
| 412 Bill Hands | .14 | .06 | .01 | 460 1974 NL Champs: | .50 | .20 | .05 |
| 413 Marty Pattin | .14 | .06 | .01 | Dodgers over Pirates | | | |
| 414 Manny Mota | .20 | .09 | .02 | (Taveras and Garvey | | | |
| 415 John Hiller | .20 | .09 | .02 | at second base) | | | |
| 416 Larry Lintz | .14 | .06 | .01 | 461 World Series Game 1 | 1.10 | .50 | .11 |
| 417 Skip Lockwood | .14 | .06 | .01 | (Reggie Jackson) | | | |
| 418 Leo Foster | .14 | .06 | .01 | 462 World Series Game 2 | .30 | .12 | .03 |
| 419 Dave Goltz | .20 | .09 | .02 | (Dodger dugout) | | | |
| 420 Larry Bowa | .30 | .12 | .03 | 463 World Series Game 3 | .50 | .22 | .05 |
| 421 Mets: Team/Mgr | .50 | .10 | .02 | (Fingers pitching) | | | |
| Yogi Berra | | | | 464 World Series Game 4 | .30 | .12 | .03 |
| 422 Brian Downing | .20 | .09 | .02 | (A's batter) | | | |
| 423 Clay Kirby | .14 | .06 | .01 | 465 World Series Game 5 | .30 | .12 | .03 |
| 424 John Lowenstein | .14 | .06 | .01 | (Rudi rounding third) | | | |
| 425 Tito Fuentes | .14 | .06 | .01 | 466 World Series Summary: | .30 | .12 | .03 |
| 426 George Medich | .20 | .09 | .01 | A's do it again | | | |
| 427 Clarence Gaston | .14 | .06 | .01 | Win 3rd straight | | | |
| 428 Dave Hamilton | .14 | .06 | .01 | (A's group) | | | |
| 429 Jim Dwyer | .14 | .06 | .01 | 467 Ed Halicki | .14 | .06 | .01 |
| 430 Luis Tiant | .30 | .12 | .03 | 468 Bobby Mitchell | .14 | .06 | .01 |
| 431 Rod Gilbreath | .14 | .06 | .01 | 469 Tom Dettore | .14 | .06 | .01 |
| 432 Ken Berry | .14 | .06 | .01 | 470 Jeff Burroughs | .20 | .09 | .02 |
| 433 Larry Demery | .14 | .06 | .01 | 471 Bob Stinson | .14 | .06 | .01 |
| 434 Bob Locker | .14 | .06 | .01 | 472 Bruce Dal Canton | .14 | .06 | .01 |
| 435 Dave Nelson | .14 | .06 | .01 | 473 Ken McMullen | .14 | .06 | .01 |
| 436 Ken Frailing | .14 | .06 | .01 | 474 Luke Walker | .14 | .06 | .01 |
| 437 Al Cowens | .45 | .20 | .04 | 475 Darrell Evans | .40 | .18 | .04 |
| 438 Don Carrithers | .14 | .06 | .01 | 476 Eduardo Figueroa | .14 | .06 | .01 |
| 439 Ed Brinkman | .14 | .06 | .01 | 477 Tom Hutton | .14 | .06 | .01 |
| 440 Andy Messersmith | .20 | .09 | .02 | 478 Tom Burgmeier | .14 | .06 | .01 |
| 441 Bobby Heise | .14 | .06 | .01 | 479 Ken Boswell | .14 | .06 | .01 |
| 442 Maximino Leon | .14 | .06 | .01 | 480 Carlos May | .14 | .06 | .01 |
| 443 Twins: Team/Mgr. | .35 | .07 | .01 | 481 Will McEnaney | .14 | .06 | .01 |
| Frank Quilici | | | | 482 Tom McCraw | .14 | .06 | .01 |
| 444 Gene Garber | .14 | .06 | .01 | 483 Steve Ontiveros | .14 | .06 | .01 |
| 445 Felix Millan | .14 | .06 | .01 | 484 Glenn Beckert | .20 | .09 | .02 |
| 446 Bart Johnson | .14 | .06 | .01 | 485 Sparky Lyle | .30 | .12 | .03 |
| 447 Terry Crowley | .14 | .06 | .01 | 486 Ray Fosse | .14 | .06 | .01 |
| 448 Frank Duffy | .14 | .06 | .01 | 487 Astros: Team/Mgr. | .35 | .07 | .01 |
| 449 Charlie Williams | .14 | .06 | .01 | Preston Gomez | | | |
| 450 Willie McCovey | 2.00 | .90 | .20 | 488 Bill Travers | .14 | .06 | .01 |
| 451 Rick Dempsey | .25 | .10 | .02 | 489 Cecil Cooper | 1.50 | .70 | .15 |
| 452 Angel Mangual | .14 | .06 | .01 | 490 Reggie Smith | .30 | .12 | .03 |
| 453 Claude Osteen | .20 | .09 | .02 | 491 Doyle Alexander | .25 | .10 | .02 |
| 454 Doug Griffin | .14 | .06 | .01 | 492 Rich Hebner | .14 | .06 | .01 |
| 455 Don Wilson | .14 | .06 | .01 | 493 Don Stanhouse | .14 | .06 | .01 |
| 456 Bob Coluccio | .14 | .06 | .01 | 494 Pete LaCock | .14 | .06 | .01 |
| 457 Mario Mendoza | .14 | .06 | .01 | 495 Nelson Briles | .14 | .06 | .01 |

|  | MINT | VG-E | F-G |
|---|---|---|---|
| ☐ 496 Pepe Frias | .14 | .06 | .01 |
| ☐ 497 Jim Nettles | .14 | .06 | .01 |
| ☐ 498 Al Downing | .14 | .06 | .01 |
| ☐ 499 Marty Perez | .14 | .06 | .01 |
| ☐ 500 Nolan Ryan | 3.25 | 1.50 | .32 |
| ☐ 501 Bill Robinson | .14 | .06 | .01 |
| ☐ 502 Pat Bourque | .14 | .06 | .01 |
| ☐ 503 Fred Stanley | .14 | .06 | .01 |
| ☐ 504 Buddy Bradford | .14 | .06 | .01 |
| ☐ 505 Chris Speier | .14 | .06 | .01 |
| ☐ 506 Leron Lee | .14 | .06 | .01 |
| ☐ 507 Tom Carroll | .14 | .06 | .01 |
| ☐ 508 Bob Hansen | .14 | .06 | .01 |
| ☐ 509 Dave Hilton | .14 | .06 | .01 |
| ☐ 510 Vida Blue | .35 | .15 | .03 |
| ☐ 511 Rangers: Team/Mgr. | .50 | .10 | .02 |
| Billy Martin | | | |
| ☐ 512 Larry Milbourne | .14 | .06 | .01 |
| ☐ 513 Dick Pole | .14 | .06 | .01 |
| ☐ 514 Jose Cruz | .50 | .22 | .05 |
| ☐ 515 Manny Sanguillen | .25 | .10 | .02 |
| ☐ 516 Don Hood | .14 | .06 | .01 |
| ☐ 517 Checklist: 397–528 | .40 | .08 | .01 |
| ☐ 518 Leo Cardenas | .14 | .06 | .01 |
| ☐ 519 Jim Todd | .14 | .06 | .01 |
| ☐ 520 Amos Otis | .30 | .12 | .03 |
| ☐ 521 Dennis Blair | .14 | .06 | .01 |
| ☐ 522 Gary Sutherland | .14 | .06 | .01 |
| ☐ 523 Tom Paciorek | .20 | .09 | .02 |
| ☐ 524 John Doherty | .14 | .06 | .01 |
| ☐ 525 Tom House | .14 | .06 | .01 |
| ☐ 526 Larry Hisle | .20 | .09 | .02 |
| ☐ 527 Mac Scarce | .14 | .06 | .01 |
| ☐ 528 Eddie Leon | .14 | .06 | .01 |
| ☐ 529 Gary Thomasson | .14 | .06 | .01 |
| ☐ 530 Gaylord Perry | 1.50 | .70 | .15 |
| ☐ 531 Reds: Team/Mgr. | .45 | .08 | .01 |
| Sparky Anderson | | | |
| ☐ 532 Gorman Thomas | .90 | .40 | .09 |
| ☐ 533 Rudy Meoli | .14 | .06 | .01 |
| ☐ 534 Alex Johnson | .14 | .06 | .01 |
| ☐ 535 Gene Tenace | .14 | .06 | .01 |
| ☐ 536 Bob Moose | .14 | .06 | .01 |
| ☐ 537 Tommy Harper | .20 | .09 | .01 |
| ☐ 538 Duffy Dyer | .14 | .06 | .01 |
| ☐ 539 Jesse Jefferson | .14 | .06 | .01 |
| ☐ 540 Lou Brock | 2.00 | .90 | .20 |
| ☐ 541 Roger Metzger | .14 | .06 | .01 |
| ☐ 542 Pete Broberg | .14 | .06 | .01 |
| ☐ 543 Larry Biittner | .14 | .06 | .01 |
| ☐ 544 Steve Mingori | .14 | .06 | .01 |
| ☐ 545 Billy Williams | .75 | .35 | .07 |
| ☐ 546 John Knox | .14 | .06 | .01 |

|  | MINT | VG-E | F-G |
|---|---|---|---|
| ☐ 547 Von Joshua | .14 | .06 | .01 |
| ☐ 548 Charlie Sands | .14 | .06 | .01 |
| ☐ 549 Bill Butler | .14 | .06 | .01 |
| ☐ 550 Ralph Garr | .20 | .09 | .02 |
| ☐ 551 Larry Christenson | .14 | .06 | .01 |
| ☐ 552 Jack Brohamer | .14 | .06 | .01 |
| ☐ 553 John Boccabella | .14 | .06 | .01 |
| ☐ 554 Rich Gossage | 1.25 | .60 | .12 |
| ☐ 555 Al Oliver | .90 | .40 | .09 |
| ☐ 556 Tim Johnson | .14 | .06 | .01 |
| ☐ 557 Larry Gura | .25 | .10 | .02 |
| ☐ 558 Dave Roberts | .14 | .06 | .01 |
| ☐ 559 Bob Montgomery | .14 | .06 | .01 |
| ☐ 560 Tony Perez | .75 | .35 | .07 |
| ☐ 561 A's: Team/Mgr. | .35 | .07 | .01 |
| Alvin Dark | | | |
| ☐ 562 Gary Nolan | .14 | .06 | .01 |
| ☐ 563 Wilbur Howard | .14 | .06 | .01 |
| ☐ 564 Tommy Davis | .20 | .09 | .02 |
| ☐ 565 Joe Torre | .50 | .22 | .05 |
| ☐ 566 Ray Burris | .20 | .09 | .01 |
| ☐ 567 Jim Sundberg | .75 | .35 | .07 |
| ☐ 568 Dale Murray | .14 | .06 | .01 |
| ☐ 569 Frank White | .40 | .18 | .04 |
| ☐ 570 Jim Wynn | .20 | .09 | .02 |
| ☐ 571 Dave Lemanczyk | .14 | .06 | .01 |
| ☐ 572 Roger Nelson | .14 | .06 | .01 |
| ☐ 573 Orlando Pena | .14 | .06 | .01 |
| ☐ 574 Tony Taylor | .14 | .06 | .01 |
| ☐ 575 Gene Clines | .14 | .06 | .01 |
| ☐ 576 Phil Roof | .14 | .06 | .01 |
| ☐ 577 John Morris | .14 | .06 | .01 |
| ☐ 578 Dave Tomlin | .14 | .06 | .01 |
| ☐ 579 Skip Pitlock | .14 | .06 | .01 |
| ☐ 580 Frank Robinson | 2.00 | .90 | .20 |
| ☐ 581 Darrel Chaney | .14 | .06 | .01 |
| ☐ 582 Eduardo Rodriguez | .14 | .06 | .01 |
| ☐ 583 Andy Etchebarren | .14 | .06 | .01 |
| ☐ 584 Mike Garman | .14 | .06 | .01 |
| ☐ 585 Chris Chambliss | .30 | .12 | .03 |
| ☐ 586 Tim McCarver | .25 | .10 | .02 |
| ☐ 587 Chris Ward | .14 | .06 | .01 |
| ☐ 588 Rick Auerbach | .14 | .06 | .01 |
| ☐ 589 Braves: Team/Mgr. | .35 | .07 | .01 |
| Clyde King | | | |
| ☐ 590 Cesar Cedeno | .30 | .12 | .03 |
| ☐ 591 Glenn Abbott | .14 | .06 | .01 |
| ☐ 592 Balor Moore | .14 | .06 | .01 |
| ☐ 593 Gene Lamont | .14 | .06 | .01 |
| ☐ 594 Jim Fuller | .14 | .06 | .01 |
| ☐ 595 Joe Niekro | .35 | .15 | .03 |
| ☐ 596 Ollie Brown | .14 | .06 | .01 |
| ☐ 597 Winston Llenas | .14 | .06 | .01 |

| | MINT | VG-E | F-G |
|---|---|---|---|
| ☐ 598 Bruce Kison | .14 | .06 | .01 |
| ☐ 599 Nate Colbert | .14 | .06 | .01 |
| ☐ 600 Rod Carew | 4.25 | 2.00 | .42 |
| ☐ 601 Juan Beniquez | .25 | .10 | .02 |
| ☐ 602 John Vukovich | .14 | .06 | .01 |
| ☐ 603 Lew Krausse | .14 | .06 | .01 |
| ☐ 604 Oscar Zamora | .14 | .06 | .01 |
| ☐ 605 John Ellis | .14 | .06 | .01 |
| ☐ 606 Bruce Miller | .14 | .06 | .01 |
| ☐ 607 Jim Holt | .14 | .06 | .01 |
| ☐ 608 Gene Michael | .20 | .09 | .02 |
| ☐ 609 Ellie Hendricks | .14 | .06 | .01 |
| ☐ 610 Ron Hunt | .14 | .06 | .01 |
| ☐ 611 Yankees: Team/Mgr. | .50 | .10 | .02 |
| Bill Virdon | | | |
| ☐ 612 Terry Hughes | .14 | .06 | .01 |
| ☐ 613 Bill Parsons | .14 | .06 | .01 |
| ☐ 614 Rookie Pitchers: | .20 | .09 | .02 |
| Jack Kucek | | | |
| Dyar Miller | | | |
| Vern Ruhle | | | |
| Paul Siebert | | | |
| ☐ 615 Rookie Pitchers: | .90 | .40 | .09 |
| Pat Darcy | | | |
| Dennis Leonard | | | |
| Tom Underwood | | | |
| Hank Webb | | | |
| ☐ 616 Rookie Outfielders: | 18.00 | 8.50 | 1.80 |
| Dave Augustine | | | |
| Pepe Mangual | | | |
| Jim Rice | | | |
| John Scott | | | |
| ☐ 617 Rookie Infielders: | 2.00 | .90 | .20 |
| Mike Cubbage | | | |
| Doug DeCinces | | | |
| Reggie Sanders | | | |
| Manny Trillo | | | |
| ☐ 618 Rookie Pitchers: | 1.75 | .85 | .17 |
| Jamie Easterly | | | |
| Tom Johnson | | | |
| Scott McGregor | | | |
| Rick Rhoden | | | |
| ☐ 619 Rookie Outfielders: | .20 | .09 | .02 |
| Benny Ayala | | | |
| Nyls Nyman | | | |
| Tommy Smith | | | |
| Jerry Turner | | | |
| ☐ 620 Rookie Catcher/OF: | 14.00 | 6.50 | 1.40 |
| Gary Carter | | | |
| Marc Hill | | | |
| Danny Meyer | | | |
| Leon Roberts | | | |

| | MINT | VG-E | F-G |
|---|---|---|---|
| ☐ 621 Rookie Pitchers: | 1.75 | .85 | .17 |
| John Denny | | | |
| Rawly Eastwick | | | |
| Jim Kern | | | |
| Juan Veintidos | | | |
| ☐ 622 Rookie Outfielders: | 9.00 | 4.25 | .90 |
| Ed Armbrister | | | |
| Fred Lynn | | | |
| Tom Poquette | | | |
| Terry Whitfield | | | |
| ☐ 623 Rookie Infielders: | 10.00 | 4.75 | 1.00 |
| Phil Garner | | | |
| Keith Hernandez | | | |
| Bob Sheldon | | | |
| Tom Veryzer | | | |
| ☐ 624 Rookie Pitchers: | .25 | .10 | .02 |
| Doug Konieczny | | | |
| Gary Lavelle | | | |
| Jim Otten | | | |
| Eddie Solomon | | | |
| ☐ 625 Boog Powell | .45 | .20 | .04 |
| ☐ 626 Larry Haney | .14 | .06 | .01 |
| (photo actually | | | |
| Dave Duncan) | | | |
| ☐ 627 Tom Walker | .14 | .06 | .01 |
| ☐ 628 Ron LeFlore | .50 | .22 | .05 |
| ☐ 629 Joe Hoerner | .14 | .06 | .01 |
| ☐ 630 Greg Luzinski | .65 | .30 | .06 |
| ☐ 631 Lee Lacy | .25 | .10 | .02 |
| ☐ 632 Morris Nettles | .14 | .06 | .01 |
| ☐ 633 Paul Casanova | .14 | .06 | .01 |
| ☐ 634 Cy Acosta | .14 | .06 | .01 |
| ☐ 635 Chuck Dobson | .14 | .06 | .01 |
| ☐ 636 Charlie Moore | .14 | .06 | .01 |
| ☐ 637 Ted Martinez | .14 | .06 | .01 |
| ☐ 638 Cubs: Team/Mgr. | .35 | .07 | .01 |
| Jim Marshall | | | |
| ☐ 639 Steve Kline | .14 | .06 | .01 |
| ☐ 640 Harmon Killebrew | 1.50 | .70 | .15 |
| ☐ 641 Jim Northrup | .14 | .06 | .01 |
| ☐ 642 Mike Phillips | .14 | .06 | .01 |
| ☐ 643 Brent Strom | .14 | .06 | .01 |
| ☐ 644 Bill Fahey | .14 | .06 | .01 |
| ☐ 645 Danny Cater | .14 | .06 | .01 |
| ☐ 646 Checklist: 529–660 | .40 | .08 | .01 |
| ☐ 647 Claudell Washington | 1.50 | .70 | .15 |
| ☐ 648 Dave Pagan | .14 | .06 | .01 |
| ☐ 649 Jack Heidemann | .14 | .06 | .01 |
| ☐ 650 Dave May | .14 | .06 | .01 |
| ☐ 651 John Morlan | .14 | .06 | .01 |
| ☐ 652 Lindy McDaniel | .14 | .06 | .01 |
| ☐ 653 Lee Richard | .14 | .06 | .01 |
| ☐ 654 Jerry Terrell | .14 | .06 | .01 |

|  | MINT | VG-E | F-G |
|---|---|---|---|
| ☐ 655 Rico Carty | .25 | .10 | .02 |
| ☐ 656 Bill Plummer | .14 | .06 | .01 |
| ☐ 657 Bob Oliver | .14 | .06 | .01 |
| ☐ 658 Vic Harris | .14 | .06 | .01 |
| ☐ 659 Bob Apodaca | .14 | .06 | .01 |
| ☐ 660 Hank Aaron | 7.50 | 2.50 | .50 |

## 1976 TOPPS

WILLIE McCOVEY
PADRES

*The 1976 Topps set of 660 cards (measuring 2½" by 3½") is known for its sharp color photographs and interesting presentation of subjects. A "Father and Son" series (66–70) spotlights five Major Leaguers whose fathers also made the "Big Show." Other series include "All Time All Stars" (341–350) and "Record Breakers" from the previous season (1–6).*

Complete Set: M-140.00; VG-E-65.00; F-G-14.00

Common Player (1–660)    .12    .05    .01

| | MINT | VG-E | F-G |
|---|---|---|---|
| ☐ 1 RB: Hank Aaron<br>Most RBI's 2262 | 5.00 | 1.25 | .25 |
| ☐ 2 RB: Bobby Bonds<br>Most leadoff homers 32;<br>Plus 3 Seasons of<br>30 HR's and 30 SB's | .25 | .10 | .02 |
| ☐ 3 RB: Mickey Lolich<br>Lefthander Most<br>Strikeouts 2679 | .25 | .10 | .02 |
| ☐ 4 RB: Dave Lopes<br>Most consecutive<br>SB attempts, 38 | .25 | .10 | .02 |
| ☐ 5 RB: Tom Seaver<br>Most cons. seasons<br>with 200 SO's, 8 | 1.25 | .60 | .12 |

| | MINT | VG-E | F-G |
|---|---|---|---|
| ☐ 6 RB: Rennie Stennett<br>Most hits in a 9<br>inning game, 7 | .16 | .07 | .01 |
| ☐ 7 Jim Umbarger | .12 | .05 | .01 |
| ☐ 8 Tito Fuentes | .12 | .05 | .01 |
| ☐ 9 Paul Lindblad | .12 | .05 | .01 |
| ☐ 10 Lou Brock | 1.50 | .70 | .15 |
| ☐ 11 Jim Hughes | .12 | .05 | .01 |
| ☐ 12 Richie Zisk | .16 | .07 | .01 |
| ☐ 13 John Wockenfuss | .12 | .05 | .01 |
| ☐ 14 Gene Garber | .12 | .05 | .01 |
| ☐ 15 George Scott | .16 | .07 | .01 |
| ☐ 16 Bob Apodaca | .12 | .05 | .01 |
| ☐ 17 New York Yankees Team | .50 | .10 | .02 |
| ☐ 18 Dale Murray | .12 | .05 | .01 |
| ☐ 19 George Brett | 7.00 | 3.25 | .70 |
| ☐ 20 Bob Watson | .16 | .07 | .01 |
| ☐ 21 Dave LaRoche | .12 | .05 | .01 |
| ☐ 22 Bill Russell | .16 | .07 | .01 |
| ☐ 23 Brian Downing | .16 | .07 | .01 |
| ☐ 24 Cesar Geronimo | .12 | .05 | .01 |
| ☐ 25 Mike Torrez | .16 | .07 | .01 |
| ☐ 26 Andy Thornton | .25 | .10 | .02 |
| ☐ 27 Ed Figueroa | .12 | .05 | .01 |
| ☐ 28 Dusty Baker | .30 | .12 | .03 |
| ☐ 29 Rick Burleson | .25 | .10 | .02 |
| ☐ 30 John Montefusco | .30 | .12 | .03 |
| ☐ 31 Len Randle | .12 | .05 | .01 |
| ☐ 32 Danny Frisella | .12 | .05 | .01 |
| ☐ 33 Bill North | .12 | .05 | .01 |
| ☐ 34 Mike Garman | .12 | .05 | .01 |
| ☐ 35 Tony Oliva | .40 | .18 | .04 |
| ☐ 36 Frank Taveras | .12 | .05 | .01 |
| ☐ 37 John Hiller | .16 | .07 | .01 |
| ☐ 38 Garry Maddox | .16 | .07 | .01 |
| ☐ 39 Pete Broberg | .12 | .05 | .01 |
| ☐ 40 Dave Kingman | .60 | .28 | .06 |
| ☐ 41 Tippy Martinez | .65 | .30 | .06 |
| ☐ 42 Barry Foote | .12 | .05 | .01 |
| ☐ 43 Paul Splittorff | .16 | .07 | .01 |
| ☐ 44 Doug Rader | .16 | .07 | .01 |
| ☐ 45 Boog Powell | .35 | .15 | .03 |
| ☐ 46 Dodgers Team | .50 | .10 | .02 |
| ☐ 47 Jesse Jefferson | .12 | .05 | .01 |
| ☐ 48 Dave Concepcion | .35 | .15 | .03 |
| ☐ 49 Dave Duncan | .12 | .05 | .01 |
| ☐ 50 Fred Lynn | 1.75 | .85 | .17 |
| ☐ 51 Ray Burris | .12 | .05 | .01 |
| ☐ 52 Dave Chalk | .12 | .05 | .01 |
| ☐ 53 Mike Beard | .12 | .05 | .01 |
| ☐ 54 Dave Radar | .12 | .05 | .01 |
| ☐ 55 Gaylord Perry | 1.25 | .60 | .12 |
| ☐ 56 Bob Tolan | .12 | .05 | .01 |

| | MINT | VG-E | F-G |
|---|---|---|---|
| ☐ 57 Phil Garner | .25 | .10 | .02 |
| ☐ 58 Ron Reed | .12 | .05 | .01 |
| ☐ 59 Larry Hisle | .16 | .07 | .01 |
| ☐ 60 Jerry Reuss | .25 | .10 | .02 |
| ☐ 61 Ron LeFlore | .25 | .10 | .02 |
| ☐ 62 Johnny Oates | .12 | .05 | .01 |
| ☐ 63 Bobby Darwin | .12 | .05 | .01 |
| ☐ 64 Jerry Koosman | .25 | .10 | .02 |
| ☐ 65 Chris Chambliss | .20 | .09 | .02 |
| **FATHER/SON CARDS (66–70)** | | | |
| ☐ 66 Father and Son: Gus Bell Buddy Bell | .35 | .15 | .03 |
| ☐ 67 Father and Son: Ray Boone Bob Boone | .20 | .09 | .02 |
| ☐ 68 Father and Son: Joe Coleman Joe Coleman Jr. | .16 | .07 | .01 |
| ☐ 69 Father and Son: Jim Hegan Mike Hegan | .16 | .07 | .01 |
| ☐ 70 Father and Son: Roy Smalley Roy Smalley Jr. | .20 | .09 | .02 |
| ☐ 71 Steve Rogers | .30 | .12 | .03 |
| ☐ 72 Hal McRae | .25 | .10 | .02 |
| ☐ 73 Orioles Team | .50 | .10 | .02 |
| ☐ 74 Oscar Gamble | .20 | .09 | .02 |
| ☐ 75 Larry Dierker | .16 | .07 | .01 |
| ☐ 76 Willie Crawford | .12 | .05 | .01 |
| ☐ 77 Pedro Borbon | .12 | .05 | .01 |
| ☐ 78 Cecil Cooper | .90 | .40 | .09 |
| ☐ 79 Jerry Morales | .12 | .05 | .01 |
| ☐ 80 Jim Kaat | .45 | .20 | .04 |
| ☐ 81 Darrell Evans | .35 | .15 | .03 |
| ☐ 82 Von Joshua | .12 | .05 | .01 |
| ☐ 83 Jim Spencer | .12 | .05 | .01 |
| ☐ 84 Brent Strom | .12 | .05 | .01 |
| ☐ 85 Mickey Rivers | .25 | .10 | .02 |
| ☐ 86 Mike Tyson | .12 | .05 | .01 |
| ☐ 87 Tom Burgmeier | .12 | .05 | .01 |
| ☐ 88 Duffy Dyer | .12 | .05 | .01 |
| ☐ 89 Vern Ruhle | .12 | .05 | .01 |
| ☐ 90 Sal Bando | .20 | .09 | .02 |
| ☐ 91 Tom Hutton | .12 | .05 | .01 |
| ☐ 92 Eduardo Rodriguez | .12 | .05 | .01 |
| ☐ 93 Mike Phillips | .12 | .05 | .01 |
| ☐ 94 Jim Dwyer | .12 | .05 | .01 |
| ☐ 95 Brooks Robinson | 1.75 | .85 | .17 |
| ☐ 96 Doug Bird | .12 | .05 | .01 |
| ☐ 97 Wilbur Howard | .12 | .05 | .01 |

| | MINT | VG-E | F-G |
|---|---|---|---|
| ☐ 98 Dennis Eckersley | 1.00 | .45 | .10 |
| ☐ 99 Lee Lacy | .20 | .09 | .02 |
| ☐ 100 Jim Hunter | .75 | .35 | .07 |
| ☐ 101 Pete LaCock | .12 | .05 | .01 |
| ☐ 102 Jim Willoughby | .12 | .05 | .01 |
| ☐ 103 Biff Pocoroba | .12 | .05 | .01 |
| ☐ 104 Reds Team | .50 | .10 | .02 |
| ☐ 105 Gary Lavelle | .16 | .07 | .01 |
| ☐ 106 Tom Grieve | .16 | .07 | .01 |
| ☐ 107 Dave Roberts | .12 | .05 | .01 |
| ☐ 108 Don Kirkwood | .12 | .05 | .01 |
| ☐ 109 Larry Lintz | .12 | .05 | .01 |
| ☐ 110 Carlos May | .12 | .05 | .01 |
| ☐ 111 Danny Thompson | .12 | .05 | .01 |
| ☐ 112 Kent Tekulve | .75 | .35 | .07 |
| ☐ 113 Gary Sutherland | .12 | .05 | .01 |
| ☐ 114 Jay Johnstone | .16 | .07 | .01 |
| ☐ 115 Ken Holtzman | .20 | .09 | .02 |
| ☐ 116 Charlie Moore | .12 | .05 | .01 |
| ☐ 117 Mike Jorgensen | .12 | .05 | .01 |
| ☐ 118 Red Sox Team | .50 | .10 | .02 |
| ☐ 119 Checklist 1–132 | .35 | .07 | .01 |
| ☐ 120 Rusty Staub | .30 | .12 | .03 |
| ☐ 121 Tony Solaita | .12 | .05 | .01 |
| ☐ 122 Mike Cosgrove | .12 | .05 | .01 |
| ☐ 123 Walt Williams | .12 | .05 | .01 |
| ☐ 124 Doug Rau | .12 | .05 | .01 |
| ☐ 125 Don Baylor | .60 | .28 | .06 |
| ☐ 126 Tom Dettore | .12 | .05 | .01 |
| ☐ 127 Larvell Blanks | .12 | .05 | .01 |
| ☐ 128 Ken Griffey | .35 | .15 | .03 |
| ☐ 129 Andy Etchebarren | .12 | .05 | .01 |
| ☐ 130 Luis Tiant | .25 | .10 | .02 |
| ☐ 131 Bill Stein | .12 | .05 | .01 |
| ☐ 132 Don Hood | .12 | .05 | .01 |
| ☐ 133 Gary Matthews | .30 | .12 | .03 |
| ☐ 134 Mike Ivie | .12 | .05 | .01 |
| ☐ 135 Bake McBride | .16 | .07 | .01 |
| ☐ 136 Dave Goltz | .16 | .07 | .01 |
| ☐ 137 Bill Robinson | .12 | .05 | .01 |
| ☐ 138 Lerrin LaGrow | .12 | .05 | .01 |
| ☐ 139 Gorman Thomas | .45 | .20 | .04 |
| ☐ 140 Vida Blue | .30 | .12 | .03 |
| ☐ 141 Larry Parrish | 1.00 | .45 | .10 |
| ☐ 142 Dick Drago | .12 | .05 | .01 |
| ☐ 143 Jerry Grote | .12 | .05 | .01 |
| ☐ 144 Al Fitzmorris | .12 | .05 | .01 |
| ☐ 145 Larry Bowa | .30 | .12 | .03 |
| ☐ 146 George Medich | .16 | .07 | .01 |
| ☐ 147 Astros Team | .35 | .07 | .01 |
| ☐ 148 Stan Thomas | .12 | .05 | .01 |
| ☐ 149 Tommy Davis | .16 | .07 | .01 |
| ☐ 150 Steve Garvey | 3.75 | 1.75 | .37 |

|  | MINT | VG-E | F-G |
|---|---|---|---|
| ☐ 151 Bill Bonham | .12 | .05 | .01 |
| ☐ 152 Leroy Stanton | .12 | .05 | .01 |
| ☐ 153 Buzz Capra | .12 | .05 | .01 |
| ☐ 154 Bucky Dent | .25 | .10 | .02 |
| ☐ 155 Jack Billingham | .12 | .05 | .01 |
| ☐ 156 Rico Carty | .20 | .09 | .02 |
| ☐ 157 Mike Caldwell | .16 | .07 | .01 |
| ☐ 158 Ken Reitz | .12 | .05 | .01 |
| ☐ 159 Jerry Terrell | .12 | .05 | .01 |
| ☐ 160 Dave Winfield | 3.50 | 1.65 | .35 |
| ☐ 161 Bruce Kison | .12 | .05 | .01 |
| ☐ 162 Jack Pierce | .12 | .05 | .01 |
| ☐ 163 Jim Slaton | .12 | .05 | .01 |
| ☐ 164 Pepe Mangual | .12 | .05 | .01 |
| ☐ 165 Gene Tenace | .12 | .05 | .01 |
| ☐ 166 Skip Lockwood | .12 | .05 | .01 |
| ☐ 167 Freddie Patek | .12 | .05 | .01 |
| ☐ 168 Tom Hilgendorf | .12 | .05 | .01 |
| ☐ 169 Graig Nettles | .85 | .40 | .08 |
| ☐ 170 Rick Wise | .16 | .07 | .01 |
| ☐ 171 Greg Gross | .12 | .05 | .01 |
| ☐ 172 Rangers Team | .35 | .07 | .01 |
| ☐ 173 Steve Swisher | .12 | .05 | .01 |
| ☐ 174 Charlie Hough | .16 | .07 | .01 |
| ☐ 175 Ken Singleton | .30 | .12 | .03 |
| ☐ 176 Dick Lange | .12 | .05 | .01 |
| ☐ 177 Marty Perez | .12 | .05 | .01 |
| ☐ 178 Tom Buskey | .12 | .05 | .01 |
| ☐ 179 George Foster | 1.50 | .70 | .15 |
| ☐ 180 Rich Gossage | 1.20 | .55 | .12 |
| ☐ 181 Willie Montanez | .12 | .05 | .01 |
| ☐ 182 Harry Rasmussen | .12 | .05 | .01 |
| ☐ 183 Steve Braun | .12 | .05 | .01 |
| ☐ 184 Bill Greif | .12 | .05 | .01 |
| ☐ 185 Dave Parker | 1.75 | .85 | .17 |
| ☐ 186 Tom Walker | .12 | .05 | .01 |
| ☐ 187 Pedro Garcia | .12 | .05 | .01 |
| ☐ 188 Fred Scherman | .12 | .05 | .01 |
| ☐ 189 Claudell Washington | .35 | .15 | .03 |
| ☐ 190 Jon Matlack | .16 | .07 | .01 |
| ☐ 191 NL Batting Leaders:<br>Bill Madlock<br>Ted Simmons<br>Manny Sanguillen | .40 | .18 | .04 |
| ☐ 192 AL Batting Leaders:<br>Rod Carew<br>Fred Lynn<br>Thurman Munson | 1.10 | .50 | .11 |
| ☐ 193 NL Home Run Leaders:<br>Mike Schmidt<br>Dave Kingman<br>Greg Luzinski | .65 | .30 | .06 |
| ☐ 194 AL Home Run Leaders:<br>Reggie Jackson<br>George Scott<br>John Mayberry | .65 | .30 | .06 |
| ☐ 195 NL RBI Leaders:<br>Greg Luzinski<br>Johnny Bench<br>Tony Perez | .45 | .20 | .04 |
| ☐ 196 AL RBI Leaders:<br>George Scott<br>John Mayberry<br>Fred Lynn | .40 | .18 | .04 |
| ☐ 197 NL Stolen Base Leaders:<br>Dave Lopes<br>Joe Morgan<br>Lou Brock | .65 | .25 | .06 |
| ☐ 198 AL Stolen Base Leaders:<br>Mickey Rivers<br>Claudell Washington<br>Amos Otis | .25 | .10 | .02 |
| ☐ 199 NL Victory Leaders:<br>Tom Seaver<br>Randy Jones<br>Andy Messersmith | .45 | .20 | .04 |
| ☐ 200 AL Victory Leaders:<br>Jim Hunter<br>Jim Palmer<br>Vida Blue | .60 | .28 | .06 |
| ☐ 201 NL ERA Leaders:<br>Randy Jones<br>Andy Messersmith<br>Tom Seaver | .45 | .20 | .04 |
| ☐ 202 AL ERA Leaders:<br>Jim Palmer<br>Jim Hunter<br>Dennis Eckersley | .50 | .22 | .05 |
| ☐ 203 NL Strikeout Leaders:<br>Tom Seaver<br>John Montefusco<br>Andy Messersmith | .45 | .20 | .04 |
| ☐ 204 AL Strikeout Leaders:<br>Frank Tanana<br>Bert Blyleven<br>Gaylord Perry | .40 | .18 | .04 |
| ☐ 205 Leading Firemen:<br>Al Hrabosky<br>Rich Gossage | .25 | .10 | .02 |
| ☐ 206 Manny Trillo | .25 | .10 | .02 |
| ☐ 207 Andy Hassler | .12 | .05 | .01 |
| ☐ 208 Mike Lum | .12 | .05 | .01 |

| | MINT | VG-E | F-G |
|---|---|---|---|
| ☐ 209 Alan Ashby | .25 | .10 | .02 |
| ☐ 210 Lee May | .25 | .10 | .02 |
| ☐ 211 Clay Carroll | .12 | .05 | .01 |
| ☐ 212 Pat Kelly | .12 | .05 | .01 |
| ☐ 213 Dave Heaverlo | .12 | .05 | .01 |
| ☐ 214 Eric Soderholm | .12 | .05 | .01 |
| ☐ 215 Reggie Smith | .30 | .12 | .03 |
| ☐ 216 Expos Team | .35 | .07 | .01 |
| ☐ 217 Dave Freisleben | .12 | .05 | .01 |
| ☐ 218 John Knox | .12 | .05 | .01 |
| ☐ 219 Tom Murphy | .12 | .05 | .01 |
| ☐ 220 Manny Sanguillen | .16 | .07 | .01 |
| ☐ 221 Jim Todd | .12 | .05 | .01 |
| ☐ 222 Wayne Garrett | .12 | .05 | .01 |
| ☐ 223 Ollie Brown | .12 | .05 | .01 |
| ☐ 224 Jim York | .12 | .05 | .01 |
| ☐ 225 Roy White | .16 | .07 | .01 |
| ☐ 226 Jim Sundberg | .20 | .09 | .02 |
| ☐ 227 Oscar Zamora | .12 | .05 | .01 |
| ☐ 228 John Hale | .12 | .05 | .01 |
| ☐ 229 Jerry Remy | .30 | .12 | .03 |
| ☐ 230 Carl Yastrzemski | 4.50 | 2.10 | .45 |
| ☐ 231 Tom House | .12 | .05 | .01 |
| ☐ 232 Frank Duffy | .12 | .05 | .01 |
| ☐ 233 Grant Jackson | .12 | .05 | .01 |
| ☐ 234 Mike Sadek | .12 | .05 | .01 |
| ☐ 235 Bert Blyleven | .45 | .20 | .04 |
| ☐ 236 Royals Team | .35 | .07 | .01 |
| ☐ 237 Dave Hamilton | .12 | .05 | .01 |
| ☐ 238 Larry Biittner | .12 | .05 | .01 |
| ☐ 239 John Curtis | .12 | .05 | .01 |
| ☐ 240 Pete Rose | 10.00 | 4.75 | 1.00 |
| ☐ 241 Hector Torres | .12 | .05 | .01 |
| ☐ 242 Dan Meyer | .12 | .05 | .01 |
| ☐ 243 Jim Rooker | .12 | .05 | .01 |
| ☐ 244 Bill Sharp | .12 | .05 | .01 |
| ☐ 245 Felix Millan | .12 | .05 | .01 |
| ☐ 246 Cesar Tovar | .12 | .05 | .01 |
| ☐ 247 Terry Harmon | .12 | .05 | .01 |
| ☐ 248 Dick Tidrow | .12 | .05 | .01 |
| ☐ 249 Cliff Johnson | .12 | .05 | .01 |
| ☐ 250 Fergie Jenkins | .40 | .18 | .04 |
| ☐ 251 Rick Monday | .16 | .07 | .01 |
| ☐ 252 Tim Nordbrook | .12 | .05 | .01 |
| ☐ 253 Bill Buckner | .40 | .15 | .03 |
| ☐ 254 Rudy Meoli | .12 | .05 | .01 |
| ☐ 255 Fritz Peterson | .12 | .05 | .01 |
| ☐ 256 Rowland Office | .12 | .05 | .01 |
| ☐ 257 Ross Grimsley | .12 | .05 | .01 |
| ☐ 258 Nyls Nyman | .12 | .05 | .01 |
| ☐ 259 Darrel Chaney | .12 | .05 | .01 |
| ☐ 260 Steve Busby | .16 | .07 | .01 |

| | MINT | VG-E | F-G |
|---|---|---|---|
| ☐ 261 Gary Thomasson | .12 | .05 | .01 |
| ☐ 262 Checklist: 133–264 | .35 | .06 | .01 |
| ☐ 263 Lyman Bostock | .45 | .20 | .04 |
| ☐ 264 Steve Renko | .12 | .05 | .01 |
| ☐ 265 Willie Davis | .16 | .07 | .01 |
| ☐ 266 Alan Foster | .12 | .05 | .01 |
| ☐ 267 Aurelio Rodriguez | .12 | .05 | .01 |
| ☐ 268 Del Unser | .12 | .05 | .01 |
| ☐ 269 Rick Austin | .12 | .05 | .01 |
| ☐ 270 Willie Stargell | 1.50 | .70 | .15 |
| ☐ 271 Jim Lonborg | .16 | .07 | .01 |
| ☐ 272 Rick Dempsey | .20 | .09 | .02 |
| ☐ 273 Joe Niekro | .25 | .10 | .02 |
| ☐ 274 Tommy Harper | .16 | .07 | .01 |
| ☐ 275 Rick Manning | .25 | .10 | .02 |
| ☐ 276 Mickey Scott | .12 | .05 | .01 |
| ☐ 277 Cubs Team | .35 | .07 | .01 |
| ☐ 278 Bernie Carbo | .12 | .05 | .01 |
| ☐ 279 Roy Howell | .12 | .05 | .01 |
| ☐ 280 Burt Hooten | .16 | .07 | .01 |
| ☐ 281 Dave May | .12 | .05 | .01 |
| ☐ 282 Dan Osborn | .12 | .05 | .01 |
| ☐ 283 Merv Rettenmund | .12 | .05 | .01 |
| ☐ 284 Steve Ontiveros | .12 | .05 | .01 |
| ☐ 285 Mike Cuellar | .16 | .07 | .01 |
| ☐ 286 Jim Wohlford | .12 | .05 | .01 |
| ☐ 287 Pete Mackanin | .12 | .05 | .01 |
| ☐ 288 Bill Campbell | .16 | .07 | .01 |
| ☐ 289 Enzo Hernandez | .12 | .05 | .01 |
| ☐ 290 Ted Simmons | .60 | .28 | .06 |
| ☐ 291 Ken Sanders | .12 | .05 | .01 |
| ☐ 292 Leon Roberts | .12 | .05 | .01 |
| ☐ 293 Bill Castro | .12 | .05 | .01 |
| ☐ 294 Ed Kirkpatrick | .12 | .05 | .01 |
| ☐ 295 Dave Cash | .12 | .05 | .01 |
| ☐ 296 Pat Dobson | .16 | .07 | .01 |
| ☐ 297 Roger Metzger | .12 | .05 | .01 |
| ☐ 298 Dick Bosman | .12 | .05 | .01 |
| ☐ 299 Champ Summers | .12 | .05 | .01 |
| ☐ 300 Johnny Bench | 3.00 | 1.40 | .30 |
| ☐ 301 Jackie Brown | .12 | .05 | .01 |
| ☐ 302 Rick Miller | .12 | .05 | .01 |
| ☐ 303 Steve Foucault | .12 | .05 | .01 |
| ☐ 304 Angels Team | .35 | .07 | .01 |
| ☐ 305 Andy Messersmith | .16 | .07 | .01 |
| ☐ 306 Rod Gilbreath | .12 | .05 | .01 |
| ☐ 307 Al Bumbry | .12 | .05 | .01 |
| ☐ 308 Jim Barr | .12 | .05 | .01 |
| ☐ 309 Bill Melton | .12 | .05 | .01 |
| ☐ 310 Randy Jones | .25 | .10 | .02 |
| ☐ 311 Cookie Rojas | .12 | .05 | .01 |
| ☐ 312 Don Carrithers | .12 | .05 | .01 |

|  | MINT | VG-E | F-G |
|---|---|---|---|
| ☐ 313 Dan Ford | .25 | .10 | .02 |
| ☐ 314 Ed Kranepool | .16 | .07 | .01 |
| ☐ 315 Al Hrabosky | .16 | .07 | .01 |
| ☐ 316 Robin Yount | 4.00 | 1.85 | .40 |
| ☐ 317 John Candelaria | 1.50 | .70 | .15 |
| ☐ 318 Bob Boone | .20 | .09 | .02 |
| ☐ 319 Larry Gura | .20 | .09 | .02 |
| ☐ 320 Willie Horton | .16 | .07 | .01 |
| ☐ 321 Jose Cruz | .40 | .18 | .04 |
| ☐ 322 Glenn Abbott | .12 | .05 | .01 |
| ☐ 323 Rob Sperring | .12 | .05 | .01 |
| ☐ 324 Jim Bibby | .16 | .07 | .01 |
| ☐ 325 Tony Perez | .45 | .20 | .04 |
| ☐ 326 Dick Pole | .12 | .05 | .01 |
| ☐ 327 Dave Moates | .12 | .05 | .01 |
| ☐ 328 Carl Morton | .12 | .05 | .01 |
| ☐ 329 Joe Ferguson | .12 | .05 | .01 |
| ☐ 330 Nolan Ryan | 2.50 | 1.15 | .25 |
| ☐ 331 Padres Team | .35 | .07 | .01 |
| ☐ 332 Charlie Williams | .12 | .05 | .01 |
| ☐ 333 Bob Coluccio | .12 | .05 | .01 |
| ☐ 334 Dennis Leonard | .25 | .10 | .02 |
| ☐ 335 Bob Grich | .25 | .10 | .02 |
| ☐ 336 Vic Albury | .12 | .05 | .01 |
| ☐ 337 Bud Harrelson | .12 | .05 | .01 |
| ☐ 338 Bob Bailey | .12 | .05 | .01 |
| ☐ 339 John Denny | .60 | .28 | .06 |
| ☐ 340 Jim Rice | 4.50 | 2.10 | .45 |
| ☐ 341 All-Time 1B: Lou Gehrig | 1.60 | .80 | .16 |
| ☐ 342 All-Time 2B: Rogers Hornsby | .90 | .40 | .09 |
| ☐ 343 All-Time 3B: Pie Traynor | .60 | .28 | .06 |
| ☐ 344 All-Time SS: Honus Wagner | .90 | .40 | .09 |
| ☐ 345 All-Time OF: Babe Ruth | 2.50 | 1.15 | .25 |
| ☐ 346 All-Time OF: Ty Cobb | 1.60 | .80 | .16 |
| ☐ 347 All-Time OF: Ted Williams | 1.60 | .80 | .16 |
| ☐ 348 All-Time C: Mickey Cochrane | .60 | .28 | .06 |
| ☐ 349 All-Time RHP: Walter Johnson | .90 | .40 | .09 |
| ☐ 350 All-Time LHP: Lefty Grove | .75 | .35 | .07 |
| ☐ 351 Randy Hundley | .12 | .05 | .01 |
| ☐ 352 Dave Giusti | .12 | .05 | .01 |
| ☐ 353 Sixto Lezcano | .30 | .12 | .03 |
| ☐ 354 Ron Blomberg | .12 | .05 | .01 |

|  | MINT | VG-E | F-G |
|---|---|---|---|
| ☐ 355 Steve Carlton | 3.50 | 1.65 | .35 |
| ☐ 356 Ted Martinez | .12 | .05 | .01 |
| ☐ 357 Ken Forsch | .16 | .07 | .01 |
| ☐ 358 Buddy Bell | .40 | .18 | .04 |
| ☐ 359 Rick Reuschel | .20 | .09 | .02 |
| ☐ 360 Jeff Burroughs | .16 | .07 | .01 |
| ☐ 361 Tigers Team | .40 | .08 | .01 |
| ☐ 362 Will McEnaney | .12 | .05 | .01 |
| ☐ 363 Dave Collins | 1.25 | .60 | .12 |
| ☐ 364 Elias Sosa | .12 | .05 | .01 |
| ☐ 365 Carlton Fisk | 1.10 | .50 | .11 |
| ☐ 366 Bobby Valentine | .16 | .07 | .01 |
| ☐ 367 Bruce Miller | .12 | .05 | .01 |
| ☐ 368 Wilbur Wood | .16 | .07 | .01 |
| ☐ 369 Frank White | .35 | .15 | .03 |
| ☐ 370 Ron Cey | .65 | .30 | .06 |
| ☐ 371 Ellie Hendricks | .12 | .05 | .01 |
| ☐ 372 Rick Baldwin | .12 | .05 | .01 |
| ☐ 373 Johnny Briggs | .12 | .05 | .01 |
| ☐ 374 Dan Warthen | .12 | .05 | .01 |
| ☐ 375 Ron Fairly | .16 | .07 | .01 |
| ☐ 376 Rich Hebner | .12 | .05 | .01 |
| ☐ 377 Mike Hegan | .12 | .05 | .01 |
| ☐ 378 Steve Stone | .20 | .09 | .02 |
| ☐ 379 Ken Boswell | .12 | .05 | .01 |
| ☐ 380 Bobby Bonds | .30 | .12 | .03 |
| ☐ 381 Denny Doyle | .12 | .05 | .01 |
| ☐ 382 Matt Alexander | .12 | .05 | .01 |
| ☐ 383 John Ellis | .12 | .05 | .01 |
| ☐ 384 Phillies Team | .35 | .07 | .01 |
| ☐ 385 Mickey Lolich | .30 | .12 | .03 |
| ☐ 386 Ed Goodson | .12 | .05 | .01 |
| ☐ 387 Mike Miley | .12 | .05 | .01 |
| ☐ 388 Stan Perzanowski | .12 | .05 | .01 |
| ☐ 389 Glenn Adams | .12 | .05 | .01 |
| ☐ 390 Don Gullett | .16 | .07 | .01 |
| ☐ 391 Jerry Hairston | .12 | .05 | .01 |
| ☐ 392 Checklist 265-396 | .35 | .06 | .01 |
| ☐ 393 Paul Mitchell | .12 | .05 | .01 |
| ☐ 394 Fran Healy | .12 | .05 | .01 |
| ☐ 395 Jim Wynn | .16 | .07 | .01 |
| ☐ 396 Bill Lee | .16 | .07 | .01 |
| ☐ 397 Tim Foli | .12 | .05 | .01 |
| ☐ 398 Dave Tomlin | .12 | .05 | .01 |
| ☐ 399 Luis Melendez | .12 | .05 | .01 |
| ☐ 400 Rod Carew | 3.50 | 1.65 | .35 |
| ☐ 401 Ken Brett | .16 | .07 | .01 |
| ☐ 402 Don Money | .16 | .07 | .01 |
| ☐ 403 Geoff Zahn | .16 | .07 | .01 |
| ☐ 404 Enos Cabell | .16 | .07 | .01 |
| ☐ 405 Rollie Fingers | .80 | .40 | .08 |
| ☐ 406 Ed Herrmann | .12 | .05 | .01 |

| | | MINT | VG-E | F-G |
|---|---|---|---|---|
| ☐ 407 | Tom Underwood | .12 | .05 | .01 |
| ☐ 408 | Charlie Spikes | .12 | .05 | .01 |
| ☐ 409 | Dave Lemanczyk | .12 | .05 | .01 |
| ☐ 410 | Ralph Garr | .16 | .07 | .01 |
| ☐ 411 | Bill Singer | .12 | .05 | .01 |
| ☐ 412 | Toby Harrah | .20 | .09 | .02 |
| ☐ 413 | Pete Varney | .12 | .05 | .01 |
| ☐ 414 | Wayne Garland | .12 | .05 | .01 |
| ☐ 415 | Vada Pinson | .25 | .10 | .02 |
| ☐ 416 | Tommy John | .70 | .32 | .07 |
| ☐ 417 | Gene Clines | .12 | .05 | .01 |
| ☐ 418 | Jose Morales | .12 | .05 | .01 |
| ☐ 419 | Reggie Cleveland | .12 | .05 | .01 |
| ☐ 420 | Joe Morgan | 2.00 | .90 | .20 |
| ☐ 421 | A's Team | .35 | .07 | .01 |
| ☐ 422 | Johnny Grubb | .12 | .05 | .01 |
| ☐ 423 | Ed Halicki | .12 | .05 | .01 |
| ☐ 424 | Phil Roof | .12 | .05 | .01 |
| ☐ 425 | Rennie Stennett | .12 | .05 | .01 |
| ☐ 426 | Bob Forsch | .16 | .07 | .01 |
| ☐ 427 | Kurt Bevacqua | .12 | .05 | .01 |
| ☐ 428 | Jim Crawford | .12 | .05 | .01 |
| ☐ 429 | Fred Stanley | .12 | .05 | .01 |
| ☐ 430 | Jose Cardenal | .12 | .05 | .01 |
| ☐ 431 | Dick Ruthven | .12 | .05 | .01 |
| ☐ 432 | Tom Veryzer | .12 | .05 | .01 |
| ☐ 433 | Rick Waits | .16 | .07 | .01 |
| ☐ 434 | Morris Nettles | .12 | .05 | .01 |
| ☐ 435 | Phil Niekro | .90 | .40 | .09 |
| ☐ 436 | Bill Fahey | .12 | .05 | .01 |
| ☐ 437 | Terry Forster | .25 | .10 | .02 |
| ☐ 438 | Doug DeCinces | .65 | .30 | .06 |
| ☐ 439 | Rick Rhoden | .30 | .12 | .03 |
| ☐ 440 | John Mayberry | .16 | .07 | .01 |
| ☐ 441 | Gary Carter | 4.50 | 2.10 | .45 |
| ☐ 442 | Hank Webb | .12 | .05 | .01 |
| ☐ 443 | Giants Team | .35 | .07 | .01 |
| ☐ 444 | Gary Nolan | .12 | .05 | .01 |
| ☐ 445 | Rico Petrocelli | .16 | .07 | .01 |
| ☐ 446 | Larry Haney | .12 | .05 | .01 |
| ☐ 447 | Gene Locklear | .12 | .05 | .01 |
| ☐ 448 | Tom Johnson | .12 | .05 | .01 |
| ☐ 449 | Bob Robertson | .12 | .05 | .01 |
| ☐ 450 | Jim Palmer | 2.25 | 1.00 | .22 |
| ☐ 451 | Buddy Bradford | .12 | .05 | .01 |
| ☐ 452 | Tom Hausman | .12 | .05 | .01 |
| ☐ 453 | Lou Piniella | .25 | .10 | .02 |
| ☐ 454 | Tom Griffin | .12 | .05 | .01 |
| ☐ 455 | Dick Allen | .30 | .12 | .03 |
| ☐ 456 | Joe Coleman | .12 | .05 | .01 |
| ☐ 457 | Ed Crosby | .12 | .05 | .01 |
| ☐ 458 | Earl Williams | .12 | .05 | .01 |

| | | MINT | VG-E | F-G |
|---|---|---|---|---|
| ☐ 459 | Jim Brewer | .12 | .05 | .01 |
| ☐ 460 | Cesar Cedeno | .25 | .10 | .02 |
| ☐ 461 | NL and AL Champs: | .40 | .18 | .04 |
| | Reds sweep Bucs | | | |
| | Bosox surprise A's | | | |
| ☐ 462 | '75 World Series: | .40 | .18 | .04 |
| | Reds Champs | | | |
| ☐ 463 | Steve Hargan | .12 | .05 | .01 |
| ☐ 464 | Ken Henderson | .12 | .05 | .01 |
| ☐ 465 | Mike Marshall | .16 | .07 | .01 |
| ☐ 466 | Bob Stinson | .12 | .05 | .01 |
| ☐ 467 | Woodie Fryman | .12 | .05 | .01 |
| ☐ 468 | Jesus Alou | .12 | .05 | .01 |
| ☐ 469 | Rawley Eastwick | .12 | .05 | .01 |
| ☐ 470 | Bobby Murcer | .40 | .18 | .04 |
| ☐ 471 | Jim Burton | .12 | .05 | .01 |
| ☐ 472 | Bob Davis | .12 | .05 | .01 |
| ☐ 473 | Paul Blair | .16 | .07 | .01 |
| ☐ 474 | Ray Corbin | .12 | .05 | .01 |
| ☐ 475 | Joe Rudi | .16 | .07 | .01 |
| ☐ 476 | Bob Moose | .12 | .05 | .01 |
| ☐ 477 | Indians Team | .35 | .07 | .01 |
| ☐ 478 | Lynn McGlothen | .12 | .05 | .01 |
| ☐ 479 | Bobby Mitchell | .12 | .05 | .01 |
| ☐ 480 | Mike Schmidt | 5.50 | 2.60 | .55 |
| ☐ 481 | Rudy May | .12 | .05 | .01 |
| ☐ 482 | Tim Hosley | .12 | .05 | .01 |
| ☐ 483 | Mickey Stanley | .12 | .05 | .01 |
| ☐ 484 | Eric Raich | .12 | .05 | .01 |
| ☐ 485 | Mike Hargrove | .16 | .07 | .01 |
| ☐ 486 | Bruce Dal Canton | .12 | .05 | .01 |
| ☐ 487 | Leron Lee | .12 | .05 | .01 |
| ☐ 488 | Claude Osteen | .16 | .07 | .01 |
| ☐ 489 | Skip Jutze | .12 | .05 | .01 |
| ☐ 490 | Frank Tanana | .25 | .10 | .02 |
| ☐ 491 | Terry Crowley | .12 | .05 | .01 |
| ☐ 492 | Martin Pattin | .12 | .05 | .01 |
| ☐ 493 | Derrel Thomas | .12 | .05 | .01 |
| ☐ 494 | Craig Swan | .16 | .07 | .01 |
| ☐ 495 | Nate Colbert | .12 | .05 | .01 |
| ☐ 496 | Juan Beniquez | .16 | .07 | .01 |
| ☐ 497 | Joe McIntosh | .12 | .05 | .01 |
| ☐ 498 | Glenn Borgmann | .12 | .05 | .01 |
| ☐ 499 | Mario Guerrero | .12 | .05 | .01 |
| ☐ 500 | Reggie Jackson | 4.50 | 2.10 | .45 |
| ☐ 501 | Billy Champion | .12 | .05 | .01 |
| ☐ 502 | Tim McCarver | .20 | .09 | .02 |
| ☐ 503 | Elliott Maddox | .12 | .05 | .01 |
| ☐ 504 | Pirates Team | .35 | .07 | .01 |
| ☐ 505 | Mark Belanger | .16 | .07 | .01 |
| ☐ 506 | George Mitterwald | .12 | .05 | .01 |
| ☐ 507 | Ray Bare | .12 | .05 | .01 |

| | MINT | VG-E | F-G |
|---|---|---|---|
| ☐ 508 Duane Kuiper | .12 | .05 | .01 |
| ☐ 509 Bill Hands | .12 | .05 | .01 |
| ☐ 510 Amos Otis | .20 | .09 | .02 |
| ☐ 511 Jamie Easterley | .12 | .05 | .01 |
| ☐ 512 Ellie Rodriguez | .12 | .05 | .01 |
| ☐ 513 Bart Johnson | .12 | .05 | .01 |
| ☐ 514 Dan Driessen | .16 | .07 | .01 |
| ☐ 515 Steve Yeager | .16 | .07 | .01 |
| ☐ 516 Wayne Granger | .12 | .05 | .01 |
| ☐ 517 John Milner | .12 | .05 | .01 |
| ☐ 518 Doug Flynn | .12 | .05 | .01 |
| ☐ 519 Steve Brye | .12 | .05 | .01 |
| ☐ 520 Willie McCovey | 1.50 | .70 | .15 |
| ☐ 521 Jim Colborn | .12 | .05 | .01 |
| ☐ 522 Ted Sizemore | .12 | .05 | .01 |
| ☐ 523 Bob Montgomery | .12 | .05 | .01 |
| ☐ 524 Pete Falcone | .12 | .05 | .01 |
| ☐ 525 Billy Williams | .65 | .30 | .06 |
| ☐ 526 Checklist 397–528 | .35 | .06 | .01 |
| ☐ 527 Mike Anderson | .12 | .05 | .01 |
| ☐ 528 Dock Ellis | .12 | .05 | .01 |
| ☐ 529 Deron Johnson | .12 | .05 | .01 |
| ☐ 530 Don Sutton | .70 | .32 | .07 |
| ☐ 531 New York Mets Team | .50 | .10 | .02 |
| ☐ 532 Milt May | .12 | .05 | .01 |
| ☐ 533 Lee Richard | .12 | .05 | .01 |
| ☐ 534 Stan Bahnsen | .12 | .05 | .01 |
| ☐ 535 Dave Nelson | .12 | .05 | .01 |
| ☐ 536 Mike Thompson | .12 | .05 | .01 |
| ☐ 537 Tony Muser | .12 | .05 | .01 |
| ☐ 538 Pat Darcy | .12 | .05 | .01 |
| ☐ 539 John Balaz | .12 | .05 | .01 |
| ☐ 540 Bill Freehan | .20 | .09 | .02 |
| ☐ 541 Steve Mingori | .12 | .05 | .01 |
| ☐ 542 Keith Hernandez | 3.00 | 1.40 | .30 |
| ☐ 543 Wayne Twitchell | .12 | .05 | .01 |
| ☐ 544 Pepe Frias | .12 | .05 | .01 |
| ☐ 545 Sparky Lyle | .25 | .10 | .02 |
| ☐ 546 Dave Rosello | .12 | .05 | .01 |
| ☐ 547 Roric Harrison | .12 | .05 | .01 |
| ☐ 548 Manny Mota | .16 | .07 | .01 |
| ☐ 549 Randy Tate | .12 | .05 | .01 |
| ☐ 550 Hank Aaron | 5.00 | 2.35 | .50 |
| ☐ 551 Jerry DaVanon | .12 | .05 | .01 |
| ☐ 552 Terry Humphrey | .12 | .05 | .01 |
| ☐ 553 Randy Moffitt | .12 | .05 | .01 |
| ☐ 554 Ray Fosse | .12 | .05 | .01 |
| ☐ 555 Dyar Miller | .12 | .05 | .01 |
| ☐ 556 Twins Team | .35 | .07 | .01 |
| ☐ 557 Dan Spillner | .12 | .05 | .01 |
| ☐ 558 Clarence Gaston | .12 | .05 | .01 |
| ☐ 559 Clyde Wright | .12 | .05 | .01 |
| ☐ 560 Jorge Orta | .12 | .05 | .01 |

| | MINT | VG-E | F-G |
|---|---|---|---|
| ☐ 561 Tom Carroll | .12 | .05 | .01 |
| ☐ 562 Adrian Garrett | .12 | .05 | .01 |
| ☐ 563 Larry Demery | .12 | .05 | .01 |
| ☐ 564 Bubble Gum Champ: | .16 | .07 | .01 |
| Kurt Bevacqua | | | |
| ☐ 565 Tug McGraw | .25 | .10 | .02 |
| ☐ 566 Ken McMullen | .12 | .05 | .01 |
| ☐ 567 George Stone | .12 | .05 | .01 |
| ☐ 568 Rob Andrews | .12 | .05 | .01 |
| ☐ 569 Nelson Briles | .12 | .05 | .01 |
| ☐ 570 George Hendrick | .25 | .10 | .02 |
| ☐ 571 Don DeMola | .12 | .05 | .01 |
| ☐ 572 Rich Coggins | .12 | .05 | .01 |
| ☐ 573 Bill Travers | .12 | .05 | .01 |
| ☐ 574 Don Kessinger | .16 | .07 | .01 |
| ☐ 575 Dwight Evans | .50 | .22 | .05 |
| ☐ 576 Maximino Leon | .12 | .05 | .01 |
| ☐ 577 Marc Hill | .12 | .05 | .01 |
| ☐ 578 Ted Kubiak | .12 | .05 | .01 |
| ☐ 579 Clay Kirby | .12 | .05 | .01 |
| ☐ 580 Bert Campaneris | .20 | .09 | .02 |
| ☐ 581 Cardinals Team | .50 | .10 | .02 |
| ☐ 582 Mike Kekich | .12 | .05 | .01 |
| ☐ 583 Tommy Helms | .12 | .05 | .01 |
| ☐ 584 Stan Wall | .12 | .05 | .01 |
| ☐ 585 Joe Torre | .40 | .18 | .04 |
| ☐ 586 Ron Schueler | .12 | .05 | .01 |
| ☐ 587 Leo Cardenas | .12 | .05 | .01 |
| ☐ 588 Kevin Kobel | .12 | .05 | .01 |
| ☐ 589 Rookie Pitchers: | 1.50 | .70 | .15 |
| Santo Alcala | | | |
| Mike Flanagan | | | |
| Joe Pactwa | | | |
| Pablo Torrealba | | | |
| ☐ 590 Rookie Outfielders: | 1.50 | .70 | .15 |
| Henry Cruz | | | |
| Chet Lemon | | | |
| Ellis Valentine | | | |
| Terry Whitfield | | | |
| ☐ 591 Rookie Pitchers: | .20 | .09 | .02 |
| Steve Grilli | | | |
| Craig Mitchell | | | |
| Jose Sosa | | | |
| George Throop | | | |
| ☐ 592 Rookie Infielders: | 1.25 | .60 | .12 |
| Willie Randolph | | | |
| Dave McKay | | | |
| Jerry Royster | | | |
| Roy Staiger | | | |
| ☐ 593 Rookie Pitchers: | .20 | .09 | .02 |
| Larry Anderson | | | |
| Ken Crosby | | | |
| Mark Littell | | | |
| Butch Metzger | | | |

|  | MINT | VG-E | F-G |
|---|---|---|---|
| ☐ 594 Rookie Catchers/OF: ... | .20 | .09 | .02 |
|    Andy Merchant | | | |
|    Ed Ott | | | |
|    Royle Stillman | | | |
|    Jerry White | | | |
| ☐ 595 Rookie Pitchers: ....... | .20 | .09 | .02 |
|    Art DeFilipis | | | |
|    Randy Lerch | | | |
|    Sid Monge | | | |
|    Steve Barr | | | |
| ☐ 596 Rookie Infielders: ..... | .35 | .15 | .03 |
|    Craig Reynolds | | | |
|    Lamar Johnson | | | |
|    Johnnie LeMaster | | | |
|    Jerry Manuel | | | |
| ☐ 597 Rookie Pitchers: ....... | .35 | .15 | .03 |
|    Don Aase | | | |
|    Jack Kucek | | | |
|    Frank LaCorte | | | |
|    Mike Pazik | | | |
| ☐ 598 Rookie Outfielders: ..... | .20 | .09 | .02 |
|    Hector Cruz | | | |
|    Jamie Quirk | | | |
|    Jerry Turner | | | |
|    Joe Wallis | | | |
| ☐ 599 Rookie Pitchers: ....... | 8.50 | 4.00 | .85 |
|    Rob Dressler | | | |
|    Ron Guidry | | | |
|    Bob McClure | | | |
|    Pat Zachry | | | |
| ☐ 600 Tom Seaver ............ | 3.00 | 1.40 | .30 |
| ☐ 601 Ken Rudolph ........... | .12 | .05 | .01 |
| ☐ 602 Doug Konieczny ........ | .12 | .05 | .01 |
| ☐ 603 Jim Holt .............. | .12 | .05 | .01 |
| ☐ 604 Joe Lovitto ............ | .12 | .05 | .01 |
| ☐ 605 Al Downing ............ | .12 | .05 | .01 |
| ☐ 606 Brewers Team .......... | .35 | .07 | .01 |
| ☐ 607 Rich Hinton ........... | .12 | .05 | .01 |
| ☐ 608 Vic Correll ............ | .12 | .05 | .01 |
| ☐ 609 Fred Norman .......... | .12 | .05 | .01 |
| ☐ 610 Greg Luzinski ......... | .40 | .18 | .04 |
| ☐ 611 Rich Folkers .......... | .12 | .05 | .01 |
| ☐ 612 Joe Lahoud ........... | .12 | .05 | .01 |
| ☐ 613 Tim Johnson .......... | .12 | .05 | .01 |
| ☐ 614 Fernando Arroyo ...... | .12 | .05 | .01 |
| ☐ 615 Mike Cubbage ........ | .12 | .05 | .01 |
| ☐ 616 Buck Martinez ........ | .12 | .05 | .01 |
| ☐ 617 Darold Knowles ....... | .12 | .05 | .01 |
| ☐ 618 Jack Brohamer ........ | .12 | .05 | .01 |
| ☐ 619 Bill Butler ............ | .12 | .05 | .01 |
| ☐ 620 Al Oliver ............. | .70 | .32 | .07 |
| ☐ 621 Tom Hall ............. | .12 | .05 | .01 |
| ☐ 622 Rick Auerbach ........ | .12 | .05 | .01 |
| ☐ 623 Bob Allietta ........... | .12 | .05 | .01 |

|  | MINT | VG-E | F-G |
|---|---|---|---|
| ☐ 624 Tony Taylor ........... | .12 | .05 | .01 |
| ☐ 625 J.R. Richard .......... | .25 | .10 | .02 |
| ☐ 626 Bob Sheldon .......... | .12 | .05 | .01 |
| ☐ 627 Bill Plummer .......... | .12 | .05 | .01 |
| ☐ 628 John D'Acquisto ...... | .12 | .05 | .01 |
| ☐ 629 Sandy Alomar ........ | .12 | .05 | .01 |
| ☐ 630 Chris Speier .......... | .12 | .05 | .01 |
| ☐ 631 Braves Team .......... | .35 | .07 | .01 |
| ☐ 632 Rogelio Moret ........ | .12 | .05 | .01 |
| ☐ 633 John Stearns ......... | .25 | .10 | .02 |
| ☐ 634 Larry Christenson .... | .12 | .05 | .01 |
| ☐ 635 Jim Fregosi .......... | .16 | .07 | .01 |
| ☐ 636 Joe Decker ........... | .12 | .05 | .01 |
| ☐ 637 Bruce Bochte ........ | .20 | .09 | .02 |
| ☐ 638 Doyle Alexander ...... | .16 | .07 | .01 |
| ☐ 639 Fred Kendall ......... | .12 | .05 | .01 |
| ☐ 640 Bill Madlock ......... | 1.25 | .60 | .12 |
| ☐ 641 Tom Paciorek ........ | .16 | .07 | .01 |
| ☐ 642 Dennis Blair ......... | .12 | .05 | .01 |
| ☐ 643 Checklist 529–660 ... | .35 | .06 | .01 |
| ☐ 644 Tom Bradley ......... | .12 | .05 | .01 |
| ☐ 645 Darrell Porter ........ | .20 | .09 | .02 |
| ☐ 646 John Lowenstein ..... | .12 | .05 | .01 |
| ☐ 647 Ramon Hernandez .... | .12 | .05 | .01 |
| ☐ 648 Al Cowens ........... | .16 | .07 | .01 |
| ☐ 649 Dave Roberts ........ | .12 | .05 | .01 |
| ☐ 650 Thurman Munson ..... | 3.25 | 1.50 | .32 |
| ☐ 651 John Odom ........... | .12 | .05 | .01 |
| ☐ 652 Ed Armbrister ........ | .12 | .05 | .01 |
| ☐ 653 Mike Norris .......... | .25 | .10 | .02 |
| ☐ 654 Doug Griffin ......... | .12 | .05 | .01 |
| ☐ 655 Mike Vail ............ | .12 | .05 | .01 |
| ☐ 656 White Sox Team ...... | .35 | .07 | .01 |
| ☐ 657 Roy Smalley .......... | .30 | .12 | .03 |
| ☐ 658 Jerry Johnson ........ | .12 | .05 | .01 |
| ☐ 659 Ben Oglivie .......... | .25 | .10 | .02 |
| ☐ 660 Dave Lopes .......... | .45 | .10 | .02 |

## 1976 TOPPS TRADED

NOV. 17 *SPORTS EXTRA* 1976
FERGIE BRINGS FASTBALL TO FENWAY
PITCHER FERGIE JENKINS

*The cards in this 44 card set measure 2½"
by 3½". The 1976 Topps Traded set contains 43 players and one unnumbered
checklist card. The individuals pictured
were traded after the Topps regular set
was printed. A "Sports Extra" heading
design is found on each picture and is also
used to introduce the biographical section
of the reverse. Each card is numbered according to the player's regular 1976 card
design with the addition of "T" to indicate his
new status.*

Complete Set: M-5.00; VG-E-2.35; F-G-.50

|  | MINT | VG-E | F-G |
|---|---|---|---|
| Common Player ....... | .10 | .04 | .01 |
| ☐ 27 T Ed Figueroa .......... | .10 | .04 | .01 |
| ☐ 28 T Dusty Baker ......... | .30 | .12 | .03 |
| ☐ 44 T Doug Rader ......... | .15 | .06 | .01 |
| ☐ 58 T Ron Reed ............ | .15 | .06 | .01 |
| ☐ 74 T Oscar Gamble ....... | .20 | .09 | .02 |
| ☐ 80 T Jim Kaat ............ | .40 | .18 | .04 |
| ☐ 83 T Jim Spencer ........ | .10 | .04 | .01 |
| ☐ 85 T Mickey Rivers ...... | .15 | .06 | .01 |
| ☐ 99 T Lee Lacy ............ | .20 | .09 | .02 |
| ☐ 120 T Rusty Staub ........ | .30 | .12 | .03 |
| ☐ 127 T Larvell Blanks ...... | .10 | .04 | .01 |
| ☐ 146 T George Medich ...... | .15 | .06 | .01 |
| ☐ 158 T Ken Reitz .......... | .10 | .04 | .01 |
| ☐ 208 T Mike Lum .......... | .10 | .04 | .01 |
| ☐ 211 T Clay Carroll ........ | .10 | .04 | .01 |
| ☐ 231 T Tom House ......... | .10 | .04 | .01 |
| ☐ 250 T Fergie Jenkins ...... | .40 | .18 | .04 |
| ☐ 259 T Darrel Chaney ...... | .10 | .04 | .01 |
| ☐ 292 T Leon Roberts ....... | .10 | .04 | .01 |
| ☐ 296 T Pat Dobson ........ | .15 | .06 | .01 |
| ☐ 309 T Bill Melton ......... | .10 | .04 | .01 |
| ☐ 338 T Bob Bailey ......... | .10 | .04 | .01 |
| ☐ 380 T Bobby Bonds ....... | .20 | .09 | .02 |
| ☐ 383 T John Ellis .......... | .10 | .04 | .01 |
| ☐ 385 T Mickey Lolich ....... | .25 | .10 | .02 |
| ☐ 401 T Ken Brett .......... | .15 | .06 | .01 |
| ☐ 410 T Ralph Garr ......... | .15 | .06 | .01 |
| ☐ 411 T Bill Singer ......... | .10 | .04 | .01 |
| ☐ 428 T Jim Crawford ....... | .10 | .04 | .01 |
| ☐ 434 T Morris Nettles ...... | .10 | .04 | .01 |
| ☐ 464 T Ken Henderson ..... | .10 | .04 | .01 |
| ☐ 497 T Joe McIntosh ....... | .10 | .04 | .01 |
| ☐ 524 T Pete Falcone ....... | .10 | .04 | .01 |
| ☐ 527 T Mike Anderson ..... | .10 | .04 | .01 |
| ☐ 528 T Dock Ellis ......... | .10 | .04 | .01 |
| ☐ 532 T Milt May .......... | .10 | .04 | .01 |
| ☐ 554 T Ray Fosse .......... | .10 | .04 | .01 |

|  | MINT | VG-E | F-G |
|---|---|---|---|
| ☐ 579 T Clay Kirby .......... | .10 | .04 | .01 |
| ☐ 583 T Tommy Helms ...... | .10 | .04 | .01 |
| ☐ 592 T Willie Randolph ...... | .40 | .18 | .04 |
| ☐ 618 T Jack Brohamer ...... | .10 | .04 | .01 |
| ☐ 632 T Rogelio Moret ...... | .10 | .04 | .01 |
| ☐ 649 T Dave Roberts ........ | .10 | .04 | .01 |
| (unnumbered) ......... | | | |

## 1977 TOPPS

*The cards in this 660 card set measure
2½" by 3½". In 1977, for the fifth consecutive year, Topps produced a 660 card
baseball set. The player's name, team affiliation and his position are compactly arranged over the picture area and a
facsimile autograph appears on the photo.
Appearing for the first time are the series
"Brothers" (631–634) and "Turn Back
The Clock" (433–437).*

Complete Set: M-140.00; VG-E-65.00; F-G-14.00

|  | MINT | VG-E | F-G |
|---|---|---|---|
| Common Player (1–660) | .10 | .04 | .01 |
| ☐ 1 Batting Leaders: ....... George Brett Bill Madlock | 1.25 | .30 | .06 |
| ☐ 2 Home Run Leaders: ..... Graig Nettles Mike Schmidt | .60 | .28 | .06 |
| ☐ 3 RBI Leaders: ........ Lee May George Foster | .30 | .12 | .03 |

|  | | MINT | VG-E | F-G |
|---|---|---|---|---|
| ☐ | 4 Stolen Base Leaders:<br>Bill North<br>Dave Lopes | .20 | .09 | .02 |
| ☐ | 5 Victory Leaders:<br>Jim Palmer<br>Randy Jones | .35 | .15 | .03 |
| ☐ | 6 Strikeout Leaders:<br>Nolan Ryan<br>Tom Seaver | .80 | .40 | .08 |
| ☐ | 7 ERA Leaders:<br>Mark Fidrych<br>John Denny | .20 | .09 | .02 |
| ☐ | 8 Leading Firemen:<br>Bill Campbell<br>Rawly Eastwick | .15 | .06 | .01 |
| ☐ | 9 Doug Rader | .15 | .06 | .01 |
| ☐ | 10 Reggie Jackson | 3.75 | 1.75 | .37 |
| ☐ | 11 Rob Dressler | .10 | .04 | .01 |
| ☐ | 12 Larry Haney | .10 | .04 | .01 |
| ☐ | 13 Luis Gomez | .10 | .04 | .01 |
| ☐ | 14 Tommy Smith | .10 | .04 | .01 |
| ☐ | 15 Don Gullett | .15 | .06 | .01 |
| ☐ | 16 Bob Jones | .10 | .04 | .01 |
| ☐ | 17 Steve Stone | .15 | .06 | .01 |
| ☐ | 18 Indians Team/Mgr.<br>Frank Robinson | .35 | .07 | .01 |
| ☐ | 19 John D'Acquisto | .10 | .04 | .01 |
| ☐ | 20 Graig Nettles | .75 | .35 | .07 |
| ☐ | 21 Ken Forsch | .15 | .06 | .01 |
| ☐ | 22 Bill Freehan | .15 | .06 | .01 |
| ☐ | 23 Dan Driessen | .15 | .06 | .01 |
| ☐ | 24 Carl Morton | .10 | .04 | .01 |
| ☐ | 25 Dwight Evans | .40 | .18 | .04 |
| ☐ | 26 Ray Sadecki | .10 | .04 | .01 |
| ☐ | 27 Bill Buckner | .35 | .15 | .03 |
| ☐ | 28 Woodie Fryman | .10 | .04 | .01 |
| ☐ | 29 Bucky Dent | .20 | .09 | .02 |
| ☐ | 30 Greg Luzinski | .35 | .15 | .03 |
| ☐ | 31 Jim Todd | .10 | .04 | .01 |
| ☐ | 32 Checklist 1 | .35 | .06 | .01 |
| ☐ | 33 Wayne Garland | .10 | .04 | .01 |
| ☐ | 34 Angels Team/Mgr.<br>Norm Sherry | .35 | .06 | .01 |
| ☐ | 35 Rennie Stennett | .10 | .04 | .01 |
| ☐ | 36 John Ellis | .10 | .04 | .01 |
| ☐ | 37 Steve Hargan | .10 | .04 | .01 |
| ☐ | 38 Craig Kusick | .10 | .04 | .01 |
| ☐ | 39 Tom Griffin | .10 | .04 | .01 |
| ☐ | 40 Bobby Murcer | .35 | .15 | .03 |
| ☐ | 41 Jim Kern | .10 | .04 | .01 |
| ☐ | 42 Jose Cruz | .35 | .15 | .03 |
| ☐ | 43 Ray Bare | .10 | .04 | .01 |
| ☐ | 44 Bud Harrelson | .10 | .04 | .01 |

|  | | MINT | VG-E | F-G |
|---|---|---|---|---|
| ☐ | 45 Rawly Eastwick | .10 | .04 | .01 |
| ☐ | 46 Buck Martinez | .10 | .04 | .01 |
| ☐ | 47 Lynn McGlothen | .10 | .04 | .01 |
| ☐ | 48 Tom Paciorek | .15 | .06 | .01 |
| ☐ | 49 Grant Jackson | .10 | .04 | .01 |
| ☐ | 50 Ron Cey | .50 | .22 | .05 |
| ☐ | 51 Brewers Team/Mgr.<br>Alex Grammas | .35 | .07 | .01 |
| ☐ | 52 Ellis Valentine | .15 | .06 | .01 |
| ☐ | 53 Paul Mitchell | .10 | .04 | .01 |
| ☐ | 54 Sandy Alomar | .10 | .04 | .01 |
| ☐ | 55 Jeff Burroughs | .15 | .06 | .01 |
| ☐ | 56 Rudy May | .10 | .04 | .01 |
| ☐ | 57 Marc Hill | .10 | .04 | .01 |
| ☐ | 58 Chet Lemon | .40 | .18 | .04 |
| ☐ | 59 Larry Christenson | .10 | .04 | .01 |
| ☐ | 60 Jim Rice | 3.25 | 1.50 | .32 |
| ☐ | 61 Manny Sanguillen | .15 | .06 | .01 |
| ☐ | 62 Eric Raich | .10 | .04 | .01 |
| ☐ | 63 Tito Fuentes | .10 | .04 | .01 |
| ☐ | 64 Larry Biittner | .10 | .04 | .01 |
| ☐ | 65 Skip Lockwood | .10 | .04 | .01 |
| ☐ | 66 Roy Smalley | .15 | .06 | .01 |
| ☐ | 67 Joaquin Andujar | 2.25 | 1.00 | .22 |
| ☐ | 68 Bruce Bochte | .15 | .06 | .01 |
| ☐ | 69 Jim Crawford | .10 | .04 | .01 |
| ☐ | 70 Johnny Bench | 2.50 | 1.15 | .25 |
| ☐ | 71 Dock Ellis | .10 | .04 | .01 |
| ☐ | 72 Mike Anderson | .10 | .04 | .01 |
| ☐ | 73 Charles Williams | .10 | .04 | .01 |
| ☐ | 74 A's Team/Mgr.<br>Jack McKeon | .35 | .07 | .01 |
| ☐ | 75 Dennis Leonard | .20 | .09 | .02 |
| ☐ | 76 Tim Foli | .10 | .04 | .01 |
| ☐ | 77 Dyar Miller | .10 | .04 | .01 |
| ☐ | 78 Bob Davis | .10 | .04 | .01 |
| ☐ | 79 Don Money | .10 | .04 | .01 |
| ☐ | 80 Andy Messersmith | .15 | .06 | .01 |
| ☐ | 81 Juan Beniquez | .15 | .06 | .01 |
| ☐ | 82 Jim Rooker | .10 | .04 | .01 |
| ☐ | 83 Kevin Bell | .10 | .04 | .01 |
| ☐ | 84 Ollie Brown | .10 | .04 | .01 |
| ☐ | 85 Duane Kuiper | .10 | .04 | .01 |
| ☐ | 86 Pat Zachry | .10 | .04 | .01 |
| ☐ | 87 Glenn Borgmann | .10 | .04 | .01 |
| ☐ | 88 Stan Wall | .10 | .04 | .01 |
| ☐ | 89 Butch Hobson | .10 | .04 | .01 |
| ☐ | 90 Cesar Cedeno | .20 | .09 | .02 |
| ☐ | 91 John Verhoeven | .10 | .04 | .01 |
| ☐ | 92 Dave Rosello | .10 | .04 | .01 |
| ☐ | 93 Tom Poquette | .10 | .04 | .01 |
| ☐ | 94 Craig Swan | .15 | .06 | .01 |
| ☐ | 95 Keith Hernandez | 2.00 | .90 | .20 |

| | MINT | VG-E | F-G |
|---|---|---|---|
| ☐ 96 Lou Piniella | .25 | .10 | .02 |
| ☐ 97 Dave Heaverlo | .10 | .04 | .01 |
| ☐ 98 Milt May | .10 | .04 | .01 |
| ☐ 99 Tom Hausman | .10 | .04 | .01 |
| ☐ 100 Joe Morgan | 1.00 | .45 | .10 |
| ☐ 101 Dick Bosman | .10 | .04 | .01 |
| ☐ 102 Jose Morales | .10 | .04 | .01 |
| ☐ 103 Mike Bacsik | .10 | .04 | .01 |
| ☐ 104 Omar Moreno | .35 | .15 | .03 |
| ☐ 105 Steve Yeager | .15 | .06 | .01 |
| ☐ 106 Mike Flanagan | .25 | .10 | .02 |
| ☐ 107 Bill Melton | .10 | .04 | .01 |
| ☐ 108 Alan Foster | .10 | .04 | .01 |
| ☐ 109 Jorge Orta | .10 | .04 | .01 |
| ☐ 110 Steve Carlton | 3.25 | 1.50 | .32 |
| ☐ 111 Rico Petrocelli | .15 | .06 | .01 |
| ☐ 112 Bill Greif | .10 | .04 | .01 |
| ☐ 113 Blue Jays Team/Mgr | .30 | .07 | .01 |
| Roy Hartsfield | | | |
| Coaches: Don Leppert | | | |
| Bob Miller | | | |
| Jackie Moore | | | |
| Harry Warner | | | |
| ☐ 114 Bruce Dal Canton | .10 | .04 | .01 |
| ☐ 115 Rick Manning | .15 | .06 | .01 |
| ☐ 116 Joe Niekro | .25 | .10 | .02 |
| ☐ 117 Frank White | .25 | .10 | .02 |
| ☐ 118 Rick Jones | .10 | .04 | .01 |
| ☐ 119 John Stearns | .15 | .06 | .01 |
| ☐ 120 Rod Carew | 3.25 | 1.50 | .32 |
| ☐ 121 Gary Nolan | .10 | .04 | .01 |
| ☐ 122 Ben Oglivie | .20 | .09 | .02 |
| ☐ 123 Fred Stanley | .10 | .04 | .01 |
| ☐ 124 George Mitterwald | .10 | .04 | .01 |
| ☐ 125 Bill Travers | .10 | .04 | .01 |
| ☐ 126 Rod Gilbreath | .10 | .04 | .01 |
| ☐ 127 Ron Fairly | .15 | .06 | .01 |
| ☐ 128 Tommy John | .70 | .32 | .07 |
| ☐ 129 Mike Sadek | .10 | .04 | .01 |
| ☐ 130 Al Oliver | .70 | .32 | .07 |
| ☐ 131 Orlando Ramirez | .10 | .04 | .01 |
| ☐ 132 Chip Lang | .10 | .04 | .01 |
| ☐ 133 Ralph Garr | .15 | .06 | .01 |
| ☐ 134 Padres Team/Mgr. | .35 | .07 | .01 |
| John McNamara | | | |
| ☐ 135 Mark Belanger | .15 | .06 | .01 |
| ☐ 136 Jerry Mumphrey | .45 | .20 | .04 |
| ☐ 137 Jeff Terpko | .10 | .04 | .01 |
| ☐ 138 Bob Stinson | .10 | .04 | .01 |
| ☐ 139 Fred Norman | .10 | .04 | .01 |
| ☐ 140 Mike Schmidt | 4.25 | 2.00 | .42 |
| ☐ 141 Mark Littell | .10 | .04 | .01 |
| ☐ 142 Steve Dillard | .10 | .04 | .01 |

| | MINT | VG-E | F-G |
|---|---|---|---|
| ☐ 143 Ed Herrmann | .10 | .04 | .01 |
| ☐ 144 Bruce Sutter | 3.75 | 1.75 | .37 |
| ☐ 145 Tom Veryzer | .10 | .04 | .01 |
| ☐ 146 Dusty Baker | .25 | .10 | .02 |
| ☐ 147 Jackie Brown | .10 | .04 | .01 |
| ☐ 148 Fran Healy | .10 | .04 | .01 |
| ☐ 149 Mike Cubbage | .10 | .04 | .01 |
| ☐ 150 Tom Seaver | 2.50 | 1.15 | .25 |
| ☐ 151 Johnny LeMaster | .10 | .04 | .01 |
| ☐ 152 Gaylord Perry | 1.10 | .50 | .11 |
| ☐ 153 Ron Jackson | .10 | .04 | .01 |
| ☐ 154 Dave Giusti | .10 | .04 | .01 |
| ☐ 155 Joe Rudi | .15 | .06 | .01 |
| ☐ 156 Pete Mackanin | .10 | .04 | .01 |
| ☐ 157 Ken Brett | .15 | .06 | .01 |
| ☐ 158 Ted Kubiak | .10 | .04 | .01 |
| ☐ 159 Bernie Carbo | .10 | .04 | .01 |
| ☐ 160 Will McEnaney | .10 | .04 | .01 |
| ☐ 161 Garry Templeton | 1.75 | .85 | .17 |
| ☐ 162 Mike Cuellar | .15 | .06 | .01 |
| ☐ 163 Dave Hilton | .10 | .04 | .01 |
| ☐ 164 Tug McGraw | .25 | .10 | .02 |
| ☐ 165 Jim Wynn | .15 | .06 | .01 |
| ☐ 166 Bill Campbell | .15 | .06 | .01 |
| ☐ 167 Rich Hebner | .10 | .04 | .01 |
| ☐ 168 Charlie Spikes | .10 | .04 | .01 |
| ☐ 169 Darold Knowles | .10 | .04 | .01 |
| ☐ 170 Thurman Munson | 2.25 | 1.00 | .22 |
| ☐ 171 Ken Sanders | .10 | .04 | .01 |
| ☐ 172 John Milner | .10 | .04 | .01 |
| ☐ 173 Chuck Scrivener | .10 | .04 | .01 |
| ☐ 174 Nelson Briles | .10 | .04 | .01 |
| ☐ 175 Butch Wynegar | .75 | .35 | .07 |
| ☐ 176 Bob Robertson | .10 | .04 | .01 |
| ☐ 177 Bart Johnson | .10 | .04 | .01 |
| ☐ 178 Bombo Rivera | .10 | .04 | .01 |
| ☐ 179 Paul Hartzell | .10 | .04 | .01 |
| ☐ 180 Dave Lopes | .25 | .10 | .02 |
| ☐ 181 Ken McMullen | .10 | .04 | .01 |
| ☐ 182 Dan Spillner | .10 | .04 | .01 |
| ☐ 183 Cardinals Team/Mgr | .35 | .07 | .01 |
| Vern Rapp | | | |
| ☐ 184 Bo McLaughlin | .10 | .04 | .01 |
| ☐ 185 Sixto Lezcano | .15 | .06 | .01 |
| ☐ 186 Doug Flynn | .10 | .04 | .01 |
| ☐ 187 Dick Pole | .10 | .04 | .01 |
| ☐ 188 Bob Tolan | .10 | .04 | .01 |
| ☐ 189 Rick Dempsey | .20 | .09 | .02 |
| ☐ 190 Ray Burris | .10 | .04 | .01 |
| ☐ 191 Doug Griffin | .10 | .04 | .01 |
| ☐ 192 Clarence Gaston | .10 | .04 | .01 |
| ☐ 193 Larry Gura | .15 | .06 | .01 |
| ☐ 194 Gary Matthews | .25 | .10 | .02 |

| | MINT | VG-E | F-G |
|---|---|---|---|
| ☐ 195 Ed Figueroa | .10 | .04 | .01 |
| ☐ 196 Len Randle | .10 | .04 | .01 |
| ☐ 197 Ed Ott | .10 | .04 | .01 |
| ☐ 198 Wilbur Wood | .15 | .06 | .01 |
| ☐ 199 Pepe Frias | .10 | .04 | .01 |
| ☐ 200 Frank Tanana | .20 | .09 | .02 |
| ☐ 201 Ed Kranepool | .15 | .06 | .01 |
| ☐ 202 Tom Johnson | .10 | .04 | .01 |
| ☐ 203 Ed Armbrister | .10 | .04 | .01 |
| ☐ 204 Jeff Newman | .10 | .04 | .01 |
| ☐ 205 Pete Falcone | .10 | .04 | .01 |
| ☐ 206 Boog Powell | .30 | .12 | .03 |
| ☐ 207 Glenn Abbott | .10 | .04 | .01 |
| ☐ 208 Checklist 2 | .35 | .06 | .01 |
| ☐ 209 Rob Andrews | .10 | .04 | .01 |
| ☐ 210 Fred Lynn | 1.50 | .70 | .15 |
| ☐ 211 Giants Team/Mgr. | .35 | .07 | .01 |
| Joe Altobelli | | | |
| ☐ 212 Jim Mason | .10 | .04 | .01 |
| ☐ 213 Maximino Leon | .10 | .04 | .01 |
| ☐ 214 Darrell Porter | .20 | .09 | .02 |
| ☐ 215 Butch Metzger | .10 | .04 | .01 |
| ☐ 216 Doug DeCinces | .40 | .18 | .04 |
| ☐ 217 Tom Underwood | .10 | .04 | .01 |
| ☐ 218 John Wathan | .25 | .10 | .02 |
| ☐ 219 Joe Coleman | .10 | .04 | .01 |
| ☐ 220 Chris Chambliss | .20 | .09 | .02 |
| ☐ 221 Bob Bailey | .10 | .04 | .01 |
| ☐ 222 Fran Barrios | .10 | .04 | .01 |
| ☐ 223 Earl Williams | .10 | .04 | .01 |
| ☐ 224 Rusty Torres | .10 | .04 | .01 |
| ☐ 225 Bob Apodaca | .10 | .04 | .01 |
| ☐ 226 Leroy Stanton | .10 | .04 | .01 |
| ☐ 227 Joe Sambito | .30 | .12 | .03 |
| ☐ 228 Twins Team/Mgr. | .35 | .07 | .01 |
| Gene Mauch | | | |
| ☐ 229 Don Kessinger | .15 | .06 | .01 |
| ☐ 230 Vida Blue | .25 | .10 | .02 |
| ☐ 231 RB: George Brett | 1.25 | .60 | .12 |
| Most cons. games | | | |
| with 3 or more hits | | | |
| ☐ 232 RB: Minnie Minoso | .20 | .09 | .02 |
| Oldest to Hit Safely | | | |
| ☐ 233 RB: Jose Morales, Most | .15 | .06 | .01 |
| pinch-hits, Season | | | |
| ☐ 234 RB: Nolan Ryan | .85 | .40 | .08 |
| Most seasons 300 | | | |
| or more Strikeouts | | | |
| ☐ 235 Cecil Cooper | .85 | .40 | .08 |
| ☐ 236 Tom Buskey | .10 | .04 | .01 |
| ☐ 237 Gene Clines | .10 | .04 | .01 |
| ☐ 238 Tippy Martinez | .20 | .09 | .02 |
| ☐ 239 Bill Plummer | .10 | .04 | .01 |

| | MINT | VG-E | F-G |
|---|---|---|---|
| ☐ 240 Ron LeFlore | .20 | .09 | .02 |
| ☐ 241 Dave Tomlin | .10 | .04 | .01 |
| ☐ 242 Ken Henderson | .10 | .04 | .01 |
| ☐ 243 Ron Reed | .10 | .04 | .01 |
| ☐ 244 John Mayberry | .20 | .09 | .02 |
| (cartoon on back | | | |
| mentions T206 Wagner) | | | |
| ☐ 245 Rick Rhoden | .15 | .06 | .01 |
| ☐ 246 Mike Vail | .10 | .04 | .01 |
| ☐ 247 Chris Knapp | .10 | .04 | .01 |
| ☐ 248 Wilbur Howard | .10 | .04 | .01 |
| ☐ 249 Pete Redfern | .10 | .04 | .01 |
| ☐ 250 Bill Madlock | .85 | .40 | .08 |
| ☐ 251 Tony Muser | .10 | .04 | .01 |
| ☐ 252 Dale Murray | .10 | .04 | .01 |
| ☐ 253 John Hale | .10 | .04 | .01 |
| ☐ 254 Doyle Alexander | .15 | .06 | .01 |
| ☐ 255 George Scott | .15 | .06 | .01 |
| ☐ 256 Joe Hoerner | .10 | .04 | .01 |
| ☐ 257 Mike Miley | .10 | .04 | .01 |
| ☐ 258 Luis Tiant | .20 | .09 | .02 |
| ☐ 259 Mets Team/Mgr. | .40 | .08 | .01 |
| Joe Frazier | | | |
| ☐ 260 J.R. Richard | .25 | .10 | .02 |
| ☐ 261 Phil Garner | .15 | .06 | .01 |
| ☐ 262 Al Cowens | .15 | .06 | .01 |
| ☐ 263 Mike Marshall | .15 | .06 | .01 |
| ☐ 264 Tom Hutton | .10 | .04 | .01 |
| ☐ 265 Mark Fidrych | .45 | .20 | .04 |
| ☐ 266 Derrel Thomas | .10 | .04 | .01 |
| ☐ 267 Ray Fosse | .10 | .04 | .01 |
| ☐ 268 Rick Sawyer | .10 | .04 | .01 |
| ☐ 269 Joe Lis | .10 | .04 | .01 |
| ☐ 270 Dave Parker | 1.25 | .60 | .12 |
| ☐ 271 Terry Forster | .25 | .10 | .02 |
| ☐ 272 Lee Lacy | .20 | .09 | .02 |
| ☐ 273 Eric Soderholm | .10 | .04 | .01 |
| ☐ 274 Don Stanhouse | .10 | .04 | .01 |
| ☐ 275 Mike Hargrove | .15 | .06 | .01 |
| ☐ 276 A.L. Champs: | .35 | .15 | .03 |
| Chambliss' homer | | | |
| decides it | | | |
| ☐ 277 N.L. Champs: | .35 | .15 | .03 |
| Reds sweep Phillies | | | |
| ☐ 278 Danny Frisella | .10 | .04 | .01 |
| ☐ 279 Joe Wallis | .10 | .04 | .01 |
| ☐ 280 Jim Hunter | .65 | .30 | .06 |
| ☐ 281 Roy Staiger | .10 | .04 | .01 |
| ☐ 282 Sid Monge | .10 | .04 | .01 |
| ☐ 283 Jerry DaVanon | .10 | .04 | .01 |
| ☐ 284 Mike Norris | .15 | .06 | .01 |
| ☐ 285 Brooks Robinson | 1.75 | .85 | .17 |
| ☐ 286 Johnny Grubb | .10 | .04 | .01 |

| | MINT | VG-E | F-G |
|---|---|---|---|
| ☐ 287 Reds Team/Mgr. Sparky Anderson | .40 | .08 | .01 |
| ☐ 288 Bob Montgomery | .10 | .04 | .01 |
| ☐ 289 Gene Garber | .10 | .04 | .01 |
| ☐ 290 Amos Otis | .20 | .09 | .02 |
| ☐ 291 Jason Thompson | .90 | .40 | .09 |
| ☐ 292 Rogelio Moret | .10 | .04 | .01 |
| ☐ 293 Jack Brohamer | .10 | .04 | .01 |
| ☐ 294 George Medich | .15 | .06 | .01 |
| ☐ 295 Gary Carter | 3.25 | 1.50 | .32 |
| ☐ 296 Don Hood | .10 | .04 | .01 |
| ☐ 297 Ken Reitz | .10 | .04 | .01 |
| ☐ 298 Charlie Hough | .15 | .06 | .01 |
| ☐ 299 Otto Velez | .10 | .04 | .01 |
| ☐ 300 Jerry Koosman | .25 | .10 | .02 |
| ☐ 301 Toby Harrah | .15 | .06 | .01 |
| ☐ 302 Mike Garman | .10 | .04 | .01 |
| ☐ 303 Gene Tenace | .10 | .04 | .01 |
| ☐ 304 Jim Hughes | .10 | .04 | .01 |
| ☐ 305 Mickey Rivers | .15 | .06 | .01 |
| ☐ 306 Rick Waits | .10 | .04 | .01 |
| ☐ 307 Gary Sutherland | .10 | .04 | .01 |
| ☐ 308 Gene Pentz | .10 | .04 | .01 |
| ☐ 309 Red Sox Team/Mgr. Don Zimmer | .35 | .07 | .01 |
| ☐ 310 Larry Bowa | .25 | .10 | .02 |
| ☐ 311 Vern Ruhle | .10 | .04 | .01 |
| ☐ 312 Rob Belloir | .10 | .04 | .01 |
| ☐ 313 Paul Blair | .15 | .06 | .01 |
| ☐ 314 Steve Mingori | .10 | .04 | .01 |
| ☐ 315 Dave Chalk | .10 | .04 | .01 |
| ☐ 316 Steve Rogers | .20 | .09 | .02 |
| ☐ 317 Kurt Bevacqua | .10 | .04 | .01 |
| ☐ 318 Duffy Dyer | .10 | .04 | .01 |
| ☐ 319 Rich Gossage | .75 | .35 | .07 |
| ☐ 320 Ken Griffey | .25 | .10 | .02 |
| ☐ 321 Dave Goltz | .15 | .06 | .01 |
| ☐ 322 Bill Russell | .15 | .06 | .01 |
| ☐ 323 Larry Lintz | .10 | .04 | .01 |
| ☐ 324 John Curtis | .10 | .04 | .01 |
| ☐ 325 Mike Ivie | .10 | .04 | .01 |
| ☐ 326 Jesse Jefferson | .10 | .04 | .01 |
| ☐ 327 Astros Team/Mgr. Bill Virdon | .35 | .07 | .01 |
| ☐ 328 Tommy Boggs | .10 | .04 | .01 |
| ☐ 329 Ron Hodges | .10 | .04 | .01 |
| ☐ 330 George Hendrick | .25 | .10 | .02 |
| ☐ 331 Jim Colborn | .10 | .04 | .01 |
| ☐ 332 Elliott Maddox | .10 | .04 | .01 |
| ☐ 333 Paul Reuschel | .10 | .04 | .01 |
| ☐ 334 Bill Stein | .10 | .04 | .01 |
| ☐ 335 Bill Robinson | .10 | .04 | .01 |
| ☐ 336 Denny Doyle | .10 | .04 | .01 |

| | MINT | VG-E | F-G |
|---|---|---|---|
| ☐ 337 Ron Schueler | .10 | .04 | .01 |
| ☐ 338 Dave Duncan | .10 | .04 | .01 |
| ☐ 339 Adrian Devine | .10 | .04 | .01 |
| ☐ 340 Hal McRae | .20 | .09 | .02 |
| ☐ 341 Joe Kerrigan | .10 | .04 | .01 |
| ☐ 342 Jerry Remy | .15 | .06 | .01 |
| ☐ 343 Ed Halicki | .10 | .04 | .01 |
| ☐ 344 Brian Downing | .15 | .06 | .01 |
| ☐ 345 Reggie Smith | .25 | .10 | .02 |
| ☐ 346 Bill Singer | .10 | .04 | .01 |
| ☐ 347 George Foster | 1.25 | .60 | .12 |
| ☐ 348 Brent Strom | .10 | .04 | .01 |
| ☐ 349 Jim Holt | .10 | .04 | .01 |
| ☐ 350 Larry Dierker | .15 | .06 | .01 |
| ☐ 351 Jim Sundberg | .15 | .06 | .01 |
| ☐ 352 Mike Phillips | .10 | .04 | .01 |
| ☐ 353 Stan Thomas | .10 | .04 | .01 |
| ☐ 354 Pirates Team/Mgr. Chuck Tanner | .35 | .07 | .01 |
| ☐ 355 Lou Brock | 1.50 | .70 | .15 |
| ☐ 356 Checklist 3 | .35 | .06 | .01 |
| ☐ 357 Tim McCarver | .20 | .09 | .02 |
| ☐ 358 Tom House | .10 | .04 | .01 |
| ☐ 359 Willie Randolph | .30 | .12 | .03 |
| ☐ 360 Rick Monday | .15 | .06 | .01 |
| ☐ 361 Ed Rodriguez | .10 | .04 | .01 |
| ☐ 362 Tommy Davis | .15 | .06 | .01 |
| ☐ 363 Dave Roberts | .10 | .04 | .01 |
| ☐ 364 Vic Correll | .10 | .04 | .01 |
| ☐ 365 Mike Torrez | .15 | .06 | .01 |
| ☐ 366 Ted Sizemore | .10 | .04 | .01 |
| ☐ 367 Dave Hamilton | .10 | .04 | .01 |
| ☐ 368 Mike Jorgensen | .10 | .04 | .01 |
| ☐ 369 Terry Humphrey | .10 | .04 | .01 |
| ☐ 370 John Montefusco | .15 | .06 | .01 |
| ☐ 371 Royals Team/Mgr. Whitey Herzog | .35 | .07 | .01 |
| ☐ 372 Rich Folkers | .10 | .04 | .01 |
| ☐ 373 Bert Campaneris | .20 | .09 | .02 |
| ☐ 374 Kent Tekulve | .20 | .09 | .02 |
| ☐ 375 Larry Hisle | .15 | .06 | .01 |
| ☐ 376 Nino Espinosa | .10 | .04 | .01 |
| ☐ 377 Dave McKay | .10 | .04 | .01 |
| ☐ 378 Jim Umbarger | .10 | .04 | .01 |
| ☐ 379 Larry Cox | .10 | .04 | .01 |
| ☐ 380 Lee May | .20 | .09 | .02 |
| ☐ 381 Bob Forsch | .15 | .06 | .01 |
| ☐ 382 Charlie Moore | .10 | .04 | .01 |
| ☐ 383 Stan Bahnsen | .10 | .04 | .01 |
| ☐ 384 Darrell Chaney | .10 | .04 | .01 |
| ☐ 385 Dave LaRoche | .10 | .04 | .01 |
| ☐ 386 Manny Mota | .15 | .06 | .01 |
| ☐ 387 Yankees Team | .40 | .08 | .01 |

| | MINT | VG-E | F-G |
|---|---|---|---|
| ☐ 388 Terry Harmon | .10 | .04 | .01 |
| ☐ 389 Ken Kravec | .10 | .04 | .01 |
| ☐ 390 Dave Winfield | 2.75 | 1.25 | .27 |
| ☐ 391 Dan Warthen | .10 | .04 | .01 |
| ☐ 392 Phil Roof | .10 | .04 | .01 |
| ☐ 393 John Lowenstein | .10 | .04 | .01 |
| ☐ 394 Bill Laxton | .10 | .04 | .01 |
| ☐ 395 Manny Trillo | .15 | .06 | .01 |
| ☐ 396 Tom Murphy | .10 | .04 | .01 |
| ☐ 397 Larry Herndon | .50 | .22 | .05 |
| ☐ 398 Tom Burgmeier | .10 | .04 | .01 |
| ☐ 399 Bruce Boisclair | .10 | .04 | .01 |
| ☐ 400 Steve Garvey | 2.75 | 1.25 | .27 |
| ☐ 401 Mickey Scott | .10 | .04 | .01 |
| ☐ 402 Tommy Helms | .10 | .04 | .01 |
| ☐ 403 Tom Grieve | .15 | .06 | .01 |
| ☐ 404 Eric Rasmussen | .10 | .04 | .01 |
| ☐ 405 Claudell Washington | .20 | .09 | .02 |
| ☐ 406 Tim Johnson | .10 | .04 | .01 |
| ☐ 407 Dave Freisleben | .10 | .04 | .01 |
| ☐ 408 Cesar Tovar | .10 | .04 | .01 |
| ☐ 409 Pete Broberg | .10 | .04 | .01 |
| ☐ 410 Willie Montanez | .10 | .04 | .01 |
| ☐ 411 W.S. Games 1 and 2 | .40 | .18 | .04 |
|    Morgan homers opener | | | |
|    Bench stars as | | | |
|    Reds take 2nd game | | | |
| ☐ 412 W.S. Games 3 and 4 | .40 | .18 | .04 |
|    Reds' stop Yankees | | | |
|    Bench's two homers | | | |
|    wrap it up | | | |
| ☐ 413 World Series Summary | .40 | .18 | .04 |
|    Cincy wins 2nd | | | |
|    straight series | | | |
| ☐ 414 Tommy Harper | .15 | .06 | .01 |
| ☐ 415 Jay Johnstone | .15 | .06 | .01 |
| ☐ 416 Chuck Hartenstein | .10 | .04 | .01 |
| ☐ 417 Wayne Garrett | .10 | .04 | .01 |
| ☐ 418 White Sox Team/Mgr. | .40 | .08 | .01 |
|    Bob Lemon | | | |
| ☐ 419 Steve Swisher | .10 | .04 | .01 |
| ☐ 420 Rusty Staub | .25 | .10 | .02 |
| ☐ 421 Doug Rau | .10 | .04 | .01 |
| ☐ 422 Freddie Patek | .10 | .04 | .01 |
| ☐ 423 Gary Lavelle | .15 | .06 | .01 |
| ☐ 424 Steve Brye | .10 | .04 | .01 |
| ☐ 425 Joe Torre | .35 | .15 | .03 |
| ☐ 426 Dick Drago | .10 | .04 | .01 |
| ☐ 427 Dave Rader | .10 | .04 | .01 |
| ☐ 428 Rangers Team/Mgr. | .35 | .07 | .01 |
|    Frank Lucchesi | | | |
| ☐ 429 Ken Boswell | .10 | .04 | .01 |
| ☐ 430 Fergie Jenkins | .35 | .15 | .03 |
| ☐ 431 Dave Collins | .25 | .10 | .02 |
|    (photo actually | | | |
|    Bobby Jones) | | | |
| ☐ 432 Buzz Capra | .10 | .04 | .01 |
| ☐ 433 Turn Back Clock 1972 | .15 | .06 | .01 |
|    Nate Colbert | | | |
| ☐ 434 Turn Back Clock 1967 | 1.35 | .60 | .12 |
|    Yaz Triple Crown | | | |
| ☐ 435 Turn Back Clock 1962 | .35 | .15 | .03 |
|    Wills 104 Steals | | | |
| ☐ 436 Turn Back Clock 1957 | .15 | .06 | .01 |
|    Keegan hurls Majors' | | | |
|    only No-Hitter | | | |
| ☐ 437 Turn Back Clock 1952 | .35 | .15 | .03 |
|    Kiner leads NL HR's | | | |
|    7th straight year | | | |
| ☐ 438 Marty Perez | .10 | .04 | .01 |
| ☐ 439 Gorman Thomas | .35 | .15 | .03 |
| ☐ 440 Jon Matlack | .15 | .06 | .01 |
| ☐ 441 Larvell Blanks | .10 | .04 | .01 |
| ☐ 442 Braves Team/Mgr. | .35 | .07 | .01 |
|    Dave Bristol | | | |
| ☐ 443 Lamar Johnson | .10 | .04 | .01 |
| ☐ 444 Wayne Twitchell | .10 | .04 | .01 |
| ☐ 445 Ken Singleton | .25 | .10 | .02 |
| ☐ 446 Bill Bonham | .10 | .04 | .01 |
| ☐ 447 Jerry Turner | .10 | .04 | .01 |
| ☐ 448 Ellie Rodriguez | .10 | .04 | .01 |
| ☐ 449 Al Fitzmorris | .10 | .04 | .01 |
| ☐ 450 Pete Rose | 6.00 | 2.80 | .60 |
| ☐ 451 Checklist 4 | .35 | .06 | .01 |
| ☐ 452 Mike Caldwell | .15 | .06 | .01 |
| ☐ 453 Pedro Garcia | .10 | .04 | .01 |
| ☐ 454 Andy Etchebarren | .10 | .04 | .01 |
| ☐ 455 Rick Wise | .15 | .06 | .01 |
| ☐ 456 Leon Roberts | .10 | .04 | .01 |
| ☐ 457 Steve Luebber | .10 | .04 | .01 |
| ☐ 458 Leo Foster | .10 | .04 | .01 |
| ☐ 459 Steve Foucault | .10 | .04 | .01 |
| ☐ 460 Willie Stargell | 1.35 | .60 | .12 |
| ☐ 461 Dick Tidrow | .10 | .04 | .01 |
| ☐ 462 Don Baylor | .50 | .22 | .05 |
| ☐ 463 Jamie Quirk | .10 | .04 | .01 |
| ☐ 464 Randy Moffitt | .10 | .04 | .01 |
| ☐ 465 Rico Carty | .15 | .06 | .01 |
| ☐ 466 Fred Holdsworth | .10 | .04 | .01 |
| ☐ 467 Phillies Team/Mgr. | .35 | .07 | .01 |
|    Danny Ozark | | | |
| ☐ 468 Ramon Hernandez | .10 | .04 | .01 |
| ☐ 469 Pat Kelly | .10 | .04 | .01 |
| ☐ 470 Ted Simmons | .50 | .22 | .05 |
| ☐ 471 Del Unser | .10 | .04 | .01 |

| | MINT | VG-E | F-G |
|---|---|---|---|
| ☐ 472 Rookie Pitchers: ....... | .30 | .12 | .03 |
| Don Aase | | | |
| Bob McClure | | | |
| Gil Patterson | | | |
| Dave Wehrmeister | | | |
| ☐ 473 Rookie Outfielders: ...... | 8.00 | 3.75 | .80 |
| Andre Dawson | | | |
| Gene Richards | | | |
| John Scott | | | |
| Denny Walling | | | |
| ☐ 474 Rookie Shortstops: ...... | .20 | .09 | .02 |
| Bob Bailor | | | |
| Kiko Garcia | | | |
| Craig Reynolds | | | |
| Alex Taveras | | | |
| ☐ 475 Rookie Pitchers: ....... | .40 | .18 | .04 |
| Chris Batton | | | |
| Rick Camp | | | |
| Scott McGregor | | | |
| Manny Sarmiento | | | |
| ☐ 476 Rookie Catchers: ...... | 38.00 | 16.00 | 3.00 |
| Gary Alexander | | | |
| Rick Cerone | | | |
| Dale Murphy | | | |
| Kevin Pasley | | | |
| ☐ 477 Rookie Infielders: ...... | .20 | .09 | .02 |
| Doug Ault | | | |
| Rich Dauer | | | |
| Orlando Gonzalez | | | |
| Phil Mankowski | | | |
| ☐ 478 Rookie Pitchers: ....... | .20 | .09 | .02 |
| Jim Gideon | | | |
| Leon Hooten | | | |
| Dave Johnson | | | |
| Mark Lemongello | | | |
| ☐ 479 Rookie Outfielders: ...... | .20 | .09 | .02 |
| Brian Asselstine | | | |
| Wayne Gross | | | |
| Sam Mejias | | | |
| Alvis Woods | | | |
| ☐ 480 Carl Yastrzemski ...... | 3.50 | 1.65 | .35 |
| ☐ 481 Roger Metzger ......... | .10 | .04 | .01 |
| ☐ 482 Tony Solaita ........... | .10 | .04 | .01 |
| ☐ 483 Richie Zisk ........... | .15 | .06 | .01 |
| ☐ 484 Burt Hooton .......... | .15 | .06 | .01 |
| ☐ 485 Roy White ........... | .15 | .06 | .01 |
| ☐ 486 Ed Bane ............ | .10 | .04 | .01 |
| ☐ 487 Rookie Pitchers: ....... | .20 | .09 | .02 |
| Larry Anderson | | | |
| Ed Glynn | | | |
| Joe Henderson | | | |
| Greg Terlecky | | | |

| | MINT | VG-E | F-G |
|---|---|---|---|
| ☐ 488 Rookie Outfielders: ...... | 6.00 | 2.80 | .60 |
| Jack Clark | | | |
| Ruppert Jones | | | |
| Lee Mazzilli | | | |
| Dan Thomas | | | |
| ☐ 489 Rookie Pitchers: ........ | .90 | .40 | .09 |
| Len Barker | | | |
| Randy Lerch | | | |
| Greg Minton | | | |
| Mike Overy | | | |
| ☐ 490 Rookie Shortstops: ...... | .20 | .09 | .02 |
| Billy Almon | | | |
| Mickey Klutts | | | |
| Tommy McMillan | | | |
| Mark Wagner | | | |
| ☐ 491 Rookie Pitchers: ........ | .30 | .12 | .03 |
| Mike Dupree | | | |
| Denny Martinez | | | |
| Craig Mitchell | | | |
| Bob Sykes | | | |
| ☐ 492 Rookie Outfielders: ...... | 6.00 | 2.80 | .60 |
| Tony Armas | | | |
| Steve Kemp | | | |
| Carlos Lopez | | | |
| Gary Woods | | | |
| ☐ 493 Rookie Pitchers: ........ | .35 | .15 | .03 |
| Mike Krukow | | | |
| Jim Otten | | | |
| Gary Wheelock | | | |
| Mike Willis | | | |
| ☐ 494 Rookie Infielders: ...... | .50 | .22 | .05 |
| Juan Bernhardt | | | |
| Mike Champion | | | |
| Jim Gantner | | | |
| Bump Wills | | | |
| ☐ 495 Al Hrabosky ............ | .15 | .06 | .01 |
| ☐ 496 Gary Thomasson ........ | .10 | .04 | .01 |
| ☐ 497 Clay Carroll ........... | .10 | .04 | .01 |
| ☐ 498 Sal Bando ............ | .20 | .09 | .02 |
| ☐ 499 Pablo Torrealba ........ | .10 | .04 | .01 |
| ☐ 500 Dave Kingman ......... | .50 | .22 | .05 |
| ☐ 501 Jim Bibby ............ | .15 | .06 | .01 |
| ☐ 502 Randy Hundley ........ | .10 | .04 | .01 |
| ☐ 503 Bill Lee .............. | .15 | .06 | .01 |
| ☐ 504 Dodgers Team/Mgr. ..... | .50 | .10 | .02 |
| Tom Lasorda | | | |
| ☐ 505 Oscar Gamble ......... | .20 | .09 | .02 |
| ☐ 506 Steve Grilli ........... | .10 | .04 | .01 |
| ☐ 507 Mike Hegan ........... | .10 | .04 | .01 |
| ☐ 508 Dave Pagan .......... | .10 | .04 | .01 |
| ☐ 509 Cookie Rojas .......... | .10 | .04 | .01 |
| ☐ 510 John Candelaria ........ | .25 | .10 | .02 |

| | MINT | VG-E | F-G |
|---|---|---|---|
| ☐ 511 Bill Fahey | .10 | .04 | .01 |
| ☐ 512 Jack Billingham | .10 | .04 | .01 |
| ☐ 513 Jerry Terrell | .10 | .04 | .01 |
| ☐ 514 Cliff Johnson | .10 | .04 | .01 |
| ☐ 515 Chris Speier | .10 | .04 | .01 |
| ☐ 516 Bake McBride | .15 | .06 | .01 |
| ☐ 517 Pete Vuckovich | .70 | .32 | .07 |
| ☐ 518 Cubs Team/Mgr. | .35 | .07 | .01 |
| Herman Franks | | | |
| ☐ 519 Don Kirkwood | .10 | .04 | .01 |
| ☐ 520 Garry Maddox | .15 | .06 | .01 |
| ☐ 521 Bob Grich | .20 | .09 | .02 |
| ☐ 522 Enzo Hernandez | .10 | .04 | .01 |
| ☐ 523 Rollie Fingers | .60 | .28 | .06 |
| ☐ 524 Rowland Office | .10 | .04 | .01 |
| ☐ 525 Dennis Eckersley | .20 | .09 | .02 |
| ☐ 526 Larry Parrish | .25 | .10 | .02 |
| ☐ 527 Dan Meyer | .10 | .04 | .01 |
| ☐ 528 Bill Castro | .10 | .04 | .01 |
| ☐ 529 Jim Essian | .10 | .04 | .01 |
| ☐ 530 Rick Reuschel | .20 | .09 | .02 |
| ☐ 531 Lyman Bostock | .25 | .10 | .02 |
| ☐ 532 Jim Willoughby | .10 | .04 | .01 |
| ☐ 533 Mickey Stanley | .10 | .04 | .01 |
| ☐ 534 Paul Splittorff | .15 | .06 | .01 |
| ☐ 535 Cesar Geronimo | .10 | .04 | .01 |
| ☐ 536 Vic Albury | .10 | .04 | .01 |
| ☐ 537 Dave Roberts | .10 | .04 | .01 |
| ☐ 538 Frank Taveras | .10 | .04 | .01 |
| ☐ 539 Mike Wallace | .10 | .04 | .01 |
| ☐ 540 Bob Watson | .15 | .06 | .01 |
| ☐ 541 John Denny | .30 | .12 | .03 |
| ☐ 542 Frank Duffy | .10 | .04 | .01 |
| ☐ 543 Ron Blomberg | .10 | .04 | .01 |
| ☐ 544 Gary Ross | .10 | .04 | .01 |
| ☐ 545 Bob Boone | .20 | .09 | .02 |
| ☐ 546 Orioles Team/Mgr. | .40 | .08 | .01 |
| Earl Weaver | | | |
| ☐ 547 Willie McCovey | 1.35 | .60 | .12 |
| ☐ 548 Joel Youngblood | .10 | .04 | .01 |
| ☐ 549 Jerry Royster | .10 | .04 | .01 |
| ☐ 550 Randy Jones | .15 | .06 | .01 |
| ☐ 551 Bill North | .10 | .04 | .01 |
| ☐ 552 Pepe Mangual | .10 | .04 | .01 |
| ☐ 553 Jack Heidemann | .10 | .04 | .01 |
| ☐ 554 Bruce Kimm | .10 | .04 | .01 |
| ☐ 555 Dan Ford | .15 | .06 | .01 |
| ☐ 556 Doug Bird | .10 | .04 | .01 |
| ☐ 557 Jerry White | .10 | .04 | .01 |
| ☐ 558 Elias Sosa | .10 | .04 | .01 |
| ☐ 559 Alan Bannister | .10 | .04 | .01 |
| ☐ 560 Dave Concepcion | .35 | .15 | .03 |

| | MINT | VG-E | F-G |
|---|---|---|---|
| ☐ 561 Pete LaCock | .10 | .04 | .01 |
| ☐ 562 Checklist 5 | .35 | .06 | .01 |
| ☐ 563 Bruce Kison | .10 | .04 | .01 |
| ☐ 564 Alan Ashby | .15 | .06 | .01 |
| ☐ 565 Mickey Lolich | .25 | .10 | .02 |
| ☐ 566 Rick Miller | .10 | .04 | .01 |
| ☐ 567 Enos Cabell | .10 | .04 | .01 |
| ☐ 568 Carlos May | .10 | .04 | .01 |
| ☐ 569 Jim Lonborg | .15 | .06 | .01 |
| ☐ 570 Bobby Bonds | .25 | .10 | .02 |
| ☐ 571 Darrell Evans | .30 | .12 | .03 |
| ☐ 572 Ross Grimsley | .10 | .04 | .01 |
| ☐ 573 Joe Ferguson | .10 | .04 | .01 |
| ☐ 574 Aurelio Rodriguez | .10 | .04 | .01 |
| ☐ 575 Dick Ruthven | .10 | .04 | .01 |
| ☐ 576 Fred Kendall | .10 | .04 | .01 |
| ☐ 577 Jerry Augustine | .10 | .04 | .01 |
| ☐ 578 Bob Randall | .10 | .04 | .01 |
| ☐ 579 Don Carrithers | .10 | .04 | .01 |
| ☐ 580 George Brett | 5.00 | 2.35 | .50 |
| ☐ 581 Pedro Borbon | .10 | .04 | .01 |
| ☐ 582 Ed Kirkpatrick | .10 | .04 | .01 |
| ☐ 583 Paul Lindblad | .10 | .04 | .01 |
| ☐ 584 Ed Goodson | .10 | .04 | .01 |
| ☐ 585 Rick Burleson | .15 | .06 | .01 |
| ☐ 586 Steve Renko | .10 | .04 | .01 |
| ☐ 587 Rick Baldwin | .10 | .04 | .01 |
| ☐ 588 Dave Moates | .10 | .04 | .01 |
| ☐ 589 Mike Cosgrove | .10 | .04 | .01 |
| ☐ 590 Buddy Bell | .35 | .15 | .03 |
| ☐ 591 Chris Arnold | .10 | .04 | .01 |
| ☐ 592 Dan Briggs | .10 | .04 | .01 |
| ☐ 593 Dennis Blair | .10 | .04 | .01 |
| ☐ 594 Biff Pocoroba | .10 | .04 | .01 |
| ☐ 595 John Hiller | .15 | .06 | .01 |
| ☐ 596 Jerry Martin | .10 | .04 | .01 |
| ☐ 597 Mariners Team/Mgr. | .35 | .07 | .01 |
| Darrell Johnson | | | |
| Coaches: Don Bryant | | | |
| Jim Busby | | | |
| Vada Pinson | | | |
| Wes Stock | | | |
| ☐ 598 Sparky Lyle | .30 | .12 | .03 |
| ☐ 599 Mike Tyson | .10 | .04 | .01 |
| ☐ 600 Jim Palmer | 1.50 | .70 | .15 |
| ☐ 601 Mike Lum | .10 | .04 | .01 |
| ☐ 602 Andy Hassler | .10 | .04 | .01 |
| ☐ 603 Willie Davis | .15 | .06 | .01 |
| ☐ 604 Jim Slaton | .10 | .04 | .01 |
| ☐ 605 Felix Millan | .10 | .04 | .01 |
| ☐ 606 Steve Braun | .10 | .04 | .01 |
| ☐ 607 Larry Demery | .10 | .04 | .01 |

|  | MINT | VG-E | F-G |
|---|---|---|---|
| ☐ 608 Roy Howell | .10 | .04 | .01 |
| ☐ 609 Jim Barr | .10 | .04 | .01 |
| ☐ 610 Jose Cardenal | .10 | .04 | .01 |
| ☐ 611 Dave Lemanczyk | .10 | .04 | .01 |
| ☐ 612 Barry Foote | .10 | .04 | .01 |
| ☐ 613 Reggie Cleveland | .10 | .04 | .01 |
| ☐ 614 Greg Gross | .10 | .04 | .01 |
| ☐ 615 Phil Niekro | .80 | .40 | .08 |
| ☐ 616 Tommy Sandt | .10 | .04 | .01 |
| ☐ 617 Bobby Darwin | .10 | .04 | .01 |
| ☐ 618 Pat Dobson | .15 | .06 | .01 |
| ☐ 619 Johnny Oates | .10 | .04 | .01 |
| ☐ 620 Don Sutton | .65 | .30 | .06 |
| ☐ 621 Tigers Team/Mgr. | .40 | .08 | .01 |
|     Ralph Houk | | | |
| ☐ 622 Jim Wohlford | .10 | .04 | .01 |
| ☐ 623 Jack Kucek | .10 | .04 | .01 |
| ☐ 624 Hector Cruz | .10 | .04 | .01 |
| ☐ 625 Ken Holtzman | .15 | .06 | .01 |
| ☐ 626 Al Bumbry | .10 | .04 | .01 |
| ☐ 627 Bob Myrick | .10 | .04 | .01 |
| ☐ 628 Mario Guerrero | .10 | .04 | .01 |
| ☐ 629 Bob Valentine | .15 | .06 | .01 |
| ☐ 630 Bert Blyleven | .40 | .18 | .04 |
| ☐ 631 Big League Brothers: | 1.10 | .50 | .11 |
|     George Brett | | | |
|     Ken Brett | | | |
| ☐ 632 Big League Brothers: | .25 | .10 | .02 |
|     Bob Forsch | | | |
|     Ken Forsch | | | |
| ☐ 633 Big League Brothers: | .25 | .10 | .02 |
|     Lee May | | | |
|     Carlos May | | | |
| ☐ 634 Big League Brothers: | .25 | .10 | .02 |
|     Paul Reuschel | | | |
|     Rick Reuschel | | | |
|     (photos switched) | | | |
| ☐ 635 Robin Yount | 3.00 | 1.40 | .30 |
| ☐ 636 Santo Alcala | .10 | .04 | .01 |
| ☐ 637 Alex Johnson | .10 | .04 | .01 |
| ☐ 638 Jim Kaat | .35 | .15 | .03 |
| ☐ 639 Jerry Morales | .10 | .04 | .01 |
| ☐ 640 Carlton Fisk | .70 | .32 | .07 |
| ☐ 641 Dan Larson | .10 | .04 | .01 |
| ☐ 642 Willie Crawford | .10 | .04 | .01 |
| ☐ 643 Mike Pazik | .10 | .04 | .01 |
| ☐ 644 Matt Alexander | .10 | .04 | .01 |
| ☐ 645 Jerry Reuss | .20 | .09 | .02 |
| ☐ 646 Andres Mora | .10 | .04 | .01 |
| ☐ 647 Expos Team/Mgr. | .35 | .07 | .01 |
|     Dick Williams | | | |
| ☐ 648 Jim Spencer | .10 | .04 | .01 |
| ☐ 649 Dave Cash | .10 | .04 | .01 |

|  | MINT | VG-E | F-G |
|---|---|---|---|
| ☐ 650 Nolan Ryan | 2.50 | 1.15 | .25 |
| ☐ 651 Von Joshua | .10 | .04 | .01 |
| ☐ 652 Tom Walker | .10 | .04 | .01 |
| ☐ 653 Diego Segui | .10 | .04 | .01 |
| ☐ 654 Ron Pruitt | .10 | .04 | .01 |
| ☐ 655 Tony Perez | .45 | .20 | .04 |
| ☐ 656 Ron Guidry | 2.25 | 1.00 | .22 |
| ☐ 657 Mick Kelleher | .10 | .04 | .01 |
| ☐ 658 Marty Pattin | .10 | .04 | .01 |
| ☐ 659 Merv Rettenmund | .10 | .04 | .01 |
| ☐ 660 Willie Horton | .20 | .09 | .02 |

## 1978 TOPPS

The cards in this 726 card set measure 2½" by 3½". The 1978 Topps set experienced an increase of cards from the previous five regular issues. Cards 1 through 7 feature record breakers (RB) of the 1977 season. While no scarcities exist, 66 of the cards are more abundant in supply. These 66 double-printed cards are noted in the checklist by DP.

Complete Set: M-100.00; VG-E-45.00; F-G-10.00

|  | MINT | VG-E | F-G |
|---|---|---|---|
|     Common Player (1–726) | .08 | .03 | .01 |
| ☐ 1 RB: Lou Brock | 1.25 | .30 | .05 |
|     Most Steals, Lifetime | | | |
| ☐ 2 RB: Sparky Lyle | .15 | .06 | .01 |
|     Most Games Pure | | | |
|     Relief, Lifetime | | | |
| ☐ 3 RB: Willie McCovey | .45 | .20 | .04 |
|     Most times 2 HR's | | | |
|     in inning, Lifetime | | | |
| ☐ 4 RB: Brooks Robinson | .65 | .30 | .06 |
|     Most consecutive | | | |
|     Seasons with one club | | | |

| | | MINT | VG-E | F-G |
|---|---|---|---|---|
| ☐ | 5 RB: Pete Rose, Most Hits Switch Hitter, Lifetime | 1.50 | .70 | .15 |
| ☐ | 6 RB: Nolan Ryan, Most Games 10 or more Strikeouts, Lifetime | .75 | .35 | .07 |
| ☐ | 7 RB: Reggie Jackson, Most Homers One World Series | 1.00 | .45 | .10 |
| ☐ | 8 Mike Sadek | .08 | .03 | .01 |
| ☐ | 9 Doug DeCinces | .25 | .10 | .02 |
| ☐ | 10 Phil Niekro | .65 | .30 | .06 |
| ☐ | 11 Rick Manning | .08 | .03 | .01 |
| ☐ | 12 Don Aase | .08 | .03 | .01 |
| ☐ | 13 Art Howe | .08 | .03 | .01 |
| ☐ | 14 Lerrin LaGrow | .08 | .03 | .01 |
| ☐ | 15 Tony Perez DP | .12 | .05 | .01 |
| ☐ | 16 Roy White | .12 | .05 | .01 |
| ☐ | 17 Mike Krukow | .08 | .03 | .01 |
| ☐ | 18 Bob Grich | .15 | .06 | .01 |
| ☐ | 19 Darrell Porter | .15 | .06 | .01 |
| ☐ | 20 Pete Rose DP | 3.00 | 1.40 | .30 |
| ☐ | 21 Steve Kemp | .35 | .15 | .03 |
| ☐ | 22 Charlie Hough | .08 | .03 | .01 |
| ☐ | 23 Bump Wills | .08 | .03 | .01 |
| ☐ | 24 Don Money DP | .04 | .01 | .00 |
| ☐ | 25 Jon Matlack | .12 | .05 | .01 |
| ☐ | 26 Rich Hebner | .08 | .03 | .01 |
| ☐ | 27 Geoff Zahn | .08 | .03 | .01 |
| ☐ | 28 Ed Ott | .08 | .03 | .01 |
| ☐ | 29 Bob Lacey | .08 | .03 | .01 |
| ☐ | 30 George Hendrick | .18 | .08 | .01 |
| ☐ | 31 Glenn Abbott | .08 | .03 | .01 |
| ☐ | 32 Garry Templeton | .40 | .18 | .04 |
| ☐ | 33 Dave Lemanczyk | .08 | .03 | .01 |
| ☐ | 34 Willie McCovey | 1.00 | .45 | .10 |
| ☐ | 35 Sparky Lyle | .18 | .08 | .01 |
| ☐ | 36 Eddie Murray | 22.00 | 10.00 | 2.20 |
| ☐ | 37 Rick Waits | .08 | .03 | .01 |
| ☐ | 38 Willie Montanez | .08 | .03 | .01 |
| ☐ | 39 Floyd Bannister | .75 | .35 | .07 |
| ☐ | 40 Carl Yastrzemski | 2.25 | 1.00 | .22 |
| ☐ | 41 Burt Hooton | .08 | .03 | .01 |
| ☐ | 42 Jorge Orta | .08 | .03 | .01 |
| ☐ | 43 Bill Atkinson | .08 | .03 | .01 |
| ☐ | 44 Toby Harrah | .12 | .05 | .01 |
| ☐ | 45 Mark Fidrych | .18 | .08 | .01 |
| ☐ | 46 Al Cowens | .12 | .05 | .01 |
| ☐ | 47 Jack Billingham | .08 | .03 | .01 |
| ☐ | 48 Don Baylor | .40 | .18 | .04 |
| ☐ | 49 Ed Kranepool | .12 | .05 | .01 |
| ☐ | 50 Rick Reuschel | .18 | .08 | .01 |
| ☐ | 51 Charlie Moore DP | .04 | .01 | .01 |
| ☐ | 52 Jim Lonborg | .08 | .03 | .01 |
| ☐ | 53 Phil Garner DP | .04 | .01 | .00 |
| ☐ | 54 Tom Johnson | .08 | .03 | .01 |
| ☐ | 55 Mitchell Page | .12 | .05 | .01 |
| ☐ | 56 Randy Jones | .12 | .05 | .01 |
| ☐ | 57 Dan Meyer | .08 | .03 | .01 |
| ☐ | 58 Bob Forsch | .12 | .05 | .01 |
| ☐ | 59 Otto Velez | .08 | .03 | .01 |
| ☐ | 60 Thurman Munson | 1.50 | .70 | .15 |
| ☐ | 61 Larvell Blanks | .08 | .03 | .01 |
| ☐ | 62 Jim Barr | .08 | .03 | .01 |
| ☐ | 63 Don Zimmer | .08 | .03 | .01 |
| ☐ | 64 Gene Pentz | .08 | .03 | .01 |
| ☐ | 65 Ken Singleton | .18 | .08 | .01 |
| ☐ | 66 White Sox Team | .30 | .05 | .01 |
| ☐ | 67 Claudell Washington | .18 | .08 | .01 |
| ☐ | 68 Steve Foucault DP | .04 | .01 | .00 |
| ☐ | 69 Mike Vail | .08 | .03 | .01 |
| ☐ | 70 Rich Gossage | .60 | .28 | .06 |
| ☐ | 71 Terry Humphrey | .08 | .03 | .01 |
| ☐ | 72 Andre Dawson | 1.50 | .70 | .15 |
| ☐ | 73 Andy Hassler | .08 | .03 | .01 |
| ☐ | 74 Checklist 1 | .20 | .03 | .00 |
| ☐ | 75 Dick Ruthven | .08 | .03 | .01 |
| ☐ | 76 Steve Ontiveros | .08 | .03 | .01 |
| ☐ | 77 Ed Kirkpatrick | .08 | .03 | .01 |
| ☐ | 78 Pablo Torrealba | .08 | .03 | .01 |
| ☐ | 79 Darrell Johnson DP | .04 | .01 | .00 |
| ☐ | 80 Ken Griffey | .18 | .08 | .01 |
| ☐ | 81 Pete Redfern | .08 | .03 | .01 |
| ☐ | 82 Giants Team | .30 | .06 | .01 |
| ☐ | 83 Bob Montgomery | .08 | .03 | .01 |
| ☐ | 84 Kent Tekulve | .15 | .06 | .01 |
| ☐ | 85 Ron Fairly | .08 | .03 | .01 |
| ☐ | 86 Dave Tomlin | .08 | .03 | .01 |
| ☐ | 87 John Lowenstein | .08 | .03 | .01 |
| ☐ | 88 Mike Phillips | .08 | .03 | .01 |
| ☐ | 89 Ken Clay | .08 | .03 | .01 |
| ☐ | 90 Larry Bowa | .20 | .09 | .02 |
| ☐ | 91 Oscar Zamora | .08 | .03 | .01 |
| ☐ | 92 Adrian Devine | .08 | .03 | .01 |
| ☐ | 93 Bobby Cox DP | .04 | .01 | .00 |
| ☐ | 94 Chuck Scrivener | .08 | .03 | .01 |
| ☐ | 95 Jamie Quirk | .08 | .03 | .01 |
| ☐ | 96 Orioles Team | .30 | .06 | .01 |
| ☐ | 97 Stan Bahnsen | .08 | .03 | .01 |
| ☐ | 98 Jim Essian | .08 | .03 | .01 |
| ☐ | 99 Willie Hernandez | 1.75 | .85 | .17 |
| ☐ | 100 George Brett | 3.25 | 1.50 | .32 |
| ☐ | 101 Sid Monge | .08 | .03 | .01 |
| ☐ | 102 Matt Alexander | .08 | .03 | .01 |
| ☐ | 103 Tom Murphy | .08 | .03 | .01 |
| ☐ | 104 Lee Lacy | .15 | .06 | .01 |

| | MINT | VG-E | F-G |
|---|---|---|---|
| ☐ 105 Reggie Cleveland | .08 | .03 | .01 |
| ☐ 106 Bill Plummer | .08 | .03 | .01 |
| ☐ 107 Ed Halicki | .08 | .03 | .01 |
| ☐ 108 Von Joshua | .08 | .03 | .01 |
| ☐ 109 Joe Torre | .20 | .09 | .02 |
| ☐ 110 Richie Zisk | .12 | .05 | .01 |
| ☐ 111 Mike Tyson | .08 | .03 | .01 |
| ☐ 112 Astros Team | .30 | .06 | .01 |
| ☐ 113 Don Carrithers | .08 | .03 | .01 |
| ☐ 114 Paul Blair | .08 | .03 | .01 |
| ☐ 115 Gary Nolan | .08 | .03 | .01 |
| ☐ 116 Tucker Ashford | .08 | .03 | .01 |
| ☐ 117 John Montague | .08 | .03 | .01 |
| ☐ 118 Terry Harmon | .08 | .03 | .01 |
| ☐ 119 Denny Martinez | .08 | .03 | .01 |
| ☐ 120 Gary Carter | 1.75 | .85 | .17 |
| ☐ 121 Alvis Woods | .08 | .03 | .01 |
| ☐ 122 Dennis Eckersley | .12 | .05 | .01 |
| ☐ 123 Manny Trillo | .12 | .05 | .01 |
| ☐ 124 Dave Rozema | .12 | .05 | .01 |
| ☐ 125 George Scott | .12 | .05 | .01 |
| ☐ 126 Paul Moskau | .08 | .03 | .01 |
| ☐ 127 Chet Lemon | .18 | .08 | .01 |
| ☐ 128 Bill Russell | .12 | .05 | .01 |
| ☐ 129 Jim Colborn | .08 | .03 | .01 |
| ☐ 130 Jeff Burroughs | .12 | .05 | .01 |
| ☐ 131 Bert Blyleven | .30 | .12 | .03 |
| ☐ 132 Enos Cabell | .08 | .03 | .01 |
| ☐ 133 Jerry Augustine | .08 | .03 | .01 |
| ☐ 134 Steve Henderson | .12 | .05 | .01 |
| ☐ 135 Ron Guidry DP | .60 | .28 | .06 |
| ☐ 136 Ted Sizemore | .08 | .03 | .01 |
| ☐ 137 Craig Kusick | .08 | .03 | .01 |
| ☐ 138 Larry Demery | .08 | .03 | .01 |
| ☐ 139 Wayne Gross | .08 | .03 | .01 |
| ☐ 140 Rollie Fingers | .50 | .22 | .05 |
| ☐ 141 Ruppert Jones | .15 | .06 | .01 |
| ☐ 142 John Montefusco | .12 | .05 | .01 |
| ☐ 143 Keith Hernandez | 1.50 | .70 | .15 |
| ☐ 144 Jesse Jefferson | .08 | .03 | .01 |
| ☐ 145 Rick Monday | .12 | .05 | .01 |
| ☐ 146 Doyle Alexander | .12 | .05 | .01 |
| ☐ 147 Lee Mazzilli | .18 | .08 | .01 |
| ☐ 148 Andre Thorton | .20 | .09 | .02 |
| ☐ 149 Dale Murray | .08 | .03 | .01 |
| ☐ 150 Bobby Bonds | .18 | .08 | .01 |
| ☐ 151 Milt Wilcox | .12 | .05 | .01 |
| ☐ 152 Ivan DeJesus | .08 | .03 | .01 |
| ☐ 153 Steve Stone | .12 | .05 | .01 |
| ☐ 154 Cecil Cooper DP | .20 | .09 | .02 |
| ☐ 155 Butch Hobson | .08 | .03 | .01 |
| ☐ 156 Andy Messersmith | .12 | .05 | .01 |
| ☐ 157 Pete LaCock DP | .04 | .01 | .00 |

| | MINT | VG-E | F-G |
|---|---|---|---|
| ☐ 158 Joaquin Andujar | .45 | .20 | .04 |
| ☐ 159 Lou Piniella | .25 | .10 | .02 |
| ☐ 160 Jim Palmer | 1.25 | .60 | .12 |
| ☐ 161 Bob Boone | .15 | .06 | .01 |
| ☐ 162 Paul Thormodsgard | .08 | .03 | .01 |
| ☐ 163 Bill North | .08 | .03 | .01 |
| ☐ 164 Bob Owchinko | .08 | .03 | .01 |
| ☐ 165 Rennie Stennett | .08 | .03 | .01 |
| ☐ 166 Carlos Lopez | .08 | .03 | .01 |
| ☐ 167 Tim Foli | .08 | .03 | .01 |
| ☐ 168 Reggie Smith | .25 | .10 | .02 |
| ☐ 169 Jerry Johnson | .08 | .03 | .01 |
| ☐ 170 Lou Brock | 1.25 | .60 | .12 |
| ☐ 171 Pat Zachry | .08 | .03 | .01 |
| ☐ 172 Mike Hargrove | .12 | .05 | .01 |
| ☐ 173 Robin Yount | 1.50 | .70 | .15 |
| ☐ 174 Wayne Garland | .08 | .03 | .01 |
| ☐ 175 Jerry Morales | .08 | .03 | .01 |
| ☐ 176 Milt May | .08 | .03 | .01 |
| ☐ 177 Gene Garber DP | .04 | .01 | .00 |
| ☐ 178 Dave Chalk | .08 | .03 | .01 |
| ☐ 179 Dick Tidrow | .08 | .03 | .01 |
| ☐ 180 Dave Concepcion | .25 | .10 | .02 |
| ☐ 181 Ken Forsch | .12 | .05 | .01 |
| ☐ 182 Jim Spencer | .08 | .03 | .01 |
| ☐ 183 Doug Bird | .08 | .03 | .01 |
| ☐ 184 Checklist 2 | .20 | .03 | .00 |
| ☐ 185 Ellis Valentine | .12 | .05 | .01 |
| ☐ 186 Bob Stanley DP | .25 | .10 | .02 |
| ☐ 187 Jerry Royster DP | .04 | .01 | .00 |
| ☐ 188 Al Bumbry | .08 | .03 | .01 |
| ☐ 189 Tom Lasorda MGR | .15 | .06 | .01 |
| ☐ 190 John Candelaria | .18 | .08 | .01 |
| ☐ 191 Rodney Scott | .08 | .03 | .01 |
| ☐ 192 Padres Team | .30 | .06 | .01 |
| ☐ 193 Rich Chiles | .08 | .03 | .01 |
| ☐ 194 Derrel Thomas | .08 | .03 | .01 |
| ☐ 195 Larry Dierker | .12 | .05 | .01 |
| ☐ 196 Bob Bailor | .08 | .03 | .01 |
| ☐ 197 Nino Espinosa | .08 | .03 | .01 |
| ☐ 198 Ron Pruitt | .08 | .03 | .01 |
| ☐ 199 Craig Reynolds | .08 | .03 | .01 |
| ☐ 200 Reggie Jackson | 2.25 | 1.00 | .22 |
| ☐ 201 Batting Leaders: Dave Parker Rod Carew | .50 | .22 | .05 |
| ☐ 202 Home Run Leaders DP: George Foster Jim Rice | .12 | .05 | .01 |
| ☐ 203 RBI Leaders: George Foster Larry Hisle | .20 | .09 | .02 |

| | MINT | VG-E | F-G |
|---|---|---|---|
| ☐ 204 Steals Leaders DP: .... | .08 | .03 | .01 |
|    Frank Taveras | | | |
|    Freddie Patek | | | |
| ☐ 205 Victory Leaders: ....... | .45 | .20 | .04 |
|    Steve Carlton | | | |
|    Dave Goltz | | | |
|    Dennis Leonard | | | |
|    Jim Palmer | | | |
| ☐ 206 Strikeout Leaders DP: .. | .12 | .05 | .01 |
|    Phil Niekro | | | |
|    Nolan Ryan | | | |
| ☐ 207 ERA Leaders DP: ...... | .08 | .03 | .01 |
|    John Candelaria | | | |
|    Frank Tanana | | | |
| ☐ 208 Top Firemen: .......... | .18 | .08 | .01 |
|    Rollie Fingers | | | |
|    Bill Campbell | | | |
| ☐ 209 Dock Ellis .......... | .08 | .03 | .01 |
| ☐ 210 Jose Cardenal .......... | .08 | .03 | .01 |
| ☐ 211 Earl Weaver MGR DP .. | .08 | .03 | .01 |
| ☐ 212 Mike Caldwell ....... | .12 | .05 | .01 |
| ☐ 213 Alan Bannister ....... | .08 | .03 | .01 |
| ☐ 214 Angels Team ........ | .30 | .06 | .01 |
| ☐ 215 Darrell Evans ....... | .25 | .10 | .02 |
| ☐ 216 Mike Paxton ........ | .08 | .03 | .01 |
| ☐ 217 Rod Gilbreath ....... | .08 | .03 | .01 |
| ☐ 218 Marty Pattin ........ | .08 | .03 | .01 |
| ☐ 219 Mike Cubbage ....... | .08 | .03 | .01 |
| ☐ 220 Pedro Borbon ....... | .08 | .03 | .01 |
| ☐ 221 Chris Speier ........ | .08 | .03 | .01 |
| ☐ 222 Jerry Martin ........ | .08 | .03 | .01 |
| ☐ 223 Bruce Kison ........ | .08 | .03 | .01 |
| ☐ 224 Jerry Tabb ......... | .08 | .03 | .01 |
| ☐ 225 Don Gullett DP ...... | .04 | .01 | .00 |
| ☐ 226 Joe Ferguson ....... | .08 | .03 | .01 |
| ☐ 227 Al Fitzmorris ....... | .08 | .03 | .01 |
| ☐ 228 Manny Mota DP ...... | .08 | .03 | .01 |
| ☐ 229 Leo Foster ......... | .08 | .03 | .01 |
| ☐ 230 Al Hrabosky ........ | .12 | .05 | .01 |
| ☐ 231 Wayne Nordhagen ..... | .08 | .03 | .01 |
| ☐ 232 Mickey Stanley ...... | .08 | .03 | .01 |
| ☐ 233 Dick Pole .......... | .08 | .03 | .01 |
| ☐ 234 Herman Franks ...... | .08 | .03 | .01 |
| ☐ 235 Tim McCarver ....... | .15 | .06 | .01 |
| ☐ 236 Terry Whitfield ...... | .08 | .03 | .01 |
| ☐ 237 Rich Dauer ........ | .08 | .03 | .01 |
| ☐ 238 Juan Beniquez ...... | .12 | .05 | .01 |
| ☐ 239 Dyar Miller ........ | .08 | .03 | .01 |
| ☐ 240 Gene Tenace ....... | .08 | .03 | .01 |
| ☐ 241 Pete Vuckovich ...... | .18 | .08 | .01 |
| ☐ 242 Barry Bonnell DP ..... | .08 | .03 | .01 |
| ☐ 243 Bob McClure ....... | .08 | .03 | .01 |

| | MINT | VG-E | F-G |
|---|---|---|---|
| ☐ 244 Expos Team DP ....... | .15 | .03 | .00 |
| ☐ 245 Rick Burleson ....... | .12 | .05 | .01 |
| ☐ 246 Dan Driessen ........ | .12 | .05 | .01 |
| ☐ 247 Larry Christenson ...... | .08 | .03 | .01 |
| ☐ 248 Frank White DP ....... | .08 | .03 | .01 |
| ☐ 249 Dave Goltz DP ....... | .04 | .01 | .00 |
| ☐ 250 Graig Nettles DP ...... | .15 | .06 | .01 |
| ☐ 251 Don Kirkwood ........ | .08 | .03 | .01 |
| ☐ 252 Steve Swisher DP ..... | .04 | .01 | .00 |
| ☐ 253 Jim Kern ........... | .08 | .03 | .01 |
| ☐ 254 Dave Collins ........ | .15 | .06 | .01 |
| ☐ 255 Jerry Reuss ......... | .18 | .08 | .01 |
| ☐ 256 Joe Altobelli MGR ..... | .08 | .03 | .01 |
| ☐ 257 Hector Cruz ......... | .08 | .03 | .01 |
| ☐ 258 John Hiller ......... | .08 | .03 | .01 |
| ☐ 259 Dodgers Team ....... | .35 | .07 | .01 |
| ☐ 260 Bert Campaneris ...... | .15 | .06 | .01 |
| ☐ 261 Tim Hosley ......... | .08 | .03 | .01 |
| ☐ 262 Rudy May .......... | .08 | .03 | .01 |
| ☐ 263 Danny Walton ........ | .08 | .03 | .01 |
| ☐ 264 Jamie Easterly ....... | .08 | .03 | .01 |
| ☐ 265 Sal Bando DP ....... | .08 | .03 | .01 |
| ☐ 266 Bob Shirley ......... | .08 | .03 | .01 |
| ☐ 267 Doug Ault .......... | .08 | .03 | .01 |
| ☐ 268 Gil Flores .......... | .08 | .03 | .01 |
| ☐ 269 Wayne Twitchell ...... | .08 | .03 | .01 |
| ☐ 270 Carlton Fisk ........ | .65 | .30 | .06 |
| ☐ 271 Randy Lerch DP ...... | .04 | .01 | .00 |
| ☐ 272 Royle Stillman ....... | .08 | .03 | .01 |
| ☐ 273 Fred Norman ........ | .08 | .03 | .01 |
| ☐ 274 Freddie Patek ....... | .08 | .03 | .01 |
| ☐ 275 Dan Ford .......... | .12 | .05 | .01 |
| ☐ 276 Bill Bonham DP ...... | .04 | .01 | .00 |
| ☐ 277 Bruce Boisclair ...... | .08 | .03 | .01 |
| ☐ 278 Enrique Romo ....... | .08 | .03 | .01 |
| ☐ 279 Bill Virdon MGR ...... | .12 | .05 | .01 |
| ☐ 280 Buddy Bell ......... | .25 | .10 | .02 |
| ☐ 281 Eric Rasmussen DP .... | .04 | .01 | .00 |
| ☐ 282 Yankees Team ....... | .40 | .08 | .01 |
| ☐ 283 Omar Moreno ....... | .12 | .05 | .01 |
| ☐ 284 Randy Moffitt ....... | .08 | .03 | .01 |
| ☐ 285 Steve Yeager DP ..... | .04 | .01 | .00 |
| ☐ 286 Ben Oglivie ........ | .15 | .06 | .01 |
| ☐ 287 Kiko Garcia ........ | .08 | .03 | .01 |
| ☐ 288 Dave Hamilton ...... | .08 | .03 | .01 |
| ☐ 289 Checklist 3 ........ | .20 | .03 | .00 |
| ☐ 290 Willie Horton ....... | .12 | .05 | .01 |
| ☐ 291 Gary Ross ......... | .08 | .03 | .01 |
| ☐ 292 Gene Richards ...... | .08 | .03 | .01 |
| ☐ 293 Mike Willis ........ | .08 | .03 | .01 |
| ☐ 294 Larry Parrish ....... | .20 | .09 | .02 |
| ☐ 295 Bill Lee ........... | .12 | .05 | .01 |

| | MINT | VG-E | F-G |
|---|---|---|---|
| ☐ 296 Biff Pocoroba | .08 | .03 | .01 |
| ☐ 297 Warren Brusstar DP | .04 | .01 | .00 |
| ☐ 298 Tony Armas | .75 | .35 | .07 |
| ☐ 299 Whitey Herzog MGR | .12 | .05 | .01 |
| ☐ 300 Joe Morgan | .85 | .40 | .08 |
| ☐ 301 Buddy Schultz | .08 | .03 | .01 |
| ☐ 302 Cubs Team | .30 | .06 | .01 |
| ☐ 303 Sam Hinds | .08 | .03 | .01 |
| ☐ 304 John Milner | .08 | .03 | .01 |
| ☐ 305 Rico Carty | .12 | .05 | .01 |
| ☐ 306 Joe Niekro | .20 | .09 | .02 |
| ☐ 307 Glenn Borgmann | .08 | .03 | .01 |
| ☐ 308 Jim Rooker | .08 | .03 | .01 |
| ☐ 309 Cliff Johnson | .08 | .03 | .01 |
| ☐ 310 Don Sutton | .50 | .22 | .05 |
| ☐ 311 Jose Baez DP | .04 | .01 | .00 |
| ☐ 312 Greg Minton | .18 | .08 | .01 |
| ☐ 313 Andy Etchebarren | .08 | .03 | .01 |
| ☐ 314 Paul Lindblad | .08 | .03 | .01 |
| ☐ 315 Mark Belanger | .12 | .05 | .01 |
| ☐ 316 Henry Cruz DP | .04 | .01 | .00 |
| ☐ 317 Dave Johnson | .12 | .05 | .01 |
| ☐ 318 Tom Griffin | .08 | .03 | .01 |
| ☐ 319 Alan Ashby | .08 | .03 | .01 |
| ☐ 320 Fred Lynn | .90 | .40 | .09 |
| ☐ 321 Santo Alcala | .08 | .03 | .01 |
| ☐ 322 Tom Paciorek | .08 | .03 | .01 |
| ☐ 323 Jim Fregosi DP | .08 | .03 | .01 |
| ☐ 324 Vern Rapp MGR | .08 | .03 | .01 |
| ☐ 325 Bruce Sutter | 1.00 | .45 | .10 |
| ☐ 326 Mike Lum DP | .04 | .01 | .00 |
| ☐ 327 Rick Langford DP | .04 | .01 | .00 |
| ☐ 328 Milwaukee Brewers Team | .30 | .06 | .01 |
| ☐ 329 John Verhoeven | .08 | .03 | .01 |
| ☐ 330 Bob Watson | .12 | .05 | .01 |
| ☐ 331 Mark Littell | .12 | .05 | .01 |
| ☐ 332 Duane Kuiper | .08 | .03 | .01 |
| ☐ 333 Jim Todd | .08 | .03 | .01 |
| ☐ 334 John Stearns | .12 | .05 | .01 |
| ☐ 335 Bucky Dent | .18 | .08 | .01 |
| ☐ 336 Steve Busby | .12 | .05 | .01 |
| ☐ 337 Tom Grieve | .12 | .05 | .01 |
| ☐ 338 Dave Heaverlo | .08 | .03 | .01 |
| ☐ 339 Mario Guerrero | .08 | .03 | .01 |
| ☐ 340 Bake McBride | .12 | .05 | .01 |
| ☐ 341 Mike Flanagan | .18 | .08 | .01 |
| ☐ 342 Aurelio Rodriguez | .08 | .03 | .01 |
| ☐ 343 John Wathan DP | .04 | .01 | .00 |
| ☐ 344 Sam Ewing | .08 | .03 | .01 |
| ☐ 345 Luis Tiant | .15 | .06 | .01 |
| ☐ 346 Larry Biittner | .08 | .03 | .01 |

| | MINT | VG-E | F-G |
|---|---|---|---|
| ☐ 347 Terry Forster | .18 | .08 | .01 |
| ☐ 348 Del Unser | .08 | .03 | .01 |
| ☐ 349 Rick Camp DP | .08 | .03 | .01 |
| ☐ 350 Steve Garvey | 2.25 | 1.00 | .22 |
| ☐ 351 Jeff Torborg | .08 | .03 | .01 |
| ☐ 352 Tony Scott | .08 | .03 | .01 |
| ☐ 353 Doug Bair | .12 | .05 | .01 |
| ☐ 354 Cesar Geronimo | .08 | .03 | .01 |
| ☐ 355 Bill Travers | .08 | .03 | .01 |
| ☐ 356 Mets Team | .35 | .07 | .01 |
| ☐ 357 Tom Poquette | .08 | .03 | .01 |
| ☐ 358 Mark Lemongello | .08 | .03 | .01 |
| ☐ 359 Marc Hill | .08 | .03 | .01 |
| ☐ 360 Mike Schmidt | 2.75 | 1.25 | .27 |
| ☐ 361 Chris Knapp | .08 | .03 | .01 |
| ☐ 362 Dave May | .08 | .03 | .01 |
| ☐ 363 Bob Randall | .08 | .03 | .01 |
| ☐ 364 Jerry Turner | .08 | .03 | .01 |
| ☐ 365 Ed Figueroa | .08 | .03 | .01 |
| ☐ 366 Larry Milbourne DP | .04 | .01 | .00 |
| ☐ 367 Rick Dempsey | .15 | .06 | .01 |
| ☐ 368 Balor Moore | .08 | .03 | .01 |
| ☐ 369 Tim Nordbrook | .08 | .03 | .01 |
| ☐ 370 Rusty Staub | .20 | .09 | .02 |
| ☐ 371 Ray Burris | .08 | .03 | .01 |
| ☐ 372 Brian Asselstine | .08 | .03 | .01 |
| ☐ 373 Jim Willoughby | .08 | .03 | .01 |
| ☐ 374 Jose Morales | .08 | .03 | .01 |
| ☐ 375 Tommy John | .55 | .25 | .05 |
| ☐ 376 Jim Wohlford | .08 | .03 | .01 |
| ☐ 377 Manny Sarmiento | .08 | .03 | .01 |
| ☐ 378 Bobby Winkles MGR | .08 | .03 | .01 |
| ☐ 379 Skip Lockwood | .08 | .03 | .01 |
| ☐ 380 Ted Simmons | .40 | .18 | .04 |
| ☐ 381 Phillies Team | .30 | .06 | .01 |
| ☐ 382 Joe Lahoud | .08 | .03 | .01 |
| ☐ 383 Mario Mendoza | .08 | .03 | .01 |
| ☐ 384 Jack Clark | 1.00 | .45 | .10 |
| ☐ 385 Tito Fuentes | .08 | .03 | .01 |
| ☐ 386 Bob Gorinski | .08 | .03 | .01 |
| ☐ 387 Ken Holtzman | .12 | .05 | .01 |
| ☐ 388 Bill Fahey DP | .04 | .01 | .00 |
| ☐ 389 Julio Gonzalez | .08 | .03 | .01 |
| ☐ 390 Oscar Gamble | .12 | .05 | .01 |
| ☐ 391 Larry Haney | .08 | .03 | .01 |
| ☐ 392 Billy Almon | .08 | .03 | .01 |
| ☐ 393 Tippy Martinez | .12 | .05 | .01 |
| ☐ 394 Roy Howell DP | .04 | .01 | .00 |
| ☐ 395 Jim Hughes | .08 | .03 | .01 |
| ☐ 396 Bob Stinson DP | .04 | .01 | .00 |
| ☐ 397 Greg Gross | .08 | .03 | .01 |
| ☐ 398 Don Hood | .08 | .03 | .01 |

| | MINT | VG-E | F-G |
|---|---|---|---|
| ☐ 399 Pete Mackanin | .08 | .03 | .01 |
| ☐ 400 Nolan Ryan | 1.50 | .70 | .15 |
| ☐ 401 Sparky Anderson MGR | .12 | .05 | .01 |
| ☐ 402 Dave Campbell | .08 | .03 | .01 |
| ☐ 403 Bud Harrelson | .08 | .03 | .01 |
| ☐ 404 Tigers Team | .35 | .07 | .01 |
| ☐ 405 Rawly Eastwick | .08 | .03 | .01 |
| ☐ 406 Mike Jorgensen | .08 | .03 | .01 |
| ☐ 407 Odell Jones | .08 | .03 | .01 |
| ☐ 408 Joe Zdeb | .08 | .03 | .01 |
| ☐ 409 Ron Schueler | .08 | .03 | .01 |
| ☐ 410 Bill Madlock | .70 | .32 | .07 |
| ☐ 411 AL Champs: | .45 | .20 | .04 |
| Yankees rally to | | | |
| defeat Royals | | | |
| ☐ 412 NL Champs: | .45 | .20 | .04 |
| Dodgers overpower | | | |
| Phillies in four | | | |
| ☐ 413 World Series: | 1.00 | .45 | .10 |
| Reggie and Yankees | | | |
| reign supreme | | | |
| ☐ 414 Darold Knowles DP | .04 | .01 | .00 |
| ☐ 415 Ray Fosse | .08 | .03 | .01 |
| ☐ 416 Jack Brohamer | .08 | .03 | .01 |
| ☐ 417 Mike Garman DP | .04 | .01 | .00 |
| ☐ 418 Tony Muser | .08 | .03 | .01 |
| ☐ 419 Jerry Garvin | .08 | .03 | .01 |
| ☐ 420 Greg Luzinski | .25 | .10 | .02 |
| ☐ 421 Junior Moore | .08 | .03 | .01 |
| ☐ 422 Steve Braun | .08 | .03 | .01 |
| ☐ 423 Dave Rosello | .08 | .03 | .01 |
| ☐ 424 Red Sox Team | .30 | .06 | .01 |
| ☐ 425 Steve Rogers DP | .08 | .03 | .01 |
| ☐ 426 Fred Kendall | .08 | .03 | .01 |
| ☐ 427 Mario Soto | 2.50 | 1.15 | .25 |
| ☐ 428 Joel Youngblood | .08 | .03 | .01 |
| ☐ 429 Mike Barlow | .08 | .03 | .01 |
| ☐ 430 Al Oliver | .50 | .22 | .05 |
| ☐ 431 Butch Metzger | .08 | .03 | .01 |
| ☐ 432 Terry Bulling | .08 | .03 | .01 |
| ☐ 433 Fernando Gonzalez | .08 | .03 | .01 |
| ☐ 434 Mike Norris | .12 | .05 | .01 |
| ☐ 435 Checklist 4 | .20 | .03 | .00 |
| ☐ 436 Vic Harris DP | .04 | .01 | .00 |
| ☐ 437 Bo McLaughlin | .08 | .03 | .01 |
| ☐ 438 John Ellis | .08 | .03 | .01 |
| ☐ 439 Ken Kravec | .08 | .03 | .01 |
| ☐ 440 Dave Lopes | .20 | .09 | .02, |
| ☐ 441 Larry Gura | .15 | .06 | .01 |
| ☐ 442 Elliott Maddox | .08 | .03 | .01 |
| ☐ 443 Darrell Chaney | .08 | .03 | .01 |
| ☐ 444 Roy Hartsfield MGR | .08 | .03 | .01 |

| | MINT | VG-E | F-G |
|---|---|---|---|
| ☐ 445 Mike Ivie | .08 | .03 | .01 |
| ☐ 446 Tug McGraw | .20 | .09 | .02 |
| ☐ 447 Leroy Stanton | .08 | .03 | .01 |
| ☐ 448 Bill Castro | .08 | .03 | .01 |
| ☐ 449 Tim Blackwell DP | .04 | .01 | .00 |
| ☐ 450 Tom Seaver | 1.50 | .70 | .15 |
| ☐ 451 Twins Team | .30 | .06 | .01 |
| ☐ 452 Jerry Mumphrey | .12 | .05 | .01 |
| ☐ 453 Doug Flynn | .08 | .03 | .01 |
| ☐ 454 Dave LaRoche | .08 | .03 | .01 |
| ☐ 455 Bill Robinson | .08 | .03 | .01 |
| ☐ 456 Vern Ruhle | .08 | .03 | .01 |
| ☐ 457 Bob Bailey | .08 | .03 | .01 |
| ☐ 458 Jeff Newman | .08 | .03 | .01 |
| ☐ 459 Charlie Spikes | .08 | .03 | .01 |
| ☐ 460 Jim Hunter | .50 | .22 | .05 |
| ☐ 461 Rob Andrews DP | .04 | .01 | .00 |
| ☐ 462 Rogelio Moret | .08 | .03 | .01 |
| ☐ 463 Kevin Bell | .08 | .03 | .01 |
| ☐ 464 Jerry Grote | .08 | .03 | .01 |
| ☐ 465 Hal McRae | .18 | .08 | .01 |
| ☐ 466 Dennis Blair | .08 | .03 | .01 |
| ☐ 467 Alvin Dark | .12 | .05 | .01 |
| ☐ 468 Warren Cromartie | .15 | .06 | .01 |
| ☐ 469 Rick Cerone | .12 | .05 | .01 |
| ☐ 470 J.R. Richard | .18 | .08 | .01 |
| ☐ 471 Roy Smalley | .12 | .05 | .01 |
| ☐ 472 Ron Reed | .08 | .03 | .01 |
| ☐ 473 Bill Buckner | .25 | .10 | .02 |
| ☐ 474 Jim Slaton | .08 | .03 | .01 |
| ☐ 475 Gary Matthews | .18 | .08 | .01 |
| ☐ 476 Bill Stein | .08 | .03 | .01 |
| ☐ 477 Doug Capilla | .08 | .03 | .01 |
| ☐ 478 Jerry Remy | .12 | .05 | .01 |
| ☐ 479 Cardinals Team | .30 | .06 | .01 |
| ☐ 480 Ron LeFlore | .15 | .06 | .01 |
| ☐ 481 Jackson Todd | .08 | .03 | .01 |
| ☐ 482 Rick Miller | .08 | .03 | .01 |
| ☐ 483 Ken Macha | .08 | .03 | .01 |
| ☐ 484 Jim Norris | .08 | .03 | .01 |
| ☐ 485 Chris Chambliss | .15 | .06 | .01 |
| ☐ 486 John Curtis | .08 | .03 | .01 |
| ☐ 487 Jim Tyrone | .08 | .03 | .01 |
| ☐ 488 Dan Spillner | .08 | .03 | .01 |
| ☐ 489 Rudy Meoli | .08 | .03 | .01 |
| ☐ 490 Amos Otis | .18 | .08 | .01 |
| ☐ 491 Scott McGregor | .18 | .08 | .01 |
| ☐ 492 Jim Sundberg | .12 | .05 | .01 |
| ☐ 493 Steve Renko | .08 | .03 | .01 |
| ☐ 494 Chuck Tanner MGR | .12 | .05 | .01 |
| ☐ 495 Dave Cash | .08 | .03 | .01 |
| ☐ 496 Jim Clancy DP | .08 | .03 | .01 |

| | MINT | VG-E | F-G | | MINT | VG-E | F-G |
|---|---|---|---|---|---|---|---|
| ☐ 497 Glenn Adams | .08 | .03 | .01 | ☐ 548 Billy Hunter MGR DP | .04 | .01 | .00 |
| ☐ 498 Joe Sambito | .12 | .05 | .01 | ☐ 549 Joe Kerrigan | .08 | .03 | .01 |
| ☐ 499 Seattle Mariners Team | .25 | .05 | .01 | ☐ 550 John Mayberry | .12 | .05 | .01 |
| ☐ 500 George Foster | 1.00 | .45 | .10 | ☐ 551 Atlanta Braves Team | .30 | .06 | .01 |
| ☐ 501 Dave Roberts | .08 | .03 | .01 | ☐ 552 Francisco Barrios | .08 | .03 | .01 |
| ☐ 502 Pat Rockett | .08 | .03 | .01 | ☐ 553 Terry Puhl | .40 | .18 | .04 |
| ☐ 503 Ike Hampton | .08 | .03 | .01 | ☐ 554 Joe Coleman | .08 | .03 | .01 |
| ☐ 504 Roger Freed | .08 | .03 | .01 | ☐ 555 Butch Wynegar | .18 | .08 | .01 |
| ☐ 505 Felix Millan | .08 | .03 | .01 | ☐ 556 Ed Armbrister | .08 | .03 | .01 |
| ☐ 506 Ron Blomberg | .08 | .03 | .01 | ☐ 557 Tony Solaita | .08 | .03 | .01 |
| ☐ 507 Willie Crawford | .08 | .03 | .01 | ☐ 558 Paul Mitchell | .08 | .03 | .01 |
| ☐ 508 Johnny Oates | .08 | .03 | .01 | ☐ 559 Phil Mankowski | .08 | .03 | .01 |
| ☐ 509 Brent Strom | .08 | .03 | .01 | ☐ 560 Dave Parker | 1.25 | .60 | .12 |
| ☐ 510 Willie Stargell | 1.00 | .45 | .10 | ☐ 561 Charlie Williams | .08 | .03 | .01 |
| ☐ 511 Frank Duffy | .08 | .03 | .01 | ☐ 562 Glenn Burke | .08 | .03 | .01 |
| ☐ 512 Larry Herndon | .15 | .06 | .01 | ☐ 563 Dave Rader | .08 | .03 | .01 |
| ☐ 513 Barry Foote | .08 | .03 | .01 | ☐ 564 Mick Kelleher | .08 | .03 | .01 |
| ☐ 514 Rob Sperring | .08 | .03 | .01 | ☐ 565 Jerry Koosman | .20 | .09 | .02 |
| ☐ 515 Tim Corcoran | .08 | .03 | .01 | ☐ 566 Merv Rettenmund | .08 | .03 | .01 |
| ☐ 516 Gary Beare | .08 | .03 | .01 | ☐ 567 Dick Drago | .08 | .03 | .01 |
| ☐ 517 Andres Mora | .08 | .03 | .01 | ☐ 568 Tom Hutton | .08 | .03 | .01 |
| ☐ 518 Tommy Boggs DP | .04 | .01 | .00 | ☐ 569 Lary Sorensen | .08 | .03 | .01 |
| ☐ 519 Brian Downing | .12 | .05 | .01 | ☐ 570 Dave Kingman | .50 | .22 | .05 |
| ☐ 520 Larry Hisle | .12 | .05 | .01 | ☐ 571 Buck Martinez | .08 | .03 | .01 |
| ☐ 521 Steve Staggs | .08 | .03 | .01 | ☐ 572 Rick Wise | .12 | .05 | .01 |
| ☐ 522 Dick Williams MGR | .12 | .05 | .01 | ☐ 573 Luis Gomez | .08 | .03 | .01 |
| ☐ 523 Donnie Moore | .65 | .30 | .06 | ☐ 574 Bob Lemon MGR | .18 | .08 | .01 |
| ☐ 524 Bernie Carbo | .08 | .03 | .01 | ☐ 575 Pat Dobson | .12 | .05 | .01 |
| ☐ 525 Jerry Terrell | .08 | .03 | .01 | ☐ 576 Sam Mejias | .08 | .03 | .01 |
| ☐ 526 Reds Team | .35 | .07 | .01 | ☐ 577 Oakland A's Team | .30 | .06 | .01 |
| ☐ 527 Vic Correll | .08 | .03 | .01 | ☐ 578 Buzz Capra | .08 | .03 | .01 |
| ☐ 528 Rob Picciolo | .08 | .03 | .01 | ☐ 579 Rance Mulliniks | .12 | .05 | .01 |
| ☐ 529 Paul Hartzell | .08 | .03 | .01 | ☐ 580 Rod Carew | 1.50 | .70 | .15 |
| ☐ 530 Dave Winfield | 1.75 | .85 | .17 | ☐ 581 Lynn McGlothen | .08 | .03 | .01 |
| ☐ 531 Tom Underwood | .08 | .03 | .01 | ☐ 582 Fran Healy | .08 | .03 | .01 |
| ☐ 532 Skip Jutze | .08 | .03 | .01 | ☐ 583 George Medich | .08 | .03 | .01 |
| ☐ 533 Sandy Alomar | .08 | .03 | .01 | ☐ 584 John Hale | .08 | .03 | .01 |
| ☐ 534 Wilbur Howard | .08 | .03 | .01 | ☐ 585 Woodie Fryman DP | .04 | .01 | .00 |
| ☐ 535 Checklist 5 | .20 | .03 | .00 | ☐ 586 Ed Goodson | .08 | .03 | .01 |
| ☐ 536 Roric Harrison | .08 | .03 | .01 | ☐ 587 John Urrea | .08 | .03 | .01 |
| ☐ 537 Bruce Bochte | .12 | .05 | .01 | ☐ 588 Jim Mason | .08 | .03 | .01 |
| ☐ 538 Johnny LeMaster | .08 | .03 | .01 | ☐ 589 Bob Knepper | .50 | .22 | .05 |
| ☐ 539 Vic Davalillo DP | .04 | .01 | .00 | ☐ 590 Bobby Murcer | .25 | .10 | .02 |
| ☐ 540 Steve Carlton | 1.75 | .85 | .17 | ☐ 591 George Zeber | .08 | .03 | .01 |
| ☐ 541 Larry Cox | .08 | .03 | .01 | ☐ 592 Bob Apodaca | .08 | .03 | .01 |
| ☐ 542 Tim Johnson | .08 | .03 | .01 | ☐ 593 Dave Skaggs | .08 | .03 | .01 |
| ☐ 543 Larry Harlow DP | .04 | .01 | .00 | ☐ 594 Dave Freisleben | .08 | .03 | .01 |
| ☐ 544 Len Randle DP | .04 | .01 | .00 | ☐ 595 Sixto Lezcano | .12 | .05 | .01 |
| ☐ 545 Bill Campbell | .12 | .05 | .01 | ☐ 596 Gary Wheelock | .08 | .03 | .01 |
| ☐ 546 Ted Martinez | .08 | .03 | .01 | ☐ 597 Steve Dillard | .08 | .03 | .01 |
| ☐ 547 John Scott | .08 | .03 | .01 | ☐ 598 Eddie Solomon | .08 | .03 | .01 |

| | MINT | VG-E | F-G |
|---|---|---|---|
| ☐ 599 Gary Woods | .08 | .03 | .01 |
| ☐ 600 Frank Tanana | .15 | .06 | .01 |
| ☐ 601 Gene Mauch MGR | .12 | .05 | .01 |
| ☐ 602 Eric Soderholm | .08 | .03 | .01 |
| ☐ 603 Will McEnaney | .08 | .03 | .01 |
| ☐ 604 Earl Williams | .08 | .03 | .01 |
| ☐ 605 Rick Rhoden | .12 | .05 | .01 |
| ☐ 606 Pirates Team | .30 | .06 | .01 |
| ☐ 607 Fernando Arroyo | .08 | .03 | .01 |
| ☐ 608 Johnny Grubb | .08 | .03 | .01 |
| ☐ 609 John Denny | .25 | .10 | .02 |
| ☐ 610 Garry Maddox | .12 | .05 | .01 |
| ☐ 611 Pat Scanlon | .08 | .03 | .01 |
| ☐ 612 Ken Henderson | .08 | .03 | .01 |
| ☐ 613 Marty Perez | .08 | .03 | .01 |
| ☐ 614 Joe Wallis | .08 | .03 | .01 |
| ☐ 615 Clay Carroll | .08 | .03 | .01 |
| ☐ 616 Pat Kelly | .08 | .03 | .01 |
| ☐ 617 Joe Nolan | .08 | .03 | .01 |
| ☐ 618 Tommy Helms | .08 | .03 | .01 |
| ☐ 619 Thad Bosley DP | .08 | .03 | .01 |
| ☐ 620 Willie Randolph | .20 | .09 | .02 |
| ☐ 621 Craig Swan DP | .08 | .03 | .01 |
| ☐ 622 Champ Summers | .08 | .03 | .01 |
| ☐ 623 Ed Rodriquez | .08 | .03 | .01 |
| ☐ 624 Gary Alexander DP | .04 | .01 | .00 |
| ☐ 625 Jose Cruz | .30 | .12 | .03 |
| ☐ 626 Blue Jays Team DP | .15 | .03 | .00 |
| ☐ 627 David Johnson | .08 | .03 | .01 |
| ☐ 628 Ralph Garr | .12 | .05 | .01 |
| ☐ 629 Don Stanhouse | .08 | .03 | .01 |
| ☐ 630 Ron Cey | .40 | .18 | .04 |
| ☐ 631 Danny Ozark MGR | .08 | .03 | .01 |
| ☐ 632 Rowland Office | .08 | .03 | .01 |
| ☐ 633 Tom Veryzer | .08 | .03 | .01 |
| ☐ 634 Len Barker | .18 | .08 | .01 |
| ☐ 635 Joe Rudi | .12 | .05 | .01 |
| ☐ 636 Jim Bibby | .12 | .05 | .01 |
| ☐ 637 Duffy Dyer | .08 | .03 | .01 |
| ☐ 638 Paul Splittorff | .12 | .05 | .01 |
| ☐ 639 Gene Clines | .08 | .03 | .01 |
| ☐ 640 Lee May DP | .08 | .03 | .01 |
| ☐ 641 Doug Rau | .08 | .03 | .01 |
| ☐ 642 Denny Doyle | .08 | .03 | .01 |
| ☐ 643 Tom House | .08 | .03 | .01 |
| ☐ 644 Jim Dwyer | .08 | .03 | .01 |
| ☐ 645 Mike Torrez | .12 | .05 | .01 |
| ☐ 646 Rick Auerbach DP | .04 | .01 | .00 |
| ☐ 647 Steve Dunning | .08 | .03 | .01 |
| ☐ 648 Gary Thomasson | .08 | .03 | .01 |
| ☐ 649 Moose Haas | .35 | .15 | .03 |
| ☐ 650 Cesar Cedeno | .20 | .09 | .02 |
| ☐ 651 Doug Rader | .12 | .05 | .01 |
| ☐ 652 Checklist 6 | .20 | .03 | .00 |
| ☐ 653 Ron Hodges DP | .04 | .01 | .00 |
| ☐ 654 Pepe Frias | .08 | .03 | .01 |
| ☐ 655 Lyman Bostock | .18 | .08 | .01 |
| ☐ 656 Dave Garcia | .08 | .03 | .01 |
| ☐ 657 Bombo Rivera | .08 | .03 | .01 |
| ☐ 658 Manny Sanguillen | .12 | .05 | .01 |
| ☐ 659 Rangers Team | .30 | .06 | .01 |
| ☐ 660 Jason Thompson | .25 | .10 | .02 |
| ☐ 661 Grant Jackson | .08 | .03 | .01 |
| ☐ 662 Paul Dade | .08 | .03 | .01 |
| ☐ 663 Paul Reuschel | .08 | .03 | .01 |
| ☐ 664 Fred Stanley | .08 | .03 | .01 |
| ☐ 665 Dennis Leonard | .15 | .06 | .01 |
| ☐ 666 Billy Smith | .08 | .03 | .01 |
| ☐ 667 Jeff Byrd | .08 | .03 | .01 |
| ☐ 668 Dusty Baker | .18 | .08 | .01 |
| ☐ 669 Pete Falcone | .08 | .03 | .01 |
| ☐ 670 Jim Rice | 2.50 | 1.15 | .25 |
| ☐ 671 Gary Lavelle | .12 | .05 | .01 |
| ☐ 672 Don Kessinger | .12 | .05 | .01 |
| ☐ 673 Steve Brye | .08 | .03 | .01 |
| ☐ 674 Ray Knight | .35 | .15 | .03 |
| ☐ 675 Jay Johnstone | .12 | .05 | .01 |
| ☐ 676 Bob Myrick | .08 | .03 | .01 |
| ☐ 677 Ed Herrmann | .08 | .03 | .01 |
| ☐ 678 Tom Burgmeier | .08 | .03 | .01 |
| ☐ 679 Wayne Garrett | .08 | .03 | .01 |
| ☐ 680 Vida Blue | .18 | .08 | .01 |
| ☐ 681 Rob Belloir | .08 | .03 | .01 |
| ☐ 682 Ken Brett | .12 | .05 | .01 |
| ☐ 683 Mike Champion | .08 | .03 | .01 |
| ☐ 684 Ralph Houk MGR | .12 | .05 | .01 |
| ☐ 685 Frank Taveras | .08 | .03 | .01 |
| ☐ 686 Gaylord Perry | 1.00 | .45 | .10 |
| ☐ 687 Julio Cruz | .35 | .15 | .03 |
| ☐ 688 George Mitterwald | .08 | .03 | .01 |
| ☐ 689 Indians Team | .30 | .06 | .01 |
| ☐ 690 Mickey Rivers | .15 | .06 | .01 |
| ☐ 691 Ross Grimsley | .08 | .03 | .01 |
| ☐ 692 Ken Reitz | .08 | .03 | .01 |
| ☐ 693 Lamar Johnson | .08 | .03 | .01 |
| ☐ 694 Elias Sosa | .08 | .03 | .01 |
| ☐ 695 Dwight Evans | .35 | .15 | .03 |
| ☐ 696 Steve Mingori | .08 | .03 | .01 |
| ☐ 697 Roger Metzger | .08 | .03 | .01 |
| ☐ 698 Juan Bernhardt | .08 | .03 | .01 |
| ☐ 699 Jackie Brown | .08 | .03 | .01 |
| ☐ 700 Johnny Bench | 1.50 | .70 | .15 |

| | | MINT | VG-E | F-G |
|---|---|---|---|---|
| ☐ 701 | Rookie Pitchers: ....... | .30 | .12 | .03 |
| | Tom Hume | | | |
| | Larry Landreth | | | |
| | Steve McCatty | | | |
| | Bruce Taylor | | | |
| ☐ 702 | Rookie Catchers: ....... | .12 | .05 | .01 |
| | Bill Nahorodny | | | |
| | Kevin Pasley | | | |
| | Rick Sweet | | | |
| | Don Werner | | | |
| ☐ 703 | Rookie Pitchers DP: .... | 2.75 | 1.25 | .27 |
| | Larry Andersen | | | |
| | Tim Jones | | | |
| | Mickey Mahler | | | |
| | Jack Morris | | | |
| ☐ 704 | Rookie 2nd Basemen: .. | 5.00 | 2.35 | .50 |
| | Garth Iorg | | | |
| | Dave Oliver | | | |
| | Sam Perlozzo | | | |
| | Lou Whitaker | | | |
| ☐ 705 | Rookie Outfielders: ..... | .30 | .12 | .03 |
| | Dave Bergman | | | |
| | Miguel Dilone | | | |
| | Clint Hurdle | | | |
| | Willie Norwood | | | |
| ☐ 706 | Rookie 1st Basemen: ... | .20 | .09 | .02 |
| | Wayne Cage | | | |
| | Ted Cox | | | |
| | Pat Putnam | | | |
| | Dave Revering | | | |
| ☐ 707 | Rookie Shortstops: ..... | 11.00 | 5.25 | 1.10 |
| | Mickey Klutts | | | |
| | Paul Molitor | | | |
| | Alan Trammell | | | |
| | U.L. Washington | | | |
| ☐ 708 | Rookie Catchers: ...... | 16.00 | 7.50 | 1.60 |
| | Bo Diaz | | | |
| | Dale Murphy | | | |
| | Lance Parrish | | | |
| | Ernie Whitt | | | |
| ☐ 709 | Rookie Pitchers: ....... | .20 | .09 | .02 |
| | Steve Burke | | | |
| | Matt Keough | | | |
| | Lance Rautzhan | | | |
| | Dan Schatzeder | | | |
| ☐ 710 | Rookie Outfielders: ..... | 1.25 | .60 | .12 |
| | Dell Alston | | | |
| | Rick Bosetti | | | |
| | Mike Easler | | | |
| | Keith Smith | | | |

| | | MINT | VG-E | F-G |
|---|---|---|---|---|
| ☐ 711 | Rookie Pitchers DP: .... | .12 | .05 | .01 |
| | Cardell Camper | | | |
| | Dennis Lamp | | | |
| | Craig Mitchell | | | |
| | Roy Thomas | | | |
| ☐ 712 | Bobby Valentine ........ | .12 | .05 | .01 |
| ☐ 713 | Bob Davis ............. | .08 | .03 | .01 |
| ☐ 714 | Mike Anderson ......... | .08 | .03 | .01 |
| ☐ 715 | Jim Kaat .............. | .25 | .10 | .02 |
| ☐ 716 | Clarence Gaston ....... | .08 | .03 | .01 |
| ☐ 717 | Nelson Briles ......... | .08 | .03 | .01 |
| ☐ 718 | Ron Jackson .......... | .08 | .03 | .01 |
| ☐ 719 | Randy Elliott ......... | .08 | .03 | .01 |
| ☐ 720 | Fergie Jenkins ........ | .25 | .10 | .02 |
| ☐ 721 | Billy Martin MGR ...... | .25 | .10 | .02 |
| ☐ 722 | Pete Broberg ......... | .08 | .03 | .01 |
| ☐ 723 | John Wockenfuss ...... | .08 | .03 | .01 |
| ☐ 724 | K.C. Royals Team ..... | .30 | .06 | .01 |
| ☐ 725 | Kurt Bevacqua ........ | .08 | .03 | .01 |
| ☐ 726 | Wilbur Wood .......... | .12 | .05 | .01 |

## 1979 TOPPS

*The cards in this 726 set measure 2½" by 3½". Topps continued with the same number of cards as in 1978. Various series spotlight "Season and Career Record Holders" (411–418), "Record Breakers of 1978" (201–206) and "Prospects" (701–726). There are 66 cards that were double-printed and these are noted in the checklist by the abbreviation DP. Bump Wills was initially depicted in a Ranger uniform but with a Blue Jays affiliation; later printings correctly labeled him with Texas.*

*The set price listed does not include the scarcer Wills (Rangers) card.*
Complete Set: M-70.00; VG-E-30.00; F-G-6.00

| | | MINT | VG-E | F-G |
|---|---|---|---|---|
| | Common Player (1–726) | .07 | .03 | .01 |
| ☐ 1 | Batting Leaders: Rod Carew Dave Parker | .75 | .20 | .04 |
| ☐ 2 | Home Run Leaders: Jim Rice George Foster | .35 | .15 | .03 |
| ☐ 3 | RBI Leaders: Jim Rice George Foster | .35 | .15 | .03 |
| ☐ 4 | Stolen Base Leaders: Ron LeFlore Omar Moreno | .12 | .05 | .01 |
| ☐ 5 | Victory Leaders: Ron Guidry Gaylord Perry | .25 | .10 | .02 |
| ☐ 6 | Strikeout Leaders: Nolan Ryan J.R. Richard | .25 | .10 | .02 |
| ☐ 7 | ERA Leaders: Ron Guidry Craig Swan | .15 | .06 | .01 |
| ☐ 8 | Leading Firemen: Rich Gossage Rollie Fingers | .20 | .09 | .01 |
| ☐ 9 | Dave Campbell | .07 | .03 | .01 |
| ☐ 10 | Lee May | .12 | .05 | .01 |
| ☐ 11 | Marc Hill | .07 | .03 | .01 |
| ☐ 12 | Dick Drago | .07 | .03 | .01 |
| ☐ 13 | Paul Dade | .07 | .03 | .01 |
| ☐ 14 | Rafael Landestoy | .07 | .03 | .01 |
| ☐ 15 | Ross Grimsley | .07 | .03 | .01 |
| ☐ 16 | Fred Stanley | .07 | .03 | .01 |
| ☐ 17 | Donnie Moore | .15 | .06 | .01 |
| ☐ 18 | Tony Solaita | .07 | .03 | .01 |
| ☐ 19 | Larry Gura DP | .07 | .03 | .01 |
| ☐ 20 | Joe Morgan DP | .15 | .06 | .01 |
| ☐ 21 | Kevin Kobel | .07 | .03 | .01 |
| ☐ 22 | Mike Jorgensen | .07 | .03 | .01 |
| ☐ 23 | Terry Forster | .12 | .05 | .01 |
| ☐ 24 | Paul Molitor | .85 | .40 | .08 |
| ☐ 25 | Steve Carlton | 1.50 | .70 | .15 |
| ☐ 26 | Jamie Quirk | .07 | .03 | .01 |
| ☐ 27 | Dave Goltz | .07 | .03 | .01 |
| ☐ 28 | Steve Brye | .07 | .03 | .01 |
| ☐ 29 | Rick Langford | .07 | .03 | .01 |
| ☐ 30 | Dave Winfield | 1.50 | .70 | .15 |

| | | MINT | VG-E | F-G |
|---|---|---|---|---|
| ☐ 31 | Tom House DP | .03 | .01 | .00 |
| ☐ 32 | Jerry Mumphrey | .12 | .05 | .01 |
| ☐ 33 | Dave Rozema | .07 | .03 | .01 |
| ☐ 34 | Rob Andrews | .07 | .03 | .01 |
| ☐ 35 | Ed Figueroa | .07 | .03 | .01 |
| ☐ 36 | Alan Ashby | .07 | .03 | .01 |
| ☐ 37 | Joe Kerrigan DP | .03 | .01 | .00 |
| ☐ 38 | Bernie Carbo | .07 | .03 | .01 |
| ☐ 39 | Dale Murphy | 3.75 | 1.75 | .37 |
| ☐ 40 | Dennis Eckersley | .12 | .05 | .01 |
| ☐ 41 | Twins Team/Mgr. Gene Mauch | .25 | .05 | .01 |
| ☐ 42 | Ron Blomberg | .07 | .03 | .01 |
| ☐ 43 | Wayne Twitchell | .07 | .03 | .01 |
| ☐ 44 | Kurt Bevacqua | .07 | .03 | .01 |
| ☐ 45 | Al Hrabosky | .12 | .05 | .01 |
| ☐ 46 | Ron Hodges | .07 | .03 | .01 |
| ☐ 47 | Fred Norman | .07 | .03 | .01 |
| ☐ 48 | Merv Rettenmund | .07 | .03 | .01 |
| ☐ 49 | Vern Ruhle | .07 | .03 | .01 |
| ☐ 50 | Steve Garvey DP | .75 | .35 | .07 |
| ☐ 51 | Ray Fosse DP | .03 | .01 | .00 |
| ☐ 52 | Randy Lerch | .07 | .03 | .01 |
| ☐ 53 | Mick Kelleher | .07 | .03 | .01 |
| ☐ 54 | Dell Alston DP | .03 | .01 | .00 |
| ☐ 55 | Willie Stargell | .90 | .40 | .09 |
| ☐ 56 | John Hale | .07 | .03 | .01 |
| ☐ 57 | Eric Rasmussen | .07 | .03 | .01 |
| ☐ 58 | Bob Randall DP | .03 | .01 | .00 |
| ☐ 59 | John Denny DP | .07 | .03 | .01 |
| ☐ 60 | Mickey Rivers | .12 | .05 | .01 |
| ☐ 61 | Bo Diaz | .15 | .06 | .01 |
| ☐ 62 | Randy Moffitt | .07 | .03 | .01 |
| ☐ 63 | Jack Brohamer | .07 | .03 | .01 |
| ☐ 64 | Tom Underwood | .07 | .03 | .01 |
| ☐ 65 | Mark Belanger | .12 | .05 | .01 |
| ☐ 66 | Tigers Team/Mgr. Les Moss | .25 | .05 | .01 |
| ☐ 67 | Jim Mason DP | .03 | .01 | .00 |
| ☐ 68 | Joe Niekro DP | .07 | .03 | .01 |
| ☐ 69 | Elliott Maddox | .07 | .03 | .01 |
| ☐ 70 | John Candelaria | .15 | .06 | .01 |
| ☐ 71 | Brian Downing | .12 | .05 | .01 |
| ☐ 72 | Steve Mingori | .07 | .03 | .01 |
| ☐ 73 | Ken Henderson | .07 | .03 | .01 |
| ☐ 74 | Shane Rawley | .50 | .22 | .05 |
| ☐ 75 | Steve Yeager | .10 | .04 | .01 |
| ☐ 76 | Warren Cromartie | .07 | .03 | .01 |
| ☐ 77 | Dan Briggs DP | .03 | .01 | .00 |
| ☐ 78 | Elias Sosa | .07 | .03 | .01 |
| ☐ 79 | Ted Cox | .07 | .03 | .01 |
| ☐ 80 | Jason Thompson | .15 | .06 | .01 |

|  | | MINT | VG-E | F-G |
|---|---|---|---|---|
| ☐ 81 | Roger Erickson | .10 | .04 | .01 |
| ☐ 82 | Mets Team/Mgr. | .25 | .05 | .01 |
| | Joe Torre | | | |
| ☐ 83 | Fred Kendall | .07 | .03 | .01 |
| ☐ 84 | Greg Minton | .12 | .05 | .01 |
| ☐ 85 | Gary Matthews | .18 | .08 | .01 |
| ☐ 86 | Rodney Scott | .07 | .03 | .01 |
| ☐ 87 | Pete Falcone | .07 | .03 | .01 |
| ☐ 88 | Bob Molinaro | .07 | .03 | .01 |
| ☐ 89 | Dick Tidrow | .07 | .03 | .01 |
| ☐ 90 | Bob Boone | .12 | .05 | .01 |
| ☐ 91 | Terry Crowley | .07 | .03 | .01 |
| ☐ 92 | Jim Bibby | .10 | .04 | .01 |
| ☐ 93 | Phil Mankowski | .07 | .03 | .01 |
| ☐ 94 | Len Barker | .15 | .06 | .01 |
| ☐ 95 | Robin Yount | 1.25 | .60 | .12 |
| ☐ 96 | Indians Team/Mgr. | .25 | .05 | .01 |
| | Jeff Torborg | | | |
| ☐ 97 | Sam Mejias | .07 | .03 | .01 |
| ☐ 98 | Ray Burris | .07 | .03 | .01 |
| ☐ 99 | John Wathan | .07 | .03 | .01 |
| ☐ 100 | Tom Seaver DP | .75 | .35 | .07 |
| ☐ 101 | Roy Howell | .07 | .03 | .01 |
| ☐ 102 | Mike Anderson | .07 | .03 | .01 |
| ☐ 103 | Jim Todd | .07 | .03 | .01 |
| ☐ 104 | Johnny Oates DP | .03 | .01 | .00 |
| ☐ 105 | Rick Camp DP | .03 | .01 | .00 |
| ☐ 106 | Frank Duffy | .07 | .03 | .01 |
| ☐ 107 | Jesus Alou DP | .03 | .01 | .00 |
| ☐ 108 | Eduardo Rodriguez | .07 | .03 | .01 |
| ☐ 109 | Joel Youngblood | .07 | .03 | .01 |
| ☐ 110 | Vida Blue | .15 | .06 | .01 |
| ☐ 111 | Roger Freed | .07 | .03 | .01 |
| ☐ 112 | Phillies Team/Mgr. | .25 | .05 | .01 |
| | Danny Ozark | | | |
| ☐ 113 | Pete Redfern | .07 | .03 | .01 |
| ☐ 114 | Cliff Johnson | .07 | .03 | .01 |
| ☐ 115 | Nolan Ryan | 1.10 | .50 | .11 |
| ☐ 116 | Ozzie Smith | 2.00 | .90 | .20 |
| ☐ 117 | Grant Jackson | .07 | .03 | .01 |
| ☐ 118 | Bud Harrelson | .07 | .03 | .01 |
| ☐ 119 | Don Stanhouse | .07 | .03 | .01 |
| ☐ 120 | Jim Sundberg | .10 | .04 | .01 |
| ☐ 121 | Checklist 1 DP | .10 | .02 | .00 |
| ☐ 122 | Mike Paxton | .07 | .03 | .01 |
| ☐ 123 | Lou Whitaker | 1.50 | .70 | .15 |
| ☐ 124 | Dan Schatzeder | .07 | .03 | .01 |
| ☐ 125 | Rick Burleson | .10 | .04 | .01 |
| ☐ 126 | Doug Bair | .07 | .03 | .01 |
| ☐ 127 | Thad Bosley | .07 | .03 | .01 |
| ☐ 128 | Ted Martinez | .07 | .03 | .01 |
| ☐ 129 | Marty Pattin DP | .03 | .01 | .00 |
| ☐ 130 | Bob Watson DP | .07 | .03 | .01 |
| ☐ 131 | Jim Clancy | .07 | .03 | .01 |
| ☐ 132 | Rowland Office | .07 | .03 | .01 |
| ☐ 133 | Bill Castro | .07 | .03 | .01 |
| ☐ 134 | Alan Bannister | .07 | .03 | .01 |
| ☐ 135 | Bobby Murcer | .15 | .06 | .01 |
| ☐ 136 | Jim Kaat | .20 | .09 | .02 |
| ☐ 137 | Larry Wolfe DP | .03 | .01 | .00 |
| ☐ 138 | Mark Lee | .07 | .03 | .01 |
| ☐ 139 | Luis Pujols | .07 | .03 | .01 |
| ☐ 140 | Don Gullett | .07 | .03 | .01 |
| ☐ 141 | Tom Paciorek | .07 | .03 | .01 |
| ☐ 142 | Charlie Williams | .07 | .03 | .01 |
| ☐ 143 | Tony Scott | .07 | .03 | .01 |
| ☐ 144 | Sandy Alomar | .07 | .03 | .01 |
| ☐ 145 | Rick Rhoden | .10 | .04 | .01 |
| ☐ 146 | Duane Kuiper | .07 | .03 | .01 |
| ☐ 147 | Dave Hamilton | .07 | .03 | .01 |
| ☐ 148 | Bruce Boisclair | .07 | .03 | .01 |
| ☐ 149 | Manny Sarmiento | .07 | .03 | .01 |
| ☐ 150 | Wayne Cage | .07 | .03 | .01 |
| ☐ 151 | John Hiller | .10 | .04 | .01 |
| ☐ 152 | Rick Cerone | .10 | .04 | .01 |
| ☐ 153 | Dennis Lamp | .07 | .03 | .01 |
| ☐ 154 | Jim Gantner DP | .07 | .03 | .01 |
| ☐ 155 | Dwight Evans | .30 | .12 | .03 |
| ☐ 156 | Buddy Solomon | .07 | .03 | .01 |
| ☐ 157 | U.L. Washington | .07 | .03 | .01 |
| ☐ 158 | Joe Sambito | .10 | .04 | .01 |
| ☐ 159 | Roy White | .10 | .04 | .01 |
| ☐ 160 | Mike Flanagan | .18 | .08 | .01 |
| ☐ 161 | Barry Foote | .07 | .03 | .01 |
| ☐ 162 | Tom Johnson | .07 | .03 | .01 |
| ☐ 163 | Glenn Burke | .07 | .03 | .01 |
| ☐ 164 | Mickey Lolich | .15 | .06 | .01 |
| ☐ 165 | Frank Taveras | .07 | .03 | .01 |
| ☐ 166 | Leon Roberts | .07 | .03 | .01 |
| ☐ 167 | Roger Metzger DP | .03 | .01 | .00 |
| ☐ 168 | Dave Freisleben | .07 | .03 | .01 |
| ☐ 169 | Bill Nahorodny | .07 | .03 | .01 |
| ☐ 170 | Don Sutton | .35 | .15 | .03 |
| ☐ 171 | Gene Clines | .07 | .03 | .01 |
| ☐ 172 | Mike Bruhert | .07 | .03 | .01 |
| ☐ 173 | John Lowenstein | .07 | .03 | .01 |
| ☐ 174 | Rick Auerbach | .07 | .03 | .01 |
| ☐ 175 | George Hendrick | .15 | .06 | .01 |
| ☐ 176 | Aurelio Rodriguez | .07 | .03 | .01 |
| ☐ 177 | Ron Reed | .07 | .03 | .01 |
| ☐ 178 | Alvis Woods | .07 | .03 | .01 |
| ☐ 179 | Jim Beattie DP | .07 | .03 | .01 |
| ☐ 180 | Larry Hisle | .10 | .04 | .01 |
| ☐ 181 | Mike Garman | .07 | .03 | .01 |
| ☐ 182 | Tim Johnson | .07 | .03 | .01 |
| ☐ 183 | Paul Splittorff | .10 | .04 | .01 |

|  |  | MINT | VG-E | F-G |
|---|---|---|---|---|
| ☐ 184 | Darrell Chaney | .07 | .03 | .01 |
| ☐ 185 | Mike Torrez | .10 | .04 | .01 |
| ☐ 186 | Eric Soderholm | .07 | .03 | .01 |
| ☐ 187 | Mark Lemongello | .07 | .03 | .01 |
| ☐ 188 | Pat Kelly | .07 | .03 | .01 |
| ☐ 189 | Eddie Whitson | .50 | .22 | .05 |
| ☐ 190 | Ron Cey | .35 | .15 | .03 |
| ☐ 191 | Mike Norris | .10 | .04 | .01 |
| ☐ 192 | Cardinals Team/Mgr. | .25 | .05 | .00 |
|  | Ken Boyer |  |  |  |
| ☐ 193 | Glenn Adams | .07 | .03 | .01 |
| ☐ 194 | Randy Jones | .10 | .04 | .01 |
| ☐ 195 | Bill Madlock | .40 | .18 | .04 |
| ☐ 196 | Steve Kemp DP | .10 | .04 | .01 |
| ☐ 197 | Bob Apodaca | .07 | .03 | .01 |
| ☐ 198 | Johnny Grubb | .07 | .03 | .01 |
| ☐ 199 | Larry Milbourne | .07 | .03 | .01 |
| ☐ 200 | Johnny Bench DP | .70 | .32 | .07 |
| ☐ 201 | RB: Mike Edwards | .10 | .04 | .01 |
|  | Most unassisted |  |  |  |
|  | 2nd basemen DP's |  |  |  |
| ☐ 202 | RB: Ron Guidry, Most | .25 | .10 | .02 |
|  | Strikeouts, Lefthander |  |  |  |
|  | 9 inning game |  |  |  |
| ☐ 203 | RB: J.R. Richard | .15 | .06 | .01 |
|  | Most Strikeouts |  |  |  |
|  | Season, Righthander |  |  |  |
| ☐ 204 | RB: Pete Rose | 1.00 | .45 | .10 |
|  | Most consecutive |  |  |  |
|  | games batting safe |  |  |  |
| ☐ 205 | RB: John Stearns | .10 | .04 | .01 |
|  | Most SB's by |  |  |  |
|  | Catcher, Season |  |  |  |
| ☐ 206 | RB: Sammy Stewart | .10 | .04 | .01 |
|  | 7 straight SO's |  |  |  |
|  | First ML Game |  |  |  |
| ☐ 207 | Dave Lemanczyk | .07 | .03 | .01 |
| ☐ 208 | Clarence Gaston | .07 | .03 | .01 |
| ☐ 209 | Reggie Cleveland | .07 | .03 | .01 |
| ☐ 210 | Larry Bowa | .16 | .07 | .01 |
| ☐ 211 | Denny Martinez | .07 | .03 | .01 |
| ☐ 212 | Carney Lansford | 1.50 | .70 | .15 |
| ☐ 213 | Bill Travers | .07 | .03 | .01 |
| ☐ 214 | Red Sox Team/Mgr. | .25 | .05 | .01 |
|  | Don Zimmer |  |  |  |
| ☐ 215 | Willie McCovey | .90 | .40 | .09 |
| ☐ 216 | Wilbur Wood | .10 | .04 | .01 |
| ☐ 217 | Steve Dillard | .07 | .03 | .01 |
| ☐ 218 | Dennis Leonard | .15 | .06 | .01 |
| ☐ 219 | Roy Smalley | .10 | .04 | .01 |
| ☐ 220 | Cesar Geronimo | .07 | .03 | .01 |
| ☐ 221 | Jesse Jefferson | .07 | .03 | .01 |
| ☐ 222 | Bob Beall | .07 | .03 | .01 |

|  |  | MINT | VG-E | F-G |
|---|---|---|---|---|
| ☐ 223 | Kent Tekulve | .15 | .06 | .01 |
| ☐ 224 | Dave Revering | .07 | .03 | .01 |
| ☐ 225 | Rich Gossage | .50 | .22 | .05 |
| ☐ 226 | Ron Pruitt | .07 | .03 | .01 |
| ☐ 227 | Steve Stone | .12 | .05 | .01 |
| ☐ 228 | Vic Davalillo | .07 | .03 | .01 |
| ☐ 229 | Doug Flynn | .07 | .03 | .01 |
| ☐ 230 | Bob Forsch | .10 | .04 | .01 |
| ☐ 231 | Johnny Wockenfuss | .07 | .03 | .01 |
| ☐ 232 | Jimmy Sexton | .07 | .03 | .01 |
| ☐ 233 | Paul Mitchell | .07 | .03 | .01 |
| ☐ 234 | Toby Harrah | .10 | .04 | .01 |
| ☐ 235 | Steve Rogers | .15 | .06 | .01 |
| ☐ 236 | Jim Dwyer | .07 | .03 | .01 |
| ☐ 237 | Billy Smith | .07 | .03 | .01 |
| ☐ 238 | Balor Moore | .07 | .03 | .01 |
| ☐ 239 | Willie Horton | .10 | .04 | .01 |
| ☐ 240 | Rick Reuschel | .12 | .05 | .01 |
| ☐ 241 | Checklist 2 DP | .10 | .02 | .00 |
| ☐ 242 | Pablo Torrealba | .07 | .03 | .01 |
| ☐ 243 | Buck Martinez DP | .03 | .01 | .00 |
| ☐ 244 | Pirates Team/Mgr. | .25 | .05 | .01 |
|  | Chuck Tanner |  |  |  |
| ☐ 245 | Jeff Burroughs | .10 | .04 | .01 |
| ☐ 246 | Darrell Jackson | .07 | .03 | .01 |
| ☐ 247 | Tucker Ashford DP | .03 | .01 | .00 |
| ☐ 248 | Pete LaCock | .07 | .03 | .01 |
| ☐ 249 | Paul Thormodsgard | .07 | .03 | .01 |
| ☐ 250 | Willie Randolph | .15 | .06 | .01 |
| ☐ 251 | Jack Morris | 1.10 | .50 | .11 |
| ☐ 252 | Bob Stinson | .07 | .03 | .01 |
| ☐ 253 | Rick Wise | .10 | .04 | .01 |
| ☐ 254 | Luis Gomez | .07 | .03 | .01 |
| ☐ 255 | Tommy John | .35 | .15 | .03 |
| ☐ 256 | Mike Sadek | .07 | .03 | .01 |
| ☐ 257 | Adrian Devine | .07 | .03 | .01 |
| ☐ 258 | Mike Phillips | .07 | .03 | .01 |
| ☐ 259 | Reds Team/Mgr. | .25 | .05 | .00 |
|  | Sparky Anderson |  |  |  |
| ☐ 260 | Richie Zisk | .10 | .04 | .01 |
| ☐ 261 | Mario Guerrero | .07 | .03 | .01 |
| ☐ 262 | Nelson Briles | .07 | .03 | .01 |
| ☐ 263 | Oscar Gamble | .10 | .04 | .01 |
| ☐ 264 | Don Robinson | .25 | .10 | .02 |
| ☐ 265 | Don Money | .07 | .03 | .01 |
| ☐ 266 | Jim Willoughby | .07 | .03 | .01 |
| ☐ 267 | Joe Rudi | .12 | .05 | .01 |
| ☐ 268 | Julio Gonzalez | .07 | .03 | .01 |
| ☐ 269 | Woodie Fryman | .07 | .03 | .01 |
| ☐ 270 | Butch Hobson | .07 | .03 | .01 |
| ☐ 271 | Rawly Eastwick | .07 | .03 | .01 |
| ☐ 272 | Tim Corcoran | .07 | .03 | .01 |
| ☐ 273 | Jerry Terrell | .07 | .03 | .01 |

|  | MINT | VG-E | F-G |
|---|---|---|---|
| ☐ 274 Willie Norwood | .07 | .03 | .01 |
| ☐ 275 Junior Moore | .07 | .03 | .01 |
| ☐ 276 Jim Colborn | .07 | .03 | .01 |
| ☐ 277 Tom Grieve | .10 | .04 | .01 |
| ☐ 278 Andy Messersmith | .10 | .04 | .01 |
| ☐ 279 Jerry Grote DP | .03 | .01 | .00 |
| ☐ 280 Andre Thornton | .15 | .06 | .01 |
| ☐ 281 Vic Correll DP | .03 | .01 | .00 |
| ☐ 282 Blue Jays Team/Mgr | .20 | .05 | .01 |
|  Roy Hartsfield |  |  |  |
| ☐ 283 Ken Kravec | .07 | .03 | .01 |
| ☐ 284 Johnnie LeMaster | .07 | .03 | .01 |
| ☐ 285 Bobby Bonds | .15 | .06 | .01 |
| ☐ 286 Duffy Dyer | .07 | .03 | .01 |
| ☐ 287 Andres Mora | .07 | .03 | .01 |
| ☐ 288 Milt Wilcox | .10 | .04 | .01 |
| ☐ 289 Jose Cruz | .25 | .10 | .02 |
| ☐ 290 Dave Lopes | .20 | .09 | .02 |
| ☐ 291 Tom Griffin | .07 | .03 | .01 |
| ☐ 292 Don Reynolds | .07 | .03 | .01 |
| ☐ 293 Jerry Garvin | .07 | .03 | .01 |
| ☐ 294 Pepe Frias | .07 | .03 | .01 |
| ☐ 295 Mitchell Page | .07 | .03 | .01 |
| ☐ 296 Preston Hanna | .07 | .03 | .01 |
| ☐ 297 Ted Sizemore | .07 | .03 | .01 |
| ☐ 298 Rich Gale | .07 | .03 | .01 |
| ☐ 299 Steve Ontiveros | .07 | .03 | .01 |
| ☐ 300 Rod Carew | 1.25 | .60 | .12 |
| ☐ 301 Tom Hume | .07 | .03 | .01 |
| ☐ 302 Braves Team/Mgr. | .25 | .05 | .01 |
|  Bobby Cox |  |  |  |
| ☐ 303 Lary Sorensen | .07 | .03 | .01 |
| ☐ 304 Steve Swisher | .07 | .03 | .01 |
| ☐ 305 Willie Montanez | .07 | .03 | .01 |
| ☐ 306 Floyd Bannister | .15 | .06 | .01 |
| ☐ 307 Larvell Blanks | .07 | .03 | .01 |
| ☐ 308 Bert Blyleven | .30 | .12 | .03 |
| ☐ 309 Ralph Garr | .10 | .04 | .01 |
| ☐ 310 Thurman Munson | 1.50 | .70 | .15 |
| ☐ 311 Gary Lavelle | .10 | .04 | .01 |
| ☐ 312 Bob Robertson | .07 | .03 | .01 |
| ☐ 313 Dyar Miller | .07 | .03 | .01 |
| ☐ 314 Larry Harlow | .07 | .03 | .01 |
| ☐ 315 Jon Matlack | .10 | .04 | .01 |
| ☐ 316 Milt May | .07 | .03 | .01 |
| ☐ 317 Jose Cardenal | .07 | .03 | .01 |
| ☐ 318 Bob Welch | 1.00 | .45 | .10 |
| ☐ 319 Wayne Garrett | .07 | .03 | .01 |
| ☐ 320 Carl Yastrzemski | 2.00 | .90 | .20 |
| ☐ 321 Gaylord Perry | .65 | .30 | .06 |
| ☐ 322 Danny Goodwin | .07 | .03 | .01 |
| ☐ 323 Lynn McGlothen | .07 | .03 | .01 |
| ☐ 324 Mike Tyson | .07 | .03 | .01 |

|  | MINT | VG-E | F-G |
|---|---|---|---|
| ☐ 325 Cecil Cooper | .55 | .25 | .05 |
| ☐ 326 Pedro Borbon | .07 | .03 | .01 |
| ☐ 327 Art Howe | .07 | .03 | .01 |
| ☐ 328 Oakland A's Team/Mgr. | .20 | .05 | .01 |
|  Jack McKeon |  |  |  |
| ☐ 329 Joe Coleman | .07 | .03 | .01 |
| ☐ 330 George Brett | 2.25 | 1.00 | .22 |
| ☐ 331 Mickey Mahler | .07 | .03 | .01 |
| ☐ 332 Gary Alexander | .07 | .03 | .01 |
| ☐ 333 Chet Lemon | .25 | .10 | .02 |
| ☐ 334 Craig Swan | .07 | .03 | .01 |
| ☐ 335 Chris Chambliss | .15 | .06 | .01 |
| ☐ 336 Bobby Thompson | .07 | .03 | .01 |
| ☐ 337 John Montague | .07 | .03 | .01 |
| ☐ 338 Vic Harris | .07 | .03 | .01 |
| ☐ 339 Ron Jackson | .07 | .03 | .01 |
| ☐ 340 Jim Palmer | 1.00 | .45 | .10 |
| ☐ 341 Willie Upshaw | 2.00 | .90 | .20 |
| ☐ 342 Dave Roberts | .07 | .03 | .01 |
| ☐ 343 Ed Glynn | .07 | .03 | .01 |
| ☐ 344 Jerry Royster | .07 | .03 | .01 |
| ☐ 345 Tug McGraw | .18 | .08 | .01 |
| ☐ 346 Bill Buckner | .20 | .09 | .02 |
| ☐ 347 Doug Rau | .07 | .03 | .01 |
| ☐ 348 Andre Dawson | 1.25 | .60 | .12 |
| ☐ 349 Jim Wright | .07 | .03 | .01 |
| ☐ 350 Garry Templeton | .25 | .10 | .02 |
| ☐ 351 Wayne Nordhagen | .07 | .03 | .01 |
| ☐ 352 Steve Renko | .07 | .03 | .01 |
| ☐ 353 Checklist 3 | .20 | .03 | .00 |
| ☐ 354 Bill Bonham | .07 | .03 | .01 |
| ☐ 355 Lee Mazzilli | .15 | .06 | .01 |
| ☐ 356 Giants Team/Mgr. | .25 | .05 | .01 |
|  Joe Altobelli |  |  |  |
| ☐ 357 Jerry Augustine | .07 | .03 | .01 |
| ☐ 358 Alan Trammell | 1.50 | .70 | .15 |
| ☐ 359 Dan Spillner DP | .07 | .03 | .01 |
| ☐ 360 Amos Otis | .15 | .06 | .01 |
| ☐ 361 Tom Dixon | .07 | .03 | .01 |
| ☐ 362 Mike Cubbage | .07 | .03 | .01 |
| ☐ 363 Craig Skok | .07 | .03 | .01 |
| ☐ 364 Gene Richards | .07 | .03 | .01 |
| ☐ 365 Sparky Lyle | .15 | .06 | .01 |
| ☐ 366 Juan Bernhardt | .07 | .03 | .01 |
| ☐ 367 Dave Skaggs | .07 | .03 | .01 |
| ☐ 368 Don Aase | .10 | .04 | .01 |
| ☐ 369 A Bump Wills ERR | 2.50 | 1.15 | .25 |
|  (Blue Jays) |  |  |  |
| ☐ 369 B Bump Wills COR | 3.75 | 1.75 | .37 |
|  (Rangers) |  |  |  |
| ☐ 370 Dave Kingman | .40 | .18 | .04 |
| ☐ 371 Jeff Holly | .07 | .03 | .01 |
| ☐ 372 Lamar Johnson | .07 | .03 | .01 |

| | MINT | VG-E | F-G |
|---|---|---|---|
| ☐ 373 Lance Rautzhan | .07 | .03 | .01 |
| ☐ 374 Ed Herrmann | .07 | .03 | .01 |
| ☐ 375 Bill Campbell | .10 | .04 | .01 |
| ☐ 376 Gorman Thomas | .25 | .10 | .02 |
| ☐ 377 Paul Moskau | .07 | .03 | .01 |
| ☐ 378 Rob Picciolo DP | .03 | .01 | .00 |
| ☐ 379 Dale Murray | .07 | .03 | .01 |
| ☐ 380 John Mayberry | .10 | .04 | .01 |
| ☐ 381 Astros Team/Mgr. | .25 | .05 | .01 |
| Bill Virdon | | | |
| ☐ 382 Jerry Martin | .07 | .03 | .01 |
| ☐ 383 Phil Garner | .10 | .04 | .01 |
| ☐ 384 Tommy Boggs | .07 | .03 | .01 |
| ☐ 385 Dan Ford | .10 | .04 | .01 |
| ☐ 386 Francisco Barrios | .07 | .03 | .01 |
| ☐ 387 Gary Thomasson | .07 | .03 | .01 |
| ☐ 388 Jack Billingham | .07 | .03 | .01 |
| ☐ 389 Joe Zdeb | .07 | .03 | .01 |
| ☐ 390 Rollie Fingers | .35 | .15 | .03 |
| ☐ 391 Al Oliver | .30 | .12 | .03 |
| ☐ 392 Doug Ault | .07 | .03 | .01 |
| ☐ 393 Scott McGregor | .15 | .06 | .01 |
| ☐ 394 Randy Stein | .07 | .03 | .01 |
| ☐ 395 Dave Cash | .07 | .03 | .01 |
| ☐ 396 Bill Plummer | .07 | .03 | .01 |
| ☐ 397 Sergio Ferrer | .07 | .03 | .01 |
| ☐ 398 Ivan DeJesus | .07 | .03 | .01 |
| ☐ 399 David Clyde | .07 | .03 | .01 |
| ☐ 400 Jim Rice | 1.75 | .85 | .17 |
| ☐ 401 Ray Knight | .15 | .06 | .01 |
| ☐ 402 Paul Hartzell | .07 | .03 | .01 |
| ☐ 403 Tim Foli | .07 | .03 | .01 |
| ☐ 404 White Sox Team/Mgr. | .25 | .05 | .01 |
| Don Kessinger | | | |
| ☐ 405 Butch Wynegar DP | .07 | .03 | .01 |
| ☐ 406 Joe Wallis DP | .03 | .01 | .00 |
| ☐ 407 Pete Vuckovich | .12 | .05 | .01 |
| ☐ 408 Charlie Moore DP | .03 | .01 | .00 |
| ☐ 409 Willie Wilson | 2.25 | 1.00 | .22 |
| ☐ 410 Darrell Evans | .25 | .10 | .02 |
| ☐ 411 Hits Record: | .40 | .18 | .04 |
| Season: George Sisler | | | |
| Career: Ty Cobb | | | |
| ☐ 412 RBI Record: | .40 | .18 | .04 |
| Season: Hack Wilson | | | |
| Career: Hank Aaron | | | |
| ☐ 413 Home Run Record: | .40 | .18 | .04 |
| Season: Roger Maris | | | |
| Career: Hank Aaron | | | |
| ☐ 414 Batting Record: | .40 | .18 | .04 |
| Season: Rogers Hornsby | | | |
| Career: Ty Cobb | | | |

| | MINT | VG-E | F-G |
|---|---|---|---|
| ☐ 415 Steals Record: | .40 | .18 | .04 |
| Season: Lou Brock | | | |
| Career: Lou Brock | | | |
| ☐ 416 Wins Record: | .20 | .09 | .02 |
| Season: Jack Chesbro | | | |
| Career: Cy Young | | | |
| ☐ 417 Strikeout Record DP: | .10 | .04 | .01 |
| Season: Nolan Ryan | | | |
| Career: Walter Johnson | | | |
| ☐ 418 ERA Record DP: | .07 | .03 | .01 |
| Season: Dutch Leonard | | | |
| Career: Walter Johnson | | | |
| ☐ 419 Dick Ruthven | .07 | .03 | .01 |
| ☐ 420 Ken Griffey | .15 | .06 | .01 |
| ☐ 421 Doug DeCinces | .18 | .08 | .01 |
| ☐ 422 Ruppert Jones | .15 | .06 | .01 |
| ☐ 423 Bob Montgomery | .07 | .03 | .01 |
| ☐ 424 Angels Team/Mgr. | .25 | .05 | .01 |
| Jim Fregosi | | | |
| ☐ 425 Rick Manning | .07 | .03 | .01 |
| ☐ 426 Chris Speier | .07 | .03 | .01 |
| ☐ 427 Andy Replogle | .07 | .03 | .01 |
| ☐ 428 Bobby Valentine | .12 | .05 | .01 |
| ☐ 429 John Urrea DP | .03 | .01 | .00 |
| ☐ 430 Dave Parker | .85 | .40 | .08 |
| ☐ 431 Glenn Borgmann | .07 | .03 | .01 |
| ☐ 432 Dave Heaverlo | .07 | .03 | .01 |
| ☐ 433 Larry Biittner | .07 | .03 | .01 |
| ☐ 434 Ken Clay | .07 | .03 | .01 |
| ☐ 435 Gene Tenace | .07 | .03 | .01 |
| ☐ 436 Hector Cruz | .07 | .03 | .01 |
| ☐ 437 Rick Williams | .07 | .03 | .01 |
| ☐ 438 Horace Speed | .07 | .03 | .01 |
| ☐ 439 Frank White | .20 | .09 | .02 |
| ☐ 440 Rusty Staub | .20 | .09 | .02 |
| ☐ 441 Lee Lacy | .15 | .06 | .01 |
| ☐ 442 Doyle Alexander | .12 | .05 | .01 |
| ☐ 443 Bruce Bochte | .10 | .04 | .01 |
| ☐ 444 Aurelio Lopez | .30 | .12 | .03 |
| ☐ 445 Steve Henderson | .10 | .04 | .01 |
| ☐ 446 Jim Lonborg | .10 | .04 | .01 |
| ☐ 447 Manny Sanguillen | .10 | .04 | .01 |
| ☐ 448 Moose Haas | .10 | .04 | .01 |
| ☐ 449 Bombo Rivera | .07 | .03 | .01 |
| ☐ 450 Dave Concepcion | .20 | .09 | .02 |
| ☐ 451 Royals Team/Mgr. | .25 | .05 | .00 |
| Whitey Herzog | | | |
| ☐ 452 Jerry Morales | .07 | .03 | .01 |
| ☐ 453 Chris Knapp | .07 | .03 | .01 |
| ☐ 454 Len Randle | .07 | .03 | .01 |
| ☐ 455 Bill Lee DP | .07 | .03 | .01 |
| ☐ 456 Chuck Baker | .07 | .03 | .01 |
| ☐ 457 Bruce Sutter | .75 | .35 | .07 |

| | MINT | VG-E | F-G |
|---|---|---|---|
| ☐ 458 Jim Essian | .07 | .03 | .01 |
| ☐ 459 Sid Monge | .07 | .03 | .01 |
| ☐ 460 Graig Nettles | .35 | .15 | .03 |
| ☐ 461 Jim Barr DP | .03 | .01 | .00 |
| ☐ 462 Otto Velez | .07 | .03 | .01 |
| ☐ 463 Steve Comer | .07 | .03 | .01 |
| ☐ 464 Joe Nolan | .07 | .03 | .01 |
| ☐ 465 Reggie Smith | .18 | .08 | .01 |
| ☐ 466 Mark Littell | .07 | .03 | .01 |
| ☐ 467 Don Kessinger DP | .07 | .03 | .01 |
| ☐ 468 Stan Bahnsen DP | .03 | .01 | .00 |
| ☐ 469 Lance Parrish | 1.50 | .70 | .15 |
| ☐ 470 Garry Maddox DP | .07 | .03 | .01 |
| ☐ 471 Joaquin Andujar | .35 | .15 | .03 |
| ☐ 472 Craig Kusick | .07 | .03 | .01 |
| ☐ 473 Dave Roberts | .07 | .03 | .01 |
| ☐ 474 Dick Davis | .07 | .03 | .01 |
| ☐ 475 Dan Driessen | .10 | .04 | .01 |
| ☐ 476 Tom Poquette | .07 | .03 | .01 |
| ☐ 477 Bob Grich | .15 | .06 | .01 |
| ☐ 478 Juan Beniquez | .10 | .04 | .01 |
| ☐ 479 Padres Team/Mgr. | .25 | .05 | .01 |
|     Roger Craig | | | |
| ☐ 480 Fred Lynn | .75 | .35 | .07 |
| ☐ 481 Skip Lockwood | .07 | .03 | .01 |
| ☐ 482 Craig Reynolds | .07 | .03 | .01 |
| ☐ 483 Checklist 4 DP | .10 | .02 | .00 |
| ☐ 484 Rick Waits | .07 | .03 | .01 |
| ☐ 485 Bucky Dent | .15 | .06 | .01 |
| ☐ 486 Bob Knepper | .15 | .06 | .01 |
| ☐ 487 Miguel Dilone | .10 | .04 | .01 |
| ☐ 488 Bob Owchinko | .07 | .03 | .01 |
| ☐ 489 Larry Cox | .07 | .03 | .01 |
| ☐ 490 Al Cowens | .10 | .04 | .01 |
| ☐ 491 Tippy Martinez | .10 | .04 | .01 |
| ☐ 492 Bob Bailor | .07 | .03 | .01 |
| ☐ 493 Larry Christenson | .07 | .03 | .01 |
| ☐ 494 Jerry White | .07 | .03 | .01 |
| ☐ 495 Tony Perez | .30 | .12 | .03 |
| ☐ 496 Barry Bonnell DP | .03 | .01 | .00 |
| ☐ 497 Glenn Abbott | .07 | .03 | .01 |
| ☐ 498 Rich Chiles | .07 | .03 | .01 |
| ☐ 499 Rangers Team/Mgr. | .25 | .05 | .00 |
|     Pat Corrales | | | |
| ☐ 500 Ron Guidry | .80 | .40 | .08 |
| ☐ 501 Junior Kennedy | .07 | .03 | .01 |
| ☐ 502 Steve Braun | .07 | .03 | .01 |
| ☐ 503 Terry Humphrey | .07 | .03 | .01 |
| ☐ 504 Larry McWilliams | .50 | .22 | .05 |
| ☐ 505 Ed Kranepool | .10 | .04 | .01 |
| ☐ 506 John D'Acquisto | .07 | .03 | .01 |
| ☐ 507 Tony Armas | .60 | .28 | .06 |
| ☐ 508 Charlie Hough | .10 | .04 | .01 |

| | MINT | VG-E | F-G |
|---|---|---|---|
| ☐ 509 Mario Mendoza | .07 | .03 | .01 |
| ☐ 510 Ted Simmons | .35 | .15 | .03 |
| ☐ 511 Paul Reuschel DP | .03 | .01 | .00 |
| ☐ 512 Jack Clark | .85 | .40 | .08 |
| ☐ 513 Dave Johnson | .07 | .03 | .01 |
| ☐ 514 Mike Proly | .07 | .03 | .01 |
| ☐ 515 Enos Cabell | .07 | .03 | .01 |
| ☐ 516 Champ Summers DP | .03 | .01 | .00 |
| ☐ 517 Al Bumbry | .07 | .03 | .01 |
| ☐ 518 Jim Umbarger | .07 | .03 | .01 |
| ☐ 519 Ben Oglivie | .15 | .06 | .01 |
| ☐ 520 Gary Carter | 1.50 | .70 | .15 |
| ☐ 521 Sam Ewing | .07 | .03 | .01 |
| ☐ 522 Ken Holtzman | .10 | .04 | .01 |
| ☐ 523 John Milner | .07 | .03 | .01 |
| ☐ 524 Tom Burgmeier | .07 | .03 | .01 |
| ☐ 525 Freddie Patek | .07 | .03 | .01 |
| ☐ 526 Dodgers Team/Mgr. | .30 | .06 | .01 |
|     Tom Lasorda | | | |
| ☐ 527 Lerrin LaGrow | .07 | .03 | .01 |
| ☐ 528 Wayne Gross DP | .03 | .01 | .00 |
| ☐ 529 Brian Asselstine | .07 | .03 | .01 |
| ☐ 530 Frank Tanana | .12 | .05 | .01 |
| ☐ 531 Fernando Gonzalez | .07 | .03 | .01 |
| ☐ 532 Buddy Schultz | .07 | .03 | .01 |
| ☐ 533 Leroy Stanton | .07 | .03 | .01 |
| ☐ 534 Ken Forsch | .07 | .03 | .01 |
| ☐ 535 Ellis Valentine | .10 | .04 | .01 |
| ☐ 536 Jerry Reuss | .15 | .06 | .01 |
| ☐ 537 Tom Veryzer | .07 | .03 | .01 |
| ☐ 538 Mike Ivie DP | .03 | .01 | .00 |
| ☐ 539 John Ellis | .07 | .03 | .01 |
| ☐ 540 Greg Luzinski | .25 | .10 | .02 |
| ☐ 541 Jim Slaton | .07 | .03 | .01 |
| ☐ 542 Rick Bosetti | .07 | .03 | .01 |
| ☐ 543 Kiko Garcia | .07 | .03 | .01 |
| ☐ 544 Fergie Jenkins | .25 | .10 | .02 |
| ☐ 545 John Stearns | .07 | .03 | .01 |
| ☐ 546 Bill Russell | .10 | .04 | .01 |
| ☐ 547 Clint Hurdle | .07 | .03 | .01 |
| ☐ 548 Enrique Romo | .07 | .03 | .01 |
| ☐ 549 Bob Bailey | .07 | .03 | .01 |
| ☐ 550 Sal Bando | .12 | .05 | .01 |
| ☐ 551 Cubs Team/Mgr. | .25 | .05 | .01 |
|     Herman Franks | | | |
| ☐ 552 Jose Morales | .07 | .03 | .01 |
| ☐ 553 Denny Walling | .07 | .03 | .01 |
| ☐ 554 Matt Keough | .10 | .04 | .01 |
| ☐ 555 Biff Pocoroba | .07 | .03 | .01 |
| ☐ 556 Mike Lum | .07 | .03 | .01 |
| ☐ 557 Ken Brett | .10 | .04 | .01 |
| ☐ 558 Jay Johnstone | .10 | .04 | .01 |
| ☐ 559 Greg Pryor | .07 | .03 | .01 |

| | MINT | VG-E | F-G |
|---|---|---|---|
| ☐ 560 John Montefusco | .10 | .04 | .01 |
| ☐ 561 Ed Ott | .07 | .03 | .01 |
| ☐ 562 Dusty Baker | .18 | .08 | .01 |
| ☐ 563 Roy Thomas | .07 | .03 | .01 |
| ☐ 564 Jerry Turner | .07 | .03 | .01 |
| ☐ 565 Rico Carty | .12 | .05 | .01 |
| ☐ 566 Nino Espinosa | .07 | .03 | .01 |
| ☐ 567 Rich Hebner | .07 | .03 | .01 |
| ☐ 568 Carlos Lopez | .07 | .03 | .01 |
| ☐ 569 Bob Sykes | .07 | .03 | .01 |
| ☐ 570 Cesar Cedeno | .18 | .08 | .01 |
| ☐ 571 Darrell Porter | .12 | .05 | .01 |
| ☐ 572 Rod Gilbreath | .07 | .03 | .01 |
| ☐ 573 Jim Kern | .07 | .03 | .01 |
| ☐ 574 Claudell Washington | .15 | .06 | .01 |
| ☐ 575 Luis Tiant | .15 | .06 | .01 |
| ☐ 576 Mike Parrott | .07 | .03 | .01 |
| ☐ 577 Brewers Team/Mgr. | .25 | .05 | .01 |
| George Bamberger | | | |
| ☐ 578 Pete Broberg | .07 | .03 | .01 |
| ☐ 579 Greg Gross | .07 | .03 | .01 |
| ☐ 580 Ron Fairly | .10 | .04 | .01 |
| ☐ 581 Darold Knowles | .07 | .03 | .01 |
| ☐ 582 Paul Blair | .10 | .04 | .01 |
| ☐ 583 Julio Cruz | .10 | .04 | .01 |
| ☐ 584 Jim Rooker | .07 | .03 | .01 |
| ☐ 585 Hal McRae | .15 | .06 | .01 |
| ☐ 586 Bob Horner | 4.00 | 1.85 | .40 |
| ☐ 587 Ken Reitz | .07 | .03 | .01 |
| ☐ 588 Tom Murphy | .07 | .03 | .01 |
| ☐ 589 Terry Whitfield | .07 | .03 | .01 |
| ☐ 590 J.R. Richard | .18 | .08 | .01 |
| ☐ 591 Mike Hargrove | .10 | .04 | .01 |
| ☐ 592 Mike Krukow | .10 | .04 | .01 |
| ☐ 593 Rick Dempsey | .12 | .05 | .01 |
| ☐ 594 Bob Shirley | .07 | .03 | .01 |
| ☐ 595 Phil Niekro | .60 | .28 | .06 |
| ☐ 596 Jim Wohlford | .07 | .03 | .01 |
| ☐ 597 Bob Stanley | .18 | .08 | .01 |
| ☐ 598 Mark Wagner | .07 | .03 | .01 |
| ☐ 599 Jim Spencer | .07 | .03 | .01 |
| ☐ 600 George Foster | .75 | .35 | .07 |
| ☐ 601 Dave LaRoche | .07 | .03 | .01 |
| ☐ 602 Checklist 5 | .20 | .03 | .00 |
| ☐ 603 Rudy May | .07 | .03 | .01 |
| ☐ 604 Jeff Newman | .07 | .03 | .01 |
| ☐ 605 Rick Monday DP | .07 | .03 | .01 |
| ☐ 606 Expos Team/Mgr. | .25 | .05 | .01 |
| Dick Williams | | | |
| ☐ 607 Omar Moreno | .10 | .04 | .01 |
| ☐ 608 Dave McKay | .07 | .03 | .01 |
| ☐ 609 Silvio Martinez | .07 | .03 | .01 |
| ☐ 610 Mike Schmidt | 2.50 | 1.15 | .25 |

| | MINT | VG-E | F-G |
|---|---|---|---|
| ☐ 611 Jim Norris | .07 | .03 | .01 |
| ☐ 612 Rick Honeycutt | .60 | .28 | .06 |
| ☐ 613 Mike Edwards | .07 | .03 | .01 |
| ☐ 614 Willie Hernandez | .60 | .28 | .06 |
| ☐ 615 Ken Singleton | .15 | .06 | .01 |
| ☐ 616 Billy Almon | .07 | .03 | .01 |
| ☐ 617 Terry Puhl | .12 | .05 | .01 |
| ☐ 618 Jerry Remy | .10 | .04 | .01 |
| ☐ 619 Ken Landreaux | .35 | .15 | .03 |
| ☐ 620 Bert Campaneris | .12 | .05 | .01 |
| ☐ 621 Pat Zachry | .07 | .03 | .01 |
| ☐ 622 Dave Collins | .15 | .06 | .01 |
| ☐ 623 Bob McClure | .07 | .03 | .01 |
| ☐ 624 Larry Herndon | .12 | .05 | .01 |
| ☐ 625 Mark Fidrych | .15 | .06 | .01 |
| ☐ 626 Yankees Team/Mgr. | .30 | .06 | .01 |
| Bob Lemon | | | |
| ☐ 627 Gary Serum | .07 | .03 | .01 |
| ☐ 628 Del Unser | .07 | .03 | .01 |
| ☐ 629 Gene Garber | .07 | .03 | .01 |
| ☐ 630 Bake McBride | .10 | .04 | .01 |
| ☐ 631 Jorge Orta | .07 | .03 | .01 |
| ☐ 632 Don Kirkwood | .07 | .03 | .01 |
| ☐ 633 Rob Wilfong DP | .03 | .01 | .00 |
| ☐ 634 Paul Lindblad | .07 | .03 | .01 |
| ☐ 635 Don Baylor | .65 | .30 | .06 |
| ☐ 636 Wayne Garland | .07 | .03 | .01 |
| ☐ 637 Bill Robinson | .07 | .03 | .01 |
| ☐ 638 Al Fitzmorris | .07 | .03 | .01 |
| ☐ 639 Manny Trillo | .10 | .04 | .01 |
| ☐ 640 Eddie Murray | 3.75 | 1.75 | .37 |
| ☐ 641 Bobby Castillo | .07 | .03 | .01 |
| ☐ 642 Wilbur Howard DP | .03 | .01 | .00 |
| ☐ 643 Tom Hausman | .07 | .03 | .01 |
| ☐ 644 Manny Mota | .10 | .04 | .01 |
| ☐ 645 George Scott DP | .07 | .03 | .01 |
| ☐ 646 Rick Sweet | .07 | .03 | .01 |
| ☐ 647 Bob Lacey | .07 | .03 | .01 |
| ☐ 648 Lou Piniella | .20 | .09 | .02 |
| ☐ 649 John Curtis | .07 | .03 | .01 |
| ☐ 650 Pete Rose | 3.50 | 1.65 | .35 |
| ☐ 651 Mike Caldwell | .10 | .04 | .01 |
| ☐ 652 Stan Papi | .07 | .03 | .01 |
| ☐ 653 Warren Brusstar DP | .03 | .01 | .00 |
| ☐ 654 Rick Miller | .07 | .03 | .01 |
| ☐ 655 Jerry Koosman | .15 | .06 | .01 |
| ☐ 656 Hosken Powell | .07 | .03 | .01 |
| ☐ 657 George Medich | .07 | .03 | .01 |
| ☐ 658 Taylor Duncan | .07 | .03 | .01 |
| ☐ 659 Mariners Team/Mgr. | .20 | .05 | .01 |
| Darrell Johnson | | | |
| ☐ 660 Ron LeFlore DP | .07 | .03 | .01 |
| ☐ 661 Bruce Kison | .07 | .03 | .01 |

|  | MINT | VG-E | F-G |
|---|---|---|---|
| ☐ 662 Kevin Bell | .07 | .03 | .01 |
| ☐ 663 Mike Vail | .07 | .03 | .01 |
| ☐ 664 Doug Bird | .07 | .03 | .01 |
| ☐ 665 Lou Brock | 1.00 | .45 | .10 |
| ☐ 666 Rich Dauer | .07 | .03 | .01 |
| ☐ 667 Don Hood | .07 | .03 | .01 |
| ☐ 668 Bill North | .07 | .03 | .01 |
| ☐ 669 Checklist 6 | .20 | .03 | .00 |
| ☐ 670 Jim Hunter DP | .15 | .06 | .01 |
| ☐ 671 Joe Ferguson DP | .03 | .01 | .00 |
| ☐ 672 Ed Halicki | .07 | .03 | .01 |
| ☐ 673 Tom Hutton | .07 | .03 | .01 |
| ☐ 674 Dave Tomlin | .07 | .03 | .01 |
| ☐ 675 Tim McCarver | .12 | .05 | .01 |
| ☐ 676 Johnny Sutton | .07 | .03 | .01 |
| ☐ 677 Larry Parrish | .12 | .05 | .01 |
| ☐ 678 Geoff Zahn | .07 | .03 | .01 |
| ☐ 679 Derrel Thomas | .07 | .03 | .01 |
| ☐ 680 Carlton Fisk | .50 | .22 | .05 |
| ☐ 681 John Henry Johnson | .07 | .03 | .01 |
| ☐ 682 Dave Chalk | .07 | .03 | .01 |
| ☐ 683 Dan Meyer DP | .03 | .01 | .00 |
| ☐ 684 Jamie Easterly DP | .03 | .01 | .00 |
| ☐ 685 Sixto Lezcano | .07 | .03 | .01 |
| ☐ 686 Ron Schueler DP | .03 | .01 | .00 |
| ☐ 687 Rennie Stennett | .07 | .03 | .01 |
| ☐ 688 Mike Willis | .07 | .03 | .01 |
| ☐ 689 Orioles Team/Mgr.: | .25 | .05 | .01 |
| Earl Weaver | | | |
| ☐ 690 Buddy Bell DP | .10 | .04 | .01 |
| ☐ 691 Dock Ellis DP | .03 | .01 | .00 |
| ☐ 692 Mickey Stanley | .07 | .03 | .01 |
| ☐ 693 Dave Rader | .07 | .03 | .01 |
| ☐ 694 Burt Hooton | .07 | .03 | .01 |
| ☐ 695 Keith Hernandez | 1.25 | .60 | .12 |
| ☐ 696 Andy Hassler | .07 | .03 | .01 |
| ☐ 697 Dave Bergman | .07 | .03 | .01 |
| ☐ 698 Bill Stein | .07 | .03 | .01 |
| ☐ 699 Hal Dues | .07 | .03 | .01 |
| ☐ 700 Reggie Jackson DP | .75 | .35 | .07 |
| ☐ 701 Orioles Prospects: | .25 | .10 | .02 |
| Mark Corey | | | |
| John Flinn | | | |
| Sammy Stewart | | | |
| ☐ 702 Red Sox Prospects: | .12 | .05 | .01 |
| Joel Finch | | | |
| Garry Hancock | | | |
| Allen Ripley | | | |
| ☐ 703 Angels Prospects: | .12 | .05 | .01 |
| Jim Anderson | | | |
| Dave Frost | | | |
| Bob Slater | | | |

|  | MINT | VG-E | F-G |
|---|---|---|---|
| ☐ 704 White Sox Prospects: | .12 | .05 | .01 |
| Ross Baumgarten | | | |
| Mike Colbern | | | |
| Mike Squires | | | |
| ☐ 705 Indians Prospects: | .65 | .30 | .06 |
| Alfredo Griffin | | | |
| Tim Norrid | | | |
| Dave Oliver | | | |
| ☐ 706 Tigers Prospects: | .12 | .05 | .01 |
| Dave Stegman | | | |
| Dave Tobik | | | |
| Kip Young | | | |
| ☐ 707 Royals Prospects: | .12 | .05 | .01 |
| Randy Bass | | | |
| Jim Gaudet | | | |
| Randy McGilberry | | | |
| ☐ 708 Brewers Prospects: | .18 | .08 | .01 |
| Kevin Bass | | | |
| Eddie Romero | | | |
| Ned Yost | | | |
| ☐ 709 Twins Prospects: | .12 | .05 | .01 |
| Sam Perlozzo | | | |
| Rick Sofield | | | |
| Kevin Stanfield | | | |
| ☐ 710 Yankees Prospects: | .25 | .10 | .02 |
| Brian Doyle | | | |
| Mike Heath | | | |
| Dave Rajsich | | | |
| ☐ 711 A's Prospects: | .80 | .30 | .01 |
| Dwayne Murphy | | | |
| Bruce Robinson | | | |
| Alan Wirth | | | |
| ☐ 712 Mariners Prospects: | .12 | .05 | .01 |
| Bud Anderson | | | |
| Greg Biercevicz | | | |
| Byron McLaughlin | | | |
| ☐ 713 Rangers Prospects: | .40 | .18 | .04 |
| Danny Darwin | | | |
| Pat Putnam | | | |
| Billy Sample | | | |
| ☐ 714 Blue Jays Prospects: | .12 | .05 | .01 |
| Victor Cruz | | | |
| Pat Kelly | | | |
| Ernie Whitt | | | |
| ☐ 715 Braves Prospects: | .50 | .22 | .05 |
| Bruce Benedict | | | |
| Glenn Hubbard | | | |
| Larry Whisenton | | | |
| ☐ 716 Cubs Prospects: | .12 | .05 | .01 |
| Dave Geisel | | | |
| Karl Pagel | | | |
| Scot Thompson | | | |

## 1980 TOPPS

| | MINT | VG-E | F-G |
|---|---|---|---|
| ☐ 717 Reds Prospects: | .40 | .18 | .04 |
| Mike LaCoss | | | |
| Ron Oester | | | |
| Harry Spilman | | | |
| ☐ 718 Astros Prospects: | .12 | .05 | .01 |
| Bruce Bochy | | | |
| Mike Fischlin | | | |
| Don Pisker | | | |
| ☐ 719 Dodgers Prospects: | 5.00 | 2.35 | .50 |
| Pedro Guerrero | | | |
| Rudy Law | | | |
| Joe Simpson | | | |
| ☐ 720 Expos Prospects: | .25 | .10 | .02 |
| Jerry Fry | | | |
| Jerry Pirtle | | | |
| Scott Sanderson | | | |
| ☐ 721 Mets Prospects: | .15 | .06 | .01 |
| Juan Berenguer | | | |
| Dwight Bernard | | | |
| Dan Norman | | | |
| ☐ 722 Phillies Prospects: | 1.25 | .60 | .12 |
| Jim Morrison | | | |
| Lonnie Smith | | | |
| Jim Wright | | | |
| ☐ 723 Pirates Prospects: | .30 | .12 | .03 |
| Dale Berra | | | |
| Eugenio Cotes | | | |
| Ben Wiltbank | | | |
| ☐ 724 Cardinals Prospects: | 1.25 | .60 | .12 |
| Tom Bruno | | | |
| George Frazier | | | |
| Terry Kennedy | | | |
| ☐ 725 Padres Prospects: | .12 | .05 | .01 |
| Jim Beswick | | | |
| Steve Mura | | | |
| Broderick Perkins | | | |
| ☐ 726 Giants Prospects: | .12 | .05 | .01 |
| Greg Johnston | | | |
| Joe Strain | | | |
| John Tamargo | | | |

*The cards in this 726 card set measure 2½" by 3½". In 1980 Topps released another set of the same size and number of cards as the previous two years. The player's name appears over the picture and his position and team are found in pennant design. Every card carries a facsimile autograph. Cards 1–6 show Highlights (HL) of the 1979 season and cards 659 through 686 feature American and National League rookie "Prospects".*
Complete Set: M-57.00; VG-E-25.00; F-G-5.00

| | | MINT | VG-E | F-G |
|---|---|---|---|---|
| | Common Player (1–726) | .06 | .02 | .00 |
| ☐ 1 | HL: Brock and Yaz, Enter 3000 hit circle | .75 | .15 | .03 |
| ☐ 2 | HL: Willie McCovey, 512th homer sets new mark for NL lefties | .40 | .18 | .04 |
| ☐ 3 | HL: Manny Mota, All-time pinch-hits 145 | .12 | .05 | .01 |
| ☐ 4 | HL: Pete Rose, Career Record 10th season with 200 or more hits | 1.00 | .45 | .10 |
| ☐ 5 | HL: Garry Templeton, 1st with 100 hits from each side of plate | .20 | .09 | .02 |
| ☐ 6 | HL: Del Unser, 3rd consecutive pinchhomer sets new ML standard | .10 | .04 | .01 |
| ☐ 7 | Mike Lum | .06 | .02 | .00 |
| ☐ 8 | Craig Swan | .06 | .02 | .00 |
| ☐ 9 | Steve Braun | .06 | .02 | .00 |
| ☐ 10 | Denny Martinez | .06 | .02 | .00 |

|  | MINT | VG-E | F-G |
|---|---|---|---|
| ☐ 11 Jimmy Sexton | .06 | .02 | .00 |
| ☐ 12 John Curtis DP | .03 | .01 | .00 |
| ☐ 13 Ron Pruitt | .06 | .02 | .00 |
| ☐ 14 Dave Cash | .06 | .02 | .00 |
| ☐ 15 Bill Campbell | .06 | .02 | .00 |
| ☐ 16 Jerry Narron | .06 | .02 | .00 |
| ☐ 17 Bruce Sutter | .50 | .22 | .05 |
| ☐ 18 Ron Jackson | .06 | .02 | .00 |
| ☐ 19 Balor Moore | .06 | .02 | .00 |
| ☐ 20 Dan Ford | .06 | .02 | .00 |
| ☐ 21 Manny Sarmiento | .06 | .02 | .00 |
| ☐ 22 Pat Putnam | .06 | .02 | .00 |
| ☐ 23 Derrel Thomas | .06 | .02 | .00 |
| ☐ 24 Jim Slaton | .06 | .02 | .00 |
| ☐ 25 Lee Mazzilli | .12 | .05 | .01 |
| ☐ 26 Marty Pattin | .06 | .02 | .00 |
| ☐ 27 Del Unser | .06 | .02 | .00 |
| ☐ 28 Bruce Kison | .06 | .02 | .00 |
| ☐ 29 Mark Wagner | .06 | .02 | .00 |
| ☐ 30 Vida Blue | .15 | .06 | .01 |
| ☐ 31 Jay Johnstone | .09 | .04 | .01 |
| ☐ 32 Julio Cruz DP | .06 | .02 | .00 |
| ☐ 33 Tony Scott | .06 | .02 | .00 |
| ☐ 34 Jeff Newman DP | .03 | .01 | .00 |
| ☐ 35 Luis Tiant | .12 | .05 | .01 |
| ☐ 36 Rusty Torres | .06 | .02 | .00 |
| ☐ 37 Kiko Garcia | .06 | .02 | .00 |
| ☐ 38 Dan Spillner DP | .03 | .01 | .00 |
| ☐ 39 Rowland Office | .06 | .02 | .00 |
| ☐ 40 Carlton Fisk | .35 | .15 | .03 |
| ☐ 41 Rangers Team/Mgr. | .20 | .04 | .01 |
| Pat Corrales | | | |
| ☐ 42 David Palmer | .25 | .10 | .02 |
| ☐ 43 Bombo Rivera | .06 | .02 | .00 |
| ☐ 44 Bill Fahey | .06 | .02 | .00 |
| ☐ 45 Frank White | .12 | .05 | .01 |
| ☐ 46 Rico Carty | .09 | .04 | .01 |
| ☐ 47 Bill Bonham DP | .03 | .01 | .00 |
| ☐ 48 Rick Miller | .06 | .02 | .00 |
| ☐ 49 Mario Guerrero | .06 | .02 | .00 |
| ☐ 50 J.R. Richard | .15 | .06 | .01 |
| ☐ 51 Joe Ferguson DP | .03 | .01 | .00 |
| ☐ 52 Warren Brusstar | .06 | .02 | .00 |
| ☐ 53 Ben Oglivie | .12 | .05 | .01 |
| ☐ 54 Dennis Lamp | .06 | .02 | .00 |
| ☐ 55 Bill Madlock | .35 | .15 | .03 |
| ☐ 56 Bobby Valentine | .09 | .04 | .01 |
| ☐ 57 Pete Vuckovich | .12 | .05 | .01 |
| ☐ 58 Doug Flynn | .06 | .02 | .00 |
| ☐ 59 Eddy Putman | .06 | .02 | .00 |
| ☐ 60 Bucky Dent | .12 | .05 | .01 |
| ☐ 61 Gary Serum | .06 | .02 | .00 |

|  | MINT | VG-E | F-G |
|---|---|---|---|
| ☐ 62 Mike Ivie | .06 | .02 | .00 |
| ☐ 63 Bob Stanley | .12 | .05 | .01 |
| ☐ 64 Joe Nolan | .06 | .02 | .00 |
| ☐ 65 Al Bumbry | .06 | .02 | .00 |
| ☐ 66 Royals Team/Mgr. | .20 | .04 | .01 |
| Jim Frey | | | |
| ☐ 67 Doyle Alexander | .09 | .04 | .01 |
| ☐ 68 Larry Harlow | .06 | .02 | .00 |
| ☐ 69 Rick Williams | .06 | .02 | .00 |
| ☐ 70 Gary Carter | 1.25 | .60 | .12 |
| ☐ 71 John Milner DP | .03 | .01 | .00 |
| ☐ 72 Fred Howard DP | .03 | .01 | .00 |
| ☐ 73 Dave Collins | .09 | .04 | .01 |
| ☐ 74 Sid Monge | .06 | .02 | .00 |
| ☐ 75 Bill Russell | .09 | .04 | .01 |
| ☐ 76 John Stearns | .06 | .02 | .00 |
| ☐ 77 Dave Stieb | 3.50 | 1.65 | .35 |
| ☐ 78 Ruppert Jones | .09 | .04 | .01 |
| ☐ 79 Bob Owchinko | .06 | .02 | .00 |
| ☐ 80 Ron LeFlore | .09 | .04 | .01 |
| ☐ 81 Ted Sizemore | .06 | .02 | .00 |
| ☐ 82 Astros Team/Mgr. | .20 | .04 | .01 |
| Bill Virdon | | | |
| ☐ 83 Steve Trout | .50 | .22 | .05 |
| ☐ 84 Gary Lavelle | .09 | .04 | .01 |
| ☐ 85 Ted Simmons | .35 | .15 | .03 |
| ☐ 86 Dave Hamilton | .06 | .02 | .00 |
| ☐ 87 Pepe Frias | .06 | .02 | .00 |
| ☐ 88 Ken Landreaux | .09 | .04 | .01 |
| ☐ 89 Don Hood | .06 | .02 | .00 |
| ☐ 90 Manny Trillo | .09 | .04 | .01 |
| ☐ 91 Rick Dempsey | .09 | .04 | .01 |
| ☐ 92 Rick Rhoden | .09 | .04 | .01 |
| ☐ 93 Dave Roberts DP | .03 | .01 | .00 |
| ☐ 94 Neil Allen | .30 | .12 | .03 |
| ☐ 95 Cecil Cooper | .35 | .15 | .03 |
| ☐ 96 A's Team/Mgr. | .20 | .04 | .01 |
| Jim Marshall | | | |
| ☐ 97 Bill Lee | .09 | .04 | .01 |
| ☐ 98 Jerry Terrell | .06 | .02 | .00 |
| ☐ 99 Victor Cruz | .06 | .02 | .00 |
| ☐ 100 Johnny Bench | 1.00 | .45 | .10 |
| ☐ 101 Aurelio Lopez | .06 | .02 | .00 |
| ☐ 102 Rich Dauer | .06 | .02 | .00 |
| ☐ 103 Bill Caudill | .60 | .28 | .06 |
| ☐ 104 Manny Mota | .09 | .04 | .01 |
| ☐ 105 Frank Tanana | .12 | .05 | .01 |
| ☐ 106 Jeff Leonard | .65 | .30 | .06 |
| ☐ 107 Francisco Barrios | .06 | .02 | .00 |
| ☐ 108 Bob Horner | .90 | .40 | .09 |
| ☐ 109 Bill Travers | .06 | .02 | .00 |
| ☐ 110 Fred Lynn DP | .25 | .10 | .02 |

|  | MINT | VG-E | F-G |
|---|---|---|---|
| ☐ 111 Bob Knepper | .12 | .05 | .01 |
| ☐ 112 White Sox Team/Mgr. Tony LaRussa | .20 | .04 | .01 |
| ☐ 113 Geoff Zahn | .06 | .02 | .00 |
| ☐ 114 Juan Beniquez | .09 | .04 | .01 |
| ☐ 115 Sparky Lyle | .15 | .06 | .01 |
| ☐ 116 Larry Cox | .06 | .02 | .00 |
| ☐ 117 Dock Ellis | .06 | .02 | .00 |
| ☐ 118 Phil Garner | .09 | .04 | .01 |
| ☐ 119 Sammy Stewart | .09 | .04 | .01 |
| ☐ 120 Greg Luzinski | .20 | .09 | .02 |
| ☐ 121 Checklist 1 | .18 | .03 | .00 |
| ☐ 122 Dave Roselio DP | .03 | .01 | .00 |
| ☐ 123 Lynn Jones | .06 | .02 | .00 |
| ☐ 124 Dave Lemanczyk | .06 | .02 | .00 |
| ☐ 125 Tony Perez | .25 | .10 | .02 |
| ☐ 126 Dave Tomlin | .06 | .02 | .00 |
| ☐ 127 Gary Thomasson | .06 | .02 | .00 |
| ☐ 128 Tom Burgmeier | .06 | .02 | .00 |
| ☐ 129 Craig Reynolds | .06 | .02 | .00 |
| ☐ 130 Amos Otis | .12 | .05 | .01 |
| ☐ 131 Paul Mitchell | .06 | .02 | .00 |
| ☐ 132 Biff Pocoroba | .06 | .02 | .00 |
| ☐ 133 Jerry Turner | .06 | .02 | .00 |
| ☐ 134 Matt Keough | .06 | .02 | .00 |
| ☐ 135 Bill Buckner | .20 | .09 | .02 |
| ☐ 136 Dick Ruthven | .06 | .02 | .00 |
| ☐ 137 John Castino | .18 | .08 | .01 |
| ☐ 138 Ross Baumgarten | .06 | .02 | .00 |
| ☐ 139 Dane Iorg | .18 | .08 | .01 |
| ☐ 140 Rich Gossage | .45 | .20 | .04 |
| ☐ 141 Gary Alexander | .06 | .02 | .00 |
| ☐ 142 Phil Huffman | .06 | .02 | .00 |
| ☐ 143 Bruce Bochte DP | .06 | .02 | .00 |
| ☐ 144 Steve Comer | .06 | .02 | .00 |
| ☐ 145 Darrell Evans | .20 | .09 | .02 |
| ☐ 146 Bob Welch | .15 | .06 | .01 |
| ☐ 147 Terry Puhl | .09 | .04 | .01 |
| ☐ 148 Manny Sanguillen | .09 | .04 | .01 |
| ☐ 149 Tom Hume | .06 | .02 | .00 |
| ☐ 150 Jason Thompson | .15 | .06 | .01 |
| ☐ 151 Tom Hausman DP | .03 | .01 | .00 |
| ☐ 152 John Fulgham | .06 | .02 | .00 |
| ☐ 153 Tim Blackwell | .06 | .02 | .00 |
| ☐ 154 Lary Sorensen | .06 | .02 | .00 |
| ☐ 155 Jerry Remy | .09 | .04 | .01 |
| ☐ 156 Tony Brizzolara | .06 | .02 | .00 |
| ☐ 157 Willie Wilson DP | .20 | .09 | .02 |
| ☐ 158 Rob Picciolo DP | .03 | .01 | .00 |
| ☐ 159 Ken Clay | .06 | .02 | .00 |
| ☐ 160 Eddie Murray | 2.75 | 1.25 | .27 |
| ☐ 161 Larry Christenson | .06 | .02 | .00 |
| ☐ 162 Bob Randall | .06 | .02 | .00 |
| ☐ 163 Steve Swisher | .06 | .02 | .00 |
| ☐ 164 Greg Pryor | .06 | .02 | .00 |
| ☐ 165 Omar Moreno | .09 | .04 | .01 |
| ☐ 166 Glenn Abbott | .06 | .02 | .00 |
| ☐ 167 Jack Clark | .60 | .28 | .06 |
| ☐ 168 Rick Waits | .06 | .02 | .00 |
| ☐ 169 Luis Gomez | .06 | .02 | .00 |
| ☐ 170 Burt Hooton | .06 | .02 | .00 |
| ☐ 171 Fernando Gonzalez | .06 | .02 | .00 |
| ☐ 172 Ron Hodges | .06 | .02 | .00 |
| ☐ 173 John Henry Johnson | .06 | .02 | .00 |
| ☐ 174 Ray Knight | .09 | .04 | .01 |
| ☐ 175 Rick Reuschel | .12 | .05 | .01 |
| ☐ 176 Champ Summers | .06 | .02 | .00 |
| ☐ 177 Dave Heaverlo | .06 | .02 | .00 |
| ☐ 178 Tim McCarver | .12 | .05 | .01 |
| ☐ 179 Ron Davis | .30 | .12 | .03 |
| ☐ 180 Warren Cromartie | .06 | .02 | .00 |
| ☐ 181 Moose Haas | .09 | .04 | .01 |
| ☐ 182 Ken Reitz | .06 | .02 | .00 |
| ☐ 183 Jim Anderson DP | .03 | .01 | .00 |
| ☐ 184 Steve Renko DP | .03 | .01 | .00 |
| ☐ 185 Hal McRae | .12 | .05 | .01 |
| ☐ 186 Junior Moore | .06 | .02 | .00 |
| ☐ 187 Alan Ashby | .06 | .02 | .00 |
| ☐ 188 Terry Crowley | .06 | .02 | .00 |
| ☐ 189 Kevin Kobel | .06 | .02 | .00 |
| ☐ 190 Buddy Bell | .18 | .08 | .01 |
| ☐ 191 Ted Martinez | .06 | .02 | .00 |
| ☐ 192 Braves Team/Mgr. Bobby Cox | .20 | .04 | .01 |
| ☐ 193 Dave Goltz | .09 | .04 | .01 |
| ☐ 194 Mike Easler | .20 | .09 | .02 |
| ☐ 195 John Montefusco | .09 | .04 | .01 |
| ☐ 196 Lance Parrish | .90 | .40 | .09 |
| ☐ 197 Byron McLaughlin | .06 | .02 | .00 |
| ☐ 198 Dell Alston DP | .03 | .01 | .00 |
| ☐ 199 Mike LaCoss | .06 | .02 | .00 |
| ☐ 200 Jim Rice | 1.50 | .70 | .15 |
| ☐ 201 Batting Leaders: Keith Hernandez Fred Lynn | .20 | .09 | .02 |
| ☐ 202 Home Run Leaders: Dave Kingman Gorman Thomas | .15 | .06 | .01 |
| ☐ 203 RBI Leaders: Dave Winfield Don Baylor | .20 | .09 | .02 |
| ☐ 204 Stolen Base Leaders: Omar Moreno Willie Wilson | .12 | .05 | .01 |

| | MINT | VG-E | F-G |
|---|---|---|---|
| ☐ 205 Victory Leaders: | .20 | .09 | .02 |
| Joe Niekro | | | |
| Phil Niekro | | | |
| Mike Flanagan | | | |
| ☐ 206 Strikeout Leaders: | .20 | .09 | .02 |
| J.R. Richard | | | |
| Nolan Ryan | | | |
| ☐ 207 ERA Leaders: | .15 | .06 | .01 |
| J.R. Richard | | | |
| Ron Guidry | | | |
| ☐ 208 Wayne Cage | .06 | .02 | .00 |
| ☐ 209 Von Joshua | .06 | .02 | .00 |
| ☐ 210 Steve Carlton | 1.50 | .70 | .15 |
| ☐ 211 Dave Skaggs DP | .03 | .01 | .00 |
| ☐ 212 Dave Roberts | .06 | .02 | .00 |
| ☐ 213 Mike Jorgensen DP | .03 | .01 | .00 |
| ☐ 214 Angels Team/Mgr.: | .20 | .04 | .01 |
| Jim Fregosi | | | |
| ☐ 215 Sixto Lezcano | .06 | .02 | .00 |
| ☐ 216 Phil Mankowski | .06 | .02 | .00 |
| ☐ 217 Ed Halicki | .06 | .02 | .00 |
| ☐ 218 Jose Morales | .06 | .02 | .00 |
| ☐ 219 Steve Mingori | .06 | .02 | .00 |
| ☐ 220 Dave Concepcion | .20 | .09 | .02 |
| ☐ 221 Joe Cannon | .06 | .02 | .00 |
| ☐ 222 Ron Hassey | .09 | .04 | .01 |
| ☐ 223 Bob Sykes | .06 | .02 | .00 |
| ☐ 224 Willie Montanez | .06 | .02 | .00 |
| ☐ 225 Lou Piniella | .18 | .08 | .01 |
| ☐ 226 Bill Stein | .06 | .02 | .00 |
| ☐ 227 Len Barker | .15 | .06 | .01 |
| ☐ 228 Johnny Oates | .06 | .02 | .00 |
| ☐ 229 Jim Bibby | .09 | .04 | .01 |
| ☐ 230 Dave Winfield | 1.25 | .60 | .12 |
| ☐ 231 Steve McCatty | .06 | .02 | .00 |
| ☐ 232 Alan Trammell | .90 | .40 | .09 |
| ☐ 233 LaRue Washington | .06 | .02 | .00 |
| ☐ 234 Vern Ruhle | .06 | .02 | .00 |
| ☐ 235 Andre Dawson | .90 | .40 | .09 |
| ☐ 236 Marc Hill | .06 | .02 | .00 |
| ☐ 237 Scott McGregor | .12 | .05 | .01 |
| ☐ 238 Rob Wilfong | .06 | .02 | .00 |
| ☐ 239 Don Aase | .06 | .02 | .00 |
| ☐ 240 Dave Kingman | .35 | .15 | .03 |
| ☐ 241 Checklist 2 | .18 | .03 | .00 |
| ☐ 242 Lamar Johnson | .06 | .02 | .00 |
| ☐ 243 Jerry Augustine | .06 | .02 | .00 |
| ☐ 244 Cardinals Team/Mgr.: | .20 | .05 | .01 |
| Ken Boyer | | | |
| ☐ 245 Phil Niekro | .45 | .20 | .04 |
| ☐ 246 Tim Foli DP | .03 | .01 | .00 |
| ☐ 247 Frank Riccelli | .06 | .02 | .00 |
| ☐ 248 Jamie Quirk | .06 | .02 | .00 |

| | MINT | VG-E | F-G |
|---|---|---|---|
| ☐ 249 Jim Clancy | .06 | .02 | .00 |
| ☐ 250 Jim Kaat | .20 | .09 | .02 |
| ☐ 251 Kip Young | .06 | .02 | .00 |
| ☐ 252 Ted Cox | .06 | .02 | .00 |
| ☐ 253 John Montague | .06 | .02 | .00 |
| ☐ 254 Paul Dade DP | .03 | .01 | .00 |
| ☐ 255 Dusty Baker DP | .06 | .02 | .00 |
| ☐ 256 Roger Erickson | .06 | .02 | .00 |
| ☐ 257 Larry Herndon | .09 | .04 | .01 |
| ☐ 258 Paul Moskau | .06 | .02 | .00 |
| ☐ 259 Mets Team/Mgr.: | .25 | .05 | .01 |
| Joe Torre | | | |
| ☐ 260 Al Oliver | .30 | .12 | .03 |
| ☐ 261 Dave Chalk | .06 | .02 | .00 |
| ☐ 262 Benny Ayala | .06 | .02 | .00 |
| ☐ 263 Dave LaRoche DP | .03 | .01 | .00 |
| ☐ 264 Bill Robinson | .06 | .02 | .00 |
| ☐ 265 Robin Yount | 1.00 | .45 | .10 |
| ☐ 266 Bernie Carbo | .06 | .02 | .00 |
| ☐ 267 Dan Schatzeder | .06 | .02 | .00 |
| ☐ 268 Rafael Landestoy | .06 | .02 | .00 |
| ☐ 269 Dave Tobik | .06 | .02 | .00 |
| ☐ 270 Mike Schmidt DP | .85 | .40 | .08 |
| ☐ 271 Dick Drago DP | .03 | .01 | .00 |
| ☐ 272 Ralph Garr | .09 | .04 | .01 |
| ☐ 273 Eduardo Rodriguez | .06 | .02 | .00 |
| ☐ 274 Dale Murphy | 3.00 | 1.40 | .30 |
| ☐ 275 Jerry Koosman | .15 | .06 | .01 |
| ☐ 276 Tom Veryzer | .06 | .02 | .00 |
| ☐ 277 Rick Bosetti | .06 | .02 | .00 |
| ☐ 278 Jim Spencer | .06 | .02 | .00 |
| ☐ 279 Rob Andrews | .06 | .02 | .00 |
| ☐ 280 Gaylord Perry | .45 | .20 | .04 |
| ☐ 281 Paul Blair | .06 | .02 | .00 |
| ☐ 282 Mariners Team/Mgr.: | .18 | .04 | .01 |
| Darrell Johnson | | | |
| ☐ 283 John Ellis | .06 | .02 | .00 |
| ☐ 284 Larry Murray DP | .03 | .01 | .00 |
| ☐ 285 Don Baylor | .30 | .12 | .03 |
| ☐ 286 Darold Knowles DP | .03 | .01 | .00 |
| ☐ 287 John Lowenstein | .06 | .02 | .00 |
| ☐ 288 Dave Rozema | .06 | .02 | .00 |
| ☐ 289 Bruce Bochy | .06 | .02 | .00 |
| ☐ 290 Steve Garvey | 1.25 | .60 | .12 |
| ☐ 291 Randy Scarberry | .06 | .02 | .00 |
| ☐ 292 Dale Berra | .09 | .04 | .01 |
| ☐ 293 Elias Sosa | .06 | .02 | .00 |
| ☐ 294 Charlie Spikes | .06 | .02 | .00 |
| ☐ 295 Larry Gura | .09 | .04 | .01 |
| ☐ 296 Dave Rader | .06 | .02 | .00 |
| ☐ 297 Tim Johnson | .06 | .02 | .00 |
| ☐ 298 Ken Holtzman | .09 | .04 | .01 |
| ☐ 299 Steve Henderson | .06 | .02 | .00 |

| | MINT | VG-E | F-G | | MINT | VG-E | F-G |
|---|---|---|---|---|---|---|---|
| 300 Ron Guidry | .65 | .30 | .06 | 351 Bob Davis | .06 | .02 | .00 |
| 301 Mike Edwards | .06 | .02 | .00 | 352 Dan Briggs | .06 | .02 | .00 |
| 302 Dodgers Team/Mgr. | .25 | .05 | .01 | 353 Andy Hassler | .06 | .02 | .00 |
| Tom Lasorda | | | | 354 Rick Auerbach | .06 | .02 | .00 |
| 303 Bill Castro | .06 | .02 | .00 | 355 Gary Matthews | .18 | .08 | .01 |
| 304 Butch Wynegar | .09 | .04 | .01 | 356 Padres Team/Mgr. | .20 | .04 | .01 |
| 305 Randy Jones | .09 | .04 | .01 | Jerry Coleman | | | |
| 306 Denny Walling | .06 | .02 | .00 | 357 Bob McClure | .06 | .02 | .00 |
| 307 Rick Honeycutt | .12 | .05 | .01 | 358 Lou Whitaker | .80 | .40 | .08 |
| 308 Mike Hargrove | .09 | .04 | .01 | 359 Randy Moffitt | .06 | .02 | .00 |
| 309 Larry McWilliams | .12 | .05 | .01 | 360 Darrell Porter DP | .06 | .02 | .00 |
| 310 Dave Parker | .65 | .30 | .06 | 361 Wayne Garland | .06 | .02 | .00 |
| 311 Roger Metzger | .06 | .02 | .00 | 362 Danny Goodwin | .06 | .02 | .00 |
| 312 Mike Barlow | .06 | .02 | .00 | 363 Wayne Gross | .06 | .02 | .00 |
| 313 Johnny Grubb | .06 | .02 | .00 | 364 Ray Burris | .06 | .02 | .00 |
| 314 Tim Stoddard | .20 | .09 | .02 | 365 Bobby Murcer | .18 | .08 | .01 |
| 315 Steve Kemp | .18 | .08 | .01 | 366 Rob Dressler | .06 | .02 | .00 |
| 316 Bob Lacey | .06 | .02 | .00 | 367 Billy Smith | .06 | .02 | .00 |
| 317 Mike Anderson DP | .03 | .01 | .00 | 368 Willie Aikens | .20 | .09 | .02 |
| 318 Jerry Reuss | .12 | .05 | .01 | 369 Jim Kern | .06 | .02 | .00 |
| 319 Chris Speier | .06 | .02 | .00 | 370 Cesar Cedeno | .15 | .06 | .01 |
| 320 Dennis Eckersley | .09 | .04 | .01 | 371 Jack Morris | .75 | .35 | .07 |
| 321 Keith Hernandez | 1.00 | .45 | .10 | 372 Joel Youngblood | .06 | .02 | .00 |
| 322 Claudell Washington | .12 | .05 | .01 | 373 Dan Petry DP | 2.00 | .90 | .20 |
| 323 Mick Kelleher | .06 | .02 | .00 | 374 Jim Gantner | .09 | .04 | .01 |
| 324 Tom Underwood | .06 | .02 | .00 | 375 Ross Grimsley | .06 | .02 | .00 |
| 325 Dan Driessen | .09 | .04 | .01 | 376 Gary Allenson | .12 | .05 | .01 |
| 326 Bo McLaughlin | .06 | .02 | .00 | 377 Junior Kennedy | .06 | .02 | .00 |
| 327 Ray Fosse DP | .03 | .01 | .00 | 378 Jerry Mumphrey | .09 | .04 | .01 |
| 328 Twins Team/Manager | .20 | .04 | .01 | 379 Kevin Bell | .06 | .02 | .00 |
| Gene Mauch | | | | 380 Garry Maddox | .09 | .04 | .01 |
| 329 Bert Roberge | .06 | .02 | .00 | 381 Cubs Team/Mgr. | .20 | .04 | .01 |
| 330 Al Cowens | .09 | .04 | .01 | Preston Gomez | | | |
| 331 Rich Hebner | .06 | .02 | .00 | 382 Dave Freisleben | .06 | .02 | .00 |
| 332 Enrique Romo | .06 | .02 | .00 | 383 Ed Ott | .06 | .02 | .00 |
| 333 Jim Norris DP | .03 | .01 | .00 | 384 Joey McLaughlin | .06 | .02 | .00 |
| 334 Jim Beattie | .06 | .02 | .00 | 385 Enos Cabell | .06 | .02 | .00 |
| 335 Willie McCovey | .75 | .35 | .07 | 386 Darrell Jackson | .06 | .02 | .00 |
| 336 George Medich | .06 | .02 | .00 | 387 Fred Stanley | .06 | .02 | .00 |
| 337 Carney Lansford | .35 | .15 | .03 | 388 Mike Paxton | .06 | .02 | .00 |
| 338 Johnny Wockenfuss | .06 | .02 | .00 | 389 Pete LaCock | .06 | .02 | .00 |
| 339 John D'Acquisto | .06 | .02 | .00 | 390 Fergie Jenkins | .25 | .10 | .02 |
| 340 Ken Singleton | .15 | .06 | .01 | 391 Tony Armas DP | .12 | .05 | .01 |
| 341 Jim Essian | .06 | .02 | .00 | 392 Milt Wilcox | .09 | .04 | .01 |
| 342 Odell Jones | .06 | .02 | .00 | 393 Ozzie Smith | .30 | .12 | .03 |
| 343 Mike Vail | .06 | .02 | .00 | 394 Reggie Cleveland | .06 | .02 | .00 |
| 344 Randy Lerch | .06 | .02 | .00 | 395 Ellis Valentine | .09 | .04 | .01 |
| 345 Larry Parrish | .12 | .05 | .01 | 396 Dan Meyer | .06 | .02 | .00 |
| 346 Buddy Solomon | .06 | .02 | .00 | 397 Roy Thomas DP | .03 | .01 | .00 |
| 347 Harry Chappas | .06 | .02 | .00 | 398 Barry Foote | .06 | .02 | .00 |
| 348 Checklist 3 | .18 | .03 | .00 | 399 Mike Proly DP | .03 | .01 | .00 |
| 349 Jack Brohamer | .06 | .02 | .00 | 400 George Foster | .50 | .22 | .05 |
| 350 George Hendrick | .15 | .06 | .01 | 401 Pete Falcone | .06 | .02 | .00 |

| | MINT | VG-E | F-G | | MINT | VG-E | F-G |
|---|---|---|---|---|---|---|---|
| ☐ 402 Merv Rettenmund | .06 | .02 | .00 | ☐ 452 Steve Dillard | .06 | .02 | .00 |
| ☐ 403 Pete Redfern DP | .03 | .01 | .00 | ☐ 453 Mike Bacsik | .06 | .02 | .00 |
| ☐ 404 Orioles Team/Mgr. | .25 | .05 | .01 | ☐ 454 Tom Donohue | .06 | .02 | .00 |
| Earl Weaver | | | | ☐ 455 Mike Torrez | .09 | .04 | .01 |
| ☐ 405 Dwight Evans | .30 | .12 | .03 | ☐ 456 Frank Taveras | .06 | .02 | .00 |
| ☐ 406 Paul Molitor | .35 | .15 | .03 | ☐ 457 Bert Blyleven | .25 | .10 | .02 |
| ☐ 407 Tony Solaita | .06 | .02 | .00 | ☐ 458 Billy Sample | .06 | .02 | .00 |
| ☐ 408 Bill North | .06 | .02 | .00 | ☐ 459 Mickey Lolich DP | .06 | .02 | .00 |
| ☐ 409 Paul Splittorff | .09 | .04 | .01 | ☐ 460 Willie Randolph | .12 | .05 | .01 |
| ☐ 410 Bobby Bonds | .15 | .06 | .01 | ☐ 461 Dwayne Murphy | .15 | .06 | .01 |
| ☐ 411 Frank LaCorte | .06 | .02 | .00 | ☐ 462 Mike Sadek DP | .03 | .01 | .00 |
| ☐ 412 Thad Bosley | .06 | .02 | .00 | ☐ 463 Jerry Royster | .06 | .02 | .00 |
| ☐ 413 Allen Ripley | .06 | .02 | .00 | ☐ 464 John Denny | .18 | .08 | .01 |
| ☐ 414 George Scott | .09 | .04 | .01 | ☐ 465 Rick Monday | .09 | .04 | .01 |
| ☐ 415 Bill Atkinson | .06 | .02 | .00 | ☐ 466 Mike Squires | .06 | .02 | .00 |
| ☐ 416 Tom Brookens | .06 | .02 | .00 | ☐ 467 Jesse Jefferson | .06 | .02 | .00 |
| ☐ 417 Craig Chamberlain DP | .03 | .01 | .00 | ☐ 468 Aurelio Rodriguez | .06 | .02 | .00 |
| ☐ 418 Roger Freed DP | .03 | .01 | .00 | ☐ 469 Randy Niemann DP | .03 | .01 | .00 |
| ☐ 419 Vic Correll | .06 | .02 | .00 | ☐ 470 Bob Boone | .09 | .04 | .01 |
| ☐ 420 Butch Hobson | .06 | .02 | .00 | ☐ 471 Hosken Powell DP | .03 | .01 | .00 |
| ☐ 421 Doug Bird | .06 | .02 | .00 | ☐ 472 Willie Hernandez | .50 | .22 | .05 |
| ☐ 422 Larry Milbourne | .06 | .02 | .00 | ☐ 473 Bump Wills | .06 | .02 | .00 |
| ☐ 423 Dave Frost | .06 | .02 | .00 | ☐ 474 Steve Busby | .09 | .04 | .01 |
| ☐ 424 Yankees Team/Mgr. | .25 | .05 | .01 | ☐ 475 Cesar Geronimo | .06 | .02 | .00 |
| Dick Howser | | | | ☐ 476 Bob Shirley | .06 | .02 | .00 |
| ☐ 425 Mark Belanger | .09 | .04 | .01 | ☐ 477 Buck Martinez | .06 | .02 | .00 |
| ☐ 426 Grant Jackson | .06 | .02 | .00 | ☐ 478 Gil Flores | .06 | .02 | .00 |
| ☐ 427 Tom Hutton DP | .03 | .01 | .00 | ☐ 479 Expos Team/Mgr. | .20 | .04 | .01 |
| ☐ 428 Pat Zachry | .06 | .02 | .00 | Dick Williams | | | |
| ☐ 429 Duane Kuiper | .06 | .02 | .00 | ☐ 480 Bob Watson | .09 | .04 | .01 |
| ☐ 430 Larry Hisle DP | .06 | .02 | .00 | ☐ 481 Tom Paciorek | .06 | .02 | .00 |
| ☐ 431 Mike Krukow | .06 | .02 | .00 | ☐ 482 Rickey Henderson | 12.00 | 5.50 | 1.20 |
| ☐ 432 Willie Norwood | .06 | .02 | .00 | ☐ 483 Bo Diaz | .09 | .04 | .01 |
| ☐ 433 Rich Gale | .06 | .02 | .00 | ☐ 484 Checklist 4 | .18 | .03 | .00 |
| ☐ 434 Johnnie LeMaster | .06 | .02 | .00 | ☐ 485 Mickey Rivers | .09 | .04 | .01 |
| ☐ 435 Don Gullett | .06 | .02 | .00 | ☐ 486 Mike Tyson DP | .03 | .01 | .00 |
| ☐ 436 Billy Almon | .06 | .02 | .00 | ☐ 487 Wayne Nordhagen | .06 | .02 | .00 |
| ☐ 437 Joe Niekro | .15 | .06 | .01 | ☐ 488 Roy Howell | .06 | .02 | .00 |
| ☐ 438 Dave Revering | .06 | .02 | .00 | ☐ 489 Preston Hanna DP | .03 | .01 | .00 |
| ☐ 439 Mike Phillips | .06 | .02 | .00 | ☐ 490 Lee May | .10 | .04 | .01 |
| ☐ 440 Don Sutton | .40 | .18 | .04 | ☐ 491 Steve Mura DP | .03 | .01 | .00 |
| ☐ 441 Eric Soderholm | .06 | .02 | .00 | ☐ 492 Todd Cruz | .09 | .04 | .01 |
| ☐ 442 Jorge Orta | .06 | .02 | .00 | ☐ 493 Jerry Martin | .06 | .02 | .00 |
| ☐ 443 Mike Parrott | .06 | .02 | .00 | ☐ 494 Craig Minetto | .06 | .02 | .00 |
| ☐ 444 Alvis Woods | .06 | .02 | .00 | ☐ 495 Bake McBride | .09 | .04 | .01 |
| ☐ 445 Mark Fidrych | .15 | .06 | .01 | ☐ 496 Silvio Martinez | .06 | .02 | .00 |
| ☐ 446 Duffy Dyer | .06 | .02 | .00 | ☐ 497 Jim Mason | .06 | .02 | .00 |
| ☐ 447 Nino Espinosa | .06 | .02 | .00 | ☐ 498 Danny Darwin | .09 | .04 | .01 |
| ☐ 448 Jim Wohlford | .06 | .02 | .00 | ☐ 499 Giants Team/Mgr. | .20 | .05 | .01 |
| ☐ 449 Doug Bair | .06 | .02 | .00 | Dave Bristol | | | |
| ☐ 450 George Brett | 2.50 | 1.15 | .25 | ☐ 500 Tom Seaver | 1.00 | .45 | .10 |
| ☐ 451 Indians Team/Mgr. | .20 | .04 | .01 | ☐ 501 Rennie Stennett | .06 | .02 | .00 |
| Dave Garcia | | | | ☐ 502 Rich Wortham DP | .03 | .01 | .00 |

| | | MINT | VG-E | F-G |
|---|---|---|---|---|
| ☐ 503 | Mike Cubbage | .06 | .02 | .00 |
| ☐ 504 | Gene Garber | .06 | .02 | .00 |
| ☐ 505 | Bert Campaneris | .09 | .04 | .01 |
| ☐ 506 | Tom Buskey | .06 | .02 | .00 |
| ☐ 507 | Leon Roberts | .06 | .02 | .00 |
| ☐ 508 | U.L. Washington | .06 | .02 | .00 |
| ☐ 509 | Ed Glynn | .06 | .02 | .00 |
| ☐ 510 | Ron Cey | .30 | .12 | .03 |
| ☐ 511 | Eric Wilkins | .06 | .02 | .00 |
| ☐ 512 | Jose Cardenal | .06 | .02 | .00 |
| ☐ 513 | Tom Dixon DP | .03 | .01 | .00 |
| ☐ 514 | Steve Ontiveros | .06 | .02 | .00 |
| ☐ 515 | Mike Caldwell | .09 | .04 | .01 |
| ☐ 516 | Hector Cruz | .06 | .02 | .00 |
| ☐ 517 | Don Stanhouse | .06 | .02 | .00 |
| ☐ 518 | Nelson Norman | .06 | .02 | .00 |
| ☐ 519 | Steve Nicosia | .06 | .02 | .00 |
| ☐ 520 | Steve Rogers | .15 | .06 | .01 |
| ☐ 521 | Ken Brett | .09 | .04 | .01 |
| ☐ 522 | Jim Morrison | .06 | .02 | .00 |
| ☐ 523 | Ken Henderson | .06 | .02 | .00 |
| ☐ 524 | Jim Wright DP | .03 | .01 | .00 |
| ☐ 525 | Clint Hurdle | .06 | .02 | .00 |
| ☐ 526 | Phillies Team/Mgr. Dallas Green | .20 | .04 | .01 |
| ☐ 527 | Doug Rau DP | .03 | .01 | .00 |
| ☐ 528 | Adrian Devine | .06 | .02 | .00 |
| ☐ 529 | Jim Barr | .06 | .02 | .00 |
| ☐ 530 | Jim Sundberg DP | .06 | .02 | .00 |
| ☐ 531 | Eric Rasmussen | .06 | .02 | .00 |
| ☐ 532 | Willie Horton | .09 | .04 | .01 |
| ☐ 533 | Checklist 5 | .18 | .03 | .00 |
| ☐ 534 | Andre Thornton | .18 | .08 | .01 |
| ☐ 535 | Bob Forsch | .09 | .04 | .01 |
| ☐ 536 | Lee Lacy | .15 | .06 | .01 |
| ☐ 537 | Alex Trevino | .15 | .06 | .01 |
| ☐ 538 | Joe Strain | .06 | .02 | .00 |
| ☐ 539 | Rudy May | .06 | .02 | .00 |
| ☐ 540 | Pete Rose | 2.75 | 1.25 | .27 |
| ☐ 541 | Miguel Dilone | .06 | .02 | .00 |
| ☐ 542 | Joe Coleman | .06 | .02 | .00 |
| ☐ 543 | Pat Kelly | .06 | .02 | .00 |
| ☐ 544 | Rick Sutcliffe | 3.25 | 1.50 | .32 |
| ☐ 545 | Jeff Burroughs | .09 | .04 | .01 |
| ☐ 546 | Rick Langford | .06 | .02 | .00 |
| ☐ 547 | John Wathan | .06 | .02 | .00 |
| ☐ 548 | Dave Rajsich | .06 | .02 | .00 |
| ☐ 549 | Larry Wolfe | .06 | .02 | .00 |
| ☐ 550 | Ken Griffey | .12 | .05 | .01 |
| ☐ 551 | Pirates Team/Mgr. Chuck Tanner | .20 | .04 | .01 |
| ☐ 552 | Bill Nahorodny | .06 | .02 | .00 |
| ☐ 553 | Dick Davis | .06 | .02 | .00 |

| | | MINT | VG-E | F-G |
|---|---|---|---|---|
| ☐ 554 | Art Howe | .06 | .02 | .00 |
| ☐ 555 | Ed Figueroa | .06 | .02 | .00 |
| ☐ 556 | Joe Rudi | .09 | .04 | .01 |
| ☐ 557 | Mark Lee | .06 | .02 | .00 |
| ☐ 558 | Alfredo Griffin | .20 | .09 | .02 |
| ☐ 559 | Dale Murray | .06 | .02 | .00 |
| ☐ 560 | Dave Lopes | .15 | .06 | .01 |
| ☐ 561 | Eddie Whitson | .12 | .05 | .01 |
| ☐ 562 | Joe Wallis | .06 | .02 | .00 |
| ☐ 563 | Will McEnaney | .06 | .02 | .00 |
| ☐ 564 | Rick Manning | .06 | .02 | .00 |
| ☐ 565 | Dennis Leonard | .12 | .05 | .01 |
| ☐ 566 | Bud Harrelson | .06 | .02 | .00 |
| ☐ 567 | Skip Lockwood | .06 | .02 | .00 |
| ☐ 568 | Gary Roenicke | .30 | .12 | .03 |
| ☐ 569 | Terry Kennedy | .30 | .12 | .03 |
| ☐ 570 | Roy Smalley | .09 | .04 | .01 |
| ☐ 571 | Joe Sambito | .09 | .04 | .01 |
| ☐ 572 | Jerry Morales DP | .03 | .01 | .00 |
| ☐ 573 | Kent Tekulve | .12 | .05 | .01 |
| ☐ 574 | Scot Thompson | .06 | .02 | .00 |
| ☐ 575 | Ken Kravec | .06 | .02 | .00 |
| ☐ 576 | Jim Dwyer | .06 | .02 | .00 |
| ☐ 577 | Blue Jays Team/Mgr Bobby Mattick | .18 | .04 | .01 |
| ☐ 578 | Scott Sanderson | .09 | .04 | .01 |
| ☐ 579 | Charlie Moore | .06 | .02 | .00 |
| ☐ 580 | Nolan Ryan | .90 | .40 | .09 |
| ☐ 581 | Bob Bailor | .06 | .02 | .00 |
| ☐ 582 | Brian Doyle | .06 | .02 | .00 |
| ☐ 583 | Bob Stinson | .06 | .02 | .00 |
| ☐ 584 | Kurt Bevacqua | .06 | .02 | .00 |
| ☐ 585 | Al Hrabosky | .09 | .04 | .01 |
| ☐ 586 | Mitchell Page | .06 | .02 | .00 |
| ☐ 587 | Garry Templeton | .20 | .09 | .02 |
| ☐ 588 | Greg Minton | .09 | .04 | .01 |
| ☐ 589 | Chet Lemon | .15 | .06 | .01 |
| ☐ 590 | Jim Palmer | .75 | .35 | .07 |
| ☐ 591 | Rick Cerone | .09 | .04 | .01 |
| ☐ 592 | Jon Matlack | .09 | .04 | .01 |
| ☐ 593 | Jesus Alou | .06 | .02 | .00 |
| ☐ 594 | Dick Tidrow | .06 | .02 | .00 |
| ☐ 595 | Don Money | .06 | .02 | .00 |
| ☐ 596 | Rick Matula | .06 | .02 | .00 |
| ☐ 597 | Tom Poquette | .06 | .02 | .00 |
| ☐ 598 | Fred Kendall DP | .03 | .01 | .00 |
| ☐ 599 | Mike Norris | .09 | .04 | .01 |
| ☐ 600 | Reggie Jackson | 1.50 | .70 | .15 |
| ☐ 601 | Buddy Schultz | .06 | .02 | .00 |
| ☐ 602 | Brian Downing | .09 | .04 | .01 |
| ☐ 603 | Jack Billingham DP | .03 | .01 | .00 |
| ☐ 604 | Glenn Adams | .06 | .02 | .00 |
| ☐ 605 | Terry Forster | .12 | .05 | .01 |

| | MINT | VG-E | F-G |
|---|---|---|---|
| ☐ 606 Reds Team/Mgr. John McNamara | .20 | .05 | .01 |
| ☐ 607 Woodie Fryman | .06 | .02 | .00 |
| ☐ 608 Alan Bannister | .06 | .02 | .00 |
| ☐ 609 Ron Reed | .06 | .02 | .00 |
| ☐ 610 Willie Stargell | .55 | .25 | .05 |
| ☐ 611 Jerry Garvin DP | .03 | .01 | .00 |
| ☐ 612 Cliff Johnson | .06 | .02 | .00 |
| ☐ 613 Randy Stein | .06 | .02 | .00 |
| ☐ 614 John Hiller | .06 | .02 | .00 |
| ☐ 615 Doug DeCinces | .20 | .09 | .02 |
| ☐ 616 Gene Richards | .06 | .02 | .00 |
| ☐ 617 Joaquin Andujar | .25 | .10 | .02 |
| ☐ 618 Bob Montgomery DP | .03 | .01 | .00 |
| ☐ 619 Sergio Ferrer | .06 | .02 | .00 |
| ☐ 620 Richie Zisk | .09 | .04 | .01 |
| ☐ 621 Bob Grich | .12 | .05 | .01 |
| ☐ 622 Mario Soto | .18 | .08 | .01 |
| ☐ 623 Gorman Thomas | .18 | .08 | .01 |
| ☐ 624 Lerrin LaGrow | .06 | .02 | .00 |
| ☐ 625 Chris Chambliss | .12 | .05 | .01 |
| ☐ 626 Tigers Team/Mgr. Sparky Anderson | .25 | .05 | .01 |
| ☐ 627 Pedro Borbon | .06 | .02 | .00 |
| ☐ 628 Doug Capilla | .06 | .02 | .00 |
| ☐ 629 Jim Todd | .06 | .02 | .00 |
| ☐ 630 Larry Bowa | .18 | .08 | .01 |
| ☐ 631 Mark Littell | .06 | .02 | .00 |
| ☐ 632 Barry Bonnell | .09 | .04 | .01 |
| ☐ 633 Bob Apodaca | .06 | .02 | .00 |
| ☐ 634 Glenn Borgmann DP | .03 | .01 | .00 |
| ☐ 635 John Candelaria | .12 | .05 | .01 |
| ☐ 636 Toby Harrah | .09 | .04 | .01 |
| ☐ 637 Joe Simpson | .06 | .02 | .00 |
| ☐ 638 Mark Clear | .25 | .10 | .02 |
| ☐ 639 Larry Biittner | .06 | .02 | .00 |
| ☐ 640 Mike Flanagan | .12 | .05 | .01 |
| ☐ 641 Ed Kranepool | .09 | .04 | .01 |
| ☐ 642 Ken Forsch DP | .06 | .02 | .00 |
| ☐ 643 John Mayberry | .09 | .04 | .01 |
| ☐ 644 Charlie Hough | .09 | .04 | .01 |
| ☐ 645 Rick Burleson | .12 | .05 | .01 |
| ☐ 646 Checklist 6 | .18 | .03 | .00 |
| ☐ 647 Milt May | .06 | .02 | .00 |
| ☐ 648 Roy White | .09 | .04 | .01 |
| ☐ 649 Tom Griffin | .06 | .02 | .00 |
| ☐ 650 Joe Morgan | .40 | .18 | .04 |
| ☐ 651 Rollie Fingers | .35 | .15 | .03 |
| ☐ 652 Mario Mendoza | .06 | .02 | .00 |
| ☐ 653 Stan Bahnsen | .06 | .02 | .00 |
| ☐ 654 Bruce Boisclair DP | .03 | .01 | .00 |
| ☐ 655 Tug McGraw | .15 | .06 | .01 |
| ☐ 656 Larvell Blanks | .06 | .02 | .00 |

| | MINT | VG-E | F-G |
|---|---|---|---|
| ☐ 657 Dave Edwards | .06 | .02 | .00 |
| ☐ 658 Chris Knapp | .06 | .02 | .00 |
| ☐ 659 Brewers Team/Mgr. George Bamberger | .20 | .04 | .01 |
| ☐ 660 Rusty Staub | .15 | .06 | .01 |
| ☐ 661 Orioles Rookies: Mark Corey Dave Ford Wayne Krenchicki | .12 | .05 | .01 |
| ☐ 662 Red Sox Rookies: Joel Finch Mike O'Berry Chuck Rainey | .12 | .05 | .01 |
| ☐ 663 Angels Rookies: Ralph Botting Bob Clark Dickie Thon | .75 | .35 | .07 |
| ☐ 664 White Sox Rookies: Mike Colbern Guy Hoffman Dewey Robinson | .12 | .05 | .01 |
| ☐ 665 Indians Rookies: Larry Anderson Bobby Cuellar Randy Wihtol | .12 | .05 | .01 |
| ☐ 666 Tigers Rookies: Mike Chris Al Greene Bruce Robbins | .12 | .05 | .01 |
| ☐ 667 Royals Rookies: Renie Martin Bill Paschall Dan Quisenberry | 3.00 | 1.40 | .30 |
| ☐ 668 Brewers Rookies: Danny Boitano Willie Mueller Lenn Sakata | .12 | .05 | .01 |
| ☐ 669 Twins Rookies: Dan Graham Rick Sofield Gary Ward | .65 | .30 | .06 |
| ☐ 670 Yankees Rookies: Bobby Brown Brad Gulden Darryl Jones | .12 | .05 | .01 |
| ☐ 671 A's Rookies: Derek Bryant Brian Kingman Mike Morgan | .20 | .09 | .02 |
| ☐ 672 Mariners Rookies: Charlie Beamon Rodney Craig Rafael Vasquez | .12 | .05 | .01 |

|  | MINT | VG-E | F-G |
|---|---|---|---|
| ☐ 673 Rangers Rookies: Brian Allard, Jerry Don Gleaton, Greg Mahlberg | .12 | .05 | .01 |
| ☐ 674 Blue Jays Rookies: Butch Edge, Pat Kelly, Ted Wilborn | .12 | .05 | .01 |
| ☐ 675 Braves Rookies: Bruce Benedict, Larry Bradford, Eddie Miller | .20 | .09 | .02 |
| ☐ 676 Cubs Rookies: Dave Geisel, Steve Macko, Karl Pagel | .12 | .05 | .01 |
| ☐ 677 Reds Rookies: Art DeFreites, Frank Pastore, Harry Spilman | .12 | .05 | .01 |
| ☐ 678 Astros Rookies: Reggie Baldwin, Alan Knicely, Pete Ladd | .20 | .09 | .02 |
| ☐ 679 Dodgers Rookies: Joe Beckwith, Mickey Hatcher, Dave Patterson | .40 | .18 | .04 |
| ☐ 680 Expos Rookies: Tony Bernazard, Randy Miller, John Tamargo | .20 | .09 | .02 |
| ☐ 681 Mets Rookies: Dan Norman, Jesse Orosco, Mike Scott | .90 | .40 | .09 |
| ☐ 682 Phillies Rookies: Ramon Aviles, Dickie Noles, Kevin Saucier | .20 | .09 | .02 |
| ☐ 683 Pirates Rookies: Dorian Boyland, Alberto Lois, Harry Saferight | .12 | .05 | .01 |
| ☐ 684 Cardinals Rookies: George Frazier, Tom Herr, Dan O'Brien | 1.50 | .70 | .15 |
| ☐ 685 Padres Rookies: Tim Flannery, Brian Greer, Jim Wilhelm | .12 | .05 | .01 |

|  | MINT | VG-E | F-G |
|---|---|---|---|
| ☐ 686 Giants Rookies: Greg Johnston, Dennis Littlejohn, Phil Nastu | .12 | .05 | .01 |
| ☐ 687 Mike Heath DP | .03 | .01 | .00 |
| ☐ 688 Steve Stone | .12 | .05 | .01 |
| ☐ 689 Red Sox Team/Mgr. Don Zimmer | .20 | .04 | .01 |
| ☐ 690 Tommy John | .30 | .12 | .03 |
| ☐ 691 Ivan DeJesus | .06 | .02 | .00 |
| ☐ 692 Rawly Eastwick DP | .03 | .01 | .00 |
| ☐ 693 Craig Kusick | .06 | .02 | .00 |
| ☐ 694 Jim Rooker | .06 | .02 | .00 |
| ☐ 695 Reggie Smith | .15 | .06 | .01 |
| ☐ 696 Julio Gonzalez | .06 | .02 | .00 |
| ☐ 697 David Clyde | .06 | .02 | .00 |
| ☐ 698 Oscar Gamble | .09 | .04 | .01 |
| ☐ 699 Floyd Bannister | .12 | .05 | .01 |
| ☐ 700 Rod Carew DP | .45 | .20 | .04 |
| ☐ 701 Ken Oberkfell | .25 | .10 | .02 |
| ☐ 702 Ed Farmer | .06 | .02 | .00 |
| ☐ 703 Otto Velez | .06 | .02 | .00 |
| ☐ 704 Gene Tenace | .06 | .02 | .00 |
| ☐ 705 Freddie Patek | .06 | .02 | .00 |
| ☐ 706 Tippy Martinez | .09 | .04 | .01 |
| ☐ 707 Elliott Maddox | .06 | .02 | .00 |
| ☐ 708 Bob Tolan | .06 | .02 | .00 |
| ☐ 709 Pat Underwood | .06 | .02 | .00 |
| ☐ 710 Graig Nettles | .25 | .10 | .02 |
| ☐ 711 Bob Galasso | .06 | .02 | .00 |
| ☐ 712 Rodney Scott | .06 | .02 | .00 |
| ☐ 713 Terry Whitfield | .06 | .02 | .00 |
| ☐ 714 Fred Norman | .06 | .02 | .00 |
| ☐ 715 Sal Bando | .09 | .04 | .01 |
| ☐ 716 Lynn McGlothen | .06 | .02 | .00 |
| ☐ 717 Mickey Klutts DP | .03 | .01 | .00 |
| ☐ 718 Greg Gross | .06 | .02 | .00 |
| ☐ 719 Don Robinson | .09 | .04 | .01 |
| ☐ 720 Carl Yastrzemski DP | .70 | .32 | .07 |
| ☐ 721 Paul Hartzell | .06 | .02 | .00 |
| ☐ 722 Jose Cruz | .20 | .09 | .02 |
| ☐ 723 Shane Rawley | .09 | .04 | .01 |
| ☐ 724 Jerry White | .06 | .02 | .00 |
| ☐ 725 Rick Wise | .09 | .04 | .01 |
| ☐ 726 Steve Yeager | .12 | .05 | .01 |

# 1981 TOPPS

The cards in this 726 card set measure 2½" by 3½". League Leaders (1–8) and Record Breakers (201–208) are two of the mini-series to be found in this set marketed by Topps in 1981. The obverses carry the player's position and team in a baseball cap design, and the company name is printed in a small baseball. The backs are red and gray. Double-printed cards are noted in the checklist by DP.
Complete Set: M-40.00; VG-E-18.00; F-G-4.00

|  | MINT | VG-E | F-G |
|---|---|---|---|
| Common Player (1–726) | .05 | .02 | .00 |
| 1 Batting Leaders: George Brett, Bill Buckner | .45 | .10 | .02 |
| 2 Home Run Leaders: Reggie Jackson, Ben Oglivie, Mike Schmidt | .20 | .09 | .02 |
| 3 RBI Leaders: Cecil Cooper, Mike Schmidt | .20 | .09 | .02 |
| 4 Stolen Base Leaders: Rickey Henderson, Ron LeFlore | .18 | .08 | .01 |
| 5 Victory Leaders: Steve Stone, Steve Carlton | .14 | .06 | .01 |
| 6 Strikeout Leaders: Len Barker, Steve Carlton | .14 | .06 | .01 |
| 7 ERA Leaders: Rudy May, Don Sutton | .08 | .03 | .01 |

|  | MINT | VG-E | F-G |
|---|---|---|---|
| 8 Leading Firemen: Dan Quisenberry, Rollie Fingers, Tom Hume | .14 | .06 | .01 |
| 9 Pete LaCock DP | .02 | .01 | .00 |
| 10 Mike Flanagan | .12 | .05 | .01 |
| 11 Jim Wohlford DP | .02 | .01 | .00 |
| 12 Mark Clear | .05 | .02 | .00 |
| 13 Joe Charboneau | .12 | .05 | .01 |
| 14 John Tudor | 1.00 | .45 | .10 |
| 15 Larry Parrish | .10 | .04 | .01 |
| 16 Ron Davis | .10 | .04 | .01 |
| 17 Cliff Johnson | .05 | .02 | .00 |
| 18 Glenn Adams | .05 | .02 | .00 |
| 19 Jim Clancy | .05 | .02 | .00 |
| 20 Jeff Burroughs | .07 | .03 | .01 |
| 21 Ron Oester | .07 | .03 | .01 |
| 22 Danny Darwin | .05 | .02 | .00 |
| 23 Alex Trevino | .05 | .02 | .00 |
| 24 Don Stanhouse | .05 | .02 | .00 |
| 25 Sixto Lezcano | .05 | .02 | .00 |
| 26 U.L. Washington | .05 | .02 | .00 |
| 27 Champ Summers DP | .02 | .01 | .00 |
| 28 Enrique Romo | .05 | .02 | .00 |
| 29 Gene Tenace | .05 | .02 | .00 |
| 30 Jack Clark | .35 | .15 | .03 |
| 31 Checklist 1–121 DP | .07 | .01 | .00 |
| 32 Ken Oberkfell | .05 | .02 | .00 |
| 33 Rick Honeycutt | .08 | .03 | .01 |
| 34 Aurelio Rodriguez | .05 | .02 | .00 |
| 35 Mitchell Page | .05 | .02 | .00 |
| 36 Ed Farmer | .05 | .02 | .00 |
| 37 Gary Roenicke | .08 | .03 | .01 |
| 38 Win Remmerswaal | .07 | .03 | .01 |
| 39 Tom Veryzer | .05 | .02 | .00 |
| 40 Tug McGraw | .12 | .05 | .01 |
| 41 Ranger Rookies: Bob Babcock, John Butcher, Jerry Don Gleaton | .25 | .10 | .02 |
| 42 Jerry White DP | .02 | .01 | .00 |
| 43 Jose Morales | .05 | .02 | .00 |
| 44 Larry McWilliams | .08 | .03 | .01 |
| 45 Enos Cabell | .05 | .02 | .00 |
| 46 Rick Bosetti | .05 | .02 | .00 |
| 47 Ken Brett | .07 | .03 | .01 |
| 48 Dave Skaggs | .05 | .02 | .00 |
| 49 Bob Shirley | .05 | .02 | .00 |
| 50 Dave Lopes | .12 | .05 | .01 |
| 51 Bill Robinson DP | .02 | .01 | .00 |
| 52 Hector Cruz | .05 | .02 | .00 |
| 53 Kevin Saucier | .05 | .02 | .00 |

| | | MINT | VG-E | F-G |
|---|---|---|---|---|
| ☐ 54 | Ivan DeJesus | .05 | .02 | .00 |
| ☐ 55 | Mike Norris | .07 | .03 | .01 |
| ☐ 56 | Buck Martinez | .05 | .02 | .00 |
| ☐ 57 | Dave Roberts | .05 | .02 | .00 |
| ☐ 58 | Joel Youngblood | .05 | .02 | .00 |
| ☐ 59 | Dan Petry | .40 | .18 | .04 |
| ☐ 60 | Willie Randolph | .12 | .05 | .01 |
| ☐ 61 | Butch Wynegar | .10 | .04 | .01 |
| ☐ 62 | Joe Pettini | .05 | .02 | .00 |
| ☐ 63 | Steve Renko DP | .02 | .01 | .00 |
| ☐ 64 | Brian Asselstine | .05 | .02 | .00 |
| ☐ 65 | Scott McGregor | .12 | .05 | .01 |
| ☐ 66 | Royals Rookies | .12 | .05 | .01 |
| | Manny Castillo | | | |
| | Tim Ireland | | | |
| | Mike Jones | | | |
| ☐ 67 | Ken Kravec | .05 | .02 | .00 |
| ☐ 68 | Matt Alexander DP | .02 | .01 | .00 |
| ☐ 69 | Ed Halicki | .05 | .02 | .00 |
| ☐ 70 | Al Oliver DP | .12 | .05 | .01 |
| ☐ 71 | Hal Dues | .05 | .02 | .00 |
| ☐ 72 | Barry Evans DP | .02 | .01 | .00 |
| ☐ 73 | Doug Bair | .05 | .02 | .00 |
| ☐ 74 | Mike Hargrove | .07 | .03 | .01 |
| ☐ 75 | Reggie Smith | .12 | .05 | .01 |
| ☐ 76 | Mario Mendoza | .05 | .02 | .00 |
| ☐ 77 | Mike Barlow | .05 | .02 | .00 |
| ☐ 78 | Steve Dillard | .05 | .02 | .00 |
| ☐ 79 | Bruce Robbins | .05 | .02 | .00 |
| ☐ 80 | Rusty Staub | .15 | .06 | .01 |
| ☐ 81 | Dave Stapleton | .15 | .06 | .01 |
| ☐ 82 | Astros Rookies DP | .10 | .04 | .01 |
| | Danny Heep | | | |
| | Alan Knicely | | | |
| | Bobby Sprowl | | | |
| ☐ 83 | Mike Proly | .05 | .02 | .00 |
| ☐ 84 | Johnnie LeMaster | .05 | .02 | .00 |
| ☐ 85 | Mike Caldwell | .08 | .03 | .01 |
| ☐ 86 | Wayne Gross | .05 | .02 | .00 |
| ☐ 87 | Rick Camp | .05 | .02 | .00 |
| ☐ 88 | Joe Lefebvre | .15 | .06 | .01 |
| ☐ 89 | Darrell Jackson | .05 | .02 | .00 |
| ☐ 90 | Bake McBride | .07 | .03 | .01 |
| ☐ 91 | Tim Stoddard DP | .05 | .02 | .00 |
| ☐ 92 | Mike Easler | .12 | .05 | .01 |
| ☐ 93 | Ed Glynn DP | .02 | .01 | .00 |
| ☐ 94 | Harry Spilman DP | .02 | .01 | .00 |
| ☐ 95 | Jim Sundberg | .07 | .03 | .01 |
| ☐ 96 | A's Rookies | .12 | .05 | .01 |
| | Dave Beard | | | |
| | Ernie Camacho | | | |
| | Pat Dempsey | | | |
| ☐ 97 | Chris Speier | .05 | .02 | .00 |
| ☐ 98 | Clint Hurdle | .05 | .02 | .00 |
| ☐ 99 | Eric Wilkins | .05 | .02 | .00 |
| ☐ 100 | Rod Carew | .90 | .40 | .09 |
| ☐ 101 | Benny Ayala | .05 | .02 | .00 |
| ☐ 102 | Dave Tobik | .05 | .02 | .00 |
| ☐ 103 | Jerry Martin | .05 | .02 | .00 |
| ☐ 104 | Terry Forster | .12 | .05 | .01 |
| ☐ 105 | Jose Cruz | .20 | .09 | .02 |
| ☐ 106 | Don Money | .05 | .02 | .00 |
| ☐ 107 | Rich Wortham | .05 | .02 | .00 |
| ☐ 108 | Bruce Benedict | .07 | .03 | .01 |
| ☐ 109 | Mike Scott | .10 | .04 | .01 |
| ☐ 110 | Carl Yastrzemski | 1.00 | .45 | .10 |
| ☐ 111 | Greg Minton | .08 | .03 | .01 |
| ☐ 112 | White Sox Rookies | .12 | .05 | .01 |
| | Rusty Kuntz | | | |
| | Fran Mullin | | | |
| | Leo Sutherland | | | |
| ☐ 113 | Mike Phillips | .05 | .02 | .00 |
| ☐ 114 | Tom Underwood | .05 | .02 | .00 |
| ☐ 115 | Roy Smalley | .07 | .03 | .01 |
| ☐ 116 | Joe Simpson | .05 | .02 | .00 |
| ☐ 117 | Pete Falcone | .05 | .02 | .00 |
| ☐ 118 | Kurt Bevacqua | .05 | .02 | .00 |
| ☐ 119 | Tippy Martinez | .07 | .03 | .01 |
| ☐ 120 | Larry Bowa | .12 | .05 | .01 |
| ☐ 121 | Larry Harlow | .05 | .02 | .00 |
| ☐ 122 | John Denny | .15 | .06 | .01 |
| ☐ 123 | Al Cowens | .07 | .03 | .01 |
| ☐ 124 | Jerry Garvin | .05 | .02 | .00 |
| ☐ 125 | Andre Dawson | .50 | .22 | .05 |
| ☐ 126 | Charlie Leibrandt | .65 | .30 | .06 |
| ☐ 127 | Rudy Law | .05 | .02 | .00 |
| ☐ 128 | Garry Allenson DP | .02 | .01 | .00 |
| ☐ 129 | Art Howe | .05 | .02 | .00 |
| ☐ 130 | Larry Gura | .08 | .03 | .01 |
| ☐ 131 | Keith Moreland | .55 | .25 | .05 |
| ☐ 132 | Tommy Boggs | .05 | .02 | .00 |
| ☐ 133 | Jeff Cox | .07 | .03 | .01 |
| ☐ 134 | Steve Mura | .05 | .02 | .00 |
| ☐ 135 | Gorman Thomas | .18 | .08 | .01 |
| ☐ 136 | Doug Capilla | .05 | .02 | .00 |
| ☐ 137 | Hosken Powell | .05 | .02 | .00 |
| ☐ 138 | Rich Dotson DP | .40 | .18 | .04 |
| ☐ 139 | Oscar Gamble | .08 | .03 | .01 |
| ☐ 140 | Bob Forsch | .07 | .03 | .01 |
| ☐ 141 | Miguel Dilone | .05 | .02 | .00 |
| ☐ 142 | Jackson Todd | .05 | .02 | .00 |
| ☐ 143 | Dan Meyer | .05 | .02 | .00 |
| ☐ 144 | Allen Ripley | .05 | .02 | .00 |
| ☐ 145 | Mickey Rivers | .10 | .04 | .01 |

| | MINT | VG-E | F-G | | | MINT | VG-E | F-G |
|---|---|---|---|---|---|---|---|---|
| 146 Bobby Castillo | .05 | .02 | .00 | 196 Duffy Dyer | .05 | .02 | .00 |
| 147 Dale Berra | .08 | .03 | .01 | 197 Jim Kern | .05 | .02 | .00 |
| 148 Randy Niemann | .05 | .02 | .00 | 198 Jerry Dybzinski | .05 | .02 | .00 |
| 149 Joe Nolan | .05 | .02 | .00 | 199 Chuck Rainey | .05 | .02 | .00 |
| 150 Mark Fidrych | .10 | .04 | .01 | 200 George Foster | .35 | .15 | .03 |
| 151 Claudell Washington | .12 | .05 | .01 | 201 RB: Johnny Bench | .25 | .10 | .02 |
| 152 John Urrea | .05 | .02 | .00 | Most HR's | | | |
| 153 Tom Poquette | .05 | .02 | .00 | lifetime catcher | | | |
| 154 Rick Langford | .05 | .02 | .00 | 202 RB: Steve Carlton | .25 | .10 | .02 |
| 155 Chris Chambliss | .10 | .04 | .01 | Most Strikeouts, | | | |
| 156 Bob McClure | .05 | .02 | .00 | Lefthander, Lifetime | | | |
| 157 John Wathan | .05 | .02 | .00 | 203 RB: Bill Gullickson | .07 | .03 | .01 |
| 158 Fergie Jenkins | .20 | .09 | .02 | Most Strikeouts | | | |
| 159 Brian Doyle | .05 | .02 | .00 | Game, Rookie | | | |
| 160 Garry Maddox | .08 | .03 | .01 | 204 RB: Ron LeFlore and | .07 | .03 | .01 |
| 161 Dan Graham | .05 | .02 | .00 | Rodney Scott | | | |
| 162 Doug Corbett | .12 | .05 | .01 | Most Stolen Bases | | | |
| 163 Billy Almon | .05 | .02 | .00 | Teammates, Season | | | |
| 164 LaMarr Hoyt | 1.10 | .50 | .11 | 205 RB: Pete Rose | .55 | .25 | .05 |
| 165 Tony Scott | .05 | .02 | .00 | Most Cons. Seasons | | | |
| 166 Floyd Bannister | .10 | .04 | .01 | 600 or More At-Bats | | | |
| 167 Terry Whitfield | .05 | .02 | .00 | 206 RB: Mike Schmidt | .30 | .12 | .03 |
| 168 Don Robinson DP | .02 | .01 | .00 | Most Home Runs | | | |
| 169 John Mayberry | .08 | .03 | .01 | Third Baseman, Season | | | |
| 170 Ross Grimsley | .05 | .02 | .00 | 207 RB: Ozzie Smith | .12 | .05 | .01 |
| 171 Gene Richards | .05 | .02 | .00 | Most Assists | | | |
| 172 Gary Woods | .05 | .02 | .00 | Season SS | | | |
| 173 Bump Wills | .05 | .02 | .00 | 208 RB: Willie Wilson | .15 | .06 | .01 |
| 174 Doug Rau | .05 | .02 | .00 | Most At-Bats Season | | | |
| 175 Dave Collins | .08 | .03 | .01 | 209 Dickie Thon DP | .07 | .03 | .01 |
| 176 Mike Krukow | .05 | .02 | .00 | 210 Jim Palmer | .05 | .22 | .05 |
| 177 Rick Peters | .05 | .02 | .00 | 211 Derrell Thomas | .05 | .02 | .00 |
| 178 Jim Essian DP | .02 | .01 | .00 | 212 Steve Nicosia | .05 | .02 | .00 |
| 179 Rudy May | .05 | .02 | .00 | 213 Al Holland | .35 | .15 | .03 |
| 180 Pete Rose | 1.75 | .85 | .17 | 214 Angels Rookies | .12 | .05 | .01 |
| 181 Elias Sosa | .05 | .02 | .00 | Ralph Botting | | | |
| 182 Bob Grich | .12 | .05 | .01 | Jim Dorsey | | | |
| 183 Dick Davis DP | .02 | .01 | .00 | John Harris | | | |
| 184 Jim Dwyer | .05 | .02 | .00 | 215 Larry Hisle | .07 | .03 | .01 |
| 185 Dennis Leonard | .10 | .04 | .01 | 216 John Henry Johnson | .05 | .02 | .00 |
| 186 Wayne Nordhagen | .05 | .02 | .00 | 217 Rich Hebner | .05 | .02 | .00 |
| 187 Mike Parrott | .05 | .02 | .00 | 218 Paul Splittorff | .07 | .03 | .01 |
| 188 Doug DeCinces | .15 | .06 | .01 | 219 Ken Landreaux | .07 | .03 | .01 |
| 189 Craig Swan | .05 | .02 | .00 | 220 Tom Seaver | .70 | .32 | .07 |
| 190 Cesar Cedeno | .12 | .05 | .01 | 221 Bob Davis | .05 | .02 | .00 |
| 191 Rick Sutcliffe | .55 | .25 | .05 | 222 Jorge Orta | .05 | .02 | .00 |
| 192 Braves Rookies | .30 | .12 | .03 | 223 Roy Lee Jackson | .07 | .03 | .01 |
| Terry Harper | | | | 224 Pat Zachry | .05 | .02 | .00 |
| Ed Miller | | | | 225 Ruppert Jones | .07 | .03 | .01 |
| Rafael Ramirez | | | | 226 Manny Sanguillen DP | .02 | .01 | .00 |
| 193 Pete Vuckovich | .12 | .05 | .01 | 227 Fred Martinez | .05 | .02 | .00 |
| 194 Rod Scurry | .12 | .05 | .01 | 228 Tom Paciorek | .05 | .02 | .00 |
| 195 Rich Murray | .08 | .03 | .01 | 229 Rollie Fingers | .35 | .15 | .03 |

| | MINT | VG-E | F-G |
|---|---|---|---|
| ☐ 230 George Hendrick | .12 | .05 | .01 |
| ☐ 231 Joe Beckwith | .05 | .02 | .00 |
| ☐ 232 Mickey Klutts | .05 | .02 | .00 |
| ☐ 233 Skip Lockwood | .05 | .02 | .00 |
| ☐ 234 Lou Whitaker | .40 | .18 | .04 |
| ☐ 235 Scott Sanderson | .08 | .03 | .01 |
| ☐ 236 Mike Ivie | .05 | .02 | .00 |
| ☐ 237 Charlie Moore | .05 | .02 | .00 |
| ☐ 238 Willie Hernandez | .30 | .12 | .03 |
| ☐ 239 Rick Miller DP | .02 | .01 | .00 |
| ☐ 240 Nolan Ryan | .60 | .28 | .06 |
| ☐ 241 Checklist 122–242 DP | .07 | .01 | .00 |
| ☐ 242 Chet Lemon | .12 | .05 | .01 |
| ☐ 243 Sal Butera | .05 | .02 | .00 |
| ☐ 244 Cardinals Rookies | .15 | .06 | .01 |
| Tito Landrum | | | |
| Al Olmsted | | | |
| Andy Rincon | | | |
| ☐ 245 Ed Figueroa | .05 | .02 | .00 |
| ☐ 246 Ed Ott DP | .02 | .01 | .00 |
| ☐ 247 Glen Hubbard DP | .02 | .01 | .00 |
| ☐ 248 Joey McLaughlin | .05 | .02 | .00 |
| ☐ 249 Larry Cox | .05 | .02 | .00 |
| ☐ 250 Ron Guidry | .35 | .15 | .03 |
| ☐ 251 Tom Brookens | .05 | .02 | .00 |
| ☐ 252 Victor Cruz | .05 | .02 | .00 |
| ☐ 253 Dave Bergman | .05 | .02 | .00 |
| ☐ 254 Ozzie Smith | .20 | .09 | .02 |
| ☐ 255 Mark Littell | .05 | .02 | .00 |
| ☐ 256 Bombo Rivera | .05 | .02 | .00 |
| ☐ 257 Rennie Stennett | .05 | .02 | .00 |
| ☐ 258 Joe Price | .08 | .03 | .01 |
| ☐ 259 Mets Rookies | 1.25 | .60 | .12 |
| Juan Berenguer | | | |
| Hubie Brooks | | | |
| Mookie Wilson | | | |
| ☐ 260 Ron Cey | .20 | .09 | .02 |
| ☐ 261 Ricky Henderson | 1.50 | .70 | .15 |
| ☐ 262 Sammy Stewart | .05 | .02 | .00 |
| ☐ 263 Brian Downing | .07 | .03 | .01 |
| ☐ 264 Jim Norris | .05 | .02 | .00 |
| ☐ 265 John Candelaria | .10 | .04 | .01 |
| ☐ 266 Tom Herr | .30 | .12 | .03 |
| ☐ 267 Stan Bahnsen | .05 | .02 | .00 |
| ☐ 268 Jerry Royster | .05 | .02 | .00 |
| ☐ 269 Ken Forsch | .07 | .03 | .01 |
| ☐ 270 Greg Luzinski | .15 | .06 | .01 |
| ☐ 271 Bill Castro | .05 | .02 | .00 |
| ☐ 272 Bruce Kimm | .05 | .02 | .00 |
| ☐ 273 Stan Papi | .05 | .02 | .00 |
| ☐ 274 Craig Chamberlain | .05 | .02 | .00 |
| ☐ 275 Dwight Evans | .25 | .10 | .02 |
| ☐ 276 Dan Spillner | .05 | .02 | .00 |

| | MINT | VG-E | F-G |
|---|---|---|---|
| ☐ 277 Alfredo Griffin | .10 | .04 | .01 |
| ☐ 278 Rick Sofield | .05 | .02 | .00 |
| ☐ 279 Bob Knepper | .08 | .03 | .01 |
| ☐ 280 Ken Griffey | .12 | .05 | .01 |
| ☐ 281 Fred Stanley | .05 | .02 | .00 |
| ☐ 282 Mariners Rookies | .07 | .03 | .01 |
| Rick Anderson | | | |
| Greg Biercevicz | | | |
| Rodney Craig | | | |
| ☐ 283 Billy Sample | .05 | .02 | .00 |
| ☐ 284 Brian Kingman | .05 | .02 | .00 |
| ☐ 285 Jerry Turner | .05 | .02 | .00 |
| ☐ 286 Dave Frost | .05 | .02 | .00 |
| ☐ 287 Lenn Sakata | .05 | .02 | .00 |
| ☐ 288 Bob Clark | .05 | .02 | .00 |
| ☐ 289 Mickey Hatcher | .07 | .03 | .01 |
| ☐ 290 Bob Boone DP | .05 | .02 | .00 |
| ☐ 291 Aurelio Lopez | .05 | .02 | .00 |
| ☐ 292 Mike Squires | .05 | .02 | .00 |
| ☐ 293 Charlie Lea | .30 | .12 | .03 |
| ☐ 294 Mike Tyson DP | .02 | .01 | .00 |
| ☐ 295 Hal McRae | .10 | .04 | .01 |
| ☐ 296 Bill Nahorodny DP | .02 | .01 | .00 |
| ☐ 297 Bob Bailor | .05 | .02 | .00 |
| ☐ 298 Buddy Solomon | .05 | .02 | .00 |
| ☐ 299 Elliott Maddox | .05 | .02 | .00 |
| ☐ 300 Paul Molitor | .25 | .10 | .02 |
| ☐ 301 Matt Keough | .05 | .02 | .00 |
| ☐ 302 Dodgers Rookies | 2.75 | 1.25 | .27 |
| Jack Perconte | | | |
| Mike Scioscia | | | |
| Fernando Valenzuela | | | |
| ☐ 303 Johnny Oates | .05 | .02 | .00 |
| ☐ 304 John Castino | .05 | .02 | .00 |
| ☐ 305 Ken Clay | .05 | .02 | .00 |
| ☐ 306 Juan Beniquez DP | .05 | .02 | .00 |
| ☐ 307 Gene Garber | .05 | .02 | .00 |
| ☐ 308 Rick Manning | .05 | .02 | .00 |
| ☐ 309 Luis Salazar | .12 | .05 | .01 |
| ☐ 310 Vida Blue DP | .07 | .03 | .01 |
| ☐ 311 Freddie Patek | .05 | .02 | .00 |
| ☐ 312 Rick Rhoden | .08 | .03 | .01 |
| ☐ 313 Luis Pujols | .05 | .02 | .00 |
| ☐ 314 Rich Dauer | .05 | .02 | .00 |
| ☐ 315 Kirk Gibson | 2.25 | 1.00 | .22 |
| ☐ 316 Craig Minetto | .05 | .02 | .00 |
| ☐ 317 Lonnie Smith | .15 | .06 | .01 |
| ☐ 318 Steve Yeager | .08 | .03 | .01 |
| ☐ 319 Rowland Office | .05 | .02 | .00 |
| ☐ 320 Tom Burgmeier | .05 | .02 | .00 |
| ☐ 321 Leon Durham | 1.75 | .85 | .17 |
| ☐ 322 Neil Allen | .08 | .03 | .01 |
| ☐ 323 Jim Morrison DP | .02 | .01 | .00 |

| | MINT | VG-E | F-G |
|---|---|---|---|
| ☐ 324 Mike Willis | .05 | .02 | .00 |
| ☐ 325 Ray Knight | .08 | .03 | .01 |
| ☐ 326 Biff Pocoroba | .05 | .02 | .00 |
| ☐ 327 Moose Haas | .07 | .03 | .01 |
| ☐ 328 Twins Rookies | .30 | .12 | .03 |
| Dave Engle | | | |
| Greg Johnston | | | |
| Gary Ward | | | |
| ☐ 329 Joaquin Andujar | .25 | .10 | .02 |
| ☐ 330 Frank White | .12 | .05 | .01 |
| ☐ 331 Dennis Lamp | .05 | .02 | .00 |
| ☐ 332 Lee Lacy DP | .05 | .02 | .00 |
| ☐ 333 Sid Monge | .05 | .02 | .00 |
| ☐ 334 Dane Iorg | .05 | .02 | .00 |
| ☐ 335 Rick Cerone | .07 | .03 | .01 |
| ☐ 336 Eddie Whitson | .10 | .04 | .01 |
| ☐ 337 Lynn Jones | .05 | .02 | .00 |
| ☐ 338 Checklist 243–363 | .11 | .01 | .00 |
| ☐ 339 John Ellis | .05 | .02 | .00 |
| ☐ 340 Bruce Kison | .05 | .02 | .00 |
| ☐ 341 Dwayne Murphy | .12 | .05 | .01 |
| ☐ 342 Eric Rasmussen DP | .02 | .01 | .00 |
| ☐ 343 Frank Taveras | .05 | .02 | .00 |
| ☐ 344 Byron McLaughlin | .05 | .02 | .00 |
| ☐ 345 Warren Cromartie | .05 | .02 | .00 |
| ☐ 346 Larry Christenson DP | .02 | .01 | .00 |
| ☐ 347 Harold Baines | 2.25 | 1.00 | .22 |
| ☐ 348 Bob Sykes | .05 | .02 | .00 |
| ☐ 349 Glenn Hoffman | .12 | .05 | .01 |
| ☐ 350 J.R. Richard | .12 | .05 | .01 |
| ☐ 351 Otto Velez | .05 | .02 | .00 |
| ☐ 352 Dick Tidrow DP | .02 | .01 | .00 |
| ☐ 353 Terry Kennedy | .18 | .08 | .01 |
| ☐ 354 Mario Soto | .15 | .06 | .01 |
| ☐ 355 Bob Horner | .40 | .18 | .04 |
| ☐ 356 Padres Rookies | .12 | .05 | .01 |
| George Stablein | | | |
| Craig Stimac | | | |
| Tom Tellmann | | | |
| ☐ 357 Jim Slaton | .05 | .02 | .00 |
| ☐ 358 Mark Wagner | .05 | .02 | .00 |
| ☐ 359 Tom Hausman | .05 | .02 | .00 |
| ☐ 360 Willie Wilson | .35 | .15 | .03 |
| ☐ 361 Joe Strain | .05 | .02 | .00 |
| ☐ 362 Bo Diaz | .08 | .03 | .01 |
| ☐ 363 Geoff Zahn | .07 | .03 | .01 |
| ☐ 364 Mike Davis | .75 | .35 | .07 |
| ☐ 365 Graig Nettles DP | .08 | .03 | .01 |
| ☐ 366 Mike Ramsey | .05 | .02 | .00 |
| ☐ 367 Denny Martinez | .05 | .02 | .00 |
| ☐ 368 Leon Roberts | .05 | .02 | .00 |
| ☐ 369 Frank Tanana | .07 | .03 | .01 |
| ☐ 370 Dave Winfield | .80 | .40 | .08 |

| | MINT | VG-E | F-G |
|---|---|---|---|
| ☐ 371 Charlie Hough | .07 | .03 | .01 |
| ☐ 372 Jay Johnstone | .07 | .03 | .01 |
| ☐ 373 Pat Underwood | .05 | .02 | .00 |
| ☐ 374 Tom Hutton | .05 | .02 | .00 |
| ☐ 375 Dave Concepcion | .15 | .06 | .01 |
| ☐ 376 Ron Reed | .05 | .02 | .00 |
| ☐ 377 Jerry Morales | .05 | .02 | .00 |
| ☐ 378 Dave Rader | .05 | .02 | .00 |
| ☐ 379 Lary Sorensen | .05 | .02 | .00 |
| ☐ 380 Willie Stargell | .40 | .18 | .04 |
| ☐ 381 Cubs Rookies | .12 | .05 | .01 |
| Carlos Lezcano | | | |
| Steve Macko | | | |
| Randy Martz | | | |
| ☐ 382 Paul Mirabella | .05 | .02 | .00 |
| ☐ 383 Eric Soderholm DP | .02 | .01 | .00 |
| ☐ 384 Mike Sadek | .05 | .02 | .00 |
| ☐ 385 Joe Sambito | .07 | .03 | .01 |
| ☐ 386 Dave Edwards | .05 | .02 | .00 |
| ☐ 387 Phil Niekro | .35 | .15 | .03 |
| ☐ 388 Andre Thornton | .15 | .06 | .01 |
| ☐ 389 Marty Pattin | .05 | .02 | .00 |
| ☐ 390 Cesar Geronimo | .05 | .02 | .00 |
| ☐ 391 Dave Lemanczyk DP | .02 | .01 | .00 |
| ☐ 392 Lance Parrish | .45 | .20 | .04 |
| ☐ 393 Broderick Perkins | .05 | .02 | .00 |
| ☐ 394 Woodie Fryman | .05 | .02 | .00 |
| ☐ 395 Scot Thompson | .05 | .02 | .00 |
| ☐ 396 Bill Campbell | .07 | .03 | .01 |
| ☐ 397 Julio Cruz | .05 | .02 | .00 |
| ☐ 398 Ross Baumgarten | .05 | .02 | .00 |
| ☐ 399 Orioles Rookies | 1.50 | .70 | .15 |
| Mike Boddicker | | | |
| Mark Corey | | | |
| Floyd Rayford | | | |
| ☐ 400 Reggie Jackson | 1.00 | .45 | .10 |
| ☐ 401 A.L. Champs: | .35 | .15 | .03 |
| Royals sweep Yanks | | | |
| (Brett swinging) | | | |
| ☐ 402 N.L. Champs: | .20 | .09 | .02 |
| Phillies squeak | | | |
| past Astros | | | |
| ☐ 403 1980 World Series: | .20 | .09 | .02 |
| Phillies beat | | | |
| Royals in 6 | | | |
| ☐ 404 1980 World Series: | .20 | .09 | .02 |
| Phillies win first | | | |
| World Series | | | |
| ☐ 405 Nino Espinosa | .05 | .02 | .00 |
| ☐ 406 Dickie Noles | .05 | .02 | .00 |
| ☐ 407 Ernie Whitt | .05 | .02 | .00 |
| ☐ 408 Fernando Arroyo | .05 | .02 | .00 |
| ☐ 409 Larry Herndon | .07 | .03 | .01 |

| | MINT | VG-E | F-G |
|---|---|---|---|
| ☐ 410 Bert Campaneris | .08 | .03 | .01 |
| ☐ 411 Terry Puhl | .05 | .02 | .00 |
| ☐ 412 Britt Burns | .55 | .25 | .05 |
| ☐ 413 Tony Bernazard | .05 | .02 | .00 |
| ☐ 414 John Pacella DP | .02 | .01 | .00 |
| ☐ 415 Ben Oglivie | .12 | .05 | .01 |
| ☐ 416 Gary Alexander | .05 | .02 | .00 |
| ☐ 417 Dan Schatzeder | .05 | .02 | .00 |
| ☐ 418 Bobby Brown | .05 | .02 | .00 |
| ☐ 419 Tom Hume | .05 | .02 | .00 |
| ☐ 420 Keith Hernandez | .45 | .20 | .04 |
| ☐ 421 Bob Stanley | .09 | .04 | .01 |
| ☐ 422 Dan Ford | .07 | .03 | .01 |
| ☐ 423 Shane Rawley | .07 | .03 | .01 |
| ☐ 424 Yankees Rookies | .30 | .12 | .03 |
| Tim Lollar | | | |
| Bruce Robinson | | | |
| Dennis Werth | | | |
| ☐ 425 Al Bumbry | .05 | .02 | .00 |
| ☐ 426 Warren Brusstar | .05 | .02 | .00 |
| ☐ 427 John D'Acquisto | .05 | .02 | .00 |
| ☐ 428 John Stearns | .05 | .02 | .00 |
| ☐ 429 Mick Kelleher | .05 | .02 | .00 |
| ☐ 430 Jim Bibby | .07 | .03 | .01 |
| ☐ 431 Dave Roberts | .05 | .02 | .00 |
| ☐ 432 Len Barker | .12 | .05 | .01 |
| ☐ 433 Rance Mulliniks | .05 | .02 | .00 |
| ☐ 434 Roger Erickson | .05 | .02 | .00 |
| ☐ 435 Jim Spencer | .05 | .02 | .00 |
| ☐ 436 Gary Lucas | .12 | .05 | .01 |
| ☐ 437 Mike Heath DP | .02 | .01 | .00 |
| ☐ 438 John Montefusco | .07 | .03 | .01 |
| ☐ 439 Denny Walling | .05 | .02 | .00 |
| ☐ 440 Jerry Reuss | .12 | .05 | .01 |
| ☐ 441 Ken Reitz | .05 | .02 | .00 |
| ☐ 442 Ron Pruitt | .05 | .02 | .00 |
| ☐ 443 Jim Beattie DP | .02 | .01 | .00 |
| ☐ 444 Garth Iorg | .05 | .02 | .00 |
| ☐ 445 Ellis Valentine | .07 | .03 | .01 |
| ☐ 446 Checklist 364–484 | .11 | .01 | .00 |
| ☐ 447 Junior Kennedy DP | .02 | .01 | .00 |
| ☐ 448 Tim Corcoran | .05 | .02 | .00 |
| ☐ 449 Paul Mitchell | .05 | .02 | .00 |
| ☐ 450 Dave Kingman DP | .09 | .04 | .01 |
| ☐ 451 Indians Rookies | .16 | .07 | .01 |
| Chris Bando | | | |
| Tom Brennan | | | |
| Sandy Wihtol | | | |
| ☐ 452 Renie Martin | .05 | .02 | .00 |
| ☐ 453 Rob Wilfong DP | .02 | .01 | .00 |
| ☐ 454 Andy Hassler | .05 | .02 | .00 |
| ☐ 455 Rick Burleson | .08 | .03 | .01 |
| ☐ 456 Jeff Reardon | .70 | .32 | .07 |

| | MINT | VG-E | F-G |
|---|---|---|---|
| ☐ 457 Mike Lum | .05 | .02 | .00 |
| ☐ 458 Randy Jones | .07 | .03 | .01 |
| ☐ 459 Greg Gross | .05 | .02 | .00 |
| ☐ 460 Rich Gossage | .35 | .15 | .03 |
| ☐ 461 Dave McKay | .05 | .02 | .00 |
| ☐ 462 Jack Brohamer | .05 | .02 | .00 |
| ☐ 463 Milt May | .05 | .02 | .00 |
| ☐ 464 Adrian Devine | .05 | .02 | .00 |
| ☐ 465 Bill Russell | .07 | .03 | .01 |
| ☐ 466 Bob Molinaro | .05 | .02 | .00 |
| ☐ 467 Dave Stieb | .65 | .30 | .06 |
| ☐ 468 Johnny Wockenfuss | .05 | .02 | .00 |
| ☐ 469 Jeff Leonard | .12 | .05 | .01 |
| ☐ 470 Manny Trillo | .07 | .03 | .01 |
| ☐ 471 Mike Vail | .05 | .02 | .00 |
| ☐ 472 Dyar Miller DP | .02 | .01 | .00 |
| ☐ 473 Jose Cardenal | .05 | .02 | .00 |
| ☐ 474 Mike LaCoss | .05 | .02 | .00 |
| ☐ 475 Buddy Bell | .20 | .09 | .02 |
| ☐ 476 Jerry Koosman | .15 | .06 | .01 |
| ☐ 477 Luis Gomez | .05 | .02 | .00 |
| ☐ 478 Juan Eichelberger | .07 | .03 | .01 |
| ☐ 479 Expos Rookies | 2.25 | 1.00 | .22 |
| Tim Raines | | | |
| Roberto Ramos | | | |
| Bobby Pate | | | |
| ☐ 480 Carlton Fisk | .35 | .15 | .03 |
| ☐ 481 Bob Lacey DP | .02 | .01 | .00 |
| ☐ 482 Jim Gantner | .07 | .03 | .01 |
| ☐ 483 Mike Griffin | .07 | .03 | .01 |
| ☐ 484 Max Venable DP | .02 | .01 | .00 |
| ☐ 485 Garry Templeton | .20 | .09 | .02 |
| ☐ 486 Marc Hill | .05 | .02 | .00 |
| ☐ 487 Dewey Robinson | .05 | .02 | .00 |
| ☐ 488 Damaso Garcia | .90 | .40 | .09 |
| ☐ 489 John Littlefield | .07 | .03 | .01 |
| ☐ 490 Eddie Murray | 1.25 | .60 | .12 |
| ☐ 491 Gordy Pladson | .07 | .03 | .01 |
| ☐ 492 Barry Foote | .05 | .02 | .00 |
| ☐ 493 Dan Quisenberry | .55 | .25 | .05 |
| ☐ 494 Bob Walk | .07 | .03 | .01 |
| ☐ 495 Dusty Baker | .12 | .05 | .01 |
| ☐ 496 Paul Dade | .05 | .02 | .00 |
| ☐ 497 Fred Norman | .05 | .02 | .00 |
| ☐ 498 Pat Putnam | .05 | .02 | .00 |
| ☐ 499 Frank Pastore | .05 | .02 | .00 |
| ☐ 500 Jim Rice | .70 | .32 | .07 |
| ☐ 501 Tim Foli DP | .02 | .01 | .00 |
| ☐ 502 Giants Rookies | .07 | .03 | .01 |
| Chris Bourjos | | | |
| Al Hargesheimer | | | |
| Mike Rowland | | | |
| ☐ 503 Steve McCatty | .05 | .02 | .00 |

| | MINT | VG-E | F-G |
|---|---|---|---|
| ☐ 504 Dale Murphy | 1.75 | .85 | .17 |
| ☐ 505 Jason Thompson | .12 | .05 | .01 |
| ☐ 506 Phil Huffman | .05 | .02 | .00 |
| ☐ 507 Jamie Quirk | .05 | .02 | .00 |
| ☐ 508 Rob Dressler | .05 | .02 | .00 |
| ☐ 509 Pete Mackanin | .05 | .02 | .00 |
| ☐ 510 Lee Mazzilli | .10 | .04 | .01 |
| ☐ 511 Wayne Garland | .05 | .02 | .00 |
| ☐ 512 Gary Thomasson | .05 | .02 | .00 |
| ☐ 513 Frank LaCorte | .05 | .02 | .00 |
| ☐ 514 George Riley | .07 | .03 | .01 |
| ☐ 515 Robin Yount | .65 | .30 | .06 |
| ☐ 516 Doug Bird | .05 | .02 | .00 |
| ☐ 517 Richie Zisk | .07 | .03 | .01 |
| ☐ 518 Grant Jackson | .05 | .02 | .00 |
| ☐ 519 John Tamargo DP | .02 | .01 | .00 |
| ☐ 520 Steve Stone | .10 | .04 | .01 |
| ☐ 521 Sam Mejias | .05 | .02 | .00 |
| ☐ 522 Mike Colbern | .05 | .02 | .00 |
| ☐ 523 John Fulgham | .05 | .02 | .00 |
| ☐ 524 Willie Aikens | .10 | .04 | .01 |
| ☐ 525 Mike Torrez | .08 | .03 | .01 |
| ☐ 526 Phillies Rookies | .18 | .08 | .01 |
|     Marty Bystrom | | | |
|     Jay Loviglio | | | |
|     Jim Wright | | | |
| ☐ 527 Danny Goodwin | .05 | .02 | .00 |
| ☐ 528 Gary Matthews | 13 | .06 | .01 |
| ☐ 529 Dave LaRoche | .05 | .02 | .00 |
| ☐ 530 Steve Garvey | .90 | .40 | .09 |
| ☐ 531 John Curtis | .05 | .02 | .00 |
| ☐ 532 Bill Stein | .05 | .02 | .00 |
| ☐ 533 Jesus Figueroa | .07 | .03 | .01 |
| ☐ 534 Dave Smith | .12 | .05 | .01 |
| ☐ 535 Omar Moreno | .07 | .03 | .01 |
| ☐ 536 Bob Owchinko DP | .02 | .01 | .00 |
| ☐ 537 Ron Hodges | .05 | .02 | .00 |
| ☐ 538 Tom Griffin | .05 | .02 | .00 |
| ☐ 539 Rodney Scott | .05 | .02 | .00 |
| ☐ 540 Mike Schmidt DP | .60 | .28 | .06 |
| ☐ 541 Steve Swisher | .05 | .02 | .00 |
| ☐ 542 Larry Bradford DP | .02 | .01 | .00 |
| ☐ 543 Terry Crowley | .05 | .02 | .00 |
| ☐ 544 Rich Gale | .05 | .02 | .00 |
| ☐ 545 Johnny Grubb | .05 | .02 | .00 |
| ☐ 546 Paul Moskau | .05 | .02 | .00 |
| ☐ 547 Mario Guerrero | .05 | .02 | .00 |
| ☐ 548 Dave Goltz | .05 | .02 | .00 |
| ☐ 549 Jerry Remy | .07 | .03 | .01 |
| ☐ 550 Tommy John | .30 | .12 | .03 |
| ☐ 551 Pirates Rookies | 1.75 | .85 | .17 |
|     Vance Law | | | |
|     Tony Pena | | | |
|     Pascual Perez | | | |

| | MINT | VG-E | F-G |
|---|---|---|---|
| ☐ 552 Steve Trout | .07 | .03 | .01 |
| ☐ 553 Tim Blackwell | .05 | .02 | .00 |
| ☐ 554 Bert Blyleven | .25 | .10 | .02 |
| ☐ 555 Cecil Cooper | .30 | .12 | .03 |
| ☐ 556 Jerry Mumphrey | .07 | .03 | .01 |
| ☐ 557 Chris Knapp | .05 | .02 | .00 |
| ☐ 558 Barry Bonnell | .07 | .03 | .01 |
| ☐ 559 Willie Montanez | .05 | .02 | .00 |
| ☐ 560 Joe Morgan | .35 | .15 | .03 |
| ☐ 561 Dennis Littlejohn | .05 | .02 | .00 |
| ☐ 562 Checklist 485–605 | .11 | .01 | .00 |
| ☐ 563 Jim Kaat | .18 | .08 | .01 |
| ☐ 564 Ron Hassey DP | .02 | .01 | .00 |
| ☐ 565 Burt Hooton | .05 | .02 | .00 |
| ☐ 566 Del Unser | .05 | .02 | .00 |
| ☐ 567 Mark Bomback | .07 | .03 | .01 |
| ☐ 568 Dave Revering | .05 | .02 | .00 |
| ☐ 569 Al Williams DP | .02 | .01 | .00 |
| ☐ 570 Ken Singleton | .12 | .05 | .01 |
| ☐ 571 Todd Cruz | .05 | .02 | .00 |
| ☐ 572 Jack Morris | .40 | .18 | .04 |
| ☐ 573 Phil Garner | .07 | .03 | .01 |
| ☐ 574 Bill Caudill | .15 | .06 | .01 |
| ☐ 575 Tony Perez | .20 | .09 | .02 |
| ☐ 576 Reggie Cleveland | .05 | .02 | .00 |
| ☐ 577 Blue Jays Rookies | .30 | .12 | .03 |
|     Luis Leal | | | |
|     Brian Milner | | | |
|     Ken Schrom | | | |
| ☐ 578 Bill Gullickson | .50 | .20 | .05 |
| ☐ 579 Tim Flannery | .05 | .02 | .00 |
| ☐ 580 Don Baylor | .30 | .12 | .03 |
| ☐ 581 Roy Howell | .05 | .02 | .00 |
| ☐ 582 Gaylord Perry | .40 | .18 | .04 |
| ☐ 583 Larry Milbourne | .05 | .02 | .00 |
| ☐ 584 Randy Lerch | .05 | .02 | .00 |
| ☐ 585 Amos Otis | .12 | .05 | .01 |
| ☐ 586 Silvio Martinez | .05 | .02 | .00 |
| ☐ 587 Jeff Newman | .05 | .02 | .00 |
| ☐ 588 Gary Lavelle | .07 | .03 | .01 |
| ☐ 589 Lamar Johnson | .05 | .02 | .00 |
| ☐ 590 Bruce Sutter | .45 | .20 | .04 |
| ☐ 591 John Lowenstein | .05 | .02 | .00 |
| ☐ 592 Steve Comer | .05 | .02 | .00 |
| ☐ 593 Steve Kemp | .18 | .08 | .01 |
| ☐ 594 Preston Hanna DP | .02 | .01 | .00 |
| ☐ 595 Butch Hobson | .05 | .02 | .00 |
| ☐ 596 Jerry Augustine | .05 | .02 | .00 |
| ☐ 597 Rafael Landestoy | .05 | .02 | .00 |
| ☐ 598 George Vukovich DP | .02 | .01 | .00 |
| ☐ 599 Dennis Kinney | .07 | .03 | .01 |
| ☐ 600 Johnny Bench | .60 | .28 | .06 |
| ☐ 601 Don Aase | .05 | .02 | .00 |
| ☐ 602 Bobby Murcer | .15 | .06 | .01 |

| | MINT | VG-E | F-G |
|---|---|---|---|
| ☐ 603 John Verhoeven | .05 | .02 | .00 |
| ☐ 604 Rob Picciolo | .05 | .02 | .00 |
| ☐ 605 Don Sutton | .25 | .10 | .02 |
| ☐ 606 Reds Rookies DP | .08 | .03 | .01 |
| Bruce Berenyi | | | |
| Geoff Combe | | | |
| Paul Householder | | | |
| ☐ 607 Dave Palmer | .07 | .03 | .01 |
| ☐ 608 Greg Pryor | .05 | .02 | .00 |
| ☐ 609 Lynn McGlothen | .05 | .02 | .00 |
| ☐ 610 Darrell Porter | .08 | .03 | .01 |
| ☐ 611 Rick Matula DP | .02 | .01 | .00 |
| ☐ 612 Duane Kuiper | .05 | .02 | .00 |
| ☐ 613 Jim Anderson | .05 | .02 | .00 |
| ☐ 614 Dave Rozema | .05 | .02 | .00 |
| ☐ 615 Rick Dempsey | .08 | .03 | .01 |
| ☐ 616 Rick Wise | .07 | .03 | .01 |
| ☐ 617 Craig Reynolds | .05 | .02 | .00 |
| ☐ 618 John Milner | .05 | .02 | .00 |
| ☐ 619 Steve Henderson | .07 | .03 | .01 |
| ☐ 620 Dennis Eckersley | .08 | .03 | .01 |
| ☐ 621 Tom Donohue | .05 | .02 | .00 |
| ☐ 622 Randy Moffitt | .05 | .02 | .00 |
| ☐ 623 Sal Bando | .08 | .03 | .01 |
| ☐ 624 Bob Welch | .13 | .06 | .01 |
| ☐ 625 Bill Buckner | .15 | .06 | .01 |
| ☐ 626 Tigers Rookies | .12 | .05 | .01 |
| Dave Steffen | | | |
| Jerry Ujdur | | | |
| Roger Weaver | | | |
| ☐ 627 Luis Tiant | .12 | .05 | .01 |
| ☐ 628 Vic Correll | .05 | .02 | .00 |
| ☐ 629 Tony Armas | .20 | .09 | .02 |
| ☐ 630 Steve Carlton | .80 | .30 | .07 |
| ☐ 631 Ron Jackson | .05 | .02 | .00 |
| ☐ 632 Alan Bannister | .05 | .02 | .00 |
| ☐ 633 Bill Lee | .08 | .03 | .01 |
| ☐ 634 Doug Flynn | .05 | .02 | .00 |
| ☐ 635 Bobby Bonds | .12 | .05 | .01 |
| ☐ 636 Al Hrabosky | .08 | .03 | .01 |
| ☐ 637 Jerry Narron | .05 | .02 | .00 |
| ☐ 638 Checklist 606–726 | .11 | .01 | .00 |
| ☐ 639 Carney Lansford | .20 | .09 | .02 |
| ☐ 640 Dave Parker | .40 | .18 | .04 |
| ☐ 641 Mark Belanger | .07 | .03 | .01 |
| ☐ 642 Vern Ruhle | .05 | .02 | .00 |
| ☐ 643 Lloyd Moseby | 1.75 | .85 | .17 |
| ☐ 644 Ramon Aviles DP | .02 | .01 | .00 |
| ☐ 645 Rick Reuschel | .08 | .03 | .01 |
| ☐ 646 Marvis Foley | .07 | .03 | .01 |
| ☐ 647 Dick Drago | .05 | .02 | .00 |
| ☐ 648 Darrell Evans | .20 | .09 | .02 |
| ☐ 649 Manny Sarmiento | .05 | .02 | .00 |
| ☐ 650 Bucky Dent | .12 | .05 | .01 |

| | MINT | VG-E | F-G |
|---|---|---|---|
| ☐ 651 Pedro Guerrero | 1.00 | .45 | .10 |
| ☐ 652 John Montague | .05 | .02 | .00 |
| ☐ 653 Bill Fahey | .05 | .02 | .00 |
| ☐ 654 Ray Burris | .05 | .02 | .00 |
| ☐ 655 Dan Driessen | .08 | .03 | .01 |
| ☐ 656 Jon Matlack | .08 | .03 | .01 |
| ☐ 657 Mike Cubbage DP | .02 | .01 | .00 |
| ☐ 658 Milt Wilcox | .07 | .03 | .01 |
| ☐ 659 Brewers Rookies: | .08 | .03 | .01 |
| John Flinn | | | |
| Ed Romero | | | |
| Ned Yost | | | |
| ☐ 660 Gary Carter | .75 | .35 | .07 |
| ☐ 661 Orioles Team/Mgr. | .18 | .03 | .01 |
| Earl Weaver | | | |
| ☐ 662 Red Sox Team/Mgr. | .18 | .03 | .01 |
| Ralph Houk | | | |
| ☐ 663 Angels Team/Mgr. | .18 | .03 | .01 |
| Jim Fregosi | | | |
| ☐ 664 White Sox Team/Mgr. | .18 | .03 | .01 |
| Tony LaRussa | | | |
| ☐ 665 Indians Team/Mgr. | .18 | .03 | .01 |
| Dave Garcia | | | |
| ☐ 666 Tigers Team/Mgr. | .18 | .03 | .01 |
| Sparky Anderson | | | |
| ☐ 667 Royals Team/Mgr. | .18 | .03 | .01 |
| Jim Frey | | | |
| ☐ 668 Brewers Team/Mgr. | .18 | .03 | .01 |
| Bob Rodgers | | | |
| ☐ 669 Twins Team/Mgr. | .15 | .03 | .01 |
| John Goryl | | | |
| ☐ 670 Yankees Team/Mgr. | .18 | .03 | .01 |
| Gene Michael | | | |
| ☐ 671 A's Team/Mgr. | .18 | .03 | .01 |
| Billy Martin | | | |
| ☐ 672 Mariners Team/Mgr. | .15 | .03 | .01 |
| Maury Wills | | | |
| ☐ 673 Rangers Team/Mgr. | .15 | .03 | .01 |
| Don Zimmer | | | |
| ☐ 674 Blue Jays Team/Mgr. | .15 | .03 | .01 |
| Bobby Mattick | | | |
| ☐ 675 Braves Team/Mgr. | .18 | .03 | .01 |
| Bobby Cox | | | |
| ☐ 676 Cubs Team/Mgr. | .18 | .03 | .01 |
| Joe Amalfitano | | | |
| ☐ 677 Reds Team/Mgr. | .18 | .03 | .01 |
| John McNamara | | | |
| ☐ 678 Astros Team/Mgr. | .18 | .03 | .01 |
| Bill Virdon | | | |
| ☐ 679 Dodgers Team/Mgr. | .18 | .03 | .01 |
| Tom Lasorda | | | |
| ☐ 680 Expos Team/Mgr. | .18 | .03 | .01 |
| Dick Williams | | | |

|  | MINT | VG-E | F-G |
|---|---|---|---|
| ☐ 681 Mets Team/Mgr. | .18 | .03 | .01 |
| Joe Torre | | | |
| ☐ 682 Phillies Team/Mgr. | .18 | .03 | .01 |
| Dallas Green | | | |
| ☐ 683 Pirates Team/Mgr. | .18 | .03 | .01 |
| Chuck Tanner | | | |
| ☐ 684 Cardinals Team/Mgr. | .18 | .03 | .01 |
| Whitey Herzog | | | |
| ☐ 685 Padres Team/Mgr. | .15 | .03 | .01 |
| Frank Howard | | | |
| ☐ 686 Giants Team/Mgr. | .18 | .03 | .01 |
| Dave Bristol | | | |
| ☐ 687 Jeff Jones | .12 | .05 | .01 |
| ☐ 688 Kiko Garcia | .05 | .02 | .00 |
| ☐ 689 Red Sox Rookies: | .30 | .12 | .03 |
| Bruce Hurst | | | |
| Keith MacWhorter | | | |
| Reid Nichols | | | |
| ☐ 690 Bob Watson | .08 | .03 | .01 |
| ☐ 691 Dick Ruthven | .05 | .02 | .00 |
| ☐ 692 Lenny Randle | .05 | .02 | .00 |
| ☐ 693 Steve Howe | .30 | .12 | .03 |
| ☐ 694 Bud Harrelson DP | .02 | .03 | .01 |
| ☐ 695 Kent Tekulve | .08 | .03 | .01 |
| ☐ 696 Alan Ashby | .05 | .02 | .00 |
| ☐ 697 Rick Waits | .05 | .02 | .00 |
| ☐ 698 Mike Jorgensen | .05 | .02 | .00 |
| ☐ 699 Glen Abbott | .05 | .02 | .00 |
| ☐ 700 George Brett | 1.50 | .70 | .15 |
| ☐ 701 Joe Rudi | .08 | .03 | .01 |
| ☐ 702 George Medich | .07 | .03 | .01 |
| ☐ 703 Alvis Woods | .05 | .02 | .00 |
| ☐ 704 Bill Travers DP | .02 | .03 | .01 |
| ☐ 705 Ted Simmons | .20 | .09 | .02 |
| ☐ 706 Dave Ford | .05 | .02 | .00 |
| ☐ 707 Dave Cash | .05 | .02 | .00 |
| ☐ 708 Doyle Alexander | .08 | .03 | .01 |
| ☐ 709 Alan Trammell DP | .12 | .05 | .01 |
| ☐ 710 Ron LeFlore DP | .05 | .02 | .00 |
| ☐ 711 Joe Ferguson | .05 | .02 | .00 |
| ☐ 712 Bill Bonham | .05 | .02 | .00 |
| ☐ 713 Bill North | .05 | .02 | .00 |
| ☐ 714 Pete Redfern | .05 | .02 | .00 |
| ☐ 715 Bill Madlock | .30 | .12 | .03 |
| ☐ 716 Glenn Borgmann | .05 | .02 | .00 |
| ☐ 717 Jim Barr DP | .02 | .03 | .01 |
| ☐ 718 Larry Biittner | .05 | .02 | .00 |
| ☐ 719 Sparky Lyle | .12 | .05 | .01 |
| ☐ 720 Fred Lynn | .35 | .15 | .03 |
| ☐ 721 Toby Harrah | .08 | .03 | .01 |
| ☐ 722 Joe Niekro | .12 | .05 | .01 |
| ☐ 723 Bruce Bochte | .08 | .03 | .01 |
| ☐ 724 Lou Piniella | .12 | .05 | .01 |

|  | MINT | VG-E | F-G |
|---|---|---|---|
| ☐ 725 Steve Rogers | .12 | .05 | .01 |
| ☐ 726 Rick Monday | .10 | .03 | .01 |

## 1981 TOPPS TRADED

*The cards in this 132 card set measure 2½" by 3½". For the first time since 1976, Topps issued a ''Traded Set'' in 1981. Unlike the small traded sets of 1974 and 1976, this set contains a larger number of cards and was sequentially numbered, alphabetically, from 727 to 858. Thus, this set gives the impression it is a continuation of their regular issue of this year. The sets were issued only through hobby card dealers and were boxed in complete sets of 132 cards.*

**Complete Set: M-17.50; VG-E-7.00; F-G-1.50**

| Common Player | .08 | .03 | .01 |
|---|---|---|---|
| ☐ 727 Danny Ainge | .45 | .20 | .04 |
| ☐ 728 Doyle Alexander | .12 | .05 | .01 |
| ☐ 729 Gary Alexander | .08 | .03 | .01 |
| ☐ 730 Billy Almon | .08 | .03 | .01 |
| ☐ 731 Joaquin Andujar | .25 | .10 | .02 |
| ☐ 732 Bob Bailor | .08 | .03 | .01 |
| ☐ 733 Juan Beniquez | .12 | .05 | .01 |
| ☐ 734 Dave Bergman | .08 | .03 | .01 |
| ☐ 735 Tony Bernazard | .08 | .03 | .01 |
| ☐ 736 Larry Biittner | .08 | .03 | .01 |
| ☐ 737 Doug Bird | .08 | .03 | .01 |
| ☐ 738 Bert Blyleven | .30 | .12 | .03 |
| ☐ 739 Mark Bomback | .08 | .03 | .01 |
| ☐ 740 Bobby Bonds | .12 | .05 | .01 |
| ☐ 741 Rick Bosetti | .08 | .03 | .01 |
| ☐ 742 Hubie Brooks | .60 | .28 | .06 |

| | MINT | VG-E | F-G |
|---|---|---|---|
| ☐ 743 Rick Burleson | .12 | .05 | .01 |
| ☐ 744 Ray Burris | .08 | .03 | .01 |
| ☐ 745 Jeff Burroughs | .12 | .05 | .01 |
| ☐ 746 Enos Cabell | .08 | .03 | .01 |
| ☐ 747 Ken Clay | .08 | .03 | .01 |
| ☐ 748 Mark Clear | .12 | .05 | .01 |
| ☐ 749 Larry Cox | .08 | .03 | .01 |
| ☐ 750 Hector Cruz | .08 | .03 | .01 |
| ☐ 751 Victor Cruz | .08 | .03 | .01 |
| ☐ 752 Mike Cubbage | .08 | .03 | .01 |
| ☐ 753 Dick Davis | .08 | .03 | .01 |
| ☐ 754 Brian Doyle | .08 | .03 | .01 |
| ☐ 755 Dick Drago | .08 | .03 | .01 |
| ☐ 756 Leon Durham | 1.25 | .60 | .12 |
| ☐ 757 Jim Dwyer | .08 | .03 | .01 |
| ☐ 758 Dave Edwards | .08 | .03 | .01 |
| ☐ 759 Jim Essian | .08 | .03 | .01 |
| ☐ 760 Bill Fahey | .08 | .03 | .01 |
| ☐ 761 Rollie Fingers | .75 | .35 | .07 |
| ☐ 762 Carlton Fisk | .75 | .35 | .07 |
| ☐ 763 Barry Foote | .08 | .03 | .01 |
| ☐ 764 Ken Forsch | .12 | .05 | .01 |
| ☐ 765 Kiko Garcia | .08 | .03 | .01 |
| ☐ 766 Cesar Geronimo | .08 | .03 | .01 |
| ☐ 767 Gary Gray | .12 | .05 | .01 |
| ☐ 768 Mickey Hatcher | .12 | .05 | .01 |
| ☐ 769 Steve Henderson | .12 | .05 | .01 |
| ☐ 770 Marc Hill | .08 | .03 | .01 |
| ☐ 771 Butch Hobson | .08 | .03 | .01 |
| ☐ 772 Rick Honeycutt | .12 | .05 | .01 |
| ☐ 773 Roy Howell | .08 | .03 | .01 |
| ☐ 774 Mike Ivie | .08 | .03 | .01 |
| ☐ 775 Roy Lee Jackson | .08 | .03 | .01 |
| ☐ 776 Cliff Johnson | .08 | .03 | .01 |
| ☐ 777 Randy Jones | .12 | .05 | .01 |
| ☐ 778 Ruppert Jones | .12 | .05 | .01 |
| ☐ 779 Mick Kelleher | .08 | .03 | .01 |
| ☐ 780 Terry Kennedy | .30 | .12 | .03 |
| ☐ 781 Dave Kingman | .35 | .15 | .03 |
| ☐ 782 Bob Knepper | .12 | .05 | .01 |
| ☐ 783 Ken Kravec | .08 | .03 | .01 |
| ☐ 784 Bob Lacey | .08 | .03 | .01 |
| ☐ 785 Dennis Lamp | .08 | .03 | .01 |
| ☐ 786 Rafael Landestoy | .08 | .03 | .01 |
| ☐ 787 Ken Landreaux | .12 | .05 | .01 |
| ☐ 788 Carney Lansford | .40 | .18 | .04 |
| ☐ 789 Dave LaRoche | .08 | .03 | .01 |
| ☐ 790 Joe LeFebvre | .08 | .03 | .01 |
| ☐ 791 Ron LeFlore | .12 | .05 | .01 |
| ☐ 792 Randy Lerch | .08 | .03 | .01 |
| ☐ 793 Sixto Lezcano | .12 | .05 | .01 |
| ☐ 794 John Littlefield | .08 | .03 | .01 |
| ☐ 795 Mike Lum | .08 | .03 | .01 |

| | MINT | VG-E | F-G |
|---|---|---|---|
| ☐ 796 Greg Luzinski | .30 | .12 | .03 |
| ☐ 797 Fred Lynn | .70 | .32 | .07 |
| ☐ 798 Jerry Martin | .08 | .03 | .01 |
| ☐ 799 Buck Martinez | .08 | .03 | .01 |
| ☐ 800 Gary Matthews | .15 | .06 | .01 |
| ☐ 801 Mario Mendoza | .08 | .03 | .01 |
| ☐ 802 Larry Milbourne | .08 | .03 | .01 |
| ☐ 803 Rick Miller | .08 | .03 | .01 |
| ☐ 804 John Montefusco | .12 | .05 | .01 |
| ☐ 805 Jerry Morales | .08 | .03 | .01 |
| ☐ 806 Jose Morales | .08 | .03 | .01 |
| ☐ 807 Joe Morgan | .90 | .40 | .09 |
| ☐ 808 Jerry Mumphrey | .12 | .05 | .01 |
| ☐ 809 Gene Nelson | .30 | .12 | .03 |
| ☐ 810 Ed Ott | .08 | .03 | .01 |
| ☐ 811 Bob Owchinko | .08 | .03 | .01 |
| ☐ 812 Gaylord Perry | .90 | .40 | .09 |
| ☐ 813 Mike Phillips | .08 | .03 | .01 |
| ☐ 814 Darrell Porter | .12 | .05 | .01 |
| ☐ 815 Mike Proly | .08 | .03 | .01 |
| ☐ 816 Tim Raines | 3.25 | 1.50 | .32 |
| ☐ 817 Len Randle | .08 | .03 | .01 |
| ☐ 818 Doug Rau | .08 | .03 | .01 |
| ☐ 819 Jeff Reardon | .35 | .15 | .03 |
| ☐ 820 Ken Reitz | .08 | .03 | .01 |
| ☐ 821 Steve Renko | .08 | .03 | .01 |
| ☐ 822 Rick Reuschel | .15 | .06 | .01 |
| ☐ 823 Dave Revering | .08 | .03 | .01 |
| ☐ 824 Dave Roberts | .08 | .03 | .01 |
| ☐ 825 Leon Roberts | .08 | .03 | .01 |
| ☐ 826 Joe Rudi | .12 | .05 | .01 |
| ☐ 827 Kevin Saucier | .08 | .03 | .01 |
| ☐ 828 Tony Scott | .08 | .03 | .01 |
| ☐ 829 Bob Shirley | .08 | .03 | .01 |
| ☐ 830 Ted Simmons | .40 | .18 | .04 |
| ☐ 831 Lary Sorensen | .08 | .03 | .01 |
| ☐ 832 Jim Spencer | .08 | .03 | .01 |
| ☐ 833 Harry Spilman | .08 | .03 | .01 |
| ☐ 834 Fred Stanley | .08 | .03 | .01 |
| ☐ 835 Rusty Staub | .20 | .09 | .02 |
| ☐ 836 Bill Stein | .08 | .03 | .01 |
| ☐ 837 Joe Strain | .08 | .03 | .01 |
| ☐ 838 Bruce Sutter | .80 | .40 | .08 |
| ☐ 839 Don Sutton | .50 | .22 | .05 |
| ☐ 840 Steve Swisher | .08 | .03 | .01 |
| ☐ 841 Frank Tanana | .12 | .05 | .01 |
| ☐ 842 Gene Tenace | .08 | .03 | .01 |
| ☐ 843 Jason Thompson | .15 | .06 | .01 |
| ☐ 844 Dickie Thon | .25 | .10 | .02 |
| ☐ 845 Bill Travers | .08 | .03 | .01 |
| ☐ 846 Tom Underwood | .08 | .03 | .01 |
| ☐ 847 John Urrea | .08 | .03 | .01 |
| ☐ 848 Mike Vail | .08 | .03 | .01 |

| | | MINT | VG-E | F-G |
|---|---|---|---|---|
| ☐ 849 | Ellis Valentine | .12 | .05 | .01 |
| ☐ 850 | Fernando Valenzuela | 3.25 | 1.50 | .32 |
| ☐ 851 | Pete Vuckovich | .15 | .06 | .01 |
| ☐ 852 | Mark Wagner | .08 | .03 | .01 |
| ☐ 853 | Bob Walk | .08 | .03 | .01 |
| ☐ 854 | Claudell Washington | .15 | .06 | .01 |
| ☐ 855 | Dave Winfield | 1.50 | .70 | .15 |
| ☐ 856 | Geoff Zahn | .12 | .05 | .01 |
| ☐ 857 | Richie Zisk | .12 | .05 | .01 |
| ☐ 858 | Checklist 727–858 | .20 | .04 | .00 |

## 1982 TOPPS

The cards in this 792 card set measure 2½" by 3½". The 1982 baseball series is the largest set Topps has ever issued at one printing. The 66 card increase from the previous year's total eliminated the "double-print" practice which had occurred in every regular issue since 1978. Cards 1–6 depict Highlights (HL) of the 1981 season and there are mini-series of A.L. (547–557) and N.L. (337–347) All Stars (AS). The abbreviation "SA" in the checklist prefaces the 40 "Super Action" cards introduced for the first time in this set.

Complete Set: M-35.00; VG-E-16.50; F-G-3.50

| | Common Player (1–792) | .04 | .02 | .00 |
|---|---|---|---|---|
| ☐ 1 | HL: Steve Carlton Sets New NL Strikeout Record | .40 | .10 | .02 |
| ☐ 2 | HL: Ron Davis, Fans 8 Straight in Relief | .06 | .02 | .00 |

| | | MINT | VG-E | F-G |
|---|---|---|---|---|
| ☐ 3 | HL: Tim Raines, Swipes 71 Bases as Rookie | .20 | .09 | .02 |
| ☐ 4 | HL: Pete Rose, Sets NL Career Hits Mark | .55 | .25 | .05 |
| ☐ 5 | HL: Nolan Ryan, Pitches 5th Career No-Hitter | .25 | .10 | .02 |
| ☐ 6 | HL: Fernando Valenzuela, 8 Shutouts as Rookie | .25 | .10 | .02 |
| ☐ 7 | Scott Sanderson | .05 | .02 | .00 |
| ☐ 8 | Rich Dauer | .04 | .02 | .00 |
| ☐ 9 | Ron Guidry | .30 | .12 | .03 |
| ☐ 10 | SA: Ron Guidry | .18 | .08 | .01 |
| ☐ 11 | Gary Alexander | .04 | .02 | .00 |
| ☐ 12 | Moose Haas | .05 | .02 | .00 |
| ☐ 13 | Lamar Johnson | .04 | .02 | .00 |
| ☐ 14 | Steve Howe | .07 | .03 | .01 |
| ☐ 15 | Ellis Valentine | .05 | .02 | .00 |
| ☐ 16 | Steve Comer | .04 | .02 | .00 |
| ☐ 17 | Darrell Evans | .15 | .06 | .01 |
| ☐ 18 | Fernando Arroyo | .04 | .02 | .00 |
| ☐ 19 | Ernie Whitt | .04 | .02 | .00 |
| ☐ 20 | Garry Maddox | .06 | .02 | .00 |
| ☐ 21 | Orioles Rookies: Bob Bonner Cal Ripken Jeff Schneider | 6.25 | 2.25 | .50 |
| ☐ 22 | Jim Beattie | .04 | .02 | .00 |
| ☐ 23 | Willie Hernandez | .35 | .15 | .03 |
| ☐ 24 | Dave Frost | .04 | .02 | .00 |
| ☐ 25 | Jerry Remy | .04 | .02 | .00 |
| ☐ 26 | Jorge Orta | .04 | .02 | .00 |
| ☐ 27 | Tom Herr | .25 | .10 | .02 |
| ☐ 28 | John Urrea | .04 | .02 | .00 |
| ☐ 29 | Dwayne Murphy | .08 | .03 | .01 |
| ☐ 30 | Tom Seaver | .50 | .22 | .05 |
| ☐ 31 | SA: Tom Seaver | .25 | .10 | .02 |
| ☐ 32 | Gene Garber | .04 | .02 | .00 |
| ☐ 33 | Jerry Morales | .04 | .02 | .00 |
| ☐ 34 | Joe Sambito | .06 | .02 | .00 |
| ☐ 35 | Willie Aikens | .08 | .03 | .01 |
| ☐ 36 | Rangers Team Mgr. Don Zimmer Batting: Al Oliver Pitching: Doc Medich | .10 | .02 | .00 |
| ☐ 37 | Dan Graham | .04 | .02 | .00 |
| ☐ 38 | Charlie Lea | .06 | .02 | .00 |
| ☐ 39 | Lou Whitaker | .35 | .15 | .03 |
| ☐ 40 | Dave Parker | .35 | .15 | .03 |
| ☐ 41 | SA: Dave Parker | .15 | .06 | .01 |
| ☐ 42 | Rick Sofield | .04 | .02 | .00 |

| | MINT | VG-E | F-G |
|---|---|---|---|
| ☐ 43 Mike Cubbage | .04 | .02 | .00 |
| ☐ 44 Britt Burns | .10 | .04 | .01 |
| ☐ 45 Rick Cerone | .06 | .02 | .00 |
| ☐ 46 Jerry Augustine | .04 | .02 | .00 |
| ☐ 47 Jeff Leonard | .08 | .03 | .01 |
| ☐ 48 Bobby Castillo | .04 | .02 | .00 |
| ☐ 49 Alvis Woods | .04 | .02 | .00 |
| ☐ 50 Buddy Bell | .15 | .06 | .01 |
| ☐ 51 Cubs Rookies: | .50 | .22 | .05 |
| Jay Howell | | | |
| Carlos Lezcano | | | |
| Ty Waller | | | |
| ☐ 52 Larry Andersen | .06 | .02 | .00 |
| ☐ 53 Greg Gross | .04 | .02 | .00 |
| ☐ 54 Ron Hassey | .04 | .02 | .00 |
| ☐ 55 Rick Burleson | .06 | .02 | .00 |
| ☐ 56 Mark Littell | .04 | .02 | .00 |
| ☐ 57 Craig Reynolds | .04 | .02 | .00 |
| ☐ 58 John D'Acquisto | .04 | .02 | .00 |
| ☐ 59 Rich Gedman | .90 | .40 | .09 |
| ☐ 60 Tony Armas | .20 | .09 | .02 |
| ☐ 61 Tommy Boggs | .04 | .02 | .00 |
| ☐ 62 Mike Tyson | .04 | .02 | .00 |
| ☐ 63 Mario Soto | .13 | .06 | .01 |
| ☐ 64 Lynn Jones | .04 | .02 | .00 |
| ☐ 65 Terry Kennedy | .13 | .06 | .01 |
| ☐ 66 Astros Team | .12 | .02 | .00 |
| Mgr. Bill Virdon | | | |
| Batting: Art Howe | | | |
| Pitching: Nolan Ryan | | | |
| ☐ 67 Rich Gale | .04 | .02 | .00 |
| ☐ 68 Roy Howell | .04 | .02 | .00 |
| ☐ 69 Al Williams | .04 | .02 | .00 |
| ☐ 70 Tim Raines | .60 | .28 | .06 |
| ☐ 71 Roy Lee Jackson | .04 | .02 | .00 |
| ☐ 72 Rick Auerbach | .04 | .02 | .00 |
| ☐ 73 Buddy Solomon | .04 | .02 | .00 |
| ☐ 74 Bob Clark | .04 | .02 | .00 |
| ☐ 75 Tommy John | .25 | .10 | .02 |
| ☐ 76 Greg Pryor | .04 | .02 | .00 |
| ☐ 77 Miguel Dilone | .04 | .02 | .00 |
| ☐ 78 George Medich | .04 | .02 | .00 |
| ☐ 79 Bob Bailor | .04 | .02 | .00 |
| ☐ 80 Jim Palmer | .35 | .15 | .03 |
| ☐ 81 SA: Jim Palmer | .18 | .08 | .01 |
| ☐ 82 Bob Welch | .08 | .03 | .01 |
| ☐ 83 Yankees Rookies: | .75 | .35 | .07 |
| Steve Balboni | | | |
| Andy McGaffigan | | | |
| Andre Robertson | | | |
| ☐ 84 Rennie Stennett | .04 | .02 | .00 |
| ☐ 85 Lynn McGlothen | .04 | .02 | .00 |

| | MINT | VG-E | F-G |
|---|---|---|---|
| ☐ 86 Dane Iorg | .04 | .02 | .00 |
| ☐ 87 Matt Keough | .06 | .02 | .00 |
| ☐ 88 Biff Pocoroba | .04 | .02 | .00 |
| ☐ 89 Steve Henderson | .04 | .02 | .00 |
| ☐ 90 Nolan Ryan | .50 | .22 | .05 |
| ☐ 91 Carney Lansford | .15 | .06 | .01 |
| ☐ 92 Brad Havens | .06 | .02 | .00 |
| ☐ 93 Larry Hisle | .06 | .02 | .00 |
| ☐ 94 Andy Hassler | .04 | .02 | .00 |
| ☐ 95 Ozzie Smith | .15 | .06 | .01 |
| ☐ 96 Royals Team | .15 | .03 | .01 |
| Mgr. Jim Frey | | | |
| Batting: George Brett | | | |
| Pitching: Larry Gura | | | |
| ☐ 97 Paul Moskau | .04 | .02 | .00 |
| ☐ 98 Terry Bulling | .04 | .02 | .00 |
| ☐ 99 Barry Bonnell | .04 | .02 | .00 |
| ☐ 100 Mike Schmidt | .80 | .40 | .08 |
| ☐ 101 SA: Mike Schmidt | .40 | .18 | .04 |
| ☐ 102 Dan Briggs | .04 | .02 | .00 |
| ☐ 103 Bob Lacey | .04 | .02 | .00 |
| ☐ 104 Rance Mulliniks | .04 | .02 | .00 |
| ☐ 105 Kirk Gibson | .60 | .28 | .06 |
| ☐ 106 Enrique Romo | .04 | .02 | .00 |
| ☐ 107 Wayne Krenchicki | .04 | .02 | .00 |
| ☐ 108 Bob Sykes | .04 | .02 | .00 |
| ☐ 109 Dave Revering | .04 | .02 | .00 |
| ☐ 110 Carlton Fisk | .25 | .10 | .02 |
| ☐ 111 SA: Carlton Fisk | .15 | .06 | .01 |
| ☐ 112 Billy Sample | .04 | .02 | .00 |
| ☐ 113 Steve McCatty | .06 | .02 | .00 |
| ☐ 114 Ken Landreaux | .06 | .02 | .00 |
| ☐ 115 Gaylord Perry | .25 | .10 | .02 |
| ☐ 116 Jim Wohlford | .04 | .02 | .00 |
| ☐ 117 Rawly Eastwick | .04 | .02 | .00 |
| ☐ 118 Expos Rookies: | .55 | .25 | .05 |
| Terry Francona | | | |
| Brad Mills | | | |
| Bryn Smith | | | |
| ☐ 119 Joe Pittman | .04 | .02 | .00 |
| ☐ 120 Gary Lucas | .04 | .02 | .00 |
| ☐ 121 Ed Lynch | .15 | .06 | .01 |
| ☐ 122 Jamie Easterly | .04 | .02 | .00 |
| ☐ 123 Danny Goodwin | .04 | .02 | .00 |
| ☐ 124 Reid Nichols | .04 | .02 | .00 |
| ☐ 125 Danny Ainge | .10 | .04 | .01 |
| ☐ 126 Braves Team Leaders: | .10 | .02 | .00 |
| Mgr. Bobby Cox | | | |
| Batting: C. Washington | | | |
| Pitching: Rick Mahler | | | |
| ☐ 127 Lonnie Smith | .12 | .05 | .01 |
| ☐ 128 Frank Pastore | .04 | .02 | .00 |

| | MINT | VG-E | F-G |
|---|---|---|---|
| ☐ 129 Checklist: 1–132 | .10 | .02 | .00 |
| ☐ 130 Julio Cruz | .04 | .02 | .00 |
| ☐ 131 Stan Bahnsen | .04 | .02 | .00 |
| ☐ 132 Lee May | .06 | .02 | .00 |
| ☐ 133 Pat Underwood | .04 | .02 | .00 |
| ☐ 134 Dan Ford | .06 | .02 | .00 |
| ☐ 135 Andy Rincon | .04 | .02 | .00 |
| ☐ 136 Lenn Sakata | .04 | .02 | .00 |
| ☐ 137 George Cappuzzello | .06 | .02 | .00 |
| ☐ 138 Tony Pena | .30 | .12 | .03 |
| ☐ 139 Jeff Jones | .04 | .02 | .00 |
| ☐ 140 Ron LeFlore | .06 | .02 | .00 |
| ☐ 141 Indians Rookies | 1.20 | .55 | .12 |
| Chris Bando | | | |
| Tom Brennan | | | |
| Von Hayes | | | |
| ☐ 142 Dave LaRoche | .04 | .02 | .00 |
| ☐ 143 Mookie Wilson | .12 | .05 | .01 |
| ☐ 144 Fred Breining | .12 | .05 | .01 |
| ☐ 145 Bob Horner | .35 | .15 | .03 |
| ☐ 146 Mike Griffin | .04 | .02 | .00 |
| ☐ 147 Denny Walling | .04 | .02 | .00 |
| ☐ 148 Mickey Klutts | .04 | .02 | .00 |
| ☐ 149 Pat Putnam | .04 | .02 | .00 |
| ☐ 150 Ted Simmons | .15 | .06 | .01 |
| ☐ 151 Dave Edwards | .04 | .02 | .00 |
| ☐ 152 Ramon Aviles | .04 | .02 | .00 |
| ☐ 153 Roger Erickson | .04 | .02 | .00 |
| ☐ 154 Dennis Werth | .04 | .02 | .00 |
| ☐ 155 Otto Velez | .04 | .02 | .00 |
| ☐ 156 A's Team Leaders: | .12 | .02 | .00 |
| Mgr. Billy Martin | | | |
| Batting: R. Henderson | | | |
| Pitching: S. McCatty | | | |
| ☐ 157 Steve Crawford | .09 | .04 | .01 |
| ☐ 158 Brian Downing | .06 | .02 | .00 |
| ☐ 159 Larry Biittner | .04 | .02 | .00 |
| ☐ 160 Luis Tiant | .10 | .04 | .01 |
| ☐ 161 Batting Leaders: | .15 | .06 | .01 |
| Bill Madlock | | | |
| Carney Lansford | | | |
| ☐ 162 Home Run Leaders: | .20 | .09 | .02 |
| Mike Schmidt | | | |
| Tony Armas | | | |
| Dwight Evans | | | |
| Bobby Grich | | | |
| Eddie Murray | | | |
| ☐ 163 RBI Leaders: | .25 | .10 | .02 |
| Mike Schmidt | | | |
| Eddie Murray | | | |
| ☐ 164 Stolen Base Leaders | .25 | .10 | .02 |
| Tim Raines | | | |
| Rickey Henderson | | | |

| | MINT | VG-E | F-G |
|---|---|---|---|
| ☐ 165 Victory Leaders | .15 | .06 | .01 |
| Tom Seaver | | | |
| Denny Martinez | | | |
| Steve McCatty | | | |
| Jack Morris | | | |
| Pete Vuckovich | | | |
| ☐ 166 Strikeout Leaders | .15 | .06 | .01 |
| Fernando Valenzuela | | | |
| Len Barker | | | |
| ☐ 167 ERA Leaders: | .15 | .06 | .01 |
| Nolan Ryan | | | |
| Steve McCatty | | | |
| ☐ 168 Leading Firemen: | .15 | .06 | .01 |
| Bruce Sutter | | | |
| Rollie Fingers | | | |
| ☐ 169 Charlie Leibrandt | .10 | .04 | .01 |
| ☐ 170 Jim Bibby | .06 | .02 | .00 |
| ☐ 171 Giants Rookies | .85 | .40 | .08 |
| Bob Brenly | | | |
| Chili Davis | | | |
| Bob Tufts | | | |
| ☐ 172 Bill Gullickson | .06 | .02 | .00 |
| ☐ 173 Jamie Quirk | .04 | .02 | .00 |
| ☐ 174 Dave Ford | .04 | .02 | .00 |
| ☐ 175 Jerry Mumphrey | .06 | .02 | .00 |
| ☐ 176 Dewey Robinson | .04 | .02 | .00 |
| ☐ 177 John Ellis | .04 | .02 | .00 |
| ☐ 178 Dyar Miller | .04 | .02 | .00 |
| ☐ 179 Steve Garvey | .65 | .30 | .06 |
| ☐ 180 SA: Steve Garvey | .35 | .15 | .03 |
| ☐ 181 Silvio Martinez | .04 | .02 | .00 |
| ☐ 182 Larry Herndon | .06 | .02 | .00 |
| ☐ 183 Mike Proly | .04 | .02 | .00 |
| ☐ 184 Mick Kelleher | .04 | .02 | .00 |
| ☐ 185 Phil Niekro | .25 | .10 | .02 |
| ☐ 186 Cardinals Team Leaders: | .11 | .02 | .00 |
| Mgr. Whitey Herzog | | | |
| Batting K. Hernandez | | | |
| Pitching Bob Forsch | | | |
| ☐ 187 Jeff Newman | .04 | .02 | .00 |
| ☐ 188 Randy Martz | .04 | .02 | .00 |
| ☐ 189 Glenn Hoffman | .04 | .02 | .00 |
| ☐ 190 J.R. Richard | .10 | .04 | .01 |
| ☐ 191 Tim Wallach | .80 | .40 | .08 |
| ☐ 192 Broderick Perkins | .04 | .02 | .00 |
| ☐ 193 Darrell Jackson | .04 | .02 | .00 |
| ☐ 194 Mike Vail | .04 | .02 | .00 |
| ☐ 195 Paul Molitor | .20 | .09 | .02 |
| ☐ 196 Willie Upshaw | .20 | .09 | .02 |
| ☐ 197 Shane Rawley | .06 | .02 | .00 |
| ☐ 198 Chris Speier | .04 | .02 | .00 |
| ☐ 199 Don Aase | .04 | .02 | .00 |

| | MINT | VG-E | F-G |
|---|---|---|---|
| ☐ 200 George Brett | 1.10 | .50 | .11 |
| ☐ 201 SA: George Brett | .50 | .22 | .05 |
| ☐ 202 Rick Manning | .03 | .01 | .00 |
| ☐ 203 Blue Jays Rookies | 1.00 | .45 | .10 |
| Jesse Barfield | | | |
| Brian Milner | | | |
| Boomer Wells | | | |
| ☐ 204 Gary Roenicke | .06 | .02 | .00 |
| ☐ 205 Neil Allen | .06 | .02 | .00 |
| ☐ 206 Tony Bernazard | .04 | .02 | .00 |
| ☐ 207 Rod Scurry | .04 | .02 | .00 |
| ☐ 208 Bobby Murcer | .12 | .05 | .01 |
| ☐ 209 Gary Lavelle | .04 | .02 | .00 |
| ☐ 210 Keith Hernandez | .40 | .18 | .04 |
| ☐ 211 Dan Petry | .25 | .10 | .02 |
| ☐ 212 Mario Mendoza | .04 | .02 | .00 |
| ☐ 213 Dave Stewart | .15 | .06 | .01 |
| ☐ 214 Brian Asselstine | .04 | .02 | .00 |
| ☐ 215 Mike Krukow | .04 | .02 | .00 |
| ☐ 216 White Sox Team | | | |
| Leaders: | .11 | .02 | .00 |
| Mgr. Tony LaRussa | | | |
| Batting: Chet Lemon | | | |
| Pitching: Dennis Lamp | | | |
| ☐ 217 Bo McLaughlin | .04 | .02 | .00 |
| ☐ 218 Dave Roberts | .04 | .02 | .00 |
| ☐ 219 John Curtis | .04 | .02 | .00 |
| ☐ 220 Manny Trillo | .06 | .02 | .00 |
| ☐ 221 Jim Slaton | .04 | .02 | .00 |
| ☐ 222 Butch Wynegar | .06 | .02 | .00 |
| ☐ 223 Lloyd Moseby | .25 | .10 | .02 |
| ☐ 224 Bruce Bochte | .06 | .02 | .00 |
| ☐ 225 Mike Torrez | .06 | .02 | .00 |
| ☐ 226 Checklist 133–264 | .11 | .02 | .00 |
| ☐ 227 Ray Burris | .04 | .02 | .00 |
| ☐ 228 Sam Mejias | .04 | .02 | .00 |
| ☐ 229 Geoff Zahn | .04 | .02 | .00 |
| ☐ 230 Willie Wilson | .25 | .10 | .02 |
| ☐ 231 Phillies Rookies | .60 | .28 | .06 |
| Mark Davis | | | |
| Bob Dernier | | | |
| Ozzie Virgil | | | |
| ☐ 232 Terry Crowley | .04 | .02 | .00 |
| ☐ 233 Duane Kuiper | .04 | .02 | .00 |
| ☐ 234 Ron Hodges | .04 | .02 | .00 |
| ☐ 235 Mike Easler | .10 | .04 | .01 |
| ☐ 236 John Martin | .06 | .02 | .00 |
| ☐ 237 Rusty Kuntz | .04 | .02 | .00 |
| ☐ 238 Kevin Saucier | .04 | .02 | .00 |
| ☐ 239 Jon Matlack | .06 | .02 | .00 |
| ☐ 240 Bucky Dent | .08 | .03 | .01 |
| ☐ 241 SA: Bucky Dent | .06 | .02 | .00 |
| ☐ 242 Milt May | .04 | .02 | .00 |

| | MINT | VG-E | F-G |
|---|---|---|---|
| ☐ 243 Bob Owchinko | .04 | .02 | .00 |
| ☐ 244 Rufino Linares | .06 | .02 | .00 |
| ☐ 245 Ken Reitz | .04 | .02 | .00 |
| ☐ 246 New York Mets Team | .11 | .02 | .00 |
| Mgr. Joe Torre | | | |
| Batting: Hubie Brooks | | | |
| Pitching: Mike Scott | | | |
| ☐ 247 Pedro Guerrero | .50 | .22 | .05 |
| ☐ 248 Frank LaCorte | .04 | .02 | .00 |
| ☐ 249 Tim Flannery | .04 | .02 | .00 |
| ☐ 250 Tug McGraw | .10 | .04 | .01 |
| ☐ 251 Fred Lynn | .30 | .12 | .03 |
| ☐ 252 SA: Fred Lynn | .15 | .06 | .01 |
| ☐ 253 Chuck Baker | .04 | .02 | .00 |
| ☐ 254 Jorge Bell | 1.50 | .70 | .15 |
| ☐ 255 Tony Perez | .18 | .08 | .01 |
| ☐ 256 SA: Tony Perez | .10 | .04 | .01 |
| ☐ 257 Larry Harlow | .04 | .02 | .00 |
| ☐ 258 Bo Diaz | .10 | .04 | .01 |
| ☐ 259 Rodney Scott | .04 | .02 | .00 |
| ☐ 260 Bruce Sutter | .30 | .12 | .03 |
| ☐ 261 Tigers Rookies: | .12 | .05 | .01 |
| Howard Bailey | | | |
| Marty Castillo | | | |
| Dave Rucker | | | |
| ☐ 262 Doug Bair | .04 | .02 | .00 |
| ☐ 263 Victor Cruz | .04 | .02 | .00 |
| ☐ 264 Dan Quisenberry | .30 | .12 | .03 |
| ☐ 265 Al Bumbry | .04 | .02 | .00 |
| ☐ 266 Rick Leach | .08 | .03 | .01 |
| ☐ 267 Kurt Bevacqua | .04 | .02 | .00 |
| ☐ 268 Rickey Keeton | .06 | .02 | .00 |
| ☐ 269 Jim Essian | .04 | .02 | .00 |
| ☐ 270 Rusty Staub | .10 | .04 | .01 |
| ☐ 271 Larry Bradford | .04 | .02 | .00 |
| ☐ 272 Bump Wills | .04 | .02 | .00 |
| ☐ 273 Doug Bird | .04 | .02 | .00 |
| ☐ 274 Bob Ojeda | .35 | .15 | .03 |
| ☐ 275 Bob Watson | .06 | .02 | .00 |
| ☐ 276 Angels Team Leaders: | .12 | .02 | .00 |
| Mgr. Gene Mauch | | | |
| Batting: Rod Carew | | | |
| Pitching: Ken Forsch | | | |
| ☐ 277 Terry Puhl | .06 | .02 | .00 |
| ☐ 278 John Littlefield | .04 | .02 | .00 |
| ☐ 279 Bill Russell | .06 | .02 | .00 |
| ☐ 280 Ben Oglivie | .10 | .04 | .01 |
| ☐ 281 John Verhoeven | .04 | .02 | .00 |
| ☐ 282 Ken Macha | .04 | .02 | .00 |
| ☐ 283 Brian Allard | .04 | .02 | .00 |
| ☐ 284 Bob Grich | .10 | .04 | .01 |
| ☐ 285 Sparky Lyle | .10 | .04 | .01 |
| ☐ 286 Bill Fahey | .04 | .02 | .00 |

|  | MINT | VG-E | F-G |
|---|---|---|---|
| ☐ 287 Alan Bannister | .04 | .02 | .00 |
| ☐ 288 Garry Templeton | .15 | .06 | .01 |
| ☐ 289 Bob Stanley | .06 | .02 | .00 |
| ☐ 290 Ken Singleton | .12 | .05 | .01 |
| ☐ 291 Pirates Rookies | .85 | .40 | .08 |
|     Vance Law | | | |
|     Bob Long | | | |
|     Johnny Ray | | | |
| ☐ 292 David Palmer | .06 | .02 | .00 |
| ☐ 293 Rob Picciolo | .04 | .02 | .00 |
| ☐ 294 Mike LaCoss | .04 | .02 | .00 |
| ☐ 295 Jason Thompson | .10 | .04 | .01 |
| ☐ 296 Bob Walk | .04 | .02 | .00 |
| ☐ 297 Clint Hurdle | .04 | .02 | .00 |
| ☐ 298 Danny Darwin | .04 | .02 | .00 |
| ☐ 299 Steve Trout | .06 | .02 | .00 |
| ☐ 300 Reggie Jackson | .75 | .35 | .07 |
| ☐ 301 SA: Reggie Jackson | .35 | .15 | .03 |
| ☐ 302 Doug Flynn | .04 | .02 | .00 |
| ☐ 303 Bill Caudill | .10 | .04 | .01 |
| ☐ 304 Johnnie LeMaster | .04 | .02 | .00 |
| ☐ 305 Don Sutton | .20 | .09 | .02 |
| ☐ 306 SA: Don Sutton | .10 | .04 | .01 |
| ☐ 307 Randy Bass | .04 | .02 | .00 |
| ☐ 308 Charlie Moore | .04 | .02 | .00 |
| ☐ 309 Pete Redfern | .04 | .02 | .00 |
| ☐ 310 Mike Hargrove | .06 | .02 | .00 |
| ☐ 311 Dodgers Team | .12 | .02 | .00 |
|     Mgr. Tom Lasorda | | | |
|     Batting: Dusty Baker | | | |
|     Pitching: Burt Hooton | | | |
| ☐ 312 Lenny Randle | .04 | .02 | .00 |
| ☐ 313 John Harris | .04 | .02 | .00 |
| ☐ 314 Buck Martinez | .04 | .02 | .00 |
| ☐ 315 Burt Hooton | .04 | .02 | .00 |
| ☐ 316 Steve Braun | .04 | .02 | .00 |
| ☐ 317 Dick Ruthven | .04 | .02 | .00 |
| ☐ 318 Mike Heath | .04 | .02 | .00 |
| ☐ 319 Dave Rozema | .04 | .02 | .00 |
| ☐ 320 Chris Chambliss | .08 | .03 | .01 |
| ☐ 321 SA: Chris Chambliss | .06 | .02 | .00 |
| ☐ 322 Garry Hancock | .04 | .02 | .00 |
| ☐ 323 Bill Lee | .06 | .02 | .00 |
| ☐ 324 Steve Dillard | .04 | .02 | .00 |
| ☐ 325 Jose Cruz | .15 | .06 | .01 |
| ☐ 326 Pete Falcone | .04 | .02 | .00 |
| ☐ 327 Joe Nolan | .04 | .02 | .00 |
| ☐ 328 Ed Farmer | .04 | .02 | .00 |
| ☐ 329 U.L. Washington | .04 | .02 | .00 |
| ☐ 330 Rick Wise | .06 | .02 | .00 |
| ☐ 331 Benny Ayala | .04 | .02 | .00 |
| ☐ 332 Don Robinson | .04 | .02 | .00 |

|  | MINT | VG-E | F-G |
|---|---|---|---|
| ☐ 333 Brewers Rookies | .16 | .07 | .01 |
|     Frank DiPino | | | |
|     Marshall Edwards | | | |
|     Chuck Porter | | | |
| ☐ 334 Aurelio Rodriguez | .04 | .02 | .00 |
| ☐ 335 Jim Sundberg | .06 | .02 | .00 |
| ☐ 336 Mariners Team | .10 | .02 | .00 |
|     Mgr. Rene Lachemann | | | |
|     Batting: Tom Paciorek | | | |
|     Pitching: Glenn Abbott | | | |
|     NL ALL-STARS | | | |
|     (337–347) | | | |
| ☐ 337 Pete Rose AS | .55 | .25 | .05 |
| ☐ 338 Dave Lopes AS | .07 | .03 | .01 |
| ☐ 339 Mike Schmidt AS | .35 | .15 | .03 |
| ☐ 340 Dave Concepcion AS | .10 | .04 | .01 |
| ☐ 341 Andre Dawson AS | .18 | .08 | .01 |
| ☐ 342 A George Foster AS | .25 | .10 | .02 |
|     (with autograph) | | | |
| ☐ 342 B George Foster AS | 2.25 | 1.00 | .22 |
|     (w/o autograph) | | | |
| ☐ 343 Dave Parker AS | .18 | .08 | .01 |
| ☐ 344 Gary Carter AS | .25 | .10 | .02 |
| ☐ 345 Fernando Valenzuela AS | .25 | .10 | .02 |
| ☐ 346 Tom Seaver AS | .25 | .10 | .02 |
| ☐ 347 Bruce Sutter AS | .15 | .06 | .01 |
| ☐ 348 Derrel Thomas | .04 | .02 | .00 |
| ☐ 349 George Frazier | .04 | .02 | .00 |
| ☐ 350 Thad Bosley | .04 | .02 | .00 |
| ☐ 351 Reds Rookies: | .09 | .04 | .01 |
|     Scott Brown | | | |
|     Geoff Coumbe | | | |
|     Paul Householder | | | |
| ☐ 352 Dick Davis | .04 | .02 | .00 |
| ☐ 353 Jack O'Connor | .08 | .03 | .01 |
| ☐ 354 Roberto Ramos | .04 | .02 | .00 |
| ☐ 355 Dwight Evans | .16 | .07 | .01 |
| ☐ 356 Denny Lewallyn | .08 | .03 | .01 |
| ☐ 357 Butch Hobson | .04 | .02 | .00 |
| ☐ 358 Mike Parrott | .04 | .02 | .00 |
| ☐ 359 Jim Dwyer | .04 | .02 | .00 |
| ☐ 360 Len Barker | .09 | .04 | .01 |
| ☐ 361 Rafael Landestoy | .04 | .02 | .00 |
| ☐ 362 Jim Wright | .04 | .02 | .00 |
| ☐ 363 Bob Molinaro | .04 | .02 | .00 |
| ☐ 364 Doyle Alexander | .06 | .02 | .00 |
| ☐ 365 Bill Madlock | .25 | .10 | .02 |
| ☐ 366 Padres Team Leaders: | .10 | .02 | .00 |
|     Mgr. Frank Howard | | | |
|     Batting: Luis Salazar | | | |
|     Pitching: Eichelberger | | | |

| | MINT | VG-E | F-G |
|---|---|---|---|
| ☐ 367 Jim Kaat | .11 | .05 | .01 |
| ☐ 368 Alex Trevino | .04 | .02 | .00 |
| ☐ 369 Champ Summers | .04 | .02 | .00 |
| ☐ 370 Mike Norris | .06 | .02 | .00 |
| ☐ 371 Jerry Don Gleaton | .04 | .02 | .00 |
| ☐ 372 Luis Gómez | .04 | .02 | .00 |
| ☐ 373 Gene Nelson | .12 | .05 | .01 |
| ☐ 374 Tim Blackwell | .04 | .02 | .00 |
| ☐ 375 Dusty Baker | .10 | .04 | .01 |
| ☐ 376 Chris Welsh | .08 | .03 | .01 |
| ☐ 377 Kiko Garcia | .04 | .02 | .00 |
| ☐ 378 Mike Caldwell | .06 | .02 | .00 |
| ☐ 379 Rob Wilfong | .04 | .02 | .00 |
| ☐ 380 Dave Stieb | .35 | .15 | .03 |
| ☐ 381 Red Sox Rookies: | .12 | .05 | .01 |
|     Bruce Hurst | | | |
|     Dave Schmidt | | | |
|     Julio Valdez | | | |
| ☐ 382 Joe Simpson | .04 | .02 | .00 |
| ☐ 383 Pascual Perez | .08 | .03 | .01 |
| ☐ 384 Keith Moreland | .06 | .02 | .00 |
| ☐ 385 Ken Forsch | .04 | .02 | .00 |
| ☐ 386 Jerry White | .04 | .02 | .00 |
| ☐ 387 Tom Veryzer | .04 | .02 | .00 |
| ☐ 388 Joe Rudi | .06 | .02 | .00 |
| ☐ 389 George Vukovich | .04 | .02 | .00 |
| ☐ 390 Eddie Murray | 1.00 | .45 | .10 |
| ☐ 391 Dave Tobik | .04 | .02 | .00 |
| ☐ 392 Rick Bosetti | .04 | .02 | .00 |
| ☐ 393 Al Hrabosky | .06 | .02 | .00 |
| ☐ 394 Checklist: 265–396 | .10 | .02 | .00 |
| ☐ 395 Omar Moreno | .06 | .02 | .00 |
| ☐ 396 Twins Team Leaders: | .10 | .02 | .00 |
|     Mgr. Billy Gardner | | | |
|     Batting: John Castino | | | |
|     Pitching: F. Arroyo | | | |
| ☐ 397 Ken Brett | .06 | .02 | .00 |
| ☐ 398 Mike Squires | .04 | .02 | .00 |
| ☐ 399 Pat Zachry | .04 | .02 | .00 |
| ☐ 400 Johnny Bench | .55 | .25 | .05 |
| ☐ 401 SA: Johnny Bench | .25 | .10 | .02 |
| ☐ 402 Bill Stein | .04 | .02 | .00 |
| ☐ 403 Jim Tracy | .04 | .02 | .00 |
| ☐ 404 Dickie Thon | .10 | .04 | .01 |
| ☐ 405 Rick Reuschel | .06 | .02 | .00 |
| ☐ 406 Al Holland | .06 | .02 | .00 |
| ☐ 407 Danny Boone | .06 | .02 | .00 |
| ☐ 408 Ed Romero | .04 | .02 | .00 |
| ☐ 409 Don Cooper | .06 | .02 | .00 |
| ☐ 410 Ron Cey | .15 | .06 | .01 |
| ☐ 411 SA: Ron Cey | .09 | .04 | .01 |
| ☐ 412 Luis Leal | .04 | .02 | .00 |
| ☐ 413 Dan Meyer | .04 | .02 | .00 |
| ☐ 414 Elias Sosa | .04 | .02 | .00 |
| ☐ 415 Don Baylor | .15 | .06 | .01 |
| ☐ 416 Marty Bystrom | .04 | .02 | .00 |
| ☐ 417 Pat Kelly | .04 | .02 | .00 |
| ☐ 418 Rangers Rookies: | .09 | .04 | .01 |
|     John Butcher | | | |
|     Bobby Johnson | | | |
|     Dave Schmidt | | | |
| ☐ 419 Steve Stone | .08 | .03 | .01 |
| ☐ 420 George Hendrick | .10 | .04 | .01 |
| ☐ 421 Mark Clear | .06 | .02 | .00 |
| ☐ 422 Cliff Johnson | .04 | .02 | .00 |
| ☐ 423 Stan Papi | .04 | .02 | .00 |
| ☐ 424 Bruce Benedict | .04 | .02 | .00 |
| ☐ 425 John Candelaria | .10 | .04 | .01 |
| ☐ 426 Orioles Team Leaders: | .12 | .02 | .00 |
|     Mgr. Earl Weaver | | | |
|     Batting: Eddie Murray | | | |
|     Pitching: Sam Stewart | | | |
| ☐ 427 Ron Oester | .06 | .02 | .00 |
| ☐ 428 LaMarr Hoyt | .15 | .06 | .01 |
| ☐ 429 John Wathan | .04 | .02 | .00 |
| ☐ 430 Vida Blue | .12 | .05 | .01 |
| ☐ 431 SA: Vida Blue | .07 | .03 | .01 |
| ☐ 432 Mike Scott | .06 | .02 | .00 |
| ☐ 433 Alan Ashby | .04 | .02 | .00 |
| ☐ 434 Joe LeFebvre | .06 | .02 | .00 |
| ☐ 435 Robin Yount | .60 | .28 | .06 |
| ☐ 436 Joe Strain | .04 | .02 | .00 |
| ☐ 437 Juan Berenguer | .04 | .02 | .00 |
| ☐ 438 Pete Mackanin | .04 | .02 | .00 |
| ☐ 439 Dave Righetti | 1.25 | .60 | .12 |
| ☐ 440 Jeff Burroughs | .06 | .02 | .00 |
| ☐ 441 Astros Rookies: | .09 | .04 | .01 |
|     Danny Heep | | | |
|     Billy Smith | | | |
|     Bobby Sprowl | | | |
| ☐ 442 Bruce Kison | .04 | .02 | .00 |
| ☐ 443 Mark Wagner | .04 | .02 | .00 |
| ☐ 444 Terry Forster | .10 | .04 | .01 |
| ☐ 445 Larry Parrish | .08 | .03 | .01 |
| ☐ 446 Wayne Garland | .04 | .02 | .00 |
| ☐ 447 Darrell Porter | .08 | .03 | .01 |
| ☐ 448 SA: Darrell Porter | .06 | .02 | .00 |
| ☐ 449 Luis Aguayo | .06 | .02 | .00 |
| ☐ 450 Jack Morris | .40 | .18 | .04 |
| ☐ 451 Ed Miller | .04 | .02 | .00 |
| ☐ 452 Lee Smith | .65 | .30 | .06 |
| ☐ 453 Art Howe | .04 | .02 | .00 |
| ☐ 454 Rick Langford | .04 | .02 | .00 |
| ☐ 455 Tom Burgmeier | .04 | .02 | .00 |

|  | MINT | VG-E | F-G |
|---|---|---|---|
| ☐ 456 Chicago Cubs Team ... | .10 | .02 | .00 |
|    Mgr. Joe Amalfitano | | | |
|    Batting: Bill Buckner | | | |
|    Pitching: Randy Martz | | | |
| ☐ 457 Tim Stoddard | .04 | .02 | .00 |
| ☐ 458 Willie Montanez | .04 | .02 | .00 |
| ☐ 459 Bruce Berenyi | .06 | .02 | .00 |
| ☐ 460 Jack Clark | .30 | .12 | .03 |
| ☐ 461 Rich Dotson | .10 | .04 | .01 |
| ☐ 462 Dave Chalk | .04 | .02 | .00 |
| ☐ 463 Jim Kern | .04 | .02 | .00 |
| ☐ 464 Juan Bonilla | .08 | .03 | .01 |
| ☐ 465 Lee Mazzilli | .06 | .02 | .00 |
| ☐ 466 Randy Lerch | .04 | .02 | .00 |
| ☐ 467 Mickey Hatcher | .06 | .02 | .00 |
| ☐ 468 Floyd Bannister | .08 | .03 | .01 |
| ☐ 469 Ed Ott | .04 | .02 | .00 |
| ☐ 470 John Mayberry | .06 | .02 | .00 |
| ☐ 471 Royals Rookies | .50 | .22 | .05 |
|    Atlee Hammaker | | | |
|    Mike Jones | | | |
|    Darryl Motley | | | |
| ☐ 472 Oscar Gamble | .06 | .02 | .00 |
| ☐ 473 Mike Stanton | .04 | .02 | .00 |
| ☐ 474 Ken Oberkfell | .06 | .02 | .00 |
| ☐ 475 Alan Trammell | .40 | .18 | .04 |
| ☐ 476 Brian Kingman | .04 | .02 | .00 |
| ☐ 477 Steve Yeager | .06 | .02 | .00 |
| ☐ 478 Ray Searage | .15 | .06 | .01 |
| ☐ 479 Rowland Office | .04 | .02 | .00 |
| ☐ 480 Steve Carlton | .55 | .25 | .05 |
| ☐ 481 SA: Steve Carlton | .30 | .12 | .03 |
| ☐ 482 Glenn Hubbard | .06 | .02 | .00 |
| ☐ 483 Gary Woods | .04 | .02 | .00 |
| ☐ 484 Ivan DeJesus | .04 | .02 | .00 |
| ☐ 485 Kent Tekulve | .08 | .03 | .01 |
| ☐ 486 Yankees Team | .12 | .02 | .00 |
|    Mgr. Bob Lemon | | | |
|    Batting: J. Mumphrey | | | |
|    Pitching: Tommy John | | | |
| ☐ 487 Bob McClure | .04 | .02 | .00 |
| ☐ 488 Ron Jackson | .04 | .02 | .00 |
| ☐ 489 Rick Dempsey | .06 | .02 | .00 |
| ☐ 490 Dennis Eckersley | .06 | .02 | .00 |
| ☐ 491 Checklist: 397–528 | .11 | .02 | .00 |
| ☐ 492 Joe Price | .04 | .02 | .00 |
| ☐ 493 Chet Lemon | .10 | .04 | .01 |
| ☐ 494 Hubie Brooks | .15 | .06 | .01 |
| ☐ 495 Dennis Leonard | .06 | .02 | .00 |
| ☐ 496 Johnny Grubb | .04 | .02 | .00 |
| ☐ 497 Jim Anderson | .04 | .02 | .00 |
| ☐ 498 Dave Bergman | .04 | .02 | .00 |
| ☐ 499 Paul Mirabella | .04 | .02 | .00 |

|  | MINT | VG-E | F-G |
|---|---|---|---|
| ☐ 500 Rod Carew | .55 | .25 | .05 |
| ☐ 501 SA: Rod Carew | .30 | .12 | .03 |
| ☐ 502 Braves Rookies: | .65 | .30 | .06 |
|    Steve Bedrosian | | | |
|    Brett Butler | | | |
|    Larry Owen | | | |
| ☐ 503 Julio Gonzalez | .04 | .02 | .00 |
| ☐ 504 Rick Peters | .04 | .02 | .00 |
| ☐ 505 Graig Nettles | .16 | .07 | .01 |
| ☐ 506 SA: Graig Nettles | .10 | .04 | .01 |
| ☐ 507 Terry Harper | .04 | .02 | .00 |
| ☐ 508 Jody Davis | .65 | .30 | .06 |
| ☐ 509 Harry Spilman | .04 | .02 | .00 |
| ☐ 510 Fernando Valenzuela | .70 | .32 | .07 |
| ☐ 511 Ruppert Jones | .06 | .02 | .00 |
| ☐ 512 Jerry Dybzinski | .04 | .02 | .00 |
| ☐ 513 Rick Rhoden | .06 | .02 | .00 |
| ☐ 514 Joe Ferguson | .04 | .02 | .00 |
| ☐ 515 Larry Bowa | .10 | .04 | .01 |
| ☐ 516 SA: Larry Bowa | .06 | .02 | .00 |
| ☐ 517 Mark Brouhard | .08 | .03 | .01 |
| ☐ 518 Garth Iorg | .04 | .02 | .00 |
| ☐ 519 Glenn Adams | .04 | .02 | .00 |
| ☐ 520 Mike Flanagan | .10 | .04 | .01 |
| ☐ 521 Billy Almon | .04 | .02 | .00 |
| ☐ 522 Chuck Rainey | .04 | .02 | .00 |
| ☐ 523 Gary Gray | .06 | .02 | .00 |
| ☐ 524 Tom Hausman | .04 | .02 | .00 |
| ☐ 525 Ray Knight | .06 | .02 | .00 |
| ☐ 526 Expos Team | .10 | .02 | .00 |
|    Mgr. Jim Fanning | | | |
|    Batting: W. Cromartie | | | |
|    Pitching: B. Gullickson | | | |
| ☐ 527 John Henry Johnson | .04 | .02 | .00 |
| ☐ 528 Matt Alexander | .04 | .02 | .00 |
| ☐ 529 Allen Ripley | .04 | .02 | .00 |
| ☐ 530 Dickie Noles | .04 | .02 | .00 |
| ☐ 531 A's Rookies: | .09 | .04 | .01 |
|    Rich Bordi | | | |
|    Mark Budaska | | | |
|    Kelvin Moore | | | |
| ☐ 532 Toby Harrah | .06 | .02 | .00 |
| ☐ 533 Joaquin Andujar | .16 | .07 | .01 |
| ☐ 534 Dave McKay | .04 | .02 | .00 |
| ☐ 535 Lance Parrish | .40 | .18 | .04 |
| ☐ 536 Rafael Ramirez | .06 | .02 | .00 |
| ☐ 537 Doug Capilla | .04 | .02 | .00 |
| ☐ 538 Lou Piniella | .10 | .04 | .01 |
| ☐ 539 Vern Ruhle | .04 | .02 | .00 |
| ☐ 540 Andre Dawson | .30 | .12 | .03 |
| ☐ 541 Barry Evans | .04 | .02 | .00 |
| ☐ 542 Ned Yost | .04 | .02 | .00 |
| ☐ 543 Bill Robinson | .04 | .02 | .00 |

| | MINT | VG-E | F-G |
|---|---|---|---|
| ☐ 544 Larry Christenson | .04 | .02 | .00 |
| ☐ 545 Reggie Smith | .10 | .04 | .01 |
| ☐ 546 SA: Reggie Smith | .06 | .02 | .00 |
| AL ALL-STARS (547-557) | | | |
| ☐ 547 Rod Carew AS | .25 | .10 | .02 |
| ☐ 548 Willie Randolph AS | .07 | .03 | .01 |
| ☐ 549 George Brett AS | .40 | .18 | .04 |
| ☐ 550 Bucky Dent AS | .07 | .03 | .01 |
| ☐ 551 Reggie Jackson AS | .35 | .15 | .03 |
| ☐ 552 Ken Singleton AS | .06 | .02 | .00 |
| ☐ 553 Dave Winfield AS | .30 | .12 | .03 |
| ☐ 554 Carlton Fisk AS | .16 | .07 | .01 |
| ☐ 555 Scott McGregor AS | .07 | .03 | .01 |
| ☐ 556 Jack Morris AS | .16 | .07 | .01 |
| ☐ 557 Rich Gossage AS | .16 | .07 | .01 |
| ☐ 558 John Tudor | .30 | .10 | .02 |
| ☐ 559 Indians Team | .10 | .02 | .00 |
| Mgr. Dave Garcia | | | |
| Batting: Mike Hargrove | | | |
| Pitching: Bert Blyleven | | | |
| ☐ 560 Doug Corbett | .04 | .02 | .00 |
| ☐ 561 Cardinals Rookies | .15 | .06 | .01 |
| Glenn Brummer | | | |
| Luis DeLeon | | | |
| Gene Roof | | | |
| ☐ 562 Mike O'Berry | .04 | .02 | .00 |
| ☐ 563 Ross Baumgarten | .04 | .02 | .00 |
| ☐ 564 Doug DeCinces | .12 | .05 | .01 |
| ☐ 565 Jackson Todd | .04 | .02 | .00 |
| ☐ 566 Mike Jorgensen | .04 | .02 | .00 |
| ☐ 567 Bob Babcock | .04 | .02 | .00 |
| ☐ 568 Joe Pettini | .04 | .02 | .00 |
| ☐ 569 Willie Randolph | .10 | .04 | .01 |
| ☐ 570 SA: Willie Randolph | .06 | .02 | .00 |
| ☐ 571 Glenn Abbott | .04 | .02 | .00 |
| ☐ 572 Juan Beniquez | .06 | .02 | .00 |
| ☐ 573 Rick Waits | .04 | .02 | .00 |
| ☐ 574 Mike Ramsey | .04 | .02 | .00 |
| ☐ 575 Al Cowens | .06 | .02 | .00 |
| ☐ 576 Giants Team | .10 | .02 | .00 |
| Mgr. Frank Robinson | | | |
| Batting: Milt May | | | |
| Pitching: Vida Blue | | | |
| ☐ 577 Rick Monday | .06 | .02 | .00 |
| ☐ 578 Shooty Babitt | .06 | .02 | .00 |
| ☐ 579 Rick Mahler | .35 | .15 | .03 |
| ☐ 580 Bobby Bonds | .10 | .04 | .01 |
| ☐ 581 Ron Reed | .04 | .02 | .00 |
| ☐ 582 Luis Pujols | .04 | .02 | .00 |
| ☐ 583 Tippy Martinez | .06 | .02 | .00 |
| ☐ 584 Hosken Powell | .04 | .02 | .00 |
| ☐ 585 Rollie Fingers | .25 | .10 | .02 |
| ☐ 586 SA: Rollie Fingers | .15 | .06 | .01 |
| ☐ 587 Tim Lollar | .08 | .03 | .01 |
| ☐ 588 Dale Berra | .06 | .02 | .00 |
| ☐ 589 Dave Stapleton | .06 | .02 | .00 |
| ☐ 590 Al Oliver | .25 | .10 | .02 |
| ☐ 591 SA: Al Oliver | .15 | .06 | .01 |
| ☐ 592 Craig Swan | .04 | .02 | .00 |
| ☐ 593 Billy Smith | .04 | .02 | .00 |
| ☐ 594 Renie Martin | .04 | .02 | .00 |
| ☐ 595 Dave Collins | .06 | .02 | .00 |
| ☐ 596 Damaso Garcia | .15 | .06 | .01 |
| ☐ 597 Wayne Nordhagen | .04 | .02 | .00 |
| ☐ 598 Bob Galasso | .04 | .02 | .00 |
| ☐ 599 White Sox Rookies | .09 | .04 | .01 |
| Jay Loviglio | | | |
| Reggie Patterson | | | |
| Leo Sutherland | | | |
| ☐ 600 Dave Winfield | .45 | .20 | .04 |
| ☐ 601 Sid Monge | .04 | .02 | .00 |
| ☐ 602 Freddie Patek | .04 | .02 | .00 |
| ☐ 603 Rich Hebner | .04 | .02 | .00 |
| ☐ 604 Orlando Sanchez | .06 | .02 | .00 |
| ☐ 605 Steve Rogers | .09 | .04 | .01 |
| ☐ 606 Blue Jays Team Leaders: | .10 | .02 | .00 |
| Mgr. Bobby Mattick | | | |
| Batting: John Mayberry | | | |
| Pitching: Dave Stieb | | | |
| ☐ 607 Leon Durham | .35 | .15 | .03 |
| ☐ 608 Jerry Royster | .04 | .02 | .00 |
| ☐ 609 Rick Sutcliffe | .35 | .15 | .03 |
| ☐ 610 Rickey Henderson | .80 | .40 | .08 |
| ☐ 611 Joe Niekro | .12 | .05 | .01 |
| ☐ 612 Gary Ward | .06 | .02 | .00 |
| ☐ 613 Jim Gantner | .06 | .02 | .00 |
| ☐ 614 Juan Eichelberger | .04 | .02 | .00 |
| ☐ 615 Bob Boone | .06 | .02 | .00 |
| ☐ 616 SA: Bob Boone | .06 | .02 | .00 |
| ☐ 617 Scott McGregor | .10 | .04 | .01 |
| ☐ 618 Tim Foli | .04 | .02 | .00 |
| ☐ 619 Bill Campbell | .06 | .02 | .00 |
| ☐ 620 Ken Griffey | .10 | .04 | .01 |
| ☐ 621 SA: Ken Griffey | .06 | .02 | .00 |
| ☐ 622 Dennis Lamp | .04 | .02 | .00 |
| ☐ 623 Mets Rookies: | .15 | .06 | .01 |
| Ron Gardenhire | | | |
| Terry Leach | | | |
| Tim Leary | | | |
| ☐ 624 Fergie Jenkins | .15 | .06 | .01 |
| ☐ 625 Hal McRae | .08 | .03 | .01 |
| ☐ 626 Randy Jones | .06 | .02 | .00 |
| ☐ 627 Enos Cabell | .04 | .02 | .00 |
| ☐ 628 Bill Travers | .04 | .02 | .00 |
| ☐ 629 Johnny Wockenfuss | .04 | .02 | .00 |

| | MINT | VG-E | F-G | | MINT | VG-E | F-G |
|---|---|---|---|---|---|---|---|
| ☐ 630 Joe Charboneau | .06 | .02 | .00 | ☐ 675 Cecil Cooper | .25 | .10 | .02 |
| ☐ 631 Gene Tenace | .04 | .02 | .00 | ☐ 676 Sal Butera | .04 | .02 | .00 |
| ☐ 632 Bryan Clark | .08 | .03 | .01 | ☐ 677 Alfredo Griffin | .10 | .04 | .01 |
| ☐ 633 Mitchell Page | .04 | .02 | .00 | ☐ 678 Tom Paciorek | .04 | .02 | .00 |
| ☐ 634 Checklist: 529–660 | .11 | .02 | .00 | ☐ 679 Sammy Stewart | .04 | .02 | .00 |
| ☐ 635 Ron Davis | .06 | .02 | .00 | ☐ 680 Gary Matthews | .10 | .04 | .01 |
| ☐ 636 Phillies Team Leaders: | .25 | .05 | .01 | ☐ 681 Dodgers Rookies | 1.25 | .60 | .12 |
| Mgr. Dallas Green | | | | Mike Marshall | | | |
| Batting: Pete Rose | | | | Ron Roenicke | | | |
| Pitching: Steve Carlton | | | | Steve Sax | | | |
| ☐ 637 Rick Camp | .04 | .02 | .00 | ☐ 682 Jesse Jefferson | .04 | .02 | .00 |
| ☐ 638 John Milner | .04 | .02 | .00 | ☐ 683 Phil Garner | .06 | .02 | .00 |
| ☐ 639 Ken Kravec | .04 | .02 | .00 | ☐ 684 Harold Baines | .50 | .22 | .05 |
| ☐ 640 Cesar Cedeno | .10 | .04 | .01 | ☐ 685 Bert Blyleven | .15 | .06 | .01 |
| ☐ 641 Steve Mura | .04 | .02 | .00 | ☐ 686 Gary Allenson | .04 | .02 | .00 |
| ☐ 642 Mike Scioscia | .04 | .02 | .00 | ☐ 687 Greg Minton | .04 | .02 | .00 |
| ☐ 643 Pete Vuckovich | .12 | .05 | .01 | ☐ 688 Leon Roberts | .04 | .02 | .00 |
| ☐ 644 John Castino | .06 | .02 | .00 | ☐ 689 Lary Sorensen | .04 | .02 | .00 |
| ☐ 645 Frank White | .08 | .03 | .01 | ☐ 690 Dave Kingman | .15 | .06 | .01 |
| ☐ 646 SA: Frank White | .06 | .02 | .00 | ☐ 691 Dan Schatzeder | .04 | .02 | .00 |
| ☐ 647 Warren Brusstar | .04 | .02 | .00 | ☐ 692 Wayne Gross | .04 | .02 | .00 |
| ☐ 648 Jose Morales | .04 | .02 | .00 | ☐ 693 Cesar Geronimo | .04 | .02 | .00 |
| ☐ 649 Ken Clay | .04 | .02 | .00 | ☐ 694 Dave Wehrmeister | .04 | .02 | .00 |
| ☐ 650 Carl Yastrzemski | .90 | .40 | .09 | ☐ 695 Warren Cromartie | .04 | .02 | .00 |
| ☐ 651 SA: Carl Yastrzemski | .45 | .20 | .04 | ☐ 696 Pirates Team Leaders: | .10 | .02 | .00 |
| ☐ 652 Steve Nicosia | .04 | .02 | .00 | Mgr. Chuck Tanner | | | |
| ☐ 653 Angels Rookies | 1.75 | .85 | .17 | Batting: Bill Madlock | | | |
| Tom Brunansky | | | | Pitching: Eddie Solomon | | | |
| Luis Sanchez | | | | ☐ 697 John Montefusco | .06 | .02 | .00 |
| Daryl Sconiers | | | | ☐ 698 Tony Scott | .04 | .02 | .00 |
| ☐ 654 Jim Morrison | .04 | .02 | .00 | ☐ 699 Dick Tidrow | .04 | .02 | .00 |
| ☐ 655 Joel Youngblood | .04 | .02 | .00 | ☐ 700 George Foster | .25 | .10 | .02 |
| ☐ 656 Eddie Whitson | .09 | .03 | .01 | ☐ 701 SA: George Foster | .15 | .06 | .01 |
| ☐ 657 Tom Poquette | .04 | .02 | .00 | ☐ 702 Steve Renko | .04 | .02 | .00 |
| ☐ 658 Tito Landrum | .06 | .02 | .00 | ☐ 703 Brewers Team | .11 | .02 | .00 |
| ☐ 659 Fred Martinez | .04 | .02 | .00 | Mgr. Bob Rodgers | | | |
| ☐ 660 Dave Concepcion | .12 | .05 | .01 | Batting: Cecil Cooper | | | |
| ☐ 661 SA: Dave Concepcion | .08 | .03 | .01 | Pitching: P. Vuckovich | | | |
| ☐ 662 Luis Salazar | .04 | .02 | .00 | ☐ 704 Mickey Rivers | .06 | .02 | .00 |
| ☐ 663 Hector Cruz | .04 | .02 | .00 | ☐ 705 SA: Mickey Rivers | .06 | .02 | .00 |
| ☐ 664 Dan Spillner | .04 | .02 | .00 | ☐ 706 Barry Foote | .04 | .02 | .00 |
| ☐ 665 Jim Clancy | .04 | .02 | .00 | ☐ 707 Mark Bomback | .04 | .02 | .00 |
| ☐ 666 Tigers Team | .10 | .02 | .00 | ☐ 708 Gene Richards | .04 | .02 | .00 |
| Mgr. Sparky Anderson | | | | ☐ 709 Don Money | .04 | .02 | .00 |
| Batting: Steve Kemp | | | | ☐ 710 Jerry Reuss | .10 | .04 | .01 |
| Pitching: Dan Petry | | | | ☐ 711 Mariners Rookies | .20 | .09 | .02 |
| ☐ 667 Jeff Reardon | .10 | .04 | .01 | Dave Edler | | | |
| ☐ 668 Dale Murphy | 1.25 | .60 | .12 | Dave Henderson | | | |
| ☐ 669 Larry Milbourne | .04 | .02 | .00 | Reggie Walton | | | |
| ☐ 670 Steve Kemp | .10 | .04 | .01 | ☐ 712 Denny Martinez | .04 | .02 | .00 |
| ☐ 671 Mike Davis | .20 | .07 | .01 | ☐ 713 Del Unser | .04 | .02 | .00 |
| ☐ 672 Bob Knepper | .06 | .02 | .00 | ☐ 714 Jerry Koosman | .10 | .04 | .01 |
| ☐ 673 Keith Drumright | .06 | .02 | .00 | ☐ 715 Willie Stargell | .30 | .12 | .03 |
| ☐ 674 Dave Goltz | .04 | .02 | .00 | ☐ 716 SA: Willie Stargell | .15 | .06 | .01 |

|  | MINT | VG-E | F-G |
|---|---|---|---|
| ☐ 717 Rick Miller | .04 | .02 | .00 |
| ☐ 718 Charlie Hough | .06 | .02 | .00 |
| ☐ 719 Jerry Narron | .04 | .02 | .00 |
| ☐ 720 Greg Luzinski | .15 | .06 | .01 |
| ☐ 721 SA: Greg Luzinski | .10 | .04 | .01 |
| ☐ 722 Jerry Martin | .04 | .02 | .00 |
| ☐ 723 Junior Kennedy | .04 | .02 | .00 |
| ☐ 724 Dave Rosello | .04 | .02 | .00 |
| ☐ 725 Amos Otis | .08 | .03 | .01 |
| ☐ 726 SA: Amos Otis | .06 | .02 | .00 |
| ☐ 727 Sixto Lezcano | .04 | .02 | .00 |
| ☐ 728 Aurelio Lopez | .04 | .02 | .00 |
| ☐ 729 Jim Spencer | .04 | .02 | .00 |
| ☐ 730 Gary Carter | .45 | .20 | .04 |
| ☐ 731 Padres Rookies: | .10 | .04 | .01 |
|     Mike Armstrong | | | |
|     Doug Gwosdz | | | |
|     Fred Kuhaulua | | | |
| ☐ 732 Mike Lum | .04 | .02 | .00 |
| ☐ 733 Larry McWilliams | .08 | .03 | .01 |
| ☐ 734 Mike Ivie | .04 | .02 | .00 |
| ☐ 735 Rudy May | .04 | .02 | .00 |
| ☐ 736 Jerry Turner | .04 | .02 | .00 |
| ☐ 737 Reggie Cleveland | .04 | .02 | .00 |
| ☐ 738 Dave Engle | .06 | .02 | .00 |
| ☐ 739 Joey McLaughlin | .04 | .02 | .00 |
| ☐ 740 Dave Lopes | .09 | .04 | .01 |
| ☐ 741 SA: Dave Lopes | .06 | .02 | .00 |
| ☐ 742 Dick Drago | .04 | .02 | .00 |
| ☐ 743 John Stearns | .04 | .02 | .00 |
| ☐ 744 Mike Witt | .65 | .30 | .06 |
| ☐ 745 Bake McBride | .04 | .02 | .00 |
| ☐ 746 Andre Thornton | .10 | .04 | .01 |
| ☐ 747 John Lowenstein | .04 | .02 | .00 |
| ☐ 748 Marc Hill | .04 | .02 | .00 |
| ☐ 749 Bob Shirley | .04 | .02 | .00 |
| ☐ 750 Jim Rice | .60 | .28 | .06 |
| ☐ 751 Rick Honeycutt | .06 | .02 | .00 |
| ☐ 752 Lee Lacy | .08 | .03 | .01 |
| ☐ 753 Tom Brookens | .04 | .02 | .00 |
| ☐ 754 Joe Morgan | .30 | .12 | .03 |
| ☐ 755 SA: Joe Morgan | .15 | .06 | .01 |
| ☐ 756 Reds Team Leaders: | .12 | .02 | .00 |
|     Mgr. John McNamara | | | |
|     Batting: Ken Griffey | | | |
|     Pitching: Tom Seaver | | | |
| ☐ 757 Tom Underwood | .04 | .02 | .00 |
| ☐ 758 Claudell Washington | .10 | .04 | .01 |
| ☐ 759 Paul Splittorff | .06 | .02 | .00 |
| ☐ 760 Bill Buckner | .14 | .06 | .01 |
| ☐ 761 Dave Smith | .06 | .02 | .00 |
| ☐ 762 Mike Phillips | .04 | .02 | .00 |
| ☐ 763 Tom Hume | .04 | .02 | .00 |
| ☐ 764 Steve Swisher | .04 | .02 | .00 |

|  | MINT | VG-E | F-G |
|---|---|---|---|
| ☐ 765 Gorman Thomas | .12 | .05 | .01 |
| ☐ 766 Twins Rookies: | 2.75 | 1.25 | .27 |
|     Lenny Faedo | | | |
|     Kent Hrbek | | | |
|     Tim Laudner | | | |
| ☐ 767 Roy Smalley | .06 | .02 | .00 |
| ☐ 768 Jerry Garvin | .04 | .02 | .00 |
| ☐ 769 Richie Zisk | .06 | .02 | .00 |
| ☐ 770 Rich Gossage | .25 | .10 | .02 |
| ☐ 771 SA: Rich Gossage | .15 | .06 | .01 |
| ☐ 772 Bert Campaneris | .06 | .02 | .00 |
| ☐ 773 John Denny | .10 | .04 | .01 |
| ☐ 774 Jay Johnstone | .06 | .02 | .00 |
| ☐ 775 Bob Forsch | .06 | .02 | .00 |
| ☐ 776 Mark Belanger | .06 | .02 | .00 |
| ☐ 777 Tom Griffin | .04 | .02 | .00 |
| ☐ 778 Kevin Hickey | .10 | .04 | .01 |
| ☐ 779 Grant Jackson | .04 | .02 | .00 |
| ☐ 780 Pete Rose | 1.50 | .70 | .15 |
| ☐ 781 SA: Pete Rose | .70 | .32 | .07 |
| ☐ 782 Frank Taveras | .04 | .02 | .00 |
| ☐ 783 Greg Harris | .10 | .04 | .01 |
| ☐ 784 Milt Wilcox | .04 | .02 | .00 |
| ☐ 785 Dan Driessen | .06 | .02 | .00 |
| ☐ 786 Red Sox Team Leaders: | .10 | .02 | .00 |
|     Mgr. Ralph Houk | | | |
|     Batting: Carney Lansford | | | |
|     Pitching: Mike Torrez | | | |
| ☐ 787 Fred Stanley | .04 | .02 | .00 |
| ☐ 788 Woodie Fryman | .04 | .02 | .00 |
| ☐ 789 Checklist 661–792 | .11 | .02 | .00 |
| ☐ 790 Larry Gura | .06 | .02 | .00 |
| ☐ 791 Bobby Brown | .04 | .02 | .00 |
| ☐ 792 Frank Tanana | .09 | .02 | .00 |

## 1982 TOPPS EXTENDED

*The cards in this 132 card set measure 2½" by 3½". The Topps "Traded" series for 1982 is distinguished by a "T" printed after the number (located on the reverse). Of the total cards, 70 players represent the American League and 61 represent the National League, with the remaining card a numbered checklist (132T). The Cubs lead the pack with 12 changes while the Red Sox are the only team in either league to have no new additions. All 131 player photos used in the set are completely new. Of this total, 112 individuals are seen in the uniform of their new team, 11 others have been elevated to single card status from "Future Stars" cards, and 8 more are entirely new to the 1982 Topps lineup. The backs are almost completely red in color with black print.*

Complete Set: M-13.50; VG-E-6.00; F-G-1.25

|  | MINT | VG-E | F-G |
|---|---|---|---|
| Common Player | .08 | .03 | .01 |
| ☐ 1 T Doyle Alexander | .12 | .05 | .01 |
| ☐ 2 T Jesse Barfield | .50 | .22 | .05 |
| ☐ 3 T Ross Baumgarten | .08 | .03 | .01 |
| ☐ 4 T Steve Bedrosian | .20 | .09 | .02 |
| ☐ 5 T Mark Belanger | .12 | .05 | .01 |
| ☐ 6 T Kurt Bevacqua | .08 | .03 | .01 |
| ☐ 7 T Tim Blackwell | .08 | .03 | .01 |
| ☐ 8 T Vida Blue | .16 | .07 | .01 |
| ☐ 9 T Bob Boone | .12 | .05 | .01 |
| ☐ 10 T Larry Bowa | .16 | .07 | .01 |
| ☐ 11 T Dan Briggs | .08 | .03 | .01 |
| ☐ 12 T Bobby Brown | .08 | .03 | .01 |
| ☐ 13 T Tom Brunansky | 1.00 | .45 | .10 |
| ☐ 14 T Jeff Burroughs | .08 | .03 | .01 |
| ☐ 15 T Enos Cabell | .08 | .03 | .01 |
| ☐ 16 T Bill Campbell | .08 | .03 | .01 |
| ☐ 17 T Bobby Castillo | .08 | .03 | .01 |
| ☐ 18 T Bill Caudill | .15 | .06 | .01 |
| ☐ 19 T Cesar Cedeno | .15 | .06 | .01 |
| ☐ 20 T Dave Collins | .15 | .06 | .01 |
| ☐ 21 T Doug Corbett | .12 | .05 | .01 |
| ☐ 22 T Al Cowens | .12 | .05 | .01 |
| ☐ 23 T Chili Davis | .55 | .25 | .05 |
| ☐ 24 T Dick Davis | .08 | .03 | .01 |
| ☐ 25 T Ron Davis | .12 | .05 | .01 |
| ☐ 26 T Doug DeCinces | .25 | .10 | .02 |
| ☐ 27 T Ivan DeJesus | .08 | .03 | .01 |
| ☐ 28 T Bob Dernier | .25 | .10 | .02 |
| ☐ 29 T Bo Diaz | .12 | .05 | .01 |

|  | MINT | VG-E | F-G |
|---|---|---|---|
| ☐ 30 T Roger Erickson | .08 | .03 | .01 |
| ☐ 31 T Jim Essian | .08 | .03 | .01 |
| ☐ 32 T Ed Farmer | .08 | .03 | .01 |
| ☐ 33 T Doug Flynn | .08 | .03 | .01 |
| ☐ 34 T Tim Foli | .08 | .03 | .01 |
| ☐ 35 T Dan Ford | .12 | .05 | .01 |
| ☐ 36 T George Foster | .40 | .18 | .04 |
| ☐ 37 T Dave Frost | .08 | .03 | .01 |
| ☐ 38 T Rich Gale | .08 | .03 | .01 |
| ☐ 39 T Ron Gardenhire | .12 | .05 | .01 |
| ☐ 40 T Ken Griffey | .16 | .07 | .01 |
| ☐ 41 T Greg Harris | .08 | .03 | .01 |
| ☐ 42 T Von Hayes | .85 | .40 | .08 |
| ☐ 43 T Larry Herndon | .12 | .05 | .01 |
| ☐ 44 T Kent Hrbek | 2.25 | 1.00 | .22 |
| ☐ 45 T Mike Ivie | .08 | .03 | .01 |
| ☐ 46 T Grant Jackson | .08 | .03 | .01 |
| ☐ 47 T Reggie Jackson | 1.25 | .60 | .12 |
| ☐ 48 T Ron Jackson | .08 | .03 | .01 |
| ☐ 49 T Fergie Jenkins | .25 | .10 | .02 |
| ☐ 50 T Lamar Johnson | .08 | .03 | .01 |
| ☐ 51 T Randy Johnson | .08 | .03 | .01 |
| ☐ 52 T Jay Johnstone | .12 | .05 | .01 |
| ☐ 53 T Mick Kelleher | .08 | .03 | .01 |
| ☐ 54 T Steve Kemp | .16 | .07 | .01 |
| ☐ 55 T Junior Kennedy | .08 | .03 | .01 |
| ☐ 56 T Jim Kern | .08 | .03 | .01 |
| ☐ 57 T Ray Knight | .12 | .05 | .01 |
| ☐ 58 T Wayne Krenchicki | .08 | .03 | .01 |
| ☐ 59 T Mike Krukow | .08 | .03 | .01 |
| ☐ 60 T Duane Kuiper | .08 | .03 | .01 |
| ☐ 61 T Mike LaCross | .08 | .03 | .01 |
| ☐ 62 T Chet Lemon | .16 | .07 | .01 |
| ☐ 63 T Sixto Lezcano | .12 | .05 | .01 |
| ☐ 64 T Dave Lopes | .16 | .07 | .01 |
| ☐ 65 T Jerry Martin | .08 | .03 | .01 |
| ☐ 66 T Renie Martin | .08 | .03 | .01 |
| ☐ 67 T John Mayberry | .12 | .05 | .01 |
| ☐ 68 T Lee Mazzilli | .12 | .05 | .01 |
| ☐ 69 T Bake McBride | .12 | .05 | .01 |
| ☐ 70 T Dan Meyer | .08 | .03 | .01 |
| ☐ 71 T Larry Milbourne | .08 | .03 | .01 |
| ☐ 72 T Eddie Milner | .25 | .10 | .02 |
| ☐ 73 T Sid Monge | .08 | .03 | .01 |
| ☐ 74 T John Montefusco | .12 | .05 | .01 |
| ☐ 75 T Jose Morales | .08 | .03 | .01 |
| ☐ 76 T Keith Moreland | .16 | .07 | .01 |
| ☐ 77 T Jim Morrison | .08 | .03 | .01 |
| ☐ 78 T Rance Mulliniks | .08 | .03 | .01 |
| ☐ 79 T Steve Mura | .08 | .03 | .01 |
| ☐ 80 T Gene Nelson | .12 | .05 | .01 |
| ☐ 81 T Joe Nolan | .08 | .03 | .01 |
| ☐ 82 T Dickie Noles | .08 | .03 | .01 |

| | MINT | VG-E | F-G |
|---|---|---|---|
| ☐ 83 T Al Oliver | .40 | .18 | .04 |
| ☐ 84 T Jorge Orta | .08 | .03 | .01 |
| ☐ 85 T Tom Paciorek | .12 | .05 | .01 |
| ☐ 86 T Larry Parrish | .16 | .07 | .01 |
| ☐ 87 T Jack Perconte | .08 | .03 | .01 |
| ☐ 88 T Gaylord Perry | .70 | .32 | .07 |
| ☐ 89 T Rob Picciolo | .08 | .03 | .01 |
| ☐ 90 T Joe Pittman | .08 | .03 | .01 |
| ☐ 91 T Hosken Powell | .08 | .03 | .01 |
| ☐ 92 T Mike Proly | .08 | .03 | .01 |
| ☐ 93 T Greg Pryor | .08 | .03 | .01 |
| ☐ 94 T Charlie Puleo | .12 | .05 | .01 |
| ☐ 95 T Shane Rawley | .16 | .07 | .01 |
| ☐ 96 T Johnny Ray | .75 | .35 | .07 |
| ☐ 97 T Dave Revering | .08 | .03 | .01 |
| ☐ 98 T Cal Ripken | 6.00 | 2.80 | .60 |
| ☐ 99 T Allen Ripley | .08 | .03 | .01 |
| ☐ 100 T Bill Robinson | .08 | .03 | .01 |
| ☐ 101 T Aurelio Rodriguez | .08 | .03 | .01 |
| ☐ 102 T Joe Rudi | .12 | .05 | .01 |
| ☐ 103 T Steve Sax | .75 | .35 | .07 |
| ☐ 104 T Dan Schatzeder | .08 | .03 | .01 |
| ☐ 105 T Bob Shirley | .08 | .03 | .01 |
| ☐ 106 T Eric Show | .50 | .22 | .05 |
| ☐ 107 T Roy Smalley | .12 | .05 | .01 |
| ☐ 108 T Lonnie Smith | .20 | .09 | .02 |
| ☐ 109 T Ozzie Smith | .30 | .12 | .03 |
| ☐ 110 T Reggie Smith | .16 | .07 | .01 |
| ☐ 111 T Larry Sorensen | .08 | .03 | .01 |
| ☐ 112 T Elias Sosa | .08 | .03 | .01 |
| ☐ 113 T Mike Stanton | .08 | .03 | .01 |
| ☐ 114 T Steve Stroughter | .12 | .05 | .01 |
| ☐ 115 T Champ Summers | .08 | .03 | .01 |
| ☐ 116 T Rick Sutcliffe | .50 | .22 | .05 |
| ☐ 117 T Frank Tanana | .12 | .05 | .01 |
| ☐ 118 T Frank Taveras | .08 | .03 | .01 |
| ☐ 119 T Garry Templeton | .20 | .09 | .02 |
| ☐ 120 T Alex Trevino | .08 | .03 | .01 |
| ☐ 121 T Jerry Turner | .08 | .03 | .01 |
| ☐ 122 T Ed VandeBerg | .30 | .12 | .03 |
| ☐ 123 T Tom Veryzer | .08 | .03 | .01 |
| ☐ 124 T Ron Washington | .12 | .05 | .01 |
| ☐ 125 T Bob Watson | .12 | .05 | .01 |
| ☐ 126 T Dennis Werth | .08 | .03 | .01 |
| ☐ 127 T Eddie Whitson | .12 | .05 | .01 |
| ☐ 128 T Rob Wilfong | .08 | .03 | .01 |
| ☐ 129 T Bump Wills | .08 | .03 | .01 |
| ☐ 130 T Gary Woods | .08 | .03 | .01 |
| ☐ 131 T Butch Wynegar | .12 | .05 | .01 |
| ☐ 132 T Checklist: 1-132 | .20 | .04 | .01 |

## 1983 TOPPS

*The cards in this 792 card set measure 2½″ by 3½″. Each regular card of the Topps set for 1983 features a large action shot of a player with a small cameo portrait at bottom right. There are special series for A.L. and N.L. All Stars (386–407), League Leaders (701–708) and Record Breakers (1–6). In addition, there are 34 "Super Veteran" (SV) cards and six numbered checklist cards. The cards are numbered on the reverse at the upper left corner.*

Complete Set: M-32.00; VG-E-15.00; F-G-3.20

| | MINT | VG-E | F-G |
|---|---|---|---|
| Common Player (1–792) | .03 | .01 | .00 |
| ☐ 1 RB: Tony Armas | .15 | .03 | .01 |
| ☐ 2 RB: Rickey Henderson | .25 | .10 | .02 |
| ☐ 3 RB: Greg Minton | .06 | .02 | .00 |
| ☐ 4 RB: Lance Parrish | .15 | .06 | .01 |
| ☐ 5 RB: Manny Trillo | .06 | .02 | .00 |
| ☐ 6 RB: John Wathan | .06 | .02 | .00 |
| ☐ 7 Gene Richards | .03 | .01 | .00 |
| ☐ 8 Steve Balboni | .06 | .02 | .00 |
| ☐ 9 Joey McLaughlin | .03 | .01 | .00 |
| ☐ 10 Gorman Thomas | .12 | .05 | .01 |
| ☐ 11 Billy Gardner | .03 | .01 | .00 |
| ☐ 12 Paul Mirabella | .03 | .01 | .00 |
| ☐ 13 Larry Herndon | .05 | .02 | .00 |
| ☐ 14 Frank LaCorte | .03 | .01 | .00 |
| ☐ 15 Ron Cey | .14 | .06 | .01 |
| ☐ 16 George Vukovich | .03 | .01 | .00 |
| ☐ 17 Kent Tekulve | .08 | .03 | .01 |
| ☐ 18 SV: Kent Tekulve | .06 | .02 | .00 |
| ☐ 19 Oscar Gamble | .06 | .02 | .00 |

| | | MINT | VG-E | F-G |
|---|---|---|---|---|
| ☐ 20 | Carlton Fisk | .20 | .09 | .02 |
| ☐ 21 | Baltimore Orioles | .16 | .04 | .01 |
| | Team Leaders: | | | |
| | BA: Eddie Murray | | | |
| | ERA: Jim Palmer | | | |
| ☐ 22 | Randy Martz | .03 | .01 | .00 |
| ☐ 23 | Mike Heath | .03 | .01 | .00 |
| ☐ 24 | Steve Mura | .03 | .01 | .00 |
| ☐ 25 | Hal McRae | .06 | .02 | .00 |
| ☐ 26 | Jerry Royster | .03 | .01 | .00 |
| ☐ 27 | Doug Corbett | .03 | .01 | .00 |
| ☐ 28 | Bruce Bochte | .03 | .01 | .00 |
| ☐ 29 | Randy Jones | .05 | .02 | .00 |
| ☐ 30 | Jim Rice | .40 | .18 | .04 |
| ☐ 31 | Bill Gullickson | .06 | .02 | .00 |
| ☐ 32 | Dave Bergman | .03 | .01 | .00 |
| ☐ 33 | Jack O'Connor | .03 | .01 | .00 |
| ☐ 34 | Paul Householder | .05 | .02 | .00 |
| ☐ 35 | Rollie Fingers | .20 | .09 | .02 |
| ☐ 36 | SV: Rollie Fingers | .14 | .06 | .01 |
| ☐ 37 | Darrell Johnson | .03 | .01 | .00 |
| ☐ 38 | Tim Flannery | .03 | .01 | .00 |
| ☐ 39 | Terry Puhl | .03 | .01 | .00 |
| ☐ 40 | Fernando Valenzuela | .35 | .15 | .03 |
| ☐ 41 | Jerry Turner | .03 | .01 | .00 |
| ☐ 42 | Dale Murray | .03 | .01 | .00 |
| ☐ 43 | Bob Dernier | .08 | .03 | .01 |
| ☐ 44 | Don Robinson | .03 | .01 | .00 |
| ☐ 45 | John Mayberry | .05 | .02 | .00 |
| ☐ 46 | Richard Dotson | .09 | .04 | .01 |
| ☐ 47 | Dave McKay | .03 | .01 | .00 |
| ☐ 48 | Lary Sorensen | .03 | .01 | .00 |
| ☐ 49 | Willie McGee | 2.50 | 1.15 | .25 |
| ☐ 50 | Bob Horner | .25 | .10 | .02 |
| ☐ 51 | Chicago Cubs | .11 | .02 | .00 |
| | Team Leaders: | | | |
| | BA: Leon Durham | | | |
| | ERA: Fergie Jenkins | | | |
| ☐ 52 | Onix Concepcion | .09 | .04 | .01 |
| ☐ 53 | Mike Witt | .09 | .04 | .01 |
| ☐ 54 | Jim Maler | .06 | .02 | .00 |
| ☐ 55 | Mookie Wilson | .08 | .03 | .01 |
| ☐ 56 | Chuck Rainey | .03 | .01 | .00 |
| ☐ 57 | Tim Blackwell | .03 | .01 | .00 |
| ☐ 58 | Al Holland | .05 | .02 | .00 |
| ☐ 59 | Benny Ayala | .03 | .01 | .00 |
| ☐ 60 | Johnny Bench | .40 | .18 | .04 |
| ☐ 61 | SV: Johnny Bench | .25 | .10 | .02 |
| ☐ 62 | Bob McClure | .03 | .01 | .00 |
| ☐ 63 | Rick Monday | .05 | .02 | .00 |
| ☐ 64 | Bill Stein | .03 | .01 | .00 |
| ☐ 65 | Jack Morris | .25 | .10 | .02 |
| ☐ 66 | Bob Lillis | .03 | .01 | .00 |

| | | MINT | VG-E | F-G |
|---|---|---|---|---|
| ☐ 67 | Sal Butera | .03 | .01 | .00 |
| ☐ 68 | Eric Show | .20 | .09 | .02 |
| ☐ 69 | Lee Lacy | .07 | .03 | .01 |
| ☐ 70 | Steve Carlton | .40 | .18 | .04 |
| ☐ 71 | SV: Steve Carlton | .20 | .09 | .02 |
| ☐ 72 | Tom Paciorek | .03 | .01 | .00 |
| ☐ 73 | Allen Ripley | .03 | .01 | .00 |
| ☐ 74 | Julio Gonzalez | .03 | .01 | .00 |
| ☐ 75 | Amos Otis | .07 | .03 | .01 |
| ☐ 76 | Rick Mahler | .06 | .02 | .00 |
| ☐ 77 | Hosken Powell | .03 | .01 | .00 |
| ☐ 78 | Bill Caudill | .08 | .03 | .01 |
| ☐ 79 | Mick Kelleher | .03 | .01 | .00 |
| ☐ 80 | George Foster | .20 | .09 | .02 |
| ☐ 81 | New York Yankees | .10 | .02 | .00 |
| | Team Leaders: | | | |
| | BA: Jerry Mumphrey | | | |
| | ERA: Dave Righetti | | | |
| ☐ 82 | Bruce Hurst | .03 | .01 | .00 |
| ☐ 83 | Ryne Sandberg | 4.00 | 1.85 | .40 |
| ☐ 84 | Milt May | .03 | .01 | .00 |
| ☐ 85 | Ken Singleton | .10 | .04 | .01 |
| ☐ 86 | Tom Hume | .03 | .01 | .00 |
| ☐ 87 | Joe Rudi | .06 | .02 | .00 |
| ☐ 88 | Jim Gantner | .05 | .02 | .00 |
| ☐ 89 | Leon Roberts | .03 | .01 | .00 |
| ☐ 90 | Jerry Reuss | .09 | .04 | .01 |
| ☐ 91 | Larry Milbourne | .03 | .01 | .00 |
| ☐ 92 | Mike LaCoss | .03 | .01 | .00 |
| ☐ 93 | John Castino | .05 | .02 | .00 |
| ☐ 94 | Dave Edwards | .03 | .01 | .00 |
| ☐ 95 | Alan Trammell | .30 | .12 | .03 |
| ☐ 96 | Dick Howser | .05 | .02 | .00 |
| ☐ 97 | Ross Baumgarten | .03 | .01 | .00 |
| ☐ 98 | Vance Law | .03 | .01 | .00 |
| ☐ 99 | Dickie Noles | .03 | .01 | .00 |
| ☐ 100 | Pete Rose | 1.00 | .45 | .10 |
| ☐ 101 | SV: Pete Rose | .50 | .22 | .05 |
| ☐ 102 | Dave Beard | .03 | .01 | .00 |
| ☐ 103 | Darrell Porter | .06 | .02 | .00 |
| ☐ 104 | Bob Walk | .03 | .01 | .00 |
| ☐ 105 | Don Baylor | .14 | .06 | .01 |
| ☐ 106 | Gene Nelson | .03 | .01 | .00 |
| ☐ 107 | Mike Jorgensen | .03 | .01 | .00 |
| ☐ 108 | Glenn Hoffman | .03 | .01 | .00 |
| ☐ 109 | Luis Leal | .03 | .01 | .00 |
| ☐ 110 | Ken Griffey | .10 | .04 | .01 |
| ☐ 111 | Montreal Expos | .12 | .02 | .00 |
| | Team Leaders: | | | |
| | BA: Al Oliver | | | |
| | ERA: Steve Rogers | | | |
| ☐ 112 | Bob Shirley | .03 | .01 | .00 |
| ☐ 113 | Ron Roenicke | .03 | .01 | .00 |

| | MINT | VG-E | F-G | | MINT | VG-E | F-G |
|---|---|---|---|---|---|---|---|
| ☐ 114 Jim Slaton | .03 | .01 | .00 | ☐ 165 Dan Driessen | .05 | .02 | .00 |
| ☐ 115 Chili Davis | .14 | .06 | .01 | ☐ 166 John Pacella | .03 | .01 | .00 |
| ☐ 116 Dave Schmidt | .03 | .01 | .00 | ☐ 167 Mark Brouhard | .03 | .01 | .00 |
| ☐ 117 Alan Knicely | .03 | .01 | .00 | ☐ 168 Juan Eichelberger | .03 | .01 | .00 |
| ☐ 118 Chris Welsh | .03 | .01 | .00 | ☐ 169 Doug Flynn | .03 | .01 | .00 |
| ☐ 119 Tom Brookens | .03 | .01 | .00 | ☐ 170 Steve Howe | .06 | .02 | .00 |
| ☐ 120 Len Barker | .06 | .02 | .00 | ☐ 171 Giants Leaders: | .09 | .02 | .00 |
| ☐ 121 Mickey Hatcher | .05 | .02 | .00 | BA: Joe Morgan | | | |
| ☐ 122 Jimmy Smith | .05 | .02 | .00 | ERA: Bill Laskey | | | |
| ☐ 123 George Frazier | .03 | .01 | .00 | | | | |
| ☐ 124 Marc Hill | .03 | .01 | .00 | ☐ 172 Vern Ruhle | .03 | .01 | .00 |
| ☐ 125 Leon Durham | .20 | .09 | .02 | ☐ 173 Jim Morrison | .03 | .01 | .00 |
| ☐ 126 Joe Torre | .07 | .03 | .01 | ☐ 174 Jerry Ujdur | .03 | .01 | .00 |
| ☐ 127 Preston Hanna | .03 | .01 | .00 | ☐ 175 Bo Diaz | .05 | .02 | .00 |
| ☐ 128 Mike Ramsey | .03 | .01 | .00 | ☐ 176 Dave Righetti | .20 | .09 | .02 |
| ☐ 129 Checklist: 1–132 | .10 | .01 | .00 | ☐ 177 Harold Baines | .30 | .12 | .03 |
| ☐ 130 Dave Stieb | .25 | .10 | .02 | ☐ 178 Luis Tiant | .08 | .03 | .01 |
| ☐ 131 Ed Ott | .03 | .01 | .00 | ☐ 179 SV: Luis Tiant | .06 | .02 | .00 |
| ☐ 132 Todd Cruz | .03 | .01 | .00 | ☐ 180 Rickey Henderson | .50 | .22 | .05 |
| ☐ 133 Jim Barr | .03 | .01 | .00 | ☐ 181 Terry Felton | .07 | .03 | .01 |
| ☐ 134 Hubie Brooks | .12 | .05 | .01 | ☐ 182 Mike Fischlin | .03 | .01 | .00 |
| ☐ 135 Dwight Evans | .16 | .07 | .01 | ☐ 183 Ed VandeBerg | .20 | .09 | .02 |
| ☐ 136 Willie Aikens | .05 | .02 | .00 | ☐ 184 Bob Clark | .03 | .01 | .00 |
| ☐ 137 Woodie Fryman | .03 | .01 | .00 | ☐ 185 Tim Lollar | .05 | .02 | .00 |
| ☐ 138 Rick Dempsey | .06 | .02 | .00 | ☐ 186 Whitey Herzog MGR | .06 | .02 | .00 |
| ☐ 139 Bruce Berenyi | .05 | .02 | .00 | ☐ 187 Terry Leach | .03 | .01 | .00 |
| ☐ 140 Willie Randolph | .07 | .03 | .01 | ☐ 188 Rick Miller | .03 | .01 | .00 |
| ☐ 141 Indians Leaders | .09 | .02 | .00 | ☐ 189 Dan Schatzeder | .03 | .01 | .00 |
| BA: Toby Harrah | | | | ☐ 190 Cecil Cooper | .18 | .08 | .01 |
| ERA: Rick Sutcliffe | | | | ☐ 191 Joe Price | .03 | .01 | .00 |
| ☐ 142 Mike Caldwell | .05 | .02 | .00 | ☐ 192 Floyd Rayford | .03 | .01 | .00 |
| ☐ 143 Joe Pettini | .03 | .01 | .00 | ☐ 193 Harry Spilman | .03 | .01 | .00 |
| ☐ 144 Mark Wagner | .03 | .01 | .00 | ☐ 194 Cesar Geronimo | .03 | .01 | .00 |
| ☐ 145 Don Sutton | .16 | .07 | .01 | ☐ 195 Bob Stoddard | .08 | .03 | .01 |
| ☐ 146 SV: Don Sutton | .10 | .04 | .01 | ☐ 196 Bill Fahey | .03 | .01 | .00 |
| ☐ 147 Rick Leach | .03 | .01 | .00 | ☐ 197 Jim Eisenreich | .09 | .04 | .01 |
| ☐ 148 Dave Roberts | .03 | .01 | .00 | ☐ 198 Kiko Garcia | .03 | .01 | .00 |
| ☐ 149 Johnny Ray | .16 | .07 | .01 | ☐ 199 Marty Bystrom | .03 | .01 | .00 |
| ☐ 150 Bruce Sutter | .20 | .09 | .02 | ☐ 200 Rod Carew | .40 | .18 | .04 |
| ☐ 151 SV: Bruce Sutter | .14 | .06 | .01 | ☐ 201 SV: Rod Carew | .20 | .09 | .02 |
| ☐ 152 Jay Johnstone | .05 | .02 | .00 | ☐ 202 Blue Jays Leaders: | .09 | .02 | .00 |
| ☐ 153 Jerry Koosman | .08 | .03 | .01 | Team Leaders: | | | |
| ☐ 154 Johnnie LeMaster | .03 | .01 | .00 | BA: Damaso Garcia | | | |
| ☐ 155 Dan Quisenberry | .25 | .10 | .02 | ERA: Dave Stieb | | | |
| ☐ 156 Billy Martin | .14 | .06 | .01 | | | | |
| ☐ 157 Steve Bedrosian | .08 | .03 | .01 | ☐ 203 Mike Morgan | .06 | .02 | .00 |
| ☐ 158 Rob Wilfong | .03 | .01 | .00 | ☐ 204 Junior Kennedy | .03 | .01 | .00 |
| ☐ 159 Mike Stanton | .03 | .01 | .00 | ☐ 205 Dave Parker | .25 | .10 | .02 |
| ☐ 160 Dave Kingman | .14 | .06 | .01 | ☐ 206 Ken Oberkfell | .05 | .02 | .00 |
| ☐ 161 SV: Dave Kingman | .10 | .04 | .01 | ☐ 207 Rick Camp | .03 | .01 | .00 |
| ☐ 162 Mark Clear | .05 | .02 | .00 | ☐ 208 Dan Meyer | .03 | .01 | .00 |
| ☐ 163 Cal Ripken | 1.50 | .70 | .15 | ☐ 209 Mike Moore | .35 | .15 | .03 |
| ☐ 164 David Palmer | .06 | .02 | .00 | ☐ 210 Jack Clark | .25 | .10 | .02 |
| | | | | ☐ 211 John Denny | .14 | .06 | .01 |
| | | | | ☐ 212 John Stearns | .03 | .01 | .00 |

|  | MINT | VG-E | F-G |
|---|---|---|---|
| ☐ 213 Tom Burgmeier | .03 | .01 | .00 |
| ☐ 214 Jerry White | .03 | .01 | .00 |
| ☐ 215 Mario Soto | .12 | .05 | .01 |
| ☐ 216 Tony LaRussa | .05 | .02 | .00 |
| ☐ 217 Tim Stoddard | .03 | .01 | .00 |
| ☐ 218 Roy Howell | .03 | .01 | .00 |
| ☐ 219 Mike Armstrong | .03 | .01 | .00 |
| ☐ 220 Dusty Baker | .09 | .04 | .01 |
| ☐ 221 Joe Niekro | .08 | .03 | .01 |
| ☐ 222 Damaso Garcia | .15 | .06 | .01 |
| ☐ 223 John Montefusco | .05 | .02 | .00 |
| ☐ 224 Mickey Rivers | .06 | .02 | .00 |
| ☐ 225 Enos Cabell | .03 | .01 | .00 |
| ☐ 226 Enrique Romo | .03 | .01 | .00 |
| ☐ 227 Chris Bando | .03 | .01 | .00 |
| ☐ 228 Joaquin Andujar | .15 | .06 | .01 |
| ☐ 229 Phillies Leaders: | .10 | .02 | .00 |
| Team Leaders: | | | |
| BA: Bo Diaz | | | |
| ☐ 230 Fergie Jenkins | .13 | .06 | .01 |
| ☐ 231 SV: Fergie Jenkins | .09 | .04 | .01 |
| ☐ 232 Tom Brunansky | .25 | .10 | .02 |
| ☐ 233 Wayne Gross | .03 | .01 | .00 |
| ☐ 234 Larry Andersen | .03 | .01 | .00 |
| ☐ 235 Claudell Washington | .10 | .04 | .01 |
| ☐ 236 Steve Renko | .03 | .01 | .00 |
| ☐ 237 Dan Norman | .03 | .01 | .00 |
| ☐ 238 Bud Black | .45 | .20 | .04 |
| ☐ 239 Dave Stapleton | .05 | .02 | .00 |
| ☐ 240 Rich Gossage | .25 | .10 | .02 |
| ☐ 241 SV: Rich Gossage | .14 | .06 | .01 |
| ☐ 242 Joe Nolan | .03 | .01 | .00 |
| ☐ 243 Duane Walker | .16 | .07 | .01 |
| ☐ 244 Dwight Bernard | .03 | .01 | .00 |
| ☐ 245 Steve Sax | .18 | .08 | .01 |
| ☐ 246 George Bamberger | .03 | .01 | .00 |
| ☐ 247 Dave Smith | .03 | .01 | .00 |
| ☐ 248 Bake McBride | .03 | .01 | .00 |
| ☐ 249 Checklist: 133–264 | .10 | .01 | .00 |
| ☐ 250 Bill Buckner | .14 | .06 | .01 |
| ☐ 251 Alan Wiggins | .45 | .20 | .04 |
| ☐ 252 Luis Aguayo | .03 | .01 | .00 |
| ☐ 253 Larry McWilliams | .06 | .02 | .00 |
| ☐ 254 Rick Cerone | .05 | .02 | .00 |
| ☐ 255 Gene Garber | .03 | .01 | .00 |
| ☐ 256 SV: Gene Garber | .03 | .01 | .00 |
| ☐ 257 Jesse Barfield | .15 | .06 | .01 |
| ☐ 258 Manny Castillo | .03 | .01 | .00 |
| ☐ 259 Jeff Jones | .03 | .01 | .00 |
| ☐ 260 Steve Kemp | .10 | .04 | .01 |
| ☐ 261 Tigers Leaders: | .10 | .02 | .00 |
| BA: Larry Herndon | | | |
| ERA: Dan Petry | | | |

|  | MINT | VG-E | F-G |
|---|---|---|---|
| ☐ 262 Ron Jackson | .03 | .01 | .00 |
| ☐ 263 Renie Martin | .03 | .01 | .00 |
| ☐ 264 Jamie Quirk | .03 | .01 | .00 |
| ☐ 265 Joel Youngblood | .03 | .01 | .00 |
| ☐ 266 Paul Boris | .06 | .02 | .00 |
| ☐ 267 Terry Francona | .07 | .03 | .01 |
| ☐ 268 Storm Davis | .55 | .25 | .05 |
| ☐ 269 Ron Oester | .05 | .02 | .00 |
| ☐ 270 Dennis Eckersley | .06 | .02 | .00 |
| ☐ 271 Ed Romero | .03 | .01 | .00 |
| ☐ 272 Frank Tanana | .05 | .02 | .00 |
| ☐ 273 Mark Belanger | .05 | .02 | .00 |
| ☐ 274 Terry Kennedy | .12 | .05 | .01 |
| ☐ 275 Ray Knight | .06 | .02 | .00 |
| ☐ 276 Gene Mauch | .03 | .01 | .00 |
| ☐ 277 Rance Mulliniks | .03 | .01 | .00 |
| ☐ 278 Kevin Hickey | .03 | .01 | .00 |
| ☐ 279 Greg Gross | .03 | .01 | .00 |
| ☐ 280 Bert Blyleven | .15 | .06 | .01 |
| ☐ 281 Andre Robertson | .03 | .01 | .00 |
| ☐ 282 Reggie Smith | .10 | .04 | .01 |
| ☐ 283 SV: Reggie Smith | .06 | .02 | .00 |
| ☐ 284 Jeff Lahti | .12 | .05 | .01 |
| ☐ 285 Lance Parrish | .35 | .15 | .03 |
| ☐ 286 Rick Langford | .03 | .01 | .00 |
| ☐ 287 Bobby Brown | .03 | .01 | .00 |
| ☐ 288 Joe Cowley | .30 | .12 | .03 |
| ☐ 289 Jerry Dybzinski | .03 | .01 | .00 |
| ☐ 290 Jeff Reardon | .09 | .04 | .01 |
| ☐ 291 Pirates Leaders: | .10 | .02 | .00 |
| BA: Bill Madlock | | | |
| ERA: John Candelaria | | | |
| ☐ 292 Craig Swan | .03 | .01 | .00 |
| ☐ 293 Glenn Gulliver | .06 | .02 | .00 |
| ☐ 294 Dave Engle | .06 | .02 | .00 |
| ☐ 295 Jerry Remy | .05 | .02 | .00 |
| ☐ 296 Greg Harris | .03 | .01 | .00 |
| ☐ 297 Ned Yost | .03 | .01 | .00 |
| ☐ 298 Floyd Chiffer | .06 | .02 | .00 |
| ☐ 299 George Wright | .15 | .06 | .01 |
| ☐ 300 Mike Schmidt | .60 | .28 | .06 |
| ☐ 301 SV: Mike Schmidt | .30 | .12 | .03 |
| ☐ 302 Ernie Whitt | .03 | .01 | .00 |
| ☐ 303 Miguel Dilone | .03 | .01 | .00 |
| ☐ 304 Dave Rucker | .03 | .01 | .00 |
| ☐ 305 Larry Bowa | .10 | .04 | .01 |
| ☐ 306 Tom Lasorda MGR | .07 | .03 | .01 |
| ☐ 307 Lou Piniella | .10 | .04 | .01 |
| ☐ 308 Jesus Vega | .07 | .03 | .01 |
| ☐ 309 Jeff Leonard | .07 | .03 | .01 |
| ☐ 310 Greg Luzinski | .14 | .06 | .01 |
| ☐ 311 Glenn Brummer | .03 | .01 | .00 |
| ☐ 312 Brian Kingman | .03 | .01 | .00 |
| ☐ 313 Gary Gray | .03 | .01 | .00 |

| | MINT | VG-E | F-G |
|---|---|---|---|
| ☐ 314 Ken Dayley | .06 | .02 | .00 |
| ☐ 315 Rick Burleson | .06 | .02 | .00 |
| ☐ 316 Paul Splittorff | .05 | .02 | .00 |
| ☐ 317 Gary Rajsich | .07 | .03 | .01 |
| ☐ 318 John Tudor | .30 | .12 | .03 |
| ☐ 319 Lenn Sakata | .03 | .01 | .00 |
| ☐ 320 Steve Rogers | .10 | .04 | .01 |
| ☐ 321 Brewers Leaders: | .12 | .02 | .00 |
|    BA: Robin Yount | | | |
|    ERA: Pete Vuckovich | | | |
| ☐ 322 Dave Van Gorder | .06 | .02 | .00 |
| ☐ 323 Luis DeLeon | .03 | .01 | .00 |
| ☐ 324 Mike Marshall | .25 | .10 | .02 |
| ☐ 325 Von Hayes | .20 | .09 | .02 |
| ☐ 326 Garth Iorg | .03 | .01 | .00 |
| ☐ 327 Bobby Castillo | .03 | .01 | .00 |
| ☐ 328 Craig Reynolds | .03 | .01 | .00 |
| ☐ 329 Randy Niemann | .03 | .01 | .00 |
| ☐ 330 Buddy Bell | .15 | .06 | .01 |
| ☐ 331 Mike Krukow | .03 | .01 | .00 |
| ☐ 332 Glenn Wilson | .75 | .35 | .07 |
| ☐ 333 Dave LaRoche | .03 | .01 | .00 |
| ☐ 334 SV: Dave LaRoche | .03 | .01 | .00 |
| ☐ 335 Steve Henderson | .03 | .01 | .00 |
| ☐ 336 Rene Lachemann MGR | .03 | .01 | .00 |
| ☐ 337 Tito Landrum | .05 | .02 | .00 |
| ☐ 338 Bob Owchinko | .03 | .01 | .00 |
| ☐ 339 Terry Harper | .03 | .01 | .00 |
| ☐ 340 Larry Gura | .06 | .02 | .00 |
| ☐ 341 Doug DeCinces | .12 | .05 | .01 |
| ☐ 342 Atlee Hammaker | .10 | .04 | .01 |
| ☐ 343 Bob Bailor | .03 | .01 | .00 |
| ☐ 344 Roger LaFrancois | .06 | .02 | .00 |
| ☐ 345 Jim Clancy | .03 | .01 | .00 |
| ☐ 346 Joe Pittman | .03 | .01 | .00 |
| ☐ 347 Sammy Stewart | .03 | .01 | .00 |
| ☐ 348 Alan Bannister | .03 | .01 | .00 |
| ☐ 349 Checklist: 265–396 | .10 | .01 | .00 |
| ☐ 350 Robin Yount | .35 | .15 | .03 |
| ☐ 351 Reds Leaders: | .09 | .02 | .00 |
|    BA: Cesar Cedeno | | | |
|    ERA: Mario Soto | | | |
| ☐ 352 Mike Scioscia | .03 | .01 | .00 |
| ☐ 353 Steve Comer | .03 | .01 | .00 |
| ☐ 354 Randy Johnson | .05 | .02 | .00 |
| ☐ 355 Jim Bibby | .05 | .02 | .00 |
| ☐ 356 Gary Woods | .03 | .01 | .00 |
| ☐ 357 Len Matuszek | .10 | .04 | .01 |
| ☐ 358 Jerry Garvin | .03 | .01 | .00 |
| ☐ 359 Dave Collins | .07 | .03 | .01 |
| ☐ 360 Nolan Ryan | .35 | .15 | .03 |
| ☐ 361 SV: Nolan Ryan | .16 | .07 | .01 |
| ☐ 362 Bill Almon | .03 | .01 | .00 |
| ☐ 363 John Stuper | .15 | .06 | .01 |

| | MINT | VG-E | F-G |
|---|---|---|---|
| ☐ 364 Bret Butler | .15 | .06 | .01 |
| ☐ 365 Dave Lopes | .07 | .03 | .01 |
| ☐ 366 Dick Williams MGR | .03 | .01 | .00 |
| ☐ 367 Bud Anderson | .03 | .01 | .00 |
| ☐ 368 Richie Zisk | .05 | .02 | .00 |
| ☐ 369 Jesse Orosco | .10 | .04 | .01 |
| ☐ 370 Gary Carter | .35 | .15 | .03 |
| ☐ 371 Mike Richardt | .07 | .03 | .01 |
| ☐ 372 Terry Crowley | .03 | .01 | .00 |
| ☐ 373 Kevin Saucier | .03 | .01 | .00 |
| ☐ 374 Wayne Krenchicki | .03 | .01 | .00 |
| ☐ 375 Pete Vuckovich | .06 | .02 | .00 |
| ☐ 376 Ken Landreaux | .05 | .02 | .00 |
| ☐ 377 Lee May | .07 | .03 | .01 |
| ☐ 378 SV: Lee May | .06 | .02 | .00 |
| ☐ 379 Guy Sularz | .07 | .03 | .01 |
| ☐ 380 Ron Davis | .06 | .02 | .00 |
| ☐ 381 Red Sox Leaders: | .12 | .02 | .00 |
|    BA: Jim Rice | | | |
|    ERA: Bob Stanley | | | |
| ☐ 382 Bob Knepper | .06 | .02 | .00 |
| ☐ 383 Ozzie Virgil | .08 | .03 | .01 |
| ☐ 384 Dave Dravecky | .45 | .20 | .04 |
| ☐ 385 Mike Easler | .06 | .02 | .00 |
|    AL ALL-STARS | | | |
|    (386–396) | | | |
| ☐ 386 Rod Carew AS | .25 | .10 | .02 |
| ☐ 387 Bob Grich AS | .07 | .03 | .01 |
| ☐ 388 George Brett AS | .35 | .15 | .03 |
| ☐ 389 Robin Yount AS | .25 | .10 | .02 |
| ☐ 390 Reggie Jackson AS | .30 | .12 | .03 |
| ☐ 391 Rickey Henderson AS | .35 | .15 | .03 |
| ☐ 392 Fred Lynn AS | .15 | .06 | .01 |
| ☐ 393 Carlton Fisk AS | .14 | .06 | .01 |
| ☐ 394 Pete Vuckovich AS | .06 | .02 | .00 |
| ☐ 395 Larry Gura AS | .06 | .02 | .00 |
| ☐ 396 Dan Quisenberry AS | .13 | .06 | .01 |
|    NL ALL-STARS | | | |
|    (397–407) | | | |
| ☐ 397 Pete Rose AS | .50 | .22 | .05 |
| ☐ 398 Manny Trillo AS | .06 | .02 | .00 |
| ☐ 399 Mike Schmidt AS | .35 | .15 | .03 |
| ☐ 400 Dave Concepcion AS | .07 | .03 | .01 |
| ☐ 401 Dale Murphy AS | .40 | .18 | .04 |
| ☐ 402 Andre Dawson AS | .18 | .08 | .01 |
| ☐ 403 Tim Raines AS | .18 | .08 | .01 |
| ☐ 404 Gary Carter AS | .25 | .10 | .02 |
| ☐ 405 Steve Rogers AS | .09 | .04 | .01 |
| ☐ 406 Steve Carlton AS | .25 | .10 | .02 |
| ☐ 407 Bruce Sutter AS | .14 | .06 | .01 |
| ☐ 408 Rudy May | .03 | .01 | .00 |
| ☐ 409 Marvis Foley | .03 | .01 | .00 |
| ☐ 410 Phil Niekro | .25 | .10 | .02 |
| ☐ 411 SV: Phil Niekro | .13 | .06 | .01 |

|  | MINT | VG-E | F-G |
|---|---|---|---|
| ☐ 412 Rangers Leaders: | .09 | .02 | .00 |
| BA: Buddy Bell | | | |
| ERA: Charlie Hough | | | |
| ☐ 413 Matt Keough | .05 | .02 | .00 |
| ☐ 414 Julio Cruz | .03 | .01 | .00 |
| ☐ 415 Bob Forsch | .05 | .02 | .00 |
| ☐ 416 Joe Ferguson | .03 | .01 | .00 |
| ☐ 417 Tom Hausman | .03 | .01 | .00 |
| ☐ 418 Greg Pryor | .03 | .01 | .00 |
| ☐ 419 Steve Crawford | .03 | .01 | .00 |
| ☐ 420 Al Oliver | .18 | .08 | .01 |
| ☐ 421 SV: Al Oliver | .10 | .04 | .01 |
| ☐ 422 George Cappuzzello | .03 | .01 | .00 |
| ☐ 423 Tom Lawless | .07 | .03 | .01 |
| ☐ 424 Jerry Augustine | .03 | .01 | .00 |
| ☐ 425 Pedro Guerrero | .35 | .15 | .03 |
| ☐ 426 Earl Weaver | .10 | .04 | .01 |
| ☐ 427 Roy Lee Jackson | .03 | .01 | .00 |
| ☐ 428 Champ Summers | .03 | .01 | .00 |
| ☐ 429 Eddie Whitson | .08 | .03 | .01 |
| ☐ 430 Kirk Gibson | .30 | .12 | .03 |
| ☐ 431 Gary Gaetti | .40 | .18 | .04 |
| ☐ 432 Porfirio Altamirano | .07 | .03 | .01 |
| ☐ 433 Dale Berra | .06 | .02 | .00 |
| ☐ 434 Dennis Lamp | .03 | .01 | .00 |
| ☐ 435 Tony Armas | .16 | .07 | .01 |
| ☐ 436 Bill Campbell | .05 | .02 | .00 |
| ☐ 437 Rick Sweet | .03 | .01 | .00 |
| ☐ 438 Dave LaPoint | .20 | .09 | .02 |
| ☐ 439 Rafael Ramirez | .05 | .02 | .00 |
| ☐ 440 Ron Guidry | .25 | .10 | .02 |
| ☐ 441 Astros Leaders: | .09 | .02 | .00 |
| BA: Ray Knight | | | |
| ERA: Joe Niekro | | | |
| ☐ 442 Brian Downing | .05 | .02 | .00 |
| ☐ 443 Don Hood | .03 | .01 | .00 |
| ☐ 444 Wally Backman | .06 | .02 | .00 |
| ☐ 445 Mike Flanagan | .08 | .03 | .01 |
| ☐ 446 Reid Nichols | .05 | .02 | .00 |
| ☐ 447 Bryn Smith | .06 | .02 | .00 |
| ☐ 448 Darrell Evans | .13 | .06 | .01 |
| ☐ 449 Eddie Milner | .14 | .06 | .01 |
| ☐ 450 Ted Simmons | .14 | .06 | .01 |
| ☐ 451 SV: Ted Simmons | .09 | .04 | .01 |
| ☐ 452 Lloyd Moseby | .15 | .06 | .01 |
| ☐ 453 Lamar Johnson | .03 | .01 | .00 |
| ☐ 454 Bob Welch | .07 | .03 | .01 |
| ☐ 455 Sixto Lezcano | .03 | .01 | .00 |
| ☐ 456 Lee Elia MGR | .03 | .01 | .00 |
| ☐ 457 Milt Wilcox | .03 | .01 | .00 |
| ☐ 458 Ron Washington | .07 | .03 | .01 |
| ☐ 459 Ed Farmer | .03 | .01 | .00 |
| ☐ 460 Roy Smalley | .05 | .02 | .00 |

|  | MINT | VG-E | F-G |
|---|---|---|---|
| ☐ 461 Steve Trout | .05 | .02 | .00 |
| ☐ 462 Steve Nicosia | .03 | .01 | .00 |
| ☐ 463 Gaylord Perry | .25 | .10 | .02 |
| ☐ 464 SV: Gaylord Perry | .13 | .06 | .01 |
| ☐ 465 Lonnie Smith | .11 | .05 | .01 |
| ☐ 466 Tom Underwood | .03 | .01 | .00 |
| ☐ 467 Rufino Linares | .03 | .01 | .00 |
| ☐ 468 Dave Goltz | .03 | .01 | .00 |
| ☐ 469 Ron Gardenhire | .03 | .01 | .00 |
| ☐ 470 Greg Minton | .05 | .02 | .00 |
| ☐ 471 Kansas City Royals | .10 | .02 | .00 |
| Team Leaders: | | | |
| BA: Willie Wilson | | | |
| ERA: Vida Blue | | | |
| ☐ 472 Gary Allenson | .03 | .01 | .00 |
| ☐ 473 John Lowenstein | .03 | .01 | .00 |
| ☐ 474 Ray Burris | .03 | .01 | .00 |
| ☐ 475 Cesar Cedeno | .10 | .04 | .01 |
| ☐ 476 Rob Picciolo | .03 | .01 | .00 |
| ☐ 477 Tom Niedenfuer | .12 | .05 | .01 |
| ☐ 478 Phil Garner | .05 | .02 | .00 |
| ☐ 479 Charlie Hough | .05 | .02 | .00 |
| ☐ 480 Toby Harrah | .05 | .02 | .00 |
| ☐ 481 Scot Thompson | .03 | .01 | .00 |
| ☐ 482 Tony Gwynn | 3.50 | 1.35 | .35 |
| ☐ 483 Lynn Jones | .03 | .01 | .00 |
| ☐ 484 Dick Ruthven | .03 | .01 | .00 |
| ☐ 485 Omar Moreno | .05 | .02 | .00 |
| ☐ 486 Clyde King | .03 | .01 | .00 |
| ☐ 487 Jerry Hairston | .03 | .01 | .00 |
| ☐ 488 Alfredo Griffin | .05 | .02 | .00 |
| ☐ 489 Tom Herr | .20 | .09 | .02 |
| ☐ 490 Jim Palmer | .30 | .12 | .03 |
| ☐ 491 SV: Jim Palmer | .15 | .06 | .01 |
| ☐ 492 Paul Serna | .05 | .02 | .00 |
| ☐ 493 Steve McCatty | .05 | .02 | .00 |
| ☐ 494 Bob Brenly | .10 | .04 | .01 |
| ☐ 495 Warren Cromartie | .03 | .01 | .00 |
| ☐ 496 Tom Veryzer | .03 | .01 | .00 |
| ☐ 497 Rick Sutcliffe | .25 | .10 | .02 |
| ☐ 498 Wade Boggs | 5.25 | 2.00 | .35 |
| ☐ 499 Jeff Little | .07 | .03 | .01 |
| ☐ 500 Reggie Jackson | .45 | .20 | .04 |
| ☐ 501 SV: Reggie Jackson | .25 | .10 | .02 |
| ☐ 502 Atlanta Braves | .15 | .03 | .01 |
| Team Leaders: | | | |
| BA: Dale Murphy | | | |
| ERA: Phil Niekro | | | |
| ☐ 503 Moose Haas | .05 | .02 | .00 |
| ☐ 504 Don Werner | .03 | .01 | .00 |
| ☐ 505 Garry Templeton | .13 | .06 | .01 |
| ☐ 506 Jim Gott | .10 | .04 | .01 |
| ☐ 507 Tony Scott | .03 | .01 | .00 |

|  | MINT | VG-E | F-G |
|---|---|---|---|
| ☐ 508 Tom Filer | .25 | .10 | .02 |
| ☐ 509 Lou Whitaker | .25 | .10 | .02 |
| ☐ 510 Tug McGraw | .10 | .04 | .01 |
| ☐ 511 SV: Tug McGraw | .07 | .03 | .01 |
| ☐ 512 Doyle Alexander | .06 | .02 | .00 |
| ☐ 513 Fred Stanley | .03 | .01 | .00 |
| ☐ 514 Rudy Law | .03 | .01 | .00 |
| ☐ 515 Gene Tenace | .03 | .01 | .00 |
| ☐ 516 Bill Virdon | .05 | .02 | .00 |
| ☐ 517 Gary Ward | .06 | .02 | .00 |
| ☐ 518 Bill Laskey | .18 | .08 | .01 |
| ☐ 519 Terry Bulling | .03 | .01 | .00 |
| ☐ 520 Fred Lynn | .20 | .09 | .02 |
| ☐ 521 Bruce Benedict | .03 | .01 | .00 |
| ☐ 522 Pat Zachry | .03 | .01 | .00 |
| ☐ 523 Carney Lansford | .14 | .06 | .01 |
| ☐ 524 Tom Brennan | .03 | .01 | .00 |
| ☐ 525 Frank White | .07 | .03 | .01 |
| ☐ 526 Checklist: 397–528 | .10 | .02 | .00 |
| ☐ 527 Larry Biittner | .03 | .01 | .00 |
| ☐ 528 Jamie Easterly | .03 | .01 | .00 |
| ☐ 529 Tim Laudner | .03 | .01 | .00 |
| ☐ 530 Eddie Murray | .50 | .22 | .05 |
| ☐ 531 Oakland A's Leaders: | .11 | .02 | .00 |
|   BA: Rickey Henderson |  |  |  |
|   ERA: Rick Langford |  |  |  |
| ☐ 532 Dave Stewart | .03 | .01 | .00 |
| ☐ 533 Luis Salazar | .03 | .01 | .00 |
| ☐ 534 John Butcher | .03 | .01 | .00 |
| ☐ 535 Manny Trillo | .05 | .02 | .00 |
| ☐ 536 Johnny Wockenfuss | .03 | .01 | .00 |
| ☐ 537 Rod Scurry | .03 | .01 | .00 |
| ☐ 538 Danny Heep | .03 | .01 | .00 |
| ☐ 539 Roger Erickson | .03 | .01 | .00 |
| ☐ 540 Ozzie Smith | .12 | .05 | .01 |
| ☐ 541 Britt Burns | .08 | .03 | .01 |
| ☐ 542 Jody Davis | .11 | .05 | .01 |
| ☐ 543 Alan Fowlkes | .07 | .03 | .01 |
| ☐ 544 Larry Whisenton | .03 | .01 | .00 |
| ☐ 545 Floyd Bannister | .08 | .03 | .01 |
| ☐ 546 Dave Garcia | .03 | .01 | .00 |
| ☐ 547 Geoff Zahn | .05 | .02 | .00 |
| ☐ 548 Brian Giles | .07 | .03 | .01 |
| ☐ 549 Charlie Puleo | .06 | .02 | .00 |
| ☐ 550 Carl Yastrzemski | .60 | .28 | .06 |
| ☐ 551 SV: Carl Yastrzemski | .30 | .12 | .03 |
| ☐ 552 Tim Wallach | .15 | .06 | .01 |
| ☐ 553 Denny Martinez | .03 | .01 | .00 |
| ☐ 554 Mike Vail | .03 | .01 | .00 |
| ☐ 555 Steve Yeager | .05 | .02 | .00 |
| ☐ 556 Willie Upshaw | .15 | .06 | .01 |
| ☐ 557 Rick Honeycutt | .05 | .02 | .00 |
| ☐ 558 Dickie Thon | .09 | .04 | .01 |

|  | MINT | VG-E | F-G |
|---|---|---|---|
| ☐ 559 Pete Redfern | .03 | .01 | .00 |
| ☐ 560 Ron LeFlore | .05 | .02 | .00 |
| ☐ 561 Cardinals Leaders: | .10 | .02 | .00 |
|   BA: Lonnie Smith |  |  |  |
|   ERA: Joaquin Andujar |  |  |  |
| ☐ 562 Dave Rozema | .03 | .01 | .00 |
| ☐ 563 Juan Bonilla | .03 | .01 | .00 |
| ☐ 564 Sid Monge | .03 | .01 | .00 |
| ☐ 565 Bucky Dent | .06 | .02 | .00 |
| ☐ 566 Manny Sarmiento | .03 | .01 | .00 |
| ☐ 567 Joe Simpson | .03 | .01 | .00 |
| ☐ 568 Willie Hernandez | .20 | .09 | .02 |
| ☐ 569 Jack Perconte | .03 | .01 | .00 |
| ☐ 570 Vida Blue | .09 | .04 | .01 |
| ☐ 571 Mickey Klutts | .03 | .01 | .00 |
| ☐ 572 Bob Watson | .05 | .02 | .00 |
| ☐ 573 Andy Hassler | .03 | .01 | .00 |
| ☐ 574 Glenn Adams | .03 | .01 | .00 |
| ☐ 575 Neil Allen | .06 | .02 | .00 |
| ☐ 576 Frank Robinson MGR | .14 | .06 | .01 |
| ☐ 577 Luis Aponte | .07 | .03 | .01 |
| ☐ 578 David Green | .25 | .10 | .02 |
| ☐ 579 Rich Dauer | .03 | .01 | .00 |
| ☐ 580 Tom Seaver | .40 | .18 | .04 |
| ☐ 581 SV: Tom Seaver | .20 | .09 | .02 |
| ☐ 582 Marshall Edwards | .03 | .01 | .00 |
| ☐ 583 Terry Forster | .09 | .04 | .01 |
| ☐ 584 Dave Hostetler | .09 | .04 | .01 |
| ☐ 585 Jose Cruz | .13 | .06 | .01 |
| ☐ 586 Frank Viola | .55 | .25 | .05 |
| ☐ 587 Ivan DeJesus | .03 | .01 | .00 |
| ☐ 588 Pat Underwood | .03 | .01 | .00 |
| ☐ 589 Alvis Woods | .03 | .01 | .00 |
| ☐ 590 Tony Pena | .16 | .07 | .01 |
| ☐ 591 White Sox Leaders: | .11 | .02 | .00 |
|   BA: Greg Luzinski |  |  |  |
|   ERA: LaMarr Hoyt |  |  |  |
| ☐ 592 Shane Rawley | .06 | .02 | .00 |
| ☐ 593 Broderick Perkins | .03 | .01 | .00 |
| ☐ 594 Eric Rasmussen | .03 | .01 | .00 |
| ☐ 595 Tim Raines | .30 | .12 | .03 |
| ☐ 596 Randy Johnson | .07 | .03 | .01 |
| ☐ 597 Mike Proly | .03 | .01 | .00 |
| ☐ 598 Dwayne Murphy | .07 | .03 | .01 |
| ☐ 599 Don Aase | .03 | .01 | .00 |
| ☐ 600 George Brett | .65 | .30 | .06 |
| ☐ 601 Ed Lynch | .03 | .01 | .00 |
| ☐ 602 Rich Gedman | .07 | .03 | .01 |
| ☐ 603 Joe Morgan | .25 | .10 | .02 |
| ☐ 604 SV: Joe Morgan | .13 | .06 | .01 |
| ☐ 605 Gary Roenicke | .05 | .02 | .00 |
| ☐ 606 Bobby Cox MGR | .03 | .01 | .00 |
| ☐ 607 Charlie Leibrandt | .07 | .03 | .01 |

| | MINT | VG-E | F-G |
|---|---|---|---|
| ☐ 608 Don Money | .03 | .01 | .00 |
| ☐ 609 Danny Darwin | .03 | .01 | .00 |
| ☐ 610 Steve Garvey | .50 | .22 | .05 |
| ☐ 611 Bert Roberge | .03 | .01 | .00 |
| ☐ 612 Steve Swisher | .03 | .01 | .00 |
| ☐ 613 Mike Ivie | .03 | .01 | .00 |
| ☐ 614 Ed Glynn | .03 | .01 | .00 |
| ☐ 615 Garry Maddox | .05 | .02 | .00 |
| ☐ 616 Bill Nahorodny | .03 | .01 | .00 |
| ☐ 617 Butch Wynegar | .06 | .02 | .00 |
| ☐ 618 LaMarr Hoyt | .15 | .06 | .01 |
| ☐ 619 Keith Moreland | .06 | .02 | .00 |
| ☐ 620 Mike Norris | .05 | .02 | .00 |
| ☐ 621 Mets Team Leaders: | .09 | .02 | .00 |
|     BA: Mookie Wilson | | | |
|     ERA: Craig Swan | | | |
| ☐ 622 Dave Edler | .03 | .01 | .00 |
| ☐ 623 Luis Sanchez | .03 | .01 | .00 |
| ☐ 624 Glenn Hubbard | .05 | .02 | .00 |
| ☐ 625 Ken Forsch | .03 | .01 | .00 |
| ☐ 626 Jerry Martin | .03 | .01 | .00 |
| ☐ 627 Doug Bair | .03 | .01 | .00 |
| ☐ 628 Julio Valdez | .03 | .01 | .00 |
| ☐ 629 Charlie Lea | .05 | .02 | .00 |
| ☐ 630 Paul Molitor | .16 | .07 | .01 |
| ☐ 631 Tippy Martinez | .06 | .02 | .00 |
| ☐ 632 Alex Trevino | .03 | .01 | .00 |
| ☐ 633 Vicente Romo | .03 | .01 | .00 |
| ☐ 634 Max Venable | .03 | .01 | .00 |
| ☐ 635 Graig Nettles | .16 | .07 | .01 |
| ☐ 636 SV: Graig Nettles | .10 | .04 | .01 |
| ☐ 637 Pat Corrales MGR | .03 | .01 | .00 |
| ☐ 638 Dan Petry | .18 | .08 | .01 |
| ☐ 639 Art Howe | .03 | .01 | .00 |
| ☐ 640 Andre Thornton | .10 | .04 | .01 |
| ☐ 641 Billy Sample | .03 | .01 | .00 |
| ☐ 642 Checklist: 529–660 | .10 | .01 | .00 |
| ☐ 643 Bump Wills | .03 | .01 | .00 |
| ☐ 644 Joe LeFebvre | .03 | .01 | .00 |
| ☐ 645 Bill Madlock | .16 | .07 | .01 |
| ☐ 646 Jim Essian | .03 | .01 | .00 |
| ☐ 647 Bobby Mitchell | .05 | .02 | .00 |
| ☐ 648 Jeff Burroughs | .05 | .02 | .00 |
| ☐ 649 Tommy Boggs | .03 | .01 | .00 |
| ☐ 650 George Hendrick | .09 | .04 | .01 |
| ☐ 651 Angels Leaders: | .12 | .02 | .00 |
|     BA: Rod Carew | | | |
|     ERA: Mike Witt | | | |
| ☐ 652 Butch Hobson | .03 | .01 | .00 |
| ☐ 653 Ellis Valentine | .03 | .01 | .00 |
| ☐ 654 Bob Ojeda | .06 | .02 | .00 |
| ☐ 655 Al Bumbry | .03 | .01 | .00 |
| ☐ 656 Dave Frost | .03 | .01 | .00 |

| | MINT | VG-E | F-G |
|---|---|---|---|
| ☐ 657 Mike Gates | .07 | .03 | .01 |
| ☐ 658 Frank Pastore | .03 | .01 | .00 |
| ☐ 659 Charlie Moore | .03 | .01 | .00 |
| ☐ 660 Mike Hargrove | .05 | .02 | .00 |
| ☐ 661 Bill Russell | .05 | .02 | .00 |
| ☐ 662 Joe Sambito | .05 | .02 | .00 |
| ☐ 663 Tom O'Malley | .09 | .04 | .01 |
| ☐ 664 Bob Molinaro | .03 | .01 | .00 |
| ☐ 665 Jim Sundberg | .06 | .02 | .00 |
| ☐ 666 Sparky Anderson MGR | .06 | .02 | .00 |
| ☐ 667 Dick Davis | .03 | .01 | .00 |
| ☐ 668 Larry Christenson | .03 | .01 | .00 |
| ☐ 669 Mike Squires | .03 | .01 | .00 |
| ☐ 670 Jerry Mumphrey | .05 | .02 | .00 |
| ☐ 671 Lenny Faedo | .03 | .01 | .00 |
| ☐ 672 Jim Kaat | .10 | .04 | .01 |
| ☐ 673 SV: Jim Kaat | .07 | .03 | .01 |
| ☐ 674 Kurt Bevacqua | .03 | .01 | .00 |
| ☐ 675 Jim Beattie | .03 | .01 | .00 |
| ☐ 676 Biff Pocoroba | .03 | .01 | .00 |
| ☐ 677 Dave Revering | .03 | .01 | .00 |
| ☐ 678 Juan Beniquez | .05 | .02 | .00 |
| ☐ 679 Mike Scott | .05 | .02 | .00 |
| ☐ 680 Andre Dawson | .30 | .12 | .03 |
| ☐ 681 Dodgers Leaders: | .15 | .04 | .01 |
|     BA: Pedro Guerrero | | | |
|     ERA: Fernando | | | |
|     Valenzuela | | | |
| ☐ 682 Bob Stanley | .06 | .02 | .00 |
| ☐ 683 Dan Ford | .05 | .02 | .00 |
| ☐ 684 Rafael Landestoy | .03 | .01 | .00 |
| ☐ 685 Lee Mazzilli | .06 | .02 | .00 |
| ☐ 686 Randy Lerch | .03 | .01 | .00 |
| ☐ 687 U.L. Washington | .03 | .01 | .00 |
| ☐ 688 Jim Wohlford | .03 | .01 | .00 |
| ☐ 689 Ron Hassey | .03 | .01 | .00 |
| ☐ 690 Kent Hrbek | .45 | .20 | .04 |
| ☐ 691 Dave Tobik | .03 | .01 | .00 |
| ☐ 692 Denny Walling | .03 | .01 | .00 |
| ☐ 693 Sparky Lyle | .10 | .04 | .01 |
| ☐ 694 SV: Sparky Lyle | .07 | .03 | .01 |
| ☐ 695 Ruppert Jones | .05 | .02 | .00 |
| ☐ 696 Chuck Tanner MGR | .03 | .01 | .00 |
| ☐ 697 Barry Foote | .03 | .01 | .00 |
| ☐ 698 Tony Bernazard | .03 | .01 | .00 |
| ☐ 699 Lee Smith | .11 | .05 | .01 |
| ☐ 700 Keith Hernandez | .35 | .15 | .03 |
| ☐ 701 Batting Leaders: | .15 | .06 | .01 |
|     AL: Willie Wilson | | | |
|     NL: Al Oliver | | | |
| ☐ 702 Home Run Leaders: | .15 | .06 | .01 |
|     AL: Reggie Jackson | | | |
|     AL: Gorman Thomas | | | |
|     NL: Dave Kingman | | | |

| | MINT | VG-E | F-G |
|---|---|---|---|
| ☐ 703 RBI Leaders: | .15 | .06 | .01 |
| AL: Hal McRae | | | |
| NL: Dale Murphy | | | |
| NL: Al Oliver | | | |
| ☐ 704 SB Leaders: | .20 | .09 | .02 |
| AL: Rickey Henderson | | | |
| NL: Tim Raines | | | |
| ☐ 705 Victory Leaders: | .15 | .06 | .01 |
| AL: LaMarr Hoyt | | | |
| NL: Steve Carlton | | | |
| ☐ 706 Strikeout Leaders: | .15 | .06 | .01 |
| AL: Floyd Bannister | | | |
| NL: Steve Carlton | | | |
| ☐ 707 ERA Leaders: | .09 | .04 | .01 |
| AL: Rick Sutcliffe | | | |
| NL: Steve Rogers | | | |
| ☐ 708 Leading Firemen: | .11 | .05 | .01 |
| AL: Dan Quisenberry | | | |
| NL: Bruce Sutter | | | |
| ☐ 709 Jimmy Sexton | .03 | .01 | .00 |
| ☐ 710 Willie Wilson | .25 | .10 | .02 |
| ☐ 711 Mariners Leaders: | .08 | .02 | .00 |
| BA: Bruce Bochte | | | |
| ERA: Jim Beattie | | | |
| ☐ 712 Bruce Kison | .03 | .01 | .00 |
| ☐ 713 Ron Hodges | .03 | .01 | .00 |
| ☐ 714 Wayne Nordhagen | .03 | .01 | .00 |
| ☐ 715 Tony Perez | .15 | .06 | .01 |
| ☐ 716 SV: Tony Perez | .10 | .04 | .01 |
| ☐ 717 Scott Sanderson | .05 | .02 | .00 |
| ☐ 718 Jim Dwyer | .03 | .01 | .00 |
| ☐ 719 Rich Gale | .03 | .01 | .00 |
| ☐ 720 Dave Concepcion | .10 | .04 | .01 |
| ☐ 721 John Martin | .03 | .01 | .00 |
| ☐ 722 Jorge Orta | .03 | .01 | .00 |
| ☐ 723 Randy Moffitt | .03 | .01 | .00 |
| ☐ 724 Johnny Grubb | .03 | .01 | .00 |
| ☐ 725 Dan Spillner | .03 | .01 | .00 |
| ☐ 726 Harvey Kuenn | .05 | .02 | .00 |
| ☐ 727 Chet Lemon | .09 | .04 | .01 |
| ☐ 728 Ron Reed | .03 | .01 | .00 |
| ☐ 729 Jerry Morales | .03 | .01 | .00 |
| ☐ 730 Jason Thompson | .09 | .04 | .01 |
| ☐ 731 Al Williams | .03 | .01 | .00 |
| ☐ 732 Dave Henderson | .05 | .02 | .00 |
| ☐ 733 Buck Martinez | .03 | .01 | .00 |
| ☐ 734 Steve Braun | .03 | .01 | .00 |
| ☐ 735 Tommy John | .16 | .07 | .01 |
| ☐ 736 SV: Tommy John | .10 | .04 | .01 |
| ☐ 737 Mitchell Page | .03 | .01 | .00 |
| ☐ 738 Tim Foli | .03 | .01 | .00 |
| ☐ 739 Rick Ownbey | .09 | .04 | .01 |
| ☐ 740 Rusty Staub | .10 | .04 | .01 |

| | MINT | VG-E | F-G |
|---|---|---|---|
| ☐ 741 SV: Rusty Staub | .07 | .03 | .01 |
| ☐ 742 Padres Leaders: | .08 | .02 | .00 |
| BA: Terry Kennedy | | | |
| ERA: Tim Lollar | | | |
| ☐ 743 Mike Torrez | .05 | .02 | .00 |
| ☐ 744 Brad Mills | .03 | .01 | .00 |
| ☐ 745 Scott McGregor | .09 | .04 | .01 |
| ☐ 746 John Wathan | .03 | .01 | .00 |
| ☐ 747 Fred Breining | .03 | .01 | .00 |
| ☐ 748 Derrel Thomas | .03 | .01 | .00 |
| ☐ 749 Jon Matlack | .05 | .02 | .00 |
| ☐ 750 Ben Oglivie | .09 | .04 | .01 |
| ☐ 751 Brad Havens | .03 | .01 | .00 |
| ☐ 752 Luis Pujols | .03 | .01 | .00 |
| ☐ 753 Elias Sosa | .03 | .01 | .00 |
| ☐ 754 Bill Robinson | .03 | .01 | .00 |
| ☐ 755 John Candelaria | .08 | .03 | .01 |
| ☐ 756 Russ Nixon | .03 | .01 | .00 |
| ☐ 757 Rick Manning | .03 | .01 | .00 |
| ☐ 758 Aurelio Rodriguez | .03 | .01 | .00 |
| ☐ 759 Doug Bird | .03 | .01 | .00 |
| ☐ 760 Dale Murphy | 1.00 | .45 | .10 |
| ☐ 761 Gary Lucas | .03 | .01 | .00 |
| ☐ 762 Cliff Johnson | .03 | .01 | .00 |
| ☐ 763 Al Cowens | .05 | .02 | .00 |
| ☐ 764 Pete Falcone | .03 | .01 | .00 |
| ☐ 765 Bob Boone | .06 | .02 | .00 |
| ☐ 766 Barry Bonnell | .03 | .01 | .00 |
| ☐ 767 Duane Kuiper | .03 | .01 | .00 |
| ☐ 768 Chris Speier | .03 | .01 | .00 |
| ☐ 769 Checklist: 661–792 | .10 | .01 | .00 |
| ☐ 770 Dave Winfield | .40 | .18 | .04 |
| ☐ 771 Twins Leaders: | .09 | .02 | .00 |
| BA: Kent Hrbek | | | |
| ERA: Bobby Castillo | | | |
| ☐ 772 Jim Kern | .03 | .01 | .00 |
| ☐ 773 Larry Hisle | .05 | .02 | .00 |
| ☐ 774 Alan Ashby | .03 | .01 | .00 |
| ☐ 775 Burt Hooton | .03 | .01 | .00 |
| ☐ 776 Larry Parrish | .06 | .02 | .00 |
| ☐ 777 John Curtis | .03 | .01 | .00 |
| ☐ 778 Rich Hebner | .03 | .01 | .00 |
| ☐ 779 Rick Waits | .03 | .01 | .00 |
| ☐ 780 Gary Matthews | .09 | .04 | .01 |
| ☐ 781 Rick Rhoden | .06 | .02 | .00 |
| ☐ 782 Bobby Murcer | .10 | .04 | .01 |
| ☐ 783 SV: Bobby Murcer | .06 | .02 | .00 |
| ☐ 784 Jeff Newman | .03 | .01 | .00 |
| ☐ 785 Dennis Leonard | .06 | .02 | .00 |
| ☐ 786 Ralph Houk MGR | .03 | .01 | .00 |
| ☐ 787 Dick Tidrow | .03 | .01 | .00 |
| ☐ 788 Dane Iorg | .03 | .01 | .00 |
| ☐ 789 Bryan Clark | .03 | .01 | .00 |

|  | MINT | VG-E | F-G |
|---|---|---|---|
| ☐ 790 Bob Grich | .07 | .03 | .01 |
| ☐ 791 Gary Lavelle | .03 | .01 | .00 |
| ☐ 792 Chris Chambliss | .07 | .02 | .00 |

## 1983 TOPPS EXTENDED

TONY ARMAS

The cards in this 132 card set measure 2½" by 3½". For the third year in a row, Topps issued a 132 card traded set featuring some of the year's top rookies and players who had changed teams during the year, but were featured with their old team in the Topps regular issue of 1983. The cards were available through hobby dealers only and were printed in Ireland by the Topps affiliate in that country. The set is numbered alphabetically by the last name of the player of the card.

Complete Set: M-14.00; VG-E-6.50; F-G-1.40

|  | MINT | VG-E | F-G |
|---|---|---|---|
| Common Player | .08 | .03 | .01 |
|  |  |  |  |
| ☐ 1 T Neil Allen | .12 | .05 | .01 |
| ☐ 2 T Bill Almon | .08 | .03 | .01 |
| ☐ 3 T Joe Altobelli MGR | .08 | .03 | .01 |
| ☐ 4 T Tony Armas | .20 | .09 | .02 |
| ☐ 5 T Doug Bair | .08 | .03 | .01 |
| ☐ 6 T Steve Baker | .12 | .05 | .01 |
| ☐ 7 T Floyd Bannister | .12 | .05 | .01 |
| ☐ 8 T Don Baylor | .20 | .09 | .02 |
| ☐ 9 T Tony Bernazard | .08 | .03 | .01 |
| ☐ 10 T Larry Biittner | .08 | .03 | .01 |
| ☐ 11 T Dann Bilardello | .12 | .05 | .01 |
| ☐ 12 T Doug Bird | .08 | .03 | .01 |
| ☐ 13 T Steve Boros MGR | .08 | .03 | .01 |
| ☐ 14 T Greg Brock | .50 | .22 | .05 |
| ☐ 15 T Mike Brown | .15 | .06 | .01 |

|  | MINT | VG-E | F-G |
|---|---|---|---|
| ☐ 16 T Tom Burgmeier | .08 | .03 | .01 |
| ☐ 17 T Randy Bush | .12 | .05 | .01 |
| ☐ 18 T Bert Campaneris | .12 | .05 | .01 |
| ☐ 19 T Ron Cey | .20 | .09 | .02 |
| ☐ 20 T Chris Codiroli | .12 | .05 | .01 |
| ☐ 21 T Dave Collins | .12 | .05 | .01 |
| ☐ 22 T Terry Crowley | .08 | .03 | .01 |
| ☐ 23 T Julio Cruz | .08 | .03 | .01 |
| ☐ 24 T Mike Davis | .25 | .10 | .02 |
| ☐ 25 T Frank DiPino | .12 | .05 | .01 |
| ☐ 26 T Bill Doran | .75 | .35 | .07 |
| ☐ 27 T Jerry Dybzinski | .08 | .03 | .01 |
| ☐ 28 T Jamie Easterly | .08 | .03 | .01 |
| ☐ 29 T Juan Eichelberger | .08 | .03 | .01 |
| ☐ 30 T Jim Essian | .08 | .03 | .01 |
| ☐ 31 T Pete Falcone | .08 | .03 | .01 |
| ☐ 32 T Mike Ferraro MGR | .08 | .03 | .01 |
| ☐ 33 T Terry Forster | .15 | .06 | .01 |
| ☐ 34 T Julio Franco | 1.00 | .45 | .10 |
| ☐ 35 T Rich Gale | .08 | .03 | .01 |
| ☐ 36 T Kiko Garcia | .08 | .03 | .01 |
| ☐ 37 T Steve Garvey | 1.00 | .45 | .10 |
| ☐ 38 T Johnny Grubb | .08 | .03 | .01 |
| ☐ 39 T Mel Hall | .50 | .22 | .05 |
| ☐ 40 T Von Hayes | .50 | .22 | .05 |
| ☐ 41 T Danny Heep | .08 | .03 | .01 |
| ☐ 42 T Steve Henderson | .08 | .03 | .01 |
| ☐ 43 T Keith Hernandez | .75 | .35 | .07 |
| ☐ 44 T Leo Hernandez | .15 | .06 | .01 |
| ☐ 45 T Willie Hernandez | .40 | .18 | .04 |
| ☐ 46 T Al Holland | .12 | .05 | .01 |
| ☐ 47 T Frank Howard | .12 | .05 | .01 |
| ☐ 48 T Bobby Johnson | .08 | .03 | .01 |
| ☐ 49 T Cliff Johnson | .08 | .03 | .01 |
| ☐ 50 T Odell Jones | .08 | .03 | .01 |
| ☐ 51 T Mike Jorgensen | .08 | .03 | .01 |
| ☐ 52 T Bob Kearney | .08 | .03 | .01 |
| ☐ 53 T Steve Kemp | .16 | .07 | .01 |
| ☐ 54 T Matt Keough | .08 | .03 | .01 |
| ☐ 55 T Ron Kittle | .75 | .35 | .07 |
| ☐ 56 T Mickey Klutts | .08 | .03 | .01 |
| ☐ 57 T Alan Knicely | .08 | .03 | .01 |
| ☐ 58 T Mike Krukow | .08 | .03 | .01 |
| ☐ 59 T Rafael Landestoy | .08 | .03 | .01 |
| ☐ 60 T Carney Lansford | .25 | .10 | .02 |
| ☐ 61 T Joe Lefebvre | .08 | .03 | .01 |
| ☐ 62 T Bryan Little | .12 | .05 | .01 |
| ☐ 63 T Aurelio Lopez | .12 | .05 | .01 |
| ☐ 64 T Mike Madden | .20 | .09 | .02 |
| ☐ 65 T Rick Manning | .08 | .03 | .01 |
| ☐ 66 T Billy Martin MGR | .16 | .07 | .01 |
| ☐ 67 T Lee Mazzilli | .12 | .05 | .01 |
| ☐ 68 T Andy McGaffigan | .08 | .03 | .01 |

|  | MINT | VG-E | F-G |
|---|---|---|---|
| ☐ 69 T Craig McMurtry | .25 | .10 | .02 |
| ☐ 70 T John McNamara MGR | .08 | .03 | .01 |
| ☐ 71 T Orlando Mercado | .12 | .05 | .01 |
| ☐ 72 T Larry Milbourne | .08 | .03 | .01 |
| ☐ 73 T Randy Moffitt | .08 | .03 | .01 |
| ☐ 74 T Sid Monge | .08 | .03 | .01 |
| ☐ 75 T Jose Morales | .08 | .03 | .01 |
| ☐ 76 T Omar Moreno | .12 | .05 | .01 |
| ☐ 77 T Joe Morgan | .55 | .25 | .05 |
| ☐ 78 T Mike Morgan | .08 | .03 | .01 |
| ☐ 79 T Dale Murray | .08 | .03 | .01 |
| ☐ 80 T Jeff Newman | .08 | .03 | .01 |
| ☐ 81 T Pete O'Brien | .65 | .30 | .06 |
| ☐ 82 T Jorge Orta | .08 | .03 | .01 |
| ☐ 83 T Alejandro Pena | .60 | .28 | .05 |
| ☐ 84 T Pascual Perez | .12 | .05 | .01 |
| ☐ 85 T Tony Perez | .30 | .12 | .03 |
| ☐ 86 T Broderick Perkins | .08 | .03 | .01 |
| ☐ 87 T Tony Phillips | .12 | .05 | .01 |
| ☐ 88 T Charlie Puleo | .08 | .03 | .01 |
| ☐ 89 T Pat Putnam | .08 | .03 | .01 |
| ☐ 90 T Jamie Quirk | .08 | .03 | .01 |
| ☐ 91 T Doug Rader MGR | .12 | .05 | .01 |
| ☐ 92 T Chuck Rainey | .08 | .03 | .01 |
| ☐ 93 T Bobby Ramos | .08 | .03 | .01 |
| ☐ 94 T Gary Redus | .55 | .25 | .05 |
| ☐ 95 T Steve Renko | .08 | .03 | .01 |
| ☐ 96 T Leon Roberts | .08 | .03 | .01 |
| ☐ 97 T Aurelio Rodriguez | .08 | .03 | .01 |
| ☐ 98 T Dick Ruthven | .08 | .03 | .01 |
| ☐ 99 T Daryl Sconiers | .12 | .05 | .01 |
| ☐ 100 T Mike Scott | .12 | .05 | .01 |
| ☐ 101 T Tom Seaver | 1.00 | .45 | .10 |
| ☐ 102 T John Shelby | .15 | .06 | .01 |
| ☐ 103 T Bob Shirley | .08 | .03 | .01 |
| ☐ 104 T Joe Simpson | .08 | .03 | .01 |
| ☐ 105 T Doug Sisk | .15 | .06 | .01 |
| ☐ 106 T Mike Smithson | .20 | .09 | .02 |
| ☐ 107 T Elias Sosa | .08 | .03 | .01 |
| ☐ 108 T Darryl Strawberry | 5.50 | 2.60 | .55 |
| ☐ 109 T Tom Tellmann | .08 | .03 | .01 |
| ☐ 110 T Gene Tenace | .08 | .03 | .01 |
| ☐ 111 T Gorman Thomas | .20 | .09 | .02 |
| ☐ 112 T Dick Tidrow | .08 | .03 | .01 |
| ☐ 113 T Dave Tobik | .08 | .03 | .01 |
| ☐ 114 T Wayne Tolleson | .12 | .05 | .01 |
| ☐ 115 T Mike Torrez | .12 | .05 | .01 |
| ☐ 116 T Manny Trillo | .12 | .05 | .01 |
| ☐ 117 T Steve Trout | .12 | .05 | .01 |
| ☐ 118 T Lee Tunnell | .15 | .06 | .01 |
| ☐ 119 T Mike Vail | .08 | .03 | .01 |
| ☐ 120 T Ellis Valentine | .12 | .05 | .01 |
| ☐ 121 T Tom Veryzer | .08 | .03 | .01 |

|  | MINT | VG-E | F-G |
|---|---|---|---|
| ☐ 122 T George Vukovich | .08 | .03 | .01 |
| ☐ 123 T Rick Waits | .08 | .03 | .01 |
| ☐ 124 T Greg Walker | 1.50 | .70 | .15 |
| ☐ 125 T Chris Welsh | .08 | .03 | .01 |
| ☐ 126 T Len Whitehouse | .12 | .05 | .01 |
| ☐ 127 T Eddie Whitson | .12 | .05 | .01 |
| ☐ 128 T Jim Wohlford | .08 | .03 | .01 |
| ☐ 129 T Matt Young | .25 | .10 | .02 |
| ☐ 130 T Joel Youngblood | .08 | .03 | .01 |
| ☐ 131 T Pat Zachry | .08 | .03 | .01 |
| ☐ 132 T Checklist 1T–132T | .20 | .04 | .01 |

## 1984 TOPPS

The cards in this 792 card set measure 2½" by 3½". For the second year in a row, Topps utilized a dual picture on the front of the card. A portrait is shown in a square insert and an action shot is featured in the main photo. Card numbers 1–6 feature 1983 Highlights (HL), card numbers 386–407 feature All Stars and card numbers 701–718 feature active Major League career leaders. Each team leader card features the team's leading hitter and pitcher. There are six checklist cards and the backs feature team logos.

Complete Set: M-28.00; VG-E-12.50; F-G-2.80

|  | MINT | VG-E | F-G |
|---|---|---|---|
| Common Player (1–792) | .03 | .01 | .00 |
| ☐ 1 HL: Steve Carlton 300th Win and All Time SO King | .25 | .08 | .02 |
| ☐ 2 HL: Rickey Henderson 100 Stolen Bases Three Times | .20 | .09 | .02 |

| | MINT | VG-E | F-G |
|---|---|---|---|
| 3 HL: Dan Quisenberry ... Sets Save Record | .12 | .05 | .01 |
| 4 HL: Nolan Ryan, ....... Steve Carlton, and Gaylord Perry (All Surpass Johnson) | .25 | .10 | .02 |
| 5 HL: Dave Righetti, ..... Bob Forsch, and Mike Warren (All Pitch No-Hitters) | .12 | .05 | .01 |
| 6 HL: Johnny Bench ..... Gaylord Perry, and Carl Yastrzemski (Superstars Retire) | .25 | .10 | .02 |
| 7 Gary Lucas ........... | .03 | .01 | .00 |
| 8 Don Mattingly ........ | 5.50 | 2.60 | .55 |
| 9 Jim Gott ............. | .03 | .01 | .00 |
| 10 Robin Yount .......... | .35 | .15 | .03 |
| 11 Minnesota Twins Leaders ............. Kent Hrbek Ken Schrom | .09 | .02 | .00 |
| 12 Billy Sample ......... | .03 | .01 | .00 |
| 13 Scott Holman ........ | .03 | .01 | .00 |
| 14 Tom Brookens ........ | .03 | .01 | .00 |
| 15 Burt Hooton ......... | .03 | .01 | .00 |
| 16 Omar Moreno ........ | .05 | .02 | .00 |
| 17 John Denny ......... | .08 | .03 | .01 |
| 18 Dale Berra .......... | .05 | .02 | .00 |
| 19 Ray Fontenot ........ | .14 | .06 | .01 |
| 20 Greg Luzinski ........ | .12 | .05 | .01 |
| 21 Joe Altobelli MGR .... | .03 | .01 | .00 |
| 22 Bryan Clark ......... | .03 | .01 | .00 |
| 23 Keith Moreland ...... | .05 | .02 | .00 |
| 24 John Martin ......... | .03 | .01 | .00 |
| 25 Glenn Hubbard ...... | .05 | .02 | .00 |
| 26 Bud Black .......... | .05 | .02 | .00 |
| 27 Daryl Sconiers ...... | .03 | .01 | .00 |
| 28 Frank Viola ......... | .07 | .03 | .01 |
| 29 Danny Heep ........ | .03 | .01 | .00 |
| 30 Wade Boggs ........ | 1.10 | .50 | .11 |
| 31 Andy McGaffigan .... | .03 | .01 | .00 |
| 32 Bobby Ramos ....... | .03 | .01 | .00 |
| 33 Tom Burgmeier ...... | .03 | .01 | .00 |
| 34 Eddie Milner ........ | .03 | .01 | .00 |
| 35 Don Sutton ......... | .14 | .06 | .01 |
| 36 Denny Walling ...... | .03 | .01 | .00 |
| 37 Texas Rangers Leaders Buddy Bell Rick Honeycutt | .08 | .02 | .00 |
| 38 Luis DeLeon ........ | .03 | .01 | .00 |
| 39 Garth Iorg ......... | .03 | .01 | .00 |
| 40 Dusty Baker ........ | .09 | .04 | .01 |

| | MINT | VG-E | F-G |
|---|---|---|---|
| 41 Tony Bernazard ....... | .03 | .01 | .00 |
| 42 Johnny Grubb ........ | .03 | .01 | .00 |
| 43 Ron Reed ........... | .03 | .01 | .00 |
| 44 Jim Morrison ........ | .03 | .01 | .00 |
| 45 Jerry Mumphrey ...... | .05 | .02 | .01 |
| 46 Ray Smith .......... | .06 | .02 | .00 |
| 47 Rudy Law ........... | .03 | .01 | .00 |
| 48 Julio Franco ......... | .25 | .10 | .02 |
| 49 John Stuper ......... | .03 | .01 | .00 |
| 50 Chris Chambliss ..... | .05 | .02 | .00 |
| 51 Jim Frey MGR ....... | .03 | .01 | .00 |
| 52 Paul Splittorff ....... | .05 | .02 | .00 |
| 53 Juan Beniquez ....... | .05 | .02 | .00 |
| 54 Jesse Orosco ........ | .07 | .03 | .01 |
| 55 Dave Concepcion ..... | .10 | .04 | .01 |
| 56 Gary Allenson ....... | .03 | .01 | .00 |
| 57 Dan Schatzeder ...... | .03 | .01 | .00 |
| 58 Max Venable ........ | .03 | .01 | .00 |
| 59 Sammy Stewart ...... | .03 | .01 | .00 |
| 60 Paul Molitor ........ | .13 | .06 | .01 |
| 61 Chris Codiroli ....... | .08 | .03 | .01 |
| 62 Dave Hostetler ...... | .03 | .01 | .00 |
| 63 Ed VandeBerg ....... | .06 | .02 | .00 |
| 64 Mike Scioscia ....... | .03 | .01 | .00 |
| 65 Kirk Gibson ......... | .25 | .10 | .02 |
| 66 Houston Astros Leaders Jose Cruz Nolan Ryan | .08 | .02 | .00 |
| 67 Gary Ward .......... | .06 | .02 | .00 |
| 68 Luis Salazar ........ | .03 | .01 | .00 |
| 69 Rod Scurry ......... | .03 | .01 | .00 |
| 70 Gary Matthews ...... | .08 | .03 | .01 |
| 71 Leo Hernandez ...... | .11 | .05 | .01 |
| 72 Mike Squires ........ | .03 | .01 | .00 |
| 73 Jody Davis ......... | .10 | .04 | .01 |
| 74 Jerry Martin ........ | .03 | .01 | .00 |
| 75 Bob Forsch ......... | .05 | .02 | .00 |
| 76 Alfredo Griffin ...... | .05 | .02 | .00 |
| 77 Brett Butler ........ | .08 | .03 | .01 |
| 78 Mike Torrez ........ | .05 | .02 | .00 |
| 79 Rob Wilfong ........ | .03 | .01 | .00 |
| 80 Steve Rogers ....... | .08 | .03 | .01 |
| 81 Billy Martin MGR .... | .12 | .05 | .01 |
| 82 Doug Bird .......... | .03 | .01 | .00 |
| 83 Richie Zisk ......... | .05 | .02 | .00 |
| 84 Lenny Faedo ........ | .03 | .01 | .00 |
| 85 Atlee Hammaker ..... | .05 | .02 | .00 |
| 86 John Shelby ........ | .09 | .04 | .01 |
| 87 Frank Pastore ....... | .03 | .01 | .00 |
| 88 Rob Picciolo ........ | .03 | .01 | .00 |
| 89 Mike Smithson ...... | .14 | .06 | .01 |
| 90 Pedro Guerrero ...... | .35 | .15 | .03 |
| 91 Dan Spillner ........ | .03 | .01 | .00 |

|  | MINT | VG-E | F-G |
|---|---|---|---|
| ☐ 92 Lloyd Moseby | .14 | .06 | .01 |
| ☐ 93 Bob Knepper | .06 | .02 | .00 |
| ☐ 94 Mario Ramirez | .06 | .02 | .00 |
| ☐ 95 Aurelio Lopez | .05 | .02 | .00 |
| ☐ 96 K.C. Royals Leaders | .08 | .02 | .00 |
| Hal McRae | | | |
| Larry Gura | | | |
| ☐ 97 LaMarr Hoyt | .12 | .05 | .01 |
| ☐ 98 Steve Nicosia | .03 | .01 | .00 |
| ☐ 99 Craig Lefferts | .18 | .08 | .01 |
| ☐ 100 Reggie Jackson | .45 | .20 | .04 |
| ☐ 101 Porfirio Altamirano | .03 | .01 | .00 |
| ☐ 102 Ken Oberkfell | .03 | .01 | .00 |
| ☐ 103 Dwayne Murphy | .07 | .03 | .01 |
| ☐ 104 Ken Dayley | .03 | .01 | .00 |
| ☐ 105 Tony Armas | .14 | .06 | .01 |
| ☐ 106 Tim Stoddard | .03 | .01 | .00 |
| ☐ 107 Ned Yost | .03 | .01 | .00 |
| ☐ 108 Randy Moffitt | .03 | .01 | .00 |
| ☐ 109 Brad Wellman | .06 | .02 | .00 |
| ☐ 110 Ron Guidry | .20 | .09 | .02 |
| ☐ 111 Bill Virdon | .05 | .02 | .00 |
| ☐ 112 Tom Niedenfuer | .07 | .03 | .01 |
| ☐ 113 Kelly Paris | .10 | .04 | .01 |
| ☐ 114 Checklist 1–132 | .08 | .01 | .00 |
| ☐ 115 Andre Thornton | .08 | .03 | .01 |
| ☐ 116 George Bjorkman | .06 | .02 | .00 |
| ☐ 117 Tom Veryzer | .03 | .01 | .00 |
| ☐ 118 Charlie Hough | .05 | .02 | .00 |
| ☐ 119 Johnny Wockenfuss | .03 | .01 | .00 |
| ☐ 120 Keith Hernandez | .35 | .15 | .03 |
| ☐ 121 Pat Sheridan | .25 | .10 | .02 |
| ☐ 122 Cecilio Guante | .05 | .02 | .00 |
| ☐ 123 Butch Wynegar | .05 | .02 | .00 |
| ☐ 124 Damaso Garcia | .09 | .04 | .01 |
| ☐ 125 Britt Burns | .08 | .03 | .01 |
| ☐ 126 Atlanta Braves Leaders | .10 | .02 | .00 |
| Dale Murphy | | | |
| Craig McMurtry | | | |
| ☐ 127 Mike Madden | .14 | .06 | .01 |
| ☐ 128 Rick Manning | .03 | .01 | .00 |
| ☐ 129 Bill Laskey | .03 | .01 | .00 |
| ☐ 130 Ozzie Smith | .12 | .05 | .01 |
| ☐ 131 Batting Leaders: | .20 | .09 | .02 |
| Bill Madlock | | | |
| Wade Boggs | | | |
| ☐ 132 Home Run Leaders: | .20 | .09 | .02 |
| Mike Schmidt | | | |
| Jim Rice | | | |
| ☐ 133 RBI Leaders: | .20 | .09 | .02 |
| Dale Murphy | | | |
| Cecil Cooper | | | |
| Jim Rice | | | |

|  | MINT | VG-E | F-G |
|---|---|---|---|
| ☐ 134 Stolen Base Leaders: | .20 | .09 | .02 |
| Tim Raines | | | |
| Rickey Henderson | | | |
| ☐ 135 Victory Leaders: | .08 | .03 | .01 |
| John Denny | | | |
| LaMarr Hoyt | | | |
| ☐ 136 Strikeout Leaders: | .14 | .06 | .01 |
| Steve Carlton | | | |
| Jack Morris | | | |
| ☐ 137 ERA Leaders: | .06 | .02 | .00 |
| Atlee Hammaker | | | |
| Rick Honeycutt | | | |
| ☐ 138 Leading Firemen: | .08 | .03 | .01 |
| Al Holland | | | |
| Dan Quisenberry | | | |
| ☐ 139 Bert Campaneris | .06 | .02 | .00 |
| ☐ 140 Storm Davis | .09 | .04 | .01 |
| ☐ 141 Pat Corrales MGR | .03 | .01 | .00 |
| ☐ 142 Rich Gale | .03 | .01 | .00 |
| ☐ 143 Jose Morales | .03 | .01 | .00 |
| ☐ 144 Brian Harper | .09 | .04 | .01 |
| ☐ 145 Gary Lavelle | .03 | .01 | .00 |
| ☐ 146 Ed Romero | .03 | .01 | .00 |
| ☐ 147 Dan Petry | .16 | .07 | .01 |
| ☐ 148 Joe Lefebvre | .03 | .01 | .00 |
| ☐ 149 Jon Matlack | .05 | .02 | .00 |
| ☐ 150 Dale Murphy | .70 | .32 | .07 |
| ☐ 151 Steve Trout | .05 | .02 | .00 |
| ☐ 152 Glenn Brummer | .03 | .01 | .00 |
| ☐ 153 Dick Tidrow | .03 | .01 | .00 |
| ☐ 154 Dave Henderson | .05 | .02 | .00 |
| ☐ 155 Frank White | .07 | .03 | .01 |
| ☐ 156 Oakland A's Leaders | .10 | .02 | .00 |
| Rickey Henderson | | | |
| Tim Conroy | | | |
| ☐ 157 Gary Gaetti | .03 | .01 | .00 |
| ☐ 158 John Curtis | .03 | .01 | .00 |
| ☐ 159 Darryl Cias | .06 | .02 | .00 |
| ☐ 160 Mario Soto | .10 | .04 | .01 |
| ☐ 161 Junior Ortiz | .07 | .03 | .01 |
| ☐ 162 Bob Ojeda | .06 | .02 | .00 |
| ☐ 163 Lorenzo Gray | .07 | .03 | .01 |
| ☐ 164 Scott Sanderson | .05 | .02 | .00 |
| ☐ 165 Ken Singleton | .09 | .04 | .01 |
| ☐ 166 Jamie Nelson | .08 | .03 | .01 |
| ☐ 167 Marshall Edwards | .03 | .01 | .00 |
| ☐ 168 Juan Bonilla | .03 | .01 | .00 |
| ☐ 169 Larry Parrish | .06 | .02 | .00 |
| ☐ 170 Jerry Reuss | .08 | .03 | .01 |
| ☐ 171 Frank Robinson MGR | .13 | .06 | .01 |
| ☐ 172 Frank DiPino | .05 | .02 | .00 |
| ☐ 173 Marvell Wynne | .15 | .06 | .01 |
| ☐ 174 Juan Berenguer | .03 | .01 | .00 |

| | MINT | VG-E | F-G |
|---|---|---|---|
| ☐ 175 Graig Nettles | .14 | .06 | .01 |
| ☐ 176 Lee Smith | .10 | .04 | .01 |
| ☐ 177 Jerry Hairston | .03 | .01 | .00 |
| ☐ 178 Bill Krueger | .08 | .03 | .01 |
| ☐ 179 Buck Martinez | .03 | .01 | .00 |
| ☐ 180 Manny Trillo | .05 | .02 | .00 |
| ☐ 181 Roy Thomas | .03 | .01 | .00 |
| ☐ 182 Darryl Strawberry | 3.50 | 1.65 | .35 |
| ☐ 183 Al Williams | .03 | .01 | .00 |
| ☐ 184 Mike O'Berry | .03 | .01 | .00 |
| ☐ 185 Sixto Lezcano | .03 | .01 | .00 |
| ☐ 186 Cardinal Leaders | .08 | .02 | .00 |
| Lonnie Smith | | | |
| John Stuper | | | |
| ☐ 187 Luis Aponte | .03 | .01 | .00 |
| ☐ 188 Bryan Little | .06 | .02 | .00 |
| ☐ 189 Tim Conroy | .08 | .03 | .01 |
| ☐ 190 Ben Ogilvie | .08 | .03 | .01 |
| ☐ 191 Mike Boddicker | .11 | .05 | .01 |
| ☐ 192 Nick Esasky | .30 | .12 | .03 |
| ☐ 193 Darrell Brown | .07 | .03 | .01 |
| ☐ 194 Domingo Ramos | .06 | .02 | .00 |
| ☐ 195 Jack Morris | .20 | .09 | .02 |
| ☐ 196 Don Slaught | .03 | .01 | .00 |
| ☐ 197 Garry Hancock | .03 | .01 | .00 |
| ☐ 198 Bill Doran | .35 | .15 | .03 |
| ☐ 199 Willie Hernandez | .30 | .12 | .03 |
| ☐ 200 Andre Dawson | .25 | .10 | .02 |
| ☐ 201 Bruce Kison | .03 | .01 | .00 |
| ☐ 202 Bobby Cox MGR | .03 | .01 | .00 |
| ☐ 203 Matt Keough | .03 | .01 | .00 |
| ☐ 204 Bobby Meacham | .30 | .12 | .03 |
| ☐ 205 Greg Minton | .05 | .02 | .00 |
| ☐ 206 Andy Van Slyke | .45 | .20 | .04 |
| ☐ 207 Donnie Moore | .08 | .03 | .01 |
| ☐ 208 Jose Oquendo | .09 | .04 | .01 |
| ☐ 209 Manny Sarmiento | .03 | .01 | .00 |
| ☐ 210 Joe Morgan | .16 | .07 | .01 |
| ☐ 211 Rick Sweet | .03 | .01 | .00 |
| ☐ 212 Broderick Perkins | .03 | .01 | .00 |
| ☐ 213 Bruce Hurst | .03 | .01 | .00 |
| ☐ 214 Paul Householder | .03 | .01 | .00 |
| ☐ 215 Tippy Martinez | .05 | .02 | .00 |
| ☐ 216 White Sox Leaders | .09 | .02 | .00 |
| Carlton Fisk | | | |
| Richard Dotson | | | |
| ☐ 217 Alan Ashby | .03 | .01 | .00 |
| ☐ 218 Rick Waits | .03 | .01 | .00 |
| ☐ 219 Joe Simpson | .03 | .01 | .00 |
| ☐ 220 Fernando Valenzuela | .35 | .15 | .03 |
| ☐ 221 Cliff Johnson | .03 | .01 | .00 |
| ☐ 222 Rick Honeycutt | .05 | .02 | .00 |
| ☐ 223 Wayne Krenchicki | .03 | .01 | .00 |

| | MINT | VG-E | F-G |
|---|---|---|---|
| ☐ 224 Sid Monge | .03 | .01 | .00 |
| ☐ 225 Lee Mazzilli | .06 | .02 | .00 |
| ☐ 226 Juan Eichelberger | .03 | .01 | .00 |
| ☐ 227 Steve Braun | .03 | .01 | .00 |
| ☐ 228 John Rabb | .12 | .05 | .01 |
| ☐ 229 Paul Owens MGR | .03 | .01 | .00 |
| ☐ 230 Rickey Henderson | .50 | .22 | .05 |
| ☐ 231 Gary Woods | .03 | .01 | .00 |
| ☐ 232 Tim Wallach | .12 | .05 | .01 |
| ☐ 233 Checklist 133–264 | .08 | .01 | .00 |
| ☐ 234 Rafael Ramirez | .05 | .02 | .00 |
| ☐ 235 Matt Young | .11 | .05 | .01 |
| ☐ 236 Ellis Valentine | .03 | .01 | .00 |
| ☐ 237 John Castino | .03 | .01 | .00 |
| ☐ 238 Reid Nichols | .03 | .01 | .00 |
| ☐ 239 Jay Howell | .07 | .03 | .01 |
| ☐ 240 Eddie Murray | .55 | .25 | .05 |
| ☐ 241 Billy Almon | .03 | .01 | .00 |
| ☐ 242 Alex Trevino | .03 | .01 | .00 |
| ☐ 243 Pete Ladd | .03 | .01 | .00 |
| ☐ 244 Candy Maldonado | .06 | .02 | .00 |
| ☐ 245 Rick Sutcliffe | .25 | .10 | .02 |
| ☐ 246 New York Mets Leaders | .10 | .02 | .00 |
| Mookie Wilson | | | |
| Tom Seaver | | | |
| ☐ 247 Onix Concepcion | .03 | .01 | .00 |
| ☐ 248 Bill Dawley | .25 | .10 | .02 |
| ☐ 249 Jay Johnstone | .05 | .02 | .00 |
| ☐ 250 Bill Madlock | .15 | .06 | .01 |
| ☐ 251 Tony Gwynn | .65 | .30 | .06 |
| ☐ 252 Larry Christenson | .03 | .01 | .00 |
| ☐ 253 Jim Wohlford | .03 | .01 | .00 |
| ☐ 254 Shane Rawley | .06 | .02 | .00 |
| ☐ 255 Bruce Benedict | .03 | .01 | .00 |
| ☐ 256 Dave Geisel | .03 | .01 | .00 |
| ☐ 257 Julio Cruz | .03 | .01 | .00 |
| ☐ 258 Luis Sanchez | .03 | .01 | .00 |
| ☐ 259 Sparky Anderson MGR | .05 | .02 | .00 |
| ☐ 260 Scott McGregor | .08 | .03 | .01 |
| ☐ 261 Bobby Brown | .03 | .01 | .00 |
| ☐ 262 Tom Candiotti | .06 | .02 | .00 |
| ☐ 263 Jack Fimple | .09 | .04 | .01 |
| ☐ 264 Doug Frobel | .09 | .04 | .01 |
| ☐ 265 Donnie Hill | .09 | .04 | .01 |
| ☐ 266 Steve Lubratich | .08 | .03 | .01 |
| ☐ 267 Carmelo Martinez | .35 | .15 | .03 |
| ☐ 268 Jack O'Connor | .03 | .01 | .00 |
| ☐ 269 Aurelio Rodriguez | .03 | .01 | .00 |
| ☐ 270 Jeff Russell | .09 | .04 | .01 |
| ☐ 271 Moose Haas | .05 | .02 | .00 |
| ☐ 272 Rick Dempsey | .05 | .02 | .00 |
| ☐ 273 Charlie Puleo | .03 | .01 | .00 |
| ☐ 274 Rick Monday | .05 | .02 | .00 |

| | MINT | VG-E | F-G |
|---|---|---|---|
| ☐ 275 Len Matuszek | .03 | .01 | .00 |
| ☐ 276 Angels Leaders | .09 | .02 | .00 |
| Rod Carew | | | |
| Geoff Zahn | | | |
| ☐ 277 Eddie Whitson | .07 | .03 | .01 |
| ☐ 278 Jorge Bell | .12 | .05 | .01 |
| ☐ 279 Ivan DeJesus | .03 | .01 | .00 |
| ☐ 280 Floyd Bannister | .08 | .03 | .01 |
| ☐ 281 Larry Milbourne | .03 | .01 | .00 |
| ☐ 282 Jim Barr | .03 | .01 | .00 |
| ☐ 283 Larry Biittner | .03 | .01 | .00 |
| ☐ 284 Howard Bailey | .03 | .01 | .00 |
| ☐ 285 Darrell Porter | .06 | .02 | .00 |
| ☐ 286 Lary Sorensen | .03 | .01 | .00 |
| ☐ 287 Warren Cromartie | .03 | .01 | .00 |
| ☐ 288 Jim Beattie | .03 | .01 | .00 |
| ☐ 289 Randy Johnson | .03 | .01 | .00 |
| ☐ 290 Dave Dravecky | .08 | .03 | .01 |
| ☐ 291 Chuck Tanner MGR | .05 | .02 | .00 |
| ☐ 292 Tony Scott | .03 | .01 | .00 |
| ☐ 293 Ed Lynch | .03 | .01 | .00 |
| ☐ 294 U.L. Washington | .03 | .01 | .00 |
| ☐ 295 Mike Flanagan | .08 | .03 | .01 |
| ☐ 296 Jeff Newman | .03 | .01 | .00 |
| ☐ 297 Bruce Berenyi | .05 | .02 | .00 |
| ☐ 298 Jim Gantner | .05 | .02 | .00 |
| ☐ 299 John Butcher | .03 | .01 | .00 |
| ☐ 300 Pete Rose | 1.00 | .45 | .10 |
| ☐ 301 Frank LaCorte | .03 | .01 | .00 |
| ☐ 302 Barry Bonnell | .03 | .01 | .00 |
| ☐ 303 Marty Castillo | .03 | .01 | .00 |
| ☐ 304 Warren Brusstar | .03 | .01 | .00 |
| ☐ 305 Roy Smalley | .05 | .02 | .00 |
| ☐ 306 Dodgers Leaders: | .09 | .02 | .00 |
| Pedro Guerrero | | | |
| Bob Welch | | | |
| ☐ 307 Bobby Mitchell | .03 | .01 | .00 |
| ☐ 308 Ron Hassey | .03 | .01 | .00 |
| ☐ 309 Tony Phillips | .06 | .02 | .00 |
| ☐ 310 Willie McGee | .50 | .22 | .05 |
| ☐ 311 Jerry Koosman | .08 | .03 | .01 |
| ☐ 312 Jorge Orta | .03 | .01 | .00 |
| ☐ 313 Mike Jorgensen | .03 | .01 | .00 |
| ☐ 314 Orlando Mercado | .06 | .02 | .00 |
| ☐ 315 Bob Grich | .07 | .03 | .01 |
| ☐ 316 Mark Bradley | .10 | .04 | .01 |
| ☐ 317 Greg Pryor | .03 | .01 | .00 |
| ☐ 318 Bill Gullickson | .06 | .02 | .00 |
| ☐ 319 Al Bumbry | .03 | .01 | .00 |
| ☐ 320 Bob Stanley | .06 | .02 | .00 |
| ☐ 321 Harvey Kuenn MGR | .05 | .02 | .00 |
| ☐ 322 Ken Schrom | .03 | .01 | .00 |
| ☐ 323 Alan Knicely | .03 | .01 | .00 |
| ☐ 324 Alejandro Pena | .30 | .12 | .03 |
| ☐ 325 Darrell Evans | .12 | .05 | .01 |
| ☐ 326 Bob Kearney | .03 | .01 | .00 |
| ☐ 327 Ruppert Jones | .05 | .02 | .00 |
| ☐ 328 Vern Ruhle | .03 | .01 | .00 |
| ☐ 329 Pat Tabler | .06 | .02 | .00 |
| ☐ 330 John Candelaria | .07 | .03 | .01 |
| ☐ 331 Bucky Dent | .06 | .02 | .00 |
| ☐ 332 Kevin Gross | .18 | .08 | .01 |
| ☐ 333 Larry Herndon | .05 | .02 | .00 |
| ☐ 334 Chuck Rainey | .03 | .01 | .00 |
| ☐ 335 Don Baylor | .12 | .05 | .01 |
| ☐ 336 Seattle Mariners Leaders | .07 | .02 | .00 |
| Pat Putnam | | | |
| Matt Young | | | |
| ☐ 337 Kevin Hagen | .08 | .03 | .01 |
| ☐ 338 Mike Warren | .12 | .05 | .01 |
| ☐ 339 Roy Lee Jackson | .03 | .01 | .00 |
| ☐ 340 Hal McRae | .06 | .02 | .00 |
| ☐ 341 Dave Tobik | .03 | .01 | .00 |
| ☐ 342 Tim Foli | .03 | .01 | .00 |
| ☐ 343 Mark Davis | .03 | .01 | .00 |
| ☐ 344 Rick Miller | .03 | .01 | .00 |
| ☐ 345 Kent Hrbek | .35 | .15 | .03 |
| ☐ 346 Kurt Bevacqua | .03 | .01 | .00 |
| ☐ 347 Allan Ramirez | .06 | .02 | .00 |
| ☐ 348 Toby Harrah | .05 | .02 | .00 |
| ☐ 349 Bob L. Gibson | .08 | .03 | .01 |
| (Brewers Pitcher) | | | |
| ☐ 350 George Foster | .16 | .07 | .01 |
| ☐ 351 Russ Nixon MGR | .03 | .01 | .00 |
| ☐ 352 Dave Stewart | .03 | .01 | .00 |
| ☐ 353 Jim Anderson | .03 | .01 | .00 |
| ☐ 354 Jeff Burroughs | .05 | .02 | .00 |
| ☐ 355 Jason Thompson | .08 | .03 | .01 |
| ☐ 356 Glenn Abbott | .03 | .01 | .00 |
| ☐ 357 Ron Cey | .12 | .05 | .01 |
| ☐ 358 Bob Dernier | .07 | .03 | .01 |
| ☐ 359 Jim Acker | .15 | .06 | .01 |
| ☐ 360 Willie Randolph | .06 | .02 | .00 |
| ☐ 361 Dave Smith | .03 | .01 | .00 |
| ☐ 362 David Green | .06 | .02 | .00 |
| ☐ 363 Tim Laudner | .03 | .01 | .00 |
| ☐ 364 Scott Fletcher | .03 | .01 | .00 |
| ☐ 365 Steve Bedrosian | .07 | .03 | .01 |
| ☐ 366 Padres Leaders | .08 | .02 | .00 |
| Terry Kennedy | | | |
| Dave Dravecky | | | |
| ☐ 367 Jamie Easterly | .03 | .01 | .00 |
| ☐ 368 Hubie Brooks | .09 | .04 | .01 |
| ☐ 369 Steve McCatty | .05 | .02 | .00 |
| ☐ 370 Tim Raines | .35 | .15 | .03 |
| ☐ 371 Dave Gumpert | .06 | .02 | .00 |

|  | MINT | VG-E | F-G |
|---|---|---|---|
| ☐ 372 Gary Roenicke | .05 | .02 | .00 |
| ☐ 373 Bill Scherrer | .09 | .04 | .01 |
| ☐ 374 Don Money | .03 | .01 | .00 |
| ☐ 375 Dennis Leonard | .06 | .02 | .00 |
| ☐ 376 Dave Anderson | .12 | .05 | .01 |
| ☐ 377 Danny Darwin | .03 | .01 | .00 |
| ☐ 378 Bob Brenly | .07 | .03 | .01 |
| ☐ 379 Checklist 265–396 | .08 | .01 | .00 |
| ☐ 380 Steve Garvey | .45 | .20 | .04 |
| ☐ 381 Ralph Houk MGR | .05 | .02 | .00 |
| ☐ 382 Chris Nyman | .07 | .03 | .01 |
| ☐ 383 Terry Puhl | .03 | .01 | .00 |
| ☐ 384 Lee Tunnell | .09 | .04 | .01 |
| ☐ 385 Tony Perez | .14 | .06 | .01 |
| NL ALL-STARS | | | |
| (386–396) | | | |
| ☐ 386 George Hendrick AS | .08 | .03 | .01 |
| ☐ 387 Johnny Ray AS | .08 | .03 | .01 |
| ☐ 388 Mike Schmidt AS | .30 | .12 | .03 |
| ☐ 389 Ozzie Smith AS | .09 | .04 | .01 |
| ☐ 390 Tim Raines AS | .20 | .09 | .02 |
| ☐ 391 Dale Murphy AS | .35 | .15 | .03 |
| ☐ 392 Andre Dawson AS | .20 | .09 | .02 |
| ☐ 393 Gary Carter AS | .25 | .10 | .02 |
| ☐ 394 Steve Rogers AS | .08 | .03 | .01 |
| ☐ 395 Steve Carlton AS | .30 | .12 | .03 |
| ☐ 396 Jesse Orosco AS | .08 | .03 | .01 |
| AL ALL-STARS | | | |
| (397–407) | | | |
| ☐ 397 Eddie Murray AS | .35 | .15 | .03 |
| ☐ 398 Lou Whitaker AS | .13 | .06 | .01 |
| ☐ 399 George Brett AS | .35 | .15 | .03 |
| ☐ 400 Cal Ripken AS | .35 | .15 | .03 |
| ☐ 401 Jim Rice AS | .25 | .10 | .02 |
| ☐ 402 Dave Winfield AS | .25 | .10 | .02 |
| ☐ 403 Lloyd Moseby AS | .11 | .05 | .01 |
| ☐ 404 Ted Simmons AS | .09 | .04 | .01 |
| ☐ 405 LaMarr Hoyt AS | .09 | .04 | .01 |
| ☐ 406 Ron Guidry AS | .14 | .06 | .01 |
| ☐ 407 Dan Quisenberry AS | .14 | .06 | .01 |
| ☐ 408 Lou Piniella | .09 | .04 | .01 |
| ☐ 409 Juan Agosto | .06 | .02 | .00 |
| ☐ 410 Claudell Washington | .08 | .03 | .01 |
| ☐ 411 Houston Jimenez | .09 | .04 | .01 |
| ☐ 412 Doug Rader MGR | .05 | .02 | .00 |
| ☐ 413 Spike Owen | .15 | .06 | .01 |
| ☐ 414 Mitchell Page | .03 | .01 | .00 |
| ☐ 415 Tommy John | .14 | .06 | .01 |
| ☐ 416 Dane Iorg | .03 | .01 | .00 |
| ☐ 417 Mike Armstrong | .03 | .01 | .00 |
| ☐ 418 Ron Hodges | .03 | .01 | .00 |
| ☐ 419 John Henry Johnson | .03 | .01 | .00 |
| ☐ 420 Cecil Cooper | .16 | .07 | .01 |
| ☐ 421 Charlie Lea | .05 | .02 | .00 |
| ☐ 422 Jose Cruz | .11 | .05 | .01 |
| ☐ 423 Mike Morgan | .03 | .01 | .00 |
| ☐ 424 Dann Bilardello | .06 | .02 | .00 |
| ☐ 425 Steve Howe | .06 | .02 | .00 |
| ☐ 426 Orioles Leaders | .12 | .02 | .00 |
| Cal Ripken | | | |
| Mike Boddicker | | | |
| ☐ 427 Rick Leach | .03 | .01 | .00 |
| ☐ 428 Fred Breining | .03 | .01 | .00 |
| ☐ 429 Randy Bush | .07 | .03 | .01 |
| ☐ 430 Rusty Staub | .09 | .04 | .01 |
| ☐ 431 Chris Bando | .03 | .01 | .00 |
| ☐ 432 Charlie Hudson | .16 | .07 | .01 |
| ☐ 433 Rich Hebner | .03 | .01 | .00 |
| ☐ 434 Harold Baines | .25 | .10 | .02 |
| ☐ 435 Neil Allen | .06 | .02 | .00 |
| ☐ 436 Rick Peters | .03 | .01 | .00 |
| ☐ 437 Mike Proly | .03 | .01 | .00 |
| ☐ 438 Biff Pocoroba | .03 | .01 | .00 |
| ☐ 439 Bob Stoddard | .03 | .01 | .00 |
| ☐ 440 Steve Kemp | .09 | .04 | .01 |
| ☐ 441 Bob Lillis MGR | .03 | .01 | .00 |
| ☐ 442 Byron McLaughlin | .03 | .01 | .00 |
| ☐ 443 Benny Ayala | .03 | .01 | .00 |
| ☐ 444 Steve Renko | .03 | .01 | .00 |
| ☐ 445 Jerry Remy | .05 | .02 | .00 |
| ☐ 446 Luis Pujols | .03 | .01 | .00 |
| ☐ 447 Tom Brunansky | .20 | .09 | .02 |
| ☐ 448 Ben Hayes | .03 | .01 | .00 |
| ☐ 449 Joe Pettini | .03 | .01 | .00 |
| ☐ 450 Gary Carter | .35 | .15 | .03 |
| ☐ 451 Bob Jones | .03 | .01 | .00 |
| ☐ 452 Chuck Porter | .03 | .01 | .00 |
| ☐ 453 Willie Upshaw | .15 | .06 | .01 |
| ☐ 454 Joe Beckwith | .03 | .01 | .00 |
| ☐ 455 Terry Kennedy | .10 | .04 | .01 |
| ☐ 456 Chicago Cubs Leaders | .08 | .02 | .00 |
| Keith Moreland | | | |
| Fergie Jenkins | | | |
| ☐ 457 Dave Rozema | .03 | .01 | .00 |
| ☐ 458 Kiko Garcia | .03 | .01 | .00 |
| ☐ 459 Kevin Hickey | .03 | .01 | .00 |
| ☐ 460 Dave Winfield | .40 | .18 | .04 |
| ☐ 461 Jim Maler | .03 | .01 | .00 |
| ☐ 462 Lee Lacy | .05 | .02 | .00 |
| ☐ 463 Dave Engle | .05 | .02 | .00 |
| ☐ 464 Jeff A. Jones | .05 | .02 | .00 |
| (A's Pitcher) | | | |
| ☐ 465 Mookie Wilson | .08 | .03 | .01 |
| ☐ 466 Gene Garber | .03 | .01 | .00 |
| ☐ 467 Mike Ramsey | .03 | .01 | .00 |
| ☐ 468 Geoff Zahn | .03 | .01 | .00 |

| | MINT | VG-E | F-G |
|---|---|---|---|
| ☐ 469 Tom O'Malley | .03 | .01 | .00 |
| ☐ 470 Nolan Ryan | .30 | .12 | .03 |
| ☐ 471 Dick Howser MGR | .05 | .02 | .00 |
| ☐ 472 Mike Brown (Red Sox Pitcher) | .06 | .02 | .00 |
| ☐ 473 Jim Dwyer | .03 | .01 | .00 |
| ☐ 474 Greg Bargar | .07 | .03 | .01 |
| ☐ 475 Gary Redus | .30 | .12 | .03 |
| ☐ 476 Tom Tellmann | .03 | .01 | .00 |
| ☐ 477 Rafael Landestoy | .03 | .01 | .00 |
| ☐ 478 Alan Bannister | .03 | .01 | .00 |
| ☐ 479 Frank Tanana | .05 | .02 | .00 |
| ☐ 480 Ron Kittle | .25 | .10 | .02 |
| ☐ 481 Mark Thurmond | .25 | .10 | .02 |
| ☐ 482 Enos Cabell | .03 | .01 | .00 |
| ☐ 483 Fergie Jenkins | .12 | .05 | .01 |
| ☐ 484 Ozzie Virgil | .06 | .02 | .00 |
| ☐ 485 Rick Rhoden | .06 | .02 | .00 |
| ☐ 486 N.Y. Yankees Leaders Don Baylor Ron Guidry | .09 | .02 | .00 |
| ☐ 487 Ricky Adams | .08 | .03 | .01 |
| ☐ 488 Jesse Barfield | .11 | .05 | .01 |
| ☐ 489 Dave Von Ohlen | .07 | .03 | .01 |
| ☐ 490 Cal Ripken | .65 | .30 | .06 |
| ☐ 491 Bobby Castillo | .03 | .01 | .00 |
| ☐ 492 Tucker Ashford | .03 | .01 | .00 |
| ☐ 493 Mike Norris | .05 | .02 | .00 |
| ☐ 494 Chili Davis | .10 | .04 | .01 |
| ☐ 495 Rollie Fingers | .20 | .09 | .02 |
| ☐ 496 Terry Francona | .06 | .02 | .00 |
| ☐ 497 Bud Anderson | .03 | .01 | .00 |
| ☐ 498 Rich Gedman | .07 | .03 | .01 |
| ☐ 499 Mike Witt | .09 | .04 | .01 |
| ☐ 500 George Brett | .55 | .25 | .05 |
| ☐ 501 Steve Henderson | .03 | .01 | .00 |
| ☐ 502 Joe Torre MGR | .07 | .03 | .01 |
| ☐ 503 Elias Sosa | .03 | .01 | .00 |
| ☐ 504 Mickey Rivers | .06 | .02 | .00 |
| ☐ 505 Pete Vuckovich | .08 | .03 | .01 |
| ☐ 506 Ernie Whitt | .03 | .01 | .00 |
| ☐ 507 Mike LaCoss | .03 | .01 | .00 |
| ☐ 508 Mel Hall | .11 | .05 | .01 |
| ☐ 509 Brad Havens | .03 | .01 | .00 |
| ☐ 510 Alan Trammell | .30 | .12 | .03 |
| ☐ 511 Marty Bystrom | .03 | .01 | .00 |
| ☐ 512 Oscar Gamble | .06 | .02 | .00 |
| ☐ 513 Dave Beard | .03 | .01 | .00 |
| ☐ 514 Floyd Rayford | .03 | .01 | .00 |
| ☐ 515 Gorman Thomas | .10 | .04 | .01 |
| ☐ 516 Montreal Expos Leaders Al Oliver Charlie Lea | .08 | .02 | .00 |

| | MINT | VG-E | F-G |
|---|---|---|---|
| ☐ 517 John Moses | .07 | .03 | .01 |
| ☐ 518 Greg Walker | .75 | .35 | .07 |
| ☐ 519 Ron Davis | .05 | .02 | .00 |
| ☐ 520 Bob Boone | .06 | .02 | .00 |
| ☐ 521 Pete Falcone | .03 | .01 | .00 |
| ☐ 522 Dave Bergman | .03 | .01 | .00 |
| ☐ 523 Glenn Hoffman | .03 | .01 | .00 |
| ☐ 524 Carlos Diaz | .03 | .01 | .00 |
| ☐ 525 Willie Wilson | .20 | .09 | .02 |
| ☐ 526 Ron Oester | .05 | .02 | .00 |
| ☐ 527 Checklist 397–528 | .08 | .01 | .00 |
| ☐ 528 Mark Brouhard | .03 | .01 | .00 |
| ☐ 529 Keith Atherton | .08 | .03 | .01 |
| ☐ 530 Dan Ford | .05 | .02 | .00 |
| ☐ 531 Steve Boros MGR | .03 | .01 | .00 |
| ☐ 532 Eric Show | .05 | .02 | .00 |
| ☐ 533 Ken Landreaux | .05 | .02 | .00 |
| ☐ 534 Pete O'Brien | .40 | .18 | .04 |
| ☐ 535 Bo Diaz | .05 | .02 | .00 |
| ☐ 536 Doug Bair | .03 | .01 | .00 |
| ☐ 537 Johnny Ray | .11 | .05 | .01 |
| ☐ 538 Kevin Bass | .03 | .01 | .00 |
| ☐ 539 George Frazier | .03 | .01 | .00 |
| ☐ 540 George Hendrick | .08 | .03 | .01 |
| ☐ 541 Dennis Lamp | .03 | .01 | .00 |
| ☐ 542 Duane Kuiper | .03 | .01 | .00 |
| ☐ 543 Craig McMurtry | .14 | .06 | .01 |
| ☐ 544 Cesar Geronimo | .03 | .01 | .00 |
| ☐ 545 Bill Buckner | .09 | .04 | .01 |
| ☐ 546 Indians Leaders Mike Hargrove Lary Sorensen | .07 | .02 | .00 |
| ☐ 547 Mike Moore | .07 | .03 | .01 |
| ☐ 548 Ron Jackson | .03 | .01 | .00 |
| ☐ 549 Walt Terrell | .30 | .12 | .03 |
| ☐ 550 Jim Rice | .35 | .15 | .03 |
| ☐ 551 Scott Ullger | .07 | .03 | .01 |
| ☐ 552 Ray Burris | .03 | .01 | .00 |
| ☐ 553 Joe Nolan | .03 | .01 | .00 |
| ☐ 554 Ted Power | .06 | .02 | .00 |
| ☐ 555 Greg Brock | .11 | .05 | .01 |
| ☐ 556 Joey McLaughlin | .03 | .01 | .00 |
| ☐ 557 Wayne Tolleson | .05 | .02 | .00 |
| ☐ 558 Mike Davis | .09 | .04 | .01 |
| ☐ 559 Mike Scott | .05 | .02 | .00 |
| ☐ 560 Carlton Fisk | .16 | .07 | .01 |
| ☐ 561 Whitey Herzog MGR | .06 | .02 | .00 |
| ☐ 562 Manny Castillo | .03 | .01 | .00 |
| ☐ 563 Glenn Wilson | .15 | .06 | .01 |
| ☐ 564 Al Holland | .06 | .02 | .00 |
| ☐ 565 Leon Durham | .18 | .08 | .01 |
| ☐ 566 Jim Bibby | .05 | .02 | .00 |
| ☐ 567 Mike Heath | .03 | .01 | .00 |

| | MINT | VG-E | F-G | | MINT | VG-E | F-G |
|---|---|---|---|---|---|---|---|
| ☐ 568 Pete Filson | .07 | .03 | .01 | ☐ 617 Rick Cerone | .05 | .02 | .00 |
| ☐ 569 Bake McBride | .03 | .01 | .00 | ☐ 618 Dickie Noles | .03 | .01 | .00 |
| ☐ 570 Dan Quisenberry | .20 | .09 | .02 | ☐ 619 Jerry Dybzinski | .03 | .01 | .00 |
| ☐ 571 Bruce Bochy | .03 | .01 | .00 | ☐ 620 Al Oliver | .18 | .08 | .01 |
| ☐ 572 Jerry Royster | .03 | .01 | .00 | ☐ 621 Frank Howard | .05 | .02 | .00 |
| ☐ 573 Dave Kingman | .13 | .06 | .01 | ☐ 622 Al Cowens | .05 | .02 | .00 |
| ☐ 574 Brian Downing | .05 | .02 | .00 | ☐ 623 Ron Washington | .03 | .01 | .00 |
| ☐ 575 Jim Clancy | .03 | .01 | .00 | ☐ 624 Terry Harper | .03 | .01 | .00 |
| ☐ 576 Giants Leaders | .07 | .02 | .00 | ☐ 625 Larry Gura | .06 | .02 | .00 |
| Jeff Leonard | | | | ☐ 626 Bob Clark | .03 | .01 | .00 |
| Atlee Hammaker | | | | ☐ 627 Dave LaPoint | .05 | .02 | .00 |
| ☐ 577 Mark Clear | .03 | .01 | .00 | ☐ 628 Ed Jurak | .06 | .02 | .00 |
| ☐ 578 Lenn Sakata | .03 | .01 | .00 | ☐ 629 Rick Langford | .03 | .01 | .00 |
| ☐ 579 Bob James | .25 | .10 | .02 | ☐ 630 Ted Simmons | .12 | .05 | .01 |
| ☐ 580 Lonnie Smith | .09 | .04 | .01 | ☐ 631 Denny Martinez | .03 | .01 | .00 |
| ☐ 581 Jose DeLeon | .25 | .10 | .02 | ☐ 632 Tom Foley | .08 | .03 | .01 |
| ☐ 582 Bob McClure | .03 | .01 | .00 | ☐ 633 Mike Krukow | .03 | .01 | .00 |
| ☐ 583 Derrel Thomas | .03 | .01 | .00 | ☐ 634 Mike Marshall | .15 | .06 | .01 |
| ☐ 584 Dave Schmidt | .03 | .01 | .00 | ☐ 635 Dave Righetti | .14 | .06 | .01 |
| ☐ 585 Dan Driessen | .05 | .02 | .00 | ☐ 636 Pat Putnam | .03 | .01 | .00 |
| ☐ 586 Joe Niekro | .07 | .03 | .01 | ☐ 637 Phillies Leaders | .08 | .02 | .00 |
| ☐ 587 Von Hayes | .13 | .06 | .01 | Gary Matthews | | | |
| ☐ 588 Milt Wilcox | .03 | .01 | .00 | John Denny | | | |
| ☐ 589 Mike Easler | .08 | .03 | .01 | ☐ 638 George Vukovich | .03 | .01 | .00 |
| ☐ 590 Dave Stieb | .25 | .10 | .02 | ☐ 639 Rick Lysander | .07 | .03 | .01 |
| ☐ 591 Tony LaRussa MGR | .05 | .02 | .00 | ☐ 640 Lance Parrish | .25 | .10 | .02 |
| ☐ 592 Andre Robertson | .03 | .01 | .00 | ☐ 641 Mike Richardt | .03 | .01 | .00 |
| ☐ 593 Jeff Lahti | .03 | .01 | .00 | ☐ 642 Tom Underwood | .03 | .01 | .00 |
| ☐ 594 Gene Richards | .03 | .01 | .00 | ☐ 643 Mike Brown | .25 | .10 | .02 |
| ☐ 595 Jeff Reardon | .08 | .03 | .01 | (Angels OF) | | | |
| ☐ 596 Ryne Sandberg | .90 | .40 | .09 | ☐ 644 Tim Lollar | .05 | .02 | .00 |
| ☐ 597 Rick Camp | .03 | .01 | .00 | ☐ 645 Tony Pena | .13 | .06 | .01 |
| ☐ 598 Rusty Kuntz | .03 | .01 | .00 | ☐ 646 Checklist 529–660 | .08 | .01 | .00 |
| ☐ 599 Doug Sisk | .15 | .06 | .01 | ☐ 647 Ron Roenicke | .03 | .01 | .00 |
| ☐ 600 Rod Carew | .35 | .15 | .03 | ☐ 648 Len Whitehouse | .07 | .03 | .01 |
| ☐ 601 John Tudor | .20 | .09 | .02 | ☐ 649 Tom Herr | .16 | .07 | .01 |
| ☐ 602 John Wathan | .03 | .01 | .00 | ☐ 650 Phil Niekro | .16 | .07 | .01 |
| ☐ 603 Renie Martin | .03 | .01 | .00 | ☐ 651 John McNamara MGR | .03 | .01 | .00 |
| ☐ 604 John Lowenstein | .03 | .01 | .00 | ☐ 652 Rudy May | .03 | .01 | .00 |
| ☐ 605 Mike Caldwell | .05 | .02 | .00 | ☐ 653 Dave Stapleton | .03 | .01 | .00 |
| ☐ 606 Blue Jays Leaders | .09 | .02 | .00 | ☐ 654 Bob Bailor | .03 | .01 | .00 |
| Lloyd Moseby | | | | ☐ 655 Amos Otis | .06 | .02 | .00 |
| Dave Stieb | | | | ☐ 656 Bryn Smith | .05 | .02 | .00 |
| ☐ 607 Tom Hume | .03 | .01 | .00 | ☐ 657 Thad Bosley | .03 | .01 | .00 |
| ☐ 608 Bobby Johnson | .03 | .01 | .00 | ☐ 658 Jerry Augustine | .03 | .01 | .00 |
| ☐ 609 Dan Meyer | .03 | .01 | .00 | ☐ 659 Duane Walker | .03 | .01 | .00 |
| ☐ 610 Steve Sax | .16 | .07 | .01 | ☐ 660 Ray Knight | .06 | .02 | .00 |
| ☐ 611 Chet Lemon | .09 | .04 | .01 | ☐ 661 Steve Yeager | .05 | .02 | .00 |
| ☐ 612 Harry Spilman | .03 | .01 | .00 | ☐ 662 Tom Brennan | .03 | .01 | .00 |
| ☐ 613 Greg Gross | .03 | .01 | .00 | ☐ 663 Johnnie LeMaster | .03 | .01 | .00 |
| ☐ 614 Len Barker | .06 | .02 | .00 | ☐ 664 Dave Stegman | .03 | .01 | .00 |
| ☐ 615 Garry Templeton | .11 | .05 | .01 | ☐ 665 Buddy Bell | .13 | .06 | .01 |
| ☐ 616 Don Robinson | .03 | .01 | .00 | | | | |

|  | MINT | VG-E | F-G |
|---|---|---|---|
| ☐ **666** Detroit Tigers Leaders .. | .10 | .02 | .00 |
| Lou Whitaker | | | |
| Jack Morris | | | |
| ☐ **667** Vance Law ............... | .03 | .01 | .00 |
| ☐ **668** Larry McWilliams ....... | .06 | .02 | .00 |
| ☐ **669** Dave Lopes ............. | .07 | .03 | .01 |
| ☐ **670** Rich Gossage .......... | .20 | .09 | .02 |
| ☐ **671** Jamie Quirk ............ | .03 | .01 | .00 |
| ☐ **672** Ricky Nelson ........... | .09 | .04 | .01 |
| ☐ **673** Mike Walters ........... | .09 | .04 | .01 |
| ☐ **674** Tim Flannery ........... | .03 | .01 | .00 |
| ☐ **675** Pascual Perez .......... | .06 | .02 | .00 |
| ☐ **676** Brian Giles ............. | .03 | .01 | .00 |
| ☐ **677** Doyle Alexander ....... | .06 | .02 | .00 |
| ☐ **678** Chris Speier ........... | .03 | .01 | .00 |
| ☐ **679** Art Howe .............. | .03 | .01 | .00 |
| ☐ **680** Fred Lynn ............. | .20 | .09 | .02 |
| ☐ **681** Tom Lasorda MGR .... | .06 | .02 | .00 |
| ☐ **682** Dan Morogiello ........ | .07 | .03 | .01 |
| ☐ **683** Marty Barrett .......... | .60 | .28 | .06 |
| ☐ **684** Bob Shirley ........... | .03 | .01 | .00 |
| ☐ **685** Willie Aikens .......... | .05 | .02 | .00 |
| ☐ **686** Joe Price ............. | .03 | .01 | .00 |
| ☐ **687** Roy Howell ............ | .03 | .01 | .00 |
| ☐ **688** George Wright ......... | .05 | .02 | .00 |
| ☐ **689** Mike Fischlin .......... | .03 | .01 | .00 |
| ☐ **690** Jack Clark ............. | .18 | .08 | .01 |
| ☐ **691** Steve Lake ............ | .07 | .03 | .01 |
| ☐ **692** Dickie Thon ........... | .07 | .03 | .01 |
| ☐ **693** Alan Wiggins .......... | .09 | .04 | .01 |
| ☐ **694** Mike Stanton .......... | .03 | .01 | .00 |
| ☐ **695** Lou Whitaker .......... | .20 | .09 | .02 |
| ☐ **696** Pirates Leaders ........ | .08 | .02 | .00 |
| Bill Madlock | | | |
| Rick Rhoden | | | |
| ☐ **697** Dale Murray ........... | .03 | .01 | .00 |
| ☐ **698** Marc Hill .............. | .03 | .01 | .00 |
| ☐ **699** Dave Rucker ........... | .03 | .01 | .00 |
| ☐ **700** Mike Schmidt .......... | .45 | .20 | .04 |
| N.L. ACTIVE LEADERS: | | | |
| ☐ **701** Active Batting: ......... | .20 | .09 | .02 |
| Bill Madlock | | | |
| Pete Rose | | | |
| Dave Parker | | | |
| ☐ **702** Active Hits: ............ | .20 | .09 | .02 |
| Pete Rose | | | |
| Rusty Staub | | | |
| Tony Perez | | | |
| ☐ **703** Active Home Run: ...... | .18 | .08 | .01 |
| Mike Schmidt | | | |
| Tony Perez | | | |
| Dave Kingman | | | |

|  | MINT | VG-E | F-G |
|---|---|---|---|
| ☐ **704** Active RBI: ............ | .13 | .06 | .01 |
| Tony Perez | | | |
| Rusty Staub | | | |
| Al Oliver | | | |
| ☐ **705** Active Stolen Bases: ... | .10 | .04 | .01 |
| Joe Morgan | | | |
| Cesar Cedeno | | | |
| Larry Bowa | | | |
| ☐ **706** Active Victory: ......... | .18 | .08 | .01 |
| Steve Carlton | | | |
| Fergie Jenkins | | | |
| Tom Seaver | | | |
| ☐ **707** Active Strikeout: ....... | .20 | .09 | .02 |
| Steve Carlton | | | |
| Nolan Ryan | | | |
| Tom Seaver | | | |
| ☐ **708** Active ERA: ........... | .18 | .08 | .01 |
| Tom Seaver | | | |
| Steve Carlton | | | |
| Steve Rogers | | | |
| ☐ **709** Active Save: .......... | .09 | .04 | .01 |
| Bruce Sutter | | | |
| Tug McGraw | | | |
| Gene Garber | | | |
| A.L. ACTIVE LEADERS: | | | |
| ☐ **710** Active Batting: ......... | .20 | .09 | .02 |
| Rod Carew | | | |
| George Brett | | | |
| Cecil Cooper | | | |
| ☐ **711** Active Hits: ........... | .18 | .08 | .01 |
| Rod Carew | | | |
| Bert Campaneris | | | |
| Reggie Jackson | | | |
| ☐ **712** Active Home Run: ...... | .18 | .08 | .01 |
| Reggie Jackson | | | |
| Graig Nettles | | | |
| Greg Luzinski | | | |
| ☐ **713** Active RBI: ........... | .18 | .08 | .01 |
| Reggie Jackson | | | |
| Ted Simmons | | | |
| Graig Nettles | | | |
| ☐ **714** Active Stolen Bases: ... | .09 | .04 | .01 |
| Bert Campaneris | | | |
| Dave Lopes | | | |
| Omar Moreno | | | |
| ☐ **715** Active Victory: ......... | .18 | .08 | .01 |
| Jim Palmer | | | |
| Don Sutton | | | |
| Tommy John | | | |
| ☐ **716** Active Strikeout: ....... | .09 | .04 | .01 |
| Don Sutton | | | |
| Bert Blyleven | | | |
| Jerry Koosman | | | |

| | MINT | VG-E | F-G |
|---|---|---|---|
| ☐ **717** Active ERA: | .18 | .08 | .01 |
| Jim Palmer | | | |
| Rollie Fingers | | | |
| Ron Guidry | | | |
| ☐ **718** Active Save: | .18 | .08 | .01 |
| Rollie Fingers | | | |
| Rich Gossage | | | |
| Dan Quisenberry | | | |
| ☐ **719** Andy Hassler | .03 | .01 | .00 |
| ☐ **720** Dwight Evans | .14 | .06 | .01 |
| ☐ **721** Del Crandall MGR | .03 | .01 | .00 |
| ☐ **722** Bob Welch | .06 | .02 | .00 |
| ☐ **723** Rich Dauer | .03 | .01 | .00 |
| ☐ **724** Eric Rasmussen | .03 | .01 | .00 |
| ☐ **725** Cesar Cedeno | .07 | .03 | .01 |
| ☐ **726** Brewers Leaders | .08 | .02 | .00 |
| Ted Simmons | | | |
| Moose Haas | | | |
| ☐ **727** Joel Youngblood | .03 | .01 | .00 |
| ☐ **728** Tug McGraw | .09 | .04 | .01 |
| ☐ **729** Gene Tenace | .03 | .01 | .00 |
| ☐ **730** Bruce Sutter | .18 | .08 | .01 |
| ☐ **731** Lynn Jones | .03 | .01 | .00 |
| ☐ **732** Terry Crowley | .03 | .01 | .00 |
| ☐ **733** Dave Collins | .06 | .02 | .00 |
| ☐ **734** Odell Jones | .03 | .01 | .00 |
| ☐ **735** Rick Burleson | .06 | .02 | .00 |
| ☐ **736** Dick Ruthven | .03 | .01 | .00 |
| ☐ **737** Jim Essian | .03 | .01 | .00 |
| ☐ **738** Bill Schroeder | .30 | .12 | .03 |
| ☐ **739** Bob Watson | .05 | .02 | .00 |
| ☐ **740** Tom Seaver | .40 | .18 | .04 |
| ☐ **741** Wayne Gross | .03 | .01 | .00 |
| ☐ **742** Dick Williams MGR | .03 | .01 | .00 |
| ☐ **743** Don Hood | .03 | .01 | .00 |
| ☐ **744** Jamie Allen | .10 | .04 | .01 |
| ☐ **745** Dennis Eckersley | .06 | .02 | .00 |
| ☐ **746** Mickey Hatcher | .05 | .02 | .00 |
| ☐ **747** Pat Zachry | .03 | .01 | .00 |
| ☐ **748** Jeff Leonard | .07 | .03 | .01 |
| ☐ **749** Doug Flynn | .03 | .01 | .00 |
| ☐ **750** Jim Palmer | .25 | .10 | .02 |
| ☐ **751** Charlie Moore | .03 | .01 | .00 |
| ☐ **752** Phil Garner | .05 | .02 | .00 |
| ☐ **753** Doug Gwosdz | .03 | .01 | .00 |
| ☐ **754** Kent Tekulve | .08 | .03 | .01 |
| ☐ **755** Garry Maddox | .05 | .02 | .00 |
| ☐ **756** Reds Leaders | .07 | .02 | .00 |
| Ron Oester | | | |
| Mario Soto | | | |
| ☐ **757** Larry Bowa | .08 | .03 | .01 |
| ☐ **758** Bill Stein | .03 | .01 | .00 |
| ☐ **759** Richard Dotson | .08 | .03 | .01 |

| | MINT | VG-E | F-G |
|---|---|---|---|
| ☐ **760** Bob Horner | .25 | .10 | .02 |
| ☐ **761** John Montefusco | .05 | .02 | .00 |
| ☐ **762** Rance Mulliniks | .03 | .01 | .00 |
| ☐ **763** Craig Swan | .03 | .01 | .00 |
| ☐ **764** Mike Hargrove | .03 | .01 | .00 |
| ☐ **765** Ken Forsch | .03 | .01 | .00 |
| ☐ **766** Mike Vail | .03 | .01 | .00 |
| ☐ **767** Carney Lansford | .10 | .04 | .01 |
| ☐ **768** Champ Summers | .03 | .01 | .00 |
| ☐ **769** Bill Caudill | .08 | .03 | .01 |
| ☐ **770** Ken Griffey | .08 | .03 | .01 |
| ☐ **771** Billy Gardner MGR | .03 | .01 | .00 |
| ☐ **772** Jim Slaton | .03 | .01 | .00 |
| ☐ **773** Todd Cruz | .03 | .01 | .00 |
| ☐ **774** Tom Gorman | .15 | .06 | .01 |
| ☐ **775** Dave Parker | .20 | .09 | .02 |
| ☐ **776** Craig Reynolds | .03 | .01 | .00 |
| ☐ **777** Tom Paciorek | .03 | .01 | .00 |
| ☐ **778** Andy Hawkins | .70 | .32 | .07 |
| ☐ **779** Jim Sundberg | .06 | .02 | .00 |
| ☐ **780** Steve Carlton | .35 | .15 | .03 |
| ☐ **781** Checklist 661–792 | .08 | .02 | .00 |
| ☐ **782** Steve Balboni | .06 | .02 | .00 |
| ☐ **783** Luis Leal | .03 | .01 | .00 |
| ☐ **784** Leon Roberts | .03 | .01 | .00 |
| ☐ **785** Joaquin Andujar | .14 | .06 | .01 |
| ☐ **786** Red Sox Leaders | .10 | .02 | .00 |
| Wade Boggs | | | |
| Bob Ojeda | | | |
| ☐ **787** Bill Campbell | .05 | .02 | .00 |
| ☐ **788** Milt May | .03 | .01 | .00 |
| ☐ **789** Bert Blyleven | .12 | .05 | .01 |
| ☐ **790** Doug DeCinces | .11 | .05 | .01 |
| ☐ **791** Terry Forster | .08 | .03 | .01 |
| ☐ **792** Bill Russell | .06 | .02 | .00 |

### 1984 TOPPS EXTENDED

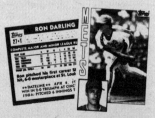

*The cards in this 132 card set measure 2½" by 3½". In its now standard procedure, Topps issued its traded set for the fourth year in a row. Because all photos and statistics of its regular set for the year were developed during the fall and winter months of the preceding year, players who changed teams during the fall, winter and spring months are portrayed with the teams they were with in 1983. The traded set amends the shortcomings of the regular set by presenting the players with their proper teams for the current year. Rookies not contained in the regular set are also picked up in the traded set. Again this year, the Topps affiliate in Ireland printed the cards, and the cards were available through hobby channels only.*

Complete Set: M-30.00; VG-E-14.00; F-G-3.00

| | MINT | VG-E | F-G |
|---|---|---|---|
| Common Player | .08 | .03 | .01 |

| | MINT | VG-E | F-G |
|---|---|---|---|
| ☐ 1 T Willie Aikens | .12 | .05 | .01 |
| ☐ 2 T Luis Aponte | .08 | .03 | .01 |
| ☐ 3 T Mike Armstrong | .08 | .03 | .01 |
| ☐ 4 T Bob Bailor | .08 | .03 | .01 |
| ☐ 5 T Dusty Baker | .12 | .05 | .01 |
| ☐ 6 T Steve Balboni | .12 | .05 | .01 |
| ☐ 7 T Alan Bannister | .08 | .03 | .01 |
| ☐ 8 T Dave Beard | .08 | .03 | .01 |
| ☐ 9 T Joe Beckwith | .08 | .03 | .01 |
| ☐ 10 T Bruce Berenyi | .12 | .05 | .01 |
| ☐ 11 T Dave Bergman | .08 | .03 | .01 |
| ☐ 12 T Tony Bernazard | .08 | .03 | .01 |
| ☐ 13 T Yogi Berra | .25 | .10 | .02 |
| ☐ 14 T Barry Bonnell | .08 | .03 | .01 |
| ☐ 15 T Phil Bradley | 2.00 | .90 | .20 |
| ☐ 16 T Fred Breining | .08 | .03 | .01 |
| ☐ 17 T Bill Buckner | .25 | .10 | .02 |
| ☐ 18 T Ray Burris | .08 | .03 | .01 |
| ☐ 19 T John Butcher | .08 | .03 | .01 |
| ☐ 20 T Brett Butler | .30 | .12 | .03 |
| ☐ 21 T Enos Cabell | .08 | .03 | .01 |
| ☐ 22 T Bill Campbell | .12 | .05 | .01 |
| ☐ 23 T Bill Caudill | .16 | .07 | .01 |
| ☐ 24 T Bob Clark | .08 | .03 | .01 |
| ☐ 25 T Bryan Clark | .08 | .03 | .01 |
| ☐ 26 T Jaime Cocanower | .16 | .07 | .01 |
| ☐ 27 T Ron Darling | 1.50 | .70 | .15 |
| ☐ 28 T Alvin Davis | 2.00 | .90 | .20 |
| ☐ 29 T Ken Dayley | .12 | .05 | .01 |
| ☐ 30 T Jeff Dedmon | .16 | .07 | .01 |
| ☐ 31 T Bob Dernier | .12 | .05 | .01 |
| ☐ 32 T Carlos Diaz | .08 | .03 | .01 |
| ☐ 33 T Mike Easler | .16 | .07 | .01 |
| ☐ 34 T Dennis Eckersley | .16 | .07 | .01 |
| ☐ 35 T Jim Essian | .08 | .03 | .01 |
| ☐ 36 T Darrell Evans | .25 | .10 | .02 |
| ☐ 37 T Mike Fitzgerald | .16 | .07 | .01 |
| ☐ 38 T Tim Foli | .08 | .03 | .01 |
| ☐ 39 T George Frazier | .08 | .03 | .01 |
| ☐ 40 T Rich Gale | .08 | .03 | .01 |
| ☐ 41 T Barbaro Garbey | .25 | .10 | .02 |
| ☐ 42 T Dwight Gooden | 16.00 | 7.50 | 1.60 |
| ☐ 43 T Rich Gossage | .30 | .12 | .03 |
| ☐ 44 T Wayne Gross | .08 | .03 | .01 |
| ☐ 45 T Mark Gubicza | .40 | .18 | .04 |
| ☐ 46 T Jackie Gutierrez | .25 | .10 | .02 |
| ☐ 47 T Mel Hall | .20 | .09 | .02 |
| ☐ 48 T Toby Harrah | .12 | .05 | .01 |
| ☐ 49 T Ron Hassey | .08 | .03 | .01 |
| ☐ 50 T Rich Hebner | .08 | .03 | .01 |
| ☐ 51 T Willie Hernandez | .35 | .15 | .03 |
| ☐ 52 T Ricky Horton | .25 | .10 | .02 |
| ☐ 53 T Art Howe | .08 | .03 | .01 |
| ☐ 54 T Dane Iorg | .08 | .03 | .01 |
| ☐ 55 T Brook Jacoby | 1.00 | .45 | .10 |
| ☐ 56 T Mike Jeffcoat | .12 | .05 | .01 |
| ☐ 57 T Dave Johnson MGR | .12 | .05 | .01 |
| ☐ 58 T Lynn Jones | .08 | .03 | .01 |
| ☐ 59 T Ruppert Jones | .12 | .05 | .01 |
| ☐ 60 T Mike Jorgensen | .08 | .03 | .01 |
| ☐ 61 T Bob Kearney | .08 | .03 | .01 |
| ☐ 62 T Jimmy Key | .85 | .40 | .08 |
| ☐ 63 T Dave Kingman | .20 | .09 | .02 |
| ☐ 64 T Jerry Koosman | .16 | .07 | .01 |
| ☐ 65 T Wayne Krenchicki | .08 | .03 | .01 |
| ☐ 66 T Rusty Kuntz | .08 | .03 | .01 |
| ☐ 67 T Rene Lachemann MGR | .08 | .03 | .01 |
| ☐ 68 T Frank LaCorte | .08 | .03 | .01 |
| ☐ 69 T Dennis Lamp | .08 | .03 | .01 |
| ☐ 70 T Mark Langston | .85 | .40 | .08 |
| ☐ 71 T Rick Leach | .08 | .03 | .01 |
| ☐ 72 T Craig Lefferts | .08 | .03 | .01 |
| ☐ 73 T Gary Lucas | .08 | .03 | .01 |
| ☐ 74 T Jerry Martin | .08 | .03 | .01 |
| ☐ 75 T Carmelo Martinez | .30 | .12 | .03 |
| ☐ 76 T Mike Mason | .20 | .09 | .02 |
| ☐ 77 T Gary Matthews | .16 | .07 | .01 |
| ☐ 78 T Andy McGaffigan | .08 | .03 | .01 |
| ☐ 79 T Larry Milbourne | .08 | .03 | .01 |
| ☐ 80 T Sid Monge | .08 | .03 | .01 |
| ☐ 81 T Jackie Moore | .08 | .03 | .01 |
| ☐ 82 T Joe Morgan | .40 | .18 | .04 |

|  |  | MINT | VG-E | F-G |
|---|---|---|---|---|
| ☐ 83 | T Graig Nettles | .30 | .12 | .03 |
| ☐ 84 | T Phil Niekro | .50 | .22 | .05 |
| ☐ 85 | T Ken Oberkfell | .12 | .05 | .01 |
| ☐ 86 | T Mike O'Berry | .08 | .03 | .01 |
| ☐ 87 | T Al Oliver | .25 | .10 | .02 |
| ☐ 88 | T Jorge Orta | .08 | .03 | .01 |
| ☐ 89 | T Amos Otis | .16 | .07 | .01 |
| ☐ 90 | T Dave Parker | .50 | .22 | .05 |
| ☐ 91 | T Tony Perez | .25 | .10 | .02 |
| ☐ 92 | T Gerald Perry | .25 | .10 | .02 |
| ☐ 93 | T Gary Pettis | .50 | .22 | .05 |
| ☐ 94 | T Rob Picciolo | .08 | .03 | .01 |
| ☐ 95 | T Vern Rapp MGR | .08 | .03 | .01 |
| ☐ 96 | T Floyd Rayford | .08 | .03 | .01 |
| ☐ 97 | T Randy Ready | .25 | .10 | .02 |
| ☐ 98 | T Ron Reed | .08 | .03 | .01 |
| ☐ 99 | T Gene Richards | .08 | .03 | .01 |
| ☐ 100 | T Jose Rijo | .25 | .10 | .02 |
| ☐ 101 | T Jeff Robinson | .20 | .09 | .02 |
| ☐ 102 | T Ron Romanick | .85 | .40 | .08 |
| ☐ 103 | T Pete Rose | 3.50 | 1.65 | .35 |
| ☐ 104 | T Bret Saberhagen | 3.50 | 1.65 | .35 |
| ☐ 105 | T Juan Samuel | 1.50 | .70 | .15 |
| ☐ 106 | T Scott Sanderson | .12 | .05 | .01 |
| ☐ 107 | T Dick Schofield | .25 | .10 | .02 |
| ☐ 108 | T Tom Seaver | .85 | .40 | .08 |
| ☐ 109 | T Jim Slaton | .08 | .03 | .01 |
| ☐ 110 | T Mike Smithson | .08 | .03 | .01 |
| ☐ 111 | T Larry Sorensen | .08 | .03 | .01 |
| ☐ 112 | T Tim Stoddard | .08 | .03 | .01 |
| ☐ 113 | T Champ Summers | .08 | .03 | .01 |
| ☐ 114 | T Jim Sundberg | .12 | .05 | .01 |
| ☐ 115 | T Rick Sutcliffe | .60 | .28 | .06 |
| ☐ 116 | T Craig Swan | .08 | .03 | .01 |
| ☐ 117 | T Tim Teufel | .40 | .18 | .04 |
| ☐ 118 | T Derrel Thomas | .08 | .03 | .01 |
| ☐ 119 | T Gorman Thomas | .16 | .07 | .01 |
| ☐ 120 | T Alex Trevino | .08 | .03 | .01 |
| ☐ 121 | T Manny Trillo | .12 | .05 | .01 |
| ☐ 122 | T John Tudor | .35 | .15 | .03 |
| ☐ 123 | T Tom Underwood | .08 | .03 | .01 |
| ☐ 124 | T Mike Vail | .08 | .03 | .01 |
| ☐ 125 | T Tom Waddell | .16 | .07 | .01 |
| ☐ 126 | T Gary Ward | .12 | .05 | .01 |
| ☐ 127 | T Curt Wilkerson | .12 | .05 | .01 |
| ☐ 128 | T Frank Williams | .16 | .07 | .01 |
| ☐ 129 | T Glenn Wilson | .25 | .10 | .02 |
| ☐ 130 | T Johnny Wockenfuss | .08 | .03 | .01 |
| ☐ 131 | T Ned Yost | .08 | .03 | .01 |
| ☐ 132 | T Checklist: 1–132 | .15 | .03 | .01 |

## 1985 TOPPS

The cards in this 792 card set measure 2½" by 3½". The 1985 Topps set contains full color cards. The fronts feature both the Topps and team logos along with the team name, player's name and his position. The backs feature player statistics with ink colors of light green and maroon on a gray stock. A trivia quiz is included on the lower portion of the backs. The first ten cards (1–10) are Record Breakers (RB), cards 131–143 are Father and Son (FS) cards, and cards 701–722 portray All Star selections (AS). Cards 271–282 represent "First Draft Picks" still active in the Major Leagues and cards 389–404 feature the coach and players on the 1984 U.S. Olympic Baseball Team.

Complete Set: M-22.00; VG-E-10.00; F-G-2.20

|  |  | MINT | VG-E | F-G |
|---|---|---|---|---|
|  | Common Player | .03 | .01 | .00 |
| ☐ 1 | Carlton Fisk RB | .15 | .04 | .01 |
| ☐ 2 | Steve Garvey RB | .18 | .08 | .01 |
| ☐ 3 | Dwight Gooden RB | 1.00 | .45 | .10 |
| ☐ 4 | Cliff Johnson RB | .05 | .02 | .00 |
| ☐ 5 | Joe Morgan RB | .12 | .05 | .01 |
| ☐ 6 | Pete Rose RB | .40 | .18 | .04 |
| ☐ 7 | Nolan Ryan RB | .18 | .08 | .01 |
| ☐ 8 | Juan Samuel RB | .15 | .06 | .01 |
| ☐ 9 | Bruce Sutter RB | .12 | .05 | .01 |
| ☐ 10 | Don Sutton RB | .09 | .04 | .01 |
| ☐ 11 | Ralph Houk MGR | .03 | .01 | .00 |
| ☐ 12 | Dave Lopes | .06 | .02 | .00 |
| ☐ 13 | Tim Lollar | .03 | .01 | .00 |
| ☐ 14 | Chris Bando | .03 | .01 | .00 |
| ☐ 15 | Jerry Koosman | .07 | .03 | .01 |

| | | MINT | VG-E | F-G | | | MINT | VG-E | F-G |
|---|---|---|---|---|---|---|---|---|---|
| ☐ | 16 Bobby Meacham | .05 | .02 | .00 | ☐ | 69 Jim Winn | .08 | .03 | .01 |
| ☐ | 17 Mike Scott | .05 | .02 | .00 | ☐ | 70 Don Baylor | .10 | .04 | .01 |
| ☐ | 18 Mickey Hatcher | .05 | .02 | .00 | ☐ | 71 Tim Laudner | .03 | .01 | .00 |
| ☐ | 19 George Frazier | .03 | .01 | .00 | ☐ | 72 Rick Sutcliffe | .16 | .07 | .01 |
| ☐ | 20 Chet Lemon | .07 | .03 | .01 | ☐ | 73 Rusty Kuntz | .03 | .01 | .00 |
| ☐ | 21 Lee Tunnell | .05 | .02 | .00 | ☐ | 74 Mike Krukow | .03 | .01 | .00 |
| ☐ | 22 Duane Kuiper | .03 | .01 | .00 | ☐ | 75 Willie Upshaw | .11 | .05 | .01 |
| ☐ | 23 Bret Saberhagen | 1.50 | .70 | .15 | ☐ | 76 Alan Bannister | .03 | .01 | .00 |
| ☐ | 24 Jesse Barfield | .09 | .04 | .01 | ☐ | 77 Joe Beckwith | .03 | .01 | .00 |
| ☐ | 25 Steve Bedrosian | .07 | .03 | .01 | ☐ | 78 Scott Fletcher | .03 | .01 | .00 |
| ☐ | 26 Roy Smalley | .03 | .01 | .00 | ☐ | 79 Rick Mahler | .05 | .02 | .00 |
| ☐ | 27 Bruce Berenyi | .03 | .01 | .00 | ☐ | 80 Keith Hernandez | .25 | .10 | .02 |
| ☐ | 28 Dann Bilardello | .03 | .01 | .00 | ☐ | 81 Lenn Sakata | .03 | .01 | .00 |
| ☐ | 29 Odell Jones | .03 | .01 | .00 | ☐ | 82 Joe Price | .03 | .01 | .00 |
| ☐ | 30 Cal Ripken | .45 | .20 | .04 | ☐ | 83 Charlie Moore | .03 | .01 | .00 |
| ☐ | 31 Terry Whitfield | .03 | .01 | .00 | ☐ | 84 Spike Owen | .05 | .02 | .00 |
| ☐ | 32 Chuck Porter | .03 | .01 | .00 | ☐ | 85 Mike Marshall | .11 | .05 | .01 |
| ☐ | 33 Tito Landrum | .03 | .01 | .00 | ☐ | 86 Don Aase | .03 | .01 | .00 |
| ☐ | 34 Ed Nunez | .09 | .04 | .01 | ☐ | 87 David Green | .06 | .02 | .00 |
| ☐ | 35 Graig Nettles | .12 | .05 | .01 | ☐ | 88 Bryn Smith | .03 | .01 | .00 |
| ☐ | 36 Fred Breining | .03 | .01 | .00 | ☐ | 89 Jackie Gutierrez | .12 | .05 | .01 |
| ☐ | 37 Reid Nichols | .03 | .01 | .00 | ☐ | 90 Rich Gossage | .16 | .07 | .01 |
| ☐ | 38 Jackie Moore MGR | .03 | .01 | .00 | ☐ | 91 Jeff Burroughs | .03 | .01 | .00 |
| ☐ | 39 John Wockenfuss | .03 | .01 | .00 | ☐ | 92 Paul Owens MGR | .03 | .01 | .00 |
| ☐ | 40 Phil Niekro | .16 | .07 | .01 | ☐ | 93 Don Schulze | .09 | .04 | .01 |
| ☐ | 41 Mike Fischlin | .03 | .01 | .00 | ☐ | 94 Toby Harrah | .05 | .02 | .00 |
| ☐ | 42 Luis Sanchez | .03 | .01 | .00 | ☐ | 95 Jose Cruz | .10 | .04 | .01 |
| ☐ | 43 Andre David | .12 | .05 | .01 | ☐ | 96 Johnny Ray | .10 | .04 | .01 |
| ☐ | 44 Dickie Thon | .07 | .03 | .01 | ☐ | 97 Pete Filson | .03 | .01 | .00 |
| ☐ | 45 Greg Minton | .03 | .01 | .00 | ☐ | 98 Steve Lake | .05 | .02 | .00 |
| ☐ | 46 Gary Woods | .03 | .01 | .00 | ☐ | 99 Milt Wilcox | .03 | .01 | .00 |
| ☐ | 47 Dave Rozema | .03 | .01 | .00 | ☐ | 100 George Brett | .45 | .20 | .04 |
| ☐ | 48 Tony Fernandez | .15 | .06 | .01 | ☐ | 101 Jim Acker | .03 | .01 | .00 |
| ☐ | 49 Butch Davis | .06 | .02 | .00 | ☐ | 102 Tommy Dunbar | .06 | .02 | .00 |
| ☐ | 50 John Candelaria | .06 | .02 | .00 | ☐ | 103 Randy Lerch | .03 | .01 | .00 |
| ☐ | 51 Bob Watson | .05 | .02 | .00 | ☐ | 104 Mike Fitzgerald | .07 | .03 | .01 |
| ☐ | 52 Jerry Dybzinski | .03 | .01 | .00 | ☐ | 105 Ron Kittle | .15 | .06 | .01 |
| ☐ | 53 Tom Gorman | .05 | .02 | .00 | ☐ | 106 Pascual Perez | .05 | .02 | .00 |
| ☐ | 54 Cesar Cedeno | .07 | .03 | .01 | ☐ | 107 Tom Foley | .03 | .01 | .00 |
| ☐ | 55 Frank Tanana | .05 | .02 | .00 | ☐ | 108 Darnell Coles | .09 | .04 | .01 |
| ☐ | 56 Jim Dwyer | .03 | .01 | .00 | ☐ | 109 Gary Roenicke | .05 | .02 | .00 |
| ☐ | 57 Pat Zachry | .03 | .01 | .00 | ☐ | 110 Alejandro Pena | .07 | .03 | .01 |
| ☐ | 58 Orlando Mercado | .03 | .01 | .00 | ☐ | 111 Doug DeCinces | .09 | .04 | .01 |
| ☐ | 59 Rick Waits | .03 | .01 | .00 | ☐ | 112 Tom Tellmann | .03 | .01 | .00 |
| ☐ | 60 George Hendrick | .07 | .03 | .01 | ☐ | 113 Tom Herr | .13 | .06 | .01 |
| ☐ | 61 Curt Kaufman | .10 | .04 | .01 | ☐ | 114 Bob James | .06 | .02 | .00 |
| ☐ | 62 Mike Ramsey | .03 | .01 | .00 | ☐ | 115 Rickey Henderson | .40 | .18 | .04 |
| ☐ | 63 Steve McCatty | .03 | .01 | .00 | ☐ | 116 Dennis Boyd | .15 | .06 | .01 |
| ☐ | 64 Mark Bailey | .10 | .04 | .01 | ☐ | 117 Greg Gross | .03 | .01 | .00 |
| ☐ | 65 Bill Buckner | .09 | .04 | .01 | ☐ | 118 Eric Show | .05 | .02 | .00 |
| ☐ | 66 Dick Williams MGR | .03 | .01 | .00 | ☐ | 119 Pat Corrales MGR | .03 | .01 | .00 |
| ☐ | 67 Rafael Santana | .15 | .06 | .01 | ☐ | 120 Steve Kemp | .07 | .03 | .01 |
| ☐ | 68 Von Hayes | .12 | .05 | .01 | ☐ | 121 Checklist: 1–132 | .08 | .01 | .00 |

| | MINT | VG-E | F-G |
|---|---|---|---|
| ☐ 122 Tom Brunansky | .16 | .07 | .01 |
| ☐ 123 Dave Smith | .05 | .02 | .00 |
| ☐ 124 Rich Hebner | .03 | .01 | .00 |
| ☐ 125 Kent Tekulve | .05 | .02 | .00 |
| ☐ 126 Ruppert Jones | .05 | .02 | .00 |
| ☐ 127 Mark Gubicza | .20 | .09 | .02 |
| ☐ 128 Ernie Whitt | .03 | .01 | .00 |
| ☐ 129 Gene Garber | .03 | .01 | .00 |
| ☐ 130 Al Oliver | .12 | .05 | .01 |
| FATHER/SON CARDS (131–143) | | | |
| ☐ 131 Buddy/Gus Bell FS | .07 | .03 | .01 |
| ☐ 132 Dale/Yogi Berra FS | .07 | .02 | .01 |
| ☐ 133 Bob/Ray Boone FS | .05 | .02 | .00 |
| ☐ 134 Terry/Tito Francona FS | .07 | .03 | .01 |
| ☐ 135 Terry/Bob Kennedy FS | .05 | .02 | .00 |
| ☐ 136 Jeff/Jim Kunkel FS | .05 | .02 | .00 |
| ☐ 137 Vance/Vern Law FS | .05 | .02 | .00 |
| ☐ 138 Dick/Dick Schofield FS | .05 | .02 | .00 |
| ☐ 139 Joel/Bob Skinner FS | .05 | .02 | .00 |
| ☐ 140 Roy/Roy Smalley FS | .05 | .02 | .00 |
| ☐ 141 Mike/Dave Stenhouse FS | .05 | .02 | .00 |
| ☐ 142 Steve/Dizzy Trout FS | .05 | .02 | .00 |
| ☐ 143 Ozzie/Ozzie Virgil FS | .05 | .02 | .00 |
| ☐ 144 Ron Gardenhire | .03 | .01 | .00 |
| ☐ 145 Alvin Davis | 1.00 | .45 | .10 |
| ☐ 146 Gary Redus | .07 | .03 | .01 |
| ☐ 147 Bill Swaggerty | .12 | .05 | .01 |
| ☐ 148 Steve Yeager | .05 | .02 | .00 |
| ☐ 149 Dickie Noles | .03 | .01 | .00 |
| ☐ 150 Jim Rice | .30 | .12 | .03 |
| ☐ 151 Moose Haas | .05 | .02 | .00 |
| ☐ 152 Steve Braun | .03 | .01 | .00 |
| ☐ 153 Frank LaCorte | .03 | .01 | .00 |
| ☐ 154 Argenis Salazar | .10 | .04 | .01 |
| ☐ 155 Yogi Berra MGR | .10 | .04 | .01 |
| ☐ 156 Craig Reynolds | .03 | .01 | .00 |
| ☐ 157 Tug McGraw | .07 | .03 | .01 |
| ☐ 158 Pat Tabler | .05 | .02 | .00 |
| ☐ 159 Carlos Diaz | .03 | .01 | .00 |
| ☐ 160 Lance Parrish | .20 | .09 | .02 |
| ☐ 161 Ken Schrom | .03 | .01 | .00 |
| ☐ 162 Benny Distefano | .15 | .06 | .01 |
| ☐ 163 Dennis Eckersley | .05 | .02 | .00 |
| ☐ 164 Jorge Orta | .03 | .01 | .00 |
| ☐ 165 Dusty Baker | .06 | .02 | .00 |
| ☐ 166 Keith Atherton | .03 | .01 | .00 |
| ☐ 167 Rufino Linares | .03 | .01 | .00 |
| ☐ 168 Garth Iorg | .03 | .01 | .00 |
| ☐ 169 Dan Spillner | .03 | .01 | .00 |
| ☐ 170 George Foster | .16 | .07 | .01 |
| ☐ 171 Bill Stein | .03 | .01 | .00 |
| ☐ 172 Jack Perconte | .03 | .01 | .00 |

| | MINT | VG-E | F-G |
|---|---|---|---|
| ☐ 173 Mike Young | .30 | .12 | .03 |
| ☐ 174 Rick Honeycutt | .05 | .02 | .00 |
| ☐ 175 Dave Parker | .18 | .08 | .01 |
| ☐ 176 Bill Schroeder | .03 | .01 | .00 |
| ☐ 177 Dave Von Ohlen | .03 | .01 | .00 |
| ☐ 178 Miguel Dilone | .03 | .01 | .00 |
| ☐ 179 Tommy John | .12 | .05 | .01 |
| ☐ 180 Dave Winfield | .30 | .12 | .03 |
| ☐ 181 Roger Clemens | .45 | .20 | .04 |
| ☐ 182 Tim Flannery | .03 | .01 | .00 |
| ☐ 183 Larry McWilliams | .05 | .02 | .00 |
| ☐ 184 Carmen Castillo | .03 | .01 | .00 |
| ☐ 185 Al Holland | .05 | .02 | .00 |
| ☐ 186 Bob Lillis MGR | .03 | .01 | .00 |
| ☐ 187 Mike Walters | .05 | .02 | .00 |
| ☐ 188 Greg Pryor | .03 | .01 | .00 |
| ☐ 189 Warren Brusstar | .03 | .01 | .00 |
| ☐ 190 Rusty Staub | .08 | .03 | .01 |
| ☐ 191 Steve Nicosia | .03 | .01 | .00 |
| ☐ 192 Howard Johnson | .05 | .02 | .00 |
| ☐ 193 Jimmy Key | .40 | .18 | .04 |
| ☐ 194 Dave Stegman | .03 | .01 | .00 |
| ☐ 195 Glenn Hubbard | .05 | .02 | .00 |
| ☐ 196 Pete O'Brien | .05 | .02 | .00 |
| ☐ 197 Mike Warren | .05 | .02 | .00 |
| ☐ 198 Eddie Milner | .05 | .02 | .00 |
| ☐ 199 Denny Martinez | .03 | .01 | .00 |
| ☐ 200 Reggie Jackson | .35 | .15 | .03 |
| ☐ 201 Burt Hooton | .03 | .01 | .00 |
| ☐ 202 Gorman Thomas | .08 | .03 | .01 |
| ☐ 203 Bob McClure | .03 | .01 | .00 |
| ☐ 204 Art Howe | .03 | .01 | .00 |
| ☐ 205 Steve Rogers | .07 | .03 | .01 |
| ☐ 206 Phil Garner | .05 | .02 | .00 |
| ☐ 207 Mark Clear | .03 | .01 | .00 |
| ☐ 208 Champ Summers | .03 | .01 | .00 |
| ☐ 209 Bill Campbell | .05 | .02 | .00 |
| ☐ 210 Gary Matthews | .07 | .03 | .01 |
| ☐ 211 Clay Christiansen | .10 | .04 | .01 |
| ☐ 212 George Vukovich | .03 | .01 | .00 |
| ☐ 213 Billy Gardner MGR | .03 | .01 | .00 |
| ☐ 214 John Tudor | .15 | .06 | .01 |
| ☐ 215 Bob Brenly | .08 | .03 | .01 |
| ☐ 216 Jerry Don Gleaton | .03 | .01 | .00 |
| ☐ 217 Leon Roberts | .03 | .01 | .00 |
| ☐ 218 Doyle Alexander | .05 | .02 | .00 |
| ☐ 219 Gerald Perry | .07 | .03 | .01 |
| ☐ 220 Fred Lynn | .15 | .06 | .01 |
| ☐ 221 Ron Reed | .03 | .01 | .00 |
| ☐ 222 Hubie Brooks | .08 | .03 | .01 |
| ☐ 223 Tom Hume | .03 | .01 | .00 |
| ☐ 224 Al Cowens | .05 | .02 | .00 |
| ☐ 225 Mike Boddicker | .10 | .04 | .01 |

| | MINT | VG-E | F-G |
|---|---|---|---|
| ☐ 226 Juan Beniquez | .05 | .02 | .00 |
| ☐ 227 Danny Darwin | .03 | .01 | .00 |
| ☐ 228 Dion James | .10 | .04 | .01 |
| ☐ 229 Dave LaPoint | .03 | .01 | .00 |
| ☐ 230 Gary Carter | .30 | .12 | .03 |
| ☐ 231 Dwayne Murphy | .07 | .03 | .01 |
| ☐ 232 Dave Beard | .03 | .01 | .00 |
| ☐ 233 Ed Jurak | .03 | .01 | .00 |
| ☐ 234 Jerry Narron | .03 | .01 | .00 |
| ☐ 235 Garry Maddox | .03 | .01 | .00 |
| ☐ 236 Mark Thurmond | .05 | .02 | .00 |
| ☐ 237 Julio Franco | .12 | .05 | .01 |
| ☐ 238 Jose Rijo | .15 | .06 | .01 |
| ☐ 239 Tim Teufel | .16 | .07 | .01 |
| ☐ 240 Dave Stieb | .16 | .07 | .01 |
| ☐ 241 Jim Frey MGR | .03 | .01 | .00 |
| ☐ 242 Greg Harris | .03 | .01 | .00 |
| ☐ 243 Barbaro Garbey | .12 | .05 | .01 |
| ☐ 244 Mike Jones | .05 | .02 | .00 |
| ☐ 245 Chili Davis | .07 | .03 | .01 |
| ☐ 246 Mike Norris | .03 | .01 | .00 |
| ☐ 247 Wayne Tolleson | .03 | .01 | .00 |
| ☐ 248 Terry Forster | .07 | .03 | .01 |
| ☐ 249 Harold Baines | .16 | .07 | .01 |
| ☐ 250 Jesse Orosco | .06 | .02 | .00 |
| ☐ 251 Brad Gulden | .03 | .01 | .00 |
| ☐ 252 Dan Ford | .05 | .02 | .00 |
| ☐ 253 Sid Bream | .16 | .07 | .01 |
| ☐ 254 Pete Vuckovich | .07 | .03 | .01 |
| ☐ 255 Lonnie Smith | .07 | .03 | .01 |
| ☐ 256 Mike Stanton | .03 | .01 | .00 |
| ☐ 257 Bryan Little | .03 | .01 | .00 |
| ☐ 258 Mike Brown | .05 | .02 | .00 |
| ☐ 259 Gary Allenson | .03 | .01 | .00 |
| ☐ 260 Dave Righetti | .12 | .05 | .01 |
| ☐ 261 Checklist: 133–264 | .08 | .01 | .00 |
| ☐ 262 Greg Booker | .10 | .04 | .01 |
| ☐ 263 Mel Hall | .10 | .04 | .01 |
| ☐ 264 Joe Sambito | .05 | .02 | .00 |
| ☐ 265 Juan Samuel | .65 | .30 | .06 |
| ☐ 266 Frank Viola | .07 | .03 | .01 |
| ☐ 267 Henry Cotto | .12 | .05 | .01 |
| ☐ 268 Chuck Tanner MGR | .03 | .01 | .00 |
| ☐ 269 Doug Baker | .10 | .04 | .01 |
| ☐ 270 Dan Quisenberry | .16 | .07 | .01 |
| FIRST DRAFT PICKS (271–282) | | | |
| ☐ 271 Tim Foli '68 | .03 | .01 | .00 |
| ☐ 272 Jeff Burroughs '69 | .03 | .01 | .00 |
| ☐ 273 Bill Almon '74 | .03 | .01 | .00 |
| ☐ 274 Floyd Bannister '76 | .05 | .02 | .00 |
| ☐ 275 Harold Baines '77 | .13 | .06 | .01 |
| ☐ 276 Bob Horner '78 | .13 | .06 | .01 |

| | MINT | VG-E | F-G |
|---|---|---|---|
| ☐ 277 Al Chambers '79 | .05 | .02 | .00 |
| ☐ 278 Darryl Strawberry '80 | .30 | .12 | .03 |
| ☐ 279 Mike Moore '81 | .07 | .03 | .01 |
| ☐ 280 Shawon Dunston '82 | .25 | .10 | .02 |
| ☐ 281 Tim Belcher '83 | .12 | .05 | .01 |
| ☐ 282 Shawn Abner '84 | .25 | .10 | .02 |
| ☐ 283 Fran Mullins | .03 | .01 | .00 |
| ☐ 284 Marty Bystrom | .03 | .01 | .00 |
| ☐ 285 Dan Driessen | .03 | .01 | .00 |
| ☐ 286 Rudy Law | .03 | .01 | .00 |
| ☐ 287 Walt Terrell | .05 | .02 | .00 |
| ☐ 288 Jeff Kunkel | .12 | .05 | .01 |
| ☐ 289 Tom Underwood | .03 | .01 | .00 |
| ☐ 290 Cecil Cooper | .13 | .06 | .01 |
| ☐ 291 Bob Welch | .06 | .02 | .00 |
| ☐ 292 Brad Komminsk | .09 | .04 | .01 |
| ☐ 293 Curt Young | .12 | .05 | .01 |
| ☐ 294 Tom Nieto | .09 | .04 | .01 |
| ☐ 295 Joe Niekro | .06 | .02 | .00 |
| ☐ 296 Ricky Nelson | .05 | .02 | .00 |
| ☐ 297 Gary Lucas | .03 | .01 | .00 |
| ☐ 298 Marty Barrett | .06 | .02 | .00 |
| ☐ 299 Andy Hawkins | .07 | .03 | .01 |
| ☐ 300 Rod Carew | .35 | .15 | .03 |
| ☐ 301 John Montefusco | .05 | .02 | .00 |
| ☐ 302 Tim Corcoran | .03 | .01 | .00 |
| ☐ 303 Mike Jeffcoat | .06 | .02 | .00 |
| ☐ 304 Gary Gaetti | .05 | .02 | .00 |
| ☐ 305 Dale Berra | .05 | .02 | .00 |
| ☐ 306 Rick Reuschel | .06 | .02 | .00 |
| ☐ 307 Sparky Anderson MGR | .05 | .02 | .00 |
| ☐ 308 John Wathan | .03 | .01 | .00 |
| ☐ 309 Mike Witt | .08 | .03 | .01 |
| ☐ 310 Manny Trillo | .05 | .02 | .00 |
| ☐ 311 Jim Gott | .03 | .01 | .00 |
| ☐ 312 Marc Hill | .03 | .01 | .00 |
| ☐ 313 Dave Schmidt | .03 | .01 | .00 |
| ☐ 314 Ron Oester | .05 | .02 | .00 |
| ☐ 315 Doug Sisk | .05 | .02 | .00 |
| ☐ 316 John Lowenstein | .03 | .01 | .00 |
| ☐ 317 Jack Lazorko | .10 | .04 | .01 |
| ☐ 318 Ted Simmons | .10 | .04 | .01 |
| ☐ 319 Jeff Jones | .03 | .01 | .00 |
| ☐ 320 Dale Murphy | .45 | .20 | .04 |
| ☐ 321 Ricky Horton | .20 | .09 | .02 |
| ☐ 322 Dave Stapleton | .05 | .02 | .00 |
| ☐ 323 Andy McGaffigan | .03 | .01 | .00 |
| ☐ 324 Bruce Bochy | .03 | .01 | .00 |
| ☐ 325 John Denny | .07 | .03 | .01 |
| ☐ 326 Kevin Bass | .03 | .01 | .00 |
| ☐ 327 Brook Jacoby | .20 | .09 | .02 |
| ☐ 328 Bob Shirley | .03 | .01 | .00 |
| ☐ 329 Ron Washington | .03 | .01 | .00 |

|  | MINT | VG-E | F-G |
|---|---|---|---|
| 330 Leon Durham | .15 | .06 | .01 |
| 331 Bill Laskey | .03 | .01 | .00 |
| 332 Brian Harper | .03 | .01 | .00 |
| 333 Willie Hernandez | .15 | .06 | .01 |
| 334 Dick Howser MGR | .03 | .01 | .00 |
| 335 Bruce Benedict | .03 | .01 | .00 |
| 336 Rance Mulliniks | .03 | .01 | .00 |
| 337 Billy Sample | .03 | .01 | .00 |
| 338 Britt Burns | .06 | .02 | .00 |
| 339 Danny Heep | .03 | .01 | .00 |
| 340 Robin Yount | .30 | .12 | .03 |
| 341 Floyd Rayford | .03 | .01 | .00 |
| 342 Ted Power | .05 | .02 | .00 |
| 343 Bill Russell | .05 | .02 | .00 |
| 344 Dave Henderson | .03 | .01 | .00 |
| 345 Charlie Lea | .05 | .02 | .00 |
| 346 Terry Pendleton | .45 | .20 | .04 |
| 347 Rick Langford | .03 | .01 | .00 |
| 348 Bob Boone | .05 | .02 | .00 |
| 349 Domingo Ramos | .03 | .01 | .00 |
| 350 Wade Boggs | .45 | .20 | .04 |
| 351 Juan Agosto | .03 | .01 | .00 |
| 352 Joe Morgan | .15 | .06 | .01 |
| 353 Julio Solano | .10 | .04 | .01 |
| 354 Andre Robertson | .03 | .01 | .00 |
| 355 Bert Blyleven | .09 | .04 | .01 |
| 356 Dave Meier | .12 | .05 | .01 |
| 357 Rich Bordi | .03 | .01 | .00 |
| 358 Tony Pena | .10 | .04 | .01 |
| 359 Pat Sheridan | .05 | .02 | .00 |
| 360 Steve Carlton | .30 | .12 | .03 |
| 361 Alfredo Griffin | .05 | .02 | .00 |
| 362 Craig McMurtry | .05 | .02 | .00 |
| 363 Ron Hodges | .03 | .01 | .00 |
| 364 Richard Dotson | .06 | .02 | .00 |
| 365 Danny Ozark MGR | .03 | .01 | .00 |
| 366 Todd Cruz | .03 | .01 | .00 |
| 367 Keefe Cato | .09 | .04 | .01 |
| 368 Dave Bergman | .03 | .01 | .00 |
| 369 R. J. Reynolds | .20 | .09 | .02 |
| 370 Bruce Sutter | .15 | .06 | .01 |
| 371 Mickey Rivers | .05 | .02 | .00 |
| 372 Roy Howell | .03 | .01 | .00 |
| 373 Mike Moore | .07 | .03 | .01 |
| 374 Brian Downing | .05 | .02 | .00 |
| 375 Jeff Reardon | .07 | .03 | .01 |
| 376 Jeff Newman | .03 | .01 | .00 |
| 377 Checklist: 265–396 | .08 | .01 | .00 |
| 378 Alan Wiggins | .09 | .04 | .01 |
| 379 Charles Hudson | .05 | .02 | .00 |
| 380 Ken Griffey | .06 | .02 | .00 |
| 381 Roy Smith | .09 | .04 | .01 |
| 382 Denny Walling | .03 | .01 | .00 |

|  | MINT | VG-E | F-G |
|---|---|---|---|
| 383 Rick Lysander | .03 | .01 | .00 |
| 384 Jody Davis | .10 | .04 | .01 |
| 385 Jose DeLeon | .05 | .02 | .00 |
| 386 Dan Gladden | .30 | .12 | .03 |
| 387 Buddy Biancalana | .12 | .05 | .01 |
| 388 Bert Roberge | .03 | .01 | .00 |
| U.S. OLYMPIANS (389–404) | | | |
| 389 Rod Dedeaux COACH | .03 | .01 | .00 |
| 390 Sid Akins | .10 | .04 | .01 |
| 391 Flavio Alfaro | .10 | .04 | .01 |
| 392 Don August | .10 | .04 | .01 |
| 393 Scott Bankhead | .10 | .04 | .01 |
| 394 Bob Caffrey | .10 | .04 | .01 |
| 395 Mike Dunne | .10 | .04 | .01 |
| 396 Gary Green | .10 | .04 | .01 |
| 397 John Hoover | .10 | .04 | .01 |
| 398 Shane Mack | .20 | .09 | .02 |
| 399 John Marzano | .10 | .04 | .01 |
| 400 Oddibe McDowell | .75 | .35 | .07 |
| 401 Mark McGwire | .15 | .06 | .01 |
| 402 Pat Pacillo | .10 | .04 | .01 |
| 403 Cory Snyder | .30 | .12 | .03 |
| 404 Billy Swift | .15 | .06 | .01 |
| 405 Tom Veryzer | .03 | .01 | .00 |
| 406 Len Whitehouse | .03 | .01 | .00 |
| 407 Bobby Ramos | .03 | .01 | .00 |
| 408 Sid Monge | .03 | .01 | .00 |
| 409 Brad Wellman | .03 | .01 | .00 |
| 410 Bob Horner | .15 | .06 | .01 |
| 411 Bobby Cox MGR | .03 | .01 | .00 |
| 412 Bud Black | .05 | .02 | .00 |
| 413 Vance Law | .03 | .01 | .00 |
| 414 Gary Ward | .05 | .02 | .00 |
| 415 Ron Darling | .40 | .18 | .04 |
| 416 Wayne Gross | .03 | .01 | .00 |
| 417 John Franco | .30 | .12 | .03 |
| 418 Ken Landreaux | .05 | .02 | .00 |
| 419 Mike Caldwell | .05 | .02 | .00 |
| 420 Andre Dawson | .20 | .09 | .02 |
| 421 Dave Rucker | .03 | .01 | .00 |
| 422 Carney Lansford | .10 | .04 | .01 |
| 423 Barry Bonnell | .03 | .01 | .00 |
| 424 Al Nipper | .20 | .09 | .02 |
| 425 Mike Hargrove | .03 | .01 | .00 |
| 426 Vern Ruhle | .03 | .01 | .00 |
| 427 Mario Ramirez | .03 | .01 | .00 |
| 428 Larry Andersen | .03 | .01 | .00 |
| 429 Rick Cerone | .05 | .02 | .00 |
| 430 Ron Davis | .05 | .02 | .00 |
| 431 U. L. Washington | .03 | .01 | .00 |
| 432 Thad Bosley | .03 | .01 | .00 |
| 433 Jim Morrison | .03 | .01 | .00 |

| | MINT | VG-E | F-G | | MINT | VG-E | F-G |
|---|---|---|---|---|---|---|---|
| ☐ 434 Gene Richards | .03 | .01 | .00 | ☐ 487 Frank Williams | .10 | .04 | .01 |
| ☐ 435 Dan Petry | .12 | .05 | .01 | ☐ 488 Joel Skinner | .08 | .03 | .01 |
| ☐ 436 Willie Aikens | .05 | .02 | .00 | ☐ 489 Bryan Clark | .03 | .01 | .00 |
| ☐ 437 Al Jones | .12 | .05 | .01 | ☐ 490 Jason Thompson | .07 | .03 | .01 |
| ☐ 438 Joe Torre MGR | .06 | .02 | .00 | ☐ 491 Rick Camp | .03 | .01 | .00 |
| ☐ 439 Junior Ortiz | .03 | .01 | .00 | ☐ 492 Dave Johnson MGR | .05 | .02 | .00 |
| ☐ 440 Fernando Valenzuela | .30 | .12 | .03 | ☐ 493 Orel Hershiser | 1.25 | .60 | .12 |
| ☐ 441 Duane Walker | .05 | .02 | .00 | ☐ 494 Rich Dauer | .03 | .01 | .00 |
| ☐ 442 Ken Forsch | .03 | .01 | .00 | ☐ 495 Mario Soto | .10 | .04 | .01 |
| ☐ 443 George Wright | .05 | .02 | .00 | ☐ 496 Donnie Scott | .08 | .03 | .01 |
| ☐ 444 Tony Phillips | .03 | .01 | .00 | ☐ 497 Gary Pettis | .35 | .15 | .03 |
| ☐ 445 Tippy Martinez | .05 | .02 | .00 | ☐ 498 Ed Romero | .03 | .01 | .00 |
| ☐ 446 Jim Sundberg | .05 | .02 | .00 | ☐ 499 Danny Cox | .20 | .09 | .02 |
| ☐ 447 Jeff Lahti | .03 | .01 | .00 | ☐ 500 Mike Schmidt | .35 | .15 | .03 |
| ☐ 448 Derrel Thomas | .03 | .01 | .00 | ☐ 501 Dan Schatzeder | .03 | .01 | .00 |
| ☐ 449 Phil Bradley | 1.00 | .45 | .10 | ☐ 502 Rick Miller | .03 | .01 | .00 |
| ☐ 450 Steve Garvey | .35 | .15 | .03 | ☐ 503 Tim Conroy | .03 | .01 | .00 |
| ☐ 451 Bruce Hurst | .03 | .01 | .00 | ☐ 504 Jerry Willard | .07 | .03 | .01 |
| ☐ 452 John Castino | .03 | .01 | .00 | ☐ 505 Jim Beattie | .03 | .01 | .00 |
| ☐ 453 Tom Waddell | .12 | .05 | .01 | ☐ 506 Franklin Stubbs | .12 | .05 | .01 |
| ☐ 454 Glenn Wilson | .10 | .04 | .01 | ☐ 507 Ray Fontenot | .03 | .01 | .00 |
| ☐ 455 Bob Knepper | .07 | .03 | .01 | ☐ 508 John Shelby | .03 | .01 | .00 |
| ☐ 456 Tim Foli | .03 | .01 | .00 | ☐ 509 Milt May | .03 | .01 | .00 |
| ☐ 457 Cecilio Guante | .03 | .01 | .00 | ☐ 510 Kent Hrbek | .30 | .12 | .03 |
| ☐ 458 Randy Johnson | .03 | .01 | .00 | ☐ 511 Lee Smith | .08 | .03 | .01 |
| ☐ 459 Charlie Leibrandt | .06 | .02 | .00 | ☐ 512 Tom Brookens | .03 | .01 | .00 |
| ☐ 460 Ryne Sandberg | .45 | .20 | .04 | ☐ 513 Lynn Jones | .03 | .01 | .00 |
| ☐ 461 Marty Castillo | .03 | .01 | .00 | ☐ 514 Jeff Cornell | .10 | .04 | .01 |
| ☐ 462 Gary Lavelle | .03 | .01 | .00 | ☐ 515 Dave Concepcion | .08 | .03 | .01 |
| ☐ 463 Dave Collins | .05 | .02 | .00 | ☐ 516 Roy Lee Jackson | .03 | .01 | .00 |
| ☐ 464 Mike Mason | .10 | .04 | .01 | ☐ 517 Jerry Martin | .03 | .01 | .00 |
| ☐ 465 Bob Grich | .07 | .03 | .01 | ☐ 518 Chris Chambliss | .05 | .02 | .00 |
| ☐ 466 Tony LaRussa MGR | .03 | .01 | .00 | ☐ 519 Doug Rader MGR | .03 | .01 | .00 |
| ☐ 467 Ed Lynch | .03 | .01 | .00 | ☐ 520 LaMarr Hoyt | .08 | .03 | .01 |
| ☐ 468 Wayne Krenchicki | .03 | .01 | .00 | ☐ 521 Rick Dempsey | .06 | .02 | .00 |
| ☐ 469 Sammy Stewart | .03 | .01 | .00 | ☐ 522 Paul Molitor | .10 | .04 | .01 |
| ☐ 470 Steve Sax | .12 | .05 | .01 | ☐ 523 Candy Maldonado | .05 | .02 | .00 |
| ☐ 471 Pete Ladd | .05 | .02 | .00 | ☐ 524 Rob Wilfong | .03 | .01 | .00 |
| ☐ 472 Jim Essian | .03 | .01 | .00 | ☐ 525 Darrell Porter | .05 | .02 | .00 |
| ☐ 473 Tim Wallach | .08 | .03 | .01 | ☐ 526 Dave Palmer | .05 | .02 | .00 |
| ☐ 474 Kurt Kepshire | .12 | .05 | .01 | ☐ 527 Checklist: 397–528 | .08 | .01 | .00 |
| ☐ 475 Andre Thornton | .08 | .03 | .01 | ☐ 528 Bill Krueger | .03 | .01 | .00 |
| ☐ 476 Jeff Stone | .25 | .10 | .02 | ☐ 529 Rich Gedman | .07 | .03 | .01 |
| ☐ 477 Bob Ojeda | .05 | .02 | .00 | ☐ 530 Dave Dravecky | .06 | .02 | .00 |
| ☐ 478 Kurt Bevacqua | .03 | .01 | .00 | ☐ 531 Joe Lefebvre | .03 | .01 | .00 |
| ☐ 479 Mike Madden | .05 | .02 | .00 | ☐ 532 Frank DiPino | .05 | .02 | .00 |
| ☐ 480 Lou Whitaker | .16 | .07 | .01 | ☐ 533 Tony Bernazard | .03 | .01 | .00 |
| ☐ 481 Dale Murray | .03 | .01 | .00 | ☐ 534 Brian Dayett | .08 | .03 | .01 |
| ☐ 482 Harry Spilman | .03 | .01 | .00 | ☐ 535 Pat Putnam | .03 | .01 | .00 |
| ☐ 483 Mike Smithson | .05 | .02 | .00 | ☐ 536 Kirby Puckett | .60 | .28 | .06 |
| ☐ 484 Larry Bowa | .07 | .03 | .01 | ☐ 537 Don Robinson | .05 | .02 | .00 |
| ☐ 485 Matt Young | .05 | .02 | .00 | ☐ 538 Keith Moreland | .05 | .02 | .00 |
| ☐ 486 Steve Balboni | .05 | .02 | .00 | ☐ 539 Aurelio Lopez | .03 | .01 | .00 |

| | MINT | VG-E | F-G | | MINT | VG-E | F-G |
|---|---|---|---|---|---|---|---|
| 540 Claudell Washington ... | .07 | .03 | .01 | 593 Rick Leach | .03 | .01 | .00 |
| 541 Mark Davis | .03 | .01 | .00 | 594 Curt Wilkerson | .06 | .02 | .00 |
| 542 Don Slaught | .03 | .01 | .00 | 595 Larry Gura | .05 | .02 | .00 |
| 543 Mike Squires | .03 | .01 | .00 | 596 Jerry Hairston | .03 | .01 | .00 |
| 544 Bruce Kison | .03 | .01 | .00 | 597 Brad Lesley | .03 | .01 | .00 |
| 545 Lloyd Moseby | .12 | .05 | .01 | 598 Jose Oquendo | .03 | .01 | .00 |
| 546 Brent Gaff | .05 | .02 | .00 | 599 Storm Davis | .07 | .03 | .01 |
| 547 Pete Rose MGR | .35 | .15 | .03 | 600 Pete Rose | .70 | .32 | .07 |
| 548 Larry Parrish | .07 | .03 | .01 | 601 Tom Lasorda MGR | .05 | .02 | .00 |
| 549 Mike Scioscia | .03 | .01 | .00 | 602 Jeff Dedmon | .09 | .04 | .01 |
| 550 Scott McGregor | .06 | .02 | .00 | 603 Rick Manning | .03 | .01 | .00 |
| 551 Andy Van Slyke | .07 | .03 | .01 | 604 Daryl Sconiers | .03 | .01 | .00 |
| 552 Chris Codiroli | .03 | .01 | .00 | 605 Ozzie Smith | .09 | .04 | .01 |
| 553 Bob Clark | .03 | .01 | .00 | 606 Rich Gale | .03 | .01 | .00 |
| 554 Doug Flynn | .03 | .01 | .00 | 607 Bill Almon | .03 | .01 | .00 |
| 555 Bob Stanley | .05 | .02 | .00 | 608 Craig Lefferts | .03 | .01 | .00 |
| 556 Sixto Lezcano | .03 | .01 | .00 | 609 Broderick Perkins | .03 | .01 | .00 |
| 557 Len Barker | .05 | .02 | .00 | 610 Jack Morris | .15 | .06 | .01 |
| 558 Carmelo Martinez | .09 | .04 | .01 | 611 Ozzie Virgil | .06 | .02 | .00 |
| 559 Jay Howell | .06 | .02 | .00 | 612 Mike Armstrong | .05 | .02 | .00 |
| 560 Bill Madlock | .12 | .05 | .01 | 613 Terry Puhl | .03 | .01 | .00 |
| 561 Darryl Motley | .05 | .02 | .00 | 614 Al Williams | .03 | .01 | .00 |
| 562 Houston Jimenez | .05 | .02 | .00 | 615 Marvell Wynne | .03 | .01 | .00 |
| 563 Dick Ruthven | .03 | .01 | .00 | 616 Scott Sanderson | .03 | .01 | .00 |
| 564 Alan Ashby | .03 | .01 | .00 | 617 Willie Wilson | .15 | .06 | .01 |
| 565 Kirk Gibson | .20 | .09 | .02 | 618 Pete Falcone | .03 | .01 | .00 |
| 566 Ed Vande Berg | .05 | .02 | .00 | 619 Jeff Leonard | .06 | .02 | .00 |
| 567 Joel Youngblood | .03 | .01 | .00 | 620 Dwight Gooden | 6.00 | 2.00 | .40 |
| 568 Cliff Johnson | .03 | .01 | .00 | 621 Marvis Foley | .03 | .01 | .00 |
| 569 Ken Oberkfell | .03 | .01 | .00 | 622 Luis Leal | .03 | .01 | .00 |
| 570 Darryl Strawberry | .40 | .18 | .04 | 623 Greg Walker | .12 | .05 | .01 |
| 571 Charlie Hough | .05 | .02 | .00 | 624 Benny Ayala | .03 | .01 | .00 |
| 572 Tom Paciorek | .03 | .01 | .00 | 625 Mark Langston | .40 | .18 | .04 |
| 573 Jay Tibbs | .18 | .08 | .01 | 626 German Rivera | .12 | .05 | .01 |
| 574 Joe Altobelli MGR | .03 | .01 | .00 | 627 Eric Davis | .30 | .12 | .03 |
| 575 Pedro Guerrero | .20 | .09 | .02 | 628 Rene Lachemann MGR | .03 | .01 | .00 |
| 576 Jaime Cocanower | .08 | .03 | .01 | 629 Dick Schofield | .08 | .03 | .01 |
| 577 Chris Speier | .03 | .01 | .00 | 630 Tim Raines | .20 | .09 | .02 |
| 578 Terry Francona | .07 | .03 | .01 | 631 Bob Forsch | .05 | .02 | .00 |
| 579 Ron Romanick | .30 | .12 | .03 | 632 Bruce Bochte | .05 | .02 | .00 |
| 580 Dwight Evans | .11 | .05 | .01 | 633 Glenn Hoffman | .03 | .01 | .00 |
| 581 Mark Wagner | .03 | .01 | .00 | 634 Bill Dawley | .05 | .02 | .00 |
| 582 Ken Phelps | .05 | .02 | .00 | 635 Terry Kennedy | .08 | .03 | .01 |
| 583 Bobby Brown | .03 | .01 | .00 | 636 Shane Rawley | .06 | .02 | .00 |
| 584 Kevin Gross | .03 | .01 | .00 | 637 Brett Butler | .08 | .03 | .01 |
| 585 Butch Wynegar | .05 | .02 | .00 | 638 Mike Pagliarulo | .25 | .10 | .02 |
| 586 Bill Scherrer | .03 | .01 | .00 | 639 Ed Hodge | .08 | .03 | .01 |
| 587 Doug Frobel | .05 | .02 | .00 | 640 Steve Henderson | .03 | .01 | .00 |
| 588 Bobby Castillo | .03 | .01 | .00 | 641 Rod Scurry | .03 | .01 | .00 |
| 589 Bob Dernier | .06 | .02 | .00 | 642 Dave Owen | .08 | .03 | .01 |
| 590 Ray Knight | .05 | .02 | .00 | 643 Johnny Grubb | .03 | .01 | .00 |
| 591 Larry Herndon | .05 | .02 | .00 | 644 Mark Huismann | .08 | .03 | .01 |
| 592 Jeff Robinson | .10 | .04 | .01 | 645 Damaso Garcia | .08 | .03 | .01 |

|  | | MINT | VG-E | F-G |
|---|---|---|---|---|
| ☐ 646 | Scot Thompson | .03 | .01 | .00 |
| ☐ 647 | Rafael Ramirez | .03 | .01 | .00 |
| ☐ 648 | Bob Jones | .03 | .01 | .00 |
| ☐ 649 | Sid Fernandez | .16 | .07 | .01 |
| ☐ 650 | Greg Luzinski | .09 | .04 | .01 |
| ☐ 651 | Jeff Russell | .03 | .01 | .00 |
| ☐ 652 | Joe Nolan | .03 | .01 | .00 |
| ☐ 653 | Mark Brouhard | .03 | .01 | .00 |
| ☐ 654 | Dave Anderson | .03 | .01 | .00 |
| ☐ 655 | Joaquin Andujar | .09 | .04 | .01 |
| ☐ 656 | Chuck Cottier MGR | .03 | .01 | .00 |
| ☐ 657 | Jim Slaton | .03 | .01 | .00 |
| ☐ 658 | Mike Stenhouse | .05 | .02 | .00 |
| ☐ 659 | Checklist: 529–660 | .08 | .01 | .00 |
| ☐ 660 | Tony Gwynn | .30 | .12 | .03 |
| ☐ 661 | Steve Crawford | .03 | .01 | .00 |
| ☐ 662 | Mike Heath | .03 | .01 | .00 |
| ☐ 663 | Luis Aguayo | .03 | .01 | .00 |
| ☐ 664 | Steve Farr | .12 | .05 | .01 |
| ☐ 665 | Don Mattingly | 1.20 | .55 | .12 |
| ☐ 666 | Mike LaCoss | .03 | .01 | .00 |
| ☐ 667 | Dave Engle | .05 | .02 | .00 |
| ☐ 668 | Steve Trout | .05 | .02 | .00 |
| ☐ 669 | Lee Lacy | .05 | .02 | .00 |
| ☐ 670 | Tom Seaver | .25 | .10 | .02 |
| ☐ 671 | Dane Iorg | .03 | .01 | .00 |
| ☐ 672 | Juan Berenguer | .03 | .01 | .00 |
| ☐ 673 | Buck Martinez | .03 | .01 | .00 |
| ☐ 674 | Atlee Hammaker | .06 | .02 | .00 |
| ☐ 675 | Tony Perez | .11 | .05 | .01 |
| ☐ 676 | Albert Hall | .12 | .05 | .01 |
| ☐ 677 | Wally Backman | .03 | .01 | .00 |
| ☐ 678 | Joe McLaughlin | .03 | .01 | .00 |
| ☐ 679 | Bob Kearney | .03 | .01 | .00 |
| ☐ 680 | Jerry Reuss | .05 | .02 | .00 |
| ☐ 681 | Ben Oglivie | .05 | .02 | .00 |
| ☐ 682 | Doug Corbett | .03 | .01 | .00 |
| ☐ 683 | Whitey Herzog MGR | .05 | .02 | .00 |
| ☐ 684 | Bill Doran | .07 | .03 | .01 |
| ☐ 685 | Bill Caudill | .07 | .03 | .01 |
| ☐ 686 | Mike Easler | .06 | .02 | .00 |
| ☐ 687 | Bill Gullickson | .05 | .02 | .00 |
| ☐ 688 | Len Matuszek | .03 | .01 | .00 |
| ☐ 689 | Luis DeLeon | .03 | .01 | .00 |
| ☐ 690 | Alan Trammell | .20 | .09 | .02 |
| ☐ 691 | Dennis Rasmussen | .08 | .03 | .01 |
| ☐ 692 | Randy Bush | .03 | .01 | .00 |
| ☐ 693 | Tim Stoddard | .03 | .01 | .00 |
| ☐ 694 | Joe Carter | .10 | .04 | .01 |
| ☐ 695 | Rick Rhoden | .05 | .02 | .00 |
| ☐ 696 | John Rabb | .05 | .02 | .00 |
| ☐ 697 | Onix Concepcion | .03 | .01 | .00 |
| ☐ 698 | Jorge Bell | .09 | .04 | .01 |

|  | | MINT | VG-E | F-G |
|---|---|---|---|---|
| ☐ 699 | Donnie Moore | .07 | .03 | .01 |
| ☐ 700 | Eddie Murray | .40 | .18 | .04 |
|  | AL ALL-STARS | | | |
|  | (701–711) | | | |
| ☐ 701 | Eddie Murray AS | .25 | .10 | .02 |
| ☐ 702 | Damaso Garcia AS | .06 | .02 | .00 |
| ☐ 703 | George Brett AS | .25 | .10 | .02 |
| ☐ 704 | Cal Ripken AS | .25 | .10 | .02 |
| ☐ 705 | Dave Winfield AS | .20 | .09 | .02 |
| ☐ 706 | Rickey Henderson AS | .25 | .10 | .02 |
| ☐ 707 | Tony Armas AS | .07 | .03 | .01 |
| ☐ 708 | Lance Parrish AS | .15 | .06 | .01 |
| ☐ 709 | Mike Boddicker AS | .07 | .03 | .01 |
| ☐ 710 | Frank Viola AS | .07 | .03 | .01 |
| ☐ 711 | Dan Quisenberry AS | .15 | .06 | .01 |
|  | NL ALL-STARS | | | |
|  | (712–722) | | | |
| ☐ 712 | Keith Hernandez AS | .16 | .07 | .01 |
| ☐ 713 | Ryne Sandberg AS | .20 | .09 | .02 |
| ☐ 714 | Mike Schmidt AS | .25 | .10 | .02 |
| ☐ 715 | Ozzie Smith AS | .07 | .03 | .01 |
| ☐ 716 | Dale Murphy AS | .25 | .10 | .02 |
| ☐ 717 | Tony Gwynn AS | .20 | .09 | .02 |
| ☐ 718 | Jeff Leonard AS | .06 | .02 | .00 |
| ☐ 719 | Gary Carter AS | .18 | .08 | .01 |
| ☐ 720 | Rick Sutcliffe AS | .14 | .06 | .01 |
| ☐ 721 | Bob Knepper AS | .06 | .02 | .00 |
| ☐ 722 | Bruce Sutter AS | .14 | .06 | .01 |
| ☐ 723 | Dave Stewart | .03 | .01 | .00 |
| ☐ 724 | Oscar Gamble | .03 | .01 | .00 |
| ☐ 725 | Floyd Bannister | .05 | .02 | .00 |
| ☐ 726 | Al Bumbry | .03 | .01 | .00 |
| ☐ 727 | Frank Pastore | .03 | .01 | .00 |
| ☐ 728 | Bob Bailor | .03 | .01 | .00 |
| ☐ 729 | Don Sutton | .11 | .05 | .01 |
| ☐ 730 | Dave Kingman | .10 | .04 | .01 |
| ☐ 731 | Neil Allen | .05 | .02 | .00 |
| ☐ 732 | John McNamara MGR | .03 | .01 | .00 |
| ☐ 733 | Tony Scott | .03 | .01 | .00 |
| ☐ 734 | John Henry Johnson | .03 | .01 | .00 |
| ☐ 735 | Garry Templeton | .10 | .04 | .01 |
| ☐ 736 | Jerry Mumphrey | .05 | .02 | .00 |
| ☐ 737 | Bo Diaz | .05 | .02 | .00 |
| ☐ 738 | Omar Moreno | .05 | .02 | .00 |
| ☐ 739 | Ernie Camacho | .03 | .01 | .00 |
| ☐ 740 | Jack Clark | .14 | .06 | .01 |
| ☐ 741 | John Butcher | .03 | .01 | .00 |
| ☐ 742 | Ron Hassey | .03 | .01 | .00 |
| ☐ 743 | Frank White | .06 | .02 | .00 |
| ☐ 744 | Doug Bair | .03 | .01 | .00 |
| ☐ 745 | Buddy Bell | .10 | .04 | .01 |
| ☐ 746 | Jim Clancy | .03 | .01 | .00 |
| ☐ 747 | Alex Trevino | .03 | .01 | .00 |

| | MINT | VG-E | F-G |
|---|---|---|---|
| ☐ **748** Lee Mazzilli | .05 | .02 | .00 |
| ☐ **749** Julio Cruz | .03 | .01 | .00 |
| ☐ **750** Rollie Fingers | .15 | .06 | .01 |
| ☐ **751** Kelvin Chapman | .12 | .05 | .01 |
| ☐ **752** Bob Owchinko | .03 | .01 | .00 |
| ☐ **753** Greg Brock | .07 | .03 | .01 |
| ☐ **754** Larry Milbourne | .03 | .01 | .00 |
| ☐ **755** Ken Singleton | .08 | .03 | .01 |
| ☐ **756** Rob Picciolo | .03 | .01 | .00 |
| ☐ **757** Willie McGee | .35 | .15 | .03 |
| ☐ **758** Ray Burris | .03 | .01 | .00 |
| ☐ **759** Jim Fanning MGR | .03 | .01 | .00 |
| ☐ **760** Nolan Ryan | .30 | .12 | .03 |
| ☐ **761** Jerry Remy | .03 | .01 | .00 |
| ☐ **762** Eddie Whitson | .06 | .02 | .00 |
| ☐ **763** Kiko Garcia | .03 | .01 | .00 |
| ☐ **764** Jamie Easterly | .03 | .01 | .00 |
| ☐ **765** Willie Randolph | .06 | .02 | .00 |
| ☐ **766** Paul Mirabella | .03 | .01 | .00 |
| ☐ **767** Darrell Brown | .03 | .01 | .00 |
| ☐ **768** Ron Cey | .10 | .04 | .01 |
| ☐ **769** Joe Cowley | .05 | .02 | .00 |
| ☐ **770** Carlton Fisk | .14 | .06 | .01 |
| ☐ **771** Geoff Zahn | .05 | .02 | .00 |
| ☐ **772** Johnnie LeMaster | .03 | .01 | .00 |
| ☐ **773** Hal McRae | .05 | .02 | .00 |
| ☐ **774** Dennis Lamp | .03 | .01 | .00 |
| ☐ **775** Mookie Wilson | .07 | .03 | .01 |
| ☐ **776** Jerry Royster | .03 | .01 | .00 |
| ☐ **777** Ned Yost | .03 | .01 | .00 |
| ☐ **778** Mike Davis | .08 | .03 | .01 |
| ☐ **779** Nick Esasky | .07 | .03 | .01 |
| ☐ **780** Mike Flanagan | .06 | .02 | .00 |
| ☐ **781** Jim Gantner | .05 | .02 | .00 |
| ☐ **782** Tom Niedenfuer | .06 | .02 | .00 |
| ☐ **783** Mike Jorgensen | .03 | .01 | .00 |
| ☐ **784** Checklist: 661–792 | .08 | .01 | .00 |
| ☐ **785** Tony Armas | .11 | .05 | .01 |
| ☐ **786** Enos Cabell | .03 | .01 | .00 |
| ☐ **787** Jim Wohlford | .03 | .01 | .00 |
| ☐ **788** Steve Comer | .03 | .01 | .00 |
| ☐ **789** Luis Salazar | .03 | .01 | .00 |
| ☐ **790** Ron Guidry | .16 | .07 | .01 |
| ☐ **791** Ivan DeJesus | .03 | .01 | .00 |
| ☐ **792** Darrell Evans | .12 | .03 | .01 |

## 1985 TOPPS EXTENDED

*The cards in this 132 card set measure 2½" by 3½". In its now standard procedure, Topps issued its traded set for the fifth year in a row. Because all photos and statistics of its regular set for the year were developed during the fall and winter months of the preceding year, players who changed teams during the fall, winter and spring months are portrayed in the 1985 regular issue set with the teams they were with in 1984. The traded set amends the shortcomings of the regular set by presenting the players with their proper teams for the current year. Rookies not contained in the regular set are also picked up in the traded set. Again this year, the Topps affiliate in Ireland printed the cards, and the cards were available through hobby channels only.*

Complete Set: M-11.00; VG-E-5.25; F-G-1.10

| | MINT | VG-E | F-G |
|---|---|---|---|
| Common Player | .06 | .02 | .00 |
| ☐ 1 T Don Aase | .10 | .02 | .00 |
| ☐ 2 T Bill Almon | .06 | .02 | .00 |
| ☐ 3 T Benny Ayala | .06 | .02 | .00 |
| ☐ 4 T Dusty Baker | .10 | .04 | .01 |
| ☐ 5 T George Bamberger MGR | .06 | .02 | .00 |
| ☐ 6 T Dale Berra | .10 | .04 | .01 |
| ☐ 7 T Rich Bordi | .06 | .02 | .00 |
| ☐ 8 T Daryl Boston | .20 | .09 | .02 |
| ☐ 9 T Hubie Brooks | .15 | .06 | .01 |
| ☐ 10 T Chris Brown | .65 | .30 | .06 |
| ☐ 11 T Tom Browning | .75 | .35 | .07 |
| ☐ 12 T Al Bumbry | .06 | .02 | .00 |

| | MINT | VG-E | F-G | | MINT | VG-E | F-G |
|---|---|---|---|---|---|---|---|
| 13 T Ray Burris | .06 | .02 | .00 | 66 T Steve Kemp | .10 | .04 | .01 |
| 14 T Jeff Burroughs | .06 | .02 | .00 | 67 T Bruce Kison | .06 | .02 | .00 |
| 15 T Bill Campbell | .06 | .02 | .00 | 68 T Alan Knicely | .06 | .02 | .00 |
| 16 T Don Carman | .20 | .09 | .02 | 69 T Mike LaCoss | .06 | .02 | .00 |
| 17 T Gary Carter | .75 | .35 | .07 | 70 T Lee Lacy | .10 | .04 | .01 |
| 18 T Bobby Castillo | .06 | .02 | .00 | 71 T Dave LaPoint | .06 | .02 | .00 |
| 19 T Bill Caudill | .10 | .04 | .01 | 72 T Gary Lavelle | .06 | .02 | .00 |
| 20 T Rick Cerone | .10 | .04 | .01 | 73 T Vance Law | .06 | .02 | .00 |
| 21 T Bryan Clark | .06 | .02 | .00 | 74 T Johnnie LeMaster | .06 | .02 | .00 |
| 22 T Jack Clark | .25 | .10 | .02 | 75 T Sixto Lezcano | .06 | .02 | .00 |
| 23 T Pat Clements | .25 | .10 | .02 | 76 T Tim Lollar | .06 | .02 | .00 |
| 24 T Vince Coleman | 2.50 | 1.15 | .25 | 77 T Fred Lynn | .20 | .09 | .02 |
| 25 T Dave Collins | .10 | .04 | .01 | 78 T Billy Martin MGR | .12 | .05 | .01 |
| 26 T Danny Darwin | .06 | .02 | .00 | 79 T Ron Mathis | .15 | .06 | .01 |
| 27 T Jim Davenport MGR | .06 | .02 | .00 | 80 T Len Matuszek | .06 | .02 | .00 |
| 28 T Jerry Davis | .12 | .05 | .01 | 81 T Gene Mauch MGR | .06 | .02 | .00 |
| 29 T Brian Dayett | .06 | .02 | .00 | 82 T Oddibe McDowell | 1.00 | .45 | .10 |
| 30 T Ivan DeJesus | .06 | .02 | .00 | 83 T Roger McDowell | .55 | .25 | .05 |
| 31 T Ken Dixon | .15 | .06 | .01 | 84 T John McNamara MGR | .06 | .02 | .00 |
| 32 T Mariano Duncan | .65 | .30 | .06 | 85 T Donnie Moore | .06 | .02 | .00 |
| 33 T John Felske MGR | .06 | .02 | .00 | 86 T Gene Nelson | .06 | .02 | .00 |
| 34 T Mike Fitzgerald | .06 | .02 | .00 | 87 T Steve Nicosia | .06 | .02 | .00 |
| 35 T Ray Fontenot | .06 | .02 | .00 | 88 T Al Oliver | .15 | .06 | .01 |
| 36 T Greg Gagne | .15 | .06 | .01 | 89 T Joe Orsulak | .30 | .12 | .03 |
| 37 T Oscar Gamble | .10 | .04 | .01 | 90 T Rob Picciolo | .06 | .02 | .00 |
| 38 T Scott Garrelts | .25 | .10 | .02 | 91 T Chris Pittaro | .20 | .09 | .02 |
| 39 T Bob L. Gibson | .06 | .02 | .00 | 92 T Jim Presley | 1.00 | .45 | .10 |
| 40 T Jim Gott | .06 | .02 | .00 | 93 T Rick Reuschel | .10 | .04 | .01 |
| 41 T David Green | .10 | .04 | .01 | 94 T Bert Roberge | .06 | .02 | .00 |
| 42 T Alfredo Griffin | .10 | .04 | .01 | 95 T Bob Rodgers MGR | .06 | .02 | .00 |
| 43 T Ozzie Guillen | .75 | .35 | .07 | 96 T Jerry Royster | .06 | .02 | .00 |
| 44 T Eddie Haas MGR | .06 | .02 | .00 | 97 T Dave Rozema | .06 | .02 | .00 |
| 45 T Terry Harper | .06 | .02 | .00 | 98 T Dave Rucker | .06 | .02 | .00 |
| 46 T Toby Harrah | .10 | .04 | .01 | 99 T Vern Ruhle | .06 | .02 | .00 |
| 47 T Greg Harris | .06 | .02 | .00 | 100 T Paul Runge | .15 | .06 | .01 |
| 48 T Ron Hassey | .06 | .02 | .00 | 101 T Mark Salas | .35 | .15 | .03 |
| 49 T Rickey Henderson | .75 | .35 | .07 | 102 T Luis Salazar | .06 | .02 | .00 |
| 50 T Steve Henderson | .06 | .02 | .00 | 103 T Joe Sambito | .10 | .04 | .01 |
| 51 T George Hendrick | .10 | .04 | .01 | 104 T Rick Schu | .15 | .10 | .02 |
| 52 T Joe Hesketh | .30 | .12 | .03 | 105 T Donnie Scott | .06 | .02 | .00 |
| 53 T Teddy Higuera | .30 | .12 | .03 | 106 T Larry Sheets | .25 | .10 | .02 |
| 54 T Donnie Hill | .06 | .02 | .00 | 107 T Don Slaught | .06 | .02 | .00 |
| 55 T Al Holland | .10 | .04 | .01 | 108 T Roy Smalley | .10 | .04 | .01 |
| 56 T Burt Hooton | .06 | .02 | .00 | 109 T Lonnie Smith | .12 | .05 | .01 |
| 57 T Jay Howell | .12 | .05 | .01 | 110 T Nate Snell | .20 | .09 | .02 |
| 58 T Ken Howell | .20 | .09 | .02 | 111 T Chris Speier | .06 | .02 | .00 |
| 59 T LaMarr Hoyt | .12 | .05 | .01 | 112 T Mike Stenhouse | .10 | .04 | .01 |
| 60 T Tim Hulett | .20 | .09 | .02 | 113 T Tim Stoddard | .06 | .02 | .00 |
| 61 T Bob James | .10 | .04 | .01 | 114 T Jim Sundberg | .10 | .04 | .01 |
| 62 T Steve Jeltz | .15 | .06 | .01 | 115 T Bruce Sutter | .25 | .10 | .02 |
| 63 T Cliff Johnson | .06 | .02 | .00 | 116 T Don Sutton | .25 | .10 | .02 |
| 64 T Howard Johnson | .15 | .06 | .01 | 117 T Kent Tekulve | .10 | .04 | .01 |
| 65 T Ruppert Jones | .10 | .04 | .01 | 118 T Tom Tellman | .06 | .02 | .00 |

|  | MINT | VG-E | F-G |
|---|---|---|---|
| ☐ 119 T Walt Terrell | .10 | .04 | .01 |
| ☐ 120 T Mickey Tettleton | .15 | .06 | .01 |
| ☐ 121 T Derrel Thomas | .06 | .02 | .00 |
| ☐ 122 T Rich Thompson | .15 | .06 | .01 |
| ☐ 123 T Alex Trevino | .06 | .02 | .00 |
| ☐ 124 T John Tudor | .20 | .09 | .02 |
| ☐ 125 T Jose Uribe | .12 | .05 | .01 |
| ☐ 126 T Bobby Valentine MGR | .10 | .04 | .01 |
| ☐ 127 T Dave Von Ohlen | .06 | .02 | .00 |
| ☐ 128 T U. L. Washington | .06 | .02 | .00 |
| ☐ 129 T Earl Weaver MGR | .10 | .04 | .01 |
| ☐ 130 T Eddie Whitson | .10 | .04 | .01 |
| ☐ 131 T Herm Winningham | .20 | .09 | .02 |
| ☐ 132 T Checklist 1–132 | .10 | .01 | .00 |

## 1986 TOPPS

DON MATTINGLY

The cards in this 792 card set are standard sized (2½" by 3½"). The first seven cards are a tribute to Pete Rose and his career. The team leader cards were done differently with a simple player action shot on a white background; the player pictured is dubbed the "Dean" of that team, i.e., the player with the longest continuous service with that team. Topps again features a "Turn Back the Clock" series (401–405). Record breakers of the previous year are acknowledged on cards 201–207. Manager cards feature the team checklist on the reverse. The backs of all the cards have a distinctive red background. Topps also printed cards on the bottoms of their wax pack boxes; there are four different boxes, each with four cards. These 16 cards ("numbered" A through P) are listed

at the end of the checklist below but are not considered an integral part of the set.
Complete Set: M-17.50; VG-E-8.00; F-G-1.50

|  | MINT | VG-E | F-G |
|---|---|---|---|
| Common Player | .03 | .01 | .00 |
| ☐ 1 Pete Rose | .80 | .20 | .04 |
| ☐ 2 Rose Special: '63–'66 | .25 | .10 | .02 |
| ☐ 3 Rose Special: '67–'70 | .25 | .10 | .02 |
| ☐ 4 Rose Special: '71–'74 | .25 | .10 | .02 |
| ☐ 5 Rose Special: '75–'78 | .25 | .10 | .02 |
| ☐ 6 Rose Special: '79–'82 | .25 | .10 | .02 |
| ☐ 7 Rose Special: '83–'85 | .25 | .10 | .02 |
| ☐ 8 Dwayne Murphy | .06 | .02 | .00 |
| ☐ 9 Roy Smith | .03 | .01 | .00 |
| ☐ 10 Tony Gwynn | .20 | .09 | .02 |
| ☐ 11 Bob Ojeda | .05 | .02 | .00 |
| ☐ 12 Jose Uribe | .12 | .05 | .01 |
| ☐ 13 Bob Kearney | .03 | .01 | .00 |
| ☐ 14 Julio Cruz | .03 | .01 | .00 |
| ☐ 15 Eddie Whitson | .05 | .02 | .00 |
| ☐ 16 Rick Schu | .07 | .03 | .01 |
| ☐ 17 Mike Stenhouse | .03 | .01 | .00 |
| ☐ 18 Brent Gaff | .03 | .01 | .00 |
| ☐ 19 Rich Hebner | .03 | .01 | .00 |
| ☐ 20 Lou Whitaker | .14 | .06 | .01 |
| ☐ 21 George Bamberger MGR (checklist back) | .07 | .01 | .00 |
| ☐ 22 Duane Walker | .03 | .01 | .00 |
| ☐ 23 Manny Lee | .12 | .05 | .01 |
| ☐ 24 Len Barker | .05 | .02 | .00 |
| ☐ 25 Willie Wilson | .15 | .06 | .01 |
| ☐ 26 Frank DiPino | .05 | .02 | .00 |
| ☐ 27 Ray Knight | .05 | .02 | .00 |
| ☐ 28 Eric Davis | .07 | .03 | .01 |
| ☐ 29 Tony Phillips | .03 | .01 | .00 |
| ☐ 30 Eddie Murray | .35 | .15 | .03 |
| ☐ 31 Jamie Easterly | .03 | .01 | .00 |
| ☐ 32 Steve Yeager | .05 | .02 | .00 |
| ☐ 33 Jeff Lahti | .03 | .01 | .00 |
| ☐ 34 Ken Phelps | .03 | .01 | .00 |
| ☐ 35 Jeff Reardon | .06 | .02 | .00 |
| ☐ 36 Tigers Leaders Lance Parrish | .13 | .06 | .01 |
| ☐ 37 Mark Thurmond | .05 | .02 | .00 |
| ☐ 38 Glenn Hoffman | .03 | .01 | .00 |
| ☐ 39 Dave Rucker | .03 | .01 | .00 |
| ☐ 40 Ken Griffey | .06 | .02 | .00 |
| ☐ 41 Brad Wellman | .03 | .01 | .00 |
| ☐ 42 Geoff Zahn | .03 | .01 | .00 |
| ☐ 43 Dave Engle | .05 | .02 | .00 |
| ☐ 44 Lance McCullers | .20 | .09 | .02 |

|  | MINT | VG-E | F-G |
|---|---|---|---|
| 45 Damaso Garcia | .07 | .03 | .01 |
| 46 Billy Hatcher | .06 | .02 | .00 |
| *47 Juan Berenguer | .03 | .01 | .00 |
| 48 Bill Almon | .03 | .01 | .00 |
| 49 Rick Manning | .03 | .01 | .00 |
| 50 Dan Quisenberry | .15 | .06 | .01 |
| 51 Bobby Wine MGR ERR | .08 | .01 | .00 |
| (checklist back) | | | |
| (number of card on | | | |
| back is actually 57) | | | |
| 52 Chris Welsh | .03 | .01 | .00 |
| 53 Len Dykstra | .20 | .09 | .02 |
| 54 John Franco | .07 | .03 | .01 |
| 55 Fred Lynn | .15 | .06 | .01 |
| 56 Tom Niedenfuer | .06 | .02 | .00 |
| 57 Bill Doran | .09 | .04 | .01 |
| (see also 51) | | | |
| 58 Bill Krueger | .03 | .01 | .00 |
| 59 Andre Thornton | .07 | .03 | .01 |
| 60 Dwight Evans | .10 | .04 | .01 |
| 61 Karl Best | .12 | .05 | .01 |
| 62 Bob Boone | .05 | .02 | .00 |
| 63 Ron Roenicke | .03 | .01 | .00 |
| 64 Floyd Bannister | .05 | .02 | .00 |
| 65 Dan Driessen | .03 | .01 | .00 |
| 66 Cardinals Leaders | .06 | .02 | .00 |
| Bob Forsch | | | |
| 67 Carmelo Martinez | .06 | .02 | .00 |
| 68 Ed Lynch | .03 | .01 | .00 |
| 69 Luis Aguayo | .03 | .01 | .00 |
| 70 Dave Winfield | .30 | .12 | .03 |
| 71 Ken Schrom | .03 | .01 | .00 |
| 72 Shawon Dunston | .06 | .02 | .00 |
| 73 Randy O'Neal | .07 | .03 | .01 |
| 74 Rance Mulliniks | .03 | .01 | .00 |
| 75 Jose DeLeon | .05 | .02 | .00 |
| 76 Dion James | .05 | .02 | .00 |
| 77 Charlie Leibrandt | .06 | .02 | .00 |
| 78 Bruce Benedict | .03 | .01 | .00 |
| 79 Dave Schmidt | .03 | .01 | .00 |
| 80 Darryl Strawberry | .30 | .12 | .03 |
| 80 Gene Mauch MGR | .07 | .01 | .00 |
| (checklist back) | | | |
| 82 Tippy Martinez | .03 | .01 | .00 |
| 83 Phil Garner | .03 | .01 | .00 |
| 84 Curt Young | .03 | .01 | .00 |
| 85 Tony Perez | .11 | .05 | .01 |
| 86 Tom Waddell | .03 | .01 | .00 |
| 87 Candy Maldonado | .03 | .01 | .00 |
| 88 Tom Nieto | .03 | .01 | .00 |
| 89 Randy St. Claire | .06 | .02 | .00 |
| 90 Garry Templeton | .09 | .04 | .01 |
| 91 Steve Crawford | .03 | .01 | .00 |

|  | MINT | VG-E | F-G |
|---|---|---|---|
| 92 Al Cowens | .05 | .02 | .00 |
| 93 Scot Thompson | .03 | .01 | .00 |
| 94 Rich Bordi | .03 | .01 | .00 |
| 95 Ozzie Virgil | .05 | .02 | .00 |
| 96 Blue Jays Leaders | .06 | .02 | .00 |
| Jim Clancy | | | |
| 97 Gary Gaetti | .05 | .02 | .00 |
| 98 Dick Ruthven | .03 | .01 | .00 |
| 99 Buddy Biancalana | .05 | .02 | .00 |
| 100 Nolan Ryan | .30 | .12 | .03 |
| 101 Dave Bergman | .03 | .01 | .00 |
| 102 Joe Orsulak | .25 | .10 | .02 |
| 103 Luis Salazar | .03 | .01 | .00 |
| 104 Sid Fernandez | .07 | .03 | .01 |
| 105 Gary Ward | .05 | .02 | .00 |
| 106 Ray Burris | .03 | .01 | .00 |
| 107 Rafael Ramirez | .03 | .01 | .00 |
| 108 Ted Power | .05 | .02 | .00 |
| 109 Len Matuszek | .03 | .01 | .00 |
| 110 Scott McGregor | .06 | .02 | .00 |
| 111 Roger Craig MGR | .07 | .01 | .00 |
| (checklist back) | | | |
| 112 Bill Campbell | .03 | .01 | .00 |
| 113 U.L. Washington | .03 | .01 | .00 |
| 114 Mike Brown | .03 | .01 | .00 |
| 115 Jay Howell | .05 | .02 | .00 |
| 116 Brook Jacoby | .09 | .04 | .01 |
| 117 Bruce Kison | .03 | .01 | .00 |
| 118 Jerry Royster | .03 | .01 | .00 |
| 119 Barry Bonnell | .03 | .01 | .00 |
| 120 Steve Carlton | .30 | .12 | .03 |
| 121 Nelson Simmons | .25 | .10 | .02 |
| 122 Pete Filson | .03 | .01 | .00 |
| 123 Greg Walker | .11 | .05 | .01 |
| 124 Luis Sanchez | .03 | .01 | .00 |
| 125 Dave Lopes | .06 | .02 | .00 |
| 126 Mets Leaders | .06 | .02 | .00 |
| Mookie Wilson | | | |
| 127 Jack Howell | .35 | .15 | .03 |
| 128 John Wathan | .03 | .01 | .00 |
| 129 Jeff Dedmon | .03 | .01 | .00 |
| 130 Alan Trammell | .18 | .08 | .01 |
| 131 Checklist: 1–132 | .07 | .01 | .00 |
| 132 Razor Shines | .06 | .02 | .00 |
| 133 Andy McGaffigan | .03 | .01 | .00 |
| 134 Carney Lansford | .09 | .04 | .01 |
| 135 Joe Niekro | .06 | .02 | .00 |
| 136 Mike Hargrove | .05 | .02 | .00 |
| 137 Charlie Moore | .03 | .01 | .00 |
| 138 Mark Davis | .03 | .01 | .00 |
| 139 Daryl Boston | .07 | .03 | .01 |
| 140 John Candelaria | .06 | .02 | .00 |

| | MINT | VG-E | F-G |
|---|---|---|---|
| ☐ 141 Chuck Cottier MGR .... (checklist back) (see also 171) | .07 | .01 | .00 |
| ☐ 142 Bob Jones | .03 | .01 | .00 |
| ☐ 143 Dave Van Gorder | .03 | .01 | .00 |
| ☐ 144 Doug Sisk | .03 | .01 | .00 |
| ☐ 145 Pedro Guerrero | .20 | .09 | .02 |
| ☐ 146 Jack Perconte | .03 | .01 | .00 |
| ☐ 147 Larry Sheets | .10 | .04 | .01 |
| ☐ 148 Mike Heath | .03 | .01 | .00 |
| ☐ 149 Brett Butler | .09 | .04 | .01 |
| ☐ 150 Joaquin Andujar | .08 | .03 | .01 |
| ☐ 151 Dave Stapleton | .03 | .01 | .00 |
| ☐ 152 Mike Morgan | .03 | .01 | .00 |
| ☐ 153 Ricky Adams | .03 | .01 | .00 |
| ☐ 154 Bert Roberge | .03 | .01 | .00 |
| ☐ 155 Bob Grich | .06 | .02 | .00 |
| ☐ 156 White Sox Leaders .... Richard Dotson | .06 | .02 | .00 |
| ☐ 157 Ron Hassey | .03 | .01 | .00 |
| ☐ 158 Derrel Thomas | .03 | .01 | .00 |
| ☐ 159 Orel Hershiser | .30 | .12 | .03 |
| ☐ 160 Chet Lemon | .06 | .02 | .00 |
| ☐ 161 Lee Tunnell | .03 | .01 | .00 |
| ☐ 162 Greg Gagne | .03 | .01 | .00 |
| ☐ 163 Pete Ladd | .03 | .01 | .00 |
| ☐ 164 Steve Balboni | .06 | .02 | .00 |
| ☐ 165 Mike Davis | .06 | .02 | .00 |
| ☐ 166 Dickie Thon | .05 | .02 | .00 |
| ☐ 167 Zane Smith | .06 | .02 | .00 |
| ☐ 168 Jeff Burroughs | .03 | .01 | .00 |
| ☐ 169 George Wright | .03 | .01 | .00 |
| ☐ 170 Gary Carter | .30 | .12 | .03 |
| ☐ 171 Bob Rodgers MGR ERR (checklist back) (number of card on back actually 141) | .09 | .01 | .00 |
| ☐ 172 Jerry Reed | .10 | .04 | .01 |
| ☐ 173 Wayne Gross | .03 | .01 | .00 |
| ☐ 174 Brian Snyder | .15 | .06 | .01 |
| ☐ 175 Steve Sax | .12 | .05 | .01 |
| ☐ 176 Jay Tibbs | .03 | .01 | .00 |
| ☐ 177 Joel Youngblood | .03 | .01 | .00 |
| ☐ 178 Ivan DeJesus | .03 | .01 | .00 |
| ☐ 179 Stu Cliburn | .20 | .09 | .02 |
| ☐ 180 Don Mattingly | .75 | .35 | .07 |
| ☐ 181 Al Nipper | .05 | .02 | .00 |
| ☐ 182 Bobby Brown | .03 | .01 | .00 |
| ☐ 183 Larry Andersen | .03 | .01 | .00 |
| ☐ 184 Tim Laudner | .03 | .01 | .00 |
| ☐ 185 Rollie Fingers | .14 | .06 | .01 |
| ☐ 186 Astros Leaders Jose Cruz | .07 | .03 | .01 |

| | MINT | VG-E | F-G |
|---|---|---|---|
| ☐ 187 Scott Fletcher | .03 | .01 | .00 |
| ☐ 188 Bob Dernier | .05 | .02 | .00 |
| ☐ 189 Mike Mason | .03 | .01 | .00 |
| ☐ 190 George Hendrick | .07 | .03 | .01 |
| ☐ 191 Wally Backman | .03 | .01 | .00 |
| ☐ 192 Milt Wilcox | .03 | .01 | .00 |
| ☐ 193 Daryl Sconiers | .03 | .01 | .00 |
| ☐ 194 Craig McMurtry | .03 | .01 | .00 |
| ☐ 195 Dave Concepcion | .07 | .03 | .01 |
| ☐ 196 Doyle Alexander | .05 | .02 | .00 |
| ☐ 197 Enos Cabell | .03 | .01 | .00 |
| ☐ 198 Ken Dixon | .07 | .03 | .01 |
| ☐ 199 Dick Howser MGR (checklist back) | .07 | .01 | .00 |
| ☐ 200 Mike Schmidt | .35 | .15 | .03 |
| ☐ 201 RB: Vince Coleman | .25 | .10 | .02 |
| ☐ 202 RB: Dwight Gooden .... Youngest 20 Game Winner | .50 | .22 | .05 |
| ☐ 203 RB: Keith Hernandez ... Most Game Winning RBI | .15 | .06 | .01 |
| ☐ 204 RB: Phil Niekro Oldest Shutout Pitcher | .13 | .06 | .01 |
| ☐ 205 RB: Tony Perez Oldest Grand Slammer | .10 | .04 | .01 |
| ☐ 206 RB: Pete Rose Most Hits, Lifetime | .35 | .15 | .03 |
| ☐ 207 RB: Fernando Valenzuela | .17 | .07 | .01 |
| ☐ 208 Ramon Romero | .10 | .04 | .01 |
| ☐ 209 Randy Ready | .07 | .03 | .01 |
| ☐ 210 Calvin Schiraldi | .07 | .03 | .01 |
| ☐ 211 Ed Wojna | .15 | .06 | .01 |
| ☐ 212 Chris Speier | .03 | .01 | .00 |
| ☐ 213 Bob Shirley | .03 | .01 | .00 |
| ☐ 214 Randy Bush | .03 | .01 | .00 |
| ☐ 215 Frank White | .06 | .02 | .00 |
| ☐ 216 A's Leaders Dwayne Murphy | .06 | .02 | .00 |
| ☐ 217 Bill Scherrer | .03 | .01 | .00 |
| ☐ 218 Randy Hunt | .10 | .04 | .01 |
| ☐ 219 Dennis Lamp | .03 | .01 | .00 |
| ☐ 220 Bob Horner | .16 | .07 | .01 |
| ☐ 221 Dave Henderson | .05 | .02 | .00 |
| ☐ 222 Craig Gerber | .12 | .05 | .01 |
| ☐ 223 Atlee Hammaker | .05 | .02 | .00 |
| ☐ 224 Cesar Cedeno | .06 | .02 | .00 |
| ☐ 225 Ron Darling | .16 | .07 | .01 |
| ☐ 226 Lee Lacy | .06 | .02 | .00 |
| ☐ 227 Al Jones | .03 | .01 | .00 |
| ☐ 228 Tom Lawless | .03 | .01 | .00 |
| ☐ 229 Bill Gullickson | .05 | .02 | .00 |
| ☐ 230 Terry Kennedy | .06 | .02 | .00 |

| | MINT | VG-E | F-G |
|---|---|---|---|
| ☐ 231 Jim Frey MGR | .07 | .01 | .00 |
| (checklist back) | | | |
| ☐ 232 Rick Rhoden | .05 | .02 | .00 |
| ☐ 233 Steve Lyons | .09 | .04 | .01 |
| ☐ 234 Doug Corbett | .03 | .01 | .00 |
| ☐ 235 Butch Wynegar | .05 | .02 | .00 |
| ☐ 236 Frank Eufemia | .12 | .05 | .01 |
| ☐ 237 Ted Simmons | .10 | .04 | .01 |
| ☐ 238 Larry Parrish | .06 | .02 | .00 |
| ☐ 239 Joel Skinner | .05 | .02 | .00 |
| ☐ 240 Tommy John | .12 | .05 | .01 |
| ☐ 241 Tony Fernandez | .08 | .03 | .01 |
| ☐ 242 Rich Thompson | .10 | .04 | .01 |
| ☐ 243 Johnny Grubb | .03 | .01 | .00 |
| ☐ 244 Craig Lefferts | .03 | .01 | .00 |
| ☐ 245 Jim Sundberg | .05 | .02 | .00 |
| ☐ 246 Phillies Leaders | .15 | .06 | .01 |
| Steve Carlton | | | |
| ☐ 247 Terry Harper | .03 | .01 | .00 |
| ☐ 248 Spike Owen | .03 | .01 | .00 |
| ☐ 249 Rob Deer | .07 | .03 | .01 |
| ☐ 250 Dwight Gooden | 1.50 | .70 | .15 |
| ☐ 251 Rich Dauer | .03 | .01 | .00 |
| ☐ 252 Bobby Castillo | .03 | .01 | .00 |
| ☐ 253 Dann Bilardello | .03 | .01 | .00 |
| ☐ 254 Ozzie Guillen | .50 | .22 | .05 |
| ☐ 255 Tony Armas | .10 | .04 | .01 |
| ☐ 256 Kurt Kepshire | .03 | .01 | .00 |
| ☐ 257 Doug DeCinces | .08 | .03 | .01 |
| ☐ 258 Tim Burke | .20 | .09 | .02 |
| ☐ 259 Dan Pasqua | .18 | .08 | .01 |
| ☐ 260 Tony Pena | .12 | .05 | .01 |
| ☐ 261 Bobby Valentine MGR | .07 | .01 | .00 |
| (checklist back) | | | |
| ☐ 262 Mario Ramirez | .03 | .01 | .00 |
| ☐ 263 Checklist: 133–264 | .07 | .01 | .00 |
| ☐ 264 Darren Daulton | .16 | .07 | .01 |
| ☐ 265 Ron Davis | .05 | .02 | .00 |
| ☐ 266 Keith Moreland | .05 | .02 | .00 |
| ☐ 267 Paul Molitor | .10 | .04 | .01 |
| ☐ 268 Mike Scott | .05 | .02 | .00 |
| ☐ 269 Dane Iorg | .03 | .01 | .00 |
| ☐ 270 Jack Morris | .14 | .06 | .01 |
| ☐ 271 Dave Collins | .05 | .02 | .00 |
| ☐ 272 Tim Tolman | .10 | .04 | .01 |
| ☐ 273 Jerry Willard | .03 | .01 | .00 |
| ☐ 274 Ron Gardenhire | .03 | .01 | .00 |
| ☐ 275 Charlie Hough | .05 | .02 | .00 |
| ☐ 276 Yankees Leaders | .06 | .02 | .00 |
| Willie Randolph | | | |
| ☐ 277 Jaime Cocanower | .03 | .01 | .00 |
| ☐ 278 Sixto Lezcano | .03 | .01 | .00 |
| ☐ 279 Al Pardo | .15 | .06 | .01 |

| | MINT | VG-E | F-G |
|---|---|---|---|
| ☐ 280 Tim Raines | .18 | .08 | .01 |
| ☐ 281 Steve Mura | .03 | .01 | .00 |
| ☐ 282 Jerry Mumphrey | .03 | .01 | .00 |
| ☐ 283 Mike Fischlin | .03 | .01 | .00 |
| ☐ 284 Brian Dayett | .03 | .01 | .00 |
| ☐ 285 Buddy Bell | .10 | .04 | .01 |
| ☐ 286 Luis DeLeon | .03 | .01 | .00 |
| ☐ 287 John Christensen | .09 | .04 | .01 |
| ☐ 288 Don Aase | .03 | .01 | .00 |
| ☐ 289 Johnnie LeMaster | .03 | .01 | .00 |
| ☐ 290 Carlton Fisk | .14 | .06 | .01 |
| ☐ 291 Tom Lasorda MGR | .09 | .01 | .00 |
| (checklist back) | | | |
| ☐ 292 Chuck Porter | .03 | .01 | .00 |
| ☐ 293 Chris Chambliss | .05 | .02 | .00 |
| ☐ 294 Danny Cox | .11 | .05 | .01 |
| ☐ 295 Kirk Gibson | .18 | .08 | .01 |
| ☐ 296 Geno Petralli | .03 | .01 | .00 |
| ☐ 297 Tim Lollar | .03 | .01 | .00 |
| ☐ 298 Craig Reynolds | .03 | .01 | .00 |
| ☐ 299 Bryn Smith | .05 | .02 | .00 |
| ☐ 300 George Brett | .40 | .18 | .04 |
| ☐ 301 Dennis Rasmussen | .03 | .01 | .00 |
| ☐ 302 Greg Gross | .03 | .01 | .00 |
| ☐ 303 Curt Wardle | .11 | .05 | .01 |
| ☐ 304 Mike Gallego | .12 | .05 | .01 |
| ☐ 305 Phil Bradley | .16 | .07 | .01 |
| ☐ 306 Padres Leaders | .06 | .02 | .00 |
| Terry Kennedy | | | |
| ☐ 307 Dave Sax | .03 | .01 | .00 |
| ☐ 308 Ray Fontenot | .03 | .01 | .00 |
| ☐ 309 John Shelby | .03 | .01 | .00 |
| ☐ 310 Greg Minton | .03 | .01 | .00 |
| ☐ 311 Dick Schofield | .05 | .02 | .00 |
| ☐ 312 Tom Filer | .05 | .02 | .00 |
| ☐ 313 Joe De Sa | .15 | .06 | .01 |
| ☐ 314 Frank Pastore | .03 | .01 | .00 |
| ☐ 315 Mookie Wilson | .06 | .02 | .00 |
| ☐ 316 Sammy Khalifa | .10 | .04 | .01 |
| ☐ 317 Ed Romero | .03 | .01 | .00 |
| ☐ 318 Terry Whitfield | .03 | .01 | .00 |
| ☐ 319 Rick Camp | .03 | .01 | .00 |
| ☐ 320 Jim Rice | .25 | .10 | .02 |
| ☐ 321 Earl Weaver MGR | .09 | .01 | .00 |
| (checklist back) | | | |
| ☐ 322 Bob Forsch | .05 | .02 | .00 |
| ☐ 323 Jerry Davis | .07 | .03 | .01 |
| ☐ 324 Dan Schatzeder | .03 | .01 | .00 |
| ☐ 325 Juan Beniquez | .05 | .02 | .00 |
| ☐ 326 Kent Tekulve | .05 | .02 | .00 |
| ☐ 327 Mike Pagliarulo | .06 | .02 | .00 |
| ☐ 328 Pete O'Brien | .05 | .02 | .00 |
| ☐ 329 Kirby Puckett | .10 | .04 | .01 |

| | MINT | VG-E | F-G |
|---|---|---|---|
| ☐ 330 Rick Sutcliffe | .13 | .06 | .01 |
| ☐ 331 Alan Ashby | .03 | .01 | .00 |
| ☐ 332 Darryl Motley | .05 | .02 | .00 |
| ☐ 333 Tom Henke | .06 | .02 | .00 |
| ☐ 334 Ken Oberkfell | .03 | .01 | .00 |
| ☐ 335 Don Sutton | .13 | .06 | .01 |
| ☐ 336 Indians Leaders | .06 | .02 | .00 |
|     Andre Thornton | | | |
| ☐ 337 Darnell Coles | .06 | .02 | .00 |
| ☐ 338 Jorge Bell | .11 | .05 | .01 |
| ☐ 339 Bruce Berenyi | .03 | .01 | .00 |
| ☐ 340 Cal Ripken | .40 | .18 | .04 |
| ☐ 341 Frank Williams | .03 | .01 | .00 |
| ☐ 342 Gary Redus | .05 | .02 | .00 |
| ☐ 343 Carlos Diaz | .03 | .01 | .00 |
| ☐ 344 Jim Wohlford | .03 | .01 | .00 |
| ☐ 345 Donnie Moore | .05 | .02 | .00 |
| ☐ 346 Bryan Little | .03 | .01 | .00 |
| ☐ 347 Teddy Higuera | .30 | .12 | .03 |
| ☐ 348 Cliff Johnson | .03 | .01 | .00 |
| ☐ 349 Mark Clear | .03 | .01 | .00 |
| ☐ 350 Jack Clark | .14 | .06 | .01 |
| ☐ 351 Chuck Tanner MGR | .07 | .01 | .00 |
|     (checklist back) | | | |
| ☐ 352 Harry Spilman | .03 | .01 | .00 |
| ☐ 353 Keith Atherton | .03 | .01 | .00 |
| ☐ 354 Tony Bernazard | .03 | .01 | .00 |
| ☐ 355 Lee Smith | .07 | .03 | .01 |
| ☐ 356 Mickey Hatcher | .05 | .02 | .00 |
| ☐ 357 Ed VandeBerg | .05 | .02 | .00 |
| ☐ 358 Rick Dempsey | .05 | .02 | .00 |
| ☐ 359 Mike LaCoss | .03 | .01 | .00 |
| ☐ 360 Lloyd Moseby | .13 | .06 | .01 |
| ☐ 361 Shane Rawley | .05 | .02 | .00 |
| ☐ 362 Tom Paciorek | .03 | .01 | .00 |
| ☐ 363 Terry Forster | .07 | .03 | .01 |
| ☐ 364 Reid Nichols | .03 | .01 | .00 |
| ☐ 365 Mike Flanagan | .07 | .03 | .01 |
| ☐ 366 Reds Leaders | .07 | .03 | .01 |
|     Dave Concepcion | | | |
| ☐ 367 Aurelio Lopez | .03 | .01 | .00 |
| ☐ 368 Greg Brock | .06 | .02 | .00 |
| ☐ 369 Al Holland | .05 | .02 | .00 |
| ☐ 370 Vince Coleman | 1.25 | .50 | .12 |
| ☐ 371 Bill Stein | .03 | .01 | .00 |
| ☐ 372 Ben Ogilvie | .06 | .02 | .00 |
| ☐ 373 Urbano Lugo | .10 | .04 | .01 |
| ☐ 374 Terry Francona | .06 | .02 | .00 |
| ☐ 375 Rich Gedman | .07 | .03 | .01 |
| ☐ 376 Bill Dawley | .05 | .02 | .00 |
| ☐ 377 Joe Carter | .06 | .02 | .00 |
| ☐ 378 Bruce Bochte | .05 | .02 | .00 |
| ☐ 379 Bobby Meacham | .05 | .02 | .00 |

| | MINT | VG-E | F-G |
|---|---|---|---|
| ☐ 380 LaMarr Hoyt | .08 | .03 | .01 |
| ☐ 381 Ray Miller MGR | .07 | .01 | .00 |
|     (checklist back) | | | |
| ☐ 382 Ivan Calderon | .20 | .09 | .02 |
| ☐ 383 Chris Brown | .30 | .12 | .03 |
| ☐ 384 Steve Trout | .05 | .02 | .00 |
| ☐ 385 Cecil Cooper | .13 | .06 | .01 |
| ☐ 386 Cecil Fielder | .25 | .10 | .02 |
| ☐ 387 Steve Kemp | .07 | .03 | .01 |
| ☐ 388 Dickie Noles | .03 | .01 | .00 |
| ☐ 389 Glenn Davis | .15 | .06 | .01 |
| ☐ 390 Tom Seaver | .30 | .12 | .03 |
| ☐ 391 Julio Franco | .09 | .04 | .01 |
| ☐ 392 John Russell | .06 | .02 | .00 |
| ☐ 393 Chris Pittaro | .15 | .06 | .01 |
| ☐ 394 Checklist: 265–396 | .07 | .01 | .00 |
| ☐ 395 Scott Garrelts | .05 | .02 | .00 |
| ☐ 396 Red Sox Leaders | .07 | .03 | .01 |
|     Dwight Evans | | | |
| ☐ 397 Steve Buechele | .10 | .04 | .01 |
| ☐ 398 Earnie Riles | .40 | .18 | .04 |
| ☐ 399 Bill Swift | .05 | .02 | .00 |
| ☐ 400 Rod Carew | .30 | .12 | .03 |
|     TURN BACK CLOCK | | | |
|     (401–405) | | | |
| ☐ 401 Turn Back 5 Years | .18 | .08 | .01 |
|     Fernando Valenzuela '81 | | | |
| ☐ 402 Turn Back 10 Years | .18 | .08 | .01 |
|     Tom Seaver '76 | | | |
| ☐ 403 Turn Back 15 Years | .18 | .08 | .01 |
|     Willie Mays '71 | | | |
| ☐ 404 Turn Back 20 Years | .11 | .05 | .01 |
|     Frank Robinson '66 | | | |
| ☐ 405 Turn Back 25 Years | .15 | .06 | .01 |
|     Roger Maris '61 | | | |
| ☐ 406 Scott Sanderson | .05 | .02 | .00 |
| ☐ 407 Sal Butera | .03 | .01 | .00 |
| ☐ 408 Dave Smith | .05 | .02 | .00 |
| ☐ 409 Paul Runge | .15 | .06 | .01 |
| ☐ 410 Dave Kingman | .10 | .04 | .01 |
| ☐ 411 Sparky Anderson MGR | .09 | .01 | .00 |
|     (checklist back) | | | |
| ☐ 412 Jim Clancy | .03 | .01 | .00 |
| ☐ 413 Tim Flannery | .03 | .01 | .00 |
| ☐ 414 Tom Gorman | .03 | .01 | .00 |
| ☐ 415 Hal McRae | .05 | .02 | .00 |
| ☐ 416 Denny Martinez | .03 | .01 | .00 |
| ☐ 417 R.J. Reynolds | .05 | .02 | .00 |
| ☐ 418 Alan Knicely | .03 | .01 | .00 |
| ☐ 419 Frank Wills | .15 | .06 | .01 |
| ☐ 420 Von Hayes | .10 | .04 | .01 |
| ☐ 421 Dave Palmer | .03 | .01 | .00 |
| ☐ 422 Mike Jorgensen | .03 | .01 | .00 |

| | MINT | VG-E | F-G |
|---|---|---|---|
| ☐ 423 Dan Spillner | .03 | .01 | .00 |
| ☐ 424 Rick Miller | .03 | .01 | .00 |
| ☐ 425 Larry McWilliams | .05 | .02 | .00 |
| ☐ 426 Brewers Leaders Charlie Moore | .05 | .02 | .00 |
| ☐ 427 Joe Cowley | .05 | .02 | .00 |
| ☐ 428 Max Venable | .03 | .01 | .00 |
| ☐ 429 Greg Booker | .03 | .01 | .00 |
| ☐ 430 Kent Hrbek | .18 | .08 | .01 |
| ☐ 431 George Frazier | .03 | .01 | .00 |
| ☐ 432 Mark Bailey | .03 | .01 | .00 |
| ☐ 433 Chris Codiroli | .03 | .01 | .00 |
| ☐ 434 Curt Wilkerson | .03 | .01 | .00 |
| ☐ 435 Bill Caudill | .06 | .02 | .00 |
| ☐ 436 Doug Flynn | .03 | .01 | .00 |
| ☐ 437 Rick Mahler | .05 | .02 | .00 |
| ☐ 438 Clint Hurdle | .03 | .01 | .00 |
| ☐ 439 Rick Honeycutt | .05 | .02 | .00 |
| ☐ 440 Alvin Davis | .18 | .08 | .01 |
| ☐ 441 Whitey Herzog MGR (checklist back) | .09 | .01 | .00 |
| ☐ 442 Ron Robinson | .03 | .01 | .00 |
| ☐ 443 Bill Buckner | .08 | .03 | .01 |
| ☐ 444 Alex Trevino | .03 | .01 | .00 |
| ☐ 445 Bert Blyleven | .09 | .04 | .01 |
| ☐ 446 Lenn Sakata | .03 | .01 | .00 |
| ☐ 447 Jerry Don Gleaton | .03 | .01 | .00 |
| ☐ 448 Herm Winningham | .15 | .06 | .01 |
| ☐ 449 Rod Scurry | .03 | .01 | .00 |
| ☐ 450 Craig Nettles | .12 | .05 | .01 |
| ☐ 451 Mark Brown | .09 | .04 | .01 |
| ☐ 452 Bob Clark | .03 | .01 | .00 |
| ☐ 453 Steve Jeltz | .07 | .03 | .01 |
| ☐ 454 Burt Hooton | .03 | .01 | .00 |
| ☐ 455 Willie Randolph | .06 | .02 | .00 |
| ☐ 456 Braves Leaders Dale Murphy | .25 | .10 | .02 |
| ☐ 457 Mickey Tettleton | .11 | .05 | .01 |
| ☐ 458 Kevin Bass | .03 | .01 | .00 |
| ☐ 459 Luis Leal | .03 | .01 | .00 |
| ☐ 460 Leon Durham | .13 | .06 | .01 |
| ☐ 461 Walt Terrell | .05 | .02 | .00 |
| ☐ 462 Domingo Ramos | .03 | .01 | .00 |
| ☐ 463 Jim Gott | .03 | .01 | .00 |
| ☐ 464 Ruppert Jones | .05 | .02 | .00 |
| ☐ 465 Jesse Orosco | .05 | .02 | .00 |
| ☐ 466 Tom Foley | .03 | .01 | .00 |
| ☐ 467 Bob James | .06 | .02 | .00 |
| ☐ 468 Mike Scioscia | .03 | .01 | .00 |
| ☐ 469 Storm Davis | .07 | .03 | .01 |
| ☐ 470 Bill Madlock | .11 | .05 | .01 |
| ☐ 471 Bobby Cox MGR (checklist back) | .07 | .01 | .00 |
| ☐ 472 Joe Hesketh | .11 | .05 | .01 |
| ☐ 473 Mark Brouhard | .03 | .01 | .00 |
| ☐ 474 John Tudor | .13 | .06 | .01 |
| ☐ 475 Juan Samuel | .13 | .06 | .01 |
| ☐ 476 Ron Mathis | .11 | .05 | .01 |
| ☐ 477 Mike Easler | .05 | .02 | .00 |
| ☐ 478 Andy Hawkins | .07 | .03 | .01 |
| ☐ 479 Bob Melvin | .11 | .05 | .01 |
| ☐ 480 Oddibe McDowell | .20 | .09 | .02 |
| ☐ 481 Scott Bradley | .08 | .03 | .01 |
| ☐ 482 Rick Lysander | .03 | .01 | .00 |
| ☐ 483 George Vukovich | .03 | .01 | .00 |
| ☐ 484 Donnie Hill | .03 | .01 | .00 |
| ☐ 485 Gary Matthews | .07 | .03 | .01 |
| ☐ 486 Angels Leaders Bobby Grich | .07 | .03 | .01 |
| ☐ 487 Bret Saberhagen | .35 | .15 | .03 |
| ☐ 488 Lou Thornton | .11 | .05 | .01 |
| ☐ 489 Jim Winn | .03 | .01 | .00 |
| ☐ 490 Jeff Leonard | .06 | .02 | .00 |
| ☐ 491 Pascual Perez | .05 | .02 | .00 |
| ☐ 492 Kelvin Chapman | .03 | .01 | .00 |
| ☐ 493 Gene Nelson | .03 | .01 | .00 |
| ☐ 494 Gary Roenicke | .05 | .02 | .00 |
| ☐ 495 Mark Langston | .07 | .03 | .01 |
| ☐ 496 Jay Johnstone | .05 | .02 | .00 |
| ☐ 497 John Stuper | .03 | .01 | .00 |
| ☐ 498 Tito Landrum | .03 | .01 | .00 |
| ☐ 499 Bob L. Gibson | .03 | .01 | .00 |
| ☐ 500 Rickey Henderson | .35 | .15 | .03 |
| ☐ 501 Dave Johnson MGR (checklist back) | .09 | .01 | .00 |
| ☐ 502 Glen Cook | .15 | .06 | .01 |
| ☐ 503 Mike Fitzgerald | .03 | .01 | .00 |
| ☐ 504 Denny Walling | .03 | .01 | .00 |
| ☐ 505 Jerry Koosman | .08 | .03 | .01 |
| ☐ 506 Bill Russell | .05 | .02 | .00 |
| ☐ 507 Steve Ontiveros | .20 | .09 | .02 |
| ☐ 508 Alan Wiggins | .08 | .03 | .01 |
| ☐ 509 Ernie Camacho | .03 | .01 | .00 |
| ☐ 510 Wade Boggs | .40 | .18 | .04 |
| ☐ 511 Ed Nunez | .05 | .02 | .00 |
| ☐ 512 Thad Bosley | .03 | .01 | .00 |
| ☐ 513 Ron Washington | .03 | .01 | .00 |
| ☐ 514 Mike Jones | .03 | .01 | .00 |
| ☐ 515 Darrell Evans | .09 | .04 | .01 |
| ☐ 516 Giants Leaders Greg Minton | .06 | .02 | .00 |
| ☐ 517 Milt Thompson | .20 | .09 | .02 |
| ☐ 518 Buck Martinez | .03 | .01 | .00 |
| ☐ 519 Danny Darwin | .03 | .01 | .00 |
| ☐ 520 Keith Hernandez | .25 | .10 | .02 |
| ☐ 521 Nate Snell | .14 | .06 | .01 |

| | MINT | VG-E | F-G |
|---|---|---|---|
| ☐ 522 Bob Bailor | .03 | .01 | .00 |
| ☐ 523 Joe Price | .03 | .01 | .00 |
| ☐ 524 Darrell Miller | .07 | .03 | .01 |
| ☐ 525 Marvell Wynne | .03 | .01 | .00 |
| ☐ 526 Charlie Lea | .05 | .02 | .00 |
| ☐ 527 Checklist: 397–528 | .07 | .01 | .00 |
| ☐ 528 Terry Pendleton | .07 | .03 | .01 |
| ☐ 529 Marc Sullivan | .10 | .04 | .01 |
| ☐ 530 Rich Gossage | .14 | .06 | .01 |
| ☐ 531 Tony LaRussa MGR | .07 | .01 | .00 |
| (checklist back) | | | |
| ☐ 532 Don Carman | .15 | .06 | .01 |
| ☐ 533 Billy Sample | .03 | .01 | .00 |
| ☐ 534 Jeff Calhoun | .12 | .05 | .01 |
| ☐ 535 Toby Harrah | .05 | .02 | .00 |
| ☐ 536 Jose Rijo | .05 | .02 | .00 |
| ☐ 537 Mark Salas | .11 | .05 | .01 |
| ☐ 538 Dennis Eckersley | .06 | .02 | .00 |
| ☐ 539 Glenn Hubbard | .05 | .02 | .00 |
| ☐ 540 Dan Petry | .12 | .05 | .01 |
| ☐ 541 Jorge Orta | .03 | .01 | .00 |
| ☐ 542 Don Schulze | .03 | .01 | .00 |
| ☐ 543 Jerry Narron | .03 | .01 | .00 |
| ☐ 544 Eddie Milner | .03 | .01 | .00 |
| ☐ 545 Jimmy Key | .09 | .04 | .01 |
| ☐ 546 Mariners Leaders | .05 | .02 | .00 |
| Dave Henderson | | | |
| ☐ 547 Roger McDowell | .30 | .12 | .03 |
| ☐ 548 Mike Young | .18 | .08 | .01 |
| ☐ 549 Bob Welch | .06 | .02 | .00 |
| ☐ 550 Tom Herr | .12 | .05 | .01 |
| ☐ 551 Dave LaPoint | .03 | .01 | .00 |
| ☐ 552 Marc Hill | .03 | .01 | .00 |
| ☐ 553 Jim Morrison | .03 | .01 | .00 |
| ☐ 554 Paul Householder | .03 | .01 | .00 |
| ☐ 555 Hubie Brooks | .07 | .03 | .01 |
| ☐ 556 John Denny | .07 | .03 | .01 |
| ☐ 557 Gerald Perry | .05 | .02 | .00 |
| ☐ 558 Tim Stoddard | .03 | .01 | .00 |
| ☐ 559 Tommy Dunbar | .03 | .01 | .00 |
| ☐ 560 Dave Righetti | .11 | .05 | .01 |
| ☐ 561 Bob Lillis MGR | .07 | .01 | .00 |
| (checklist back) | | | |
| ☐ 562 Joe Beckwith | .03 | .01 | .00 |
| ☐ 563 Alejandro Sanchez | .08 | .03 | .01 |
| ☐ 564 Warren Brusstar | .03 | .01 | .00 |
| ☐ 565 Tom Brunansky | .12 | .05 | .01 |
| ☐ 566 Alfredo Griffin | .05 | .02 | .00 |
| ☐ 567 Jeff Barkley | .11 | .05 | .01 |
| ☐ 568 Donnie Scott | .03 | .01 | .00 |
| ☐ 569 Jim Acker | .03 | .01 | .00 |
| ☐ 570 Rusty Staub | .08 | .03 | .01 |

| | MINT | VG-E | F-G |
|---|---|---|---|
| ☐ 571 Mike Jeffcoat | .03 | .01 | .00 |
| ☐ 572 Paul Zuvella | .08 | .03 | .01 |
| ☐ 573 Tom Hume | .03 | .01 | .00 |
| ☐ 574 Ron Kittle | .12 | .05 | .01 |
| ☐ 575 Mike Boddicker | .09 | .04 | .01 |
| ☐ 576 Expos Leaders | .13 | .06 | .01 |
| Andre Dawson | | | |
| ☐ 577 Jerry Reuss | .06 | .02 | .00 |
| ☐ 578 Lee Mazzilli | .05 | .02 | .00 |
| ☐ 579 Jim Slaton | .05 | .02 | .00 |
| ☐ 580 Willie McGee | .25 | .10 | .02 |
| ☐ 581 Bruce Hurst | .03 | .01 | .00 |
| ☐ 582 Jim Gantner | .05 | .02 | .00 |
| ☐ 583 Al Bumbry | .03 | .01 | .00 |
| ☐ 584 Brian Fisher | .30 | .12 | .03 |
| ☐ 585 Garry Maddox | .03 | .01 | .00 |
| ☐ 586 Greg Harris | .03 | .01 | .00 |
| ☐ 587 Rafael Santana | .03 | .01 | .00 |
| ☐ 588 Steve Lake | .03 | .01 | .00 |
| ☐ 589 Sid Bream | .03 | .01 | .00 |
| ☐ 590 Bob Knepper | .05 | .02 | .00 |
| ☐ 591 Jackie Moore MGR | .07 | .01 | .00 |
| (checklist back) | | | |
| ☐ 592 Frank Tanana | .05 | .02 | .00 |
| ☐ 593 Jesse Barfield | .11 | .05 | .01 |
| ☐ 594 Chris Bando | .03 | .01 | .00 |
| ☐ 595 Dave Parker | .18 | .08 | .01 |
| ☐ 596 Onix Concepcion | .03 | .01 | .00 |
| ☐ 597 Sammy Stewart | .03 | .01 | .00 |
| ☐ 598 Jim Presley | .20 | .09 | .02 |
| ☐ 599 Rick Aguilera | .20 | .09 | .02 |
| ☐ 600 Dale Murphy | .40 | .18 | .04 |
| ☐ 601 Gary Lucas | .03 | .01 | .00 |
| ☐ 602 Mariano Duncan | .40 | .18 | .04 |
| ☐ 603 Bill Laskey | .03 | .01 | .00 |
| ☐ 604 Gary Pettis | .07 | .03 | .01 |
| ☐ 605 Dennis Boyd | .06 | .02 | .00 |
| ☐ 606 Royals Leaders | .06 | .02 | .00 |
| Hal McRae | | | |
| ☐ 607 Ken Dayley | .03 | .01 | .00 |
| ☐ 608 Bruce Bochy | .03 | .01 | .00 |
| ☐ 609 Barbaro Garbey | .03 | .01 | .00 |
| ☐ 610 Ron Guidry | .14 | .06 | .01 |
| ☐ 611 Gary Woods | .03 | .01 | .00 |
| ☐ 612 Richard Dotson | .06 | .02 | .00 |
| ☐ 613 Roy Smalley | .05 | .02 | .00 |
| ☐ 614 Rick Waits | .03 | .01 | .00 |
| ☐ 615 Johnny Ray | .09 | .04 | .01 |
| ☐ 616 Glenn Brummer | .03 | .01 | .00 |
| ☐ 617 Lonnie Smith | .08 | .03 | .01 |
| ☐ 618 Jim Pankovits | .06 | .02 | .00 |
| ☐ 619 Danny Heep | .03 | .01 | .00 |

| | MINT | VG-E | F-G | | | MINT | VG-E | F-G |
|---|---|---|---|---|---|---|---|---|
| ☐ 620 Bruce Sutter | .14 | .06 | .01 | ☐ 668 Cecilio Guante | .03 | .01 | .00 |
| ☐ 621 John Felske MGR | .07 | .01 | .00 | ☐ 669 Ron Cey | .10 | .04 | .01 |
| (checklist back) | | | | ☐ 670 Willie Hernandez | .12 | .05 | .01 |
| ☐ 622 Gary Lavelle | .03 | .01 | .00 | ☐ 671 Lynn Jones | .03 | .01 | .00 |
| ☐ 623 Floyd Rayford | .03 | .01 | .00 | ☐ 672 Rob Picciolo | .03 | .01 | .00 |
| ☐ 624 Steve McCatty | .03 | .01 | .00 | ☐ 673 Ernie Whitt | .03 | .01 | .00 |
| ☐ 625 Bob Brenly | .05 | .02 | .00 | ☐ 674 Pat Tabler | .05 | .02 | .00 |
| ☐ 626 Roy Thomas | .03 | .01 | .00 | ☐ 675 Claudell Washington | .06 | .02 | .00 |
| ☐ 627 Ron Oester | .05 | .02 | .00 | ☐ 676 Matt Young | .05 | .02 | .00 |
| ☐ 628 Kirk McCaskill | .20 | .09 | .02 | ☐ 677 Nick Esasky | .06 | .02 | .00 |
| ☐ 629 Mitch Webster | .12 | .05 | .01 | ☐ 678 Dan Gladden | .06 | .02 | .00 |
| ☐ 630 Fernando Valenzuela | .30 | .12 | .03 | ☐ 679 Britt Burns | .07 | .03 | .01 |
| ☐ 631 Steve Braun | .03 | .01 | .00 | ☐ 680 George Foster | .14 | .06 | .01 |
| ☐ 632 Dave Von Ohlen | .03 | .01 | .00 | ☐ 681 Dick Williams MGR | .07 | .01 | .00 |
| ☐ 633 Jackie Gutierrez | .03 | .01 | .00 | (checklist back) | | | |
| ☐ 634 Roy Lee Jackson | .03 | .01 | .00 | ☐ 682 Junior Ortiz | .03 | .01 | .00 |
| ☐ 635 Jason Thompson | .06 | .02 | .00 | ☐ 683 Andy Van Slyke | .06 | .02 | .00 |
| ☐ 636 Cubs Leaders | .07 | .03 | .01 | ☐ 684 Bob McClure | .03 | .01 | .00 |
| Lee Smith | | | | ☐ 685 Tim Wallach | .09 | .04 | .01 |
| ☐ 637 Rudy Law | .03 | .01 | .00 | ☐ 686 Jeff Stone | .06 | .02 | .00 |
| ☐ 638 John Butcher | .03 | .01 | .00 | ☐ 687 Mike Trujillo | .09 | .04 | .01 |
| ☐ 639 Bo Diaz | .05 | .02 | .00 | ☐ 688 Larry Herndon | .05 | .02 | .00 |
| ☐ 640 Jose Cruz | .09 | .04 | .01 | ☐ 689 Dave Stewart | .03 | .01 | .00 |
| ☐ 641 Wayne Tolleson | .03 | .01 | .00 | ☐ 690 Ryne Sandberg | .30 | .12 | .03 |
| ☐ 642 Ray Searage | .03 | .01 | .00 | ☐ 691 Mike Madden | .05 | .02 | .00 |
| ☐ 643 Tom Brookens | .03 | .01 | .00 | ☐ 692 Dale Berra | .05 | .02 | .00 |
| ☐ 644 Mark Gubicza | .06 | .02 | .00 | ☐ 693 Tom Tellmann | .03 | .01 | .00 |
| ☐ 645 Dusty Baker | .06 | .02 | .00 | ☐ 694 Garth Iorg | .03 | .01 | .00 |
| ☐ 646 Mike Moore | .05 | .02 | .00 | ☐ 695 Mike Smithson | .03 | .01 | .00 |
| ☐ 647 Mel Hall | .07 | .03 | .01 | ☐ 696 Dodgers Leaders | .05 | .02 | .00 |
| ☐ 648 Steve Bedrosian | .06 | .02 | .00 | Bill Russell | | | |
| ☐ 649 Ronn Reynolds | .11 | .05 | .01 | ☐ 697 Bud Black | .05 | .02 | .00 |
| ☐ 650 Dave Stieb | .14 | .06 | .01 | ☐ 698 Brad Komminsk | .06 | .02 | .00 |
| ☐ 651 Billy Martin MGR | .09 | .01 | .00 | ☐ 699 Pat Corrales MGR | .07 | .01 | .00 |
| (checklist back) | | | | (checklist back) | | | |
| ☐ 652 Tom Browning | .15 | .06 | .01 | ☐ 700 Reggie Jackson | .35 | .15 | .03 |
| ☐ 653 Jim Dwyer | .03 | .01 | .00 | NL ALL-STARS | | | |
| ☐ 654 Ken Howell | .08 | .03 | .01 | (701–711) | | | |
| ☐ 655 Manny Trillo | .05 | .02 | .00 | ☐ 701 Keith Hernandez AS | .16 | .07 | .01 |
| ☐ 656 Brian Harper | .03 | .01 | .00 | ☐ 702 Tom Herr AS | .08 | .03 | .01 |
| ☐ 657 Juan Agosto | .03 | .01 | .00 | ☐ 703 Tim Wallach AS | .08 | .03 | .01 |
| ☐ 658 Rob Wilfong | .03 | .01 | .00 | ☐ 704 Ozzie Smith AS | .08 | .03 | .01 |
| ☐ 659 Checklist: 529–660 | .07 | .01 | .00 | ☐ 705 Dale Murphy AS | .30 | .12 | .03 |
| ☐ 660 Steve Garvey | .35 | .15 | .01 | ☐ 706 Pedro Guerrero AS | .16 | .07 | .01 |
| ☐ 661 Roger Clemens | .07 | .03 | .01 | ☐ 707 Willie McGee AS | .16 | .07 | .01 |
| ☐ 662 Bill Schroeder | .03 | .01 | .00 | ☐ 708 Gary Carter AS | .20 | .09 | .02 |
| ☐ 663 Neil Allen | .05 | .02 | .00 | ☐ 709 Dwight Gooden AS | .50 | .22 | .05 |
| ☐ 664 Tim Corcoran | .03 | .01 | .00 | ☐ 710 John Tudor AS | .08 | .03 | .01 |
| ☐ 665 Alejandro Pena | .06 | .02 | .00 | ☐ 711 Jeff Reardon AS | .06 | .02 | .00 |
| ☐ 666 Rangers Leaders | .05 | .02 | .00 | AL ALL-STARS | | | |
| Charlie Hough | | | | (712–722) | | | |
| ☐ 667 Tim Teufel | .08 | .03 | .01 | ☐ 712 Don Mattingly AS | .40 | .18 | .04 |

| | | MINT | VG-E | F-G |
|---|---|---|---|---|
| ☐ 713 | Damaso Garcia AS | .07 | .03 | .01 |
| ☐ 714 | George Brett AS | .30 | .12 | .03 |
| ☐ 715 | Cal Ripken AS | .30 | .12 | .03 |
| ☐ 716 | Rickey Henderson AS | .25 | .10 | .02 |
| ☐ 717 | Dave Winfield AS | .20 | .09 | .02 |
| ☐ 718 | Jorge Bell AS | .08 | .03 | .01 |
| ☐ 719 | Carlton Fisk AS | .10 | .04 | .01 |
| ☐ 720 | Bret Saberhagen AS | .20 | .09 | .02 |
| ☐ 721 | Ron Guidry AS | .12 | .05 | .01 |
| ☐ 722 | Dan Quisenberry AS | .11 | .05 | .01 |
| ☐ 723 | Marty Bystrom | .03 | .01 | .00 |
| ☐ 724 | Tim Hulett | .08 | .03 | .01 |
| ☐ 725 | Mario Soto | .09 | .04 | .01 |
| ☐ 726 | Orioles Leaders | .05 | .02 | .00 |
| | Rick Dempsey | | | |
| ☐ 727 | David Green | .05 | .02 | .00 |
| ☐ 728 | Mike Marshall | .12 | .05 | .01 |
| ☐ 729 | Jim Beattie | .03 | .01 | .00 |
| ☐ 730 | Ozzie Smith | .09 | .04 | .01 |
| ☐ 731 | Don Robinson | .03 | .01 | .00 |
| ☐ 732 | Floyd Youmans | .25 | .10 | .02 |
| ☐ 733 | Ron Romanick | .06 | .02 | .00 |
| ☐ 734 | Marty Barrett | .05 | .02 | .00 |
| ☐ 735 | Dave Dravecky | .06 | .02 | .00 |
| ☐ 736 | Glenn Wilson | .09 | .04 | .01 |
| ☐ 737 | Pete Vuckovich | .05 | .02 | .00 |
| ☐ 738 | Andre Robertson | .03 | .01 | .00 |
| ☐ 739 | Dave Rozema | .03 | .01 | .00 |
| ☐ 740 | Lance Parrish | .20 | .09 | .02 |
| ☐ 741 | Pete Rose MGR | .30 | .10 | .02 |
| | (checklist back) | | | |
| ☐ 742 | Frank Viola | .05 | .02 | .00 |
| ☐ 743 | Pat Sheridan | .03 | .01 | .00 |
| ☐ 744 | Lary Sorensen | .03 | .01 | .00 |
| ☐ 745 | Willie Upshaw | .09 | .04 | .01 |
| ☐ 746 | Denny Gonzalez | .08 | .03 | .01 |
| ☐ 747 | Rick Cerone | .05 | .02 | .00 |
| ☐ 748 | Steve Henderson | .03 | .01 | .00 |
| ☐ 749 | Ed Jurak | .03 | .01 | .00 |
| ☐ 750 | Gorman Thomas | .08 | .03 | .01 |
| ☐ 751 | Howard Johnson | .05 | .02 | .00 |
| ☐ 752 | Mike Krukow | .03 | .01 | .00 |
| ☐ 753 | Dan Ford | .03 | .01 | .00 |
| ☐ 754 | Pat Clements | .20 | .09 | .02 |
| ☐ 755 | Harold Baines | .18 | .08 | .01 |
| ☐ 756 | Pirates Leaders | .05 | .02 | .00 |
| | Rick Rhoden | | | |
| ☐ 757 | Darrell Porter | .05 | .02 | .00 |
| ☐ 758 | Dave Anderson | .03 | .01 | .00 |
| ☐ 759 | Moose Haas | .05 | .02 | .00 |
| ☐ 760 | Andre Dawson | .18 | .08 | .01 |
| ☐ 761 | Don Slaught | .03 | .01 | .00 |
| ☐ 762 | Eric Show | .05 | .02 | .00 |
| ☐ 763 | Terry Puhl | .05 | .02 | .00 |
| ☐ 764 | Kevin Gross | .03 | .01 | .00 |
| ☐ 765 | Don Baylor | .10 | .04 | .01 |
| ☐ 766 | Rick Langford | .03 | .01 | .00 |
| ☐ 767 | Jody Davis | .08 | .03 | .01 |
| ☐ 768 | Vern Ruhle | .03 | .01 | .00 |
| ☐ 769 | Harold Reynolds | .14 | .06 | .01 |
| ☐ 770 | Vida Blue | .08 | .03 | .01 |
| ☐ 771 | John McNamara MGR | .07 | .01 | .00 |
| | (checklist back) | | | |
| ☐ 772 | Brian Downing | .05 | .02 | .00 |
| ☐ 773 | Greg Pryor | .03 | .01 | .00 |
| ☐ 774 | Terry Leach | .03 | .01 | .00 |
| ☐ 775 | Al Oliver | .13 | .06 | .01 |
| ☐ 776 | Gene Garber | .03 | .01 | .00 |
| ☐ 777 | Wayne Krenchicki | .03 | .01 | .00 |
| ☐ 778 | Jerry Hairston | .03 | .01 | .00 |
| ☐ 779 | Rick Reuschel | .05 | .02 | .00 |
| ☐ 780 | Robin Yount | .25 | .10 | .02 |
| ☐ 779 | Rick Reuschel | .05 | .02 | .00 |
| ☐ 780 | Robin Yount | .25 | .10 | .02 |
| ☐ 781 | Joe Nolan | .03 | .01 | .00 |
| ☐ 782 | Ken Landreaux | .05 | .02 | .00 |
| ☐ 783 | Ricky Horton | .03 | .01 | .00 |
| ☐ 784 | Alan Bannister | .03 | .01 | .00 |
| ☐ 785 | Bob Stanley | .05 | .02 | .00 |
| ☐ 786 | Twins Leaders | .05 | .02 | .00 |
| | Mickey Hatcher | | | |
| ☐ 787 | Vance Law | .03 | .01 | .00 |
| ☐ 788 | Marty Castillo | .03 | .01 | .00 |
| ☐ 789 | Kurt Bevacqua | .03 | .01 | .00 |
| ☐ 790 | Phil Niekro | .14 | .06 | .01 |
| ☐ 791 | Checklist: 661–792 | .07 | .01 | .00 |
| ☐ 792 | Charles Hudson | .06 | .02 | .00 |
| | WAX PACK BOX | | | |
| | BOTTOM CARDS | | | |
| ☐ A | Jorge Bell | .15 | .06 | .01 |
| ☐ B | Wade Boggs | .75 | .35 | .07 |
| ☐ C | George Brett | .75 | .35 | .07 |
| ☐ D | Vince Coleman | .75 | .35 | .07 |
| ☐ E | Carlton Fisk | .20 | .09 | .02 |
| ☐ F | Dwight Gooden | 1.25 | .60 | .12 |
| ☐ G | Pedro Guerrero | .25 | .10 | .02 |
| ☐ H | Ron Guidry | .25 | .10 | .02 |
| ☐ I | Reggie Jackson | .50 | .22 | .05 |
| ☐ J | Don Mattingly | .75 | .35 | .07 |
| ☐ K | Oddibe McDowell | .25 | .10 | .02 |
| ☐ L | Willie McGee | .25 | .10 | .02 |
| ☐ M | Dale Murphy | .75 | .35 | .07 |
| ☐ N | Pete Rose | 1.00 | .45 | .10 |
| ☐ O | Bret Saberhagen | .50 | .22 | .05 |
| ☐ P | Fernando Valenzuela | .35 | .15 | .03 |

# 1981 DONRUSS

The cards in this 605 set measure 2½" by 3½". In 1981 Donruss launched itself into the baseball card market with a set containing 600 numbered cards and five un-numbered checklists. The cards are printed on thin stock, and more than one pose exists for several popular players. The numerous errors of the first print run were later corrected by the company. These are marked P1 and P2 in the checklist.

Complete Set: M-20.00; VG-E-9.00; F-G-2.00

|  | MINT | VG-E | F-G |
|---|---|---|---|
| Common Player(1–605) | .03 | .01 | .00 |
| ☐ 1 Ozzie Smith | .25 | .05 | .01 |
| ☐ 2 Rollie Fingers | .30 | .12 | .03 |
| ☐ 3 Rick Wise | .06 | .02 | .00 |
| ☐ 4 Gene Richards | .03 | .01 | .00 |
| ☐ 5 Alan Trammell | .35 | .15 | .03 |
| ☐ 6 Tom Brookens | .03 | .01 | .00 |
| ☐ 7 A Duffy Dyer P1 | .05 | .02 | .00 |
| 1980 batting average has decimal point | | | |
| ☐ 7 B Duffy Dyer P2 | .05 | .02 | .00 |
| 1980 batting average has no decimal point | | | |
| ☐ 8 Mark Fidrych | .07 | .03 | .01 |
| ☐ 9 Dave Rozema | .03 | .01 | .00 |
| ☐ 10 Ricky Peters | .05 | .02 | .00 |
| ☐ 11 Mike Schmidt | .80 | .40 | .08 |
| ☐ 12 Willie Stargell | .30 | .12 | .03 |
| ☐ 13 Tim Foli | .03 | .01 | .00 |
| ☐ 14 Manny Sanguillen | .05 | .02 | .00 |

|  | MINT | VG-E | F-G |
|---|---|---|---|
| ☐ 15 Grant Jackson | .03 | .01 | .00 |
| ☐ 16 Eddie Solomon | .03 | .01 | .00 |
| ☐ 17 Omar Moreno | .05 | .02 | .00 |
| ☐ 18 Joe Morgan | .25 | .10 | .02 |
| ☐ 19 Rafael Landestoy | .03 | .01 | .00 |
| ☐ 20 Bruce Bochy | .03 | .01 | .00 |
| ☐ 21 Joe Sambito | .05 | .02 | .00 |
| ☐ 22 Manny Trillo | .05 | .02 | .00 |
| ☐ 23 A Dave Smith P1 | .10 | .04 | .01 |
| Line box around stats is not complete | | | |
| ☐ 23 B Dave Smith P2 | .10 | .04 | .01 |
| Box totally encloses stats at top | | | |
| ☐ 24 Terry Puhl | .05 | .02 | .00 |
| ☐ 25 Bump Wills | .03 | .01 | .00 |
| ☐ 26 A John Ellis P1 ERR | .40 | .18 | .04 |
| Photo on front shows Danny Walton | | | |
| ☐ 26 B John Ellis P2 COR | .09 | .04 | .01 |
| ☐ 27 Jim Kern | .03 | .01 | .00 |
| ☐ 28 Richie Zisk | .05 | .02 | .00 |
| ☐ 29 John Mayberry | .05 | .02 | .00 |
| ☐ 30 Bob Davis | .03 | .01 | .00 |
| ☐ 31 Jackson Todd | .03 | .01 | .00 |
| ☐ 32 Al Woods | .03 | .01 | .00 |
| ☐ 33 Steve Carlton | .55 | .25 | .05 |
| ☐ 34 Lee Mazzilli | .07 | .03 | .01 |
| ☐ 35 John Stearns | .03 | .01 | .00 |
| ☐ 36 Roy Lee Jackson | .05 | .02 | .00 |
| ☐ 37 Mike Scott | .05 | .02 | .00 |
| ☐ 38 Lamar Johnson | .03 | .01 | .00 |
| ☐ 39 Kevin Bell | .03 | .01 | .00 |
| ☐ 40 Ed Farmer | .03 | .01 | .00 |
| ☐ 41 Ross Baumgarten | .03 | .01 | .00 |
| ☐ 42 Leo Sutherland | .05 | .02 | .00 |
| ☐ 43 Dan Meyer | .03 | .01 | .00 |
| ☐ 44 Ron Reed | .03 | .01 | .00 |
| ☐ 45 Mario Mendoza | .03 | .01 | .00 |
| ☐ 46 Rick Honeycutt | .05 | .02 | .00 |
| ☐ 47 Glenn Abbott | .03 | .01 | .00 |
| ☐ 48 Leon Roberts | .03 | .01 | .00 |
| ☐ 49 Rod Carew | .50 | .22 | .05 |
| ☐ 50 Bert Campaneris | .05 | .02 | .00 |
| ☐ 51 A Tom Donahue P1 ERR | .09 | .04 | .01 |
| Name on front misspelled Donahue | | | |
| ☐ 51 B Tom Donohue P2 COR | .09 | .04 | .01 |
| ☐ 52 Dave Frost | .03 | .01 | .00 |
| ☐ 53 Ed Halicki | .03 | .01 | .00 |
| ☐ 54 Dan Ford | .05 | .02 | .00 |
| ☐ 55 Garry Maddox | .05 | .02 | .00 |

| | MINT | VG-E | F-G |
|---|---|---|---|
| ☐ 56 A Steve Garvey P1 "Surpassed 25 HR" | .60 | .28 | .06 |
| ☐ 56 B Steve Garvey P2 "Surpassed 21 HR" | .60 | .28 | .06 |
| ☐ 57 Bill Russell | .06 | .02 | .00 |
| ☐ 58 Don Sutton | .20 | .09 | .02 |
| ☐ 59 Reggie Smith | .08 | .03 | .01 |
| ☐ 60 Rick Monday | .06 | .02 | .00 |
| ☐ 61 Ray Knight | .05 | .02 | .00 |
| ☐ 62 Johnny Bench | .50 | .22 | .05 |
| ☐ 63 Mario Soto | .10 | .04 | .01 |
| ☐ 64 Doug Bair | .03 | .01 | .00 |
| ☐ 65 George Foster | .25 | .10 | .02 |
| ☐ 66 Jeff Burroughs | .05 | .02 | .00 |
| ☐ 67 Keith Hernandez | .35 | .15 | .03 |
| ☐ 68 Tom Herr | .15 | .06 | .01 |
| ☐ 69 Bob Forsch | .05 | .02 | .00 |
| ☐ 70 John Fulgham | .03 | .01 | .00 |
| ☐ 71 A Bobby Bonds P1 ERR 986 lifetime HR | .20 | .09 | .02 |
| ☐ 71 B Bobby Bonds P2 COR 326 lifetime HR | .09 | .04 | .01 |
| ☐ 72 A Rennie Stennett P1 "breaking broke leg" | .08 | .03 | .01 |
| ☐ 72 B Rennie Stennett P2 Word "broke" deleted | .08 | .03 | .01 |
| ☐ 73 Joe Strain | .03 | .01 | .00 |
| ☐ 74 Ed Whitson | .07 | .03 | .01 |
| ☐ 75 Tom Griffin | .03 | .01 | .00 |
| ☐ 76 Billy North | .03 | .01 | .00 |
| ☐ 77 Gene Garber | .03 | .01 | .00 |
| ☐ 78 Mike Hargrove | .05 | .02 | .00 |
| ☐ 79 Dave Rosello | .03 | .01 | .00 |
| ☐ 80 Ron Hassey | .03 | .01 | .00 |
| ☐ 81 Sid Monge | .03 | .01 | .00 |
| ☐ 82 A Joe Charboneau P1 '78 highlights, "For some reason" | .15 | .06 | .01 |
| ☐ 82 B Joe Charboneau P2 phrase "For some reason" deleted | .10 | .04 | .01 |
| ☐ 83 Cecil Cooper | .20 | .09 | .02 |
| ☐ 84 Sal Bando | .06 | .02 | .00 |
| ☐ 85 Moose Haas | .05 | .02 | .00 |
| ☐ 86 Mike Caldwell | .05 | .02 | .00 |
| ☐ 87 A Larry Hisle P1 '77 highlights, line ends with "28 RBI" | .12 | .05 | .01 |
| ☐ 87 B Larry Hisle P2 correct line "28 HR" | .08 | .03 | .01 |
| ☐ 88 Luis Gomez | .03 | .01 | .00 |
| ☐ 89 Larry Parrish | .06 | .02 | .00 |
| ☐ 90 Gary Carter | .40 | .18 | .04 |

| | MINT | VG-E | F-G |
|---|---|---|---|
| ☐ 91 Bill Gullickson | .35 | .15 | .03 |
| ☐ 92 Fred Norman | .03 | .01 | .00 |
| ☐ 93 Tommy Hutton | .03 | .01 | .00 |
| ☐ 94 Carl Yastrzemski | .80 | .40 | .08 |
| ☐ 95 Glenn Hoffman | .10 | .04 | .01 |
| ☐ 96 Dennis Eckersley | .06 | .02 | .00 |
| ☐ 97 A Tom Burgmeier P1 ERR Throws: Right | .06 | .02 | .00 |
| ☐ 97 B Tom Burgmeier P2 COR Throws: Left | .06 | .02 | .00 |
| ☐ 98 Win Remmerswaal | .05 | .02 | .00 |
| ☐ 99 Bob Horner | .25 | .10 | .02 |
| ☐ 100 George Brett | .80 | .40 | .08 |
| ☐ 101 Dave Chalk | .03 | .01 | .00 |
| ☐ 102 Dennis Leonard | .07 | .03 | .01 |
| ☐ 103 Renie Martin | .03 | .01 | .00 |
| ☐ 104 Amos Otis | .07 | .03 | .01 |
| ☐ 105 Graig Nettles | .16 | .07 | .01 |
| ☐ 106 Eric Soderholm | .03 | .01 | .00 |
| ☐ 107 Tommy John | .20 | .09 | .02 |
| ☐ 108 Tom Underwood | .03 | .01 | .00 |
| ☐ 109 Lou Piniella | .12 | .05 | .01 |
| ☐ 110 Mickey Klutts | .03 | .01 | .00 |
| ☐ 111 Bobby Murcer | .10 | .04 | .01 |
| ☐ 112 Eddie Murray | .80 | .40 | .08 |
| ☐ 113 Rick Dempsey | .05 | .02 | .00 |
| ☐ 114 Scott McGregor | .07 | .03 | .01 |
| ☐ 115 Ken Singleton | .09 | .04 | .01 |
| ☐ 116 Gary Roenicke | .05 | .02 | .00 |
| ☐ 117 Dave Revering | .03 | .01 | .00 |
| ☐ 118 Mike Norris | .03 | .01 | .00 |
| ☐ 119 Rickey Henderson | .70 | .32 | .07 |
| ☐ 120 Mike Heath | .03 | .01 | .00 |
| ☐ 121 Dave Cash | .03 | .01 | .00 |
| ☐ 122 Randy Jones | .05 | .02 | .00 |
| ☐ 123 Eric Rasmussen | .03 | .01 | .00 |
| ☐ 124 Jerry Mumphrey | .05 | .02 | .00 |
| ☐ 125 Richie Hebner | .03 | .01 | .00 |
| ☐ 126 Mark Wagner | .03 | .01 | .00 |
| ☐ 127 Jack Morris | .25 | .10 | .02 |
| ☐ 128 Dan Petry | .20 | .09 | .02 |
| ☐ 129 Bruce Robbins | .03 | .01 | .00 |
| ☐ 130 Champ Summers | .03 | .01 | .00 |
| ☐ 131 A Pete Rose P1 last line ends with "see card 251" | 1.25 | .60 | .12 |
| ☐ 131 B Pete Rose P2 last line corrected "see card 371" | 1.25 | .60 | .12 |
| ☐ 132 Willie Stargell | .30 | .12 | .03 |
| ☐ 133 Ed Ott | .03 | .01 | .00 |

| | MINT | VG-E | F-G | | | MINT | VG-E | F-G |
|---|---|---|---|---|---|---|---|---|
| ☐ 134 Jim Bibby | .05 | .02 | .00 | ☐ 183 Mike LaCoss | | .03 | .01 | .00 |
| ☐ 135 Bert Blyleven | .15 | .06 | .01 | ☐ 184 Ken Griffey | | .09 | .04 | .01 |
| ☐ 136 Dave Parker | .30 | .12 | .03 | ☐ 185 Dave Collins | | .07 | .03 | .01 |
| ☐ 137 Bill Robinson | .03 | .01 | .00 | ☐ 186 Brian Asselstine | | .03 | .01 | .00 |
| ☐ 138 Enos Cabell | .03 | .01 | .00 | ☐ 187 Garry Templeton | | .12 | .05 | .01 |
| ☐ 139 Dave Bergman | .03 | .01 | .00 | ☐ 188 Mike Phillips | | .03 | .01 | .00 |
| ☐ 140 J.R. Richard | .09 | .04 | .01 | ☐ 189 Pete Vuckovich | | .08 | .03 | .01 |
| ☐ 141 Ken Forsch | .03 | .01 | .00 | ☐ 190 John Urrea | | .03 | .01 | .00 |
| ☐ 142 Larry Bowa | .08 | .03 | .01 | ☐ 191 Tony Scott | | .03 | .01 | .00 |
| ☐ 143 Frank LaCorte | .03 | .01 | .00 | ☐ 192 Darrell Evans | | .12 | .05 | .01 |
| ☐ 144 Dennis Walling | .03 | .01 | .00 | ☐ 193 Milt May | | .03 | .01 | .00 |
| ☐ 145 Buddy Bell | .14 | .06 | .01 | ☐ 194 Bob Knepper | | .09 | .04 | .01 |
| ☐ 146 Ferguson Jenkins | .14 | .06 | .01 | ☐ 195 Randy Moffitt | | .03 | .01 | .00 |
| ☐ 147 Danny Darwin | .05 | .02 | .00 | ☐ 196 Larry Herndon | | .05 | .02 | .00 |
| ☐ 148 John Grubb | .03 | .01 | .00 | ☐ 197 Rick Camp | | .03 | .01 | .00 |
| ☐ 149 Alfredo Griffin | .10 | .04 | .01 | ☐ 198 Andre Thornton | | .10 | .04 | .01 |
| ☐ 150 Jerry Garvin | .03 | .01 | .00 | ☐ 199 Tom Veryzer | | .03 | .01 | .00 |
| ☐ 151 Paul Mirabella | .05 | .02 | .00 | ☐ 200 Gary Alexander | | .03 | .01 | .00 |
| ☐ 152 Rick Bosetti | .03 | .01 | .00 | ☐ 201 Rick Waits | | .03 | .01 | .00 |
| ☐ 153 Dick Ruthven | .03 | .01 | .00 | ☐ 202 Rick Manning | | .03 | .01 | .00 |
| ☐ 154 Frank Taveras | .03 | .01 | .00 | ☐ 203 Paul Molitor | | .20 | .09 | .02 |
| ☐ 155 Craig Swan | .05 | .02 | .00 | ☐ 204 Jim Gantner | | .03 | .01 | .00 |
| ☐ 156 Jeff Reardon | .50 | .22 | .05 | ☐ 205 Paul Mitchell | | .03 | .01 | .00 |
| ☐ 157 Steve Henderson | .03 | .01 | .00 | ☐ 206 Reggie Cleveland | | .03 | .01 | .00 |
| ☐ 158 Jim Morrison | .03 | .01 | .00 | ☐ 207 Sixto Lezcano | | .03 | .01 | .00 |
| ☐ 159 Glenn Borgmann | .03 | .01 | .00 | ☐ 208 Bruce Benedict | | .03 | .01 | .00 |
| ☐ 160 LaMarr Hoyt | .80 | .40 | .08 | ☐ 209 Rodney Scott | | .03 | .01 | .00 |
| ☐ 161 Rich Wortham | .03 | .01 | .00 | ☐ 210 John Tamargo | | .03 | .01 | .00 |
| ☐ 162 Thad Bosley | .03 | .01 | .00 | ☐ 211 Bill Lee | | .05 | .02 | .00 |
| ☐ 163 Julio Cruz | .03 | .01 | .00 | ☐ 212 Andre Dawson | | .30 | .12 | .03 |
| ☐ 164 A Del Unser P1 | .06 | .02 | .00 | ☐ 213 Rowland Office | | .03 | .01 | .00 |
| no "3B" heading | | | | ☐ 214 Carl Yastrzemski | | .80 | .40 | .08 |
| ☐ 164 B Del Unser P2 | .06 | .02 | .00 | ☐ 215 Jerry Remy | | .05 | .02 | .00 |
| Batting record on back | | | | ☐ 216 Mike Torrez | | .05 | .02 | .00 |
| corrected ("3B") | | | | ☐ 217 Skip Lockwood | | .03 | .01 | .00 |
| ☐ 165 Jim Anderson | .03 | .01 | .00 | ☐ 218 Fred Lynn | | .25 | .10 | .02 |
| ☐ 166 Jim Beattie | .03 | .01 | .00 | ☐ 219 Chris Chambliss | | .08 | .03 | .01 |
| ☐ 167 Shane Rawley | .06 | .02 | .00 | ☐ 220 Willie Aikens | | .05 | .02 | .00 |
| ☐ 168 Joe Simpson | .03 | .01 | .00 | ☐ 221 John Wathan | | .03 | .01 | .00 |
| ☐ 169 Rod Carew | .50 | .22 | .05 | ☐ 222 Dan Quisenberry | | .30 | .12 | .03 |
| ☐ 170 Fred Patek | .03 | .01 | .00 | ☐ 223 Willie Wilson | | .30 | .12 | .03 |
| ☐ 171 Frank Tanana | .06 | .02 | .00 | ☐ 224 Clint Hurdle | | .03 | .01 | .00 |
| ☐ 172 Alfredo Martinez | .05 | .02 | .00 | ☐ 225 Bob Watson | | .05 | .02 | .00 |
| ☐ 173 Chris Knapp | .03 | .01 | .00 | ☐ 226 Jim Spencer | | .03 | .01 | .00 |
| ☐ 174 Joe Rudi | .05 | .02 | .00 | ☐ 227 Ron Guidry | | .30 | .12 | .03 |
| ☐ 175 Greg Luzinski | .14 | .06 | .01 | ☐ 228 Reggie Jackson | | .70 | .32 | .07 |
| ☐ 176 Steve Garvey | .60 | .28 | .06 | ☐ 229 Oscar Gamble | | .06 | .02 | .00 |
| ☐ 177 Joe Ferguson | .03 | .01 | .00 | ☐ 230 Jeff Cox | | .05 | .02 | .00 |
| ☐ 178 Bob Welch | .08 | .03 | .01 | ☐ 231 Luis Tiant | | .08 | .03 | .01 |
| ☐ 179 Dusty Baker | .09 | .04 | .01 | ☐ 232 Rich Dauer | | .03 | .01 | .00 |
| ☐ 180 Rudy Law | .03 | .01 | .00 | ☐ 233 Dan Graham | | .03 | .01 | .00 |
| ☐ 181 Dave Concepcion | .14 | .06 | .01 | ☐ 234 Mike Flanagan | | .08 | .03 | .01 |
| ☐ 182 Johnny Bench | .50 | .22 | .05 | ☐ 235 John Lowenstein | | .03 | .01 | .00 |

| | MINT | VG-E | F-G |
|---|---|---|---|
| ☐ 236 Benny Ayala | .03 | .01 | .00 |
| ☐ 237 Wayne Gross | .03 | .01 | .00 |
| ☐ 238 Rick Langford | .03 | .01 | .00 |
| ☐ 239 Tony Armas | .16 | .07 | .01 |
| ☐ 240 A Bob Lacy P1 ERR | .12 | .05 | .01 |
| Name misspelled | | | |
| Bob "Lacy" | | | |
| ☐ 240 B Bob Lacey P2 COR | .08 | .03 | .01 |
| ☐ 241 Gene Tenace | .03 | .01 | .00 |
| ☐ 242 Bob Shirley | .03 | .01 | .00 |
| ☐ 243 Gary Lucas | .10 | .04 | .01 |
| ☐ 244 Jerry Turner | .03 | .01 | .00 |
| ☐ 245 John Wockenfuss | .03 | .01 | .00 |
| ☐ 246 Stan Papi | .03 | .01 | .00 |
| ☐ 247 Milt Wilcox | .05 | .02 | .00 |
| ☐ 248 Dan Schatzeder | .03 | .01 | .00 |
| ☐ 249 Steve Kemp | .12 | .05 | .01 |
| ☐ 250 Jim Lentine | .05 | .02 | .00 |
| ☐ 251 Pete Rose | 1.25 | .60 | .12 |
| ☐ 252 Bill Madlock | .25 | .10 | .02 |
| ☐ 253 Dale Berra | .05 | .02 | .00 |
| ☐ 254 Kent Tekulve | .08 | .03 | .01 |
| ☐ 255 Enrique Romo | .03 | .01 | .00 |
| ☐ 256 Mike Easler | .08 | .03 | .01 |
| ☐ 257 Chuck Tanner MGR | .05 | .02 | .00 |
| ☐ 258 Art Howe | .03 | .01 | .00 |
| ☐ 259 Alan Ashby | .03 | .01 | .00 |
| ☐ 260 Nolan Ryan | .40 | .18 | .04 |
| ☐ 261 A Vern Ruhle P1 ERR | .40 | .18 | .04 |
| Photo on front | | | |
| actually Ken Forsch | | | |
| ☐ 261 B Vern Ruhle P2 COR | .10 | .04 | .01 |
| ☐ 262 Bob Boone | .06 | .02 | .00 |
| ☐ 263 Cesar Cedeno | .09 | .04 | .01 |
| ☐ 264 Jeff Leonard | .08 | .03 | .01 |
| ☐ 265 Pat Putnam | .03 | .01 | .00 |
| ☐ 266 Jon Matlack | .06 | .02 | .00 |
| ☐ 267 Dave Rajsich | .03 | .01 | .00 |
| ☐ 268 Bill Sample | .03 | .01 | .00 |
| ☐ 269 Damaso Garcia | .65 | .30 | .06 |
| ☐ 270 Tom Buskey | .03 | .01 | .00 |
| ☐ 271 Joey McLaughlin | .03 | .01 | .00 |
| ☐ 272 Barry Bonnell | .05 | .02 | .00 |
| ☐ 273 Tug McGraw | .09 | .04 | .01 |
| ☐ 274 Mike Jorgensen | .03 | .01 | .00 |
| ☐ 275 Pat Zachry | .03 | .01 | .00 |
| ☐ 276 Neil Allen | .06 | .02 | .00 |
| ☐ 277 Joel Youngblood | .03 | .01 | .00 |
| ☐ 278 Greg Pryor | .03 | .01 | .00 |
| ☐ 279 Britt Burns | .60 | .28 | .06 |
| ☐ 280 Rich Dotson | .35 | .15 | .03 |
| ☐ 281 Chet Lemon | .09 | .04 | .01 |
| ☐ 282 Rusty Kuntz | .05 | .02 | .00 |

| | MINT | VG-E | F-G |
|---|---|---|---|
| ☐ 283 Ted Cox | .03 | .01 | .00 |
| ☐ 284 Sparky Lyle | .09 | .04 | .01 |
| ☐ 285 Larry Cox | .03 | .01 | .00 |
| ☐ 286 Floyd Bannister | .07 | .03 | .01 |
| ☐ 287 Byron McLaughlin | .03 | .01 | .00 |
| ☐ 288 Rodney Craig | .03 | .01 | .00 |
| ☐ 289 Bobby Grich | .09 | .04 | .01 |
| ☐ 290 Dickie Thon | .12 | .05 | .01 |
| ☐ 291 Mark Clear | .05 | .02 | .00 |
| ☐ 292 Dave Lemanczyk | .03 | .01 | .00 |
| ☐ 293 Jason Thompson | .08 | .03 | .01 |
| ☐ 294 Rick Miller | .03 | .01 | .00 |
| ☐ 295 Lonnie Smith | .09 | .04 | .01 |
| ☐ 296 Ron Cey | .15 | .06 | .01 |
| ☐ 297 Steve Yeager | .06 | .02 | .00 |
| ☐ 298 Bobby Castillo | .03 | .01 | .00 |
| ☐ 299 Manny Mota | .06 | .02 | .00 |
| ☐ 300 Jay Johnstone | .05 | .02 | .00 |
| ☐ 301 Dan Driessen | .05 | .02 | .00 |
| ☐ 302 Joe Nolan | .03 | .01 | .00 |
| ☐ 303 Paul Householder | .10 | .04 | .01 |
| ☐ 304 Harry Spilman | .03 | .01 | .00 |
| ☐ 305 Cesar Geronimo | .03 | .01 | .00 |
| ☐ 306 A Gary Mathews P1 ERR | .12 | .05 | .01 |
| Name misspelled | | | |
| ☐ 306 B Gary Matthews P2 COR | .08 | .03 | .01 |
| ☐ 307 Ken Reitz | .03 | .01 | .00 |
| ☐ 308 Ted Simmons | .14 | .06 | .01 |
| ☐ 309 John Littlefield | .05 | .02 | .00 |
| ☐ 310 George Frazier | .03 | .01 | .00 |
| ☐ 311 Dane Iorg | .03 | .01 | .00 |
| ☐ 312 Mike Ivie | .03 | .01 | .00 |
| ☐ 313 Dennis Littlejohn | .03 | .01 | .00 |
| ☐ 314 Gary Lavelle | .03 | .01 | .00 |
| ☐ 315 Jack Clark | .20 | .09 | .02 |
| ☐ 316 Jim Wohlford | .03 | .01 | .00 |
| ☐ 317 Rick Matula | .03 | .01 | .00 |
| ☐ 318 Toby Harrah | .05 | .02 | .00 |
| ☐ 319 A Dwane Kuiper P1 ERR | .12 | .05 | .01 |
| Name misspelled | | | |
| ☐ 319 B Duane Kuiper P2 COR | .08 | .03 | .01 |
| ☐ 320 Len Barker | .08 | .03 | .01 |
| ☐ 321 Victor Cruz | .03 | .01 | .00 |
| ☐ 322 Dell Alston | .03 | .01 | .00 |
| ☐ 323 Robin Yount | .45 | .20 | .04 |
| ☐ 324 Charlie Moore | .03 | .01 | .00 |
| ☐ 325 Lary Sorensen | .03 | .01 | .00 |
| ☐ 326 A Gorman Thomas P1 | .18 | .08 | .01 |
| 2nd line on back: | | | |
| "30 HR mark 4th" | | | |

| | | MINT | VG-E | F-G |
|---|---|---|---|---|
| ☐ 326 | **B** Gorman Thomas P2 .. "30 HR mark 3rd" | .12 | .05 | .01 |
| ☐ 327 | Bob Rodgers | .03 | .01 | .00 |
| ☐ 328 | Phil Niekro | .25 | .10 | .02 |
| ☐ 329 | Chris Speier | .03 | .01 | .00 |
| ☐ 330 | **A** Steve Rodgers P1 ERR Name misspelled | .15 | .06 | .01 |
| ☐ 330 | **B** Steve Rogers P2 COR | .10 | .04 | .01 |
| ☐ 331 | Woodie Fryman | .03 | .01 | .00 |
| ☐ 332 | Warren Cromartie | .03 | .01 | .00 |
| ☐ 333 | Jerry White | .03 | .01 | .00 |
| ☐ 334 | Tony Perez | .15 | .06 | .01 |
| ☐ 335 | Carlton Fisk | .25 | .10 | .02 |
| ☐ 336 | Dick Drago | .03 | .01 | .00 |
| ☐ 337 | Steve Renko | .03 | .01 | .00 |
| ☐ 338 | Jim Rice | .45 | .20 | .04 |
| ☐ 339 | Jerry Royster | .03 | .01 | .00 |
| ☐ 340 | Frank White | .08 | .03 | .01 |
| ☐ 341 | Jamie Quirk | .03 | .01 | .00 |
| ☐ 342 | **A** Paul Spittorff P1 ERR Name misspelled | .08 | .03 | .01 |
| ☐ 342 | **B** Paul Splittorff P2 COR | .08 | .03 | .01 |
| ☐ 343 | Marty Pattin | .03 | .01 | .00 |
| ☐ 344 | Pete LaCock | .03 | .01 | .00 |
| ☐ 345 | Willie Randolph | .09 | .04 | .01 |
| ☐ 346 | Rick Cerone | .06 | .02 | .00 |
| ☐ 347 | Rich Gossage | .25 | .10 | .02 |
| ☐ 348 | Reggie Jackson | .70 | .32 | .07 |
| ☐ 349 | Ruppert Jones | .05 | .02 | .00 |
| ☐ 350 | Dave McKay | .03 | .01 | .00 |
| ☐ 351 | Yogi Berra | .20 | .09 | .02 |
| ☐ 352 | Doug DeCinces | .10 | .04 | .01 |
| ☐ 353 | Jim Palmer | .35 | .15 | .03 |
| ☐ 354 | Tippy Martinez | .06 | .02 | .00 |
| ☐ 355 | Al Bumbry | .03 | .01 | .00 |
| ☐ 356 | Earl Weaver | .09 | .04 | .01 |
| ☐ 357 | **A** Bob Picciolo P1 ERR Name misspelled | .07 | .03 | .01 |
| ☐ 357 | **B** Rob Picciolo P2 COR | .06 | .02 | .00 |
| ☐ 358 | Matt Keough | .05 | .02 | .00 |
| ☐ 359 | Dwayne Murphy | .07 | .03 | .01 |
| ☐ 360 | Brian Kingman | .03 | .01 | .00 |
| ☐ 361 | Bill Fahey | .03 | .01 | .00 |
| ☐ 362 | Steve Mura | .03 | .01 | .00 |
| ☐ 363 | Dennis Kinney | .03 | .01 | .00 |
| ☐ 364 | Dave Winfield | .50 | .22 | .05 |
| ☐ 365 | Lou Whitaker | .25 | .10 | .02 |
| ☐ 366 | Lance Parrish | .35 | .15 | .03 |
| ☐ 367 | Tim Corcoran | .03 | .01 | .00 |
| ☐ 368 | Pat Underwood | .03 | .01 | .00 |
| ☐ 369 | Al Cowens | .05 | .02 | .00 |
| ☐ 370 | Sparky Anderson MGR | .07 | .03 | .01 |
| ☐ 371 | Pete Rose | 1.25 | .60 | .12 |
| ☐ 372 | Phil Garner | .05 | .02 | .00 |
| ☐ 373 | Steve Nicosia | .03 | .01 | .00 |
| ☐ 374 | John Candelaria | .08 | .03 | .01 |
| ☐ 375 | Don Robinson | .03 | .01 | .00 |
| ☐ 376 | Lee Lacy | .05 | .02 | .00 |
| ☐ 377 | John Milner | .03 | .01 | .00 |
| ☐ 378 | Craig Reynolds | .03 | .01 | .00 |
| ☐ 379 | **A** Luis Pujois P1 ERR Name misspelled | .10 | .04 | .01 |
| ☐ 379 | **B** Luis Pujols P2 COR | .07 | .03 | .01 |
| ☐ 380 | Joe Niekro | .07 | .03 | .01 |
| ☐ 381 | Joaquin Andujar | .18 | .08 | .01 |
| ☐ 382 | Keith Moreland | .40 | .18 | .04 |
| ☐ 383 | Jose Cruz | .14 | .06 | .01 |
| ☐ 384 | Bill Virdon | .05 | .02 | .00 |
| ☐ 385 | Jim Sundberg | .05 | .02 | .00 |
| ☐ 386 | Doc Medich | .03 | .01 | .00 |
| ☐ 387 | Al Oliver | .20 | .09 | .02 |
| ☐ 388 | Jim Norris | .03 | .01 | .00 |
| ☐ 389 | Bob Bailor | .03 | .01 | .00 |
| ☐ 390 | Ernie Whitt | .03 | .01 | .00 |
| ☐ 391 | Otto Velez | .03 | .01 | .00 |
| ☐ 392 | Roy Howell | .03 | .01 | .00 |
| ☐ 393 | Bob Walk | .05 | .02 | .00 |
| ☐ 394 | Doug Flynn | .03 | .01 | .00 |
| ☐ 395 | Pete Falcone | .03 | .01 | .00 |
| ☐ 396 | Tom Hausman | .03 | .01 | .00 |
| ☐ 397 | Elliott Maddox | .03 | .01 | .00 |
| ☐ 398 | Mike Squires | .03 | .01 | .00 |
| ☐ 399 | Marvis Foley | .05 | .02 | .00 |
| ☐ 400 | Steve Trout | .05 | .02 | .00 |
| ☐ 401 | Wayne Nordhagen | .03 | .01 | .00 |
| ☐ 402 | Tony LaRussa MGR | .05 | .02 | .00 |
| ☐ 403 | Bruce Bochte | .05 | .02 | .00 |
| ☐ 404 | Bake McBride | .05 | .02 | .00 |
| ☐ 405 | Jerry Narron | .03 | .01 | .00 |
| ☐ 406 | Rob Dressler | .03 | .01 | .00 |
| ☐ 407 | Dave Heaverlo | .03 | .01 | .00 |
| ☐ 408 | Tom Paciorek | .05 | .02 | .00 |
| ☐ 409 | Carney Lansford | .14 | .06 | .01 |
| ☐ 410 | Brian Downing | .05 | .02 | .00 |
| ☐ 411 | Don Aase | .03 | .01 | .00 |
| ☐ 412 | Jim Barr | .03 | .01 | .00 |
| ☐ 413 | Don Baylor | .20 | .09 | .02 |
| ☐ 414 | Jim Fregosi | .05 | .02 | .00 |
| ☐ 415 | Dallas Green MGR | .05 | .02 | .00 |
| ☐ 416 | Dave Lopes | .09 | .04 | .01 |
| ☐ 417 | Jerry Reuss | .08 | .03 | .01 |
| ☐ 418 | Rick Sutcliffe | .35 | .15 | .03 |
| ☐ 419 | Derrel Thomas | .03 | .01 | .00 |
| ☐ 420 | Tommy Lasorda MGR | .09 | .04 | .01 |
| ☐ 421 | Charles Leibrandt | .45 | .20 | .04 |

| | MINT | VG-E | F-G |
|---|---|---|---|
| ☐ 422 Tom Seaver | .40 | .18 | .04 |
| ☐ 423 Ron Oester | .05 | .02 | .00 |
| ☐ 424 Junior Kennedy | .03 | .01 | .00 |
| ☐ 425 Tom Seaver | .40 | .18 | .04 |
| ☐ 426 Bobby Cox MGR | .03 | .01 | .00 |
| ☐ 427 Leon Durham | 1.20 | .55 | .12 |
| ☐ 428 Terry Kennedy | .14 | .06 | .01 |
| ☐ 429 Silvio Martinez | .03 | .01 | .00 |
| ☐ 430 George Hendrick | .09 | .04 | .01 |
| ☐ 431 Red Schoendienst MGR | .06 | .02 | .00 |
| ☐ 432 Johnnie LeMaster | .03 | .01 | .00 |
| ☐ 433 Vida Blue | .09 | .04 | .01 |
| ☐ 434 John Montefusco | .05 | .02 | .00 |
| ☐ 435 Terry Whitfield | .03 | .01 | .00 |
| ☐ 436 Dave Bristol MGR | .03 | .01 | .00 |
| ☐ 437 Dale Murphy | 1.00 | .45 | .10 |
| ☐ 438 Jerry Dybzinski | .03 | .01 | .00 |
| ☐ 439 Jorge Orta | .03 | .01 | .00 |
| ☐ 440 Wayne Garland | .03 | .01 | .00 |
| ☐ 441 Miguel Dilone | .03 | .01 | .00 |
| ☐ 442 Dave Garcia MGR | .03 | .01 | .00 |
| ☐ 443 Don Money | .03 | .01 | .00 |
| ☐ 444 A Buck Martinez P1 ERR reverse negative | .12 | .05 | .01 |
| ☐ 444 B Buck Martinez P2 COR | .07 | .03 | .01 |
| ☐ 445 Jerry Augustine | .03 | .01 | .00 |
| ☐ 446 Ben Oglivie | .09 | .04 | .01 |
| ☐ 447 Jim Slaton | .05 | .02 | .00 |
| ☐ 448 Doyle Alexander | .05 | .02 | .00 |
| ☐ 449 Tony Bernazard | .03 | .01 | .00 |
| ☐ 450 Scott Sanderson | .03 | .01 | .00 |
| ☐ 451 Dave Palmer | .05 | .02 | .00 |
| ☐ 452 Stan Bahnsen | .03 | .01 | .00 |
| ☐ 453 Dick Williams | .05 | .02 | .00 |
| ☐ 454 Rick Burleson | .05 | .02 | .00 |
| ☐ 455 Gary Allenson | .03 | .01 | .00 |
| ☐ 456 Bob Stanley | .09 | .04 | .01 |
| ☐ 457 A John Tudor P1 ERR lifetime W-L "9.7" | .75 | .35 | .07 |
| ☐ 457 B John Tudor P2 COR corrected "9–7" | .75 | .35 | .07 |
| ☐ 458 Dwight Evans | .15 | .06 | .01 |
| ☐ 459 Glenn Hubbard | .05 | .02 | .00 |
| ☐ 460 U.L. Washington | .03 | .01 | .00 |
| ☐ 461 Larry Gura | .06 | .02 | .00 |
| ☐ 462 Rich Gale | .03 | .01 | .00 |
| ☐ 463 Hal McRae | .06 | .02 | .00 |
| ☐ 464 Jim Frey | .03 | .01 | .00 |
| ☐ 465 Bucky Dent | .08 | .03 | .01 |
| ☐ 466 Dennis Werth | .05 | .02 | .00 |
| ☐ 467 Ron Davis | .05 | .02 | .00 |
| ☐ 468 Reggie Jackson | .70 | .32 | .07 |
| ☐ 469 Bobby Brown | .03 | .01 | .00 |
| ☐ 470 Mike Davis | .40 | .18 | .04 |
| ☐ 471 Gaylord Perry | .30 | .12 | .03 |
| ☐ 472 Mark Belanger | .05 | .02 | .00 |
| ☐ 473 Jim Palmer | .35 | .15 | .03 |
| ☐ 474 Sammy Stewart | .03 | .01 | .00 |
| ☐ 475 Tim Stoddard | .03 | .01 | .00 |
| ☐ 476 Steve Stone | .05 | .02 | .00 |
| ☐ 477 Jeff Newman | .03 | .01 | .00 |
| ☐ 478 Steve McCatty | .05 | .02 | .00 |
| ☐ 479 Billy Martin | .15 | .06 | .01 |
| ☐ 480 Mitchell Page | .03 | .01 | .00 |
| ☐ 481 Cy Young Winner 1980 Steve Carlton | .35 | .15 | .03 |
| ☐ 482 Bill Buckner | .14 | .06 | .01 |
| ☐ 483 A Ivan DeJesus P1 ERR lifetime hits "702" | .07 | .03 | .01 |
| ☐ 483 B Ivan DeJesus P2 COR lifetime hits "642" | .07 | .03 | .01 |
| ☐ 484 Cliff Johnson | .03 | .01 | .00 |
| ☐ 485 Lenny Randle | .03 | .01 | .00 |
| ☐ 486 Larry Milbourne | .03 | .01 | .00 |
| ☐ 487 Roy Smalley | .05 | .02 | .00 |
| ☐ 488 John Castino | .05 | .02 | .00 |
| ☐ 489 Ron Jackson | .03 | .01 | .00 |
| ☐ 490 A Dave Roberts P1 Career Highlights: "Showed pop in" | .06 | .02 | .00 |
| ☐ 490 B Dave Roberts P2 "Declared himself" | .06 | .02 | .00 |
| ☐ 491 MVP: George Brett | .50 | .22 | .05 |
| ☐ 492 Mike Cubbage | .03 | .01 | .00 |
| ☐ 493 Rob Wilfong | .03 | .01 | .00 |
| ☐ 494 Danny Goodwin | .03 | .01 | .00 |
| ☐ 495 Jose Morales | .03 | .01 | .00 |
| ☐ 496 Mickey Rivers | .07 | .03 | .01 |
| ☐ 497 Mike Edwards | .03 | .01 | .00 |
| ☐ 498 Mike Sadek | .03 | .01 | .00 |
| ☐ 499 Lenn Sakata | .03 | .01 | .00 |
| ☐ 500 Gene Michael | .05 | .02 | .00 |
| ☐ 501 Dave Roberts | .03 | .01 | .00 |
| ☐ 502 Steve Dillard | .03 | .01 | .00 |
| ☐ 503 Jim Essian | .03 | .01 | .00 |
| ☐ 504 Rance Mulliniks | .03 | .01 | .00 |
| ☐ 505 Darrell Porter | .07 | .03 | .01 |
| ☐ 506 Joe Torre | .09 | .04 | .01 |
| ☐ 507 Terry Crowley | .03 | .01 | .00 |
| ☐ 508 Bill Travers | .03 | .01 | .00 |
| ☐ 509 Nelson Norman | .03 | .01 | .00 |
| ☐ 510 Bob McClure | .03 | .01 | .00 |
| ☐ 511 Steve Howe | .20 | .09 | .02 |
| ☐ 512 Dave Rader | .03 | .01 | .00 |
| ☐ 513 Mick Kelleher | .03 | .01 | .00 |
| ☐ 514 Kiko Garcia | .03 | .01 | .00 |

| | MINT | VG-E | F-G |
|---|---|---|---|
| ☐ 515 Larry Biittner | .03 | .01 | .00 |
| ☐ 516 A Willie Norwood P1 | .07 | .03 | .01 |
| Career Highlights: | | | |
| "Spent most of" | | | |
| ☐ 516 B Willie Norwood P2 | .07 | .03 | .01 |
| "Traded to Seattle" | | | |
| ☐ 517 Bo Diaz | .08 | .03 | .01 |
| ☐ 518 Juan Beniquez | .05 | .02 | .00 |
| ☐ 519 Scot Thompson | .03 | .01 | .00 |
| ☐ 520 Jim Tracy | .05 | .02 | .00 |
| ☐ 521 Carlos Lezcano | .05 | .02 | .00 |
| ☐ 522 Joe Amalfitano | .03 | .01 | .00 |
| ☐ 523 Preston Hanna | .03 | .01 | .00 |
| ☐ 524 A Ray Burris P1 | .08 | .03 | .01 |
| Career Highlights: | | | |
| "Went on . . ." | | | |
| ☐ 524 B Ray Burris P2 | .08 | .03 | .01 |
| "Drafted by . . ." | | | |
| ☐ 525 Broderick Perkins | .03 | .01 | .00 |
| ☐ 526 Mickey Hatcher | .05 | .02 | .00 |
| ☐ 527 John Goryl | .03 | .01 | .00 |
| ☐ 528 Dick Davis | .03 | .01 | .00 |
| ☐ 529 Butch Wynegar | .06 | .02 | .00 |
| ☐ 530 Sal Butera | .05 | .02 | .00 |
| ☐ 531 Jerry Koosman | .09 | .04 | .01 |
| ☐ 532 A Geoff Zahn P1 | .09 | .04 | .01 |
| Career Highlights: | | | |
| "Was 2nd in" | | | |
| ☐ 532 B Geoff Zahn P2 | .09 | .04 | .01 |
| "Signed a 3 year" | | | |
| ☐ 533 Dennis Martinez | .03 | .01 | .00 |
| ☐ 534 Gary Thomasson | .03 | .01 | .00 |
| ☐ 535 Steve Macko | .03 | .01 | .00 |
| ☐ 536 Jim Kaat | .14 | .06 | .01 |
| ☐ 537 Best Hitters: | 1.00 | .45 | .10 |
| George Brett | | | |
| Rod Carew | | | |
| ☐ 538 Tim Raines | 1.50 | .70 | .15 |
| ☐ 539 Keith Smith | .03 | .01 | .00 |
| ☐ 540 Ken Macha | .03 | .01 | .00 |
| ☐ 541 Burt Hooton | .03 | .01 | .00 |
| ☐ 542 Butch Hobson | .03 | .01 | .00 |
| ☐ 543 Bill Stein | .03 | .01 | .00 |
| ☐ 544 Dave Stapleton | .15 | .06 | .01 |
| ☐ 545 Bob Pate | .05 | .02 | .00 |
| ☐ 546 Doug Corbett | .08 | .03 | .01 |
| ☐ 547 Darrell Jackson | .03 | .01 | .00 |
| ☐ 548 Pete Redfern | .03 | .01 | .00 |
| ☐ 549 Roger Erickson | .03 | .01 | .00 |
| ☐ 550 Al Hrabosky | .06 | .02 | .00 |
| ☐ 551 Dick Tidrow | .03 | .01 | .00 |
| ☐ 552 Dave Ford | .03 | .01 | .00 |
| ☐ 553 Dave Kingman | .14 | .06 | .01 |
| ☐ 554 A Mike Vail P1 | .07 | .03 | .01 |
| Career Highlights: | | | |
| "After two . . ." | | | |
| ☐ 554 B Mike Vail P2 | .07 | .03 | .01 |
| "Traded to . . ." | | | |
| ☐ 555 A Jerry Martin P1 | .07 | .03 | .01 |
| Career Highlights: | | | |
| "Overcame . . ." | | | |
| ☐ 555 B Jerry Martin P2 | .07 | .03 | .01 |
| "Traded to . . ." | | | |
| ☐ 556 A Jesus Figueroa P1 | .06 | .02 | .00 |
| Career Highlights: | | | |
| "Had an . . ." | | | |
| ☐ 556 B Jesus Figueroa P2 | .06 | .02 | .00 |
| "Traded to . . ." | | | |
| ☐ 557 Don Stanhouse | .03 | .01 | .00 |
| ☐ 558 Barry Foote | .03 | .01 | .00 |
| ☐ 559 Tim Blackwell | .03 | .01 | .00 |
| ☐ 560 Bruce Sutter | .30 | .12 | .03 |
| ☐ 561 Rick Reuschel | .06 | .02 | .00 |
| ☐ 562 Lynn McGlothen | .03 | .01 | .00 |
| ☐ 563 A Bob Owchinko P1 | .07 | .03 | .01 |
| Career Highlights: | | | |
| "Traded to . . ." | | | |
| ☐ 563 B Bob Owchinko P2 | .07 | .03 | .01 |
| "Involved in a . . ." | | | |
| ☐ 564 John Verhoeven | .03 | .01 | .00 |
| ☐ 565 Ken Landreaux | .06 | .02 | .00 |
| ☐ 566 A Glen Adams P1 ERR | .10 | .04 | .01 |
| Name misspelled | | | |
| ☐ 566 B Glenn Adams P2 COR | .07 | .03 | .01 |
| ☐ 567 Hosken Powell | .03 | .01 | .00 |
| ☐ 568 Dick Noles | .03 | .01 | .00 |
| ☐ 569 Danny Ainge | .25 | .10 | .02 |
| ☐ 570 Bobby Mattick | .03 | .01 | .00 |
| ☐ 571 Joe LeFebvre | .12 | .05 | .01 |
| ☐ 572 Bobby Clark | .03 | .01 | .00 |
| ☐ 573 Dennis Lamp | .03 | .01 | .00 |
| ☐ 574 Randy Lerch | .03 | .01 | .00 |
| ☐ 575 Mookie Wilson | .40 | .18 | .04 |
| ☐ 576 Ron LeFlore | .06 | .02 | .00 |
| ☐ 577 Jim Dwyer | .03 | .01 | .00 |
| ☐ 578 Bill Castro | .03 | .01 | .00 |
| ☐ 579 Greg Minton | .05 | .02 | .00 |
| ☐ 580 Mark Littell | .03 | .01 | .00 |
| ☐ 581 Andy Hassler | .03 | .01 | .00 |
| ☐ 582 Dave Stieb | .35 | .15 | .03 |
| ☐ 583 Ken Oberkfell | .05 | .02 | .00 |
| ☐ 584 Larry Bradford | .03 | .01 | .00 |
| ☐ 585 Fred Stanley | .03 | .01 | .00 |
| ☐ 586 Bill Caudill | .10 | .04 | .01 |
| ☐ 587 Doug Capilla | .03 | .01 | .00 |
| ☐ 588 George Riley | .05 | .02 | .00 |

|  | | MINT | VG-E | F-G |
|---|---|---|---|---|
| ☐ 589 | Willie Hernandez | .25 | .10 | .02 |
| ☐ 590 | MVP: Mike Schmidt | .45 | .20 | .04 |
| ☐ 591 | Cy Young Winner 1980: Steve Stone | .08 | .03 | .01 |
| ☐ 592 | Rick Sofield | .03 | .01 | .00 |
| ☐ 593 | Bombo Rivera | .03 | .01 | .00 |
| ☐ 594 | Gary Ward | .09 | .04 | .01 |
| ☐ 595 A | Dave Edwards P1 Career Highlights: "Sidelined the" | .07 | .03 | .01 |
| ☐ 595 B | Dave Edwards P2 "Traded to . . ." | .07 | .03 | .01 |
| ☐ 596 | Mike Proly | .03 | .01 | .00 |
| ☐ 597 | Tommy Boggs | .03 | .01 | .00 |
| ☐ 598 | Greg Gross | .03 | .01 | .00 |
| ☐ 599 | Elias Sosa | .03 | .01 | .00 |
| ☐ 600 | Pat Kelly | .03 | .01 | .00 |
|  | UNNUMBERED CHECKLISTS | | | |
| ☐ 601 A | Checklist 1 P1 ERR 51 Donahue | .10 | .02 | .00 |
| ☐ 601 B | Checklist 1 P2 COR 51 Donohue | .70 | .10 | .02 |
| ☐ 602 | Checklist 2 | .10 | .02 | .00 |
| ☐ 603 A | Checklist 3 P1 ERR 306 Mathews | .10 | .02 | .00 |
| ☐ 603 B | Checklist 3 P2 COR 306 Mathews | .10 | .02 | .00 |
| ☐ 604 A | Checklist 4 P1 ERR 379 Pujois | .10 | .02 | .00 |
| ☐ 604 B | Checklist 4 P2 COR 379 Pujois | .10 | .02 | .00 |
| ☐ 605 A | Checklist 5 P1 ERR 566 Glen Adams | .10 | .02 | .00 |
| ☐ 605 B | Checklist 5 P2 COR 566 Glenn Adams | .10 | .02 | .00 |

## 1982 DONRUSS

The 1982 Donruss set contains 653 numbered cards and the seven unnumbered checklists; each card measures 2½" by 3½". The first 26 cards of this set are entitled Donruss Diamond Kings (DK) and feature the artwork of Dick Perez of Perez-Steele Galleries. The set was marketed with puzzle pieces rather than with bubble gum. There are 63 pieces to the puzzle, which when put together make a collage of Babe Ruth entitled "Hall of Fame Diamond King." The card stock in this year's Donruss cards is considerably thicker than that of the 1981 cards.

Complete Set: M-17.00; VG-E-8.00; F-G-1.70

|  | | MINT | VG-E | F-G |
|---|---|---|---|---|
|  | Common Player (1–660) | .03 | .01 | .00 |
|  | DIAMOND KINGS (1–26) | | | |
| ☐ 1 | Pete Rose DK | 1.25 | .60 | .12 |
| ☐ 2 | Gary Carter DK | .45 | .20 | .04 |
| ☐ 3 | Steve Garvey DK | .50 | .22 | .05 |
| ☐ 4 | Vida Blue DK | .13 | .06 | .01 |
| ☐ 5 A | Alan Trammel DK ERR (name misspelled) | .55 | .25 | .05 |
| ☐ 5 B | Alan Trammell DK COR | .35 | .15 | .03 |
| ☐ 6 | Len Barker DK | .09 | .04 | .01 |
| ☐ 7 | Dwight Evans DK | .14 | .06 | .01 |
| ☐ 8 | Rod Carew DK | .45 | .20 | .04 |
| ☐ 9 | George Hendrick DK | .09 | .04 | .01 |
| ☐ 10 | Phil Niekro DK | .30 | .12 | .03 |
| ☐ 11 | Richie Zisk DK | .09 | .04 | .01 |
| ☐ 12 | Dave Parker DK | .30 | .12 | .03 |
| ☐ 13 | Nolan Ryan DK | .40 | .18 | .04 |
| ☐ 14 | Ivan DeJesus DK | .09 | .04 | .01 |
| ☐ 15 | George Brett DK | .65 | .30 | .06 |
| ☐ 16 | Tom Seaver DK | .40 | .18 | .04 |
| ☐ 17 | Dave Kingman DK | .14 | .06 | .01 |
| ☐ 18 | Dave Winfield DK | .45 | .20 | .04 |
| ☐ 19 | Mike Norris DK | .09 | .04 | .01 |
| ☐ 20 | Carlton Fisk DK | .25 | .10 | .02 |
| ☐ 21 | Ozzie Smith DK | .14 | .06 | .01 |
| ☐ 22 | Roy Smalley DK | .09 | .04 | .01 |
| ☐ 23 | Buddy Bell DK | .12 | .05 | .01 |
| ☐ 24 | Ken Singleton DK | .09 | .04 | .01 |
| ☐ 25 | John Mayberry DK | .09 | .04 | .01 |
| ☐ 26 | Gorman Thomas DK | .12 | .05 | .01 |
| ☐ 27 | Earl Weaver MGR | .08 | .03 | .01 |
| ☐ 28 | Rollie Fingers | .20 | .09 | .02 |
| ☐ 29 | Sparky Anderson MGR | .08 | .03 | .01 |

| | | MINT | VG-E | F-G |
|---|---|---|---|---|
| ☐ 30 | Dennis Eckersley | .06 | .02 | .00 |
| ☐ 31 | Dave Winfield | .45 | .20 | .04 |
| ☐ 32 | Burt Hooton | .03 | .01 | .00 |
| ☐ 33 | Rick Waits | .03 | .01 | .00 |
| ☐ 34 | George Brett | .65 | .30 | .06 |
| ☐ 35 | Steve McCatty | .03 | .01 | .00 |
| ☐ 36 | Steve Rogers | .08 | .03 | .01 |
| ☐ 37 | Bill Stein | .03 | .01 | .00 |
| ☐ 38 | Steve Renko | .03 | .01 | .00 |
| ☐ 39 | Mike Squires | .03 | .01 | .00 |
| ☐ 40 | George Hendrick | .08 | .03 | .01 |
| ☐ 41 | Bob Knepper | .06 | .02 | .00 |
| ☐ 42 | Steve Carlton | .50 | .22 | .05 |
| ☐ 43 | Larry Bittner | .03 | .01 | .00 |
| ☐ 44 | Chris Welsh | .07 | .03 | .01 |
| ☐ 45 | Steve Nicosia | .03 | .01 | .00 |
| ☐ 46 | Jack Clark | .18 | .08 | .01 |
| ☐ 47 | Chris Chambliss | .05 | .02 | .00 |
| ☐ 48 | Ivan DeJesus | .03 | .01 | .00 |
| ☐ 49 | Lee Mazzilli | .06 | .02 | .00 |
| ☐ 50 | Julio Cruz | .03 | .01 | .00 |
| ☐ 51 | Pete Redfern | .03 | .01 | .00 |
| ☐ 52 | Dave Stieb | .25 | .10 | .02 |
| ☐ 53 | Doug Corbett | .05 | .02 | .00 |
| ☐ 54 | Jorge Bell | .85 | .40 | .08 |
| ☐ 55 | Joe Simpson | .03 | .01 | .00 |
| ☐ 56 | Rusty Staub | .09 | .04 | .01 |
| ☐ 57 | Hector Cruz | .03 | .01 | .00 |
| ☐ 58 | Claudell Washington | .08 | .03 | .01 |
| ☐ 59 | Enrique Romo | .03 | .01 | .00 |
| ☐ 60 | Gary Lavelle | .03 | .01 | .00 |
| ☐ 61 | Tim Flannery | .03 | .01 | .00 |
| ☐ 62 | Joe Nolan | .03 | .01 | .00 |
| ☐ 63 | Larry Bowa | .09 | .04 | .01 |
| ☐ 64 | Sixto Lezcano | .03 | .01 | .00 |
| ☐ 65 | Joe Sambito | .05 | .02 | .00 |
| ☐ 66 | Bruce Kison | .03 | .01 | .00 |
| ☐ 67 | Wayne Nordhagen | .03 | .01 | .00 |
| ☐ 68 | Woodie Fryman | .03 | .01 | .00 |
| ☐ 69 | Billy Sample | .03 | .01 | .00 |
| ☐ 70 | Amos Otis | .07 | .03 | .01 |
| ☐ 71 | Matt Keough | .03 | .01 | .00 |
| ☐ 72 | Toby Harrah | .06 | .02 | .00 |
| ☐ 73 | Dave Righetti | .70 | .32 | .07 |
| ☐ 74 | Carl Yastrzemski | .65 | .30 | .06 |
| ☐ 75 | Bob Welch | .09 | .04 | .01 |
| ☐ 76 A | Alan Trammel ERR (name misspelled) | .55 | .25 | .05 |
| ☐ 76 B | Alan Trammell CORR | .30 | .12 | .03 |
| ☐ 77 | Rick Dempsey | .05 | .02 | .00 |
| ☐ 78 | Paul Molitor | .16 | .07 | .01 |
| ☐ 79 | Dennis Martinez | .03 | .01 | .00 |
| ☐ 80 | Jim Slaton | .03 | .01 | .00 |

| | | MINT | VG-E | F-G |
|---|---|---|---|---|
| ☐ 81 | Champ Summers | .03 | .01 | .00 |
| ☐ 82 | Carney Lansford | .13 | .06 | .01 |
| ☐ 83 | Barry Foote | .03 | .01 | .00 |
| ☐ 84 | Steve Garvey | .45 | .20 | .04 |
| ☐ 85 | Rick Manning | .03 | .01 | .00 |
| ☐ 86 | John Wathan | .03 | .01 | .00 |
| ☐ 87 | Brian Kingman | .03 | .01 | .00 |
| ☐ 88 | Andre Dawson | .25 | .10 | .02 |
| ☐ 89 | Jim Kern | .03 | .01 | .00 |
| ☐ 90 | Bobby Grich | .08 | .03 | .01 |
| ☐ 91 | Bob Forsch | .05 | .02 | .00 |
| ☐ 92 | Art Howe | .03 | .01 | .00 |
| ☐ 93 | Marty Bystrom | .03 | .01 | .00 |
| ☐ 94 | Ozzie Smith | .12 | .05 | .01 |
| ☐ 95 | Dave Parker | .25 | .10 | .02 |
| ☐ 96 | Doyle Alexander | .06 | .02 | .00 |
| ☐ 97 | Al Hrabosky | .06 | .02 | .00 |
| ☐ 98 | Frank Taveras | .03 | .01 | .00 |
| ☐ 99 | Tim Blackwell | .03 | .01 | .00 |
| ☐ 100 | Floyd Bannister | .07 | .03 | .01 |
| ☐ 101 | Alfredo Griffin | .08 | .03 | .01 |
| ☐ 102 | Dave Engle | .07 | .03 | .01 |
| ☐ 103 | Mario Soto | .13 | .06 | .01 |
| ☐ 104 | Ross Baumgarten | .03 | .01 | .00 |
| ☐ 105 | Ken Singleton | .09 | .04 | .01 |
| ☐ 106 | Ted Simmons | .14 | .06 | .01 |
| ☐ 107 | Jack Morris | .25 | .10 | .02 |
| ☐ 108 | Bob Watson | .06 | .01 | .00 |
| ☐ 109 | Dwight Evans | .15 | .06 | .01 |
| ☐ 110 | Tom LaSorda | .09 | .04 | .01 |
| ☐ 111 | Bert Blyleven | .15 | .06 | .01 |
| ☐ 112 | Dan Quisenberry | .25 | .10 | .02 |
| ☐ 113 | Rickey Henderson | .55 | .25 | .05 |
| ☐ 114 | Gary Carter | .40 | .18 | .04 |
| ☐ 115 | Brian Downing | .05 | .02 | .00 |
| ☐ 116 | Al Oliver | .18 | .08 | .01 |
| ☐ 117 | LaMarr Hoyt | .14 | .06 | .01 |
| ☐ 118 | Cesar Cedeno | .09 | .04 | .01 |
| ☐ 119 | Keith Moreland | .05 | .02 | .00 |
| ☐ 120 | Bob Shirley | .03 | .01 | .00 |
| ☐ 121 | Terry Kennedy | .11 | .05 | .01 |
| ☐ 122 | Frank Pastore | .03 | .01 | .00 |
| ☐ 123 | Gene Garber | .03 | .01 | .00 |
| ☐ 124 | Tony Pena | .16 | .07 | .01 |
| ☐ 125 | Allen Ripley | .03 | .01 | .00 |
| ☐ 126 | Randy Martz | .03 | .01 | .00 |
| ☐ 127 | Richie Zisk | .05 | .02 | .00 |
| ☐ 128 | Mike Scott | .05 | .02 | .00 |
| ☐ 129 | Lloyd Moseby | .16 | .07 | .01 |
| ☐ 130 | Rob Wilfong | .03 | .01 | .00 |
| ☐ 131 | Tim Stoddard | .03 | .01 | .00 |
| ☐ 132 | Gorman Thomas | .13 | .06 | .01 |
| ☐ 133 | Dan Petry | .18 | .08 | .01 |

| | MINT | VG-E | F-G | | MINT | VG-E | F-G |
|---|---|---|---|---|---|---|---|
| ☐ 134 Bob Stanley | .07 | .03 | .01 | ☐ 187 Danny Boone | .05 | .02 | .00 |
| ☐ 135 Lou Piniella | .10 | .04 | .01 | ☐ 188 Junior Kennedy | .03 | .01 | .00 |
| ☐ 136 Pedro Guerrero | .35 | .15 | .03 | ☐ 189 Sparky Lyle | .09 | .04 | .01 |
| ☐ 137 Len Barker | .08 | .03 | .01 | ☐ 190 Whitey Herzog MGR | .05 | .02 | .00 |
| ☐ 138 Rich Gale | .03 | .01 | .00 | ☐ 191 Dave Smith | .03 | .01 | .00 |
| ☐ 139 Wayne Gross | .03 | .01 | .00 | ☐ 192 Ed Ott | .03 | .01 | .00 |
| ☐ 140 Tim Wallach | .65 | .30 | .06 | ☐ 193 Greg Luzinski | .13 | .06 | .01 |
| ☐ 141 Gene Mauch | .03 | .01 | .00 | ☐ 194 Bill Lee | .05 | .02 | .00 |
| ☐ 142 Doc Medich | .03 | .01 | .00 | ☐ 195 Don Zimmer | .03 | .01 | .00 |
| ☐ 143 Tony Bernazard | .03 | .01 | .00 | ☐ 196 Hal McRae | .07 | .03 | .01 |
| ☐ 144 Bill Virdon | .03 | .01 | .00 | ☐ 197 Mike Norris | .05 | .02 | .00 |
| ☐ 145 John Littlefield | .03 | .01 | .00 | ☐ 198 Duane Kuiper | .03 | .01 | .00 |
| ☐ 146 Dave Bergman | .03 | .01 | .00 | ☐ 199 Rick Cerone | .05 | .02 | .00 |
| ☐ 147 Dick Davis | .03 | .01 | .00 | ☐ 200 Jim Rice | .35 | .15 | .03 |
| ☐ 148 Tom Seaver | .40 | .18 | .04 | ☐ 201 Steve Yeager | .05 | .02 | .00 |
| ☐ 149 Matt Sinatro | .05 | .02 | .00 | ☐ 202 Tom Brookens | .03 | .01 | .00 |
| ☐ 150 Chuck Tanner | .03 | .01 | .00 | ☐ 203 Jose Morales | .03 | .01 | .00 |
| ☐ 151 Leon Durham | .25 | .10 | .02 | ☐ 204 Roy Howell | .03 | .01 | .00 |
| ☐ 152 Gene Tenace | .03 | .01 | .00 | ☐ 205 Tippy Martinez | .05 | .02 | .00 |
| ☐ 153 Al Bumbry | .03 | .01 | .00 | ☐ 206 Moose Haas | .05 | .02 | .00 |
| ☐ 154 Mark Brouhard | .05 | .02 | .00 | ☐ 207 Al Cowens | .05 | .02 | .00 |
| ☐ 155 Rick Peters | .03 | .01 | .00 | ☐ 208 Dave Stapleton | .03 | .01 | .00 |
| ☐ 156 Jerry Remy | .05 | .02 | .00 | ☐ 209 Bucky Dent | .08 | .03 | .01 |
| ☐ 157 Rick Reuschel | .06 | .02 | .00 | ☐ 210 Ron Cey | .15 | .06 | .01 |
| ☐ 158 Steve Howe | .06 | .02 | .00 | ☐ 211 Jorge Orta | .03 | .01 | .00 |
| ☐ 159 Alan Bannister | .03 | .01 | .00 | ☐ 212 Jamie Quirk | .03 | .01 | .00 |
| ☐ 160 U.L. Washington | .03 | .01 | .00 | ☐ 213 Jeff Jones | .03 | .01 | .00 |
| ☐ 161 Rick Langford | .03 | .01 | .00 | ☐ 214 Tim Raines | .40 | .18 | .04 |
| ☐ 162 Bill Gullickson | .06 | .02 | .00 | ☐ 215 Jon Matlack | .05 | .02 | .00 |
| ☐ 163 Mark Wagner | .03 | .01 | .00 | ☐ 216 Rod Carew | .45 | .20 | .04 |
| ☐ 164 Geoff Zahn | .05 | .02 | .00 | ☐ 217 Jim Kaat | .12 | .05 | .01 |
| ☐ 165 Ron LeFlore | .06 | .02 | .00 | ☐ 218 Joe Pittman | .05 | .02 | .00 |
| ☐ 166 Dane Iorg | .03 | .01 | .00 | ☐ 219 Larry Christenson | .03 | .01 | .00 |
| ☐ 167 Joe Niekro | .07 | .03 | .01 | ☐ 220 Juan Bonilla | .07 | .03 | .01 |
| ☐ 168 Pete Rose | 1.00 | .45 | .10 | ☐ 221 Mike Easler | .06 | .02 | .00 |
| ☐ 169 Dave Collins | .07 | .03 | .01 | ☐ 222 Vida Blue | .09 | .04 | .01 |
| ☐ 170 Rick Wise | .05 | .02 | .00 | ☐ 223 Rick Camp | .03 | .01 | .00 |
| ☐ 171 Jim Bibby | .05 | .02 | .00 | ☐ 224 Mike Jorgensen | .03 | .01 | .00 |
| ☐ 172 Larry Herndon | .05 | .02 | .00 | ☐ 225 Jody Davis | .50 | .22 | .05 |
| ☐ 173 Bob Horner | .25 | .10 | .02 | ☐ 226 Mike Parrott | .03 | .01 | .00 |
| ☐ 174 Steve Dillard | .03 | .01 | .00 | ☐ 227 Jim Clancy | .03 | .01 | .00 |
| ☐ 175 Mookie Wilson | .10 | .04 | .01 | ☐ 228 Hosken Powell | .03 | .01 | .00 |
| ☐ 176 Dan Meyer | .03 | .01 | .00 | ☐ 229 Tom Hume | .03 | .01 | .00 |
| ☐ 177 Fernando Arroyo | .03 | .01 | .00 | ☐ 230 Britt Burns | .08 | .03 | .01 |
| ☐ 178 Jackson Todd | .03 | .01 | .00 | ☐ 231 Jim Palmer | .30 | .12 | .03 |
| ☐ 179 Darrell Jackson | .03 | .01 | .00 | ☐ 232 Bob Rodgers | .03 | .01 | .00 |
| ☐ 180 Al Woods | .03 | .01 | .00 | ☐ 233 Milt Wilcox | .03 | .01 | .00 |
| ☐ 181 Jim Anderson | .03 | .01 | .00 | ☐ 234 Dave Revering | .03 | .01 | .00 |
| ☐ 182 Dave Kingman | .14 | .06 | .01 | ☐ 235 Mike Torrez | .06 | .02 | .00 |
| ☐ 183 Steve Henderson | .03 | .01 | .00 | ☐ 236 Robert Castillo | .03 | .01 | .00 |
| ☐ 184 Brian Asselstine | .03 | .01 | .00 | ☐ 237 Von Hayes | .75 | .35 | .07 |
| ☐ 185 Rod Scurry | .03 | .01 | .00 | ☐ 238 Renie Martin | .03 | .01 | .00 |
| ☐ 186 Fred Breining | .10 | .04 | .01 | ☐ 239 Dwayne Murphy | .07 | .03 | .01 |

| | MINT | VG-E | F-G |
|---|---|---|---|
| ☐ 240 Rodney Scott | .03 | .01 | .00 |
| ☐ 241 Fred Patek | .03 | .01 | .00 |
| ☐ 242 Mickey Rivers | .06 | .02 | .00 |
| ☐ 243 Steve Trout | .05 | .02 | .00 |
| ☐ 244 Jose Cruz | .14 | .06 | .01 |
| ☐ 245 Manny Trillo | .05 | .02 | .00 |
| ☐ 246 Lary Sorensen | .03 | .01 | .00 |
| ☐ 247 Dave Edwards | .03 | .01 | .00 |
| ☐ 248 Dan Driessen | .05 | .02 | .00 |
| ☐ 249 Tommy Boggs | .03 | .01 | .00 |
| ☐ 250 Dale Berra | .05 | .02 | .00 |
| ☐ 251 Ed Whitson | .07 | .03 | .01 |
| ☐ 252 Lee Smith | .50 | .22 | .05 |
| ☐ 253 Tom Paciorek | .03 | .01 | .00 |
| ☐ 254 Pat Zachry | .03 | .01 | .00 |
| ☐ 255 Luis Leal | .05 | .02 | .00 |
| ☐ 256 John Castino | .03 | .01 | .00 |
| ☐ 257 Rich Dauer | .03 | .01 | .00 |
| ☐ 258 Cecil Cooper | .18 | .08 | .01 |
| ☐ 259 Dave Rozema | .03 | .01 | .00 |
| ☐ 260 John Tudor | .15 | .06 | .01 |
| ☐ 261 Jerry Mumphrey | .05 | .02 | .00 |
| ☐ 262 Jay Johnstone | .05 | .02 | .00 |
| ☐ 263 Bo Diaz | .05 | .02 | .00 |
| ☐ 264 Dennis Leonard | .07 | .03 | .01 |
| ☐ 265 Jim Spencer | .03 | .01 | .00 |
| ☐ 266 John Milner | .03 | .01 | .00 |
| ☐ 267 Don Aase | .03 | .01 | .00 |
| ☐ 268 Jim Sundberg | .06 | .02 | .00 |
| ☐ 269 Lamar Johnson | .03 | .01 | .00 |
| ☐ 270 Frank LaCorte | .03 | .01 | .00 |
| ☐ 271 Barry Evans | .03 | .01 | .00 |
| ☐ 272 Enos Cabell | .03 | .01 | .00 |
| ☐ 273 Del Unser | .03 | .01 | .00 |
| ☐ 274 George Foster | .18 | .08 | .01 |
| ☐ 275 Brett Butler | .60 | .28 | .06 |
| ☐ 276 Lee Lacy | .06 | .02 | .00 |
| ☐ 277 Ken Reitz | .03 | .01 | .00 |
| ☐ 278 Keith Hernandez | .30 | .12 | .03 |
| ☐ 279 Doug DeCinces | .10 | .04 | .01 |
| ☐ 280 Charlie Moore | .03 | .01 | .00 |
| ☐ 281 Lance Parrish | .30 | .12 | .03 |
| ☐ 282 Ralph Houk | .06 | .02 | .00 |
| ☐ 283 Rich Gossage | .25 | .10 | .02 |
| ☐ 284 Jerry Reuss | .06 | .02 | .00 |
| ☐ 285 Mike Stanton | .03 | .01 | .00 |
| ☐ 286 Frank White | .08 | .03 | .01 |
| ☐ 287 Bob Owchinko | .03 | .01 | .00 |
| ☐ 288 Scott Sanderson | .05 | .02 | .00 |
| ☐ 289 Bump Wills | .03 | .01 | .00 |
| ☐ 290 Dave Frost | .03 | .01 | .00 |
| ☐ 291 Chet Lemon | .08 | .03 | .01 |
| ☐ 292 Tito Landrum | .05 | .02 | .00 |
| ☐ 293 Vern Ruhle | .03 | .01 | .00 |
| ☐ 294 Mike Schmidt | .55 | .25 | .05 |
| ☐ 295 Sam Mejias | .03 | .01 | .00 |
| ☐ 296 Gary Lucas | .03 | .01 | .00 |
| ☐ 297 John Candelaria | .06 | .02 | .00 |
| ☐ 298 Jerry Martin | .03 | .01 | .00 |
| ☐ 299 Dale Murphy | .85 | .40 | .08 |
| ☐ 300 Mike Lum | .03 | .01 | .00 |
| ☐ 301 Tom Hausman | .03 | .01 | .00 |
| ☐ 302 Glenn Abbott | .03 | .01 | .00 |
| ☐ 303 Roger Erickson | .03 | .01 | .00 |
| ☐ 304 Otto Velez | .03 | .01 | .00 |
| ☐ 305 Danny Goodwin | .03 | .01 | .00 |
| ☐ 306 John Mayberry | .05 | .02 | .00 |
| ☐ 307 Lenny Randle | .03 | .01 | .00 |
| ☐ 308 Bob Bailor | .03 | .01 | .00 |
| ☐ 309 Jerry Morales | .03 | .01 | .00 |
| ☐ 310 Rufino Linares | .05 | .02 | .00 |
| ☐ 311 Kent Tekulve | .06 | .02 | .00 |
| ☐ 312 Joe Morgan | .20 | .09 | .02 |
| ☐ 313 John Urrea | .03 | .01 | .00 |
| ☐ 314 Paul Householder | .03 | .01 | .00 |
| ☐ 315 Garry Maddox | .05 | .02 | .00 |
| ☐ 316 Mike Ramsey | .03 | .01 | .00 |
| ☐ 317 Alan Ashby | .03 | .01 | .00 |
| ☐ 318 Bob Clark | .03 | .01 | .00 |
| ☐ 319 Tony LaRussa | .05 | .02 | .00 |
| ☐ 320 Charlie Lea | .05 | .02 | .00 |
| ☐ 321 Danny Darwin | .03 | .01 | .00 |
| ☐ 322 Cesar Geronimo | .03 | .01 | .00 |
| ☐ 323 Tom Underwood | .03 | .01 | .00 |
| ☐ 324 Andre Thornton | .08 | .03 | .01 |
| ☐ 325 Rudy May | .03 | .01 | .00 |
| ☐ 326 Frank Tanana | .05 | .02 | .00 |
| ☐ 327 Davey Lopes | .07 | .03 | .01 |
| ☐ 328 Richie Hebner | .03 | .01 | .00 |
| ☐ 329 Mike Flanagan | .08 | .03 | .01 |
| ☐ 330 Mike Caldwell | .05 | .02 | .00 |
| ☐ 331 Scott McGregor | .08 | .03 | .01 |
| ☐ 332 Jerry Augustine | .03 | .01 | .00 |
| ☐ 333 Stan Papi | .03 | .01 | .00 |
| ☐ 334 Rick Miller | .03 | .01 | .00 |
| ☐ 335 Graig Nettles | .14 | .06 | .01 |
| ☐ 336 Dusty Baker | .09 | .04 | .01 |
| ☐ 337 Dave Garcia | .03 | .01 | .00 |
| ☐ 338 Larry Gura | .06 | .02 | .00 |
| ☐ 339 Cliff Johnson | .03 | .01 | .00 |
| ☐ 340 Warren Cromartie | .03 | .01 | .00 |
| ☐ 341 Steve Comer | .03 | .01 | .00 |
| ☐ 342 Rick Burleson | .06 | .02 | .00 |
| ☐ 343 John Martin | .05 | .02 | .00 |
| ☐ 344 Craig Reynolds | .03 | .01 | .00 |
| ☐ 345 Mike Proly | .03 | .01 | .00 |

| | MINT | VG-E | F-G |
|---|---|---|---|
| ☐ 346 Ruppert Jones | .05 | .02 | .00 |
| ☐ 347 Omar Moreno | .05 | .02 | .00 |
| ☐ 348 Greg Minton | .05 | .02 | .00 |
| ☐ 349 Rick Mahler | .25 | .10 | .02 |
| ☐ 350 Alex Trevino | .03 | .01 | .00 |
| ☐ 351 Mike Krukow | .03 | .01 | .00 |
| ☐ 352 A Shane Rawley ERR | .50 | .22 | .05 |
| (photo actually | | | |
| Jim Anderson) | | | |
| ☐ 352 B Shane Rawley COR | .10 | .04 | .01 |
| ☐ 353 Garth Iorg | .03 | .01 | .00 |
| ☐ 354 Pete Mackanin | .03 | .01 | .00 |
| ☐ 355 Paul Moskau | .03 | .01 | .00 |
| ☐ 356 Richard Dotson | .07 | .03 | .01 |
| ☐ 357 Steve Stone | .06 | .02 | .00 |
| ☐ 358 Larry Hisle | .06 | .02 | .00 |
| ☐ 359 Aurelio Lopez | .05 | .02 | .00 |
| ☐ 360 Oscar Gamble | .06 | .02 | .00 |
| ☐ 361 Tom Burgmeier | .03 | .01 | .00 |
| ☐ 362 Terry Forster | .09 | .04 | .01 |
| ☐ 363 Joe Charboneau | .06 | .02 | .00 |
| ☐ 364 Ken Brett | .05 | .02 | .00 |
| ☐ 365 Tony Armas | .14 | .06 | .01 |
| ☐ 366 Chris Speier | .03 | .01 | .00 |
| ☐ 367 Fred Lynn | .20 | .09 | .02 |
| ☐ 368 Buddy Bell | .13 | .06 | .01 |
| ☐ 369 Jim Essian | .03 | .01 | .00 |
| ☐ 370 Terry Puhl | .03 | .01 | .00 |
| ☐ 371 Greg Gross | .03 | .01 | .00 |
| ☐ 372 Bruce Sutter | .25 | .10 | .02 |
| ☐ 373 Joe LeFebvre | .05 | .02 | .00 |
| ☐ 374 Ray Knight | .05 | .02 | .00 |
| ☐ 375 Bruce Benedict | .03 | .01 | .00 |
| ☐ 376 Tim Foli | .03 | .01 | .00 |
| ☐ 377 Al Holland | .05 | .02 | .00 |
| ☐ 378 Ken Kravec | .03 | .01 | .00 |
| ☐ 379 Jeff Burroughs | .05 | .02 | .00 |
| ☐ 380 Pete Falcone | .03 | .01 | .00 |
| ☐ 381 Ernie Whitt | .03 | .01 | .00 |
| ☐ 382 Brad Havens | .07 | .03 | .01 |
| ☐ 383 Terry Crowley | .03 | .01 | .00 |
| ☐ 384 Don Money | .03 | .01 | .00 |
| ☐ 385 Dan Schatzeder | .03 | .01 | .00 |
| ☐ 386 Gary Allenson | .03 | .01 | .00 |
| ☐ 387 Yogi Berra | .15 | .06 | .01 |
| ☐ 388 Ken Landreaux | .05 | .02 | .00 |
| ☐ 389 Mike Hargrove | .05 | .02 | .00 |
| ☐ 390 Darryl Motley | .25 | .10 | .02 |
| ☐ 391 Dave McKay | .03 | .01 | .00 |
| ☐ 392 Stan Bahnsen | .03 | .01 | .00 |
| ☐ 393 Ken Forsch | .03 | .01 | .00 |
| ☐ 394 Mario Mendoza | .03 | .01 | .00 |
| ☐ 395 Jim Morrison | .03 | .01 | .00 |

| | MINT | VG-E | F-G |
|---|---|---|---|
| ☐ 396 Mike Ivie | .03 | .01 | .00 |
| ☐ 397 Broderick Perkins | .03 | .01 | .00 |
| ☐ 398 Darrell Evans | .12 | .05 | .01 |
| ☐ 399 Ron Reed | .03 | .01 | .00 |
| ☐ 400 Johnny Bench | .40 | .18 | .04 |
| ☐ 401 Steve Bedrosian | .30 | .12 | .03 |
| ☐ 402 Bill Robinson | .03 | .01 | .00 |
| ☐ 403 Bill Buckner | .13 | .06 | .01 |
| ☐ 404 Ken Oberkfell | .03 | .01 | .00 |
| ☐ 405 Cal Ripken Jr. | 4.00 | 1.85 | .40 |
| ☐ 406 Jim Gantner | .05 | .02 | .00 |
| ☐ 407 Kirk Gibson | .35 | .15 | .03 |
| ☐ 408 Tony Perez | .15 | .06 | .01 |
| ☐ 409 Tommy John | .18 | .08 | .01 |
| ☐ 410 Dave Stewart | .12 | .05 | .01 |
| ☐ 411 Dan Spillner | .03 | .01 | .00 |
| ☐ 412 Willie Aikens | .05 | .02 | .00 |
| ☐ 413 Mike Heath | .03 | .01 | .00 |
| ☐ 414 Ray Burris | .03 | .01 | .00 |
| ☐ 415 Leon Roberts | .03 | .01 | .00 |
| ☐ 416 Mike Witt | .40 | .18 | .04 |
| ☐ 417 Bob Molinaro | .03 | .01 | .00 |
| ☐ 418 Steve Braun | .03 | .01 | .00 |
| ☐ 419 Nolan Ryan | .35 | .15 | .03 |
| ☐ 420 Tug McGraw | .08 | .03 | .01 |
| ☐ 421 Dave Concepcion | .10 | .04 | .01 |
| ☐ 422 A Juan Eichelberger | | | |
| ERR | .50 | .22 | .05 |
| (photo actually | | | |
| Gary Lucas) | | | |
| ☐ 422 B Juan Eichelberger | | | |
| COR | .07 | .03 | .01 |
| ☐ 423 Rick Rhoden | .06 | .02 | .00 |
| ☐ 424 Frank Robinson | .16 | .07 | .01 |
| ☐ 425 Eddie Miller | .03 | .01 | .00 |
| ☐ 426 Bill Caudill | .07 | .03 | .01 |
| ☐ 427 Doug Flynn | .03 | .01 | .00 |
| ☐ 428 Larry Andersen | .05 | .02 | .00 |
| ☐ 429 Al Williams | .03 | .01 | .00 |
| ☐ 430 Jerry Garvin | .03 | .01 | .00 |
| ☐ 431 Glenn Adams | .03 | .01 | .00 |
| ☐ 432 Barry Bonnell | .03 | .01 | .00 |
| ☐ 433 Jerry Narron | .03 | .01 | .00 |
| ☐ 434 John Stearns | .03 | .01 | .00 |
| ☐ 435 Mike Tyson | .03 | .01 | .00 |
| ☐ 436 Glenn Hubbard | .05 | .02 | .00 |
| ☐ 437 Eddie Solomon | .03 | .01 | .00 |
| ☐ 438 Jeff Leonard | .07 | .03 | .01 |
| ☐ 439 Randy Bass | .03 | .01 | .00 |
| ☐ 440 Mike LaCoss | .03 | .01 | .00 |
| ☐ 441 Gary Matthews | .08 | .03 | .01 |
| ☐ 442 Mark Littell | .03 | .01 | .00 |
| ☐ 443 Don Sutton | .15 | .06 | .01 |

| | MINT | VG-E | F-G |
|---|---|---|---|
| ☐ 444 John Harris | .03 | .01 | .00 |
| ☐ 445 Vada Pinson | .06 | .02 | .00 |
| ☐ 446 Elias Sosa | .03 | .01 | .00 |
| ☐ 447 Charlie Hough | .06 | .02 | .00 |
| ☐ 448 Willie Wilson | .25 | .10 | .02 |
| ☐ 449 Fred Stanley | .03 | .01 | .00 |
| ☐ 450 Tom Veryzer | .03 | .01 | .00 |
| ☐ 451 Ron Davis | .05 | .02 | .00 |
| ☐ 452 Mark Clear | .05 | .02 | .00 |
| ☐ 453 Bill Russell | .05 | .02 | .00 |
| ☐ 454 Lou Whitaker | .20 | .09 | .02 |
| ☐ 455 Dan Graham | .03 | .01 | .00 |
| ☐ 456 Reggie Cleveland | .03 | .01 | .00 |
| ☐ 457 Sammy Stewart | .03 | .01 | .00 |
| ☐ 458 Pete Vuckovich | .10 | .04 | .01 |
| ☐ 459 John Wockenfuss | .03 | .01 | .00 |
| ☐ 460 Glen Hoffman | .03 | .01 | .00 |
| ☐ 461 Willie Randolph | .06 | .02 | .00 |
| ☐ 462 Fernando Valenzuela | .40 | .18 | .04 |
| ☐ 463 Ron Hassey | .03 | .01 | .00 |
| ☐ 464 Paul Splittorff | .05 | .02 | .00 |
| ☐ 465 Rob Picciolo | .03 | .01 | .00 |
| ☐ 466 Larry Parrish | .06 | .02 | .00 |
| ☐ 467 Johnny Grubb | .03 | .01 | .00 |
| ☐ 468 Dan Ford | .05 | .02 | .00 |
| ☐ 469 Silvio Martinez | .03 | .01 | .00 |
| ☐ 470 Kiko Garcia | .03 | .01 | .00 |
| ☐ 471 Bob Boone | .05 | .02 | .00 |
| ☐ 472 Luis Salazar | .03 | .01 | .00 |
| ☐ 473 Randy Niemann | .03 | .01 | .00 |
| ☐ 474 Tom Griffin | .03 | .01 | .00 |
| ☐ 475 Phil Niekro | .20 | .09 | .02 |
| ☐ 476 Hubie Brooks | .12 | .05 | .01 |
| ☐ 477 Dick Tidrow | .03 | .01 | .00 |
| ☐ 478 Jim Beattie | .03 | .01 | .00 |
| ☐ 479 Damaso Garcia | .12 | .05 | .01 |
| ☐ 480 Mickey Hatcher | .05 | .02 | .00 |
| ☐ 481 Joe Price | .03 | .01 | .00 |
| ☐ 482 Ed Farmer | .03 | .01 | .00 |
| ☐ 483 Eddie Murray | .65 | .30 | .06 |
| ☐ 484 Ben Oglivie | .09 | .04 | .01 |
| ☐ 485 Kevin Saucier | .03 | .01 | .00 |
| ☐ 486 Bobby Murcer | .10 | .04 | .01 |
| ☐ 487 Bill Campbell | .05 | .02 | .00 |
| ☐ 488 Reggie Smith | .09 | .04 | .01 |
| ☐ 489 Wayne Garland | .03 | .01 | .00 |
| ☐ 490 Jim Wright | .03 | .01 | .00 |
| ☐ 491 Billy Martin MGR | .14 | .06 | .01 |
| ☐ 492 Jim Fanning MGR | .03 | .01 | .00 |
| ☐ 493 Don Baylor | .13 | .06 | .01 |
| ☐ 494 Rick Honeycutt | .05 | .02 | .00 |
| ☐ 495 Carlton Fisk | .20 | .09 | .02 |
| ☐ 496 Denny Walling | .03 | .01 | .00 |

| | MINT | VG-E | F-G |
|---|---|---|---|
| ☐ 497 Bake McBride | .03 | .01 | .00 |
| ☐ 498 Darrell Porter | .06 | .02 | .00 |
| ☐ 499 Gene Richards | .03 | .01 | .00 |
| ☐ 500 Ron Oester | .05 | .02 | .00 |
| ☐ 501 Ken Dayley | .20 | .09 | .02 |
| ☐ 502 Jason Thompson | .08 | .03 | .01 |
| ☐ 503 Milt May | .03 | .01 | .00 |
| ☐ 504 Doug Bird | .03 | .01 | .00 |
| ☐ 505 Bruce Bochte | .05 | .02 | .00 |
| ☐ 506 Neil Allen | .06 | .02 | .00 |
| ☐ 507 Joey McLaughlin | .03 | .01 | .00 |
| ☐ 508 Butch Wynegar | .06 | .02 | .00 |
| ☐ 509 Gary Roenicke | .05 | .02 | .00 |
| ☐ 510 Robin Yount | .50 | .22 | .05 |
| ☐ 511 Dave Tobik | .03 | .01 | .00 |
| ☐ 512 Rich Gedman | .55 | .25 | .05 |
| ☐ 513 Gene Nelson | .10 | .04 | .01 |
| ☐ 514 Rick Monday | .05 | .02 | .00 |
| ☐ 515 Miguel Dilone | .03 | .01 | .00 |
| ☐ 516 Clint Hurdle | .03 | .01 | .00 |
| ☐ 517 Jeff Newman | .03 | .01 | .00 |
| ☐ 518 Grant Jackson | .03 | .01 | .00 |
| ☐ 519 Andy Hassler | .03 | .01 | .00 |
| ☐ 520 Pat Putnam | .03 | .01 | .00 |
| ☐ 521 Greg Pryor | .03 | .01 | .00 |
| ☐ 522 Tony Scott | .03 | .01 | .00 |
| ☐ 523 Steve Mura | .03 | .01 | .00 |
| ☐ 524 Johnnie LeMaster | .03 | .01 | .00 |
| ☐ 525 Dick Ruthven | .03 | .01 | .00 |
| ☐ 526 John McNamara MGR | .03 | .01 | .00 |
| ☐ 527 Larry McWilliams | .06 | .03 | .00 |
| ☐ 528 Johnny Ray | .65 | .30 | .06 |
| ☐ 529 Pat Tabler | .45 | .20 | .04 |
| ☐ 530 Tom Herr | .12 | .05 | .01 |
| ☐ 531 A San Diego Chicken (with TM) | .90 | .40 | .09 |
| ☐ 531 B San Diego Chicken (without TM) | .90 | .40 | .09 |
| ☐ 532 Sal Butera | .03 | .01 | .00 |
| ☐ 533 Mike Griffin | .03 | .01 | .00 |
| ☐ 534 Kelvin Moore | .07 | .03 | .01 |
| ☐ 535 Reggie Jackson | .45 | .20 | .04 |
| ☐ 536 Ed Romero | .03 | .01 | .00 |
| ☐ 537 Derrel Thomas | .03 | .01 | .00 |
| ☐ 538 Mike O'Berry | .03 | .01 | .00 |
| ☐ 539 Jack O'Connor | .07 | .03 | .01 |
| ☐ 540 Bob Ojeda | .30 | .12 | .03 |
| ☐ 541 Roy Lee Jackson | .03 | .01 | .00 |
| ☐ 542 Lynn Jones | .03 | .01 | .00 |
| ☐ 543 Gaylord Perry | .25 | .10 | .02 |
| ☐ 544 A Phil Garner ERR (reverse negative) | .40 | .18 | .04 |
| ☐ 544 B Phil Garner COR | .07 | .03 | .01 |

| | MINT | VG-E | F-G |
|---|---|---|---|
| ☐ 545 Garry Templeton | .13 | .06 | .01 |
| ☐ 546 Rafael Ramirez | .05 | .02 | .00 |
| ☐ 547 Jeff Reardon | .10 | .04 | .01 |
| ☐ 548 Ron Guidry | .20 | .09 | .02 |
| ☐ 549 Tim Laudner | .15 | .06 | .01 |
| ☐ 550 John Henry Johnson | .03 | .01 | .00 |
| ☐ 551 Chris Bando | .03 | .01 | .00 |
| ☐ 552 Bobby Brown | .03 | .01 | .00 |
| ☐ 553 Larry Bradford | .03 | .01 | .00 |
| ☐ 554 Scot Fletcher | .05 | .02 | .00 |
| ☐ 555 Jerry Royster | .03 | .01 | .00 |
| ☐ 556 Shooty Babitt | .05 | .02 | .00 |
| ☐ 557 Kent Hrbek | 2.00 | .90 | .20 |
| ☐ 558 Yankee Winners | .15 | .06 | .01 |
| Ron Guidry | | | |
| Tommy John | | | |
| ☐ 559 Mark Bomback | .03 | .01 | .00 |
| ☐ 560 Julio Valdez | .07 | .03 | .01 |
| ☐ 561 Buck Martinez | .03 | .01 | .00 |
| ☐ 562 Mike Marshall | 1.00 | .45 | .10 |
| (Dodger hitter) | | | |
| ☐ 563 Rennie Stennett | .03 | .01 | .00 |
| ☐ 564 Steve Crawford | .07 | .03 | .01 |
| ☐ 565 Bob Babcock | .03 | .01 | .00 |
| ☐ 566 Johnny Podres | .06 | .02 | .00 |
| ☐ 567 Paul Serna | .07 | .03 | .01 |
| ☐ 568 Harold Baines | .30 | .12 | .03 |
| ☐ 569 Dave LaRoche | .03 | .01 | .00 |
| ☐ 570 Lee May | .06 | .02 | .00 |
| ☐ 571 Gary Ward | .06 | .02 | .00 |
| ☐ 572 John Denny | .09 | .04 | .01 |
| ☐ 573 Roy Smalley | .05 | .02 | .00 |
| ☐ 574 Bob Brenly | .30 | .12 | .03 |
| ☐ 575 Bronx Bombers: | .35 | .15 | .03 |
| Reggie Jackson | | | |
| Dave Winfield | | | |
| ☐ 576 Luis Pujols | .03 | .01 | .00 |
| ☐ 577 Butch Hobson | .03 | .01 | .00 |
| ☐ 578 Harvey Kuenn | .05 | .02 | .00 |
| ☐ 579 Cal Ripken Sr. | .05 | .02 | .00 |
| (Orioles coach) | | | |
| ☐ 580 Juan Berenguer | .03 | .01 | .00 |
| ☐ 581 Benny Ayala | .03 | .01 | .00 |
| ☐ 582 Vance Law | .03 | .01 | .00 |
| ☐ 583 Rick Leach | .07 | .03 | .01 |
| ☐ 584 George Frazier | .03 | .01 | .00 |
| ☐ 585 Phillies Finest | .55 | .25 | .05 |
| Pete Rose | | | |
| Mike Schmidt | | | |
| ☐ 586 Joe Rudi | .06 | .02 | .00 |
| ☐ 587 Juan Beniquez | .05 | .02 | .00 |
| ☐ 588 Luis DeLeon | .12 | .05 | .01 |
| ☐ 589 Craig Swan | .03 | .01 | .00 |

| | MINT | VG-E | F-G |
|---|---|---|---|
| ☐ 590 Dave Chalk | .03 | .01 | .00 |
| ☐ 591 Billy Gardner | .03 | .01 | .00 |
| ☐ 592 Sal Bando | .06 | .02 | .00 |
| ☐ 593 Bert Campaneris | .06 | .02 | .00 |
| ☐ 594 Steve Kemp | .09 | .04 | .01 |
| ☐ 595 A Randy Lerch ERR | .40 | .18 | .04 |
| (Braves) | | | |
| ☐ 595 B Rand dy Lerch COR | .07 | .03 | .01 |
| (Brewers) | | | |
| ☐ 596 Bryan Clark | .07 | .03 | .01 |
| ☐ 597 David Ford | .03 | .01 | .00 |
| ☐ 598 Mike Scioscia | .03 | .01 | .00 |
| ☐ 599 John Lowenstein | .03 | .01 | .00 |
| ☐ 600 Rene Lachemann MGR | .03 | .01 | .00 |
| ☐ 601 Mick Kelleher | .03 | .01 | .00 |
| ☐ 602 Ron Jackson | .03 | .01 | .00 |
| ☐ 603 Jerry Koosman | .07 | .03 | .01 |
| ☐ 604 Dave Goltz | .03 | .01 | .00 |
| ☐ 605 Ellis Valentine | .05 | .02 | .00 |
| ☐ 606 Lonnie Smith | .09 | .04 | .01 |
| ☐ 607 Joaquin Andujar | .16 | .07 | .01 |
| ☐ 608 Garry Hancock | .03 | .01 | .00 |
| ☐ 609 Jerry Turner | .03 | .01 | .00 |
| ☐ 610 Bob Bonner | .05 | .02 | .00 |
| ☐ 611 Jim Dwyer | .03 | .01 | .00 |
| ☐ 612 Terry Bulling | .03 | .01 | .00 |
| ☐ 613 Joel Youngblood | .03 | .01 | .00 |
| ☐ 614 Larry Milbourne | .03 | .01 | .00 |
| ☐ 615 Gene Roof | .10 | .04 | .01 |
| ☐ 616 Keith Drumright | .05 | .02 | .00 |
| ☐ 617 Dave Rosello | .03 | .01 | .00 |
| ☐ 618 Rickey Keeton | .05 | .02 | .00 |
| ☐ 619 Dennis Lamp | .03 | .01 | .00 |
| ☐ 620 Sid Monge | .03 | .01 | .00 |
| ☐ 621 Jerry White | .03 | .01 | .00 |
| ☐ 622 Luis Aguayo | .05 | .02 | .00 |
| ☐ 623 Jamie Easterly | .03 | .01 | .00 |
| ☐ 624 Steve Sax | .65 | .30 | .06 |
| ☐ 625 Dave Roberts | .03 | .01 | .00 |
| ☐ 626 Rick Bosetti | .03 | .01 | .00 |
| ☐ 627 Terry Francona | .45 | .20 | .04 |
| ☐ 628 Pride of Reds: | .30 | .12 | .03 |
| Tom Seaver | | | |
| Johnny Bench | | | |
| ☐ 629 Paul Mirabella | .03 | .01 | .00 |
| ☐ 630 Rance Mulliniks | .03 | .01 | .00 |
| ☐ 631 Kevin Hickey | .07 | .03 | .01 |
| ☐ 632 Reid Nichols | .03 | .01 | .00 |
| ☐ 633 Dave Geisel | .03 | .01 | .00 |
| ☐ 634 Ken Griffey | .09 | .04 | .01 |
| ☐ 635 Bob Lemon MGR | .09 | .04 | .01 |
| ☐ 636 Orlando Sanchez | .05 | .02 | .00 |
| ☐ 637 Bill Almon | .03 | .01 | .00 |

| | MINT | VG-E | F-G |
|---|---|---|---|
| ☐ 638 Danny Ainge | .09 | .04 | .01 |
| ☐ 639 Willie Stargell | .25 | .10 | .02 |
| ☐ 640 Bob Sykes | .03 | .01 | .00 |
| ☐ 641 Ed Lynch | .13 | .06 | .01 |
| ☐ 642 John Ellis | .03 | .01 | .00 |
| ☐ 643 Ferguson Jenkins | .13 | .06 | .01 |
| ☐ 644 Lenn Sakata | .03 | .01 | .00 |
| ☐ 645 Julio Gonzalez | .03 | .01 | .00 |
| ☐ 646 Jesse Orosco | .10 | .04 | .01 |
| ☐ 647 Jerry Dybzinski | .03 | .01 | .00 |
| ☐ 648 Tommy Davis | .05 | .02 | .00 |
| ☐ 649 Ron Gardenhire | .12 | .05 | .01 |
| ☐ 650 Felipe Alou | .05 | .02 | .00 |
| ☐ 651 Harvey Haddix | .05 | .02 | .00 |
| ☐ 652 Willie Upshaw | .13 | .06 | .01 |
| ☐ 653 Bill Madlock | .18 | .08 | .01 |
| **UNNUMBERED CHECKLISTS** | | | |
| ☐ 654 A DK Checklist (with Trammell) | .11 | .01 | .00 |
| ☐ 654 B DK Checklist (with Trammell) | .11 | .01 | .00 |
| ☐ 655 Checklist 1 | .07 | .01 | .00 |
| ☐ 656 Checklist 2 | .07 | .01 | .00 |
| ☐ 657 Checklist 3 | .07 | .01 | .00 |
| ☐ 658 Checklist 4 | .07 | .01 | .00 |
| ☐ 659 Checklist 5 | .07 | .01 | .00 |
| ☐ 660 Checklist 6 | .07 | .01 | .00 |

## 1983 DONRUSS

*FRED LYNN*

*The cards in this 660 card set measure 2½" × 3½". The 1983 Donruss baseball set, issued with a 63 piece Diamond King puzzle, again leads off with a 26 card Diamond Kings (DK) series. Of the remaining*

*634 cards, two are combination cards, one portrays the San Diego Chicken, one shows the completed Ty Cobb puzzle, and seven are unnumbered checklist cards. The Donruss logo and the year of issue are shown in the upper left corner of the obverse. The card backs have black print on yellow and white and are numbered on a small ball design.*

Complete Set: M-16.00; VG-E-7.50; F-G-1.60

| | MINT | VG-E | F-G |
|---|---|---|---|
| Common Player(1–160) | .03 | .01 | .00 |
| **DIAMOND KINGS (1–26)** | | | |
| ☐ 1 Fernando Valenzuela DK | .50 | .12 | .02 |
| ☐ 2 Rollie Fingers DK | .25 | .10 | .02 |
| ☐ 3 Reggie Jackson DK | .45 | .20 | .04 |
| ☐ 4 Jim Palmer DK | .35 | .15 | .03 |
| ☐ 5 Jack Morris DK | .30 | .12 | .03 |
| ☐ 6 George Foster DK | .20 | .09 | .02 |
| ☐ 7 Jim Sundberg DK | .09 | .04 | .01 |
| ☐ 8 Willie Stargell DK | .25 | .10 | .02 |
| ☐ 9 Dave Stieb DK | .30 | .12 | .03 |
| ☐ 10 Joe Niekro DK | .10 | .04 | .01 |
| ☐ 11 Rickey Henderson DK | .50 | .22 | .05 |
| ☐ 12 Dale Murphy DK | .65 | .30 | .06 |
| ☐ 13 Toby Harrah DK | .09 | .04 | .01 |
| ☐ 14 Bill Buckner DK | .14 | .06 | .01 |
| ☐ 15 Willie Wilson DK | .25 | .10 | .02 |
| ☐ 16 Steve Carlton DK | .40 | .18 | .04 |
| ☐ 17 Ron Guidry DK | .30 | .12 | .03 |
| ☐ 18 Steve Rogers DK | .09 | .04 | .01 |
| ☐ 19 Kent Hrbek DK | .35 | .15 | .03 |
| ☐ 20 Keith Hernandez DK | .35 | .15 | .03 |
| ☐ 21 Floyd Bannister DK | .09 | .04 | .01 |
| ☐ 22 John Bench DK | .40 | .18 | .04 |
| ☐ 23 Britt Burns DK | .09 | .04 | .01 |
| ☐ 24 Joe Morgan DK | .25 | .10 | .02 |
| ☐ 25 Carl Yastrzemski DK | .65 | .30 | .06 |
| ☐ 26 Terry Kennedy DK | .12 | .05 | .01 |
| ☐ 27 Gary Roenicke | .06 | .02 | .00 |
| ☐ 28 Dwight Bernard | .03 | .01 | .00 |
| ☐ 29 Pat Underwood | .03 | .01 | .00 |
| ☐ 30 Gary Allenson | .03 | .01 | .00 |
| ☐ 31 Ron Guidry | .20 | .09 | .02 |
| ☐ 32 Burt Hooton | .03 | .01 | .00 |
| ☐ 33 Chris Bando | .03 | .01 | .00 |
| ☐ 34 Vida Blue | .09 | .04 | .01 |
| ☐ 35 Rickey Henderson | .45 | .20 | .04 |
| ☐ 36 Ray Burris | .03 | .01 | .00 |
| ☐ 37 John Butcher | .03 | .01 | .00 |

| | | MINT | VG-E | F-G |
|---|---|---|---|---|
| ☐ 38 | Don Aase | .03 | .01 | .00 |
| ☐ 39 | Jerry Koosman | .07 | .03 | .01 |
| ☐ 40 | Bruce Sutter | .20 | .09 | .02 |
| ☐ 41 | Jose Cruz | .10 | .04 | .01 |
| ☐ 42 | Pete Rose | .80 | .40 | .08 |
| ☐ 43 | Cesar Cedeno | .09 | .04 | .01 |
| ☐ 44 | Floyd Chiffer | .06 | .02 | .00 |
| ☐ 45 | Larry McWilliams | .06 | .02 | .00 |
| ☐ 46 | Alan Fowlkes | .06 | .02 | .00 |
| ☐ 47 | Dale Murphy | .65 | .30 | .06 |
| ☐ 48 | Doug Bird | .03 | .01 | .00 |
| ☐ 49 | Hubie Brooks | .09 | .04 | .01 |
| ☐ 50 | Floyd Bannister | .08 | .03 | .01 |
| ☐ 51 | Jack O'Connor | .03 | .01 | .00 |
| ☐ 52 | Steve Senteney | .05 | .02 | .00 |
| ☐ 53 | Gary Gaetti | .25 | .10 | .02 |
| ☐ 54 | Damaso Garcia | .09 | .04 | .01 |
| ☐ 55 | Gene Nelson | .03 | .01 | .00 |
| ☐ 56 | Mookie Wilson | .08 | .03 | .01 |
| ☐ 57 | Allen Ripley | .03 | .01 | .00 |
| ☐ 58 | Bob Horner | .20 | .09 | .02 |
| ☐ 59 | Tony Pena | .13 | .06 | .01 |
| ☐ 60 | Gary Lavelle | .03 | .01 | .00 |
| ☐ 61 | Tim Lollar | .05 | .02 | .00 |
| ☐ 62 | Frank Pastore | .03 | .01 | .00 |
| ☐ 63 | Garry Maddox | .05 | .02 | .00 |
| ☐ 64 | Bob Forsch | .05 | .02 | .00 |
| ☐ 65 | Harry Spilman | .03 | .01 | .00 |
| ☐ 66 | Geoff Zahn | .05 | .02 | .00 |
| ☐ 67 | Salome Barojas | .07 | .03 | .01 |
| ☐ 68 | David Palmer | .05 | .02 | .00 |
| ☐ 69 | Charlie Hough | .05 | .02 | .00 |
| ☐ 70 | Dan Quisenberry | .20 | .09 | .02 |
| ☐ 71 | Tony Armas | .15 | .06 | .01 |
| ☐ 72 | Rick Sutcliffe | .20 | .09 | .02 |
| ☐ 73 | Steve Balboni | .08 | .03 | .01 |
| ☐ 74 | Jerry Remy | .05 | .02 | .00 |
| ☐ 75 | Mike Scioscia | .03 | .01 | .00 |
| ☐ 76 | John Wockenfuss | .03 | .01 | .00 |
| ☐ 77 | Jim Palmer | .25 | .10 | .02 |
| ☐ 78 | Rollie Fingers | .20 | .09 | .02 |
| ☐ 79 | Joe Nolan | .03 | .01 | .00 |
| ☐ 80 | Pete Vuckovich | .08 | .03 | .01 |
| ☐ 81 | Rick Leach | .03 | .01 | .00 |
| ☐ 82 | Rick Miller | .03 | .01 | .00 |
| ☐ 83 | Graig Nettles | .14 | .06 | .01 |
| ☐ 84 | Ron Cey | .13 | .06 | .01 |
| ☐ 85 | Miguel Dilone | .03 | .01 | .00 |
| ☐ 86 | John Wathan | .03 | .01 | .00 |
| ☐ 87 | Kelvin Moore | .03 | .01 | .00 |
| ☐ 88 | Bryn Smith | .08 | .03 | .01 |
| ☐ 89 | Dave Hostetler | .08 | .03 | .01 |
| ☐ 90 | Rod Carew | .40 | .18 | .04 |
| ☐ 91 | Lonnie Smith | .08 | .03 | .01 |
| ☐ 92 | Bob Knepper | .06 | .02 | .00 |
| ☐ 93 | Marty Bystrom | .03 | .01 | .00 |
| ☐ 94 | Chris Welsh | .03 | .01 | .00 |
| ☐ 95 | Jason Thompson | .08 | .03 | .01 |
| ☐ 96 | Tom O'Malley | .08 | .03 | .01 |
| ☐ 97 | Phil Niekro | .20 | .09 | .02 |
| ☐ 98 | Neil Allen | .06 | .02 | .00 |
| ☐ 99 | Bill Buckner | .10 | .04 | .01 |
| ☐ 100 | Ed VandeBerg | .12 | .05 | .01 |
| ☐ 101 | Jim Clancy | .03 | .01 | .00 |
| ☐ 102 | Robert Castillo | .03 | .01 | .00 |
| ☐ 103 | Bruce Berenyi | .05 | .02 | .00 |
| ☐ 104 | Carlton Fisk | .20 | .09 | .02 |
| ☐ 105 | Mike Flanagan | .09 | .04 | .01 |
| ☐ 106 | Cecil Cooper | .16 | .07 | .01 |
| ☐ 107 | Jack Morris | .20 | .09 | .02 |
| ☐ 108 | Mike Morgan | .03 | .01 | .00 |
| ☐ 109 | Luis Aponte | .06 | .02 | .00 |
| ☐ 110 | Pedro Guerrero | .30 | .12 | .03 |
| ☐ 111 | Len Barker | .08 | .03 | .01 |
| ☐ 112 | Willie Wilson | .20 | .09 | .02 |
| ☐ 113 | Dave Beard | .03 | .01 | .00 |
| ☐ 114 | Mike Gates | .07 | .03 | .01 |
| ☐ 115 | Reggie Jackson | .40 | .18 | .04 |
| ☐ 116 | George Wright | .15 | .06 | .01 |
| ☐ 117 | Vance Law | .03 | .01 | .00 |
| ☐ 118 | Nolan Ryan | .30 | .12 | .03 |
| ☐ 119 | Mike Krukow | .03 | .01 | .00 |
| ☐ 120 | Ozzie Smith | .12 | .05 | .01 |
| ☐ 121 | Broderick Perkins | .03 | .01 | .00 |
| ☐ 122 | Tom Seaver | .30 | .12 | .03 |
| ☐ 123 | Chris Chambliss | .06 | .02 | .00 |
| ☐ 124 | Chuck Tanner | .03 | .01 | .00 |
| ☐ 125 | Johnnie LeMaster | .03 | .01 | .00 |
| ☐ 126 | Mel Hall | .40 | .18 | .04 |
| ☐ 127 | Bruce Bochte | .05 | .02 | .00 |
| ☐ 128 | Charlie Puleo | .05 | .02 | .00 |
| ☐ 129 | Luis Leal | .03 | .01 | .00 |
| ☐ 130 | John Pacella | .03 | .01 | .00 |
| ☐ 131 | Glenn Gulliver | .06 | .02 | .00 |
| ☐ 132 | Don Money | .03 | .01 | .00 |
| ☐ 133 | Dave Rozema | .03 | .01 | .00 |
| ☐ 134 | Bruce Hurst | .03 | .01 | .00 |
| ☐ 135 | Rudy May | .03 | .01 | .00 |
| ☐ 136 | Tom LaSorda MGR | .06 | .02 | .00 |
| ☐ 137 | Dan Spillner | .08 | .03 | .01 |
| | (photo actually | | | |
| | Ed Whitson) | | | |
| ☐ 138 | Jerry Martin | .03 | .01 | .00 |
| ☐ 139 | Mike Norris | .05 | .02 | .00 |

| | | MINT | VG-E | F-G |
|---|---|---|---|---|
| ☐ 140 | Al Oliver | .16 | .07 | .01 |
| ☐ 141 | Daryl Sconiers | .05 | .02 | .00 |
| ☐ 142 | Lamar Johnson | .03 | .01 | .00 |
| ☐ 143 | Harold Baines | .25 | .10 | .02 |
| ☐ 144 | Alan Ashby | .03 | .01 | .00 |
| ☐ 145 | Garry Templeton | .12 | .05 | .01 |
| ☐ 146 | Al Holland | .06 | .02 | .00 |
| ☐ 147 | Bo Diaz | .06 | .02 | .00 |
| ☐ 148 | Dave Concepcion | .10 | .04 | .01 |
| ☐ 149 | Rick Camp | .03 | .01 | .00 |
| ☐ 150 | Jim Morrison | .03 | .01 | .00 |
| ☐ 151 | Randy Martz | .03 | .01 | .00 |
| ☐ 152 | Keith Hernandez | .30 | .12 | .03 |
| ☐ 153 | John Lowenstein | .03 | .01 | .00 |
| ☐ 154 | Mike Caldwell | .05 | .02 | .00 |
| ☐ 155 | Milt Wilcox | .03 | .01 | .00 |
| ☐ 156 | Rich Gedman | .07 | .03 | .01 |
| ☐ 157 | Rich Gossage | .20 | .09 | .02 |
| ☐ 158 | Jerry Reuss | .06 | .02 | .00 |
| ☐ 159 | Ron Hassey | .03 | .01 | .00 |
| ☐ 160 | Larry Gura | .06 | .02 | .00 |
| ☐ 161 | Dwayne Murphy | .07 | .03 | .01 |
| ☐ 162 | Woodie Fryman | .03 | .01 | .00 |
| ☐ 163 | Steve Comer | .03 | .01 | .00 |
| ☐ 164 | Ken Forsch | .03 | .01 | .00 |
| ☐ 165 | Dennis Lamp | .03 | .01 | .00 |
| ☐ 166 | David Green | .20 | .09 | .02 |
| ☐ 167 | Terry Puhl | .03 | .01 | .00 |
| ☐ 168 | Mike Schmidt | .45 | .20 | .04 |
| ☐ 169 | Eddie Milner | .10 | .04 | .01 |
| ☐ 170 | John Curtis | .03 | .01 | .00 |
| ☐ 171 | Don Robinson | .03 | .01 | .00 |
| ☐ 172 | Rich Gale | .03 | .01 | .00 |
| ☐ 173 | Steve Bedrosian | .08 | .03 | .01 |
| ☐ 174 | Willie Hernandez | .20 | .09 | .02 |
| ☐ 175 | Ron Gardenhire | .03 | .01 | .00 |
| ☐ 176 | Jim Beattie | .03 | .01 | .00 |
| ☐ 177 | Tim Laudner | .03 | .01 | .00 |
| ☐ 178 | Buck Martinez | .03 | .01 | .00 |
| ☐ 179 | Kent Hrbek | .35 | .15 | .03 |
| ☐ 180 | Alfredo Griffin | .07 | .03 | .01 |
| ☐ 181 | Larry Andersen | .03 | .01 | .00 |
| ☐ 182 | Pete Falcone | .03 | .01 | .00 |
| ☐ 183 | Jody Davis | .10 | .04 | .01 |
| ☐ 184 | Glen Hubbard | .05 | .02 | .00 |
| ☐ 185 | Dale Berra | .05 | .02 | .00 |
| ☐ 186 | Greg Minton | .05 | .02 | .00 |
| ☐ 187 | Gary Lucas | .03 | .01 | .00 |
| ☐ 188 | Dave Van Gorder | .06 | .02 | .00 |
| ☐ 189 | Bob Dernier | .06 | .02 | .00 |
| ☐ 190 | Willie McGee | 1.50 | .70 | .15 |
| ☐ 191 | Dickie Thon | .09 | .04 | .01 |
| ☐ 192 | Bob Boone | .06 | .02 | .00 |
| ☐ 193 | Britt Burns | .06 | .02 | .00 |
| ☐ 194 | Jeff Reardon | .09 | .04 | .01 |
| ☐ 195 | Jon Matlack | .05 | .02 | .00 |
| ☐ 196 | Don Slaught | .25 | .10 | .02 |
| ☐ 197 | Fred Stanley | .03 | .01 | .00 |
| ☐ 198 | Rick Manning | .03 | .01 | .00 |
| ☐ 199 | Dave Righetti | .13 | .06 | .01 |
| ☐ 200 | Dave Stapleton | .03 | .01 | .00 |
| ☐ 201 | Steve Yeager | .05 | .02 | .00 |
| ☐ 202 | Enos Cabell | .03 | .01 | .00 |
| ☐ 203 | Sammy Stewart | .03 | .01 | .00 |
| ☐ 204 | Moose Haas | .05 | .02 | .00 |
| ☐ 205 | Lenn Sakata | .03 | .01 | .00 |
| ☐ 206 | Charlie Moore | .03 | .01 | .00 |
| ☐ 207 | Alan Trammell | .25 | .10 | .02 |
| ☐ 208 | Jim Rice | .35 | .15 | .03 |
| ☐ 209 | Roy Smalley | .05 | .02 | .00 |
| ☐ 210 | Bill Russell | .05 | .02 | .00 |
| ☐ 211 | Andre Thornton | .08 | .03 | .01 |
| ☐ 212 | Willie Aikens | .05 | .02 | .00 |
| ☐ 213 | Dave McKay | .03 | .01 | .00 |
| ☐ 214 | Tim Blackwell | .03 | .01 | .00 |
| ☐ 215 | Buddy Bell | .12 | .05 | .01 |
| ☐ 216 | Doug DeCinces | .13 | .06 | .01 |
| ☐ 217 | Tom Herr | .14 | .06 | .01 |
| ☐ 218 | Frank LaCorte | .03 | .01 | .00 |
| ☐ 219 | Steve Carlton | .35 | .15 | .03 |
| ☐ 220 | Terry Kennedy | .12 | .05 | .01 |
| ☐ 221 | Mike Easler | .06 | .02 | .00 |
| ☐ 222 | Jack Clark | .18 | .08 | .01 |
| ☐ 223 | Gene Garber | .03 | .01 | .00 |
| ☐ 224 | Scott Holman | .06 | .02 | .00 |
| ☐ 225 | Mike Proly | .03 | .01 | .00 |
| ☐ 226 | Terry Bulling | .03 | .01 | .00 |
| ☐ 227 | Jerry Garvin | .03 | .01 | .00 |
| ☐ 228 | Ron Davis | .05 | .02 | .00 |
| ☐ 229 | Tom Hume | .03 | .01 | .00 |
| ☐ 230 | Marc Hill | .03 | .01 | .00 |
| ☐ 231 | Dennis Martinez | .03 | .01 | .00 |
| ☐ 232 | Jim Gantner | .05 | .02 | .00 |
| ☐ 233 | Larry Pashnick | .06 | .02 | .00 |
| ☐ 234 | Dave Collins | .06 | .02 | .00 |
| ☐ 235 | Tom Burgmeier | .03 | .01 | .00 |
| ☐ 236 | Ken Landreaux | .05 | .02 | .00 |
| ☐ 237 | John Denny | .12 | .05 | .01 |
| ☐ 238 | Hal McRae | .07 | .03 | .01 |
| ☐ 239 | Matt Keough | .05 | .02 | .00 |
| ☐ 240 | Doug Flynn | .03 | .01 | .00 |
| ☐ 241 | Fred Lynn | .20 | .09 | .02 |
| ☐ 242 | Billy Sample | .03 | .01 | .00 |
| ☐ 243 | Tom Paciorek | .03 | .01 | .00 |

| | MINT | VG-E | F-G |
|---|---|---|---|
| ☐ 244 Joe Sambito | .03 | .01 | .00 |
| ☐ 245 Sid Monge | .03 | .01 | .00 |
| ☐ 246 Ken Oberkfell | .03 | .01 | .00 |
| ☐ 247 Joe Pittman | .08 | .03 | .01 |
| (photo actually | | | |
| Juan Eichelberger) | | | |
| ☐ 248 Mario Soto | .09 | .04 | .01 |
| ☐ 249 Claudell Washington | .09 | .04 | .01 |
| ☐ 250 Rick Rhoden | .06 | .02 | .00 |
| ☐ 251 Darrell Evans | .12 | .05 | .01 |
| ☐ 252 Steve Henderson | .03 | .01 | .00 |
| ☐ 253 Manny Castillo | .03 | .01 | .00 |
| ☐ 254 Craig Swan | .03 | .01 | .00 |
| ☐ 255 Joey McLaughlin | .03 | .01 | .00 |
| ☐ 256 Pete Redfern | .03 | .01 | .00 |
| ☐ 257 Ken Singleton | .09 | .04 | .01 |
| ☐ 258 Robin Yount | .30 | .12 | .03 |
| ☐ 259 Elias Sosa | .03 | .01 | .00 |
| ☐ 260 Bob Ojeda | .06 | .02 | .00 |
| ☐ 261 Bobby Murcer | .09 | .04 | .01 |
| ☐ 262 Candy Maldonado | .20 | .09 | .02 |
| ☐ 263 Rick Waits | .03 | .01 | .00 |
| ☐ 264 Greg Pryor | .03 | .01 | .00 |
| ☐ 265 Bob Owchinko | .03 | .01 | .00 |
| ☐ 266 Chris Speier | .03 | .01 | .00 |
| ☐ 267 Bruce Kison | .03 | .01 | .00 |
| ☐ 268 Mark Wagner | .03 | .01 | .00 |
| ☐ 269 Steve Kemp | .08 | .03 | .01 |
| ☐ 270 Phil Garner | .05 | .02 | .00 |
| ☐ 271 Gene Richards | .03 | .01 | .00 |
| ☐ 272 Renie Martin | .03 | .01 | .00 |
| ☐ 273 Dave Roberts | .03 | .01 | .00 |
| ☐ 274 Dan Driessen | .05 | .02 | .00 |
| ☐ 275 Rufino Linares | .03 | .01 | .00 |
| ☐ 276 Lee Lacy | .06 | .02 | .00 |
| ☐ 277 Ryne Sandberg | 2.50 | 1.15 | .25 |
| ☐ 278 Darrell Porter | .06 | .02 | .00 |
| ☐ 279 Cal Ripken | .75 | .35 | .07 |
| ☐ 280 Jamie Easterly | .03 | .01 | .00 |
| ☐ 281 Bill Fahey | .03 | .01 | .00 |
| ☐ 282 Glenn Hoffman | .03 | .01 | .00 |
| ☐ 283 Willie Randolph | .06 | .02 | .00 |
| ☐ 284 Fernando Valenzuela | .35 | .15 | .03 |
| ☐ 285 Alan Bannister | .03 | .01 | .00 |
| ☐ 286 Paul Splittorff | .05 | .02 | .00 |
| ☐ 287 Joe Rudi | .05 | .02 | .00 |
| ☐ 288 Bill Gullickson | .05 | .02 | .00 |
| ☐ 289 Danny Darwin | .03 | .01 | .00 |
| ☐ 290 Andy Hassler | .03 | .01 | .00 |
| ☐ 291 Ernesto Escarrega | .06 | .02 | .00 |
| ☐ 292 Steve Mura | .03 | .01 | .00 |
| ☐ 293 Tony Scott | .03 | .01 | .00 |
| ☐ 294 Manny Trillo | .05 | .02 | .00 |

| | MINT | VG-E | F-G |
|---|---|---|---|
| ☐ 295 Greg Harris | .03 | .01 | .00 |
| ☐ 296 Luis DeLeon | .03 | .01 | .00 |
| ☐ 297 Kent Tekulve | .07 | .03 | .01 |
| ☐ 298 Atlee Hammaker | .07 | .03 | .01 |
| ☐ 299 Bruce Benedict | .03 | .01 | .00 |
| ☐ 300 Fergie Jenkins | .12 | .05 | .01 |
| ☐ 301 Dave Kingman | .12 | .05 | .01 |
| ☐ 302 Bill Caudill | .07 | .03 | .01 |
| ☐ 303 John Castino | .03 | .01 | .00 |
| ☐ 304 Ernie Whitt | .03 | .01 | .00 |
| ☐ 305 Randy Johnson | .05 | .02 | .00 |
| ☐ 306 Garth Iorg | .03 | .01 | .00 |
| ☐ 307 Gaylord Perry | .20 | .09 | .02 |
| ☐ 308 Ed Lynch | .03 | .01 | .00 |
| ☐ 309 Keith Moreland | .05 | .02 | .00 |
| ☐ 310 Rafael Ramirez | .05 | .02 | .00 |
| ☐ 311 Bill Madlock | .16 | .07 | .01 |
| ☐ 312 Milt May | .03 | .01 | .00 |
| ☐ 313 John Montefusco | .05 | .02 | .00 |
| ☐ 314 Wayne Krenchicki | .03 | .01 | .00 |
| ☐ 315 George Vukovich | .03 | .01 | .00 |
| ☐ 316 Joaquin Andujar | .12 | .05 | .01 |
| ☐ 317 Craig Reynolds | .03 | .01 | .00 |
| ☐ 318 Rick Burleson | .06 | .02 | .00 |
| ☐ 319 Richard Dotson | .07 | .03 | .01 |
| ☐ 320 Steve Rogers | .08 | .03 | .01 |
| ☐ 321 Dave Schmidt | .03 | .01 | .00 |
| ☐ 322 Bud Black | .30 | .02 | .03 |
| ☐ 323 Jeff Burroughs | .05 | .01 | .00 |
| ☐ 324 Von Hayes | .15 | .06 | .01 |
| ☐ 325 Butch Wynegar | .06 | .02 | .00 |
| ☐ 326 Carl Yastrzemski | .50 | .22 | .05 |
| ☐ 327 Ron Roenicke | .05 | .02 | .00 |
| ☐ 328 Howard Johnson | .15 | .06 | .01 |
| ☐ 329 Rick Dempsey | .06 | .02 | .00 |
| ☐ 330 Jim Slaton | .03 | .01 | .00 |
| ☐ 331 Benny Ayala | .03 | .01 | .00 |
| ☐ 332 Ted Simmons | .13 | .06 | .01 |
| ☐ 333 Lou Whitaker | .20 | .09 | .02 |
| ☐ 334 Chuck Rainey | .03 | .01 | .00 |
| ☐ 335 Lou Piniella | .10 | .04 | .01 |
| ☐ 336 Steve Sax | .16 | .07 | .01 |
| ☐ 337 Toby Harrah | .06 | .02 | .00 |
| ☐ 338 George Brett | .45 | .20 | .04 |
| ☐ 339 Davey Lopes | .07 | .03 | .01 |
| ☐ 340 Gary Carter | .35 | .15 | .03 |
| ☐ 341 John Grubb | .03 | .01 | .00 |
| ☐ 342 Tim Foli | .03 | .01 | .00 |
| ☐ 343 Jim Kaat | .08 | .03 | .01 |
| ☐ 344 Mike LaCoss | .03 | .01 | .00 |
| ☐ 345 Larry Christenson | .03 | .01 | .00 |
| ☐ 346 Juan Bonilla | .03 | .01 | .00 |
| ☐ 347 Omar Moreno | .05 | .02 | .00 |

|  | MINT | VG-E | F-G |
|---|---|---|---|
| ☐ 348 Chili Davis | .12 | .05 | .01 |
| ☐ 349 Tommy Boggs | .03 | .01 | .00 |
| ☐ 350 Rusty Staub | .10 | .04 | .01 |
| ☐ 351 Bump Wills | .03 | .01 | .00 |
| ☐ 352 Rick Sweet | .03 | .01 | .00 |
| ☐ 353 Jim Gott | .09 | .04 | .01 |
| ☐ 354 Terry Felton | .06 | .02 | .00 |
| ☐ 355 Jim Kern | .03 | .01 | .00 |
| ☐ 356 Bill Almon | .03 | .01 | .00 |
| ☐ 357 Tippy Martinez | .05 | .02 | .00 |
| ☐ 358 Roy Howell | .03 | .01 | .00 |
| ☐ 359 Dan Petry | .16 | .07 | .01 |
| ☐ 360 Jerry Mumphrey | .05 | .02 | .00 |
| ☐ 361 Mark Clear | .05 | .02 | .00 |
| ☐ 362 Mike Marshall | .20 | .09 | .02 |
| ☐ 363 Lary Sorensen | .03 | .01 | .00 |
| ☐ 364 Amos Otis | .07 | .03 | .01 |
| ☐ 365 Rick Langford | .03 | .01 | .00 |
| ☐ 366 Brad Mills | .03 | .01 | .00 |
| ☐ 367 Brian Downing | .03 | .01 | .00 |
| ☐ 368 Mike Richardt | .06 | .02 | .00 |
| ☐ 369 Aurelio Rodriguez | .03 | .01 | .00 |
| ☐ 370 Dave Smith | .03 | .01 | .00 |
| ☐ 371 Tug McGraw | .09 | .04 | .01 |
| ☐ 372 Doug Bair | .03 | .01 | .00 |
| ☐ 373 Ruppert Jones | .05 | .02 | .00 |
| ☐ 374 Alex Trevino | .03 | .01 | .00 |
| ☐ 375 Ken Dayley | .03 | .01 | .00 |
| ☐ 376 Rod Scurry | .03 | .01 | .00 |
| ☐ 377 Bob Brenly | .07 | .03 | .01 |
| ☐ 378 Scot Thompson | .03 | .01 | .00 |
| ☐ 379 Julio Cruz | .03 | .01 | .00 |
| ☐ 380 John Stearns | .03 | .01 | .00 |
| ☐ 381 Dale Murray | .03 | .01 | .00 |
| ☐ 382 Frank Viola | .50 | .22 | .05 |
| ☐ 383 Al Bumbry | .03 | .01 | .00 |
| ☐ 384 Ben Oglivie | .08 | .03 | .01 |
| ☐ 385 Dave Tobik | .03 | .01 | .00 |
| ☐ 386 Bob Stanley | .06 | .02 | .00 |
| ☐ 387 Andre Robertson | .03 | .01 | .00 |
| ☐ 388 Jorge Orta | .03 | .01 | .00 |
| ☐ 389 Ed Whitson | .07 | .03 | .01 |
| ☐ 390 Don Hood | .03 | .01 | .00 |
| ☐ 391 Tom Underwood | .03 | .01 | .00 |
| ☐ 392 Tim Wallach | .12 | .05 | .01 |
| ☐ 393 Steve Renko | .03 | .01 | .00 |
| ☐ 394 Mickey Rivers | .06 | .02 | .00 |
| ☐ 395 Greg Luzinski | .12 | .05 | .01 |
| ☐ 396 Art Howe | .03 | .01 | .00 |
| ☐ 397 Alan Wiggins | .30 | .12 | .03 |
| ☐ 398 Jim Barr | .03 | .01 | .00 |
| ☐ 399 Ivan DeJesus | .03 | .01 | .00 |
| ☐ 400 Tom Lawless | .07 | .03 | .01 |

|  | MINT | VG-E | F-G |
|---|---|---|---|
| ☐ 401 Bob Walk | .03 | .01 | .00 |
| ☐ 402 Jimmy Smith | .05 | .02 | .00 |
| ☐ 403 Lee Smith | .09 | .04 | .01 |
| ☐ 404 George Hendrick | .09 | .04 | .01 |
| ☐ 405 Eddie Murray | .50 | .22 | .05 |
| ☐ 406 Marshall Edwards | .03 | .01 | .00 |
| ☐ 407 Lance Parrish | .30 | .12 | .03 |
| ☐ 408 Carney Lansford | .12 | .05 | .01 |
| ☐ 409 Dave Winfield | .35 | .15 | .03 |
| ☐ 410 Bob Welch | .07 | .03 | .01 |
| ☐ 411 Larry Milbourne | .03 | .01 | .00 |
| ☐ 412 Dennis Leonard | .06 | .02 | .00 |
| ☐ 413 Dan Meyer | .03 | .01 | .00 |
| ☐ 414 Charlie Lea | .05 | .02 | .00 |
| ☐ 415 Rick Honeycutt | .05 | .02 | .00 |
| ☐ 416 Mike Witt | .09 | .04 | .01 |
| ☐ 417 Steve Trout | .05 | .02 | .00 |
| ☐ 418 Glenn Brummer | .03 | .01 | .00 |
| ☐ 419 Denny Walling | .03 | .01 | .00 |
| ☐ 420 Gary Matthews | .09 | .04 | .01 |
| ☐ 421 Charlie Leibrandt | .06 | .02 | .00 |
| ☐ 422 Juan Eichelberger | .03 | .01 | .00 |
| ☐ 423 Matt Guante | .07 | .03 | .01 |
| ☐ 424 Bill Laskey | .15 | .06 | .01 |
| ☐ 425 Jerry Royster | .03 | .01 | .00 |
| ☐ 426 Dickie Noles | .03 | .01 | .00 |
| ☐ 427 George Foster | .20 | .09 | .02 |
| ☐ 428 Mike Moore | .25 | .10 | .01 |
| ☐ 429 Gary Ward | .06 | .02 | .00 |
| ☐ 430 Barry Bonnell | .05 | .02 | .00 |
| ☐ 431 Ron Washington | .06 | .02 | .00 |
| ☐ 432 Rance Mulliniks | .03 | .01 | .00 |
| ☐ 433 Mike Stanton | .03 | .01 | .00 |
| ☐ 434 Jesse Orosco | .08 | .03 | .01 |
| ☐ 435 Larry Bowa | .09 | .04 | .01 |
| ☐ 436 Biff Pocoroba | .03 | .01 | .00 |
| ☐ 437 Johnny Ray | .12 | .05 | .01 |
| ☐ 438 Joe Morgan | .20 | .09 | .02 |
| ☐ 439 Eric Show | .16 | .07 | .01 |
| ☐ 440 Larry Biittner | .03 | .01 | .00 |
| ☐ 441 Greg Gross | .03 | .01 | .00 |
| ☐ 442 Gene Tenace | .03 | .01 | .00 |
| ☐ 443 Danny Heep | .03 | .01 | .00 |
| ☐ 444 Bobby Clark | .03 | .01 | .00 |
| ☐ 445 Kevin Hickey | .03 | .01 | .00 |
| ☐ 446 Scott Sanderson | .03 | .01 | .00 |
| ☐ 447 Frank Tanana | .05 | .02 | .00 |
| ☐ 448 Cesar Geronimo | .03 | .01 | .00 |
| ☐ 449 Jimmy Sexton | .03 | .01 | .00 |
| ☐ 450 Mike Hargrove | .05 | .02 | .00 |
| ☐ 451 Doyle Alexander | .05 | .02 | .00 |
| ☐ 452 Dwight Evans | .14 | .06 | .01 |
| ☐ 453 Terry Forster | .07 | .03 | .01 |

| | | MINT | VG-E | F-G | | | MINT | VG-E | F-G |
|---|---|---|---|---|---|---|---|---|---|
| ☐ 454 | Tom Brookens | .03 | .01 | .00 | ☐ 506 | Bob Bailor | .03 | .01 | .00 |
| ☐ 455 | Rich Dauer | .03 | .01 | .00 | ☐ 507 | Dave Stieb | .20 | .09 | .02 |
| ☐ 456 | Rob Picciolo | .03 | .01 | .00 | ☐ 508 | Al Williams | .03 | .01 | .00 |
| ☐ 457 | Terry Crowley | .03 | .01 | .00 | ☐ 509 | Dan Ford | .05 | .02 | .00 |
| ☐ 458 | Ned Yost | .03 | .01 | .00 | ☐ 510 | Gorman Thomas | .12 | .05 | .01 |
| ☐ 459 | Kirk Gibson | .25 | .10 | .02 | ☐ 511 | Chet Lemon | .09 | .04 | .01 |
| ☐ 460 | Reid Nichols | .03 | .01 | .00 | ☐ 512 | Mike Torrez | .06 | .02 | .00 |
| ☐ 461 | Oscar Gamble | .06 | .02 | .00 | ☐ 513 | Shane Rawley | .05 | .02 | .00 |
| ☐ 462 | Dusty Baker | .08 | .03 | .01 | ☐ 514 | Mark Belanger | .05 | .02 | .00 |
| ☐ 463 | Jack Perconte | .03 | .01 | .00 | ☐ 515 | Rodney Craig | .03 | .01 | .00 |
| ☐ 464 | Frank White | .07 | .03 | .01 | ☐ 516 | Onix Concepcion | .08 | .03 | .01 |
| ☐ 465 | Mickey Klutts | .03 | .01 | .00 | ☐ 517 | Mike Heath | .03 | .01 | .00 |
| ☐ 466 | Warren Cromartie | .03 | .01 | .00 | ☐ 518 | Andre Dawson | .20 | .09 | .02 |
| ☐ 467 | Larry Parrish | .06 | .02 | .00 | ☐ 519 | Luis Sanchez | .03 | .01 | .00 |
| ☐ 468 | Bobby Grich | .08 | .03 | .01 | ☐ 520 | Terry Bogener | .06 | .02 | .00 |
| ☐ 469 | Dane Iorg | .03 | .01 | .00 | ☐ 521 | Rudy Law | .03 | .01 | .00 |
| ☐ 470 | Joe Niekro | .07 | .03 | .01 | ☐ 522 | Ray Knight | .06 | .02 | .00 |
| ☐ 471 | Ed Farmer | .03 | .01 | .00 | ☐ 523 | Joe LeFebvre | .05 | .02 | .00 |
| ☐ 472 | Tim Flannery | .03 | .01 | .00 | ☐ 524 | Jim Wohlford | .03 | .01 | .00 |
| ☐ 473 | Dave Parker | .25 | .10 | .02 | ☐ 525 | Julio Franco | 1.00 | .45 | .10 |
| ☐ 474 | Jeff Leonard | .08 | .03 | .01 | ☐ 526 | Ron Oester | .05 | .02 | .00 |
| ☐ 475 | Al Hrabosky | .05 | .02 | .00 | ☐ 527 | Rick Mahler | .07 | .03 | .01 |
| ☐ 476 | Ron Hodges | .03 | .01 | .00 | ☐ 528 | Steve Nicosia | .03 | .01 | .00 |
| ☐ 477 | Leon Durham | .18 | .08 | .01 | ☐ 529 | Junior Kennedy | .03 | .01 | .00 |
| ☐ 478 | Jim Essian | .03 | .01 | .00 | ☐ 530 | Whitey Herzog MGR | .06 | .02 | .00 |
| ☐ 479 | Roy Lee Jackson | .03 | .01 | .00 | ☐ 531 | Don Sutton | .16 | .07 | .01 |
| ☐ 480 | Brad Havens | .03 | .01 | .00 | ☐ 532 | Mark Brouhard | .03 | .01 | .00 |
| ☐ 481 | Joe Price | .03 | .01 | .00 | ☐ 533 | Sparky Anderson | .08 | .03 | .01 |
| ☐ 482 | Tony Bernazard | .03 | .01 | .00 | ☐ 534 | Roger LaFrancois | .06 | .02 | .00 |
| ☐ 483 | Scott McGregor | .08 | .03 | .01 | ☐ 535 | George Frazier | .03 | .01 | .00 |
| ☐ 484 | Paul Molitor | .14 | .06 | .01 | ☐ 536 | Tom Niedenfuer | .08 | .03 | .01 |
| ☐ 485 | Mike Ivie | .03 | .01 | .00 | ☐ 537 | Ed Glynn | .03 | .01 | .00 |
| ☐ 486 | Ken Griffey | .09 | .04 | .01 | ☐ 538 | Lee May | .06 | .02 | .00 |
| ☐ 487 | Dennis Eckersley | .06 | .02 | .00 | ☐ 539 | Bob Kearney | .10 | .04 | .01 |
| ☐ 488 | Steve Garvey | .40 | .18 | .04 | ☐ 540 | Tim Raines | .30 | .12 | .03 |
| ☐ 489 | Mike Fischlin | .03 | .01 | .00 | ☐ 541 | Paul Mirabella | .03 | .01 | .00 |
| ☐ 490 | U.L. Washington | .03 | .01 | .00 | ☐ 542 | Luis Tiant | .06 | .02 | .00 |
| ☐ 491 | Steve McCatty | .05 | .02 | .00 | ☐ 543 | Ron LeFlore | .06 | .02 | .00 |
| ☐ 492 | Roy Johnson | .03 | .01 | .00 | ☐ 544 | Dave LaPoint | .18 | .08 | .01 |
| ☐ 493 | Don Baylor | .12 | .05 | .01 | ☐ 545 | Randy Moffitt | .03 | .01 | .00 |
| ☐ 494 | Bobby Johnson | .03 | .01 | .00 | ☐ 546 | Luis Aguayo | .03 | .01 | .00 |
| ☐ 495 | Mike Squires | .03 | .01 | .00 | ☐ 547 | Brad Lesley | .10 | .04 | .01 |
| ☐ 496 | Bert Roberge | .03 | .01 | .00 | ☐ 548 | Luis Salazar | .03 | .01 | .00 |
| ☐ 497 | Dick Ruthven | .03 | .01 | .00 | ☐ 549 | John Candelaria | .07 | .03 | .01 |
| ☐ 498 | Tito Landrum | .05 | .02 | .00 | ☐ 550 | Dave Bergman | .03 | .01 | .00 |
| ☐ 499 | Sixto Lezcano | .03 | .01 | .00 | ☐ 551 | Bob Watson | .06 | .02 | .00 |
| ☐ 500 | Johnny Bench | .35 | .15 | .03 | ☐ 552 | Pat Tabler | .07 | .03 | .01 |
| ☐ 501 | Larry Whisenton | .03 | .01 | .00 | ☐ 553 | Brent Gaff | .06 | .02 | .00 |
| ☐ 502 | Manny Sarmiento | .03 | .01 | .00 | ☐ 554 | Al Cowens | .05 | .02 | .00 |
| ☐ 503 | Fred Breining | .03 | .01 | .00 | ☐ 555 | Tom Brunansky | .25 | .10 | .02 |
| ☐ 504 | Bill Campbell | .05 | .02 | .00 | ☐ 556 | Lloyd Moseby | .14 | .06 | .01 |
| ☐ 505 | Todd Cruz | .03 | .01 | .00 | ☐ 557 | Pascual Perez | .06 | .02 | .00 |

| | MINT | VG-E | F-G |
|---|---|---|---|
| ☐ 558 Willie Upshaw | .14 | .06 | .01 |
| ☐ 559 Richie Zisk | .05 | .02 | .00 |
| ☐ 560 Pat Zachry | .03 | .01 | .00 |
| ☐ 561 Jay Johnstone | .05 | .02 | .00 |
| ☐ 562 Carlos Diaz | .12 | .05 | .01 |
| ☐ 563 John Tudor | .16 | .07 | .01 |
| ☐ 564 Frank Robinson MGR | .14 | .06 | .01 |
| ☐ 565 Dave Edwards | .03 | .01 | .00 |
| ☐ 566 Paul Householder | .05 | .02 | .00 |
| ☐ 567 Ron Reed | .03 | .01 | .00 |
| ☐ 568 Mike Ramsey | .03 | .01 | .00 |
| ☐ 569 Kiko Garcia | .03 | .01 | .00 |
| ☐ 570 Tommy John | .14 | .06 | .01 |
| ☐ 571 Tony LaRussa MGR | .05 | .02 | .00 |
| ☐ 572 Joel Youngblood | .03 | .01 | .00 |
| ☐ 573 Wayne Tolleson | .07 | .03 | .01 |
| ☐ 574 Keith Creel | .06 | .02 | .00 |
| ☐ 575 Billy Martin MGR | .13 | .06 | .01 |
| ☐ 576 Jerry Dybzinski | .03 | .01 | .00 |
| ☐ 577 Rick Cerone | .05 | .02 | .00 |
| ☐ 578 Tony Perez | .13 | .06 | .01 |
| ☐ 579 Greg Brock | .50 | .22 | .05 |
| ☐ 580 Glen Wilson | .65 | .30 | .06 |
| ☐ 581 Tim Stoddard | .03 | .01 | .00 |
| ☐ 582 Bob McClure | .03 | .01 | .00 |
| ☐ 583 Jim Dwyer | .03 | .01 | .00 |
| ☐ 584 Ed Romero | .03 | .01 | .00 |
| ☐ 585 Larry Herndon | .05 | .02 | .00 |
| ☐ 586 Wade Boggs | 3.75 | 1.25 | .25 |
| ☐ 587 Jay Howell | .06 | .02 | .00 |
| ☐ 588 Dave Stewart | .03 | .01 | .00 |
| ☐ 589 Bert Blyleven | .12 | .05 | .01 |
| ☐ 590 Dick Howser MGR | .05 | .02 | .00 |
| ☐ 591 Wayne Gross | .03 | .01 | .00 |
| ☐ 592 Terry Francona | .09 | .04 | .01 |
| ☐ 593 Don Werner | .03 | .01 | .00 |
| ☐ 594 Bill Stein | .03 | .01 | .00 |
| ☐ 595 Jesse Barfield | .09 | .04 | .01 |
| ☐ 596 Bobby Molinaro | .03 | .01 | .00 |
| ☐ 597 Mike Vail | .03 | .01 | .00 |
| ☐ 598 Tony Gwynn | 2.50 | 1.00 | .25 |
| ☐ 599 Gary Rajsich | .06 | .02 | .00 |
| ☐ 600 Jerry Ujdur | .03 | .01 | .00 |
| ☐ 601 Cliff Johnson | .03 | .01 | .00 |
| ☐ 602 Jerry White | .03 | .01 | .00 |
| ☐ 603 Bryan Clark | .03 | .01 | .00 |
| ☐ 604 Joe Ferguson | .03 | .01 | .00 |
| ☐ 605 Guy Sularz | .06 | .02 | .00 |
| ☐ 606 Ozzie Virgil | .05 | .02 | .00 |
| ☐ 607 Terry Harper | .03 | .01 | .00 |
| ☐ 608 Harvey Kuenn MGR | .05 | .02 | .00 |
| ☐ 609 Jim Sundberg | .06 | .02 | .00 |
| ☐ 610 Willie Stargell | .20 | .09 | .02 |
| ☐ 611 Reggie Smith | .09 | .04 | .01 |
| ☐ 612 Rob Wilfong | .03 | .01 | .00 |
| ☐ 613 Niekro Brothers | .12 | .05 | .01 |
| Joe and Phil | | | |
| ☐ 614 Lee Elia | .03 | .01 | .00 |
| ☐ 615 Mickey Hatcher | .05 | .02 | .00 |
| ☐ 616 Jerry Hairston | .03 | .01 | .00 |
| ☐ 617 John Martin | .03 | .01 | .00 |
| ☐ 618 Wally Backman | .05 | .02 | .00 |
| ☐ 619 Storm Davis | .45 | .20 | .04 |
| ☐ 620 Alan Knicely | .03 | .01 | .00 |
| ☐ 621 John Stuper | .12 | .05 | .01 |
| ☐ 622 Matt Sinatro | .03 | .01 | .00 |
| ☐ 623 Gene Petralli | .05 | .02 | .00 |
| ☐ 624 Duane Walker | .15 | .06 | .01 |
| ☐ 625 Dick Williams MGR | .03 | .01 | .00 |
| ☐ 626 Pat Corrales MGR | .03 | .01 | .00 |
| ☐ 627 Vern Ruhle | .03 | .01 | .00 |
| ☐ 628 Joe Torre MGR | .07 | .03 | .01 |
| ☐ 629 Anthony Johnson | .07 | .03 | .01 |
| ☐ 630 Steve Howe | .06 | .02 | .00 |
| ☐ 631 Gary Woods | .03 | .01 | .00 |
| ☐ 632 LaMarr Hoyt | .13 | .06 | .01 |
| ☐ 633 Steve Swisher | .03 | .01 | .00 |
| ☐ 634 Terry Leach | .03 | .01 | .00 |
| ☐ 635 Jeff Newman | .03 | .01 | .00 |
| ☐ 636 Brett Butler | .10 | .04 | .01 |
| ☐ 637 Gary Gray | .03 | .01 | .00 |
| ☐ 638 Lee Mazzilli | .05 | .02 | .00 |
| ☐ 639 Ron Jackson | .03 | .01 | .00 |
| ☐ 640 Juan Beniquez | .05 | .02 | .00 |
| ☐ 641 Dave Rucker | .03 | .01 | .00 |
| ☐ 642 Luis Pujols | .03 | .01 | .00 |
| ☐ 643 Rick Monday | .05 | .02 | .00 |
| ☐ 644 Hosken Powell | .03 | .01 | .00 |
| ☐ 645 The Chicken | .25 | .10 | .02 |
| ☐ 646 Dave Engle | .06 | .02 | .00 |
| ☐ 647 Dick Davis | .03 | .01 | .00 |
| ☐ 648 Frank Robinson | .13 | .06 | .01 |
| Vida Blue | | | |
| Joe Morgan | | | |
| ☐ 649 Al Chambers | .10 | .04 | .01 |
| ☐ 650 Jesus Vega | .07 | .03 | .01 |
| ☐ 651 Jeff Jones | .03 | .01 | .00 |
| ☐ 652 Marvis Foley | .03 | .01 | .00 |
| ☐ 653 Ty Cobb Puzzle Card | .20 | .09 | .02 |
| UNNUMBERED | | | |
| CHECKLISTS | | | |
| ☐ 654 Dick Perez/Diamond | .10 | .01 | .00 |
| Kings Checklist | | | |
| ☐ 655 Checklist 1 | .07 | .01 | .00 |

| | MINT | VG-E | F-G |
|---|---|---|---|
| ☐ 656 Checklist 2 | .07 | .01 | .00 |
| ☐ 657 Checklist 3 | .07 | .01 | .00 |
| ☐ 658 Checklist 4 | .07 | .01 | .00 |
| ☐ 659 Checklist 5 | .07 | .01 | .00 |
| ☐ 660 Checklist 6 | .07 | .01 | .00 |

## 1984 DONRUSS

The 1984 Donruss set contains a total of 660 cards, each measuring 2½" by 3½"; however, only 658 are numbered. Two "Living Legend" cards designated A (featuring Gaylord Perry and Rollie Fingers) and B (featuring Johnny Bench and Carl Yastrzemski) were issued as bonus cards in wax packs, but were not issued in the vending sets sold to hobby dealers. The designs on the fronts of the Donruss cards changed considerably from the past two years. The backs contain statistics and are printed in green and black ink. The cards were distributed with a 63 piece puzzle of Duke Snider.

Complete Set (658): M-35.00; VG-E-16.50; F-G-3.50

| | MINT | VG-E | F-G |
|---|---|---|---|
| Common Player (1–660) | .04 | .02 | .00 |

DIAMOND KINGS (1–26)

| | MINT | VG-E | F-G |
|---|---|---|---|
| ☐ 1 Robin Yount DK | .45 | .15 | .03 |
| ☐ 2 Dave Concepcion DK | .14 | .06 | .01 |
| ☐ 3 Dwayne Murphy DK | .12 | .05 | .01 |
| ☐ 4 John Castino DK | .08 | .03 | .01 |
| ☐ 5 Leon Durham DK | .25 | .10 | .02 |
| ☐ 6 Rusty Staub DK | .12 | .05 | .01 |
| ☐ 7 Jack Clark DK | .25 | .10 | .02 |

| | MINT | VG-E | F-G |
|---|---|---|---|
| ☐ 8 Dave Dravecky DK | .10 | .04 | .01 |
| ☐ 9 Al Oliver DK | .20 | .09 | .02 |
| ☐ 10 Dave Righetti DK | .18 | .08 | .01 |
| ☐ 11 Hal McRae DK | .12 | .05 | .01 |
| ☐ 12 Ray Knight DK | .10 | .04 | .01 |
| ☐ 13 Bruce Sutter DK | .20 | .09 | .02 |
| ☐ 14 Bob Horner DK | .25 | .10 | .02 |
| ☐ 15 Lance Parrish DK | .30 | .12 | .03 |
| ☐ 16 Matt Young DK | .12 | .05 | .01 |
| ☐ 17 Fred Lynn DK | .20 | .09 | .02 |
| ☐ 18 Ron Kittle DK | .20 | .09 | .02 |
| ☐ 19 Jim Clancy DK | .09 | .04 | .01 |
| ☐ 20 Bill Madlock DK | .18 | .08 | .01 |
| ☐ 21 Larry Parrish DK | .13 | .06 | .01 |
| ☐ 22 Eddie Murray DK | .55 | .25 | .05 |
| ☐ 23 Mike Schmidt DK | .50 | .22 | .05 |
| ☐ 24 Pedro Guerrero DK | .35 | .15 | .03 |
| ☐ 25 Andre Thornton DK | .13 | .06 | .01 |
| ☐ 26 Wade Boggs DK | .60 | .28 | .06 |
| RATED ROOKIES (27–46) | | | |
| ☐ 27 Joel Skinner RR | .14 | .06 | .01 |
| ☐ 28 Tommy Dunbar RR | .09 | .04 | .01 |
| ☐ 29 A Mike Stenhouse RR ERR (no number on back) | .15 | .06 | .01 |
| ☐ 29 B Mike Stenhouse RR COR | .60 | .28 | .06 |
| ☐ 30 A Ron Darling RR ERR (no number on back) | 1.25 | .60 | .12 |
| ☐ 30 B Ron Darling RR COR | 2.50 | 1.15 | .25 |
| ☐ 31 Dion James RR | .25 | .10 | .02 |
| ☐ 32 Tony Fernandez RR | .50 | .22 | .05 |
| ☐ 33 Angel Salazar RR | .08 | .03 | .01 |
| ☐ 34 Kevin McReynolds RR | 1.00 | .45 | .10 |
| ☐ 35 Dick Schofield RR | .16 | .07 | .01 |
| ☐ 36 Brad Komminsk RR | .25 | .10 | .02 |
| ☐ 37 Tim Teufel RR | .45 | .20 | .04 |
| ☐ 38 Doug Frobel RR | .08 | .03 | .01 |
| ☐ 39 Greg Gagne RR | .15 | .06 | .01 |
| ☐ 40 Mike Fuentes RR | .08 | .03 | .01 |
| ☐ 41 Joe Carter RR | .35 | .15 | .03 |
| ☐ 42 Mike Brown RR (Red Sox OF) | .25 | .10 | .02 |
| ☐ 43 Mike Jeffcoat RR | .10 | .04 | .01 |
| ☐ 44 Sid Fernandez RR | .60 | .28 | .06 |
| ☐ 45 Brian Dayett RR | .15 | .06 | .01 |
| ☐ 46 Chris Smith RR | .08 | .03 | .01 |
| ☐ 47 Eddie Murray | .55 | .25 | .05 |
| ☐ 48 Robin Yount | .35 | .15 | .03 |
| ☐ 49 Lance Parrish | .30 | .12 | .03 |
| ☐ 50 Jim Rice | .40 | .18 | .04 |
| ☐ 51 Dave Winfield | .40 | .18 | .04 |

| | | MINT | VG-E | F-G | | | MINT | VG-E | F-G |
|---|---|---|---|---|---|---|---|---|---|
| ☐ | 52 Fernando Valenzuela ... | .35 | .15 | .03 | ☐ 105 Dan Petry ............. | | .18 | .08 | .01 |
| ☐ | 53 George Brett .......... | .55 | .25 | .05 | ☐ 106 Cal Ripken .......... | | .60 | .28 | .06 |
| ☐ | 54 Rickey Henderson ..... | .50 | .22 | .05 | ☐ 107 Paul Molitor ......... | | .14 | .06 | .01 |
| ☐ | 55 Gary Carter .......... | .35 | .15 | .03 | ☐ 108 Fred Lynn .......... | | .18 | .08 | .01 |
| ☐ | 56 Buddy Bell ........... | .13 | .06 | .01 | ☐ 109 Neil Allen .......... | | .06 | .02 | .00 |
| ☐ | 57 Reggie Jackson ....... | .40 | .18 | .04 | ☐ 110 Joe Niekro ......... | | .06 | .02 | .00 |
| ☐ | 58 Harold Baines ........ | .25 | .10 | .02 | ☐ 111 Steve Carlton ....... | | .35 | .15 | .03 |
| ☐ | 59 Ozzie Smith .......... | .12 | .05 | .01 | ☐ 112 Terry Kennedy ...... | | .10 | .04 | .01 |
| ☐ | 60 Nolan Ryan ........... | .35 | .15 | .03 | ☐ 113 Bill Madlock ........ | | .14 | .06 | .01 |
| ☐ | 61 Pete Rose ............ | .85 | .40 | .08 | ☐ 114 Chili Davis ......... | | .10 | .04 | .01 |
| ☐ | 62 Ron Oester ........... | .06 | .02 | .00 | ☐ 115 Jim Gantner ........ | | .06 | .02 | .00 |
| ☐ | 63 Steve Garvey ......... | .45 | .20 | .04 | ☐ 116 Tom Seaver ......... | | .35 | .15 | .03 |
| ☐ | 64 Jason Thompson ...... | .09 | .04 | .01 | ☐ 117 Bill Buckner ........ | | .12 | .05 | .01 |
| ☐ | 65 Jack Clark ........... | .18 | .08 | .01 | ☐ 118 Bill Caudill ......... | | .08 | .03 | .01 |
| ☐ | 66 Dale Murphy .......... | .65 | .30 | .06 | ☐ 119 Jim Clancy ......... | | .04 | .02 | .00 |
| ☐ | 67 Leon Durham ......... | .20 | .09 | .02 | ☐ 120 John Castino ....... | | .04 | .02 | .00 |
| ☐ | 68 Darryl Strawberry ..... | 3.50 | 1.25 | .35 | ☐ 121 Dave Concepcion .... | | .10 | .04 | .01 |
| ☐ | 69 Richie Zisk .......... | .06 | .02 | .00 | ☐ 122 Greg Luzinski ....... | | .12 | .05 | .01 |
| ☐ | 70 Kent Hrbek .......... | .35 | .15 | .03 | ☐ 123 Mike Boddicker ..... | | .12 | .05 | .01 |
| ☐ | 71 Dave Stieb .......... | .25 | .10 | .02 | ☐ 124 Pete Ladd .......... | | .04 | .02 | .00 |
| ☐ | 72 Ken Schrom .......... | .04 | .02 | .00 | ☐ 125 Juan Berenguer ..... | | .04 | .02 | .00 |
| ☐ | 73 George Bell .......... | .10 | .04 | .01 | ☐ 126 John Montefusco .... | | .06 | .02 | .00 |
| ☐ | 74 John Moses .......... | .07 | .03 | .01 | ☐ 127 Ed Jurak .......... | | .06 | .02 | .00 |
| ☐ | 75 Ed Lynch ............ | .04 | .02 | .00 | ☐ 128 Tom Niedenfuer ..... | | .07 | .03 | .01 |
| ☐ | 76 Chuck Rainey ........ | .04 | .02 | .00 | ☐ 129 Bert Blyleven ....... | | .12 | .05 | .01 |
| ☐ | 77 Biff Pocoroba ........ | .04 | .02 | .00 | ☐ 130 Bud Black .......... | | .06 | .02 | .00 |
| ☐ | 78 Cecilio Guante ........ | .04 | .02 | .00 | ☐ 131 Gorman Heimueller .. | | .06 | .02 | .00 |
| ☐ | 79 Jim Barr ............ | .04 | .02 | .00 | ☐ 132 Dan Schatzeder ..... | | .04 | .02 | .00 |
| ☐ | 80 Kurt Bevacqua ....... | .04 | .02 | .00 | ☐ 133 Ron Jackson ........ | | .04 | .02 | .00 |
| ☐ | 81 Tom Foley ........... | .08 | .03 | .01 | ☐ 134 Tom Henke ......... | | .35 | .15 | .03 |
| ☐ | 82 Joe LeFebvre ........ | .04 | .02 | .00 | ☐ 135 Kevin Hickey ....... | | .04 | .02 | .00 |
| ☐ | 83 Andy Van Slyke ...... | .30 | .12 | .03 | ☐ 136 Mike Scott ......... | | .04 | .02 | .00 |
| ☐ | 84 Bob Lillis ........... | .04 | .02 | .00 | ☐ 137 Bo Diaz ........... | | .06 | .02 | .00 |
| ☐ | 85 Rick Adams .......... | .07 | .03 | .01 | ☐ 138 Glenn Brummer ..... | | .04 | .02 | .00 |
| ☐ | 86 Jerry Hairston ....... | .04 | .02 | .00 | ☐ 139 Sid Monge ......... | | .04 | .02 | .00 |
| ☐ | 87 Bob James .......... | .25 | .10 | .02 | ☐ 140 Rich Gale .......... | | .04 | .02 | .00 |
| ☐ | 88 Joe Altobelli ......... | .04 | .02 | .00 | ☐ 141 Brett Butler ........ | | .08 | .03 | .01 |
| ☐ | 89 Ed Romero .......... | .04 | .02 | .00 | ☐ 142 Brian Harper ....... | | .08 | .03 | .01 |
| ☐ | 90 John Grubb .......... | .04 | .02 | .00 | ☐ 143 John Rabb ......... | | .10 | .04 | .01 |
| ☐ | 91 John H. Johnson ...... | .04 | .02 | .00 | ☐ 144 Gary Woods ........ | | .04 | .02 | .00 |
| ☐ | 92 Juan Espino ......... | .07 | .03 | .01 | ☐ 145 Pat Putnam ........ | | .04 | .02 | .00 |
| ☐ | 93 Candy Maldonado ..... | .06 | .02 | .01 | ☐ 146 Jim Acker .......... | | .13 | .06 | .01 |
| ☐ | 94 Andre Thornton ...... | .08 | .03 | .01 | ☐ 147 Mickey Hatcher ..... | | .06 | .02 | .00 |
| ☐ | 95 Onix Concepcion ..... | .04 | .02 | .00 | ☐ 148 Todd Cruz ......... | | .04 | .02 | .00 |
| ☐ | 96 Don Hill ............. | .07 | .03 | .01 | ☐ 149 Tom Tellmann ...... | | .04 | .02 | .00 |
| ☐ | 97 Andre Dawson ....... | .20 | .09 | .02 | ☐ 150 John Wockenfuss ... | | .04 | .02 | .00 |
| ☐ | 98 Frank Tanana ........ | .06 | .02 | .00 | ☐ 151 Wade Boggs ....... | | .65 | .30 | .06 |
| ☐ | 99 Curt Wilkerson ....... | .09 | .04 | .01 | ☐ 152 Don Baylor ........ | | .13 | .06 | .01 |
| ☐ | 100 Larry Gura ........... | .06 | .02 | .00 | ☐ 153 Bob Welch ......... | | .07 | .03 | .01 |
| ☐ | 101 Dwayne Murphy ...... | .08 | .03 | .01 | ☐ 154 Alan Bannister ..... | | .04 | .02 | .00 |
| ☐ | 102 Tom Brennan ........ | .04 | .02 | .00 | ☐ 155 Willie Aikens ....... | | .06 | .02 | .00 |
| ☐ | 103 Dave Righetti ........ | .14 | .06 | .01 | ☐ 156 Jeff Burroughs ..... | | .06 | .02 | .00 |
| ☐ | 104 Steve Sax ........... | .16 | .07 | .01 | ☐ 157 Bryan Little ........ | | .06 | .02 | .00 |

| | MINT | VG-E | F-G |
|---|---|---|---|
| ☐ 158 Bob Boone | .06 | .02 | .00 |
| ☐ 159 Dave Hostetler | .04 | .02 | .00 |
| ☐ 160 Jerry Dybzinski | .04 | .02 | .00 |
| ☐ 161 Mike Madden | .13 | .06 | .01 |
| ☐ 162 Luis DeLeon | .04 | .02 | .00 |
| ☐ 163 Willie Hernandez | .25 | .10 | .02 |
| ☐ 164 Frank Pastore | .04 | .02 | .00 |
| ☐ 165 Rick Camp | .04 | .02 | .00 |
| ☐ 166 Lee Mazzilli | .06 | .02 | .00 |
| ☐ 167 Scot Thompson | .04 | .02 | .00 |
| ☐ 168 Bob Forsch | .06 | .02 | .00 |
| ☐ 169 Mike Flanagan | .08 | .03 | .01 |
| ☐ 170 Rick Manning | .04 | .02 | .00 |
| ☐ 171 Chet Lemon | .08 | .03 | .01 |
| ☐ 172 Jerry Remy | .06 | .02 | .00 |
| ☐ 173 Ron Guidry | .20 | .09 | .02 |
| ☐ 174 Pedro Guerrero | .35 | .15 | .03 |
| ☐ 175 Willie Wilson | .20 | .09 | .02 |
| ☐ 176 Carney Lansford | .11 | .05 | .01 |
| ☐ 177 Al Oliver | .16 | .07 | .01 |
| ☐ 178 Jim Sundberg | .06 | .02 | .00 |
| ☐ 179 Bobby Grich | .08 | .03 | .01 |
| ☐ 180 Rich Dotson | .08 | .03 | .01 |
| ☐ 181 Joaquin Andujar | .14 | .06 | .01 |
| ☐ 182 Jose Cruz | .12 | .05 | .01 |
| ☐ 183 Mike Schmidt | .50 | .22 | .05 |
| ☐ 184 Gary Redus | .25 | .10 | .02 |
| ☐ 185 Garry Templeton | .12 | .05 | .01 |
| ☐ 186 Tony Pena | .14 | .06 | .01 |
| ☐ 187 Greg Minton | .06 | .02 | .00 |
| ☐ 188 Phil Niekro | .18 | .08 | .01 |
| ☐ 189 Ferguson Jenkins | .11 | .05 | .01 |
| ☐ 190 Mookie Wilson | .09 | .04 | .01 |
| ☐ 191 Jim Beattie | .04 | .02 | .00 |
| ☐ 192 Gary Ward | .06 | .02 | .00 |
| ☐ 193 Jesse Barfield | .10 | .04 | .01 |
| ☐ 194 Pete Filson | .06 | .02 | .00 |
| ☐ 195 Roy Lee Jackson | .04 | .02 | .00 |
| ☐ 196 Rick Sweet | .04 | .02 | .00 |
| ☐ 197 Jesse Orosco | .09 | .04 | .01 |
| ☐ 198 Steve Lake | .06 | .02 | .00 |
| ☐ 199 Ken Dayley | .04 | .02 | .00 |
| ☐ 200 Manny Sarmiento | .04 | .02 | .00 |
| ☐ 201 Mark Davis | .04 | .02 | .00 |
| ☐ 202 Tim Flannery | .04 | .02 | .00 |
| ☐ 203 Bill Scherrer | .08 | .03 | .01 |
| ☐ 204 Al Holland | .06 | .02 | .00 |
| ☐ 205 Dave Von Ohlen | .06 | .02 | .00 |
| ☐ 206 Mike LaCoss | .04 | .02 | .00 |
| ☐ 207 Juan Beniquez | .06 | .02 | .00 |
| ☐ 208 Juan Agosto | .06 | .02 | .00 |
| ☐ 209 Bobby Ramos | .04 | .02 | .00 |

| | MINT | VG-E | F-G |
|---|---|---|---|
| ☐ 210 Al Bumbry | .04 | .02 | .00 |
| ☐ 211 Mark Brouhard | .04 | .02 | .00 |
| ☐ 212 Howard Bailey | .04 | .02 | .00 |
| ☐ 213 Bruce Hurst | .04 | .02 | .00 |
| ☐ 214 Bob Shirley | .04 | .02 | .00 |
| ☐ 215 Pat Zachry | .04 | .02 | .00 |
| ☐ 216 Julio Franco | .15 | .06 | .01 |
| ☐ 217 Mike Armstrong | .04 | .02 | .00 |
| ☐ 218 Dave Beard | .04 | .02 | .00 |
| ☐ 219 Steve Rogers | .08 | .03 | .01 |
| ☐ 220 John Butcher | .04 | .02 | .00 |
| ☐ 221 Mike Smithson | .13 | .06 | .01 |
| ☐ 222 Frank White | .07 | .03 | .01 |
| ☐ 223 Mike Heath | .04 | .02 | .00 |
| ☐ 224 Chris Bando | .04 | .02 | .00 |
| ☐ 225 Roy Smalley | .06 | .02 | .00 |
| ☐ 226 Dusty Baker | .09 | .04 | .01 |
| ☐ 227 Lou Whitaker | .20 | .09 | .02 |
| ☐ 228 John Lowenstein | .04 | .02 | .00 |
| ☐ 229 Ben Oglivie | .08 | .03 | .01 |
| ☐ 230 Doug DeCinces | .10 | .04 | .01 |
| ☐ 231 Lonnie Smith | .10 | .04 | .01 |
| ☐ 232 Ray Knight | .06 | .02 | .00 |
| ☐ 233 Gary Matthews | .09 | .04 | .01 |
| ☐ 234 Juan Bonilla | .04 | .02 | .00 |
| ☐ 235 Rod Scurry | .04 | .02 | .00 |
| ☐ 236 Atlee Hammaker | .06 | .02 | .00 |
| ☐ 237 Mike Caldwell | .04 | .02 | .00 |
| ☐ 238 Keith Hernandez | .30 | .12 | .03 |
| ☐ 239 Larry Bowa | .09 | .04 | .01 |
| ☐ 240 Tony Bernazard | .04 | .02 | .00 |
| ☐ 241 Damaso Garcia | .10 | .04 | .01 |
| ☐ 242 Tom Brunansky | .20 | .09 | .02 |
| ☐ 243 Dan Driessen | .06 | .02 | .00 |
| ☐ 244 Ron Kittle | .20 | .09 | .02 |
| ☐ 245 Tim Stoddard | .04 | .02 | .00 |
| ☐ 246 Bob L. Gibson | .08 | .03 | .01 |
| (Brewers Pitcher) | | | |
| ☐ 247 Marty Castillo | .04 | .02 | .00 |
| ☐ 248 Don Mattingly | 5.50 | 2.00 | .40 |
| ☐ 249 Jeff Newman | .04 | .02 | .00 |
| ☐ 250 Alejandro Pena | .25 | .10 | .02 |
| ☐ 251 Toby Harrah | .06 | .02 | .00 |
| ☐ 252 Cesar Geronimo | .04 | .02 | .00 |
| ☐ 253 Tom Underwood | .04 | .02 | .00 |
| ☐ 254 Doug Flynn | .04 | .02 | .00 |
| ☐ 255 Andy Hassler | .04 | .02 | .00 |
| ☐ 256 Odell Jones | .04 | .02 | .00 |
| ☐ 257 Rudy Law | .04 | .02 | .00 |
| ☐ 258 Harry Spilman | .04 | .02 | .00 |
| ☐ 259 Marty Bystrom | .04 | .02 | .00 |
| ☐ 260 Dave Rucker | .04 | .02 | .00 |

| | MINT | VG-E | F-G |
|---|---|---|---|
| ☐ 261 Ruppert Jones | .06 | .02 | .00 |
| ☐ 262 Jeff R. Jones | .08 | .03 | .01 |
| (Reds OF) | | | |
| ☐ 263 Gerald Perry | .15 | .06 | .01 |
| ☐ 264 Gene Tenace | .04 | .02 | .00 |
| ☐ 265 Brad Wellman | .07 | .03 | .01 |
| ☐ 266 Dickie Noles | .04 | .02 | .00 |
| ☐ 267 Jamie Allen | .09 | .04 | .01 |
| ☐ 268 Jim Gott | .04 | .02 | .00 |
| ☐ 269 Ron Davis | .06 | .02 | .00 |
| ☐ 270 Benny Ayala | .04 | .02 | .00 |
| ☐ 271 Ned Yost | .04 | .02 | .00 |
| ☐ 272 Dave Rozema | .04 | .02 | .00 |
| ☐ 273 Dave Stapleton | .06 | .02 | .00 |
| ☐ 274 Lou Piniella | .10 | .04 | .01 |
| ☐ 275 Jose Morales | .04 | .02 | .00 |
| ☐ 276 Brod Perkins | .04 | .02 | .00 |
| ☐ 277 Butch Davis | .10 | .04 | .01 |
| ☐ 278 Tony Phillips | .07 | .03 | .01 |
| ☐ 279 Jeff Reardon | .08 | .03 | .01 |
| ☐ 280 Ken Forsch | .04 | .02 | .00 |
| ☐ 281 Pete O'Brien | .30 | .12 | .03 |
| ☐ 282 Tom Paciorek | .04 | .02 | .00 |
| ☐ 283 Frank LaCorte | .04 | .02 | .00 |
| ☐ 284 Tim Lollar | .06 | .02 | .00 |
| ☐ 285 Greg Gross | .04 | .02 | .00 |
| ☐ 286 Alex Trevino | .04 | .02 | .00 |
| ☐ 287 Gene Garber | .04 | .02 | .00 |
| ☐ 288 Dave Parker | .25 | .10 | .02 |
| ☐ 289 Lee Smith | .10 | .04 | .01 |
| ☐ 290 Dave LaPoint | .06 | .02 | .00 |
| ☐ 291 John Shelby | .09 | .04 | .01 |
| ☐ 292 Charlie Moore | .04 | .02 | .00 |
| ☐ 293 Alan Trammell | .25 | .10 | .02 |
| ☐ 294 Tony Armas | .15 | .06 | .01 |
| ☐ 295 Shane Rawley | .06 | .02 | .00 |
| ☐ 296 Greg Brock | .08 | .03 | .01 |
| ☐ 297 Hal McRae | .07 | .03 | .01 |
| ☐ 298 Mike Davis | .10 | .04 | .01 |
| ☐ 299 Tim Raines | .30 | .12 | .03 |
| ☐ 300 Bucky Dent | .06 | .02 | .00 |
| ☐ 301 Tommy John | .15 | .06 | .01 |
| ☐ 302 Carlton Fisk | .16 | .07 | .01 |
| ☐ 303 Darrell Porter | .06 | .02 | .00 |
| ☐ 304 Dickie Thon | .08 | .03 | .01 |
| ☐ 305 Garry Maddox | .06 | .02 | .00 |
| ☐ 306 Cesar Cedeno | .07 | .03 | .01 |
| ☐ 307 Gary Lucas | .04 | .02 | .00 |
| ☐ 308 Johnny Ray | .13 | .06 | .01 |
| ☐ 309 Andy McGaffigan | .04 | .02 | .00 |
| ☐ 310 Claudell Washington | .09 | .04 | .01 |
| ☐ 311 Ryne Sandberg | .85 | .40 | .08 |
| ☐ 312 George Foster | .18 | .08 | .01 |
| ☐ 313 Spike Owen | .16 | .07 | .01 |
| ☐ 314 Garry Gaetti | .06 | .02 | .00 |
| ☐ 315 Willie Upshaw | .14 | .06 | .01 |
| ☐ 316 Al Williams | .04 | .02 | .00 |
| ☐ 317 Jorge Orta | .04 | .02 | .00 |
| ☐ 318 Orlando Mercado | .07 | .03 | .01 |
| ☐ 319 Junior Ortiz | .07 | .03 | .01 |
| ☐ 320 Mike Proly | .04 | .02 | .00 |
| ☐ 321 Randy Johnson | .04 | .02 | .00 |
| ☐ 322 Jim Morrison | .04 | .02 | .00 |
| ☐ 323 Max Venable | .04 | .02 | .00 |
| ☐ 324 Tony Gwynn | .50 | .22 | .05 |
| ☐ 325 Duane Walker | .04 | .02 | .00 |
| ☐ 326 Ozzie Virgil | .04 | .02 | .00 |
| ☐ 327 Jeff Lahti | .04 | .02 | .00 |
| ☐ 328 Bill Dawley | .15 | .06 | .01 |
| ☐ 329 Rob Wilfong | .04 | .02 | .00 |
| ☐ 330 Marc Hill | .04 | .02 | .00 |
| ☐ 331 Ray Burris | .04 | .02 | .00 |
| ☐ 332 Allan Ramirez | .07 | .03 | .01 |
| ☐ 333 Chuck Porter | .04 | .02 | .00 |
| ☐ 334 Wayne Krenchicki | .04 | .02 | .00 |
| ☐ 335 Gary Allenson | .04 | .02 | .00 |
| ☐ 336 Bobby Meacham | .25 | .10 | .02 |
| ☐ 337 Joe Beckwith | .04 | .02 | .00 |
| ☐ 338 Rick Sutcliffe | .25 | .10 | .02 |
| ☐ 339 Mark Huismann | .13 | .06 | .01 |
| ☐ 340 Tim Conroy | .09 | .04 | .01 |
| ☐ 341 Scott Sanderson | .06 | .02 | .00 |
| ☐ 342 Larry Biittner | .04 | .02 | .00 |
| ☐ 343 Dave Stewart | .04 | .02 | .00 |
| ☐ 344 Darryl Motley | .06 | .02 | .00 |
| ☐ 345 Chris Codiroli | .08 | .03 | .01 |
| ☐ 346 Rich Behenna | .07 | .03 | .01 |
| ☐ 347 Andre Robertson | .04 | .02 | .00 |
| ☐ 348 Mike Marshall | .16 | .07 | .01 |
| ☐ 349 Larry Herndon | .06 | .02 | .00 |
| ☐ 350 Rich Dauer | .04 | .02 | .00 |
| ☐ 351 Cecil Cooper | .16 | .07 | .01 |
| ☐ 352 Rod Carew | .40 | .18 | .04 |
| ☐ 353 Willie McGee | .35 | .15 | .03 |
| ☐ 354 Phil Garner | .06 | .02 | .00 |
| ☐ 355 Joe Morgan | .16 | .07 | .01 |
| ☐ 356 Luis Salazar | .04 | .02 | .00 |
| ☐ 357 John Candelaria | .08 | .03 | .01 |
| ☐ 358 Bill Laskey | .04 | .02 | .00 |
| ☐ 359 Bob McClure | .04 | .02 | .00 |
| ☐ 360 Dave Kingman | .14 | .06 | .01 |
| ☐ 361 Ron Cey | .13 | .06 | .01 |
| ☐ 362 Matt Young | .13 | .06 | .01 |
| ☐ 363 Lloyd Moseby | .14 | .06 | .01 |

| | MINT | VG-E | F-G |
|---|---|---|---|
| ☐ 364 Frank Viola | .08 | .03 | .01 |
| ☐ 365 Eddie Milner | .04 | .02 | .00 |
| ☐ 366 Floyd Bannister | .08 | .03 | .01 |
| ☐ 367 Dan Ford | .06 | .02 | .00 |
| ☐ 368 Moose Haas | .06 | .02 | .00 |
| ☐ 369 Doug Bair | .04 | .02 | .00 |
| ☐ 370 Ray Fontenot | .12 | .05 | .01 |
| ☐ 371 Luis Aponte | .04 | .02 | .00 |
| ☐ 372 Jack Fimple | .09 | .04 | .01 |
| ☐ 373 Neal Heaton | .10 | .04 | .01 |
| ☐ 374 Greg Pryor | .04 | .02 | .00 |
| ☐ 375 Wayne Gross | .04 | .02 | .00 |
| ☐ 376 Charlie Lea | .06 | .02 | .00 |
| ☐ 377 Steve Lubratich | .08 | .03 | .01 |
| ☐ 378 Jon Matlack | .06 | .02 | .00 |
| ☐ 379 Julio Cruz | .04 | .02 | .00 |
| ☐ 380 John Mizerock | .07 | .03 | .01 |
| ☐ 381 Kevin Gross | .13 | .06 | .01 |
| ☐ 382 Mike Ramsey | .04 | .02 | .00 |
| ☐ 383 Doug Gwosdz | .04 | .02 | .00 |
| ☐ 384 Kelly Paris | .09 | .04 | .01 |
| ☐ 385 Pete Falcone | .04 | .02 | .00 |
| ☐ 386 Milt May | .04 | .02 | .00 |
| ☐ 387 Fred Breining | .04 | .02 | .00 |
| ☐ 388 Craig Lefferts | .14 | .06 | .01 |
| ☐ 389 Steve Henderson | .04 | .02 | .00 |
| ☐ 390 Randy Moffitt | .04 | .02 | .00 |
| ☐ 391 Ron Washington | .04 | .02 | .00 |
| ☐ 392 Gary Roenicke | .06 | .02 | .00 |
| ☐ 393 Tom Candiotti | .07 | .03 | .01 |
| ☐ 394 Larry Pashnick | .04 | .02 | .00 |
| ☐ 395 Dwight Evans | .15 | .06 | .01 |
| ☐ 396 Goose Gossage | .20 | .09 | .02 |
| ☐ 397 Derrel Thomas | .04 | .02 | .00 |
| ☐ 398 Juan Eichelberger | .04 | .02 | .00 |
| ☐ 399 Leon Roberts | .04 | .02 | .00 |
| ☐ 400 Davey Lopes | .07 | .03 | .01 |
| ☐ 401 Bill Gullickson | .06 | .02 | .00 |
| ☐ 402 Geoff Zahn | .06 | .02 | .00 |
| ☐ 403 Billy Sample | .04 | .02 | .00 |
| ☐ 404 Mike Squires | .04 | .02 | .00 |
| ☐ 405 Craig Reynolds | .04 | .02 | .00 |
| ☐ 406 Eric Show | .06 | .02 | .00 |
| ☐ 407 John Denny | .09 | .04 | .01 |
| ☐ 408 Dann Bilardello | .07 | .03 | .01 |
| ☐ 409 Bruce Benedict | .04 | .02 | .00 |
| ☐ 410 Kent Tekulve | .08 | .03 | .01 |
| ☐ 411 Mel Hall | .10 | .04 | .01 |
| ☐ 412 John Stuper | .04 | .02 | .00 |
| ☐ 413 Rick Dempsey | .06 | .02 | .00 |
| ☐ 414 Don Sutton | .13 | .06 | .01 |
| ☐ 415 Jack Morris | .20 | .09 | .02 |
| ☐ 416 John Tudor | .15 | .06 | .01 |

| | MINT | VG-E | F-G |
|---|---|---|---|
| ☐ 417 Willie Randolph | .07 | .03 | .01 |
| ☐ 418 Jerry Reuss | .09 | .04 | .01 |
| ☐ 419 Don Slaught | .04 | .02 | .00 |
| ☐ 420 Steve McCatty | .04 | .02 | .00 |
| ☐ 421 Tim Wallach | .12 | .05 | .01 |
| ☐ 422 Larry Parrish | .07 | .03 | .01 |
| ☐ 423 Brian Downing | .06 | .02 | .00 |
| ☐ 424 Britt Burns | .08 | .03 | .01 |
| ☐ 425 David Green | .07 | .03 | .01 |
| ☐ 426 Jerry Mumphrey | .06 | .02 | .00 |
| ☐ 427 Ivan DeJesus | .04 | .02 | .00 |
| ☐ 428 Mario Soto | .10 | .04 | .01 |
| ☐ 429 Gene Richards | .04 | .02 | .00 |
| ☐ 430 Dale Berra | .06 | .02 | .00 |
| ☐ 431 Darrell Evans | .12 | .05 | .01 |
| ☐ 432 Glenn Hubbard | .06 | .02 | .00 |
| ☐ 433 Jody Davis | .10 | .04 | .01 |
| ☐ 434 Danny Heep | .04 | .02 | .00 |
| ☐ 435 Ed Nunez | .15 | .06 | .01 |
| ☐ 436 Bobby Castillo | .04 | .02 | .00 |
| ☐ 437 Ernie Whitt | .04 | .02 | .00 |
| ☐ 438 Scott Ullger | .07 | .03 | .01 |
| ☐ 439 Doyle Alexander | .06 | .02 | .00 |
| ☐ 440 Domingo Ramos | .07 | .03 | .01 |
| ☐ 441 Craig Swan | .04 | .02 | .00 |
| ☐ 442 Warren Brusstar | .04 | .02 | .00 |
| ☐ 443 Len Barker | .09 | .04 | .01 |
| ☐ 444 Mike Easler | .08 | .03 | .01 |
| ☐ 445 Renie Martin | .04 | .02 | .00 |
| ☐ 446 Dennis Rasmussen | .15 | .06 | .01 |
| ☐ 447 Ted Power | .06 | .02 | .00 |
| ☐ 448 Charlie Hudson | .15 | .06 | .01 |
| ☐ 449 Danny Cox | .40 | .18 | .04 |
| ☐ 450 Kevin Bass | .04 | .02 | .00 |
| ☐ 451 Daryl Sconiers | .04 | .02 | .00 |
| ☐ 452 Scott Fletcher | .04 | .02 | .00 |
| ☐ 453 Bryn Smith | .06 | .02 | .00 |
| ☐ 454 Jim Dwyer | .04 | .02 | .00 |
| ☐ 455 Rob Picciolo | .04 | .02 | .00 |
| ☐ 456 Enos Cabell | .04 | .02 | .00 |
| ☐ 457 Dennis Boyd | .45 | .20 | .04 |
| ☐ 458 Butch Wynegar | .06 | .02 | .00 |
| ☐ 459 Burt Hooton | .04 | .02 | .00 |
| ☐ 460 Ron Hassey | .04 | .02 | .00 |
| ☐ 461 Danny Jackson | .45 | .20 | .04 |
| ☐ 462 Bob Kearney | .04 | .02 | .00 |
| ☐ 463 Terry Francona | .07 | .03 | .01 |
| ☐ 464 Wayne Tolleson | .04 | .02 | .00 |
| ☐ 465 Mickey Rivers | .06 | .02 | .00 |
| ☐ 466 John Wathan | .04 | .02 | .00 |
| ☐ 467 Bill Almon | .04 | .02 | .00 |
| ☐ 468 George Vukovich | .04 | .02 | .00 |
| ☐ 469 Steve Kemp | .09 | .04 | .01 |

| | MINT | VG-E | F-G | | MINT | VG-E | F-G |
|---|---|---|---|---|---|---|---|
| ☐ 470 Ken Landreaux | .06 | .02 | .00 | ☐ 523 Chris Speier | .04 | .02 | .00 |
| ☐ 471 Milt Wilcox | .04 | .02 | .00 | ☐ 524 Bobby Clark | .04 | .02 | .00 |
| ☐ 472 Tippy Martinez | .06 | .02 | .00 | ☐ 525 George Wright | .06 | .02 | .00 |
| ☐ 473 Ted Simmons | .12 | .05 | .01 | ☐ 526 Dennis Lamp | .04 | .02 | .00 |
| ☐ 474 Tim Foli | .04 | .02 | .00 | ☐ 527 Tony Scott | .04 | .02 | .00 |
| ☐ 475 George Hendrick | .09 | .04 | .01 | ☐ 528 Ed Whitson | .08 | .03 | .01 |
| ☐ 476 Terry Puhl | .04 | .02 | .00 | ☐ 529 Ron Reed | .04 | .02 | .00 |
| ☐ 477 Von Hayes | .11 | .05 | .01 | ☐ 530 Charlie Puleo | .04 | .02 | .00 |
| ☐ 478 Bobby Brown | .04 | .02 | .00 | ☐ 531 Jerry Royster | .04 | .02 | .00 |
| ☐ 479 Lee Lacy | .06 | .02 | .00 | ☐ 532 Don Robinson | .04 | .02 | .00 |
| ☐ 480 Joel Youngblood | .04 | .02 | .00 | ☐ 533 Steve Trout | .06 | .02 | .00 |
| ☐ 481 Jim Slaton | .04 | .02 | .00 | ☐ 534 Bruce Sutter | .20 | .09 | .02 |
| ☐ 482 Mike Fitzgerald | .10 | .04 | .01 | ☐ 535 Bob Horner | .20 | .09 | .02 |
| ☐ 483 Keith Moreland | .06 | .02 | .00 | ☐ 536 Pat Tabler | .06 | .02 | .00 |
| ☐ 484 Ron Roenicke | .04 | .02 | .00 | ☐ 537 Chris Chambliss | .06 | .02 | .00 |
| ☐ 485 Luis Leal | .04 | .02 | .00 | ☐ 538 Bob Ojeda | .06 | .02 | .00 |
| ☐ 486 Bryan Oelkers | .07 | .03 | .01 | ☐ 539 Alan Ashby | .04 | .02 | .00 |
| ☐ 487 Bruce Berenyi | .06 | .02 | .00 | ☐ 540 Jay Johnstone | .06 | .02 | .00 |
| ☐ 488 LaMarr Hoyt | .12 | .05 | .01 | ☐ 541 Bob Dernier | .08 | .03 | .01 |
| ☐ 489 Joe Nolan | .04 | .02 | .00 | ☐ 542 Brook Jacoby | .75 | .35 | .07 |
| ☐ 490 Marshall Edwards | .04 | .02 | .00 | ☐ 543 U.L. Washington | .04 | .02 | .00 |
| ☐ 491 Mike Laga | .08 | .03 | .01 | ☐ 544 Danny Darwin | .04 | .02 | .00 |
| ☐ 492 Rick Cerone | .06 | .02 | .00 | ☐ 545 Kiko Garcia | .04 | .02 | .00 |
| ☐ 493 Rick Miller | .04 | .02 | .00 | ☐ 546 Vance Law | .04 | .02 | .00 |
| ☐ 494 Rick Honeycutt | .06 | .02 | .00 | ☐ 547 Tug McGraw | .09 | .04 | .01 |
| ☐ 495 Mike Hargrove | .06 | .02 | .00 | ☐ 548 Dave Smith | .04 | .02 | .00 |
| ☐ 496 Joe Simpson | .04 | .02 | .00 | ☐ 549 Len Matuszek | .04 | .02 | .00 |
| ☐ 497 Keith Atherton | .07 | .03 | .01 | ☐ 550 Tom Hume | .04 | .02 | .00 |
| ☐ 498 Chris Welsh | .04 | .02 | .00 | ☐ 551 Dave Dravecky | .08 | .03 | .01 |
| ☐ 499 Bruce Kison | .04 | .02 | .00 | ☐ 552 Rick Rhoden | .06 | .02 | .00 |
| ☐ 500 Bobby Johnson | .04 | .02 | .00 | ☐ 553 Duane Kuiper | .04 | .02 | .00 |
| ☐ 501 Jerry Koosman | .07 | .03 | .01 | ☐ 554 Rusty Staub | .10 | .04 | .01 |
| ☐ 502 Frank DiPino | .06 | .02 | .00 | ☐ 555 Bill Campbell | .06 | .02 | .00 |
| ☐ 503 Tony Perez | .13 | .06 | .01 | ☐ 556 Mike Torrez | .06 | .02 | .00 |
| ☐ 504 Ken Oberkfell | .04 | .02 | .00 | ☐ 557 Dave Henderson | .06 | .02 | .00 |
| ☐ 505 Mark Thurmond | .20 | .09 | .02 | ☐ 558 Len Whitehouse | .07 | .03 | .01 |
| ☐ 506 Joe Price | .04 | .02 | .00 | ☐ 559 Barry Bonnell | .04 | .02 | .00 |
| ☐ 507 Pascual Perez | .06 | .02 | .00 | ☐ 560 Rick Lysander | .07 | .03 | .01 |
| ☐ 508 Marvell Wynne | .15 | .06 | .01 | ☐ 561 Garth Iorg | .04 | .02 | .00 |
| ☐ 509 Mike Krukow | .04 | .02 | .00 | ☐ 562 Bryan Clark | .04 | .02 | .00 |
| ☐ 510 Dick Ruthven | .04 | .02 | .00 | ☐ 563 Brian Giles | .04 | .02 | .00 |
| ☐ 511 Al Cowens | .06 | .02 | .00 | ☐ 564 Vern Ruhle | .04 | .02 | .00 |
| ☐ 512 Cliff Johnson | .04 | .02 | .00 | ☐ 565 Steve Bedrosian | .07 | .03 | .01 |
| ☐ 513 Randy Bush | .04 | .02 | .00 | ☐ 566 Larry McWilliams | .06 | .02 | .00 |
| ☐ 514 Sammy Stewart | .04 | .02 | .00 | ☐ 567 Jeff Leonard | .07 | .03 | .01 |
| ☐ 515 Bill Schroeder | .20 | .09 | .02 | ☐ 568 Alan Wiggins | .10 | .04 | .01 |
| ☐ 516 Aurelio Lopez | .06 | .02 | .00 | ☐ 569 Jeff Russell | .08 | .03 | .01 |
| ☐ 517 Mike Brown | .08 | .03 | .01 | ☐ 570 Salome Barojas | .04 | .02 | .00 |
| ☐ 518 Graig Nettles | .14 | .06 | .01 | ☐ 571 Dane Iorg | .04 | .02 | .00 |
| ☐ 519 Dave Sax | .07 | .03 | .01 | ☐ 572 Bob Knepper | .06 | .02 | .00 |
| ☐ 520 Gerry Willard | .16 | .07 | .01 | ☐ 573 Gary Lavelle | .04 | .02 | .00 |
| ☐ 521 Paul Splittorff | .06 | .02 | .00 | ☐ 574 Gorman Thomas | .10 | .04 | .01 |
| ☐ 522 Tom Burgmeier | .04 | .02 | .00 | ☐ 575 Manny Trillo | .06 | .02 | .00 |

| | | MINT | VG-E | F-G |
|---|---|---|---|---|
| ☐ 576 | Jim Palmer | .25 | .10 | .02 |
| ☐ 577 | Dale Murray | .04 | .02 | .00 |
| ☐ 578 | Tom Brookens | .04 | .02 | .00 |
| ☐ 579 | Rich Gedman | .07 | .03 | .01 |
| ☐ 580 | Bill Doran | .30 | .12 | .03 |
| ☐ 581 | Steve Yeager | .06 | .02 | .00 |
| ☐ 582 | Dan Spillner | .04 | .02 | .00 |
| ☐ 583 | Dan Quisenberry | .20 | .09 | .02 |
| ☐ 584 | Rance Mulliniks | .04 | .02 | .00 |
| ☐ 585 | Storm Davis | .09 | .04 | .01 |
| ☐ 586 | Dave Schmidt | .04 | .02 | .00 |
| ☐ 587 | Bill Russell | .06 | .02 | .00 |
| ☐ 588 | Pat Sheridan | .20 | .09 | .02 |
| ☐ 589 | Rafael Ramirez | .06 | .02 | .00 |
| ☐ 590 | Bud Anderson | .04 | .02 | .00 |
| ☐ 591 | George Frazier | .04 | .02 | .00 |
| ☐ 592 | Lee Tunnell | .09 | .04 | .01 |
| ☐ 593 | Kirk Gibson | .25 | .10 | .02 |
| ☐ 594 | Scott McGregor | .08 | .03 | .01 |
| ☐ 595 | Bob Bailor | .04 | .02 | .00 |
| ☐ 596 | Tommy Herr | .13 | .05 | .01 |
| ☐ 597 | Luis Sanchez | .04 | .02 | .00 |
| ☐ 598 | Dave Engle | .06 | .02 | .00 |
| ☐ 599 | Craig McMurtry | .12 | .05 | .01 |
| ☐ 600 | Carlos Diaz | .04 | .02 | .00 |
| ☐ 601 | Tom O'Malley | .04 | .02 | .00 |
| ☐ 602 | Nick Esasky | .30 | .12 | .03 |
| ☐ 603 | Ron Hodges | .04 | .02 | .00 |
| ☐ 604 | Ed Vande Berg | .06 | .02 | .00 |
| ☐ 605 | Alfredo Griffin | .06 | .02 | .00 |
| ☐ 606 | Glen Hoffman | .04 | .02 | .00 |
| ☐ 607 | Hubie Brooks | .09 | .04 | .01 |
| ☐ 608 | Richard Barnes | .07 | .03 | .01 |
| ☐ 609 | Greg Walker | .75 | .35 | .07 |
| ☐ 610 | Ken Singleton | .09 | .04 | .01 |
| ☐ 611 | Mark Clear | .06 | .02 | .00 |
| ☐ 612 | Buck Martinez | .04 | .02 | .00 |
| ☐ 613 | Ken Griffey | .09 | .04 | .01 |
| ☐ 614 | Reid Nichols | .04 | .02 | .00 |
| ☐ 615 | Doug Sisk | .12 | .05 | .01 |
| ☐ 616 | Bob Brenly | .08 | .03 | .01 |
| ☐ 617 | Joey McLaughlin | .04 | .02 | .00 |
| ☐ 618 | Glenn Wilson | .10 | .04 | .01 |
| ☐ 619 | Bob Stoddard | .04 | .02 | .00 |
| ☐ 620 | Lenn Sakata | .04 | .02 | .00 |
| ☐ 621 | Mike Young | 1.25 | .60 | .12 |
| ☐ 622 | John Stefero | .07 | .03 | .01 |
| ☐ 623 | Carmelo Martinez | .30 | .12 | .03 |
| ☐ 624 | Dave Bergman | .04 | .02 | .00 |

| | | MINT | VG-E | F-G |
|---|---|---|---|---|
| ☐ 625 | Runnin' Reds | .15 | .06 | .01 |
| | David Green | | | |
| | Willie McGee | | | |
| | Lonnie Smith | | | |
| | Ozzie Smith | | | |
| | (sic, Redbirds) | | | |
| ☐ 626 | Rudy May | .04 | .02 | .00 |
| ☐ 627 | Matt Keough | .04 | .02 | .00 |
| ☐ 628 | Jose DeLeon | .20 | .09 | .02 |
| ☐ 629 | Jim Essian | .04 | .02 | .00 |
| ☐ 630 | Darnell Coles | .20 | .09 | .02 |
| ☐ 631 | Mike Warren | .12 | .05 | .01 |
| ☐ 632 | Del Crandall | .04 | .02 | .00 |
| ☐ 633 | Dennis Martinez | .04 | .02 | .00 |
| ☐ 634 | Mike Moore | .06 | .02 | .00 |
| ☐ 635 | Lary Sorensen | .04 | .02 | .00 |
| ☐ 636 | Rick Nelson | .09 | .04 | .01 |
| ☐ 637 | Omar Moreno | .06 | .02 | .00 |
| ☐ 638 | Charlie Hough | .06 | .02 | .00 |
| ☐ 639 | Dennis Eckersley | .06 | .02 | .00 |
| ☐ 640 | Walt Terrell | .30 | .12 | .03 |
| ☐ 641 | Denny Walling | .04 | .02 | .00 |
| ☐ 642 | Dave Anderson | .12 | .05 | .01 |
| ☐ 643 | Jose Oquendo | .08 | .03 | .01 |
| ☐ 644 | Bob Stanley | .06 | .02 | .00 |
| ☐ 645 | Dave Geisel | .04 | .02 | .00 |
| ☐ 646 | Scott Garrelts | .30 | .12 | .03 |
| ☐ 647 | Gary Pettis | .45 | .20 | .04 |
| ☐ 648 | Duke Snider Puzzle | .15 | .06 | .01 |
| ☐ 649 | Johnnie LeMaster | .04 | .02 | .00 |
| ☐ 650 | Dave Collins | .06 | .02 | .00 |
| ☐ 651 | The Chicken | .25 | .10 | .02 |
| | UNNUMBERED | | | |
| | CHECKLISTS | | | |
| ☐ 652 | DK Checklist | .10 | .02 | .00 |
| ☐ 653 | Checklist 1–130 | .08 | .01 | .00 |
| ☐ 654 | Checklist 131–234 | .08 | .01 | .00 |
| ☐ 655 | Checklist 235–338 | .08 | .01 | .00 |
| ☐ 656 | Checklist 339–442 | .08 | .01 | .00 |
| ☐ 657 | Checklist 443–546 | .08 | .01 | .00 |
| ☐ 658 | Checklist 547–651 | .08 | .01 | .00 |
| | LIVING LEGENDS | | | |
| ☐ A | Living Legends: | 1.40 | .60 | .14 |
| | Gaylord Perry | | | |
| | Rollie Fingers | | | |
| ☐ B | Living Legends: | 2.10 | .80 | .15 |
| | Carl Yastrzemski | | | |
| | Johnny Bench | | | |

# 1985 DONRUSS

The cards in this 660 card set measure 2½" by 3½". The 1985 Donruss regular issue cards have fronts that feature jet black borders on which orange lines have been placed. The fronts contain the standard team logo, player's name, position, and Donruss logo. The cards were distributed with puzzle pieces from a Dick Perez rendition of Lou Gehrig. The first 26 cards of the set are again entitled Diamond Kings (DK), for the fourth year in a row; the artwork on the Diamond Kings was again produced by the Perez-Steele Galleries. Cards 27–46 feature Rated Rookies (RR). The boxes in which the wax packs were contained feature four baseball cards, with backs. The price of the set below does not include these cards; however, these cards are priced at the end of the set below.

Complete Set: M-25.00; VG-E-11.00; F-G-2.50

|  | | MINT | VG-E | F-G |
|---|---|---|---|---|
|  | Common Player | .03 | .01 | .00 |
|  | DIAMOND KINGS (1–26) | | | |
| ☐ | 1 Ryne Sandberg DK | .45 | .15 | .03 |
| ☐ | 2 Doug DeCinces DK | .10 | .04 | .01 |
| ☐ | 3 Richard Dotson DK | .07 | .03 | .01 |
| ☐ | 4 Bert Blyleven DK | .12 | .05 | .01 |
| ☐ | 5 Lou Whitaker DK | .20 | .09 | .02 |
| ☐ | 6 Dan Quisenberry DK | .20 | .09 | .02 |
| ☐ | 7 Don Mattingly DK | .60 | .28 | .06 |
| ☐ | 8 Carney Lansford DK | .11 | .05 | .01 |

| ☐ | 9 Frank Tanana DK | .07 | .03 | .01 |
|---|---|---|---|---|
| ☐ | 10 Willie Upshaw DK | .11 | .05 | .01 |
| ☐ | 11 Claudell Washington DK | .10 | .04 | .01 |
| ☐ | 12 Mike Marshall DK | .16 | .07 | .01 |
| ☐ | 13 Joaquin Andujar DK | .11 | .05 | .01 |
| ☐ | 14 Cal Ripken DK | .45 | .20 | .04 |
| ☐ | 15 Jim Rice DK | .35 | .15 | .03 |
| ☐ | 16 Don Sutton DK | .13 | .06 | .01 |
| ☐ | 17 Frank Viola DK | .11 | .05 | .01 |
| ☐ | 18 Alvin Davis DK | .45 | .20 | .04 |
| ☐ | 19 Mario Soto DK | .11 | .05 | .01 |
| ☐ | 20 Jose Cruz DK | .12 | .05 | .01 |
| ☐ | 21 Charlie Lea DK | .07 | .03 | .01 |
| ☐ | 22 Jesse Orosco DK | .07 | .03 | .01 |
| ☐ | 23 Juan Samuel DK | .30 | .12 | .03 |
| ☐ | 24 Tony Pena DK | .12 | .05 | .01 |
| ☐ | 25 Tony Gwynn DK | .35 | .15 | .03 |
| ☐ | 26 Bob Brenly DK | .12 | .05 | .01 |
|  | RATED ROOKIES (27–46) | | | |
| ☐ | 27 Danny Tartabull RR | .30 | .12 | .03 |
| ☐ | 28 Mike Bielecki RR | .10 | .04 | .01 |
| ☐ | 29 Steve Lyons RR | .25 | .10 | .02 |
| ☐ | 30 Jeff Reed RR | .10 | .04 | .01 |
| ☐ | 31 Tony Brewer RR | .10 | .04 | .01 |
| ☐ | 32 John Morris RR | .15 | .06 | .01 |
| ☐ | 33 Daryl Boston RR | .15 | .06 | .01 |
| ☐ | 34 Alfonso Pulido RR | .10 | .04 | .01 |
| ☐ | 35 Steve Kiefer RR | .10 | .04 | .01 |
| ☐ | 36 Larry Sheets RR | .30 | .12 | .03 |
| ☐ | 37 Scott Bradley RR | .20 | .09 | .02 |
| ☐ | 38 Calvin Schiraldi RR | .20 | .09 | .02 |
| ☐ | 39 Shawon Dunston RR | .20 | .09 | .02 |
| ☐ | 40 Charlie Mitchell RR | .10 | .04 | .01 |
| ☐ | 41 Billy Hatcher RR | .10 | .04 | .01 |
| ☐ | 42 Russ Stephans RR | .10 | .04 | .01 |
| ☐ | 43 Alejandro Sanchez RR | .12 | .05 | .01 |
| ☐ | 44 Steve Jeltz RR | .15 | .06 | .01 |
| ☐ | 45 Jim Traber RR | .10 | .04 | .01 |
| ☐ | 46 Doug Loman RR | .30 | .12 | .03 |
| ☐ | 47 Eddie Murray | .40 | .18 | .04 |
| ☐ | 48 Robin Yount | .25 | .10 | .02 |
| ☐ | 49 Lance Parrish | .20 | .09 | .02 |
| ☐ | 50 Jim Rice | .30 | .12 | .03 |
| ☐ | 51 Dave Winfield | .30 | .12 | .03 |
| ☐ | 52 Fernando Valenzuela | .30 | .12 | .03 |
| ☐ | 53 George Brett | .45 | .20 | .04 |
| ☐ | 54 Dave Kingman | .12 | .05 | .01 |
| ☐ | 55 Gary Carter | .30 | .12 | .03 |
| ☐ | 56 Buddy Bell | .11 | .05 | .01 |
| ☐ | 57 Reggie Jackson | .35 | .15 | .03 |
| ☐ | 58 Harold Baines | .20 | .09 | .02 |
| ☐ | 59 Ozzie Smith | .10 | .04 | .01 |

| | MINT | VG-E | F-G |
|---|---|---|---|
| ☐ 60 Nolan Ryan | .25 | .10 | .02 |
| ☐ 61 Mike Schmidt | .35 | .15 | .03 |
| ☐ 62 Dave Parker | .20 | .09 | .02 |
| ☐ 63 Tony Gwynn | .30 | .12 | .03 |
| ☐ 64 Tony Pena | .13 | .06 | .01 |
| ☐ 65 Jack Clark | .17 | .07 | .01 |
| ☐ 66 Dale Murphy | .50 | .22 | .05 |
| ☐ 67 Ryne Sandberg | .45 | .20 | .04 |
| ☐ 68 Keith Hernandez | .25 | .10 | .02 |
| ☐ 69 Alvin Davis | .85 | .40 | .08 |
| ☐ 70 Kent Hrbek | .30 | .12 | .03 |
| ☐ 71 Willie Upshaw | .13 | .06 | .01 |
| ☐ 72 Dave Engle | .06 | .02 | .00 |
| ☐ 73 Alfredo Griffin | .06 | .02 | .00 |
| ☐ 74 Jack Perconte | .15 | .06 | .01 |
| ☐ 75 Jesse Orosco | .07 | .03 | .01 |
| ☐ 76 Jody Davis | .12 | .05 | .01 |
| ☐ 77 Bob Horner | .17 | .07 | .01 |
| ☐ 78 Larry McWilliams | .05 | .02 | .00 |
| ☐ 79 Joel Youngblood | .03 | .01 | .00 |
| ☐ 80 Alan Wiggins | .10 | .04 | .01 |
| ☐ 81 Ron Oester | .05 | .02 | .00 |
| ☐ 82 Ozzie Virgil | .05 | .02 | .00 |
| ☐ 83 Ricky Horton | .18 | .08 | .01 |
| ☐ 84 Bill Doran | .07 | .03 | .01 |
| ☐ 85 Rod Carew | .35 | .15 | .03 |
| ☐ 86 LaMarr Hoyt | .12 | .05 | .01 |
| ☐ 87 Tim Wallach | .10 | .04 | .01 |
| ☐ 88 Mike Flanagan | .07 | .03 | .01 |
| ☐ 89 Jim Sundberg | .06 | .02 | .00 |
| ☐ 90 Chet Lemon | .07 | .03 | .01 |
| ☐ 91 Bob Stanley | .06 | .02 | .00 |
| ☐ 92 Willie Randolph | .06 | .02 | .00 |
| ☐ 93 Bill Russell | .05 | .02 | .00 |
| ☐ 94 Julio Franco | .13 | .06 | .01 |
| ☐ 95 Dan Quisenberry | .18 | .08 | .01 |
| ☐ 96 Bill Caudill | .07 | .03 | .01 |
| ☐ 97 Bill Gullickson | .05 | .02 | .00 |
| ☐ 98 Danny Darwin | .03 | .01 | .00 |
| ☐ 99 Curtis Wilkerson | .03 | .01 | .00 |
| ☐ 100 Bud Black | .05 | .02 | .00 |
| ☐ 101 Tony Phillips | .03 | .01 | .00 |
| ☐ 102 Tony Bernazard | .03 | .01 | .00 |
| ☐ 103 Jay Howell | .05 | .02 | .00 |
| ☐ 104 Burt Hooton | .03 | .01 | .00 |
| ☐ 105 Milt Wilcox | .03 | .01 | .00 |
| ☐ 106 Rich Dauer | .03 | .01 | .00 |
| ☐ 107 Don Sutton | .13 | .06 | .01 |
| ☐ 108 Mike Witt | .10 | .04 | .01 |
| ☐ 109 Bruce Sutter | .16 | .07 | .01 |
| ☐ 110 Enos Cabell | .03 | .01 | .00 |
| ☐ 111 John Denny | .07 | .03 | .01 |
| ☐ 112 Dave Dravecky | .06 | .02 | .00 |
| ☐ 113 Marvell Wynne | .05 | .02 | .00 |
| ☐ 114 Johnnie LeMaster | .03 | .01 | .00 |
| ☐ 115 Chuck Porter | .03 | .01 | .00 |
| ☐ 116 John Gibbons | .10 | .04 | .01 |
| ☐ 117 Keith Moreland | .06 | .02 | .00 |
| ☐ 118 Darnell Coles | .07 | .03 | .01 |
| ☐ 119 Dennis Lamp | .03 | .01 | .00 |
| ☐ 120 Ron Davis | .05 | .02 | .00 |
| ☐ 121 Nick Esasky | .08 | .03 | .01 |
| ☐ 122 Vance Law | .03 | .01 | .00 |
| ☐ 123 Gary Roenicke | .05 | .02 | .00 |
| ☐ 124 Bill Schroeder | .03 | .01 | .00 |
| ☐ 125 Dave Rozema | .03 | .01 | .00 |
| ☐ 126 Bobby Meacham | .05 | .02 | .00 |
| ☐ 127 Marty Barrett | .08 | .03 | .01 |
| ☐ 128 R.J. Reynolds | .15 | .06 | .01 |
| ☐ 129 Ernie Camacho | .03 | .01 | .00 |
| ☐ 130 Jorge Orta | .03 | .01 | .00 |
| ☐ 131 Lary Sorensen | .03 | .01 | .00 |
| ☐ 132 Terry Francona | .07 | .03 | .01 |
| ☐ 133 Fred Lynn | .17 | .07 | .01 |
| ☐ 134 Bob Jones | .03 | .01 | .00 |
| ☐ 135 Jerry Hairston | .03 | .01 | .00 |
| ☐ 136 Kevin Bass | .03 | .01 | .00 |
| ☐ 137 Garry Maddox | .05 | .02 | .00 |
| ☐ 138 Dave LaPoint | .03 | .01 | .00 |
| ☐ 139 Kevin McReynolds | .15 | .06 | .01 |
| ☐ 140 Wayne Krenchicki | .03 | .01 | .00 |
| ☐ 141 Rafael Ramirez | .05 | .02 | .00 |
| ☐ 142 Rod Scurry | .03 | .01 | .00 |
| ☐ 143 Greg Minton | .05 | .02 | .00 |
| ☐ 144 Tim Stoddard | .03 | .01 | .00 |
| ☐ 145 Steve Henderson | .03 | .01 | .00 |
| ☐ 146 George Bell | .11 | .05 | .01 |
| ☐ 147 Dave Meier | .12 | .05 | .01 |
| ☐ 148 Sammy Stewart | .03 | .01 | .00 |
| ☐ 149 Mark Brouhard | .03 | .01 | .00 |
| ☐ 150 Larry Herndon | .05 | .02 | .00 |
| ☐ 151 Oil Can Boyd | .06 | .02 | .00 |
| ☐ 152 Brian Dayett | .05 | .02 | .00 |
| ☐ 153 Tom Niedenfuer | .06 | .02 | .00 |
| ☐ 154 Brook Jacoby | .09 | .04 | .01 |
| ☐ 155 Onix Concepcion | .03 | .01 | .00 |
| ☐ 156 Tim Conroy | .03 | .01 | .00 |
| ☐ 157 Joe Hesketh | .30 | .12 | .03 |
| ☐ 158 Brian Downing | .03 | .01 | .00 |
| ☐ 159 Tommy Dunbar | .05 | .02 | .00 |
| ☐ 160 Marc Hill | .03 | .01 | .00 |
| ☐ 161 Phil Garner | .05 | .02 | .00 |
| ☐ 162 Jerry Davis | .12 | .05 | .01 |
| ☐ 163 Bill Campbell | .05 | .02 | .00 |
| ☐ 164 John Franco | .35 | .15 | .03 |
| ☐ 165 Len Barker | .06 | .02 | .00 |

|  | MINT | VG-E | F-G |
|---|---|---|---|
| ☐ 166 Benny Distefano | .12 | .05 | .01 |
| ☐ 167 George Frazier | .03 | .01 | .00 |
| ☐ 168 Tito Landrum | .05 | .02 | .00 |
| ☐ 169 Cal Ripken | .40 | .18 | .04 |
| ☐ 170 Cecil Cooper | .15 | .06 | .01 |
| ☐ 171 Alan Trammell | .20 | .09 | .02 |
| ☐ 172 Wade Boggs | .50 | .22 | .05 |
| ☐ 173 Don Baylor | .12 | .05 | .01 |
| ☐ 174 Pedro Guerrero | .25 | .10 | .02 |
| ☐ 175 Frank White | .07 | .03 | .01 |
| ☐ 176 Rickey Henderson | .45 | .20 | .04 |
| ☐ 177 Charlie Lea | .07 | .03 | .01 |
| ☐ 178 Pete O'Brien | .05 | .02 | .00 |
| ☐ 179 Doug DeCinces | .09 | .04 | .01 |
| ☐ 180 Ron Kittle | .15 | .06 | .01 |
| ☐ 181 George Hendrick | .07 | .03 | .01 |
| ☐ 182 Joe Niekro | .07 | .03 | .01 |
| ☐ 183 Juan Samuel | .25 | .10 | .02 |
| ☐ 184 Mario Soto | .09 | .04 | .01 |
| ☐ 185 Goose Gossage | .16 | .07 | .01 |
| ☐ 186 Johnny Ray | .11 | .05 | .01 |
| ☐ 187 Bob Brenly | .09 | .04 | .01 |
| ☐ 188 Craig McMurtry | .06 | .02 | .00 |
| ☐ 189 Leon Durham | .14 | .06 | .01 |
| ☐ 190 Dwight Gooden | 6.00 | 1.50 | .25 |
| ☐ 191 Barry Bonnell | .03 | .01 | .00 |
| ☐ 192 Tim Teufel | .07 | .03 | .01 |
| ☐ 193 Dave Stieb | .16 | .07 | .01 |
| ☐ 194 Mickey Hatcher | .05 | .02 | .00 |
| ☐ 195 Jesse Barfield | .11 | .05 | .01 |
| ☐ 196 Al Cowens | .05 | .02 | .00 |
| ☐ 197 Hubie Brooks | .09 | .04 | .01 |
| ☐ 198 Steve Trout | .05 | .02 | .00 |
| ☐ 199 Glenn Hubbard | .05 | .02 | .00 |
| ☐ 200 Bill Madlock | .12 | .05 | .01 |
| ☐ 201 Jeff Robinson | .10 | .04 | .01 |
| ☐ 202 Eric Show | .05 | .02 | .00 |
| ☐ 203 Dave Concepcion | .09 | .04 | .01 |
| ☐ 204 Ivan DeJesus | .03 | .01 | .00 |
| ☐ 205 Neil Allen | .05 | .02 | .00 |
| ☐ 206 Jerry Mumphrey | .03 | .01 | .00 |
| ☐ 207 Mike Brown | .07 | .03 | .01 |
| ☐ 208 Carlton Fisk | .16 | .07 | .01 |
| ☐ 209 Bryn Smith | .06 | .02 | .00 |
| ☐ 210 Tippy Martinez | .05 | .02 | .00 |
| ☐ 211 Dion James | .07 | .03 | .01 |
| ☐ 212 Willie Hernandez | .15 | .06 | .01 |
| ☐ 213 Mike Easler | .06 | .02 | .00 |
| ☐ 214 Ron Guidry | .17 | .07 | .01 |
| ☐ 215 Rick Honeycutt | .05 | .02 | .00 |
| ☐ 216 Brett Butler | .09 | .04 | .01 |
| ☐ 217 Larry Gura | .05 | .02 | .00 |
| ☐ 218 Ray Burris | .03 | .01 | .00 |

|  | MINT | VG-E | F-G |
|---|---|---|---|
| ☐ 219 Steve Rogers | .07 | .03 | .01 |
| ☐ 220 Frank Tanana | .05 | .02 | .00 |
| ☐ 221 Ned Yost | .03 | .01 | .00 |
| ☐ 222 Bret Saberhagen | 1.75 | .65 | .17 |
| ☐ 223 Mike Davis | .07 | .03 | .01 |
| ☐ 224 Bert Blyleven | .11 | .05 | .01 |
| ☐ 225 Steve Kemp | .08 | .03 | .01 |
| ☐ 226 Jerry Reuss | .07 | .03 | .01 |
| ☐ 227 Darrell Evans | .12 | .05 | .01 |
| ☐ 228 Wayne Gross | .03 | .01 | .00 |
| ☐ 229 Jim Gantner | .05 | .02 | .00 |
| ☐ 230 Bob Boone | .06 | .02 | .00 |
| ☐ 231 Lonnie Smith | .07 | .03 | .01 |
| ☐ 232 Frank DiPino | .05 | .02 | .00 |
| ☐ 233 Jerry Koosman | .07 | .03 | .01 |
| ☐ 234 Graig Nettles | .13 | .06 | .01 |
| ☐ 235 John Tudor | .15 | .06 | .01 |
| ☐ 236 John Rabb | .05 | .02 | .00 |
| ☐ 237 Rick Manning | .03 | .01 | .00 |
| ☐ 238 Mike Fitzgerald | .05 | .02 | .00 |
| ☐ 239 Gary Matthews | .07 | .03 | .01 |
| ☐ 240 Jim Presley | .85 | .40 | .08 |
| ☐ 241 Dave Collins | .05 | .02 | .00 |
| ☐ 242 Gary Gaetti | .05 | .02 | .00 |
| ☐ 243 Dann Bilardello | .03 | .01 | .00 |
| ☐ 244 Rudy Law | .03 | .01 | .00 |
| ☐ 245 John Lowenstein | .03 | .01 | .00 |
| ☐ 246 Tom Tellman | .03 | .01 | .00 |
| ☐ 247 Howard Johnson | .05 | .02 | .00 |
| ☐ 248 Ray Fontenot | .05 | .02 | .00 |
| ☐ 249 Tony Armas | .12 | .05 | .01 |
| ☐ 250 Candy Maldonado | .05 | .02 | .00 |
| ☐ 251 Mike Jeffcoat | .05 | .02 | .00 |
| ☐ 252 Dane Iorg | .03 | .01 | .00 |
| ☐ 253 Bruce Bochte | .05 | .02 | .00 |
| ☐ 254 Pete Rose | .80 | .40 | .08 |
| ☐ 255 Don Aase | .03 | .01 | .00 |
| ☐ 256 George Wright | .05 | .02 | .00 |
| ☐ 257 Britt Burns | .07 | .03 | .01 |
| ☐ 258 Mike Scott | .05 | .02 | .00 |
| ☐ 259 Len Matuszek | .03 | .01 | .00 |
| ☐ 260 Dave Rucker | .03 | .01 | .00 |
| ☐ 261 Craig Lefferts | .05 | .02 | .00 |
| ☐ 262 Jay Tibbs | .15 | .06 | .01 |
| ☐ 263 Bruce Benedict | .03 | .01 | .00 |
| ☐ 264 Don Robinson | .05 | .02 | .00 |
| ☐ 265 Gary Lavelle | .03 | .01 | .00 |
| ☐ 266 Scott Sanderson | .05 | .02 | .00 |
| ☐ 267 Matt Young | .05 | .02 | .00 |
| ☐ 268 Ernie Whitt | .03 | .01 | .00 |
| ☐ 269 Houston Jimenez | .05 | .02 | .00 |
| ☐ 270 Ken Dixon | .20 | .09 | .02 |
| ☐ 271 Peter Ladd | .03 | .01 | .00 |

| | MINT | VG-E | F-G |
|---|---|---|---|
| ☐ 272 Juan Berenguer | .03 | .01 | .00 |
| ☐ 273 Roger Clemens | .35 | .15 | .03 |
| ☐ 274 Rick Cerone | .03 | .01 | .00 |
| ☐ 275 Dave Anderson | .03 | .01 | .00 |
| ☐ 276 George Vukovich | .03 | .01 | .00 |
| ☐ 277 Greg Pryor | .03 | .01 | .00 |
| ☐ 278 Mike Warren | .05 | .02 | .00 |
| ☐ 279 Bob James | .03 | .01 | .00 |
| ☐ 280 Bobby Grich | .08 | .03 | .01 |
| ☐ 281 Mike Mason | .10 | .04 | .01 |
| ☐ 282 Ron Reed | .03 | .01 | .00 |
| ☐ 283 Alan Ashby | .03 | .01 | .00 |
| ☐ 284 Mark Thurmond | .05 | .02 | .00 |
| ☐ 285 Joe Lefebvre | .03 | .01 | .00 |
| ☐ 286 Ted Power | .06 | .02 | .00 |
| ☐ 287 Chris Chambliss | .06 | .02 | .00 |
| ☐ 288 Lee Tunnell | .03 | .01 | .00 |
| ☐ 289 Rich Bordi | .03 | .01 | .00 |
| ☐ 290 Glenn Brummer | .03 | .01 | .00 |
| ☐ 291 Mike Boddicker | .10 | .04 | .01 |
| ☐ 292 Rollie Fingers | .16 | .07 | .01 |
| ☐ 293 Lou Whitaker | .18 | .08 | .01 |
| ☐ 294 Dwight Evans | .12 | .05 | .01 |
| ☐ 295 Don Mattingly | .90 | .40 | .09 |
| ☐ 296 Mike Marshall | .15 | .06 | .01 |
| ☐ 297 Willie Wilson | .17 | .07 | .01 |
| ☐ 298 Mike Heath | .03 | .01 | .00 |
| ☐ 299 Tim Raines | .25 | .10 | .02 |
| ☐ 300 Larry Parrish | .07 | .03 | .01 |
| ☐ 301 Geoff Zahn | .03 | .01 | .00 |
| ☐ 302 Rich Dotson | .07 | .03 | .01 |
| ☐ 303 David Green | .06 | .02 | .00 |
| ☐ 304 Jose Cruz | .11 | .05 | .01 |
| ☐ 305 Steve Carlton | .30 | .12 | .03 |
| ☐ 306 Gary Redus | .07 | .03 | .01 |
| ☐ 307 Steve Garvey | .35 | .15 | .03 |
| ☐ 308 Jose DeLeon | .05 | .02 | .00 |
| ☐ 309 Randy Lerch | .03 | .01 | .00 |
| ☐ 310 Claudell Washington | .07 | .03 | .01 |
| ☐ 311 Lee Smith | .08 | .03 | .01 |
| ☐ 312 Darryl Strawberry | .45 | .20 | .04 |
| ☐ 313 Jim Beattie | .03 | .01 | .00 |
| ☐ 314 John Butcher | .03 | .01 | .00 |
| ☐ 315 Damaso Garcia | .08 | .03 | .01 |
| ☐ 316 Mike Smithson | .03 | .01 | .00 |
| ☐ 317 Luis Leal | .03 | .01 | .00 |
| ☐ 318 Ken Phelps | .05 | .02 | .00 |
| ☐ 319 Wally Backman | .03 | .01 | .00 |
| ☐ 320 Ron Cey | .10 | .04 | .01 |
| ☐ 321 Brad Komminsk | .10 | .04 | .01 |
| ☐ 322 Jason Thompson | .07 | .03 | .01 |
| ☐ 323 Frank Williams | .10 | .04 | .01 |
| ☐ 324 Tim Lollar | .03 | .01 | .00 |

| | MINT | VG-E | F-G |
|---|---|---|---|
| ☐ 325 Eric Davis | .25 | .10 | .02 |
| ☐ 326 Von Hayes | .11 | .05 | .01 |
| ☐ 327 Andy Van Slyke | .07 | .03 | .01 |
| ☐ 328 Craig Reynolds | .03 | .01 | .00 |
| ☐ 329 Dick Schofield | .05 | .02 | .00 |
| ☐ 330 Scott Fletcher | .03 | .01 | .00 |
| ☐ 331 Jeff Reardon | .08 | .03 | .01 |
| ☐ 332 Rick Dempsey | .05 | .02 | .00 |
| ☐ 333 Ben Oglivie | .07 | .03 | .01 |
| ☐ 334 Dan Petry | .13 | .06 | .01 |
| ☐ 335 Jackie Gutierrez | .10 | .04 | .01 |
| ☐ 336 Dave Righetti | .13 | .06 | .01 |
| ☐ 337 Alejandro Pena | .06 | .02 | .00 |
| ☐ 338 Mel Hall | .09 | .04 | .01 |
| ☐ 339 Pat Sheridan | .06 | .02 | .00 |
| ☐ 340 Keith Atherton | .03 | .01 | .00 |
| ☐ 341 David Palmer | .05 | .02 | .00 |
| ☐ 342 Gary Ward | .05 | .02 | .00 |
| ☐ 343 Dave Stewart | .03 | .01 | .00 |
| ☐ 344 Mark Gubicza | .20 | .09 | .02 |
| ☐ 345 Carney Lansford | .11 | .05 | .01 |
| ☐ 346 Jerry Willard | .03 | .01 | .00 |
| ☐ 347 Ken Griffey | .06 | .02 | .00 |
| ☐ 348 Franklin Stubbs | .15 | .06 | .01 |
| ☐ 349 Aurelio Lopez | .03 | .01 | .00 |
| ☐ 350 Al Bumbry | .03 | .01 | .00 |
| ☐ 351 Charlie Moore | .03 | .01 | .00 |
| ☐ 352 Luis Sanchez | .03 | .01 | .00 |
| ☐ 353 Darrell Porter | .05 | .02 | .00 |
| ☐ 354 Bill Dawley | .05 | .02 | .00 |
| ☐ 355 Charles Hudson | .03 | .01 | .00 |
| ☐ 356 Garry Templeton | .10 | .04 | .01 |
| ☐ 357 Cecilio Guante | .03 | .01 | .00 |
| ☐ 358 Jeff Leonard | .06 | .02 | .00 |
| ☐ 359 Paul Molitor | .12 | .05 | .01 |
| ☐ 360 Ron Gardenhire | .03 | .01 | .00 |
| ☐ 361 Larry Bowa | .07 | .03 | .01 |
| ☐ 362 Bob Kearney | .03 | .01 | .00 |
| ☐ 363 Garth Iorg | .03 | .01 | .00 |
| ☐ 364 Tom Brunansky | .14 | .06 | .01 |
| ☐ 365 Brad Gulden | .03 | .01 | .00 |
| ☐ 366 Greg Walker | .12 | .05 | .01 |
| ☐ 367 Mike Young | .20 | .09 | .02 |
| ☐ 368 Rick Waits | .03 | .01 | .00 |
| ☐ 369 Doug Bair | .03 | .01 | .00 |
| ☐ 370 Bob Shirley | .03 | .01 | .00 |
| ☐ 371 Bob Ojeda | .05 | .02 | .00 |
| ☐ 372 Bob Welch | .06 | .02 | .00 |
| ☐ 373 Neal Heaton | .05 | .02 | .00 |
| ☐ 374 Danny Jackson | .07 | .03 | .01 |
| ☐ 375 Donnie Hill | .03 | .01 | .00 |
| ☐ 376 Mike Stenhouse | .05 | .02 | .00 |
| ☐ 377 Bruce Kison | .03 | .01 | .00 |

| | MINT | VG-E | F-G |
|---|---|---|---|
| ☐ 378 Wayne Tolleson | .03 | .01 | .00 |
| ☐ 379 Floyd Bannister | .05 | .02 | .00 |
| ☐ 380 Vern Ruhle | .03 | .01 | .00 |
| ☐ 381 Tim Corcoran | .03 | .01 | .00 |
| ☐ 382 Kurt Kepshire | .12 | .05 | .01 |
| ☐ 383 Bobby Brown | .03 | .01 | .00 |
| ☐ 384 Dave Van Gorder | .03 | .01 | .00 |
| ☐ 385 Rick Mahler | .06 | .02 | .00 |
| ☐ 386 Lee Mazzilli | .05 | .02 | .00 |
| ☐ 387 Bill Laskey | .03 | .01 | .00 |
| ☐ 388 Thad Bosley | .03 | .01 | .00 |
| ☐ 389 Al Chambers | .03 | .01 | .00 |
| ☐ 390 Tony Fernandez | .10 | .04 | .01 |
| ☐ 391 Ron Washington | .03 | .01 | .00 |
| ☐ 392 Bill Swaggerty | .12 | .05 | .01 |
| ☐ 393 Bob L. Gibson | .03 | .01 | .00 |
| ☐ 394 Marty Castillo | .03 | .01 | .00 |
| ☐ 395 Steve Crawford | .03 | .01 | .00 |
| ☐ 396 Clay Christiansen | .10 | .04 | .01 |
| ☐ 397 Bob Bailor | .03 | .01 | .00 |
| ☐ 398 Mike Hargrove | .05 | .02 | .00 |
| ☐ 399 Charlie Leibrandt | .07 | .03 | .01 |
| ☐ 400 Tom Burgmeier | .03 | .01 | .00 |
| ☐ 401 Razor Shines | .10 | .04 | .01 |
| ☐ 402 Rob Wilfong | .03 | .01 | .00 |
| ☐ 403 Tom Henke | .08 | .03 | .01 |
| ☐ 404 Al Jones | .10 | .04 | .01 |
| ☐ 405 Mike LaCoss | .03 | .01 | .00 |
| ☐ 406 Luis DeLeon | .03 | .01 | .00 |
| ☐ 407 Greg Gross | .03 | .01 | .00 |
| ☐ 408 Tom Hume | .03 | .01 | .00 |
| ☐ 409 Rick Camp | .03 | .01 | .00 |
| ☐ 410 Milt May | .03 | .01 | .00 |
| ☐ 411 Henry Cotto | .12 | .05 | .01 |
| ☐ 412 David Von Ohlen | .03 | .01 | .00 |
| ☐ 413 Scott McGregor | .08 | .03 | .01 |
| ☐ 414 Ted Simmons | .11 | .05 | .01 |
| ☐ 415 Jack Morris | .16 | .07 | .01 |
| ☐ 416 Bill Buckner | .08 | .03 | .01 |
| ☐ 417 Butch Wynegar | .06 | .02 | .00 |
| ☐ 418 Steve Sax | .11 | .05 | .01 |
| ☐ 419 Steve Balboni | .06 | .02 | .00 |
| ☐ 420 Dwayne Murphy | .06 | .02 | .00 |
| ☐ 421 Andre Dawson | .20 | .09 | .02 |
| ☐ 422 Charlie Hough | .05 | .02 | .00 |
| ☐ 423 Tommy John | .13 | .06 | .01 |
| ☐ 424 A Tom Seaver ERR | .75 | .35 | .07 |
| (photo actually | | | |
| Floyd Bannister) | | | |
| ☐ 424 B Tom Seaver COR | 3.00 | 1.40 | .30 |
| ☐ 425 Tommy Herr | .12 | .05 | .01 |
| ☐ 426 Terry Puhl | .05 | .02 | .00 |
| ☐ 427 Al Holland | .05 | .02 | .00 |
| ☐ 428 Eddie Milner | .05 | .02 | .00 |
| ☐ 429 Terry Kennedy | .08 | .03 | .01 |
| ☐ 430 John Candelaria | .07 | .03 | .01 |
| ☐ 431 Manny Trillo | .05 | .02 | .00 |
| ☐ 432 Ken Oberkfell | .03 | .01 | .00 |
| ☐ 433 Rick Sutcliffe | .15 | .06 | .01 |
| ☐ 434 Ron Darling | .18 | .08 | .01 |
| ☐ 435 Spike Owen | .05 | .02 | .00 |
| ☐ 436 Frank Viola | .08 | .03 | .01 |
| ☐ 437 Lloyd Moseby | .12 | .05 | .01 |
| ☐ 438 Kirby Puckett | .45 | .20 | .04 |
| ☐ 439 Jim Clancy | .03 | .01 | .00 |
| ☐ 440 Mike Moore | .06 | .02 | .00 |
| ☐ 441 Doug Sisk | .05 | .02 | .00 |
| ☐ 442 Dennis Eckersley | .05 | .02 | .00 |
| ☐ 443 Gerald Perry | .05 | .02 | .00 |
| ☐ 444 Dale Berra | .05 | .02 | .00 |
| ☐ 445 Dusty Baker | .05 | .02 | .00 |
| ☐ 446 Ed Whitson | .05 | .02 | .00 |
| ☐ 447 Cesar Cedeno | .07 | .03 | .01 |
| ☐ 448 Rick Schu | .20 | .09 | .02 |
| ☐ 449 Joaquin Andujar | .11 | .05 | .01 |
| ☐ 450 Mark Bailey | .10 | .04 | .01 |
| ☐ 451 Ron Romanick | .30 | .12 | .03 |
| ☐ 452 Julio Cruz | .03 | .01 | .00 |
| ☐ 453 Miguel Dilone | .03 | .01 | .00 |
| ☐ 454 Storm Davis | .07 | .03 | .01 |
| ☐ 455 Jaime Cocanower | .10 | .04 | .01 |
| ☐ 456 Barbaro Garbey | .15 | .06 | .01 |
| ☐ 457 Rich Gedman | .07 | .03 | .01 |
| ☐ 458 Phil Niekro | .15 | .06 | .01 |
| ☐ 459 Mike Scioscia | .03 | .01 | .00 |
| ☐ 460 Pat Tabler | .03 | .01 | .00 |
| ☐ 461 Darryl Motley | .05 | .02 | .00 |
| ☐ 462 Chris Codiroli | .03 | .01 | .00 |
| ☐ 463 Doug Flynn | .03 | .01 | .00 |
| ☐ 464 Billy Sample | .03 | .01 | .00 |
| ☐ 465 Mickey Rivers | .05 | .02 | .00 |
| ☐ 466 John Wathan | .03 | .01 | .00 |
| ☐ 467 Bill Krueger | .03 | .01 | .00 |
| ☐ 468 Andre Thornton | .07 | .03 | .01 |
| ☐ 469 Rex Hudler | .12 | .05 | .01 |
| ☐ 470 Sid Bream | .15 | .06 | .01 |
| ☐ 471 Kirk Gibson | .20 | .09 | .02 |
| ☐ 472 John Shelby | .03 | .01 | .00 |
| ☐ 473 Moose Haas | .05 | .02 | .00 |
| ☐ 474 Doug Corbett | .03 | .01 | .00 |
| ☐ 475 Willie McGee | .25 | .10 | .02 |
| ☐ 476 Bob Knepper | .06 | .02 | .00 |
| ☐ 477 Kevin Gross | .03 | .01 | .00 |
| ☐ 478 Carmelo Martinez | .09 | .04 | .01 |
| ☐ 479 Kent Tekulve | .05 | .02 | .00 |
| ☐ 480 Chili Davis | .08 | .03 | .01 |

| | MINT | VG-E | F-G |
|---|---|---|---|
| ☐ 481 Bobby Clark | .03 | .01 | .00 |
| ☐ 482 Mookie Wilson | .07 | .03 | .01 |
| ☐ 483 Dave Owen | .10 | .04 | .01 |
| ☐ 484 Ed Nunez | .05 | .02 | .00 |
| ☐ 485 Rance Mulliniks | .03 | .01 | .00 |
| ☐ 486 Ken Schrom | .03 | .01 | .00 |
| ☐ 487 Jeff Russell | .03 | .01 | .00 |
| ☐ 488 Tom Paciorek | .03 | .01 | .00 |
| ☐ 489 Dan Ford | .03 | .01 | .00 |
| ☐ 490 Mike Caldwell | .05 | .02 | .00 |
| ☐ 491 Scottie Earl | .10 | .04 | .01 |
| ☐ 492 Jose Rijo | .20 | .09 | .02 |
| ☐ 493 Bruce Hurst | .03 | .01 | .00 |
| ☐ 494 Ken Landreaux | .05 | .02 | .00 |
| ☐ 495 Mike Fischlin | .03 | .01 | .00 |
| ☐ 496 Don Slaught | .03 | .01 | .00 |
| ☐ 497 Steve McCatty | .03 | .01 | .00 |
| ☐ 498 Gary Lucas | .03 | .01 | .00 |
| ☐ 499 Gary Pettis | .08 | .03 | .01 |
| ☐ 500 Marvis Foley | .03 | .01 | .00 |
| ☐ 501 Mike Squires | .03 | .01 | .00 |
| ☐ 502 Jim Pankovitz | .08 | .03 | .01 |
| ☐ 503 Luis Aguayo | .03 | .01 | .00 |
| ☐ 504 Ralph Citarella | .08 | .03 | .01 |
| ☐ 505 Bruce Bochy | .03 | .01 | .00 |
| ☐ 506 Bob Owchinko | .03 | .01 | .00 |
| ☐ 507 Pascual Perez | .05 | .02 | .00 |
| ☐ 508 Lee Lacy | .05 | .02 | .00 |
| ☐ 509 Atlee Hammaker | .06 | .02 | .00 |
| ☐ 510 Bob Dernier | .06 | .02 | .00 |
| ☐ 511 Ed Vande Berg | .05 | .02 | .00 |
| ☐ 512 Cliff Johnson | .03 | .01 | .00 |
| ☐ 513 Len Whitehouse | .03 | .01 | .00 |
| ☐ 514 Dennis Martinez | .03 | .01 | .00 |
| ☐ 515 Ed Romero | .03 | .01 | .00 |
| ☐ 516 Rusty Kuntz | .03 | .01 | .00 |
| ☐ 517 Rick Miller | .03 | .01 | .00 |
| ☐ 518 Dennis Rasmussen | .05 | .02 | .00 |
| ☐ 519 Steve Yeager | .05 | .02 | .00 |
| ☐ 520 Chris Bando | .03 | .01 | .00 |
| ☐ 521 U.L. Washington | .03 | .01 | .00 |
| ☐ 522 Curt Young | .10 | .04 | .01 |
| ☐ 523 Angel Salazar | .05 | .02 | .00 |
| ☐ 524 Curt Kaufman | .10 | .04 | .01 |
| ☐ 525 Odell Jones | .03 | .01 | .00 |
| ☐ 526 Juan Agosto | .03 | .01 | .00 |
| ☐ 527 Denny Walling | .03 | .01 | .00 |
| ☐ 528 Andy Hawkins | .07 | .03 | .01 |
| ☐ 529 Sixto Lezcano | .03 | .01 | .00 |
| ☐ 530 Skeeter Barnes | .08 | .03 | .01 |
| ☐ 531 Randy Johnson | .03 | .01 | .00 |
| ☐ 532 Jim Morrison | .03 | .01 | .00 |
| ☐ 533 Warren Brusstar | .03 | .01 | .00 |

| | MINT | VG-E | F-G |
|---|---|---|---|
| ☐ 534 A Jeff Pendleton ERR (wrong first name) | .40 | .18 | .04 |
| ☐ 534 B Terry Pendleton COR | 1.50 | .70 | .15 |
| ☐ 535 Vic Rodriguez | .15 | .06 | .01 |
| ☐ 536 Bob McClure | .03 | .01 | .00 |
| ☐ 537 Dave Bergman | .03 | .01 | .00 |
| ☐ 538 Mark Clear | .05 | .02 | .00 |
| ☐ 539 Mike Pagliarulo | .25 | .10 | .02 |
| ☐ 540 Terry Whitfield | .03 | .01 | .00 |
| ☐ 541 Joe Beckwith | .03 | .01 | .00 |
| ☐ 542 Jeff Burroughs | .05 | .02 | .00 |
| ☐ 543 Dan Schatzeder | .03 | .01 | .00 |
| ☐ 544 Donnie Scott | .08 | .03 | .01 |
| ☐ 545 Jim Slaton | .05 | .02 | .00 |
| ☐ 546 Greg Luzinski | .10 | .04 | .01 |
| ☐ 547 Mark Salas | .40 | .18 | .04 |
| ☐ 548 Dave Smith | .05 | .02 | .00 |
| ☐ 549 John Wockenfuss | .03 | .01 | .00 |
| ☐ 550 Frank Pastore | .03 | .01 | .00 |
| ☐ 551 Tim Flannery | .03 | .01 | .00 |
| ☐ 552 Rick Rhoden | .05 | .02 | .00 |
| ☐ 553 Mark Davis | .05 | .02 | .00 |
| ☐ 554 Jeff Dedmon | .10 | .04 | .01 |
| ☐ 555 Gary Woods | .03 | .01 | .00 |
| ☐ 556 Danny Heep | .03 | .01 | .00 |
| ☐ 557 Mark Langston | .40 | .18 | .04 |
| ☐ 558 Darrell Brown | .03 | .01 | .00 |
| ☐ 559 Jimmy Key | .40 | .18 | .04 |
| ☐ 560 Rick Lysander | .03 | .01 | .00 |
| ☐ 561 Doyle Alexander | .06 | .02 | .00 |
| ☐ 562 Mike Stanton | .03 | .01 | .00 |
| ☐ 563 Sid Fernandez | .08 | .03 | .01 |
| ☐ 564 Richie Hebner | .03 | .01 | .00 |
| ☐ 565 Alex Trevino | .03 | .01 | .00 |
| ☐ 566 Brian Harper | .03 | .01 | .00 |
| ☐ 567 Dan Gladden | .25 | .10 | .02 |
| ☐ 568 Luis Salazar | .03 | .01 | .00 |
| ☐ 569 Tom Foley | .03 | .01 | .00 |
| ☐ 570 Larry Anderson | .03 | .01 | .00 |
| ☐ 571 Danny Cox | .11 | .05 | .01 |
| ☐ 572 Joe Sambito | .05 | .02 | .00 |
| ☐ 573 Juan Beniquez | .05 | .02 | .00 |
| ☐ 574 Joel Skinner | .05 | .02 | .00 |
| ☐ 575 Randy St. Claire | .10 | .04 | .01 |
| ☐ 576 Floyd Rayford | .05 | .02 | .00 |
| ☐ 577 Roy Howell | .03 | .01 | .00 |
| ☐ 578 John Grubb | .03 | .01 | .00 |
| ☐ 579 Ed Jurak | .03 | .01 | .00 |
| ☐ 580 John Montefusco | .05 | .02 | .00 |
| ☐ 581 Orel Hershiser | 1.25 | .40 | .12 |
| ☐ 582 Tom Waddell | .10 | .04 | .01 |
| ☐ 583 Mark Huismann | .05 | .02 | .00 |
| ☐ 584 Joe Morgan | .15 | .06 | .01 |

| | MINT | VG-E | F-G |
|---|---|---|---|
| ☐ 585 Jim Wohlford | .03 | .01 | .00 |
| ☐ 586 Dave Schmidt | .03 | .01 | .00 |
| ☐ 587 Jeff Kunkel | .15 | .06 | .01 |
| ☐ 588 Hal McRae | .06 | .02 | .00 |
| ☐ 589 Bill Almon | .03 | .01 | .00 |
| ☐ 590 Carmen Castillo | .03 | .01 | .00 |
| ☐ 591 Omar Moreno | .05 | .02 | .00 |
| ☐ 592 Ken Howell | .20 | .09 | .02 |
| ☐ 593 Tom Brookens | .03 | .01 | .00 |
| ☐ 594 Joe Nolan | .03 | .01 | .00 |
| ☐ 595 Willie Lozado | .10 | .04 | .01 |
| ☐ 596 Tom Nieto | .10 | .04 | .01 |
| ☐ 597 Walt Terrell | .06 | .02 | .00 |
| ☐ 598 Al Oliver | .12 | .05 | .01 |
| ☐ 599 Shane Rawley | .05 | .02 | .00 |
| ☐ 600 Denny Gonzalez | .10 | .04 | .01 |
| ☐ 601 Mark Grant | .10 | .04 | .01 |
| ☐ 602 Mike Armstrong | .03 | .01 | .00 |
| ☐ 603 George Foster | .15 | .06 | .01 |
| ☐ 604 Davey Lopes | .06 | .02 | .00 |
| ☐ 605 Salome Barojas | .03 | .01 | .00 |
| ☐ 606 Roy Lee Jackson | .03 | .01 | .00 |
| ☐ 607 Pete Filson | .03 | .01 | .00 |
| ☐ 608 Duane Walker | .05 | .02 | .00 |
| ☐ 609 Glenn Wilson | .09 | .04 | .01 |
| ☐ 610 Rafael Santana | .12 | .05 | .01 |
| ☐ 611 Roy Smith | .10 | .04 | .01 |
| ☐ 612 Ruppert Jones | .05 | .02 | .00 |
| ☐ 613 Joe Cowley | .05 | .02 | .00 |
| ☐ 614 Al Nipper | .20 | .09 | .02 |
| ☐ 615 Gene Nelson | .03 | .01 | .00 |
| ☐ 616 Joe Carter | .08 | .03 | .01 |
| ☐ 617 Ray Knight | .06 | .02 | .00 |
| ☐ 618 Chuck Rainey | .03 | .01 | .00 |
| ☐ 619 Dan Driessen | .03 | .01 | .00 |
| ☐ 620 Daryl Sconiers | .03 | .01 | .00 |
| ☐ 621 Bill Stein | .03 | .01 | .00 |
| ☐ 622 Roy Smalley | .05 | .02 | .00 |
| ☐ 623 Ed Lynch | .03 | .01 | .00 |
| ☐ 624 Jeff Stone | .25 | .10 | .02 |
| ☐ 625 Bruce Berenyi | .05 | .02 | .00 |
| ☐ 626 Kelvin Chapman | .10 | .04 | .01 |
| ☐ 627 Joe Price | .03 | .01 | .00 |
| ☐ 628 Steve Bedrosian | .05 | .02 | .00 |
| ☐ 629 Vic Mata | .15 | .06 | .01 |
| ☐ 630 Mike Krukow | .03 | .01 | .00 |
| ☐ 631 Phil Bradley | .90 | .40 | .09 |
| ☐ 632 Jim Gott | .03 | .01 | .00 |
| ☐ 633 Randy Bush | .03 | .01 | .00 |
| ☐ 634 Tom Browning | .90 | .40 | .09 |
| ☐ 635 Lou Gehrig Puzzle | .12 | .05 | .01 |
| ☐ 636 Reid Nichols | .03 | .01 | .00 |
| ☐ 637 Dan Pasqua | .35 | .15 | .03 |
| ☐ 638 German Rivera | .12 | .05 | .01 |
| ☐ 639 Don Schulze | .10 | .04 | .01 |
| ☐ 640 Mike Jones | .15 | .06 | .01 |
| ☐ 641 Pete Rose | .75 | .35 | .07 |
| ☐ 642 Wade Towdon | .10 | .04 | .01 |
| ☐ 643 Jerry Narron | .03 | .01 | .00 |
| ☐ 644 Darrell Miller | .15 | .06 | .01 |
| ☐ 645 Tim Hulett | .20 | .09 | .02 |
| ☐ 646 Andy McGaffigan | .03 | .01 | .00 |
| ☐ 647 Kurt Bevacqua | .03 | .01 | .00 |
| ☐ 648 John Russell | .20 | .09 | .02 |
| ☐ 649 Ron Robinson | .10 | .04 | .01 |
| ☐ 650 Donnie Moore | .03 | .01 | .00 |
| ☐ 651 Winfield/Mattingly Two for the Title | 1.00 | .45 | .10 |
| ☐ 652 Tim Laudner | .03 | .01 | .00 |
| ☐ 653 Steve Farr | .10 | .04 | .01 |
| UNNUMBERED CHECKLISTS (654–660) | | | |
| ☐ 654 DK Checklist 1–26 | .09 | .01 | .00 |
| ☐ 655 Checklist 27–130 | .07 | .01 | .00 |
| ☐ 656 Checklist 131–234 | .07 | .01 | .00 |
| ☐ 657 Checklist 235–338 | .07 | .01 | .00 |
| ☐ 658 Checklist 339–442 | .07 | .01 | .00 |
| ☐ 659 Checklist 443–546 | .07 | .01 | .00 |
| ☐ 660 Checklist 547–653 | .07 | .01 | .00 |
| WAX PACK BOX CARDS | | | |
| ☐ PC1 Dwight Gooden | 3.50 | 1.25 | .35 |
| ☐ PC2 Ryne Sandberg | .50 | .22 | .05 |
| ☐ PC3 Ron Kittle | .20 | .09 | .02 |
| ☐ PUZ Lou Gehrig Puzzle | .10 | .04 | .01 |

## 1985 DONRUSS HIGHLIGHTS

This 56 card set features the players and pitchers of the month for each league as well as a number of highlight cards commemorating the 1985 season. The Donruss Company dedicated the last two cards to their own selections for Rookies of the Year (ROY). This set proved to be much more popular than the Donruss Company had predicted, as their first and only print run was exhausted even before card dealers' initial orders were filled.

Complete Set: M-30.00; VG-E-14.00; F-G-3.00

|  | MINT | VG-E | F-G |
|---|---|---|---|
| Common Player | .15 | .06 | .01 |
| ☐ 1 Tom Seaver: Sets Opening Day Record | .50 | .22 | .05 |
| ☐ 2 Rollie Fingers: Establishes AL Save Mark | .30 | .12 | .03 |
| ☐ 3 Mike Davis: AL Player for April | .15 | .06 | .01 |
| ☐ 4 Charlie Leibrandt: AL Pitcher for April | .15 | .06 | .01 |
| ☐ 5 Dale Murphy: NL Player for April | 1.25 | .60 | .12 |
| ☐ 6 Fernando Valenzuela: NL Pitcher for April | .50 | .22 | .05 |
| ☐ 7 Larry Bowa: NL Shortstop Record | .15 | .06 | .01 |
| ☐ 8 Dave Concepcion: Joins Reds' 2000 Hit Club | .15 | .06 | .01 |
| ☐ 9 Tony Perez: Eldest Grand Slammer | .25 | .10 | .02 |
| ☐ 10 Pete Rose: NL Career Run Leader | 2.50 | 1.15 | .25 |
| ☐ 11 George Brett: AL Player for May | 1.25 | .60 | .12 |
| ☐ 12 Dave Stieb: AL Pitcher for May | .30 | .12 | .03 |
| ☐ 13 Dave Parker: NL Player for May | .40 | .18 | .04 |
| ☐ 14 Andy Hawkins: NL Pitcher for May | .15 | .06 | .01 |
| ☐ 15 Andy Hawkins: Records 11th Straight Win | .15 | .06 | .01 |
| ☐ 16 Von Hayes: Two Homers in First Inning | .25 | .10 | .02 |
| ☐ 17 Rickey Henderson: AL Player for June | 1.00 | .45 | .10 |
| ☐ 18 Jay Howell: AL Pitcher for June | .15 | .06 | .01 |

|  | MINT | VG-E | F-G |
|---|---|---|---|
| ☐ 19 Pedro Guerrero: NL Player for June | .50 | .22 | .05 |
| ☐ 20 John Tudor: NL Pitcher for June | .25 | .10 | .02 |
| ☐ 21 Hernandez/Carter: Marathon Game Iron Men | .50 | .22 | .05 |
| ☐ 22 Nolan Ryan: Records 4000th K | .50 | .22 | .05 |
| ☐ 23 LaMarr Hoyt: All-Star Game MVP | .20 | .09 | .02 |
| ☐ 24 Oddibe McDowell: 1st Ranger to Hit for Cycle | .75 | .35 | .07 |
| ☐ 25 George Brett: AL Player for July | 1.25 | .60 | .12 |
| ☐ 26 Bret Saberhagen: AL Pitcher for July | 1.00 | .45 | .10 |
| ☐ 27 Keith Hernandez: NL Player for July | .50 | .22 | .05 |
| ☐ 28 Fernando Valenzuela: NL Pitcher for July | .50 | .22 | .05 |
| ☐ 29 McGee/Coleman: Record Setting Base Stealers | 1.25 | .60 | .12 |
| ☐ 30 Tom Seaver: Notches 300th Career Win | .50 | .22 | .05 |
| ☐ 31 Rod Carew: Strokes 3000th Hit | .60 | .28 | .06 |
| ☐ 32 Dwight Gooden: Establishes Met Record | 3.50 | 1.65 | .35 |
| ☐ 33 Dwight Gooden: Achieves Strikeout Milestone | 3.50 | 1.65 | .35 |
| ☐ 34 Eddie Murray: Explodes for 9 RBI | 1.00 | .45 | .10 |
| ☐ 35 Don Baylor: AL Career HBP Leader | .20 | .09 | .02 |
| ☐ 36 Don Mattingly: AL Player for August | 2.00 | .90 | .20 |
| ☐ 37 Dave Righetti: AL Pitcher for August | .20 | .09 | .02 |
| ☐ 38 Willie McGee: NL Player for August | .50 | .22 | .05 |
| ☐ 39 Shane Rawley: NL Pitcher for August | .15 | .06 | .01 |
| ☐ 40 Pete Rose: Ty-Breaking Hit | 2.50 | 1.15 | .25 |
| ☐ 41 Andre Dawson: Hits 3 HR's Drives in 8 Runs | .40 | .18 | .04 |
| ☐ 42 Rickey Henderson: Sets Yankee Theft Mark | 1.00 | .45 | .10 |
| ☐ 43 Tom Browning: 20 Wins in Rookie Season | .50 | .22 | .05 |

| | | MINT | VG-E | F-G |
|---|---|---|---|---|
| ☐ | 44 Don Mattingly: Yankee . Milestone for Hits | 2.00 | .90 | .20 |
| ☐ | 45 Don Mattingly: AL ...... Player for September | 2.00 | .90 | .20 |
| ☐ | 46 Charlie Leibrandt: AL ... Pitcher for September | .15 | .06 | .01 |
| ☐ | 47 Gary Carter: NL ........ Player for September | .50 | .22 | .05 |
| ☐ | 48 Dwight Gooden: NL .... Pitcher for September | 3.50 | 1.65 | .35 |
| ☐ | 49 Wade Boggs: Major .... League Record Setter | 1.50 | .70 | .15 |
| ☐ | 50 Phil Niekro: Hurls ...... Shutout for 300th Win | .50 | .22 | .05 |
| ☐ | 51 Darrell Evans: ......... Venerable HR King | .20 | .09 | .02 |
| ☐ | 52 Willie McGee: NL ...... Switch-Hitting Record | .50 | .22 | .05 |
| ☐ | 53 Dave Winfield: ........ Equals DiMaggio Feat | .60 | .28 | .06 |
| ☐ | 54 Vince Coleman: ....... Donruss NL ROY | 2.50 | 1.15 | .25 |
| ☐ | 55 Ozzie Guillen: ........ Dunruss AL ROY | .50 | .22 | .05 |
| ☐ | 56 Unnumbered Checklist . | .15 | .03 | .00 |

## 1986 DONRUSS

The cards in this 660 card set measure 2½" by 3½". The 1986 Donruss regular issue cards have fronts that feature blue borders. The fronts contain the standard team logo, player's name, position, and Donruss logo. The cards were distributed with puzzle pieces from a Dick Perez rendition of Hank Aaron. The first 26 cards of

the set are again entitled Diamond Kings (DK), for the fifth year in a row; the artwork on the Diamond Kings was again produced by the Perez-Steele Galleries. Cards 27–46 again feature Rated Rookies (RR). The boxes in which the wax packs were contained feature four baseball cards, with backs. The price of the set below does not include these cards; however, these cards are priced at the end of the set below.

Complete Set: M-18.00; VG-E-8.50; F-G-1.80

| | | MINT | VG-E | F-G |
|---|---|---|---|---|
| | Common Player ........ | .03 | .01 | .00 |
| | DIAMOND KINGS (1–26) | | | |
| ☐ | 1 Kirk Gibson DK ....... | .25 | .08 | .02 |
| ☐ | 2 Goose Gossage DK .... | .16 | .07 | .01 |
| ☐ | 3 Willie McGee DK ...... | .25 | .10 | .02 |
| ☐ | 4 George Bell DK ....... | .12 | .05 | .01 |
| ☐ | 5 Tony Armas DK ....... | .12 | .05 | .01 |
| ☐ | 6 Chili Davis DK ....... | .09 | .04 | .01 |
| ☐ | 7 Cecil Cooper DK ...... | .14 | .06 | .01 |
| ☐ | 8 Mike Boddicker DK .... | .10 | .04 | .01 |
| ☐ | 9 Davey Lopes DK ...... | .08 | .03 | .01 |
| ☐ | 10 Bill Doran DK ....... | .09 | .04 | .01 |
| ☐ | 11 Bret Saberhagen DK ... | .35 | .15 | .03 |
| ☐ | 12 Brett Butler DK ...... | .11 | .05 | .01 |
| ☐ | 13 Harold Baines DK ..... | .18 | .08 | .01 |
| ☐ | 14 Mike Davis DK ....... | .10 | .04 | .01 |
| ☐ | 15 Tony Perez DK ....... | .13 | .06 | .01 |
| ☐ | 16 Willie Randolph DK .... | .09 | .04 | .01 |
| ☐ | 17 Bob Boone DK ....... | .08 | .03 | .01 |
| ☐ | 18 Orel Hershiser DK ..... | .30 | .12 | .03 |
| ☐ | 19 Johnny Ray DK ....... | .11 | .05 | .01 |
| ☐ | 20 Gary Ward DK ....... | .08 | .03 | .01 |
| ☐ | 21 Rick Mahler DK ...... | .08 | .03 | .01 |
| ☐ | 22 Phil Bradley DK ...... | .20 | .09 | .02 |
| ☐ | 23 Jerry Koosman DK .... | .08 | .03 | .01 |
| ☐ | 24 Tom Brunansky DK .... | .12 | .05 | .01 |
| ☐ | 25 Andre Dawson DK ..... | .20 | .09 | .02 |
| ☐ | 26 Dwight Gooden DK .... | 1.00 | .45 | .10 |
| | RATED ROOKIES (27–46) | | | |
| ☐ | 27 Kal Daniels ......... | .25 | .10 | .02 |
| ☐ | 28 Fred McGriff ........ | .10 | .04 | .01 |
| ☐ | 29 Cory Snyder ........ | .15 | .06 | .01 |
| ☐ | 30 Jose Guzman ........ | .15 | .06 | .01 |
| ☐ | 31 Ty Gainey .......... | .15 | .06 | .01 |
| ☐ | 32 Johnny Abrego ...... | .10 | .04 | .01 |
| ☐ | 33 Andres Galarraga ..... | .15 | .06 | .01 |
| ☐ | 34 Dave Shipanoff ...... | .15 | .06 | .01 |

| | | MINT | VG-E | F-G |
|---|---|---|---|---|
| ☐ 35 | Mark McLemore | .10 | .04 | .01 |
| ☐ 36 | Marty Clary | .10 | .04 | .01 |
| ☐ 37 | Paul O'Neill | .15 | .06 | .01 |
| ☐ 38 | Danny Tartabull | .10 | .04 | .01 |
| ☐ 39 | Jose Canseco | .75 | .35 | .07 |
| ☐ 40 | Juan Nieves | .20 | .09 | .02 |
| ☐ 41 | Lance McCullers | .20 | .09 | .02 |
| ☐ 42 | Rick Surhoff | .10 | .04 | .01 |
| ☐ 43 | Todd Worrell | .25 | .10 | .02 |
| ☐ 44 | Bob Kipper | .20 | .09 | .02 |
| ☐ 45 | John Habyan | .15 | .06 | .01 |
| ☐ 46 | Mike Woodard | .10 | .04 | .01 |
| ☐ 47 | Mike Boddicker | .09 | .04 | .01 |
| ☐ 48 | Robin Yount | .25 | .10 | .02 |
| ☐ 49 | Lou Whitaker | .16 | .07 | .01 |
| ☐ 50 | Oil Can Boyd | .07 | .03 | .01 |
| ☐ 51 | Rickey Henderson | .35 | .15 | .03 |
| ☐ 52 | Mike Marshall | .12 | .05 | .01 |
| ☐ 53 | George Brett | .40 | .18 | .04 |
| ☐ 54 | Dave Kingman | .10 | .04 | .01 |
| ☐ 55 | Hubie Brooks | .08 | .03 | .01 |
| ☐ 56 | Oddibe McDowell | .18 | .08 | .01 |
| ☐ 57 | Doug DeCinces | .09 | .04 | .01 |
| ☐ 58 | Britt Burns | .06 | .02 | .00 |
| ☐ 59 | Ozzie Smith | .10 | .04 | .01 |
| ☐ 60 | Jose Cruz | .11 | .05 | .01 |
| ☐ 61 | Mike Schmidt | .35 | .15 | .03 |
| ☐ 62 | Pete Rose | .55 | .25 | .05 |
| ☐ 63 | Steve Garvey | .35 | .15 | .03 |
| ☐ 64 | Tony Pena | .11 | .05 | .01 |
| ☐ 65 | Chili Davis | .08 | .03 | .01 |
| ☐ 66 | Dale Murphy | .40 | .18 | .04 |
| ☐ 67 | Ryne Sandberg | .25 | .10 | .02 |
| ☐ 68 | Gary Carter | .25 | .10 | .02 |
| ☐ 69 | Alvin Davis | .13 | .06 | .01 |
| ☐ 70 | Kent Hrbek | .17 | .07 | .01 |
| ☐ 71 | George Bell | .11 | .05 | .01 |
| ☐ 72 | Kirby Puckett | .08 | .03 | .01 |
| ☐ 73 | Lloyd Moseby | .13 | .06 | .01 |
| ☐ 74 | Bob Kearney | .03 | .01 | .00 |
| ☐ 75 | Dwight Gooden | 1.50 | .50 | .15 |
| ☐ 76 | Gary Matthews | .07 | .03 | .01 |
| ☐ 77 | Rick Mahler | .05 | .02 | .00 |
| ☐ 78 | Benny Distefano | .05 | .02 | .00 |
| ☐ 79 | Jeff Leonard | .05 | .02 | .00 |
| ☐ 80 | Kevin McReynolds | .07 | .03 | .01 |
| ☐ 81 | Ron Oester | .05 | .02 | .00 |
| ☐ 82 | John Russell | .03 | .01 | .00 |
| ☐ 83 | Tommy Herr | .12 | .05 | .01 |
| ☐ 84 | Jerry Mumphrey | .05 | .02 | .00 |
| ☐ 85 | Ron Romanick | .07 | .03 | .01 |
| ☐ 86 | Daryl Boston | .05 | .02 | .00 |
| ☐ 87 | Andre Dawson | .20 | .09 | .02 |
| ☐ 88 | Eddie Murray | .35 | .15 | .03 |
| ☐ 89 | Dion James | .06 | .02 | .00 |
| ☐ 90 | Chet Lemon | .06 | .02 | .00 |
| ☐ 91 | Bob Stanley | .06 | .02 | .00 |
| ☐ 92 | Willie Randolph | .06 | .02 | .00 |
| ☐ 93 | Mike Scioscia | .03 | .01 | .00 |
| ☐ 94 | Tom Waddell | .03 | .01 | .00 |
| ☐ 95 | Danny Jackson | .06 | .02 | .00 |
| ☐ 96 | Mike Davis | .09 | .04 | .01 |
| ☐ 97 | Mike Fitzgerald | .03 | .01 | .00 |
| ☐ 98 | Gary Ward | .06 | .02 | .00 |
| ☐ 99 | Pete O'Brien | .05 | .02 | .00 |
| ☐ 100 | Bret Saberhagen | .35 | .15 | .03 |
| ☐ 101 | Alfredo Griffin | .06 | .02 | .00 |
| ☐ 102 | Brett Butler | .08 | .03 | .01 |
| ☐ 103 | Ron Guidry | .16 | .07 | .01 |
| ☐ 104 | Jerry Reuss | .05 | .02 | .00 |
| ☐ 105 | Jack Morris | .15 | .06 | .01 |
| ☐ 106 | Rick Dempsey | .05 | .02 | .00 |
| ☐ 107 | Ray Burris | .03 | .01 | .00 |
| ☐ 108 | Brian Downing | .03 | .01 | .00 |
| ☐ 109 | Willie McGee | .20 | .09 | .02 |
| ☐ 110 | Bill Doran | .07 | .03 | .01 |
| ☐ 111 | Kent Tekulve | .05 | .02 | .00 |
| ☐ 112 | Tony Gwynn | .20 | .09 | .02 |
| ☐ 113 | Marvell Wynne | .03 | .01 | .00 |
| ☐ 114 | David Green | .03 | .01 | .00 |
| ☐ 115 | Jim Gantner | .03 | .01 | .00 |
| ☐ 116 | George Foster | .15 | .06 | .01 |
| ☐ 117 | Steve Trout | .05 | .02 | .00 |
| ☐ 118 | Mark Langston | .07 | .03 | .01 |
| ☐ 119 | Tony Fernandez | .09 | .04 | .01 |
| ☐ 120 | John Butcher | .03 | .01 | .00 |
| ☐ 121 | Ron Robinson | .03 | .01 | .00 |
| ☐ 122 | Dan Spillner | .03 | .01 | .00 |
| ☐ 123 | Mike Young | .14 | .06 | .01 |
| ☐ 124 | Paul Molitor | .12 | .05 | .01 |
| ☐ 125 | Kirk Gibson | .17 | .07 | .01 |
| ☐ 126 | Ken Griffey | .06 | .02 | .00 |
| ☐ 127 | Tony Armas | .10 | .04 | .01 |
| ☐ 128 | Mariano Duncan | .45 | .20 | .04 |
| ☐ 129 | Pat Tabler | .05 | .02 | .00 |
| ☐ 130 | Frank White | .06 | .02 | .00 |
| ☐ 131 | Carney Lansford | .10 | .04 | .01 |
| ☐ 132 | Vance Law | .03 | .01 | .00 |
| ☐ 133 | Dick Schofield | .05 | .02 | .00 |
| ☐ 134 | Wayne Tolleson | .03 | .01 | .00 |
| ☐ 135 | Greg Walker | .12 | .05 | .01 |
| ☐ 136 | Denny Walling | .03 | .01 | .00 |
| ☐ 137 | Ozzie Virgil | .03 | .01 | .00 |
| ☐ 138 | Ricky Horton | .03 | .01 | .00 |
| ☐ 139 | LaMarr Hoyt | .10 | .04 | .01 |
| ☐ 140 | Wayne Krenchicki | .03 | .01 | .00 |

| | MINT | VG-E | F-G | | MINT | VG-E | F-G |
|---|---|---|---|---|---|---|---|
| ☐ 141 Glenn Hubbard | .03 | .01 | .00 | ☐ 194 Frank Viola | .07 | .03 | .01 |
| ☐ 142 Cecilio Guante | .03 | .01 | .00 | ☐ 195 Willie Upshaw | .11 | .05 | .01 |
| ☐ 143 Mike Krukow | .03 | .01 | .00 | ☐ 196 Jim Beattie | .03 | .01 | .00 |
| ☐ 144 Lee Smith | .08 | .03 | .01 | ☐ 197 Darryl Strawberry | .30 | .12 | .03 |
| ☐ 145 Edwin Nunez | .05 | .02 | .00 | ☐ 198 Ron Cey | .09 | .04 | .01 |
| ☐ 146 Dave Stieb | .14 | .06 | .01 | ☐ 199 Steve Bedrosian | .05 | .02 | .00 |
| ☐ 147 Mike Smithson | .03 | .01 | .00 | ☐ 200 Steve Kemp | .06 | .02 | .00 |
| ☐ 148 Ken Dixon | .05 | .02 | .00 | ☐ 201 Manny Trillo | .05 | .02 | .00 |
| ☐ 149 Danny Darwin | .03 | .01 | .00 | ☐ 202 Garry Templeton | .08 | .03 | .01 |
| ☐ 150 Chris Pittaro | .12 | .05 | .01 | ☐ 203 Dave Parker | .17 | .07 | .01 |
| ☐ 151 Bill Buckner | .08 | .03 | .01 | ☐ 204 John Denny | .06 | .02 | .00 |
| ☐ 152 Mike Pagliarulo | .05 | .02 | .00 | ☐ 205 Terry Pendleton | .07 | .03 | .01 |
| ☐ 153 Bill Russell | .05 | .02 | .00 | ☐ 206 Terry Puhl | .05 | .02 | .00 |
| ☐ 154 Brook Jacoby | .10 | .04 | .01 | ☐ 207 Bobby Grich | .06 | .02 | .00 |
| ☐ 155 Pat Sheridan | .03 | .01 | .00 | ☐ 208 Ozzie Guillen | .45 | .20 | .04 |
| ☐ 156 Mike Gallego | .12 | .05 | .01 | ☐ 209 Jeff Reardon | .08 | .03 | .01 |
| ☐ 157 Jim Wohlford | .03 | .01 | .00 | ☐ 210 Cal Ripken | .35 | .15 | .03 |
| ☐ 158 Gary Pettis | .07 | .03 | .01 | ☐ 211 Bill Schroeder | .05 | .02 | .00 |
| ☐ 159 Toby Harrah | .05 | .02 | .00 | ☐ 212 Dan Petry | .12 | .05 | .01 |
| ☐ 160 Richard Dotson | .06 | .02 | .00 | ☐ 213 Jim Rice | .25 | .10 | .02 |
| ☐ 161 Bob Knepper | .05 | .02 | .00 | ☐ 214 Dave Righetti | .12 | .05 | .01 |
| ☐ 162 Dave Dravecky | .07 | .03 | .01 | ☐ 215 Fernando Valenzuela | .25 | .10 | .02 |
| ☐ 163 Greg Gross | .03 | .01 | .00 | ☐ 216 Julio Franco | .10 | .04 | .01 |
| ☐ 164 Eric Davis | .07 | .03 | .01 | ☐ 217 Darryl Motley | .05 | .02 | .00 |
| ☐ 165 Gerald Perry | .05 | .02 | .00 | ☐ 218 Dave Collins | .05 | .02 | .00 |
| ☐ 166 Rick Rhoden | .05 | .02 | .00 | ☐ 219 Tim Wallach | .09 | .04 | .01 |
| ☐ 167 Keith Moreland | .05 | .02 | .00 | ☐ 220 George Wright | .03 | .01 | .00 |
| ☐ 168 Jack Clark | .13 | .06 | .01 | ☐ 221 Tommy Dunbar | .03 | .01 | .00 |
| ☐ 169 Storm Davis | .06 | .02 | .00 | ☐ 222 Steve Balboni | .05 | .02 | .00 |
| ☐ 170 Cecil Cooper | .14 | .06 | .01 | ☐ 223 Jay Howell | .05 | .02 | .00 |
| ☐ 171 Alan Trammell | .16 | .07 | .01 | ☐ 224 Joe Carter | .06 | .02 | .00 |
| ☐ 172 Roger Clemens | .08 | .03 | .01 | ☐ 225 Ed Whitson | .05 | .02 | .00 |
| ☐ 173 Don Mattingly | .75 | .35 | .07 | ☐ 226 Orel Hershiser | .30 | .12 | .03 |
| ☐ 174 Pedro Guerrero | .25 | .10 | .02 | ☐ 227 Willie Hernandez | .15 | .06 | .01 |
| ☐ 175 Willie Wilson | .17 | .07 | .01 | ☐ 228 Lee Lacy | .05 | .02 | .00 |
| ☐ 176 Dwayne Murphy | .06 | .02 | .00 | ☐ 229 Rollie Fingers | .14 | .06 | .01 |
| ☐ 177 Tim Raines | .20 | .09 | .02 | ☐ 230 Bob Boone | .06 | .02 | .00 |
| ☐ 178 Larry Parrish | .06 | .02 | .00 | ☐ 231 Joaquin Andujar | .09 | .04 | .01 |
| ☐ 179 Mike Witt | .10 | .04 | .01 | ☐ 232 Craig Reynolds | .03 | .01 | .00 |
| ☐ 180 Harold Baines | .20 | .09 | .02 | ☐ 233 Shane Rawley | .05 | .02 | .00 |
| ☐ 181 Vince Coleman | 1.25 | .50 | .12 | ☐ 234 Eric Show | .05 | .02 | .00 |
| ☐ 182 Jeff Heathcock | .10 | .04 | .01 | ☐ 235 Jose DeLeon | .05 | .02 | .00 |
| ☐ 183 Steve Carlton | .25 | .10 | .02 | ☐ 236 Jose Uribe | .10 | .04 | .01 |
| ☐ 184 Mario Soto | .09 | .04 | .01 | ☐ 237 Moose Haas | .05 | .02 | .00 |
| ☐ 185 Goose Gossage | .15 | .06 | .01 | ☐ 238 Wally Backman | .05 | .02 | .00 |
| ☐ 186 Johnny Ray | .11 | .05 | .01 | ☐ 239 Dennis Eckersley | .06 | .02 | .00 |
| ☐ 187 Dan Gladden | .07 | .03 | .01 | ☐ 240 Mike Moore | .06 | .02 | .00 |
| ☐ 188 Bob Horner | .16 | .07 | .01 | ☐ 241 Damaso Garcia | .06 | .02 | .00 |
| ☐ 189 Rick Sutcliffe | .14 | .06 | .01 | ☐ 242 Tim Teufel | .06 | .02 | .00 |
| ☐ 190 Keith Hernandez | .25 | .10 | .02 | ☐ 243 Dave Concepcion | .08 | .03 | .01 |
| ☐ 191 Phil Bradley | .20 | .09 | .02 | ☐ 244 Floyd Bannister | .06 | .02 | .00 |
| ☐ 192 Tom Brunansky | .12 | .05 | .01 | ☐ 245 Fred Lynn | .14 | .06 | .01 |
| ☐ 193 Jesse Barfield | .11 | .05 | .01 | ☐ 246 Charlie Moore | .03 | .01 | .00 |

| | | MINT | VG-E | F-G |
|---|---|---|---|---|
| ☐ 247 | Walt Terrell | .05 | .02 | .00 |
| ☐ 248 | Dave Winfield | .25 | .10 | .02 |
| ☐ 249 | Dwight Evans | .12 | .05 | .01 |
| ☐ 250 | Dennis Powell | .10 | .04 | .01 |
| ☐ 251 | Andre Thornton | .07 | .03 | .01 |
| ☐ 252 | Onix Concepcion | .03 | .01 | .00 |
| ☐ 253 | Mike Heath | .03 | .01 | .00 |
| ☐ 254 | David Palmer | .05 | .02 | .00 |
| ☐ 255 | Donnie Moore | .06 | .02 | .00 |
| ☐ 256 | Curtis Wilkerson | .03 | .01 | .00 |
| ☐ 257 | Julio Cruz | .03 | .01 | .00 |
| ☐ 258 | Nolan Ryan | .25 | .10 | .02 |
| ☐ 259 | Jeff Stone | .06 | .02 | .00 |
| ☐ 260 | John Tudor | .15 | .06 | .01 |
| ☐ 261 | Mark Thurmond | .05 | .02 | .00 |
| ☐ 262 | Jay Tibbs | .03 | .01 | .00 |
| ☐ 263 | Rafael Ramirez | .05 | .02 | .00 |
| ☐ 264 | Larry McWilliams | .05 | .02 | .00 |
| ☐ 265 | Mark Davis | .05 | .02 | .00 |
| ☐ 266 | Bob Dernier | .05 | .02 | .00 |
| ☐ 267 | Matt Young | .05 | .02 | .00 |
| ☐ 268 | Jim Clancy | .03 | .01 | .00 |
| ☐ 269 | Mickey Hatcher | .05 | .02 | .00 |
| ☐ 270 | Sammy Stewart | .03 | .01 | .00 |
| ☐ 271 | Bob L. Gibson | .03 | .01 | .00 |
| ☐ 272 | Nelson Simmons | .30 | .12 | .03 |
| ☐ 273 | Rich Gedman | .07 | .03 | .01 |
| ☐ 274 | Butch Wynegar | .05 | .02 | .00 |
| ☐ 275 | Ken Howell | .06 | .02 | .00 |
| ☐ 276 | Mel Hall | .07 | .03 | .01 |
| ☐ 277 | Jim Sundberg | .06 | .02 | .00 |
| ☐ 278 | Chris Codiroli | .03 | .01 | .00 |
| ☐ 279 | Herman Winningham | .15 | .06 | .01 |
| ☐ 280 | Rod Carew | .30 | .12 | .03 |
| ☐ 281 | Don Slaught | .03 | .01 | .00 |
| ☐ 282 | Scott Fletcher | .03 | .01 | .00 |
| ☐ 283 | Bill Dawley | .05 | .02 | .00 |
| ☐ 284 | Andy Hawkins | .07 | .03 | .01 |
| ☐ 285 | Glenn Wilson | .10 | .04 | .01 |
| ☐ 286 | Nick Esasky | .07 | .03 | .01 |
| ☐ 287 | Claudell Washington | .08 | .03 | .01 |
| ☐ 288 | Lee Mazzilli | .05 | .02 | .00 |
| ☐ 289 | Jody Davis | .08 | .03 | .01 |
| ☐ 290 | Darrell Porter | .05 | .02 | .00 |
| ☐ 291 | Scott McGregor | .07 | .03 | .01 |
| ☐ 292 | Ted Simmons | .10 | .04 | .01 |
| ☐ 293 | Aurelio Lopez | .03 | .01 | .00 |
| ☐ 294 | Marty Barrett | .06 | .02 | .00 |
| ☐ 295 | Dale Berra | .05 | .02 | .00 |
| ☐ 296 | Greg Brock | .06 | .02 | .00 |
| ☐ 297 | Charlie Leibrandt | .08 | .03 | .01 |
| ☐ 298 | Bill Krueger | .03 | .01 | .00 |
| ☐ 299 | Bryn Smith | .05 | .02 | .00 |
| ☐ 300 | Burt Hooton | .03 | .01 | .00 |
| ☐ 301 | Stu Cliburn | .20 | .09 | .02 |
| ☐ 302 | Luis Salazar | .03 | .01 | .00 |
| ☐ 303 | Ken Dayley | .05 | .02 | .00 |
| ☐ 304 | Frank DiPino | .05 | .02 | .00 |
| ☐ 305 | Von Hayes | .10 | .04 | .01 |
| ☐ 306 | Gary Redus | .05 | .02 | .00 |
| ☐ 307 | Craig Lefferts | .03 | .01 | .00 |
| ☐ 308 | Sammy Khalifa | .10 | .04 | .01 |
| ☐ 309 | Scott Garrelts | .05 | .02 | .00 |
| ☐ 310 | Rick Cerone | .03 | .01 | .00 |
| ☐ 311 | Shawon Dunston | .05 | .02 | .00 |
| ☐ 312 | Howard Johnson | .05 | .02 | .00 |
| ☐ 313 | Jim Presley | .18 | .08 | .01 |
| ☐ 314 | Gary Gaetti | .05 | .02 | .00 |
| ☐ 315 | Luis Leal | .03 | .01 | .00 |
| ☐ 316 | Mark Salas | .06 | .02 | .00 |
| ☐ 317 | Bill Caudill | .06 | .02 | .00 |
| ☐ 318 | Dave Henderson | .05 | .02 | .00 |
| ☐ 319 | Rafael Santana | .03 | .01 | .00 |
| ☐ 320 | Leon Durham | .13 | .06 | .01 |
| ☐ 321 | Bruce Sutter | .15 | .06 | .01 |
| ☐ 322 | Jason Thompson | .06 | .02 | .00 |
| ☐ 323 | Bob Brenly | .06 | .02 | .00 |
| ☐ 324 | Carmelo Martinez | .06 | .02 | .00 |
| ☐ 325 | Eddie Milner | .05 | .02 | .00 |
| ☐ 326 | Juan Samuel | .12 | .05 | .01 |
| ☐ 327 | Tomo Nieto | .03 | .01 | .00 |
| ☐ 328 | Dave Smith | .05 | .02 | .00 |
| ☐ 329 | Urbano Lugo | .10 | .04 | .01 |
| ☐ 330 | Joel Skinner | .05 | .02 | .00 |
| ☐ 331 | Bill Gullickson | .05 | .02 | .00 |
| ☐ 332 | Floyd Rayford | .05 | .02 | .00 |
| ☐ 333 | Ben Oglivie | .05 | .02 | .00 |
| ☐ 334 | Lance Parrish | .16 | .07 | .01 |
| ☐ 335 | Jackie Gutierrez | .03 | .01 | .00 |
| ☐ 336 | Dennis Rasmussen | .03 | .01 | .00 |
| ☐ 337 | Terry Whitfield | .03 | .01 | .00 |
| ☐ 338 | Neal Heaton | .03 | .01 | .00 |
| ☐ 339 | Jorge Orta | .03 | .01 | .00 |
| ☐ 340 | Donnie Hill | .03 | .01 | .00 |
| ☐ 341 | Joe Hesketh | .09 | .04 | .01 |
| ☐ 342 | Charlie Hough | .05 | .02 | .00 |
| ☐ 343 | Dave Rozema | .03 | .01 | .00 |
| ☐ 344 | Greg Pryor | .03 | .01 | .00 |
| ☐ 345 | Mickey Tettleton | .08 | .03 | .01 |
| ☐ 346 | George Vukovich | .03 | .01 | .00 |
| ☐ 347 | Don Baylor | .11 | .05 | .00 |
| ☐ 348 | Carlos Diaz | .03 | .01 | .00 |
| ☐ 349 | Barbaro Garbey | .05 | .02 | .00 |
| ☐ 350 | Larry Sheets | .11 | .05 | .01 |
| ☐ 351 | Ted Higuera | .30 | .12 | .03 |
| ☐ 352 | Juan Beniquez | .05 | .02 | .00 |

|  | MINT | VG-E | F-G |
|---|---|---|---|
| ☐ 353 Bob Forsch | .05 | .02 | .00 |
| ☐ 354 Mark Bailey | .03 | .01 | .00 |
| ☐ 355 Larry Andersen | .03 | .01 | .00 |
| ☐ 356 Terry Kennedy | .07 | .03 | .01 |
| ☐ 357 Don Robinson | .03 | .01 | .00 |
| ☐ 358 Jim Gott | .03 | .01 | .00 |
| ☐ 359 Ernie Riles | .40 | .18 | .04 |
| ☐ 360 John Christensen | .08 | .03 | .01 |
| ☐ 361 Ray Fontenot | .03 | .01 | .00 |
| ☐ 362 Spike Owen | .05 | .02 | .00 |
| ☐ 363 Jim Acker | .03 | .01 | .00 |
| ☐ 364 Ron Davis | .05 | .02 | .00 |
| ☐ 365 Tom Hume | .03 | .01 | .00 |
| ☐ 366 Carlton Fisk | .16 | .07 | .01 |
| ☐ 367 Nate Snell | .12 | .05 | .01 |
| ☐ 368 Rick Manning | .03 | .01 | .00 |
| ☐ 369 Darrell Evans | .10 | .04 | .01 |
| ☐ 370 Ron Hassey | .03 | .01 | .00 |
| ☐ 371 Wade Boggs | .40 | .18 | .04 |
| ☐ 372 Rick Honeycutt | .05 | .02 | .00 |
| ☐ 373 Chris Bando | .03 | .01 | .00 |
| ☐ 374 Bud Black | .05 | .02 | .00 |
| ☐ 375 Steve Henderson | .03 | .01 | .00 |
| ☐ 376 Charlie Lea | .05 | .02 | .00 |
| ☐ 377 Reggie Jackson | .30 | .12 | .03 |
| ☐ 378 Dave Schmidt | .03 | .01 | .00 |
| ☐ 379 Bob James | .05 | .02 | .00 |
| ☐ 380 Glenn Davis | .12 | .05 | .01 |
| ☐ 381 Tim Corcoran | .03 | .01 | .00 |
| ☐ 382 Danny Cox | .09 | .04 | .01 |
| ☐ 383 Tim Flannery | .03 | .01 | .00 |
| ☐ 384 Tom Browning | .17 | .07 | .01 |
| ☐ 385 Rick Camp | .03 | .01 | .00 |
| ☐ 386 Jim Morrison | .03 | .01 | .00 |
| ☐ 387 Dave LaPoint | .03 | .01 | .00 |
| ☐ 388 Davey Lopes | .06 | .02 | .00 |
| ☐ 389 Al Cowens | .05 | .02 | .00 |
| ☐ 390 Doyle Alexander | .05 | .02 | .00 |
| ☐ 391 Tim Laudner | .03 | .01 | .00 |
| ☐ 392 Don Aase | .03 | .01 | .00 |
| ☐ 393 Jaime Cocanower | .03 | .01 | .00 |
| ☐ 394 Randy O'Neal | .05 | .02 | .00 |
| ☐ 395 Mike Easler | .05 | .02 | .00 |
| ☐ 396 Scott Bradley | .05 | .02 | .00 |
| ☐ 397 Tom Niedenfuer | .06 | .02 | .00 |
| ☐ 398 Jerry Willard | .03 | .01 | .00 |
| ☐ 399 Lonnie Smith | .07 | .03 | .01 |
| ☐ 400 Bruce Bochte | .05 | .02 | .00 |
| ☐ 401 Terry Francona | .05 | .02 | .00 |
| ☐ 402 Jim Slaton | .05 | .02 | .00 |
| ☐ 403 Bill Stein | .03 | .01 | .00 |
| ☐ 404 Tim Hulett | .06 | .02 | .00 |
| ☐ 405 Alan Ashby | .03 | .01 | .00 |

|  | MINT | VG-E | F-G |
|---|---|---|---|
| ☐ 406 Tim Stoddard | .03 | .01 | .00 |
| ☐ 407 Garry Maddox | .05 | .02 | .00 |
| ☐ 408 Ted Power | .06 | .02 | .00 |
| ☐ 409 Len Barker | .06 | .02 | .00 |
| ☐ 410 Denny Gonzalez | .05 | .02 | .00 |
| ☐ 411 George Frazier | .03 | .01 | .00 |
| ☐ 412 Andy Van Slyke | .06 | .02 | .00 |
| ☐ 413 Jim Dwyer | .03 | .01 | .00 |
| ☐ 414 Paul Householder | .03 | .01 | .00 |
| ☐ 415 Alejandro Sanchez | .05 | .02 | .00 |
| ☐ 416 Steve Crawford | .03 | .01 | .00 |
| ☐ 417 Dan Pasqua | .12 | .05 | .01 |
| ☐ 418 Enos Cabell | .03 | .01 | .00 |
| ☐ 419 Mike Jones | .03 | .01 | .00 |
| ☐ 420 Steve Kiefer | .03 | .01 | .00 |
| ☐ 421 Tim Burke | .20 | .09 | .02 |
| ☐ 422 Mike Mason | .03 | .01 | .00 |
| ☐ 423 Ruppert Jones | .05 | .02 | .00 |
| ☐ 424 Jerry Hairston | .03 | .01 | .00 |
| ☐ 425 Tito Landrum | .05 | .02 | .00 |
| ☐ 426 Jeff Calhoun | .10 | .04 | .01 |
| ☐ 427 Don Carman | .15 | .06 | .01 |
| ☐ 428 Tony Perez | .13 | .06 | .01 |
| ☐ 429 Jerry Davis | .03 | .01 | .00 |
| ☐ 430 Bob Walk | .03 | .01 | .00 |
| ☐ 431 Brad Wellman | .03 | .01 | .00 |
| ☐ 432 Terry Forster | .06 | .02 | .00 |
| ☐ 433 Billy Hatcher | .05 | .02 | .00 |
| ☐ 434 Clint Hurdle | .03 | .01 | .00 |
| ☐ 435 Ivan Calderon | .25 | .10 | .02 |
| ☐ 436 Pete Filson | .03 | .01 | .00 |
| ☐ 437 Tom Henke | .07 | .03 | .01 |
| ☐ 438 Dave Engle | .05 | .02 | .00 |
| ☐ 439 Tom Filer | .06 | .02 | .00 |
| ☐ 440 Gorman Thomas | .09 | .04 | .01 |
| ☐ 441 Rick Aguilera | .20 | .09 | .02 |
| ☐ 442 Scott Sanderson | .05 | .02 | .00 |
| ☐ 443 Jeff Dedmon | .03 | .01 | .00 |
| ☐ 444 Joe Orsulak | .25 | .10 | .02 |
| ☐ 445 Atlee Hammaker | .05 | .02 | .00 |
| ☐ 446 Jerry Royster | .03 | .01 | .00 |
| ☐ 447 Buddy Bell | .10 | .04 | .01 |
| ☐ 448 Ivan DeJesus | .03 | .01 | .00 |
| ☐ 450 Jim Pankovits | .03 | .01 | .00 |
| ☐ 451 Jerry Narron | .03 | .01 | .00 |
| ☐ 452 Bryan Little | .03 | .01 | .00 |
| ☐ 453 Gary Lucas | .03 | .01 | .00 |
| ☐ 454 Dennis Martinez | .03 | .01 | .00 |
| ☐ 455 Ed Romero | .03 | .01 | .00 |
| ☐ 456 Bob Melvin | .10 | .04 | .01 |
| ☐ 457 Glenn Hoffman | .03 | .01 | .00 |
| ☐ 458 Bob Shirley | .03 | .01 | .00 |
| ☐ 459 Bob Welch | .05 | .02 | .00 |

|  | MINT | VG-E | F-G |
|---|---|---|---|
| 460 Carmen Castillo | .03 | .01 | .00 |
| 461 Dave Leeper | .10 | .04 | .01 |
| 462 Tim Birtsas | .15 | .06 | .01 |
| 463 Randy St. Claire | .03 | .01 | .00 |
| 464 Chris Welsh | .03 | .01 | .00 |
| 465 Greg Harris | .03 | .01 | .00 |
| 466 Lynn Jones | .03 | .01 | .00 |
| 467 Dusty Baker | .06 | .02 | .00 |
| 468 Roy Smith | .03 | .01 | .00 |
| 469 Andre Robertson | .03 | .01 | .00 |
| 470 Ken Landreaux | .05 | .02 | .00 |
| 471 Dave Bergman | .03 | .01 | .00 |
| 472 Gary Roenicke | .05 | .02 | .00 |
| 473 Pete Vuckovich | .05 | .02 | .00 |
| 474 Kirk McCaskill | .25 | .10 | .02 |
| 475 Jeff Lahti | .03 | .01 | .00 |
| 476 Mike Scott | .05 | .02 | .00 |
| 477 Darren Daulton | .15 | .06 | .01 |
| 478 Graig Nettles | .12 | .05 | .01 |
| 479 Bill Almon | .03 | .01 | .00 |
| 480 Greg Minton | .05 | .02 | .00 |
| 481 Randy Ready | .03 | .01 | .00 |
| 482 Lenny Dykstra | .25 | .10 | .02 |
| 483 Thad Bosley | .03 | .01 | .00 |
| 484 Harold Reynolds | .15 | .06 | .01 |
| 485 Al Oliver | .12 | .05 | .01 |
| 486 Roy Smalley | .05 | .02 | .00 |
| 487 John Franco | .06 | .02 | .00 |
| 488 Juan Agosto | .03 | .01 | .00 |
| 489 Al Pardo | .15 | .06 | .01 |
| 490 Bill Wegman | .15 | .06 | .01 |
| 491 Frank Tanana | .06 | .02 | .00 |
| 492 Brian Fisher | .30 | .12 | .03 |
| 493 Mark Clear | .05 | .02 | .00 |
| 494 Len Matuszek | .03 | .01 | .00 |
| 495 Ramon Romero | .08 | .03 | .01 |
| 496 John Wathan | .03 | .01 | .00 |
| 497 Rob Picciolo | .03 | .01 | .00 |
| 498 U.L. Washington | .03 | .01 | .00 |
| 499 John Candelaria | .07 | .03 | .01 |
| 500 Duane Walker | .03 | .01 | .00 |
| 501 Gene Nelson | .03 | .01 | .00 |
| 502 John Mizerock | .03 | .01 | .00 |
| 503 Luis Aguayo | .03 | .01 | .00 |
| 504 Kurt Kepshire | .03 | .01 | .00 |
| 505 Ed Wojna | .15 | .06 | .01 |
| 506 Joe Price | .03 | .01 | .00 |
| 507 Milt Thompson | .25 | .10 | .02 |
| 508 Junior Ortiz | .03 | .01 | .00 |
| 509 Vida Blue | .08 | .03 | .01 |
| 510 Steve Engel | .10 | .04 | .01 |
| 511 Karl Best | .10 | .04 | .01 |
| 512 Cecil Fielder | .25 | .10 | .02 |
| 513 Frank Eufemia | .15 | .06 | .01 |
| 514 Tippy Martinez | .05 | .02 | .00 |
| 515 Billy Robidoux | .25 | .10 | .02 |
| 516 Bill Scherrer | .03 | .01 | .00 |
| 517 Bruce Hurst | .03 | .01 | .00 |
| 518 Rich Bordi | .03 | .01 | .00 |
| 519 Steve Yeager | .05 | .02 | .00 |
| 520 Tony Bernazard | .03 | .01 | .00 |
| 521 Hal McRae | .06 | .02 | .00 |
| 522 Jose Rijo | .05 | .02 | .00 |
| 523 Mitch Webster | .12 | .05 | .01 |
| 524 Jack Howell | .35 | .15 | .03 |
| 525 Alan Bannister | .03 | .01 | .00 |
| 526 Ron Kittle | .11 | .05 | .01 |
| 527 Phil Garner | .05 | .02 | .00 |
| 528 Kurt Bevacqua | .03 | .01 | .00 |
| 529 Kevin Gross | .03 | .01 | .00 |
| 530 Bo Diaz | .03 | .01 | .00 |
| 531 Ken Oberkfell | .03 | .01 | .00 |
| 532 Rick Reuschel | .05 | .02 | .00 |
| 533 Ron Meridith | .10 | .04 | .01 |
| 534 Steve Braun | .03 | .01 | .00 |
| 535 Wayne Gross | .03 | .01 | .00 |
| 536 Ray Searage | .03 | .01 | .00 |
| 537 Tom Brookens | .03 | .01 | .00 |
| 538 Al Nipper | .05 | .02 | .00 |
| 539 Billy Sample | .03 | .01 | .00 |
| 540 Steve Sax | .11 | .05 | .01 |
| 541 Dan Quisenberry | .15 | .06 | .01 |
| 542 Tony Phillips | .03 | .01 | .00 |
| 543 Floyd Youmans | .25 | .10 | .02 |
| 544 Steve Buechele | .10 | .04 | .01 |
| 545 Craig Gerber | .10 | .04 | .01 |
| 546 Joe DeSa | .15 | .06 | .01 |
| 547 Brian Harper | .03 | .01 | .00 |
| 548 Kevin Bass | .03 | .01 | .00 |
| 549 Tom Foley | .03 | .01 | .00 |
| 550 Dave Van Gorder | .03 | .01 | .00 |
| 551 Bruce Bochy | .03 | .01 | .00 |
| 552 R.J. Reynolds | .03 | .01 | .00 |
| 553 Chris Brown | .35 | .15 | .03 |
| 554 Bruce Benedict | .03 | .01 | .00 |
| 555 Warren Brusstar | .03 | .01 | .00 |
| 556 Danny Heep | .03 | .01 | .00 |
| 557 Darnell Coles | .06 | .02 | .00 |
| 558 Greg Gagne | .03 | .01 | .00 |
| 559 Ernie Whitt | .03 | .01 | .00 |
| 560 Ron Washington | .03 | .01 | .00 |
| 561 Jimmy Key | .08 | .03 | .01 |
| 562 Billy Swift | .05 | .02 | .00 |
| 563 Ron Darling | .14 | .06 | .01 |

| | MINT | VG-E | F-G |
|---|---|---|---|
| ☐ 564 Dick Ruthven | .03 | .01 | .00 |
| ☐ 565 Zane Smith | .05 | .02 | .00 |
| ☐ 566 Sid Bream | .05 | .02 | .00 |
| ☐ 567 Joel Youngblood | .03 | .01 | .00 |
| ☐ 568 Mario Ramirez | .03 | .01 | .00 |
| ☐ 569 Tom Runnels | .10 | .04 | .01 |
| ☐ 570 Rick Schu | .05 | .02 | .00 |
| ☐ 571 Bill Campbell | .05 | .02 | .00 |
| ☐ 572 Dickie Thon | .06 | .02 | .00 |
| ☐ 573 Al Holland | .05 | .02 | .00 |
| ☐ 574 Reid Nichols | .03 | .01 | .00 |
| ☐ 575 Bert Roberge | .03 | .01 | .00 |
| ☐ 576 Mike Flanagan | .07 | .03 | .01 |
| ☐ 577 Tim Leary | .03 | .01 | .00 |
| ☐ 578 Mike Laga | .03 | .01 | .00 |
| ☐ 579 Steve Lyons | .06 | .02 | .00 |
| ☐ 580 Phil Niekro | .13 | .06 | .01 |
| ☐ 581 Gilberto Reyes | .15 | .06 | .01 |
| ☐ 582 Jamie Easterly | .03 | .01 | .00 |
| ☐ 583 Mark Gubicza | .07 | .03 | .01 |
| ☐ 584 Stan Javier | .30 | .12 | .03 |
| ☐ 585 Bill Laskey | .03 | .01 | .00 |
| ☐ 586 Jeff Russell | .03 | .01 | .00 |
| ☐ 587 Dickie Noles | .03 | .01 | .00 |
| ☐ 588 Steve Farr | .03 | .01 | .00 |
| ☐ 589 Steve Ontiveros | .20 | .09 | .02 |
| ☐ 590 Mike Hargrove | .05 | .02 | .00 |
| ☐ 591 Marty Bystrom | .05 | .02 | .00 |
| ☐ 592 Franklin Stubbs | .03 | .01 | .00 |
| ☐ 593 Larry Herndon | .05 | .02 | .00 |
| ☐ 594 Bill Swaggerty | .05 | .02 | .00 |
| ☐ 595 Carlos Ponce | .08 | .03 | .01 |
| ☐ 596 Pat Perry | .08 | .03 | .01 |
| ☐ 597 Ray Knight | .06 | .02 | .00 |
| ☐ 598 Steve Lombardozzi | .20 | .09 | .02 |
| ☐ 599 Brad Havens | .03 | .01 | .00 |
| ☐ 600 Pat Clements | .20 | .09 | .02 |
| ☐ 601 Joe Niekro | .07 | .03 | .01 |
| ☐ 602 Hank Aaron Puzzle Card | .15 | .06 | .01 |
| ☐ 603 Dwayne Henry | .10 | .04 | .01 |
| ☐ 604 Mookie Wilson | .07 | .03 | .01 |
| ☐ 605 Buddy Biancalana | .05 | .02 | .00 |
| ☐ 606 Rance Mulliniks | .03 | .01 | .00 |
| ☐ 607 Alan Wiggins | .08 | .03 | .01 |
| ☐ 608 Joe Cowley | .05 | .02 | .00 |
| ☐ 609 Tom Seaver | .25 | .10 | .02 |
| ☐ 610 Neil Allen | .05 | .02 | .00 |
| ☐ 611 Don Sutton | .12 | .05 | .01 |
| ☐ 612 Fred Toliver | .15 | .06 | .01 |
| ☐ 613 Jay Baller | .15 | .06 | .01 |
| ☐ 614 Marc Sullivan | .10 | .04 | .01 |
| ☐ 615 John Grubb | .03 | .01 | .00 |
| ☐ 616 Bruce Kison | .03 | .01 | .00 |
| ☐ 617 Bill Madlock | .12 | .05 | .01 |
| ☐ 618 Chris Chambliss | .06 | .02 | .00 |
| ☐ 619 Dave Steward | .03 | .01 | .00 |
| ☐ 620 Tim Lollar | .03 | .01 | .00 |
| ☐ 621 Gary Lavelle | .03 | .01 | .00 |
| ☐ 622 Charlie Hudson | .03 | .01 | .00 |
| ☐ 623 Joel Davis | .20 | .09 | .02 |
| ☐ 624 Joe Johnson | .20 | .09 | .02 |
| ☐ 625 Sid Fernandez | .07 | .03 | .01 |
| ☐ 626 Dennis Lamp | .03 | .01 | .00 |
| ☐ 627 Terry Harper | .03 | .01 | .00 |
| ☐ 628 Jack Lazorko | .03 | .01 | .00 |
| ☐ 629 Roger McDowell | .35 | .15 | .03 |
| ☐ 630 Mark Funderburk | .25 | .10 | .02 |
| ☐ 631 Ed Lynch | .03 | .01 | .00 |
| ☐ 632 Rudy Law | .03 | .01 | .00 |
| ☐ 633 Roger Mason | .15 | .06 | .01 |
| ☐ 634 Mike Felder | .15 | .06 | .01 |
| ☐ 635 Ken Schrom | .03 | .01 | .00 |
| ☐ 636 Bob Ojeda | .05 | .02 | .00 |
| ☐ 637 Ed Vande Berg | .05 | .02 | .00 |
| ☐ 638 Bobby Meacham | .05 | .02 | .00 |
| ☐ 639 Cliff Johnson | .03 | .01 | .00 |
| ☐ 640 Garth Lorg | .03 | .01 | .00 |
| ☐ 641 Dan Driessen | .03 | .01 | .00 |
| ☐ 642 Mike Brown | .05 | .02 | .00 |
| ☐ 643 John Shelby | .03 | .01 | .00 |
| ☐ 644 Pete Rose | .30 | .12 | .03 |
| Ty-Breaking | | | |
| ☐ 645 Knuckle Brothers | .11 | .05 | .01 |
| Phil and Joe Niekro | | | |
| ☐ 646 Jesse Orosco | .06 | .02 | .00 |
| ☐ 647 Billy Beane | .25 | .10 | .02 |
| ☐ 648 Cesar Cedeno | .07 | .03 | .01 |
| ☐ 649 Bert Blyleven | .10 | .04 | .01 |
| ☐ 650 Max Venable | .03 | .01 | .00 |
| ☐ 651 Fleet Feet | .30 | .12 | .03 |
| ☐ 652 Calvin Schiraldi | .05 | .02 | .00 |
| ☐ 653 King of Kings | .65 | .30 | .06 |
| Pete Rose | | | |
| UNNUMBERED | | | |
| CHECKLISTS | | | |
| ☐ 654 CL: Diamond Kings | .08 | .01 | .00 |
| ☐ 655 CL1: 27–130 | .06 | .01 | .00 |
| ☐ 656 CL2: 131–234 | .06 | .01 | .00 |
| ☐ 657 CL3: 235–338 | .06 | .01 | .00 |
| ☐ 658 CL4: 339–442 | .06 | .01 | .00 |
| ☐ 659 CL5: 443–546 | .06 | .01 | .00 |
| ☐ 660 CL6: 547–653 | .06 | .01 | .00 |
| WAX PACK BOX | | | |
| CARDS (REGULAR) | | | |

|  | | MINT | VG-E | F-G |
|---|---|---|---|---|
| ☐ PC4 | Kirk Gibson .......... | .50 | .22 | .05 |
| ☐ PC5 | Willie Hernandez ...... | .25 | .10 | .02 |
| ☐ PC6 | Doug DeCinces ....... | .15 | .06 | .01 |
| ☐ PUZ | Hank Aaron Puzzle .... | .10 | .04 | .01 |
|  | WAX PACK BOX | | | |
|  | CARDS (ALL-STAR) | | | |
| ☐ PC7 | Wade Boggs .......... | 1.50 | .70 | .15 |
| ☐ PC8 | Lee Smith ........... | .15 | .06 | .01 |
| ☐ PC9 | Cecil Cooper ......... | .20 | .09 | .02 |
| ☐ PUZ | Hank Aaron Puzzle .... | .10 | .04 | .01 |

## 1959 FLEER

*The cards in this 80 card set measure 2½"
by 3½". The 1959 Fleer set, designated as
R418-1 in the ACC, portrays the life of
Ted Williams. The wording of the wrapper,
"Baseball's Greatest Series," has led to
speculation that Fleer contemplated similar sets honoring other baseball immor-
tals, but chose to develop instead the
format of the 1960 and 1961 issues. Card
number 68, which was withdrawn early in
production, is considered scarce and has
even been counterfeited; the fake has a
rosy coloration and a cross-hatch pattern
visible over the picture area.*

| | MINT | VG-E | F-G |
|---|---|---|---|
| Complete Set: | M-140.00; VG-E-65.00; F-G-14.00 | | |
| Common Cards ........ | .75 | .35 | .07 |

| | | MINT | VG-E | F-G |
|---|---|---|---|---|
| ☐ 1 | The Early Years ...... | 2.25 | .50 | .10 |
| ☐ 2 | Ted's Idol Babe Ruth ... | 1.50 | .70 | .15 |
| ☐ 3 | Practice Makes Perfect . | .75 | .35 | .07 |
| ☐ 4 | Learns Fine Points ..... | .75 | .35 | .07 |
| ☐ 5 | Ted's Fame Spreads ... | .75 | .35 | .07 |

| | | MINT | VG-E | F-G |
|---|---|---|---|---|
| ☐ 6 | Ted Turns Pro ......... | .75 | .35 | .07 |
| ☐ 7 | From Mound to Plate ... | .75 | .35 | .07 |
| ☐ 8 | 1937 First Full Season .. | .75 | .35 | .07 |
| ☐ 9 | First Step to Majors .... | .75 | .35 | .07 |
| ☐ 10 | Gunning as Pasttime ... | .75 | .35 | .07 |
| ☐ 11 | First Spring Training .... | 1.00 | .45 | .10 |
| ☐ 12 | Burning Up Minors ..... | .75 | .35 | .07 |
| ☐ 13 | 1939 Shows Will Stay ... | .75 | .35 | .07 |
| ☐ 14 | Outstanding Rookie '39 . | .75 | .35 | .07 |
| ☐ 15 | Licks Sophomore Jinx .. | .75 | .35 | .07 |
| ☐ 16 | 1941 Greatest Year ..... | .75 | .35 | .07 |
| ☐ 17 | How Ted Hit .400 ...... | .75 | .35 | .07 |
| ☐ 18 | 1941 All Star Hero ..... | .75 | .35 | .07 |
| ☐ 19 | Ted Wins Triple Crown .. | .75 | .35 | .07 |
| ☐ 20 | On to Naval Training ... | .75 | .35 | .07 |
| ☐ 21 | Honors for Williams .... | .75 | .35 | .07 |
| ☐ 22 | 1944 Ted Solos ........ | .75 | .35 | .07 |
| ☐ 23 | Williams Wins Wings ... | .75 | .35 | .07 |
| ☐ 24 | 1945 Sharpshooter ..... | .75 | .35 | .07 |
| ☐ 25 | 1945 Ted Discharged ... | .75 | .35 | .07 |
| ☐ 26 | Off to Flying Start ..... | .75 | .35 | .07 |
| ☐ 27 | 7 / 9 / 46 One Man Show | .75 | .35 | .07 |
| ☐ 28 | The Williams Shift ..... | .75 | .35 | .07 |
| ☐ 29 | Ted Hits for Cycle ...... | .75 | .35 | .07 |
| ☐ 30 | Beating Williams Shift .. | .75 | .35 | .07 |
| ☐ 31 | Sox Lose Series ....... | .75 | .35 | .07 |
| ☐ 32 | Most Valuable Player ... | .75 | .35 | .07 |
| ☐ 33 | Another Triple Crown ... | .75 | .35 | .07 |
| ☐ 34 | Runs Scored Record .... | .75 | .35 | .07 |
| ☐ 35 | Sox Miss Pennant ..... | .75 | .35 | .07 |
| ☐ 36 | Banner Year for Ted ... | .75 | .35 | .07 |
| ☐ 37 | 1949 Sox Miss Again .. | .75 | .35 | .07 |
| ☐ 38 | 1949 Power Rampage ... | .75 | .35 | .07 |
| ☐ 39 | 1950 Great Start ....... | .75 | .35 | .07 |
| ☐ 40 | Ted Crashes into Wall .. | .75 | .35 | .07 |
| ☐ 41 | 1950 Ted Recovers ..... | .75 | .35 | .07 |
| ☐ 42 | Slowed by Injury ...... | .75 | .35 | .07 |
| ☐ 43 | Double Play Lead ...... | .75 | .35 | .07 |
| ☐ 44 | Back to Marines ....... | .75 | .35 | .07 |
| ☐ 45 | Farewell to Baseball? ... | .75 | .35 | .07 |
| ☐ 46 | Ready for Combat ...... | .75 | .35 | .07 |
| ☐ 47 | Ted Crash Lands Jet ... | .75 | .35 | .07 |
| ☐ 48 | 1953 Ted Returns ...... | .75 | .35 | .07 |
| ☐ 49 | Smash Return ......... | .75 | .35 | .07 |
| ☐ 50 | 1954 Spring Injury ..... | .75 | .35 | .07 |
| ☐ 51 | Ted is Patched Up ..... | .75 | .35 | .07 |
| ☐ 52 | 1954 Ted's Comeback .. | .75 | .35 | .07 |
| ☐ 53 | Comeback is Success .. | .75 | .35 | .07 |
| ☐ 54 | Ted Hooks Big One .... | .75 | .35 | .07 |
| ☐ 55 | Retirement "No Go" .... | .75 | .35 | .07 |
| ☐ 56 | 2000th Hit ........... | .75 | .35 | .07 |
| ☐ 57 | 400th Homer ......... | .75 | .35 | .07 |
| ☐ 58 | Williams Hits .388 ...... | .75 | .35 | .07 |

|                              | MINT  | VG-E  | F-G  |
|------------------------------|-------|-------|------|
| ☐ 59 Hot September for Ted   | .75   | .35   | .07  |
| ☐ 60 More Records for Ted    | .75   | .35   | .07  |
| ☐ 61 1957 Outfielder Ted     | .75   | .35   | .07  |
| ☐ 62 1958 6th Batting Title  | .75   | .35   | .07  |
| ☐ 63 Ted's All-Star Record   | .75   | .35   | .07  |
| ☐ 64 Daughter and Daddy      | .75   | .35   | .07  |
| ☐ 65 1958 August 30          | .75   | .35   | .07  |
| ☐ 66 1958 Powerhouse         | .75   | .35   | .07  |
| ☐ 67 Two Famous Fishermen    | 1.00  | .45   | .10  |
| ☐ 68 Ted Signs for 1959      | 90.00 | 42.00 | 9.00 |
| ☐ 69 A Future Ted Williams?  | .75   | .35   | .07  |
| ☐ 70 Williams and Thorpe     | 1.25  | .60   | .12  |
| ☐ 71 Hitting Fund 1          | .75   | .35   | .07  |
| ☐ 72 Hitting Fund 2          | .75   | .35   | .07  |
| ☐ 73 Hitting Fund 3          | .75   | .35   | .07  |
| ☐ 74 Here's How              | .75   | .35   | .07  |
| ☐ 75 Williams' Value to Sox  | .75   | .35   | .07  |
| ☐ 76 On Base Record          | .75   | .35   | .07  |
| ☐ 77 Ted Relaxes             | .75   | .35   | .07  |
| ☐ 78 Honors for Williams     | .75   | .35   | .07  |
| ☐ 79 Where Ted Stands        | .75   | .35   | .07  |
| ☐ 80 Ted's Goals for 1959    | 1.00  | .45   | .10  |

## 1960 FLEER

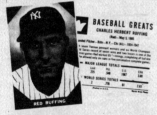

**BASEBALL GREATS**
**CHARLES HERBERT RUFFING**

RED RUFFING

The cards in this 79 card set measure 2½″ × 3½″. The cards from the 1960 Fleer series of Baseball Greats are sometimes mistaken for 1930's cards by collectors not familiar with this set. The cards each contain a tinted photo of a baseball immortal, and were issued in one series. There are no known scarcities, although a number 80 card (Pepper Martin reverse with either a Tinker, Collins, or Grove obverse) exists (this is not considered part of the set). The

catalog designation for 1960 Fleer is R418-2.
Complete Set: **M-90.00; VG-E-42.00; F-G-9.00**

|                              | MINT  | VG-E  | F-G  |
|------------------------------|-------|-------|------|
| Common Player (1–79)         | .75   | .35   | .07  |
| ☐ 1 Napoleon Lajoie          | 2.50  | .50   | .10  |
| ☐ 2 Christy Mathewson        | 2.00  | .90   | .20  |
| ☐ 3 George H. Ruth           | 9.00  | 4.25  | .90  |
| ☐ 4 Carl Hubbell             | 1.20  | .55   | .12  |
| ☐ 5 Grover Alexander         | 1.50  | .70   | .15  |
| ☐ 6 Walter P. Johnson        | 2.50  | 1.15  | .25  |
| ☐ 7 Charles A. Bender        | .75   | .35   | .07  |
| ☐ 8 Roger P. Bresnahan       | .75   | .35   | .07  |
| ☐ 9 Mordecai P. Brown        | .75   | .35   | .07  |
| ☐ 10 Tristram Speaker        | 1.25  | .60   | .12  |
| ☐ 11 Joseph (Arky) Vaughan   | .75   | .35   | .07  |
| ☐ 12 Zachariah Wheat         | .75   | .35   | .07  |
| ☐ 13 George Sisler           | 1.00  | .45   | .10  |
| ☐ 14 Connie Mack             | 1.00  | .45   | .10  |
| ☐ 15 Clark C. Griffith       | .75   | .35   | .07  |
| ☐ 16 Louis Boudreau          | 1.10  | .50   | .11  |
| ☐ 17 Ernest Lombardi         | .75   | .35   | .07  |
| ☐ 18 Henry Manush            | .75   | .35   | .07  |
| ☐ 19 Martin Marion           | .75   | .35   | .07  |
| ☐ 20 Edward Collins          | .75   | .35   | .07  |
| ☐ 21 James Maranville        | .75   | .35   | .07  |
| ☐ 22 Joseph Medwick          | .75   | .35   | .07  |
| ☐ 23 Edward Barrow           | .75   | .35   | .07  |
| ☐ 24 Gordon Cochrane         | 1.00  | .45   | .10  |
| ☐ 25 James J. Collins        | .75   | .35   | .07  |
| ☐ 26 Robert Feller           | 2.50  | 1.15  | .25  |
| ☐ 27 Lucius Appling          | 1.10  | .50   | .11  |
| ☐ 28 Lou Gehrig              | 6.00  | 2.80  | .60  |
| ☐ 29 Charles Hartnett        | .75   | .35   | .07  |
| ☐ 30 Charles Klein           | .75   | .35   | .07  |
| ☐ 31 Anthony Lazzeri         | .75   | .35   | .07  |
| ☐ 32 Aloysius Simmons        | .75   | .35   | .07  |
| ☐ 33 Wilbert Robinson        | .75   | .35   | .07  |
| ☐ 34 Edgar Rice              | .75   | .35   | .07  |
| ☐ 35 Herbert Pennock         | .75   | .35   | .07  |
| ☐ 36 Melvin Ott              | 1.10  | .50   | .11  |
| ☐ 37 Frank O'Doul            | .75   | .35   | .07  |
| ☐ 38 John Mize               | 1.10  | .50   | .11  |
| ☐ 39 Edmund Miller           | .75   | .35   | .07  |
| ☐ 40 Joseph Tinker           | .75   | .35   | .07  |
| ☐ 41 John Baker              | .75   | .35   | .07  |
| ☐ 42 Tyrus Cobb              | 7.00  | .25   | .70  |
| ☐ 43 Paul Derringer          | .75   | .35   | .07  |
| ☐ 44 Adrian Anson            | 1.10  | .50   | .11  |
| ☐ 45 James Bottomley         | .75   | .35   | .07  |
| ☐ 46 Edward S. Plank         | 1.00  | .45   | .10  |
| ☐ 47 Denton (Cy) Young       | 2.00  | .90   | .20  |

| | MINT | VG-E | F-G |
|---|---|---|---|
| ☐ 48 Hack Wilson | 1.00 | .45 | .10 |
| ☐ 49 Edward Walsh | .75 | .35 | .07 |
| ☐ 50 Frank Chance | .75 | .35 | .07 |
| ☐ 51 Arthur Vance | .75 | .35 | .07 |
| ☐ 52 William Terry | 1.00 | .45 | .10 |
| ☐ 53 James Foxx | 2.00 | .90 | .20 |
| ☐ 54 Vernon Gomez | 1.00 | .45 | .10 |
| ☐ 55 Branch Rickey | .75 | .35 | .07 |
| ☐ 56 Raymond Schalk | .75 | .35 | .07 |
| ☐ 57 John Evers | .75 | .35 | .07 |
| ☐ 58 Charles Gehringer | 1.00 | .45 | .10 |
| ☐ 59 Burleigh Grimes | .75 | .35 | .07 |
| ☐ 60 Robert (Lefty) Grove | 1.25 | .60 | .12 |
| ☐ 61 George Waddell | .75 | .35 | .07 |
| ☐ 62 John (Honus) Wagner | 2.00 | .90 | .20 |
| ☐ 63 Charles (Red) Ruffing | .75 | .35 | .07 |
| ☐ 64 Kenesaw M. Landis | .75 | .35 | .07 |
| ☐ 65 Harry Heilmann | .75 | .35 | .07 |
| ☐ 66 John McGraw | 1.00 | .45 | .10 |
| ☐ 67 Hugh Jennings | .75 | .35 | .07 |
| ☐ 68 Harold Newhouser | .75 | .35 | .07 |
| ☐ 69 Waite Hoyt | .75 | .35 | .07 |
| ☐ 70 Louis (Bobo) Newsom | .75 | .35 | .07 |
| ☐ 71 Howard (Earl) Averill | .75 | .35 | .07 |
| ☐ 72 Theodore Williams | 6.00 | 2.80 | .60 |
| ☐ 73 Warren Giles | .75 | .35 | .07 |
| ☐ 74 Ford Frick | .75 | .35 | .07 |
| ☐ 75 Hazen (Kiki) Cuyler | .75 | .35 | .07 |
| ☐ 76 Paul Waner | .75 | .35 | .07 |
| ☐ 77 Harold (Pie) Traynor | 1.00 | .45 | .10 |
| ☐ 78 Lloyd Waner | .75 | .35 | .07 |
| ☐ 79 Ralph Kiner | 1.25 | .60 | .12 |
| ☐ 80 Pepper Martin* | 65.00 | 30.00 | 6.50 |
| (Collins, Tinker, | | | |
| or Grove pictured) | | | |

**1961 FLEER**

The cards in this 154 card set measure 2½" by 3½". In 1961, Fleer continued its Baseball Greats format by issuing this series of cards. The set was released in two distinct series, 1–88 and 89–154 (of which the last is more difficult to obtain). The players within each series are conveniently numbered in alphabetical order. It appears that this set continued to be issued the following year by Fleer. The catalog number is F418-3.

Complete Set: M-225.00; VG-E-100.00; F-G-22.00

| | MINT | VG-E | F-G |
|---|---|---|---|
| Common Player (1–88) | .75 | .35 | .07 |
| Common Player (89–154) | 1.75 | .85 | .17 |
| ☐ 1 Baker/Cobb/Wheat (checklist back) | 5.00 | 1 1.00 | .20 |
| ☐ 2 Grover C. Alexander | 1.25 | .60 | .12 |
| ☐ 3 Nick Altrock | .75 | .35 | .07 |
| ☐ 4 Cap Anson | 1.10 | .50 | .11 |
| ☐ 5 Earl Averill | .75 | .35 | .07 |
| ☐ 6 Frank Baker | .75 | .35 | .07 |
| ☐ 7 Dave Bancroft | .75 | .35 | .07 |
| ☐ 8 Chief Bender | .75 | .35 | .07 |
| ☐ 9 Jim Bottomley | .75 | .35 | .07 |
| ☐ 10 Roger Bresnahan | .75 | .35 | .07 |
| ☐ 11 Mordecai Brown | .75 | .35 | .07 |
| ☐ 12 Max Carey | .75 | .35 | .07 |
| ☐ 13 Jack Chesbro | .75 | .35 | .07 |
| ☐ 14 Ty Cobb | 7.00 | 3.25 | .70 |
| ☐ 15 Mickey Cochrane | 1.00 | .45 | .10 |
| ☐ 16 Eddie Collins | .75 | .35 | .07 |
| ☐ 17 Earle Combs | .75 | .35 | .07 |
| ☐ 18 Charles Comiskey | .75 | .35 | .07 |
| ☐ 19 Kiki Cuyler | .75 | .35 | .07 |
| ☐ 20 Paul Derringer | .75 | .35 | .07 |
| ☐ 21 Howard Ehmke | .75 | .35 | .07 |
| ☐ 22 W. Evans | .75 | .35 | .07 |
| ☐ 23 Johnny Evers | .75 | .35 | .07 |
| ☐ 24 Urban Faber | .75 | .35 | .07 |
| ☐ 25 Bob Feller | 2.50 | 1.15 | .25 |
| ☐ 26 Wes Ferrell | .75 | .35 | .07 |
| ☐ 27 Lew Fonseca | .75 | .35 | .07 |
| ☐ 28 Jimmy Foxx | 2.00 | .90 | .20 |
| ☐ 29 Ford Frick | .75 | .35 | .07 |
| ☐ 30 Frank Frisch | 1.10 | .50 | .11 |
| ☐ 31 Lou Gehrig | 6.00 | 2.80 | .60 |
| ☐ 32 Charlie Gehringer | 1.00 | .45 | .10 |
| ☐ 33 Warren Giles | .75 | .35 | .07 |
| ☐ 34 Lefty Gomez | 1.00 | .45 | .10 |

| | MINT | VG-E | F-G |
|---|---|---|---|
| ☐ 35 Goose Goslin | .75 | .35 | .07 |
| ☐ 36 Clark Griffith | .75 | .35 | .07 |
| ☐ 37 Burleigh Grimes | .75 | .35 | .07 |
| ☐ 38 Lefty Grove | 1.25 | .60 | .12 |
| ☐ 39 Chick Hafey | .75 | .35 | .07 |
| ☐ 40 Jesse Haines | .75 | .35 | .07 |
| ☐ 41 Gabby Hartnett | .75 | .35 | .07 |
| ☐ 42 Harry Heilmann | .75 | .35 | .07 |
| ☐ 43 Rogers Hornsby | 1.75 | .85 | .17 |
| ☐ 44 Waite Hoyt | .75 | .35 | .07 |
| ☐ 45 Carl Hubbell | 1.10 | .50 | .11 |
| ☐ 46 Miller Huggins | .75 | .35 | .07 |
| ☐ 47 Hugh Jennings | .75 | .35 | .07 |
| ☐ 48 Ban Johnson | .75 | .35 | .07 |
| ☐ 49 Walter Johnson | 2.50 | 1.15 | .25 |
| ☐ 50 Ralph Kiner | 1.25 | .60 | .12 |
| ☐ 51 Chuck Klein | .75 | .35 | .07 |
| ☐ 52 Johnny Kling | .75 | .35 | .07 |
| ☐ 53 K.M. Landis | .75 | .35 | .07 |
| ☐ 54 Tony Lazzeri | .75 | .35 | .07 |
| ☐ 55 Ernie Lombardi | .75 | .35 | .07 |
| ☐ 56 Dolf Luque | .75 | .35 | .07 |
| ☐ 57 Heine Manush | .75 | .35 | .07 |
| ☐ 58 Marty Marion | .75 | .35 | .07 |
| ☐ 59 Christy Mathewson | 2.25 | 1.00 | .22 |
| ☐ 60 John McGraw | 1.00 | .45 | .09 |
| ☐ 61 Joe Medwick | .75 | .35 | .07 |
| ☐ 62 E. (Bing) Miller | .75 | .35 | .07 |
| ☐ 63 Johnny Mize | 1.10 | .50 | .11 |
| ☐ 64 John Mostil | .75 | .35 | .07 |
| ☐ 65 Art Nehf | .75 | .35 | .07 |
| ☐ 66 Hal Newhouser | .75 | .35 | .07 |
| ☐ 67 D. (Bobo) Newsom | .75 | .35 | .07 |
| ☐ 68 Mel Ott | 1.25 | .60 | .12 |
| ☐ 69 Allie Reynolds | .75 | .35 | .07 |
| ☐ 70 Sam Rice | .75 | .35 | .07 |
| ☐ 71 Eppa Rixey | .75 | .35 | .07 |
| ☐ 72 Edd Roush | .75 | .35 | .07 |
| ☐ 73 Schoolboy Rowe | .75 | .35 | .07 |
| ☐ 74 Red Ruffing | .75 | .35 | .07 |
| ☐ 75 Babe Ruth | 9.00 | 4.25 | .90 |
| ☐ 76 Joe Sewell | .75 | .35 | .07 |
| ☐ 77 Al Simmons | .75 | .35 | .07 |
| ☐ 78 George Sisler | 1.00 | .45 | .10 |
| ☐ 79 Tris Speaker | 1.25 | .60 | .12 |
| ☐ 80 Fred Toney | .75 | .35 | .07 |
| ☐ 81 Dazzy Vance | .75 | .35 | .07 |
| ☐ 82 Jim Vaughn | .75 | .35 | .07 |
| ☐ 83 Ed Walsh | .75 | .35 | .07 |
| ☐ 84 Lloyd Waner | .75 | .35 | .07 |
| ☐ 85 Paul Waner | .75 | .35 | .07 |
| ☐ 86 Zack Wheat | .75 | .35 | .07 |
| ☐ 87 Hack Wilson | 1.00 | .45 | .10 |

| | MINT | VG-E | F-G |
|---|---|---|---|
| ☐ 88 Jimmy Wilson | .75 | .35 | .07 |
| ☐ 89 Sisler and Traynor | 5.00 | 1.00 | .20 |
| (checklist back) | | | |
| ☐ 90 Babe Adams | 1.75 | .85 | .17 |
| ☐ 91 Dale Alexander | 1.75 | .85 | .17 |
| ☐ 92 Jim Bagby | 1.75 | .85 | .17 |
| ☐ 93 Ossie Bluege | 1.75 | .85 | .17 |
| ☐ 94 Lou Boudreau | 2.75 | 1.25 | .27 |
| ☐ 95 Tom Bridges | 1.75 | .85 | .17 |
| ☐ 96 Donie Bush | 1.75 | .85 | .17 |
| ☐ 97 Dolph Camilli | 1.75 | .85 | .17 |
| ☐ 98 Frank Chance | 2.25 | 1.00 | .22 |
| ☐ 99 Jimmy Collins | 2.25 | 1.00 | .22 |
| ☐ 100 Stan Coveleskie | 2.25 | 1.00 | .22 |
| ☐ 101 Hugh Critz | 1.75 | .85 | .17 |
| ☐ 102 Alvin Crowder | 1.75 | .85 | .17 |
| ☐ 103 Joe Dugan | 1.75 | .85 | .17 |
| ☐ 104 Bibb Falk | 1.75 | .85 | .17 |
| ☐ 105 Rick Ferrell | 2.25 | 1.00 | .22 |
| ☐ 106 Art Fletcher | 1.75 | .85 | .17 |
| ☐ 107 Dennis Galehouse | 1.75 | .85 | .17 |
| ☐ 108 Chick Galloway | 1.75 | .85 | .17 |
| ☐ 109 Mule Haas | 1.75 | .85 | .17 |
| ☐ 110 Stan Hack | 1.75 | .85 | .17 |
| ☐ 111 Bump Hadley | 1.75 | .85 | .17 |
| ☐ 112 Billy B. Hamilton | 2.25 | 1.00 | .22 |
| ☐ 113 Joe Hauser | 1.75 | .85 | .17 |
| ☐ 114 Babe Herman | 1.75 | .85 | .17 |
| ☐ 115 Travis Jackson | 2.25 | 1.00 | .22 |
| ☐ 116 Eddie Joost | 1.75 | .85 | .17 |
| ☐ 117 Addie Joss | 2.75 | 1.25 | .27 |
| ☐ 118 Joe Judge | 1.75 | .85 | .17 |
| ☐ 119 Joe Kuhel | 1.75 | .85 | .17 |
| ☐ 120 Napoleon Lajoie | 4.00 | 1.85 | .40 |
| ☐ 121 Dutch Leonard | 1.75 | .85 | .17 |
| ☐ 122 Ted Lyons | 2.25 | 1.00 | .22 |
| ☐ 123 Connie Mack | 4.00 | 1.85 | .40 |
| ☐ 124 Rabbit Maranville | 2.25 | 1.00 | .22 |
| ☐ 125 Fred Marberry | 1.75 | .85 | .17 |
| ☐ 126 Joe McGinnity | 2.25 | 1.00 | .22 |
| ☐ 127 Oscar Melillo | 1.75 | .85 | .17 |
| ☐ 128 Ray Mueller | 1.75 | .85 | .17 |
| ☐ 129 Kid Nichols | 2.25 | 1.00 | .22 |
| ☐ 130 Lefty O'Doul | 1.75 | .85 | .17 |
| ☐ 131 Bob O'Farrell | 1.75 | .85 | .17 |
| ☐ 132 Roger Peckinpaugh | 1.75 | .85 | .17 |
| ☐ 133 Herb Pennock | 2.25 | 1.00 | .22 |
| ☐ 134 George Pipgras | 1.75 | .85 | .17 |
| ☐ 135 Eddie Plank | 2.75 | 1.25 | .27 |
| ☐ 136 Ray Schalk | 2.25 | 1.00 | .22 |
| ☐ 137 Hal Schumacher | 1.75 | .85 | .17 |
| ☐ 138 Luke Sewell | 1.75 | .85 | .17 |
| ☐ 139 Bob Shawkey | 1.75 | .85 | .17 |

| | | MINT | VG-E | F-G |
|---|---|---|---|---|
| ☐ 140 | Riggs Stephenson | 1.75 | .85 | .17 |
| ☐ 141 | Billy Sullivan | 1.75 | .85 | .17 |
| ☐ 142 | Bill Terry | 3.25 | 1.50 | .32 |
| ☐ 143 | Joe Tinker | 2.25 | 1.00 | .22 |
| ☐ 144 | Pie Traynor | 3.25 | 1.50 | .32 |
| ☐ 145 | Hal Trosky | 1.75 | .85 | .17 |
| ☐ 146 | George Uhle | 1.75 | .85 | .17 |
| ☐ 147 | Johnny VanderMeer | 1.75 | .85 | .17 |
| ☐ 148 | Arky Vaughan | 2.25 | 1.00 | .22 |
| ☐ 149 | Rube Waddell | 2.25 | 1.00 | .22 |
| ☐ 150 | Honus Wagner | 6.50 | 3.00 | .65 |
| ☐ 151 | Dixie Walker | 1.75 | .85 | .17 |
| ☐ 152 | Ted Williams | 10.00 | 4.75 | 1.00 |
| ☐ 153 | Cy Young | 4.00 | 1.85 | .40 |
| ☐ 154 | Ross Young | 2.75 | 1.25 | .27 |

## 1963 FLEER

ROBERTO CLEMENTE
Pittsburgh Pirates—Outfield

Unquestionably one of the NL's standout stars, Roberto batted over .300 for the fourth time, his third year in a row. The native Puerto Rican, who led the NL in batting in 1961, was named to the All-Star team for the third straight season. Flashy fielder and owner of perhaps the best arm in baseball, Roberto has been Pittsburgh's regular right fielder since 1955 when he was drafted for $4,000 from Montreal.

*The cards in this 66 card set measure 2½" by 3½". The Fleer set of current baseball players ws marketed in 1963 in a gum card style waxed wrapper package which contained a cherry cookie instead of gum. The cards were printed in sheets of 66 with the scarce card of Adcock apparently being replaced by the unnumbered checklist card for the final press run. The complete set price includes the checklist card. The catalog designation is R418-4.*

**Complete Set: M-180.00; VG-E-85.00; F-G-18.00**

| | | | |
|---|---|---|---|
| Common Player (1–66) | .80 | .40 | .08 |

| | | MINT | VG-E | F-G |
|---|---|---|---|---|
| ☐ 1 | Steve Barber | 1.75 | .40 | .08 |
| ☐ 2 | Ron Hansen | .80 | .40 | .08 |
| ☐ 3 | Milt Pappas | .90 | .40 | .09 |
| ☐ 4 | Brooks Robinson | 8.00 | 3.75 | .80 |
| ☐ 5 | Willie Mays | 12.50 | 5.75 | 1.25 |

| | | MINT | VG-E | F-G |
|---|---|---|---|---|
| ☐ 6 | Lou Clinton | .80 | .40 | .08 |
| ☐ 7 | Bill Monbouquette | .80 | .40 | .08 |
| ☐ 8 | Carl Yastrzemski | 14.00 | 6.00 | 1.50 |
| ☐ 9 | Ray Herbert | .80 | .40 | .08 |
| ☐ 10 | Jim Landis | .80 | .40 | .08 |
| ☐ 11 | Dick Donovan | .80 | .40 | .08 |
| ☐ 12 | Tito Francona | .90 | .40 | .09 |
| ☐ 13 | Jerry Kindall | .80 | .40 | .08 |
| ☐ 14 | Frank Lary | 1.00 | .45 | .10 |
| ☐ 15 | Dick Howser | .90 | .40 | .09 |
| ☐ 16 | Jerry Lumpe | .80 | .40 | .08 |
| ☐ 17 | Norm Siebern | .80 | .40 | .08 |
| ☐ 18 | Don Lee | .80 | .40 | .08 |
| ☐ 19 | Albie Pearson | .80 | .40 | .08 |
| ☐ 20 | Bob Rodgers | .80 | .40 | .08 |
| ☐ 21 | Leon Wagner | .80 | .40 | .08 |
| ☐ 22 | Jim Kaat | 2.25 | 1.00 | .22 |
| ☐ 23 | Vic Power | .90 | .40 | .09 |
| ☐ 24 | Rich Rollins | .80 | .40 | .08 |
| ☐ 25 | Bobby Richardson | 1.50 | .70 | .15 |
| ☐ 26 | Ralph Terry | 1.00 | .45 | .10 |
| ☐ 27 | Tom Cheney | .80 | .40 | .08 |
| ☐ 28 | Chuck Cottier | 1.00 | .45 | .10 |
| ☐ 29 | Jim Piersall | 1.00 | .45 | .10 |
| ☐ 30 | Dave Stenhouse | .80 | .40 | .08 |
| ☐ 31 | Glen Hobbie | .80 | .40 | .08 |
| ☐ 32 | Ron Santo | 1.00 | .45 | .10 |
| ☐ 33 | Gene Freese | .80 | .40 | .08 |
| ☐ 34 | Vada Pinson | 1.25 | .60 | .12 |
| ☐ 35 | Bob Purkey | .80 | .40 | .08 |
| ☐ 36 | Joe Amalfitano | .80 | .40 | .08 |
| ☐ 37 | Bob Aspromonte | .80 | .40 | .08 |
| ☐ 38 | Dick Farrell | .80 | .40 | .08 |
| ☐ 39 | Al Spangler | .80 | .40 | .08 |
| ☐ 40 | Tommy Davis | 1.25 | .60 | .12 |
| ☐ 41 | Don Drysdale | 5.00 | 2.35 | .50 |
| ☐ 42 | Sandy Koufax | 12.50 | 5.75 | 1.25 |
| ☐ 43 | Maury Wills | 12.50 | 5.75 | 1.25 |
| ☐ 44 | Frank Bolling | .80 | .40 | .08 |
| ☐ 45 | Warren Spahn | 5.50 | 2.60 | .55 |
| ☐ 46 | Joe Adcock | 40.00 | 18.00 | 4.00 |
| ☐ 47 | Roger Craig | 1.00 | .45 | .10 |
| ☐ 48 | Al Jackson | .80 | .40 | .08 |
| ☐ 49 | Rod Kanehl | .80 | .40 | .08 |
| ☐ 50 | Ruben Amaro | .80 | .40 | .08 |
| ☐ 51 | John Callison | .90 | .40 | .09 |
| ☐ 52 | Clay Dalrymple | .80 | .40 | .08 |
| ☐ 53 | Don Demeter | .80 | .40 | .08 |
| ☐ 54 | Art Mahaffey | .80 | .40 | .08 |
| ☐ 55 | Smokey Burgess | .80 | .40 | .08 |
| ☐ 56 | Roberto Clemente | 12.50 | 5.75 | 1.25 |
| ☐ 57 | Roy Face | .90 | .40 | .09 |
| ☐ 58 | Vernon Law | .90 | .40 | .09 |

| | MINT | VG-E | F-G |
|---|---|---|---|
| ☐ 59 Bill Mazeroski | 1.25 | .60 | .12 |
| ☐ 60 Ken Boyer | 1.25 | .60 | .12 |
| ☐ 61 Bob Gibson | 5.50 | 2.60 | .55 |
| ☐ 62 Gene Oliver | .80 | .40 | .08 |
| ☐ 63 Bill White | 1.00 | .45 | .10 |
| ☐ 64 Orlando Cepeda | 1.50 | .70 | .15 |
| ☐ 65 Jim Davenport | 1.00 | .45 | .10 |
| ☐ 66 Bill O'Dell | 1.00 | .45 | .10 |
| Checklist (unnumbered) | 48.00 | 8.00 | .100 |

## 1981 FLEER

*The cards in this 660 card set measure 2½" by 3½". This issue of cards marks Fleer's first entry into the current player baseball card market since 1963. Players from the same team are conveniently grouped together by number in the set. There were three distinct printings: the two following the primary run were designed to correct numerous errors. The variations caused by these multiple printings are noted in the checklist below (P1, P2 or P3).*

| Complete Set: M-19.00; VG-E-8.00; F-G-1.50 | | | |
|---|---|---|---|
| Common Player (1–660) | .03 | .01 | .00 |

### PHILADELPHIA PHILLIES

| | | | |
|---|---|---|---|
| ☐ 1 Pete Rose | 1.75 | .50 | .10 |
| ☐ 2 Larry Bowa | .08 | .03 | .01 |
| ☐ 3 Manny Trillo | .05 | .02 | .00 |
| ☐ 4 Bob Boone | .05 | .02 | .00 |
| ☐ 5 Mike Schmidt | .75 | .35 | .07 |
| See 640A | | | |

| | MINT | VG-E | F-G |
|---|---|---|---|
| ☐ 6 A Steve Carlton P1 | .50 | .22 | .05 |
| Pitcher of Year | | | |
| See also 660A | | | |
| Back "1066 Cardinals" | | | |
| ☐ 6 B Steve Carlton P2 | .50 | .22 | .05 |
| Pitcher of Year | | | |
| Back "1066 Cardinals" | | | |
| ☐ 6 C Steve Carlton P3 | 1.50 | .70 | .15 |
| "1966 Cardinals" | | | |
| ☐ 7 Tug McGraw | .08 | .03 | .01 |
| See 657A | | | |
| ☐ 8 Larry Christenson | .03 | .01 | .00 |
| ☐ 9 Bake McBride | .05 | .02 | .00 |
| ☐ 10 Greg Luzinski | .14 | .06 | .01 |
| ☐ 11 Ron Reed | .03 | .01 | .00 |
| ☐ 12 Dickie Noles | .03 | .01 | .00 |
| ☐ 13 Keith Moreland | .35 | .15 | .03 |
| ☐ 14 Bob Walk | .05 | .02 | .00 |
| ☐ 15 Lonnie Smith | .09 | .04 | .01 |
| ☐ 16 Dick Ruthven | .03 | .01 | .00 |
| ☐ 17 Sparky Lyle | .09 | .04 | .01 |
| ☐ 18 Greg Gross | .03 | .01 | .00 |
| ☐ 19 Garry Maddox | .05 | .02 | .00 |
| ☐ 20 Nino Espinosa | .03 | .01 | .00 |
| ☐ 21 George Vukovich | .05 | .02 | .00 |
| ☐ 22 John Vukovich | .03 | .01 | .00 |
| ☐ 23 Ramon Aviles | .03 | .01 | .00 |
| ☐ 24 A Ken Saucier P1 | .07 | .03 | .01 |
| Name on front "Ken" | | | |
| ☐ 24 B Ken Saucier P2 | .07 | .03 | .01 |
| Name on front "Ken" | | | |
| ☐ 24 C Kevin Saucier P3 | .35 | .15 | .03 |
| Name on front "Kevin" | | | |
| ☐ 25 Randy Lerch | .03 | .01 | .00 |
| ☐ 26 Del Unser | .03 | .01 | .00 |
| ☐ 27 Tim McCarver | .07 | .03 | .01 |
| **KANSAS CITY ROYALS** | | | |
| ☐ 28 George Brett | .80 | .40 | .08 |
| See 655A | | | |
| ☐ 29 Willie Wilson | .30 | .12 | .03 |
| See 653A | | | |
| ☐ 30 Paul Splittorff | .05 | .02 | .00 |
| ☐ 31 Dan Quisenberry | .30 | .12 | .03 |
| ☐ 32 A Amos Otis P1 | .08 | .03 | .01 |
| Batting Pose | | | |
| "Outfield" | | | |
| (32 on back) | | | |
| ☐ 32 B Amos Otis P2 | .08 | .03 | .01 |
| "Series Starter" | | | |
| (483 on back) | | | |
| ☐ 33 Steve Busby | .05 | .02 | .00 |
| ☐ 34 U.L. Washington | .03 | .01 | .00 |

| | MINT | VG-E | F-G |
|---|---|---|---|
| ☐ 35 Dave Chalk | .03 | .01 | .00 |
| ☐ 36 Darrell Porter | .07 | .03 | .01 |
| ☐ 37 Marty Pattin | .03 | .01 | .00 |
| ☐ 38 Larry Gura | .06 | .02 | .00 |
| ☐ 39 Renie Martin | .03 | .01 | .00 |
| ☐ 40 Rich Gale | .03 | .01 | .00 |
| ☐ 41 A Hal McRae P1 | .50 | .22 | .05 |
| "Royals" on front in black letters | | | |
| ☐ 41 B Hal McRae P2 | .10 | .04 | .01 |
| "Royals" on front in blue letters | | | |
| ☐ 42 Dennis Leonard | .06 | .02 | .00 |
| ☐ 43 Willie Aikens | .06 | .02 | .00 |
| ☐ 44 Frank White | .08 | .03 | .01 |
| ☐ 45 Clint Hurdle | .03 | .01 | .00 |
| ☐ 46 John Wathan | .03 | .01 | .00 |
| ☐ 47 Pete LaCock | .03 | .01 | .00 |
| ☐ 48 Rance Mulliniks | .03 | .01 | .00 |
| ☐ 49 Jeff Twitty | .05 | .02 | .00 |
| ☐ 50 Jamie Quirk | .03 | .01 | .00 |
| HOUSTON ASTROS | | | |
| ☐ 51 Art Howe | .03 | .01 | .00 |
| ☐ 52 Ken Forsch | .03 | .01 | .00 |
| ☐ 53 Vern Ruhle | .03 | .01 | .00 |
| ☐ 54 Joe Niekro | .07 | .03 | .01 |
| ☐ 55 Frank LaCorte | .03 | .01 | .00 |
| ☐ 56 J.R. Richard | .09 | .04 | .01 |
| ☐ 57 Nolan Ryan | .40 | .18 | .04 |
| ☐ 58 Enos Cabell | .03 | .01 | .00 |
| ☐ 59 Cesar Cedeno | .09 | .04 | .01 |
| ☐ 60 Jose Cruz | .14 | .06 | .01 |
| ☐ 61 Bill Virdon | .05 | .02 | .00 |
| ☐ 62 Terry Puhl | .05 | .02 | .00 |
| ☐ 63 Joaquin Andujar | .15 | .06 | .01 |
| ☐ 64 Alan Ashby | .03 | .01 | .00 |
| ☐ 65 Joe Sambito | .05 | .02 | .00 |
| ☐ 66 Denny Walling | .03 | .01 | .00 |
| ☐ 67 Jeff Leonard | .07 | .03 | .01 |
| ☐ 68 Luis Pujols | .03 | .01 | .00 |
| ☐ 69 Bruce Bochy | .03 | .01 | .00 |
| ☐ 70 Rafael Landestoy | .03 | .01 | .00 |
| ☐ 71 Dave Smith | .08 | .03 | .01 |
| ☐ 72 Danny Heep | .05 | .02 | .00 |
| ☐ 73 Julio Gonzalez | .03 | .01 | .00 |
| ☐ 74 Craig Reynolds | .03 | .01 | .00 |
| ☐ 75 Gary Woods | .03 | .01 | .00 |
| ☐ 76 Dave Bergman | .03 | .01 | .00 |
| ☐ 77 Randy Niemann | .03 | .01 | .00 |
| ☐ 78 Joe Morgan | .25 | .10 | .02 |
| NEW YORK YANKEES | | | |
| ☐ 79 Reggie Jackson | .65 | .30 | .06 |
| See 650A | | | |

| | MINT | VG-E | F-G |
|---|---|---|---|
| ☐ 80 Bucky Dent | .08 | .03 | .01 |
| ☐ 81 Tommy John | .20 | .09 | .02 |
| ☐ 82 Luis Tiant | .08 | .03 | .01 |
| ☐ 83 Rick Cerone | .05 | .02 | .00 |
| ☐ 84 Dick Howser | .05 | .02 | .00 |
| ☐ 85 Lou Piniella | .10 | .04 | .01 |
| ☐ 86 Ron Davis | .05 | .02 | .00 |
| ☐ 87 A Craig Nettles P1 ERR | 10.00 | 4.75 | 1.00 |
| Name on back misspelled "Craig" | | | |
| ☐ 87 B Graig Nettles P2 COR | .25 | .10 | .02 |
| "Graig" | | | |
| ☐ 88 Ron Guidry | .25 | .10 | .02 |
| ☐ 89 Rich Gossage | .25 | .10 | .02 |
| ☐ 90 Rudy May | .03 | .01 | .00 |
| ☐ 91 Gaylord Perry | .25 | .10 | .02 |
| ☐ 92 Eric Soderholm | .03 | .01 | .00 |
| ☐ 93 Bob Watson | .05 | .02 | .00 |
| ☐ 94 Bobby Murcer | .10 | .04 | .01 |
| ☐ 95 Bobby Brown | .03 | .01 | .00 |
| ☐ 96 Jim Spencer | .03 | .01 | .00 |
| ☐ 97 Tom Underwood | .03 | .01 | .00 |
| ☐ 98 Oscar Gamble | .06 | .02 | .00 |
| ☐ 99 Johnny Oates | .03 | .01 | .00 |
| ☐ 100 Fred Stanley | .03 | .01 | .00 |
| ☐ 101 Ruppert Jones | .05 | .02 | .00 |
| ☐ 102 Dennis Werth | .05 | .02 | .00 |
| ☐ 103 Joe LeFebvre | .12 | .05 | .01 |
| ☐ 104 Brian Doyle | .05 | .02 | .00 |
| ☐ 105 Aurelio Rodriguez | .03 | .01 | .00 |
| ☐ 106 Doug Bird | .03 | .01 | .00 |
| ☐ 107 Mike Griffin | .05 | .02 | .00 |
| ☐ 108 Tim Lollar | .20 | .09 | .02 |
| ☐ 109 Willie Randolph | .09 | .04 | .01 |
| LOS ANGELES DODGERS | | | |
| ☐ 110 Steve Garvey | .50 | .22 | .05 |
| ☐ 111 Reggie Smith | .09 | .04 | .01 |
| ☐ 112 Don Sutton | .20 | .09 | .02 |
| ☐ 113 Burt Hooton | .03 | .01 | .00 |
| ☐ 114 A Dave Lopes P1 | .50 | .22 | .05 |
| Small hand on back | | | |
| ☐ 114 B Dave Lopes P2 | .09 | .04 | .01 |
| no hand | | | |
| ☐ 115 Dusty Baker | .09 | .04 | .01 |
| ☐ 116 Tom Lasorda | .09 | .04 | .01 |
| ☐ 117 Bill Russell | .06 | .02 | .00 |
| ☐ 118 Jerry Reuss | .08 | .03 | .01 |
| ☐ 119 Terry Forster | .07 | .03 | .01 |
| ☐ 120 A Bob Welch P1 | .14 | .06 | .01 |
| Name on back Bob | | | |
| ☐ 120 B Bob Welch P2 | .14 | .06 | .01 |
| Name on back Robert | | | |

| | | MINT | VG-E | F-G |
|---|---|---|---|---|
| ☐ 121 | Don Stanhouse | .03 | .01 | .00 |
| ☐ 122 | Rick Monday | .06 | .02 | .00 |
| ☐ 123 | Derrel Thomas | .03 | .01 | .00 |
| ☐ 124 | Joe Ferguson | .03 | .01 | .00 |
| ☐ 125 | Rick Sutcliffe | .30 | .12 | .03 |
| ☐ 126 A | Ron Cey P1 small hand on back | .50 | .22 | .05 |
| ☐ 126 B | Ron Cey P2 no hand | .14 | .06 | .01 |
| ☐ 127 | Dave Goltz | .03 | .01 | .00 |
| ☐ 128 | Jay Johnstone | .05 | .02 | .00 |
| ☐ 129 | Steve Yeager | .06 | .02 | .00 |
| ☐ 130 | Gary Weiss | .05 | .02 | .00 |
| ☐ 131 | Mike Scioscia | .09 | .04 | .01 |
| ☐ 132 | Vic Davalillo | .03 | .01 | .00 |
| ☐ 133 | Doug Rau | .03 | .01 | .00 |
| ☐ 134 | Pepe Frias | .03 | .01 | .00 |
| ☐ 135 | Mickey Hatcher | .05 | .02 | .00 |
| ☐ 136 | Steve Howe | .20 | .09 | .02 |
| ☐ 137 | Robert Castillo | .03 | .01 | .00 |
| ☐ 138 | Gary Thomasson | .03 | .01 | .00 |
| ☐ 139 | Rudy Law | .03 | .01 | .00 |
| ☐ 140 | Fernand Valenzuela | 2.25 | 1.00 | .22 |
| ☐ 141 | Manny Mota | .06 | .02 | .00 |
| | MONTREAL EXPOS | | | |
| ☐ 142 | Gary Carter | .35 | .15 | .03 |
| ☐ 143 | Steve Rogers | .08 | .03 | .01 |
| ☐ 144 | Warren Cromartie | .03 | .01 | .00 |
| ☐ 145 | Andre Dawson | .25 | .10 | .02 |
| ☐ 146 | Larry Parrish | .06 | .02 | .00 |
| ☐ 147 | Rowland Office | .03 | .01 | .00 |
| ☐ 148 | Ellis Valentine | .05 | .02 | .00 |
| ☐ 149 | Dick Williams | .05 | .02 | .00 |
| ☐ 150 | Bill Gullickson | .30 | .12 | .03 |
| ☐ 151 | Elias Sosa | .03 | .01 | .00 |
| ☐ 152 | John Tamargo | .03 | .01 | .00 |
| ☐ 153 | Chris Speier | .03 | .01 | .00 |
| ☐ 154 | Ron LeFlore | .06 | .02 | .00 |
| ☐ 155 | Rodney Scott | .03 | .01 | .00 |
| ☐ 156 | Stan Bahnsen | .03 | .01 | .00 |
| ☐ 157 | Bill Lee | .05 | .02 | .00 |
| ☐ 158 | Fred Norman | .03 | .01 | .00 |
| ☐ 159 | Woodie Fryman | .03 | .01 | .00 |
| ☐ 160 | Dave Palmer | .06 | .02 | .00 |
| ☐ 161 | Jerry White | .03 | .01 | .00 |
| ☐ 162 | Roberto Ramos | .05 | .02 | .00 |
| ☐ 163 | John D'Acquisto | .03 | .01 | .00 |
| ☐ 164 | Tommy Hutton | .03 | .01 | .00 |
| ☐ 165 | Charlie Lea | .25 | .10 | .02 |
| ☐ 166 | Scott Sanderson | .03 | .01 | .00 |
| ☐ 167 | Ken Macha | .03 | .01 | .00 |
| ☐ 168 | Tony Bernazard | .03 | .01 | .00 |
| | BALTIMORE ORIOLES | | | |
| ☐ 169 | Jim Palmer | .30 | .12 | .03 |
| ☐ 170 | Steve Stone | .06 | .02 | .00 |
| ☐ 171 | Mike Flanagan | .08 | .03 | .01 |
| ☐ 172 | Al Bumbry | .03 | .01 | .00 |
| ☐ 173 | Doug DeCinces | .10 | .04 | .01 |
| ☐ 174 | Scott McGregor | .08 | .03 | .01 |
| ☐ 175 | Mark Belanger | .05 | .02 | .00 |
| ☐ 176 | Tim Stoddard | .03 | .01 | .00 |
| ☐ 177 A | Rick Dempsey P1 small hand on front | .35 | .15 | .03 |
| ☐ 177 B | Rick Dempsey P2 no hand | .08 | .03 | .01 |
| ☐ 178 | Earl Weaver | .09 | .04 | .01 |
| ☐ 179 | Tippy Martinez | .05 | .02 | .00 |
| ☐ 180 | Dennis Martinez | .03 | .01 | .00 |
| ☐ 181 | Sammy Stewart | .03 | .01 | .00 |
| ☐ 182 | Rich Dauer | .03 | .01 | .00 |
| ☐ 183 | Lee May | .06 | .02 | .00 |
| ☐ 184 | Eddie Murray | .70 | .32 | .07 |
| ☐ 185 | Benny Ayala | .03 | .01 | .00 |
| ☐ 186 | John Lowenstein | .03 | .01 | .00 |
| ☐ 187 | Gary Roenicke | .05 | .02 | .00 |
| ☐ 188 | Ken Singleton | .09 | .04 | .01 |
| ☐ 189 | Dan Graham | .03 | .01 | .00 |
| ☐ 190 | Terry Crowley | .03 | .01 | .00 |
| ☐ 191 | Kiko Garcia | .03 | .01 | .00 |
| ☐ 192 | Dave Ford | .03 | .01 | .00 |
| ☐ 193 | Mark Corey | .03 | .01 | .00 |
| ☐ 194 | Lenn Sakata | .03 | .01 | .00 |
| ☐ 195 | Doug DeCinces | .10 | .04 | .01 |
| | CINCINNATI REDS | | | |
| ☐ 196 | Johnny Bench | .45 | .20 | .04 |
| ☐ 197 | Dave Concepcion | .14 | .06 | .01 |
| ☐ 198 | Ray Knight | .07 | .03 | .01 |
| ☐ 199 | Ken Griffey | .09 | .04 | .01 |
| ☐ 200 | Tom Seaver | .35 | .15 | .03 |
| ☐ 201 | Dave Collins | .07 | .03 | .01 |
| ☐ 202 A | George Foster P1 Slugger number on back 216 | .20 | .09 | .02 |
| ☐ 202 B | George Foster P2 Slugger number on back 202 | .20 | .09 | .02 |
| ☐ 203 | Junior Kennedy | .03 | .01 | .00 |
| ☐ 204 | Frank Pastore | .03 | .01 | .00 |
| ☐ 205 | Dan Driessen | .05 | .02 | .00 |
| ☐ 206 | Hector Cruz | .03 | .01 | .00 |
| ☐ 207 | Paul Moskau | .03 | .01 | .00 |
| ☐ 208 | Charlie Leibrandt | .40 | .18 | .04 |
| ☐ 209 | Harry Spilman | .03 | .01 | .00 |
| ☐ 210 | Joe Price | .05 | .02 | .00 |
| ☐ 211 | Tom Hume | .03 | .01 | .00 |
| ☐ 212 | Joe Nolan | .03 | .01 | .00 |

| | MINT | VG-E | F-G |
|---|---|---|---|
| ☐ 213 Doug Bair | .03 | .01 | .00 |
| ☐ 214 Mario Soto | .12 | .05 | .01 |
| ☐ 215 A Bill Bonham P1 | .35 | .15 | .03 |
| small hand on back | | | |
| ☐ 215 B Bill Bonham P2 | .06 | .02 | .00 |
| no hand | | | |
| ☐ 216 George Foster | .20 | .09 | .02 |
| See 202 | | | |
| ☐ 217 Paul Householder | .10 | .04 | .01 |
| ☐ 218 Ron Oester | .05 | .02 | .00 |
| ☐ 219 Sam Mejias | .03 | .01 | .00 |
| ☐ 220 Sheldon Burnside | .05 | .02 | .00 |
| BOSTON RED SOX | | | |
| ☐ 221 Carl Yastrzemski | .75 | .35 | .07 |
| ☐ 222 Jim Rice | .45 | .20 | .04 |
| ☐ 223 Fred Lynn | .25 | .10 | .02 |
| ☐ 224 Carlton Fisk | .25 | .10 | .02 |
| ☐ 225 Rick Burleson | .06 | .02 | .00 |
| ☐ 226 Dennis Eckersley | .06 | .02 | .00 |
| ☐ 227 Butch Hobson | .03 | .01 | .00 |
| ☐ 228 Tom Burgmeier | .03 | .01 | .00 |
| ☐ 229 Garry Hancock | .03 | .01 | .00 |
| ☐ 230 Don Zimmer | .03 | .01 | .00 |
| ☐ 231 Steve Renko | .03 | .01 | .00 |
| ☐ 232 Dwight Evans | .15 | .06 | .01 |
| ☐ 233 Mike Torrez | .06 | .02 | .00 |
| ☐ 234 Bob Stanley | .09 | .04 | .01 |
| ☐ 235 Jim Dwyer | .03 | .01 | .00 |
| ☐ 236 Dave Stapleton | .14 | .06 | .01 |
| ☐ 237 Glen Hoffman | .09 | .04 | .01 |
| ☐ 238 Jerry Remy | .05 | .02 | .00 |
| ☐ 239 Dick Drago | .03 | .01 | .00 |
| ☐ 240 Bill Campbell | .05 | .02 | .00 |
| ☐ 241 Tony Perez | .15 | .06 | .01 |
| ATLANTA BRAVES | | | |
| ☐ 242 Phil Niekro | .25 | .10 | .02 |
| ☐ 243 Dale Murphy | 1.00 | .45 | .10 |
| ☐ 244 Bob Horner | .25 | .10 | .02 |
| ☐ 245 Jeff Burroughs | .05 | .02 | .00 |
| ☐ 246 Rick Camp | .03 | .01 | .00 |
| ☐ 247 Bob Cox MGR | .03 | .01 | .00 |
| ☐ 248 Bruce Benedict | .03 | .01 | .00 |
| ☐ 249 Gene Garber | .03 | .01 | .00 |
| ☐ 250 Jerry Royster | .03 | .01 | .00 |
| ☐ 251 A Gary Matthews P1 | .35 | .15 | .03 |
| small hand on back | | | |
| ☐ 251 B Gary Matthews P2 | .08 | .03 | .01 |
| no hand | | | |
| ☐ 252 Chris Chambliss | .08 | .03 | .01 |
| ☐ 253 Luis Gomez | .03 | .01 | .00 |
| ☐ 254 Bill Nahorodny | .03 | .01 | .00 |
| ☐ 255 Doyle Alexander | .06 | .02 | .00 |
| ☐ 256 Brian Asselstine | .03 | .01 | .00 |

| | MINT | VG-E | F-G |
|---|---|---|---|
| ☐ 257 Biff Pocoroba | .03 | .01 | .00 |
| ☐ 258 Mike Lum | .03 | .01 | .00 |
| ☐ 259 Charlie Spikes | .03 | .01 | .00 |
| ☐ 260 Glen Hubbard | .05 | .02 | .00 |
| ☐ 261 Tommy Boggs | .03 | .01 | .00 |
| ☐ 262 Al Hrabosky | .05 | .02 | .00 |
| ☐ 263 Rick Matula | .03 | .01 | .00 |
| ☐ 264 Preston Hanna | .03 | .01 | .00 |
| ☐ 265 Larry Bradford | .03 | .01 | .00 |
| ☐ 266 Rafael Ramirez | .20 | .09 | .02 |
| ☐ 267 Larry McWilliams | .06 | .02 | .00 |
| CALIFORNIA ANGELS | | | |
| ☐ 268 Rod Carew | .50 | .22 | .05 |
| ☐ 269 Bobby Grich | .09 | .04 | .01 |
| ☐ 270 Carney Lansford | .14 | .06 | .01 |
| ☐ 271 Don Baylor | .20 | .09 | .02 |
| ☐ 272 Joe Rudi | .06 | .02 | .00 |
| ☐ 273 Dan Ford | .03 | .01 | .00 |
| ☐ 274 Jim Fregosi | .05 | .02 | .00 |
| ☐ 275 Dave Frost | .03 | .01 | .00 |
| ☐ 276 Frank Tanana | .06 | .02 | .00 |
| ☐ 277 Dickie Thon | .10 | .04 | .01 |
| ☐ 278 Jason Thompson | .08 | .03 | .01 |
| ☐ 279 Rick Miller | .03 | .01 | .00 |
| ☐ 280 Bert Campaneris | .06 | .02 | .00 |
| ☐ 281 Tom Donohue | .03 | .01 | .00 |
| ☐ 282 Brian Downing | .05 | .02 | .00 |
| ☐ 283 Fred Patek | .03 | .01 | .00 |
| ☐ 284 Bruce Kison | .03 | .01 | .00 |
| ☐ 285 Dave LaRoche | .03 | .01 | .00 |
| ☐ 286 Don Aase | .03 | .01 | .00 |
| ☐ 287 Jim Barr | .03 | .01 | .00 |
| ☐ 288 Alfredo Martinez | .05 | .02 | .00 |
| ☐ 289 Larry Harlow | .03 | .01 | .00 |
| ☐ 290 Andy Hassler | .03 | .01 | .00 |
| CHICAGO CUBS | | | |
| ☐ 291 Dave Kingman | .14 | .06 | .01 |
| ☐ 292 Bill Buckner | .14 | .06 | .01 |
| ☐ 293 Rick Reuschel | .06 | .02 | .00 |
| ☐ 294 Bruce Sutter | .25 | .10 | .02 |
| ☐ 295 Jerry Martin | .03 | .01 | .00 |
| ☐ 296 Scot Thompson | .03 | .01 | .00 |
| ☐ 297 Ivan DeJesus | .03 | .01 | .00 |
| ☐ 298 Steve Dillard | .03 | .01 | .00 |
| ☐ 299 Dick Tidrow | .03 | .01 | .00 |
| ☐ 300 Randy Martz | .03 | .01 | .00 |
| ☐ 301 Lenny Randle | .03 | .01 | .00 |
| ☐ 302 Lynn McGlothen | .03 | .01 | .00 |
| ☐ 303 Cliff Johnson | .03 | .01 | .00 |
| ☐ 304 Tim Blackwell | .03 | .01 | .00 |
| ☐ 305 Dennis Lamp | .03 | .01 | .00 |
| ☐ 306 Bill Caudill | .10 | .04 | .01 |
| ☐ 307 Carlos Lezcano | .05 | .02 | .00 |

| | MINT | VG-E | F-G |
|---|---|---|---|
| ☐ 308 Jim Tracy | .05 | .02 | .00 |
| ☐ 309 Doug Capilla | .03 | .01 | .00 |
| ☐ 310 Willie Hernandez | .25 | .10 | .02 |
| ☐ 311 Mike Vail | .03 | .01 | .00 |
| ☐ 312 Mike Krukow | .03 | .01 | .00 |
| ☐ 313 Barry Foote | .03 | .01 | .00 |
| ☐ 314 Larry Biittner | .03 | .01 | .00 |
| ☐ 315 Mike Tyson | .03 | .01 | .00 |
| **NEW YORK METS** | | | |
| ☐ 316 Lee Mazzilli | .06 | .02 | .00 |
| ☐ 317 John Stearns | .03 | .01 | .00 |
| ☐ 318 Alex Trevino | .03 | .01 | .00 |
| ☐ 319 Craig Swan | .03 | .01 | .00 |
| ☐ 320 Frank Taveras | .03 | .01 | .00 |
| ☐ 321 Steve Henderson | .03 | .01 | .00 |
| ☐ 322 Neil Allen | .06 | .02 | .00 |
| ☐ 323 Mark Bomback | .05 | .02 | .00 |
| ☐ 324 Mike Jorgensen | .03 | .01 | .00 |
| ☐ 325 Joe Torre | .08 | .03 | .01 |
| ☐ 326 Elliott Maddox | .03 | .01 | .00 |
| ☐ 327 Pete Falcone | .03 | .01 | .00 |
| ☐ 328 Ray Burris | .03 | .01 | .00 |
| ☐ 329 Claudell Washington | .08 | .03 | .01 |
| ☐ 330 Doug Flynn | .03 | .01 | .00 |
| ☐ 331 Joel Youngblood | .03 | .01 | .00 |
| ☐ 332 Bill Almon | .03 | .01 | .00 |
| ☐ 333 Tom Hausman | .03 | .01 | .00 |
| ☐ 334 Pat Zachry | .03 | .01 | .00 |
| ☐ 335 Jeff Reardon | .50 | .22 | .05 |
| ☐ 336 Wally Backman | .35 | .15 | .03 |
| ☐ 337 Dan Norman | .03 | .01 | .00 |
| ☐ 338 Jerry Morales | .03 | .01 | .00 |
| **CHICAGO WHITE SOX** | | | |
| ☐ 339 Ed Farmer | .03 | .01 | .00 |
| ☐ 340 Bob Molinaro | .03 | .01 | .00 |
| ☐ 341 Todd Cruz | .03 | .01 | .00 |
| ☐ 342 A Britt Burns P1 small hand on front | .50 | .22 | .05 |
| ☐ 342 B Britt Burns P2 no hand | .40 | .18 | .04 |
| ☐ 343 Kevin Bell | .03 | .01 | .00 |
| ☐ 344 Tony LaRussa | .05 | .02 | .00 |
| ☐ 345 Steve Trout | .05 | .02 | .00 |
| ☐ 346 Harold Baines | 1.50 | .70 | .15 |
| ☐ 347 Richard Wortham | .03 | .01 | .00 |
| ☐ 348 Wayne Nordhagen | .03 | .01 | .00 |
| ☐ 349 Mike Squires | .03 | .01 | .00 |
| ☐ 350 Lamar Johnson | .03 | .01 | .00 |
| ☐ 351 Rickey Henderson | .65 | .30 | .06 |
| ☐ 352 Francisco Barrios | .03 | .01 | .00 |
| ☐ 353 Thad Bosley | .03 | .01 | .00 |
| ☐ 354 Chet Lemon | .09 | .04 | .01 |
| ☐ 355 Bruce Kimm | .03 | .01 | .00 |

| | MINT | VG-E | F-G |
|---|---|---|---|
| ☐ 356 Richard Dotson | .30 | .12 | .03 |
| ☐ 357 Jim Morrison | .03 | .01 | .00 |
| ☐ 358 Mike Proly | .03 | .01 | .00 |
| ☐ 359 Greg Pryor | .03 | .01 | .00 |
| **PITTSBURGH PIRATES** | | | |
| ☐ 360 Dave Parker | .30 | .12 | .03 |
| ☐ 361 Omar Moreno | .05 | .02 | .00 |
| ☐ 362 A Kent Tekulve P1 Back "1071 Waterbury" and "1078 Pirates" | .12 | .05 | .01 |
| ☐ 362 B Kent Tekulve P2 "171 Waterbury" and "1978 Pirates" | .08 | .03 | .01 |
| ☐ 363 Willie Stargell | .30 | .12 | .03 |
| ☐ 364 Phil Garner | .05 | .02 | .00 |
| ☐ 365 Ed Ott | .03 | .01 | .00 |
| ☐ 366 Don Robinson | .03 | .01 | .00 |
| ☐ 367 Chuck Tanner | .05 | .02 | .00 |
| ☐ 368 Jim Rooker | .03 | .01 | .00 |
| ☐ 369 Dale Berra | .05 | .02 | .00 |
| ☐ 370 Jim Bibby | .05 | .02 | .00 |
| ☐ 371 Steve Nicosia | .03 | .01 | .00 |
| ☐ 372 Mike Easler | .08 | .03 | .01 |
| ☐ 373 Bill Robinson | .03 | .01 | .00 |
| ☐ 374 Lee Lacy | .06 | .02 | .00 |
| ☐ 375 John Candelaria | .08 | .03 | .01 |
| ☐ 376 Manny Sanguillen | .05 | .02 | .00 |
| ☐ 377 Rick Rhoden | .06 | .02 | .00 |
| ☐ 378 Grant Jackson | .03 | .01 | .00 |
| ☐ 379 Tim Foli | .03 | .01 | .00 |
| ☐ 380 Rod Scurry | .08 | .03 | .01 |
| ☐ 381 Bill Madlock | .20 | .09 | .02 |
| ☐ 382 A Kurt Bevacqua P1 ERR P on cap backwards | .20 | .09 | .02 |
| ☐ 382 B Kurt Bevacqua P2 COR P on cap is correct | .07 | .03 | .01 |
| ☐ 383 Bert Blyleven | .15 | .06 | .01 |
| ☐ 384 Eddie Solomon | .03 | .01 | .00 |
| ☐ 385 Enrique Romo | .03 | .01 | .00 |
| ☐ 386 John Milner | .03 | .01 | .00 |
| **CLEVELAND INDIANS** | | | |
| ☐ 387 Mike Hargrove | .05 | .02 | .00 |
| ☐ 388 Jorge Orta | .03 | .01 | .00 |
| ☐ 389 Toby Harrah | .05 | .02 | .00 |
| ☐ 390 Tom Veryzer | .03 | .01 | .00 |
| ☐ 391 Miguel Dilone | .03 | .01 | .00 |
| ☐ 392 Dan Spillner | .03 | .01 | .00 |
| ☐ 393 Jack Brohamer | .03 | .01 | .00 |
| ☐ 394 Wayne Garland | .03 | .01 | .00 |
| ☐ 395 Sid Monge | .03 | .01 | .00 |
| ☐ 396 Rick Waits | .03 | .01 | .00 |

| | MINT | VG-E | F-G |
|---|---|---|---|
| ☐ 397 Joe Charboneau | .09 | .04 | .01 |
| ☐ 398 Gary Alexander | .03 | .01 | .00 |
| ☐ 399 Jerry Dybzinski | .03 | .01 | .00 |
| ☐ 400 Mike Stanton | .03 | .01 | .00 |
| ☐ 401 Mike Paxton | .03 | .01 | .00 |
| ☐ 402 Gary Gray | .07 | .03 | .01 |
| ☐ 403 Rick Manning | .03 | .01 | .00 |
| ☐ 404 Bo Diaz | .08 | .03 | .01 |
| ☐ 405 Ron Hassey | .03 | .01 | .00 |
| ☐ 406 Ross Grimsley | .03 | .01 | .00 |
| ☐ 407 Victor Cruz | .03 | .01 | .00 |
| ☐ 408 Len Barker | .08 | .03 | .01 |
| **TORONTO BLUE JAYS** | | | |
| ☐ 409 Bob Bailor | .03 | .01 | .00 |
| ☐ 410 Otto Velez | .03 | .01 | .00 |
| ☐ 411 Ernie Whitt | .03 | .01 | .00 |
| ☐ 412 Jim Clancy | .03 | .01 | .00 |
| ☐ 413 Barry Bonnell | .05 | .02 | .00 |
| ☐ 414 Dave Stieb | .35 | .15 | .03 |
| ☐ 415 Damaso Garcia | .65 | .30 | .06 |
| ☐ 416 John Mayberry | .05 | .02 | .00 |
| ☐ 417 Roy Howell | .03 | .01 | .00 |
| ☐ 418 Dan Ainge | .25 | .10 | .02 |
| ☐ 419 A Jesse Jefferson P1 | .06 | .02 | .00 |
| Back says Pirates | | | |
| ☐ 419 B Jesse Jefferson P2 | .06 | .02 | .00 |
| Back says Pirates | | | |
| ☐ 419 C Jesse Jefferson P3 | .35 | .15 | .03 |
| Back says Blue Jays | | | |
| ☐ 420 Joey McLaughlin | .03 | .01 | .00 |
| ☐ 421 Lloyd Moseby | 1.00 | .45 | .10 |
| ☐ 422 Al Woods | .03 | .01 | .00 |
| ☐ 423 Garth Iorg | .03 | .01 | .00 |
| ☐ 424 Doug Ault | .03 | .01 | .00 |
| ☐ 425 Ken Schrom | .06 | .02 | .00 |
| ☐ 426 Mike Willis | .03 | .01 | .00 |
| ☐ 427 Steve Braun | .03 | .01 | .00 |
| ☐ 428 Bob Davis | .03 | .01 | .00 |
| ☐ 429 Jerry Garvin | .03 | .01 | .00 |
| ☐ 430 Alfredo Griffin | .07 | .03 | .01 |
| ☐ 431 Bob Mattick MGR | .03 | .01 | .00 |
| **SAN FRANCISCO GIANTS** | | | |
| ☐ 432 Vida Blue | .09 | .04 | .01 |
| ☐ 433 Jack Clark | .20 | .09 | .02 |
| ☐ 434 Willie McCovey | .30 | .12 | .03 |
| ☐ 435 Mike Ivie | .03 | .01 | .00 |
| ☐ 436 A Darrel Evans P1 ERR | .30 | .12 | .03 |
| Name on front "Darrel" | | | |
| ☐ 436 B Darrell Evans P2 | .12 | .05 | .01 |
| Name on front "Darrell" | | | |
| ☐ 437 Terry Whitfield | .03 | .01 | .00 |
| ☐ 438 Rennie Stennett | .03 | .01 | .00 |

| | MINT | VG-E | F-G |
|---|---|---|---|
| ☐ 439 John Montefusco | .05 | .02 | .00 |
| ☐ 440 Jim Wohlford | .03 | .01 | .00 |
| ☐ 441 Bill North | .03 | .01 | .00 |
| ☐ 442 Milt May | .03 | .01 | .00 |
| ☐ 443 Max Venable | .05 | .02 | .00 |
| ☐ 444 Ed Whitson | .07 | .03 | .01 |
| ☐ 445 Al Holland | .25 | .10 | .02 |
| ☐ 446 Randy Moffitt | .03 | .01 | .00 |
| ☐ 447 Bob Knepper | .09 | .04 | .01 |
| ☐ 448 Gary Lavelle | .05 | .02 | .00 |
| ☐ 449 Greg Minton | .05 | .02 | .00 |
| ☐ 450 Johnnie LeMaster | .03 | .01 | .00 |
| ☐ 451 Larry Herndon | .05 | .02 | .00 |
| ☐ 452 Rich Murray | .05 | .02 | .00 |
| ☐ 453 Joe Pettini | .05 | .02 | .00 |
| ☐ 454 Allen Ripley | .03 | .01 | .00 |
| ☐ 455 Dennis Littlejohn | .03 | .01 | .00 |
| ☐ 456 Tom Griffin | .03 | .01 | .00 |
| ☐ 457 Alan Hargesheimer | .05 | .02 | .00 |
| ☐ 458 Joe Strain | .03 | .01 | .00 |
| **DETROIT TIGERS** | | | |
| ☐ 459 Steve Kemp | .12 | .05 | .01 |
| ☐ 460 Sparky Anderson MGR | .07 | .03 | .01 |
| ☐ 461 Alan Trammell | .35 | .15 | .03 |
| ☐ 462 Mark Fidrych | .07 | .03 | .01 |
| ☐ 463 Lou Whitaker | .25 | .10 | .02 |
| ☐ 464 Dave Rozema | .03 | .01 | .00 |
| ☐ 465 Milt Wilcox | .05 | .02 | .00 |
| ☐ 466 Champ Summers | .03 | .01 | .00 |
| ☐ 467 Lance Parrish | .35 | .15 | .03 |
| ☐ 468 Dan Petry | .20 | .09 | .02 |
| ☐ 469 Pat Underwood | .03 | .01 | .00 |
| ☐ 470 Rick Peters | .05 | .02 | .00 |
| ☐ 471 Al Cowens | .05 | .02 | .00 |
| ☐ 472 John Wockenfuss | .03 | .01 | .00 |
| ☐ 473 Tom Brookens | .03 | .01 | .00 |
| ☐ 474 Richie Hebner | .03 | .01 | .00 |
| ☐ 475 Jack Morris | .30 | .12 | .03 |
| ☐ 476 Jim Lentine | .05 | .02 | .00 |
| ☐ 477 Bruce Robbins | .03 | .01 | .00 |
| ☐ 478 Mark Wanger | .03 | .01 | .00 |
| ☐ 479 Tim Corcoran | .03 | .01 | .00 |
| ☐ 480 A Stan Papi P1 | .12 | .05 | .01 |
| Front as Pitcher | | | |
| ☐ 480 B Stan Papi P2 | .07 | .03 | .01 |
| Front as Shortstop | | | |
| ☐ 481 Kirk Gibson | 1.50 | .70 | .15 |
| ☐ 482 Dan Schatzeder | .03 | .01 | .00 |
| ☐ 483 A Amos Otis P1 | .09 | .04 | .01 |
| See card 32 | | | |
| ☐ 483 B Amos Otis P2 | .09 | .04 | .01 |
| See card 32 | | | |
| **SAN DIEGO PADRES** | | | |

| | MINT | VG-E | F-G |
|---|---|---|---|
| ☐ 484 Dave Winfield | .50 | .22 | .05 |
| ☐ 485 Rollie Fingers | .30 | .12 | .03 |
| ☐ 486 Gene Richards | .03 | .01 | .00 |
| ☐ 487 Randy Jones | .05 | .02 | .00 |
| ☐ 488 Ozzie Smith | .14 | .06 | .01 |
| ☐ 489 Gene Tenace | .03 | .01 | .00 |
| ☐ 490 Bill Fahey | .03 | .01 | .00 |
| ☐ 491 John Curtis | .03 | .01 | .00 |
| ☐ 492 Dave Cash | .03 | .01 | .00 |
| ☐ 493 A Tim Flannery P1 | .12 | .05 | .01 |
|    Batting right | | | |
| ☐ 493 B Tim Flannery P2 | .07 | .03 | .01 |
|    Batting left | | | |
| ☐ 494 Jerry Mumphrey | .05 | .02 | .00 |
| ☐ 495 Bob Shirley | .03 | .01 | .00 |
| ☐ 496 Steve Mura | .03 | .01 | .00 |
| ☐ 497 Eric Rasmussen | .03 | .01 | .00 |
| ☐ 498 Broderick Perkins | .03 | .01 | .00 |
| ☐ 499 Barry Evans | .05 | .02 | .00 |
| ☐ 500 Chuck Baker | .03 | .01 | .00 |
| ☐ 501 Luis Salazar | .07 | .03 | .01 |
| ☐ 502 Gary Lucas | .10 | .04 | .01 |
| ☐ 503 Mike Armstrong | .09 | .04 | .01 |
| ☐ 504 Jerry Turner | .03 | .01 | .00 |
| ☐ 505 Dennis Kinney | .05 | .02 | .00 |
| ☐ 506 Willie Montanez | .03 | .01 | .00 |
| **MILWAUKEE BREWERS** | | | |
| ☐ 507 Gorman Thomas | .14 | .06 | .01 |
| ☐ 508 Ben Oglivie | .09 | .04 | .01 |
| ☐ 509 Larry Hisle | .05 | .02 | .00 |
| ☐ 510 Sal Bando | .06 | .02 | .00 |
| ☐ 511 Robin Yount | .45 | .20 | .04 |
| ☐ 512 Mike Caldwell | .05 | .02 | .00 |
| ☐ 513 Sixto Lezcano | .03 | .01 | .00 |
| ☐ 514 A Bill Travers P1 ERR | .15 | .06 | .01 |
|    "Jerry Augustine" | | | |
|    with Augustine back | | | |
| ☐ 514 B Bill Travers P2 COR | .08 | .03 | .01 |
| ☐ 515 Paul Molitor | .20 | .09 | .02 |
| ☐ 516 Moose Haas | .05 | .02 | .00 |
| ☐ 517 Bill Castro | .03 | .01 | .00 |
| ☐ 518 Jim Slaton | .05 | .02 | .00 |
| ☐ 519 Lary Sorensen | .03 | .01 | .00 |
| ☐ 520 Bob McClure | .03 | .01 | .00 |
| ☐ 521 Charlie Moore | .03 | .01 | .00 |
| ☐ 522 Jim Gantner | .05 | .02 | .00 |
| ☐ 523 Reggie Cleveland | .03 | .01 | .00 |
| ☐ 524 Don Money | .03 | .01 | .00 |
| ☐ 525 Bill Travers | .03 | .01 | .00 |
| ☐ 526 Buck Martinez | .03 | .01 | .00 |
| ☐ 527 Dick Davis | .03 | .01 | .00 |
| **ST. LOUIS CARDINALS** | | | |
| ☐ 528 Ted Simmons | .14 | .06 | .01 |

| | MINT | VG-E | F-G |
|---|---|---|---|
| ☐ 529 Garry Templeton | .14 | .06 | .01 |
| ☐ 530 Ken Reitz | .03 | .01 | .00 |
| ☐ 531 Tony Scott | .03 | .01 | .00 |
| ☐ 532 Ken Oberkfell | .03 | .01 | .00 |
| ☐ 533 Bob Sykes | .03 | .01 | .00 |
| ☐ 534 Keith Smith | .03 | .01 | .00 |
| ☐ 535 John Littlefield | .05 | .02 | .00 |
| ☐ 536 Jim Kaat | .14 | .06 | .01 |
| ☐ 537 Bob Forsch | .05 | .02 | .00 |
| ☐ 538 Mike Phillips | .03 | .01 | .00 |
| ☐ 539 Terry Landrum | .10 | .04 | .01 |
| ☐ 540 Leon Durham | 1.20 | .55 | .12 |
| ☐ 541 Terry Kennedy | .12 | .05 | .01 |
| ☐ 542 George Hendrick | .09 | .04 | .01 |
| ☐ 543 Dane Iorg | .03 | .01 | .00 |
| ☐ 544 Mark Littell | .03 | .01 | .00 |
| ☐ 545 Keith Hernandez | .30 | .12 | .03 |
| ☐ 546 Silvio Martinez | .03 | .01 | .00 |
| ☐ 547 A Don Hood P1 ERR | .20 | .09 | .02 |
|    "Pete Vuckovich" | | | |
|    with Vuckovich back | | | |
| ☐ 547 B Don Hood P2 COR | .09 | .04 | .01 |
| ☐ 548 Bobby Bonds | .09 | .04 | .01 |
| ☐ 549 Mike Ramsey | .03 | .01 | .00 |
| ☐ 550 Tom Herr | .15 | .06 | .01 |
| **MINNESOTA TWINS** | | | |
| ☐ 551 Roy Smalley | .05 | .02 | .00 |
| ☐ 552 Jerry Koosman | .08 | .03 | .01 |
| ☐ 553 Ken Landreaux | .06 | .02 | .00 |
| ☐ 554 John Castino | .05 | .02 | .00 |
| ☐ 555 Doug Corbett | .10 | .04 | .01 |
| ☐ 556 Bombo Rivera | .03 | .01 | .00 |
| ☐ 557 Ron Jackson | .03 | .01 | .00 |
| ☐ 558 Butch Wynegar | .06 | .02 | .00 |
| ☐ 559 Hosken Powell | .03 | .01 | .00 |
| ☐ 560 Pete Redfern | .03 | .01 | .00 |
| ☐ 561 Roger Erickson | .03 | .01 | .00 |
| ☐ 562 Glenn Adams | .03 | .01 | .00 |
| ☐ 563 Rick Sofield | .03 | .01 | .00 |
| ☐ 564 Geoff Zahn | .05 | .02 | .00 |
| ☐ 565 Pete Mackanin | .03 | .01 | .00 |
| ☐ 566 Mike Cubbage | .03 | .01 | .00 |
| ☐ 567 Darrell Jackson | .03 | .01 | .00 |
| ☐ 568 Dave Edwards | .03 | .01 | .00 |
| ☐ 569 Rob Wilfong | .03 | .01 | .00 |
| ☐ 570 Sal Butera | .05 | .02 | .00 |
| ☐ 571 Jose Morales | .03 | .01 | .00 |
| **OAKLAND A'S** | | | |
| ☐ 572 Rick Langford | .03 | .01 | .00 |
| ☐ 573 Mike Norris | .05 | .02 | .00 |
| ☐ 574 Rickey Henderson | .65 | .30 | .06 |
| ☐ 575 Tony Armas | .15 | .06 | .01 |
| ☐ 576 Dave Revering | .03 | .01 | .00 |

|  | MINT | VG-E | F-G |
|---|---|---|---|
| ☐ 577 Jeff Newman | .03 | .01 | .00 |
| ☐ 578 Bob Lacey | .03 | .01 | .00 |
| ☐ 579 Brian Kingman | .03 | .01 | .00 |
| ☐ 580 Mitchell Page | .03 | .01 | .00 |
| ☐ 581 Billy Martin | .10 | .04 | .01 |
| ☐ 582 Rob Picciolo | .03 | .01 | .00 |
| ☐ 583 Mike Heath | .03 | .01 | .00 |
| ☐ 584 Mickey Klutts | .03 | .01 | .00 |
| ☐ 585 Orlando Gonzalez | .03 | .01 | .00 |
| ☐ 586 Mike Davis | .40 | .18 | .04 |
| ☐ 587 Wayne Gross | .03 | .01 | .00 |
| ☐ 588 Matt Keough | .05 | .02 | .00 |
| ☐ 589 Steve McCatty | .05 | .02 | .00 |
| ☐ 590 Dwayne Murphy | .08 | .03 | .01 |
| ☐ 591 Mario Guerrero | .03 | .01 | .00 |
| ☐ 592 Dave McKay | .03 | .01 | .00 |
| ☐ 593 Jim Essian | .03 | .01 | .00 |
| ☐ 594 Dave Heaverlo | .03 | .01 | .00 |
| **SEATTLE MARINERS** | | | |
| ☐ 595 Maury Wills MGR | .09 | .04 | .01 |
| ☐ 596 Juan Beniquez | .05 | .02 | .00 |
| ☐ 597 Rodney Craig | .03 | .01 | .00 |
| ☐ 598 Jim Anderson | .03 | .01 | .00 |
| ☐ 599 Floyd Bannister | .08 | .03 | .01 |
| ☐ 600 Bruce Bochte | .05 | .02 | .00 |
| ☐ 601 Julio Cruz | .05 | .02 | .00 |
| ☐ 602 Ted Cox | .03 | .01 | .00 |
| ☐ 603 Dan Meyer | .03 | .01 | .00 |
| ☐ 604 Larry Cox | .03 | .01 | .00 |
| ☐ 605 Bill Stein | .03 | .01 | .00 |
| ☐ 606 Steve Garvey | .50 | .22 | .05 |
| ☐ 607 Dave Roberts | .03 | .01 | .00 |
| ☐ 608 Leon Roberts | .03 | .01 | .00 |
| ☐ 609 Reggie Walton | .05 | .02 | .00 |
| ☐ 610 Dave Edler | .05 | .02 | .00 |
| ☐ 611 Larry Milbourne | .03 | .01 | .00 |
| ☐ 612 Kim Allen | .05 | .02 | .00 |
| ☐ 613 Mario Mendoza | .03 | .01 | .00 |
| ☐ 614 Tom Paciorek | .03 | .01 | .00 |
| ☐ 615 Glenn Abbott | .03 | .01 | .00 |
| ☐ 616 Joe Simpson | .03 | .01 | .00 |
| **TEXAS RANGERS** | | | |
| ☐ 617 Mickey Rivers | .08 | .03 | .01 |
| ☐ 618 Jim Kern | .03 | .01 | .00 |
| ☐ 619 Jim Sundberg | .06 | .02 | .00 |
| ☐ 620 Richie Zisk | .05 | .02 | .00 |
| ☐ 621 Jon Matlack | .06 | .02 | .00 |
| ☐ 622 Ferguson Jenkins | .12 | .05 | .01 |
| ☐ 623 Pat Corrales | .05 | .02 | .00 |
| ☐ 624 Ed Figueroa | .03 | .01 | .00 |
| ☐ 625 Buddy Bell | .14 | .06 | .01 |
| ☐ 626 Al Oliver | .20 | .09 | .02 |

|  | MINT | VG-E | F-G |
|---|---|---|---|
| ☐ 627 Doc Medich | .03 | .01 | .00 |
| ☐ 628 Bump Wills | .03 | .01 | .00 |
| ☐ 629 Rusty Staub | .09 | .04 | .01 |
| ☐ 630 Pat Putnam | .03 | .01 | .00 |
| ☐ 631 John Grubb | .03 | .01 | .00 |
| ☐ 632 Danny Darwin | .05 | .02 | .00 |
| ☐ 633 Ken Clay | .03 | .01 | .00 |
| ☐ 634 Jim Norris | .03 | .01 | .00 |
| ☐ 635 John Butcher | .20 | .09 | .02 |
| ☐ 636 Dave Roberts | .03 | .01 | .00 |
| ☐ 637 Billy Sample | .03 | .01 | .00 |
| ☐ 638 Carl Yastrzemski | .75 | .35 | .07 |
| ☐ 639 Cecil Cooper | .20 | .09 | .02 |
| ☐ 640 A Mike Schmidt P1 | .85 | .40 | .08 |
| (Portrait) "Third Base" (number on back 5) | | | |
| ☐ 640 B Mike Schmidt P2 | .75 | .35 | .07 |
| "1980 Home Run King" (640 on back) | | | |
| ☐ 641 A CL: Phils/Royals P1 | .07 | .01 | .00 |
| 41 is Hal McRae | | | |
| ☐ 641 B CL: Phils/Royals P2 | .07 | .01 | .00 |
| 41 McRae Double Threat | | | |
| ☐ 642 CL: Astros/Yankees | .07 | .01 | .00 |
| ☐ 643 CL: Expos/Dodgers | .07 | .01 | .00 |
| ☐ 644 A CL: Reds/Orioles P1 | .07 | .01 | .00 |
| 202 is George Foster | | | |
| ☐ 645 A Rose/Bowa/Schmidt | 1.60 | .80 | .16 |
| Triple Threat P1 (No number on back) | | | |
| ☐ 645 B Rose/Bowa/Schmidt | .80 | .40 | .08 |
| Triple Threat P2 (Back numbered 645) | | | |
| ☐ 646 CL: Braves/Red Sox | .07 | .01 | .00 |
| ☐ 647 CL: Cubs/Angels | .07 | .01 | .00 |
| ☐ 648 CL: Mets/White Sox | .07 | .01 | .00 |
| ☐ 649 CL: Indians/Pirates | .07 | .01 | .00 |
| ☐ 650 A Reggie Jackson P1 | .80 | .40 | .08 |
| Mr. Baseball Number on back 79 | | | |
| ☐ 650 B Reggie Jackson P2 | .55 | .25 | .05 |
| Mr. Baseball Number on back 650 | | | |
| ☐ 651 CL: Giants/Blue Jays | .07 | .01 | .00 |
| ☐ 652 A CL: Tigers/Padres P1 | .07 | .01 | .00 |
| 483 is listed | | | |
| ☐ 652 B CL: Tigers/Padres P2 | .07 | .01 | .00 |
| 483 is deleted | | | |
| ☐ 653 A Willie Wilson P1 | .25 | .10 | .02 |
| Most Hits and Most Runs Number on back 29 | | | |

|  | MINT | VG-E | F-G |
|---|---|---|---|
| ☐ 653 B Willie Wilson P2 ..... Most Hits and Most Runs Number on back 653 | .25 | .10 | .02 |
| ☐ 654 A CL: Brewers/Cards P1 514 Jerry Augustine and 547 Pete Vuckovich | .07 | .01 | .00 |
| ☐ 654 B CL: Brewers/Cards P2 514 Billy Travers and 547 Don Hood | .07 | .01 | .00 |
| ☐ 655 A George Brett P1 ..... .390 Average Number on back 28 | .70 | .32 | .07 |
| ☐ 655 B George Brett P2 ..... .390 Average Number on back 655 | .70 | .32 | .07 |
| ☐ 656 CL: Twins/Oakland A's . | .07 | .01 | .00 |
| ☐ 657 A Tug McGraw P1 ..... Game Saver Number on back 7 | .08 | .03 | .01 |
| ☐ 657 B Tug McGraw P2 ..... Game Saver Number on back 657 | .08 | .03 | .01 |
| ☐ 658 CL: Rangers/Mariners .. | .07 | .01 | .00 |
| ☐ 659 A Checklist P1 ........ of Special Cards Last lines on front Wilson Most Hits | .07 | .01 | .00 |
| ☐ 659 B Checklist P2 ........ of Special Cards Last lines on front Otis Series Starter | .07 | .01 | .00 |
| ☐ 660 A Steve Carlton P1 .... Golden Arm Back "1066 Cardinals" Number on back 6 | .60 | .28 | .06 |
| ☐ 660 B Steve Carlton P2 .... Golden Arm Number on back 660 Back "1066 Cardinals" | .60 | .28 | .06 |
| ☐ 660 C Steve Carlton P3 .... Golden Arm "1966 Cardinals" | 1.75 | .85 | .17 |

## 1982 FLEER

The cards in this 660 card set measure 2½" by 3½". The 1982 Fleer set includes the last 14 cards which are checklist cards. Cards number 628 through 646 are special cards highlighting some of the stars and leaders of the 1981 season. The backs feature player statistics and a full color team logo in the upper right hand corner of each card.

Complete Set: M-17.00; VG-E-8.00; F-G-1.70

|  | MINT | VG-E | F-G |
|---|---|---|---|
| Common Player (1–660) | .03 | .01 | .00 |
| **LOS ANGELES DODGERS** |  |  |  |
| ☐ 1 Dusty Baker ........... | .12 | .03 | .01 |
| ☐ 2 Robert Castillo ........ | .03 | .01 | .00 |
| ☐ 3 Ron Cey .............. | .13 | .06 | .01 |
| ☐ 4 Terry Forster .......... | .06 | .02 | .00 |
| ☐ 5 Steve Garvey ......... | .40 | .18 | .04 |
| ☐ 6 Dave Goltz ........... | .06 | .02 | .00 |
| ☐ 7 Pedro Guerrero ....... | .35 | .15 | .03 |
| ☐ 8 Burt Hooton .......... | .03 | .01 | .00 |
| ☐ 9 Steve Howe .......... | .06 | .02 | .00 |
| ☐ 10 Jay Johnstone ........ | .05 | .02 | .00 |
| ☐ 11 Ken Landreaux ........ | .05 | .02 | .00 |
| ☐ 12 Davey Lopes .......... | .07 | .03 | .01 |
| ☐ 13 Mike Marshall ........ | 1.00 | .45 | .10 |
| ☐ 14 Bobby Mitchell ....... | .05 | .02 | .00 |
| ☐ 15 Rick Monday ......... | .05 | .02 | .00 |
| ☐ 16 Tom Niedenfuer ...... | .60 | .28 | .06 |
| ☐ 17 Ted Power .......... | .30 | .12 | .03 |
| ☐ 18 Jerry Reuss .......... | .07 | .03 | .01 |
| ☐ 19 Ron Roenicke ........ | .07 | .03 | .01 |
| ☐ 20 Bill Russell .......... | .05 | .02 | .00 |

| | | MINT | VG-E | F-G |
|---|---|---|---|---|
| ☐ 21 | Steve Sax | .60 | .28 | .06 |
| ☐ 22 | Mike Scioscia | .03 | .01 | .00 |
| ☐ 23 | Reggie Smith | .08 | .03 | .01 |
| ☐ 24 | Dave Stewart | .12 | .05 | .01 |
| ☐ 25 | Rick Sutcliffe | .25 | .10 | .02 |
| ☐ 26 | Derrel Thomas | .03 | .01 | .00 |
| ☐ 27 | Fernando Valenzuela | .40 | .18 | .04 |
| ☐ 28 | Bob Welch | .06 | .02 | .00 |
| ☐ 29 | Steve Yeager | .05 | .02 | .00 |
| | **NEW YORK YANKEES** | | | |
| ☐ 30 | Bobby Brown | .03 | .01 | .00 |
| ☐ 31 | Rick Cerone | .05 | .02 | .00 |
| ☐ 32 | Ron Davis | .05 | .02 | .00 |
| ☐ 33 | Bucky Dent | .08 | .03 | .01 |
| ☐ 34 | Barry Foote | .03 | .01 | .00 |
| ☐ 35 | George Frazier | .03 | .01 | .00 |
| ☐ 36 | Oscar Gamble | .06 | .02 | .00 |
| ☐ 37 | Rich Gossage | .20 | .09 | .02 |
| ☐ 38 | Ron Guidry | .20 | .09 | .02 |
| ☐ 39 | Reggie Jackson | .45 | .20 | .04 |
| ☐ 40 | Tommy John | .18 | .08 | .01 |
| ☐ 41 | Rudy May | .03 | .01 | .00 |
| ☐ 42 | Larry Milbourne | .03 | .01 | .00 |
| ☐ 43 | Jerry Mumphrey | .05 | .02 | .00 |
| ☐ 44 | Bobby Murcer | .09 | .04 | .01 |
| ☐ 45 | Gene Nelson | .10 | .04 | .01 |
| ☐ 46 | Graig Nettles | .15 | .06 | .01 |
| ☐ 47 | Johnny Oates | .03 | .01 | .00 |
| ☐ 48 | Lou Piniella | .10 | .04 | .01 |
| ☐ 49 | Willie Randolph | .06 | .02 | .00 |
| ☐ 50 | Rick Reuschel | .06 | .02 | .00 |
| ☐ 51 | Dave Revering | .03 | .01 | .00 |
| ☐ 52 | Dave Righetti | .75 | .35 | .07 |
| ☐ 53 | Aurelio Rodriguez | .03 | .01 | .00 |
| ☐ 54 | Bob Watson | .06 | .02 | .00 |
| ☐ 55 | Dennis Werth | .03 | .01 | .00 |
| ☐ 56 | Dave Winfield | .40 | .18 | .04 |
| | **CINCINNATI REDS** | | | |
| ☐ 57 | Johnny Bench | .40 | .18 | .04 |
| ☐ 58 | Bruce Berenyi | .05 | .02 | .00 |
| ☐ 59 | Larry Biittner | .03 | .01 | .00 |
| ☐ 60 | Scott Brown | .07 | .03 | .01 |
| ☐ 61 | Dave Collins | .06 | .02 | .00 |
| ☐ 62 | Geoff Combe | .03 | .01 | .00 |
| ☐ 63 | Dave Concepcion | .10 | .04 | .01 |
| ☐ 64 | Dan Driessen | .05 | .02 | .00 |
| ☐ 65 | Joe Edelen | .05 | .02 | .00 |
| ☐ 66 | George Foster | .18 | .08 | .01 |
| ☐ 67 | Ken Griffey | .09 | .04 | .01 |
| ☐ 68 | Paul Householder | .03 | .01 | .00 |
| ☐ 69 | Tom Hume | .03 | .01 | .00 |
| ☐ 70 | Junior Kennedy | .03 | .01 | .00 |
| ☐ 71 | Ray Knight | .06 | .02 | .00 |

| | | MINT | VG-E | F-G |
|---|---|---|---|---|
| ☐ 72 | Mike LaCoss | .03 | .01 | .00 |
| ☐ 73 | Rafael Landestoy | .03 | .01 | .00 |
| ☐ 74 | Charlie Leibrandt | .08 | .03 | .01 |
| ☐ 75 | Sam Mejias | .03 | .01 | .00 |
| ☐ 76 | Paul Moskau | .03 | .01 | .00 |
| ☐ 77 | Joe Nolan | .03 | .01 | .00 |
| ☐ 78 | Mike O'Berry | .03 | .01 | .00 |
| ☐ 79 | Ron Oester | .05 | .02 | .00 |
| ☐ 80 | Frank Pastore | .03 | .01 | .00 |
| ☐ 81 | Joe Price | .03 | .01 | .00 |
| ☐ 82 | Tom Seaver | .35 | .15 | .03 |
| ☐ 83 | Mario Soto | .12 | .05 | .01 |
| ☐ 84 | Mike Vail | .03 | .01 | .00 |
| | **OAKLAND A'S** | | | |
| ☐ 85 | Tony Armas | .15 | .06 | .01 |
| ☐ 86 | Shooty Babitt | .05 | .02 | .00 |
| ☐ 87 | Dave Beard | .03 | .01 | .00 |
| ☐ 88 | Rick Bosetti | .03 | .01 | .00 |
| ☐ 89 | Keith Drumright | .05 | .02 | .00 |
| ☐ 90 | Wayne Gross | .03 | .01 | .00 |
| ☐ 91 | Mike Heath | .03 | .01 | .00 |
| ☐ 92 | Rickey Henderson | .50 | .22 | .05 |
| ☐ 93 | Cliff Johnson | .03 | .01 | .00 |
| ☐ 94 | Jeff Jones | .03 | .01 | .00 |
| ☐ 95 | Matt Keough | .05 | .02 | .00 |
| ☐ 96 | Brian Kingman | .03 | .01 | .00 |
| ☐ 97 | Mickey Klutts | .03 | .01 | .00 |
| ☐ 98 | Rick Langford | .03 | .01 | .00 |
| ☐ 99 | Steve McCatty | .05 | .02 | .00 |
| ☐ 100 | Dave McKay | .03 | .01 | .00 |
| ☐ 101 | Dwayne Murphy | .08 | .03 | .01 |
| ☐ 102 | Jeff Newman | .03 | .01 | .00 |
| ☐ 103 | Mike Norris | .05 | .02 | .00 |
| ☐ 104 | Bob Owchinko | .03 | .01 | .00 |
| ☐ 105 | Mitchell Page | .03 | .01 | .00 |
| ☐ 106 | Rob Picciolo | .03 | .01 | .00 |
| ☐ 107 | Jim Spencer | .03 | .01 | .00 |
| ☐ 108 | Fred Stanley | .03 | .01 | .00 |
| ☐ 109 | Tom Underwood | .03 | .01 | .00 |
| | **ST. LOUIS CARDINALS** | | | |
| ☐ 110 | Joaquin Andujar | .15 | .06 | .01 |
| ☐ 111 | Steve Braun | .03 | .01 | .00 |
| ☐ 112 | Bob Forsch | .05 | .02 | .00 |
| ☐ 113 | George Hendrick | .09 | .04 | .01 |
| ☐ 114 | Keith Hernandez | .30 | .12 | .03 |
| ☐ 115 | Tom Herr | .14 | .06 | .01 |
| ☐ 116 | Dane Iorg | .03 | .01 | .00 |
| ☐ 117 | Jim Kaat | .13 | .06 | .01 |
| ☐ 118 | Tito Landrum | .05 | .02 | .00 |
| ☐ 119 | Sixto Lezcano | .03 | .01 | .00 |
| ☐ 120 | Mark Littell | .03 | .01 | .00 |
| ☐ 121 | John Martin | .05 | .02 | .00 |
| ☐ 122 | Silvio Martinez | .03 | .01 | .00 |

|  | MINT | VG-E | F-G |
|---|---|---|---|
| ☐ 123 Ken Oberkfell | .05 | .02 | .00 |
| ☐ 124 Darrell Porter | .06 | .02 | .00 |
| ☐ 125 Mike Ramsey | .03 | .01 | .00 |
| ☐ 126 Orlando Sanchez | .05 | .02 | .00 |
| ☐ 127 Bob Shirley | .03 | .01 | .00 |
| ☐ 128 Lary Sorensen | .03 | .01 | .00 |
| ☐ 129 Bruce Sutter | .25 | .10 | .02 |
| ☐ 130 Bob Sykes | .03 | .01 | .00 |
| ☐ 131 Garry Templeton | .12 | .05 | .01 |
| ☐ 132 Gene Tenace | .03 | .01 | .00 |
| **MILWAUKEE BREWERS** | | | |
| ☐ 133 Jerry Augustine | .03 | .01 | .00 |
| ☐ 134 Sal Bando | .06 | .02 | .00 |
| ☐ 135 Mark Brouhard | .05 | .02 | .00 |
| ☐ 136 Mike Caldwell | .05 | .02 | .00 |
| ☐ 137 Reggie Cleveland | .03 | .01 | .00 |
| ☐ 138 Cecil Cooper | .18 | .08 | .01 |
| ☐ 139 Jamie Easterly | .03 | .01 | .00 |
| ☐ 140 Marshall Edwards | .07 | .03 | .01 |
| ☐ 141 Rollie Fingers | .20 | .09 | .02 |
| ☐ 142 Jim Gantner | .05 | .02 | .00 |
| ☐ 143 Moose Haas | .05 | .02 | .00 |
| ☐ 144 Larry Hisle | .05 | .02 | .00 |
| ☐ 145 Roy Howell | .03 | .01 | .00 |
| ☐ 146 Rickey Keeton | .03 | .01 | .00 |
| ☐ 147 Randy Lerch | .03 | .01 | .00 |
| ☐ 148 Paul Molitor | .15 | .06 | .01 |
| ☐ 149 Don Money | .03 | .01 | .00 |
| ☐ 150 Charlie Moore | .03 | .01 | .00 |
| ☐ 151 Ben Oglivie | .08 | .03 | .01 |
| ☐ 152 Ted Simmons | .13 | .06 | .01 |
| ☐ 153 Jim Slaton | .05 | .02 | .00 |
| ☐ 154 Gorman Thomas | .13 | .06 | .01 |
| ☐ 155 Robin Yount | .50 | .22 | .05 |
| ☐ 156 Pete Vuckovich | .10 | .04 | .01 |
| **BALTIMORE ORIOLES** | | | |
| ☐ 157 Benny Ayala | .03 | .01 | .00 |
| ☐ 158 Mark Belanger | .05 | .02 | .00 |
| ☐ 159 Al Bumbry | .03 | .01 | .00 |
| ☐ 160 Terry Crowley | .03 | .01 | .00 |
| ☐ 161 Rich Dauer | .03 | .01 | .00 |
| ☐ 162 Doug DeCinces | .10 | .04 | .01 |
| ☐ 163 Rick Dempsey | .05 | .02 | .00 |
| ☐ 164 Jim Dwyer | .03 | .01 | .00 |
| ☐ 165 Mike Flanagan | .08 | .03 | .01 |
| ☐ 166 Dave Ford | .03 | .01 | .00 |
| ☐ 167 Dan Graham | .03 | .01 | .00 |
| ☐ 168 Wayne Krenchicki | .03 | .01 | .00 |
| ☐ 169 John Lowenstein | .03 | .01 | .00 |
| ☐ 170 Dennis Martinez | .03 | .01 | .00 |
| ☐ 171 Tippy Martinez | .05 | .02 | .00 |
| ☐ 172 Scott McGregor | .08 | .03 | .01 |
| ☐ 173 Jose Morales | .03 | .01 | .00 |

|  | MINT | VG-E | F-G |
|---|---|---|---|
| ☐ 174 Eddie Murray | .55 | .25 | .05 |
| ☐ 175 Jim Palmer | .30 | .12 | .03 |
| ☐ 176 Cal Ripken | 4.00 | 1.85 | .40 |
| ☐ 177 Gary Roenicke | .05 | .02 | .00 |
| ☐ 178 Lenn Sakata | .03 | .01 | .00 |
| ☐ 179 Ken Singleton | .09 | .04 | .01 |
| ☐ 180 Sammy Stewart | .03 | .01 | .00 |
| ☐ 181 Tim Stoddard | .03 | .01 | .00 |
| ☐ 182 Steve Stone | .06 | .02 | .00 |
| **MONTREAL EXPOS** | | | |
| ☐ 183 Stan Bahnsen | .03 | .01 | .00 |
| ☐ 184 Ray Burris | .03 | .01 | .00 |
| ☐ 185 Gary Carter | .40 | .18 | .04 |
| ☐ 186 Warren Cromartie | .03 | .01 | .00 |
| ☐ 187 Andre Dawson | .25 | .10 | .02 |
| ☐ 188 Terry Francona | .45 | .20 | .04 |
| ☐ 189 Woodie Fryman | .03 | .01 | .00 |
| ☐ 190 Bill Gullickson | .06 | .02 | .00 |
| ☐ 191 Grant Jackson | .03 | .01 | .00 |
| ☐ 192 Wallace Johnson | .07 | .03 | .01 |
| ☐ 193 Charlie Lea | .06 | .02 | .00 |
| ☐ 194 Bill Lee | .05 | .02 | .00 |
| ☐ 195 Jerry Manuel | .03 | .01 | .00 |
| ☐ 196 Brad Mills | .07 | .03 | .01 |
| ☐ 197 John Milner | .03 | .01 | .00 |
| ☐ 198 Rowland Office | .03 | .01 | .00 |
| ☐ 199 David Palmer | .05 | .02 | .00 |
| ☐ 200 Larry Parrish | .06 | .02 | .00 |
| ☐ 201 Mike Phillips | .03 | .01 | .00 |
| ☐ 202 Tim Raines | .40 | .18 | .04 |
| ☐ 203 Bobby Ramos | .03 | .01 | .00 |
| ☐ 204 Jeff Reardon | .09 | .04 | .01 |
| ☐ 205 Steve Rogers | .09 | .04 | .01 |
| ☐ 206 Scott Sanderson | .05 | .02 | .00 |
| ☐ 207 Rodney Scott | .03 | .01 | .00 |
| ☐ 208 Elias Sosa | .03 | .01 | .00 |
| ☐ 209 Chris Speier | .03 | .01 | .00 |
| ☐ 210 Tim Wallach | .55 | .25 | .05 |
| ☐ 211 Jerry White | .03 | .01 | .00 |
| **HOUSTON ASTROS** | | | |
| ☐ 212 Alan Ashby | .03 | .01 | .00 |
| ☐ 213 Cesar Cedeno | .09 | .04 | .01 |
| ☐ 214 Jose Cruz | .13 | .06 | .01 |
| ☐ 215 Kiko Garcia | .03 | .01 | .00 |
| ☐ 216 Phil Garner | .05 | .02 | .00 |
| ☐ 217 Danny Heep | .03 | .01 | .00 |
| ☐ 218 Art Howe | .03 | .01 | .00 |
| ☐ 219 Bob Knepper | .07 | .03 | .01 |
| ☐ 220 Frank LaCorte | .03 | .01 | .00 |
| ☐ 221 Joe Niekro | .07 | .03 | .01 |
| ☐ 222 Joe Pittman | .05 | .02 | .00 |
| ☐ 223 Terry Puhl | .05 | .02 | .00 |
| ☐ 224 Luis Pujols | .03 | .01 | .00 |

| | MINT | VG-E | F-G |
|---|---|---|---|
| ☐ 225 Craig Reynolds | .03 | .01 | .00 |
| ☐ 226 J.R. Richard | .10 | .04 | .01 |
| ☐ 227 Dave Roberts | .03 | .01 | .00 |
| ☐ 228 Vern Ruhle | .03 | .01 | .00 |
| ☐ 229 Nolan Ryan | .30 | .12 | .03 |
| ☐ 230 Joe Sambito | .05 | .02 | .00 |
| ☐ 231 Tony Scott | .03 | .01 | .00 |
| ☐ 232 Dave Smith | .05 | .02 | .00 |
| ☐ 233 Harry Spilman | .03 | .01 | .00 |
| ☐ 234 Don Sutton | .15 | .06 | .01 |
| ☐ 235 Dickie Thon | .10 | .04 | .01 |
| ☐ 236 Denny Walling | .03 | .01 | .00 |
| ☐ 237 Gary Woods | .03 | .01 | .00 |
| **PHILADELPHIA PHILLIES** | | | |
| ☐ 238 Luis Aguayo | .05 | .02 | .00 |
| ☐ 239 Ramon Aviles | .03 | .01 | .00 |
| ☐ 240 Bob Boone | .06 | .02 | .00 |
| ☐ 241 Larry Bowa | .09 | .04 | .01 |
| ☐ 242 Warren Brusstar | .03 | .01 | .00 |
| ☐ 243 Steve Carlton | .45 | .20 | .04 |
| ☐ 244 Larry Christenson | .03 | .01 | .00 |
| ☐ 245 Dick Davis | .03 | .01 | .00 |
| ☐ 246 Greg Gross | .03 | .01 | .00 |
| ☐ 247 Sparky Lyle | .09 | .04 | .01 |
| ☐ 248 Garry Maddox | .05 | .02 | .00 |
| ☐ 249 Gary Matthews | .09 | .04 | .01 |
| ☐ 250 Bake McBride | .03 | .01 | .00 |
| ☐ 251 Tug McGraw | .09 | .04 | .01 |
| ☐ 252 Keith Moreland | .05 | .02 | .00 |
| ☐ 253 Dickie Noles | .03 | .01 | .00 |
| ☐ 254 Mike Proly | .03 | .01 | .00 |
| ☐ 255 Ron Reed | .03 | .01 | .00 |
| ☐ 256 Pete Rose | 1.00 | .45 | .10 |
| ☐ 257 Dick Ruthven | .03 | .01 | .00 |
| ☐ 258 Mike Schmidt | .55 | .25 | .05 |
| ☐ 259 Lonnie Smith | .09 | .04 | .01 |
| ☐ 260 Manny Trillo | .06 | .02 | .00 |
| ☐ 261 Del Unser | .03 | .01 | .00 |
| ☐ 262 George Vukovich | .03 | .01 | .00 |
| **DETROIT TIGERS** | | | |
| ☐ 263 Tom Brookens | .03 | .01 | .00 |
| ☐ 264 George Cappuzzello | .05 | .02 | .00 |
| ☐ 265 Marty Castillo | .07 | .03 | .01 |
| ☐ 266 Al Cowens | .05 | .02 | .00 |
| ☐ 267 Kirk Gibson | .35 | .15 | .03 |
| ☐ 268 Richie Hebner | .03 | .01 | .00 |
| ☐ 269 Ron Jackson | .03 | .01 | .00 |
| ☐ 270 Lynn Jones | .03 | .01 | .00 |
| ☐ 271 Steve Kemp | .12 | .05 | .01 |
| ☐ 272 Rick Leach | .07 | .03 | .01 |
| ☐ 273 Aurelio Lopez | .05 | .02 | .00 |
| ☐ 274 Jack Morris | .25 | .10 | .02 |

| | MINT | VG-E | F-G |
|---|---|---|---|
| ☐ 275 Kevin Saucier | .03 | .01 | .00 |
| ☐ 276 Lance Parrish | .30 | .12 | .03 |
| ☐ 277 Rick Peters | .03 | .01 | .00 |
| ☐ 278 Dan Petry | .18 | .08 | .01 |
| ☐ 279 David Rozema | .03 | .01 | .00 |
| ☐ 280 Stan Papi | .03 | .01 | .00 |
| ☐ 281 Dan Schatzeder | .03 | .01 | .00 |
| ☐ 282 Champ Summers | .03 | .01 | .00 |
| ☐ 283 Alan Trammell | .25 | .10 | .02 |
| ☐ 284 Lou Whitaker | .20 | .09 | .02 |
| ☐ 285 Milt Wilcox | .05 | .02 | .00 |
| ☐ 286 John Wockenfuss | .03 | .01 | .00 |
| **BOSTON RED SOX** | | | |
| ☐ 287 Gary Allenson | .03 | .01 | .00 |
| ☐ 288 Tom Burgmeier | .03 | .01 | .00 |
| ☐ 289 Bill Campbell | .05 | .02 | .00 |
| ☐ 290 Mark Clear | .05 | .02 | .00 |
| ☐ 291 Steve Crawford | .07 | .03 | .01 |
| ☐ 292 Dennis Eckersley | .06 | .02 | .00 |
| ☐ 293 Dwight Evans | .15 | .06 | .01 |
| ☐ 294 Rich Gedman | .55 | .25 | .05 |
| ☐ 295 Garry Hancock | .03 | .01 | .00 |
| ☐ 296 Glenn Hoffman | .03 | .01 | .00 |
| ☐ 297 Bruce Hurst | .03 | .01 | .00 |
| ☐ 298 Carney Lansford | .14 | .06 | .01 |
| ☐ 299 Rick Miller | .03 | .01 | .00 |
| ☐ 300 Reid Nichols | .03 | .01 | .00 |
| ☐ 301 Bob Ojeda | .25 | .10 | .02 |
| ☐ 302 Tony Perez | .14 | .06 | .01 |
| ☐ 303 Chuck Rainey | .03 | .01 | .00 |
| ☐ 304 Jerry Remy | .05 | .02 | .00 |
| ☐ 305 Jim Rice | .40 | .18 | .04 |
| ☐ 306 Joe Rudi | .05 | .02 | .00 |
| ☐ 307 Bob Stanley | .06 | .02 | .00 |
| ☐ 308 Dave Stapleton | .03 | .01 | .00 |
| ☐ 309 Frank Tanana | .05 | .02 | .00 |
| ☐ 310 Mike Torrez | .05 | .02 | .00 |
| ☐ 311 John Tudor | .15 | .06 | .01 |
| ☐ 312 Carl Yastrzemski | .65 | .30 | .06 |
| **TEXAS RANGERS** | | | |
| ☐ 313 Buddy Bell | .14 | .06 | .01 |
| ☐ 314 Steve Comer | .03 | .01 | .00 |
| ☐ 315 Danny Darwin | .03 | .01 | .00 |
| ☐ 316 John Ellis | .03 | .01 | .00 |
| ☐ 317 John Grubb | .03 | .01 | .00 |
| ☐ 318 Rick Honeycutt | .05 | .02 | .00 |
| ☐ 319 Charlie Hough | .05 | .02 | .00 |
| ☐ 320 Ferguson Jenkins | .13 | .06 | .01 |
| ☐ 321 John Henry Johnson | .03 | .01 | .00 |
| ☐ 322 Jim Kern | .03 | .01 | .00 |
| ☐ 323 Jon Matlack | .05 | .02 | .00 |
| ☐ 324 Doc Medich | .03 | .01 | .00 |
| ☐ 325 Mario Mendoza | .03 | .01 | .00 |

| | MINT | VG-E | F-G |
|---|---|---|---|
| ☐ 326 Al Oliver | .18 | .08 | .01 |
| ☐ 327 Pat Putnam | .03 | .01 | .00 |
| ☐ 328 Mickey Rivers | .06 | .02 | .00 |
| ☐ 329 Leon Roberts | .03 | .01 | .00 |
| ☐ 330 Billy Sample | .03 | .01 | .00 |
| ☐ 331 Bill Stein | .03 | .01 | .00 |
| ☐ 332 Jim Sundberg | .06 | .02 | .00 |
| ☐ 333 Mark Wagner | .03 | .01 | .00 |
| ☐ 334 Bump Wills | .03 | .01 | .00 |
| **CHICAGO WHITE SOX** | | | |
| ☐ 335 Bill Almon | .03 | .01 | .00 |
| ☐ 336 Harold Baines | .30 | .12 | .03 |
| ☐ 337 Ross Baumgarten | .03 | .01 | .00 |
| ☐ 338 Tony Bernazard | .03 | .01 | .00 |
| ☐ 339 Britt Burns | .10 | .04 | .01 |
| ☐ 340 Richard Dotson | .10 | .04 | .01 |
| ☐ 341 Jim Essian | .03 | .01 | .00 |
| ☐ 342 Ed Farmer | .03 | .01 | .00 |
| ☐ 343 Carlton Fisk | .18 | .08 | .01 |
| ☐ 344 Kevin Hickey | .07 | .03 | .01 |
| ☐ 345 LaMarr Hoyt | .13 | .06 | .01 |
| ☐ 346 Lamar Johnson | .03 | .01 | .00 |
| ☐ 347 Jerry Koosman | .07 | .03 | .01 |
| ☐ 348 Rusty Kuntz | .03 | .01 | .00 |
| ☐ 349 Dennis Lamp | .03 | .01 | .00 |
| ☐ 350 Ron LeFlore | .05 | .02 | .00 |
| ☐ 351 Chet Lemon | .09 | .04 | .01 |
| ☐ 352 Greg Luzinski | .13 | .06 | .01 |
| ☐ 353 Bob Molinaro | .03 | .01 | .00 |
| ☐ 354 Jim Morrison | .03 | .01 | .00 |
| ☐ 355 Wayne Nordhagen | .03 | .01 | .00 |
| ☐ 356 Greg Pryor | .03 | .01 | .00 |
| ☐ 357 Mike Squires | .03 | .01 | .00 |
| ☐ 358 Steve Trout | .05 | .02 | .00 |
| **CLEVELAND INDIANS** | | | |
| ☐ 359 Alan Bannister | .03 | .01 | .00 |
| ☐ 360 Len Barker | .08 | .03 | .01 |
| ☐ 361 Bert Blyleven | .15 | .06 | .01 |
| ☐ 362 Joe Charboneau | .06 | .02 | .00 |
| ☐ 363 John Denny | .12 | .05 | .01 |
| ☐ 364 Bo Diaz | .06 | .02 | .00 |
| ☐ 365 Miguel Dilone | .03 | .01 | .00 |
| ☐ 366 Jerry Dybzinski | .03 | .01 | .00 |
| ☐ 367 Wayne Garland | .03 | .01 | .00 |
| ☐ 368 Mike Hargrove | .05 | .02 | .00 |
| ☐ 369 Toby Harrah | .06 | .02 | .00 |
| ☐ 370 Ron Hassey | .03 | .01 | .00 |
| ☐ 371 Von Hayes | .75 | .35 | .07 |
| ☐ 372 Pat Kelly | .03 | .01 | .00 |
| ☐ 373 Duane Kuiper | .03 | .01 | .00 |
| ☐ 374 Rick Manning | .03 | .01 | .00 |
| ☐ 375 Sid Monge | .03 | .01 | .00 |
| ☐ 376 Jorge Orta | .03 | .01 | .00 |

| | MINT | VG-E | F-G |
|---|---|---|---|
| ☐ 377 Dave Rosello | .03 | .01 | .00 |
| ☐ 378 Dan Spillner | .03 | .01 | .00 |
| ☐ 379 Mike Stanton | .03 | .01 | .00 |
| ☐ 380 Andre Thornton | .09 | .04 | .01 |
| ☐ 381 Tom Veryzer | .03 | .01 | .00 |
| ☐ 382 Rick Waits | .03 | .01 | .00 |
| **SAN FRANCISCO GIANTS** | | | |
| ☐ 383 Doyle Alexander | .05 | .02 | .00 |
| ☐ 384 Vida Blue | .09 | .04 | .01 |
| ☐ 385 Fred Breining | .10 | .04 | .01 |
| ☐ 386 Enos Cabell | .03 | .01 | .00 |
| ☐ 387 Jack Clark | .18 | .08 | .01 |
| ☐ 388 Darrell Evans | .12 | .05 | .01 |
| ☐ 389 Tom Griffin | .03 | .01 | .00 |
| ☐ 390 Larry Herndon | .05 | .02 | .00 |
| ☐ 391 Al Holland | .07 | .03 | .01 |
| ☐ 392 Gary Lavelle | .03 | .01 | .00 |
| ☐ 393 Johnnie LeMaster | .03 | .01 | .00 |
| ☐ 394 Jerry Martin | .03 | .01 | .00 |
| ☐ 395 Milt May | .03 | .01 | .00 |
| ☐ 396 Greg Minton | .05 | .02 | .00 |
| ☐ 397 Joe Morgan | .20 | .09 | .02 |
| ☐ 398 Joe Pettini | .03 | .01 | .00 |
| ☐ 399 Alan Ripley | .03 | .01 | .00 |
| ☐ 400 Billy Smith | .03 | .01 | .00 |
| ☐ 401 Rennie Stennett | .03 | .01 | .00 |
| ☐ 402 Ed Whitson | .07 | .03 | .01 |
| ☐ 403 Jim Wohlford | .03 | .01 | .00 |
| **KANSAS CITY ROYALS** | | | |
| ☐ 404 Willie Aikens | .05 | .02 | .00 |
| ☐ 405 George Brett | .65 | .30 | .06 |
| ☐ 406 Ken Brett | .05 | .02 | .00 |
| ☐ 407 Dave Chalk | .03 | .01 | .00 |
| ☐ 408 Rich Gale | .03 | .01 | .00 |
| ☐ 409 Cesar Geronimo | .03 | .01 | .00 |
| ☐ 410 Larry Gura | .06 | .02 | .00 |
| ☐ 411 Clint Hurdle | .03 | .01 | .00 |
| ☐ 412 Mike Jones | .03 | .01 | .00 |
| ☐ 413 Dennis Leonard | .06 | .02 | .00 |
| ☐ 414 Renie Martin | .03 | .01 | .00 |
| ☐ 415 Lee May | .06 | .02 | .00 |
| ☐ 416 Hal McRae | .06 | .02 | .00 |
| ☐ 417 Darryl Motley | .25 | .10 | .02 |
| ☐ 418 Rance Mulliniks | .03 | .01 | .00 |
| ☐ 419 Amos Otis | .06 | .02 | .00 |
| ☐ 420 Ken Phelps | .25 | .10 | .02 |
| ☐ 421 Jamie Quirk | .03 | .01 | .00 |
| ☐ 422 Dan Quisenberry | .25 | .10 | .02 |
| ☐ 423 Paul Splittorff | .05 | .02 | .00 |
| ☐ 424 U.L. Washington | .03 | .01 | .00 |
| ☐ 425 John Wathan | .03 | .01 | .00 |
| ☐ 426 Frank White | .07 | .03 | .01 |

| | MINT | VG-E | F-G |
|---|---|---|---|
| ☐ 427 Willie Wilson | .25 | .10 | .02 |
| ATLANTA BRAVES | | | |
| ☐ 428 Brian Asselstine | .03 | .01 | .00 |
| ☐ 429 Bruce Benedict | .03 | .01 | .00 |
| ☐ 430 Tom Boggs | .03 | .01 | .00 |
| ☐ 431 Larry Bradford | .03 | .01 | .00 |
| ☐ 432 Rick Camp | .03 | .01 | .00 |
| ☐ 433 Chris Chambliss | .05 | .02 | .00 |
| ☐ 434 Gene Garber | .03 | .01 | .00 |
| ☐ 435 Preston Hanna | .03 | .01 | .00 |
| ☐ 436 Bob Horner | .25 | .10 | .02 |
| ☐ 437 Glenn Hubbard | .05 | .02 | .00 |
| ☐ 438 A Al Hrabosky | 12.00 | 5.50 | 1.20 |
| (height 5'1") | | | |
| ☐ 438 B Al Hrabosky | .45 | .20 | .04 |
| (height 5'1") | | | |
| ☐ 438 C Al Hrabosky | .08 | .03 | .01 |
| (height 5'10") | | | |
| ☐ 439 Rufino Linares | .05 | .02 | .00 |
| ☐ 440 Rick Mahler | .25 | .10 | .02 |
| ☐ 441 Ed Miller | .03 | .01 | .00 |
| ☐ 442 John Montefusco | .05 | .02 | .00 |
| ☐ 443 Dale Murphy | .85 | .40 | .08 |
| ☐ 444 Phil Niekro | .20 | .09 | .02 |
| ☐ 445 Gaylord Perry | .20 | .09 | .02 |
| ☐ 446 Biff Pocoroba | .03 | .01 | .00 |
| ☐ 447 Rafael Ramirez | .05 | .02 | .00 |
| ☐ 448 Jerry Royster | .03 | .01 | .00 |
| ☐ 449 Claudell Washington | .07 | .03 | .01 |
| CALIFORNIA ANGELS | | | |
| ☐ 450 Don Aase | .03 | .01 | .00 |
| ☐ 451 Don Baylor | .13 | .06 | .01 |
| ☐ 452 Juan Beniquez | .05 | .02 | .00 |
| ☐ 453 Rick Burleson | .05 | .02 | .00 |
| ☐ 454 Bert Campaneris | .06 | .02 | .00 |
| ☐ 455 Rod Carew | .45 | .20 | .04 |
| ☐ 456 Bob Clark | .03 | .01 | .00 |
| ☐ 457 Brian Downing | .05 | .02 | .00 |
| ☐ 458 Dan Ford | .05 | .02 | .00 |
| ☐ 459 Ken Forsch | .05 | .02 | .00 |
| ☐ 460 A Dave Frost (5 mm | | | |
| space) | .35 | .15 | .03 |
| (before ERA on back) | | | |
| ☐ 460 B Dave Frost | .05 | .02 | .00 |
| (1 mm space) | | | |
| ☐ 461 Bobby Grich | .09 | .04 | .01 |
| ☐ 462 Larry Harlow | .03 | .01 | .00 |
| ☐ 463 John Harris | .03 | .01 | .00 |
| ☐ 464 Andy Hassler | .03 | .01 | .00 |
| ☐ 465 Butch Hobson | .03 | .01 | .00 |
| ☐ 466 Jesse Jefferson | .03 | .01 | .00 |
| ☐ 467 Bruce Kison | .03 | .01 | .00 |

| | MINT | VG-E | F-G |
|---|---|---|---|
| ☐ 468 Fred Lynn | .25 | .10 | .02 |
| ☐ 469 Angel Moreno | .05 | .02 | .00 |
| ☐ 470 Ed Ott | .03 | .01 | .00 |
| ☐ 471 Fred Patek | .03 | .01 | .00 |
| ☐ 472 Steve Renko | .03 | .01 | .00 |
| ☐ 473 Mike Witt | .40 | .18 | .04 |
| ☐ 474 Geoff Zahn | .05 | .02 | .00 |
| PITTSBURGH PIRATES | | | |
| ☐ 475 Gary Alexander | .03 | .01 | .00 |
| ☐ 476 Dale Berra | .05 | .02 | .00 |
| ☐ 477 Kurt Bevacqua | .03 | .01 | .00 |
| ☐ 478 Jim Bibby | .05 | .02 | .00 |
| ☐ 479 John Candelaria | .08 | .03 | .01 |
| ☐ 480 Victor Cruz | .03 | .01 | .00 |
| ☐ 481 Mike Easler | .06 | .02 | .00 |
| ☐ 482 Tim Foli | .03 | .01 | .00 |
| ☐ 483 Lee Lacey | .06 | .02 | .00 |
| ☐ 484 Vance Law | .03 | .01 | .00 |
| ☐ 485 Bill Madlock | .18 | .08 | .01 |
| ☐ 486 Willie Montanez | .03 | .01 | .00 |
| ☐ 487 Omar Moreno | .05 | .02 | .00 |
| ☐ 488 Steve Nicosia | .03 | .01 | .00 |
| ☐ 489 Dave Parker | .25 | .10 | .02 |
| ☐ 490 Tony Pena | .15 | .06 | .01 |
| ☐ 491 Pascual Perez | .08 | .03 | .01 |
| ☐ 492 Johnny Ray | .60 | .28 | .06 |
| ☐ 493 Rick Rhoden | .06 | .02 | .00 |
| ☐ 494 Bill Robinson | .03 | .01 | .00 |
| ☐ 495 Don Robinson | .03 | .01 | .00 |
| ☐ 496 Enrique Romo | .03 | .01 | .00 |
| ☐ 497 Rod Scurry | .03 | .01 | .00 |
| ☐ 498 Eddie Solomon | .03 | .01 | .00 |
| ☐ 499 Willie Stargell | .25 | .10 | .02 |
| ☐ 500 Kent Tekulve | .08 | .03 | .01 |
| ☐ 501 Jason Thompson | .08 | .03 | .01 |
| SEATTLE MARINERS | | | |
| ☐ 502 Glenn Abbott | .03 | .01 | .00 |
| ☐ 503 Jim Anderson | .03 | .01 | .00 |
| ☐ 504 Floyd Bannister | .07 | .03 | .01 |
| ☐ 505 Bruce Bochte | .05 | .02 | .00 |
| ☐ 506 Jeff Burroughs | .05 | .02 | .00 |
| ☐ 507 Bryan Clark | .06 | .02 | .00 |
| ☐ 508 Ken Clay | .03 | .01 | .00 |
| ☐ 509 Julio Cruz | .03 | .01 | .00 |
| ☐ 510 Dick Drago | .03 | .01 | .00 |
| ☐ 511 Gary Gray | .03 | .01 | .00 |
| ☐ 512 Dan Meyer | .03 | .01 | .00 |
| ☐ 513 Jerry Narron | .03 | .01 | .00 |
| ☐ 514 Tom Paciorek | .03 | .01 | .00 |
| ☐ 515 Casey Parsons | .05 | .02 | .00 |
| ☐ 516 Lenny Randle | .03 | .01 | .00 |
| ☐ 517 Shane Rawley | .05 | .02 | .00 |

| | MINT | VG-E | F-G |
|---|---|---|---|
| ☐ 518 Joe Simpson | .03 | .01 | .00 |
| ☐ 519 Richie Zisk | .05 | .02 | .00 |
| **NEW YORK METS** | | | |
| ☐ 520 Neil Allen | .06 | .02 | .00 |
| ☐ 521 Bob Bailor | .03 | .01 | .00 |
| ☐ 522 Hubie Brooks | .12 | .05 | .01 |
| ☐ 523 Mike Cubbage | .03 | .01 | .00 |
| ☐ 524 Pete Falcone | .03 | .01 | .00 |
| ☐ 525 Doug Flynn | .03 | .01 | .00 |
| ☐ 526 Tom Hausman | .03 | .01 | .00 |
| ☐ 527 Ron Hodges | .03 | .01 | .00 |
| ☐ 528 Randy Jones | .05 | .02 | .00 |
| ☐ 529 Mike Jorgensen | .03 | .01 | .00 |
| ☐ 530 Dave Kingman | .14 | .06 | .01 |
| ☐ 531 Ed Lynch | .12 | .05 | .01 |
| ☐ 532 Mike Marshall | .06 | .02 | .00 |
| (screwball pitcher) | | | |
| ☐ 533 Lee Mazzilli | .06 | .02 | .00 |
| ☐ 534 Dyar Miller | .03 | .01 | .00 |
| ☐ 535 Mike Scott | .05 | .02 | .00 |
| ☐ 536 Rusty Staub | .09 | .04 | .01 |
| ☐ 537 John Stearns | .03 | .01 | .00 |
| ☐ 538 Craig Swan | .03 | .01 | .00 |
| ☐ 539 Frank Taveras | .03 | .01 | .00 |
| ☐ 540 Alex Trevino | .03 | .01 | .00 |
| ☐ 541 Ellis Valentine | .05 | .02 | .00 |
| ☐ 542 Mookie Wilson | .09 | .04 | .01 |
| ☐ 543 Joel Youngblood | .03 | .01 | .00 |
| ☐ 544 Pat Zachry | .03 | .01 | .00 |
| **MINNESOTA TWINS** | | | |
| ☐ 545 Glenn Adams | .03 | .01 | .00 |
| ☐ 546 Fernando Arroyo | .03 | .01 | .00 |
| ☐ 547 John Verhoeven | .03 | .01 | .00 |
| ☐ 548 Sal Butera | .03 | .01 | .00 |
| ☐ 549 John Castino | .03 | .01 | .00 |
| ☐ 550 Don Cooper | .05 | .02 | .00 |
| ☐ 551 Doug Corbett | .03 | .01 | .00 |
| ☐ 552 Dave Engle | .06 | .02 | .00 |
| ☐ 553 Roger Erickson | .03 | .01 | .00 |
| ☐ 554 Danny Goodwin | .03 | .01 | .00 |
| ☐ 555 A Darrell Jackson | 1.25 | .60 | .12 |
| (black hat) | | | |
| ☐ 555 B Darrell Jackson | .09 | .04 | .01 |
| (red hat) | | | |
| ☐ 556 Pete Mackanin | .03 | .01 | .00 |
| ☐ 557 Jack O'Connor | .07 | .03 | .01 |
| ☐ 558 Hosken Powell | .03 | .01 | .00 |
| ☐ 559 Pete Redfern | .03 | .01 | .00 |
| ☐ 560 Roy Smalley | .05 | .02 | .00 |
| ☐ 561 Chuck Baker | .03 | .01 | .00 |
| ☐ 562 Gary Ward | .06 | .02 | .00 |
| ☐ 563 Rob Wilfong | .03 | .01 | .00 |

| | MINT | VG-E | F-G |
|---|---|---|---|
| ☐ 564 Al Williams | .03 | .01 | .00 |
| ☐ 565 Butch Wynegar | .06 | .02 | .00 |
| **SAN DIEGO PADRES** | | | |
| ☐ 566 Randy Bass | .03 | .01 | .00 |
| ☐ 567 Juan Bonilla | .07 | .03 | .01 |
| ☐ 568 Danny Boone | .05 | .02 | .00 |
| ☐ 569 John Curtis | .03 | .01 | .00 |
| ☐ 570 Juan Eichelberger | .03 | .01 | .00 |
| ☐ 571 Barry Evans | .03 | .01 | .00 |
| ☐ 572 Tim Flannery | .03 | .01 | .00 |
| ☐ 573 Ruppert Jones | .05 | .02 | .00 |
| ☐ 574 Terry Kennedy | .10 | .04 | .01 |
| ☐ 575 Joe LeFebvre | .05 | .02 | .00 |
| ☐ 576 A John Littlefield ERR | 40.00 | 18.00 | 4.00 |
| (left handed) | | | |
| ☐ 576 B John Littlefield COR | .08 | .03 | .01 |
| (right handed) | | | |
| ☐ 577 Gary Lucas | .05 | .02 | .00 |
| ☐ 578 Steve Mura | .03 | .01 | .00 |
| ☐ 579 Broderick Perkins | .03 | .01 | .00 |
| ☐ 580 Gene Richards | .03 | .01 | .00 |
| ☐ 581 Luis Salazar | .03 | .01 | .00 |
| ☐ 582 Ozzie Smith | .12 | .05 | .01 |
| ☐ 583 John Urrea | .03 | .01 | .00 |
| ☐ 584 Chris Welsh | .07 | .03 | .01 |
| ☐ 585 Rick Wise | .05 | .02 | .00 |
| **CHICAGO CUBS** | | | |
| ☐ 586 Doug Bird | .03 | .01 | .00 |
| ☐ 587 Tim Blackwell | .03 | .01 | .00 |
| ☐ 588 Bobby Bonds | .08 | .03 | .01 |
| ☐ 589 Bill Buckner | .13 | .06 | .01 |
| ☐ 590 Bill Caudill | .07 | .03 | .01 |
| ☐ 591 Hector Cruz | .03 | .01 | .00 |
| ☐ 592 Jody Davis | .50 | .22 | .05 |
| ☐ 593 Ivan DeJesus | .03 | .01 | .00 |
| ☐ 594 Steve Dillard | .03 | .01 | .00 |
| ☐ 595 Leon Durham | .25 | .10 | .02 |
| ☐ 596 Rawly Eastwick | .03 | .01 | .00 |
| ☐ 597 Steve Henderson | .03 | .01 | .00 |
| ☐ 598 Mike Krukow | .03 | .01 | .00 |
| ☐ 599 Mike Lum | .03 | .01 | .00 |
| ☐ 600 Randy Martz | .03 | .01 | .00 |
| ☐ 601 Jerry Morales | .03 | .01 | .00 |
| ☐ 602 Ken Reitz | .03 | .01 | .00 |
| ☐ 603 A Lee Smith ERR | .65 | .30 | .06 |
| (Cubs logo reversed) | | | |
| ☐ 603 B Lee Smith COR | .45 | .20 | .04 |
| ☐ 604 Dick Tidrow | .03 | .01 | .00 |
| ☐ 605 Jim Tracy | .03 | .01 | .00 |
| ☐ 606 Mike Tyson | .03 | .01 | .00 |
| ☐ 607 Ty Waller | .07 | .03 | .01 |
| **TORONTO BLUE JAYS** | | | |

|  | MINT | VG-E | F-G |
|---|---|---|---|
| ☐ 608 Danny Ainge | .09 | .04 | .01 |
| ☐ 609 Jorge Bell | .85 | .40 | .08 |
| ☐ 610 Mark Bomback | .03 | .01 | .00 |
| ☐ 611 Barry Bonnell | .03 | .01 | .00 |
| ☐ 612 Jim Clancy | .03 | .01 | .00 |
| ☐ 613 Damaso Garcia | .10 | .04 | .01 |
| ☐ 614 Jerry Garvin | .03 | .01 | .00 |
| ☐ 615 Alfredo Griffin | .06 | .03 | .01 |
| ☐ 616 Garth Iorg | .03 | .01 | .00 |
| ☐ 617 Luis Leal | .03 | .01 | .00 |
| ☐ 618 Ken Macha | .03 | .01 | .00 |
| ☐ 619 John Mayberry | .05 | .02 | .00 |
| ☐ 620 Joey McLaughlin | .03 | .01 | .00 |
| ☐ 621 Lloyd Moseby | .13 | .06 | .01 |
| ☐ 622 Dave Stieb | .20 | .09 | .02 |
| ☐ 623 Jackson Todd | .03 | .01 | .00 |
| ☐ 624 Willie Upshaw | .13 | .06 | .01 |
| ☐ 625 Otto Velez | .03 | .01 | .00 |
| ☐ 626 Ernie Whitt | .03 | .01 | .00 |
| ☐ 627 Al Woods | .03 | .01 | .00 |
| **SPECIAL CARDS (628–646)** | | | |
| ☐ 628 All Star Game Cleveland, Ohio | .06 | .02 | .00 |
| ☐ 629 All Star Infielders Frank White and Bucky Dent | .06 | .02 | .00 |
| ☐ 630 Big Red Machine Dan Driessen Dave Concepcion George Foster | .09 | .04 | .01 |
| ☐ 631 Bruce Sutter Top NL Relief Pitcher | .13 | .06 | .01 |
| ☐ 632 "Steve and Carlton" Steve Carlton and Carlton Fisk | .20 | .09 | .02 |
| ☐ 633 Carl Yastrzemski 3000th Game | .30 | .12 | .03 |
| ☐ 634 Dynamic Duo Johnny Bench and Tom Seaver | .25 | .10 | .02 |
| ☐ 635 West Meets East Fernando Valenzuela and Gary Carter | .25 | .10 | .02 |
| ☐ 636 A Fernando Valenzuela: NL SO King ("the" NL) | .35 | .15 | .03 |
| ☐ 636 B Fernando Valenzuela: NL SO King ("the" NL) | .30 | .12 | .03 |
| ☐ 637 Mike Schmidt Home Run King | .35 | .15 | .03 |
| ☐ 638 NL All Stars Gary Carter and Dave Parker | .20 | .09 | .02 |

|  | MINT | VG-E | F-G |
|---|---|---|---|
| ☐ 639 Perfect Game Len Barker and Bo Diaz | .09 | .04 | .01 |
| ☐ 640 Pete and Re-Pete Pete Rose and Son | .85 | .40 | .08 |
| ☐ 641 Phillies Finest Lonnie Smith Mike Schmidt Steve Carlton | .30 | .12 | .03 |
| ☐ 642 Red Sox Reunion Fred Lynn and Dwight Evans | .12 | .05 | .01 |
| ☐ 643 Rickey Henderson Most Hits and Runs | .30 | .12 | .03 |
| ☐ 644 Rollie Fingers Most Saves AL | .12 | .05 | .01 |
| ☐ 645 Tom Seaver Most 1981 Wins | .20 | .09 | .02 |
| ☐ 646 A Yankee Powerhouse Reggie Jackson and Dave Winfield (comma on back after outfielder) | .50 | .22 | .05 |
| ☐ 646 B Yankee Powerhouse Reggie Jackson and Dave Winfield (no comma) | .40 | .18 | .04 |
| **CHECKLISTS (647–660)** | | | |
| ☐ 647 CL: Yankees/Dodgers | .08 | .01 | .00 |
| ☐ 648 CL: A's/Reds | .07 | .01 | .00 |
| ☐ 649 CL: Cards/Brewers | .07 | .01 | .00 |
| ☐ 650 CL: Expos/Orioles | .07 | .01 | .00 |
| ☐ 651 CL: Astros/Phillies | .07 | .01 | .00 |
| ☐ 652 CL: Tigers/Red Sox | .07 | .01 | .00 |
| ☐ 653 CL: Rangers/White Sox | .07 | .01 | .00 |
| ☐ 654 CL: Giants/Indians | .07 | .01 | .00 |
| ☐ 655 CL: Royals/Braves | .07 | .01 | .00 |
| ☐ 656 CL: Angels/Pirates | .07 | .01 | .00 |
| ☐ 657 CL: Mariners/Mets | .07 | .01 | .00 |
| ☐ 658 CL: Padres/Twins | .07 | .01 | .00 |
| ☐ 659 CL: Blue Jays/Cubs | .07 | .01 | .00 |
| ☐ 660 Specials Checklist | .10 | .01 | .00 |

# 1983 FLEER

Goose Gossage

The cards in this 660 card set measure
2½" by 3½". In 1983, for the third straight
year, Fleer has produced a baseball series
numbering 660 cards. Of these, 1–628 are
player cards, 629–646 are special cards,
and 647–660 are checklist cards. The front
of each card has a colorful team logo at
bottom left and the player's name and
position at lower right. The reverses are
done in shades of brown on white. The
cards are numbered on the back next to a
small black and white photo of the player.
Complete Set: **M-16.00; VG-E-7.50; F-G1.60**

|  | MINT | VG-E | F-G |
|---|---|---|---|
| Common Player (1–660) | .03 | .01 | .00 |

### ST. LOUIS CARDINALS

|  |  | MINT | VG-E | F-G |
|---|---|---|---|---|
| ☐ | 1 Joaquin Andujar | .18 | .04 | .01 |
| ☐ | 2 Doug Bair | .03 | .01 | .00 |
| ☐ | 3 Steve Braun | .03 | .01 | .00 |
| ☐ | 4 Glenn Brummer | .03 | .01 | .00 |
| ☐ | 5 Bob Forsch | .05 | .02 | .00 |
| ☐ | 6 David Green | .20 | .09 | .02 |
| ☐ | 7 George Hendrick | .09 | .04 | .01 |
| ☐ | 8 Keith Hernandez | .30 | .12 | .03 |
| ☐ | 9 Tom Herr | .14 | .06 | .01 |
| ☐ | 10 Dane Iorg | .03 | .01 | .00 |
| ☐ | 11 Jim Kaat | .09 | .04 | .01 |
| ☐ | 12 Jeff Lahti | .07 | .03 | .01 |
| ☐ | 13 Tito Landrum | .05 | .02 | .00 |
| ☐ | 14 Dave LaPoint | .18 | .08 | .01 |
| ☐ | 15 Willie McGee | 1.50 | .70 | .15 |
| ☐ | 16 Steve Mura | .03 | .01 | .00 |
| ☐ | 17 Ken Oberkfell | .05 | .02 | .00 |
| ☐ | 18 Darrell Porter | .06 | .02 | .00 |
| ☐ | 19 Mike Ramsey | .03 | .01 | .00 |
| ☐ | 20 Gene Roof | .06 | .02 | .00 |
| ☐ | 21 Lonnie Smith | .09 | .04 | .01 |
| ☐ | 22 Ozzie Smith | .12 | .05 | .01 |
| ☐ | 23 John Stuper | .10 | .04 | .01 |
| ☐ | 24 Bruce Sutter | .20 | .09 | .02 |
| ☐ | 25 Gene Tenace | .03 | .01 | .00 |

### MILWAUKEE BREWERS

|  |  | MINT | VG-E | F-G |
|---|---|---|---|---|
| ☐ | 26 Jerry Augustine | .03 | .01 | .00 |
| ☐ | 27 Dwight Bernard | .03 | .01 | .00 |
| ☐ | 28 Mark Brouhard | .03 | .01 | .00 |
| ☐ | 29 Mike Caldwell | .05 | .02 | .00 |
| ☐ | 30 Cecil Cooper | .16 | .07 | .01 |
| ☐ | 31 Jamie Easterly | .03 | .01 | .00 |
| ☐ | 32 Marshall Edwards | .03 | .01 | .00 |
| ☐ | 33 Rollie Fingers | .18 | .08 | .01 |
| ☐ | 34 Jim Gantner | .05 | .02 | .00 |
| ☐ | 35 Moose Haas | .05 | .02 | .00 |
| ☐ | 36 Roy Howell | .03 | .01 | .00 |
| ☐ | 37 Peter Ladd | .03 | .01 | .00 |
| ☐ | 38 Bob McClure | .03 | .01 | .00 |
| ☐ | 39 Doc Medich | .03 | .01 | .00 |
| ☐ | 40 Paul Molitor | .15 | .06 | .01 |
| ☐ | 41 Don Money | .03 | .01 | .00 |
| ☐ | 42 Charlie Moore | .03 | .01 | .00 |
| ☐ | 43 Ben Oglivie | .08 | .03 | .01 |
| ☐ | 44 Ed Romero | .03 | .01 | .00 |
| ☐ | 45 Ted Simmons | .12 | .05 | .01 |
| ☐ | 46 Jim Slaton | .03 | .01 | .00 |
| ☐ | 47 Don Sutton | .14 | .06 | .01 |
| ☐ | 48 Gorman Thomas | .12 | .05 | .01 |
| ☐ | 49 Pete Vuckovich | .08 | .03 | .01 |
| ☐ | 50 Ned Yost | .03 | .01 | .00 |
| ☐ | 51 Robin Yount | .30 | .12 | .03 |

### BALTIMORE ORIOLES

|  |  | MINT | VG-E | F-G |
|---|---|---|---|---|
| ☐ | 52 Benny Ayala | .03 | .01 | .00 |
| ☐ | 53 Bob Bonner | .03 | .01 | .00 |
| ☐ | 54 Al Bumbry | .03 | .01 | .00 |
| ☐ | 55 Terry Crowley | .03 | .01 | .00 |
| ☐ | 56 Storm Davis | .45 | .20 | .04 |
| ☐ | 57 Rich Dauer | .03 | .01 | .00 |
| ☐ | 58 Rick Dempsey | .05 | .02 | .00 |
| ☐ | 59 Jim Dwyer | .03 | .01 | .00 |
| ☐ | 60 Mike Flanagan | .08 | .03 | .01 |
| ☐ | 61 Dan Ford | .05 | .02 | .00 |
| ☐ | 62 Glenn Gulliver | .03 | .01 | .00 |
| ☐ | 63 John Lowenstein | .03 | .01 | .00 |
| ☐ | 64 Dennis Martinez | .03 | .01 | .00 |
| ☐ | 65 Tippy Martinez | .05 | .02 | .00 |
| ☐ | 66 Scott McGregor | .08 | .03 | .01 |
| ☐ | 67 Eddie Murray | .55 | .25 | .05 |
| ☐ | 68 Joe Nolan | .03 | .01 | .00 |

| | MINT | VG-E | F-G |
|---|---|---|---|
| 69 Jim Palmer | .25 | .10 | .02 |
| 70 Cal Ripken Jr. | .75 | .35 | .07 |
| 71 Gary Roenicke | .05 | .02 | .00 |
| 72 Lenn Sakata | .03 | .01 | .00 |
| 73 Ken Singleton | .08 | .03 | .01 |
| 74 Sammy Stewart | .03 | .01 | .00 |
| 75 Tim Stoddard | .03 | .01 | .00 |
| **CALIFORNIA ANGELS** | | | |
| 76 Don Aase | .03 | .01 | .00 |
| 77 Don Baylor | .12 | .05 | .01 |
| 78 Juan Beniquez | .05 | .02 | .00 |
| 79 Bob Boone | .06 | .02 | .00 |
| 80 Rick Burleson | .06 | .02 | .00 |
| 81 Rod Carew | .40 | .18 | .04 |
| 82 Bobby Clark | .03 | .01 | .00 |
| 83 Doug Corbett | .03 | .01 | .00 |
| 84 John Curtis | .03 | .01 | .00 |
| 85 Doug DeCinces | .10 | .04 | .01 |
| 86 Brian Downing | .05 | .02 | .00 |
| 87 Joe Ferguson | .03 | .01 | .00 |
| 88 Tim Foli | .03 | .01 | .00 |
| 89 Ken Forsch | .03 | .01 | .00 |
| 90 Dave Goltz | .03 | .01 | .00 |
| 91 Bobby Grich | .07 | .03 | .01 |
| 92 Andy Hassler | .03 | .01 | .00 |
| 93 Reggie Jackson | .45 | .20 | .04 |
| 94 Ron Jackson | .03 | .01 | .00 |
| 95 Tommy John | .15 | .06 | .01 |
| 96 Bruce Kison | .03 | .01 | .00 |
| 97 Fred Lynn | .18 | .08 | .01 |
| 98 Ed Ott | .03 | .01 | .00 |
| 99 Steve Renko | .03 | .01 | .00 |
| 100 Luis Sanchez | .03 | .01 | .00 |
| 101 Rob Wilfong | .03 | .01 | .00 |
| 102 Mike Witt | .09 | .04 | .01 |
| 103 Geoff Zahn | .05 | .02 | .00 |
| **KANSAS CITY ROYALS** | | | |
| 104 Willie Aikens | .05 | .02 | .00 |
| 105 Mike Armstrong | .03 | .01 | .00 |
| 106 Vida Blue | .09 | .04 | .01 |
| 107 Bud Black | .30 | .12 | .03 |
| 108 George Brett | .50 | .22 | .05 |
| 109 Bill Castro | .03 | .01 | .00 |
| 110 Onix Concepcion | .09 | .04 | .01 |
| 111 Dave Frost | .03 | .01 | .00 |
| 112 Cesar Geronimo | .03 | .01 | .00 |
| 113 Larry Gura | .06 | .02 | .00 |
| 114 Steve Hammond | .06 | .02 | .00 |
| 115 Don Hood | .03 | .01 | .00 |
| 116 Dennis Leonard | .06 | .02 | .00 |
| 117 Jerry Martin | .03 | .01 | .00 |
| 118 Lee May | .06 | .02 | .00 |
| 119 Hal McRae | .07 | .03 | .01 |

| | MINT | VG-E | F-G |
|---|---|---|---|
| 120 Amos Otis | .07 | .03 | .01 |
| 121 Greg Pryor | .03 | .01 | .00 |
| 122 Dan Quisenberry | .20 | .09 | .02 |
| 123 Don Slaught | .20 | .09 | .02 |
| 124 Paul Splittorff | .05 | .02 | .00 |
| 125 U.L. Washington | .03 | .01 | .00 |
| 126 John Wathan | .03 | .01 | .00 |
| 127 Frank White | .07 | .03 | .01 |
| 128 Willie Wilson | .20 | .09 | .02 |
| **ATLANTA BRAVES** | | | |
| 129 Steve Bedrosian | .07 | .03 | .01 |
| 130 Bruce Benedict | .03 | .01 | .00 |
| 131 Tommy Boggs | .03 | .01 | .00 |
| 132 Brett Butler | .09 | .04 | .01 |
| 133 Rick Camp | .03 | .01 | .00 |
| 134 Chris Chambliss | .06 | .02 | .00 |
| 135 Ken Dayley | .03 | .01 | .00 |
| 136 Gene Garber | .03 | .01 | .00 |
| 137 Terry Harper | .03 | .01 | .00 |
| 138 Bob Horner | .20 | .09 | .02 |
| 139 Glenn Hubbard | .05 | .02 | .00 |
| 140 Rufino Linares | .03 | .01 | .00 |
| 141 Rick Mahler | .06 | .02 | .00 |
| 142 Dale Murphy | .75 | .35 | .07 |
| 143 Phil Niekro | .20 | .09 | .02 |
| 144 Pascual Perez | .08 | .03 | .01 |
| 145 Biff Pocoroba | .03 | .01 | .00 |
| 146 Rafael Ramirez | .05 | .02 | .00 |
| 147 Jerry Royster | .03 | .01 | .00 |
| 148 Ken Smith | .06 | .02 | .00 |
| 149 Bob Walk | .03 | .01 | .00 |
| 150 Claudell Washington | .08 | .03 | .01 |
| 151 Bob Watson | .06 | .02 | .00 |
| 152 Larry Whisenton | .03 | .01 | .00 |
| **PHILADELPHIA PHILLIES** | | | |
| 153 Porfirio Altamirano | .06 | .02 | .00 |
| 154 Marty Bystrom | .03 | .01 | .00 |
| 155 Steve Carlton | .35 | .15 | .03 |
| 156 Larry Christenson | .03 | .01 | .00 |
| 157 Ivan DeJesus | .03 | .01 | .00 |
| 158 John Denny | .10 | .04 | .01 |
| 159 Bob Dernier | .07 | .03 | .01 |
| 160 Bo Diaz | .06 | .02 | .00 |
| 161 Ed Farmer | .03 | .01 | .00 |
| 162 Greg Gross | .03 | .01 | .00 |
| 163 Mike Krukow | .03 | .01 | .00 |
| 164 Gary Maddox | .05 | .02 | .00 |
| 165 Gary Matthews | .08 | .03 | .01 |
| 166 Tug McGraw | .09 | .04 | .01 |
| 167 Bob Molinaro | .03 | .01 | .00 |
| 168 Sid Monge | .03 | .01 | .00 |
| 169 Ron Reed | .03 | .01 | .00 |

| | MINT | VG-E | F-G | | | MINT | VG-E | F-G |
|---|---|---|---|---|---|---|---|---|
| ☐ 170 Bill Robinson | .03 | .01 | .00 | ☐ 220 Steve Sax | .15 | .06 | .01 |
| ☐ 171 Pete Rose | .80 | .40 | .08 | ☐ 221 Mike Scioscia | .03 | .01 | .00 |
| ☐ 172 Dick Ruthven | .03 | .01 | .00 | ☐ 222 Dave Stewart | .03 | .01 | .00 |
| ☐ 173 Mike Schmidt | .45 | .20 | .04 | ☐ 223 Derrel Thomas | .03 | .01 | .00 |
| ☐ 174 Manny Trillo | .05 | .02 | .00 | ☐ 224 Fernando Valenzuela | .30 | .12 | .03 |
| ☐ 175 Ozzie Virgil | .06 | .02 | .00 | ☐ 225 Bob Welch | .07 | .03 | .01 |
| ☐ 176 George Vuckovich | .03 | .01 | .00 | ☐ 226 Ricky Wright | .07 | .03 | .01 |
| **BOSTON RED SOX** | | | | ☐ 227 Steve Yeager | .05 | .02 | .00 |
| ☐ 177 Gary Allenson | .03 | .01 | .00 | **CHICAGO WHITE SOX** | | | |
| ☐ 178 Luis Aponte | .06 | .02 | .00 | | | | |
| ☐ 179 Wade Boggs | 3.50 | 1.65 | .35 | ☐ 228 Bill Almon | .03 | .01 | .00 |
| ☐ 180 Tom Burgmeier | .03 | .01 | .00 | ☐ 229 Harold Baines | .25 | .10 | .02 |
| ☐ 181 Mark Clear | .05 | .02 | .00 | ☐ 230 Salome Barojas | .06 | .02 | .00 |
| ☐ 182 Dennis Eckersley | .06 | .02 | .00 | ☐ 231 Tony Bernazard | .03 | .01 | .00 |
| ☐ 183 Dwight Evans | .14 | .06 | .01 | ☐ 232 Britt Burns | .08 | .03 | .01 |
| ☐ 184 Rich Gedman | .08 | .03 | .01 | ☐ 233 Richard Dotson | .08 | .03 | .01 |
| ☐ 185 Glenn Hoffman | .03 | .01 | .00 | ☐ 234 Ernesto Escarrega | .06 | .02 | .00 |
| ☐ 186 Bruce Hurst | .03 | .01 | .00 | ☐ 235 Carlton Fisk | .18 | .08 | .01 |
| ☐ 187 Carney Lansford | .12 | .05 | .01 | ☐ 236 Jerry Hairston | .03 | .01 | .00 |
| ☐ 188 Rick Miller | .03 | .01 | .00 | ☐ 237 Kevin Hickey | .03 | .01 | .00 |
| ☐ 189 Reid Nichols | .05 | .02 | .00 | ☐ 238 LaMarr Hoyt | .13 | .06 | .01 |
| ☐ 190 Bob Ojeda | .05 | .02 | .00 | ☐ 239 Steve Kemp | .09 | .04 | .01 |
| ☐ 191 Tony Perez | .13 | .06 | .01 | ☐ 240 Jim Kern | .03 | .01 | .00 |
| ☐ 192 Chuck Rainey | .03 | .01 | .00 | ☐ 241 Ron Kittle | .75 | .35 | .07 |
| ☐ 193 Jerry Remy | .05 | .02 | .00 | ☐ 242 Jerry Koosman | .07 | .03 | .01 |
| ☐ 194 Jim Rice | .35 | .15 | .03 | ☐ 243 Dennis Lamp | .03 | .01 | .00 |
| ☐ 195 Bob Stanley | .06 | .02 | .00 | ☐ 244 Rudy Law | .03 | .01 | .00 |
| ☐ 196 Dave Stapleton | .05 | .02 | .00 | ☐ 245 Vance Law | .03 | .01 | .00 |
| ☐ 197 Mike Torrez | .05 | .02 | .00 | ☐ 246 Ron LeFlore | .06 | .02 | .00 |
| ☐ 198 John Tudor | .15 | .06 | .01 | ☐ 247 Greg Luzinski | .12 | .05 | .01 |
| ☐ 199 Julio Valdez | .03 | .01 | .00 | ☐ 248 Tom Paciorek | .03 | .01 | .00 |
| ☐ 200 Carl Yastrzemski | .55 | .25 | .05 | ☐ 249 Aurelio Rodriguez | .03 | .01 | .00 |
| **LOS ANGELES** | | | | ☐ 250 Mike Squires | .03 | .01 | .00 |
| **DODGERS** | | | | ☐ 251 Steve Trout | .05 | .02 | .00 |
| ☐ 201 Dusty Baker | .09 | .04 | .01 | **SAN FRANCISCO** | | | |
| ☐ 202 Joe Beckwith | .03 | .01 | .00 | **GIANTS** | | | |
| ☐ 203 Greg Brock | .50 | .22 | .05 | ☐ 252 Jim Barr | .03 | .01 | .00 |
| ☐ 204 Ron Cey | .13 | .06 | .01 | ☐ 253 Dave Bergman | .03 | .01 | .00 |
| ☐ 205 Terry Forster | .07 | .03 | .01 | ☐ 254 Fred Breining | .03 | .01 | .00 |
| ☐ 206 Steve Garvey | .40 | .18 | .04 | ☐ 255 Bob Brenly | .07 | .03 | .01 |
| ☐ 207 Pedro Guerrero | .30 | .12 | .03 | ☐ 256 Jack Clark | .18 | .08 | .01 |
| ☐ 208 Burt Hooton | .03 | .01 | .00 | ☐ 257 Chili Davis | .13 | .06 | .01 |
| ☐ 209 Steve Howe | .06 | .02 | .00 | ☐ 258 Darrell Evans | .12 | .05 | .01 |
| ☐ 210 Ken Landreaux | .05 | .02 | .00 | ☐ 259 Alan Fowlkes | .06 | .02 | .00 |
| ☐ 211 Mike Marshall | .20 | .09 | .02 | ☐ 260 Rich Gale | .03 | .01 | .00 |
| ☐ 212 Candy Maldonado | .20 | .09 | .02 | ☐ 261 Atlee Hammaker | .06 | .02 | .00 |
| ☐ 213 Rick Monday | .05 | .02 | .00 | ☐ 262 Al Holland | .05 | .02 | .00 |
| ☐ 214 Tom Niedenfuer | .08 | .03 | .01 | ☐ 263 Duane Kuiper | .03 | .01 | .00 |
| ☐ 215 Jorge Orta | .03 | .01 | .00 | ☐ 264 Bill Laskey | .15 | .06 | .01 |
| ☐ 216 Jerry Reuss | .07 | .03 | .01 | ☐ 265 Gary Lavelle | .03 | .01 | .00 |
| ☐ 217 Ron Roenicke | .03 | .01 | .00 | ☐ 266 Johnnie LeMaster | .03 | .01 | .00 |
| ☐ 218 Vicente Romo | .03 | .01 | .00 | ☐ 267 Renie Martin | .03 | .01 | .00 |
| ☐ 219 Bill Russell | .05 | .02 | .00 | ☐ 268 Milt May | .03 | .01 | .00 |
| | | | | ☐ 269 Greg Minton | .05 | .02 | .00 |

| | MINT | VG-E | F-G |
|---|---|---|---|
| ☐ 270 Joe Morgan | .20 | .09 | .02 |
| ☐ 271 Tom O'Malley | .09 | .04 | .01 |
| ☐ 272 Reggie Smith | .09 | .04 | .01 |
| ☐ 273 Guy Sularz | .06 | .02 | .00 |
| ☐ 274 Champ Summers | .03 | .01 | .00 |
| ☐ 275 Max Venable | .03 | .01 | .00 |
| ☐ 276 Jim Wohlford | .03 | .01 | .00 |
| **MONTREAL EXPOS** | | | |
| ☐ 277 Ray Burris | .03 | .01 | .00 |
| ☐ 278 Gary Carter | .40 | .18 | .04 |
| ☐ 279 Warren Cromartie | .03 | .01 | .00 |
| ☐ 280 Andre Dawson | .25 | .10 | .02 |
| ☐ 281 Terry Francona | .08 | .03 | .01 |
| ☐ 282 Doug Flynn | .03 | .01 | .00 |
| ☐ 283 Woody Fryman | .03 | .01 | .00 |
| ☐ 284 Bill Gullickson | .06 | .02 | .00 |
| ☐ 285 Wallace Johnson | .06 | .02 | .00 |
| ☐ 286 Charlie Lea | .05 | .02 | .00 |
| ☐ 287 Randy Lerch | .03 | .01 | .00 |
| ☐ 288 Brad Mills | .03 | .01 | .00 |
| ☐ 289 Dan Norman | .03 | .01 | .00 |
| ☐ 290 Al Oliver | .18 | .08 | .01 |
| ☐ 291 David Palmer | .06 | .02 | .00 |
| ☐ 292 Tim Raines | .30 | .12 | .03 |
| ☐ 293 Jeff Reardon | .10 | .04 | .01 |
| ☐ 294 Steve Rogers | .08 | .03 | .01 |
| ☐ 295 Scott Sanderson | .05 | .02 | .00 |
| ☐ 296 Dan Schatzeder | .03 | .01 | .00 |
| ☐ 297 Bryn Smith | .06 | .02 | .00 |
| ☐ 298 Chris Speier | .03 | .01 | .00 |
| ☐ 299 Tim Wallach | .12 | .05 | .01 |
| ☐ 300 Jerry White | .03 | .01 | .00 |
| ☐ 301 Joel Youngblood | .03 | .01 | .00 |
| **PITTSBURGH PIRATES** | | | |
| ☐ 302 Ross Baumgarten | .03 | .01 | .00 |
| ☐ 303 Dale Berra | .06 | .02 | .00 |
| ☐ 304 John Candelaria | .07 | .03 | .01 |
| ☐ 305 Dick Davis | .03 | .01 | .00 |
| ☐ 306 Mike Easler | .06 | .02 | .00 |
| ☐ 307 Richie Hebner | .03 | .01 | .00 |
| ☐ 308 Lee Lacy | .06 | .02 | .00 |
| ☐ 309 Bill Madlock | .15 | .06 | .01 |
| ☐ 310 Larry McWilliams | .06 | .02 | .00 |
| ☐ 311 John Milner | .03 | .01 | .00 |
| ☐ 312 Omar Moreno | .05 | .02 | .00 |
| ☐ 313 Jim Morrison | .03 | .01 | .00 |
| ☐ 314 Steve Nicosia | .03 | .01 | .00 |
| ☐ 315 Dave Parker | .20 | .09 | .02 |
| ☐ 316 Tony Pena | .14 | .06 | .01 |
| ☐ 317 Johnny Ray | .12 | .05 | .01 |
| ☐ 318 Rick Rhoden | .06 | .02 | .00 |
| ☐ 319 Don Robinson | .03 | .01 | .00 |
| ☐ 320 Enrique Romo | .03 | .01 | .00 |

| | MINT | VG-E | F-G |
|---|---|---|---|
| ☐ 321 Manny Sarmiento | .03 | .01 | .00 |
| ☐ 322 Rod Scurry | .03 | .01 | .00 |
| ☐ 323 Jim Smith | .05 | .02 | .00 |
| ☐ 324 Willie Stargell | .20 | .09 | .02 |
| ☐ 325 Jason Thompson | .08 | .03 | .01 |
| ☐ 326 Kent Tekulve | .08 | .03 | .01 |
| **DETROIT TIGERS** | | | |
| ☐ 327 Tom Brookens | .03 | .01 | .00 |
| ☐ 328 Enos Cabell | .03 | .01 | .00 |
| ☐ 329 Kirk Gibson | .25 | .10 | .02 |
| ☐ 330 Larry Herndon | .05 | .02 | .00 |
| ☐ 331 Mike Ivie | .03 | .01 | .00 |
| ☐ 332 Howard Johnson | .15 | .06 | .01 |
| ☐ 333 Lynn Jones | .03 | .01 | .00 |
| ☐ 334 Rick Leach | .03 | .01 | .00 |
| ☐ 335 Chet Lemon | .08 | .03 | .01 |
| ☐ 336 Jack Morris | .20 | .09 | .02 |
| ☐ 337 Lance Parrish | .25 | .10 | .02 |
| ☐ 338 Larry Pashnick | .06 | .02 | .00 |
| ☐ 339 Dan Petry | .16 | .07 | .01 |
| ☐ 340 Dave Rozema | .03 | .01 | .00 |
| ☐ 341 Dave Rucker | .03 | .01 | .00 |
| ☐ 342 Elias Sosa | .03 | .01 | .00 |
| ☐ 343 Dave Tobik | .03 | .01 | .00 |
| ☐ 344 Alan Trammell | .25 | .10 | .02 |
| ☐ 345 Jerry Turner | .03 | .01 | .00 |
| ☐ 346 Jerry Ujdur | .03 | .01 | .00 |
| ☐ 347 Pat Underwood | .03 | .01 | .00 |
| ☐ 348 Lou Whitaker | .20 | .09 | .02 |
| ☐ 349 Milt Wilcox | .05 | .02 | .00 |
| ☐ 350 Glenn Wilson | .65 | .30 | .06 |
| ☐ 351 John Wockenfuss | .03 | .01 | .00 |
| **SAN DIEGO PADRES** | | | |
| ☐ 352 Kurt Bevacqua | .03 | .01 | .00 |
| ☐ 353 Juan Bonilla | .03 | .01 | .00 |
| ☐ 354 Floyd Chiffer | .06 | .02 | .00 |
| ☐ 355 Luis DeLeon | .03 | .01 | .00 |
| ☐ 356 Dave Dravecky | .40 | .18 | .04 |
| ☐ 357 Dave Edwards | .03 | .01 | .00 |
| ☐ 358 Juan Eichelberger | .03 | .01 | .00 |
| ☐ 359 Tim Flannery | .03 | .01 | .00 |
| ☐ 360 Tony Gwynn | 2.50 | 1.15 | .25 |
| ☐ 361 Ruppert Jones | .05 | .02 | .00 |
| ☐ 362 Terry Kennedy | .11 | .05 | .01 |
| ☐ 363 Joe Lefebvre | .03 | .01 | .00 |
| ☐ 364 Sixto Lezcano | .03 | .01 | .00 |
| ☐ 365 Tim Lollar | .05 | .02 | .00 |
| ☐ 366 Gary Lucas | .03 | .01 | .00 |
| ☐ 367 John Montefusco | .05 | .02 | .00 |
| ☐ 368 Broderick Perkins | .03 | .01 | .00 |
| ☐ 369 Joe Pittman | .03 | .01 | .00 |
| ☐ 370 Gene Richards | .03 | .01 | .00 |
| ☐ 371 Luis Salazar | .03 | .01 | .00 |

| | MINT | VG-E | F-G |
|---|---|---|---|
| ☐ 372 Eric Show | .15 | .06 | .01 |
| ☐ 373 Garry Templeton | .12 | .05 | .01 |
| ☐ 374 Chris Welsh | .03 | .01 | .00 |
| ☐ 375 Alan Wiggins | .30 | .12 | .03 |
| **NEW YORK YANKEES** | | | |
| ☐ 376 Rick Cerone | .05 | .02 | .00 |
| ☐ 377 Dave Collins | .06 | .02 | .00 |
| ☐ 378 Roger Erickson | .03 | .01 | .00 |
| ☐ 379 George Frazier | .03 | .01 | .00 |
| ☐ 380 Oscar Gamble | .06 | .02 | .00 |
| ☐ 381 Goose Gossage | .20 | .09 | .02 |
| ☐ 382 Ken Griffey | .09 | .04 | .01 |
| ☐ 383 Ron Guidry | .20 | .09 | .02 |
| ☐ 384 Dave LaRoche | .03 | .01 | .00 |
| ☐ 385 Rudy May | .03 | .01 | .00 |
| ☐ 386 John Mayberry | .06 | .02 | .00 |
| ☐ 387 Lee Mazzilli | .06 | .02 | .00 |
| ☐ 388 Mike Morgan | .03 | .01 | .00 |
| ☐ 389 Jerry Mumphrey | .05 | .02 | .00 |
| ☐ 390 Bobby Murcer | .10 | .04 | .01 |
| ☐ 391 Graig Nettles | .14 | .06 | .01 |
| ☐ 392 Lou Piniella | .10 | .04 | .01 |
| ☐ 393 Willie Randolph | .06 | .02 | .00 |
| ☐ 394 Shane Rawley | .05 | .02 | .00 |
| ☐ 395 Dave Righetti | .14 | .06 | .01 |
| ☐ 396 Andre Robertson | .03 | .01 | .00 |
| ☐ 397 Roy Smalley | .05 | .02 | .00 |
| ☐ 398 Dave Winfield | .35 | .15 | .03 |
| ☐ 399 Butch Wynegar | .06 | .02 | .00 |
| **CLEVELAND INDIANS** | | | |
| ☐ 400 Chris Bando | .03 | .01 | .00 |
| ☐ 401 Alan Bannister | .03 | .01 | .00 |
| ☐ 402 Len Barker | .06 | .02 | .00 |
| ☐ 403 Tom Brennan | .03 | .01 | .00 |
| ☐ 404 Carmelo Castillo | .10 | .04 | .01 |
| ☐ 405 Miguel Dilone | .03 | .01 | .00 |
| ☐ 406 Jerry Dybzinski | .03 | .01 | .00 |
| ☐ 407 Mike Fischlin | .03 | .01 | .00 |
| ☐ 408 Ed Glynn | .03 | .01 | .00 |
| ☐ 409 Mike Hargrove | .05 | .02 | .00 |
| ☐ 410 Toby Harrah | .06 | .02 | .00 |
| ☐ 411 Ron Hassey | .03 | .01 | .00 |
| ☐ 412 Von Hayes | .12 | .05 | .01 |
| ☐ 413 Rick Manning | .03 | .01 | .00 |
| ☐ 414 Bake McBride | .03 | .01 | .00 |
| ☐ 415 Larry Milbourne | .03 | .01 | .00 |
| ☐ 416 Bill Nahorodny | .03 | .01 | .00 |
| ☐ 417 Jack Perconte | .03 | .01 | .00 |
| ☐ 418 Lary Sorensen | .03 | .01 | .00 |
| ☐ 419 Dan Spillner | .03 | .01 | .00 |
| ☐ 420 Rick Sutcliffe | .20 | .09 | .02 |
| ☐ 421 Andre Thornton | .08 | .03 | .01 |
| ☐ 422 Rick Waits | .03 | .01 | .00 |

| | MINT | VG-E | F-G |
|---|---|---|---|
| ☐ 423 Eddie Whitson | .07 | .03 | .01 |
| **TORONTO BLUE JAYS** | | | |
| ☐ 424 Jesse Barfield | .10 | .04 | .01 |
| ☐ 425 Barry Bonnell | .05 | .02 | .00 |
| ☐ 426 Jim Clancy | .03 | .01 | .00 |
| ☐ 427 Damaso Garcia | .10 | .04 | .01 |
| ☐ 428 Jerry Garvin | .03 | .01 | .00 |
| ☐ 429 Alfredo Griffin | .05 | .02 | .00 |
| ☐ 430 Garth Iorg | .03 | .01 | .00 |
| ☐ 431 Roy Lee Jackson | .03 | .01 | .00 |
| ☐ 432 Luis Leal | .03 | .01 | .00 |
| ☐ 433 Buck Martinez | .03 | .01 | .00 |
| ☐ 434 Joey McLaughlin | .03 | .01 | .00 |
| ☐ 435 Lloyd Moseby | .14 | .06 | .01 |
| ☐ 436 Rance Mulliniks | .03 | .01 | .00 |
| ☐ 437 Dale Murray | .03 | .01 | .00 |
| ☐ 438 Wayne Nordhagen | .03 | .01 | .00 |
| ☐ 439 Gene Petralli | .05 | .02 | .00 |
| ☐ 440 Hosken Powell | .03 | .01 | .00 |
| ☐ 441 Dave Stieb | .20 | .09 | .02 |
| ☐ 442 Willie Upshaw | .13 | .06 | .01 |
| ☐ 443 Ernie Whitt | .03 | .01 | .00 |
| ☐ 444 Al Woods | .03 | .01 | .00 |
| **HOUSTON ASTROS** | | | |
| ☐ 445 Alan Ashby | .03 | .01 | .00 |
| ☐ 446 Jose Cruz | .14 | .06 | .01 |
| ☐ 447 Kiko Garcia | .03 | .01 | .00 |
| ☐ 448 Phil Garner | .05 | .02 | .00 |
| ☐ 449 Danny Heep | .03 | .01 | .00 |
| ☐ 450 Art Howe | .03 | .01 | .00 |
| ☐ 451 Bob Knepper | .06 | .02 | .00 |
| ☐ 452 Alan Knicely | .03 | .01 | .00 |
| ☐ 453 Ray Knight | .05 | .02 | .00 |
| ☐ 454 Frank LaCorte | .03 | .01 | .00 |
| ☐ 455 Mike LaCoss | .03 | .01 | .00 |
| ☐ 456 Randy Moffitt | .03 | .01 | .00 |
| ☐ 457 Joe Niekro | .06 | .02 | .00 |
| ☐ 458 Terry Puhl | .03 | .01 | .00 |
| ☐ 459 Luis Pujols | .03 | .01 | .00 |
| ☐ 460 Craig Reynolds | .03 | .01 | .00 |
| ☐ 461 Bert Roberge | .03 | .01 | .00 |
| ☐ 462 Vern Ruhle | .03 | .01 | .00 |
| ☐ 463 Nolan Ryan | .25 | .10 | .02 |
| ☐ 464 Joe Sambito | .05 | .02 | .00 |
| ☐ 465 Tony Scott | .03 | .01 | .00 |
| ☐ 466 Dave Smith | .03 | .01 | .00 |
| ☐ 467 Harry Spilman | .03 | .01 | .00 |
| ☐ 468 Dickie Thon | .08 | .03 | .01 |
| ☐ 469 Denny Walling | .03 | .01 | .00 |
| **SEATTLE MARINERS** | | | |
| ☐ 470 Larry Andersen | .03 | .01 | .00 |
| ☐ 471 Floyd Bannister | .08 | .03 | .01 |
| ☐ 472 Jim Beattie | .03 | .01 | .00 |

| | | MINT | VG-E | F-G |
|---|---|---|---|---|
| ☐ 473 | Bruce Bochte | .05 | .02 | .00 |
| ☐ 474 | Manny Castillo | .03 | .01 | .00 |
| ☐ 475 | Bill Caudill | .07 | .03 | .01 |
| ☐ 476 | Bryan Clark | .05 | .02 | .00 |
| ☐ 477 | Al Cowens | .05 | .02 | .00 |
| ☐ 478 | Julio Cruz | .03 | .01 | .00 |
| ☐ 479 | Todd Cruz | .03 | .01 | .00 |
| ☐ 480 | Gary Gray | .03 | .01 | .00 |
| ☐ 481 | Dave Henderson | .05 | .02 | .00 |
| ☐ 482 | Mike Moore | .25 | .10 | .02 |
| ☐ 483 | Gaylord Perry | .20 | .09 | .02 |
| ☐ 484 | Dave Revering | .03 | .01 | .00 |
| ☐ 485 | Joe Simpson | .03 | .01 | .00 |
| ☐ 486 | Mike Stanton | .03 | .01 | .00 |
| ☐ 487 | Rick Sweet | .03 | .01 | .00 |
| ☐ 488 | Ed VandeBerg | .15 | .06 | .01 |
| ☐ 489 | Richie Zisk | .05 | .02 | .00 |
| | CHICAGO CUBS | | | |
| ☐ 490 | Doug Bird | .03 | .01 | .00 |
| ☐ 491 | Larry Bowa | .09 | .04 | .01 |
| ☐ 492 | Bill Buckner | .11 | .05 | .01 |
| ☐ 493 | Bill Campbell | .05 | .02 | .00 |
| ☐ 494 | Jody Davis | .11 | .05 | .01 |
| ☐ 495 | Leon Durham | .18 | .08 | .01 |
| ☐ 496 | Steve Henderson | .03 | .01 | .00 |
| ☐ 497 | Willie Hernandez | .20 | .09 | .02 |
| ☐ 498 | Ferguson Jenkins | .13 | .06 | .01 |
| ☐ 499 | Jay Johnstone | .05 | .02 | .00 |
| ☐ 500 | Junior Kennedy | .03 | .01 | .00 |
| ☐ 501 | Randy Martz | .03 | .01 | .00 |
| ☐ 502 | Jerry Morales | .03 | .01 | .00 |
| ☐ 503 | Keith Moreland | .05 | .02 | .00 |
| ☐ 504 | Dickie Noles | .03 | .01 | .00 |
| ☐ 505 | Mike Proly | .03 | .01 | .00 |
| ☐ 506 | Allen Ripley | .03 | .01 | .00 |
| ☐ 507 | Ryne Sandberg | 2.75 | 1.25 | .27 |
| ☐ 508 | Lee Smith | .10 | .04 | .01 |
| ☐ 509 | Pat Tabler | .06 | .02 | .00 |
| ☐ 510 | Dick Tidrow | .03 | .01 | .00 |
| ☐ 511 | Bump Wills | .03 | .01 | .00 |
| ☐ 512 | Gary Woods | .03 | .01 | .00 |
| | OAKLAND A'S | | | |
| ☐ 513 | Tony Armas | .15 | .06 | .01 |
| ☐ 514 | Dave Beard | .03 | .01 | .00 |
| ☐ 515 | Jeff Burroughs | .05 | .02 | .00 |
| ☐ 516 | John D'Acquisto | .03 | .01 | .00 |
| ☐ 517 | Wayne Gross | .03 | .01 | .00 |
| ☐ 518 | Mike Heath | .03 | .01 | .00 |
| ☐ 519 | Rickey Henderson | .50 | .22 | .05 |
| ☐ 520 | Cliff Johnson | .03 | .01 | .00 |
| ☐ 521 | Matt Keough | .05 | .02 | .00 |
| ☐ 522 | Brian Kingman | .03 | .01 | .00 |
| ☐ 523 | Rick Langford | .03 | .01 | .00 |
| ☐ 524 | Davey Lopes | .06 | .02 | .00 |
| ☐ 525 | Steve McCatty | .05 | .02 | .00 |
| ☐ 526 | Dave McKay | .03 | .01 | .00 |
| ☐ 527 | Dan Meyer | .03 | .01 | .00 |
| ☐ 528 | Dwayne Murphy | .06 | .02 | .00 |
| ☐ 529 | Jeff Newman | .03 | .01 | .00 |
| ☐ 530 | Mike Norris | .05 | .02 | .00 |
| ☐ 531 | Bob Owchinko | .03 | .01 | .00 |
| ☐ 532 | Joe Rudi | .06 | .02 | .00 |
| ☐ 533 | Jimmy Sexton | .03 | .01 | .00 |
| ☐ 534 | Fred Stanley | .03 | .01 | .00 |
| ☐ 535 | Tom Underwood | .03 | .01 | .00 |
| | NEW YORK METS | | | |
| ☐ 536 | Neil Allen | .06 | .02 | .00 |
| ☐ 537 | Wally Backman | .05 | .02 | .00 |
| ☐ 538 | Bob Bailor | .03 | .01 | .00 |
| ☐ 539 | Hube Brooks | .10 | .04 | .01 |
| ☐ 540 | Carlos Diaz | .12 | .05 | .01 |
| ☐ 541 | Pete Falcone | .03 | .01 | .00 |
| ☐ 542 | George Foster | .18 | .08 | .01 |
| ☐ 543 | Ron Gardenhire | .03 | .01 | .00 |
| ☐ 544 | Brian Giles | .06 | .02 | .00 |
| ☐ 545 | Ron Hodges | .03 | .01 | .00 |
| ☐ 546 | Randy Jones | .05 | .02 | .00 |
| ☐ 547 | Mike Jorgensen | .03 | .01 | .00 |
| ☐ 548 | Dave Kingman | .13 | .06 | .01 |
| ☐ 549 | Ed Lynch | .03 | .01 | .00 |
| ☐ 550 | Jesse Orosco | .08 | .03 | .01 |
| ☐ 551 | Rick Ownbey | .09 | .04 | .01 |
| ☐ 552 | Charlie Puleo | .06 | .02 | .00 |
| ☐ 553 | Gary Rajsich | .06 | .02 | .00 |
| ☐ 554 | Mike Scott | .06 | .02 | .00 |
| ☐ 555 | Rusty Staub | .10 | .04 | .01 |
| ☐ 556 | John Stearns | .03 | .01 | .00 |
| ☐ 557 | Craig Swan | .03 | .01 | .00 |
| ☐ 558 | Ellis Valentine | .03 | .01 | .00 |
| ☐ 559 | Tom Veryzer | .03 | .01 | .00 |
| ☐ 560 | Mookie Wilson | .09 | .04 | .01 |
| ☐ 561 | Pat Zachry | .03 | .01 | .00 |
| | TEXAS RANGERS | | | |
| ☐ 562 | Buddy Bell | .13 | .06 | .01 |
| ☐ 563 | John Butcher | .03 | .01 | .00 |
| ☐ 564 | Steve Comer | .03 | .01 | .00 |
| ☐ 565 | Danny Darwin | .03 | .01 | .00 |
| ☐ 566 | Bucky Dent | .06 | .02 | .00 |
| ☐ 567 | John Grubb | .03 | .01 | .00 |
| ☐ 568 | Rick Honeycutt | .05 | .02 | .00 |
| ☐ 569 | Dave Hostetler | .09 | .04 | .01 |
| ☐ 570 | Charlie Hough | .05 | .02 | .00 |
| ☐ 571 | Lamar Johnson | .03 | .01 | .00 |
| ☐ 572 | Jon Matlack | .05 | .02 | .00 |
| ☐ 573 | Paul Mirabella | .03 | .01 | .00 |
| ☐ 574 | Larry Parrish | .06 | .02 | .00 |

| | MINT | VG-E | F-G |
|---|---|---|---|
| ☐ 575 Mike Richardt | .06 | .02 | .00 |
| ☐ 576 Mickey Rivers | .06 | .02 | .00 |
| ☐ 577 Billy Sample | .03 | .01 | .00 |
| ☐ 578 Dave Schmidt | .03 | .01 | .00 |
| ☐ 579 Bill Stein | .03 | .01 | .00 |
| ☐ 580 Jim Sundberg | .06 | .02 | .00 |
| ☐ 581 Frank Tanana | .05 | .02 | .00 |
| ☐ 582 Mark Wagner | .03 | .01 | .00 |
| ☐ 583 George Wright | .15 | .06 | .01 |
| **CINCINNATI REDS** | | | |
| ☐ 584 Johnny Bench | .35 | .15 | .03 |
| ☐ 585 Bruce Berenyi | .05 | .02 | .00 |
| ☐ 586 Larry Biittner | .03 | .01 | .00 |
| ☐ 587 Cesar Cedeno | .09 | .04 | .01 |
| ☐ 588 Dave Concepcion | .10 | .04 | .01 |
| ☐ 589 Dan Driessen | .05 | .02 | .00 |
| ☐ 590 Greg Harris | .03 | .01 | .00 |
| ☐ 591 Ben Hayes | .06 | .02 | .00 |
| ☐ 592 Paul Householder | .05 | .02 | .00 |
| ☐ 593 Tom Hume | .03 | .01 | .00 |
| ☐ 594 Wayne Krenchicki | .03 | .01 | .00 |
| ☐ 595 Rafael Landestoy | .03 | .01 | .00 |
| ☐ 596 Charlie Leibrandt | .08 | .03 | .01 |
| ☐ 597 Eddie Milner | .12 | .05 | .01 |
| ☐ 598 Ron Oester | .05 | .02 | .00 |
| ☐ 599 Frank Pastore | .03 | .01 | .00 |
| ☐ 600 Joe Price | .03 | .01 | .00 |
| ☐ 601 Tom Seaver | .30 | .12 | .03 |
| ☐ 602 Bob Shirley | .03 | .01 | .00 |
| ☐ 603 Mario Soto | .11 | .05 | .01 |
| ☐ 604 Alex Trevino | .03 | .01 | .00 |
| ☐ 605 Mike Vail | .03 | .01 | .00 |
| ☐ 606 Duane Walker | .15 | .06 | .01 |
| **MINNESOTA TWINS** | | | |
| ☐ 607 Tom Brunansky | .20 | .09 | .02 |
| ☐ 608 Bobby Castillo | .03 | .01 | .00 |
| ☐ 609 John Castino | .03 | .01 | .00 |
| ☐ 610 Ron Davis | .05 | .02 | .00 |
| ☐ 611 Lenny Faedo | .03 | .01 | .00 |
| ☐ 612 Terry Felton | .06 | .02 | .00 |
| ☐ 613 Gary Gaetti | .25 | .10 | .02 |
| ☐ 614 Mickey Hatcher | .05 | .02 | .00 |
| ☐ 615 Brad Havens | .03 | .01 | .00 |
| ☐ 616 Kent Hrbek | .35 | .15 | .03 |
| ☐ 617 Randy Johnson | .05 | .02 | .00 |
| ☐ 618 Tim Laudner | .03 | .01 | .00 |
| ☐ 619 Jeff Little | .06 | .02 | .00 |
| ☐ 620 Bob Mitchell | .03 | .01 | .00 |
| ☐ 621 Jack O'Connor | .03 | .01 | .00 |
| ☐ 622 John Pacella | .03 | .01 | .00 |
| ☐ 623 Pete Redfern | .03 | .01 | .00 |
| ☐ 624 Jesus Vega | .06 | .02 | .00 |
| ☐ 625 Frank Viola | .50 | .22 | .05 |

| | MINT | VG-E | F-G |
|---|---|---|---|
| ☐ 626 Ron Washington | .10 | .04 | .01 |
| ☐ 627 Gary Ward | .06 | .02 | .00 |
| ☐ 628 Al Williams | .03 | .01 | .00 |
| **SPECIALS (629–646)** | | | |
| ☐ 629 Red Sox All-Stars: | .18 | .08 | .01 |
| Carl Yastrzemski | | | |
| Dennis Eckersley | | | |
| Mark Clear | | | |
| ☐ 630 "300 Career Wins" | .13 | .06 | .01 |
| Gaylord Perry and | | | |
| Terry Bulling 5 / 6 / 82 | | | |
| ☐ 631 Pride of Venezuela | .08 | .03 | .01 |
| Dave Concepcion and | | | |
| Manny Trillo | | | |
| ☐ 632 All-Star Infielders | .15 | .06 | .01 |
| Robin Yount and | | | |
| Buddy Bell | | | |
| ☐ 633 Mr. Vet and Mr. Rookie: | .20 | .08 | .01 |
| Dave Winfield and | | | |
| Kent Hrbek | | | |
| ☐ 634 Fountain of Youth: | .50 | .22 | .05 |
| Willie Stargell and | | | |
| Pete Rose | | | |
| ☐ 635 Big Chiefs: | .08 | .03 | .01 |
| Toby Harrah and | | | |
| Andre Thornton | | | |
| ☐ 636 Smith Brothers: | .09 | .04 | .01 |
| Ozzie and Lonnie | | | |
| ☐ 637 Base Stealers' Threat: | .12 | .05 | .01 |
| Bo Diaz and | | | |
| Gary Carter | | | |
| ☐ 638 All-Star Catchers: | .15 | .06 | .01 |
| Carlton Fisk and | | | |
| Gary Carter | | | |
| ☐ 639 The Silver Shoe: | .30 | .12 | .03 |
| Rickey Henderson | | | |
| ☐ 640 Home Run Threats: | .18 | .08 | .01 |
| Ben Oglivie and | | | |
| Reggie Jackson | | | |
| ☐ 641 Two Teams on Same | | | |
| Day: | .06 | .02 | .00 |
| Joel Youngblood | | | |
| 8 / 4 / 82 | | | |
| ☐ 642 Last Perfect Game: | .07 | .03 | .01 |
| Ron Hassey and | | | |
| Len Barker | | | |
| ☐ 643 Black and Blue: | .07 | .03 | .01 |
| Bud Black | | | |
| ☐ 644 Black and Blue: | .07 | .03 | .01 |
| Vida Blue | | | |
| ☐ 645 Speed and Power: | .30 | .12 | .03 |
| Reggie Jackson | | | |

|  | MINT | VG-E | F-G |
|---|---|---|---|
| ☐ 646 Speed and Power: ...... Rickey Henderson ..... | .30 | .12 | .03 |
| CHECKLISTS (647-660) | | | |
| ☐ 647 CL: Cards/Brewers ... | .07 | .01 | .00 |
| ☐ 648 CL: Orioles/Angels ... | .07 | .01 | .00 |
| ☐ 649 CL: Royals/Braves .... | .07 | .01 | .00 |
| ☐ 650 CL: Phillies/Red Sox . | .07 | .01 | .00 |
| ☐ 651 CL: Dodgers/White Sox . | .07 | .01 | .00 |
| ☐ 652 CL: Giants/Expos .... | .07 | .01 | .00 |
| ☐ 653 CL: Pirates/Tigers .... | .07 | .01 | .00 |
| ☐ 654 CL: Padres/Yankees ... | .07 | .01 | .00 |
| ☐ 655 CL: Indians/Blue Jays ... | .07 | .01 | .00 |
| ☐ 656 CL: Astros/Mariners ... | .07 | .01 | .00 |
| ☐ 657 CL: Cubs/A's .......... | .07 | .01 | .00 |
| ☐ 658 CL: Mets/Rangers .... | .07 | .01 | .00 |
| ☐ 659 CL: Reds/Twins ...... | .07 | .01 | .00 |
| ☐ 660 CL: Specials/Teams .... | .09 | .01 | .00 |

## 1984 FLEER

The cards in this 660 card set measure 2½" by 3½". The 1984 Fleer card set featured fronts with full color team logos along with the player's name and position and the Fleer identification. The set features many imaginative photos, several multi-player cards, and many more action shots than the 1983 card set. The backs are quite similar to the 1983 backs except that blue rather than brown ink is used.

Complete Set: M-18.00; VG-E-8.50; F-G-1.80

| Common Player (1–660) | .03 | .01 | .00 |
|---|---|---|---|

BALTIMORE ORIOLES

|  | MINT | VG-E | F-G |
|---|---|---|---|
| ☐ 1 Mike Boddicker ........ | .18 | .05 | .01 |
| ☐ 2 Al Bumbry ............. | .03 | .01 | .00 |

|  | MINT | VG-E | F-G |
|---|---|---|---|
| ☐ 3 Todd Cruz ............. | .03 | .01 | .00 |
| ☐ 4 Rich Dauer ............ | .03 | .01 | .00 |
| ☐ 5 Storm Davis ........... | .09 | .04 | .01 |
| ☐ 6 Rick Dempsey ......... | .05 | .02 | .00 |
| ☐ 7 Jim Dwyer ............ | .03 | .01 | .00 |
| ☐ 8 Mike Flanagan ........ | .08 | .03 | .01 |
| ☐ 9 Dan Ford ............. | .05 | .02 | .00 |
| ☐ 10 John Lowenstein ...... | .03 | .01 | .00 |
| ☐ 11 Dennis Martinez ...... | .03 | .01 | .00 |
| ☐ 12 Tippy Martinez ....... | .05 | .02 | .00 |
| ☐ 13 Scott McGregor ....... | .08 | .03 | .01 |
| ☐ 14 Eddie Murray ......... | .50 | .22 | .05 |
| ☐ 15 Joe Nolan ........... | .03 | .01 | .00 |
| ☐ 16 Jim Palmer .......... | .25 | .10 | .02 |
| ☐ 17 Cal Ripken .......... | .60 | .28 | .06 |
| ☐ 18 Gary Roenicke ....... | .05 | .02 | .00 |
| ☐ 19 Lenn Sakata ......... | .03 | .01 | .00 |
| ☐ 20 John Shelby ......... | .09 | .04 | .01 |
| ☐ 21 Ken Singleton ....... | .09 | .04 | .01 |
| ☐ 22 Sammy Stewart ...... | .03 | .01 | .00 |
| ☐ 23 Tim Stoddard ........ | .03 | .01 | .00 |
| PHILADELPHIA PHILLIES | | | |
| ☐ 24 Marty Bystrom ....... | .03 | .01 | .00 |
| ☐ 25 Steve Carlton ........ | .30 | .12 | .03 |
| ☐ 26 Ivan DeJesus ........ | .03 | .01 | .00 |
| ☐ 27 John Denny .......... | .08 | .03 | .01 |
| ☐ 28 Bob Dernier ......... | .07 | .03 | .01 |
| ☐ 29 Bo Diaz ............. | .06 | .02 | .00 |
| ☐ 30 Kiko Garcia .......... | .03 | .01 | .00 |
| ☐ 31 Greg Gross .......... | .03 | .01 | .00 |
| ☐ 32 Kevin Gross ......... | .13 | .06 | .01 |
| ☐ 33 Von Hayes .......... | .11 | .05 | .01 |
| ☐ 34 Willie Hernandez ..... | .20 | .09 | .02 |
| ☐ 35 Al Holland .......... | .06 | .02 | .00 |
| ☐ 36 Charles Hudson ...... | .12 | .05 | .01 |
| ☐ 37 Joe Lefebvre ........ | .03 | .01 | .00 |
| ☐ 38 Sixto Lezcano ....... | .03 | .01 | .00 |
| ☐ 39 Garry Maddox ....... | .05 | .02 | .00 |
| ☐ 40 Gary Matthews ...... | .09 | .04 | .01 |
| ☐ 41 Len Matuszek ....... | .03 | .01 | .00 |
| ☐ 42 Tug McGraw ........ | .09 | .04 | .01 |
| ☐ 43 Joe Morgan ......... | .16 | .07 | .01 |
| ☐ 44 Tony Perez ......... | .13 | .06 | .01 |
| ☐ 45 Ron Reed ........... | .03 | .01 | .00 |
| ☐ 46 Pete Rose .......... | .65 | .30 | .06 |
| ☐ 47 Juan Samuel ........ | 2.00 | .90 | .20 |
| ☐ 48 Mike Schmidt ........ | .40 | .18 | .04 |
| ☐ 49 Ozzie Virgil ......... | .03 | .01 | .00 |
| CHICAGO WHITE SOX | | | |
| ☐ 50 Juan Agosto ......... | .07 | .03 | .01 |
| ☐ 51 Harold Baines ....... | .20 | .09 | .02 |
| ☐ 52 Floyd Bannister ...... | .08 | .03 | .01 |

|  | MINT | VG-E | F-G |
|---|---|---|---|
| 53 Salome Barojas | .03 | .01 | .00 |
| 54 Britt Burns | .08 | .03 | .01 |
| 55 Julio Cruz | .03 | .01 | .00 |
| 56 Richard Dotson | .08 | .03 | .01 |
| 57 Jerry Dybzinski | .03 | .01 | .00 |
| 58 Carlton Fisk | .16 | .07 | .01 |
| 59 Scott Fletcher | .03 | .01 | .00 |
| 60 Jerry Hairston | .03 | .01 | .00 |
| 61 Kevin Hickey | .03 | .01 | .00 |
| 62 Marc Hill | .03 | .01 | .00 |
| 63 LaMarr Hoyt | .11 | .05 | .01 |
| 64 Ron Kittle | .18 | .08 | .01 |
| 65 Jerry Koosman | .07 | .03 | .01 |
| 66 Dennis Lamp | .03 | .01 | .00 |
| 67 Rudy Law | .03 | .01 | .00 |
| 68 Vance Law | .03 | .01 | .00 |
| 69 Greg Luzinski | .11 | .05 | .01 |
| 70 Tom Paciorek | .03 | .01 | .00 |
| 71 Mike Squires | .03 | .01 | .00 |
| 72 Dick Tidrow | .03 | .01 | .00 |
| 73 Greg Walker | .55 | .25 | .05 |
| DETROIT TIGERS | | | |
| 74 Glenn Abbott | .03 | .01 | .00 |
| 75 Howard Bailey | .03 | .01 | .00 |
| 76 Doug Bair | .03 | .01 | .00 |
| 77 Juan Berenguer | .03 | .01 | .00 |
| 78 Tom Brookens | .03 | .01 | .00 |
| 79 Enos Cabell | .03 | .01 | .00 |
| 80 Kirk Gibson | .25 | .10 | .02 |
| 81 John Grubb | .03 | .01 | .00 |
| 82 Larry Herndon | .05 | .02 | .00 |
| 83 Wayne Krenchicki | .03 | .01 | .00 |
| 84 Rick Leach | .03 | .01 | .00 |
| 85 Chet Lemon | .08 | .03 | .01 |
| 86 Aurelio Lopez | .05 | .02 | .00 |
| 87 Jack Morris | .20 | .09 | .02 |
| 88 Lance Parrish | .25 | .10 | .02 |
| 89 Dan Petry | .16 | .07 | .01 |
| 90 Dave Rozema | .03 | .01 | .00 |
| 91 Alan Trammell | .25 | .10 | .02 |
| 92 Lou Whitaker | .20 | .09 | .02 |
| 93 Milt Wilcox | .03 | .01 | .00 |
| 94 Glenn Wilson | .10 | .04 | .01 |
| 95 John Wockenfuss | .03 | .01 | .00 |
| LOS ANGELES DODGERS | | | |
| 96 Dusty Baker | .09 | .04 | .01 |
| 97 Joe Beckwith | .03 | .01 | .00 |
| 98 Greg Brock | .09 | .04 | .01 |
| 99 Jack Fimple | .08 | .03 | .01 |
| 100 Pedro Guerrero | .25 | .10 | .02 |
| 101 Rick Honeycutt | .05 | .02 | .00 |
| 102 Burt Hooton | .03 | .01 | .00 |

|  | MINT | VG-E | F-G |
|---|---|---|---|
| 103 Steve Howe | .05 | .02 | .00 |
| 104 Ken Landreaux | .05 | .02 | .00 |
| 105 Mike Marshall | .15 | .06 | .01 |
| 106 Rick Monday | .05 | .02 | .00 |
| 107 Jose Morales | .03 | .01 | .00 |
| 108 Tom Niedenfuer | .07 | .03 | .01 |
| 109 Alejandro Pena | .20 | .09 | .02 |
| 110 Jerry Reuss | .08 | .03 | .01 |
| 111 Bill Russell | .05 | .02 | .00 |
| 112 Steve Sax | .14 | .06 | .01 |
| 113 Mike Scioscia | .03 | .01 | .00 |
| 114 Derrel Thomas | .03 | .01 | .00 |
| 115 Fernando Valenzuela | .30 | .12 | .03 |
| 116 Bob Welch | .07 | .03 | .01 |
| 117 Steve Yeager | .05 | .02 | .00 |
| 118 Pat Zachry | .03 | .01 | .00 |
| NEW YORK YANKEES | | | |
| 119 Don Baylor | .12 | .05 | .01 |
| 120 Bert Campaneris | .06 | .02 | .00 |
| 121 Rick Cerone | .05 | .02 | .00 |
| 122 Ray Fontenot | .12 | .05 | .01 |
| 123 George Frazier | .03 | .01 | .00 |
| 124 Oscar Gamble | .06 | .02 | .00 |
| 125 Goose Gossage | .16 | .07 | .01 |
| 126 Ken Griffey | .09 | .04 | .01 |
| 127 Ron Guidry | .16 | .07 | .01 |
| 128 Jay Howell | .06 | .02 | .00 |
| 129 Steve Kemp | .08 | .03 | .01 |
| 130 Matt Keough | .05 | .02 | .00 |
| 131 Don Mattingly | 3.75 | 1.25 | .25 |
| 132 John Montefusco | .05 | .02 | .00 |
| 133 Omar Moreno | .05 | .02 | .00 |
| 134 Dale Murray | .03 | .01 | .00 |
| 135 Graig Nettles | .13 | .06 | .01 |
| 136 Lou Piniella | .09 | .04 | .01 |
| 137 Willie Randolph | .07 | .03 | .01 |
| 138 Shane Rawley | .05 | .02 | .00 |
| 139 Dave Righetti | .13 | .06 | .01 |
| 140 Andre Robertson | .03 | .01 | .00 |
| 141 Bob Shirley | .03 | .01 | .00 |
| 142 Roy Smalley | .05 | .02 | .00 |
| 143 Dave Winfield | .30 | .12 | .03 |
| 144 Butch Wynegar | .06 | .02 | .00 |
| TORONTO BLUE JAYS | | | |
| 145 Jim Acker | .13 | .06 | .01 |
| 146 Doyle Alexander | .06 | .02 | .00 |
| 147 Jesse Barfield | .10 | .04 | .01 |
| 148 Jorge Bell | .10 | .04 | .01 |
| 149 Barry Bonnell | .03 | .01 | .00 |
| 150 Jim Clancy | .03 | .01 | .00 |
| 151 Dave Collins | .05 | .02 | .00 |
| 152 Tony Fernandez | .40 | .18 | .04 |
| 153 Damaso Garcia | .09 | .04 | .01 |

|  | MINT | VG-E | F-G |
|---|---|---|---|
| ☐ 154 Dave Geisel | .03 | .01 | .00 |
| ☐ 155 Jim Gott | .03 | .01 | .00 |
| ☐ 156 Alfredo Griffin | .05 | .02 | .00 |
| ☐ 157 Garth Iorg | .03 | .01 | .00 |
| ☐ 158 Roy Lee Jackson | .03 | .01 | .00 |
| ☐ 159 Cliff Johnson | .03 | .01 | .00 |
| ☐ 160 Luis Leal | .03 | .01 | .00 |
| ☐ 161 Buck Martinez | .03 | .01 | .00 |
| ☐ 162 Joey McLaughlin | .03 | .01 | .00 |
| ☐ 163 Randy Moffitt | .03 | .01 | .00 |
| ☐ 164 Lloyd Moseby | .13 | .06 | .01 |
| ☐ 165 Rance Mulliniks | .03 | .01 | .00 |
| ☐ 166 Jorge Orta | .03 | .01 | .00 |
| ☐ 167 Dave Stieb | .20 | .09 | .02 |
| ☐ 168 Willie Upshaw | .13 | .06 | .01 |
| ☐ 169 Ernie Whitt | .03 | .01 | .00 |
| **ATLANTA BRAVES** | | | |
| ☐ 170 Len Barker | .08 | .03 | .01 |
| ☐ 171 Steve Bedrosian | .07 | .03 | .01 |
| ☐ 172 Bruce Benedict | .03 | .01 | .00 |
| ☐ 173 Brett Butler | .09 | .04 | .01 |
| ☐ 174 Rick Camp | .03 | .01 | .00 |
| ☐ 175 Chris Chambliss | .05 | .02 | .00 |
| ☐ 176 Ken Dayley | .03 | .01 | .00 |
| ☐ 177 Pete Falcone | .03 | .01 | .00 |
| ☐ 178 Terry Forster | .07 | .03 | .01 |
| ☐ 179 Gene Garber | .03 | .01 | .00 |
| ☐ 180 Terry Harper | .03 | .01 | .00 |
| ☐ 181 Bob Horner | .20 | .09 | .02 |
| ☐ 182 Glenn Hubbard | .05 | .02 | .00 |
| ☐ 183 Randy Johnson | .03 | .01 | .00 |
| ☐ 184 Craig McMurtry | .12 | .05 | .01 |
| ☐ 185 Donnie Moore | .08 | .03 | .01 |
| ☐ 186 Dale Murphy | .60 | .28 | .06 |
| ☐ 187 Phil Niekro | .16 | .07 | .01 |
| ☐ 188 Pascual Perez | .06 | .02 | .00 |
| ☐ 189 Biff Pocoroba | .03 | .01 | .00 |
| ☐ 190 Rafael Ramirez | .05 | .02 | .00 |
| ☐ 191 Jerry Royster | .03 | .01 | .00 |
| ☐ 192 Claudell Washington | .09 | .04 | .01 |
| ☐ 193 Bob Watson | .06 | .02 | .00 |
| **MILWAUKEE BREWERS** | | | |
| ☐ 194 Jerry Augustine | .03 | .01 | .00 |
| ☐ 195 Mark Brouhard | .03 | .01 | .00 |
| ☐ 196 Mike Caldwell | .05 | .02 | .00 |
| ☐ 197 Tom Candiotti | .07 | .03 | .01 |
| ☐ 198 Cecil Cooper | .16 | .07 | .01 |
| ☐ 199 Rollie Fingers | .16 | .07 | .01 |
| ☐ 200 Jim Gantner | .05 | .02 | .00 |
| ☐ 201 Bob L. Gibson | .08 | .03 | .01 |
| ☐ 202 Moose Haas | .05 | .02 | .00 |
| ☐ 203 Roy Howell | .03 | .01 | .00 |
| ☐ 204 Pete Ladd | .03 | .01 | .00 |
| ☐ 205 Rick Manning | .03 | .01 | .00 |
| ☐ 206 Bob McClure | .03 | .01 | .00 |
| ☐ 207 Paul Molitor | .12 | .05 | .01 |
| ☐ 208 Don Money | .03 | .01 | .00 |
| ☐ 209 Charlie Moore | .03 | .01 | .00 |
| ☐ 210 Ben Oglivie | .08 | .03 | .01 |
| ☐ 211 Chuck Porter | .03 | .01 | .00 |
| ☐ 212 Ed Romero | .03 | .01 | .00 |
| ☐ 213 Ted Simmons | .12 | .05 | .01 |
| ☐ 214 Jim Slaton | .03 | .01 | .00 |
| ☐ 215 Don Sutton | .13 | .06 | .01 |
| ☐ 216 Tom Tellmann | .03 | .01 | .00 |
| ☐ 217 Pete Vuckovich | .08 | .03 | .01 |
| ☐ 218 Ned Yost | .03 | .01 | .00 |
| ☐ 219 Robin Yount | .30 | .12 | .03 |
| **HOUSTON ASTROS** | | | |
| ☐ 220 Alan Ashby | .03 | .01 | .00 |
| ☐ 221 Kevin Bass | .05 | .02 | .00 |
| ☐ 222 Jose Cruz | .11 | .05 | .01 |
| ☐ 223 Bill Dawley | .16 | .07 | .01 |
| ☐ 224 Frank DiPino | .05 | .02 | .00 |
| ☐ 225 Bill Doran | .30 | .12 | .03 |
| ☐ 226 Phil Garner | .05 | .02 | .00 |
| ☐ 227 Art Howe | .03 | .01 | .00 |
| ☐ 228 Bob Knepper | .05 | .02 | .00 |
| ☐ 229 Ray Knight | .06 | .02 | .00 |
| ☐ 230 Frank LaCorte | .03 | .01 | .00 |
| ☐ 231 Mike LaCoss | .03 | .01 | .00 |
| ☐ 232 Mike Madden | .14 | .06 | .01 |
| ☐ 233 Jerry Mumphrey | .05 | .02 | .00 |
| ☐ 234 Joe Niekro | .06 | .02 | .00 |
| ☐ 235 Terry Puhl | .03 | .01 | .00 |
| ☐ 236 Luis Pujols | .03 | .01 | .00 |
| ☐ 237 Craig Reynolds | .03 | .01 | .00 |
| ☐ 238 Vern Ruhle | .03 | .01 | .00 |
| ☐ 239 Nolan Ryan | .25 | .10 | .02 |
| ☐ 240 Mike Scott | .05 | .02 | .00 |
| ☐ 241 Tony Scott | .03 | .01 | .00 |
| ☐ 242 Dave Smith | .03 | .01 | .00 |
| ☐ 243 Dickie Thon | .08 | .03 | .01 |
| ☐ 244 Denny Walling | .03 | .01 | .00 |
| **PITTSBURGH PIRATES** | | | |
| ☐ 245 Dale Berra | .06 | .02 | .00 |
| ☐ 246 Jim Bibby | .05 | .02 | .00 |
| ☐ 247 John Candelaria | .07 | .03 | .01 |
| ☐ 248 Jose DeLeon | .20 | .09 | .02 |
| ☐ 249 Mike Easler | .08 | .03 | .01 |
| ☐ 250 Cecilio Guante | .03 | .01 | .00 |
| ☐ 251 Richie Hebner | .03 | .01 | .00 |
| ☐ 252 Lee Lacy | .06 | .02 | .00 |
| ☐ 253 Bill Madlock | .14 | .06 | .01 |
| ☐ 254 Milt May | .03 | .01 | .00 |
| ☐ 255 Lee Mazzilli | .06 | .02 | .00 |

| | MINT | VG-E | F-G |
|---|---|---|---|
| ☐ 256 Larry McWilliams | .06 | .02 | .00 |
| ☐ 257 Jim Morrison | .03 | .01 | .00 |
| ☐ 258 Dave Parker | .20 | .09 | .02 |
| ☐ 259 Tony Pena | .14 | .06 | .01 |
| ☐ 260 Johnny Ray | .11 | .05 | .01 |
| ☐ 261 Rick Rhoden | .06 | .02 | .00 |
| ☐ 262 Don Robinson | .03 | .01 | .00 |
| ☐ 263 Manny Sarmiento | .03 | .01 | .00 |
| ☐ 264 Rod Scurry | .03 | .01 | .00 |
| ☐ 265 Kent Tekulve | .08 | .03 | .01 |
| ☐ 266 Gene Tenace | .03 | .01 | .00 |
| ☐ 267 Jason Thompson | .08 | .03 | .01 |
| ☐ 268 Lee Tunnell | .09 | .04 | .01 |
| ☐ 269 Marvell Wynne | .15 | .06 | .01 |
| **MONTREAL EXPOS** | | | |
| ☐ 270 Ray Burris | .03 | .01 | .00 |
| ☐ 271 Gary Carter | .35 | .15 | .03 |
| ☐ 272 Warren Cromartie | .03 | .01 | .00 |
| ☐ 273 Andre Dawson | .20 | .09 | .02 |
| ☐ 274 Doug Flynn | .03 | .01 | .00 |
| ☐ 275 Terry Francona | .08 | .03 | .01 |
| ☐ 276 Bill Gullickson | .06 | .02 | .00 |
| ☐ 277 Bob James | .20 | .09 | .02 |
| ☐ 278 Charlie Lea | .06 | .02 | .00 |
| ☐ 279 Bryan Little | .06 | .02 | .00 |
| ☐ 280 Al Oliver | .16 | .07 | .01 |
| ☐ 281 Tim Raines | .25 | .10 | .02 |
| ☐ 282 Bobby Ramos | .03 | .01 | .00 |
| ☐ 283 Jeff Reardon | .09 | .04 | .01 |
| ☐ 284 Steve Rogers | .08 | .03 | .01 |
| ☐ 285 Scott Sanderson | .05 | .02 | .00 |
| ☐ 286 Dan Schatzeder | .03 | .01 | .00 |
| ☐ 287 Bryn Smith | .05 | .02 | .00 |
| ☐ 288 Chris Speier | .03 | .01 | .00 |
| ☐ 289 Manny Trillo | .05 | .02 | .00 |
| ☐ 290 Mike Vail | .03 | .01 | .00 |
| ☐ 291 Tim Wallach | .11 | .05 | .01 |
| ☐ 292 Chris Welsh | .03 | .01 | .00 |
| ☐ 293 Jim Wohlford | .03 | .01 | .00 |
| **SAN DIEGO PADRES** | | | |
| ☐ 294 Kurt Bevacqua | .03 | .01 | .00 |
| ☐ 295 Juan Bonilla | .03 | .01 | .00 |
| ☐ 296 Bobby Brown | .03 | .01 | .00 |
| ☐ 297 Luis DeLeon | .03 | .01 | .00 |
| ☐ 298 Dave Dravecky | .09 | .04 | .01 |
| ☐ 299 Tim Flannery | .03 | .01 | .00 |
| ☐ 300 Steve Garvey | .40 | .18 | .04 |
| ☐ 301 Tony Gwynn | .45 | .20 | .04 |
| ☐ 302 Andy Hawkins | .55 | .25 | .05 |
| ☐ 303 Ruppert Jones | .05 | .02 | .00 |
| ☐ 304 Terry Kennedy | .10 | .04 | .01 |
| ☐ 305 Tim Lollar | .05 | .02 | .00 |
| ☐ 306 Gary Lucas | .03 | .01 | .00 |

| | MINT | VG-E | F-G |
|---|---|---|---|
| ☐ 307 Kevin McReynolds | 1.00 | .45 | .10 |
| ☐ 308 Sid Monge | .03 | .01 | .00 |
| ☐ 309 Mario Ramirez | .07 | .03 | .01 |
| ☐ 310 Gene Richards | .03 | .01 | .00 |
| ☐ 311 Luis Salazar | .03 | .01 | .00 |
| ☐ 312 Eric Show | .06 | .02 | .00 |
| ☐ 313 Elias Sosa | .03 | .01 | .00 |
| ☐ 314 Garry Templeton | .11 | .05 | .01 |
| ☐ 315 Mark Thurmond | .20 | .09 | .02 |
| ☐ 316 Ed Whitson | .08 | .03 | .01 |
| ☐ 317 Alan Wiggins | .10 | .04 | .01 |
| **ST. LOUIS CARDINALS** | | | |
| ☐ 318 Neil Allen | .06 | .02 | .00 |
| ☐ 319 Joaquin Andujar | .12 | .05 | .01 |
| ☐ 320 Steve Braun | .03 | .01 | .00 |
| ☐ 321 Glenn Brummer | .03 | .01 | .00 |
| ☐ 322 Bob Forsch | .05 | .02 | .00 |
| ☐ 323 David Green | .07 | .03 | .01 |
| ☐ 324 George Hendrick | .08 | .03 | .01 |
| ☐ 325 Tom Herr | .12 | .05 | .01 |
| ☐ 326 Dane Iorg | .03 | .01 | .00 |
| ☐ 327 Jeff Lahti | .03 | .01 | .00 |
| ☐ 328 Dave LaPoint | .06 | .02 | .00 |
| ☐ 329 Willie McGee | .25 | .10 | .02 |
| ☐ 330 Ken Oberkfell | .03 | .01 | .00 |
| ☐ 331 Darrell Porter | .06 | .02 | .00 |
| ☐ 332 Jamie Quirk | .03 | .01 | .00 |
| ☐ 333 Mike Ramsey | .03 | .01 | .00 |
| ☐ 334 Floyd Rayford | .03 | .01 | .00 |
| ☐ 335 Lonnie Smith | .09 | .04 | .01 |
| ☐ 336 Ozzie Smith | .11 | .05 | .01 |
| ☐ 337 John Stuper | .03 | .01 | .00 |
| ☐ 338 Bruce Sutter | .16 | .07 | .01 |
| ☐ 339 Andy Van Slyke | .30 | .12 | .03 |
| ☐ 340 Dave Von Ohlen | .07 | .03 | .01 |
| **KANSAS CITY ROYALS** | | | |
| ☐ 341 Willie Aikens | .05 | .02 | .00 |
| ☐ 342 Mike Armstrong | .03 | .01 | .00 |
| ☐ 343 Bud Black | .06 | .02 | .00 |
| ☐ 344 George Brett | .45 | .20 | .04 |
| ☐ 345 Onix Concepcion | .03 | .01 | .00 |
| ☐ 346 Keith Creel | .03 | .01 | .00 |
| ☐ 347 Larry Gura | .06 | .02 | .00 |
| ☐ 348 Don Hood | .03 | .01 | .00 |
| ☐ 349 Dennis Leonard | .06 | .02 | .00 |
| ☐ 350 Hal McRae | .07 | .03 | .01 |
| ☐ 351 Amos Otis | .07 | .03 | .01 |
| ☐ 352 Gaylord Perry | .16 | .07 | .01 |
| ☐ 353 Greg Pryor | .03 | .01 | .00 |
| ☐ 354 Dan Quisenberry | .18 | .08 | .01 |
| ☐ 355 Steve Renko | .03 | .01 | .00 |
| ☐ 356 Leon Roberts | .03 | .01 | .00 |
| ☐ 357 Pat Sheridan | .20 | .09 | .02 |

| | MINT | VG-E | F-G |
|---|---|---|---|
| ☐ 358 Joe Simpson | .03 | .01 | .00 |
| ☐ 359 Don Slaught | .03 | .01 | .00 |
| ☐ 360 Paul Splittorff | .05 | .02 | .00 |
| ☐ 361 U.L. Washington | .03 | .01 | .00 |
| ☐ 362 John Wathan | .03 | .01 | .00 |
| ☐ 363 Frank White | .07 | .03 | .01 |
| ☐ 364 Willie Wilson | .18 | .08 | .01 |
| **SAN FRANCISCO GIANTS** | | | |
| ☐ 365 Jim Barr | .03 | .01 | .00 |
| ☐ 366 Dave Bergman | .03 | .01 | .00 |
| ☐ 367 Fred Breining | .03 | .01 | .00 |
| ☐ 368 Bob Brenly | .07 | .03 | .01 |
| ☐ 369 Jack Clark | .18 | .08 | .01 |
| ☐ 370 Chili Davis | .10 | .04 | .01 |
| ☐ 371 Mark Davis | .03 | .01 | .00 |
| ☐ 372 Darrell Evans | .11 | .05 | .01 |
| ☐ 373 Atlee Hammaker | .06 | .02 | .00 |
| ☐ 374 Mike Krukow | .03 | .01 | .00 |
| ☐ 375 Duane Kuiper | .03 | .01 | .00 |
| ☐ 376 Bill Laskey | .03 | .01 | .00 |
| ☐ 377 Gary Lavelle | .03 | .01 | .00 |
| ☐ 378 Johnnie LeMaster | .03 | .01 | .00 |
| ☐ 379 Jeff Leonard | .08 | .03 | .01 |
| ☐ 380 Randy Lerch | .03 | .01 | .00 |
| ☐ 381 Renie Martin | .03 | .01 | .00 |
| ☐ 382 Andy McGaffigan | .03 | .01 | .00 |
| ☐ 383 Greg Minton | .05 | .02 | .00 |
| ☐ 384 Tom O'Malley | .03 | .01 | .00 |
| ☐ 385 Max Venable | .03 | .01 | .00 |
| ☐ 386 Brad Wellman | .07 | .03 | .01 |
| ☐ 387 Joel Youngblood | .03 | .01 | .00 |
| **BOSTON RED SOX** | | | |
| ☐ 388 Gary Allenson | .03 | .01 | .00 |
| ☐ 389 Luis Aponte | .03 | .01 | .00 |
| ☐ 390 Tony Armas | .13 | .06 | .01 |
| ☐ 391 Doug Bird | .03 | .01 | .00 |
| ☐ 392 Wade Boggs | .65 | .30 | .06 |
| ☐ 393 Dennis Boyd | .40 | .18 | .04 |
| ☐ 394 Mike Brown | .07 | .03 | .01 |
| ☐ 395 Mark Clear | .05 | .02 | .00 |
| ☐ 396 Dennis Eckersley | .06 | .02 | .00 |
| ☐ 397 Dwight Evans | .13 | .06 | .01 |
| ☐ 398 Rich Gedman | .07 | .03 | .01 |
| ☐ 399 Glenn Hoffman | .03 | .01 | .00 |
| ☐ 400 Bruce Hurst | .07 | .03 | .01 |
| ☐ 401 John Henry Johnson | .03 | .01 | .00 |
| ☐ 402 Ed Jurak | .06 | .02 | .00 |
| ☐ 403 Rick Miller | .03 | .01 | .00 |
| ☐ 404 Jeff Newman | .03 | .01 | .00 |
| ☐ 405 Reid Nichols | .05 | .02 | .00 |
| ☐ 406 Bob Ojeda | .06 | .02 | .00 |
| ☐ 407 Jerry Remy | .05 | .02 | .00 |
| ☐ 408 Jim Rice | .35 | .15 | .03 |
| ☐ 409 Bob Stanley | .06 | .02 | .00 |
| ☐ 410 Dave Stapleton | .05 | .02 | .00 |
| ☐ 411 John Tudor | .15 | .06 | .01 |
| ☐ 412 Carl Yastrzemski | .45 | .20 | .04 |
| **TEXAS RANGERS** | | | |
| ☐ 413 Buddy Bell | .13 | .06 | .01 |
| ☐ 414 Larry Biittner | .03 | .01 | .00 |
| ☐ 415 John Butcher | .03 | .01 | .00 |
| ☐ 416 Danny Darwin | .03 | .01 | .00 |
| ☐ 417 Bucky Dent | .06 | .02 | .00 |
| ☐ 418 Dave Hostetler | .03 | .01 | .00 |
| ☐ 419 Charlie Hough | .05 | .02 | .00 |
| ☐ 420 Bobby Johnson | .03 | .01 | .00 |
| ☐ 421 Odell Jones | .03 | .01 | .00 |
| ☐ 422 Jon Matlack | .05 | .02 | .00 |
| ☐ 423 Pete O'Brien | .25 | .10 | .02 |
| ☐ 424 Larry Parrish | .06 | .02 | .00 |
| ☐ 425 Mickey Rivers | .06 | .02 | .00 |
| ☐ 426 Billy Sample | .03 | .01 | .00 |
| ☐ 427 Dave Schmidt | .03 | .01 | .00 |
| ☐ 428 Mike Smithson | .13 | .06 | .01 |
| ☐ 429 Bill Stein | .03 | .01 | .00 |
| ☐ 430 Dave Stewart | .03 | .01 | .00 |
| ☐ 431 Jim Sundberg | .06 | .02 | .00 |
| ☐ 432 Frank Tanana | .05 | .02 | .00 |
| ☐ 433 Dave Tobik | .03 | .01 | .00 |
| ☐ 434 Wayne Tolleson | .03 | .01 | .00 |
| ☐ 435 George Wright | .05 | .02 | .00 |
| **OAKLAND A's** | | | |
| ☐ 436 Bill Almon | .03 | .01 | .00 |
| ☐ 437 Keith Atherton | .07 | .03 | .01 |
| ☐ 438 Dave Beard | .03 | .01 | .00 |
| ☐ 439 Tom Burgmeier | .03 | .01 | .00 |
| ☐ 440 Jeff Burroughs | .05 | .02 | .00 |
| ☐ 441 Chris Codiroli | .08 | .03 | .01 |
| ☐ 442 Tim Conroy | .08 | .03 | .01 |
| ☐ 443 Mike Davis | .10 | .04 | .01 |
| ☐ 444 Wayne Gross | .03 | .01 | .00 |
| ☐ 445 Garry Hancock | .03 | .01 | .00 |
| ☐ 446 Mike Heath | .03 | .01 | .00 |
| ☐ 447 Rickey Henderson | .45 | .20 | .04 |
| ☐ 448 Don Hill | .08 | .03 | .01 |
| ☐ 449 Bob Kearney | .03 | .01 | .00 |
| ☐ 450 Bill Krueger | .08 | .03 | .01 |
| ☐ 451 Rick Langford | .03 | .01 | .00 |
| ☐ 452 Carney Lansford | .10 | .04 | .01 |
| ☐ 453 Davey Lopes | .07 | .03 | .01 |
| ☐ 454 Steve McCatty | .05 | .02 | .00 |
| ☐ 455 Dan Meyer | .03 | .01 | .00 |
| ☐ 456 Dwayne Murphy | .07 | .03 | .01 |
| ☐ 457 Mike Norris | .05 | .02 | .00 |
| ☐ 458 Ricky Peters | .03 | .01 | .00 |

| | | MINT | VG-E | F-G |
|---|---|---|---|---|
| ☐ 459 | Tony Phillips | .07 | .03 | .01 |
| ☐ 460 | Tom Underwood | .03 | .01 | .00 |
| ☐ 461 | Mike Warren | .12 | .05 | .01 |
| | **CINCINNATI REDS** | | | |
| ☐ 462 | Johnny Bench | .35 | .15 | .03 |
| ☐ 463 | Bruce Berenyi | .05 | .02 | .00 |
| ☐ 464 | Dann Bilardello | .06 | .02 | .00 |
| ☐ 465 | Cesar Cedeno | .07 | .03 | .01 |
| ☐ 466 | Dave Concepcion | .09 | .04 | .01 |
| ☐ 467 | Dan Driessen | .05 | .02 | .00 |
| ☐ 468 | Nick Esasky | .25 | .10 | .02 |
| ☐ 469 | Rich Gale | .03 | .01 | .00 |
| ☐ 470 | Ben Hayes | .03 | .01 | .00 |
| ☐ 471 | Paul Householder | .03 | .01 | .00 |
| ☐ 472 | Tom Hume | .03 | .01 | .00 |
| ☐ 473 | Alan Knicely | .03 | .01 | .00 |
| ☐ 474 | Eddie Milner | .03 | .01 | .00 |
| ☐ 475 | Ron Oester | .05 | .02 | .00 |
| ☐ 476 | Kelly Paris | .09 | .04 | .01 |
| ☐ 477 | Frank Pastore | .03 | .01 | .00 |
| ☐ 478 | Ted Power | .06 | .02 | .00 |
| ☐ 479 | Joe Price | .03 | .01 | .00 |
| ☐ 480 | Charlie Puleo | .03 | .01 | .00 |
| ☐ 481 | Gary Redus | .20 | .09 | .02 |
| ☐ 482 | Bill Scherrer | .09 | .04 | .01 |
| ☐ 483 | Mario Soto | .10 | .04 | .01 |
| ☐ 484 | Alex Trevino | .03 | .01 | .00 |
| ☐ 485 | Duane Walker | .03 | .01 | .00 |
| | **CHICAGO CUBS** | | | |
| ☐ 486 | Larry Bowa | .09 | .04 | .01 |
| ☐ 487 | Warren Brusstar | .03 | .01 | .00 |
| ☐ 488 | Bill Buckner | .10 | .04 | .01 |
| ☐ 489 | Bill Campbell | .05 | .02 | .00 |
| ☐ 490 | Ron Cey | .12 | .05 | .01 |
| ☐ 491 | Jody Davis | .10 | .04 | .01 |
| ☐ 492 | Leon Durham | .16 | .07 | .01 |
| ☐ 493 | Mel Hall | .11 | .05 | .01 |
| ☐ 494 | Ferguson Jenkins | .12 | .05 | .01 |
| ☐ 495 | Jay Johnstone | .05 | .02 | .00 |
| ☐ 496 | Craig Lefferts | .14 | .06 | .01 |
| ☐ 497 | Carmelo Martinez | .30 | .12 | .03 |
| ☐ 498 | Jerry Morales | .03 | .01 | .00 |
| ☐ 499 | Keith Moreland | .05 | .02 | .00 |
| ☐ 500 | Dickie Noles | .03 | .01 | .00 |
| ☐ 501 | Mike Proly | .03 | .01 | .00 |
| ☐ 502 | Chuck Rainey | .03 | .01 | .00 |
| ☐ 503 | Dick Ruthven | .03 | .01 | .00 |
| ☐ 504 | Ryne Sandberg | .70 | .32 | .07 |
| ☐ 505 | Lee Smith | .09 | .04 | .01 |
| ☐ 506 | Steve Trout | .05 | .02 | .00 |
| ☐ 507 | Gary Woods | .03 | .01 | .00 |
| | **CALIFORNIA ANGELS** | | | |
| ☐ 508 | Juan Beniquez | .05 | .02 | .00 |
| ☐ 509 | Bob Boone | .06 | .02 | .00 |
| ☐ 510 | Rick Burleson | .06 | .02 | .00 |
| ☐ 511 | Rod Carew | .35 | .15 | .03 |
| ☐ 512 | Bobby Clark | .03 | .01 | .00 |
| ☐ 513 | John Curtis | .03 | .01 | .00 |
| ☐ 514 | Doug DeCinces | .10 | .04 | .01 |
| ☐ 515 | Brian Downing | .05 | .02 | .00 |
| ☐ 516 | Tim Foli | .03 | .01 | .00 |
| ☐ 517 | Ken Forsch | .03 | .01 | .00 |
| ☐ 518 | Bobby Grich | .07 | .03 | .01 |
| ☐ 519 | Andy Hassler | .03 | .01 | .00 |
| ☐ 520 | Reggie Jackson | .40 | .18 | .04 |
| ☐ 521 | Ron Jackson | .03 | .01 | .00 |
| ☐ 522 | Tommy John | .15 | .06 | .01 |
| ☐ 523 | Bruce Kison | .03 | .01 | .00 |
| ☐ 524 | Steve Lubratich | .07 | .03 | .01 |
| ☐ 525 | Fred Lynn | .18 | .08 | .01 |
| ☐ 526 | Gary Pettis | .35 | .15 | .03 |
| ☐ 527 | Luis Sanchez | .03 | .01 | .00 |
| ☐ 528 | Daryl Sconiers | .03 | .01 | .00 |
| ☐ 529 | Ellis Valentine | .03 | .01 | .00 |
| ☐ 530 | Rob Wilfong | .03 | .01 | .00 |
| ☐ 531 | Mike Witt | .09 | .04 | .01 |
| ☐ 532 | Geoff Zahn | .03 | .01 | .00 |
| | **CLEVELAND INDIANS** | | | |
| ☐ 533 | Bud Anderson | .03 | .01 | .00 |
| ☐ 534 | Chris Bando | .03 | .01 | .00 |
| ☐ 535 | Alan Bannister | .03 | .01 | .00 |
| ☐ 536 | Bert Blyleven | .11 | .05 | .01 |
| ☐ 537 | Tom Brennan | .03 | .01 | .00 |
| ☐ 538 | Jamie Easterly | .03 | .01 | .00 |
| ☐ 539 | Juan Eichelberger | .03 | .01 | .00 |
| ☐ 540 | Jim Essian | .03 | .01 | .00 |
| ☐ 541 | Mike Fischlin | .03 | .01 | .00 |
| ☐ 542 | Julio Franco | .12 | .05 | .01 |
| ☐ 543 | Mike Hargrove | .05 | .02 | .00 |
| ☐ 544 | Toby Harrah | .05 | .02 | .00 |
| ☐ 545 | Ron Hassey | .03 | .01 | .00 |
| ☐ 546 | Neal Heaton | .10 | .04 | .01 |
| ☐ 547 | Bake McBride | .03 | .01 | .00 |
| ☐ 548 | Broderick Perkins | .03 | .01 | .00 |
| ☐ 549 | Lary Sorensen | .03 | .01 | .00 |
| ☐ 550 | Dan Spillner | .03 | .01 | .00 |
| ☐ 551 | Rick Sutcliffe | .20 | .09 | .02 |
| ☐ 552 | Pat Tabler | .06 | .02 | .00 |
| ☐ 553 | Gorman Thomas | .11 | .05 | .01 |
| ☐ 554 | Andre Thornton | .08 | .03 | .01 |
| ☐ 555 | George Vukovich | .03 | .01 | .00 |
| | **MINNESOTA TWINS** | | | |
| ☐ 556 | Darrell Brown | .07 | .03 | .01 |
| ☐ 557 | Tom Brunansky | .16 | .07 | .01 |
| ☐ 558 | Randy Busch | .03 | .01 | .00 |
| ☐ 559 | Bobby Castillo | .03 | .01 | .00 |

| | MINT | VG-E | F-G |
|---|---|---|---|
| ☐ 560 John Castino | .03 | .01 | .00 |
| ☐ 561 Ron Davis | .05 | .02 | .00 |
| ☐ 562 Dave Engle | .06 | .02 | .00 |
| ☐ 563 Lenny Faedo | .03 | .01 | .00 |
| ☐ 564 Pete Filson | .07 | .03 | .01 |
| ☐ 565 Gary Gaetti | .06 | .02 | .00 |
| ☐ 566 Mickey Hatcher | .05 | .02 | .00 |
| ☐ 567 Kent Hrbek | .30 | .12 | .03 |
| ☐ 568 Rusty Kuntz | .03 | .01 | .00 |
| ☐ 569 Tim Laudner | .03 | .01 | .00 |
| ☐ 570 Rick Lysander | .06 | .02 | .00 |
| ☐ 571 Bobby Mitchell | .03 | .01 | .00 |
| ☐ 572 Ken Schrom | .03 | .01 | .00 |
| ☐ 573 Ray Smith | .05 | .02 | .00 |
| ☐ 574 Tim Teufel | .45 | .20 | .04 |
| ☐ 575 Frank Viola | .06 | .02 | .00 |
| ☐ 576 Gary Ward | .06 | .02 | .00 |
| ☐ 577 Ron Washington | .05 | .02 | .00 |
| ☐ 578 Len Whitehouse | .07 | .03 | .01 |
| ☐ 579 Al Williams | .03 | .01 | .00 |
| **NEW YORK METS** | | | |
| ☐ 580 Bob Bailor | .03 | .01 | .00 |
| ☐ 581 Mark Bradley | .10 | .04 | .01 |
| ☐ 582 Hubie Brooks | .08 | .03 | .01 |
| ☐ 583 Carlos Diaz | .03 | .01 | .00 |
| ☐ 584 George Foster | .16 | .07 | .01 |
| ☐ 585 Brian Giles | .03 | .01 | .00 |
| ☐ 586 Danny Heep | .03 | .01 | .00 |
| ☐ 587 Keith Hernandez | .25 | .10 | .02 |
| ☐ 588 Ron Hodges | .03 | .01 | .00 |
| ☐ 589 Scott Holman | .03 | .01 | .00 |
| ☐ 590 Dave Kingman | .13 | .06 | .01 |
| ☐ 591 Ed Lynch | .03 | .01 | .00 |
| ☐ 592 Jose Oquendo | .08 | .03 | .01 |
| ☐ 593 Jesse Orosco | .08 | .03 | .01 |
| ☐ 594 Junior Ortiz | .07 | .03 | .01 |
| ☐ 595 Tom Seaver | .25 | .10 | .02 |
| ☐ 596 Doug Sisk | .13 | .06 | .01 |
| ☐ 597 Rusty Staub | .09 | .04 | .01 |
| ☐ 598 John Stearns | .03 | .01 | .00 |
| ☐ 599 Darryl Strawberry | 2.50 | 1.00 | .25 |
| ☐ 600 Craig Swan | .03 | .01 | .00 |
| ☐ 601 Walt Terrell | .25 | .10 | .02 |
| ☐ 602 Mike Torrez | .06 | .02 | .00 |
| ☐ 603 Mookie Wilson | .08 | .03 | .01 |
| **SEATTLE MARINERS** | | | |
| ☐ 604 Jamie Allen | .09 | .04 | .01 |
| ☐ 605 Jim Beattie | .03 | .01 | .00 |
| ☐ 606 Tony Bernazard | .03 | .01 | .00 |
| ☐ 607 Manny Castillo | .03 | .01 | .00 |
| ☐ 608 Bill Caudill | .07 | .03 | .01 |
| ☐ 609 Bryan Clark | .03 | .01 | .00 |
| ☐ 610 Al Cowens | .05 | .02 | .00 |

| | MINT | VG-E | F-G |
|---|---|---|---|
| ☐ 611 Dave Henderson | .05 | .02 | .00 |
| ☐ 612 Steve Henderson | .03 | .01 | .00 |
| ☐ 613 Orlando Mercado | .07 | .03 | .01 |
| ☐ 614 Mike Moore | .06 | .02 | .00 |
| ☐ 615 Ricky Nelson | .08 | .03 | .01 |
| ☐ 616 Spike Owen | .15 | .06 | .01 |
| ☐ 617 Pat Putnam | .03 | .01 | .00 |
| ☐ 618 Ron Roenicke | .03 | .01 | .00 |
| ☐ 619 Mike Stanton | .03 | .01 | .00 |
| ☐ 620 Bob Stoddard | .03 | .01 | .00 |
| ☐ 621 Rick Sweet | .03 | .01 | .00 |
| ☐ 622 Roy Thomas | .03 | .01 | .00 |
| ☐ 623 Ed Vande Berg | .05 | .02 | .00 |
| ☐ 624 Matt Young | .12 | .05 | .01 |
| ☐ 625 Richie Zisk | .05 | .02 | .00 |
| **SPECIALS (626-645)** | | | |
| ☐ 626 Fred Lynn: 1982 AS Game RB | .12 | .05 | .01 |
| ☐ 627 Manny Trillo: 1983 AS Game RB | .06 | .02 | .00 |
| ☐ 628 Steve Garvey: NL Iron Man | .20 | .09 | .02 |
| ☐ 629 Rod Carew: AL Batting Runner-Up | .20 | .09 | .02 |
| ☐ 630 Wade Boggs: AL Batting Champion | .30 | .12 | .03 |
| ☐ 631 Tim Raines: Letting Go Of The Raines | .16 | .07 | .01 |
| ☐ 632 Al Oliver: Double Trouble | .12 | .05 | .01 |
| ☐ 633 Steve Sax: AS Second Base | .11 | .05 | .01 |
| ☐ 634 Dickie Thon: AS Shortstop | .08 | .03 | .01 |
| ☐ 635 Ace Firemen: Dan Quisenberry and Tippy Martinez | .08 | .03 | .01 |
| ☐ 636 Reds Reunited: Joe Morgan Pete Rose Tony Perez | .30 | .12 | .03 |
| ☐ 637 Backstop Stars: Lance Parrish Bob Boone | .08 | .03 | .01 |
| ☐ 638 Geo. Brett and G. Perry: Pine Tar 7 / 24 / 83 | .25 | .10 | .02 |
| ☐ 639 1983 No Hitters: Dave Righetti Mike Warren Bob Forsch | .10 | .04 | .01 |
| ☐ 640 Bench and Yaz: Retiring Superstars | .25 | .10 | .02 |

| | MINT | VG-E | F-G |
|---|---|---|---|
| ☐ 641 Gaylord Perry: Going Out In Style | .12 | .05 | .01 |
| ☐ 642 Steve Carlton: 300 Club and Strikeout Record | .20 | .09 | .02 |
| ☐ 643 Altobelli and Owens: WS Managers | .05 | .02 | .00 |
| ☐ 644 Rick Dempsey: World Series MVP | .05 | .02 | .00 |
| ☐ 645 Mike Boddicker: WS Rookie Winner | .08 | .03 | .01 |
| ☐ 646 Scott McGregor: WS Clincher | .07 | .03 | .01 |
| **Checklists (647–660)** | | | |
| ☐ 647 CL: Orioles/Royals | .08 | .01 | .00 |
| ☐ 648 CL: Phillies/Giants | .07 | .01 | .00 |
| ☐ 649 CL: White Sox/Red Sox | .07 | .01 | .00 |
| ☐ 650 CL: Tigers/Rangers | .07 | .01 | .00 |
| ☐ 651 CL: Dodgers/A's | .07 | .01 | .00 |
| ☐ 652 CL: Yankees/Reds | .07 | .01 | .00 |
| ☐ 653 CL: Blue Jays/Cubs | .07 | .01 | .00 |
| ☐ 654 CL: Braves/Angels | .07 | .01 | .00 |
| ☐ 655 CL: Brewers/Indians | .07 | .01 | .00 |
| ☐ 656 CL: Astros/Twins | .07 | .01 | .00 |
| ☐ 657 CL: Pirates/Mets | .07 | .01 | .00 |
| ☐ 658 CL: Expos/Mariners | .07 | .01 | .00 |
| ☐ 659 CL: Padres/Specials | .07 | .01 | .00 |
| ☐ 660 CL: Cardinals/Teams | .08 | .01 | .00 |

## 1984 FLEER EXTENDED

The cards in this 132 card set measure 2½" by 3½". For the first time, the Fleer Gum Company issued a traded or update set. The purpose of the set was the same as the traded sets issued by Topps over the past four years, i.e., to portray players

with their proper team for the current year and to portray rookies who were not in their regular issue. Like the Topps traded sets of the past four years, the Fleer traded sets were distributed through hobby channels only. The set was quite popular with collectors, and apparently, the print run was relatively short, as the set was quickly in short supply and exhibited a rapid and dramatic price increase.

Complete Set: M-65.00; VG-E-20.00; F-G-3.00

| | MINT | VG-E | F-G |
|---|---|---|---|
| Common Player | .12 | .04 | .01 |
| ☐ 1 U Willie Aikens | .16 | .07 | .01 |
| ☐ 2 U Luis Aponte | .12 | .04 | .01 |
| ☐ 3 U Mark Bailey | .16 | .07 | .01 |
| ☐ 4 U Bob Bailor | .12 | .04 | .01 |
| ☐ 5 U Dusty Baker | .16 | .07 | .01 |
| ☐ 6 U Steve Balboni | .16 | .07 | .01 |
| ☐ 7 U Alan Bannister | .12 | .04 | .01 |
| ☐ 8 U Marty Barrett | .70 | .32 | .07 |
| ☐ 9 U Dave Beard | .12 | .04 | .01 |
| ☐ 10 U Joe Beckwith | .12 | .04 | .01 |
| ☐ 11 U Dave Bergman | .12 | .04 | .01 |
| ☐ 12 U Tony Bernazard | .12 | .04 | .01 |
| ☐ 13 U Bruce Bochte | .12 | .04 | .01 |
| ☐ 14 U Barry Bonnell | .12 | .04 | .01 |
| ☐ 15 U Phil Bradley | 3.50 | 1.25 | .35 |
| ☐ 16 U Fred Breining | .12 | .04 | .01 |
| ☐ 17 U Mike Brown | .20 | .09 | .02 |
| ☐ 18 U Bill Buckner | .20 | .09 | .02 |
| ☐ 19 U Ray Burris | .12 | .04 | .01 |
| ☐ 20 U John Butcher | .12 | .04 | .01 |
| ☐ 21 U Brett Butler | .30 | .12 | .03 |
| ☐ 22 U Enos Cabell | .12 | .04 | .01 |
| ☐ 23 U Bill Campbell | .12 | .04 | .01 |
| ☐ 24 U Bill Caudill | .16 | .07 | .01 |
| ☐ 25 U Bobby Clark | .12 | .04 | .01 |
| ☐ 26 U Bryan Clark | .12 | .04 | .01 |
| ☐ 27 U Roger Clemens | 1.00 | .45 | .10 |
| ☐ 28 U Jaime Cocanower | .20 | .09 | .02 |
| ☐ 29 U Ron Darling | 2.50 | 1.00 | .25 |
| ☐ 30 U Alvin Davis | 3.50 | 1.25 | .35 |
| ☐ 31 U Bob Dernier | .16 | .07 | .01 |
| ☐ 32 U Carlos Diaz | .12 | .04 | .01 |
| ☐ 33 U Mike Easler | .16 | .07 | .01 |
| ☐ 34 U Dennis Eckersley | .16 | .07 | .01 |
| ☐ 35 U Jim Essian | .12 | .04 | .01 |
| ☐ 36 U Darrell Evans | .30 | .12 | .03 |
| ☐ 37 U Mike Fitzgerald | .20 | .09 | .02 |
| ☐ 38 U Tim Foli | .12 | .04 | .01 |

| | | MINT | VG-E | F-G |
|---|---|---|---|---|
| ☐ 39 | U John Franco | 1.50 | .50 | .15 |
| ☐ 40 | U George Frazier | .12 | .04 | .01 |
| ☐ 41 | U Rich Gale | .12 | .04 | .01 |
| ☐ 42 | U Barbaro Garbey | .30 | .12 | .03 |
| ☐ 43 | U Dwight Gooden | 35.00 | 10.00 | 3.50 |
| ☐ 44 | U Goose Gossage | .50 | .22 | .05 |
| ☐ 45 | U Wayne Gross | .12 | .04 | .01 |
| ☐ 46 | U Mark Gubicza | .75 | .35 | .07 |
| ☐ 47 | U Jackie Gutierrez | .30 | .12 | .03 |
| ☐ 48 | U Toby Harrah | .16 | .07 | .01 |
| ☐ 49 | U Ron Hassey | .12 | .04 | .01 |
| ☐ 50 | U Richie Hebner | .12 | .04 | .01 |
| ☐ 51 | U Willie Hernandez | .60 | .25 | .05 |
| ☐ 52 | U Ed Hodge | .16 | .07 | .01 |
| ☐ 53 | U Ricky Horton | .50 | .22 | .05 |
| ☐ 54 | U Art Howe | .12 | .04 | .01 |
| ☐ 55 | U Dane Iorg | .12 | .04 | .01 |
| ☐ 56 | U Brook Jacoby | 2.50 | 1.00 | .25 |
| ☐ 57 | U Dion James | .35 | .15 | .03 |
| ☐ 58 | U Mike Jeffcoat | .16 | .07 | .01 |
| ☐ 59 | U Ruppert Jones | .16 | .05 | .01 |
| ☐ 60 | U Bob Kearney | .12 | .04 | .01 |
| ☐ 61 | U Jimmy Key | 1.50 | .50 | .15 |
| ☐ 62 | U Dave Kingman | .25 | .10 | .02 |
| ☐ 63 | U Brad Komminsk | .50 | .22 | .05 |
| ☐ 64 | U Jerry Koosman | .20 | .09 | .02 |
| ☐ 65 | U Wayne Krenchicki | .12 | .04 | .01 |
| ☐ 66 | U Rusty Kuntz | .12 | .04 | .01 |
| ☐ 67 | U Frank LaCorte | .12 | .04 | .01 |
| ☐ 68 | U Dennis Lamp | .12 | .04 | .01 |
| ☐ 69 | U Tito Landrum | .12 | .04 | .01 |
| ☐ 70 | U Mark Langston | 1.50 | .50 | .15 |
| ☐ 71 | U Rick Leach | .12 | .04 | .01 |
| ☐ 72 | U Craig Lefferts | .12 | .04 | .01 |
| ☐ 73 | U Gary Lucas | .12 | .04 | .01 |
| ☐ 74 | U Jerry Martin | .12 | .04 | .01 |
| ☐ 75 | U Carmelo Martinez | .25 | .10 | .02 |
| ☐ 76 | U Mike Mason | .25 | .10 | .02 |
| ☐ 77 | U Gary Matthews | .20 | .09 | .02 |
| ☐ 78 | U Andy McGaffigan | .12 | .04 | .01 |
| ☐ 79 | U Joey McLaughlin | .12 | .04 | .01 |
| ☐ 80 | U Joe Morgan | 1.00 | .40 | .10 |
| ☐ 81 | U Darryl Motley | .25 | .10 | .02 |
| ☐ 82 | U Graig Nettles | .35 | .15 | .03 |
| ☐ 83 | U Phil Niekro | 1.00 | .40 | .10 |
| ☐ 84 | U Ken Oberkfell | .12 | .04 | .03 |
| ☐ 85 | U Al Oliver | .35 | .15 | .03 |
| ☐ 86 | U Jorge Orta | .12 | .04 | .01 |
| ☐ 87 | U Amos Otis | .16 | .07 | .01 |
| ☐ 88 | U Bob Owchinko | .12 | .04 | .01 |
| ☐ 89 | U Dave Parker | 1.00 | .40 | .10 |
| ☐ 90 | U Jack Perconte | .12 | .04 | .01 |
| ☐ 91 | U Tony Perez | .35 | .15 | .03 |

| | | MINT | VG-E | F-G |
|---|---|---|---|---|
| ☐ 92 | U Gerald Perry | .25 | .10 | .02 |
| ☐ 93 | U Kirby Puckett | 2.50 | 1.00 | .25 |
| ☐ 94 | U Shane Rawley | .25 | .10 | .02 |
| ☐ 95 | U Floyd Rayford | .12 | .04 | .01 |
| ☐ 96 | U Ron Reed | .12 | .04 | .01 |
| ☐ 97 | U R.J. Reynolds | .40 | .18 | .04 |
| ☐ 98 | U Gene Richards | .12 | .04 | .01 |
| ☐ 99 | U Jose Rijo | .30 | .12 | .03 |
| ☐ 100 | U Jeff Robinson | .25 | .10 | .02 |
| ☐ 101 | U Ron Romanick | 1.50 | .50 | .15 |
| ☐ 102 | U Pete Rose | 6.00 | 2.00 | .60 |
| ☐ 103 | U Bret Saberhagen | 8.00 | 3.00 | .80 |
| ☐ 104 | U Scott Sanderson | .16 | .07 | .01 |
| ☐ 105 | U Dick Schofield | .25 | .10 | .02 |
| ☐ 106 | U Tom Seaver | 1.50 | .50 | .15 |
| ☐ 107 | U Jim Slaton | .12 | .04 | .01 |
| ☐ 108 | U Mike Smithson | .12 | .04 | .01 |
| ☐ 109 | U Lary Sorensen | .12 | .04 | .01 |
| ☐ 110 | U Tim Stoddard | .12 | .04 | .01 |
| ☐ 111 | U Jeff Stone | .60 | .28 | .06 |
| ☐ 112 | U Champ Summers | .12 | .04 | .01 |
| ☐ 113 | U Jim Sundberg | .16 | .07 | .01 |
| ☐ 114 | U Rick Sutcliffe | .75 | .30 | .07 |
| ☐ 115 | U Craig Swan | .12 | .04 | .01 |
| ☐ 116 | U Derrel Thomas | .12 | .04 | .01 |
| ☐ 117 | U Gorman Thomas | .20 | .09 | .02 |
| ☐ 118 | U Alex Trevino | .12 | .04 | .01 |
| ☐ 119 | U Manny Trillo | .16 | .07 | .01 |
| ☐ 120 | U John Tudor | .35 | .15 | .03 |
| ☐ 121 | U Tom Underwood | .12 | .04 | .01 |
| ☐ 122 | U Mike Vail | .12 | .04 | .01 |
| ☐ 123 | U Tom Waddell | .20 | .09 | .02 |
| ☐ 124 | U Gary Ward | .20 | .09 | .02 |
| ☐ 125 | U Terry Whitfield | .12 | .04 | .01 |
| ☐ 126 | U Curtis Wilkerson | .16 | .07 | .01 |
| ☐ 127 | U Frank Williams | .20 | .09 | .02 |
| ☐ 128 | U Glenn Wilson | .30 | .12 | .03 |
| ☐ 129 | U John Wockenfuss | .12 | .04 | .01 |
| ☐ 130 | U Ned Yost | .12 | .04 | .01 |
| ☐ 131 | U Mike Young | 2.50 | 1.00 | .25 |
| ☐ 132 | U Checklist: 1–132 | .20 | .04 | .01 |

# 1985 FLEER

The cards in this 660 card set measure 2½" by 3½". The 1985 Fleer set features fronts which contain the team logo along with the player's name and position. The borders enclosing the photo are color-coded to correspond to the player's team. In each case, the color is one of the standard colors of that team, e.g., orange for Baltimore, red for St. Louis, etc. The backs feature the same name, number, and statistics format that Fleer has been using over the past few years. The black and white photo on the reverse is included for the third straight year.

Complete Set: M-16.00; VG-E-7.50; F-G-1.60

|  | | MINT | VG-E | F-G |
|---|---|---|---|---|
| | Common Player ........ | .03 | .01 | .00 |
| | **DETROIT TIGERS** | | | |
| ☐ | 1 Doug Bair ............. | .07 | .03 | .01 |
| ☐ | 2 Juan Berenguer ....... | .03 | .01 | .00 |
| ☐ | 3 Dave Bergman ........ | .03 | .01 | .00 |
| ☐ | 4 Tom Brookens ......... | .03 | .01 | .00 |
| ☐ | 5 Marty Castillo ........ | .03 | .01 | .00 |
| ☐ | 6 Darrell Evans ......... | .10 | .04 | .01 |
| ☐ | 7 Barbaro Garbey ....... | .15 | .06 | .01 |
| ☐ | 8 Kirk Gibson .......... | .20 | .09 | .02 |
| ☐ | 9 John Grubb .......... | .03 | .01 | .00 |
| ☐ | 10 Willie Hernandez ..... | .15 | .06 | .01 |
| ☐ | 11 Larry Herndon ....... | .05 | .02 | .00 |
| ☐ | 12 Howard Johnson ..... | .05 | .02 | .00 |
| ☐ | 13 Ruppert Jones ....... | .05 | .02 | .00 |
| ☐ | 14 Rusty Kuntz ........ | .03 | .01 | .00 |
| ☐ | 15 Chet Lemon ......... | .07 | .03 | .01 |
| ☐ | 16 Aurelio Lopez ....... | .03 | .01 | .00 |
| ☐ | 17 Sid Monge .......... | .03 | .01 | .00 |
| ☐ | 18 Jack Morris ......... | .16 | .07 | .01 |
| ☐ | 19 Lance Parrish ....... | .20 | .09 | .02 |
| ☐ | 20 Dan Petry .......... | .13 | .06 | .01 |
| ☐ | 21 Dave Rozema ....... | .03 | .01 | .00 |
| ☐ | 22 Bill Scherrer ........ | .03 | .01 | .00 |
| ☐ | 23 Alan Trammell ...... | .20 | .09 | .02 |
| ☐ | 24 Lou Whitaker ....... | .16 | .07 | .01 |
| ☐ | 25 Milt Wilcox ........ | .03 | .01 | .00 |
| | **SAN DIEGO PADRES** | | | |
| ☐ | 26 Kurt Bevacqua ...... | .03 | .01 | .00 |
| ☐ | 27 Greg Booker ........ | .09 | .04 | .01 |
| ☐ | 28 Bobby Brown ....... | .03 | .01 | .00 |
| ☐ | 29 Luis DeLeon ........ | .03 | .01 | .00 |
| ☐ | 30 Dave Dravecky ...... | .06 | .02 | .00 |
| ☐ | 31 Tim Flannery ....... | .03 | .01 | .00 |
| ☐ | 32 Steve Garvey ....... | .35 | .15 | .03 |
| ☐ | 33 Goose Gossage ..... | .16 | .07 | .01 |
| ☐ | 34 Tony Gwynn ........ | .30 | .12 | .03 |
| ☐ | 35 Greg Harris ........ | .03 | .01 | .00 |
| ☐ | 36 Andy Hawkins ...... | .07 | .03 | .01 |
| ☐ | 37 Terry Kennedy ...... | .08 | .03 | .01 |
| ☐ | 38 Craig Lefferts ...... | .03 | .01 | .00 |
| ☐ | 39 Tim Lollar ......... | .03 | .01 | .00 |
| ☐ | 40 Carmelo Martinez ... | .07 | .03 | .01 |
| ☐ | 41 Kevin McReynolds ... | .15 | .06 | .01 |
| ☐ | 42 Graig Nettles ...... | .12 | .05 | .01 |
| ☐ | 43 Luis Salazar ....... | .03 | .01 | .00 |
| ☐ | 44 Eric Show ......... | .05 | .02 | .00 |
| ☐ | 45 Garry Templeton .... | .09 | .04 | .01 |
| ☐ | 46 Mark Thurmond ..... | .06 | .02 | .00 |
| ☐ | 47 Ed Whitson ........ | .06 | .02 | .00 |
| ☐ | 48 Alan Wiggins ....... | .09 | .04 | .01 |
| | **CHICAGO CUBS** | | | |
| ☐ | 49 Rich Bordi ......... | .03 | .01 | .00 |
| ☐ | 50 Larry Bowa ........ | .07 | .03 | .01 |
| ☐ | 51 Warren Brusstar .... | .03 | .01 | .00 |
| ☐ | 52 Ron Cey .......... | .10 | .04 | .01 |
| ☐ | 53 Henry Cotto ....... | .12 | .05 | .01 |
| ☐ | 54 Jody Davis ........ | .11 | .05 | .01 |
| ☐ | 55 Bob Dernier ....... | .06 | .02 | .00 |
| ☐ | 56 Leon Durham ...... | .14 | .06 | .01 |
| ☐ | 57 Dennis Eckersley ... | .05 | .02 | .00 |
| ☐ | 58 George Frazier ..... | .03 | .01 | .00 |
| ☐ | 59 Richie Hebner ...... | .03 | .01 | .00 |
| ☐ | 60 Dave Lopes ........ | .06 | .02 | .00 |
| ☐ | 61 Gary Matthews ..... | .07 | .03 | .01 |
| ☐ | 62 Keith Moreland .... | .06 | .02 | .00 |
| ☐ | 63 Rick Reuschel ...... | .06 | .02 | .00 |
| ☐ | 64 Dick Ruthven ...... | .03 | .01 | .00 |
| ☐ | 65 Ryne Sandberg ..... | .40 | .18 | .04 |
| ☐ | 66 Scott Sanderson ... | .05 | .02 | .00 |
| ☐ | 67 Lee Smith ........ | .08 | .03 | .01 |
| ☐ | 68 Tim Stoddard ...... | .03 | .01 | .00 |

| | MINT | VG-E | F-G |
|---|---|---|---|
| 69 Rick Sutcliffe | .15 | .06 | .01 |
| 70 Steve Trout | .05 | .02 | .00 |
| 71 Gary Woods | .03 | .01 | .00 |
| **NEW YORK METS** | | | |
| 72 Wally Backman | .05 | .02 | .00 |
| 73 Bruce Berenyi | .03 | .01 | .00 |
| 74 Hubie Brooks | .08 | .03 | .01 |
| 75 Kelvin Chapman | .10 | .04 | .01 |
| 76 Ron Darling | .25 | .10 | .02 |
| 77 Sid Fernandez | .08 | .03 | .01 |
| 78 Mike Fitzgerald | .03 | .01 | .00 |
| 79 George Foster | .15 | .06 | .01 |
| 80 Brent Gaff | .03 | .01 | .00 |
| 81 Ron Gardenhire | .03 | .01 | .00 |
| 82 Dwight Gooden | 4.50 | 1.50 | .45 |
| 83 Tom Gorman | .03 | .01 | .00 |
| 84 Danny Heep | .03 | .01 | .00 |
| 85 Keith Hernandez | .25 | .10 | .02 |
| 86 Ray Knight | .05 | .02 | .00 |
| 87 Ed Lynch | .03 | .01 | .00 |
| 88 Jose Oquendo | .03 | .01 | .00 |
| 89 Jesse Orosco | .06 | .02 | .00 |
| 90 Rafael Santana | .12 | .05 | .01 |
| 91 Doug Sisk | .03 | .01 | .00 |
| 92 Rusty Staub | .07 | .03 | .01 |
| 93 Darryl Strawberry | .40 | .18 | .04 |
| 94 Walt Terrell | .06 | .02 | .00 |
| 95 Mookie Wilson | .07 | .03 | .01 |
| **TORONTO BLUE JAYS** | | | |
| 96 Jim Acker | .03 | .01 | .00 |
| 97 Willie Aikens | .05 | .02 | .00 |
| 98 Doyle Alexander | .05 | .02 | .00 |
| 99 Jesse Barfield | .11 | .05 | .01 |
| 100 George Bell | .11 | .05 | .01 |
| 101 Jim Clancy | .03 | .01 | .00 |
| 102 Dave Collins | .05 | .02 | .00 |
| 103 Tony Fernandez | .10 | .04 | .01 |
| 104 Damaso Garcia | .08 | .03 | .01 |
| 105 Jim Gott | .03 | .01 | .00 |
| 106 Alfredo Griffin | .05 | .02 | .00 |
| 107 Darth Iorg | .03 | .01 | .00 |
| 108 Roy Lee Jackson | .03 | .01 | .00 |
| 109 Cliff Johnson | .03 | .01 | .00 |
| 110 Jimmy Key | .30 | .12 | .03 |
| 111 Dennis Lamp | .03 | .01 | .00 |
| 112 Rick Leach | .03 | .01 | .00 |
| 113 Luis Leal | .03 | .01 | .00 |
| 114 Buck Martinez | .03 | .01 | .00 |
| 115 Lloyd Moseby | .12 | .05 | .01 |
| 116 Rance Mulliniks | .03 | .01 | .00 |
| 117 Dave Stieb | .15 | .06 | .01 |
| 118 Willie Upshaw | .12 | .05 | .01 |

| | MINT | VG-E | F-G |
|---|---|---|---|
| 119 Ernie Whitt | .03 | .01 | .00 |
| **NEW YORK YANKEES** | | | |
| 120 Mike Armstrong | .03 | .01 | .00 |
| 121 Don Baylor | .12 | .05 | .01 |
| 122 Marty Bystrom | .03 | .01 | .00 |
| 123 Rick Cerone | .03 | .01 | .00 |
| 124 Joe Cowley | .03 | .01 | .00 |
| 125 Brian Dayett | .03 | .01 | .00 |
| 126 Tim Foli | .03 | .01 | .00 |
| 127 Ray Fontenot | .03 | .01 | .00 |
| 128 Ken Griffey | .05 | .02 | .00 |
| 129 Ron Guidry | .16 | .07 | .01 |
| 130 Toby Harrah | .05 | .02 | .00 |
| 131 Jay Howell | .06 | .02 | .00 |
| 132 Steve Kemp | .09 | .04 | .01 |
| 133 Don Mattingly | .85 | .40 | .08 |
| 134 Bobby Meacham | .03 | .01 | .00 |
| 135 John Montefusco | .05 | .02 | .00 |
| 136 Omar Moreno | .05 | .02 | .00 |
| 137 Dale Murray | .03 | .01 | .00 |
| 138 Phil Niekro | .15 | .06 | .01 |
| 139 Mike Pagliarulo | .25 | .10 | .02 |
| 140 Willie Randolph | .06 | .02 | .00 |
| 141 Dennis Rasmussen | .03 | .01 | .00 |
| 142 Dave Righetti | .11 | .05 | .01 |
| 143 Jose Rijo | .20 | .09 | .02 |
| 144 Andre Robertson | .03 | .01 | .00 |
| 145 Bob Shirley | .03 | .01 | .00 |
| 146 Dave Winfield | .35 | .15 | .03 |
| 147 Butch Wynegar | .05 | .02 | .00 |
| **BOSTON RED SOX** | | | |
| 148 Gary Allenson | .03 | .01 | .00 |
| 149 Tony Armas | .11 | .05 | .01 |
| 150 Marty Barrett | .07 | .03 | .01 |
| 151 Wade Boggs | .45 | .20 | .04 |
| 152 Dennis Boyd | .05 | .02 | .00 |
| 153 Bill Buckner | .07 | .03 | .01 |
| 154 Mark Clear | .03 | .01 | .00 |
| 155 Roger Clemens | .35 | .15 | .03 |
| 156 Steve Crawford | .03 | .01 | .00 |
| 157 Mike Easler | .05 | .02 | .00 |
| 158 Dwight Evans | .10 | .04 | .01 |
| 159 Rich Gedman | .07 | .03 | .01 |
| 160 Jackie Gutierrez | .08 | .03 | .01 |
| 161 Bruce Hurst | .03 | .01 | .00 |
| 162 John H. Johnson | .03 | .01 | .00 |
| 163 Rick Miller | .03 | .01 | .00 |
| 164 Reid Nichols | .03 | .01 | .00 |
| 165 Al Nipper | .20 | .09 | .02 |
| 166 Bob Ojeda | .05 | .02 | .00 |
| 167 Jerry Remy | .03 | .01 | .00 |
| 168 Jim Rice | .30 | .12 | .03 |

| | | MINT | VG-E | F-G |
|---|---|---|---|---|
| ☐ 169 | Bob Stanely | .05 | .02 | .00 |
| | **BALTIMORE ORIOLES** | | | |
| ☐ 170 | Mike Boddicker | .10 | .04 | .01 |
| ☐ 171 | Al Bumbry | .03 | .01 | .00 |
| ☐ 172 | Todd Cruz | .03 | .01 | .00 |
| ☐ 173 | Rich Dauer | .03 | .01 | .00 |
| ☐ 174 | Storm Davis | .07 | .03 | .01 |
| ☐ 175 | Rick Dempsey | .05 | .02 | .00 |
| ☐ 176 | Jim Dwyer | .03 | .01 | .00 |
| ☐ 177 | Mike Flanagan | .06 | .02 | .00 |
| ☐ 178 | Dan Ford | .03 | .01 | .00 |
| ☐ 179 | Wayne Gross | .03 | .01 | .00 |
| ☐ 180 | John Lowenstein | .03 | .01 | .00 |
| ☐ 181 | Dennis Martinez | .03 | .01 | .00 |
| ☐ 182 | Tippy Martinez | .05 | .02 | .00 |
| ☐ 183 | Scott McGregor | .07 | .03 | .01 |
| ☐ 184 | Eddie Murray | .40 | .18 | .04 |
| ☐ 185 | Joe Nolan | .03 | .01 | .00 |
| ☐ 186 | Floyd Rayford | .03 | .01 | .00 |
| ☐ 187 | Cal Ripken | .40 | .18 | .04 |
| ☐ 188 | Gary Roenicke | .05 | .02 | .00 |
| ☐ 189 | Lenn Sakata | .03 | .01 | .00 |
| ☐ 190 | John Shelby | .03 | .01 | .00 |
| ☐ 191 | Ken Singleton | .07 | .03 | .01 |
| ☐ 192 | Sammy Stewart | .03 | .01 | .00 |
| ☐ 193 | Bill Swaggerty | .10 | .04 | .01 |
| ☐ 194 | Tom Underwood | .03 | .01 | .00 |
| ☐ 195 | Mike Young | .18 | .08 | .01 |
| | **KANSAS CITY ROYALS** | | | |
| ☐ 196 | Steve Balboni | .07 | .03 | .01 |
| ☐ 197 | Joe Beckwith | .03 | .01 | .00 |
| ☐ 198 | Bud Black | .05 | .02 | .00 |
| ☐ 199 | George Brett | .40 | .18 | .04 |
| ☐ 200 | Onix Concepcion | .03 | .01 | .00 |
| ☐ 201 | Mark Gubicza | .18 | .08 | .01 |
| ☐ 202 | Larry Gura | .05 | .02 | .00 |
| ☐ 203 | Mark Huismann | .05 | .02 | .00 |
| ☐ 204 | Dane Iorg | .03 | .01 | .00 |
| ☐ 205 | Danny Jackson | .06 | .02 | .00 |
| ☐ 206 | Charlie Leibrandt | .06 | .02 | .00 |
| ☐ 207 | Hal McRae | .06 | .02 | .00 |
| ☐ 208 | Darryl Motley | .05 | .02 | .00 |
| ☐ 209 | Jorge Orta | .03 | .01 | .00 |
| ☐ 210 | Greg Pryor | .03 | .01 | .00 |
| ☐ 211 | Dan Quisenberry | .15 | .06 | .01 |
| ☐ 212 | Bret Saberhagen | 1.00 | .45 | .10 |
| ☐ 213 | Pat Sheridan | .03 | .01 | .00 |
| ☐ 214 | Don Slaught | .03 | .01 | .00 |
| ☐ 215 | U.L. Washington | .03 | .01 | .00 |
| ☐ 216 | John Wathan | .03 | .01 | .00 |
| ☐ 217 | Frank White | .06 | .02 | .00 |
| ☐ 218 | Willie Wilson | .15 | .06 | .01 |
| | **ST. LOUIS CARDINALS** | | | |
| ☐ 219 | Neil Allen | .05 | .02 | .00 |
| ☐ 220 | Joaquin Andujar | .08 | .03 | .01 |
| ☐ 221 | Steve Braun | .03 | .02 | .00 |
| ☐ 222 | Danny Cox | .08 | .03 | .01 |
| ☐ 223 | Bob Forsch | .05 | .02 | .00 |
| ☐ 224 | David Green | .06 | .02 | .00 |
| ☐ 225 | George Hendrick | .07 | .03 | .01 |
| ☐ 226 | Tom Herr | .11 | .05 | .01 |
| ☐ 227 | Ricky Horton | .15 | .06 | .01 |
| ☐ 228 | Art Howe | .03 | .01 | .00 |
| ☐ 229 | Mike Jorgensen | .03 | .01 | .00 |
| ☐ 230 | Kurt Kepshire | .10 | .04 | .01 |
| ☐ 231 | Jeff Lahti | .03 | .01 | .00 |
| ☐ 232 | Tito Landrum | .05 | .02 | .00 |
| ☐ 233 | Dave LaPoint | .03 | .01 | .00 |
| ☐ 234 | Willie McGee | .25 | .10 | .02 |
| ☐ 235 | Tom Nieto | .08 | .03 | .01 |
| ☐ 236 | Terry Pendleton | .40 | .18 | .04 |
| ☐ 237 | Darrell Porter | .05 | .02 | .00 |
| ☐ 238 | Dave Rucker | .03 | .01 | .00 |
| ☐ 239 | Lonnie Smith | .07 | .03 | .01 |
| ☐ 240 | Ozzie Smith | .09 | .04 | .01 |
| ☐ 241 | Bruce Sutter | .15 | .06 | .01 |
| ☐ 242 | Andy Van Slyke | .08 | .03 | .01 |
| ☐ 243 | Dave Von Ohlen | .03 | .01 | .00 |
| | **PHILADELPHIA PHILLIES** | | | |
| ☐ 244 | Larry Andersen | .03 | .01 | .00 |
| ☐ 245 | Bill Campbell | .05 | .02 | .00 |
| ☐ 246 | Steve Carlton | .30 | .12 | .03 |
| ☐ 247 | Tim Corcoran | .03 | .01 | .00 |
| ☐ 248 | Ivan DeJesus | .03 | .01 | .00 |
| ☐ 249 | John Denny | .07 | .03 | .01 |
| ☐ 250 | Bo Diaz | .05 | .02 | .00 |
| ☐ 251 | Greg Gross | .03 | .01 | .00 |
| ☐ 252 | Kevin Gross | .03 | .01 | .00 |
| ☐ 253 | Von Hayes | .11 | .05 | .01 |
| ☐ 254 | Al Holland | .05 | .02 | .00 |
| ☐ 255 | Charles Hudson | .05 | .02 | .00 |
| ☐ 256 | Jerry Koosman | .07 | .03 | .01 |
| ☐ 257 | Joe Lefebvre | .03 | .01 | .00 |
| ☐ 258 | Sixto Lezcano | .03 | .01 | .00 |
| ☐ 259 | Garry Maddox | .05 | .02 | .00 |
| ☐ 260 | Len Matuszek | .03 | .01 | .00 |
| ☐ 261 | Tug McGraw | .08 | .03 | .01 |
| ☐ 262 | Al Oliver | .10 | .04 | .01 |
| ☐ 263 | Shane Rawley | .06 | .02 | .00 |
| ☐ 264 | Juan Samuel | .30 | .12 | .03 |
| ☐ 265 | Mike Schmidt | .35 | .15 | .03 |
| ☐ 266 | Jeff Stone | .25 | .10 | .02 |
| ☐ 267 | Ozzie Virgil | .07 | .03 | .01 |

| | MINT | VG-E | F-G |
|---|---|---|---|
| ☐ 268 Glenn Wilson | .09 | .04 | .01 |
| ☐ 269 John Wockenfuss | .03 | .01 | .00 |
| **MINNESOTA TWINS** | | | |
| ☐ 270 Darrell Brown | .03 | .01 | .00 |
| ☐ 271 Tom Brunansky | .12 | .05 | .01 |
| ☐ 272 Randy Bush | .03 | .01 | .00 |
| ☐ 273 John Butcher | .03 | .01 | .00 |
| ☐ 274 Bobby Castillo | .03 | .01 | .00 |
| ☐ 275 Ron Davis | .05 | .02 | .00 |
| ☐ 276 Dave Engle | .05 | .02 | .00 |
| ☐ 277 Pete Filson | .03 | .01 | .00 |
| ☐ 278 Gary Gaetti | .05 | .02 | .00 |
| ☐ 279 Mickey Hatcher | .03 | .01 | .00 |
| ☐ 280 Ed Hodge | .08 | .03 | .01 |
| ☐ 281 Kent Hrbek | .25 | .10 | .02 |
| ☐ 282 Houston Jimenez | .03 | .01 | .00 |
| ☐ 283 Tim Laudner | .03 | .01 | .00 |
| ☐ 284 Rick Lysander | .03 | .01 | .00 |
| ☐ 285 Dave Meier | .12 | .05 | .01 |
| ☐ 286 Kirby Puckett | .35 | .15 | .03 |
| ☐ 287 Pat Putnam | .03 | .01 | .00 |
| ☐ 288 Ken Schrom | .03 | .01 | .00 |
| ☐ 289 Mike Smithson | .05 | .02 | .00 |
| ☐ 290 Tim Teufel | .07 | .03 | .01 |
| ☐ 291 Frank Viola | .08 | .03 | .01 |
| ☐ 292 Ron Washington | .03 | .01 | .00 |
| **CALIFORNIA ANGELS** | | | |
| ☐ 293 Don Aase | .03 | .01 | .00 |
| ☐ 294 Juan Beniquez | .05 | .02 | .00 |
| ☐ 295 Bob Boone | .05 | .02 | .00 |
| ☐ 296 Mike Brown | .07 | .03 | .01 |
| ☐ 297 Rod Carew | .30 | .12 | .03 |
| ☐ 298 Doug Corbett | .03 | .01 | .00 |
| ☐ 299 Doug DeCinces | .08 | .03 | .01 |
| ☐ 300 Brian Downing | .05 | .02 | .00 |
| ☐ 301 Ken Forsch | .05 | .02 | .00 |
| ☐ 302 Bobby Grich | .07 | .03 | .01 |
| ☐ 303 Reggie Jackson | .35 | .15 | .03 |
| ☐ 304 Tommy John | .13 | .06 | .01 |
| ☐ 305 Curt Kaufman | .10 | .04 | .01 |
| ☐ 306 Bruce Kison | .03 | .01 | .00 |
| ☐ 307 Fred Lynn | .15 | .06 | .01 |
| ☐ 308 Gary Pettis | .07 | .03 | .01 |
| ☐ 309 Ron Romanick | .30 | .12 | .03 |
| ☐ 310 Luis Sanchez | .03 | .01 | .00 |
| ☐ 311 Dick Schofield | .07 | .03 | .01 |
| ☐ 312 Daryl Sconiers | .03 | .01 | .00 |
| ☐ 313 Jim Slaton | .03 | .01 | .00 |
| ☐ 314 Derrel Thomas | .03 | .01 | .00 |
| ☐ 315 Rob Wilfong | .03 | .01 | .00 |
| ☐ 316 Mike Witt | .09 | .04 | .01 |
| ☐ 317 Geoff Zahn | .05 | .02 | .00 |
| **ATLANTA BRAVES** | | | |

| | MINT | VG-E | F-G |
|---|---|---|---|
| ☐ 318 Len Barker | .05 | .02 | .00 |
| ☐ 319 Steve Bedrosian | .07 | .03 | .01 |
| ☐ 320 Bruce Benedict | .03 | .01 | .00 |
| ☐ 321 Rick Camp | .03 | .01 | .00 |
| ☐ 322 Chris Chambliss | .05 | .02 | .00 |
| ☐ 323 Jeff Dedmon | .08 | .03 | .01 |
| ☐ 324 Terry Forster | .07 | .03 | .01 |
| ☐ 325 Gene Garber | .03 | .01 | .00 |
| ☐ 326 Albert Hall | .10 | .04 | .01 |
| ☐ 327 Terry Harper | .03 | .01 | .00 |
| ☐ 328 Bob Horner | .15 | .06 | .01 |
| ☐ 329 Glenn Hubbard | .05 | .02 | .00 |
| ☐ 330 Randy Johnson | .03 | .01 | .00 |
| ☐ 331 Brad Komminsk | .08 | .03 | .01 |
| ☐ 332 Rick Mahler | .06 | .02 | .00 |
| ☐ 333 Craig McMurtry | .05 | .02 | .00 |
| ☐ 334 Donnie Moore | .06 | .02 | .00 |
| ☐ 335 Dale Murphy | .45 | .20 | .04 |
| ☐ 336 Ken Oberkfell | .03 | .01 | .00 |
| ☐ 337 Pascual Perez | .05 | .02 | .00 |
| ☐ 338 Gerald Perry | .05 | .02 | .00 |
| ☐ 339 Rafael Ramirez | .03 | .01 | .00 |
| ☐ 340 Jerry Royster | .03 | .01 | .00 |
| ☐ 341 Alex Trevino | .03 | .01 | .00 |
| ☐ 342 Claudell Washington | .07 | .03 | .01 |
| **HOUSTON ASTROS** | | | |
| ☐ 343 Alan Ashby | .03 | .01 | .00 |
| ☐ 344 Mark Bailey | .08 | .03 | .01 |
| ☐ 345 Kevin Bass | .03 | .01 | .00 |
| ☐ 346 Enos Cabell | .03 | .01 | .00 |
| ☐ 347 Jose Cruz | .11 | .05 | .01 |
| ☐ 348 Bill Dawley | .05 | .02 | .00 |
| ☐ 349 Frank DiPino | .05 | .02 | .00 |
| ☐ 350 Bill Doran | .06 | .02 | .00 |
| ☐ 351 Phil Garner | .05 | .02 | .00 |
| ☐ 352 Bob Knepper | .07 | .03 | .01 |
| ☐ 353 Mike LaCoss | .03 | .01 | .00 |
| ☐ 354 Jerry Mumphrey | .03 | .01 | .00 |
| ☐ 355 Joe Niekro | .07 | .03 | .01 |
| ☐ 356 Terry Puhl | .05 | .02 | .00 |
| ☐ 357 Craig Reynolds | .03 | .01 | .00 |
| ☐ 358 Vern Ruhle | .03 | .01 | .00 |
| ☐ 359 Nolan Ryan | .25 | .10 | .02 |
| ☐ 360 Joe Sambito | .05 | .02 | .00 |
| ☐ 361 Mike Scott | .05 | .02 | .00 |
| ☐ 362 Dave Smith | .05 | .02 | .00 |
| ☐ 363 Julio Solano | .10 | .04 | .01 |
| ☐ 364 Dickie Thon | .06 | .02 | .00 |
| ☐ 365 Denny Walling | .03 | .01 | .00 |
| **LOS ANGELES DODGERS** | | | |
| ☐ 366 Dave Anderson | .03 | .01 | .00 |
| ☐ 367 Bob Bailor | .03 | .01 | .00 |

| | MINT | VG-E | F-G | | | MINT | VG-E | F-G |
|---|---|---|---|---|---|---|---|---|
| ☐ 368 Greg Brock | .07 | .03 | .01 | ☐ 419 Bill Caudill | | .07 | .03 | .01 |
| ☐ 369 Carlos Diaz | .03 | .07 | .00 | ☐ 420 Chris Codiroli | | .03 | .01 | .00 |
| ☐ 370 Pedro Guerrero | .25 | .10 | .02 | ☐ 421 Tim Conroy | | .03 | .01 | .00 |
| ☐ 371 Orel Hershiser | 1.00 | .45 | .10 | ☐ 422 Mike Heath | | .03 | .01 | .00 |
| ☐ 372 Rick Honeycutt | .05 | .02 | .00 | ☐ 423 Jim Essian | | .03 | .01 | .00 |
| ☐ 373 Burt Hooton | .03 | .01 | .00 | ☐ 424 Mike Heath | | .03 | .01 | .00 |
| ☐ 374 Ken Howell | .20 | .09 | .02 | ☐ 425 Rickey Henderson | | .40 | .18 | .04 |
| ☐ 375 Ken Landreaux | .05 | .02 | .00 | ☐ 426 Donnie Hill | | .03 | .01 | .00 |
| ☐ 376 Candy Maldonado | .05 | .02 | .00 | ☐ 427 Dave Kingman | | .09 | .04 | .01 |
| ☐ 377 Mike Marshall | .11 | .05 | .01 | ☐ 428 Bill Krueger | | .03 | .01 | .00 |
| ☐ 378 Tom Niedenfuer | .06 | .02 | .00 | ☐ 429 Carney Lansford | | .10 | .04 | .01 |
| ☐ 379 Alejandro Pena | .05 | .02 | .00 | ☐ 430 Steve McCatty | | .03 | .01 | .00 |
| ☐ 380 Jerry Reuss | .05 | .02 | .00 | ☐ 431 Joe Morgan | | .15 | .06 | .01 |
| ☐ 381 R.J. Reynolds | .15 | .06 | .01 | ☐ 432 Dwayne Murphy | | .07 | .03 | .01 |
| ☐ 382 German Rivera | .12 | .05 | .01 | ☐ 433 Tony Phillips | | .03 | .01 | .00 |
| ☐ 383 Bill Russell | .05 | .02 | .00 | ☐ 434 Lary Sorensen | | .03 | .01 | .00 |
| ☐ 384 Steve Sax | .11 | .05 | .01 | ☐ 435 Mike Warren | | .05 | .02 | .00 |
| ☐ 385 Mike Scioscia | .03 | .01 | .00 | ☐ 436 Curt Young | | .12 | .05 | .01 |
| ☐ 386 Franklin Stubbs | .12 | .05 | .01 | **CLEVELAND INDIANS** | | | | |
| ☐ 387 Fernando Valenzuela | .30 | .12 | .03 | ☐ 437 Luis Aponte | | .03 | .01 | .00 |
| ☐ 388 Bob Welch | .06 | .02 | .00 | ☐ 438 Chris Bando | | .03 | .01 | .00 |
| ☐ 389 Terry Whitfield | .03 | .01 | .00 | ☐ 439 Tony Bernazard | | .03 | .01 | .00 |
| ☐ 390 Steve Yeager | .05 | .02 | .00 | ☐ 440 Bert Blyleven | | .11 | .05 | .01 |
| ☐ 391 Pat Zachry | .03 | .01 | .00 | ☐ 441 Brett Butler | | .09 | .04 | .01 |
| **MONTREAL EXPOS** | | | | ☐ 442 Ernie Camacho | | .03 | .01 | .00 |
| ☐ 392 Fred Breining | .03 | .01 | .00 | ☐ 443 Joe Carter | | .07 | .03 | .01 |
| ☐ 393 Gary Carter | .30 | .12 | .03 | ☐ 444 Carmelo Castillo | | .03 | .01 | .00 |
| ☐ 394 Andre Dawson | .20 | .09 | .02 | ☐ 445 Jamie Easterly | | .03 | .01 | .00 |
| ☐ 395 Miguel Dilone | .03 | .01 | .00 | ☐ 446 Steve Farr | | .10 | .04 | .01 |
| ☐ 396 Dan Driessen | .05 | .02 | .00 | ☐ 447 Mike Fischlin | | .03 | .01 | .00 |
| ☐ 397 Doug Flynn | .03 | .01 | .00 | ☐ 448 Julio Franco | | .10 | .04 | .01 |
| ☐ 398 Terry Francona | .06 | .02 | .00 | ☐ 449 Mel Hall | | .08 | .03 | .01 |
| ☐ 399 Bill Gullickson | .05 | .02 | .00 | ☐ 450 Mike Hargrove | | .05 | .02 | .00 |
| ☐ 400 Bob James | .06 | .02 | .00 | ☐ 451 Neal Heaton | | .05 | .02 | .00 |
| ☐ 401 Charlie Lea | .05 | .02 | .00 | ☐ 452 Brook Jacoby | | .09 | .04 | .01 |
| ☐ 402 Bryan Little | .03 | .01 | .00 | ☐ 453 Mike Jeffcoat | | .05 | .02 | .00 |
| ☐ 403 Gary Lucas | .03 | .01 | .00 | ☐ 454 Don Schulze | | .08 | .03 | .01 |
| ☐ 404 David Palmer | .05 | .02 | .00 | ☐ 455 Roy Smith | | .08 | .03 | .01 |
| ☐ 405 Tim Raines | .20 | .09 | .02 | ☐ 456 Pat Tabler | | .05 | .02 | .00 |
| ☐ 406 Mike Ramsey | .03 | .01 | .00 | ☐ 457 Andre Thornton | | .07 | .03 | .01 |
| ☐ 407 Jeff Reardon | .07 | .03 | .01 | ☐ 458 George Vukovich | | .03 | .01 | .00 |
| ☐ 408 Steve Rogers | .07 | .03 | .01 | ☐ 459 Tom Waddell | | .10 | .04 | .01 |
| ☐ 409 Dan Schatzeder | .03 | .01 | .00 | ☐ 460 Jerry Willard | | .03 | .01 | .00 |
| ☐ 410 Bryn Smith | .05 | .02 | .00 | **PITTSBURGH PIRATES** | | | | |
| ☐ 411 Mike Stenhouse | .05 | .02 | .00 | ☐ 461 Dale Berra | | .05 | .02 | .00 |
| ☐ 412 Tim Wallach | .09 | .04 | .01 | ☐ 462 John Candelaria | | .06 | .02 | .00 |
| ☐ 413 Jim Wohlford | .03 | .01 | .00 | ☐ 463 Jose DeLeon | | .05 | .02 | .00 |
| **OAKLAND A'S** | | | | ☐ 464 Doug Frobel | | .03 | .01 | .00 |
| ☐ 414 Bill Almon | .03 | .01 | .00 | ☐ 465 Cecilio Guante | | .03 | .01 | .00 |
| ☐ 415 Keith Atherton | .03 | .01 | .00 | ☐ 466 Brian Harper | | .03 | .01 | .00 |
| ☐ 416 Bruce Bochte | .05 | .02 | .00 | ☐ 467 Lee Lacy | | .05 | .02 | .00 |
| ☐ 417 Tom Burgmeier | .03 | .01 | .00 | ☐ 468 Bill Madlock | | .12 | .05 | .01 |
| ☐ 418 Ray Burris | .03 | .01 | .00 | ☐ 469 Lee Mazzilli | | .05 | .02 | .00 |

| | MINT | VG-E | F-G |
|---|---|---|---|
| ☐ 470 Larry McWilliams | .05 | .02 | .00 |
| ☐ 471 Jim Morrison | .03 | .01 | .00 |
| ☐ 472 Tony Pena | .12 | .05 | .01 |
| ☐ 473 Johnny Ray | .10 | .04 | .01 |
| ☐ 474 Rick Rhoden | .05 | .02 | .00 |
| ☐ 475 Don Robinson | .03 | .01 | .00 |
| ☐ 476 Rod Scurry | .03 | .01 | .00 |
| ☐ 477 Kent Tekulve | .06 | .02 | .00 |
| ☐ 478 Jason Thompson | .07 | .03 | .01 |
| ☐ 479 John Tudor | .15 | .06 | .01 |
| ☐ 480 Lee Tunnell | .03 | .01 | .00 |
| ☐ 481 Marvell Wynne | .05 | .02 | .00 |
| **SEATTLE MARINERS** | | | |
| ☐ 482 Salome Barojas | .03 | .01 | .00 |
| ☐ 483 Dave Beard | .03 | .01 | .00 |
| ☐ 484 Jim Beattie | .03 | .01 | .00 |
| ☐ 485 Barry Bonnell | .03 | .01 | .00 |
| ☐ 486 Phil Bradley | .70 | .32 | .07 |
| ☐ 487 Al Cowens | .05 | .02 | .00 |
| ☐ 488 Alvin Davis | .70 | .32 | .07 |
| ☐ 489 Dave Henderson | .05 | .02 | .00 |
| ☐ 490 Steve Henderson | .03 | .01 | .00 |
| ☐ 491 Bob Kearney | .03 | .01 | .00 |
| ☐ 492 Mark Langston | .35 | .15 | .03 |
| ☐ 493 Larry Milbourne | .03 | .01 | .00 |
| ☐ 494 Paul Mirabella | .03 | .01 | .00 |
| ☐ 495 Mike Moore | .06 | .02 | .00 |
| ☐ 496 Edwin Nunez | .05 | .02 | .00 |
| ☐ 497 Spike Owen | .05 | .02 | .00 |
| ☐ 498 Jack Perconte | .03 | .01 | .00 |
| ☐ 499 Ken Phelps | .05 | .02 | .00 |
| ☐ 500 Jim Presley | .70 | .32 | .07 |
| ☐ 501 Mike Stanton | .03 | .01 | .00 |
| ☐ 502 Bob Stoddard | .03 | .01 | .00 |
| ☐ 503 Gorman Thomas | .10 | .04 | .01 |
| ☐ 504 Ed VandeBerg | .05 | .02 | .00 |
| ☐ 505 Matt Young | .05 | .02 | .00 |
| **CHICAGO WHITE SOX** | | | |
| ☐ 506 Juan Agosto | .03 | .01 | .00 |
| ☐ 507 Harold Baines | .20 | .09 | .02 |
| ☐ 508 Floyd Bannister | .05 | .02 | .00 |
| ☐ 509 Britt Burns | .07 | .03 | .01 |
| ☐ 510 Julio Cruz | .03 | .01 | .00 |
| ☐ 511 Richard Dotson | .06 | .02 | .00 |
| ☐ 512 Jerry Dybzinski | .03 | .01 | .00 |
| ☐ 513 Carlton Fisk | .14 | .05 | .01 |
| ☐ 514 Scott Fletcher | .03 | .01 | .00 |
| ☐ 515 Jerry Hairston | .03 | .01 | .00 |
| ☐ 516 Marc Hill | .03 | .01 | .00 |
| ☐ 517 LaMarr Hoyt | .08 | .03 | .01 |
| ☐ 518 Ron Kittle | .15 | .06 | .01 |
| ☐ 519 Rudy Law | .03 | .01 | .00 |
| ☐ 520 Vance Law | .03 | .01 | .00 |

| | MINT | VG-E | F-G |
|---|---|---|---|
| ☐ 521 Greg Luzinski | .10 | .04 | .01 |
| ☐ 522 Gene Nelson | .03 | .01 | .00 |
| ☐ 523 Tom Paciorek | .03 | .01 | .00 |
| ☐ 524 Ron Reed | .03 | .01 | .00 |
| ☐ 525 Bert Roberge | .03 | .01 | .00 |
| ☐ 526 Tom Seaver | .25 | .10 | .02 |
| ☐ 527 Roy Smalley | .05 | .02 | .00 |
| ☐ 528 Dan Spillner | .03 | .01 | .00 |
| ☐ 529 Mike Squires | .03 | .01 | .00 |
| ☐ 530 Greg Walker | .13 | .06 | .01 |
| **CINCINNATI REDS** | | | |
| ☐ 531 Cesar Cedeno | .07 | .03 | .01 |
| ☐ 532 Dave Concepcion | .08 | .03 | .01 |
| ☐ 533 Eric Davis | .25 | .10 | .02 |
| ☐ 534 Nick Esasky | .07 | .03 | .01 |
| ☐ 535 Tom Foley | .03 | .01 | .00 |
| ☐ 536 John Franco | .30 | .12 | .03 |
| ☐ 537 Brad Gulden | .03 | .01 | .00 |
| ☐ 538 Tom Hume | .03 | .01 | .00 |
| ☐ 539 Wayne Krenchicki | .03 | .01 | .00 |
| ☐ 540 Andy McGaffigan | .03 | .01 | .00 |
| ☐ 541 Eddie Milner | .05 | .02 | .00 |
| ☐ 542 Ron Oester | .05 | .02 | .00 |
| ☐ 543 Bob Owchinko | .03 | .01 | .00 |
| ☐ 544 Dave Parker | .17 | .07 | .01 |
| ☐ 545 Frank Pastore | .03 | .01 | .00 |
| ☐ 546 Tony Perez | .12 | .05 | .01 |
| ☐ 547 Ted Power | .06 | .02 | .00 |
| ☐ 548 Joe Price | .03 | .01 | .00 |
| ☐ 649 Gary Redus | .07 | .03 | .01 |
| ☐ 550 Pete Rose | .60 | .28 | .06 |
| ☐ 551 Jeff Russell | .03 | .01 | .00 |
| ☐ 552 Mario Soto | .07 | .03 | .01 |
| ☐ 553 Jay Tibbs | .15 | .06 | .01 |
| ☐ 554 Duane Walker | .03 | .01 | .00 |
| **TEXAS RANGERS** | | | |
| ☐ 555 Alan Bannister | .03 | .01 | .00 |
| ☐ 556 Buddy Bell | .10 | .04 | .01 |
| ☐ 557 Danny Darwin | .03 | .01 | .00 |
| ☐ 558 Charlie Hough | .05 | .02 | .00 |
| ☐ 559 Bobby Jones | .03 | .01 | .00 |
| ☐ 560 Odell Jones | .03 | .01 | .00 |
| ☐ 561 Jeff Kunkel | .15 | .06 | .01 |
| ☐ 562 Mike Mason | .12 | .05 | .01 |
| ☐ 563 Pete O'Brien | .05 | .02 | .00 |
| ☐ 564 Larry Parrish | .07 | .03 | .01 |
| ☐ 565 Mickey Rivers | .05 | .02 | .00 |
| ☐ 566 Billy Sample | .03 | .01 | .00 |
| ☐ 567 Dave Schmidt | .03 | .01 | .00 |
| ☐ 568 Donnie Scott | .08 | .03 | .01 |
| ☐ 569 Dave Stewart | .03 | .01 | .00 |
| ☐ 570 Frank Tanana | .05 | .02 | .00 |
| ☐ 571 Wayne Tolleson | .03 | .01 | .00 |

| | MINT | VG-E | F-G |
|---|---|---|---|
| ☐ 572 Gary Ward | .06 | .02 | .00 |
| ☐ 573 Curtis Wilkerson | .05 | .02 | .00 |
| ☐ 574 George Wright | .05 | .02 | .00 |
| ☐ 575 Ned Yost | .03 | .01 | .00 |
| **MILWAUKEE BREWERS** | | | |
| ☐ 576 Mark Brouhard | .03 | .01 | .00 |
| ☐ 577 Mike Caldwell | .05 | .02 | .00 |
| ☐ 578 Bobby Clark | .03 | .01 | .00 |
| ☐ 579 Jaime Cocanower | .08 | .03 | .01 |
| ☐ 580 Cecil Cooper | .13 | .06 | .01 |
| ☐ 581 Rollie Fingers | .15 | .06 | .01 |
| ☐ 582 Jim Gantner | .05 | .02 | .00 |
| ☐ 583 Moose Haas | .05 | .02 | .00 |
| ☐ 584 Dion James | .07 | .03 | .01 |
| ☐ 585 Pete Ladd | .03 | .01 | .00 |
| ☐ 586 Rick Manning | .03 | .01 | .00 |
| ☐ 587 Bob McClure | .03 | .01 | .00 |
| ☐ 588 Paul Molitor | .11 | .05 | .01 |
| ☐ 589 Charlie Moore | .03 | .01 | .00 |
| ☐ 590 Ben Oglivie | .07 | .03 | .01 |
| ☐ 591 Chuck Porter | .03 | .01 | .00 |
| ☐ 592 Randy Ready | .15 | .06 | .01 |
| ☐ 593 Ed Romero | .03 | .01 | .00 |
| ☐ 594 Bill Schroeder | .03 | .01 | .00 |
| ☐ 595 Ray Searage | .03 | .01 | .00 |
| ☐ 596 Ted Simmons | .11 | .05 | .01 |
| ☐ 597 Jim Sundberg | .06 | .02 | .00 |
| ☐ 598 Don Sutton | .12 | .05 | .01 |
| ☐ 599 Tom Tellmann | .03 | .01 | .00 |
| ☐ 600 Rick Waits | .03 | .01 | .00 |
| ☐ 601 Robin Yount | .25 | .10 | .02 |
| **SAN FRANCISCO GIANTS** | | | |
| ☐ 602 Dusty Baker | .05 | .02 | .00 |
| ☐ 603 Bob Brenly | .07 | .03 | .01 |
| ☐ 604 Jack Clark | .12 | .05 | .01 |
| ☐ 605 Chili Davis | .08 | .03 | .01 |
| ☐ 606 Mark Davis | .03 | .01 | .00 |
| ☐ 607 Dan Gladden | .25 | .10 | .02 |
| ☐ 608 Atlee Hammaker | .07 | .03 | .01 |
| ☐ 609 Mike Krukow | .03 | .01 | .00 |
| ☐ 610 Duane Kuiper | .03 | .01 | .00 |
| ☐ 611 Bob Lacey | .03 | .01 | .00 |
| ☐ 612 Bill Laskey | .03 | .01 | .00 |
| ☐ 613 Gary Lavelle | .03 | .01 | .00 |
| ☐ 614 Johnnie LeMaster | .03 | .01 | .00 |
| ☐ 615 Jeff Leonard | .06 | .02 | .00 |
| ☐ 616 Randy Lerch | .03 | .01 | .00 |
| ☐ 617 Greg Minton | .05 | .02 | .00 |
| ☐ 618 Steve Nicosia | .03 | .01 | .00 |
| ☐ 619 Gene Richards | .03 | .01 | .00 |
| ☐ 620 Jeff Robinson | .10 | .04 | .01 |
| ☐ 621 Scot Thompson | .03 | .01 | .00 |
| ☐ 622 Manny Trillo | .05 | .02 | .00 |
| ☐ 623 Brad Wellman | .03 | .01 | .00 |
| ☐ 624 Frank Williams | .10 | .04 | .01 |
| ☐ 625 Joel Youngblood | .03 | .01 | .00 |
| **SPECIAL CARDS (626–643)** | | | |
| ☐ 626 Cal Ripken IA | .25 | .10 | .02 |
| ☐ 627 Mike Schmidt IA | .25 | .10 | .02 |
| ☐ 628 Giving The Signs: Sparky Anderson | .05 | .02 | .00 |
| ☐ 629 AL Pitcher's Nightmare: Dave Winfield Rickey Henderson | .25 | .10 | .02 |
| ☐ 630 NL Pitcher's Nightmare: Mike Schmidt Ryne Sandberg | .25 | .10 | .02 |
| ☐ 631 NL All-Stars: Darryl Strawberry Gary Carter Steve Garvey Ozzie Smith | .25 | .10 | .02 |
| ☐ 632 A-S Winning Battery: Gary Carter Charlie Lea | .10 | .04 | .01 |
| ☐ 633 NL Pennant Clinchers: Steve Garvey Goose Gossage | .15 | .06 | .01 |
| ☐ 634 NL Rookie Phenoms: Dwight Gooden Juan Samuel | 1.00 | .45 | .10 |
| ☐ 635 Toronto's Big Guns: Willie Upshaw | .08 | .03 | .01 |
| ☐ 636 Toronto's Big Guns: Lloyd Moseby | .08 | .03 | .01 |
| ☐ 637 HOLLAND: Al Holland | .05 | .02 | .00 |
| ☐ 638 TUNNELL: Lee Tunnell | .05 | .02 | .00 |
| ☐ 639 500th Homer: Reggie Jackson | .25 | .10 | .02 |
| ☐ 640 4000th Hit: Pete Rose | .35 | .15 | .03 |
| ☐ 641 Father and Son: Cal Ripken Jr. and Sr. | .25 | .10 | .02 |
| ☐ 642 Cubs: Division Champs | .05 | .02 | .00 |
| ☐ 643 Two Perfect Games and One No-Hitter: Mike Witt David Palmer Jack Morris | .10 | .04 | .01 |
| **ROOKIE PAIRS (644–653)** | | | |
| ☐ 644 Willie Lozado and Vic Mata | .12 | .05 | .01 |

| | MINT | VG-E | F-G |
|---|---|---|---|
| ☐ 645 Kelly Gruber and Randy O'Neal | .25 | .10 | .02 |
| ☐ 646 Jose Roman and Joel Skinner | .15 | .06 | .01 |
| ☐ 647 Steve Kiefer and Danny Tartabull | .25 | .10 | .02 |
| ☐ 648 Rob Deer and Alejandro Sanchez | .20 | .09 | .02 |
| ☐ 649 Bill Hatcher and Shawon Dunston | .25 | .10 | .02 |
| ☐ 650 Ron Robinson and Mike Bielecki | .15 | .06 | .01 |
| ☐ 651 Zane Smith and Paul Zuvella | .20 | .09 | .02 |
| ☐ 652 Joe Hesketh and Glenn Davis | .60 | .28 | .06 |
| ☐ 653 John Russell and Steve Jeltz | .25 | .10 | .02 |
| **TEAM CHECKLISTS (654—660)** | | | |
| ☐ 654 CL: Tigers/Padres and Cubs/Mets | .07 | .01 | .00 |
| ☐ 655 CL: Blue Jays/Yankees and Red Sox/Orioles | .07 | .01 | .00 |
| ☐ 656 CL: Royals/Cardinals and Phillies/Twins | .07 | .01 | .00 |
| ☐ 657 CL: Angels/Braves and Astros/Dodgers | .07 | .01 | .00 |
| ☐ 658 CL: Expos/A's and Indians/Pirates | .07 | .01 | .00 |
| ☐ 659 CL: Mariners/White Sox and Reds/Rangers | .07 | .01 | .00 |
| ☐ 660 CL: Brewers/Giants and Special Cards | .07 | .01 | .00 |

## 1985 FLEER UPDATE

This 132 card set was issued late in the collecting year and features new players and players on new teams compared to the 1985 Fleer regular issue cards. Cards measure 2½" by 3½" and were distributed together as a complete set within a special box.

Complete Set: M-11.00; VG-E-5.25; F-G-1.10

| | MINT | VG-E | F-G |
|---|---|---|---|
| Common Player (1–132) | .05 | .02 | .00 |
| ☐ U 1 Don Aase | .05 | .02 | .00 |
| ☐ U 2 Bill Almon | .05 | .02 | .00 |
| ☐ U 3 Dusty Baker | .07 | .03 | .01 |
| ☐ U 4 Dale Berra | .07 | .03 | .01 |
| ☐ U 5 Karl Best | .11 | .05 | .01 |
| ☐ U 6 Tim Birtsas | .30 | .12 | .03 |
| ☐ U 7 Vida Blue | .07 | .03 | .01 |
| ☐ U 8 Rich Bordi | .05 | .02 | .00 |
| ☐ U 9 Daryl Boston | .15 | .06 | .01 |
| ☐ U 10 Hubie Brooks | .15 | .06 | .01 |
| ☐ U 11 Chris Brown | .60 | .28 | .06 |
| ☐ U 12 Tom Browning | .65 | .30 | .06 |
| ☐ U 13 Al Bumbry | .05 | .02 | .00 |
| ☐ U 14 Tim Burke | .20 | .09 | .02 |
| ☐ U 15 Ray Burris | .05 | .02 | .00 |
| ☐ U 16 Jeff Burroughs | .05 | .02 | .00 |
| ☐ U 17 Ivan Calderon | .25 | .10 | .02 |
| ☐ U 18 Jeff Calhoun | .15 | .06 | .01 |
| ☐ U 19 Bill Campbell | .05 | .02 | .00 |
| ☐ U 20 Don Carman | .25 | .10 | .02 |
| ☐ U 21 Gary Carter | .65 | .30 | .06 |
| ☐ U 22 Bobby Castillo | .05 | .02 | .00 |
| ☐ U 23 Bill Caudill | .07 | .03 | .01 |
| ☐ U 24 Rick Cerone | .05 | .02 | .00 |
| ☐ U 25 Jack Clark | .25 | .10 | .02 |
| ☐ U 26 Pat Clements | .25 | .10 | .02 |
| ☐ U 27 Stewart Cliburn | .25 | .10 | .02 |
| ☐ U 28 Vince Coleman | 2.50 | 1.00 | .25 |
| ☐ U 29 Dave Collins | .07 | .03 | .01 |
| ☐ U 30 Fritz Connally | .11 | .05 | .01 |
| ☐ U 31 Henry Cotto | .05 | .02 | .00 |
| ☐ U 32 Danny Darwin | .05 | .02 | .00 |
| ☐ U 33 Darren Daulton | .15 | .06 | .01 |
| ☐ U 34 Jerry Davis | .15 | .06 | .01 |
| ☐ U 35 Brian Dayett | .15 | .06 | .01 |
| ☐ U 36 Ken Dixon | .20 | .09 | .02 |
| ☐ U 37 Tommy Dunbar | .12 | .05 | .01 |
| ☐ U 38 Mariano Duncan | .65 | .30 | .06 |
| ☐ U 39 Bob Fallon | .12 | .05 | .01 |
| ☐ U 40 Brian Fisher | .40 | .18 | .04 |
| ☐ U 41 Mike Fitzgerald | .05 | .02 | .00 |

| | MINT | VG-E | F-G | | MINT | VG-E | F-G |
|---|---|---|---|---|---|---|---|
| ☐ U 42 Ray Fontenot | .05 | .02 | .00 | ☐ U 95 Luis Salazar | .05 | .02 | .00 |
| ☐ U 43 Greg Gagne | .12 | .05 | .01 | ☐ U 96 Joe Sambito | .07 | .03 | .01 |
| ☐ U 44 Oscar Gamble | .07 | .03 | .01 | ☐ U 97 Billy Sample | .05 | .02 | .00 |
| ☐ U 45 Jim Gott | .05 | .02 | .00 | ☐ U 98 Alex Sanchez | .07 | .03 | .01 |
| ☐ U 46 David Green | .07 | .03 | .01 | ☐ U 99 Calvin Schiraldi | .25 | .10 | .02 |
| ☐ U 47 Alfredo Griffin | .07 | .03 | .01 | ☐ U 100 Rick Schu | .25 | .10 | .02 |
| ☐ U 48 Ozzie Guillen | .75 | .35 | .07 | ☐ U 101 Larry Sheets | .30 | .12 | .03 |
| ☐ U 49 Toby Harrah | .07 | .03 | .01 | ☐ U 102 Ron Shephard | .12 | .05 | .01 |
| ☐ U 50 Ron Hassey | .05 | .02 | .00 | ☐ U 103 Nelson Simmons | .35 | .15 | .03 |
| ☐ U 51 Rickey Henderson | .75 | .35 | .07 | ☐ U 104 Don Slaught | .05 | .02 | .00 |
| ☐ U 52 Steve Henderson | .05 | .02 | .00 | ☐ U 105 Roy Smalley | .07 | .03 | .01 |
| ☐ U 53 George Hendrick | .07 | .03 | .01 | ☐ U 106 Lonnie Smith | .09 | .04 | .01 |
| ☐ U 54 Teddy Higuera | .35 | .15 | .03 | ☐ U 107 Nate Snell | .20 | .09 | .02 |
| ☐ U 55 Al Holland | .07 | .03 | .01 | ☐ U 108 Lary Sorensen | .05 | .02 | .00 |
| ☐ U 56 Burt Hooton | .05 | .02 | .00 | ☐ U 109 Chris Speier | .05 | .02 | .00 |
| ☐ U 57 Jay Howell | .12 | .05 | .01 | ☐ U 110 Mike Stenhouse | .10 | .04 | .01 |
| ☐ U 58 LaMarr Hoyt | .12 | .05 | .01 | ☐ U 111 Tim Stoddard | .05 | .02 | .00 |
| ☐ U 59 Tim Hulett | .15 | .06 | .01 | ☐ U 112 John Stuper | .05 | .02 | .00 |
| ☐ U 60 Bob James | .10 | .04 | .01 | ☐ U 113 Jim Sundberg | .07 | .03 | .01 |
| ☐ U 61 Cliff Johnson | .05 | .02 | .00 | ☐ U 114 Bruce Sutter | .25 | .10 | .02 |
| ☐ U 62 Howard Johnson | .07 | .03 | .01 | ☐ U 115 Don Sutton | .25 | .10 | .02 |
| ☐ U 63 Ruppert Jones | .07 | .03 | .01 | ☐ U 116 Bruce Tanner | .15 | .06 | .01 |
| ☐ U 64 Steve Kemp | .07 | .03 | .01 | ☐ U 117 Kent Tekulve | .09 | .04 | .01 |
| ☐ U 65 Bruce Kison | .05 | .02 | .00 | ☐ U 118 Walt Terrell | .07 | .03 | .01 |
| ☐ U 66 Mike LaCoss | .05 | .02 | .00 | ☐ U 119 Mickey Tettleton | .12 | .05 | .01 |
| ☐ U 67 Lee Lacy | .07 | .03 | .01 | ☐ U 120 Rich Thompson | .10 | .04 | .01 |
| ☐ U 68 Dave LaPoint | .05 | .02 | .00 | ☐ U 121 Louis Thornton | .12 | .05 | .01 |
| ☐ U 69 Gary Lavelle | .05 | .02 | .00 | ☐ U 122 Alex Trevino | .05 | .02 | .00 |
| ☐ U 70 Vance Law | .05 | .02 | .00 | ☐ U 123 John Tudor | .25 | .10 | .02 |
| ☐ U 71 Manny Lee | .15 | .06 | .01 | ☐ U 124 Jose Uribe | .10 | .04 | .01 |
| ☐ U 72 Sixto Lezcano | .05 | .02 | .00 | ☐ U 125 Dave Valle | .10 | .04 | .01 |
| ☐ U 73 Tim Lollar | .05 | .02 | .00 | ☐ U 126 Dave Von Ohlen | .05 | .02 | .00 |
| ☐ U 74 Urbano Lugo | .12 | .05 | .01 | ☐ U 127 Curt Wardle | .05 | .02 | .00 |
| ☐ U 75 Fred Lynn | .20 | .09 | .02 | ☐ U 128 U.L. Washington | .05 | .02 | .00 |
| ☐ U 76 Steve Lyons | .25 | .10 | .02 | ☐ U 129 Ed Whitson | .07 | .03 | .01 |
| ☐ U 77 Mickey Mahler | .05 | .02 | .00 | ☐ U 130 Herm Winningham | .20 | .09 | .02 |
| ☐ U 78 Ron Mathis | .15 | .06 | .01 | ☐ U 131 Rich Yett | .12 | .05 | .01 |
| ☐ U 79 Len Matuszek | .10 | .04 | .01 | ☐ U 132 Checklist U1–U132 | .05 | .01 | .00 |
| ☐ U 80 Odibbe McDowell | .85 | .40 | .08 | | | | |
| ☐ U 81 Roger McDowell | .55 | .25 | .05 | | | | |
| ☐ U 82 Donnie Moore | .11 | .05 | .01 | | | | |
| ☐ U 83 Ron Musselman | .12 | .05 | .01 | | | | |
| ☐ U 84 Al Oliver | .15 | .06 | .01 | | | | |
| ☐ U 85 Joe Orsulak | .25 | .10 | .02 | | | | |
| ☐ U 86 Dan Pasqua | .50 | .22 | .05 | | | | |
| ☐ U 87 Chris Pittaro | .15 | .06 | .01 | | | | |
| ☐ U 88 Rick Reuschel | .10 | .04 | .01 | | | | |
| ☐ U 89 Earnie Riles | .60 | .28 | .06 | | | | |
| ☐ U 90 Jerry Royster | .05 | .02 | .00 | | | | |
| ☐ U 91 Dave Rozema | .05 | .02 | .00 | | | | |
| ☐ U 92 Dave Rucker | .05 | .02 | .00 | | | | |
| ☐ U 93 Vern Ruhle | .05 | .02 | .00 | | | | |
| ☐ U 94 Mark Salas | .40 | .18 | .04 | | | | |

## 1986 FLEER

The cards in this 660 card set measure 2½" by 3½". The 1986 Fleer set features fronts which contain the team logo along with the player's name and position. The border enclosing the photo is dark blue. The backs feature the same name, number, and statistics format that Fleer has been using over the past few years. Wax pack and cello pack boxes contained a four card panel on the bottom; these cards were numbered C-1 through C-8 and are listed at the end of the list of regular issue cards below. The set is considered complete without the box bottom cards.

Complete Set: M-16.00; VG-E-7.50; F-G-1.60

|  | MINT | VG-E | F-G |
|---|---|---|---|
| Common Player ....... | .03 | .01 | .00 |
| **KANSAS CITY ROYALS** | | | |
| ☐ 1 Steve Balboni .......... | .08 | .02 | .00 |
| ☐ 2 Joe Beckwith .......... | .03 | .01 | .00 |
| ☐ 3 Buddy Biancalana ..... | .03 | .01 | .00 |
| ☐ 4 Bud Black ............ | .03 | .01 | .00 |
| ☐ 5 George Brett .......... | .35 | .15 | .03 |
| ☐ 6 Onix Concepcion ...... | .03 | .01 | .00 |
| ☐ 7 Steve Farr ............ | .03 | .01 | .00 |
| ☐ 8 Mark Gubicza ......... | .06 | .02 | .00 |
| ☐ 9 Dane Iorg ............ | .03 | .01 | .00 |
| ☐ 10 Danny Jackson ....... | .06 | .02 | .00 |
| ☐ 11 Lynn Jones .......... | .03 | .01 | .00 |
| ☐ 12 Mike Jones .......... | .03 | .01 | .00 |
| ☐ 13 Charlie Leibrandt ..... | .06 | .02 | .00 |
| ☐ 14 Hal McRae .......... | .06 | .02 | .00 |
| ☐ 15 Omar Moreno ........ | .05 | .02 | .00 |

|  | MINT | VG-E | F-G |
|---|---|---|---|
| ☐ 16 Darryl Motley .......... | .05 | .02 | .00 |
| ☐ 17 Jorge Orta ........... | .03 | .01 | .00 |
| ☐ 18 Dan Quisenberry ...... | .15 | .06 | .01 |
| ☐ 19 Bret Saberhagen ..... | .35 | .15 | .03 |
| ☐ 20 Pat Sheridan ........ | .03 | .01 | .00 |
| ☐ 21 Lonnie Smith ........ | .07 | .03 | .01 |
| ☐ 22 Jim Sundberg ....... | .06 | .02 | .00 |
| ☐ 23 John Wathan ........ | .03 | .01 | .00 |
| ☐ 24 Frank White ......... | .06 | .02 | .00 |
| ☐ 25 Willie Wilson ........ | .15 | .06 | .01 |
| **ST. LOUIS CARDINALS** | | | |
| ☐ 26 Joaquin Andujar ...... | .08 | .03 | .01 |
| ☐ 27 Steve Braun ......... | .03 | .01 | .00 |
| ☐ 28 Bill Campbell ........ | .03 | .01 | .00 |
| ☐ 29 Cesar Cedeno ....... | .06 | .02 | .00 |
| ☐ 30 Jack Clark ......... | .13 | .06 | .01 |
| ☐ 31 Vince Coleman ...... | 1.00 | .40 | .10 |
| ☐ 32 Danny Cox ......... | .08 | .03 | .01 |
| ☐ 33 Ken Dayley ......... | .03 | .01 | .00 |
| ☐ 34 Ivan DeJesus ....... | .03 | .01 | .00 |
| ☐ 35 Bob Forsch ........ | .05 | .02 | .00 |
| ☐ 36 Brian Harper ....... | .03 | .01 | .00 |
| ☐ 37 Tom Herr .......... | .12 | .05 | .01 |
| ☐ 38 Ricky Horton ....... | .05 | .02 | .00 |
| ☐ 39 Kurt Kepshire ...... | .03 | .01 | .00 |
| ☐ 40 Jeff Lahti .......... | .03 | .01 | .00 |
| ☐ 41 Tito Landrum ....... | .05 | .02 | .00 |
| ☐ 42 Willie McGee ....... | .20 | .09 | .02 |
| ☐ 43 Tom Nieto ......... | .03 | .01 | .00 |
| ☐ 44 Terry Pendleton .... | .07 | .03 | .01 |
| ☐ 45 Darrell Porter ...... | .05 | .02 | .00 |
| ☐ 46 Ozzie Smith ........ | .10 | .04 | .01 |
| ☐ 47 John Tudor ........ | .12 | .05 | .01 |
| ☐ 48 Andy Van Slyke ..... | .06 | .02 | .00 |
| ☐ 49 Todd Worrell ....... | .25 | .10 | .02 |
| **TORONTO BLUE JAYS** | | | |
| ☐ 50 Jim Acker ......... | .03 | .01 | .00 |
| ☐ 51 Doyle Alexander ..... | .05 | .02 | .00 |
| ☐ 52 Jesse Barfield ...... | .11 | .05 | .01 |
| ☐ 53 George Bell ........ | .11 | .05 | .01 |
| ☐ 54 Jeff Burroughs ...... | .03 | .01 | .00 |
| ☐ 55 Bill Caudill ........ | .06 | .02 | .00 |
| ☐ 56 Jim Clancy ........ | .03 | .01 | .00 |
| ☐ 57 Tony Fernandez ..... | .10 | .04 | .01 |
| ☐ 58 Tom Filer ......... | .05 | .02 | .00 |
| ☐ 59 Damaso Garcia ..... | .08 | .03 | .01 |
| ☐ 60 Tom Henke ........ | .06 | .02 | .00 |
| ☐ 61 Garth Iorg ........ | .03 | .01 | .00 |
| ☐ 62 Cliff Johnson ...... | .03 | .01 | .00 |
| ☐ 63 Jimmy Key ........ | .08 | .03 | .01 |
| ☐ 64 Dennis Lamp ...... | .03 | .01 | .00 |
| ☐ 65 Gary Lavelle ....... | .03 | .01 | .00 |
| ☐ 66 Buck Martinez ...... | .03 | .01 | .00 |

|  |  | MINT | VG-E | F-G |
|---|---|---|---|---|
| ☐ 67 | Lloyd Moseby | .12 | .05 | .01 |
| ☐ 68 | Rance Mulliniks | .03 | .01 | .00 |
| ☐ 69 | Al Oliver | .12 | .05 | .01 |
| ☐ 70 | Dave Stieb | .13 | .06 | .01 |
| ☐ 71 | Louis Thornton | .12 | .05 | .01 |
| ☐ 72 | Willie Upshaw | .12 | .05 | .01 |
| ☐ 73 | Ernie Whitt | .03 | .01 | .00 |
| | **NEW YORK METS** | | | |
| ☐ 74 | Rick Aguilera | .20 | .09 | .02 |
| ☐ 75 | Wally Backman | .05 | .02 | .00 |
| ☐ 76 | Gary Carter | .30 | .12 | .03 |
| ☐ 77 | Ron Darling | .15 | .06 | .01 |
| ☐ 78 | Len Dykstra | .20 | .09 | .02 |
| ☐ 79 | Sid Fernandez | .06 | .02 | .00 |
| ☐ 80 | George Foster | .11 | .05 | .01 |
| ☐ 81 | Dwight Gooden | 1.25 | .60 | .12 |
| ☐ 82 | Tom Gorman | .03 | .01 | .00 |
| ☐ 83 | Danny Heep | .03 | .01 | .00 |
| ☐ 84 | Keith Hernandez | .25 | .10 | .02 |
| ☐ 85 | Howard Johnson | .05 | .02 | .00 |
| ☐ 86 | Ray Knight | .05 | .02 | .00 |
| ☐ 87 | Terry Leach | .03 | .01 | .00 |
| ☐ 88 | Ed Lynch | .03 | .01 | .00 |
| ☐ 89 | Roger McDowell | .30 | .12 | .03 |
| ☐ 90 | Jesse Orosco | .06 | .02 | .00 |
| ☐ 91 | Tom Paciorek | .03 | .01 | .00 |
| ☐ 92 | Ronn Reynolds | .12 | .05 | .01 |
| ☐ 93 | Rafael Santana | .03 | .01 | .00 |
| ☐ 94 | Doug Sisk | .03 | .01 | .00 |
| ☐ 95 | Rusty Staub | .07 | .03 | .01 |
| ☐ 96 | Darryl Strawberry | .30 | .12 | .03 |
| ☐ 97 | Mookie Wilson | .06 | .02 | .00 |
| | **NEW YORK YANKEES** | | | |
| ☐ 98 | Neil Allen | .05 | .02 | .00 |
| ☐ 99 | Don Baylor | .10 | .04 | .01 |
| ☐ 100 | Dale Berra | .03 | .01 | .00 |
| ☐ 101 | Rich Bordi | .03 | .01 | .00 |
| ☐ 102 | Marty Bystrom | .03 | .01 | .00 |
| ☐ 103 | Joe Cowley | .03 | .01 | .00 |
| ☐ 104 | Brian Fisher | .30 | .12 | .03 |
| ☐ 105 | Ken Griffey | .06 | .02 | .00 |
| ☐ 106 | Ron Guidry | .14 | .06 | .01 |
| ☐ 107 | Ron Hassey | .03 | .01 | .00 |
| ☐ 108 | Rickey Henderson | .35 | .15 | .03 |
| ☐ 109 | Don Mattingly | .70 | .32 | .07 |
| ☐ 110 | Bobby Meacham | .03 | .01 | .00 |
| ☐ 111 | John Montefusco | .05 | .02 | .00 |
| ☐ 112 | Phil Niekro | .13 | .06 | .01 |
| ☐ 113 | Mike Pagliarulo | .05 | .02 | .00 |
| ☐ 114 | Dan Pasqua | .12 | .05 | .01 |
| ☐ 115 | Willie Randolph | .06 | .02 | .00 |
| ☐ 116 | Dave Righetti | .11 | .05 | .01 |
| ☐ 117 | Andre Robertson | .03 | .01 | .00 |

|  |  | MINT | VG-E | F-G |
|---|---|---|---|---|
| ☐ 118 | Billy Sample | .03 | .01 | .00 |
| ☐ 119 | Bob Shirley | .03 | .01 | .00 |
| ☐ 120 | Ed Whitson | .05 | .02 | .00 |
| ☐ 121 | Dave Winfield | .30 | .12 | .03 |
| ☐ 122 | Butch Wynegar | .05 | .02 | .00 |
| | **LOS ANGELES DODGERS** | | | |
| ☐ 123 | Dave Anderson | .03 | .01 | .00 |
| ☐ 124 | Bob Bailor | .03 | .01 | .00 |
| ☐ 125 | Greg Brock | .05 | .02 | .00 |
| ☐ 126 | Enos Cabell | .03 | .01 | .00 |
| ☐ 127 | Bobby Castillo | .03 | .01 | .00 |
| ☐ 128 | Carlos Diaz | .03 | .01 | .00 |
| ☐ 129 | Mariano Duncan | .45 | .20 | .04 |
| ☐ 130 | Pedro Guerrero | .25 | .10 | .02 |
| ☐ 131 | Orel Hershiser | .30 | .12 | .03 |
| ☐ 132 | Rick Honeycutt | .05 | .02 | .00 |
| ☐ 133 | Ken Howell | .05 | .02 | .00 |
| ☐ 134 | Ken Landreaux | .05 | .02 | .00 |
| ☐ 135 | Bill Madlock | .11 | .05 | .01 |
| ☐ 136 | Candy Maldonado | .03 | .01 | .00 |
| ☐ 137 | Mike Marshall | .11 | .05 | .01 |
| ☐ 138 | Len Matuszek | .03 | .01 | .00 |
| ☐ 139 | Tom Niedenfuer | .06 | .02 | .00 |
| ☐ 140 | Alejandro Pena | .06 | .02 | .00 |
| ☐ 141 | Jerry Reuss | .06 | .02 | .00 |
| ☐ 142 | Bill Russell | .05 | .02 | .00 |
| ☐ 143 | Steve Sax | .09 | .04 | .01 |
| ☐ 144 | Mike Scioscia | .03 | .01 | .00 |
| ☐ 145 | Fernando Valenzuela | .30 | .12 | .03 |
| ☐ 146 | Bob Welch | .06 | .02 | .00 |
| ☐ 147 | Terry Whitfield | .03 | .01 | .00 |
| | **CALIFORNIA ANGELS** | | | |
| ☐ 148 | Juan Beniquez | .05 | .02 | .00 |
| ☐ 149 | Bob Boone | .05 | .02 | .00 |
| ☐ 150 | John Candelaria | .06 | .02 | .00 |
| ☐ 151 | Rod Carew | .30 | .12 | .03 |
| ☐ 152 | Stewart Cliburn | .20 | .09 | .02 |
| ☐ 153 | Doug DeCinces | .08 | .03 | .01 |
| ☐ 154 | Brian Downing | .05 | .02 | .00 |
| ☐ 155 | Ken Forsch | .05 | .02 | .00 |
| ☐ 156 | Craig Gerber | .12 | .05 | .01 |
| ☐ 157 | Bobby Grich | .08 | .03 | .01 |
| ☐ 158 | George Hendrick | .06 | .02 | .00 |
| ☐ 159 | Al Holland | .05 | .02 | .00 |
| ☐ 160 | Reggie Jackson | .30 | .12 | .03 |
| ☐ 161 | Ruppert Jones | .05 | .02 | .00 |
| ☐ 162 | Urbano Lugo | .10 | .04 | .01 |
| ☐ 163 | Kirk McCaskill | .20 | .09 | .02 |
| ☐ 164 | Donnie Moore | .07 | .03 | .01 |
| ☐ 165 | Gary Pettis | .07 | .03 | .01 |
| ☐ 166 | Ron Romanick | .07 | .03 | .01 |
| ☐ 167 | Dick Schofield | .06 | .02 | .00 |

| | MINT | VG-E | F-G |
|---|---|---|---|
| ☐ 168 Darly Sconiers | .03 | .01 | .00 |
| ☐ 169 Jim Slaton | .05 | .02 | .00 |
| ☐ 170 Don Sutton | .11 | .05 | .01 |
| ☐ 171 Mike Witt | .09 | .04 | .01 |
| **CINCINNATI REDS** | | | |
| ☐ 172 Buddy Bell | .10 | .04 | .01 |
| ☐ 173 Tom Browning | .15 | .06 | .01 |
| ☐ 174 Dave Concepcion | .09 | .04 | .01 |
| ☐ 175 Eric Davis | .08 | .03 | .01 |
| ☐ 176 Bo Diaz | .05 | .02 | .00 |
| ☐ 177 Nick Esasky | .06 | .02 | .00 |
| ☐ 178 John Franco | .08 | .03 | .01 |
| ☐ 179 Tom Hume | .03 | .01 | .00 |
| ☐ 180 Wayne Krenchicki | .03 | .01 | .00 |
| ☐ 181 Andy McGaffigan | .03 | .01 | .00 |
| ☐ 182 Eddie Milner | .03 | .01 | .00 |
| ☐ 183 Ron Oester | .05 | .02 | .00 |
| ☐ 184 Dave Parker | .15 | .06 | .01 |
| ☐ 185 Frank Pastore | .03 | .01 | .00 |
| ☐ 186 Tony Perez | .11 | .05 | .01 |
| ☐ 187 Ted Power | .06 | .02 | .00 |
| ☐ 188 Joe Price | .03 | .01 | .00 |
| ☐ 189 Gary Redus | .06 | .02 | .00 |
| ☐ 190 Ron Robinson | .03 | .01 | .00 |
| ☐ 191 Pete Rose | .45 | .20 | .04 |
| ☐ 192 Mario Soto | .08 | .03 | .01 |
| ☐ 193 John Stuper | .03 | .01 | .00 |
| ☐ 194 Jay Tibbs | .03 | .01 | .00 |
| ☐ 195 Dave Van Gorder | .03 | .01 | .00 |
| ☐ 196 Max Venable | .03 | .01 | .00 |
| **CHICAGO WHITE SOX** | | | |
| ☐ 197 Juan Agosto | .03 | .01 | .00 |
| ☐ 198 Harold Baines | .16 | .07 | .01 |
| ☐ 199 Floyd Bannister | .06 | .02 | .00 |
| ☐ 200 Britt Burns | .07 | .03 | .01 |
| ☐ 201 Julio Cruz | .03 | .01 | .00 |
| ☐ 202 Joel Davis | .20 | .09 | .02 |
| ☐ 203 Richard Dotson | .06 | .02 | .00 |
| ☐ 204 Carlton Fisk | .15 | .06 | .01 |
| ☐ 205 Scott Fletcher | .03 | .01 | .00 |
| ☐ 206 Ozzie Guillen | .45 | .20 | .04 |
| ☐ 207 Jerry Hairston | .03 | .01 | .00 |
| ☐ 208 Tim Hulett | .05 | .02 | .00 |
| ☐ 209 Bob James | .06 | .02 | .00 |
| ☐ 210 Ron Kittle | .11 | .05 | .01 |
| ☐ 211 Rudy Law | .03 | .01 | .00 |
| ☐ 212 Bryan Little | .03 | .01 | .00 |
| ☐ 213 Gene Nelson | .03 | .01 | .00 |
| ☐ 214 Reid Nichols | .03 | .01 | .00 |
| ☐ 215 Luis Salazar | .03 | .01 | .00 |
| ☐ 216 Tom Seaver | .25 | .10 | .02 |
| ☐ 217 Dan Spillner | .03 | .01 | .00 |
| ☐ 218 Bruce Tanner | .15 | .06 | .01 |
| ☐ 219 Greg Walker | .12 | .05 | .01 |
| ☐ 220 Dave Wehrmeister | .03 | .01 | .00 |
| **DETROIT TIGERS** | | | |
| ☐ 221 Juan Berenguer | .03 | .01 | .00 |
| ☐ 222 Dave Bergman | .03 | .01 | .00 |
| ☐ 223 Tom Brookens | .03 | .01 | .00 |
| ☐ 224 Darrell Evans | .10 | .04 | .01 |
| ☐ 225 Barbaro Garbey | .05 | .02 | .00 |
| ☐ 226 Kirk Gibson | .16 | .07 | .01 |
| ☐ 227 John Grubb | .03 | .01 | .00 |
| ☐ 228 Willie Hernandez | .13 | .06 | .01 |
| ☐ 229 Larry Herndon | .05 | .02 | .00 |
| ☐ 230 Chet Lemon | .07 | .03 | .01 |
| ☐ 231 Aurelio Lopez | .03 | .01 | .00 |
| ☐ 232 Jack Morris | .14 | .06 | .01 |
| ☐ 233 Randy O'Neal | .05 | .02 | .00 |
| ☐ 234 Lance Parrish | .18 | .08 | .01 |
| ☐ 235 Dan Petry | .12 | .05 | .01 |
| ☐ 236 Alex Sanchez | .05 | .02 | .00 |
| ☐ 237 Bill Scherrer | .03 | .01 | .00 |
| ☐ 238 Nelson Simmons | .25 | .10 | .02 |
| ☐ 239 Frank Tanana | .05 | .02 | .00 |
| ☐ 240 Walt Terrell | .05 | .02 | .00 |
| ☐ 241 Alan Trammell | .18 | .08 | .01 |
| ☐ 242 Lou Whitaker | .15 | .06 | .01 |
| ☐ 243 Milt Wilcox | .03 | .01 | .00 |
| **MONTREAL EXPOS** | | | |
| ☐ 244 Hubie Brooks | .08 | .03 | .01 |
| ☐ 245 Tim Burke | .20 | .09 | .02 |
| ☐ 246 Andre Dawson | .20 | .09 | .02 |
| ☐ 247 Mike Fitzgerald | .03 | .01 | .00 |
| ☐ 248 Terry Francona | .05 | .02 | .00 |
| ☐ 249 Bill Gullickson | .05 | .02 | .00 |
| ☐ 250 Joe Hesketh | .08 | .03 | .01 |
| ☐ 251 Bill Laskey | .03 | .01 | .00 |
| ☐ 252 Vance Law | .03 | .01 | .00 |
| ☐ 253 Charlie Lea | .05 | .02 | .00 |
| ☐ 254 Gary Lucas | .03 | .01 | .00 |
| ☐ 255 David Palmer | .05 | .02 | .00 |
| ☐ 256 Tim Raines | .20 | .08 | .01 |
| ☐ 257 Jeff Reardon | .07 | .03 | .01 |
| ☐ 258 Bert Roberge | .03 | .01 | .00 |
| ☐ 259 Dan Schatzeder | .03 | .01 | .00 |
| ☐ 260 Bryn Smith | .05 | .02 | .00 |
| ☐ 261 Randy St. Claire | .03 | .01 | .00 |
| ☐ 262 Scot Thompson | .03 | .01 | .00 |
| ☐ 263 Tim Wallach | .09 | .04 | .01 |
| ☐ 264 U.L. Washington | .03 | .01 | .00 |
| ☐ 265 Mitch Webster | .12 | .05 | .01 |
| ☐ 266 Herm Winningham | .15 | .06 | .01 |
| ☐ 267 Floyd Youmans | .25 | .10 | .02 |
| **BALTIMORE ORIOLES** | | | |
| ☐ 268 Don Aase | .03 | .01 | .00 |

| | | MINT | VG-E | F-G |
|---|---|---|---|---|
| ☐ 269 | Mike Boddicker | .09 | .04 | .01 |
| ☐ 270 | Rich Dauer | .03 | .01 | .00 |
| ☐ 271 | Storm Davis | .07 | .03 | .01 |
| ☐ 272 | Rick Dempsey | .05 | .02 | .00 |
| ☐ 273 | Ken Dixon | .06 | .02 | .01 |
| ☐ 274 | Jim Dwyer | .03 | .01 | .00 |
| ☐ 275 | Mike Flanagan | .07 | .03 | .01 |
| ☐ 276 | Wayne Gross | .03 | .01 | .00 |
| ☐ 277 | Lee Lacy | .06 | .02 | .00 |
| ☐ 278 | Fred Lynn | .15 | .06 | .01 |
| ☐ 279 | Dennis Martinez | .03 | .01 | .00 |
| ☐ 280 | Tippy Martinez | .05 | .02 | .00 |
| ☐ 281 | Scott McGregor | .07 | .03 | .01 |
| ☐ 282 | Eddie Murray | .35 | .15 | .03 |
| ☐ 283 | Floyd Rayford | .03 | .01 | .00 |
| ☐ 284 | Cal Ripken | .35 | .15 | .03 |
| ☐ 285 | Gary Roenicke | .05 | .02 | .00 |
| ☐ 286 | Larry Sheets | .08 | .03 | .01 |
| ☐ 287 | John Shelby | .03 | .01 | .00 |
| ☐ 288 | Nate Snell | .15 | .06 | .01 |
| ☐ 289 | Sammy Stewart | .03 | .01 | .00 |
| ☐ 290 | Alan Wiggins | .07 | .03 | .01 |
| ☐ 291 | Mike Young | .15 | .06 | .01 |
| | **HOUSTON ASTROS** | | | |
| ☐ 292 | Alan Ashby | .03 | .01 | .00 |
| ☐ 293 | Mark Bailey | .03 | .01 | .00 |
| ☐ 294 | Kevin Bass | .03 | .01 | .00 |
| ☐ 295 | Jeff Calhoun | .12 | .05 | .01 |
| ☐ 296 | Jose Cruz | .10 | .04 | .01 |
| ☐ 297 | Glenn Davis | .09 | .04 | .01 |
| ☐ 298 | Bill Dawley | .05 | .02 | .00 |
| ☐ 299 | Frank DiPino | .05 | .02 | .00 |
| ☐ 300 | Bill Doran | .07 | .03 | .01 |
| ☐ 301 | Phil Garner | .05 | .02 | .00 |
| ☐ 302 | Jeff Heathcock | .10 | .04 | .01 |
| ☐ 303 | Charlie Kerfeld | .12 | .05 | .01 |
| ☐ 304 | Bob Knepper | .06 | .02 | .00 |
| ☐ 305 | Ron Mathis | .12 | .05 | .01 |
| ☐ 306 | Jerry Mumphrey | .03 | .01 | .00 |
| ☐ 307 | Jim Pankovits | .03 | .01 | .00 |
| ☐ 308 | Terry Puhl | .05 | .02 | .00 |
| ☐ 309 | Craig Reynolds | .03 | .01 | .00 |
| ☐ 310 | Nolan Ryan | .25 | .10 | .02 |
| ☐ 311 | Mike Scott | .05 | .02 | .00 |
| ☐ 312 | Dave Smith | .05 | .02 | .00 |
| ☐ 313 | Dickie Thon | .05 | .02 | .00 |
| ☐ 314 | Denny Walling | .03 | .01 | .00 |
| | **SAN DIEGO PADRES** | | | |
| ☐ 315 | Kurt Bevacqua | .03 | .01 | .00 |
| ☐ 316 | Al Bumbry | .03 | .01 | .00 |
| ☐ 317 | Jerry Davis | .03 | .01 | .00 |
| ☐ 318 | Luis DeLeon | .03 | .01 | .00 |
| ☐ 319 | Dave Dravecky | .06 | .02 | .00 |
| ☐ 320 | Tim Flannery | .03 | .01 | .00 |
| ☐ 321 | Steve Garvey | .35 | .15 | .03 |
| ☐ 322 | Goose Gossage | .15 | .06 | .01 |
| ☐ 323 | Tony Gwynn | .20 | .09 | .02 |
| ☐ 324 | Andy Hawkins | .07 | .03 | .01 |
| ☐ 325 | LaMarr Hoyt | .09 | .04 | .01 |
| ☐ 326 | Roy Lee Jackson | .03 | .01 | .00 |
| ☐ 327 | Terry Kennedy | .08 | .03 | .01 |
| ☐ 328 | Craig Lefferts | .03 | .01 | .00 |
| ☐ 329 | Carmelo Martinez | .05 | .02 | .00 |
| ☐ 330 | Lance McCullers | .25 | .10 | .02 |
| ☐ 331 | Kevin McReynolds | .09 | .04 | .01 |
| ☐ 332 | Graig Nettles | .11 | .05 | .01 |
| ☐ 333 | Jerry Royster | .03 | .01 | .00 |
| ☐ 334 | Eric Show | .05 | .02 | .00 |
| ☐ 335 | Tim Stoddard | .03 | .01 | .00 |
| ☐ 336 | Garry Templeton | .08 | .03 | .01 |
| ☐ 337 | Mark Thurmond | .05 | .02 | .00 |
| ☐ 338 | Ed Wojna | .15 | .06 | .01 |
| | **BOSTON RED SOX** | | | |
| ☐ 339 | Tony Armas | .11 | .05 | .01 |
| ☐ 340 | Marty Barrett | .07 | .03 | .01 |
| ☐ 341 | Wade Boggs | .40 | .18 | .04 |
| ☐ 342 | Dennis Boyd | .05 | .02 | .00 |
| ☐ 343 | Bill Buckner | .08 | .03 | .01 |
| ☐ 344 | Mark Clear | .05 | .02 | .00 |
| ☐ 345 | Roger Clemens | .07 | .03 | .01 |
| ☐ 346 | Steve Crawford | .03 | .01 | .00 |
| ☐ 347 | Mike Easler | .05 | .02 | .00 |
| ☐ 348 | Dwight Evans | .10 | .04 | .01 |
| ☐ 349 | Rich Gedman | .07 | .03 | .01 |
| ☐ 350 | Jackie Gutierrez | .03 | .01 | .00 |
| ☐ 351 | Glenn Hoffman | .03 | .01 | .00 |
| ☐ 352 | Bruce Hurst | .03 | .01 | .00 |
| ☐ 353 | Bruce Kison | .03 | .01 | .00 |
| ☐ 354 | Tim Lollar | .03 | .01 | .00 |
| ☐ 355 | Steve Lyons | .06 | .02 | .00 |
| ☐ 356 | Al Nipper | .06 | .02 | .00 |
| ☐ 357 | Bob Ojeda | .05 | .02 | .00 |
| ☐ 358 | Jim Rice | .25 | .10 | .02 |
| ☐ 359 | Bob Stanley | .06 | .02 | .00 |
| ☐ 360 | Mike Trujillo | .10 | .04 | .01 |
| | **CHICAGO CUBS** | | | |
| ☐ 361 | Thad Bosley | .03 | .01 | .00 |
| ☐ 362 | Warren Brusstar | .03 | .01 | .00 |
| ☐ 363 | Ron Cey | .10 | .04 | .01 |
| ☐ 364 | Jody Davis | .09 | .04 | .01 |
| ☐ 365 | Bob Dernier | .05 | .02 | .00 |
| ☐ 366 | Shawon Dunston | .07 | .03 | .01 |
| ☐ 367 | Leon Durham | .12 | .05 | .01 |
| ☐ 368 | Dennis Eckersley | .05 | .02 | .00 |
| ☐ 369 | Ray Fontenot | .03 | .01 | .00 |
| ☐ 370 | George Frazier | .03 | .01 | .00 |

|  | MINT | VG-E | F-G |
|---|---|---|---|
| ☐ 371 Bill Hatcher | .05 | .02 | .00 |
| ☐ 372 Dave Lopes | .06 | .02 | .00 |
| ☐ 374 Ron Meredith | .10 | .04 | .01 |
| ☐ 375 Keith Moreland | .05 | .02 | .00 |
| ☐ 376 Reggie Patterson | .03 | .01 | .00 |
| ☐ 377 Dick Ruthven | .03 | .01 | .00 |
| ☐ 378 Ryne Sandberg | .25 | .10 | .02 |
| ☐ 379 Scott Sanderson | .05 | .02 | .00 |
| ☐ 380 Lee Smith | .08 | .03 | .01 |
| ☐ 381 Lary Sorensen | .03 | .01 | .00 |
| ☐ 382 Chris Speier | .03 | .01 | .00 |
| ☐ 383 Rick Sutcliffe | .13 | .05 | .01 |
| ☐ 384 Steve Trout | .05 | .02 | .00 |
| ☐ 385 Gary Woods | .03 | .01 | .00 |
| **MINNESOTA TWINS** | | | |
| ☐ 386 Bert Blyleven | .10 | .04 | .01 |
| ☐ 387 Tom Brunansky | .12 | .05 | .01 |
| ☐ 388 Randy Bush | .03 | .01 | .00 |
| ☐ 389 John Butcher | .03 | .01 | .00 |
| ☐ 390 Ron Davis | .05 | .02 | .00 |
| ☐ 391 Dave Engle | .05 | .02 | .00 |
| ☐ 392 Frank Eufemia | .15 | .06 | .01 |
| ☐ 393 Pete Filson | .03 | .01 | .00 |
| ☐ 394 Gary Gaetti | .05 | .02 | .00 |
| ☐ 395 Greg Gagne | .05 | .02 | .00 |
| ☐ 396 Mickey Hatcher | .05 | .02 | .00 |
| ☐ 397 Kent Hrbek | .18 | .08 | .01 |
| ☐ 398 Tim Laudner | .03 | .01 | .00 |
| ☐ 399 Rick Lysander | .03 | .01 | .00 |
| ☐ 400 Dave Meier | .05 | .02 | .00 |
| ☐ 401 Kirby Puckett | .10 | .04 | .01 |
| ☐ 402 Mark Salas | .07 | .03 | .01 |
| ☐ 403 Ken Schrom | .03 | .01 | .00 |
| ☐ 404 Roy Smalley | .05 | .02 | .00 |
| ☐ 405 Mike Smithson | .05 | .02 | .00 |
| ☐ 406 Mike Stenhouse | .05 | .02 | .00 |
| ☐ 407 Tim Teufel | .06 | .02 | .00 |
| ☐ 408 Frank Viola | .07 | .03 | .01 |
| ☐ 409 Ron Washington | .03 | .01 | .00 |
| **OAKLAND A'S** | | | |
| ☐ 410 Keith Atherton | .03 | .01 | .00 |
| ☐ 411 Dusty Baker | .06 | .02 | .00 |
| ☐ 412 Tim Birtsas | .20 | .09 | .02 |
| ☐ 413 Bruce Bochte | .05 | .02 | .00 |
| ☐ 414 Chris Codiroli | .03 | .01 | .00 |
| ☐ 415 Dave Collins | .05 | .02 | .00 |
| ☐ 416 Mike Heath | .03 | .01 | .00 |
| ☐ 419 Steve Henderson | .03 | .01 | .00 |
| ☐ 420 Donnie Hill | .03 | .01 | .00 |
| ☐ 421 Jay Howell | .06 | .02 | .00 |
| ☐ 422 Tommy John | .12 | .05 | .01 |
| ☐ 423 Dave Kingman | .09 | .04 | .01 |
| ☐ 424 Bill Krueger | .03 | .01 | .00 |

|  | MINT | VG-E | F-G |
|---|---|---|---|
| ☐ 425 Rick Langford | .03 | .01 | .00 |
| ☐ 426 Carney Lansford | .09 | .04 | .01 |
| ☐ 427 Steve McCatty | .03 | .01 | .00 |
| ☐ 428 Dwayne Murphy | .07 | .03 | .01 |
| ☐ 429 Steve Ontiveros | .20 | .09 | .02 |
| ☐ 430 Tony Phillips | .03 | .01 | .00 |
| ☐ 431 Jose Rijo | .05 | .02 | .00 |
| ☐ 432 Mickey Tettleton | .12 | .05 | .01 |
| **PHILADELPHIA PHILLIES** | | | |
| ☐ 433 Luis Aguayo | .03 | .01 | .00 |
| ☐ 434 Larry Andersen | .03 | .01 | .00 |
| ☐ 435 Steve Carlton | .30 | .12 | .03 |
| ☐ 436 Don Carman | .15 | .06 | .01 |
| ☐ 437 Tim Corcoran | .03 | .01 | .00 |
| ☐ 438 Darren Daulton | .15 | .06 | .01 |
| ☐ 439 John Denny | .07 | .03 | .01 |
| ☐ 440 Tom Foley | .03 | .01 | .00 |
| ☐ 441 Greg Gross | .03 | .01 | .00 |
| ☐ 442 Kevin Gross | .03 | .01 | .00 |
| ☐ 443 Von Hayes | .10 | .04 | .01 |
| ☐ 444 Charles Hudson | .05 | .02 | .00 |
| ☐ 445 Garry Maddox | .05 | .02 | .00 |
| ☐ 446 Shane Rawley | .06 | .02 | .00 |
| ☐ 447 Dave Rucker | .03 | .01 | .00 |
| ☐ 448 John Russell | .06 | .02 | .00 |
| ☐ 449 Juan Samuel | .12 | .05 | .01 |
| ☐ 450 Mike Schmidt | .35 | .15 | .03 |
| ☐ 451 Rick Schu | .06 | .02 | .00 |
| ☐ 452 Dave Shipanoff | .15 | .06 | .01 |
| ☐ 453 Dave Stewart | .03 | .01 | .00 |
| ☐ 454 Jeff Stone | .05 | .02 | .00 |
| ☐ 455 Kent Tekulve | .05 | .02 | .00 |
| ☐ 456 Ozzie Virgil | .06 | .02 | .00 |
| ☐ 457 Glenn Wilson | .10 | .04 | .01 |
| **SEATTLE MARINERS** | | | |
| ☐ 458 Jim Beattie | .03 | .01 | .00 |
| ☐ 459 Karl Best | .10 | .04 | .01 |
| ☐ 460 Barry Bonnell | .03 | .01 | .00 |
| ☐ 461 Phil Bradley | .16 | .07 | .01 |
| ☐ 462 Ivan Calderon | .20 | .09 | .02 |
| ☐ 463 Al Cowens | .05 | .02 | .00 |
| ☐ 464 Alvin Davis | .16 | .07 | .01 |
| ☐ 465 Dave Henderson | .05 | .02 | .00 |
| ☐ 466 Bob Kearney | .03 | .01 | .00 |
| ☐ 467 Mark Langston | .07 | .03 | .01 |
| ☐ 468 Bob Long | .03 | .01 | .00 |
| ☐ 469 Mike Moore | .06 | .02 | .00 |
| ☐ 470 Edwin Nunez | .05 | .02 | .00 |
| ☐ 471 Spike Owen | .05 | .02 | .00 |
| ☐ 472 Jack Perconte | .03 | .01 | .00 |
| ☐ 473 Jim Presley | .16 | .07 | .01 |
| ☐ 474 Donnie Scott | .03 | .01 | .00 |

|  | MINT | VG-E | F-G |
|---|---|---|---|
| ☐ 475 Bill Swift | .05 | .02 | .00 |
| ☐ 476 Danny Tartabull | .08 | .03 | .01 |
| ☐ 477 Gorman Thomas | .09 | .04 | .01 |
| ☐ 478 Roy Thomas | .03 | .01 | .00 |
| ☐ 479 Ed VandeBerg | .05 | .02 | .00 |
| ☐ 480 Frank Wills | .15 | .06 | .01 |
| ☐ 481 Matt Young | .05 | .02 | .00 |
| **MILWAUKEE BREWERS** | | | |
| ☐ 482 Ray Burris | .03 | .01 | .00 |
| ☐ 483 Jaime Cocanower | .03 | .01 | .00 |
| ☐ 484 Cecil Cooper | .13 | .06 | .01 |
| ☐ 485 Danny Darwin | .03 | .01 | .00 |
| ☐ 486 Rollie Fingers | .15 | .06 | .01 |
| ☐ 487 Jim Gantner | .05 | .02 | .00 |
| ☐ 488 Bob L. Gibson | .03 | .01 | .00 |
| ☐ 489 Moose Haas | .05 | .02 | .00 |
| ☐ 490 Teddy Higuera | .35 | .15 | .03 |
| ☐ 491 Paul Householder | .03 | .01 | .00 |
| ☐ 492 Pete Ladd | .03 | .01 | .00 |
| ☐ 493 Rick Manning | .03 | .01 | .00 |
| ☐ 494 Bob McClure | .03 | .01 | .00 |
| ☐ 495 Paul Molitor | .11 | .05 | .01 |
| ☐ 496 Charlie Moore | .03 | .01 | .00 |
| ☐ 497 Ben Oglivie | .06 | .02 | .00 |
| ☐ 498 Randy Ready | .05 | .02 | .00 |
| ☐ 499 Earnie Riles | .40 | .18 | .04 |
| ☐ 500 Ed Romero | .03 | .01 | .00 |
| ☐ 501 Bill Schroeder | .03 | .01 | .00 |
| ☐ 502 Ray Searage | .03 | .01 | .00 |
| ☐ 503 Ted Simmons | .11 | .05 | .01 |
| ☐ 504 Pete Vuckovich | .06 | .02 | .00 |
| ☐ 505 Rick Waits | .03 | .01 | .00 |
| ☐ 506 Robin Yount | .25 | .10 | .02 |
| **ATLANTA BRAVES** | | | |
| ☐ 507 Len Barker | .06 | .02 | .00 |
| ☐ 508 Steve Bedrosian | .06 | .02 | .00 |
| ☐ 509 Bruce Benedict | .03 | .01 | .00 |
| ☐ 510 Rick Camp | .03 | .01 | .00 |
| ☐ 511 Rick Cerone | .03 | .01 | .00 |
| ☐ 512 Chris Chambliss | .05 | .02 | .00 |
| ☐ 513 Jeff Dedmon | .03 | .01 | .00 |
| ☐ 514 Terry Forester | .06 | .02 | .00 |
| ☐ 515 Gene Garber | .03 | .01 | .00 |
| ☐ 516 Terry Harper | .03 | .01 | .00 |
| ☐ 517 Bob Horner | .15 | .06 | .01 |
| ☐ 518 Glenn Hubbard | .03 | .01 | .00 |
| ☐ 519 Joe Johnson | .20 | .09 | .02 |
| ☐ 520 Brad Komminsk | .07 | .03 | .01 |
| ☐ 521 Rick Mahler | .06 | .02 | .00 |
| ☐ 522 Dale Murphy | .45 | .20 | .04 |
| ☐ 523 Ken Oberkfell | .03 | .01 | .00 |
| ☐ 524 Pascual Perez | .05 | .02 | .00 |
| ☐ 525 Gerald Perry | .05 | .02 | .00 |

|  | MINT | VG-E | F-G |
|---|---|---|---|
| ☐ 526 Rafael Ramirez | .03 | .01 | .00 |
| ☐ 527 Steve Shields | .12 | .05 | .01 |
| ☐ 528 Zane Smith | .05 | .02 | .00 |
| ☐ 529 Bruce Sutter | .14 | .06 | .01 |
| ☐ 530 Milt Thompson | .20 | .09 | .02 |
| ☐ 531 Claudell Washington | .06 | .02 | .00 |
| ☐ 532 Paul Zuvella | .05 | .02 | .00 |
| ☐ 533 Vida Blue | .07 | .03 | .01 |
| ☐ 534 Bob Brenly | .05 | .02 | .00 |
| ☐ 535 Chris Brown | .30 | .13 | .03 |
| ☐ 536 Chili Davis | .08 | .03 | .01 |
| ☐ 537 Mark Davis | .03 | .01 | .00 |
| ☐ 538 Rob Deer | .05 | .02 | .00 |
| ☐ 539 Dan Driessen | .03 | .01 | .00 |
| ☐ 540 Scott Garrelts | .06 | .02 | .00 |
| ☐ 541 Dan Gladden | .06 | .02 | .00 |
| ☐ 542 Jim Gott | .03 | .01 | .00 |
| ☐ 543 David Green | .06 | .02 | .00 |
| ☐ 544 Atlee Hammaker | .06 | .02 | .00 |
| ☐ 545 Mike Jeffcoat | .03 | .01 | .00 |
| ☐ 546 Mike Krukow | .03 | .01 | .00 |
| ☐ 547 Dave LaPoint | .03 | .01 | .00 |
| ☐ 548 Jeff Leonard | .05 | .02 | .00 |
| ☐ 549 Greg Minton | .05 | .02 | .00 |
| ☐ 550 Alex Trevino | .03 | .01 | .00 |
| ☐ 551 Manny Trillo | .05 | .02 | .00 |
| ☐ 552 Jose Uribe | .10 | .04 | .01 |
| ☐ 553 Brad Wellman | .03 | .01 | .00 |
| ☐ 554 Frank Williams | .03 | .01 | .00 |
| ☐ 555 Joel Youngblood | .03 | .01 | .00 |
| **TEXAS RANGERS** | | | |
| ☐ 556 Alan Bannister | .03 | .01 | .00 |
| ☐ 557 Glenn Brummer | .03 | .01 | .00 |
| ☐ 558 Steve Buechele | .10 | .04 | .01 |
| ☐ 559 Jose Guzman | .15 | .06 | .01 |
| ☐ 560 Toby Harrah | .05 | .02 | .00 |
| ☐ 561 Greg Harris | .03 | .01 | .00 |
| ☐ 562 Dwayne Henry | .12 | .05 | .01 |
| ☐ 563 Burt Hooton | .03 | .01 | .00 |
| ☐ 564 Charlie Hough | .05 | .02 | .00 |
| ☐ 565 Mike Mason | .03 | .01 | .00 |
| ☐ 566 Oddibe McDowell | .20 | .09 | .02 |
| ☐ 567 Dickie Noles | .03 | .01 | .00 |
| ☐ 568 Pete O'Brien | .05 | .02 | .00 |
| ☐ 569 Larry Parrish | .07 | .03 | .01 |
| ☐ 570 Dave Rozema | .03 | .01 | .00 |
| ☐ 571 Dave Schmidt | .03 | .01 | .00 |
| ☐ 572 Don Slaught | .03 | .01 | .00 |
| ☐ 573 Wayne Tolleson | .03 | .01 | .00 |
| ☐ 574 Duane Walker | .03 | .01 | .00 |
| ☐ 575 Gary Ward | .06 | .02 | .00 |
| ☐ 576 Chris Welsh | .03 | .01 | .00 |
| ☐ 577 Curtis Wilkerson | .03 | .01 | .00 |

|  | MINT | VG-E | F-G |
|---|---|---|---|
| ☐ **578** George Wright | .03 | .01 | .00 |
| **CLEVELAND INDIANS** | | | |
| ☐ **579** Chris Bando | .03 | .01 | .00 |
| ☐ **580** Tony Bernazard | .03 | .01 | .00 |
| ☐ **581** Brett Butler | .09 | .04 | .01 |
| ☐ **582** Ernie Camacho | .03 | .01 | .00 |
| ☐ **583** Joe Carter | .07 | .03 | .01 |
| ☐ **584** Carmen Castillo | .03 | .01 | .00 |
| ☐ **585** Jamie Easterly | .03 | .01 | .00 |
| ☐ **586** Julio Franco | .10 | .04 | .01 |
| ☐ **587** Mel Hall | .07 | .03 | .01 |
| ☐ **588** Mike Hargrove | .05 | .02 | .00 |
| ☐ **589** Neal Heaton | .03 | .01 | .00 |
| ☐ **590** Brook Jacoby | .10 | .04 | .01 |
| ☐ **591** Otis Nixon | .20 | .09 | .02 |
| ☐ **592** Jerry Reed | .10 | .04 | .01 |
| ☐ **593** Vern Ruhle | .03 | .01 | .00 |
| ☐ **594** Pat Tabler | .05 | .02 | .00 |
| ☐ **595** Rich Thompson | .10 | .04 | .01 |
| ☐ **596** Andre Thornton | .07 | .03 | .01 |
| ☐ **597** Dave Von Ohlen | .03 | .01 | .00 |
| ☐ **598** George Vukovich | .03 | .01 | .00 |
| ☐ **599** Tom Waddell | .03 | .01 | .00 |
| ☐ **600** Curt Wardle | .10 | .04 | .01 |
| ☐ **601** Jerry Willard | .03 | .01 | .00 |
| **PITTSBURGH PIRATES** | | | |
| ☐ **602** Bill Almon | .03 | .01 | .00 |
| ☐ **603** Mike Bielecki | .05 | .02 | .00 |
| ☐ **604** Sid Bream | .05 | .02 | .00 |
| ☐ **605** Mike Brown | .05 | .02 | .00 |
| ☐ **606** Pat Clements | .20 | .09 | .02 |
| ☐ **607** Jose DeLeon | .05 | .02 | .00 |
| ☐ **608** Denny Gonzalez | .05 | .02 | .00 |
| ☐ **609** Cecilio Guante | .03 | .01 | .00 |
| ☐ **610** Steve Kemp | .06 | .02 | .00 |
| ☐ **611** Sam Khalifa | .10 | .04 | .01 |
| ☐ **612** Lee Mazzilli | .05 | .02 | .00 |
| ☐ **613** Larry McWilliams | .05 | .02 | .00 |
| ☐ **614** Jim Morrison | .03 | .01 | .00 |
| ☐ **615** Joe Orsulak | .25 | .10 | .02 |
| ☐ **616** Tony Pena | .11 | .05 | .01 |
| ☐ **617** Johnny Ray | .10 | .04 | .01 |
| ☐ **618** Rick Reuschel | .05 | .02 | .00 |
| ☐ **619** R.J. Reynolds | .05 | .02 | .00 |
| ☐ **620** Rick Rhoden | .05 | .02 | .00 |
| ☐ **621** Don Robinson | .03 | .01 | .00 |
| ☐ **622** Jason Thompson | .06 | .02 | .00 |
| ☐ **623** Lee Tunnell | .03 | .01 | .00 |
| ☐ **624** Jim Winn | .03 | .01 | .00 |
| ☐ **625** Marvell Wynne | .03 | .01 | .00 |
| **SPECIAL CARDS** | | | |
| **(626–643)** | | | |
| ☐ **626** Gooden in Action | .45 | .20 | .04 |

|  | MINT | VG-E | F-G |
|---|---|---|---|
| ☐ **627** Mattingly in Action | .35 | .15 | .03 |
| ☐ **628** 4192! (Pete Rose) | .35 | .15 | .03 |
| ☐ **629** 3000 Career Hits | .20 | .09 | .02 |
| Rod Carew | | | |
| ☐ **630** 300 Career Wins | .15 | .06 | .01 |
| Tom Seaver | | | |
| Phil Niekro | | | |
| ☐ **631** Ouch! Don Baylor | .10 | .04 | .01 |
| ☐ **632** Instant Offense | .20 | .09 | .02 |
| Darryl Strawberry | | | |
| Tim Raines | | | |
| ☐ **633** Shortstops Supreme | .20 | .09 | .02 |
| Cal Ripken | | | |
| Alan Trammell | | | |
| ☐ **634** Boggs and "Hero" | .40 | .18 | .04 |
| Wade Boggs | | | |
| George Brett | | | |
| ☐ **635** Braves Dynamic Duo | .25 | .10 | .02 |
| Bob Horner | | | |
| Dale Murphy | | | |
| ☐ **636** Cardinal Ignitors | .35 | .15 | .03 |
| Willie McGee | | | |
| Vince Coleman | | | |
| ☐ **637** Terror on the Basepaths | .35 | .15 | .03 |
| Vince Coleman | | | |
| ☐ **638** Charlie Hustle and Dr. K | .75 | .25 | .06 |
| Pete Rose | | | |
| Dwight Gooden | | | |
| ☐ **639** 1984 and 1985 AL | .50 | .22 | .05 |
| Batting Champs | | | |
| Wade Boggs | | | |
| Don Mattingly | | | |
| ☐ **640** NL West Sluggers | .25 | .10 | .02 |
| Dale Murphy | | | |
| Steve Garvey | | | |
| Dave Parker | | | |
| ☐ **641** Staff Aces | .50 | .22 | .05 |
| Fernando Valenzuela | | | |
| Dwight Gooden | | | |
| ☐ **642** Blue Jay Stoppers | .10 | .04 | .01 |
| Jimmy Key | | | |
| Dave Stieb | | | |
| ☐ **643** AL All-Star Backstops | .10 | .04 | .01 |
| Carlton Fisk | | | |
| Rich Gedman | | | |
| **ROOKIE PAIRS** | | | |
| **(644–653)** | | | |
| ☐ **644** Gene Walter and | .15 | .06 | .01 |
| Benito Santiago | | | |
| ☐ **645** Mike Woodard and | .15 | .06 | .01 |
| Collin Ward | | | |
| ☐ **646** Kal Daniels and | .30 | .12 | .03 |
| Paul O'Neill | | | |

| | | MINT | VG-E | F-G |
|---|---|---|---|---|
| ☐ | **647** Andres Galarraga and .. Fred Toliver | .20 | .09 | .02 |
| ☐ | **648** Bob Kipper and ........ Curt Ford | .20 | .09 | .02 |
| ☐ | **649** Jose Canseco and ..... Eric Plunk | .75 | .25 | .07 |
| ☐ | **650** Mark McLemore and ... Gus Polidor | .15 | .06 | .01 |
| ☐ | **651** Rob Woodward and .... Mickey Brantley | .15 | .06 | .01 |
| ☐ | **652** Billy Joe Robidoux and . Mark Funderburk | .25 | .10 | .02 |
| ☐ | **653** Cecil Fielder and ...... Cory Snyder | .30 | .12 | .03 |
| | **CHECKLISTS (654–660)** | | | |
| ☐ | **654** CL: Royals/Cardinals ... Blue Jays/Mets | .07 | .01 | .00 |
| ☐ | **655** CL: Yankees/Dodgers .. Angels/Reds | .07 | .01 | .00 |
| ☐ | **656** CL: White Sox/Tigers .. Expos/Orioles | .07 | .01 | .00 |
| ☐ | **657** CL: Astros/Padres ..... Red Sox/Cubs | .07 | .01 | .00 |
| ☐ | **658** CL: Twins/A's ......... Phillies/Mariners | .07 | .01 | .00 |
| ☐ | **659** CL: Brewers/Braves .... Giants/Rangers | .07 | .01 | .00 |
| ☐ | **660** CL: Indians/Pirates .... Special Cards | .07 | .01 | .00 |
| | **DISPLAY BOX CARDS** | | | |
| ☐ | **C1** Royals Logo ......... | .10 | .04 | .01 |
| ☐ | **C2** George Brett ......... | 1.00 | .40 | .10 |
| ☐ | **C3** Ozzie Guillen ........ | .50 | .22 | .05 |
| ☐ | **C4** Dale Murphy ......... | 1.00 | .40 | .10 |
| ☐ | **C5** Cardinals Logo ...... | .10 | .04 | .01 |
| ☐ | **C6** Tom Browning ........ | .40 | .18 | .04 |
| ☐ | **C7** Gary Carter ......... | .50 | .22 | .05 |
| ☐ | **C8** Carlton Fisk ......... | .25 | .10 | .02 |

## 1948 BOWMAN

The 48 card Bowman set of 1948 was the first major set of the post-war period. Each 2¹⁄₁₆″ by 2½″ card had a black and white photo of a current player, with his biographical information printed in black ink on a gray back. Due to the printing process and the 36 card sheet size upon which Bowman was then printing, the 12 cards marked with an SP in the checklist are scarcer numerically, as they were removed from the printing sheet in order to make room for the 12 high numbers (37–48). Many cards are found with overprinted, transposed, or blank backs.

Complete Set: M–525.00; VG-E–225.00; F-G–55.00

| | MINT | VG-E | F-G |
|---|---|---|---|
| Common Player (1–36) . | 4.25 | 1.80 | .45 |
| Common Player (37–48) | 7.00 | 3.25 | .70 |
| Common Player SP .... | 9.00 | 4.25 | .90 |

| | | MINT | VG-E | F-G |
|---|---|---|---|---|
| ☐ | 1 Bob Elliott ............ | 15.00 | 3.00 | .60 |
| ☐ | 2 Ewell Blackwell ........ | 5.00 | 2.35 | .50 |
| ☐ | 3 Ralph Kiner .......... | 15.00 | 7.00 | 1.50 |
| ☐ | 4 Johnny Mize .......... | 14.00 | 6.50 | 1.40 |
| ☐ | 5 Bob Feller ........... | 30.00 | 14.00 | 3.00 |
| ☐ | 6 Yogi Berra ........... | 55.00 | 25.00 | 5.50 |
| ☐ | 7 Peter Reiser SP ....... | 12.00 | 5.50 | 1.20 |
| ☐ | 8 Phil Rizzuto SP ....... | 45.00 | 20.00 | 4.50 |
| ☐ | 9 Walker Cooper ........ | 4.25 | 1.80 | .45 |
| ☐ | 10 Buddy Rosar ......... | 4.25 | 1.80 | .45 |
| ☐ | 11 Johnny Lindell ....... | 4.25 | 1.80 | .45 |
| ☐ | 12 Johnny Sain ......... | 6.50 | 3.00 | .65 |
| ☐ | 13 Willard Marshall SP ... | 9.00 | 4.25 | .90 |
| ☐ | 14 Allie Reynolds ........ | 7.50 | 3.50 | .75 |
| ☐ | 15 Eddie Joost ......... | 4.25 | 1.80 | .45 |

| | MINT | VG-E | F-G |
|---|---|---|---|
| ☐ 16 Jack Lohrke SP ........ | 9.00 | 4.25 | .90 |
| ☐ 17 Enos Slaughter ....... | 14.00 | 6.50 | 1.40 |
| ☐ 18 Warren Spahn ......... | 30.00 | 14.00 | 3.00 |
| ☐ 19 Tommy Henrich ........ | 6.50 | 3.00 | .65 |
| ☐ 20 Buddy Kerr SP ........ | 9.00 | 4.25 | .90 |
| ☐ 21 Ferris Fain ........... | 5.00 | 2.35 | .50 |
| ☐ 22 Floyd Bevens SP ...... | 9.00 | 4.25 | .90 |
| ☐ 23 Larry Jansen ......... | 4.25 | 1.80 | .45 |
| ☐ 24 Dutch Leonard SP ..... | 9.00 | 4.25 | .90 |
| ☐ 25 Barney McCosky ...... | 4.25 | 1.80 | .45 |
| ☐ 26 Frank Shea SP ........ | 9.00 | 4.25 | .90 |
| ☐ 27 Sid Gordon .......... | 4.25 | 2.00 | .42 |
| ☐ 28 Emil Verban SP ....... | 9.00 | 4.25 | .90 |
| ☐ 29 Joe Page SP ......... | 10.00 | 4.75 | 1.00 |
| ☐ 30 Whitey Lockman SP .... | 9.50 | 4.50 | .95 |
| ☐ 31 Bill McCahan ......... | 4.25 | 1.80 | .45 |
| ☐ 32 Bill Rigney .......... | 4.25 | 1.80 | .45 |
| ☐ 33 Bill Johnson ......... | 4.25 | 1.80 | .45 |
| ☐ 34 Sheldon Jones SP ..... | 9.00 | 4.25 | .90 |
| ☐ 35 Snuffy Stirnweiss ..... | 4.25 | 1.80 | .45 |
| ☐ 36 Stan Musial .......... | 90.00 | 42.00 | 9.00 |
| ☐ 37 Clint Hartung ........ | 7.00 | 3.25 | .70 |
| ☐ 38 Red Schoendienst ..... | 10.00 | 4.75 | 1.00 |
| ☐ 39 Augie Galan ......... | 7.00 | 3.25 | .70 |
| ☐ 40 Marty Marion ........ | 10.00 | 4.75 | 1.00 |
| ☐ 41 Rex Barney .......... | 7.00 | 3.25 | .70 |
| ☐ 42 Ray Poat ........... | 7.00 | 3.25 | .70 |
| ☐ 43 Bruce Edwards ....... | 7.00 | 3.25 | .70 |
| ☐ 44 Johnny Wyrostek ..... | 7.00 | 3.25 | .70 |
| ☐ 45 Hank Sauer .......... | 8.00 | 3.75 | .80 |
| ☐ 46 Herman Wehmeier ..... | 7.00 | 3.25 | .70 |
| ☐ 47 Bobby Thomson ....... | 10.00 | 4.75 | 1.00 |
| ☐ 48 Dave Koslo .......... | 9.00 | 4.25 | .90 |

## 1949 BOWMAN

AL "Red" SCHOENDIENST

*The cards in this 240 card set measure 2¹⁄₁₆" by 2½". In 1949 Bowman took an intermediate step between black and white and full color with this set of tinted photos on colored backgrounds. Collectors should note the series price variations which reflect some inconsistencies in the printing process. There are four major varieties in name printing which are noted in the checklist below: NOF: name on front; NNOF: no name on front; PR: printed name on back; and SCR: script name on back.*

Complete Set: M-3300.00; VG-E-1500.00; F-G-300.00

| | MINT | VG-E | F-G |
|---|---|---|---|
| Common Player (1–3, 5–37) ...... | 4.50 | 2.10 | .45 |
| Common Player (38–73) | 5.00 | 2.35 | .50 |
| Common Player (4, 74–108) ........ | 4.00 | 1.85 | .40 |
| Common Player (109–144) ........ | 3.00 | 1.40 | .30 |
| Common Player (145–180) ........ | 20.00 | 9.00 | 2.00 |
| Common Player (181–240) ........ | 18.00 | 8.50 | 1.80 |

| | MINT | VG-E | F-G |
|---|---|---|---|
| ☐ 1 Vern Bickford ......... | 15.00 | 3.00 | .50 |
| ☐ 2 Whitey Lockman ....... | 4.50 | 2.10 | .45 |
| ☐ 3 Bob Porterfield ....... | 4.50 | 2.10 | .45 |
| ☐ 4 A Jerry Priddy NNOF ... | 4.50 | 2.10 | .45 |
| ☐ 4 B Jerry Priddy NOF .... | 15.00 | 7.00 | 1.50 |
| ☐ 5 Hank Sauer .......... | 4.50 | 2.10 | .45 |
| ☐ 6 Phil Cavaretta ........ | 4.50 | 2.10 | .45 |
| ☐ 7 Joe Dobson .......... | 4.50 | 2.10 | .45 |
| ☐ 8 Murray Dickson ....... | 4.50 | 2.10 | .45 |
| ☐ 9 Ferris Fain .......... | 5.00 | 2.35 | .50 |
| ☐ 10 Ted Gray ........... | 4.50 | 2.10 | .45 |
| ☐ 11 Lou Boudreau ........ | 10.00 | 4.75 | 1.00 |
| ☐ 12 Cass Michaels ....... | 4.50 | 2.10 | .45 |
| ☐ 13 Bob Chesnes ........ | 4.50 | 2.10 | .45 |
| ☐ 14 Curt Simmons ....... | 6.50 | 3.00 | .65 |
| ☐ 15 Ned Garver ......... | 4.50 | 2.10 | .45 |
| ☐ 16 Al Kozar ........... | 4.50 | 2.10 | .45 |
| ☐ 17 Earl Torgeson ....... | 4.50 | 2.10 | .45 |
| ☐ 18 Bobby Thomson ...... | 5.50 | 2.60 | .55 |
| ☐ 19 Bobby Brown ........ | 7.00 | 3.25 | .70 |
| ☐ 20 Gene Hermanski ..... | 4.50 | 2.10 | .45 |
| ☐ 21 Frank Baumholtz ..... | 4.50 | 2.10 | .45 |
| ☐ 22 Peanuts Lowrey ...... | 4.50 | 2.10 | .45 |
| ☐ 23 Bobby Doerr ......... | 5.00 | 2.35 | .50 |

| | MINT | VG-E | F-G | | MINT | VG-E | F-G |
|---|---|---|---|---|---|---|---|
| ☐ 24 Stan Musial | 85.00 | 40.00 | 8.50 | ☐ 77 Ernie Donham | 4.00 | 1.85 | .40 |
| ☐ 25 Carl Scheib | 4.50 | 2.10 | .45 | ☐ 78 A Sam Zoldak NNOF | 4.50 | 2.10 | .45 |
| ☐ 26 George Kell | 8.50 | 4.00 | .85 | ☐ 78 B Sam Zoldak NOF | 15.00 | 7.00 | 1.50 |
| ☐ 27 Bob Feller | 25.00 | 11.00 | 2.50 | ☐ 79 Ron Northey | 4.00 | 1.85 | .40 |
| ☐ 28 Don Kolloway | 4.50 | 2.10 | .45 | ☐ 80 Bill McCahan | 4.00 | 1.85 | .40 |
| ☐ 29 Ralph Kiner | 12.00 | 5.50 | 1.20 | ☐ 81 Virgil Stallcup | 4.00 | 1.85 | .40 |
| ☐ 30 Andy Seminick | 4.50 | 2.10 | .45 | ☐ 82 Joe Page | 5.00 | 2.35 | .50 |
| ☐ 31 Dick Kokos | 4.50 | 2.10 | .45 | ☐ 83 A Bob Scheffing NNOF | 4.50 | 2.10 | .45 |
| ☐ 32 Eddie Yost | 4.50 | 2.10 | .45 | ☐ 83 B Bob Scheffing NOF | 15.00 | 7.00 | 1.50 |
| ☐ 33 Warren Spahn | 21.00 | 9.50 | 2.10 | ☐ 84 Roy Campanella | 65.00 | 30.00 | 6.50 |
| ☐ 34 Dave Koslo | 4.50 | 2.10 | .45 | ☐ 85 A Johnny Mize NNOF | 12.00 | 5.50 | 1.20 |
| ☐ 35 Vic Raschi | 6.00 | 2.80 | .60 | ☐ 85 B Johnny Mize NOF | 30.00 | 14.00 | 3.00 |
| ☐ 36 Pee Wee Reese | 21.00 | 9.50 | 2.10 | ☐ 86 Johnny Pesky | 4.50 | 2.10 | .45 |
| ☐ 37 John Wyrostek | 4.50 | 2.10 | .45 | ☐ 87 Randy Gumpert | 4.00 | 1.85 | .40 |
| ☐ 38 Emil Verban | 5.00 | 2.35 | .50 | ☐ 88 A Bill Salkeld NNOF | 4.50 | 2.10 | .45 |
| ☐ 39 Billy Goodman | 5.50 | 2.60 | .55 | ☐ 88 B Bill Salkeld NOF | 15.00 | 7.00 | 1.50 |
| ☐ 40 Red Munger | 5.00 | 2.35 | .50 | ☐ 89 Mizell Platt | 4.00 | 1.85 | .40 |
| ☐ 41 Lou Brissie | 5.00 | 2.35 | .50 | ☐ 90 Gil Coan | 4.00 | 1.85 | .40 |
| ☐ 42 Hoot Evers | 5.00 | 2.35 | .50 | ☐ 91 Dick Wakefield | 4.00 | 1.85 | .40 |
| ☐ 43 Dale Mitchell | 5.50 | 2.60 | .55 | ☐ 92 Willie Jones | 4.00 | 1.85 | .40 |
| ☐ 44 Dave Philley | 5.00 | 2.35 | .50 | ☐ 93 Ed Stevens | 4.00 | 1.85 | .40 |
| ☐ 45 Wally Westlake | 5.00 | 2.35 | .50 | ☐ 94 Mickey Vernon | 6.00 | 2.80 | .60 |
| ☐ 46 Robin Roberts | 21.00 | 9.50 | 2.10 | ☐ 95 Howie Pollet | 4.00 | 1.85 | .40 |
| ☐ 47 Johnny Sain | 6.50 | 3.00 | .65 | ☐ 96 Taft Wright | 4.00 | 1.85 | .40 |
| ☐ 48 Willard Marshall | 5.00 | 2.35 | .50 | ☐ 97 Danny Litwhiler | 4.00 | 1.85 | .40 |
| ☐ 49 Frank Shea | 5.50 | 2.60 | .55 | ☐ 98 A Phil Rizzuto NNOF | 16.00 | 7.50 | 1.60 |
| ☐ 50 Jackie Robinson | 80.00 | 37.00 | 8.00 | ☐ 98 B Phil Rizzuto NOF | 40.00 | 18.00 | 4.00 |
| ☐ 51 Herman Wehmeier | 5.00 | 2.35 | .50 | ☐ 99 Frank Gustine | 4.00 | 1.85 | .40 |
| ☐ 52 Johnny Schmitz | 5.00 | 2.35 | .50 | ☐ 100 Gil Hodges | 21.00 | 9.50 | 2.10 |
| ☐ 53 Jack Kramer | 5.00 | 2.35 | .50 | ☐ 101 Sid Gordon | 4.00 | 1.85 | .40 |
| ☐ 54 Marty Marion | 6.00 | 2.80 | .60 | ☐ 102 Stan Spence | 4.00 | 1.85 | .40 |
| ☐ 55 Eddie Joost | 5.00 | 2.35 | .50 | ☐ 103 Joe Tipton | 4.00 | 1.85 | .40 |
| ☐ 56 Pat Mullin | 5.00 | 2.35 | .50 | ☐ 104 Ed Stanky | 5.00 | 2.35 | .50 |
| ☐ 57 Gene Bearden | 5.50 | 2.60 | .55 | ☐ 105 Bill Kennedy | 4.00 | 1.85 | .40 |
| ☐ 58 Bob Elliott | 5.00 | 2.35 | .50 | ☐ 106 Jake Early | 4.00 | 1.85 | .40 |
| ☐ 59 Jack Lohrke | 5.00 | 2.35 | .50 | ☐ 107 Eddie Lake | 4.00 | 1.85 | .40 |
| ☐ 60 Yogi Berra | 40.00 | 18.00 | 4.00 | ☐ 108 Ken Heintzleman | 4.00 | 1.85 | .40 |
| ☐ 61 Rex Barney | 5.00 | 2.35 | .50 | ☐ 109 A Ed Fitzgerald SCR | 3.00 | 1.40 | .30 |
| ☐ 62 Grady Hatton | 5.00 | 2.35 | .50 | ☐ 109 B Ed Fitzgerald PR | 12.00 | 5.50 | 1.20 |
| ☐ 63 Andy Pafko | 5.00 | 2.35 | .50 | ☐ 110 Early Wynn | 18.00 | 8.50 | 1.80 |
| ☐ 64 Dom DiMaggio | 7.00 | 3.25 | .70 | ☐ 111 Red Schoendienst | 5.00 | 2.35 | .50 |
| ☐ 65 Enos Slaughter | 10.00 | 4.75 | 1.00 | ☐ 112 Sam Chapman | 3.00 | 1.40 | .30 |
| ☐ 66 Elmer Valo | 5.00 | 2.35 | .50 | ☐ 113 Ray LaManno | 3.00 | 1.40 | .30 |
| ☐ 67 Alvin Dark | 6.00 | 2.80 | .60 | ☐ 114 Allie Reynolds | 5.50 | 2.60 | .55 |
| ☐ 68 Sheldon Jones | 5.00 | 2.35 | .50 | ☐ 115 Dutch Leonard | 3.00 | 1.40 | .30 |
| ☐ 69 Tommy Henrich | 6.50 | 3.00 | .65 | ☐ 116 Joe Hatton | 3.50 | 1.65 | .35 |
| ☐ 70 Carl Furillo | 9.50 | 4.50 | .95 | ☐ 117 Walker Cooper | 3.00 | 1.40 | .30 |
| ☐ 71 Vern Stephens | 5.00 | 2.35 | .50 | ☐ 118 Sam Mele | 3.00 | 1.40 | .30 |
| ☐ 72 Tommy Holmes | 5.50 | 2.60 | .55 | ☐ 119 Floyd Baker | 3.00 | 1.40 | .30 |
| ☐ 73 Billy Cox | 5.50 | 2.60 | .55 | ☐ 120 Cliff Fannin | 3.00 | 1.40 | .30 |
| ☐ 74 Tom McBride | 4.00 | 1.85 | .40 | ☐ 121 Mark Christman | 3.00 | 1.40 | .30 |
| ☐ 75 Eddie Mayo | 4.00 | 1.85 | .40 | ☐ 122 George Vico | 3.00 | 1.40 | .30 |
| ☐ 76 Bill Nicholson | 4.00 | 1.85 | .40 | ☐ 123 Johnny Blatnick | 3.00 | 1.40 | .30 |

| | MINT | VG-E | F-G |
|---|---|---|---|
| ☐ 124 A Danny Murtaugh SCR | 3.50 | 1.65 | .35 |
| ☐ 124 B Danny Murtaugh PR | 12.00 | 5.50 | 1.20 |
| ☐ 125 Ken Keltner | 3.50 | 1.65 | .35 |
| ☐ 126 A Al Brazle SCR | 3.50 | 1.65 | .35 |
| ☐ 126 B Al Brazle PR | 12.00 | 5.50 | 1.20 |
| ☐ 127 A Hank Majeski SCR | 3.50 | 1.65 | .35 |
| ☐ 127 B Hank Majeski PR | 12.00 | 5.50 | 1.20 |
| ☐ 128 Johnny VanderMeer | 5.00 | 2.35 | .50 |
| ☐ 129 Bill Johnson | 3.50 | 1.65 | .35 |
| ☐ 130 Harry Walker | 3.00 | 1.40 | .30 |
| ☐ 131 Paul Lehner | 3.00 | 1.40 | .30 |
| ☐ 132 A Al Evans SCR | 3.50 | 1.65 | .35 |
| ☐ 132 B Al Evans PR | 12.00 | 5.50 | 1.20 |
| ☐ 133 Aaron Robinson | 3.00 | 1.40 | .30 |
| ☐ 134 Hank Borowy | 3.00 | 1.40 | .30 |
| ☐ 135 Stan Rojek | 3.00 | 1.40 | .30 |
| ☐ 136 Hank Edwards | 3.00 | 1.40 | .30 |
| ☐ 137 Ted Wilks | 3.00 | 1.40 | .30 |
| ☐ 138 Buddy Rosar | 3.00 | 1.40 | .30 |
| ☐ 139 Hank Arft | 3.00 | 1.40 | .30 |
| ☐ 140 Rae Scarborough | 3.00 | 1.40 | .30 |
| ☐ 141 Ulysses Lupien | 3.00 | 1.40 | .30 |
| ☐ 142 Eddie Waitkus | 3.00 | 1.40 | .30 |
| ☐ 143 A Bob Dillinger SCR | 3.50 | 1.65 | .35 |
| ☐ 143 B Bob Dillinger PR | 12.00 | 5.50 | 1.20 |
| ☐ 144 Mickey Haefner | 3.00 | 1.40 | .30 |
| ☐ 145 Sylvester Donnelly | 20.00 | 9.00 | 2.00 |
| ☐ 146 Mike McCormick | 20.00 | 9.00 | 2.00 |
| ☐ 147 Bert Singleton | 20.00 | 9.00 | 2.00 |
| ☐ 148 Bob Swift | 20.00 | 9.00 | 2.00 |
| ☐ 149 Roy Partee | 20.00 | 9.00 | 2.00 |
| ☐ 150 Allie Clark | 20.00 | 9.00 | 2.00 |
| ☐ 151 Mickey Harris | 20.00 | 9.00 | 2.00 |
| ☐ 152 Clarence Maddern | 20.00 | 9.00 | 2.00 |
| ☐ 153 Phil Masi | 20.00 | 9.00 | 2.00 |
| ☐ 154 Clint Hartung | 20.00 | 9.00 | 2.00 |
| ☐ 155 Mickey Guerra | 20.00 | 9.00 | 2.00 |
| ☐ 156 Al Zarilla | 20.00 | 9.00 | 2.00 |
| ☐ 157 Walt Masterson | 20.00 | 9.00 | 2.00 |
| ☐ 158 Harry Brecheen | 21.00 | 9.50 | 2.10 |
| ☐ 159 Glen Moulder | 20.00 | 9.00 | 2.00 |
| ☐ 160 Jim Blackburn | 20.00 | 9.00 | 2.00 |
| ☐ 161 Jocko Thompson | 20.00 | 9.00 | 2.00 |
| ☐ 162 Preacher Roe | 28.00 | 12.50 | 2.80 |
| ☐ 163 Clyde McCullough | 20.00 | 9.00 | 2.00 |
| ☐ 164 Vic Wertz | 21.00 | 9.50 | 2.10 |
| ☐ 165 Snuffy Stirnweiss | 21.00 | 9.50 | 2.10 |
| ☐ 166 Mike Tresh | 20.00 | 9.00 | 2.00 |
| ☐ 167 Babe Martin | 20.00 | 9.00 | 2.00 |
| ☐ 168 Doyle Lade | 20.00 | 9.00 | 2.00 |
| ☐ 169 Jeff Heath | 20.00 | 9.00 | 2.00 |
| ☐ 170 Bill Rigney | 21.00 | 9.50 | 2.10 |
| ☐ 171 Dick Fowler | 20.00 | 9.00 | 2.00 |
| ☐ 172 Eddie Pellagrini | 20.00 | 9.00 | 2.00 |
| ☐ 173 Eddie Stewart | 20.00 | 9.00 | 2.00 |
| ☐ 174 Terry Moore | 22.00 | 10.00 | 2.20 |
| ☐ 175 Luke Appling | 32.00 | 15.00 | 3.20 |
| ☐ 176 Ken Raffensberger | 20.00 | 9.00 | 2.00 |
| ☐ 177 Stan Lopata | 20.00 | 9.00 | 2.00 |
| ☐ 178 Tom Brown | 20.00 | 9.00 | 2.00 |
| ☐ 179 Hugh Casey | 21.00 | 9.50 | 2.10 |
| ☐ 180 Connie Berry | 20.00 | 9.00 | 2.00 |
| ☐ 181 Gus Niarhos | 18.00 | 8.50 | 1.80 |
| ☐ 182 Hall Peck | 18.00 | 8.50 | 1.80 |
| ☐ 183 Lou Stringer | 18.00 | 8.50 | 1.80 |
| ☐ 184 Bob Chipman | 18.00 | 8.50 | 1.80 |
| ☐ 185 Pete Reiser | 20.00 | 9.00 | 2.00 |
| ☐ 186 Buddy Kerr | 18.00 | 8.50 | 1.80 |
| ☐ 187 Phil Marchildon | 18.00 | 8.50 | 1.80 |
| ☐ 188 Karl Drews | 18.00 | 8.50 | 1.80 |
| ☐ 189 Earl Wooten | 18.00 | 8.50 | 1.80 |
| ☐ 190 Jim Hearn | 18.00 | 8.50 | 1.80 |
| ☐ 191 Joe Haynes | 18.00 | 8.50 | 1.80 |
| ☐ 192 Harry Gumbert | 18.00 | 8.50 | 1.80 |
| ☐ 193 Ken Trinkle | 18.00 | 8.50 | 1.80 |
| ☐ 194 Ralph Branca | 20.00 | 9.00 | 2.00 |
| ☐ 195 Eddie Bockman | 18.00 | 8.50 | 1.80 |
| ☐ 196 Fred Hutchinson | 21.00 | 9.50 | 2.10 |
| ☐ 197 Johnny Lindell | 18.00 | 8.50 | 1.80 |
| ☐ 198 Steve Gromek | 18.00 | 8.50 | 1.80 |
| ☐ 199 Tex Hughson | 18.00 | 8.50 | 1.80 |
| ☐ 200 Jess Dobernic | 18.00 | 8.50 | 1.80 |
| ☐ 201 Sibby Sisti | 18.00 | 8.50 | 1.80 |
| ☐ 202 Larry Jansen | 18.00 | 8.50 | 1.80 |
| ☐ 203 Barney McCosky | 18.00 | 8.50 | 1.80 |
| ☐ 204 Bob Savage | 18.00 | 8.50 | 1.80 |
| ☐ 205 Dick Sisler | 18.00 | 8.50 | 1.80 |
| ☐ 206 Bruce Edwards | 18.00 | 8.50 | 1.80 |
| ☐ 207 Johnny Hopp | 20.00 | 9.00 | 2.00 |
| ☐ 208 Dizzy Trout | 20.00 | 9.00 | 2.00 |
| ☐ 209 Charlie Keller | 20.00 | 9.00 | 2.00 |
| ☐ 210 Joe Gordon | 20.00 | 9.00 | 2.00 |
| ☐ 211 Boo Ferriss | 18.00 | 8.50 | 1.80 |
| ☐ 212 Ralph Hamner | 18.00 | 8.50 | 1.80 |
| ☐ 213 Red Barrett | 18.00 | 8.50 | 1.80 |
| ☐ 214 Richie Ashburn | 55.00 | 25.00 | 5.50 |
| ☐ 215 Kirby Higbe | 18.00 | 8.50 | 1.80 |
| ☐ 216 Schoolboy Rowe | 20.00 | 9.00 | 2.00 |
| ☐ 217 Marion Pieretti | 18.00 | 8.50 | 1.80 |
| ☐ 218 Dick Kryhoski | 18.00 | 8.50 | 1.80 |
| ☐ 219 Virgil Fire Trucks | 20.00 | 9.00 | 2.00 |
| ☐ 220 Johnny McCarthy | 18.00 | 8.50 | 1.80 |
| ☐ 221 Bob Muncrief | 18.00 | 8.50 | 1.80 |
| ☐ 222 Alex Kellner | 18.00 | 8.50 | 1.80 |
| ☐ 223 Bobby Hofmann | 18.00 | 8.50 | 1.80 |
| ☐ 224 Satchell Paige | 400.00 | 180.00 | 40.00 |

| | | MINT | VG-E | F-G |
|---|---|---|---|---|
| ☐ 225 | Gerry Coleman | 20.00 | 9.00 | 2.00 |
| ☐ 226 | Duke Snider | 250.00 | 110.00 | 25.00 |
| ☐ 227 | Fritz Ostermueller | 18.00 | 8.50 | 1.80 |
| ☐ 228 | Jackie Mayo | 18.00 | 8.50 | 1.80 |
| ☐ 229 | Ed Lopat | 27.00 | 12.00 | 2.70 |
| ☐ 230 | Augie Galan | 18.00 | 8.50 | 1.80 |
| ☐ 231 | Earl Johnson | 18.00 | 8.50 | 1.80 |
| ☐ 232 | George McQuinn | 18.00 | 8.50 | 1.80 |
| ☐ 233 | Larry Doby | 27.00 | 12.00 | 2.70 |
| ☐ 234 | Rip Sewell | 18.00 | 8.50 | 1.80 |
| ☐ 235 | Jim Russell | 18.00 | 8.50 | 1.80 |
| ☐ 236 | Fred Sanford | 18.00 | 8.50 | 1.80 |
| ☐ 237 | Monte Kennedy | 18.00 | 8.50 | 1.80 |
| ☐ 238 | Bob Lemon | 75.00 | 35.00 | 7.50 |
| ☐ 239 | Frank McCormick | 18.00 | 8.50 | 1.80 |
| ☐ 240 | Babe Young | 27.00 | 9.00 | 2.00 |

## 1950 BOWMAN

LEO DUROCHER

York Giants
gfield, Mass., July

925 as a shortstop with
ne Eastern League. Played
the Yankees, Reds, Card-
gers. Playing career came
finish in 1941, but Leo
few games in 1943 and
manager of Brooklyn Dod-
nd Flatbush team 8½ sea-
nager, Giants, July, 1948.
'ES of BASEBALL Picture Cards
man Gum, Inc., Phila., Pa., U.S.A.

*The cards in this 252 card set measure 2¹⁄₁₆" by 2½". This set, marketed in 1950 by Bowman, represented a major improvement in terms of quality over their previous efforts. Each card was a beautifully colored line drawing developed from a simple photograph. The first 72 cards are the scarcest in the set while the final 72 cards may be found with or without the copyright line. This was the only Bowman sports set to carry the famous "5-Star" logo.*

**Complete Set:** M-1350.00; VG-E-600.00; F-G-120.00

| | MINT | VG-E | F-G |
|---|---|---|---|
| Common Player (1–72) | 8.00 | 3.75 | .80 |
| Common Player (73–252) | 3.00 | 1.40 | .30 |

| | | MINT | VG-E | F-G |
|---|---|---|---|---|
| ☐ 1 | Mel Parnell | 35.00 | 5.00 | 1.00 |

| | | MINT | VG-E | F-G |
|---|---|---|---|---|
| ☐ 2 | Vern Stephens | 8.00 | 3.75 | .80 |
| ☐ 3 | Dom DiMaggio | 11.00 | 5.25 | 1.10 |
| ☐ 4 | Gus Zernial | 9.00 | 4.25 | .90 |
| ☐ 5 | Bob Kuzava | 8.00 | 3.75 | .80 |
| ☐ 6 | Bob Feller | 32.00 | 15.00 | 3.20 |
| ☐ 7 | Jim Hegan | 8.00 | 3.75 | .80 |
| ☐ 8 | George Kell | 13.00 | 6.00 | 1.30 |
| ☐ 9 | Vic Wertz | 8.00 | 3.75 | .80 |
| ☐ 10 | Tommy Henrich | 9.00 | 4.25 | .90 |
| ☐ 11 | Phil Rizzuto | 25.00 | 11.00 | 2.50 |
| ☐ 12 | Joe Page | 9.00 | 4.25 | .90 |
| ☐ 13 | Ferris Fain | 9.00 | 4.25 | .90 |
| ☐ 14 | Alex Kellner | 8.00 | 3.75 | .80 |
| ☐ 15 | Al Kozar | 8.00 | 3.75 | .80 |
| ☐ 16 | Roy Sievers | 9.00 | 4.25 | .90 |
| ☐ 17 | Sid Hudson | 8.00 | 3.75 | .80 |
| ☐ 18 | Eddie Robinson | 8.00 | 3.75 | .80 |
| ☐ 19 | Warren Spahn | 25.00 | 11.00 | 2.50 |
| ☐ 20 | Bob Elliott | 8.00 | 3.75 | .80 |
| ☐ 21 | Pee Wee Reese | 25.00 | 11.00 | 2.50 |
| ☐ 22 | Jackie Robinson | 75.00 | 35.00 | 7.50 |
| ☐ 23 | Don Newcombe | 13.00 | 6.00 | 1.30 |
| ☐ 24 | Johnny Schmitz | 8.00 | 3.75 | .80 |
| ☐ 25 | Hank Sauer | 9.00 | 4.25 | .90 |
| ☐ 26 | Grady Hatton | 8.00 | 3.75 | .80 |
| ☐ 27 | Herman Wehmeier | 8.00 | 3.75 | .80 |
| ☐ 28 | Bobby Thomson | 10.00 | 4.75 | 1.00 |
| ☐ 29 | Eddie Stanky | 9.00 | 4.25 | .90 |
| ☐ 30 | Eddie Waitkus | 8.00 | 3.75 | .80 |
| ☐ 31 | Del Ennis | 9.00 | 4.25 | .90 |
| ☐ 32 | Robin Roberts | 18.00 | 8.50 | 1.80 |
| ☐ 33 | Ralph Kiner | 16.00 | 7.50 | 1.60 |
| ☐ 34 | Murry Dickson | 8.00 | 3.75 | .80 |
| ☐ 35 | Enos Slaughter | 15.00 | 7.00 | 1.50 |
| ☐ 36 | Eddie Kazak | 8.00 | 3.75 | .80 |
| ☐ 37 | Luke Appling | 12.00 | 5.50 | 1.20 |
| ☐ 38 | Bill Wight | 8.00 | 3.75 | .80 |
| ☐ 39 | Larry Doby | 10.00 | 4.75 | 1.00 |
| ☐ 40 | Bob Lemon | 15.00 | 7.00 | 1.50 |
| ☐ 41 | Hoot Evers | 8.00 | 3.75 | .80 |
| ☐ 42 | Art Houtteman | 8.00 | 3.75 | .80 |
| ☐ 43 | Bobby Doerr | 9.00 | 4.25 | .90 |
| ☐ 44 | Joe Dobson | 8.00 | 3.75 | .80 |
| ☐ 45 | Al Zarilla | 8.00 | 3.75 | .80 |
| ☐ 46 | Yogi Berra | 45.00 | 20.00 | 4.50 |
| ☐ 47 | Jerry Coleman | 9.00 | 4.25 | .90 |
| ☐ 48 | Lou Brissie | 8.00 | 3.75 | .80 |
| ☐ 49 | Elmer Valo | 8.00 | 3.75 | .80 |
| ☐ 50 | Dick Kokos | 8.00 | 3.75 | .80 |
| ☐ 51 | Ned Garver | 8.00 | 3.75 | .80 |
| ☐ 52 | Sam Mele | 8.00 | 3.75 | .80 |
| ☐ 53 | Clyde Vollmer | 8.00 | 3.75 | .80 |
| ☐ 54 | Gil Coan | 8.00 | 3.75 | .80 |

| | MINT | VG-E | F-G | | MINT | VG-E | F-G |
|---|---|---|---|---|---|---|---|
| ☐ 55 Buddy Kerr | 8.00 | 3.75 | .80 | ☐ 108 Ray Scarborough | 3.00 | 1.40 | .30 |
| ☐ 56 Del Crandall | 9.00 | 4.25 | .90 | ☐ 109 Sid Gordon | 3.00 | 1.40 | .30 |
| ☐ 57 Vern Bickford | 8.00 | 3.75 | .80 | ☐ 110 Tommy Holmes | 3.50 | 1.65 | .35 |
| ☐ 58 Carl Furillo | 11.00 | 5.25 | 1.10 | ☐ 111 Walker Cooper | 3.00 | 1.40 | .30 |
| ☐ 59 Ralph Branca | 9.00 | 4.25 | .90 | ☐ 112 Gil Hodges | 18.00 | 8.50 | 1.80 |
| ☐ 60 Andy Pafko | 8.00 | 3.75 | .80 | ☐ 113 Gene Hermanski | 3.00 | 1.40 | .30 |
| ☐ 61 Bob Rush | 8.00 | 3.75 | .80 | ☐ 114 Wayne Terwilliger | 3.00 | 1.40 | .30 |
| ☐ 62 Ted Kluszewski | 11.00 | 5.25 | 1.10 | ☐ 115 Roy Smalley | 3.00 | 1.40 | .30 |
| ☐ 63 Ewell Blackwell | 9.00 | 4.25 | .90 | ☐ 116 Virgil Stallcup | 3.00 | 1.40 | .30 |
| ☐ 64 Al Dark | 10.00 | 4.75 | 1.00 | ☐ 117 Bill Rigney | 3.00 | 1.40 | .30 |
| ☐ 65 Dave Koslo | 8.00 | 3.75 | .80 | ☐ 118 Clint Hartung | 3.00 | 1.40 | .30 |
| ☐ 66 Larry Jansen | 8.00 | 3.75 | .80 | ☐ 119 Dick Sisler | 3.00 | 1.40 | .30 |
| ☐ 67 Willie Jones | 8.00 | 3.75 | .80 | ☐ 120 John Thompson | 3.00 | 1.40 | .30 |
| ☐ 68 Curt Simmons | 9.00 | 4.25 | .90 | ☐ 121 Andy Seminick | 3.00 | 1.40 | .30 |
| ☐ 69 Wally Westlake | 8.00 | 3.75 | .80 | ☐ 122 Johnny Hopp | 3.00 | 1.40 | .30 |
| ☐ 70 Bob Chesnes | 8.00 | 3.75 | .80 | ☐ 123 Dino Restelli | 3.00 | 1.40 | .30 |
| ☐ 71 Red Schoendienst | 11.00 | 5.25 | 1.10 | ☐ 124 Clyde McCullough | 3.00 | 1.40 | .30 |
| ☐ 72 Howie Pollett | 8.00 | 3.75 | .80 | ☐ 125 Del Rice | 3.00 | 1.40 | .30 |
| ☐ 73 Willard Marshall | 3.00 | 1.40 | .30 | ☐ 126 Al Brazle | 3.00 | 1.40 | .30 |
| ☐ 74 Johnny Antonelli | 4.00 | 1.85 | .40 | ☐ 127 Dave Philley | 3.00 | 1.40 | .30 |
| ☐ 75 Roy Campanella | 45.00 | 20.00 | 4.50 | ☐ 128 Phil Masi | 3.00 | 1.40 | .30 |
| ☐ 76 Rex Barney | 3.00 | 1.40 | .30 | ☐ 129 Joe Gordon | 3.50 | 1.65 | .35 |
| ☐ 77 Duke Snider | 32.00 | 15.00 | 3.20 | ☐ 130 Dale Mitchell | 3.00 | 1.40 | .30 |
| ☐ 78 Mickey Owen | 3.00 | 1.40 | .30 | ☐ 131 Steve Gromek | 3.00 | 1.40 | .30 |
| ☐ 79 Johnny VanderMeer | 4.00 | 1.85 | .40 | ☐ 132 James Mickey Vernon | 4.00 | 1.85 | .40 |
| ☐ 80 Howard Fox | 3.00 | 1.40 | .30 | ☐ 133 Don Kolloway | 3.00 | 1.40 | .30 |
| ☐ 81 Ron Northey | 3.00 | 1.40 | .30 | ☐ 134 Paul Trout | 3.00 | 1.40 | .30 |
| ☐ 82 Whitey Lockman | 3.00 | 1.40 | .30 | ☐ 135 Pat Mullin | 3.00 | 1.40 | .30 |
| ☐ 83 Sheldon Jones | 3.00 | 1.40 | .30 | ☐ 136 Warren Rosar | 3.00 | 1.40 | .30 |
| ☐ 84 Richie Ashburn | 8.50 | 4.00 | .85 | ☐ 137 Johnny Pesky | 3.50 | 1.65 | .35 |
| ☐ 85 Ken Heintzleman | 3.00 | 1.40 | .30 | ☐ 138 Allie Reynolds | 5.00 | 2.35 | .50 |
| ☐ 86 Stan Rojek | 3.00 | 1.40 | .30 | ☐ 139 Johnny Mize | 11.00 | 5.25 | 1.10 |
| ☐ 87 Bill Werle | 3.00 | 1.40 | .30 | ☐ 140 Pete Suder | 3.00 | 1.40 | .30 |
| ☐ 88 Marty Marion | 4.00 | 1.85 | .40 | ☐ 141 Joe Coleman | 3.00 | 1.40 | .30 |
| ☐ 89 Red Munger | 3.00 | 1.40 | .30 | ☐ 142 Sherman Lollar | 4.00 | 1.85 | .40 |
| ☐ 90 Harry Brecheen | 3.00 | 1.40 | .30 | ☐ 143 Eddie Stewart | 3.00 | 1.40 | .30 |
| ☐ 91 Cass Michaels | 3.00 | 1.40 | .30 | ☐ 144 Al Evans | 3.00 | 1.40 | .30 |
| ☐ 92 Hank Majeski | 3.00 | 1.40 | .30 | ☐ 145 Jack Graham | 3.00 | 1.40 | .30 |
| ☐ 93 Gene Bearden | 3.00 | 1.40 | .30 | ☐ 146 Floyd Baker | 3.00 | 1.40 | .30 |
| ☐ 94 Lou Boudreau | 9.00 | 4.25 | .90 | ☐ 147 Mike Garcia | 4.00 | 1.85 | .40 |
| ☐ 95 Aaron Robinson | 3.00 | 1.40 | .30 | ☐ 148 Early Wynn | 11.00 | 5.25 | 1.10 |
| ☐ 96 Virgil Trucks | 3.00 | 1.40 | .30 | ☐ 149 Bob Swift | 3.00 | 1.40 | .30 |
| ☐ 97 Maurice McDermott | 3.00 | 1.40 | .30 | ☐ 150 George Vico | 3.00 | 1.40 | .30 |
| ☐ 98 Ted Williams | 100.00 | 45.00 | 10.00 | ☐ 151 Fred Hutchinson | 3.50 | 1.65 | .35 |
| ☐ 99 Billy Goodman | 3.50 | 1.65 | .35 | ☐ 152 Ellis Kinder | 3.00 | 1.40 | .30 |
| ☐ 100 Vic Raschi | 4.00 | 1.85 | .40 | ☐ 153 Walt Masterson | 3.00 | 1.40 | .30 |
| ☐ 101 Bobby Brown | 5.00 | 2.35 | .50 | ☐ 154 Gus Niarhos | 3.00 | 1.40 | .30 |
| ☐ 102 Billy Johnson | 3.00 | 1.40 | .30 | ☐ 155 Frank Shea | 3.00 | 1.40 | .30 |
| ☐ 103 Eddie Joost | 3.00 | 1.40 | .30 | ☐ 156 Fred Sanford | 3.00 | 1.40 | .30 |
| ☐ 104 Sam Chapman | 3.00 | 1.40 | .30 | ☐ 157 Mike Guerra | 3.00 | 1.40 | .30 |
| ☐ 105 Bob Dillinger | 3.00 | 1.40 | .30 | ☐ 158 Paul Lehner | 3.00 | 1.40 | .30 |
| ☐ 106 Cliff Fannin | 3.00 | 1.40 | .30 | ☐ 159 Joe Tipton | 3.00 | 1.40 | .30 |
| ☐ 107 Sam Dente | 3.00 | 1.40 | .30 | ☐ 160 Mickey Harris | 3.00 | 1.40 | .30 |

| | MINT | VG-E | F-G |
|---|---|---|---|
| ☐ 161 Sherry Robertson | 3.00 | 1.40 | .30 |
| ☐ 162 Eddie Yost | 3.00 | 1.40 | .30 |
| ☐ 163 Earl Torgeson | 3.00 | 1.40 | .30 |
| ☐ 164 Sibby Sisti | 3.00 | 1.40 | .30 |
| ☐ 165 Bruce Edwards | 3.00 | 1.40 | .30 |
| ☐ 166 Joe Hatton | 3.00 | 1.40 | .30 |
| ☐ 167 Preacher Roe | 5.00 | 2.35 | .50 |
| ☐ 168 Bob Scheffing | 3.00 | 1.40 | .30 |
| ☐ 169 Hank Edwards | 3.00 | 1.40 | .30 |
| ☐ 170 Dutch Leonard | 3.00 | 1.40 | .30 |
| ☐ 171 Harry Gumbert | 3.00 | 1.40 | .30 |
| ☐ 172 Peanuts Lowrey | 3.00 | 1.40 | .30 |
| ☐ 173 Lloyd Merriman | 3.00 | 1.40 | .30 |
| ☐ 174 Hank Thompson | 3.50 | 1.65 | .35 |
| ☐ 175 Monte Kennedy | 3.00 | 1.40 | .30 |
| ☐ 176 Sylvester Donnelly | 3.00 | 1.40 | .30 |
| ☐ 177 Hank Borowy | 3.00 | 1.40 | .30 |
| ☐ 178 Eddie Fitzgerald | 3.00 | 1.40 | .30 |
| ☐ 179 Chuck Diering | 3.00 | 1.40 | .30 |
| ☐ 180 Harry Walker | 3.00 | 1.40 | .30 |
| ☐ 181 Marino Pieretti | 3.00 | 1.40 | .30 |
| ☐ 182 Sam Zoldak | 3.00 | 1.40 | .30 |
| ☐ 183 Mickey Haefner | 3.00 | 1.40 | .30 |
| ☐ 184 Randy Gumpert | 3.00 | 1.40 | .30 |
| ☐ 185 Howie Judson | 3.00 | 1.40 | .30 |
| ☐ 186 Ken Keltner | 3.50 | 1.65 | .35 |
| ☐ 187 Lou Stringer | 3.00 | 1.40 | .30 |
| ☐ 188 Earl Johnson | 3.00 | 1.40 | .30 |
| ☐ 189 Owen Friend | 3.00 | 1.40 | .30 |
| ☐ 190 Ken Wood | 3.00 | 1.40 | .30 |
| ☐ 191 Dick Starr | 3.00 | 1.40 | .30 |
| ☐ 192 Bob Chipman | 3.00 | 1.40 | .30 |
| ☐ 193 Pete Reiser | 3.50 | 1.65 | .35 |
| ☐ 194 Billy Cox | 3.50 | 1.65 | .35 |
| ☐ 195 Phil Cavaretta | 3.50 | 1.65 | .35 |
| ☐ 196 Doyle Lade | 3.00 | 1.40 | .30 |
| ☐ 197 Johnny Wyrostek | 3.00 | 1.40 | .30 |
| ☐ 198 Danny Litwiler | 3.00 | 1.40 | .30 |
| ☐ 199 Jack Kramer | 3.00 | 1.40 | .30 |
| ☐ 200 Kirby Higbe | 3.00 | 1.40 | .30 |
| ☐ 201 Pete Castiglione | 3.00 | 1.40 | .30 |
| ☐ 202 Cliff Chambers | 3.00 | 1.40 | .30 |
| ☐ 203 Danny Murtaugh | 3.50 | 1.65 | .35 |
| ☐ 204 Granny Hamner | 3.00 | 1.40 | .30 |
| ☐ 205 Mike Goliat | 3.00 | 1.40 | .30 |
| ☐ 206 Stan Lopata | 3.00 | 1.40 | .30 |
| ☐ 207 Max Lanier | 3.00 | 1.40 | .30 |
| ☐ 208 Jim Hearn | 3.00 | 1.40 | .30 |
| ☐ 209 Johnny Lindell | 3.00 | 1.40 | .30 |
| ☐ 210 Ted Gray | 3.00 | 1.40 | .30 |
| ☐ 211 Charley Keller | 3.50 | 1.65 | .35 |
| ☐ 212 Gerry Priddy | 3.00 | 1.40 | .30 |
| ☐ 213 Carl Scheib | 3.00 | 1.40 | .30 |
| ☐ 214 Dick Fowler | 3.00 | 1.40 | .30 |
| ☐ 215 Ed Lopat | 5.00 | 2.35 | .50 |
| ☐ 216 Bob Porterfield | 3.00 | 1.40 | .30 |
| ☐ 217 Casey Stengel MGR | 25.00 | 11.00 | 2.50 |
| ☐ 218 Cliff Mapes | 3.00 | 1.40 | .30 |
| ☐ 219 Hank Bauer | 6.50 | 3.00 | .65 |
| ☐ 220 Leo Durocher MGR | 8.50 | 4.00 | .85 |
| ☐ 221 Don Mueller | 3.50 | 1.65 | .35 |
| ☐ 222 Bobby Morgan | 3.00 | 1.40 | .30 |
| ☐ 223 Jim Russell | 3.00 | 1.40 | .30 |
| ☐ 224 Jack Banta | 3.00 | 1.40 | .30 |
| ☐ 225 Eddie Sawyer MGR | 3.00 | 1.40 | .30 |
| ☐ 226 Jim Konstanty | 7.00 | 3.25 | .70 |
| ☐ 227 Bob Miller | 3.00 | 1.40 | .30 |
| ☐ 228 Bill Nicholson | 3.00 | 1.40 | .30 |
| ☐ 229 Frank Frisch | 9.00 | 4.25 | .90 |
| ☐ 230 Bill Serena | 3.00 | 1.40 | .30 |
| ☐ 231 Preston Ward | 3.00 | 1.40 | .30 |
| ☐ 232 Al Rosen | 9.00 | 4.25 | .90 |
| ☐ 233 Allie Clark | 3.00 | 1.40 | .30 |
| ☐ 234 Bobby Shantz | 5.50 | 2.60 | .55 |
| ☐ 235 Harold Gilbert | 3.00 | 1.40 | .30 |
| ☐ 236 Bob Cain | 3.00 | 1.40 | .30 |
| ☐ 237 Bill Salkeld | 3.00 | 1.40 | .30 |
| ☐ 238 Vernal Jones | 3.00 | 1.40 | .30 |
| ☐ 239 Bill Howerton | 3.00 | 1.40 | .30 |
| ☐ 240 Eddie Lake | 3.00 | 1.40 | .30 |
| ☐ 241 Neil Berry | 3.00 | 1.40 | .30 |
| ☐ 242 Dick Kryhoski | 3.00 | 1.40 | .30 |
| ☐ 243 Johnny Groth | 3.00 | 1.40 | .30 |
| ☐ 244 Dale Coogan | 3.00 | 1.40 | .30 |
| ☐ 245 Al Papai | 3.00 | 1.40 | .30 |
| ☐ 246 Walt Dropo | 3.50 | 1.65 | .35 |
| ☐ 247 Irv Noren | 3.50 | 1.65 | .35 |
| ☐ 248 Sam Jethroe | 3.50 | 1.65 | .35 |
| ☐ 249 Snuffy Stirnweiss | 3.00 | 1.40 | .30 |
| ☐ 250 Ray Coleman | 3.00 | 1.40 | .30 |
| ☐ 251 John Moss | 3.00 | 1.40 | .30 |
| ☐ 252 Billy DeMars | 10.00 | 2.00 | .40 |

## 1951 BOWMAN

**BOBBY BROWN**
Third Base—New York Yankees
Born: Oct. 25, 1924
Weight: 180
Bats: Left
Throws: Right

Batted .267 in 95 games in 1950. Hit well in the World Series. Bobby had graduated from medical school, and had started his internship, when he signed with the Yankees for a reported $50,000 bonus. Farmed to Newark for first season (1946). In a utility role for Yanks, 1947. Hit .300 in 1948; .283 in 1949. Now completing hospital internship in preparation for medical branch of service.

No. 110 in the 1951 SERIES

**BASEBALL**
**PICTURE CARDS**
2196) Bowman Gum, Inc. Phila. Pa. U S.A

*The cards in this 324 card set measure 2 1/16" by 3 1/8". Many of the obverses of the cards appearing in the 1951 Bowman set are enlargements of those appearing in the previous year. The high number series (253 to 324) is highly valued and contains the rookie cards of Mickey Mantle and Willie Mays. Card number 195 depicts Paul Richards in caricature. George Kell's card (#46) incorrectly lists him as being in the "1941" Bowman series. Player names are found printed in a panel on the front of the card. These cards were also sold in sheets in variety stores in the Philadelphia area.*

Complete Set: M-2250.00; VG-E-1000.00; F-G-200.00

|  | MINT | VG-E | F-G |
|---|---|---|---|
| Common Player (1–36) | 4.00 | 1.85 | .40 |
| Common Player (37–72) | 3.50 | 1.65 | .35 |
| Common Player (73–252) | 3.00 | 1.40 | .30 |
| Common Player (253–324) | 10.00 | 4.75 | 1.00 |

|  |  | MINT | VG-E | F-G |
|---|---|---|---|---|
| ☐ | 1 Whitey Ford | 120.00 | 20.00 | 4.00 |
| ☐ | 2 Yogi Berra | 45.00 | 20.00 | 4.50 |
| ☐ | 3 Robin Roberts | 14.00 | 6.50 | 1.40 |
| ☐ | 4 Del Ennis | 4.00 | 1.85 | .40 |
| ☐ | 5 Dale Mitchell | 4.00 | 1.85 | .40 |
| ☐ | 6 Don Newcombe | 7.00 | 3.25 | .70 |
| ☐ | 7 Gil Hodges | 16.00 | 7.50 | 1.60 |
| ☐ | 8 Paul Lehner | 4.00 | 1.85 | .40 |
| ☐ | 9 Sam Chapman | 4.00 | 1.85 | .40 |
| ☐ | 10 Red Schoendienst | 5.50 | 2.60 | .55 |

|  |  | MINT | VG-E | F-G |
|---|---|---|---|---|
| ☐ | 11 Red Munger | 4.00 | 1.85 | .40 |
| ☐ | 12 Hank Majeski | 4.00 | 1.85 | .40 |
| ☐ | 13 Eddie Stanky | 4.50 | 2.10 | .45 |
| ☐ | 14 Al Dark | 5.00 | 2.35 | .50 |
| ☐ | 15 Johnny Pesky | 4.50 | 2.10 | .45 |
| ☐ | 16 Maurice McDermott | 4.00 | 1.85 | .40 |
| ☐ | 17 Pete Castiglione | 4.00 | 1.85 | .40 |
| ☐ | 18 Gil Coan | 4.00 | 1.85 | .40 |
| ☐ | 19 Sid Gordon | 4.00 | 1.85 | .40 |
| ☐ | 20 Del Crandall | 4.50 | 2.10 | .45 |
| ☐ | 21 Snuffy Stirnweiss | 4.00 | 1.85 | .40 |
| ☐ | 22 Hank Sauer | 4.50 | 2.10 | .45 |
| ☐ | 23 Hoot Evers | 4.00 | 1.85 | .40 |
| ☐ | 24 Ewell Blackwell | 4.50 | 2.10 | .45 |
| ☐ | 25 Vic Raschi | 5.00 | 2.35 | .50 |
| ☐ | 26 Phil Rizzuto | 16.00 | 7.50 | 1.60 |
| ☐ | 27 Jim Konstanty | 4.50 | 2.10 | .45 |
| ☐ | 28 Eddie Waitkus | 4.00 | 1.85 | .40 |
| ☐ | 29 Allie Clark | 4.00 | 1.85 | .40 |
| ☐ | 30 Bob Feller | 24.00 | 11.00 | 2.40 |
| ☐ | 31 Roy Campanella | 40.00 | 18.00 | 4.00 |
| ☐ | 32 Duke Snider | 28.00 | 12.50 | 2.80 |
| ☐ | 33 Bob Hooper | 4.00 | 1.85 | .40 |
| ☐ | 34 Marty Marion | 4.50 | 2.10 | .45 |
| ☐ | 35 Al Zarilla | 4.00 | 1.85 | .40 |
| ☐ | 36 Joe Dobson | 4.00 | 1.85 | .40 |
| ☐ | 37 Whitey Lockman | 3.50 | 1.65 | .35 |
| ☐ | 38 Al Evans | 3.50 | 1.65 | .35 |
| ☐ | 39 Ray Scarborough | 3.50 | 1.65 | .35 |
| ☐ | 40 Gus Bell | 4.50 | 2.10 | .45 |
| ☐ | 41 Eddie Yost | 3.50 | 1.65 | .35 |
| ☐ | 42 Vern Bickford | 3.50 | 1.65 | .35 |
| ☐ | 43 Billy DeMars | 3.50 | 1.65 | .35 |
| ☐ | 44 Roy Smalley | 3.50 | 1.65 | .35 |
| ☐ | 45 Art Houtteman | 3.50 | 1.65 | .35 |
| ☐ | 46 George Kell 1941 | 12.00 | 5.50 | 1.20 |
| ☐ | 47 Grady Hatton | 3.50 | 1.65 | .35 |
| ☐ | 48 Ken Raffensberger | 3.50 | 1.65 | .35 |
| ☐ | 49 Jerry Coleman | 4.00 | 1.85 | .40 |
| ☐ | 50 Johnny Mize | 11.00 | 5.25 | 1.10 |
| ☐ | 51 Andy Seminick | 3.50 | 1.65 | .35 |
| ☐ | 52 Dick Sisler | 3.50 | 1.65 | .35 |
| ☐ | 53 Bob Lemon | 11.00 | 5.25 | 1.10 |
| ☐ | 54 Ray Boone | 4.00 | 1.85 | .40 |
| ☐ | 55 Gene Hermanski | 3.50 | 1.65 | .35 |
| ☐ | 56 Ralph Branca | 4.00 | 1.85 | .40 |
| ☐ | 57 Alex Kellner | 3.50 | 1.65 | .35 |
| ☐ | 58 Enos Slaughter | 11.00 | 5.25 | 1.10 |
| ☐ | 59 Randy Gumpert | 3.50 | 1.65 | .35 |
| ☐ | 60 Chico Carrasquel | 3.50 | 1.65 | .35 |
| ☐ | 61 Jim Hearn | 3.50 | 1.65 | .35 |
| ☐ | 62 Lou Boudreau | 10.00 | 4.75 | 1.00 |
| ☐ | 63 Bob Dillinger | 3.50 | 1.65 | .35 |

|  | MINT | VG-E | F-G |
|---|---|---|---|
| ☐ 64 Bill Werle | 3.50 | 1.65 | .35 |
| ☐ 65 Mickey Vernon | 4.00 | 1.85 | .40 |
| ☐ 66 Bob Elliott | 3.50 | 1.65 | .35 |
| ☐ 67 Roy Sievers | 4.00 | 1.85 | .40 |
| ☐ 68 Dick Kokos | 3.50 | 1.65 | .35 |
| ☐ 69 Johnny Schmitz | 3.50 | 1.65 | .35 |
| ☐ 70 Ron Northey | 3.50 | 1.65 | .35 |
| ☐ 71 Jerry Priddy | 3.50 | 1.65 | .35 |
| ☐ 72 Lloyd Merriman | 3.50 | 1.65 | .35 |
| ☐ 73 Tommy Byrne | 3.50 | 1.65 | .35 |
| ☐ 74 Billy Johnson | 3.00 | 1.40 | .30 |
| ☐ 75 Russ Meyer | 3.00 | 1.40 | .30 |
| ☐ 76 Stan Lopata | 3.00 | 1.40 | .30 |
| ☐ 77 Mike Goliat | 3.00 | 1.40 | .30 |
| ☐ 78 Early Wynn | 11.00 | 5.25 | 1.10 |
| ☐ 79 Jim Hegan | 3.00 | 1.40 | .30 |
| ☐ 80 Pee Wee Reese | 18.00 | 8.50 | 1.80 |
| ☐ 81 Carl Furillo | 6.00 | 2.80 | .60 |
| ☐ 82 Joe Tipton | 3.00 | 1.40 | .30 |
| ☐ 83 Carl Scheib | 3.00 | 1.40 | .30 |
| ☐ 84 Barney McCoskey | 3.00 | 1.40 | .30 |
| ☐ 85 Eddie Kazak | 3.00 | 1.40 | .30 |
| ☐ 86 Harry Brecheen | 3.00 | 1.40 | .30 |
| ☐ 87 Floyd Baker | 3.00 | 1.40 | .30 |
| ☐ 88 Eddie Robinson | 3.00 | 1.40 | .30 |
| ☐ 89 Hank Thompson | 3.00 | 1.40 | .30 |
| ☐ 90 Dave Koslo | 3.00 | 1.40 | .30 |
| ☐ 91 Clyde Vollmer | 3.00 | 1.40 | .30 |
| ☐ 92 Vern Stephens | 3.00 | 1.40 | .30 |
| ☐ 93 Danny O'Connell | 3.00 | 1.40 | .30 |
| ☐ 94 Clyde McCullough | 3.00 | 1.40 | .30 |
| ☐ 95 Sherry Robertson | 3.00 | 1.40 | .30 |
| ☐ 96 Sandy Consuegra | 3.00 | 1.40 | .30 |
| ☐ 97 Bob Kuzava | 3.00 | 1.40 | .30 |
| ☐ 98 Willard Marshall | 3.00 | 1.40 | .30 |
| ☐ 99 Earl Torgeson | 3.00 | 1.40 | .30 |
| ☐ 100 Sherm Lollar | 3.00 | 1.40 | .30 |
| ☐ 101 Owen Friend | 3.00 | 1.40 | .30 |
| ☐ 102 Dutch Leonard | 3.00 | 1.40 | .30 |
| ☐ 103 Andy Pafko | 3.00 | 1.40 | .30 |
| ☐ 104 Virgil Trucks | 3.00 | 1.40 | .30 |
| ☐ 105 Don Kolloway | 3.00 | 1.40 | .30 |
| ☐ 106 Pat Mullin | 3.00 | 1.40 | .30 |
| ☐ 107 Johnny Wyrostek | 3.00 | 1.40 | .30 |
| ☐ 108 Virgil Stallcup | 3.00 | 1.40 | .30 |
| ☐ 109 Allie Reynolds | 5.00 | 2.35 | .50 |
| ☐ 110 Bobby Brown | 5.00 | 2.35 | .50 |
| ☐ 111 Curt Simmons | 3.50 | 1.65 | .35 |
| ☐ 112 Willie Jones | 3.00 | 1.40 | .30 |
| ☐ 113 Bill Nicholson | 3.00 | 1.40 | .30 |
| ☐ 114 Sam Zoldak | 3.00 | 1.40 | .30 |
| ☐ 115 Steve Gromek | 3.00 | 1.40 | .30 |
| ☐ 116 Bruce Edwards | 3.00 | 1.40 | .30 |

|  | MINT | VG-E | F-G |
|---|---|---|---|
| ☐ 117 Eddie Miksis | 3.00 | 1.40 | .30 |
| ☐ 118 Preacher Roe | 5.00 | 2.35 | .50 |
| ☐ 119 Eddie Joost | 3.00 | 1.40 | .30 |
| ☐ 120 Joe Coleman | 3.50 | 1.65 | .35 |
| ☐ 121 Gerry Staley | 3.00 | 1.40 | .30 |
| ☐ 122 Joe Garagiola | 15.00 | 7.00 | 1.50 |
| ☐ 123 Howie Judson | 3.00 | 1.40 | .30 |
| ☐ 124 Gus Niarhos | 3.00 | 1.40 | .30 |
| ☐ 125 Bill Rigney | 3.00 | 1.40 | .30 |
| ☐ 126 Bobby Thomson | 5.00 | 2.35 | .50 |
| ☐ 127 Sal Maglie | 5.50 | 2.60 | .55 |
| ☐ 128 Ellis Kinder | 3.00 | 1.40 | .30 |
| ☐ 129 Matt Batts | 3.00 | 1.40 | .30 |
| ☐ 130 Tom Saffell | 3.00 | 1.40 | .30 |
| ☐ 131 Cliff Chambers | 3.00 | 1.40 | .30 |
| ☐ 132 Cass Michaels | 3.00 | 1.40 | .30 |
| ☐ 133 Sam Dente | 3.00 | 1.40 | .30 |
| ☐ 134 Warren Spahn | 18.00 | 8.50 | 1.80 |
| ☐ 135 Walker Cooper | 3.00 | 1.40 | .30 |
| ☐ 136 Ray Coleman | 3.00 | 1.40 | .30 |
| ☐ 137 Dick Starr | 3.00 | 1.40 | .30 |
| ☐ 138 Phil Cavaretta | 3.50 | 1.65 | .35 |
| ☐ 139 Doyle Lade | 3.00 | 1.40 | .30 |
| ☐ 140 Eddie Lake | 3.00 | 1.40 | .30 |
| ☐ 141 Fred Hutchinson | 3.50 | 1.65 | .35 |
| ☐ 142 Aaron Robinson | 3.00 | 1.40 | .30 |
| ☐ 143 Ted Kluszewski | 5.50 | 2.60 | .55 |
| ☐ 144 Herman Wehmeier | 3.00 | 1.40 | .30 |
| ☐ 145 Fred Sanford | 3.00 | 1.40 | .30 |
| ☐ 146 Johnny Hopp | 3.00 | 1.40 | .30 |
| ☐ 147 Ken Heintzelman | 3.00 | 1.40 | .30 |
| ☐ 148 Granny Hamner | 3.00 | 1.40 | .30 |
| ☐ 149 Bubba Church | 3.00 | 1.40 | .30 |
| ☐ 150 Mike Garcia | 3.50 | 1.65 | .35 |
| ☐ 151 Larry Doby | 5.00 | 2.35 | .50 |
| ☐ 152 Cal Abrams | 3.00 | 1.40 | .30 |
| ☐ 153 Rex Barney | 3.00 | 1.40 | .30 |
| ☐ 154 Pete Suder | 3.00 | 1.40 | .30 |
| ☐ 155 Lou Brissie | 3.00 | 1.40 | .30 |
| ☐ 156 Del Rice | 3.00 | 1.40 | .30 |
| ☐ 157 Al Brazle | 3.00 | 1.40 | .30 |
| ☐ 158 Chuck Diering | 3.00 | 1.40 | .30 |
| ☐ 159 Eddie Stewart | 3.00 | 1.40 | .30 |
| ☐ 160 Phil Masi | 3.00 | 1.40 | .30 |
| ☐ 161 Wes Westrum | 3.00 | 1.40 | .30 |
| ☐ 162 Larry Jansen | 3.00 | 1.40 | .30 |
| ☐ 163 Monte Kennedy | 3.00 | 1.40 | .30 |
| ☐ 164 Bill Wight | 3.00 | 1.40 | .30 |
| ☐ 165 Ted Williams | 85.00 | 40.00 | 8.50 |
| ☐ 166 Stan Rojek | 3.00 | 1.40 | .30 |
| ☐ 167 Murry Dickson | 3.00 | 1.40 | .30 |
| ☐ 168 Sam Mele | 3.00 | 1.40 | .30 |
| ☐ 169 Sid Hudson | 3.00 | 1.40 | .30 |

| | MINT | VG-E | F-G |
|---|---|---|---|
| ☐ 170 Sibby Sisti | 3.00 | 1.40 | .30 |
| ☐ 171 Buddy Kerr | 3.00 | 1.40 | .30 |
| ☐ 172 Ned Garver | 3.00 | 1.40 | .30 |
| ☐ 173 Hank Arft | 3.00 | 1.40 | .30 |
| ☐ 174 Mickey Owen | 3.00 | 1.40 | .30 |
| ☐ 175 Wayne Terwilliger | 3.00 | 1.40 | .30 |
| ☐ 176 Vic Wertz | 3.00 | 1.40 | .30 |
| ☐ 177 Charlie Keller | 3.50 | 1.65 | .35 |
| ☐ 178 Ted Gray | 3.00 | 1.40 | .30 |
| ☐ 179 Danny Litwiler | 3.00 | 1.40 | .30 |
| ☐ 180 Howie Fox | 3.00 | 1.40 | .30 |
| ☐ 181 Casey Stengel | 20.00 | 9.00 | 2.00 |
| ☐ 182 Tom Ferrick | 3.00 | 1.40 | .30 |
| ☐ 183 Hank Bauer | 4.50 | 2.10 | .45 |
| ☐ 184 Eddie Sawyer | 3.00 | 1.40 | .30 |
| ☐ 185 Jimmy Bloodworth | 3.00 | 1.40 | .30 |
| ☐ 186 Richie Ashburn | 6.50 | 3.00 | .65 |
| ☐ 187 Al Rosen | 5.50 | 2.60 | .55 |
| ☐ 188 Bobby Avila | 3.50 | 1.65 | .35 |
| ☐ 189 Erv Palica | 3.00 | 1.40 | .30 |
| ☐ 190 Joe Hatton | 3.00 | 1.40 | .30 |
| ☐ 191 Billy Hitchcock | 3.00 | 1.40 | .30 |
| ☐ 192 Hank Wyse | 3.00 | 1.40 | .30 |
| ☐ 193 Ted Wilks | 3.00 | 1.40 | .30 |
| ☐ 194 Peanuts Lowrey | 3.00 | 1.40 | .30 |
| ☐ 195 Paul Richards | 5.00 | 2.35 | .50 |
| ☐ 196 Billy Pierce | 5.50 | 2.60 | .55 |
| ☐ 197 Bob Cain | 3.00 | 1.40 | .30 |
| ☐ 198 Monte Irvin | 14.00 | 6.50 | 1.40 |
| ☐ 199 Sheldon Jones | 3.00 | 1.40 | .30 |
| ☐ 200 Jack Kramer | 3.00 | 1.40 | .30 |
| ☐ 201 Steve O'Neill | 3.00 | 1.40 | .30 |
| ☐ 202 Mike Guerra | 3.00 | 1.40 | .30 |
| ☐ 203 Vernon Law | 4.50 | 2.10 | .45 |
| ☐ 204 Vic Lombardi | 3.00 | 1.40 | .30 |
| ☐ 205 Mickey Grasso | 3.00 | 1.40 | .30 |
| ☐ 206 Conrado Marrero | 3.00 | 1.40 | .30 |
| ☐ 207 Billy Southworth | 3.00 | 1.40 | .30 |
| ☐ 208 Blix Donnelly | 3.00 | 1.40 | .30 |
| ☐ 209 Ken Wood | 3.00 | 1.40 | .30 |
| ☐ 210 Les Moss | 3.00 | 1.40 | .30 |
| ☐ 211 Hal Jeffcoat | 3.00 | 1.40 | .30 |
| ☐ 212 Bob Rush | 3.00 | 1.40 | .30 |
| ☐ 213 Neil Berry | 3.00 | 1.40 | .30 |
| ☐ 214 Bob Swift | 3.00 | 1.40 | .30 |
| ☐ 215 Ken Peterson | 3.00 | 1.40 | .30 |
| ☐ 216 Connie Ryan | 3.00 | 1.40 | .30 |
| ☐ 217 Joe Page | 4.00 | 1.85 | .40 |
| ☐ 218 Ed Lopat | 5.00 | 2.35 | .50 |
| ☐ 219 Gene Woodling | 4.50 | 2.10 | .45 |
| ☐ 220 Bob Miller | 3.00 | 1.40 | .30 |
| ☐ 221 Dick Whitman | 3.00 | 1.40 | .30 |
| ☐ 222 Thurman Tucker | 3.00 | 1.40 | .30 |

| | MINT | VG-E | F-G |
|---|---|---|---|
| ☐ 223 Johnny VanderMeer | 4.00 | 1.85 | .40 |
| ☐ 224 Billy Cox | 3.50 | 1.65 | .35 |
| ☐ 225 Dan Bankhead | 3.00 | 1.40 | .30 |
| ☐ 226 Jimmy Dykes | 3.50 | 1.65 | .35 |
| ☐ 227 Bobby Shantz | 4.00 | 1.85 | .40 |
| ☐ 228 Cloyd Boyer | 3.00 | 1.40 | .30 |
| ☐ 229 Bill Howerton | 3.00 | 1.40 | .30 |
| ☐ 230 Max Lanier | 3.00 | 1.40 | .30 |
| ☐ 231 Luis Aloma | 3.00 | 1.40 | .30 |
| ☐ 232 Nelson Fox | 10.00 | 4.75 | 1.00 |
| ☐ 233 Leo Durocher | 7.00 | 3.25 | .70 |
| ☐ 234 Clint Hartung | 3.00 | 1.40 | .30 |
| ☐ 235 Jack Lohrke | 3.00 | 1.40 | .30 |
| ☐ 236 Warren Rosar | 3.00 | 1.40 | .30 |
| ☐ 237 Billy Goodman | 3.50 | 1.65 | .35 |
| ☐ 238 Peter Reiser | 3.50 | 1.65 | .35 |
| ☐ 239 Bill MacDonald | 3.00 | 1.40 | .30 |
| ☐ 240 Joe Haynes | 3.00 | 1.40 | .30 |
| ☐ 241 Irv Noren | 3.00 | 1.40 | .30 |
| ☐ 242 Sam Jethroe | 3.00 | 1.40 | .30 |
| ☐ 243 Johnny Antonelli | 3.50 | 1.65 | .35 |
| ☐ 244 Cliff Fannin | 3.00 | 1.40 | .30 |
| ☐ 245 John Berardino | 3.50 | 1.65 | .35 |
| ☐ 246 Bill Serena | 3.00 | 1.40 | .30 |
| ☐ 247 Bob Ramazotti | 3.00 | 1.40 | .30 |
| ☐ 248 Johnny Klippstein | 3.00 | 1.40 | .30 |
| ☐ 249 Johnny Groth | 3.00 | 1.40 | .30 |
| ☐ 250 Hank Borowy | 3.00 | 1.40 | .30 |
| ☐ 251 Billy Ramsdell | 3.00 | 1.40 | .30 |
| ☐ 252 Dixie Howell | 3.00 | 1.40 | .30 |
| ☐ 253 Mickey Mantle | 500.00 | 225.00 | 50.00 |
| ☐ 254 Jackie Jensen | 18.00 | 8.50 | 1.80 |
| ☐ 255 Milo Candini | 10.00 | 4.75 | 1.00 |
| ☐ 256 Ken Sylvestri | 10.00 | 4.75 | 1.00 |
| ☐ 257 Birdie Tebbetts | 10.00 | 4.75 | 1.00 |
| ☐ 258 Luke Easter | 11.00 | 5.25 | 1.10 |
| ☐ 259 Chuck Dressen | 12.00 | 5.50 | 1.20 |
| ☐ 260 Carl Erskine | 16.00 | 7.50 | 1.60 |
| ☐ 261 Wally Moses | 10.00 | 4.75 | 1.00 |
| ☐ 262 Gus Zernial | 10.00 | 4.75 | 1.00 |
| ☐ 263 Howie Pollet | 10.00 | 4.75 | 1.00 |
| ☐ 264 Don Richmond | 10.00 | 4.75 | 1.00 |
| ☐ 265 Steve Bilko | 10.00 | 4.75 | 1.00 |
| ☐ 266 Harry Dorish | 10.00 | 4.75 | 1.00 |
| ☐ 267 Ken Holcomb | 10.00 | 4.75 | 1.00 |
| ☐ 268 Don Mueller | 11.00 | 5.25 | 1.10 |
| ☐ 269 Ray Noble | 10.00 | 4.75 | 1.00 |
| ☐ 270 Willard Nixon | 10.00 | 4.75 | 1.00 |
| ☐ 271 Tommy Wright | 10.00 | 4.75 | 1.00 |
| ☐ 272 Billy Meyer | 10.00 | 4.75 | 1.00 |
| ☐ 273 Danny Murtaugh | 11.00 | 5.25 | 1.10 |
| ☐ 274 George Metkovich | 10.00 | 4.75 | 1.00 |
| ☐ 275 Bucky Harris MGR | 15.00 | 7.00 | 1.50 |

| | | MINT | VG-E | F-G |
|---|---|---|---|---|
| ☐ 276 | Frank Quinn | 10.00 | 4.75 | 1.00 |
| ☐ 277 | Roy Hartsfield | 10.00 | 4.75 | 1.00 |
| ☐ 278 | Norman Roy | 10.00 | 4.75 | 1.00 |
| ☐ 279 | Jim Delsing | 10.00 | 4.75 | 1.00 |
| ☐ 280 | Frank Overmire | 10.00 | 4.75 | 1.00 |
| ☐ 281 | Al Widmar | 10.00 | 4.75 | 1.00 |
| ☐ 282 | Frank Frisch | 18.00 | 8.50 | 1.80 |
| ☐ 283 | Walt Dubiel | 10.00 | 4.75 | 1.00 |
| ☐ 284 | Gene Bearden | 10.00 | 4.75 | 1.00 |
| ☐ 285 | Johnny Lipon | 10.00 | 4.75 | 1.00 |
| ☐ 286 | Bob Usher | 10.00 | 4.75 | 1.00 |
| ☐ 287 | Jim Blackburn | 10.00 | 4.75 | 1.00 |
| ☐ 288 | Bobby Adams | 10.00 | 4.75 | 1.00 |
| ☐ 289 | Cliff Mapes | 10.00 | 4.75 | 1.00 |
| ☐ 290 | Bill Dickey | 35.00 | 16.50 | 3.50 |
| ☐ 291 | Tommy Henrich | 14.00 | 6.50 | 1.40 |
| ☐ 292 | Eddie Pellegrini | 10.00 | 4.75 | 1.00 |
| ☐ 293 | Ken Johnson | 10.00 | 4.75 | 1.00 |
| ☐ 294 | Jocko Thompson | 10.00 | 4.75 | 1.00 |
| ☐ 295 | Al Lopez | 18.00 | 8.50 | 1.80 |
| ☐ 296 | Bob Kennedy | 11.00 | 5.25 | 1.10 |
| ☐ 297 | Dave Philley | 10.00 | 4.75 | 1.00 |
| ☐ 298 | Joe Astroth | 10.00 | 4.75 | 1.00 |
| ☐ 299 | Clyde King | 10.00 | 4.75 | 1.00 |
| ☐ 300 | Hal Rice | 10.00 | 4.75 | 1.00 |
| ☐ 301 | Tommy Glaviano | 10.00 | 4.75 | 1.00 |
| ☐ 302 | Jim Busby | 10.00 | 4.75 | 1.00 |
| ☐ 303 | Marv Rotblatt | 10.00 | 4.75 | 1.00 |
| ☐ 304 | Al Gettel | 10.00 | 4.75 | 1.00 |
| ☐ 305 | Willie Mays | 400.00 | 180.00 | 40.00 |
| ☐ 306 | Jim Piersall | 18.00 | 8.50 | 1.80 |
| ☐ 307 | Walt Masterson | 10.00 | 4.75 | 1.00 |
| ☐ 308 | Ted Beard | 10.00 | 4.75 | 1.00 |
| ☐ 309 | Mel Queen | 10.00 | 4.75 | 1.00 |
| ☐ 310 | Erv Dusak | 10.00 | 4.75 | 1.00 |
| ☐ 311 | Mickey Harris | 10.00 | 4.75 | 1.00 |
| ☐ 312 | Gene Mauch | 15.00 | 7.00 | 1.50 |
| ☐ 313 | Ray Mueller | 10.00 | 4.75 | 1.00 |
| ☐ 314 | Johnny Sain | 15.00 | 7.00 | 1.50 |
| ☐ 315 | Zack Taylor | 10.00 | 4.75 | 1.00 |
| ☐ 316 | Duane Pillette | 10.00 | 4.75 | 1.00 |
| ☐ 317 | Smokey Burgess | 13.00 | 6.00 | 1.30 |
| ☐ 318 | Warren Hacker | 10.00 | 4.75 | 1.00 |
| ☐ 319 | Red Rolfe | 11.00 | 5.25 | 1.10 |
| ☐ 320 | Hal White | 10.00 | 4.75 | 1.00 |
| ☐ 321 | Earl Johnson | 10.00 | 4.75 | 1.00 |
| ☐ 322 | Luke Sewell | 11.00 | 5.25 | 1.10 |
| ☐ 323 | Joe Adcock | 15.00 | 7.00 | 1.50 |
| ☐ 324 | Johnny Pramesa | 20.00 | 5.00 | 1.00 |

## 1952 BOWMAN

**BOBBY THOMSON**

Third Base—New York Giants
Bats: Right  Throws: Right
Height: 6.1  Weight: 190
Born: Glasgow, Scotland, Oct. 25, 1923

Fans are not going to forget Bobby's one out, last of the ninth home run in the third playoff game against the Dodgers last fall. It drove in 3 runs, gave the Giants the game, 5-4, and, with it, the pennant. Bobby hit .293 for the 1951 season. Drove in 101 runs. Had 32 homers.

**No. 2 in the 1952 SERIES**

**BASEBALL**

*The cards in this 252 card set measure 2¹⁄₁₆" by 3⅛". While the Bowman set of 1952 retained the card size introduced in 1951, it employed a modification of color tones from the two preceding years. The cards also appeared with a facsimile autograph on the front and, for the first time since 1949, premium advertising on the back. The 1952 set was sold in sheets as well as in gum packs. Artwork for 15 cards that were never issued was recently discovered.*

Complete Set: M-1400.00; VG-E-650.00; F-G-125.00

| | | MINT | VG-E | F-G |
|---|---|---|---|---|
| | Common Player (1–36) | 3.50 | 1.65 | .35 |
| | Common Player (37–180) | 3.00 | 1.40 | .30 |
| | Common Player (181–216) | 2.50 | 1.15 | .25 |
| | Common Player (217–252) | 6.00 | 2.80 | .60 |
| ☐ 1 | Yogi Berra | 90.00 | 20.00 | 4.00 |
| ☐ 2 | Bobby Thomson | 5.00 | 2.35 | .50 |
| ☐ 3 | Fred Hutchinson | 4.00 | 1.85 | .40 |
| ☐ 4 | Robin Roberts | 12.00 | 5.50 | 1.20 |
| ☐ 5 | Minnie Minoso | 7.00 | 3.25 | .70 |
| ☐ 6 | Virgil Stallcup | 3.50 | 1.65 | .35 |
| ☐ 7 | Mike Garcia | 4.00 | 1.85 | .40 |
| ☐ 8 | Pee Wee Reese | 16.00 | 7.50 | 1.60 |
| ☐ 9 | Vern Stephens | 3.50 | 1.65 | .35 |
| ☐ 10 | Bob Hooper | 3.50 | 1.65 | .35 |
| ☐ 11 | Ralph Kiner | 12.00 | 5.50 | 1.20 |
| ☐ 12 | Max Surkont | 3.50 | 1.65 | .35 |
| ☐ 13 | Cliff Mapes | 3.50 | 1.65 | .35 |

| | | MINT | VG-E | F-G |
|---|---|---|---|---|
| ☐ | 14 Cliff Chambers | 3.50 | 1.65 | .35 |
| ☐ | 15 Sam Mele | 3.50 | 1.65 | .35 |
| ☐ | 16 Turk Lown | 3.50 | 1.65 | .35 |
| ☐ | 17 Ed Lopat | 5.00 | 2.35 | .50 |
| ☐ | 18 Don mueller | 4.00 | 1.85 | .40 |
| ☐ | 19 Bob Cain | 3.50 | 1.65 | .35 |
| ☐ | 20 Willie Jones | 3.50 | 1.65 | .35 |
| ☐ | 21 Nelson Fox | 6.00 | 2.80 | .60 |
| ☐ | 22 Willard Ramsdell | 3.50 | 1.65 | .35 |
| ☐ | 23 Bob Lemon | 12.00 | 5.50 | 1.20 |
| ☐ | 24 Carl Furillo | 5.50 | 2.60 | .55 |
| ☐ | 25 Mickey McDermott | 3.50 | 1.65 | .35 |
| ☐ | 26 Eddie Joost | 3.50 | 1.65 | .35 |
| ☐ | 27 Joe Garagiola | 12.00 | 5.50 | 1.20 |
| ☐ | 28 Ray Hartsfield | 3.50 | 1.65 | .35 |
| ☐ | 29 Ned Garver | 3.50 | 1.65 | .35 |
| ☐ | 30 Red Schoendienst | 4.00 | 1.85 | .40 |
| ☐ | 31 Eddie Yost | 3.50 | 1.65 | .35 |
| ☐ | 32 Eddie Miksis | 3.50 | 1.65 | .35 |
| ☐ | 33 Gil McDougald | 5.50 | 2.60 | .55 |
| ☐ | 34 Alvin Dark | 4.00 | 1.85 | .40 |
| ☐ | 35 Granny Hamner | 3.50 | 1.65 | .35 |
| ☐ | 36 Cass Michaels | 3.50 | 1.65 | .35 |
| ☐ | 37 Vic Raschi | 4.00 | 1.85 | .40 |
| ☐ | 38 Whitey Lockman | 3.50 | 1.65 | .35 |
| ☐ | 39 Vic Wertz | 3.50 | 1.65 | .35 |
| ☐ | 40 Bubba Church | 3.00 | 1.40 | .30 |
| ☐ | 41 Chico Carrasquel | 3.00 | 1.40 | .30 |
| ☐ | 42 Johnny Wyrostek | 3.00 | 1.40 | .30 |
| ☐ | 43 Bob Feller | 24.00 | 11.00 | 2.40 |
| ☐ | 44 Roy Campanella | 40.00 | 18.00 | 4.00 |
| ☐ | 45 Johnny Pesky | 3.50 | 1.65 | .35 |
| ☐ | 46 Carl Scheib | 3.00 | 1.40 | .30 |
| ☐ | 47 Pete Castiglione | 3.00 | 1.40 | .30 |
| ☐ | 48 Vern Bickford | 3.00 | 1.40 | .30 |
| ☐ | 49 Jim Hearn | 3.00 | 1.40 | .30 |
| ☐ | 50 Gerry Staley | 3.00 | 1.40 | .30 |
| ☐ | 51 Gil Coan | 3.00 | 1.40 | .30 |
| ☐ | 52 Phil Rizzuto | 16.00 | 7.50 | 1.60 |
| ☐ | 53 Richie Ashburn | 6.00 | 2.80 | .60 |
| ☐ | 54 Billy Pierce | 4.00 | 1.85 | .40 |
| ☐ | 55 Ken Raffensberger | 3.00 | 1.40 | .30 |
| ☐ | 56 Clyde King | 3.00 | 1.40 | .30 |
| ☐ | 57 Clyde Vollmer | 3.00 | 1.40 | .30 |
| ☐ | 58 Hank Majeski | 3.00 | 1.40 | .30 |
| ☐ | 59 Murry Dickson | 3.00 | 1.40 | .30 |
| ☐ | 60 Sid Gordon | 3.00 | 1.40 | .30 |
| ☐ | 61 Tommy Byrne | 3.00 | 1.40 | .30 |
| ☐ | 62 Joe Presko | 3.00 | 1.40 | .30 |
| ☐ | 63 Irv Noren | 3.00 | 1.40 | .30 |
| ☐ | 64 Roy Smalley | 3.00 | 1.40 | .30 |
| ☐ | 65 Hank Bauer | 4.00 | 1.85 | .40 |
| ☐ | 66 Sal Maglie | 4.00 | 1.85 | .40 |

| | | MINT | VG-E | F-G |
|---|---|---|---|---|
| ☐ | 67 Johnny Groth | 3.00 | 1.40 | .30 |
| ☐ | 68 Jim Busby | 3.00 | 1.40 | .30 |
| ☐ | 69 Joe Adcock | 3.50 | 1.65 | .35 |
| ☐ | 70 Carl Erskine | 4.00 | 1.85 | .40 |
| ☐ | 71 Vernon Law | 3.50 | 1.65 | .35 |
| ☐ | 72 Earl Torgeson | 3.00 | 1.40 | .30 |
| ☐ | 73 Gerry Coleman | 3.50 | 1.65 | .35 |
| ☐ | 74 Wes Westrum | 3.00 | 1.40 | .30 |
| ☐ | 75 George Kell | 8.00 | 3.75 | .80 |
| ☐ | 76 Del Ennis | 3.50 | 1.65 | .35 |
| ☐ | 77 Eddie Robinson | 3.00 | 1.40 | .30 |
| ☐ | 78 Lloyd Merriman | 3.00 | 1.40 | .30 |
| ☐ | 79 Lou Brissie | 3.00 | 1.40 | .30 |
| ☐ | 80 Gil Hodges | 14.00 | 6.50 | 1.40 |
| ☐ | 81 Billy Goodman | 3.50 | 1.65 | .35 |
| ☐ | 82 Gus Zernial | 3.00 | 1.40 | .30 |
| ☐ | 83 Howie Pollet | 3.00 | 1.40 | .30 |
| ☐ | 84 Sam Jethroe | 3.00 | 1.40 | .30 |
| ☐ | 85 Marty Marion | 4.00 | 1.85 | .40 |
| ☐ | 86 Cal Abrams | 3.00 | 1.40 | .30 |
| ☐ | 87 Mickey Vernon | 3.50 | 1.65 | .35 |
| ☐ | 88 Bruce Edwards | 3.00 | 1.40 | .30 |
| ☐ | 89 Billy Hitchcock | 3.00 | 1.40 | .30 |
| ☐ | 90 Larry Jansen | 3.00 | 1.40 | .30 |
| ☐ | 91 Don Kolloway | 3.00 | 1.40 | .30 |
| ☐ | 92 Eddie Waitkus | 3.00 | 1.40 | .30 |
| ☐ | 93 Paul Richards | 3.00 | 1.40 | .30 |
| ☐ | 94 Luke Sewell | 3.00 | 1.40 | .30 |
| ☐ | 95 Luke Easter | 3.00 | 1.40 | .30 |
| ☐ | 96 Ralph Branca | 3.50 | 1.65 | .35 |
| ☐ | 97 Willard Marshall | 3.00 | 1.40 | .30 |
| ☐ | 98 Jimmy Dykes | 3.00 | 1.40 | .30 |
| ☐ | 99 Clyde McCullough | 3.00 | 1.40 | .30 |
| ☐ | 100 Sibby Sisti | 3.00 | 1.40 | .30 |
| ☐ | 101 Mickey Mantle | 300.00 | 130.00 | 30.00 |
| ☐ | 102 Peanuts Lowrey | 3.00 | 1.40 | .30 |
| ☐ | 103 Joe Haynes | 3.00 | 1.40 | .30 |
| ☐ | 104 Hal Jeffcoat | 3.00 | 1.40 | .30 |
| ☐ | 105 Bobby Brown | 5.00 | 2.35 | .50 |
| ☐ | 106 Randy Gumpert | 3.00 | 1.40 | .30 |
| ☐ | 107 Del Rice | 3.00 | 1.40 | .30 |
| ☐ | 108 George Metkovich | 3.00 | 1.40 | .30 |
| ☐ | 109 Tom Morgan | 3.00 | 1.40 | .30 |
| ☐ | 110 Max Lanier | 3.00 | 1.40 | .30 |
| ☐ | 111 Hoot Evers | 3.00 | 1.40 | .30 |
| ☐ | 112 Smokey Burgess | 3.50 | 1.65 | .35 |
| ☐ | 113 Al Zarilla | 3.00 | 1.40 | .30 |
| ☐ | 114 Frank Hiller | 3.00 | 1.40 | .30 |
| ☐ | 115 Larry Doby | 5.00 | 2.35 | .50 |
| ☐ | 116 Duke Snider | 25.00 | 11.00 | 2.50 |
| ☐ | 117 Bill Wight | 3.00 | 1.40 | .30 |
| ☐ | 118 Ray Murray | 3.00 | 1.40 | .30 |
| ☐ | 119 Bill Howerton | 3.00 | 1.40 | .30 |

| | | MINT | VG-E | F-G |
|---|---|---|---|---|
| ☐ 120 | Chet Nichols | 3.00 | 1.40 | .30 |
| ☐ 121 | Al Corwin | 3.00 | 1.40 | .30 |
| ☐ 122 | Billy Johnson | 3.00 | 1.40 | .30 |
| ☐ 123 | Sid Hudson | 3.00 | 1.40 | .30 |
| ☐ 124 | Birdie Tebbets | 3.00 | 1.40 | .30 |
| ☐ 125 | Howie Fox | 3.00 | 1.40 | .30 |
| ☐ 126 | Phil Cavaretta | 3.50 | 1.65 | .35 |
| ☐ 127 | Dick Sisler | 3.00 | 1.40 | .30 |
| ☐ 128 | Don Newcombe | 5.50 | 2.60 | .55 |
| ☐ 129 | Gus Niarhos | 3.00 | 1.40 | .30 |
| ☐ 130 | Allie Clark | 3.00 | 1.40 | .30 |
| ☐ 131 | Bob Swift | 3.00 | 1.40 | .30 |
| ☐ 132 | Dave Cole | 3.00 | 1.40 | .30 |
| ☐ 133 | Dick Kryhoski | 3.00 | 1.40 | .30 |
| ☐ 134 | Al Brazle | 3.00 | 1.40 | .30 |
| ☐ 135 | Mickey Harris | 3.00 | 1.40 | .30 |
| ☐ 136 | Gene Hermanski | 3.00 | 1.40 | .30 |
| ☐ 137 | Stan Rojek | 3.00 | 1.40 | .30 |
| ☐ 138 | Ted Wilks | 3.00 | 1.40 | .30 |
| ☐ 139 | Jerry Priddy | 3.00 | 1.40 | .30 |
| ☐ 140 | Ray Scarborough | 3.00 | 1.40 | .30 |
| ☐ 141 | Hank Edwards | 3.00 | 1.40 | .30 |
| ☐ 142 | Early Wynn | 10.00 | 4.75 | 1.00 |
| ☐ 143 | Sandy Consuegra | 3.00 | 1.40 | .30 |
| ☐ 144 | Joe Hatton | 3.00 | 1.40 | .30 |
| ☐ 145 | Johnny Mize | 11.00 | 5.25 | 1.10 |
| ☐ 146 | Leo Durocher | 6.50 | 3.00 | .65 |
| ☐ 147 | Marlin Stuart | 3.00 | 1.40 | .30 |
| ☐ 148 | Ken Heintzelman | 3.00 | 1.40 | .30 |
| ☐ 149 | Howie Judson | 3.00 | 1.40 | .30 |
| ☐ 150 | Herman Wehmeier | 3.00 | 1.40 | .30 |
| ☐ 151 | Al Rosen | 5.00 | 2.35 | .50 |
| ☐ 152 | Billy Cox | 3.50 | 1.65 | .35 |
| ☐ 153 | Fred Hatfield | 3.00 | 1.40 | .30 |
| ☐ 154 | Ferris Fain | 3.50 | 1.65 | .35 |
| ☐ 155 | Billy Meyer | 3.00 | 1.40 | .30 |
| ☐ 156 | Warren Spahn | 15.00 | 7.00 | 1.50 |
| ☐ 157 | Jim Delsing | 3.00 | 1.40 | .30 |
| ☐ 158 | Bucky Harris | 7.00 | 3.25 | .70 |
| ☐ 159 | Dutch Leonard | 3.00 | 1.40 | .30 |
| ☐ 160 | Eddie Stanky | 3.50 | 1.65 | .35 |
| ☐ 161 | Jackie Jensen | 4.00 | 1.85 | .40 |
| ☐ 162 | Monte Irvin | 9.00 | 4.25 | .90 |
| ☐ 163 | Johnny Lipon | 3.00 | 1.40 | .30 |
| ☐ 164 | Connie Ryan | 3.00 | 1.40 | .30 |
| ☐ 165 | Saul Rogovin | 3.00 | 1.40 | .30 |
| ☐ 166 | Bobby Adams | 3.00 | 1.40 | .30 |
| ☐ 167 | Bobby Avila | 3.50 | 1.65 | .35 |
| ☐ 168 | Preacher Roe | 5.00 | 2.35 | .50 |
| ☐ 169 | Walt Dropo | 3.00 | 1.40 | .30 |
| ☐ 170 | Joe Astroth | 3.00 | 1.40 | .30 |
| ☐ 171 | Mel Queen | 3.00 | 1.40 | .30 |
| ☐ 172 | Ebba St. Claire | 3.00 | 1.40 | .30 |

| | | MINT | VG-E | F-G |
|---|---|---|---|---|
| ☐ 173 | Gene Bearden | 3.00 | 1.40 | .30 |
| ☐ 174 | Mickey Grasso | 3.00 | 1.40 | .30 |
| ☐ 175 | Ransom Jackson | 3.00 | 1.40 | .30 |
| ☐ 176 | Harry Brecheen | 3.00 | 1.40 | .30 |
| ☐ 177 | Gene Woodling | 3.50 | 1.65 | .35 |
| ☐ 178 | Dave Williams | 3.50 | 1.65 | .35 |
| ☐ 179 | Pete Suder | 3.00 | 1.40 | .30 |
| ☐ 180 | Eddie Fitzgerald | 3.00 | 1.40 | .30 |
| ☐ 181 | Joe Collins | 3.00 | 1.40 | .30 |
| ☐ 182 | Dave Koslo | 2.50 | 1.15 | .25 |
| ☐ 183 | Pat Mullin | 2.50 | 1.15 | .25 |
| ☐ 184 | Curt Simmons | 3.00 | 1.40 | .30 |
| ☐ 185 | Eddie Stewart | 2.50 | 1.15 | .25 |
| ☐ 186 | Frank Smith | 2.50 | 1.15 | .25 |
| ☐ 187 | Jim Hegan | 2.50 | 1.15 | .25 |
| ☐ 188 | Charlie Dressen | 3.00 | 1.40 | .30 |
| ☐ 189 | Jim Piersall | 3.50 | 1.65 | .35 |
| ☐ 190 | Dick Fowler | 2.50 | 1.15 | .25 |
| ☐ 191 | Bob Friend | 3.50 | 1.65 | .35 |
| ☐ 192 | John Cusick | 2.50 | 1.15 | .25 |
| ☐ 193 | Bobby Young | 2.50 | 1.15 | .25 |
| ☐ 194 | Bob Porterfield | 2.50 | 1.15 | .25 |
| ☐ 195 | Frank Baumholtz | 2.50 | 1.15 | .25 |
| ☐ 196 | Stan Musial | 90.00 | 42.00 | 9.00 |
| ☐ 197 | Charlie Silvera | 2.50 | 1.15 | .25 |
| ☐ 198 | Chuck Diering | 2.50 | 1.15 | .25 |
| ☐ 199 | Ted Gray | 2.50 | 1.15 | .25 |
| ☐ 200 | Ken Silvestri | 2.50 | 1.15 | .25 |
| ☐ 201 | Ray Coleman | 2.50 | 1.15 | .25 |
| ☐ 202 | Harry Perkowski | 2.50 | 1.15 | .25 |
| ☐ 203 | Steve Gromek | 2.50 | 1.15 | .25 |
| ☐ 204 | Andy Pafko | 2.50 | 1.15 | .25 |
| ☐ 205 | Walt Masterson | 2.50 | 1.15 | .25 |
| ☐ 206 | Elmer Valo | 2.50 | 1.15 | .25 |
| ☐ 207 | George Strickland | 2.50 | 1.15 | .25 |
| ☐ 208 | Walker Cooper | 2.50 | 1.15 | .25 |
| ☐ 209 | Dick Littlefield | 2.50 | 1.15 | .25 |
| ☐ 210 | Archie Wilson | 2.50 | 1.15 | .25 |
| ☐ 211 | Paul Minner | 2.50 | 1.15 | .25 |
| ☐ 212 | Solly Hemus | 2.50 | 1.15 | .25 |
| ☐ 213 | Monte Kennedy | 2.50 | 1.15 | .25 |
| ☐ 214 | Ray Boone | 2.50 | 1.15 | .25 |
| ☐ 215 | Sheldon Jones | 2.50 | 1.15 | .25 |
| ☐ 216 | Matt Batts | 2.50 | 1.15 | .25 |
| ☐ 217 | Casey Stengel | 28.00 | 12.50 | 2.80 |
| ☐ 218 | Willie Mays | 225.00 | 100.00 | 22.00 |
| ☐ 219 | Neil Berry | 6.00 | 2.80 | .60 |
| ☐ 220 | Russ Meyer | 6.00 | 2.80 | .60 |
| ☐ 221 | Lou Kretlow | 6.00 | 2.80 | .60 |
| ☐ 222 | Dixie Howell | 6.00 | 2.80 | .60 |
| ☐ 223 | Harry Simpson | 6.00 | 2.80 | .60 |
| ☐ 224 | Johnny Schmitz | 6.00 | 2.80 | .60 |
| ☐ 225 | Del Wilber | 6.00 | 2.80 | .60 |

|  | MINT | VG-E | F-G |
|---|---|---|---|
| ☐ 226 Alex Kellner | 6.00 | 2.80 | .60 |
| ☐ 227 Clyde Sukeforth | 6.00 | 2.80 | .60 |
| ☐ 228 Bob Chipman | 6.00 | 2.80 | .60 |
| ☐ 229 Hank Arft | 6.00 | 2.80 | .60 |
| ☐ 230 Frank Shea | 6.00 | 2.80 | .60 |
| ☐ 231 Dee Fondy | 6.00 | 2.80 | .60 |
| ☐ 232 Enos Slaughter | 18.00 | 8.50 | 1.80 |
| ☐ 233 Bob Kuzava | 6.00 | 2.80 | .60 |
| ☐ 234 Fred Fitzsimmons | 6.00 | 2.80 | .60 |
| ☐ 235 Steve Souchock | 6.00 | 2.80 | .60 |
| ☐ 236 Tommy Brown | 6.00 | 2.80 | .60 |
| ☐ 237 Sherman Lollar | 6.50 | 3.00 | .65 |
| ☐ 238 Roy McMillan | 6.50 | 3.00 | .65 |
| ☐ 239 Dale Mitchell | 6.50 | 3.00 | .65 |
| ☐ 240 Billy Loes | 6.50 | 3.00 | .65 |
| ☐ 241 Mel Parnell | 6.50 | 3.00 | .65 |
| ☐ 242 Everett Kell | 6.00 | 2.80 | .60 |
| ☐ 243 Red Munger | 6.00 | 2.80 | .60 |
| ☐ 244 Lew Burdette | 14.00 | 6.50 | 1.40 |
| ☐ 245 George Schmees | 6.00 | 2.80 | .60 |
| ☐ 246 Jerry Snyder | 6.00 | 2.80 | .60 |
| ☐ 247 John Pramesa | 6.00 | 2.80 | .60 |
| ☐ 248 Bill Werle | 6.00 | 2.80 | .60 |
| ☐ 249 Hank Thompson | 7.00 | 3.25 | .70 |
| ☐ 250 Ivan Delock | 6.00 | 2.80 | .60 |
| ☐ 251 Jack Lohrke | 6.00 | 2.80 | .60 |
| ☐ 252 Frank Crosetti | 25.00 | 5.00 | 1.00 |

## 1953 BOWMAN COLOR

The cards in this 160 card set measure 2½" by 3¾". The 1953 Bowman color set, considered by many to be the best looking set of the modern era, contains Kodachrome photographs with no names or facsimile autographs on the face. Numbers 113 to 160 are somewhat more diffi-

cult to obtain. There are two cards of Al Corwin (126 and 149). Card number 159 is actually a picture of Floyd Baker.

Complete Set: M-2250.00; VG-E-1000.00; F-G-200.00

|  | MINT | VG-E | F-G |
|---|---|---|---|
| Common Player (1–96) | 6.00 | 2.80 | .60 |
| Common Player (97–112) | 7.00 | 3.25 | .70 |
| Common Player (113–128) | 15.00 | 7.00 | 1.50 |
| Common Player (129–160) | 10.00 | 4.75 | 1.00 |

|  | MINT | VG-E | F-G |
|---|---|---|---|
| ☐ 1 Dave Williams | 25.00 | 5.00 | 1.00 |
| ☐ 2 Vic Wertz | 6.00 | 2.80 | .60 |
| ☐ 3 Sam Jethroe | 6.00 | 2.80 | .60 |
| ☐ 4 Art Houtteman | 6.00 | 2.80 | .60 |
| ☐ 5 Sid Gordon | 6.00 | 2.80 | .60 |
| ☐ 6 Joe Ginsberg | 6.00 | 2.80 | .60 |
| ☐ 7 Harry Chiti | 6.00 | 2.80 | .60 |
| ☐ 8 Al Rosen | 9.00 | 4.25 | .90 |
| ☐ 9 Phil Rizzuto | 24.00 | 11.00 | 2.40 |
| ☐ 10 Richie Ashburn | 11.00 | 5.25 | 1.10 |
| ☐ 11 Bobby Shantz | 7.00 | 3.25 | .70 |
| ☐ 12 Carl Erskine | 8.00 | 3.75 | .80 |
| ☐ 13 Gus Zernial | 6.00 | 2.80 | .60 |
| ☐ 14 Billy Loes | 7.00 | 3.25 | .70 |
| ☐ 15 Jim Busby | 6.00 | 2.80 | .60 |
| ☐ 16 Bob Friend | 6.50 | 3.00 | .65 |
| ☐ 17 Jerry Staley | 6.00 | 2.80 | .60 |
| ☐ 18 Nelson Fox | 10.00 | 4.75 | 1.00 |
| ☐ 19 Alvin Dark | 7.00 | 3.25 | .70 |
| ☐ 20 Don Lenhardt | 6.00 | 2.80 | .60 |
| ☐ 21 Joe Garagiola | 15.00 | 7.00 | 1.50 |
| ☐ 22 Bob Porterfield | 6.00 | 2.80 | .60 |
| ☐ 23 Herman Wehmeier | 6.00 | 2.80 | .60 |
| ☐ 24 Jackie Jensen | 8.00 | 3.75 | .80 |
| ☐ 25 Hoot Evers | 6.00 | 2.80 | .60 |
| ☐ 26 Roy McMillan | 6.00 | 2.80 | .60 |
| ☐ 27 Vic Raschi | 8.00 | 3.75 | .80 |
| ☐ 28 Smokey Burgess | 6.50 | 3.00 | .65 |
| ☐ 29 Bobby Avila | 6.50 | 3.00 | .65 |
| ☐ 30 Phil Cavaretta | 6.50 | 3.00 | .65 |
| ☐ 31 Jimmy Dykes | 6.50 | 3.00 | .65 |
| ☐ 32 Stan Musial | 110.00 | 50.00 | 11.00 |
| ☐ 33 Pee Wee Reese HOR | 35.00 | 16.50 | 3.50 |
| ☐ 34 Gil Coan | 6.00 | 2.80 | .60 |
| ☐ 35 Maurice McDermott | 6.00 | 2.80 | .60 |
| ☐ 36 Minnie Minoso | 9.00 | 4.25 | .90 |
| ☐ 37 Jim Wilson | 6.00 | 2.80 | .60 |
| ☐ 38 Harry Byrd | 6.00 | 2.80 | .60 |
| ☐ 39 Paul Richards | 6.50 | 3.00 | .65 |

| | | MINT | VG-E | F-G |
|---|---|---|---|---|
| ☐ 40 | Larry Doby | 8.00 | 3.75 | .80 |
| ☐ 41 | Sammy White | 6.00 | 2.80 | .60 |
| ☐ 42 | Tommy Brown | 6.00 | 2.80 | .60 |
| ☐ 43 | Mike Garcia | 6.50 | 3.00 | .65 |
| ☐ 44 | Berra/Bauer/Mantle | 70.00 | 32.00 | 7.00 |
| ☐ 45 | Walt Dropo | 6.00 | 2.80 | .60 |
| ☐ 46 | Roy Campanella | 60.00 | 27.00 | 6.00 |
| ☐ 47 | Ned Garver | 6.00 | 2.80 | .60 |
| ☐ 48 | Hank Sauer | 6.50 | 3.00 | .65 |
| ☐ 49 | Eddie Stanky | 6.50 | 3.00 | .65 |
| ☐ 50 | Lou Kretlow | 6.00 | 2.80 | .60 |
| ☐ 51 | Monte Irvin | 12.00 | 5.50 | 1.20 |
| ☐ 52 | Marty Marion | 8.00 | 3.75 | .80 |
| ☐ 53 | Del Rice | 6.00 | 2.80 | .60 |
| ☐ 54 | Chico Carrasquel | 6.00 | 2.80 | .60 |
| ☐ 55 | Leo Durocher MGR | 9.00 | 4.25 | .90 |
| ☐ 56 | Bob Cain | 6.00 | 2.80 | .60 |
| ☐ 57 | Lou Boudreau | 11.00 | 5.25 | 1.10 |
| ☐ 58 | Willard Marshall | 6.00 | 2.80 | .60 |
| ☐ 59 | Mickey Mantle | 325.00 | 140.00 | 32.00 |
| ☐ 60 | Granny Hamner | 6.00 | 2.80 | .60 |
| ☐ 61 | George Kell | 13.00 | 6.00 | 1.30 |
| ☐ 62 | Ted Kluszewski | 10.00 | 4.75 | 1.00 |
| ☐ 63 | Gil McDougald | 9.00 | 4.25 | .90 |
| ☐ 64 | Curt Simmons | 7.00 | 3.25 | .70 |
| ☐ 65 | Robin Roberts | 16.00 | 7.50 | 1.60 |
| ☐ 66 | Mel Parnell | 6.00 | 2.80 | .60 |
| ☐ 67 | Mel Clark | 6.00 | 2.80 | .60 |
| ☐ 68 | Allie Reynolds | 9.00 | 4.25 | .90 |
| ☐ 69 | Charley Grimm | 6.50 | 3.00 | .65 |
| ☐ 70 | Clint Courtney | 6.00 | 2.80 | .60 |
| ☐ 71 | Paul Minner | 6.00 | 2.80 | .60 |
| ☐ 72 | Ted Gray | 6.00 | 2.80 | .60 |
| ☐ 73 | Billy Pierce | 7.00 | 3.25 | .70 |
| ☐ 74 | Don Mueller | 6.50 | 3.00 | .65 |
| ☐ 75 | Saul Rogovin | 6.00 | 2.80 | .60 |
| ☐ 76 | Jim Hearn | 6.00 | 2.80 | .60 |
| ☐ 77 | Mickey Grasso | 6.00 | 2.80 | .60 |
| ☐ 78 | Carl Furillo | 9.00 | 4.25 | .90 |
| ☐ 79 | Ray Boone | 6.00 | 2.80 | .60 |
| ☐ 80 | Ralph Kiner | 14.00 | 6.50 | 1.40 |
| ☐ 81 | Enos Slaughter | 14.00 | 6.50 | 1.40 |
| ☐ 82 | Joe Astroth | 6.00 | 2.80 | .60 |
| ☐ 83 | Jack Daniels | 6.00 | 2.80 | .60 |
| ☐ 84 | Hank Bauer | 8.50 | 4.00 | .85 |
| ☐ 85 | Solly Hemus | 6.00 | 2.80 | .60 |
| ☐ 86 | Harry Simpson | 6.00 | 2.80 | .60 |
| ☐ 87 | Harry Perkowski | 6.00 | 2.80 | .60 |
| ☐ 88 | Joe Dobson | 6.00 | 2.80 | .60 |
| ☐ 89 | Sandy Consuegra | 6.00 | 2.80 | .60 |
| ☐ 90 | Joe Nuxhall | 6.50 | 3.00 | .65 |
| ☐ 91 | Steve Souchock | 6.00 | 2.80 | .60 |
| ☐ 92 | Gil Hodges | 25.00 | 11.00 | 2.50 |
| ☐ 93 | Rizzuto and Martin | 45.00 | 20.00 | 4.50 |
| ☐ 94 | Bob Addis | 6.00 | 2.80 | .60 |
| ☐ 95 | Wally Moses | 6.00 | 2.80 | .60 |
| ☐ 96 | Sal Maglie | 7.00 | 3.25 | .70 |
| ☐ 97 | Ed Mathews | 25.00 | 11.00 | 2.50 |
| ☐ 98 | Hector Rodriguez | 7.00 | 3.25 | .70 |
| ☐ 99 | Warren Spahn | 25.00 | 11.00 | 2.50 |
| ☐ 100 | Bill Wight | 7.00 | 3.25 | .70 |
| ☐ 101 | Red Schoendienst | 8.00 | 3.75 | .80 |
| ☐ 102 | Jim Hegan | 7.00 | 3.25 | .70 |
| ☐ 103 | Del Ennis | 8.00 | 3.75 | .80 |
| ☐ 104 | Luke Easter | 7.00 | 3.25 | .70 |
| ☐ 105 | Eddie Joost | 7.00 | 3.25 | .70 |
| ☐ 106 | Ken Raffensberger | 7.00 | 3.25 | .70 |
| ☐ 107 | Alex Kellner | 7.00 | 3.25 | .70 |
| ☐ 108 | Bobby Adams | 7.00 | 3.25 | .70 |
| ☐ 109 | Ken Wood | 7.00 | 3.25 | .70 |
| ☐ 110 | Bob Rush | 7.00 | 3.25 | .70 |
| ☐ 111 | Jim Dyck | 7.00 | 3.25 | .70 |
| ☐ 112 | Toby Atwell | 7.00 | 3.25 | .70 |
| ☐ 113 | Karl Drews | 15.00 | 7.00 | 1.50 |
| ☐ 114 | Bob Feller | 75.00 | 35.00 | 7.50 |
| ☐ 115 | Cloyd Boyer | 15.00 | 7.00 | 1.50 |
| ☐ 116 | Eddie Yost | 15.00 | 7.00 | 1.50 |
| ☐ 117 | Duke Snider | 200.00 | 90.00 | 20.00 |
| ☐ 118 | Billy Martin | 50.00 | 22.00 | 5.00 |
| ☐ 119 | Dale Mitchell | 15.00 | 7.00 | 1.50 |
| ☐ 120 | Marlin Stuart | 15.00 | 7.00 | 1.50 |
| ☐ 121 | Yogi Berra | 150.00 | 70.00 | 15.00 |
| ☐ 122 | Bill Serena | 15.00 | 7.00 | 1.50 |
| ☐ 123 | Johnny Lipon | 15.00 | 7.00 | 1.50 |
| ☐ 124 | Charlie Dressen | 20.00 | 9.00 | 2.00 |
| ☐ 125 | Fred Hatfield | 15.00 | 7.00 | 1.50 |
| ☐ 126 | Al Corwin | 15.00 | 7.00 | 1.50 |
| ☐ 127 | Dick Kryhoski | 15.00 | 7.00 | 1.50 |
| ☐ 128 | Whitey Lockman | 15.00 | 7.00 | 1.50 |
| ☐ 129 | Russ Meyer | 10.00 | 4.75 | 1.00 |
| ☐ 130 | Cass Michaels | 10.00 | 4.75 | 1.00 |
| ☐ 131 | Connie Ryan | 10.00 | 4.75 | 1.00 |
| ☐ 132 | Fred Hutchinson | 11.00 | 5.25 | 1.10 |
| ☐ 133 | Willie Jones | 10.00 | 4.75 | 1.00 |
| ☐ 134 | Johnny Pesky | 11.00 | 5.25 | 1.10 |
| ☐ 135 | Bobby Morgan | 10.00 | 4.75 | 1.00 |
| ☐ 136 | Jim Brideweser | 10.00 | 4.75 | 1.00 |
| ☐ 137 | Sam Dente | 10.00 | 4.75 | 1.00 |
| ☐ 138 | Bubba Church | 10.00 | 4.75 | 1.00 |
| ☐ 139 | Pete Runnels | 11.00 | 5.25 | 1.10 |
| ☐ 140 | Al Brazle | 10.00 | 4.75 | 1.00 |
| ☐ 141 | Frank Shea | 10.00 | 4.75 | 1.00 |
| ☐ 142 | Larry Miggins | 10.00 | 4.75 | 1.00 |
| ☐ 143 | Al Lopez | 16.00 | 7.50 | 1.60 |
| ☐ 144 | Warren Hacker | 10.00 | 4.75 | 1.00 |
| ☐ 145 | George Shuba | 11.00 | 5.25 | 1.10 |

| | MINT | VG-E | F-G |
|---|---|---|---|
| ☐ 146 Early Wynn | 40.00 | 18.00 | 4.00 |
| ☐ 147 Clem Koshorek | 10.00 | 4.75 | 1.00 |
| ☐ 148 Billy Goodman | 11.00 | 5.25 | 1.10 |
| ☐ 149 Al Corwin | 10.00 | 4.75 | 1.00 |
| ☐ 150 Carl Scheib | 10.00 | 4.75 | 1.00 |
| ☐ 151 Joe Adcock | 13.00 | 6.00 | 1.30 |
| ☐ 152 Clyde Vollmer | 10.00 | 4.75 | 1.00 |
| ☐ 153 Whitey Ford | 75.00 | 35.00 | 7.50 |
| ☐ 154 Turk Lown | 10.00 | 4.75 | 1.00 |
| ☐ 155 Allie Clark | 10.00 | 4.75 | 1.00 |
| ☐ 156 Max Surkont | 10.00 | 4.75 | 1.00 |
| ☐ 157 Sherman Lollar | 11.00 | 5.25 | 1.10 |
| ☐ 158 Howard Fox | 10.00 | 4.75 | 1.00 |
| ☐ 159 Mickey Vernon (photo actually Floyd Baker) | 12.00 | 5.50 | 1.20 |
| ☐ 160 Cal Abrams | 15.00 | 5.00 | 1.00 |

## 1953 BOWMAN B&W

The cards in this 64 card set measure 2½"
by 3¾". Some collectors believe that the
high cost of producing the 1953 color series forced Bowman to issue this set in
black and white, since the two sets are
identical in design except for the element
of color. This set was also produced in
fewer numbers than its color counterpart,
and is popular among collectors for the
challenge involved in completing it.

Complete Set: M-900.00; VG-E-400.00; F-G-90.00

| | MINT | VG-E | F-G |
|---|---|---|---|
| Common Player (1–64) | 11.00 | 5.25 | 1.10 |
| ☐ 1 Gus Bell | 27.00 | 6.00 | 1.00 |
| ☐ 2 Willard Nixon | 11.00 | 5.25 | 1.10 |
| ☐ 3 Bill Rigney | 11.00 | 5.25 | 1.10 |

| | MINT | VG-E | F-G |
|---|---|---|---|
| ☐ 4 Pat Mullin | 11.00 | 5.25 | 1.10 |
| ☐ 5 Dee Fondy | 11.00 | 5.25 | 1.10 |
| ☐ 6 Ray Murray | 11.00 | 5.25 | 1.10 |
| ☐ 7 Andy Seminick | 11.00 | 5.25 | 1.10 |
| ☐ 8 Pete Suder | 11.00 | 5.25 | 1.10 |
| ☐ 9 Walt Masterson | 11.00 | 5.25 | 1.10 |
| ☐ 10 Dick Sisler | 11.00 | 5.25 | 1.10 |
| ☐ 11 Dick Gernert | 11.00 | 5.25 | 1.10 |
| ☐ 12 Randy Jackson | 11.00 | 5.25 | 1.10 |
| ☐ 13 Joe Tipton | 11.00 | 5.25 | 1.10 |
| ☐ 14 Bill Nicholson | 11.00 | 5.25 | 1.10 |
| ☐ 15 Johnny Mize | 35.00 | 16.50 | 3.50 |
| ☐ 16 Stu Miller | 11.00 | 5.25 | 1.10 |
| ☐ 17 Virgil Trucks | 11.00 | 5.25 | 1.10 |
| ☐ 18 Billy Hoeft | 11.00 | 5.25 | 1.10 |
| ☐ 19 Paul LaPalme | 11.00 | 5.25 | 1.10 |
| ☐ 20 Eddie Robinson | 11.00 | 5.25 | 1.10 |
| ☐ 21 Clarence Podbielan | 11.00 | 5.25 | 1.10 |
| ☐ 22 Matt Batts | 11.00 | 5.25 | 1.10 |
| ☐ 23 Wilmer Mizell | 12.00 | 5.50 | 1.20 |
| ☐ 24 Del Wilber | 11.00 | 5.25 | 1.10 |
| ☐ 25 Johnny Sain | 22.00 | 10.00 | 2.20 |
| ☐ 26 Preacher Roe | 22.00 | 10.00 | 2.20 |
| ☐ 27 Bob Lemon | 35.00 | 16.50 | 3.50 |
| ☐ 28 Hoyt Wilhelm | 35.00 | 16.50 | 3.50 |
| ☐ 29 Sid Hudson | 11.00 | 5.25 | 1.10 |
| ☐ 30 Walker Cooper | 11.00 | 5.25 | 1.10 |
| ☐ 31 Gene Woodling | 12.00 | 5.50 | 1.20 |
| ☐ 32 Rocky Bridges | 11.00 | 5.25 | 1.10 |
| ☐ 33 Bob Kuzava | 11.00 | 5.25 | 1.10 |
| ☐ 34 Ebba St. Claire | 11.00 | 5.25 | 1.10 |
| ☐ 35 Johnny Wyrostek | 11.00 | 5.25 | 1.10 |
| ☐ 36 Jim Piersall | 18.00 | 8.50 | 1.80 |
| ☐ 37 Hal Jeffcoat | 11.00 | 5.25 | 1.10 |
| ☐ 38 Dave Cole | 11.00 | 5.25 | 1.10 |
| ☐ 39 Casey Stengel | 120.00 | 55.00 | 12.00 |
| ☐ 40 Larry Jansen | 11.00 | 5.25 | 1.10 |
| ☐ 41 Bob Ramazotti | 11.00 | 5.25 | 1.10 |
| ☐ 42 Howie Judson | 11.00 | 5.25 | 1.10 |
| ☐ 43 Hal Bevan | 11.00 | 5.25 | 1.10 |
| ☐ 44 Jim Delsing | 11.00 | 5.25 | 1.10 |
| ☐ 45 Irv Noren | 11.00 | 5.25 | 1.10 |
| ☐ 46 Bucky Harris | 20.00 | 9.00 | 2.00 |
| ☐ 47 Jack Lohrke | 11.00 | 5.25 | 1.10 |
| ☐ 48 Steve Ridzek | 11.00 | 5.25 | 1.10 |
| ☐ 49 Floyd Baker | 11.00 | 5.25 | 1.10 |
| ☐ 50 Dutch Leonard | 11.00 | 5.25 | 1.10 |
| ☐ 51 Lou Burdette | 16.00 | 7.50 | 1.60 |
| ☐ 52 Ralph Branca | 12.00 | 5.50 | 1.20 |
| ☐ 53 Morris Martin | 11.00 | 5.25 | 1.10 |
| ☐ 54 Billy Miller | 11.00 | 5.25 | 1.10 |
| ☐ 55 Don Johnson | 11.00 | 5.25 | 1.10 |
| ☐ 56 Roy Smalley | 11.00 | 5.25 | 1.10 |

| | MINT | VG-E | F-G |
|---|---|---|---|
| ☐ 57 Andy Pafko .......... | 11.00 | 5.25 | 1.10 |
| ☐ 58 Jim Konstanty ........ | 12.00 | 5.50 | 1.20 |
| ☐ 59 Duane Pillette ....... | 11.00 | 5.25 | 1.10 |
| ☐ 60 Billy Cox ........... | 12.00 | 5.50 | 1.20 |
| ☐ 61 Tom Gorman ......... | 11.00 | 5.25 | 1.10 |
| ☐ 62 Keith Thomas ........ | 11.00 | 5.25 | 1.10 |
| ☐ 63 Steve Gromek ........ | 11.00 | 5.25 | 1.10 |
| ☐ 64 Andy Hansen ........ | 15.00 | 7.00 | 1.50 |

## 1954 BOWMAN

*The cards in this 224 card set measure 2½" by 3¾". A contractual problem apparently resulted in the deletion of the number 66 Ted Williams card from this Bowman set, thereby creating a scarcity which is highly valued among collectors. The set price below does NOT include number 66 Williams. Many errors in players' statistics exist (and some were corrected) while a few players' names were printed on the front, instead of appearing as a facsimile autograph.*

Complete Set: M-700.00; VG-E-320.00; F-G-70.00

| | MINT | VG-E | F-G |
|---|---|---|---|
| Common Player (1–128) | 1.35 | .60 | .15 |
| Common Player (129–224) | 1.80 | .90 | .18 |
| ☐ 1 Phil Rizzuto ......... | 35.00 | 8.00 | 1.25 |
| ☐ 2 Jackie Jensen ....... | 2.50 | 1.15 | .25 |
| ☐ 3 Marion Fricano ....... | 1.35 | .60 | .15 |
| ☐ 4 Bob Hooper ......... | 1.35 | .60 | .15 |
| ☐ 5 Bill Hunter ......... | 1.35 | .60 | .15 |
| ☐ 6 Nelson Fox ......... | 3.50 | 1.65 | .35 |
| ☐ 7 Walt Dropo ......... | 1.35 | .60 | .15 |
| ☐ 8 Jim Busby ......... | 1.35 | .60 | .15 |
| ☐ 9 Davey Williams ...... | 1.35 | .60 | .15 |

| | MINT | VG-E | F-G |
|---|---|---|---|
| ☐ 10 Carl Erskine ......... | 3.00 | 1.40 | .30 |
| ☐ 11 Sid Gordon ......... | 1.35 | .60 | .15 |
| ☐ 12 Roy McMillan ....... | 1.35 | .60 | .15 |
| ☐ 13 Paul Minner ......... | 1.35 | .60 | .15 |
| ☐ 14 Gerry Staley ......... | 1.35 | .60 | .15 |
| ☐ 15 Richie Ashburn ...... | 4.00 | 1.85 | .40 |
| ☐ 16 Jim Wilson ......... | 1.35 | .60 | .15 |
| ☐ 17 Tom Gorman ........ | 1.35 | .60 | .15 |
| ☐ 18 Hoot Evers ......... | 1.35 | .60 | .15 |
| ☐ 19 Bobby Shantz ....... | 1.75 | .85 | .17 |
| ☐ 20 Art Houtteman ...... | 1.35 | .60 | .15 |
| ☐ 21 Vic Wertz ......... | 1.35 | .60 | .15 |
| ☐ 22 Sam Mele ......... | 1.35 | .60 | .15 |
| ☐ 23 Harvey Kuenn ...... | 5.00 | 2.35 | .50 |
| ☐ 24 Bob Porterfield ...... | 1.35 | .60 | .15 |
| ☐ 25 Wes Westrum ....... | 1.35 | .60 | .15 |
| ☐ 26 Billy Cox ......... | 1.75 | .85 | .17 |
| ☐ 27 Dick Cole ......... | 1.35 | .60 | .15 |
| ☐ 28 Jim Greengrass ...... | 1.35 | .60 | .15 |
| ☐ 29 Johnny Klippstein .... | 1.35 | .60 | .15 |
| ☐ 30 Del Rice ......... | 1.35 | .60 | .15 |
| ☐ 31 Smokey Burgess ..... | 1.50 | .70 | .15 |
| ☐ 32 Del Crandall ....... | 1.50 | .70 | .15 |
| ☐ 33 A Vic Raschi ....... | 2.00 | .90 | .20 |
| (no mention of | | | |
| trade on back) | | | |
| ☐ 33 B Vic Raschi ....... | 9.00 | 4.25 | .90 |
| (traded to St. Louis) | | | |
| ☐ 34 Sammy White ....... | 1.35 | .60 | .15 |
| ☐ 35 Eddie Joost ........ | 1.35 | .60 | .15 |
| ☐ 36 George Strickland .... | 1.35 | .60 | .15 |
| ☐ 37 Dick Kokos ......... | 1.35 | .60 | .15 |
| ☐ 38 Minnie Minoso ...... | 3.00 | 1.40 | .30 |
| ☐ 39 Ned Garver ......... | 1.35 | .60 | .15 |
| ☐ 40 Gil Coan ......... | 1.35 | .60 | .15 |
| ☐ 41 Alvin Dark ......... | 1.75 | .85 | .17 |
| ☐ 42 Billy Loes ......... | 1.50 | .70 | .15 |
| ☐ 43 Bob Friend ......... | 1.50 | .70 | .15 |
| ☐ 44 Harry Perkowski ..... | 1.35 | .60 | .15 |
| ☐ 45 Ralph Kiner ........ | 9.00 | 4.25 | .90 |
| ☐ 46 Rip Repulski ....... | 1.35 | .60 | .15 |
| ☐ 47 Granny Hamner ...... | 1.35 | .60 | .15 |
| ☐ 48 Jack Dittmer ....... | 1.35 | .60 | .15 |
| ☐ 49 Harry Byrd ......... | 1.35 | .60 | .15 |
| ☐ 50 George Kell ........ | 6.00 | 2.80 | .60 |
| ☐ 51 Alex Kellner ....... | 1.35 | .60 | .15 |
| ☐ 52 Joe Ginsberg ....... | 1.35 | .60 | .15 |
| ☐ 53 Don Lenhardt ....... | 1.35 | .60 | .15 |
| ☐ 54 Chico Carrasquel .... | 1.35 | .60 | .15 |
| ☐ 55 Jim Delsing ....... | 1.35 | .60 | .15 |
| ☐ 56 Maurice McDermott ... | 1.35 | .60 | .15 |
| ☐ 57 Hoyt Wilhelm ...... | 6.00 | 2.80 | .60 |
| ☐ 58 Pee Wee Reese ..... | 13.00 | 6.00 | 1.30 |

|  | | MINT | VG-E | F-G |
|---|---|---|---|---|
| ☐ 59 | Bob Schultz | 1.35 | .60 | .15 |
| ☐ 60 | Fred Baczewski | 1.35 | .60 | .15 |
| ☐ 61 | Eddie Miksis | 1.35 | .60 | .15 |
| ☐ 62 | Enos Slaughter | 7.00 | 3.25 | .70 |
| ☐ 63 | Earl Torgeson | 1.35 | .60 | .15 |
| ☐ 64 | Eddie Mathews | 10.00 | 4.75 | 1.00 |
| ☐ 65 | Mickey Mantle | 120.00 | 55.00 | 12.00 |
| ☐ 66 A | Jim Piersall | 50.00 | 22.00 | 5.00 |
| ☐ 66 B | Ted Williams | 650.00 | 250.00 | 50.00 |
| ☐ 67 | Carl Scheib | 1.35 | .60 | .15 |
| ☐ 68 | Bobby Avila | 1.50 | .70 | .15 |
| ☐ 69 | Clint Courtney | 1.35 | .60 | .15 |
| ☐ 70 | Willard Marshall | 1.35 | .60 | .15 |
| ☐ 71 | Ted Gray | 1.35 | .60 | .15 |
| ☐ 72 | Eddie Yost | 1.35 | .60 | .15 |
| ☐ 73 | Don Mueller | 1.50 | .70 | .15 |
| ☐ 74 | Jim Gilliam | 3.00 | 1.40 | .30 |
| ☐ 75 | Max Surkont | 1.35 | .60 | .15 |
| ☐ 76 | Joe Nuxhall | 1.50 | .70 | .15 |
| ☐ 77 | Bob Rush | 1.35 | .60 | .15 |
| ☐ 78 | Sal Yvars | 1.35 | .60 | .15 |
| ☐ 79 | Curt Simmons | 1.50 | .70 | .15 |
| ☐ 80 | Johnny Logan | 1.50 | .70 | .15 |
| ☐ 81 | Jerry Coleman | 1.50 | .70 | .15 |
| ☐ 82 | Billy Goodman | 1.50 | .70 | .15 |
| ☐ 83 | Ray Murray | 1.35 | .60 | .15 |
| ☐ 84 | Larry Doby | 3.00 | 1.40 | .30 |
| ☐ 85 | Jim Dyck | 1.35 | .60 | .15 |
| ☐ 86 | Harry Dorish | 1.35 | .60 | .15 |
| ☐ 87 | Don Lund | 1.35 | .60 | .15 |
| ☐ 88 | Tom Umphlett | 1.35 | .60 | .15 |
| ☐ 89 | Willie Mays | 80.00 | 37.00 | 8.00 |
| ☐ 90 | Roy Campanella | 28.00 | 12.50 | 2.80 |
| ☐ 91 | Cal Abrams | 1.35 | .60 | .15 |
| ☐ 92 | Ken Raffensberger | 1.35 | .60 | .15 |
| ☐ 93 | Bill Serena | 1.35 | .60 | .15 |
| ☐ 94 | Solly Hemus | 1.35 | .60 | .15 |
| ☐ 95 | Robin Roberts | 8.00 | 3.75 | .80 |
| ☐ 96 | Joe Adcock | 1.75 | .85 | .17 |
| ☐ 97 | Gil McDougald | 2.50 | 1.15 | .25 |
| ☐ 98 | Ellis Kinder | 1.35 | .60 | .15 |
| ☐ 99 | Pete Suder | 1.35 | .60 | .15 |
| ☐ 100 | Mike Garcia | 1.50 | .70 | .15 |
| ☐ 101 | Don Larsen | 3.50 | 1.65 | .35 |
| ☐ 102 | Billy Pierce | 2.00 | .90 | .20 |
| ☐ 103 | Steve Souchock | 1.35 | .60 | .15 |
| ☐ 104 | Frank Shea | 1.35 | .60 | .15 |
| ☐ 105 | Sal Maglie | 2.00 | .90 | .20 |
| ☐ 106 | Clem Labine | 1.50 | .70 | .15 |
| ☐ 107 | Paul LaPalme | 1.35 | .60 | .15 |
| ☐ 108 | Bobby Adams | 1.35 | .60 | .15 |
| ☐ 109 | Roy Smalley | 1.35 | .60 | .15 |

|  | | MINT | VG-E | F-G |
|---|---|---|---|---|
| ☐ 110 | Red Schoendienst | 2.50 | 1.15 | .25 |
| ☐ 111 | Murry Dickson | 1.35 | .60 | .15 |
| ☐ 112 | Andy Pafko | 1.35 | .60 | .15 |
| ☐ 113 | Allie Reynolds | 3.50 | 1.65 | .35 |
| ☐ 114 | Willard Nixon | 1.35 | .60 | .15 |
| ☐ 115 | Don Bollweg | 1.35 | .60 | .15 |
| ☐ 116 | Luke Easter | 1.35 | .60 | .15 |
| ☐ 117 | Dick Kryhoski | 1.35 | .60 | .15 |
| ☐ 118 | Bob Boyd | 1.35 | .60 | .15 |
| ☐ 119 | Fred Hatfield | 1.35 | .60 | .15 |
| ☐ 120 | Mel Hoderlein | 1.35 | .60 | .15 |
| ☐ 121 | Ray Katt | 1.35 | .60 | .15 |
| ☐ 122 | Carl Furillo | 3.50 | 1.65 | .35 |
| ☐ 123 | Toby Atwell | 1.35 | .60 | .15 |
| ☐ 124 | Gus Bell | 1.50 | .70 | .15 |
| ☐ 125 | Warren Hacker | 1.35 | .60 | .15 |
| ☐ 126 | Cliff Chambers | 1.35 | .60 | .15 |
| ☐ 127 | Del Ennis | 1.50 | .70 | .15 |
| ☐ 128 | Ebba St. Claire | 1.35 | .60 | .15 |
| ☐ 129 | Hank Bauer | 3.50 | 1.65 | .35 |
| ☐ 130 | Milt Bolling | 1.80 | .90 | .18 |
| ☐ 131 | Joe Astroth | 1.80 | .90 | .18 |
| ☐ 132 | Bob Feller | 17.00 | 8.00 | 1.70 |
| ☐ 133 | Duane Pillette | 1.80 | .90 | .18 |
| ☐ 134 | Luis Aloma | 1.80 | .90 | .18 |
| ☐ 135 | Johnny Pesky | 2.00 | .90 | .20 |
| ☐ 136 | Clyde Vollmer | 1.80 | .90 | .18 |
| ☐ 137 | Al Corwin | 1.80 | .90 | .18 |
| ☐ 138 | Gil Hodges | 13.00 | 6.00 | 1.30 |
| ☐ 139 | Preston Ward | 1.80 | .90 | .18 |
| ☐ 140 | Saul Rogovin | 1.80 | .90 | .18 |
| ☐ 141 | Joe Garagiola | 11.00 | 5.25 | 1.10 |
| ☐ 142 | Al Brazle | 1.80 | .90 | .18 |
| ☐ 143 | Willie Jones | 1.80 | .90 | .18 |
| ☐ 144 | Ernie Johnson | 1.80 | .90 | .18 |
| ☐ 145 | Billy Martin | 13.00 | 6.00 | 1.30 |
| ☐ 146 | Dick Gernert | 1.80 | .90 | .18 |
| ☐ 147 | Joe DeMaestri | 1.80 | .90 | .18 |
| ☐ 148 | Dale Mitchell | 2.00 | .90 | .20 |
| ☐ 149 | Bob Young | 1.80 | .90 | .18 |
| ☐ 150 | Cass Michaels | 1.80 | .90 | .18 |
| ☐ 151 | Pat Mullin | 1.80 | .90 | .18 |
| ☐ 152 | Mickey Vernon | 2.25 | 1.00 | .22 |
| ☐ 153 | Whitey Lockman | 2.00 | .90 | .20 |
| ☐ 154 | Don Newcombe | 3.50 | 1.65 | .35 |
| ☐ 155 | Frank Thomas | 1.80 | .90 | .18 |
| ☐ 156 | Rocky Bridges | 1.80 | .90 | .18 |
| ☐ 157 | Turk Lown | 1.80 | .90 | .18 |
| ☐ 158 | Stu Miller | 1.80 | .90 | .18 |
| ☐ 159 | Johnny Lindell | 1.80 | .90 | .18 |
| ☐ 160 | Danny O'Connell | 1.80 | .90 | .18 |
| ☐ 161 | Yogi Berra | 30.00 | 14.00 | 3.00 |

| | MINT | VG-E | F-G |
|---|---|---|---|
| ☐ 162 Ted Lepcio | 1.80 | .90 | .18 |
| ☐ 163 A Dave Philley (no mention of trade on back) | 2.25 | 1.00 | .22 |
| ☐ 163 B Dave Philley (traded to Cleveland) | 9.00 | 4.25 | .90 |
| ☐ 164 Early Wynn | 9.00 | 4.25 | .90 |
| ☐ 165 Johnny Groth | 1.80 | .90 | .18 |
| ☐ 166 Sandy Consuegra | 1.80 | .90 | .18 |
| ☐ 167 Billy Hoeft | 1.80 | .90 | .18 |
| ☐ 168 Ed Fitzgerald | 1.80 | .90 | .18 |
| ☐ 169 Larry Jansen | 1.80 | .90 | .18 |
| ☐ 170 Duke Snider | 25.00 | 11.00 | 2.50 |
| ☐ 171 Carlos Bernier | 1.80 | .90 | .18 |
| ☐ 172 Andy Seminick | 1.80 | .90 | .18 |
| ☐ 173 Dee Fondy | 1.80 | .90 | .18 |
| ☐ 174 Pete Castiglione | 1.80 | .90 | .18 |
| ☐ 175 Mel Clark | 1.80 | .90 | .18 |
| ☐ 176 Vern Bickford | 1.80 | .90 | .18 |
| ☐ 177 Whitey Ford | 18.00 | 8.50 | 1.80 |
| ☐ 178 Del Wilber | 1.80 | .90 | .18 |
| ☐ 179 Morris Martin | 1.80 | .90 | .18 |
| ☐ 180 Joe Tipton | 1.80 | .90 | .18 |
| ☐ 181 Les Moss | 1.80 | .90 | .18 |
| ☐ 182 Sherman Lollar | 2.00 | .90 | .20 |
| ☐ 183 Matt Batts | 1.80 | .90 | .18 |
| ☐ 184 Mickey Grasso | 1.80 | .90 | .18 |
| ☐ 185 Daryl Spencer | 1.80 | .90 | .18 |
| ☐ 186 Russ Meyer | 1.80 | .90 | .18 |
| ☐ 187 Vernon Law | 2.00 | .90 | .20 |
| ☐ 188 Frank Smith | 1.80 | .90 | .18 |
| ☐ 189 Randy Jackson | 1.80 | .90 | .18 |
| ☐ 190 Joe Presko | 1.80 | .90 | .18 |
| ☐ 191 Karl Drews | 1.80 | .90 | .18 |
| ☐ 192 Lou Burdette | 3.00 | 1.40 | .30 |
| ☐ 193 Eddie Robinson | 1.80 | .90 | .18 |
| ☐ 194 Sid Hudson | 1.80 | .90 | .18 |
| ☐ 195 Bob Cain | 1.80 | .90 | .18 |
| ☐ 196 Bob Lemon | 9.00 | 4.25 | .90 |
| ☐ 197 Lou Kretlow | 1.80 | .90 | .18 |
| ☐ 198 Virgil Trucks | 1.80 | .90 | .18 |
| ☐ 199 Steve Gromek | 1.80 | .90 | .18 |
| ☐ 200 Conrado Marrero | 1.80 | .90 | .18 |
| ☐ 201 Bobby Thomson | 3.00 | 1.40 | .30 |
| ☐ 202 George Shuba | 2.00 | .90 | .20 |
| ☐ 203 Vic Janowicz | 2.00 | .90 | .20 |
| ☐ 204 Jackie Collum | 1.80 | .90 | .18 |
| ☐ 205 Hal Jeffcoat | 1.80 | .90 | .18 |
| ☐ 206 Steve Bilko | 1.80 | .90 | .18 |
| ☐ 207 Stan Lopata | 1.80 | .90 | .18 |
| ☐ 208 Johnny Antonelli | 2.00 | .90 | .20 |

| | MINT | VG-E | F-G |
|---|---|---|---|
| ☐ 209 Gene Woodling | 2.25 | 1.00 | .22 |
| ☐ 210 Jim Piersall | 3.50 | 1.65 | .35 |
| ☐ 211 Al Robertson | 1.80 | .90 | .18 |
| ☐ 212 Owen Friend | 1.80 | .90 | .18 |
| ☐ 213 Dick Littlefield | 1.80 | .90 | .18 |
| ☐ 214 Ferris Fain | 2.00 | .90 | .20 |
| ☐ 215 Johnny Bucha | 1.80 | .90 | .18 |
| ☐ 216 Jerry Snyder | 1.80 | .90 | .18 |
| ☐ 217 Henry Thompson | 2.00 | .90 | .20 |
| ☐ 218 Preacher Roe | 3.00 | 1.40 | .30 |
| ☐ 219 Hal Rice | 1.80 | .90 | .18 |
| ☐ 220 Hobie Landrith | 1.80 | .90 | .18 |
| ☐ 221 Frank Baumholtz | 1.80 | .90 | .18 |
| ☐ 222 Memo Luna | 1.80 | .90 | .18 |
| ☐ 223 Steve Ridzik | 1.80 | .90 | .18 |
| ☐ 224 Bill Bruton | 3.00 | 1.40 | .30 |

## 1955 BOWMAN

The cards in this 320 card set measure 2½" by 3¾". The Bowman set of 1955 is known as the "TV set" because each player photograph is cleverly shown within a television set design. The set contains umpire pictures, some transposed pictures (e.g., Johnsons and Bollings), an incorrect spelling for Harvey Kuenn, and a traded line for Palica (all of which are noted in the checklist below). Some three-card advertising strips exist.

Complete Set: M-725.00; VG-E-300.00; F-G-60.00

| | MINT | VG-E | F-G |
|---|---|---|---|
| Common Player (1–96) | .90 | .40 | .09 |
| Common Player (97–224) | .65 | .30 | .06 |
| Common Player (225–320) | 3.25 | 1.50 | .32 |
| ☐ 1 Hoyt Wilhelm | 20.00 | 4.00 | .75 |

| | MINT | VG-E | F-G |
|---|---|---|---|
| ☐ 2 Alvin Dark | 1.50 | .70 | .15 |
| ☐ 3 Joe Coleman | .90 | .40 | .09 |
| ☐ 4 Eddie Waitkus | .90 | .40 | .09 |
| ☐ 5 Jim Robertson | .90 | .40 | .09 |
| ☐ 6 Pete Suder | .90 | .40 | .09 |
| ☐ 7 Gene Baker | .90 | .40 | .09 |
| ☐ 8 Warren Hacker | .90 | .40 | .09 |
| ☐ 9 Gil McDougald | 2.25 | 1.00 | .22 |
| ☐ 10 Phil Rizzuto | 12.00 | 5.50 | 1.20 |
| ☐ 11 Billy Bruton | .90 | .40 | .09 |
| ☐ 12 Andy Pafko | .90 | .40 | .09 |
| ☐ 13 Clyde Vollmer | .90 | .40 | .09 |
| ☐ 14 Gus Keriazakos | .90 | .40 | .09 |
| ☐ 15 Frank Sullivan | .90 | .40 | .09 |
| ☐ 16 Jim Piersall | 2.00 | .90 | .20 |
| ☐ 17 Del Ennis | 1.00 | .45 | .10 |
| ☐ 18 Stan Lopata | .90 | .40 | .09 |
| ☐ 19 Bobby Avila | 1.00 | .45 | .10 |
| ☐ 20 Al Smith | .90 | .40 | .09 |
| ☐ 21 Don Hoak | .90 | .40 | .09 |
| ☐ 22 Roy Campanella | 24.00 | 11.00 | 2.40 |
| ☐ 23 Al Kaline | 15.00 | 7.00 | 1.50 |
| ☐ 24 Al Aber | .90 | .40 | .09 |
| ☐ 25 Minnie Minoso | 2.50 | 1.15 | .25 |
| ☐ 26 Virgil Trucks | .90 | .40 | .09 |
| ☐ 27 Preston Ward | .90 | .40 | .09 |
| ☐ 28 Dick Cole | .90 | .40 | .09 |
| ☐ 29 Red Schoendienst | 2.00 | .90 | .20 |
| ☐ 30 Bill Sarni | .90 | .40 | .09 |
| ☐ 31 Johnny Temple | 1.00 | .45 | .10 |
| ☐ 32 Wally Post | .90 | .40 | .09 |
| ☐ 33 Nelson Fox | 3.25 | 1.50 | .32 |
| ☐ 34 Clint Courtney | .90 | .40 | .09 |
| ☐ 35 Bill Tuttle | .90 | .40 | .09 |
| ☐ 36 Wayne Belardi | .90 | .40 | .09 |
| ☐ 37 Pee Wee Reese | 14.00 | 6.50 | 1.40 |
| ☐ 38 Early Wynn | 7.00 | 3.25 | .70 |
| ☐ 39 Bob Darnell | .90 | .40 | .09 |
| ☐ 40 Vic Wertz | 1.00 | .45 | .10 |
| ☐ 41 Mel Clark | .90 | .40 | .09 |
| ☐ 42 Bob Greenwood | .90 | .40 | .09 |
| ☐ 43 Bob Buhl | 1.00 | .45 | .10 |
| ☐ 44 Danny O'Connell | .90 | .40 | .09 |
| ☐ 45 Tom Umphlett | .90 | .40 | .09 |
| ☐ 46 Mickey Vernon | 1.25 | .60 | .12 |
| ☐ 47 Sammy White | .90 | .40 | .09 |
| ☐ 48 A Milt Bolling ERR | 1.00 | .45 | .10 |
| (photo actually Frank Bolling) | | | |
| ☐ 48 B Milt Bolling COR | 5.00 | 2.35 | .50 |
| ☐ 49 Jim Greengrass | .90 | .40 | .09 |
| ☐ 50 Hobie Landrith | .90 | .40 | .09 |
| ☐ 51 Elvin Tappe | .90 | .40 | .09 |
| ☐ 52 Hal Rice | .90 | .40 | .09 |
| ☐ 53 Alex Kellner | .90 | .40 | .09 |
| ☐ 54 Don Bollweg | .90 | .40 | .09 |
| ☐ 55 Cal Abrams | .90 | .40 | .09 |
| ☐ 56 Billy Cox | 1.00 | .45 | .10 |
| ☐ 57 Bob Friend | 1.00 | .45 | .10 |
| ☐ 58 Frank Thomas | 1.00 | .45 | .10 |
| ☐ 59 Whitey Ford | 13.00 | 6.00 | 1.30 |
| ☐ 60 Enos Slaughter | 7.00 | 3.25 | .70 |
| ☐ 61 Paul LaPalme | .90 | .40 | .09 |
| ☐ 62 Royce Lint | .90 | .40 | .09 |
| ☐ 63 Irv Noren | .90 | .40 | .09 |
| ☐ 64 Curt Simmons | 1.00 | .45 | .10 |
| ☐ 65 Don Zimmer | 2.00 | .90 | .20 |
| ☐ 66 George Shuba | 1.00 | .45 | .10 |
| ☐ 67 Don Larsen | 2.50 | 1.15 | .25 |
| ☐ 68 Elston Howard | 5.50 | 2.60 | .55 |
| ☐ 69 Bill Hunter | .90 | .40 | .09 |
| ☐ 70 Lou Burdette | 2.00 | .90 | .20 |
| ☐ 71 Dave Jolly | .90 | .40 | .09 |
| ☐ 72 Chet Nichols | .90 | .40 | .09 |
| ☐ 73 Eddie Yost | .90 | .40 | .09 |
| ☐ 74 Jerry Snyder | .90 | .40 | .09 |
| ☐ 75 Brooks Lawrence | .90 | .40 | .09 |
| ☐ 76 Tom Poholsky | .90 | .40 | .09 |
| ☐ 77 Jim McDonald | .90 | .40 | .09 |
| ☐ 78 Gil Coan | .90 | .40 | .09 |
| ☐ 79 Willie Miranda | .90 | .40 | .09 |
| ☐ 80 Lou Limmer | .90 | .40 | .09 |
| ☐ 81 Bob Morgan | .90 | .40 | .09 |
| ☐ 82 Lee Walls | .90 | .40 | .09 |
| ☐ 83 Max Surkont | .90 | .40 | .09 |
| ☐ 84 George Freese | .90 | .40 | .09 |
| ☐ 85 Cass Michaels | .90 | .40 | .09 |
| ☐ 86 Ted Gray | .90 | .40 | .09 |
| ☐ 87 Randy Jackson | .90 | .40 | .09 |
| ☐ 88 Steve Bilko | .90 | .40 | .09 |
| ☐ 89 Lou Boudreau MGR | 6.50 | 3.00 | .65 |
| ☐ 90 Art Ditmar | .90 | .40 | .09 |
| ☐ 91 Dick Marlowe | .90 | .40 | .09 |
| ☐ 92 George Zuverink | .90 | .40 | .09 |
| ☐ 93 Andy Seminick | .90 | .40 | .09 |
| ☐ 94 Hank Thompson | 1.00 | .45 | .10 |
| ☐ 95 Sal Maglie | 1.50 | .70 | .15 |
| ☐ 96 Ray Narleski | .90 | .40 | .09 |
| ☐ 97 Johnny Podres | 2.00 | .90 | .20 |
| ☐ 98 Jim Gilliam | 2.50 | 1.15 | .25 |
| ☐ 99 Jerry Coleman | .90 | .40 | .09 |
| ☐ 100 Tom Morgan | .65 | .30 | .06 |
| ☐ 101 A Don Johnson ERR | .90 | .40 | .09 |
| (photo actually Ernie Johnson) | | | |
| ☐ 101 B Don Johnson COR | 3.25 | 1.50 | .32 |

| | MINT | VG-E | F-G |
|---|---|---|---|
| ☐ 102 Bobby Thomson | 2.25 | 1.00 | .22 |
| ☐ 103 Eddie Mathews | 8.00 | 3.75 | .80 |
| ☐ 104 Bob Porterfield | .65 | .30 | .06 |
| ☐ 105 Johnny Schmitz | .65 | .30 | .06 |
| ☐ 106 Del Rice | .65 | .30 | .06 |
| ☐ 107 Solly Hemus | .65 | .30 | .06 |
| ☐ 108 Lou Kretlow | .65 | .30 | .06 |
| ☐ 109 Vern Stephens | .65 | .30 | .06 |
| ☐ 110 Bob Miller | .65 | .30 | .06 |
| ☐ 111 Steve Ridzik | .65 | .30 | .06 |
| ☐ 112 Granny Hamner | .65 | .30 | .06 |
| ☐ 113 Bob Hall | .65 | .30 | .06 |
| ☐ 114 Vic Janowicz | .75 | .35 | .07 |
| ☐ 115 Roger Bowman | .65 | .30 | .06 |
| ☐ 116 Sandy Consuegra | .65 | .30 | .06 |
| ☐ 117 Johnny Groth | .65 | .30 | .06 |
| ☐ 118 Bobby Adams | .65 | .30 | .06 |
| ☐ 119 Joe Astroth | .65 | .30 | .06 |
| ☐ 120 Ed Burtschy | .65 | .30 | .06 |
| ☐ 121 Rufus Crawford | .65 | .30 | .06 |
| ☐ 122 Al Corwin | .65 | .30 | .06 |
| ☐ 123 Marv Grissom | .65 | .30 | .06 |
| ☐ 124 Johnny Antonelli | .90 | .40 | .09 |
| ☐ 125 Paul Giel | .65 | .30 | .06 |
| ☐ 126 Billy Goodman | .75 | .35 | .07 |
| ☐ 127 Hank Majeski | .65 | .30 | .06 |
| ☐ 128 Mike Garcia | .90 | .40 | .09 |
| ☐ 129 Hal Naragon | .65 | .30 | .06 |
| ☐ 130 Richie Ashburn | 3.25 | 1.50 | .32 |
| ☐ 131 Willard Marshall | .65 | .30 | .06 |
| ☐ 132 A Harvey Kueen ERR | 2.00 | .90 | .20 |
| ☐ 132 B Harvey Kuenn COR | 4.50 | 2.10 | .45 |
| ☐ 133 Charles King | .65 | .30 | .06 |
| ☐ 134 Bob Feller | 15.00 | 7.00 | 1.50 |
| ☐ 135 Lloyd Merriman | .65 | .30 | .06 |
| ☐ 136 Rocky Bridges | .65 | .30 | .06 |
| ☐ 137 Bob Talbot | .65 | .30 | .06 |
| ☐ 138 Davey Williams | .75 | .35 | .07 |
| ☐ 139 Shantz Brothers | 1.50 | .70 | .15 |
|     Wilmer and Bobby | | | |
| ☐ 140 Bobby Shantz | 1.00 | .45 | .10 |
| ☐ 141 Wes Westrum | .65 | .30 | .06 |
| ☐ 142 Rudy Regalado | .65 | .30 | .06 |
| ☐ 143 Don Newcombe | 3.50 | 1.65 | .35 |
| ☐ 144 Art Houtteman | .65 | .30 | .06 |
| ☐ 145 Bob Nieman | .65 | .30 | .06 |
| ☐ 146 Don Liddle | .65 | .30 | .06 |
| ☐ 147 Sam Mele | .65 | .30 | .06 |
| ☐ 148 Bob Chakales | .65 | .30 | .06 |
| ☐ 149 Cloyd Boyer | .65 | .30 | .06 |
| ☐ 150 Bill Klaus | .65 | .30 | .06 |
| ☐ 151 Jim Brideweser | .65 | .30 | .06 |
| ☐ 152 Johnny Klippstein | .65 | .30 | .06 |

| | MINT | VG-E | F-G |
|---|---|---|---|
| ☐ 153 Eddie Robinson | .65 | .30 | .06 |
| ☐ 154 Frank Lary | 1.00 | .45 | .10 |
| ☐ 155 Gerry Staley | .65 | .30 | .06 |
| ☐ 156 Jim Hughes | .65 | .30 | .06 |
| ☐ 157 A Ernie Johnson ERR | .90 | .40 | .09 |
|     (photo actually | | | |
|     Don Johnson) | | | |
| ☐ 157 B Ernie Johnson COR | 3.25 | 1.50 | .32 |
| ☐ 158 Gil Hodges | 9.00 | 4.25 | .90 |
| ☐ 159 Harry Byrd | .65 | .30 | .06 |
| ☐ 160 Bill Skowron | 2.50 | 1.15 | .25 |
| ☐ 161 Matt Batts | .65 | .30 | .06 |
| ☐ 162 Charlie Maxwell | .65 | .30 | .06 |
| ☐ 163 Sid Gordon | .65 | .30 | .06 |
| ☐ 164 Toby Atwell | .65 | .30 | .06 |
| ☐ 165 Maurice McDermott | .65 | .30 | .06 |
| ☐ 166 Jim Busby | .65 | .30 | .06 |
| ☐ 167 Bob Grim | .75 | .35 | .07 |
| ☐ 168 Yogi Berra | 18.00 | 8.50 | 1.80 |
| ☐ 169 Carl Furillo | 2.50 | 1.15 | .25 |
| ☐ 170 Carl Erskine | 2.25 | 1.00 | .22 |
| ☐ 171 Robin Roberts | 6.50 | 3.00 | .65 |
| ☐ 172 Willie Jones | .65 | .30 | .06 |
| ☐ 173 Chico Carrasquel | .65 | .30 | .06 |
| ☐ 174 Sherman Lollar | .65 | .30 | .06 |
| ☐ 175 Wilmer Shantz | .65 | .30 | .06 |
| ☐ 176 Joe DeMaestri | .65 | .30 | .06 |
| ☐ 177 Willard Nixon | .65 | .30 | .06 |
| ☐ 178 Tom Brewer | .65 | .30 | .06 |
| ☐ 179 Hank Aaron | 40.00 | 18.00 | 4.00 |
| ☐ 180 Johnny Logan | .75 | .35 | .07 |
| ☐ 181 Eddie Miksis | .65 | .30 | .06 |
| ☐ 182 Bob Rush | .65 | .30 | .06 |
| ☐ 183 Ray Katt | .65 | .30 | .06 |
| ☐ 184 Willie Mays | 40.00 | 18.00 | 4.00 |
| ☐ 185 Vic Raschi | 1.50 | .70 | .15 |
| ☐ 186 Alex Grammas | .65 | .30 | .06 |
| ☐ 187 Fred Hatfield | .65 | .30 | .06 |
| ☐ 188 Ned Garver | .65 | .30 | .06 |
| ☐ 189 Jack Collum | .65 | .30 | .06 |
| ☐ 190 Fred Baczewski | .65 | .30 | .06 |
| ☐ 191 Bob Lemon | 7.00 | 3.25 | .70 |
| ☐ 192 George Strickland | .65 | .30 | .06 |
| ☐ 193 Howie Judson | .65 | .30 | .06 |
| ☐ 194 Joe Nuxhall | .90 | .40 | .09 |
| ☐ 195 A Erv Palica | .90 | .40 | .09 |
|     (without trade) | | | |
| ☐ 195 B Erv Palica | 6.00 | 2.80 | .60 |
|     (with trade) | | | |
| ☐ 196 Russ Meyer | .65 | .30 | .06 |
| ☐ 197 Ralph Kiner | 7.50 | 3.50 | .75 |
| ☐ 198 Dave Pope | .65 | .30 | .06 |
| ☐ 199 Vernon Law | .90 | .40 | .09 |

| | MINT | VG-E | F-G |
|---|---|---|---|
| ☐ 200 Dick Littlefield | .65 | .30 | .06 |
| ☐ 201 Allie Reynolds | 2.50 | 1.15 | .25 |
| ☐ 202 Mickey Mantle | 60.00 | 27.00 | 6.00 |
| ☐ 203 Steve Gromek | .65 | .30 | .06 |
| ☐ 204 A Frank Bolling ERR | .90 | .40 | .09 |
| (photo actually | | | |
| Milt Bolling) | | | |
| ☐ 204 B Frank Bolling COR | 3.25 | 1.50 | .32 |
| ☐ 205 Rip Repulski | .65 | .30 | .06 |
| ☐ 206 Ralph Beard | .65 | .30 | .06 |
| ☐ 207 Frank Shea | .65 | .30 | .06 |
| ☐ 208 Eddy Fitzgerald | .65 | .30 | .06 |
| ☐ 209 Smokey Burgess | .75 | .35 | .07 |
| ☐ 210 Earl Torgeson | .65 | .30 | .06 |
| ☐ 211 Sonny Dixon | .65 | .30 | .06 |
| ☐ 212 Jack Dittmer | .65 | .30 | .06 |
| ☐ 213 George Kell | 5.50 | 2.60 | .55 |
| ☐ 214 Billy Pierce | 1.50 | .70 | .15 |
| ☐ 215 Bob Kuzava | .65 | .30 | .06 |
| ☐ 216 Preacher Roe | 2.00 | .90 | .20 |
| ☐ 217 Del Crandall | .90 | .40 | .09 |
| ☐ 218 Joe Adcock | 1.50 | .70 | .15 |
| ☐ 219 Whitey Lockman | .75 | .35 | .07 |
| ☐ 220 Jim Hearn | .65 | .30 | .06 |
| ☐ 221 Hector Brown | .65 | .30 | .06 |
| ☐ 222 Russ Kemmerer | .65 | .30 | .06 |
| ☐ 223 Hal Jeffcoat | .65 | .30 | .06 |
| ☐ 224 Dee Fondy | .65 | .30 | .06 |
| ☐ 225 Paul Richards | 4.00 | 1.85 | .40 |
| ☐ 226 W. McKinley UMP | 5.00 | 2.35 | .50 |
| ☐ 227 Frank Baumholtz | 3.25 | 1.50 | .32 |
| ☐ 228 John Phillips | 3.25 | 1.50 | .32 |
| ☐ 229 Jim Brosnan | 4.00 | 1.85 | .40 |
| ☐ 230 Al Brazle | 3.25 | 1.50 | .32 |
| ☐ 231 Jim Konstanty | 4.00 | 1.85 | .40 |
| ☐ 232 Birdie Tebbetts | 3.25 | 1.50 | .32 |
| ☐ 233 Bill Serena | 3.25 | 1.50 | .32 |
| ☐ 234 Dick Bartell | 3.25 | 1.50 | .32 |
| ☐ 235 J. Paparella UMP | 5.00 | 2.35 | .50 |
| ☐ 236 Murry Dickson | 3.25 | 1.50 | .32 |
| ☐ 237 Johnny Wyrostek | 3.25 | 1.50 | .32 |
| ☐ 238 Eddie Stanky | 4.00 | 1.85 | .40 |
| ☐ 239 Edwin Rommel UMP | 5.00 | 2.35 | .50 |
| ☐ 240 Billy Loes | 4.00 | 1.85 | .40 |
| ☐ 241 Johnny Pesky | 4.00 | 1.85 | .40 |
| ☐ 242 Ernie Banks | 60.00 | 27.00 | 6.00 |
| ☐ 243 Gus Bell | 4.00 | 1.85 | .40 |
| ☐ 244 Duane Pillette | 3.25 | 1.50 | .32 |
| ☐ 245 Bill Miller | 3.25 | 1.50 | .32 |
| ☐ 246 Hank Bauer | 8.00 | 3.75 | .80 |
| ☐ 247 Dutch Leonard | 3.25 | 1.50 | .32 |
| ☐ 248 Harry Dorish | 3.25 | 1.50 | .32 |
| ☐ 249 Billy Gardner | 4.50 | 2.10 | .45 |
| ☐ 250 Larry Napp UMP | 5.00 | 2.35 | .50 |
| ☐ 251 Stan Jok | 3.25 | 1.50 | .32 |
| ☐ 252 Roy Smalley | 3.25 | 1.50 | .32 |
| ☐ 253 Jim Wilson | 3.25 | 1.50 | .32 |
| ☐ 254 Bennett Flowers | 3.25 | 1.50 | .32 |
| ☐ 255 Pete Runnels | 4.00 | 1.85 | .40 |
| ☐ 256 Owen Friend | 3.25 | 1.50 | .32 |
| ☐ 257 Tom Alston | 3.25 | 1.50 | .32 |
| ☐ 258 John Stevens UMP | 5.00 | 2.35 | .50 |
| ☐ 259 Don Mossi | 4.00 | 1.85 | .40 |
| ☐ 260 Edwin Hurley UMP | 5.00 | 2.35 | .50 |
| ☐ 261 Walt Moryn | 3.25 | 1.50 | .32 |
| ☐ 262 Jim Lemon | 4.00 | 1.85 | .40 |
| ☐ 263 Eddie Joost | 3.25 | 1.50 | .32 |
| ☐ 264 Bill Henry | 3.25 | 1.50 | .32 |
| ☐ 265 Albert Barlick UMP | 5.00 | 2.35 | .50 |
| ☐ 266 Mike Fornieles | 3.25 | 1.50 | .32 |
| ☐ 267 Jim Honochick UMP | 10.00 | 4.75 | 1.00 |
| ☐ 268 Roy Lee Hawes | 3.25 | 1.50 | .32 |
| ☐ 269 Joe Amalfitano | 3.25 | 1.50 | .32 |
| ☐ 270 Chico Fernandez | 3.25 | 1.50 | .32 |
| ☐ 271 Bob Hooper | 3.25 | 1.50 | .32 |
| ☐ 272 John Flaherty UMP | 5.00 | 2.35 | .50 |
| ☐ 273 Bubba Church | 3.25 | 1.50 | .32 |
| ☐ 274 Jim Delsing | 3.25 | 1.50 | .32 |
| ☐ 275 William Grieve UMP | 5.00 | 2.35 | .50 |
| ☐ 276 Ike Delock | 3.25 | 1.50 | .32 |
| ☐ 277 Ed Runge UMP | 5.00 | 2.35 | .50 |
| ☐ 278 Charles Neal | 4.00 | 1.85 | .40 |
| ☐ 279 Hank Soar UMP | 5.00 | 2.35 | .50 |
| ☐ 280 Clyde McCullough | 3.25 | 1.50 | .32 |
| ☐ 281 Charles Berry UMP | 5.00 | 2.35 | .50 |
| ☐ 282 Phil Cavaretta | 4.00 | 1.85 | .40 |
| ☐ 283 Nestor Chylak UMP | 5.00 | 2.35 | .50 |
| ☐ 284 Bill Jackowski UMP | 5.00 | 2.35 | .50 |
| ☐ 285 Walt Dropo | 4.00 | 1.85 | .40 |
| ☐ 286 Frank Secory UMP | 5.00 | 2.35 | .50 |
| ☐ 287 Ron Mrozinski | 3.25 | 1.50 | .32 |
| ☐ 288 Dick Smith | 3.25 | 1.50 | .32 |
| ☐ 289 Arthur Gore UMP | 5.00 | 2.35 | .50 |
| ☐ 290 Hershell Freeman | 3.25 | 1.50 | .32 |
| ☐ 291 Frank Dascoli UMP | 5.00 | 2.35 | .50 |
| ☐ 292 Marv Blaylock | 3.25 | 1.50 | .32 |
| ☐ 293 Thomas Gorman UMP | 5.00 | 2.35 | .50 |
| ☐ 294 Wally Moses | 4.00 | 1.85 | .40 |
| ☐ 295 Lee Ballanfant UMP | 5.00 | 2.35 | .50 |
| ☐ 296 Bill Virdon | 10.00 | 4.75 | 1.00 |
| ☐ 297 Dusty Boggess UMP | 5.00 | 2.35 | .50 |
| ☐ 298 Charlie Grimm | 4.00 | 1.85 | .40 |
| ☐ 299 Lon Warneke UMP | 5.00 | 2.35 | .50 |
| ☐ 300 Tommy Byrne | 4.00 | 1.85 | .40 |
| ☐ 301 William Engeln UMP | 5.00 | 2.35 | .50 |
| ☐ 302 Frank Malzone | 4.50 | 2.10 | .45 |

|  | | MINT | VG-E | F-G |
|---|---|---|---|---|
| ☐ 303 | Jocko Conlan UMP | 12.00 | 5.50 | 1.20 |
| ☐ 304 | Harry Chiti | 3.25 | 1.50 | .32 |
| ☐ 305 | Frank Umont UMP | 5.00 | 2.35 | .50 |
| ☐ 306 | Bob Cerv | 4.00 | 1.85 | .40 |
| ☐ 307 | Babe Pinelli UMP | 5.00 | 2.35 | .50 |
| ☐ 308 | Al Lopez | 10.00 | 4.75 | 1.00 |
| ☐ 309 | Hal Dixon UMP | 5.00 | 2.35 | .50 |
| ☐ 310 | Ken Lehman | 3.25 | 1.50 | .32 |
| ☐ 311 | Lawrence Goetz UMP | 5.00 | 2.35 | .50 |
| ☐ 312 | Bill Wight | 3.25 | 1.50 | .32 |
| ☐ 313 | Augie Donatelli UMP | 6.00 | 2.80 | .60 |
| ☐ 314 | Dale Mitchell | 4.00 | 1.85 | .40 |
| ☐ 315 | Cal Hubbard UMP | 14.00 | 6.50 | 1.40 |
| ☐ 316 | Marion Fricano | 3.25 | 1.50 | .32 |
| ☐ 317 | William Summers UMP | 5.00 | 2.35 | .50 |
| ☐ 318 | Sid Hudson | 3.25 | 1.50 | .32 |
| ☐ 319 | Albert Schroll | 3.25 | 1.50 | .32 |
| ☐ 320 | George Susce Jr. | 5.00 | 2.35 | .50 |

## 1970 KELLOGG

*The cards in this 75 card set measure 2¼" by 3½". The 1970 Kellogg set was Kellogg's first venture into the baseball card producing field. The design incorporates a brilliant color photo of the player set against an indistinct background, which is then covered with a layer of plastic to simulate a 3-D look. Cards 16–30 seem to be in shorter supply than the others in the set.*

Complete Set: M-60.00; VG-E-27.00; F-G-6.00

|  | | MINT | VG-E | F-G |
|---|---|---|---|---|
| | Common Player (1–15) | .50 | .22 | .05 |
| | Common Player (16–30) | .75 | .35 | .07 |
| | Common Player (31–75) | .50 | .22 | .05 |
| ☐ 1 | Ed Kranepool | .50 | .22 | .05 |
| ☐ 2 | Pete Rose | 9.00 | 3.00 | .50 |

|  | | MINT | VG-E | F-G |
|---|---|---|---|---|
| ☐ 3 | Cleon Jones | .50 | .22 | .05 |
| ☐ 4 | Willie McCovey | 2.50 | 1.15 | .25 |
| ☐ 5 | Mel Stottlemyre | .60 | .28 | .06 |
| ☐ 6 | Frank Howard | .60 | .28 | .06 |
| ☐ 7 | Tom Seaver | 3.00 | 1.40 | .30 |
| ☐ 8 | Don Sutton | .90 | .40 | .09 |
| ☐ 9 | Jim Wynn | .50 | .22 | .05 |
| ☐ 10 | Jim Maloney | .60 | .28 | .06 |
| ☐ 11 | Tommie Agee | .50 | .22 | .05 |
| ☐ 12 | Willie Mays | 4.00 | 1.85 | .40 |
| ☐ 13 | Juan Marichal | 2.00 | .90 | .20 |
| ☐ 14 | Dave McNally | .60 | .28 | .06 |
| ☐ 15 | Frank Robinson | 2.50 | 1.15 | .25 |
| ☐ 16 | Carlos May | .75 | .35 | .07 |
| ☐ 17 | Bill Singer | .75 | .35 | .07 |
| ☐ 18 | Rick Reichardt | .75 | .35 | .07 |
| ☐ 19 | Boog Powell | 1.00 | .45 | .10 |
| ☐ 20 | Gaylord Perry | 2.50 | 1.15 | .25 |
| ☐ 21 | Brooks Robinson | 4.00 | 1.85 | .40 |
| ☐ 22 | Luis Aparicio | 2.50 | 1.15 | .25 |
| ☐ 23 | Joel Horlen | .75 | .35 | .07 |
| ☐ 24 | Mike Epstein | .75 | .35 | .07 |
| ☐ 25 | Tom Haller | .75 | .35 | .07 |
| ☐ 26 | Willie Crawford | .75 | .35 | .07 |
| ☐ 27 | Roberto Clemente | 5.00 | 2.35 | .50 |
| ☐ 28 | Matty Alou | .75 | .35 | .07 |
| ☐ 29 | Willie Stargell | 2.50 | 1.15 | .25 |
| ☐ 30 | Tim Cullen | .75 | .35 | .07 |
| ☐ 31 | Randy Hundley | .50 | .22 | .05 |
| ☐ 32 | Reggie Jackson | 4.50 | 2.10 | .45 |
| ☐ 33 | Rich Allen | .60 | .28 | .06 |
| ☐ 34 | Tim McCarver | .60 | .28 | .06 |
| ☐ 35 | Ray Culp | .50 | .22 | .05 |
| ☐ 36 | Jim Fregosi | .60 | .28 | .06 |
| ☐ 37 | Billy Williams | 1.00 | .45 | .10 |
| ☐ 38 | Johnny Odom | .50 | .22 | .05 |
| ☐ 39 | Bert Campaneris | .60 | .28 | .06 |
| ☐ 40 | Ernie Banks | 2.50 | 1.15 | .25 |
| ☐ 41 | Chris Short | .50 | .22 | .05 |
| ☐ 42 | Ron Santo | .75 | .35 | .07 |
| ☐ 43 | Glenn Beckert | .50 | .22 | .05 |
| ☐ 44 | Lou Brock | 2.50 | 1.15 | .25 |
| ☐ 45 | Larry Hisle | .60 | .28 | .06 |
| ☐ 46 | Reggie Smith | .60 | .28 | .06 |
| ☐ 47 | Rod Carew | 2.50 | 1.15 | .25 |
| ☐ 48 | Curt Flood | .60 | .28 | .06 |
| ☐ 49 | Jim Lonborg | .60 | .28 | .06 |
| ☐ 50 | Sam McDowell | .60 | .28 | .06 |
| ☐ 51 | Sal Bando | .60 | .28 | .06 |
| ☐ 52 | Al Kaline | 2.50 | 1.15 | .25 |
| ☐ 53 | Gary Nolan | .50 | .22 | .05 |
| ☐ 54 | Rico Petrocelli | .50 | .22 | .05 |
| ☐ 55 | Ollie Brown | .50 | .22 | .05 |

| | MINT | VG-E | F-G |
|---|---|---|---|
| ☐ 56 Luis Tiant | .60 | .28 | .06 |
| ☐ 57 Bill Freehan | .60 | .28 | .06 |
| ☐ 58 Johnny Bench | 3.00 | 1.40 | .30 |
| ☐ 59 Joe Pepitone | .60 | .28 | .06 |
| ☐ 60 Bobby Murcer | .75 | .35 | .07 |
| ☐ 61 Harmon Killebrew | 2.50 | 1.15 | .25 |
| ☐ 62 Don Wilson | .50 | .22 | .05 |
| ☐ 63 Tony Oliva | .90 | .40 | .09 |
| ☐ 64 Jim Perry | .60 | .28 | .06 |
| ☐ 65 Mickey Lolich | .60 | .28 | .06 |
| ☐ 66 Jose Laboy | .50 | .22 | .05 |
| ☐ 67 Dean Chance | .50 | .22 | .05 |
| ☐ 68 Bud Harrelson | .50 | .22 | .05 |
| ☐ 69 Willie Horton | .60 | .28 | .06 |
| ☐ 70 Wally Bunker | .50 | .22 | .05 |
| ☐ 71 Bob Gibson | 2.50 | 1.15 | .25 |
| ☐ 72 Joe Morgan | 2.00 | .90 | .20 |
| ☐ 73 Denny McLain | .75 | .35 | .07 |
| ☐ 74 Tommy Harper | .50 | .22 | .05 |
| ☐ 75 Don Mincher | .50 | .22 | .05 |

## 1971 KELLOGG

The cards in this 75 card set measure 2¼" by 3½". The 1971 set of 3-D cards marketed by Kellogg is the scarcest of all that company's issues. It was distributed as single cards, one in each package of cereal, without the usual complete set mail in offer. In addition, card dealers were unable to obtain this set in quantity, as they have in other years.

Complete Set: M-375.00; VG-E-135.00; F-G-30.00

Common Player (1-75) . 3.00 1.00 .20

| | MINT | VG-E | F-G |
|---|---|---|---|
| ☐ 1 Wayne Simpson | 3.00 | 1.00 | .20 |

| | MINT | VG-E | F-G |
|---|---|---|---|
| ☐ 2 Tom Seaver | 10.00 | 4.75 | 1.00 |
| ☐ 3 Jim Perry | 3.50 | 1.65 | .35 |
| ☐ 4 Bob Robertson | 3.00 | 1.00 | .20 |
| ☐ 5 Roberto Clemente | 14.00 | 6.50 | 1.40 |
| ☐ 6 Gaylord Perry | 7.00 | 3.25 | .70 |
| ☐ 7 Felipe Alou | 3.00 | 1.00 | .20 |
| ☐ 8 Denis Menke | 3.00 | 1.00 | .20 |
| ☐ 9 Don Kessinger | 3.00 | 1.00 | .20 |
| ☐ 10 Willie Mays | 14.00 | 6.50 | 1.40 |
| ☐ 11 Jim Hickman | 3.00 | 1.00 | .20 |
| ☐ 12 Tony Oliva | 4.00 | 1.85 | .40 |
| ☐ 13 Manny Sanguillen | 3.00 | 1.00 | .20 |
| ☐ 14 Frank Howard | 3.50 | 1.65 | .35 |
| ☐ 15 Frank Robinson | 8.00 | 3.75 | .80 |
| ☐ 16 Willie Davis | 3.50 | 1.65 | .35 |
| ☐ 17 Lou Brock | 8.00 | 3.75 | .80 |
| ☐ 18 Cesar Tovar | 3.00 | 1.00 | .20 |
| ☐ 19 Luis Aparicio | 7.00 | 3.25 | .70 |
| ☐ 20 Boog Powell | 3.50 | 1.65 | .35 |
| ☐ 21 Dick Selma | 3.00 | 1.00 | .20 |
| ☐ 22 Danny Walton | 3.00 | 1.00 | .20 |
| ☐ 23 Carl Morton | 3.00 | 1.00 | .20 |
| ☐ 24 Sonny Siebert | 3.00 | 1.00 | .20 |
| ☐ 25 Jim Merritt | 3.00 | 1.00 | .20 |
| ☐ 26 Jose Cardenal | 3.00 | 1.00 | .20 |
| ☐ 27 Don Mincher | 3.00 | 1.00 | .20 |
| ☐ 28 Clyde Wright | 3.00 | 1.00 | .20 |
| ☐ 29 Les Cain | 3.00 | 1.00 | .20 |
| ☐ 30 Danny Cater | 3.00 | 1.00 | .20 |
| ☐ 31 Don Sutton | 4.50 | 2.10 | .45 |
| ☐ 32 Chuck Dobson | 3.00 | 1.00 | .20 |
| ☐ 33 Willie McCovey | 9.00 | 4.25 | .90 |
| ☐ 34 Mike Epstein | 3.00 | 1.00 | .20 |
| ☐ 35 Paul Blair | 3.00 | 1.00 | .20 |
| ☐ 36 Gary Nolan | 3.00 | 1.00 | .20 |
| ☐ 37 Sam McDowell | 3.00 | 1.00 | .20 |
| ☐ 38 Amos Otis | 3.00 | 1.00 | .20 |
| ☐ 39 Ray Fosse | 3.00 | 1.00 | .20 |
| ☐ 40 Mel Stottlemyre | 3.00 | 1.00 | .20 |
| ☐ 41 Clarence Gaston | 3.00 | 1.00 | .20 |
| ☐ 42 Dick Dietz | 3.00 | 1.00 | .20 |
| ☐ 43 Roy White | 3.00 | 1.00 | .20 |
| ☐ 44 Al Kaline | 9.00 | 4.25 | .90 |
| ☐ 45 Carlos May | 3.00 | 1.00 | .20 |
| ☐ 46 Tommie Agee | 3.00 | 1.00 | .20 |
| ☐ 47 Tommy Harper | 3.00 | 1.00 | .20 |
| ☐ 48 Larry Dierker | 3.00 | 1.00 | .20 |
| ☐ 49 Mike Cuellar | 3.00 | 1.00 | .20 |
| ☐ 50 Ernie Banks | 9.00 | 4.25 | .90 |
| ☐ 51 Bob Gibson | 8.00 | 3.75 | .80 |
| ☐ 52 Reggie Smith | 3.50 | 1.65 | .35 |
| ☐ 53 Matty Alou | 3.00 | 1.00 | .20 |
| ☐ 54 Alex Johnson | 3.00 | 1.00 | .20 |

| | | MINT | VG-E | F-G |
|---|---|---|---|---|
| ☐ | 55 Harmon Killebrew | 8.00 | 3.75 | .80 |
| ☐ | 56 Bill Grabarkewitz | 3.00 | 1.00 | .20 |
| ☐ | 57 Richie Allen | 3.50 | 1.65 | .35 |
| ☐ | 58 Tony Perez | 4.00 | 1.85 | .40 |
| ☐ | 59 Dave McNally | 3.00 | 1.00 | .20 |
| ☐ | 60 Jim Palmer | 8.00 | 3.75 | .80 |
| ☐ | 61 Billy Williams | 6.00 | 2.80 | .60 |
| ☐ | 62 Joe Torre | 4.00 | 1.85 | .40 |
| ☐ | 63 Jim Northrup | 3.00 | 1.00 | .20 |
| ☐ | 64 Jim Fregosi | 3.00 | 1.00 | .20 |
| ☐ | 65 Pete Rose | 25.00 | 8.00 | 1.50 |
| ☐ | 66 Bud Harrelson | 3.00 | 1.00 | .20 |
| ☐ | 67 Tony Taylor | 3.00 | 1.00 | .20 |
| ☐ | 68 Willie Stargell | 7.00 | 3.25 | .70 |
| ☐ | 69 Tony Horton | 3.00 | 1.00 | .20 |
| ☐ | 70 Claude Osteen | 3.00 | 1.00 | .20 |
| ☐ | 71 Glenn Beckert | 3.00 | 1.00 | .20 |
| ☐ | 72 Nate Colbert | 3.00 | 1.00 | .20 |
| ☐ | 73 Rick Monday | 3.00 | 1.00 | .20 |
| ☐ | 74 Tommy John | 6.00 | 2.80 | .60 |
| ☐ | 75 Chris Short | 3.00 | 1.00 | .20 |

## 1972 KELLOGG

The cards in this 54 card set measure 2⅛" by 3¼". The dimensions of the cards in the 1972 Kellogg set were reduced in comparison to those of the 1971 series. In addition, the length of the set was set at 54 cards rather than the 75 of the previous year. The cards of this Kellogg set are characterized by the diagonal bands found on the obverse.

**Complete Set: M-36.00; VG-E-15.00; F-G-3.00**

| | | | | |
|---|---|---|---|---|
| Common Player (1–54) | | .40 | .18 | .04 |
| ☐ 1 Tom Seaver | | 3.00 | 1.40 | .30 |

| | | MINT | VG-E | F-G |
|---|---|---|---|---|
| ☐ | 2 Amos Otis | .50 | .22 | .05 |
| ☐ | 3 Willie Davis | .50 | .22 | .05 |
| ☐ | 4 Wilbur Wood | .40 | .18 | .04 |
| ☐ | 5 Bill Parsons | .40 | .18 | .04 |
| ☐ | 6 Pete Rose | 6.50 | 3.00 | .65 |
| ☐ | 7 Willie McCovey | 2.50 | 1.15 | .25 |
| ☐ | 8 Ferguson Jenkins | .60 | .28 | .06 |
| ☐ | 9 Vida Blue | .50 | .22 | .05 |
| ☐ | 10 Joe Torre | .65 | .30 | .06 |
| ☐ | 11 Merv Rettenmund | .40 | .18 | .04 |
| ☐ | 12 Bill Melton | .40 | .18 | .04 |
| ☐ | 13 Jim Palmer | 2.00 | .90 | .20 |
| ☐ | 14 Doug Rader | .40 | .18 | .04 |
| ☐ | 15 Dave Roberts | .40 | .18 | .04 |
| ☐ | 16 Bobby Murcer | .50 | .22 | .05 |
| ☐ | 17 Wes Parker | .40 | .18 | .04 |
| ☐ | 18 Joe Coleman | .40 | .18 | .04 |
| ☐ | 19 Manny Sanguillen | .40 | .18 | .04 |
| ☐ | 20 Reggie Jackson | 3.50 | 1.65 | .35 |
| ☐ | 21 Ralph Garr | .40 | .18 | .04 |
| ☐ | 22 Jim Hunter | 1.00 | .45 | .10 |
| ☐ | 23 Rick Wise | .40 | .18 | .04 |
| ☐ | 24 Glenn Beckert | .40 | .18 | .04 |
| ☐ | 25 Tony Oliva | .65 | .30 | .06 |
| ☐ | 26 Bob Gibson | 1.50 | .70 | .15 |
| ☐ | 27 Mike Cuellar | .40 | .18 | .04 |
| ☐ | 28 Chris Speier | .40 | .18 | .04 |
| ☐ | 29 Dave McNally | .50 | .22 | .05 |
| ☐ | 30 Leo Cardenas | .40 | .18 | .04 |
| ☐ | 31 Bill Freehan | .50 | .22 | .05 |
| ☐ | 32 Bud Harrelson | .40 | .18 | .04 |
| ☐ | 33 Sam McDowell | .50 | .22 | .05 |
| ☐ | 34 Claude Osteen | .50 | .22 | .05 |
| ☐ | 35 Reggie Smith | .50 | .22 | .05 |
| ☐ | 36 Sonny Siebert | .40 | .18 | .04 |
| ☐ | 37 Lee May | .50 | .22 | .05 |
| ☐ | 38 Mickey Lolich | .60 | .28 | .06 |
| ☐ | 39 Cookie Rojas | .40 | .18 | .04 |
| ☐ | 40 Dick Drago | .40 | .18 | .04 |
| ☐ | 41 Nate Colbert | .40 | .18 | .04 |
| ☐ | 42 Andy Messersmith | .50 | .22 | .05 |
| ☐ | 43 Dave Johnson | .50 | .22 | .05 |
| ☐ | 44 Steve Blass | .40 | .18 | .04 |
| ☐ | 45 Bob Robertson | .40 | .18 | .04 |
| ☐ | 46 Billy Williams | 1.00 | .45 | .10 |
| ☐ | 47 Juan Marichal | 1.50 | .70 | .15 |
| ☐ | 48 Lou Brock | 2.00 | .90 | .20 |
| ☐ | 49 Roberto Clemente | 4.00 | 1.85 | .40 |
| ☐ | 50 Mel Stottlemyre | .50 | .22 | .05 |
| ☐ | 51 Don Wilson | .40 | .18 | .04 |
| ☐ | 52 Sal Bando | .50 | .22 | .05 |
| ☐ | 53 Willie Stargell | 1.50 | .70 | .15 |
| ☐ | 54 Willie Mays | 4.00 | 1.85 | .40 |

## 1972 KELLOGG ATG

The cards in this 15 card set measure 2¼" by 3½". The 1972 All-Time Greats 3-D set was issued with Kellogg's Danish Go Rounds. The set is a reissue of a 1970 set issued by Rold Gold Pretzels to commemorate baseball's first 100 years.

Complete Set: M-9.00; VG-E-4.25; F-G-.90

|  | MINT | VG-E | F-G |
|---|---|---|---|
| Common Player (1–15) . | .40 | .18 | .04 |
| ☐ 1 Walter Johnson ........ | .80 | .40 | .08 |
| ☐ 2 Rogers Hornsby ........ | .60 | .28 | .06 |
| ☐ 3 John McGraw .......... | .40 | .18 | .04 |
| ☐ 4 Mickey Cochrane ...... | .50 | .22 | .05 |
| ☐ 5 George Sisler ......... | .40 | .18 | .04 |
| ☐ 6 Babe Ruth ............. | 1.60 | .80 | .16 |
| ☐ 7 Lefty Grove ........... | .50 | .22 | .05 |
| ☐ 8 Pie Traynor ........... | .40 | .18 | .04 |
| ☐ 9 Honus Wagner ......... | .80 | .40 | .08 |
| ☐ 10 Eddie Collins ......... | .40 | .18 | .04 |
| ☐ 11 Tris Speaker ......... | .50 | .22 | .05 |
| ☐ 12 Cy Young ............. | .60 | .28 | .06 |
| ☐ 13 Lou Gehrig ........... | 1.20 | .55 | .12 |
| ☐ 14 Babe Ruth ............ | 1.60 | .80 | .16 |
| ☐ 15 Ty Cobb .............. | 1.20 | .55 | .12 |

## 1973 KELLOGG 2D

The cards in this 54 card set measure 2¼" by 3½". The 1973 Kellogg set is the only non 3-D set produced by Kellogg. The complete set could be obtained from the company through a box top redemption procedure. The card size is slightly larger than the previous year.

Complete Set: M-32.00; VG-E-15.00; F-G-3.20

|  | MINT | VG-E | F-G |
|---|---|---|---|
| Common Player (1–54) . | .40 | .18 | .04 |
| ☐ 1 Amos Otis ............. | .50 | .22 | .05 |
| ☐ 2 Ellie Rodriguez ....... | .40 | .18 | .04 |
| ☐ 3 Mickey Lolich ......... | .60 | .28 | .06 |
| ☐ 4 Tony Oliva ............ | .60 | .28 | .06 |
| ☐ 5 Don Sutton ........... | .80 | .40 | .08 |
| ☐ 6 Pete Rose ............ | 6.50 | 3.00 | .65 |
| ☐ 7 Steve Carlton ........ | 3.00 | 1.40 | .30 |
| ☐ 8 Bobby Bonds ......... | .50 | .22 | .05 |
| ☐ 9 Wilbur Wood .......... | .40 | .18 | .04 |
| ☐ 10 Billy Williams ........ | .90 | .40 | .09 |
| ☐ 11 Steve Blass ......... | .40 | .18 | .04 |
| ☐ 12 Jon Matlack ......... | .50 | .22 | .05 |
| ☐ 13 Cesar Cedeno ....... | .50 | .22 | .05 |
| ☐ 14 Bob Gibson .......... | 1.75 | .85 | .17 |
| ☐ 15 Sparky Lyle .......... | .50 | .22 | .05 |
| ☐ 16 Nolan Ryan .......... | 2.25 | 1.00 | .22 |
| ☐ 17 Jim Palmer .......... | 1.75 | .85 | .17 |
| ☐ 18 Ray Fosse ........... | .40 | .18 | .04 |
| ☐ 19 Bobby Murcer ....... | .50 | .22 | .05 |
| ☐ 20 Jim Hunter .......... | .80 | .40 | .08 |
| ☐ 21 Tom McCraw ........ | .40 | .18 | .04 |
| ☐ 22 Reggie Jackson ...... | 3.00 | 1.40 | .30 |
| ☐ 23 Bill Stoneman ....... | .40 | .18 | .04 |
| ☐ 24 Lou Piniella ......... | .60 | .28 | .06 |

|  | MINT | VG-E | F-G |
|---|---|---|---|
| ☐ 25 Willie Stargell | 1.50 | .70 | .15 |
| ☐ 26 Dick Allen | .60 | .28 | .06 |
| ☐ 27 Carlton Fisk | 1.10 | .50 | .11 |
| ☐ 28 Ferguson Jenkins | .65 | .30 | .06 |
| ☐ 29 Phil Niekro | 1.20 | .55 | .12 |
| ☐ 30 Gary Nolan | .40 | .18 | .04 |
| ☐ 31 Joe Torre | .60 | .28 | .06 |
| ☐ 32 Bobby Tolan | .40 | .18 | .04 |
| ☐ 33 Nate Colbert | .40 | .18 | .04 |
| ☐ 34 Joe Morgan | 1.50 | .70 | .15 |
| ☐ 35 Bert Blyleven | .60 | .28 | .06 |
| ☐ 36 Joe Rudi | .50 | .22 | .05 |
| ☐ 37 Ralph Garr | .40 | .18 | .04 |
| ☐ 38 Gaylord Perry | 1.50 | .70 | .15 |
| ☐ 39 Bobby Grich | .50 | .22 | .05 |
| ☐ 40 Lou Brock | 2.00 | .90 | .20 |
| ☐ 41 Pete Broberg | .40 | .18 | .04 |
| ☐ 42 Manny Sanguillen | .40 | .18 | .04 |
| ☐ 43 Willie Davis | .50 | .22 | .05 |
| ☐ 44 Dave Kingman | .75 | .35 | .07 |
| ☐ 45 Carlos May | .40 | .18 | .04 |
| ☐ 46 Tom Seaver | 2.25 | 1.00 | .22 |
| ☐ 47 Mike Cuellar | .50 | .22 | .05 |
| ☐ 48 Joe Coleman | .40 | .18 | .04 |
| ☐ 49 Claude Osteen | .40 | .18 | .04 |
| ☐ 50 Steve Kline | .40 | .18 | .04 |
| ☐ 51 Rod Carew | 2.25 | 1.00 | .22 |
| ☐ 52 Al Kaline | 2.25 | 1.00 | .22 |
| ☐ 53 Larry Dierker | .40 | .18 | .04 |
| ☐ 54 Ron Santo | .60 | .28 | .06 |

## 1974 KELLOGG

*The cards in this 54 card set measure 2⅛"
by 3¼". In 1974 Kellogg returned to its 3-D
format; it also returned to the smaller-*

*sized card. Complete sets could be ob-
tained from the company through a box
top offer.*

Complete Set: M-32.00; VG-E-15.00; F-G-3.20

|  | MINT | VG-E | F-G |
|---|---|---|---|
| Common Player (1–54) . | .30 | .12 | .03 |
| ☐ 1 Bob Gibson | 1.50 | .70 | .15 |
| ☐ 2 Rick Monday | .40 | .18 | .04 |
| ☐ 3 Joe Coleman | .30 | .12 | .03 |
| ☐ 4 Bert Campaneris | .40 | .18 | .04 |
| ☐ 5 Carlton Fisk | .90 | .40 | .09 |
| ☐ 6 Jim Palmer | 1.50 | .70 | .15 |
| ☐ 7 Ron Santo | .50 | .22 | .05 |
| ☐ 8 Nolan Ryan | 2.25 | 1.00 | .22 |
| ☐ 9 Greg Luzinski | .70 | .32 | .07 |
| ☐ 10 Buddy Bell | .70 | .32 | .07 |
| ☐ 11 Bob Watson | .30 | .12 | .03 |
| ☐ 12 Bill Singer | .30 | .12 | .03 |
| ☐ 13 Dave May | .30 | .12 | .03 |
| ☐ 14 Jim Brewer | .30 | .12 | .03 |
| ☐ 15 Manny Sanguillen | .30 | .12 | .03 |
| ☐ 16 Jeff Burroughs | .30 | .12 | .03 |
| ☐ 17 Amos Otis | .40 | .18 | .04 |
| ☐ 18 Ed Goodson | .30 | .12 | .03 |
| ☐ 19 Nate Colbert | .30 | .12 | .03 |
| ☐ 20 Reggie Jackson | 3.00 | 1.40 | .30 |
| ☐ 21 Ted Simmons | .70 | .32 | .07 |
| ☐ 22 Bobby Murcer | .40 | .18 | .04 |
| ☐ 23 Willie Horton | .40 | .18 | .04 |
| ☐ 24 Orlando Cepeda | .50 | .22 | .05 |
| ☐ 25 Ron Hunt | .30 | .12 | .03 |
| ☐ 26 Wayne Twitchell | .30 | .12 | .03 |
| ☐ 27 Ron Fairly | .30 | .12 | .03 |
| ☐ 28 Johnny Bench | 2.50 | 1.15 | .25 |
| ☐ 29 John Mayberry | .30 | .12 | .03 |
| ☐ 30 Rod Carew | 2.50 | 1.15 | .25 |
| ☐ 31 Ken Holtzman | .40 | .18 | .04 |
| ☐ 32 Billy Williams | .80 | .40 | .08 |
| ☐ 33 Dick Allen | .50 | .22 | .05 |
| ☐ 34 Wilbur Wood | .30 | .12 | .03 |
| ☐ 35 Danny Thompson | .30 | .12 | .03 |
| ☐ 36 Joe Morgan | 1.50 | .70 | .15 |
| ☐ 37 Willie Stargell | 1.50 | .70 | .15 |
| ☐ 38 Pete Rose | 6.00 | 2.80 | .60 |
| ☐ 39 Bobby Bonds | .40 | .18 | .04 |
| ☐ 40 Chris Speier | .30 | .12 | .03 |
| ☐ 41 Sparky Lyle | .40 | .18 | .04 |
| ☐ 42 Cookie Rojas | .30 | .12 | .03 |
| ☐ 43 Tommy Davis | .40 | .18 | .04 |
| ☐ 44 Jim Hunter | .80 | .40 | .08 |
| ☐ 45 Willie Davis | .40 | .18 | .04 |

| | MINT | VG-E | F-G |
|---|---|---|---|
| ☐ 46 Bert Blyleven | .50 | .22 | .05 |
| ☐ 47 Pat Kelly | .30 | .12 | .03 |
| ☐ 48 Ken Singleton | .40 | .18 | .04 |
| ☐ 49 Manny Mota | .40 | .18 | .04 |
| ☐ 50 Dave Johnson | .40 | .18 | .04 |
| ☐ 51 Sal Bando | .40 | .18 | .04 |
| ☐ 52 Tom Seaver | 2.50 | 1.15 | .25 |
| ☐ 53 Felix Millan | .30 | .12 | .03 |
| ☐ 54 Ron Blomberg | .30 | .12 | .03 |

## 1975 KELLOGG

The cards in this 57 card set measure 2⅛" by 3¼". The 1975 Kellogg 3-D set could be obtained card by card in cereal boxes or as a set from a box top offer from the company. Card number 44 Jim Hunter exists with the A's emblem or the Yankee's emblem on the back of the card.

Complete Set: M-80.00; VG-E-37.00; F-G-8.00

| | | MINT | VG-E | F-G |
|---|---|---|---|---|
| | Common Player (1–57) | .50 | .22 | .05 |
| ☐ | 1 Roy White | .60 | .28 | .06 |
| ☐ | 2 Ross Grimsley | .50 | .22 | .05 |
| ☐ | 3 Reggie Smith | .60 | .28 | .06 |
| ☐ | 4 Bob Grich | .60 | .28 | .06 |
| ☐ | 5 Greg Gross | .50 | .22 | .05 |
| ☐ | 6 Bob Watson | .60 | .28 | .06 |
| ☐ | 7 Johnny Bench | 4.00 | 1.85 | .40 |
| ☐ | 8 Jeff Burroughs | .60 | .28 | .06 |
| ☐ | 9 Elliott Maddox | .50 | .22 | .05 |
| ☐ | 10 Jon Matlack | .60 | .28 | .06 |
| ☐ | 11 Pete Rose | 9.00 | 4.25 | .90 |
| ☐ | 12 Lee Stanton | .50 | .22 | .05 |
| ☐ | 13 Bake McBride | .50 | .22 | .05 |
| ☐ | 14 Jorge Orta | .50 | .22 | .05 |
| ☐ | 15 Al Oliver | 1.25 | .60 | .12 |

| | MINT | VG-E | F-G |
|---|---|---|---|
| ☐ 16 John Briggs | .50 | .22 | .05 |
| ☐ 17 Steve Garvey | 4.00 | 1.85 | .40 |
| ☐ 18 Brooks Robinson | 4.00 | 1.85 | .40 |
| ☐ 19 John Hiller | .50 | .22 | .05 |
| ☐ 20 Lynn McGlothen | .50 | .22 | .05 |
| ☐ 21 Cleon Jones | .50 | .22 | .05 |
| ☐ 22 Fergie Jenkins | .90 | .40 | .09 |
| ☐ 23 Bill North | .50 | .22 | .05 |
| ☐ 24 Steve Busby | .50 | .22 | .05 |
| ☐ 25 Richie Zisk | .60 | .28 | .06 |
| ☐ 26 Nolan Ryan | 4.00 | 1.85 | .40 |
| ☐ 27 Joe Morgan | 2.50 | 1.15 | .25 |
| ☐ 28 Joe Rudi | .60 | .28 | .06 |
| ☐ 29 Jose Cardenal | .50 | .22 | .05 |
| ☐ 30 Andy Messersmith | .50 | .22 | .05 |
| ☐ 31 Willie Montanez | .50 | .22 | .05 |
| ☐ 32 Bill Buckner | .90 | .40 | .09 |
| ☐ 33 Rod Carew | 4.00 | 1.85 | .40 |
| ☐ 34 Lou Piniella | .75 | .35 | .07 |
| ☐ 35 Ralph Garr | .60 | .28 | .06 |
| ☐ 36 Mike Marshall | .60 | .28 | .06 |
| ☐ 37 Garry Maddox | .60 | .28 | .06 |
| ☐ 38 Dwight Evans | 1.00 | .45 | .10 |
| ☐ 39 Lou Brock | 4.00 | 1.85 | .40 |
| ☐ 40 Ken Singleton | .80 | .40 | .08 |
| ☐ 41 Steve Braun | .50 | .22 | .05 |
| ☐ 42 Rich Allen | .90 | .40 | .09 |
| ☐ 43 John Grubb | .50 | .22 | .05 |
| ☐ 44 Jim Hunter (2) | 2.00 | .90 | .20 |
| ☐ 45 Gaylord Perry | 2.00 | .90 | .20 |
| ☐ 46 George Hendrick | .80 | .40 | .08 |
| ☐ 47 Sparky Lyle | .75 | .35 | .07 |
| ☐ 48 Dave Cash | .50 | .22 | .05 |
| ☐ 49 Luis Tiant | .75 | .35 | .07 |
| ☐ 50 Cesar Geronimo | .50 | .22 | .05 |
| ☐ 51 Carl Yastrzemski | 6.00 | 2.80 | .60 |
| ☐ 52 Ken Brett | .50 | .22 | .05 |
| ☐ 53 Hal McRae | .80 | .40 | .08 |
| ☐ 54 Reggie Jackson | 5.00 | 2.35 | .50 |
| ☐ 55 Rollie Fingers | 1.50 | .70 | .15 |
| ☐ 56 Mike Schmidt | 5.00 | 2.35 | .50 |
| ☐ 57 Richie Hebner | .50 | .22 | .05 |

# 1976 KELLOGG

The cards in this 57 card set measure 2⅛"
by 3¼". The 1976 Kellogg 3-D set could
be obtained card by card in cereal boxes
or as a set from the company for box tops.
Card number 6, that of Clay Carroll, exists
with both a Reds or White Sox emblem on
the back. Cards 1–3 were apparently
printed apart from the other 54 and are in
shorter supply.

Complete Set: M-42.00; VG-E-17.00; F-G-4.00

|  |  | MINT | VG-E | F-G |
|---|---|---|---|---|
| | Common Player (1–3) | | | |
| | SP | 6.00 | 2.80 | .60 |
| | Common Player (4–57) | .30 | .12 | .03 |
| ☐ | 1 Steve Hargan SP | 6.00 | 2.80 | .60 |
| ☐ | 2 Claudell Washington SP | 6.00 | 2.80 | .60 |
| ☐ | 3 Don Gullett SP | 6.00 | 2.80 | .60 |
| ☐ | 4 Randy Jones | .40 | .18 | .04 |
| ☐ | 5 Jim Hunter | .80 | .40 | .08 |
| ☐ | 6 Clay Carroll (2) | .50 | .22 | .05 |
| ☐ | 7 Joe Rudi | .40 | .18 | .04 |
| ☐ | 8 Reggie Jackson | 2.50 | 1.15 | .25 |
| ☐ | 9 Felix Millan | .30 | .12 | .03 |
| ☐ | 10 Jim Rice | 1.75 | .85 | .17 |
| ☐ | 11 Bert Blyleven | .50 | .20 | .05 |
| ☐ | 12 Ken Singleton | .40 | .18 | .04 |
| ☐ | 13 Don Sutton | .50 | .22 | .05 |
| ☐ | 14 Joe Morgan | 1.50 | .70 | .15 |
| ☐ | 15 Dave Parker | 1.00 | .45 | .10 |
| ☐ | 16 Dave Cash | .30 | .12 | .03 |
| ☐ | 17 Ron LeFlore | .40 | .18 | .04 |
| ☐ | 18 Greg Luzinski | .60 | .28 | .06 |
| ☐ | 19 Dennis Eckersley | .40 | .18 | .04 |
| ☐ | 20 Bill Madlock | .90 | .40 | .09 |

|  |  | MINT | VG-E | F-G |
|---|---|---|---|---|
| ☐ | 21 George Scott | .30 | .12 | .03 |
| ☐ | 22 Willie Stargell | 1.25 | .60 | .12 |
| ☐ | 23 Al Hrabosky | .40 | .18 | .04 |
| ☐ | 24 Carl Yastrzemski | 3.00 | 1.40 | .30 |
| ☐ | 25 Jim Kaat | .60 | .28 | .06 |
| ☐ | 26 Marty Perez | .30 | .12 | .03 |
| ☐ | 27 Bob Watson | .30 | .12 | .03 |
| ☐ | 28 Eric Soderholm | .30 | .12 | .03 |
| ☐ | 29 Bill Lee | .30 | .12 | .03 |
| ☐ | 30 Frank Tanana | .40 | .18 | .04 |
| ☐ | 31 Fred Lynn | 1.25 | .60 | .12 |
| ☐ | 32 Tom Seaver | 2.00 | .90 | .20 |
| ☐ | 33 Steve Busby | .30 | .12 | .03 |
| ☐ | 34 Gary Carter | 2.00 | .90 | .20 |
| ☐ | 35 Rick Wise | .30 | .12 | .03 |
| ☐ | 36 Johnny Bench | 2.00 | .90 | .20 |
| ☐ | 37 Jim Palmer | 1.50 | .70 | .15 |
| ☐ | 38 Bobby Murcer | .40 | .18 | .04 |
| ☐ | 39 Von Joshua | .30 | .12 | .03 |
| ☐ | 40 Lou Brock | 2.00 | .90 | .20 |
| ☐ | 41 Mickey Rivers (2) | .40 | .18 | .04 |
| ☐ | 42 Manny Sanguillen | .30 | .12 | .03 |
| ☐ | 43 Jerry Reuss | .40 | .18 | .04 |
| ☐ | 44 Ken Griffey | .40 | .18 | .04 |
| ☐ | 45 Jorge Orta | .30 | .12 | .03 |
| ☐ | 46 John Mayberry | .30 | .12 | .03 |
| ☐ | 47 Vida Blue (2) | .40 | .18 | .04 |
| ☐ | 48 Rod Carew | 2.00 | .90 | .20 |
| ☐ | 49 Jon Matlack | .40 | .18 | .04 |
| ☐ | 50 Boog Powell | .40 | .18 | .04 |
| ☐ | 51 Mike Hargrove | .30 | .12 | .03 |
| ☐ | 52 Paul Lindblad | .30 | .12 | .03 |
| ☐ | 53 Thurman Munson | 2.00 | .90 | .20 |
| ☐ | 54 Steve Garvey | 2.00 | .90 | .20 |
| ☐ | 55 Pete Rose | 5.50 | 2.60 | .55 |
| ☐ | 56 Greg Gross | .30 | .12 | .03 |
| ☐ | 57 Ted Simmons | .70 | .32 | .07 |

# 1977 KELLOGG

The cards in this 57 card set measure 2⅛"
by 3¼". The 1977 Kellogg series of 3-D
Baseball player cards could be obtained
card by card from cereal boxes or by send-
ing in box tops and money. Each player's
picture appears in miniature form on the
reverse, an idea begun in 1971 and replaced in subsequent years by the use of a
picture of the Kellogg mascot.

**Complete Set: M-25.00; VG-E-11.00; F-G-2.50**

| | MINT | VG-E | F-G |
|---|---|---|---|
| Common Player (1–57) . | .25 | .10 | .02 |
| 1 George Foster . . . . . . . . | .90 | .40 | .09 |
| 2 Bert Campaneris . . . . . . | .30 | .12 | .03 |
| 3 Fergie Jenkins . . . . . . . | .50 | .22 | .05 |
| 4 Dock Ellis . . . . . . . . . . | .25 | .10 | .02 |
| 5 John Montefusco . . . . . | .25 | .10 | .02 |
| 6 George Brett . . . . . . . . | 3.25 | 1.50 | .32 |
| 7 John Candelaria . . . . . . | .30 | .12 | .03 |
| 8 Fred Norman . . . . . . . . | .25 | .10 | .02 |
| 9 Bill Travers . . . . . . . . . | .25 | .10 | .02 |
| 10 Hal McRae . . . . . . . . . | .30 | .12 | .03 |
| 11 Doug Rau . . . . . . . . . . | .25 | .10 | .02 |
| 12 Greg Luzinski . . . . . . . | .60 | .28 | .06 |
| 13 Ralph Garr . . . . . . . . . | .25 | .10 | .02 |
| 14 Steve Garvey . . . . . . . | 2.25 | 1.00 | .22 |
| 15 Rick Manning . . . . . . . | .25 | .10 | .02 |
| 16 Lyman Bostock . . . . . . | .30 | .12 | .03 |
| 17 Randy Jones . . . . . . . . | .30 | .12 | .03 |
| 18 Ron Cey . . . . . . . . . . . | .50 | .22 | .05 |
| 19 Dave Parker . . . . . . . . | .90 | .40 | .09 |
| 20 Pete Rose . . . . . . . . . | 5.00 | 2.00 | .40 |
| 21 Wayne Garland . . . . . . | .25 | .10 | .02 |
| 22 Bill North . . . . . . . . . . | .25 | .10 | .02 |
| 23 Thurman Munson . . . . . | 1.50 | .70 | .15 |
| 24 Tom Poquette . . . . . . . | .25 | .10 | .02 |
| 25 Ron LeFlore . . . . . . . . | .30 | .12 | .03 |
| 26 Mark Fidrych . . . . . . . | .30 | .12 | .03 |
| 27 Sixto Lezcano . . . . . . . | .25 | .10 | .02 |
| 28 Dave Winfield . . . . . . . | 2.25 | 1.00 | .22 |
| 29 Jerry Koosman . . . . . . | .30 | .12 | .03 |
| 30 Mike Hargrove . . . . . . | .25 | .10 | .02 |
| 31 Willie Montanez . . . . . | .25 | .10 | .02 |
| 32 Don Stanhouse . . . . . . | .25 | .10 | .02 |
| 33 Jay Johnstone . . . . . . | .25 | .10 | .02 |
| 34 Bake McBride . . . . . . . | .25 | .10 | .02 |
| 35 Dave Kingman . . . . . . | .60 | .28 | .06 |
| 36 Fred Patek . . . . . . . . . | .25 | .10 | .02 |
| 37 Garry Maddox . . . . . . | .30 | .12 | .03 |
| 38 Ken Reitz . . . . . . . . . . | .25 | .10 | .02 |
| 39 Bobby Grich . . . . . . . . | .30 | .12 | .03 |

| | MINT | VG-E | F-G |
|---|---|---|---|
| 40 Cesar Geronimo . . . . . . | .25 | .10 | .02 |
| 41 Jim Lonborg . . . . . . . . | .25 | .10 | .02 |
| 42 Ed Figueroa . . . . . . . . | .25 | .10 | .02 |
| 43 Bill Madlock . . . . . . . . | .80 | .40 | .08 |
| 44 Jerry Remy . . . . . . . . . | .25 | .10 | .02 |
| 45 Frank Tanana . . . . . . . | .30 | .12 | .03 |
| 46 Al Oliver . . . . . . . . . . . | .80 | .40 | .08 |
| 47 Charlie Hough . . . . . . . | .30 | .12 | .03 |
| 48 Lou Piniella . . . . . . . . | .40 | .18 | .04 |
| 49 Ken Griffey . . . . . . . . . | .30 | .12 | .03 |
| 50 Jose Cruz . . . . . . . . . . | .60 | .28 | .06 |
| 51 Rollie Fingers . . . . . . . | .80 | .40 | .08 |
| 52 Chris Chambliss . . . . . | .30 | .12 | .03 |
| 53 Rod Carew . . . . . . . . . | 2.00 | .90 | .20 |
| 54 Andy Messersmith . . . . | .30 | .12 | .03 |
| 55 Mickey Rivers . . . . . . . | .30 | .12 | .03 |
| 56 Butch Wynegar . . . . . . | .25 | .10 | .02 |
| 57 Steve Carlton . . . . . . . | 2.00 | .90 | .20 |

## 1978 KELLOGG

The cards in this 57 card set measure 2⅛"
by 3¼". This 1978 3-D Kellogg series
marks the first year in which Tony the Ti-
ger appears on the reverse of each card
next to the team and MLB logos. Once
again, the set could be obtained as individually wrapped cards in cereal boxes or as
a set via a mail in offer.

**Complete Set: M-21.00; VG-E-9.50; F-G-2.10**

| | MINT | VG-E | F-G |
|---|---|---|---|
| Common Player (1–57) . | .20 | .09 | .02 |
| 1 Steve Carlton . . . . . . . | 1.50 | .70 | .15 |
| 2 Bucky Dent . . . . . . . . . | .25 | .10 | .02 |
| 3 Mike Schmidt . . . . . . . | 2.00 | .90 | .20 |
| 4 Ken Griffey . . . . . . . . . | .25 | .10 | .02 |
| 5 Al Cowens . . . . . . . . . | .20 | .09 | .02 |

|  | MINT | VG-E | F-G |
|---|---|---|---|
| ☐ 6 George Brett | 2.50 | 1.15 | .25 |
| ☐ 7 Lou Brock | 1.25 | .60 | .12 |
| ☐ 8 Rich Gossage | .65 | .30 | .06 |
| ☐ 9 Tom Johnson | .20 | .09 | .02 |
| ☐ 10 George Foster | .65 | .30 | .06 |
| ☐ 11 Dave Winfield | 1.75 | .85 | .17 |
| ☐ 12 Dan Meyer | .20 | .09 | .02 |
| ☐ 13 Chris Chambliss | .25 | .10 | .02 |
| ☐ 14 Paul Dade | .20 | .09 | .02 |
| ☐ 15 Jeff Burroughs | .20 | .09 | .02 |
| ☐ 16 Jose Cruz | .35 | .15 | .03 |
| ☐ 17 Mickey Rivers | .25 | .10 | .02 |
| ☐ 18 John Candelaria | .25 | .10 | .02 |
| ☐ 19 Ellis Valentine | .20 | .09 | .02 |
| ☐ 20 Hal McRae | .25 | .10 | .02 |
| ☐ 21 Dave Rozema | .20 | .09 | .02 |
| ☐ 22 Lenny Randle | .20 | .09 | .02 |
| ☐ 23 Willie McCovey | 1.25 | .60 | .12 |
| ☐ 24 Ron Cey | .50 | .22 | .05 |
| ☐ 25 Eddie Murray | 4.00 | 1.85 | .40 |
| ☐ 26 Larry Bowa | .35 | .15 | .03 |
| ☐ 27 Tom Seaver | 1.50 | .70 | .15 |
| ☐ 28 Garry Maddox | .25 | .10 | .02 |
| ☐ 29 Rod Carew | 1.50 | .70 | .15 |
| ☐ 30 Thurman Munson | 1.50 | .70 | .15 |
| ☐ 31 Gary Templeton | .50 | .22 | .05 |
| ☐ 32 Eric Soderholm | .20 | .09 | .02 |
| ☐ 33 Greg Luzinski | .50 | .22 | .05 |
| ☐ 34 Reggie Smith | .25 | .10 | .02 |
| ☐ 35 Dave Goltz | .20 | .09 | .02 |
| ☐ 36 Tommy John | .60 | .28 | .06 |
| ☐ 37 Ralph Garr | .20 | .09 | .02 |
| ☐ 38 Alan Bannister | .20 | .09 | .02 |
| ☐ 39 Bob Bailor | .20 | .09 | .02 |
| ☐ 40 Reggie Jackson | 2.00 | .90 | .20 |
| ☐ 41 Cecil Cooper | .65 | .30 | .06 |
| ☐ 42 Burt Hooton | .20 | .09 | .02 |
| ☐ 43 Sparky Lyle | .30 | .12 | .03 |
| ☐ 44 Steve Ontiveros | .20 | .09 | .02 |
| ☐ 45 Rick Reuschel | .25 | .10 | .02 |
| ☐ 46 Lyman Bostock | .25 | .10 | .02 |
| ☐ 47 Mitchell Page | .20 | .09 | .02 |
| ☐ 48 Bruce Sutter | .75 | .35 | .07 |
| ☐ 49 Jim Rice | 1.25 | .60 | .12 |
| ☐ 50 Ken Forsch | .25 | .10 | .02 |
| ☐ 51 Nolan Ryan | 1.25 | .60 | .12 |
| ☐ 52 Dave Parker | .75 | .35 | .07 |
| ☐ 53 Bert Blyleven | .35 | .15 | .03 |
| ☐ 54 Frank Tanana | .25 | .10 | .02 |
| ☐ 55 Ken Singleton | .35 | .15 | .03 |
| ☐ 56 Mike Hargrove | .20 | .09 | .02 |
| ☐ 57 Don Sutton | .60 | .28 | .06 |

## 1979 KELLOGG

*The cards in this 60 card set measure 1 15/16" by 3 1/4". The 1979 edition of Kellogg's 3-D baseball cards have a 3/16" reduced width from the previous year; a nicely designed curved panel above the picture gives this set a distinctive appearance. The set contains the largest number of cards issued by Kellogg since the 1971 series.*

Complete Set: M-17.00; VG-E-8.00; F-G-1.70

|  | MINT | VG-E | F-G |
|---|---|---|---|
| Common Player (1–60) | .15 | .06 | .01 |
| ☐ 1 Bruce Sutter | .70 | .32 | .07 |
| ☐ 2 Ted Simmons | .40 | .18 | .04 |
| ☐ 3 Ross Grimsley | .15 | .06 | .01 |
| ☐ 4 Wayne Nordhagen | .15 | .06 | .01 |
| ☐ 5 Jim Palmer | 1.00 | .45 | .10 |
| ☐ 6 John Henry Johnson | .15 | .06 | .01 |
| ☐ 7 Jason Thompson | .30 | .12 | .03 |
| ☐ 8 Pat Zachry | .15 | .06 | .01 |
| ☐ 9 Dennis Eckersley | .20 | .09 | .02 |
| ☐ 10 Paul Splittorff | .20 | .09 | .02 |
| ☐ 11 Ron Guidry | 1.00 | .45 | .10 |
| ☐ 12 Jeff Burroughs | .15 | .06 | .01 |
| ☐ 13 Rod Carew | 1.50 | .70 | .15 |
| ☐ 14 Buddy Bell | .30 | .12 | .03 |
| ☐ 15 Jim Rice | 1.50 | .70 | .15 |
| ☐ 16 Garry Maddox | .20 | .09 | .02 |
| ☐ 17 Willie McCovey | 1.25 | .60 | .12 |
| ☐ 18 Steve Carlton | 1.50 | .70 | .15 |
| ☐ 19 J.R. Richard | .30 | .12 | .03 |
| ☐ 20 Paul Molitor | .40 | .18 | .04 |
| ☐ 21 Dave Parker | .60 | .28 | .06 |
| ☐ 22 Pete Rose | 3.50 | 1.65 | .35 |
| ☐ 23 Vida Blue | .30 | .12 | .03 |

|  | MINT | VG-E | F-G |
|---|---|---|---|
| ☐ 24 Richie Zisk ............. | .20 | .09 | .02 |
| ☐ 25 Darrell Porter ......... | .20 | .09 | .02 |
| ☐ 26 Dan Driessen ......... | .20 | .09 | .02 |
| ☐ 27 Jeff Zahn ............. | .15 | .06 | .01 |
| ☐ 28 Phil Niekro ........... | .75 | .35 | .07 |
| ☐ 29 Tom Seaver .......... | 1.25 | .60 | .12 |
| ☐ 30 Fred Lynn ............ | .60 | .28 | .06 |
| ☐ 31 Bill Bonham ......... | .15 | .06 | .01 |
| ☐ 32 George Foster ........ | .60 | .28 | .06 |
| ☐ 33 Terry Puhl ........... | .20 | .09 | .02 |
| ☐ 34 John Candelaria ...... | .20 | .09 | .02 |
| ☐ 35 Bob Knepper ......... | .20 | .09 | .02 |
| ☐ 36 Fred Patek ........... | .15 | .06 | .01 |
| ☐ 37 Chris Chambliss ...... | .20 | .09 | .02 |
| ☐ 38 Bob Forsch .......... | .15 | .06 | .01 |
| ☐ 39 Ken Griffey .......... | .20 | .09 | .02 |
| ☐ 40 Jack Clark ........... | .60 | .28 | .06 |
| ☐ 41 Dwight Evans ........ | .50 | .22 | .05 |
| ☐ 42 Lee Mazzilli ......... | .20 | .09 | .02 |
| ☐ 43 Mario Guerrero ...... | .15 | .06 | .01 |
| ☐ 44 Larry Bowa .......... | .30 | .12 | .03 |
| ☐ 45 Carl Yastrzemski .... | 2.00 | .90 | .20 |
| ☐ 46 Reggie Jackson ...... | 1.50 | .70 | .15 |
| ☐ 47 Rick Reuschel ....... | .20 | .09 | .02 |
| ☐ 48 Mike Flanagan ....... | .25 | .10 | .02 |
| ☐ 49 Gaylord Perry ....... | .60 | .28 | .06 |
| ☐ 50 George Brett ......... | 2.00 | .90 | .20 |
| ☐ 51 Craig Reynolds ...... | .15 | .06 | .01 |
| ☐ 52 Dave Lopes .......... | .25 | .10 | .02 |
| ☐ 53 Bill Almon ........... | .15 | .06 | .01 |
| ☐ 54 Roy Howell .......... | .15 | .06 | .01 |
| ☐ 55 Frank Tanana ........ | .20 | .09 | .02 |
| ☐ 56 Doug Rau ............ | .15 | .06 | .01 |
| ☐ 57 Rick Monday ......... | .20 | .09 | .02 |
| ☐ 58 Jon Matlack ......... | .20 | .09 | .02 |
| ☐ 59 Ron Jackson ......... | .15 | .06 | .01 |
| ☐ 60 Jim Sundberg ........ | .20 | .09 | .02 |

## 1980 KELLOGG

3-D SUPER STARS

The cards in this 60 card set measure 1⅞"
by 3¼". The 1980 Kellogg's 3-D set is
quite similar to, but smaller than, the other
recent Kellogg's issues. Sets could be obtained card by card from cereal boxes or
as a set from a box top offer from the company.

Complete Set: **M-13.00; VG-E-6.00; F-G-1.30**

|  | MINT | VG-E | F-G |
|---|---|---|---|
| Common Player (1–60) . | .15 | .06 | .01 |
| ☐ 1 Ross Grimsley ......... | .15 | .06 | .01 |
| ☐ 2 Mike Schmidt ......... | 1.25 | .60 | .12 |
| ☐ 3 Mike Flanagan ........ | .20 | .09 | .02 |
| ☐ 4 Ron Guidry ........... | .80 | .40 | .08 |
| ☐ 5 Bert Blyleven ......... | .30 | .12 | .03 |
| ☐ 6 Dave Kingman ........ | .35 | .15 | .03 |
| ☐ 7 Jeff Newman ......... | .15 | .06 | .01 |
| ☐ 8 Steve Rogers ........ | .25 | .10 | .02 |
| ☐ 9 George Brett ......... | 1.50 | .70 | .15 |
| ☐ 10 Bruce Sutter ......... | .65 | .30 | .06 |
| ☐ 11 Gorman Thomas ...... | .30 | .12 | .03 |
| ☐ 12 Darrell Porter ........ | .20 | .09 | .02 |
| ☐ 13 Roy Smalley ......... | .20 | .09 | .02 |
| ☐ 14 Steve Carlton ........ | 1.25 | .60 | .12 |
| ☐ 15 Jim Palmer .......... | .80 | .40 | .08 |
| ☐ 16 Bob Bailor .......... | .15 | .06 | .01 |
| ☐ 17 Jason Thompson ..... | .25 | .10 | .02 |
| ☐ 18 Graig Nettles ........ | .35 | .15 | .03 |
| ☐ 19 Ron Cey ............ | .30 | .12 | .03 |
| ☐ 20 Nolan Ryan .......... | 1.00 | .45 | .10 |
| ☐ 21 Ellis Valentine ....... | .15 | .06 | .01 |
| ☐ 22 Larry Hisle .......... | .20 | .09 | .02 |
| ☐ 23 Dave Parker ......... | .60 | .28 | .06 |
| ☐ 24 Eddie Murray ........ | 1.50 | .70 | .15 |
| ☐ 25 Willie Stargell ....... | .60 | .28 | .06 |
| ☐ 26 Reggie Jackson ...... | 1.50 | .70 | .15 |
| ☐ 27 Carl Yastrzemski .... | 1.50 | .70 | .15 |
| ☐ 28 Andre Thorton ....... | .25 | .10 | .02 |
| ☐ 29 Dave Lopes .......... | .20 | .09 | .02 |
| ☐ 30 Ken Singleton ....... | .25 | .10 | .02 |
| ☐ 31 Steve Garvey ........ | 1.25 | .60 | .12 |
| ☐ 32 Dave Winfield ........ | 1.25 | .60 | .12 |
| ☐ 33 Steve Kemp ......... | .20 | .09 | .02 |
| ☐ 34 Claudell Washington . | .20 | .09 | .02 |
| ☐ 35 Pete Rose ........... | 3.00 | 1.40 | .30 |
| ☐ 36 Cesar Cedeno ....... | .20 | .09 | .02 |
| ☐ 37 John Stearns ........ | .15 | .06 | .01 |
| ☐ 38 Lee Mazzilli ......... | .15 | .06 | .01 |
| ☐ 39 Larry Bowa .......... | .25 | .10 | .02 |
| ☐ 40 Fred Lynn ........... | .50 | .22 | .05 |
| ☐ 41 Carlton Fisk ......... | .60 | .28 | .06 |

|  | | MINT | VG-E | F-G |
|---|---|---|---|---|
| ☐ 42 | Vida Blue | .25 | .10 | .02 |
| ☐ 43 | Keith Hernandez | .80 | .40 | .08 |
| ☐ 44 | Ted Simmons | .35 | .15 | .03 |
| ☐ 45 | Chet Lemon | .20 | .09 | .02 |
| ☐ 46 | Jim Rice | .80 | .40 | .08 |
| ☐ 47 | Ferguson Jenkins | .25 | .10 | .02 |
| ☐ 48 | Gary Matthews | .20 | .09 | .02 |
| ☐ 49 | Tom Seaver | 1.00 | .45 | .10 |
| ☐ 50 | George Foster | .60 | .28 | .06 |
| ☐ 51 | Phil Niekro | .75 | .35 | .07 |
| ☐ 52 | Johnny Bench | 1.00 | .45 | .10 |
| ☐ 53 | Buddy Bell | .30 | .12 | .03 |
| ☐ 54 | Lance Parrish | .75 | .30 | .07 |
| ☐ 55 | Joaquin Andujar | .25 | .10 | .02 |
| ☐ 56 | Don Baylor | .35 | .15 | .03 |
| ☐ 57 | Jack Clark | .50 | .22 | .05 |
| ☐ 58 | J.R. Richard | .25 | .10 | .02 |
| ☐ 59 | Bruce Bochte | .20 | .09 | .02 |
| ☐ 60 | Rod Carew | 1.00 | .45 | .10 |

## 1981 KELLOGG

*The cards in this 66 card set measure 2½" by 3½". The 1981 Kellogg set witnessed an increase in both the size of the card and the size of the set. For the first time, cards were not packed in cereal sizes but available only by mail in procedure. The offer for the card set was advertised on boxes of Kellogg's Corn Flakes. The cards were printed on a different stock than in previous years, presumably to prevent the cracking problem which has plagued all Kellogg's 3-D issues.*

Complete Set: M-5.50; VG-E-2.60; F-G-.55

Common Player ....... .06 .02 .00

|  | | MINT | VG-E | F-G |
|---|---|---|---|---|
| ☐ 1 | George Foster | .15 | .06 | .01 |
| ☐ 2 | Jim Palmer | .25 | .10 | .02 |
| ☐ 3 | Reggie Jackson | .60 | .28 | .06 |
| ☐ 4 | Al Oliver | .10 | .04 | .01 |
| ☐ 5 | Mike Schmidt | .60 | .28 | .06 |
| ☐ 6 | Nolan Ryan | .25 | .10 | .02 |
| ☐ 7 | Bucky Dent | .07 | .03 | .01 |
| ☐ 8 | George Brett | .60 | .28 | .06 |
| ☐ 9 | Jim Rice | .25 | .10 | .02 |
| ☐ 10 | Steve Garvey | .40 | .18 | .04 |
| ☐ 11 | Willie Stargell | .15 | .06 | .01 |
| ☐ 12 | Phil Niekro | .15 | .06 | .01 |
| ☐ 13 | Dave Parker | .15 | .06 | .01 |
| ☐ 14 | Cesar Cedeno | .07 | .03 | .01 |
| ☐ 15 | Don Baylor | .08 | .03 | .01 |
| ☐ 16 | J.R. Richard | .07 | .03 | .01 |
| ☐ 17 | Tony Perez | .10 | .04 | .01 |
| ☐ 18 | Eddie Murray | .50 | .22 | .05 |
| ☐ 19 | Chet Lemon | .08 | .03 | .01 |
| ☐ 20 | Ben Oglivie | .07 | .03 | .01 |
| ☐ 21 | Dave Winfield | .40 | .18 | .04 |
| ☐ 22 | Joe Morgan | .20 | .09 | .02 |
| ☐ 23 | Vida Blue | .07 | .03 | .01 |
| ☐ 24 | Willie Wilson | .15 | .06 | .01 |
| ☐ 25 | Steve Henderson | .06 | .02 | .00 |
| ☐ 26 | Rod Carew | .40 | .18 | .04 |
| ☐ 27 | Garry Templeton | .10 | .04 | .01 |
| ☐ 28 | Dave Concepcion | .10 | .04 | .01 |
| ☐ 29 | Dave Lopes | .07 | .03 | .01 |
| ☐ 30 | Ken Landreaux | .06 | .02 | .00 |
| ☐ 31 | Keith Hernandez | .30 | .12 | .03 |
| ☐ 32 | Cecil Cooper | .15 | .06 | .01 |
| ☐ 33 | Rickey Henderson | .40 | .18 | .04 |
| ☐ 34 | Frank White | .08 | .03 | .01 |
| ☐ 35 | George Hendrick | .08 | .03 | .01 |
| ☐ 36 | Reggie Smith | .07 | .03 | .01 |
| ☐ 37 | Tug McGraw | .06 | .02 | .00 |
| ☐ 38 | Tom Seaver | .40 | .18 | .04 |
| ☐ 39 | Ken Singleton | .09 | .04 | .01 |
| ☐ 40 | Fred Lynn | .15 | .06 | .01 |
| ☐ 41 | Rich Gossage | .15 | .06 | .01 |
| ☐ 42 | Terry Puhl | .06 | .02 | .00 |
| ☐ 43 | Larry Bowa | .07 | .03 | .01 |
| ☐ 44 | Phil Garner | .06 | .02 | .00 |
| ☐ 45 | Ron Guidry | .20 | .09 | .02 |
| ☐ 46 | Lee Mazzilli | .06 | .02 | .00 |
| ☐ 47 | Dave Kingman | .10 | .04 | .01 |
| ☐ 48 | Carl Yastrzemski | .60 | .28 | .06 |
| ☐ 49 | Rick Burleson | .07 | .03 | .01 |
| ☐ 50 | Steve Carlton | .40 | .18 | .04 |
| ☐ 51 | Alan Trammell | .20 | .09 | .02 |
| ☐ 52 | Tommy John | .15 | .06 | .01 |
| ☐ 53 | Paul Molitor | .15 | .06 | .01 |

| | | MINT | VG-E | F-G |
|---|---|---|---|---|
| ☐ 54 | Joe Charbonneau | .07 | .03 | .01 |
| ☐ 55 | Rick Langford | .06 | .02 | .00 |
| ☐ 56 | Bruce Sutter | .15 | .06 | .01 |
| ☐ 57 | Robin Yount | .25 | .10 | .02 |
| ☐ 58 | Steve Stone | .06 | .02 | .00 |
| ☐ 59 | Larry Gura | .06 | .02 | .00 |
| ☐ 60 | Mike Flanagan | .07 | .03 | .01 |
| ☐ 61 | Bob Horner | .20 | .09 | .02 |
| ☐ 62 | Bruce Bochte | .06 | .02 | .00 |
| ☐ 63 | Pete Rose | .90 | .40 | .09 |
| ☐ 64 | Buddy Bell | .10 | .04 | .01 |
| ☐ 65 | Johnny Bench | .35 | .15 | .03 |
| ☐ 66 | Mike Hargrove | .06 | .02 | .00 |

## 1982 KELLOGG

The cards in this 64 card set measure 2⅛"
by 3¼". The 1982 version of 3-D cards
prepared for Kellogg by Visual Pan-
ographics, Inc., is not only smaller in physical dimensions from the 1981 series
(which was standard card size at 2½" by
3½") but is also two cards shorter in length
(64 in '82 and 66 in '81). In addition, while
retaining the policy of not inserting single
cards into cereal packages and offering
the sets through box top mail-ins only, Kellogg accepted box tops from four types of
cereals, as opposed to only one type the
previous year. Each card features a color
3-D ballplayer picture with a vertical line of
white stars on each side set upon a blue
background. The player's name and the
word Kellogg's are printed in red on the
obverse, and the card number is found on
the bottom right of the reverse.
Complete Set: M-8.00; VG-E-3.75; F-G-.80

| | | MINT | VG-E | F-G |
|---|---|---|---|---|
| | Common Player | .06 | .02 | .00 |
| ☐ 1 | Richie Zisk | .07 | .03 | .01 |
| ☐ 2 | Bill Buckner | .10 | .04 | .01 |
| ☐ 3 | George Brett | .60 | .28 | .06 |
| ☐ 4 | Rickey Henderson | .50 | .22 | .05 |
| ☐ 5 | Jack Morris | .12 | .05 | .01 |
| ☐ 6 | Ozzie Smith | .10 | .04 | .01 |
| ☐ 7 | Rollie Fingers | .15 | .06 | .01 |
| ☐ 8 | Tom Seaver | .40 | .18 | .04 |
| ☐ 9 | Fernando Valuenzuela | .30 | .12 | .03 |
| ☐ 10 | Hubie Brooks | .08 | .03 | .01 |
| ☐ 11 | Nolan Ryan | .35 | .15 | .03 |
| ☐ 12 | Dave Winfield | .35 | .15 | .03 |
| ☐ 13 | Bob Horner | .20 | .09 | .02 |
| ☐ 14 | Reggie Jackson | .50 | .22 | .05 |
| ☐ 15 | Burt Hooton | .06 | .02 | .00 |
| ☐ 16 | Mike Schmidt | .50 | .22 | .05 |
| ☐ 17 | Bruce Sutter | .15 | .06 | .01 |
| ☐ 18 | Pete Rose | .90 | .40 | .09 |
| ☐ 19 | Dave Kingman | .12 | .05 | .01 |
| ☐ 20 | Neil Allen | .06 | .02 | .00 |
| ☐ 21 | Don Sutton | .15 | .06 | .01 |
| ☐ 22 | Dave Concepcion | .10 | .04 | .01 |
| ☐ 23 | Keith Hernandez | .25 | .10 | .02 |
| ☐ 24 | Gary Carter | .35 | .15 | .03 |
| ☐ 25 | Carlton Fisk | .20 | .09 | .02 |
| ☐ 26 | Ron Guidry | .20 | .09 | .02 |
| ☐ 27 | Steve Carlton | .30 | .12 | .03 |
| ☐ 28 | Robin Yount | .25 | .10 | .02 |
| ☐ 29 | John Castino | .07 | .03 | .01 |
| ☐ 30 | Johnny Bench | .30 | .12 | .03 |
| ☐ 31 | Bob Knepper | .07 | .03 | .01 |
| ☐ 32 | Rich Gossage | .15 | .06 | .01 |
| ☐ 33 | Buddy Bell | .10 | .04 | .01 |
| ☐ 34 | Art Howe | .06 | .02 | .00 |
| ☐ 35 | Tony Armas | .10 | .04 | .01 |
| ☐ 36 | Phil Niekro | .15 | .06 | .01 |
| ☐ 37 | Len Barker | .07 | .03 | .01 |
| ☐ 38 | Bob Grich | .09 | .04 | .01 |
| ☐ 39 | Steve Kemp | .10 | .04 | .01 |
| ☐ 40 | Kirk Gibson | .20 | .09 | .02 |
| ☐ 41 | Carney Lansford | .11 | .05 | .01 |
| ☐ 42 | Jim Palmer | .25 | .10 | .02 |
| ☐ 43 | Carl Yastrzemski | .50 | .22 | .05 |
| ☐ 44 | Rick Burleson | .07 | .03 | .01 |
| ☐ 45 | Dwight Evans | .10 | .04 | .01 |
| ☐ 46 | Ron Cey | .10 | .04 | .01 |
| ☐ 47 | Steve Garvey | .45 | .20 | .04 |
| ☐ 48 | Dave Parker | .20 | .09 | .02 |
| ☐ 49 | Mike Easler | .07 | .03 | .01 |
| ☐ 50 | Dusty Baker | .08 | .03 | .01 |
| ☐ 51 | Rod Carew | .35 | .15 | .03 |

| | MINT | VG-E | F-G |
|---|---|---|---|
| 52 Chris Chambliss | .07 | .03 | .01 |
| 53 Tim Raines | .25 | .10 | .02 |
| 54 Chet Lemon | .08 | .03 | .01 |
| 55 Bill Madlock | .15 | .06 | .01 |
| 56 George Foster | .15 | .06 | .01 |
| 57 Dwayne Murphy | .07 | .03 | .01 |
| 58 Ken Singleton | .10 | .04 | .01 |
| 59 Mike Norris | .06 | .02 | .00 |
| 60 Cecil Cooper | .15 | .06 | .01 |
| 61 Al Oliver | .15 | .06 | .01 |
| 62 Willie Wilson | .15 | .06 | .01 |
| 63 Vida Blue | .10 | .04 | .01 |
| 64 Eddie Murray | .50 | .22 | .05 |

## 1983 KELLOGG

*The cards in this 60 card set measure 1⅞"*
*by 3¼". For the 14th year in a row, Kellogg*
*issued a card set of Major League players.*
*The set of 3-D cards contains the photo,*
*player's autograph, Kellogg's logo, and*
*name and position of the player on the*
*front of the card. The backs feature the*
*player's team logo, career statistics,*
*player biography, and a narrative on the*
*player's career.*

Complete Set: M-9.00; VG-E-4.25; F-G-.90

| Common Player | .06 | .02 | .00 |
|---|---|---|---|
| 1 Rod Carew | .40 | .18 | .04 |
| 2 Rollie Fingers | .15 | .06 | .01 |
| 3 Reggie Jackson | .50 | .22 | .05 |
| 4 George Brett | .60 | .28 | .06 |
| 5 Hal McRae | .08 | .03 | .01 |
| 6 Pete Rose | .80 | .40 | .08 |
| 7 Fernando Valenzuela | .25 | .10 | .02 |

| | MINT | VG-E | F-G |
|---|---|---|---|
| 8 Rickey Henderson | .40 | .18 | .04 |
| 9 Carl Yastrzemski | .50 | .22 | .05 |
| 10 Rich Gossage | .15 | .06 | .01 |
| 11 Eddie Murray | .45 | .20 | .04 |
| 12 Buddy Bell | .10 | .04 | .01 |
| 13 Jim Rice | .25 | .10 | .02 |
| 14 Robin Yount | .25 | .10 | .02 |
| 15 Dave Winfield | .30 | .12 | .03 |
| 16 Harold Baines | .15 | .06 | .01 |
| 17 Garry Templeton | .08 | .03 | .01 |
| 18 Bill Madlock | .15 | .06 | .01 |
| 19 Pete Vuckovich | .08 | .03 | .01 |
| 20 Pedro Guerrero | .20 | .09 | .02 |
| 21 Ozzie Smith | .10 | .04 | .01 |
| 22 George Foster | .15 | .06 | .01 |
| 23 Willie Wilson | .15 | .06 | .01 |
| 24 Johnny Ray | .10 | .04 | .01 |
| 25 George Hendrick | .08 | .03 | .01 |
| 26 Andre Thorton | .10 | .04 | .01 |
| 27 Leon Durham | .12 | .05 | .01 |
| 28 Cecil Cooper | .15 | .06 | .01 |
| 29 Don Baylor | .10 | .04 | .01 |
| 30 Lonnie Smith | .10 | .04 | .01 |
| 31 Nolan Ryan | .25 | .10 | .02 |
| 32 Dan Quisenberry | .15 | .06 | .01 |
| 33 Len Barker | .08 | .03 | .01 |
| 34 Neil Allen | .08 | .03 | .01 |
| 35 Jack Morris | .15 | .06 | .01 |
| 36 Dave Stieb | .15 | .06 | .01 |
| 37 Bruce Sutter | .15 | .06 | .01 |
| 38 Jim Sundberg | .06 | .02 | .00 |
| 39 Jim Palmer | .25 | .10 | .02 |
| 40 Lance Parrish | .20 | .09 | .02 |
| 41 Floyd Bannister | .08 | .03 | .01 |
| 42 Larry Gura | .06 | .02 | .00 |
| 43 Britt Burns | .08 | .03 | .01 |
| 44 Toby Harrah | .08 | .03 | .01 |
| 45 Steve Carlton | .30 | .12 | .03 |
| 46 Greg Minton | .06 | .02 | .00 |
| 47 Gorman Thomas | .08 | .03 | .01 |
| 48 Jack Clark | .15 | .06 | .01 |
| 49 Keith Hernandez | .20 | .09 | .02 |
| 50 Greg Luzinski | .10 | .04 | .01 |
| 51 Fred Lynn | .15 | .06 | .01 |
| 52 Dale Murphy | .50 | .22 | .05 |
| 53 Kent Hrbek | .25 | .10 | .02 |
| 54 Bob Horner | .20 | .09 | .02 |
| 55 Gary Carter | .30 | .12 | .03 |
| 56 Carlton Fisk | .15 | .06 | .01 |
| 57 Dave Concepcion | .10 | .04 | .01 |
| 58 Mike Schmidt | .45 | .20 | .04 |
| 59 Bill Buckner | .10 | .04 | .01 |
| 60 Bob Grich | .08 | .03 | .01 |

## 1975 HOSTESS

er Edward Rose

PETE ROSE
OUTFIELD
**Cincinnati REDS**

*The cards in this 150 card set measure 2¼" by 3¼" individually, or 3¼" by 7¼" as panels of three. The 1975 Hostess set was issued in panels of three cards each on the backs of family-sized packages of Hostess cakes. Card number 125, Bill Madlock, was listed correctly as an infielder and incorrectly as a pitcher. Number 11, Burt Hooten, and number 89, Dave Radar, are spelled two different ways. Some panels are more scarce than others as they were issued only on the backs of less popular Hostess products. These scarcer panels are shown with asterisks in the checklist. Although complete panel prices are not explicitly listed, they would generally have a value 25% greater than the sum of the values of the individual players on that panel.*

**Complete Indiv. Set: M-100.00; VG-E-45.00; F-G-10.00**

|  | MINT | VG-E | F-G |
|---|---|---|---|
| Common Player ........ | .30 | .12 | .03 |
| ☐ 1 Bob Tolan ............ | .30 | .12 | .03 |
| ☐ 2 Cookie Rojas ......... | .30 | .12 | .03 |
| ☐ 3 Darrell Evans ........ | .40 | .18 | .04 |
| ☐ 4 Sal Bando ........... | .30 | .12 | .03 |
| ☐ 5 Joe Morgan .......... | 1.50 | .70 | .15 |
| ☐ 6 Mickey Lolich ........ | .40 | .18 | .04 |
| ☐ 7 Don Sutton .......... | .60 | .28 | .06 |
| ☐ 8 Bill Melton .......... | .30 | .12 | .03 |
| ☐ 9 Tim Foli ............ | .30 | .12 | .03 |
| ☐ 10 Joe Lahoud ......... | .30 | .12 | .03 |
| ☐ 11 A Bert Hooten (sic) .. | 1.00 | .45 | .10 |
| ☐ 11 B Burt Hooten ...... | 1.00 | .45 | .10 |

|  | MINT | VG-E | F-G |
|---|---|---|---|
| ☐ 12 Paul Blair ........... | .30 | .12 | .03 |
| ☐ 13 Jim Barr ........... | .30 | .12 | .03 |
| ☐ 14 Toby Harrah ........ | .40 | .18 | .04 |
| ☐ 15 John Milner ......... | .30 | .12 | .03 |
| ☐ 16 Ken Holtzman ....... | .40 | .18 | .04 |
| ☐ 17 Cesar Cedeno ....... | .40 | .18 | .04 |
| ☐ 18 Dwight Evans ....... | .60 | .28 | .06 |
| ☐ 19 Willie McCovey ...... | 2.00 | .90 | .20 |
| ☐ 20 Tony Oliva ......... | .60 | .28 | .06 |
| ☐ 21 Manny Sanguillen ... | .30 | .12 | .03 |
| ☐ 22 Mickey Rivers ....... | .30 | .12 | .03 |
| ☐ 23 Lou Brock .......... | 2.00 | .90 | .20 |
| ☐ 24 Graig Nettles ....... | .60 | .28 | .06 |
| ☐ 25 Jim Wynn .......... | .30 | .12 | .03 |
| ☐ 26 George Scott ....... | .30 | .12 | .03 |
| ☐ 27 Greg Luzinski ....... | .50 | .22 | .05 |
| ☐ 28 Bert Campaneris .... | .40 | .18 | .04 |
| ☐ 29 Pete Rose .......... | 6.00 | 2.80 | .60 |
| ☐ 30 Buddy Bell ......... | .50 | .22 | .05 |
| ☐ 31 Gary Matthews ..... | .40 | .18 | .04 |
| ☐ 32 Freddie Patek ...... | .30 | .12 | .03 |
| ☐ 33 Mike Lum .......... | .30 | .12 | .03 |
| ☐ 34 Ellie Rodriguez ..... | .30 | .12 | .03 |
| ☐ 35 Milt May .......... | .50 | .22 | .05 |
| (photo actually Lee May) | | | |
| ☐ 36 Willie Horton ....... | .40 | .18 | .04 |
| ☐ 37 Dave Winfield ...... | 3.00 | 1.40 | .30 |
| ☐ 38 Tom Grieve ........ | .40 | .18 | .04 |
| ☐ 39 Barry Foote ........ | .30 | .12 | .03 |
| ☐ 40 Joe Rudi ........... | .30 | .12 | .03 |
| ☐ 41 Bake McBride ...... | .30 | .12 | .03 |
| ☐ 42 Mike Cuellar ....... | .40 | .18 | .04 |
| ☐ 43 Garry Maddox ...... | .30 | .12 | .03 |
| ☐ 44 Carlos May ........ | .30 | .12 | .03 |
| ☐ 45 Bud Harrelson ..... | .30 | .12 | .03 |
| ☐ 46 Dave Chalk ........ | .30 | .12 | .03 |
| ☐ 47 Dave Concepcion ... | .40 | .18 | .04 |
| ☐ 48 Carl Yastrzemski ... | 4.00 | 1.85 | .40 |
| ☐ 49 Steve Garvey ...... | 3.00 | 1.40 | .30 |
| ☐ 50 Amos Otis ......... | .40 | .18 | .04 |
| ☐ 51 Rick Reuschel ...... | .40 | .18 | .04 |
| ☐ 52 Rollie Fingers ...... | .80 | .40 | .08 |
| ☐ 53 Bob Watson ........ | .40 | .18 | .04 |
| ☐ 54 John Ellis ......... | .30 | .12 | .03 |
| ☐ 55 Bob Bailey ......... | .30 | .12 | .03 |
| ☐ 56 Rod Carew ........ | 3.00 | 1.40 | .30 |
| ☐ 57 Rich Hebner ....... | .30 | .12 | .03 |
| ☐ 58 Nolan Ryan ........ | 3.00 | 1.40 | .30 |
| ☐ 59 Reggie Smith ...... | .40 | .18 | .04 |
| ☐ 60 Joe Coleman ....... | .30 | .12 | .03 |
| ☐ 61 Ron Cey .......... | .50 | .22 | .05 |
| ☐ 62 Darrell Porter ...... | .40 | .18 | .04 |

| | MINT | VG-E | F-G |
|---|---|---|---|
| ☐ 63 Steve Carlton | 3.00 | 1.40 | .30 |
| ☐ 64 Gene Tenace | .30 | .12 | .03 |
| ☐ 65 Jose Cardenal | .30 | .12 | .03 |
| ☐ 66 Bill Lee | .30 | .12 | .03 |
| ☐ 67 Dave Lopes | .40 | .18 | .04 |
| ☐ 68 Wilbur Wood | .30 | .12 | .03 |
| ☐ 69 Steve Renko | .30 | .12 | .03 |
| ☐ 70 Joe Torre | .50 | .22 | .05 |
| ☐ 71 Ted Sizemore | .30 | .12 | .03 |
| ☐ 72 Bobby Grich | .40 | .18 | .04 |
| ☐ 73 Chris Speier | .30 | .12 | .03 |
| ☐ 74 Bert Blyleven | .60 | .28 | .06 |
| ☐ 75 Tom Seaver | 3.00 | 1.40 | .30 |
| ☐ 76 Nate Colbert | .30 | .12 | .03 |
| ☐ 77 Don Kessinger | .30 | .12 | .03 |
| ☐ 78 George Medich | .30 | .12 | .03 |
| ☐ 79 Andy Messersmith* | .50 | .22 | .05 |
| ☐ 80 Robin Yount* | 5.00 | 2.35 | .50 |
| ☐ 81 Al Oliver* | 1.25 | .60 | .12 |
| ☐ 82 Bill Singer* | .40 | .18 | .04 |
| ☐ 83 Johnny Bench* | 4.00 | 1.85 | .40 |
| ☐ 84 Gaylord Perry* | 2.00 | .90 | .20 |
| ☐ 85 Dave Kingman* | 1.00 | .45 | .10 |
| ☐ 86 Ed Herrmann* | .40 | .18 | .04 |
| ☐ 87 Ralph Garr* | .40 | .18 | .04 |
| ☐ 88 Reggie Jackson* | 5.00 | 2.35 | .50 |
| ☐ 89 A Doug Radar ERR* | 1.00 | .40 | .10 |
| (sic, Rader) | | | |
| ☐ 89 B Doug Rader COR* | 2.00 | .90 | .20 |
| ☐ 90 Elliott Maddox* | .40 | .18 | .04 |
| ☐ 91 Bill Russell* | .50 | .22 | .05 |
| ☐ 92 John Mayberry* | .40 | .18 | .04 |
| ☐ 93 Dave Cash* | .40 | .18 | .04 |
| ☐ 94 Jeff Burroughs* | .40 | .18 | .04 |
| ☐ 95 Ted Simmons* | 1.00 | .45 | .10 |
| ☐ 96 Joe Decker* | .40 | .18 | .04 |
| ☐ 97 Bill Buckner* | 1.00 | .45 | .10 |
| ☐ 98 Bobby Darwin* | .40 | .18 | .04 |
| ☐ 99 Phil Niekro* | 2.00 | .90 | .20 |
| ☐ 100 Jim Sundberg | .40 | .18 | .04 |
| ☐ 101 Greg Gross | .30 | .12 | .03 |
| ☐ 102 Luis Tiant | .40 | .18 | .04 |
| ☐ 103 Glenn Beckert | .30 | .12 | .03 |
| ☐ 104 Hal McRae | .40 | .18 | .04 |
| ☐ 105 Mike Jorgensen | .30 | .12 | .03 |
| ☐ 106 Mike Hargrove | .30 | .12 | .03 |
| ☐ 107 Don Gullett | .30 | .12 | .03 |
| ☐ 108 Tito Fuentes | .30 | .12 | .03 |
| ☐ 109 John Grubb | .30 | .12 | .03 |
| ☐ 110 Jim Kaat | .60 | .28 | .06 |
| ☐ 111 Felix Millan | .30 | .12 | .03 |
| ☐ 112 Don Money | .30 | .12 | .03 |
| ☐ 113 Rick Monday | .40 | .18 | .04 |

| | MINT | VG-E | F-G |
|---|---|---|---|
| ☐ 114 Dick Bosman | .30 | .12 | .03 |
| ☐ 115 Roger Metzger | .30 | .12 | .03 |
| ☐ 116 Fergie Jenkins | .60 | .28 | .06 |
| ☐ 117 Dusty Baker | .50 | .22 | .05 |
| ☐ 118 Billy Champion* | .40 | .18 | .04 |
| ☐ 119 Bob Gibson* | 2.50 | 1.15 | .25 |
| ☐ 120 Bill Freehan* | .50 | .22 | .05 |
| ☐ 121 Cesar Geronimo | .30 | .12 | .03 |
| ☐ 122 Jorge Orta | .30 | .12 | .03 |
| ☐ 123 Cleon Jones | .30 | .12 | .03 |
| ☐ 124 Steve Busby | .30 | .12 | .03 |
| ☐ 125 A Bill Madlock ERR | 1.50 | .70 | .15 |
| ☐ 125 B Bill Madlock COR | 1.50 | .70 | .15 |
| ☐ 126 Jim Palmer | 2.00 | .90 | .20 |
| ☐ 127 Tony Perez | .60 | .28 | .06 |
| ☐ 128 Larry Hisle | .40 | .18 | .04 |
| ☐ 129 Rusty Staub | .50 | .22 | .05 |
| ☐ 130 Hank Aaron* | 5.00 | 2.35 | .50 |
| ☐ 131 Rennie Stennett* | .40 | .18 | .04 |
| ☐ 132 Rico Petrocelli* | .50 | .22 | .05 |
| ☐ 133 Mike Schmidt | 3.50 | 1.65 | .35 |
| ☐ 134 Sparky Lyle | .50 | .22 | .05 |
| ☐ 135 Willie Stargell | 1.50 | .70 | .15 |
| ☐ 136 Ken Henderson | .30 | .12 | .03 |
| ☐ 137 Willie Montanez | .30 | .12 | .03 |
| ☐ 138 Thurman Munson | 2.50 | 1.15 | .25 |
| ☐ 139 Richie Zisk | .40 | .18 | .04 |
| ☐ 140 George Hendrick | .40 | .18 | .04 |
| ☐ 141 Bobby Murcer | .50 | .22 | .05 |
| ☐ 142 Lee May | .40 | .18 | .04 |
| ☐ 143 Carlton Fisk | .75 | .35 | .07 |
| ☐ 144 Brooks Robinson | 2.50 | 1.15 | .25 |
| ☐ 145 Bobby Bonds | .40 | .18 | .04 |
| ☐ 146 Gary Sutherland | .30 | .12 | .03 |
| ☐ 147 Oscar Gamble | .30 | .12 | .03 |
| ☐ 148 Jim Hunter | .90 | .40 | .09 |
| ☐ 149 Tug McGraw | .50 | .22 | .05 |
| ☐ 150 Dave McNally | .40 | .18 | .04 |

## 1976 HOSTESS

David Gene Parker

**DAVE PARKER**
Pittsburgh PIRATES

The cards in this 150 card set measure 2¼" by 3¼" individually, or 3¼" by 7¼" as panels of three. The 1976 Hostess set contains color, numbered cards issued in panels of three each each contained in family sized packages of Hostess cakes. Scarcer panels (those only found on less popular Hostess products) are listed in the checklist below with asterisks. Complete panels of three have a value 25% more than the sum of the individual cards on the panel.

Complete Indiv. Set: M-100.00; VG-E-45.00; F-G-10.00

| | | MINT | VG-E | F-G |
|---|---|---|---|---|
| | Common Player | .30 | .12 | .03 |
| ☐ 1 | Fred Lynn | 1.50 | .70 | .15 |
| ☐ 2 | Joe Morgan | 1.50 | .70 | .15 |
| ☐ 3 | Phil Niekro | 1.50 | .70 | .15 |
| ☐ 4 | Gaylord Perry | 1.50 | .70 | .15 |
| ☐ 5 | Bob Watson | .40 | .18 | .04 |
| ☐ 6 | Bill Freehan | .40 | .18 | .04 |
| ☐ 7 | Lou Brock | 2.00 | .90 | .20 |
| ☐ 8 | Al Fitzmorris | .30 | .12 | .03 |
| ☐ 9 | Rennie Stennett | .30 | .12 | .03 |
| ☐ 10 | Tony Oliva | .60 | .28 | .06 |
| ☐ 11 | Robin Yount | 2.50 | 1.15 | .25 |
| ☐ 12 | Rick Manning | .30 | .12 | .03 |
| ☐ 13 | Bobby Grich | .40 | .18 | .04 |
| ☐ 14 | Terry Forster | .40 | .18 | .04 |
| ☐ 15 | Dave Kingman | .60 | .28 | .06 |
| ☐ 16 | Thurman Munson | 2.50 | 1.15 | .25 |
| ☐ 17 | Rick Reuschel | .40 | .18 | .04 |
| ☐ 18 | Bobby Bonds | .40 | .18 | .04 |
| ☐ 19 | Steve Garvey | 3.00 | 1.40 | .30 |
| ☐ 20 | Vida Blue | .40 | .18 | .04 |
| ☐ 21 | Dave Rader | .30 | .12 | .03 |

| | | MINT | VG-E | F-G |
|---|---|---|---|---|
| ☐ 22 | Johnny Bench | 2.50 | 1.15 | .25 |
| ☐ 23 | Luis Tiant | .50 | .22 | .05 |
| ☐ 24 | Darrell Evans | .50 | .22 | .05 |
| ☐ 25 | Larry Dierker | .30 | .12 | .03 |
| ☐ 26 | Willie Horton | .40 | .18 | .04 |
| ☐ 27 | John Ellis | .30 | .12 | .03 |
| ☐ 28 | Al Cowens | .40 | .18 | .04 |
| ☐ 29 | Jerry Reuss | .40 | .18 | .04 |
| ☐ 30 | Reggie Smith | .40 | .18 | .04 |
| ☐ 31 | Bobby Darwin* | .40 | .18 | .04 |
| ☐ 32 | Fritz Peterson* | .40 | .18 | .04 |
| ☐ 33 | Rod Carew* | 4.00 | 1.85 | .40 |
| ☐ 34 | Carlos May* | .40 | .18 | .04 |
| ☐ 35 | Tom Seaver* | 4.00 | 1.85 | .40 |
| ☐ 36 | Brooks Robinson* | 4.00 | 1.85 | .40 |
| ☐ 37 | Jose Cardenal | .30 | .12 | .03 |
| ☐ 38 | Ron Blomberg | .30 | .12 | .03 |
| ☐ 39 | Leroy Stanton | .30 | .12 | .03 |
| ☐ 40 | Dave Cash | .30 | .12 | .03 |
| ☐ 41 | John Montefusco | .30 | .12 | .03 |
| ☐ 42 | Bob Tolan | .30 | .12 | .03 |
| ☐ 43 | Carl Morton | .30 | .12 | .03 |
| ☐ 44 | Rick Burleson | .40 | .18 | .04 |
| ☐ 45 | Don Gullett | .30 | .12 | .03 |
| ☐ 46 | Vern Ruhle | .30 | .12 | .03 |
| ☐ 47 | Cesar Cedeno | .40 | .18 | .04 |
| ☐ 48 | Toby Harrah | .40 | .18 | .04 |
| ☐ 49 | Willie Stargell | 1.50 | .70 | .15 |
| ☐ 50 | Al Hrabosky | .40 | .18 | .04 |
| ☐ 51 | Amos Otis | .40 | .18 | .04 |
| ☐ 52 | Bud Harrelson | .30 | .12 | .03 |
| ☐ 53 | Jim Hughes | .30 | .12 | .03 |
| ☐ 54 | George Scott | .30 | .12 | .03 |
| ☐ 55 | Mike Vail | .40 | .18 | .04 |
| ☐ 56 | Jim Palmer* | 2.50 | 1.15 | .25 |
| ☐ 57 | Jorge Orta* | .40 | .18 | .04 |
| ☐ 58 | Chris Chambliss* | .50 | .22 | .05 |
| ☐ 59 | Dave Chalk* | .40 | .18 | .04 |
| ☐ 60 | Ray Burris* | .40 | .18 | .04 |
| ☐ 61 | Bert Campaneris* | .50 | .22 | .05 |
| ☐ 62 | Gary Carter* | 3.00 | 1.40 | .30 |
| ☐ 63 | Ron Cey* | .75 | .35 | .07 |
| ☐ 64 | Carlton Fisk* | 1.00 | .45 | .10 |
| ☐ 65 | Marty Perez* | .40 | .18 | .04 |
| ☐ 66 | Pete Rose* | 6.00 | 2.80 | .60 |
| ☐ 67 | Roger Metzger* | .40 | .18 | .04 |
| ☐ 68 | Jim Sundberg* | .40 | .18 | .04 |
| ☐ 69 | Ron LeFlore* | .40 | .18 | .04 |
| ☐ 70 | Ted Sizemore* | .40 | .18 | .04 |
| ☐ 71 | Steve Busby* | .40 | .18 | .04 |
| ☐ 72 | Manny Sanguillen* | .40 | .18 | .04 |
| ☐ 73 | Larry Hisle* | .40 | .18 | .04 |
| ☐ 74 | Pete Broberg* | .40 | .18 | .04 |

| | MINT | VG-E | F-G |
|---|---|---|---|
| ☐ 75 Boog Powell* | .60 | .28 | .06 |
| ☐ 76 Ken Singleton* | .60 | .28 | .06 |
| ☐ 77 Rich Gossage* | 1.50 | .70 | .15 |
| ☐ 78 Jerry Grote* | .40 | .18 | .04 |
| ☐ 79 Nolan Ryan* | 3.00 | 1.40 | .30 |
| ☐ 80 Rick Monday* | .50 | .22 | .05 |
| ☐ 81 Graig Nettles* | .75 | .35 | .07 |
| ☐ 82 Chris Speier | .30 | .12 | .03 |
| ☐ 83 Dave Winfield | 3.00 | 1.40 | .30 |
| ☐ 84 Mike Schmidt | 3.50 | 1.65 | .35 |
| ☐ 85 Buzz Capra | .30 | .12 | .03 |
| ☐ 86 Tony Perez | .60 | .28 | .06 |
| ☐ 87 Dwight Evans | .60 | .28 | .06 |
| ☐ 88 Mike Hargrove | .30 | .12 | .03 |
| ☐ 89 Joe Coleman | .30 | .12 | .03 |
| ☐ 90 Greg Gross | .30 | .12 | .03 |
| ☐ 91 John Mayberry | .40 | .18 | .04 |
| ☐ 92 John Candelaria | .40 | .18 | .04 |
| ☐ 93 Bake McBride | .30 | .12 | .03 |
| ☐ 94 Hank Aaron | 4.00 | 1.85 | .40 |
| ☐ 95 Buddy Bell | .50 | .22 | .05 |
| ☐ 96 Steve Braun | .30 | .12 | .03 |
| ☐ 97 Jon Matlack | .40 | .18 | .04 |
| ☐ 98 Lee May | .40 | .18 | .04 |
| ☐ 99 Wilbur Wood | .30 | .12 | .03 |
| ☐ 100 Bill Madlock | .75 | .35 | .07 |
| ☐ 101 Frank Tanana | .40 | .18 | .04 |
| ☐ 102 Mickey Rivers | .30 | .12 | .03 |
| ☐ 103 Mike Ivie | .30 | .12 | .03 |
| ☐ 104 Rollie Fingers | .80 | .40 | .08 |
| ☐ 105 Dave Lopes | .40 | .18 | .04 |
| ☐ 106 George Foster | 1.00 | .45 | .10 |
| ☐ 107 Denny Doyle | .30 | .12 | .03 |
| ☐ 108 Earl Williams | .30 | .12 | .03 |
| ☐ 109 Tom Veryzer | .30 | .12 | .03 |
| ☐ 110 J.R. Richard | .40 | .18 | .04 |
| ☐ 111 Jeff Burroughs | .30 | .12 | .03 |
| ☐ 112 Al Oliver | .80 | .40 | .08 |
| ☐ 113 Ted Simmons | .75 | .35 | .07 |
| ☐ 114 George Brett | 4.00 | 1.85 | .40 |
| ☐ 115 Frank Duffy | .30 | .12 | .03 |
| ☐ 116 Bert Blyleven | .50 | .22 | .05 |
| ☐ 117 Darrell Porter | .30 | .12 | .03 |
| ☐ 118 Don Baylor | .50 | .22 | .05 |
| ☐ 119 Bucky Dent | .40 | .18 | .04 |
| ☐ 120 Felix Millan | .30 | .12 | .03 |
| ☐ 121 Mike Cuellar | .30 | .12 | .03 |
| ☐ 122 Gene Tenace | .30 | .12 | .03 |
| ☐ 123 Bobby Murcer | .50 | .22 | .05 |
| ☐ 124 Willie McCovey | 1.50 | .70 | .15 |
| ☐ 125 Greg Luzinski | .50 | .22 | .05 |
| ☐ 126 Larry Parrish | .60 | .28 | .06 |
| ☐ 127 Jim Rice | 3.00 | 1.40 | .30 |

| | MINT | VG-E | F-G |
|---|---|---|---|
| ☐ 128 Dave Concepcion | .50 | .22 | .05 |
| ☐ 129 Jim Wynn | .40 | .18 | .04 |
| ☐ 130 Tom Grieve | .40 | .18 | .04 |
| ☐ 131 Mike Cosgrove | .30 | .12 | .03 |
| ☐ 132 Dan Meyer | .30 | .12 | .03 |
| ☐ 133 Dave Parker | 1.50 | .70 | .15 |
| ☐ 134 Don Kessinger | .30 | .12 | .03 |
| ☐ 135 Hal McRae | .40 | .18 | .04 |
| ☐ 136 Don Money | .30 | .12 | .03 |
| ☐ 137 Dennis Eckersley | .40 | .18 | .04 |
| ☐ 138 Fergie Jenkins | .60 | .28 | .06 |
| ☐ 139 Mike Torrez | .40 | .18 | .04 |
| ☐ 140 Jerry Morales | .30 | .12 | .03 |
| ☐ 141 Jim Hunter | .90 | .40 | .09 |
| ☐ 142 Gary Matthews | .40 | .18 | .04 |
| ☐ 143 Randy Jones | .40 | .18 | .04 |
| ☐ 144 Mike Jorgensen | .30 | .12 | .03 |
| ☐ 145 Larry Bowa | .40 | .18 | .04 |
| ☐ 146 Reggie Jackson | 3.50 | 1.65 | .35 |
| ☐ 147 Steve Yeager | .30 | .12 | .03 |
| ☐ 148 Dave May | .30 | .12 | .03 |
| ☐ 149 Carl Yastrzemski | 4.00 | 1.85 | .40 |
| ☐ 150 Cesar Geronimo | .30 | .12 | .03 |

## 1977 HOSTESS

*The cards in this 150 card set measure 2¼" by 3¼" individually, or 3¼" by 7¼" as panels of three. The 1977 Hostess set contains color, numbered cards issued in panels of three cards each with Hostess family-sized cake products. Scarcer panels are listed in the checklist below with asterisks. Although complete panel prices are not explicitly listed below, they would generally have a value 25% greater than*

the sum of the individual players on the panel.

Complete Indiv. Set: M-100.00; VG-E-45.00; F-G-10.00

| | | MINT | VG-E | F-G |
|---|---|---|---|---|
| | Common Player | .30 | .12 | .03 |
| ☐ 1 | Jim Palmer | 2.00 | .90 | .20 |
| ☐ 2 | Joe Morgan | 1.50 | .70 | .15 |
| ☐ 3 | Reggie Jackson | 3.50 | 1.65 | .35 |
| ☐ 4 | Carl Yastrzemski | 4.00 | 1.85 | .40 |
| ☐ 5 | Thurman Munson | 2.50 | 1.15 | .25 |
| ☐ 6 | Johnny Bench | 3.00 | 1.40 | .30 |
| ☐ 7 | Tom Seaver | 2.50 | 1.15 | .25 |
| ☐ 8 | Pete Rose | 6.00 | 2.80 | .60 |
| ☐ 9 | Rod Carew | 3.00 | 1.40 | .30 |
| ☐ 10 | Luis Tiant | .40 | .18 | .04 |
| ☐ 11 | Phil Garner | .30 | .12 | .03 |
| ☐ 12 | Sixto Lezcano | .30 | .12 | .03 |
| ☐ 13 | Mike Torrez | .30 | .12 | .03 |
| ☐ 14 | Dave Lopes | .40 | .18 | .04 |
| ☐ 15 | Doug DeCinces | .40 | .18 | .04 |
| ☐ 16 | Jim Spencer | .30 | .12 | .03 |
| ☐ 17 | Hal McRae | .40 | .18 | .04 |
| ☐ 18 | Mike Hargrove | .30 | .12 | .03 |
| ☐ 19 | Willie Montanez* | .40 | .18 | .04 |
| ☐ 20 | Roger Metzger* | .40 | .18 | .04 |
| ☐ 21 | Dwight Evans* | 1.00 | .45 | .10 |
| ☐ 22 | Steve Rogers* | 1.00 | .45 | .10 |
| ☐ 23 | Jim Rice* | 3.00 | 1.40 | .30 |
| ☐ 24 | Pete Falcone* | .40 | .18 | .04 |
| ☐ 25 | Greg Luzinski* | 1.00 | .45 | .10 |
| ☐ 26 | Randy Jones* | .50 | .20 | .05 |
| ☐ 27 | Willie Stargell* | 2.00 | .90 | .20 |
| ☐ 28 | John Hiller* | .40 | .18 | .04 |
| ☐ 29 | Bobby Murcer* | .50 | .22 | .05 |
| ☐ 30 | Rick Monday* | .50 | .22 | .05 |
| ☐ 31 | John Montefusco* | .40 | .18 | .04 |
| ☐ 32 | Lou Brock* | 2.50 | 1.15 | .25 |
| ☐ 33 | Bill North* | .40 | .18 | .04 |
| ☐ 34 | Robin Yount* | 3.00 | 1.40 | .30 |
| ☐ 35 | Steve Garvey* | 4.00 | 1.85 | .40 |
| ☐ 36 | George Brett* | 5.00 | 2.35 | .50 |
| ☐ 37 | Toby Harrah* | .50 | .22 | .05 |
| ☐ 38 | Jerry Royster* | .40 | .18 | .04 |
| ☐ 39 | Bob Watson* | .40 | .18 | .04 |
| ☐ 40 | George Foster* | 1.00 | .45 | .10 |
| ☐ 41 | Gary Carter* | 2.50 | 1.15 | .25 |
| ☐ 42 | John Denny | .50 | .22 | .05 |
| ☐ 43 | Mike Schmidt | 3.50 | 1.65 | .35 |
| ☐ 44 | Dave Winfield | 3.00 | 1.40 | .30 |
| ☐ 45 | Al Oliver | .80 | .40 | .08 |
| ☐ 46 | Mark Fidrych | .50 | .22 | .05 |

| | | MINT | VG-E | F-G |
|---|---|---|---|---|
| ☐ 47 | Larry Herndon | .30 | .12 | .03 |
| ☐ 48 | Dave Goltz | .30 | .12 | .03 |
| ☐ 49 | Jerry Morales | .30 | .12 | .03 |
| ☐ 50 | Ron LeFlore | .40 | .18 | .04 |
| ☐ 51 | Fred Lynn | 1.50 | .70 | .15 |
| ☐ 52 | Vida Blue | .40 | .18 | .04 |
| ☐ 53 | Rick Manning | .30 | .12 | .03 |
| ☐ 54 | Bill Buckner | .60 | .28 | .06 |
| ☐ 55 | Lee May | .40 | .18 | .04 |
| ☐ 56 | John Mayberry | .40 | .18 | .04 |
| ☐ 57 | Darrel Chaney | .30 | .12 | .03 |
| ☐ 58 | Cesar Cedeno | .40 | .18 | .04 |
| ☐ 59 | Ken Griffey | .40 | .18 | .04 |
| ☐ 60 | Dave Kingman | .60 | .28 | .06 |
| ☐ 61 | Ted Simmons | .75 | .35 | .07 |
| ☐ 62 | Larry Bowa | .40 | .18 | .04 |
| ☐ 63 | Frank Tanana | .40 | .18 | .04 |
| ☐ 64 | Jason Thompson | .50 | .22 | .05 |
| ☐ 65 | Ken Brett | .30 | .12 | .03 |
| ☐ 66 | Roy Smalley | .30 | .12 | .03 |
| ☐ 67 | Ray Burris | .30 | .12 | .03 |
| ☐ 68 | Rick Burleson | .40 | .18 | .04 |
| ☐ 69 | Buddy Bell | .50 | .22 | .05 |
| ☐ 70 | Don Sutton | .60 | .28 | .06 |
| ☐ 71 | Mark Belanger | .40 | .18 | .04 |
| ☐ 72 | Dennis Leonard | .40 | .18 | .04 |
| ☐ 73 | Gaylord Perry | 1.50 | .70 | .15 |
| ☐ 74 | Dick Ruthven | .30 | .12 | .03 |
| ☐ 75 | Jose Cruz | .50 | .22 | .05 |
| ☐ 76 | Cesar Geronimo | .30 | .12 | .03 |
| ☐ 77 | Jerry Koosman | .50 | .22 | .05 |
| ☐ 78 | Garry Templeton | 1.00 | .45 | .10 |
| ☐ 79 | Jim Hunter | .90 | .40 | .09 |
| ☐ 80 | John Candelaria | .40 | .18 | .04 |
| ☐ 81 | Nolan Ryan | 2.50 | 1.15 | .25 |
| ☐ 82 | Rusty Staub | .50 | .22 | .05 |
| ☐ 83 | Jim Barr | .30 | .12 | .03 |
| ☐ 84 | Butch Wynegar | .40 | .18 | .04 |
| ☐ 85 | Jose Cardenal | .30 | .12 | .03 |
| ☐ 86 | Claudell Washington | .40 | .18 | .04 |
| ☐ 87 | Bill Travers | .30 | .12 | .03 |
| ☐ 88 | Rick Waits | .30 | .12 | .03 |
| ☐ 89 | Ron Cey | .50 | .22 | .05 |
| ☐ 90 | Al Bumbry | .30 | .12 | .03 |
| ☐ 91 | Bucky Dent | .40 | .18 | .04 |
| ☐ 92 | Amos Otis | .40 | .18 | .04 |
| ☐ 93 | Tom Grieve | .40 | .18 | .04 |
| ☐ 94 | Enos Cabell | .30 | .12 | .03 |
| ☐ 95 | Dave Concepcion | .40 | .18 | .04 |
| ☐ 96 | Felix Millan | .30 | .12 | .03 |
| ☐ 97 | Bake McBride | .30 | .12 | .03 |
| ☐ 98 | Chris Chambliss | .40 | .18 | .04 |
| ☐ 99 | Butch Metzger | .30 | .12 | .03 |

|  | MINT | VG-E | F-G |
|---|---|---|---|
| ☐ 100 Rennie Stennett | .30 | .12 | .03 |
| ☐ 101 Dave Roberts | .30 | .12 | .03 |
| ☐ 102 Lyman Bostock | .40 | .18 | .04 |
| ☐ 103 Rick Reuschel | .40 | .18 | .04 |
| ☐ 104 Carlton Fisk | .75 | .35 | .07 |
| ☐ 105 Jim Slaton | .30 | .12 | .03 |
| ☐ 106 Dennis Eckersley | .40 | .18 | .04 |
| ☐ 107 Ken Singleton | .50 | .22 | .05 |
| ☐ 108 Ralph Garr | .30 | .12 | .03 |
| ☐ 109 Freddie Patek* | .40 | .18 | .04 |
| ☐ 110 Jim Sundberg* | .40 | .18 | .04 |
| ☐ 111 Phil Niekro* | 2.00 | .90 | .20 |
| ☐ 112 J.R. Richard* | .50 | .22 | .05 |
| ☐ 113 Gary Nolan* | .40 | .18 | .04 |
| ☐ 114 Jon Matlack* | .50 | .22 | .05 |
| ☐ 115 Keith Hernandez* | 2.50 | 1.15 | .25 |
| ☐ 116 Graig Nettles* | .90 | .40 | .09 |
| ☐ 117 Steve Carlton* | 3.00 | 1.40 | .30 |
| ☐ 118 Bill Madlock* | 1.50 | .70 | .15 |
| ☐ 119 Jerry Reuss* | .60 | .28 | .06 |
| ☐ 120 Aurelio Rodriguez* | .40 | .18 | .04 |
| ☐ 121 Dan Ford* | .40 | .18 | .04 |
| ☐ 122 Ray Fosse* | .40 | .18 | .04 |
| ☐ 123 George Hendrick* | .50 | .22 | .05 |
| ☐ 124 Alan Ashby | .30 | .12 | .03 |
| ☐ 125 Joe Lis | .30 | .12 | .03 |
| ☐ 126 Sal Bando | .40 | .18 | .04 |
| ☐ 127 Richie Zisk | .40 | .18 | .04 |
| ☐ 128 Rich Gossage | .80 | .40 | .08 |
| ☐ 129 Don Baylor | .50 | .22 | .05 |
| ☐ 130 Dave McKay | .30 | .12 | .03 |
| ☐ 131 Bob Grich | .40 | .18 | .04 |
| ☐ 132 Dave Pagan | .30 | .12 | .03 |
| ☐ 133 Dave Cash | .30 | .12 | .03 |
| ☐ 134 Steve Braun | .30 | .12 | .03 |
| ☐ 135 Dan Meyer | .30 | .12 | .03 |
| ☐ 136 Bill Stein | .30 | .12 | .03 |
| ☐ 137 Rollie Fingers | .90 | .40 | .09 |
| ☐ 138 Brian Downing | .40 | .18 | .04 |
| ☐ 139 Bill Singer | .30 | .12 | .03 |
| ☐ 140 Doyle Alexander | .40 | .18 | .04 |
| ☐ 141 Gene Tenace | .30 | .12 | .03 |
| ☐ 142 Gary Matthews | .40 | .18 | .04 |
| ☐ 143 Don Gullett | .30 | .12 | .03 |
| ☐ 144 Wayne Garland | .30 | .12 | .03 |
| ☐ 145 Pete Broberg | .30 | .12 | .03 |
| ☐ 146 Joe Rudi | .40 | .18 | .04 |
| ☐ 147 Glenn Abbott | .30 | .12 | .03 |
| ☐ 148 George Scott | .30 | .12 | .03 |
| ☐ 149 Bert Campaneris | .40 | .18 | .04 |
| ☐ 150 Andy Messersmith | .40 | .18 | .04 |

## 1978 HOSTESS

KEITH HERNANDEZ
1b

*The cards in this 150 card set measure 2¼" by 3¼" individually, or 3¼" by 7¼" as panels of three. The 1978 Hostess set contains full color, numbered cards issued in panels of three cards each on family packages of Hostess cake products. Scarcer panels are listed in the checklist with asterisks. The 1978 Hostess panels are considered by some collectors to be somewhat more difficult to obtain than Hostess panels of other years. Although complete panel prices are not explicitly listed below, they would generally have a value 25% greater than the sum of the individual players on the panel.*

Complete Indiv. Set: M-100.00; VG-E-45.00; F-G-10.00

|  | MINT | VG-E | F-G |
|---|---|---|---|
| Common Player | .30 | .12 | .03 |
| ☐ 1 Butch Hobson | .40 | .18 | .04 |
| ☐ 2 George Foster | 1.00 | .45 | .10 |
| ☐ 3 Bob Forsch | .30 | .12 | .03 |
| ☐ 4 Tony Perez | .60 | .28 | .06 |
| ☐ 5 Bruce Sutter | 1.00 | .45 | .10 |
| ☐ 6 Hal McRae | .40 | .18 | .04 |
| ☐ 7 Tommy John | .75 | .35 | .07 |
| ☐ 8 Greg Luzinski | .50 | .22 | .05 |
| ☐ 9 Enos Cabell | .30 | .12 | .03 |
| ☐ 10 Doug DeCinces | .40 | .18 | .04 |
| ☐ 11 Willie Stargell | 1.25 | .60 | .12 |
| ☐ 12 Ed Halicki | .30 | .12 | .03 |
| ☐ 13 Larry Hisle | .40 | .18 | .04 |
| ☐ 14 Jim Slaton | .30 | .12 | .03 |
| ☐ 15 Buddy Bell | .50 | .22 | .05 |
| ☐ 16 Earl Williams | .30 | .12 | .03 |

| | MINT | VG-E | F-G | | MINT | VG-E | F-G |
|---|---|---|---|---|---|---|---|
| ☐ 17 Glenn Abbott | .30 | .12 | .03 | ☐ 70 Don Sutton | .60 | .28 | .06 |
| ☐ 18 Dan Ford | .30 | .12 | .03 | ☐ 71 Larry Bowa | .40 | .18 | .04 |
| ☐ 19 Gary Matthews | .40 | .18 | .04 | ☐ 72 Jose Cruz | .50 | .22 | .05 |
| ☐ 20 Eric Soderholm | .30 | .12 | .03 | ☐ 73 Willie McCovey | 1.50 | .70 | .15 |
| ☐ 21 Bump Wills | .30 | .12 | .03 | ☐ 74 Bert Blyleven | .60 | .28 | .06 |
| ☐ 22 Keith Hernandez | 2.00 | .90 | .20 | ☐ 75 Ken Singleton | .50 | .22 | .05 |
| ☐ 23 Dave Cash | .30 | .12 | .03 | ☐ 76 Bill North | .30 | .12 | .03 |
| ☐ 24 George Scott | .30 | .12 | .03 | ☐ 77 Jason Thompson | .40 | .18 | .04 |
| ☐ 25 Ron Guidry | 1.25 | .60 | .12 | ☐ 78 Dennis Eckersley | .40 | .18 | .04 |
| ☐ 26 Dave Kingman | .60 | .28 | .06 | ☐ 79 Jim Sundberg | .40 | .18 | .04 |
| ☐ 27 George Brett | 4.00 | 1.85 | .40 | ☐ 80 Jerry Koosman | .40 | .18 | .04 |
| ☐ 28 Bob Watson* | .40 | .18 | .04 | ☐ 81 Bruce Bochte | .30 | .12 | .03 |
| ☐ 29 Bob Boone* | .40 | .18 | .04 | ☐ 82 George Hendrick | .40 | .18 | .04 |
| ☐ 30 Reggie Smith | .50 | .22 | .05 | ☐ 83 Nolan Ryan | 2.50 | 1.15 | .25 |
| ☐ 31 Eddie Murray* | 4.00 | 1.85 | .40 | ☐ 84 Roy Howell | .30 | .12 | .03 |
| ☐ 32 Gary Lavelle* | .40 | .18 | .04 | ☐ 85 Roger Metzger | .30 | .12 | .03 |
| ☐ 33 Rennie Stennett* | .40 | .18 | .04 | ☐ 86 Doc Medich | .30 | .12 | .03 |
| ☐ 34 Duane Kuiper* | .40 | .18 | .04 | ☐ 87 Joe Morgan | 1.50 | .70 | .15 |
| ☐ 35 Sixto Lezcano* | .40 | .18 | .04 | ☐ 88 Dennis Leonard | .40 | .18 | .04 |
| ☐ 36 Dave Rozema* | .40 | .18 | .04 | ☐ 89 Willie Randolph | .40 | .18 | .04 |
| ☐ 37 Butch Wynegar* | .50 | .22 | .05 | ☐ 90 Bobby Murcer | .50 | .22 | .05 |
| ☐ 38 Mitchell Page* | .40 | .18 | .04 | ☐ 91 Rick Manning | .30 | .12 | .03 |
| ☐ 39 Bill Stein* | .40 | .18 | .04 | ☐ 92 J.R. Richard | .40 | .18 | .04 |
| ☐ 40 Elliott Maddox | .30 | .12 | .03 | ☐ 93 Ron Cey | .50 | .22 | .05 |
| ☐ 41 Mike Hargrove | .30 | .12 | .03 | ☐ 94 Sal Bando | .40 | .18 | .04 |
| ☐ 42 Bobby Bonds | .40 | .18 | .04 | ☐ 95 Ron LeFlore | .30 | .12 | .03 |
| ☐ 43 Garry Templeton | .60 | .28 | .06 | ☐ 96 Dave Goltz | .30 | .12 | .03 |
| ☐ 44 Johnny Bench | 3.00 | 1.40 | .30 | ☐ 97 Dan Meyer | .30 | .12 | .03 |
| ☐ 45 Jim Rice | 3.00 | 1.40 | .30 | ☐ 98 Chris Chambliss | .40 | .18 | .04 |
| ☐ 46 Bill Buckner | .60 | .28 | .06 | ☐ 99 Biff Pocoroba | .30 | .12 | .03 |
| ☐ 47 Reggie Jackson | 3.50 | 1.65 | .35 | ☐ 100 Oscar Gamble | .40 | .18 | .04 |
| ☐ 48 Freddie Patek | .30 | .12 | .03 | ☐ 101 Frank Tanana | .40 | .18 | .04 |
| ☐ 49 Steve Carlton | 3.00 | 1.40 | .30 | ☐ 102 Len Randle | .30 | .12 | .03 |
| ☐ 50 Cesar Cedeno | .40 | .18 | .04 | ☐ 103 Tommy Hutton | .30 | .12 | .03 |
| ☐ 51 Steve Yeager | .30 | .12 | .03 | ☐ 104 John Candelaria | .40 | .18 | .04 |
| ☐ 52 Phil Garner | .30 | .12 | .03 | ☐ 105 George Orta | .30 | .12 | .03 |
| ☐ 53 Lee May | .40 | .18 | .04 | ☐ 106 Ken Reitz | .30 | .12 | .03 |
| ☐ 54 Darrell Evans | .50 | .22 | .05 | ☐ 107 Bill Campbell | .30 | .12 | .03 |
| ☐ 55 Steve Kemp | .50 | .22 | .05 | ☐ 108 Dave Concepcion | .40 | .18 | .04 |
| ☐ 56 Dusty Baker | .50 | .22 | .05 | ☐ 109 Joe Ferguson | .30 | .12 | .03 |
| ☐ 57 Ray Fosse | .30 | .12 | .03 | ☐ 110 Mickey Rivers | .30 | .12 | .03 |
| ☐ 58 Manny Sanguillen | .30 | .12 | .03 | ☐ 111 Paul Splittorff | .30 | .12 | .03 |
| ☐ 59 Tom Johnson | .30 | .12 | .03 | ☐ 112 Dave Lopes | .40 | .18 | .04 |
| ☐ 60 Lee Stanton | .30 | .12 | .03 | ☐ 113 Mike Schmidt | 3.50 | 1.65 | .35 |
| ☐ 61 Jeff Burroughs | .30 | .12 | .03 | ☐ 114 Joe Rudi | .40 | .18 | .04 |
| ☐ 62 Bobby Grich | .40 | .18 | .04 | ☐ 115 Milt May | .30 | .12 | .03 |
| ☐ 63 Dave Winfield | 3.00 | 1.40 | .30 | ☐ 116 Jim Palmer | 2.00 | .90 | .20 |
| ☐ 64 Dan Driessen | .30 | .12 | .03 | ☐ 117 Bill Madlock | 1.00 | .45 | .10 |
| ☐ 65 Ted Simmons | .75 | .35 | .07 | ☐ 118 Roy Smalley | .30 | .12 | .03 |
| ☐ 66 Jerry Remy | .30 | .12 | .03 | ☐ 119 Cecil Cooper | .90 | .40 | .09 |
| ☐ 67 Al Cowens | .40 | .18 | .04 | ☐ 120 Rick Langford | .30 | .12 | .03 |
| ☐ 68 Sparky Lyle | .50 | .22 | .05 | ☐ 121 Ruppert Jones | .40 | .18 | .04 |
| ☐ 69 Manny Trillo | .40 | .18 | .04 | ☐ 122 Phil Niekro | 1.00 | .45 | .10 |

|  |  | MINT | VG-E | F-G |
|---|---|---|---|---|
| ☐ 123 | Toby Harrah | .40 | .18 | .04 |
| ☐ 124 | Chet Lemon | .40 | .18 | .04 |
| ☐ 125 | Gene Tenace | .30 | .12 | .03 |
| ☐ 126 | Steve Henderson | .30 | .12 | .03 |
| ☐ 127 | Mike Torrez | .30 | .12 | .03 |
| ☐ 128 | Pete Rose | 6.00 | 2.80 | .60 |
| ☐ 129 | John Denny | .50 | .22 | .05 |
| ☐ 130 | Darrell Porter | .40 | .18 | .04 |
| ☐ 131 | Rick Reuschel | .40 | .18 | .04 |
| ☐ 132 | Graig Nettles | .75 | .35 | .07 |
| ☐ 133 | Garry Maddox | .30 | .12 | .03 |
| ☐ 134 | Mike Flanagan | .40 | .18 | .04 |
| ☐ 135 | Dave Parker | 1.50 | .70 | .15 |
| ☐ 136 | Terry Whitfield | .30 | .12 | .03 |
| ☐ 137 | Wayne Garland | .30 | .12 | .03 |
| ☐ 138 | Robin Yount | 2.50 | 1.15 | .25 |
| ☐ 139 | Gaylord Perry | 1.50 | .70 | .15 |
| ☐ 140 | Rod Carew | 3.00 | 1.40 | .30 |
| ☐ 141 | Greg Gross | .30 | .12 | .03 |
| ☐ 142 | Barry Bonnell | .30 | .12 | .03 |
| ☐ 143 | Willie Montanez | .30 | .12 | .03 |
| ☐ 144 | Rollie Fingers | .90 | .40 | .09 |
| ☐ 145 | Lyman Bostock | .40 | .18 | .04 |
| ☐ 146 | Gary Carter | 2.50 | 1.15 | .25 |
| ☐ 147 | Ron Blomberg | .30 | .12 | .03 |
| ☐ 148 | Bob Bailor | .30 | .12 | .03 |
| ☐ 149 | Tom Seaver | 2.50 | 1.15 | .25 |
| ☐ 150 | Thurman Munson | 2.50 | 1.15 | .25 |

## 1979 HOSTESS

*The cards in this 150 card set measure 3¼" by 7¼" as panels of three. The 1979 Hostess set contains full color, numbered cards issued in panels of three cards each on the backs of family-sized Hostess cake products. Scarcer panels*

*are listed in the checklist below with asterisks. Although complete panel prices are not explicitly listed below, they would generally have a value 25% greater than the sum of the individual players on the panel.*

Complete Indiv. Set: M-100.00; VG-E-45.00; F-G-10.00

|  |  | MINT | VG-E | F-G |
|---|---|---|---|---|
| | Common Player | .30 | .12 | .03 |
| ☐ 1 | John Denny | .60 | .28 | .06 |
| ☐ 2 | Jim Rice | 3.00 | 1.40 | .30 |
| ☐ 3 | Doug Bair | .30 | .12 | .03 |
| ☐ 4 | Darrell Porter | .40 | .18 | .04 |
| ☐ 5 | Ross Grimsley | .30 | .12 | .03 |
| ☐ 6 | Bobby Murcer | .50 | .22 | .05 |
| ☐ 7 | Lee Mazzilli | .30 | .12 | .03 |
| ☐ 8 | Steve Garvey | 3.00 | 1.40 | .30 |
| ☐ 9 | Mike Schmidt | 3.50 | 1.65 | .35 |
| ☐ 10 | Terry Whitfield | .30 | .12 | .03 |
| ☐ 11 | Jim Palmer | 2.00 | .90 | .20 |
| ☐ 12 | Omar Moreno | .30 | .12 | .03 |
| ☐ 13 | Duane Kuiper | .30 | .12 | .03 |
| ☐ 14 | Mike Caldwell | .30 | .12 | .03 |
| ☐ 15 | Steve Kemp | .50 | .22 | .05 |
| ☐ 16 | Dave Goltz | .30 | .12 | .03 |
| ☐ 17 | Mitchell Page | .30 | .12 | .03 |
| ☐ 18 | Bill Stein | .30 | .12 | .03 |
| ☐ 19 | Gene Tenace | .30 | .12 | .03 |
| ☐ 20 | Jeff Burroughs | .30 | .12 | .03 |
| ☐ 21 | Francisco Barrios | .30 | .12 | .03 |
| ☐ 22 | Mike Torrez | .30 | .12 | .03 |
| ☐ 23 | Ken Reitz | .30 | .12 | .03 |
| ☐ 24 | Gary Carter | 2.50 | 1.15 | .25 |
| ☐ 25 | Al Hrabosky | .40 | .18 | .04 |
| ☐ 26 | Thurman Munson | 2.50 | 1.15 | .25 |
| ☐ 27 | Bill Buckner | .60 | .28 | .06 |
| ☐ 28 | Ron Cey* | .60 | .28 | .06 |
| ☐ 29 | J.R. Richard* | .50 | .22 | .05 |
| ☐ 30 | Greg Luzinski* | 1.00 | .45 | .10 |
| ☐ 31 | Ed Ott* | .40 | .18 | .04 |
| ☐ 32 | Dennis Martinez* | .40 | .18 | .04 |
| ☐ 33 | Darrell Evans* | .60 | .28 | .06 |
| ☐ 34 | Ron LeFlore | .30 | .12 | .03 |
| ☐ 35 | Rick Waits | .30 | .12 | .03 |
| ☐ 36 | Cecil Cooper | .90 | .40 | .09 |
| ☐ 37 | Leon Roberts | .30 | .12 | .03 |
| ☐ 38 | Rod Carew | 2.50 | 1.15 | .25 |
| ☐ 39 | John Henry Johnson | .30 | .12 | .03 |
| ☐ 40 | Chet Lemon | .40 | .18 | .04 |
| ☐ 41 | Craig Swan | .30 | .12 | .03 |
| ☐ 42 | Gary Matthews | .40 | .18 | .04 |

| | | MINT | VG-E | F-G |
|---|---|---|---|---|
| ☐ 43 | Lamar Johnson | .30 | .12 | .03 |
| ☐ 44 | Ted Simmons | .60 | .28 | .06 |
| ☐ 45 | Ken Griffey | .40 | .18 | .04 |
| ☐ 46 | Fred Patek | .30 | .12 | .03 |
| ☐ 47 | Frank Tanana | .40 | .18 | .04 |
| ☐ 48 | Goose Gossage | 1.00 | .45 | .10 |
| ☐ 49 | Burt Hooten | .30 | .12 | .03 |
| ☐ 50 | Ellis Valentine | .30 | .12 | .03 |
| ☐ 51 | Ken Forsch | .30 | .12 | .03 |
| ☐ 52 | Bob Knepper | .40 | .18 | .04 |
| ☐ 53 | Dave Parker | 1.50 | .70 | .15 |
| ☐ 54 | Doug DeCinces | .40 | .18 | .04 |
| ☐ 55 | Robin Yount | 2.50 | 1.15 | .25 |
| ☐ 56 | Rusty Staub | .50 | .22 | .05 |
| ☐ 57 | Gary Alexander | .30 | .12 | .03 |
| ☐ 58 | Julio Cruz | .30 | .12 | .03 |
| ☐ 59 | Matt Keough | .30 | .12 | .03 |
| ☐ 60 | Roy Smalley | .30 | .12 | .03 |
| ☐ 61 | Joe Morgan | 1.50 | .70 | .15 |
| ☐ 62 | Phil Niekro | 1.00 | .45 | .10 |
| ☐ 63 | Don Baylor | .50 | .22 | .05 |
| ☐ 64 | Dwight Evans | .50 | .22 | .05 |
| ☐ 65 | Tom Seaver | 2.50 | 1.15 | .25 |
| ☐ 66 | George Hendrick | .40 | .18 | .04 |
| ☐ 67 | Rick Reuschel | .40 | .18 | .04 |
| ☐ 68 | George Brett | 4.00 | 1.85 | .40 |
| ☐ 69 | Lou Piniella | .50 | .22 | .05 |
| ☐ 70 | Enos Cabell | .30 | .12 | .03 |
| ☐ 71 | Steve Carlton | 2.50 | 1.15 | .25 |
| ☐ 72 | Reggie Smith | .40 | .18 | .04 |
| ☐ 73 | Rick Dempsey* | .50 | .22 | .05 |
| ☐ 74 | Vida Blue* | .50 | .22 | .05 |
| ☐ 75 | Phil Garner* | .40 | .18 | .04 |
| ☐ 76 | Rick Manning* | .40 | .18 | .04 |
| ☐ 77 | Mark Fidrych* | .50 | .22 | .05 |
| ☐ 78 | Mario Guerrero* | .40 | .18 | .04 |
| ☐ 79 | Bob Stinson* | .40 | .18 | .04 |
| ☐ 80 | Al Oliver* | 1.00 | .45 | .10 |
| ☐ 81 | Doug Flynn* | .40 | .18 | .04 |
| ☐ 82 | John Mayberry | .30 | .12 | .03 |
| ☐ 83 | Gaylord Perry | 1.50 | .70 | .15 |
| ☐ 84 | Joe Rudi | .40 | .18 | .04 |
| ☐ 85 | Dave Concepcion | .40 | .18 | .04 |
| ☐ 86 | John Candelaria | .40 | .18 | .04 |
| ☐ 87 | Pete Vuckovich | .40 | .18 | .04 |
| ☐ 88 | Ivan DeJesus | .30 | .12 | .03 |
| ☐ 89 | Ron Guidry | 1.25 | .60 | .12 |
| ☐ 90 | Hal McRae | .40 | .18 | .04 |
| ☐ 91 | Cesar Cedeno | .40 | .18 | .04 |
| ☐ 92 | Don Sutton | .60 | .28 | .06 |
| ☐ 93 | Andre Thornton | .40 | .18 | .04 |
| ☐ 94 | Roger Erickson | .30 | .12 | .03 |
| ☐ 95 | Larry Hisle | .40 | .18 | .04 |

| | | MINT | VG-E | F-G |
|---|---|---|---|---|
| ☐ 96 | Jason Thompson | .40 | .18 | .04 |
| ☐ 97 | Jim Sundberg | .40 | .18 | .04 |
| ☐ 98 | Bob Horner | 2.50 | 1.15 | .25 |
| ☐ 99 | Ruppert Jones | .30 | .12 | .03 |
| ☐ 100 | Willie Montanez | .30 | .12 | .03 |
| ☐ 101 | Nolan Ryan | 2.50 | 1.15 | .25 |
| ☐ 102 | Ozzie Smith | .75 | .35 | .07 |
| ☐ 103 | Eric Soderholm | .30 | .12 | .03 |
| ☐ 104 | Willie Stargell | 1.25 | .60 | .12 |
| ☐ 105 | Bob Bailor | .30 | .12 | .03 |
| ☐ 106 | Carlton Fisk | .90 | .40 | .09 |
| ☐ 107 | George Foster | 1.00 | .45 | .10 |
| ☐ 108 | Keith Hernandez | 2.00 | .90 | .20 |
| ☐ 109 | Dennis Leonard | .40 | .18 | .04 |
| ☐ 110 | Graig Nettles | .75 | .35 | .07 |
| ☐ 111 | Jose Cruz | .50 | .22 | .05 |
| ☐ 112 | Bobby Grich | .40 | .18 | .04 |
| ☐ 113 | Bob Boone | .30 | .12 | .03 |
| ☐ 114 | Dave Lopes | .40 | .18 | .04 |
| ☐ 115 | Eddie Murray | 3.50 | 1.65 | .35 |
| ☐ 116 | Jack Clark | .90 | .40 | .09 |
| ☐ 117 | Lou Whitaker | .75 | .35 | .07 |
| ☐ 118 | Miguel Dilone | .30 | .12 | .03 |
| ☐ 119 | Sal Bando | .40 | .18 | .04 |
| ☐ 120 | Reggie Jackson | 3.50 | 1.65 | .35 |
| ☐ 121 | Dale Murphy | 5.00 | 2.35 | .50 |
| ☐ 122 | Jon Matlack | .40 | .18 | .04 |
| ☐ 123 | Bruce Bochte | .30 | .12 | .03 |
| ☐ 124 | John Stearns | .30 | .12 | .03 |
| ☐ 125 | Dave Winfield | 3.00 | 1.40 | .30 |
| ☐ 126 | Jorge Orta | .30 | .12 | .03 |
| ☐ 127 | Garry Templeton | .50 | .22 | .05 |
| ☐ 128 | Johnny Bench | 3.00 | 1.40 | .30 |
| ☐ 129 | Butch Hobson | .30 | .12 | .03 |
| ☐ 130 | Bruce Sutter | 1.00 | .45 | .10 |
| ☐ 131 | Bucky Dent | .40 | .18 | .04 |
| ☐ 132 | Amos Otis | .40 | .18 | .04 |
| ☐ 133 | Bert Blyleven | .50 | .22 | .05 |
| ☐ 134 | Larry Bowa | .40 | .18 | .04 |
| ☐ 135 | Ken Singleton | .40 | .18 | .04 |
| ☐ 136 | Sixto Lezcano | .30 | .12 | .03 |
| ☐ 137 | Roy Howell | .30 | .12 | .03 |
| ☐ 138 | Bill Madlock | .90 | .40 | .09 |
| ☐ 139 | Dave Revering | .30 | .12 | .03 |
| ☐ 140 | Richie Zisk | .40 | .18 | .04 |
| ☐ 141 | Butch Wynegar | .40 | .18 | .04 |
| ☐ 142 | Alan Ashby | .30 | .12 | .03 |
| ☐ 143 | Sparky Lyle | .50 | .22 | .05 |
| ☐ 144 | Pete Rose | 6.00 | 2.80 | .60 |
| ☐ 145 | Dennis Eckersley | .40 | .18 | .04 |
| ☐ 146 | Dave Kingman | .60 | .28 | .06 |
| ☐ 147 | Buddy Bell | .50 | .22 | .05 |
| ☐ 148 | Mike Hargrove | .30 | .12 | .03 |

|  | MINT | VG-E | F-G |
|---|---|---|---|
| ☐ 149 Jerry Koosman ........ | .40 | .18 | .04 |
| ☐ 150 Toby Harrah ........ | .40 | .18 | .04 |

## 1986 SPORTFLICS

This 200 card set was marketed with 133 small trivia cards. The set features 139 single player "magic motion" cards (which can be tilted to show three different pictures of the same player), 50 "Tri-Stars" (which show three different players), 10 "Big Six" cards (which show six players who share similar achievements), and one World Champs card featuring 12 members of the victorious Kansas City Royals. All cards measure 2½" by 3½".

**Note:** The above photo appears distorted because it is a "magic motion" card.

Complete Set: M-35.00; VG-E-15.00; F-G-3.00

|  | Common Player ........ | .15 | .06 | .01 |
|---|---|---|---|---|

|  |  | MINT | VG-E | F-G |
|---|---|---|---|---|
| ☐ | 1 George Brett .......... | 1.25 | .60 | .12 |
| ☐ | 2 Don Mattingly ........ | 1.75 | .85 | .17 |
| ☐ | 3 Wade Boggs .......... | 1.25 | .60 | .12 |
| ☐ | 4 Eddie Murray .......... | 1.25 | .60 | .12 |
| ☐ | 5 Dale Murphy .......... | 1.25 | .60 | .12 |
| ☐ | 6 Rickey Henderson .... | 1.25 | .60 | .12 |
| ☐ | 7 Harold Baines ........ | .45 | .20 | .04 |
| ☐ | 8 Cal Ripken .......... | 1.25 | .60 | .12 |
| ☐ | 9 Orel Hershiser ........ | .75 | .35 | .07 |
| ☐ | 10 Bret Saberhagen ...... | 1.00 | .45 | .10 |
| ☐ | 11 Tim Raines .......... | .55 | .25 | .05 |
| ☐ | 12 Fernando Valenzuela .. | .55 | .25 | .05 |
| ☐ | 13 Tony Gwynn .......... | .55 | .25 | .05 |
| ☐ | 14 Pedro Guerrero ...... | .45 | .20 | .04 |

|  |  | MINT | VG-E | F-G |
|---|---|---|---|---|
| ☐ | 15 Keith Hernandez ...... | .45 | .20 | .04 |
| ☐ | 16 Ernie Riles .......... | .45 | .20 | .04 |
| ☐ | 17 Jim Rice .......... | .55 | .25 | .05 |
| ☐ | 18 Ron Guidry .......... | .45 | .20 | .04 |
| ☐ | 19 Willie McGee ........ | .75 | .35 | .07 |
| ☐ | 20 Ryne Sandberg ...... | .75 | .35 | .07 |
| ☐ | 21 Kirk Gibson .......... | .45 | .20 | .04 |
| ☐ | 22 Ozzie Guillen ........ | .75 | .35 | .07 |
| ☐ | 23 Dave Parker .......... | .45 | .20 | .04 |
| ☐ | 24 Vince Coleman ...... | 1.50 | .70 | .15 |
| ☐ | 25 Tom Seaver .......... | .75 | .35 | .07 |
| ☐ | 26 Brett Butler .......... | .25 | .10 | .02 |
| ☐ | 27 Steve Carlton ........ | .75 | .35 | .07 |
| ☐ | 28 Gary Carter .......... | .75 | .35 | .07 |
| ☐ | 29 Cecil Cooper ........ | .35 | .15 | .03 |
| ☐ | 30 Jose Cruz .......... | .25 | .10 | .02 |
| ☐ | 31 Alvin Davis .......... | .25 | .10 | .02 |
| ☐ | 32 Dwight Evans ........ | .25 | .10 | .02 |
| ☐ | 33 Julio Franco .......... | .25 | .10 | .02 |
| ☐ | 34 Damaso Garcia ...... | .20 | .09 | .02 |
| ☐ | 35 Steve Garvey ........ | 1.00 | .45 | .10 |
| ☐ | 36 Kent Hrbek .......... | .35 | .15 | .03 |
| ☐ | 37 Reggie Jackson ...... | 1.00 | .45 | .10 |
| ☐ | 38 Fred Lynn .......... | .35 | .15 | .03 |
| ☐ | 39 Paul Molitor .......... | .25 | .10 | .02 |
| ☐ | 40 Jim Presley .......... | .35 | .15 | .03 |
| ☐ | 41 Dave Righetti ........ | .25 | .10 | .02 |
| ☐ | 42 Robin Yount .......... | .45 | .20 | .04 |
| ☐ | 43 Nolan Ryan .......... | .65 | .30 | .06 |
| ☐ | 44 Mike Schmidt ........ | .90 | .40 | .09 |
| ☐ | 45 Lee Smith .......... | .25 | .10 | .02 |
| ☐ | 46 Rick Sutcliffe ........ | .25 | .10 | .02 |
| ☐ | 47 Bruce Sutter ........ | .35 | .15 | .03 |
| ☐ | 48 Lou Whitaker ........ | .35 | .15 | .03 |
| ☐ | 49 Dave Winfield ........ | .75 | .35 | .07 |
| ☐ | 50 Pete Rose .......... | 2.25 | 1.00 | .22 |
| ☐ | 51 National League MVP's: | 1.25 | .60 | .12 |
| ☐ |     Ryne Sandberg |  |  |  |
| ☐ |     Steve Garvey |  |  |  |
| ☐ |     Pete Rose |  |  |  |
| ☐ | 52 Slugging Stars: | 1.00 | .45 | .10 |
| ☐ |     George Brett |  |  |  |
| ☐ |     Harold Baines |  |  |  |
| ☐ |     Jim Rice |  |  |  |
| ☐ | 53 No-Hitters: .......... | .25 | .10 | .02 |
| ☐ |     Phil Niekro |  |  |  |
| ☐ |     Jerry Reuss |  |  |  |
| ☐ |     Mike Witt |  |  |  |
| ☐ | 54 Big Hitters .......... | 1.25 | .60 | .12 |
| ☐ |     Don Mattingly |  |  |  |
| ☐ |     Cal Ripken |  |  |  |
| ☐ |     Robin Yount |  |  |  |

|  | MINT | VG-E | F-G |
|---|---|---|---|
| ☐ 55 Bullpen Aces: | .25 | .10 | .02 |
| Dan Quisenberry | | | |
| Goose Gossage | | | |
| Lee Smith | | | |
| ☐ 56 Double Award Winners: | .45 | .20 | .04 |
| Fernando Valenzuela | | | |
| Rick Sutcliffe | | | |
| Tom Seaver | | | |
| ☐ 57 Cy Young Winners: | .25 | .10 | .02 |
| LaMarr Hoyt | | | |
| Mike Flanagan | | | |
| Ron Guidry | | | |
| ☐ 58 Repeat Batting Champs: | 1.00 | .45 | .10 |
| Dave Parker | | | |
| Bill Madlock | | | |
| Pete Rose | | | |
| ☐ 59 American League MVP's: | .75 | .35 | .07 |
| Cal Ripken | | | |
| Don Baylor | | | |
| Reggie Jackson | | | |
| ☐ 60 Rookies of The Year: | 1.25 | .60 | .12 |
| Darryl Strawberry | | | |
| Steve Sax | | | |
| Pete Rose | | | |
| ☐ 61 Home Run Champs: | .75 | .35 | .07 |
| Reggie Jackson | | | |
| Jim Rice | | | |
| Tony Armas | | | |
| ☐ 62 National League MVP's: | 1.00 | .45 | .10 |
| Keith Hernandez | | | |
| Dale Murphy | | | |
| Mike Schmidt | | | |
| ☐ 63 American League MVP's: | .75 | .35 | .07 |
| Robin Yount | | | |
| George Brett | | | |
| Fred Lynn | | | |
| ☐ 64 Comeback Players: | .20 | .09 | .02 |
| Bert Blyleven | | | |
| Dave Kingman | | | |
| John Denny | | | |
| ☐ 65 Cy Young Relievers: | .25 | .10 | .02 |
| Willie Hernandez | | | |
| Rollie Fingers | | | |
| Bruce Sutter | | | |
| ☐ 66 Rookies of The Year: | .25 | .10 | .02 |
| Bob Horner | | | |
| Andre Dawson | | | |
| Gary Matthews | | | |
| ☐ 67 Rookies of The Year: | .35 | .15 | .03 |
| Ron Kittle | | | |
| Carlton Fisk | | | |
| Tom Seaver | | | |

|  | MINT | VG-E | F-G |
|---|---|---|---|
| ☐ 68 Home Run Champs: | .35 | .15 | .03 |
| Mike Schmidt | | | |
| George Foster | | | |
| Dave Kingman | | | |
| ☐ 69 Double Award Winners: | 1.25 | .60 | .12 |
| Cal Ripken | | | |
| Rod Carew | | | |
| Pete Rose | | | |
| ☐ 70 Cy Young Winners: | .45 | .20 | .04 |
| Rick Sutcliffe | | | |
| Steve Carlton | | | |
| Tom Seaver | | | |
| ☐ 71 Top Sluggers: | .45 | .20 | .04 |
| Reggie Jackson | | | |
| Fred Lynn | | | |
| Robin Yount | | | |
| ☐ 72 Rookies of The Year: | .35 | .15 | .03 |
| Dave Righetti | | | |
| Fernando Valenzuela | | | |
| Rick Sutcliffe | | | |
| ☐ 73 Rookies of The Year: | 1.00 | .45 | .10 |
| Fred Lynn | | | |
| Eddie Murray | | | |
| Cal Ripken | | | |
| ☐ 74 Rookies of The Year: | .35 | .15 | .03 |
| Alvin Davis | | | |
| Lou Whitaker | | | |
| Rod Carew | | | |
| ☐ 75 Batting Champs: | 1.50 | .70 | .15 |
| Don Mattingly | | | |
| Wade Boggs | | | |
| Carney Lansford | | | |
| ☐ 76 Jesse Barfield | .25 | .10 | .02 |
| ☐ 77 Phil Bradley | .35 | .15 | .03 |
| ☐ 78 Chris Brown | .35 | .15 | .03 |
| ☐ 79 Tom Browning | .35 | .15 | .03 |
| ☐ 80 Tom Brunansky | .25 | .10 | .02 |
| ☐ 81 Bill Buckner | .20 | .09 | .02 |
| ☐ 82 Chili Davis | .20 | .09 | .02 |
| ☐ 83 Mike Davis | .20 | .09 | .02 |
| ☐ 84 Rich Gedman | .20 | .09 | .02 |
| ☐ 85 Willie Hernandez | .25 | .10 | .02 |
| ☐ 86 Ron Kittle | .25 | .10 | .02 |
| ☐ 87 Lee Lacy | .15 | .06 | .01 |
| ☐ 88 Bill Madlock | .25 | .10 | .02 |
| ☐ 89 Mike Marshall | .25 | .10 | .02 |
| ☐ 90 Keith Moreland | .15 | .06 | .01 |
| ☐ 91 Graig Nettles | .25 | .10 | .02 |
| ☐ 92 Lance Parrish | .35 | .15 | .03 |
| ☐ 93 Kirby Puckett | .25 | .10 | .02 |
| ☐ 94 Juan Samuel | .25 | .10 | .02 |
| ☐ 95 Steve Sax | .25 | .10 | .02 |

|  |  | MINT | VG-E | F-G |
|---|---|---|---|---|
| ☐ | 96 Dave Stieb | .35 | .15 | .03 |
| ☐ | 97 Darryl Strawberry | 1.00 | .45 | .10 |
| ☐ | 98 Willie Upshaw | .20 | .09 | .02 |
| ☐ | 99 Frank Viola | .20 | .09 | .02 |
| ☐ | 100 Dwight Gooden | 3.25 | 1.50 | .32 |
| ☐ | 101 Joaquin Andujar | .25 | .10 | .02 |
| ☐ | 102 George Bell | .25 | .10 | .02 |
| ☐ | 103 Bert Blyleven | .20 | .09 | .02 |
| ☐ | 104 Mike Boddicker | .20 | .09 | .02 |
| ☐ | 105 Britt Burns | .20 | .09 | .02 |
| ☐ | 106 Rod Carew | .75 | .35 | .07 |
| ☐ | 107 Jack Clark | .35 | .15 | .03 |
| ☐ | 108 Danny Cox | .25 | .10 | .02 |
| ☐ | 109 Ron Darling | .35 | .15 | .03 |
| ☐ | 110 Andre Dawson | .45 | .20 | .04 |
| ☐ | 111 Leon Durham | .25 | .10 | .02 |
| ☐ | 112 Tony Fernandez | .25 | .10 | .02 |
| ☐ | 113 Tommy Herr | .25 | .10 | .02 |
| ☐ | 114 Teddy Higuera | .35 | .15 | .03 |
| ☐ | 115 Bob Horner | .35 | .15 | .03 |
| ☐ | 116 Dave Kingman | .25 | .10 | .02 |
| ☐ | 117 Jack Morris | .35 | .13 | .03 |
| ☐ | 118 Dan Quisenberry | .45 | .20 | .04 |
| ☐ | 119 Jeff Reardon | .25 | .10 | .02 |
| ☐ | 120 Bryn Smith | .15 | .06 | .01 |
| ☐ | 121 Ozzie Smith | .25 | .10 | .02 |
| ☐ | 122 John Tudor | .25 | .10 | .02 |
| ☐ | 123 Tim Wallach | .25 | .10 | .02 |
| ☐ | 124 Willie Wilson | .35 | .15 | .03 |
| ☐ | 125 Carlton Fisk | .45 | .20 | .04 |
| ☐ | 126 RBI Sluggers: | .35 | .15 | .03 |
|  | Gary Carter |  |  |  |
|  | Al Oliver |  |  |  |
|  | George Foster |  |  |  |
| ☐ | 127 Run Scorers: | .65 | .30 | .06 |
|  | Tim Raines |  |  |  |
|  | Ryne Sandberg |  |  |  |
|  | Keith Hernandez |  |  |  |
| ☐ | 128 Run Scorers: | .65 | .30 | .06 |
|  | Paul Molitor |  |  |  |
|  | Cal Ripken |  |  |  |
|  | Willie Wilson |  |  |  |
| ☐ | 129 No-Hitters: | .20 | .09 | .02 |
|  | John Candelaria |  |  |  |
|  | Dennis Eckersley |  |  |  |
|  | Bob Forsch |  |  |  |
| ☐ | 130 Veteran Pitchers: | .45 | .20 | .04 |
|  | Tom Seaver |  |  |  |
|  | Phil Niekro |  |  |  |
|  | Don Sutton |  |  |  |

|  |  | MINT | VG-E | F-G |
|---|---|---|---|---|
| ☐ | 131 All-Star Game MVPs: | .20 | .09 | .02 |
|  | Dave Concepcion |  |  |  |
|  | George Foster |  |  |  |
|  | Bill Madlock |  |  |  |
| ☐ | 132 Cy Young Winners: | .25 | .10 | .02 |
|  | John Denny |  |  |  |
|  | Fernando Valenzuela |  |  |  |
|  | Vida Blue |  |  |  |
| ☐ | 133 Comeback Players: | .20 | .09 | .02 |
|  | Rich Dotson |  |  |  |
|  | Joaquin Andujar |  |  |  |
|  | Doyle Alexander |  |  |  |
| ☐ | 134 Big Winners: | .45 | .20 | .04 |
|  | Rick Sutcliffe |  |  |  |
|  | Tom Seaver |  |  |  |
|  | John Denny |  |  |  |
| ☐ | 135 Batting Champs: | .35 | .*5 | .03 |
|  | Tony Gwynn |  |  |  |
|  | Al Oliver |  |  |  |
|  | Bill Buckner |  |  |  |
| ☐ | 136 Rookies of The Year: | 1.50 | .70 | .15 |
|  | Dwight Gooden |  |  |  |
|  | Vince Coleman |  |  |  |
|  | Alfredo Griffin |  |  |  |
| ☐ | 137 All-Star Game MVPs: | .45 | .20 | .04 |
|  | Gary Carter |  |  |  |
|  | Fred Lynn |  |  |  |
|  | Steve Garvey |  |  |  |
| ☐ | 138 Veteran Hitters: | .85 | .40 | .08 |
|  | Pete Rose |  |  |  |
|  | Rusty Staub |  |  |  |
|  | Tony Perez |  |  |  |
| ☐ | 139 Power Hitters: | .50 | .22 | .05 |
|  | Mike Schmidt |  |  |  |
|  | Jim Rice |  |  |  |
|  | George Foster |  |  |  |
| ☐ | 140 RBI Sluggers: | .50 | .22 | .05 |
|  | Tony Armas |  |  |  |
|  | Cecil Cooper |  |  |  |
|  | Eddie Murray |  |  |  |
| ☐ | 141 No-Hitters: | .35 | .15 | .03 |
|  | Nol Ian Ryan |  |  |  |
|  | Jack Morris |  |  |  |
|  | Dave Righetti |  |  |  |
| ☐ | 142 No-Hitters: | .35 | .15 | .03 |
|  | T Tom Seaver |  |  |  |
|  | Bert Blyleven |  |  |  |
|  | Vida Blue |  |  |  |
| ☐ | 143 Strikeout Kings: | 1.50 | .70 | .15 |
|  | Nolan Ryan |  |  |  |
|  | Fernando Valenzuela |  |  |  |
|  | Dwight Gooden |  |  |  |

|  | | MINT | VG-E | F-G |
|---|---|---|---|---|
| ☐ 144 | Base Stealers:<br>Tim Raines<br>Willie Wilson<br>Davey Lopes | .45 | .20 | .04 |
| ☐ 145 | Comeback Players:<br>Reggie Jackson<br>Dave Kingman<br>Fred Lynn | .45 | .20 | .04 |
| ☐ 146 | American League MVP's:<br>Rod Carew<br>Jim Rice<br>Rollie Fingers | .45 | .20 | .04 |
| ☐ 147 | World Series MVP's:<br>Alan Trammell<br>Rick Dempsey<br>Reggie Jackson | .45 | .20 | .04 |
| ☐ 148 | World Series MVP's:<br>Darrell Porter<br>Pedro Guerrero<br>Mike Schmidt | .45 | .20 | .04 |
| ☐ 149 | ERA Leaders:<br>Mike Boddicker<br>Rick Sutcliffe<br>Ron Guidry | .25 | .10 | .02 |
| ☐ 150 | World Series MVP's:<br>Pete Rose<br>Ron Cey<br>Rollie Fingers | .85 | .40 | .08 |
| ☐ 151 | Buddy Bell | .20 | .09 | .02 |
| ☐ 152 | Dennis Boyd | .15 | .06 | .01 |
| ☐ 153 | Dave Concepcion | .20 | .09 | .02 |
| ☐ 154 | Brian Downing | .15 | .06 | .01 |
| ☐ 155 | Shawon Dunston | .15 | .06 | .01 |
| ☐ 156 | John Franco | .20 | .09 | .02 |
| ☐ 157 | Scott Garrelts | .20 | .09 | .02 |
| ☐ 158 | Bob James | .20 | .09 | .02 |
| ☐ 159 | Charlie Leibrandt | .20 | .09 | .02 |
| ☐ 160 | Oddibe McDowell | .65 | .30 | .06 |
| ☐ 161 | Roger McDowell | .35 | .15 | .03 |
| ☐ 162 | Mike Moore | .20 | .09 | .02 |
| ☐ 163 | Phil Niekro | .45 | .20 | .04 |
| ☐ 164 | Al Oliver | .25 | .10 | .02 |
| ☐ 165 | Tony Pena | .25 | .10 | .02 |
| ☐ 166 | Ted Power | .20 | .09 | .02 |
| ☐ 167 | Mike Scioscia | .15 | .06 | .01 |
| ☐ 168 | Mario Soto | .20 | .09 | .02 |
| ☐ 169 | Bob Stanley | .20 | .09 | .02 |
| ☐ 170 | Gary Templeton | .20 | .09 | .02 |
| ☐ 171 | Andre Thornton | .20 | .09 | .02 |
| ☐ 172 | Alan Trammell | .35 | .15 | .03 |
| ☐ 173 | Doug DeCinces | .25 | .10 | .02 |
| ☐ 174 | Greg Walker | .25 | .10 | .02 |
| ☐ 175 | Don Sutton | .35 | .15 | .03 |

|  | | MINT | VG-E | F-G |
|---|---|---|---|---|
| ☐ 176 | 1985 Award Winners:<br>Ozzie Guillen<br>Bret Saberhagen<br>Don Mattingly<br>Vince Coleman<br>Dwight Gooden<br>Willie McGee | 1.50 | .70 | .15 |
| ☐ 177 | 1985 Hot Rookies:<br>Stew Cliburn<br>Brian Fisher<br>Joe Hesketh<br>Joe Orsulak<br>Mark Salas<br>Larry Sheets | .45 | .20 | .04 |
| ☐ 178 | 1986 Rookies To Watch:<br>Jose Canseco<br>Mark Funderburk<br>Mike Greenwell<br>Steve Lombardozzi<br>Billy Joe Robidoux<br>Dan Tartabull | 1.50 | .70 | .15 |
| ☐ 179 | 1985 Gold Glovers:<br>George Brett<br>Ron Guidry<br>Keith Hernandez<br>Don Mattingly<br>Willie McGee<br>Dale Murphy | 1.00 | .45 | .10 |
| ☐ 180 | Active Lifetime .300<br>Wade Boggs<br>George Brett<br>Rod Carew<br>Cecil Cooper<br>Don Mattingly<br>Willie Wilson | 1.00 | .45 | .10 |
| ☐ 181 | Active Lifetime .300<br>Pedro Guerrero<br>Tony Gwynn<br>Keith Hernandez<br>Bill Madlock<br>Dave Parker<br>Pete Rose | 1.00 | .45 | .10 |
| ☐ 182 | 1985 Milestones:<br>Rod Carew<br>Phil Niekro<br>Mike Schmidt<br>Tom Seaver<br>Pete Rose<br>Nolan Ryan | 1.00 | .45 | .10 |

|  | | MINT | VG-E | F-G |
|---|---|---|---|---|
| ☐ 183 | 1985 Triple Crown: ..... | 1.00 | .45 | .10 |
| | Wade Boggs | | | |
| | Darrell Evans | | | |
| | Don Mattingly | | | |
| | Willie McGee | | | |
| | Dale Murphy | | | |
| | Dave Parker | | | |
| ☐ 184 | 1985 Highlights: ........ | 2.00 | .90 | .20 |
| | Wade Boggs | | | |
| | Dwight Gooden | | | |
| | Rickey Henderson | | | |
| | Don Mattingly | | | |
| | Willie McGee | | | |
| | John Tudor | | | |
| ☐ 185 | 1985 20 Game Winners: | 1.50 | .70 | .15 |
| | Dwight Gooden | | | |
| | Ron Guidry | | | |
| | John Tudor | | | |
| | Joaquin Andujar | | | |
| | Bret Saberhagen | | | |
| | Tom Browning | | | |

|  | | MINT | VG-E | F-G |
|---|---|---|---|---|
| ☐ 186 | World Series Champs .. | .45 | .20 | .04 |
| | L. Smith, Dane Iorg | | | |
| | W. Wilson, C. Leibrandt | | | |
| | G. Brett, B. Saberhagen | | | |
| | D. Motley, D. | | | |
| | Quisenberry | | | |
| | D. Jackson, J. Sundberg | | | |
| | S. Balboni, F. White | | | |
| ☐ 187 | Hubie Brooks ......... | .25 | .10 | .02 |
| ☐ 188 | Glen Davis ........... | .25 | .10 | .02 |
| ☐ 189 | Darrell Evans ......... | .25 | .10 | .02 |
| ☐ 190 | Rich Gossage ........ | .35 | .15 | .03 |
| ☐ 191 | Andy Hawkins ........ | .20 | .09 | .02 |
| ☐ 192 | Jay Howell ........... | .20 | .09 | .02 |
| ☐ 193 | LaMarr Hoyt .......... | .25 | .10 | .02 |
| ☐ 194 | Davey Lopes .......... | .20 | .09 | .02 |
| ☐ 195 | Mike Scott ........... | .15 | .06 | .01 |
| ☐ 196 | Ted Simmons ......... | .25 | .10 | .02 |
| ☐ 197 | Gary Ward ........... | .15 | .06 | .01 |
| ☐ 198 | Bob Welch ........... | .15 | .06 | .01 |
| ☐ 199 | Mike Young ........... | .35 | .15 | .03 |
| ☐ 200 | Buddy Biancalana ..... | .15 | .06 | .01 |

☐ Please send me the following price guides—
☐ I would like the most current edition of the books listed below.

### THE OFFICIAL PRICE GUIDES TO:

☐ 465-8 American Silver & Silver Plate 4th Ed. — 10.95
☐ 482-8 Antique Clocks 3rd Ed. — 10.95
☐ 455-0 Antique & Modern Dolls 2nd Ed. — 9.95
☐ 483-6 Antique & Modern Firearms 5th Ed. — 10.95
☐ 271-X Antiques & Other Collectibles 8th Ed. — 9.95
☐ 466-6 Antique Jewelry 4th Ed. — 10.95
☐ 270-1 Beer Cans & Collectibles, 3rd Ed. — 7.95
☐ 262-0 Bottles Old & New 9th Ed. — 10.95
☐ 255-8 Carnival Glass 1st Ed. — 10.95
☐ 453-4 Collectible Cameras 1st Ed. — 10.95
☐ 277-9 Collectibles of the Third Reich 2nd Ed. — 10.95
☐ 454-2 Collectible Toys 1st Ed. — 10.95
☐ 490-9 Collector Cars 6th Ed. — 9.95
☐ 267-1 Collector Handguns 3rd Ed. — 11.95
☐ 459-3 Collector Knives 7th Ed. — 11.95
☐ 266-3 Collector Plates 4th Ed. — 10.95
☐ 476-3 Collector Prints 6th Ed. — 11.95
☐ 489-5 Comic Books & Collectibles 8th Ed. — 9.95
☐ 433-X Depression Glass 1st Ed. — 9.95
☐ 472-0 Glassware 2nd Ed. — 10.95
☐ 492-5 Hummel Figurines & Plates 5th Ed. — 9.95
☐ 451-8 Kitchen Collectibles 2nd Ed. — 10.95

☐ 460-7 Military Collectibles 4th Ed. — 10.95
☐ 268-X Music Collectibles 6th Ed. — 11.95
☐ 491-7 Old Books & Autographs 6th Ed. — 10.95
☐ 452-6 Oriental Collectibles 2nd Ed. — 11.95
☐ 461-5 Paper Collectibles 4th Ed. — 10.95
☐ 276-0 Pottery & Porcelain 5th Ed. — 11.95
☐ 263-9 Radio, TV, & Movie Memorabilia 2nd Ed. — 11.95
☐ 484-4 Records 6th Ed. — 9.95
☐ 485-2 Royal Doulton 4th Ed. — 10.95
☐ 418-6 Science Fiction & Fantasy Collectibles 1st Ed. — 9.95
☐ 477-1 Wicker 3rd Ed. — 10.95

### THE OFFICIAL:

☐ 445-3 Collector's Journal 1st Ed. — 4.95
☐ 413-5 Identification Guide to Glassware 1st Ed. — 9.95
☐ 448-8 Identification Guide to Gunmarks 2nd Ed. — 9.95
☐ 412-7 Identification Guide to Pottery & Porcelain 1st Ed. — 9.95
☐ 415-1 Identification Guide to Victorian Furniture 1st Ed. — 9.95

### THE OFFICIAL (POCKET SIZE) PRICE GUIDES TO:

☐ 473-9 Antiques & Flea Markets 3rd Ed. — 3.95
☐ 442-9 Antique Jewelry 2nd Ed. — 3.95
☐ 264-7 Baseball Cards 5th Ed. — 4.95
☐ 488-7 Bottles 2nd Ed. — 4.95

☐ 468-2 Cars & Trucks 2nd Ed. — 4.95
☐ 260-4 Collectible Americana 2nd Ed. — 4.95
☐ 463-1 Collectible Records 2nd Ed. — 3.95
☐ 469-0 Collector Guns 2nd Ed. — 4.95
☐ 474-7 Comic Books 3rd Ed. — 3.95
☐ 486-0 Dolls 3rd Ed. — 4.95
☐ 292-2 Football Cards 5th Ed. — 4.95
☐ 258-2 Glassware 2nd Ed. — 4.95
☐ 487-9 Hummels 3rd Ed. — 4.95
☐ 441-0 Military Collectibles 2nd Ed. — 3.95
☐ 480-1 Paperbacks & Magazines 3rd Ed. — 4.95
☐ 443-7 Pocket Knives 3rd Ed. — 3.95
☐ 479-8 Scouting Collectibles 3rd Ed. — 4.95
☐ 439-9 Sports Collectibles 2nd Ed. — 3.95
☐ 494-1 Star Trek/Star Wars Collectibles 2nd Ed. — 3.95
☐ 493-3 Toys 3rd Ed. — 4.95

### THE OFFICIAL BLACKBOOK PRICE GUIDES TO:

☐ 284-1 U.S. Coins 24th Ed. — 3.95
☐ 286-8 U.S. Paper Money 18th Ed. — 3.95
☐ 285-X U.S. Postage Stamps 8th Ed. — 3.95

### THE OFFICIAL INVESTORS GUIDE TO BUYING & SELLING:

☐ 496-8 Gold, Silver and Diamonds 2nd Ed. — 9.95
☐ 497-6 Gold Coins 2nd Ed. — 9.95
☐ 498-4 Silver Coins 2nd Ed. — 9.95

TOTAL

*SEE REVERSE SIDE FOR ORDERING INSTRUCTIONS*

# BILL HENDERSON'S CARDS
## "King of the Commons"

1113 COLUMBUS CIRCLE - PG8
JANESVILLE, WISCONSIN 53545
1-608-755-0922

"ALWAYS BUYING"
Call or Write
for Quote

"ALWAYS BUYING"
Call or Write
for Quote

| | HI NOS. | COMMONS EACH | EX/MT TO MINT CONDITION GROUP LOTS FOR SALE | | | | VG Condition | | |
|---|---|---|---|---|---|---|---|---|---|
| | | | 50 Diff. | 100 Diff. | 300 Asst. | 500 Asst. | 50 | 100 | 200 Different |
| 1948 BOWMAN | | 4.00 | | | | | | | |
| 1949 BOWMAN | | 4.00 | | | | | | | |
| 50-51 BOWMAN | 8.50 | 3.00 | | 140. | | | | 80. | |
| 1952 TOPPS | 60.00 | 5.00 (2-80) 6.00 | 230. | | | | | 130. | |
| 1952 BOWMAN | 5.00 | 3.00 (2-72) 3.75 | 140. | | | | | 80. | |
| 1953 TOPPS | 12.00 | 2.50 | | 115. | | | | 70. | |
| 1953 BOWMAN | 9.00 | 3.00 (113-128) 12.00 | 235. | | | | | 135. | |
| 1954 TOPPS | | 1.50 (51-75) 2.00 | 70. | 135. | | | | 45. | |
| 1954 BOWMAN | | 1.50 (129-224) 2.00 | 70. | 135. | | | | 45. | |
| 1955 TOPPS | 3.50 | 1.50 (150-160) 2.50 | 70. | 135. | 390. | | | 45. | |
| 1955 BOWMAN | 2.50-5. Umps | .75 | | 35. | 68. | 200. | 20. | 40. | |
| 1956 TOPPS | | 1.25 (181-260) 2.00 | 58. | 112. | 320. | | 35. | 68. | |
| 1957 TOPPS | 3.50 | .75 (353-407) .85 | 35. | 68. | 200. | | 20. | 40. | |
| 1958 TOPPS | | .65 (1-110) .85 | 30. | 58. | 170. | 275. | | 35. | 68. |
| 1959 TOPPS | 2.00 | .40 (1-110) .50 | 20. | 38. | 110. | 175. | | 20. | 38. |
| 1960 TOPPS | (553-572 2.00) 1.75 | .35 (441-506) .60 | 17. | 32. | 92. | 150. | | 18. | 34. |
| 1961 TOPPS | 6.50-8.50 S.N. | .35 (371-522) .40 | 17. | 32. | 92. | 150. | | 18. | 34. |
| 1962 TOPPS | 1.75-5.00 RKS. | .35 (371-522) .50 | 17. | 32. | 92. | 150. | | 18. | 34. |
| 1963 TOPPS | 1.75 | .30 (197-446) .50 | 14. | 28. | 80. | | | 17. | |
| 1964 TOPPS | 1.00 | .25 (371-522) .40 | 12. | 24. | 70. | 110. | | 15. | 28. |
| 1965 TOPPS | (447-552 .50) .75 | .25 (199-446) .35 | 12. | 24. | 70. | 110. | | 15. | 28. |
| 1966 TOPPS | 3.00 | .25 (447-522) .60 | 12. | 24. | 70. | 110. | | 15. | 28. |
| 1967 TOPPS | 2.50 | .25 (458-533) 1.00 | 12. | 24. | 70. | 110. | | 15. | 28. |
| 1968 TOPPS | (13-110 .25) .40 | .25 (458-533) .30 | 12. | 24 | *70. | 110. | | 15. | 28. |
| 1969 TOPPS | | .25 (219-327) .40 | | 24. | *70. | 110. | | 15. | 28. |
| 1970 TOPPS | .90 | .25 (553-636) .40 | | 24. | *70. | 110. | | 15. | 28. |
| 1971 TOPPS | .90 | .25 (524-643) .50 | | 24. | *70. | 110. | | 15. | 28. |
| 1972 TOPPS | (395-525 .25) .90 | .20 (526-656) .40 | | 18. | *52. | 85. | | 10. | 19. |
| 1973 TOPPS | .50 | .20 (397-528) .25 | | 18. | *52. | 85. | | 10. | 19. |
| 1974 TOPPS | | .20 | | 18. | *52. | *85. | | 10. | 19. |
| 1975 TOPPS | (8-132 .25) | .20 | | 18. | *52. | *85. | | 10. | 19. |
| 1976-77 | | .15 | | 14. | *42. | *68. | | 9. | 16. |
| 1978-1980 | | .10 | | 8. | *22. | *35. | | 5. | 9. |
| 1981 thru 1986 TOPPS, FLEER, or DONRUS Specify Year & Company | | .10 | | 5. Per Yr. | *14. Per Yr. | *20. Per Yr. | | 3. | 6. |

SPECIAL IN VG
CONDITION-POSTPAID

| | | |
|---|---|---|
| 250 | 54-59 | $88.00 |
| 500 | 54-59 | 160.00 |
| 250 | 60-69 | 35.00 |
| 500 | 60-69 | 65.00 |
| 1000 | 60-69 | 125.00 |
| 250 | 70-74 | 20.00 |
| 500 | 70-74 | 40.00 |
| 1000 | 70-74 | 75.00 |

*These lots are all different.
Special 1 Different from each year 1950-86 from above $28.00 postpaid.
Special 100 Different from each year 1954-86 from above $845.00 postpaid.
Special 10 Different from each year 1954-86 from above $90.00 postpaid.
All lot groups are my choice.
All assorted lots will contain as many different as possible.
Please list alternates whenever possible.
Send your want list and I will fill them at the above price for commons. High numbers, specials, scarce series, and stars extra.

Minimum order $7.50 - Postage and handling .50 per 100 cards (minimum $1.75)
Have thousands of star and super star cards. Call or send for star list.
Also interested in purchasing your collection.
Groups include various years of my choice.

SETS AVAILABLE
POSTAGE 2.50 PER SET

| | |
|---|---|
| 1979 Topps | $65.00 |
| 1980 Topps | 55.00 |
| 1981 Topps | 40.00 |
| 1981 Donrus | 17.00 |
| 1981 Fleer | 14.00 |
| 1982 Topps | 38.00 |
| 1982 or 83 Donrus | 14.00 |
| 1982 Fleer | 14.00 |
| 1983 Topps | 32.00 |
| 1984 Topps | 28.00 |
| 1985 Topps | 24.00 |
| 1986 Topps | 18.00 |
| 1986 Donrus | 16.00 |
| 1986 Fleer | 16.00 |

ANY CARD NOT LISTED ON PRICE SHEET IS PRICED AT BECKETT-SPORTS AMERICANA PRICE GUIDE VIII.

# San Diego Sports Collectibles

## Super Card Lots

We have good quantities of all lots listed below. This is an excellent way of obtaining a major portion of a set at low prices.

**1. TOPPS 1958-1976** — 1500 Different cards, approximately 80 each year, including: Aaron, Adcock, Allen, Alston, Aparicio, Ashburn, Banks, Bauer, Berra, Boyer, Brock, Bunning, Burdette, Carew, Cash, Cepeda, Clemente, Colavito, Dark, Davis, Drysdale, Face, Flood, Ford, Fox, Gibson, Gilliam, Groat, Hodges, Houk, E. Howard, F. Howard, Jenkins, John, Kaat, Kaline, Killebrew, Kluszewski, Koufax, Kubek, Kuenn, Larsen, Lopez, Mantle, Maris, Martin, Mathews, Mays, Mazeroski, McCovey, McGraw, Mclain, Minoso, Moon, Morgan, Murcer, Niekro, Oliva, Perez, Perry, Pierce, Piniella, Piersall, Pinson, Podres, Powell, Richardson, B. Robby, F. Robby, Rose, Santo, Schoendienst, Score, Shantz, Skowron, Snider, Spahn, Stargell, Staub, Sutton, Tlanson, Tiant, Torre, Turley, Virdon, Wilhelm, Williams, Wills, Zimmer, and Yaz. Very Good to Excellent condition. $295.00.

**2. TOPPS 1957-1962** — 150 Different cards including: Clemente, Mantle, Aaron, Drysdale, Ford, Killebrew, Wynn, Hodges, Spahn, Banks, Mathews, Roberts, Aparicio, Fox, Minoso and many more. Very Good to Excellent condition. $89.00.

**3. TOPPS 1962-1970** — 150 Different cards including: Aaron, Banks, Clemente, Drysdale, Ford, Gibson, Hodges, Kaline, Killebrew, Mantle, Mathews, Mays, McCovey, Morgan, Roberts, Aparicio, Hunter, F. Robby, and many more. Very Good to Excellent condition. $89.00.

**5. TOPPS/FLEER/DONRUSS 1981-1986** — 800 Assorted including: Valenzuela, Boggs, Henderson, Schmidt, Carlton, Seaver, Bench, Murphy, Carew, Ripken, Palmer, Brett, Winfield, Rice, Strawberry, Jackson, Guerrero, Garvey, Lynn, Bench, Carter, Morgan, Perry, Dawson, Murray and Yaz. Mint condition. $19.95.

MIKE SCHMIDT

**4. TOPPS 1970-1977** — 200 Different including: Aaron, Oliva, Brock, Carew, Carlton, Garvey, Gibson, Hodges, Hunter, Kaline, Killebrew, Robinson, Seaver, Yount, Aparicio, McCovey, Morgan, Munson, Palmer, Perry, Stargell. About Excellent condition. $39.00.

## Complete Mint Baseball Sets

| | | | |
|---|---|---|---|
| Topps 1986 | $19.50 | Fleer 1986 | 19.50 |
| Topps 1985 | 23.50 | Fleer 1985 | 16.50 |
| Topps 1984 | 27.00 | Fleer 1984 | 16.50 |
| Topps 1983 | 35.00 | Fleer 1983 | 16.50 |
| Topps 1982 | 37.00 | Fleer 1982 | 16.50 |
| Topps 1981 | 45.00 | Fleer 1981 | 16.95 |
| Topps 1980 | 63.00 | Donruss 1986 | 28.50 |
| Topps 1979 | 68.00 | Donruss 1985 | 29.50 |
| Topps 1981 (Traded) | 17.50 | Donruss 1983 | 18.00 |
| Topps 1982 (Traded) | 17.50 | Donruss 1982 | 18.00 |
| Topps 1983 (Traded) | 21.50 | Donruss 1981 | 22.00 |
| Topps 1985 (Traded) | 12.95 | Drakes 1984 | 6.50 |
| Fleer 1985 (Traded) | 15.95 | Ralston 1984 | 6.50 |

### Free Catalog!

Please send 3 stamps to receive our next three 48-page illustrated catalogues listing thousands of old baseball cards from the early 1900s to present. Includes Topps sets, singles and stars as well as Bowman, Fleer, Donruss, Goudey, Tobacco, Leaf and many other regional and miscellaneous issues. Also featured are football cards and sports memorabilia of all types. Issued 3 times yearly.

## Mail Order Instructions

Credit Card Holders call toll free for instant service 10 a.m. - 5 p.m. (West Coast time) Mon-Sat (Orders only).

**1-800-621-0852 Ext. 561**

For other inquiries and on Sunday call (619) 236-0600.

Send Payment to:

## San Diego Sports Collectibles
5043 Westminster Terrace Dept. V
San Diego, California 92116

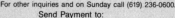

## Shipping & Insurance
Baseball Cards

| | |
|---|---|
| 1-25 cards | $1.95 |
| 26-100 cads | 2.50 |
| 101-800 cards | 4.95 |
| 801 or more | 9.95 |
| Complete Sets | 2.50 |

CALIF. RES. ADD 6% SALES TAX

# San Diego Sports Collectibles

THE WEST COAST'S LARGEST BASEBALL CARD STORE

## Topps Hall of Famer Lots

Over the years we have built a large inventory of these popular **regular issue Topps** cards. All cards are in very good condition or better and are **guaranteed** originals. All cards are our choice but we will do our best to send your **three** preferences.

| Player | Years | 3 Diff |
|---|---|---|
| Henry Aaron | 1968-1972 | $14.95 |
| Henry Aaron | 1973-1976 | 9.95 |
| Ernie Banks | 1966-1971 | 6.25 |
| Johnny Bench | 1977-1980 | 3.25 |
| Lou Brock | 1966-1971 | 8.00 |
| Lou Brock | 1972-1977 | 3.00 |
| Rod Carew | 1973-1977 | 6.50 |
| Rod Carew | 1978-1980 | 3.00 |
| Steve Carlton | 1971-1976 | 8.25 |
| Steve Carlton | 1977-1980 | 2.75 |
| R. Clemente | 1968-1973 | 12.95 |
| Don Drysdale | 1965-1969 | 7.25 |
| Whitey Ford | 1964-1967 | 7.95 |
| Steve Garvey | 1973-1976 | 7.95 |
| Steve Garvey | 1977-1980 | 4.50 |
| Bob Gibson | 1965-1969 | 6.25 |
| Bob Gibson | 1970-1975 | 3.95 |
| Gil Hodges | 1967-1972 | 2.95 |
| Catfish Hunter | 1971-1975 | 1.95 |
| R. Jackson | 1971-1975 | 9.50 |
| R. Jackson | 1976-1980 | 3.70 |
| Al Kaline | 1964-1969 | 6.00 |
| Al Kaline | 1971-1975 | 3.75 |
| H. Killebrew | 1966-1971 | 5.95 |
| H. Killebrew | 1972-1975 | 2.20 |
| Sandy Koufax | 1959-1966 | 19.95 |
| Fred Lynn | 1976-1980 | 2.25 |

| Player | Years | 3 Diff |
|---|---|---|
| Willie Mays | 1969-1973 | 14.95 |
| W. McCovey | 1972-1976 | 2.95 |
| W. McCovey | 1977-1980 | 1.95 |
| Joe Morgan | 1966-1970 | 5.75 |
| Joe Morgan | 1971-1975 | 2.50 |
| T. Munson | 1971-1975 | 4.75 |
| Stan Musial | 1959-1963 | 19.95 |

| Player | Years | 3 Diff |
|---|---|---|
| M. Mantle | 1964-1969 | 49.95 |
| Juan Marichal | 1967-1970 | 5.50 |
| Juan Marichal | 1971-1974 | 2.75 |
| Roger Maris | 1959-1963 | 15.95 |
| Roger Maris | 1964-1968 | 8.75 |
| Ed Mathews | 1959-1964 | 6.95 |
| Ed Mathews | 1965-1968 | 5.50 |
| Willie Mays | 1964-1968 | 24.50 |

| Player | Years | 3 Diff |
|---|---|---|
| Jim Palmer | 1967-1971 | 8.95 |
| Jim Palmer | 1972-1976 | 2.25 |
| Gaylord Perry | 1967-1971 | 5.75 |
| Gaylord Perry | 1972-1976 | 2.75 |
| Jim Rice | 1976-1980 | 3.75 |
| Robin Roberts | 1959-1965 | 4.75 |
| B. Robinson | 1964-1969 | 7.50 |
| B. Robinson | 1970-1973 | 5.95 |
| Frank Robinson | 1965-1971 | 8.50 |
| Frank Robinson | 1972-1975 | 3.25 |
| Pete Rose | 1966-1969 | 59.00 |
| Pete Rose | 1973-1976 | 19.95 |
| Pete Rose | 1977-1980 | 8.25 |
| Nolan Ryan | 1977-1980 | 1.95 |
| Mike Schmidt | 1974-1976 | 13.25 |
| Mike Schmidt | 1977-1980 | 5.50 |
| Tom Seaver | 1968-1970 | 19.95 |
| Tom Seaver | 1971-1975 | 6.50 |
| Duke Snider | 1959-1964 | 10.50 |
| Warren Spahn | 1959-1965 | 8.75 |
| Willie Stargell | 1964-1969 | 7.95 |
| Willie Stargell | 1970-1975 | 2.95 |
| Dave Winfield | 1975-1977 | 4.95 |
| Dave Winfield | 1978-1980 | 2.95 |
| Early Wynn | 1959-1962 | 6.25 |
| C. Yastrzemski | 1970-1973 | 12.95 |
| C. Yastrzemski | 1974-1977 | 7.75 |
| Robin Yount | 1976-1980 | 2.75 |

# CLASSIFIED ADS

# COMPLETE MINT
# BASEBALL CARD SETS

| | |
|---|---|
| 1986 Topps (792) ...................................... | $20.00 |
| 1986 Fleer (660) ...................................... | $17.00 |
| 1986 Donruss (660) ...................................... | $23.00 |
| 1986 Sportflics (200 w/Trivia) ...................... | $37.00 |
| All Four Above 1986 Sets ............................ | $90.00 |
| 1986 Topps GLossy All-Star (22) .................. | $5.00 |
| 1986 Donruss All-Stars (60) ......................... | $8.00 |
| 1986 Donruss All-Star Pop-Ups (18) ............ | $7.00 |
| 1986 Donruss Diamond Kings (5x7) (28) ...... | $9.00 |
| 1986 Donruss-Leaf (264) ............................. | $14.00 |
| 1985 Topps (All 924 Cards) ......................... | $35.00 |
| 1985 Topps (792) ...................................... | $25.00 |
| 1985 Topps Traded (132) ............................ | $12.00 |
| 1985 Fleer (All 792 Cards) .......................... | $30.00 |
| 1985 Fleer (660) ...................................... | $19.00 |
| 1985 Fleer Update (132) ............................. | $13.00 |
| 1985 Topps Glossy All-Star (22) .................. | $6.00 |
| 1985 Topps Pete Rose Set (120) .................. | $16.00 |
| 1985 Topps Home Run Kings (33) ................ | $5.00 |
| 1985 Donruss Diamond Kings (5X7) (28) ...... | $8.00 |
| 1985 Donruss Highlight (56) ........................ | $45.00 |

| | |
|---|---|
| 1984 Topps (792) ...................................... | $28.00 |
| 1984 Topps Glossy All-Star (22) .................. | $6.00 |
| 1984 O.P.C. (396) ..................................... | $15.00 |
| 1983 Topps (792) ...................................... | $35.00 |
| 1983 Donruss (660) ................................... | $15.00 |
| 1982 Topps (792) ...................................... | $40.00 |
| 1982 Topps Traded (132) ............................ | $14.00 |
| 1982 Fleer(660) ........................................ | $14.00 |
| 1982 Donruss (660) ................................... | $14.00 |
| 1982 Topps Sticker (260 w/album) ............... | $10.00 |
| 1982 Fleer Stamps (Box of 600) .................. | $10.00 |
| 1981 Topps (726) ...................................... | $44.00 |
| 1981 Fleer (660) ....................................... | $17.00 |
| 1981 Topps Sticker (262 w/Album) ............... | $10.00 |
| 1980 Topps Supers (60 Grey Backs) ............ | $ 8.00 |

All prices include postage and handling; all orders
shipped via UPS or first class mail; payment in U.S.
funds only; Alaska, Hawaii, and foreign orders add
25%; No COD's or credit cards.

**BILL DODGE**
592 Yarmouth Lane
Bay Village, OH 44140

**METS** — Dwight Gooden, Pitcher

# THE TENTH INNING
## 2211 W. Mercury Blvd.
## Hampton, VA 23666

We have the world's largest selection of T.C.M.A. minor league cards dating from 1974 to 1984. Send $2.00 for a complete list of sets and prices.

| | | |
|---|---|---|
| A. Tidewater Tides w/Strawberry | ...................... | $14.95 |
| B. Lynchburg Mets w/Gooden | ............................ | $26.50 |
| C. Ogden A's w/Henderson | .............................. | $19.95 |
| D. Pawtucket Red Sox w/Boggs | ........................ | $19.95 |
| E. El Paso Diablos w/Riles | .............................. | $9.95 |
| F. Anderson Braves w/Butler | ........................... | $8.95 |
| G. Oklahoma City 89'ers w/Sandberg | ................ | $14.95 |
| H. Rochester Red Wings w/Ripken | ................... | $19.95 |

Don't forget to add $2.50 postage and handling. Hawaii, Alaska, and Canada add $5.00. Prices subject to change without notice. **These cards are one of the hottest items in the hobby, so order now!**

The Tenth Inning T.C.M.A. minor league checklist book, 1972-1985. Only $6.95 plus 95 cents postage and handling.

Telephone orders welcome. We take Visa and Mastercard. Call (804) 827-1667. Open Monday through Friday 10am to 8pm and Saturday 10am to 6pm. Send $2.00 for our new 50 page catalog. Win a case of 1986 Donruss cards. Please send self addressed stamped envelope for official contest form.

**TIDES** — Darryl Strawberry, Outfield

### OTHER MAJOR/MINOR SETS

| | | |
|---|---|---|
| Arkansas Travelers w/Worrell | ...................... | $7.95 |
| Waterbury Reds w/E. Davis | ....................... | $8.95 |
| Beaumont Golden Gators w/Guillen | ............ | $8.95 |
| Jackson Mets w/Strawberry | ...................... | $49.95 |
| Omaha Royals w/Biancalana | ..................... | $8.95 |
| Durham Bulls w/M.Yastrzemski | ................. | $7.95 |
| West Haven Yankees w/McGee | .................. | $35.00 |
| Portland Beavers w/Pena and Perez | .......... | $7.95 |

**RICKEY HENDERSON** — Outfielder

## Virginia's Largest
## Card and Comic Store

# FIRST BASE

## SPORTS NOSTALGIA SHOP

**231 Webb Chapel Village**
**Dallas, Texas 75229**
**(214) 243-5271**

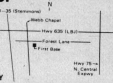

OPEN: TUESDAY THROUGH SATURDAY
11 A.M. to 7 P.M.

We are located on the Southeast corner of Webb Chapel and Forest just 15 minutes from the airport. Our large (1650 square foot showroom) store is convenient to all parts of Dallas being only one block south of the LBJ (635) Freeway at the Webb Chapel exit. Many collectors (and dealers) have told us that our store is the most complete they've ever seen. Just look on the opposite page for a few of our offers. We want you for a customer — please stop in and see for yourself.

Sincerely,

Wayne Grove
Gervise Ford

**FIRST BASE**

P.S.  We are always interested in buying your cards — let us know what you have.

## SPECIAL OFFERS

**#1:** Type set: One card from each year of Topps baseball 1952 through 1986, our choice of cards 35 cards for $9.95.

**#2:** Baseball cigarette card from 1910, our choice $5.95.

**#3:** 500 assorted (mostly different) baseball cards from 1978 to 1984 in excellent condition for $16.95

**#4:** Dallas Cowboy Weekly: 20 different back issues, our choice, for $14.95. We also have most single issues from 1977 to date available from $1.00 to $2.00 each. Send your want list. Some older issues also available.

**#5:** Poster: Robert Redford as "The Natural" plus a free Bucky Dent "Best Little Shortstop in Texas" poster for $6.95 postpaid.

**#6:** 1978 Topps baseball cards 50 different in excellent to mint condition $2.50.

**#7:** 1979 Topps baseball cards 50 different in excellent to mint condition includes some stars $2.95.

**#8:** 1980 Topps baseball cards 50 different in excellent to mint condition includes some stars $2.95.

**#9:** 1981 Topps baseball cards 50 different in excellent to mint condition includes some stars $2.95.

**#10:** 89 different 1984-85 Topps hockey cards in excellent to mint condition includes some stars $2.50.

**#11:** 66 different 1981-82 Topps basketball cards in excellent to mint condition includes stars (Bird, Magic, Kareem, Dr. J, etc.) $3.50.

**#12:** 115 different 1983 Topps football cards in excellent to mint condition includes many stars $2.95.

**#13:** Donruss puzzle sets: Complete set of all seven puzzle card sets (Ruth, Cobb, Mantle, Williams, Snider, Gehrig, Aaron) for $9.95.

**#14:** 1985 Dallas Cowboy Media Guide (not issued to the public) $4.95; Cowboy Bluebook $12.95.

### COMPLETE SETS

1985 Performance Rangers (28) ................ $4.95
1984 Jarvis Press Rangers (28) ................ $4.95
1983 Affiliated Foods Rangers (28) ........... $4.95
1984 Ralston-Purina Baseball (33) ........... $4.95
1983 Seven-Eleven 3-D Coins (12) .......... $12.95
1981 Topps 5x7 Dodgers/Angels (18) ...... $4.95
1978 Tucson Toros (Sample/Darwin) (24)  $3.50
1980 Tucson Toros (Heep/Knicely) (24) .. $3.00
1983 Dallas Cowboy Police (28) ................ $9.95
1981 Dallas Cowboy Police (14) ................ $7.95
1980 Dallas Cowboy Police (14) ................ $9.95
1979 Dallas Cowboy Police (15) .............. $13.95
1981 Shell Dallas Cowboys Portraits (6) .. $6.95
1981 Shell National Set Portraits (6) ....... $6.95
    includes Walter Payton and Earl Campbell

### BASEBALL CARD LOTS

1958 Topps 25 diff (f-vg) $4.95
1959 Topps 25 diff (f-vg) $3.95
1960 Topps 25 diff (f-vg) $3.50
1961 Topps 25 diff (f-vg) $3.50
1962 Topps 25 diff (f-vg) $3.50
1963 Topps 25 diff (f-vg) $3.25
1964 Topps 25 diff (f-vg) $3.25
1965 Topps 25 diff (f-vg) $3.25
1966 Topps 25 diff (f-vg) $2.95
1967 Topps 25 diff (f-vg) $2.95
1968 Topps 25 diff (f-vg) $2.95
1969 Topps 25 diff (f-vg) $2.75
1970 Topps 25 diff (f-vg) $1.95
1971 Topps 25 diff (f-vg) $1.75
1972 Topps 25 diff (f-vg) $1.75

# FIRST BASE

## — FOR SALE — MAIL ORDER —

### First Base

231 Webb Chapel Village
Dallas, Texas 75229

# BECKETT
# BASEBALL CAR[D]
## MONTHLY

$2

**Dwight Gooden**
METS • RIGHT HAND PITCHER

FLEER ALL STAR TEAM

1986 Cards He

**Curren**
**Price Guid**

Who's
& Who's N

# Now! Get
# BECKETT
# BASEBALL
# CARD
# MONTHLY
## for up to
# ½ OFF
## the cover price!

### BECKETT BASEBALL CARD MONTHLY'S
## Weather Report

The temperature rankings of the cards and players listed below are determined solely by reader input and represent the combined tabulated opinions of the contributors from all over the country) over the past month.

Many (but not all) of the "Who's Hot" have been printed in the Readers Write section as limited space does not permit publication of everything we receive. In the lists below, following each name in parentheses is the player's rank in the previous issue. The abbreviation NR is used for those players who were "not ranked" in the previous issue. It is essential to compile a player may fall into both the hot and cold top ten.

**Hot**
1. Dwight Gooden (1)
2. Pete Rose (2)
3. Don Mattingly (3)
4. Wade Boggs (4)
5. Bret Saberhagen (5)
6. George Brett (14)
7. Willie McGee (7)
8. Vince Coleman (20)
9. Dale Murphy (8)
10. Rickey Henderson (6)

11. Darryl Strawberry (9)
12. Eddie Murray (10)
13. Ryne Sandberg (9)
14. Mickey Mantle (15)
15. Cal Ripken (11)
16. Pedro Guerrero (NR)
17. Oddibe McDowell (12)
18. Orel Hershiser (18)
19. Reggie Jackson (NR)
20. Tom Seaver (13)

**Cold**
C10. Alan Wiggins (NR)
C9. Fred Lynn (C9)
C8. Ryne Sandberg (NR)
C7. Fernando Valenzuela (NR)
C6. Steve Sax (C3)
C5. Steve Carlton (C7)
C4. Reggie Jackson (NR)
C3. Mike Schmidt (C2)
C2. Robin Yount (C4)
C1. Ron Kittle (C1)

HOT          WARM          COLD

### BASEBALL CARD MONTHLY
## Price Guide

1950 Bowman

1951 Bowman